BEST OF EUROPE 2008

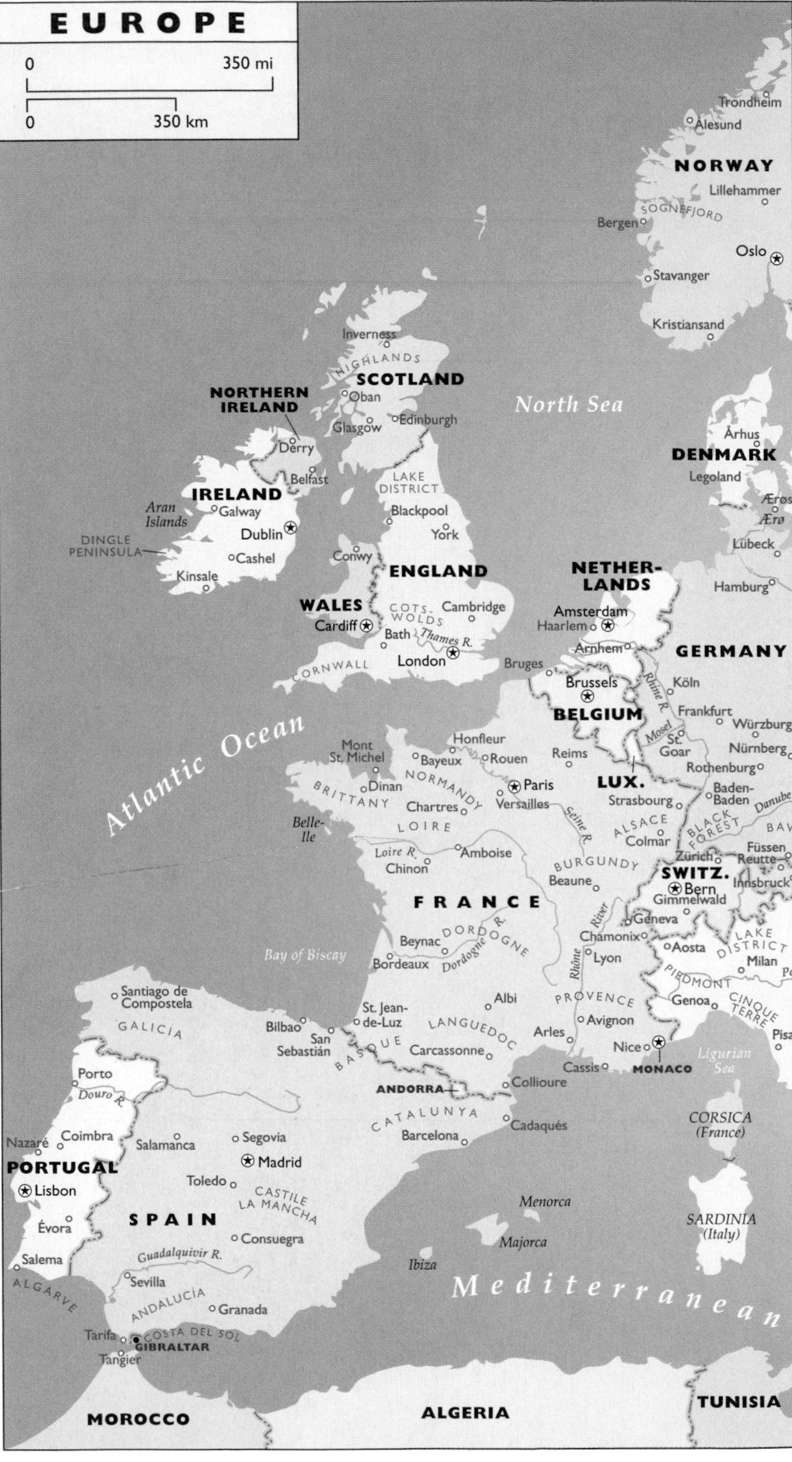
EUROPE
0
350 mi
0
350 km
NORWAY
Trondheim
Ålesund
Lillehammer
SOGNEFJORD
Bergen
Oslo
Stavanger
Kristiansand
North Sea
DENMARK
Århus
Legoland
Ærøskøbing
Ærø
Lübeck
Hamburg
SCOTLAND
Inverness
HIGHLANDS
Oban
Glasgow
Edinburgh
NORTHERN IRELAND
Derry
Belfast
IRELAND
Galway
Aran Islands
Dublin
DINGLE PENINSULA
Cashel
Kinsale
LAKE DISTRICT
Blackpool
York
Conwy
ENGLAND
WALES
Cardiff
COTSWOLDS
Cambridge
Bath
Thames R.
London
CORNWALL
NETHERLANDS
Amsterdam
Haarlem
Arnhem
GERMANY
Bruges
Brussels
BELGIUM
Köln
Rhine R.
Frankfurt
Würzburg
Mosel
St. Goar
Nürnberg
Rothenburg
LUX.
Baden-Baden
Danube
Atlantic Ocean
Mont St. Michel
Honfleur
Bayeux
Rouen
Reims
NORMANDY
Dinan
Paris
BRITTANY
Chartres
Versailles
Strasbourg
Seine R.
ALSACE
Colmar
BLACK FOREST
BAV
Belle-Ile
LOIRE
Loire R.
Amboise
Chinon
BURGUNDY
Zürich
Füssen
Reutte
SWITZ.
Bern
Innsbruck
Beaune
Gimmelwald
FRANCE
Geneva
Chamonix
Aosta
LAKE DISTRICT
Milan
Po
DORDOGNE
Dordogne R.
Beynac
Bordeaux
Bay of Biscay
Rhône River
Lyon
PIEDMONT
Genoa
CINQUE TERRE
Pisa
Santiago de Compostela
GALICIA
Albi
PROVENCE
Avignon
Bilbao
St. Jean-de-Luz
San Sebastián
LANGUEDOC
BASQUE
Arles
Carcassonne
Nice
MONACO
Cassis
Ligurian Sea
Porto
Douro R.
ANDORRA
Collioure
CATALUNYA
Barcelona
Cadaqués
CORSICA (France)
Nazaré
Coimbra
Salamanca
Segovia
PORTUGAL
Madrid
Lisbon
Toledo
CASTILE LA MANCHA
Menorca
SPAIN
Évora
Consuegra
Majorca
SARDINIA (Italy)
Salema
Guadalquivir R.
Ibiza
ALGARVE
Sevilla
Mediterranean
ANDALUCÍA
Granada
Tarifa
COSTA DEL SOL
GIBRALTAR
Tangier
MOROCCO
ALGERIA
TUNISIA

SWEDEN
FINLAND
Savonlinna
Gulf of Bothnia
Turku
Helsinki
St. Petersburg
Volga River
Uppsala
Tallinn
Stockholm
ESTONIA
RUSSIA
Moscow
LATVIA
Göteborg
Visby
Riga
Kalmar
Växjö
Öland
Baltic Sea
LITHUANIA
Don River
Copenhagen
Malmö
Vilnius
købing
RUSSIA
Minsk
Gdańsk
BELARUS
Poznań
Toruń
Warsaw
Berlin
POLAND
Kiev
Elbe R.
Dnieper River
Oder
Vistula R.
Dresden
L'viv
UKRAINE
Auschwitz
Kraków
Prague
TATRA MTNS
CZECH REPUBLIC
Levoča
Český Krumlov
Brno
SLOVAKIA
MOLDOVA
Chişinău
Odessa
Munich
Melk
Bratislava
Eger
Vienna
Segesta
Salzburg
Budapest
Hallstatt
Sigisoara
AUSTRIA
HUNGARY
Pécs
ROMANIA
SLOVENIA
DOLOMITES
Bled
Bran
Venice
Ljubljana
CROATIA
Zagreb
Bucharest
Plitvice
Belgrade
ISTRIA
Pula
BOSNIA & HERZ.
Danube R.
Black Sea
Ravenna
SAN MARINO
Sarajevo
SERBIA
Split
BULGARIA
Florence
Ancona
DALMATIAN COAST
Siena
Mostar
Podgorica
Sofia
Plovdiv
TUSCANY
Istanbul
Assisi
KOSOVO
Rila
Dubrovnik
MONT.
Adriatic Sea
UMBRIA
Kotor
Skopje
Civita
MACEDONIA
Rome
Tiranë
Thessaloniki
VATICAN CITY
ITALY
Bari
ALBANIA
Naples
Brindisi
Meteora
TURKEY
Sorrento
Aegean Sea
GREECE
AMALFI COAST
Paestum
Corfu
Ephesus
Tyrrhenian Sea
Delphi
Sámos
Ionian Sea
Athens
Bodrum
Mykonos
Nafplion
Hydra
Naxos
Paros
Cefalù
PELOPONNESE
Palermo
Rhodes
SICILY
Taormina
Santorini
Finikoundas
Agrigento
Sea
Valletta
MALTA
CRETE
GORGE OF SAMARIA

NETHERLANDS
Bergen-Belsen
Celle
Wolfsburg
Hannover
Braunschweig
Bad Bentheim
Hengelo
Rheine
Osnabrück
Hameln
Magdeburg
Bielefeld
Münster
Goslar
Halberstadt
Arnhem
Nijmegen
Emmerich
Paderborn
Aschersleben
HARZ MOUNTAINS
Göttingen
Essen
Duisburg
Dortmund
Kassel
Venlo
Korbach
Düsseldorf
Naumburg
GERMANY
Erfurt
Weimar
Bebra
Eisenach
Maastricht
Köln
Marburg
Aachen
Bonn
Suhl
Liege
Fulda
Remagen
Rhine
Wetzlar
BELGIUM
Burg Eltz
Koblenz
Coburg
Boppard
Cochem
St. Goar
Frankfurt
Beilstein
Wiesbaden
Zell
Bacharach
Bamberg
Bayreuth
Bingen
Mainz
Main
LUXEMBOURG
Mosel
Rudesheim
Würzburg
Weiden
Trier
Steinach
Worms
Luxembourg City
Mannheim
Nürnberg
Heidelberg
Thionville
Kaiserslautern
Rothenburg
Castle Road
Saarbrücken
Metz
Dinkelsbühl
Karlsruhe
Romantic Road
LORRAINE
Nördlingen
Ingolstadt
Baden-Baden
Stuttgart
Schwäbisch Gmünd
Donauworth
Toul
Nancy
BAVA
Strasbourg
Kehl
Reutlingen
Augsburg
St Dié
ALSACE
BLACK FOREST
Tübingen
Ulm
Dachau
Ribeauvillé
Hausach Open-Air Museum
Munich
Kaysersberg
Colmar
Triberg
Danube
Herrsching
LES VOSGES
Eguisheim
Furtwangen
Landsberg
Andechs Monastery
Freiburg
Bad Krozingen
Ravensburg
Ronchamp
Meersburg
Lake Constance
Oberammergau
Isar
Mulhouse
Staufen
Kempten
Rhinefalls
Konstanz
Neuschwanstein
Stein
Lindau
Füssen
Belfort
FRANCE
Basel
Reutte
Bregenz
Zugspitze
Ehrenberg
Fallerschein
Zürich
APPENZELL
Feldkirch
JURA MTNS.
Appenzell
Lech
Innsbruck
Besançon
Ebenalp
SWITZERLAND
LIECHTENSTEIN
Stubai Glacier
Buchs
Vaduz
Bludenz
TIROL
Luzern
Zug
Brenner Pass
Neuchâtel
Vipiteno
Murten
Bern
Lac de Neuchâtel
Ballenberg Museum
Fluelen
Avenches
Chur
Reifenstein Castle
Frasne
Inter-laken
Susten Pass
Scuol
Fribourg
Spiez
Glacier Express
Merano
Gruyères
BERNER OBERLAND
Grindelwald
Samedan
Bolzano
Lausanne
Jungfrau
St. Moritz
Glurns
Montreux
Chillon
Gimmelwald
TICINO
Pontresina
Lac Léman
Schilthorn
ITALY
Geneva
Saas-Fee
Locarno
Sondrio
Martigny
Trento
Zermatt
Lugano
Lago Como
Bernina Express
Matterhorn
Lago Maggiore
Varenna
Annecy
Chamonix
Mont Blanc
Lago Lugano
Bellagio

GERMANY, AUSTRIA, SWITZERLAND & CZECH REPUBLIC
A24 Freeway/Autobahn
Major Roads
Major Rail Line
Airport
St. Goar Recommended Location*
Bebra Just Passing Through**
Ruin, Museum, other Point of Interest
Castle/Monument/Palace
* Black locations are places of interest to tourists, sized by importance.
** Gray locations are not places of interest to tourists and are sized by population.
0 km 50 100 km
0 miles 50 miles
POLAND
CZECH REPUBLIC
AUSTRIA
SLOVAKIA
HUNGARY
CROATIA
SLOVENIA
SAXONY
BOHEMIA
MORAVIA
WACHAU
SALZKAMMERGUT
DOLOMITES
FRIULI
VENETO
JULIAN ALPS
ALPE DI SIUSI
Berlin
Tegel
Frankfurt an der Oder
Rzepin
Brandenburg
Potsdam
Sanssouci Palace
Zielona Góra
Wittenberg
Cottbus
Zary
Elbe
Lauchhammer
Boleslawiec
Halle
Leipzig
Moritzburg
Zgorzelec
Gorlitz
Meissen
Dresden
Bad Schandau
Zittau
Glauchau
Chemnitz
Seiffen
Decin
Usti nad Labem
Litoměřice
Terezín
Plauen
Ruzyně
Karlovy Vary
Prague
Kutná Hora
Cheb
Marianské Lazne
Marktredwitz
Karlstejn Castle
Olomouc
Plzen
Kromeriz
Tabor
Zlín
Český Kubice
Telc
Brno
Furth
Veseli nad Luznici
Slavonice
Český Budejovice
Český Velenice
Gmund
Breclav
Regensburg
Kuty
Obertraubling
Český Krumlov
Passau
Summerau
Durnstein
Krems
Danube
Vienna
Grinzing
Bratislava
Linz
Mauthausen
Melk
Schönbrunn Palace
St. Valentin
Attnang Puchheim
Puchberg
Eisenstadt
Salzach
Schneeberg
Herrenchiemsee
Chiemsee
Salzburg
Bad Ischl
Sopron
Esterhazy Palace
Rosenheim
Berchtesgaden
Hallstatt
Selzthal
Kufstein
Hallein
Bruck an der Mur
Leoben
Szombathely
Worgl
Stainach Irdning
Zell am See
Hinterhornalm
Hall
Kitzbuhel
Piber
Graz
Badgastein
Grossglockner Pass
Spielfeld
Spittal
Klagenfurt
Nagykanizsa
Dobbiaco
Lienz
Maribor
Villach
Jesenice
Castelrotto
Cortina
Tarvisio
Vršič Pass
Bled/Lesce
Koprivnica
Brnik
Lake Bohinj
Lake Bled
Calalzo
Ljubljana
Belluno
Zagreb
Udine
Pordenone
Palmanova
Postojna Caves
Škocjan Caves
A10
A12
A2
A9
A13
A15
A4
A72
A93
E50
E65
A3
A92
A1
M1
A8
A12
A22
A23
A27

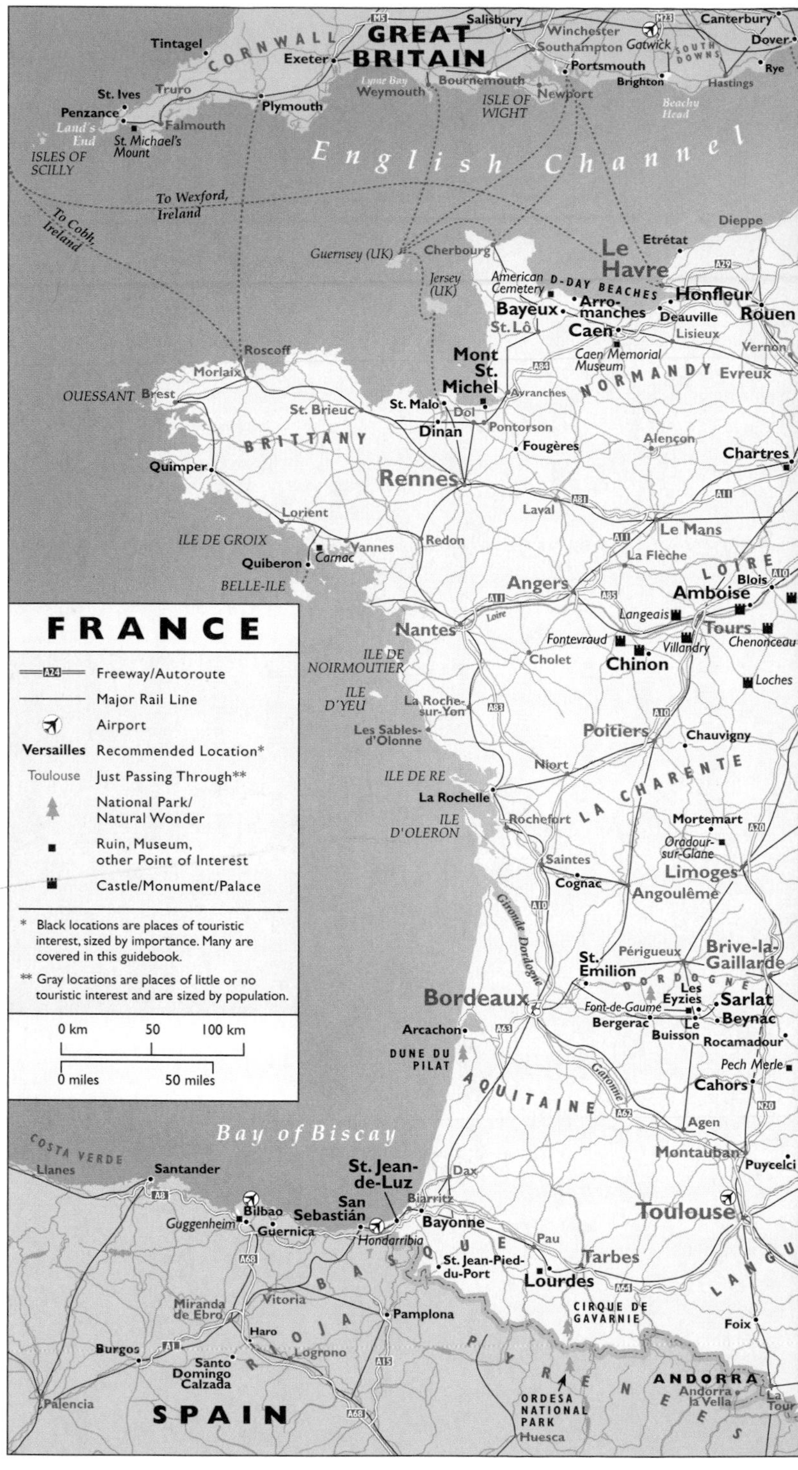
FRANCE
Freeway/Autoroute
Major Rail Line
Airport
Versailles Recommended Location*
Toulouse Just Passing Through**
National Park/ Natural Wonder
Ruin, Museum, other Point of Interest
Castle/Monument/Palace
* Black locations are places of touristic interest, sized by importance. Many are covered in this guidebook.
** Gray locations are places of little or no touristic interest and are sized by population.
0 km 50 100 km
0 miles 50 miles
GREAT BRITAIN
English Channel
Bay of Biscay
SPAIN
CORNWALL
BRITTANY
NORMANDY
LOIRE
LA CHARENTE
DORDOGNE
AQUITAINE
BASQUE
RIOJA
PYRENEES
D-DAY BEACHES
Salisbury
Winchester
Southampton
Gatwick
Canterbury
Dover
Rye
Hastings
Brighton
Portsmouth
Tintagel
Exeter
St. Ives
Penzance
Truro
Falmouth
Plymouth
Weymouth
Bournemouth
Newport
ISLE OF WIGHT
St. Michael's Mount
ISLES OF SCILLY
To Wexford, Ireland
To Cobh, Ireland
Guernsey (UK)
Jersey (UK)
Cherbourg
Dieppe
Etrétat
Le Havre
Honfleur
Rouen
Deauville
Lisieux
American Cemetery
Bayeux
Arromanches
St. Lô
Caen
Caen Memorial Museum
Vernon
Evreux
Mont St. Michel
Avranches
Roscoff
Morlaix
Brest
OUESSANT
St. Brieuc
St. Malo
Dinan
Dol
Pontorson
Fougères
Alençon
Chartres
Quimper
Rennes
Laval
Le Mans
Lorient
ILE DE GROIX
Vannes
Carnac
Quiberon
BELLE-ILE
Redon
La Flèche
Angers
Blois
Amboise
Langeais
Tours
Chenonceau
Nantes
Loire
Fontevraud
Villandry
Chinon
Cholet
Loches
ILE DE NOIRMOUTIER
ILE D'YEU
La Roche-sur-Yon
Les Sables-d'Olonne
Poitiers
Chauvigny
Niort
ILE DE RE
La Rochelle
ILE D'OLERON
Rochefort
Mortemart
Oradour-sur-Glane
Limoges
Saintes
Cognac
Angoulême
Gironde
Dordogne
Périgueux
Brive-la-Gaillarde
St. Emilion
Les Eyzies
Sarlat
Bordeaux
Font-de-Gaume
Beynac
Bergerac
Le Buisson
Arcachon
Rocamadour
DUNE DU PILAT
Pech Merle
Cahors
Garonne
Agen
Montauban
Puycelci
Toulouse
Dax
St. Jean-de-Luz
Biarritz
San Sebastián
Bayonne
Hondarribia
Pau
Tarbes
St. Jean-Pied-du-Port
Lourdes
CIRQUE DE GAVARNIE
Foix
ANDORRA
Andorra la Vella
La Tour
ORDESA NATIONAL PARK
Huesca
COSTA VERDE
Llanes
Santander
Bilbao
Guggenheim
Guernica
Vitoria
Miranda de Ebro
Pamplona
Haro
Logrono
Burgos
Santo Domingo Calzada
Palencia
LANGU

Ostende
Bruges
Antwerp
Düsseldorf
Channel Tunnel
Dunkerque
Ghent
Calais
Brussels
Köln
Marburg
Boulogne
St. Omer
Waterloo
Aachen
Bonn
FLANDERS
Lille
BELGIUM
Liege
Wetzlar
Rhine
Namur
Arras
Cambrai
Aulnoye
WALLONIE
Cochem
St. Goar
Frankfurt
Abbeville
Zell
Mosel
Bacharach
Amiens
Rudesheim
ARDENNES
St. Quentin
Charleville Mézières
LUXEMBOURG
Trier
GERMANY
Beauvais
Laon
Luxembourg City
Mannheim
Senlis
Longwy
Kaiserslautern
Chantilly
Soissons
Reims
Verdun Battlefield
Thionville
Heidelberg
Giverny
Charles de Gaulle
Metz
Saarbrücken
Seine
Epernay
CHAMPAGNE
Karlsruhe
Paris
Châlons
LORRAINE
Stuttgart
Versailles
Disneyland Paris
Baden-Baden
Orly
Nancy
Vaux-le-Vicomte
Seine
St. Dizier
Toul
Strasbourg
BLACK FOREST
Fontainebleau
ALSACE
Freudenstadt
VOSGES
Troyes
Ribeauvillé
Chaumont
Kaysersberg
Rhein
Triberg
Chablis
Colmar
Orléans
Laroche
BURGUNDY
Eguisheim
Freiburg
Auxerre
Culmont
Mulhouse
Cheverny
Loire
Avallon
Abbey of Fontenay
Ronchamp
Meersburg
Staufen
Chambord
Guedelon
Vézelay
LES VOSGES
Semur-en-Auxois
Belfort
Basel
Zürich
JURA MTNS.
Sancerre
Vierzon
Besançon
Bourges
Autun
Dijon
SWITZERLAND
Châteauneuf-en-Auxois
Luzern
Beaune
Dol
Neuchâtel
Bern
Lake Luzern
Châteauroux
Nevers
Le Creusot
Lac de Neuchâtel
Avenches
Châlon-sur-Saône
Frasne
Fribourg
Interlaken
Moulins
Brançion
Gruyères
Tournus
Vallorbe
BERNER OBERLAND
Lausanne
Cluny
Gimmelwald
Montluçon
Montreux
Vichy
Mâcon
Bourg-en-Bresse
Guéret
Locarno
Geneva
BEAUJOLAIS
FRANCE
Roanne
Martigny
Lugano
Chamonix
Rhône
Annecy
Lago Maggiore
Clermont-Ferrand
Mont Blanc
Stresa
Lyon
Mont Blanc Tunnel
Lago di Orta
SAVOIE
AUVERGNE
Aosta
Chambéry
Malpensa
Bourg S.M.
St. Etienne
Vienne
Milan
PIEDMONT
Loire
Modane
Grenoble
Po
Torino
ITALY
Le Puy-en-Velay
Gouffre Padirac
Valence
Briançon
Lot
Pinerolo
Rhône
Clelles
LE LANGHE
Rodez
Mende
Barolo
St. Cirq Lapopie
Montélimar
Gap
PROVENCE
Cuneo
Genoa
Savona
GORGES DU TARN
GORGE DE L'ARDECHE
Vaison la Romaine
Cordes
Orange
Digne
Finale
Tarn
Millau
Pont du Gard
Châteauneuf-du-Pape
Avignon
Albi
Uzès
Isle-sur-la-Sorgue
Nîmes
Les Baux
Roussillon
Vence
Menton
Castres
St. Rémy
St. Paul
MONACO
Ligurian Sea
Montpellier
Arles
LUBERON
Grasse
Villefranche
Caunes-Minervois
Minerve
CAMARGUE
GRAND CANYON DU VERDON
Nice
Aix-en-Provence
Antibes
To Bastia, Corsica
Carcassonne
Béziers
Cannes
Marseille
Narbonne
St-Tropez
CÔTE D'AZUR
Queribus & Peyrepertuse
Cassis
Toulon
Mediterranean Sea
Perpignan
To Porto Torres, Sardinia
L'Ile Rousse
Collioure
To Ajaccio, Corsica
Port Bou
CORSICA (France)
Figueres
Cadaqués

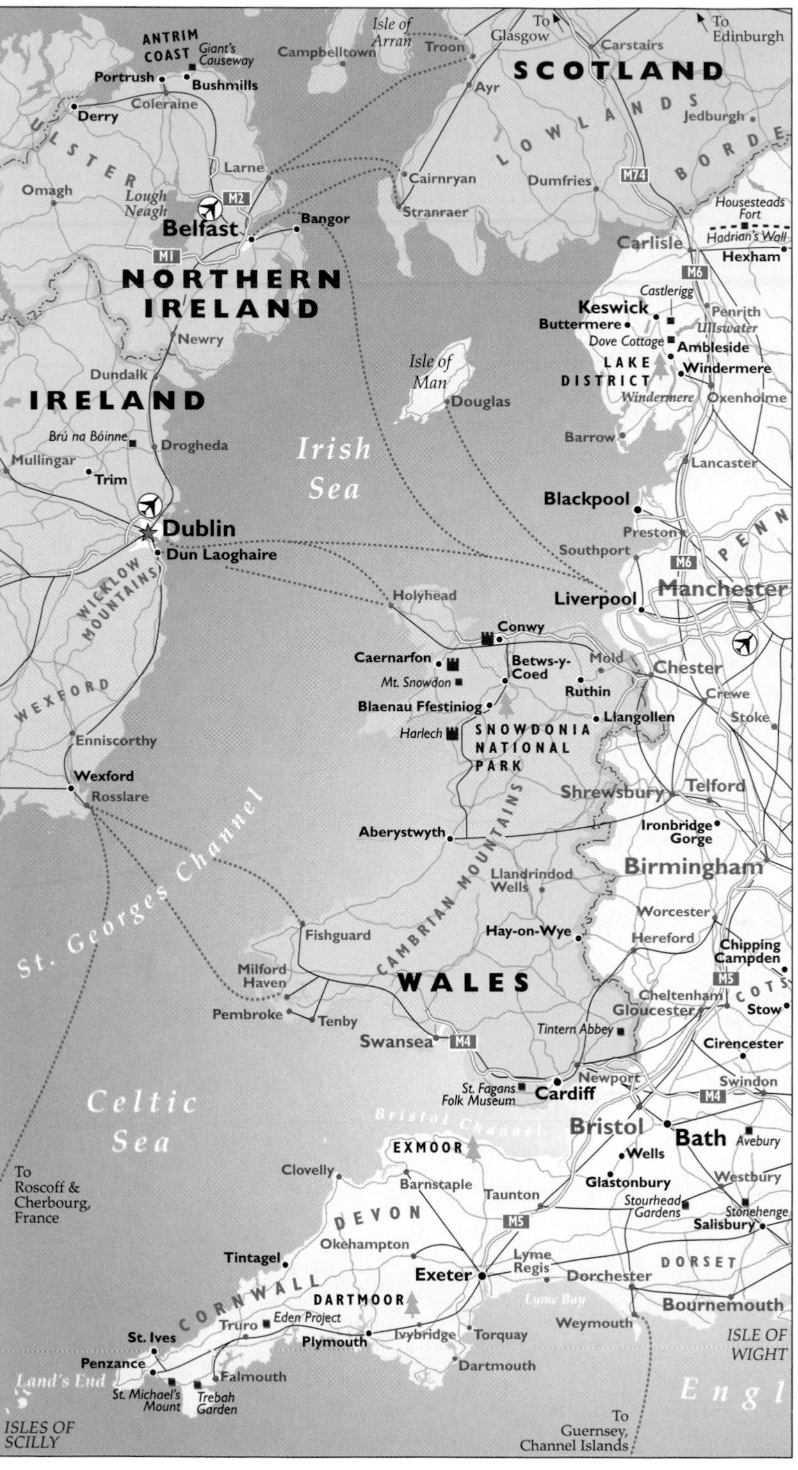

SCOTLAND
NORTHERN IRELAND
IRELAND
WALES
Irish Sea
St. Georges Channel
Celtic Sea
Bristol Channel
Engl
ANTRIM COAST
Giant's Causeway
Portrush
Bushmills
Coleraine
Derry
ULSTER
Larne
Omagh
Lough Neagh
Belfast
Bangor
Newry
Dundalk
Brú na Bóinne
Drogheda
Mullingar
Trim
Dublin
Dun Laoghaire
WICKLOW MOUNTAINS
WEXFORD
Enniscorthy
Wexford
Rosslare
Isle of Arran
Campbelltown
Troon
To Glasgow
Ayr
To Edinburgh
Carstairs
LOWLANDS
BORDE
Jedburgh
Cairnryan
Stranraer
Dumfries
Housesteads Fort
Hadrian's Wall
Carlisle
Hexham
Castlerigg
Keswick
Penrith
Buttermere
Ullswater
Dove Cottage
Ambleside
LAKE DISTRICT
Windermere
Oxenholme
Isle of Man
Douglas
Barrow
Lancaster
Blackpool
Preston
Southport
PENN
Liverpool
Manchester
Holyhead
Conwy
Caernarfon
Mt. Snowdon
Betws-y-Coed
Mold
Chester
Ruthin
Crewe
Blaenau Ffestiniog
Llangollen
Stoke
Harlech
SNOWDONIA NATIONAL PARK
Shrewsbury
Telford
Aberystwyth
Ironbridge Gorge
Birmingham
CAMBRIAN MOUNTAINS
Llandrindod Wells
Worcester
Hay-on-Wye
Hereford
Chipping Campden
Fishguard
Milford Haven
Pembroke
Tenby
Swansea
Cheltenham
COTS
Gloucester
Stow
Tintern Abbey
Cirencester
St. Fagans Folk Museum
Cardiff
Newport
Swindon
Bristol
Bath
Avebury
EXMOOR
Wells
Clovelly
Barnstaple
Glastonbury
Taunton
Westbury
Stourhead Gardens
Stonehenge
Salisbury
DEVON
Okehampton
Tintagel
Exeter
Lyme Regis
DORSET
Dorchester
Lyme Bay
Bournemouth
CORNWALL
DARTMOOR
Eden Project
Truro
Weymouth
St. Ives
Plymouth
Ivybridge
Torquay
ISLE OF WIGHT
Penzance
Dartmouth
Land's End
Falmouth
St. Michael's Mount
Trebah Garden
ISLES OF SCILLY
To Roscoff & Cherbourg, France
To Guernsey, Channel Islands
M1
M2
M74
M6
M5
M4

ENGLAND
Freeway/Motorway
Major Rail Line
Airport
York Recommended Location*
Bristol Just Passing Through**
National Park/ Natural Wonder
Ruin, Museum, other Point of Interest
Castle/Monument/Palace
* Black locations are places of touristic interest, sized by importance.
** Gray locations are places of little or no touristic interest and are sized by population.
0 km 50 km 100 km
0 miles 50 miles
To Bergen, Norway
Berwick-upon-Tweed
Holy Island
Bamburgh Castle
Alnwick
Newcastle-upon-Tyne
Beamish Open-Air Museum
Durham
A1
Middlesbrough
Staithes
Whitby
NORTH YORK MOORS
Robin Hood's Bay
Thirsk
Pickering
Scarborough
Eden Camp
Castle Howard
Bridlington
York
Leeds
Doncaster
M62
Kingston-upon-Hull
Sheffield
M1
Great Grimsby
North Sea
MIDLANDS
Lincoln
Newark
Skegness
Derby
Nottingham
Boston
ENGLAND
Cromer
Leicester
Stamford
King's Lynn
Peterborough
Norwich
To Esbjerg, Denmark
Coventry
Great Yarmouth
Warwick
Ely
EAST ANGLIA
Stratford
Northampton
Cambridge
WOLDS
Moreton
Luton
Ipswich
M40
Stansted
To Hoek van Holland, Netherlands
Blenheim Palace
Oxford
Hertford
Harwich
M11
Colchester
Didcot
London
Windsor
Reading
City
Southend-on-Sea
Greenwich
Heathrow
Whitstable
M3
Ramsgate
M23
M20
M2
KENT
Canterbury
Ostende
Bruges
Dover
Winchester
Gatwick
Ashford
E40
Sissinghurst Gardens
Southampton
Arundel Castle
Folkestone
Dunkerque
Channel Tunnel
BELGIUM
Portsmouth
Brighton
Battle
Rye
Calais
Hastings
Newport
Newhaven
Eastbourne
E17
Boulogne
Beachy Head
FRANCE
Channel
Lille
E42
A26
A16
To Cherbourg, France
To Ouistreham, France
To Dieppe, France
To Paris

SWITZERLAND
LIECH.
ITALY
FRANCE
MONACO
Ligurian Sea
Mediterranean Sea
CORSICA (France)
SARDINIA (Italy)
Neuchâtel
Murten
Bern
Luzern
Lake Luzern
Vaduz
Brenner Pass
Vipiteno
Reifenstein Castle
Lac de Neuchâtel
Avenches
Fribourg
Brienz
Interlaken
Spiez
Gruyères
Lausanne
BERNER OBERLAND
Mt. Schilthorn
Gimmelwald
Mt. Jungfrau
Glacier Express
Lac Léman
Montreux
Château Chillon
TICINO
St. Moritz
Pontresina
Glurns
Merano
Castelrotto
Bolzano
ALPE DI SIUSI
Bernina Express
TRENTINO ALTO ADIGE
Adige
Trento
Locarno
Saas Fee
Domodossola
Matterhorn
Zermatt
Lugano
Lago di Como
Menaggio
Varenna
Bellagio
Lago Lugano
Lago Maggiore
Chamonix
Aiguille du Midi
Breuil-Cervinia
Mont Blanc
Courmayeur
Stresa
Chiasso
Como
Lecco
Lago d'Iseo
Lago di Garda
Riva
Lago di Orta
Pré Didier
Aosta
AOSTA
Bergamo
Orio al Serio
Monza
Malpensa
Milan
Linate
Brescia
Sirmione
Verona
Vicenza
Desenzano
Catullo
LOMBARDY
Mantua
Cremona
Po
Modane
Turin
Piacenza
Briançon
PIEDMONT
Asti
Parma
EMILIA ROMAGNA
Modena
Reggio Emilia
Bologna
Alba
Barolo
Monte Viso
Genoa
Cuneo
Santa Margherita Ligure
Sestri Levante
Levanto
Monterosso
Vernazza
Camogli
San Fruttuoso
Portofino
CINQUE TERRE
APUAN ALPS
La Spezia
Carrara
Portovenere
LIGURIA
Colle di Tonda Pass
Finale
Pistoia
Amerigo Vespucci
Fiesole
Lucca
Florence
Viareggio
Pisa
Arno
CHIANTI
Galileo
Livorno
San Gimignano
Volterra
TUSCANY
Siena
Montalcino
Vence
St. Paul
Ventimiglia
Nice
Villefranche
Antibes
Cannes
St. Tropez
COTE D'AZUR
CAPRAIA
VIA AURELIA
ELBA
Bastia
L'Ile Rousse
To Marseille, France
Ajaccio
Bonifacio
MADDALENA
S. Teresa
EMERALD COAST
ASINARA
Porto Torres
Sassari
Grotto of Neptune
A1
A3
A12
A2
A9
A40
A22
A5
A8
A4
A21
A32
A6
A7
A26
A15
A13
A14
A10
A11
S68
S222

ITALY
Freeway/Autostrada
Major Road
Major Rail Line
Airport
Naples Recommended Location*
Genoa Just Passing Through**
Ruin, Museum, other Point of Interest
0 km
50 kilometers
0 miles
50 miles
AUSTRIA
Klagenfurt
San Candido
Cortina
Tarvisio
JULIAN ALPS
Bled
Brnik Airport
Lake Bohinj
Lake Bled
Ljubljana
DOLOMITES
Calalzo
FRIULI
Udine
SLOVENIA
Palmanova
Postojna Caves
Aquileia
Skocjan Caves
Asolo
Grado
Lipica
Trieste
Treviso
Piran
Marco Polo
Venice
Padua
Rijeka
Pazin
ISTRIA
KRK
Chioggia
Po
Pula
CRES
RAB
BOSNIA & HERZ.
Ferrara
CROATIA
Ravenna
Adriatic Sea
Zadar
DUGI OTOK
Rimini
SAN MARINO
Pesaro
Sibenik
Split
Trogir
San Leo
Rubicon
Urbino
Falconara
Ancona
LE MARCHE
Sansepolcro
BRAC
HVAR
Arezzo
Gubbio
Macerata
Cortona
To Dubrovnik, Croatia
Monte-pulciano
L. Trasimeno
Assisi
Perugia
Spello
Pienza
Deruta
Ascoli Piceno
Bevagna
Montefalco
Chiusi
UMBRIA
Orvieto
Todi
Spoleto
Mt. Gran Sasso
Pitigliano
Bagnoregio & Civita
Pescara
To Patras, Greece
Lago di Bolsena
Terni
ABRUZZO
Viterbo
Rieti
L'Aquila
Chieti
Orte
Tiber
Tarquinia
Termoli
LAZIO
Cerveteri
Tivoli
Hadrian's Villa
ABRUZZO NAT'L PARK
GARGANO PENINSULA
VATICAN CITY
Rome
MOLISE
Manfredonia
Fiumicino
Ostia Antica
Ciampino
Isernia
Campobasso
Foggia
Montecassino
Tyrrenhian Sea
Latina
Anzio
PUGLIA
Formia
Caserta
CAMPANIA
BASILICATA
Naples
Mt. Vesuvius
Pompeii
Herculaneum
Potenza
PONZA
ISCHIA
Positano
Sorrento
Amalfi
CAPRI
AMALFI COAST
Paestum
to Sicily

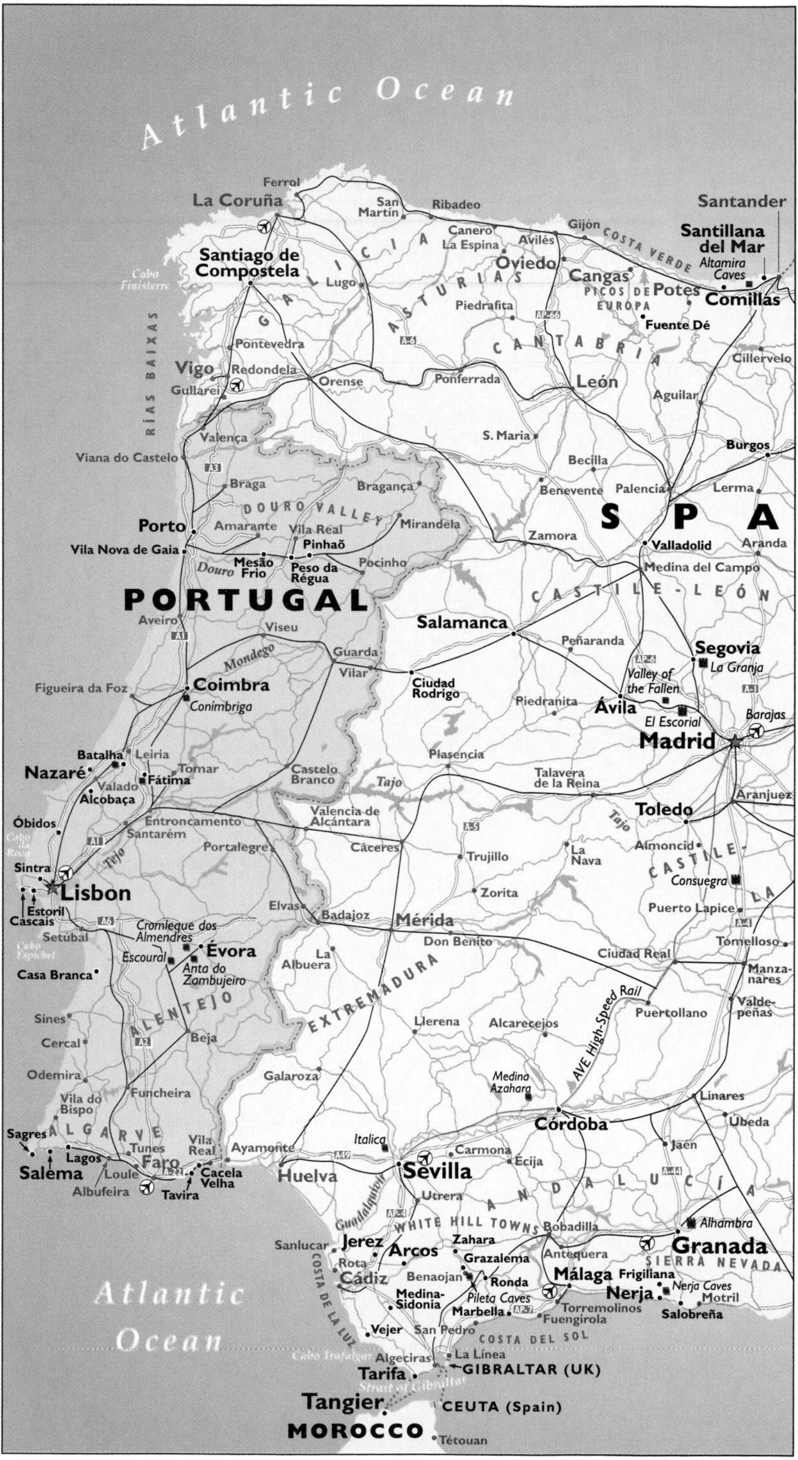

Atlantic Ocean
Ferrol
La Coruña
San Martín
Ribadeo
Santander
Santiago de Compostela
Cabo Finisterre
GALICIA
Lugo
Canero
La Espina
Gijón
COSTA VERDE
Avilés
Oviedo
ASTURIAS
Santillana del Mar
Altamira Caves
Cangas
PICOS DE EUROPA
Potes
Comillas
Piedrafita
AP-66
Fuente Dé
RÍAS BAIXAS
Pontevedra
A-6
CANTABRIA
Cillervelo
Vigo
Redondela
Gullarei
Orense
Ponferrada
León
Aguilar
Valença
S. Maria
Burgos
Viana do Castelo
A3
Becilla
Braga
Bragança
Benevente
Palencia
Lerma
DOURO VALLEY
Mirandela
SPA
Porto
Amarante
Vila Real
Zamora
Pinhaõ
Valladolid
Aranda
Vila Nova de Gaia
Mesão Frio
Peso da Régua
Pocinho
Medina del Campo
Douro
PORTUGAL
CASTILE-LEÓN
Aveiro
Viseu
Salamanca
A1
Peñaranda
Segovia
Mondego
Guarda
AP-6
La Granja
Vilar
Ciudad Rodrigo
Valley of the Fallen
Figueira da Foz
Coimbra
A-1
Conímbriga
Piedranita
Ávila
Barajas
El Escorial
Madrid
Batalha
Leiria
Plasencia
Nazaré
Tomar
Castelo Branco
Valado
Fátima
Talavera de la Reina
Tajo
Alcobaça
Aranjuez
Valencia de Alcántara
Toledo
Óbidos
Entroncamento
Cabo da Roca
A1
Santarém
A-5
Tajo
Portalegre
Cáceres
Almoncid
Tejo
Trujillo
La Nava
CASTILE-LA
Sintra
Consuegra
Lisbon
Zorita
Estoril
Cascais
Elvas
Badajoz
Mérida
Puerto Lapice
A6
Cromleque dos Almendres
A-4
Setúbal
Don Benito
Tomelloso
Cabo Espichel
Évora
La Albuera
Ciudad Real
Escoural
Anta do Zambujeiro
Manzanares
Casa Branca
EXTREMADURA
Rail
Valdepeñas
ALENTEJO
AVE High-Speed
Puertollano
Sines
Llerena
Alcarecejos
A2
Beja
Cercal
Odemira
Galaroza
Medina Azahara
Vila do Bispo
Funcheira
Linares
Sagres
ALGARVE
Córdoba
Úbeda
Tunes
Vila Real
Ayamonte
Italica
Carmona
Jaén
Lagos
Salema
Faro
A49
Écija
Loule
A-22
Cacela Velha
Huelva
Sevilla
A-44
Albufeira
Tavira
Utrera
ANDALUCÍA
Guadalquivir
AP-4
WHITE HILL TOWNS
Bobadilla
Alhambra
Sanlucar
Jerez
Zahara
Granada
Arcos
Rota
Grazalema
Antequera
SIERRA NEVADA
COSTA DE LA LUZ
Cádiz
Benaojan
Ronda
Málaga
Frigiliana
Atlantic Ocean
Medina-Sidonia
Pileta Caves
Nerja
Nerja Caves
Motril
Marbella
AP-7
Torremolinos
Salobreña
Fuengirola
Vejer
San Pedro
COSTA DEL SOL
Cabo Trafalgar
Algeciras
La Línea
Tarifa
GIBRALTAR (UK)
Strait of Gibraltar
Tangier
CEUTA (Spain)
MOROCCO
Tétouan

SPAIN
To Plymouth, England
To Portsmouth, England
To Paris
To Lyon and Paris
Bay of Biscay
Bordeaux
Libourne
St. Emilion
Périgueux
Brive-la-Gaillarde
DORDOGNE
Dordogne
Sarlat
Le Buisson
Beynac
Aurillac
Lot
Rodez
Cahors
DUNE DU PILAT
Garonne
AQUITAINE
Agen
Montauban
Millau
Tarn
Albi
St. Jean-de-Luz
Dax
FRANCE
Toulouse
Castres
To Nice
Lekeitio
Bilbao
San Sebastián
Biarritz
Bayonne
Guérnica
Irun
Hendaye
Bilbao Guggenheim Museum
BASQUE
St. Jean-Pied-du-Port
Pau
Lourdes
Tarbes
LANGUEDOC
Minerve
Carcassonne
Narbonne
Miranda de Ebro
Vitoria
Pamplona
Canfranc
CIRQUE DE GAVARNIE
Foix
Haro
RIOJA
Logroño
PYRENÉES
Jaca
ORDESA NAT'L PARK
Perpignan
ANDORRA
Santo Domingo de la Calzada
Torla
Ainsa
Andorra la Vella
La Tour
Collioure
Castejón
Cerbère
Puigcerda
Portbou
IN
ARAGÓN
Ebro
Huesca
Figueres
Dali Museum
Cadaqués
Soria
Barbastro
Girona
Tossa
Duero
Zaragoza
Lérida
CATALUNYA
COSTA BRAVA
AVE High-Speed Rail
Almazan
Calatayud
Montserrat
Mataró
Siguenza
Ebro
Vilafranca
Barcelona
Daroca
El Prat de Llobregat
Sitges
Molina
Alcañiz
Tarragona
Montalbán
Guadalajara
Monreal
Tortosa
COSTA DORADA
Delta del Ebro
Sacedon
Morella
Teruel
Vinarós
Cuenca
Torrebaja
Alcazar
Ferries to Menorca
MANCHA
Castelló de la Plana
Motilla
BALEARIC ISLANDS
Requena
Sagunto
MALLORCA
Valencia
Palma
Sotuélamos
Albacete
IBIZA
Alzira
Gandla
CABRERA
Alcaraz
Dénia
Ibiza
Alcoy
Jávea
Elche
FORMENTERA
Jumilla
Elda
Benidorm
MURCIA
Alicante
Caravaca
Elche
COSTA BLANCA
Murcia
Cúllar Baza
Lorca
Cartagena
La Manga
MTNS.
Mojacar
Almería
Mediterranean Sea
A8
A68
AP-1
A15
A63
A62
N20
A71
A61
A64
A9
AP-7
A-2
A2
A31
A24 Freeway
Major Rail Line
Airport
Tarifa Recommended Location
Cádiz Just Passing Through
National Park/Natural Wonder
Ruin, Museum, other Point of Interest
Castle, Monument, Palace
0 50 100 km
0 50 100 mi

LOW COUNTRIES
A7 Freeway
Major Rail Line
Ferry Lines
Airport
Haarlem Recommended Location*
Nijmegen Just Passing Through**
Ruin, Museum, other Point of Interest
* Black locations are places of interest to tourists, sized by importance. Many are covered in this guidebook.
** Gray locations are places of little or no interest to tourists and are sized by population.
0 km
50 km
100 km
0 mi
50 mi
North Sea
Wadden Islands
Waddenzee
Emden
Groningen
Leeuwarden
Afsluitdijk
Den Helder
Hindeloopen
NETHERLANDS
Medemblik
Open-Air Museum
Enkhuizen
Alkmaar
Hoorn
Edam
Zaanse Schans
Lelystad
Flevoland
Haarlem
Keukenhof
Amsterdam
Bad Bentheim
Aalsmeer
Schiphol
Hengelo
Scheveningen
Leiden
The Hague
Utrecht
Kröller-Muller Museum
Delft
Open-Air Museum
To Harwich, England
Hoek van Holland
Rotterdam
Arnhem
Waal
Nijmegen
Emmerich
Maas
Rhine
Delta Expo
Middelburg
Eindhoven
Essen
Duisburg
To Dover, England
Zeebrugge
Bruges
Ostende
Antwerp
Venlo
Düsseldorf
FLANDERS
Flanders Fields Museum
Ieper
Ghent
Brussels
GERMANY
Hasselt
Maastricht
Köln
Waterloo
Leuven
Aachen
Tournai
Lille
BELGIUM
Liege
Rhine
Remagen
Meuse
Namur
Mons
Arras
Cambrai
Aulnoye
Dinant
WALLONIE
La Roche
Cochem
Bastogne
Zell
FRANCE
Vianden
ARDENNES
LUXEMBOURG
Mosel
St. Quentin
Charleville Mézières
Trier
Laon
Luxembourg City
Soissons
Longwy
Senlis
Thionville
Reims
Verdun Battlefield
Saarbrücken
Charles de Gaulle
A7
A28
A31
A1
A30
A2
A12
A15
A16
A27
A3
A57
A58
A73
A67
E40
E313
E17
E42
A26
E25
A4
A61

Rick Steves'®

BEST OF EUROPE 2008

CONTENTS

INTRODUCTION

Big Ben, the Eiffel Tower, and the Roman Colosseum. Yodeling in the Alps, biking down cobblestone paths, and taking a canal ride under the stars. Michelangelo's *David* and "Mad" King Ludwig's castles. Sunny Riviera beaches, medieval German towns, and Spanish streets that teem with people at night. Pasta and bratwurst, strudel and scones, Parisian crêpes and Tuscan grapes....

Europe offers a rich smorgasbord of cultures. To wrestle it down to a manageable size, this book breaks Europe into its top destinations. It then gives you all the information and opinions necessary to wring the maximum value out of your limited time and money in each location. If you plan to stay for two months or less in Europe, this book is all you need for a blitz trip.

Experiencing Europe's culture, people, and natural wonders economically and hassle-free has been my goal for 30 years of traveling, tour guiding, and travel writing. With this book, I pass on to you the lessons I've learned, updated for 2008.

Rick Steves' Best of Europe is the crème de la crème of places featured in my Country Guides. It's balanced to include a comfortable mix of exciting cities and cozy towns: from Paris, London, and Rome to traffic-free Italian Riviera ports, alpine villages, and mom-and-pop châteaux. It covers the predictable biggies and mixes in a healthy dose of Back Door intimacy. Along with Leonardo in the Louvre, you'll enjoy Caterina in her cantina. I've been selective. For example, rather than listing countless medieval towns, I recommend only the best.

The best is, of course, only my opinion. But after three decades of travel research, I've developed a sixth sense for what travelers enjoy.

About This Book

This book is organized by destinations. I cover each destination as a mini-vacation on its own, filled with exciting sights and homey, affordable places to stay. In each chapter, you'll find:

Planning Your Time contains a suggested schedule, with thoughts on how to best use your limited time.

Orientation includes tourist information, city transportation, and an easy-to-read map designed to make the text clear and your arrival smooth.

Sights are rated as follows:

▲▲▲—Don't miss.
▲▲—Try hard to see.
▲—Worthwhile if you can make it.
No rating—Worth knowing about.

Sleeping and Eating includes descriptions, addresses, and phone numbers of my favorite good-value hotels and restaurants.

Transportation Connections covers how to reach nearby destinations by train or bus.

The **appendix** has a climate chart, a calendar, and information on US embassies for the countries in this book.

Browse through this book, choose your favorite destinations, and create your own itinerary. Then have a great trip! You'll travel like a temporary local, getting the most out of every mile, minute, and dollar.

PLANNING

Trip Costs

Five components make up your trip cost: airfare, surface transportation, room and board, sightseeing and entertainment, and shopping and miscellany.

Airfare: A basic round-trip US-to-Europe flight costs around $700–1,000 (cheaper in winter), depending on where you fly from and when. Consider saving time and money in Europe by flying "open jaw" (flying into one city and out of another, such as flying into London and out of Rome).

Surface Transportation: Your best mode of travel depends on the time you have and the scope of your trip. For many, the best option is a Eurailpass. Note that train passes are generally only available outside of Europe. You may save money by simply buying tickets as you go (for more information, see "Traveling by Train," on page 8).

Drivers can figure $250 per person per week (based on two people splitting the cost of the car, tolls, gas, and insurance). For trips over three weeks, leasing is cheaper. Car rental is cheapest to arrange from the US; for trips over three weeks.

European Almanac

Population: The European Union (EU) has 496 million (the US has 301 million, and all of Europe, including the non-EU countries, numbers 728 million).

Area: The EU countries measure 915,000 square miles (roughly half of the continental US).

Languages: Three main groups: Romance (Italian, Spanish, French), Slavic (Eastern Europe and Russia), and Germanic (German, Dutch, Scandinavian...and English). Most popular second languages are English and French.

Climate: Moderate, warmed by prevailing westerly sea winds. Average of about 65°F in summer, 40°F in winter.

Vegetation: In the north, a mix of conifers (pine and fir) and deciduous trees (oak, elm, and maple). Along the Mediterranean, there are olives, figs, and grapes.

Major Rivers: Danube, Rhine, Rhône, Po, and Seine.

Life Expectancy: About 77 years, among the highest in the world.

Religion: Largely Protestant in the North, Catholic in the South. Many Europeans claim no church affiliation.

Government: The EU is a federation of independent nations. Formed as an economic trade bloc, it is increasingly a political body with elected representatives.

Gross Domestic Product: The EU's nominal GDP is $13 trillion (about the same as the US).

Room and Board: You can easily manage in Europe in 2008 on an overall average of $100 a day per person for room and board (more for cities, less for towns). A $100-a-day budget allows $10 for lunch, $5 for snacks, $20 for dinner, and $65 for lodging (based on two people splitting the cost of a $130 double room that includes breakfast). That's doable. Students and tightwads can do it on $50 ($25 per bed, $25 for meals and snacks).

Sightseeing and Entertainment: In big cities, figure $5–10 per major sight, $3 for minor ones, and $25 for splurge experiences (e.g., tours, concerts, gelato binges). An overall average of $15 a day works for most. Don't skimp here. After all, this category is the driving force behind your trip—you came to sightsee, enjoy, and experience Europe.

Shopping and Miscellany: Figure $1 per postcard and $2 per coffee, beer, and ice-cream cone. Shopping can vary in cost from nearly nothing to a small fortune. Good budget travelers find that this category has little to do with assembling a trip full of lifelong and wonderful memories.

When to Go

May, June, September, and October are the best travel months. Peak season, July and August, offers the sunniest weather and the most exciting slate of activities—but the worst crowds. During this busy time, it's best to reserve rooms well in advance, particularly in big cities.

During the off-season, October through April, expect generally shorter hours at attractions, more closures for lunchtime (especially at smaller sights), fewer activities, and fewer—if any—guided tours in English. Especially off-season, be sure to confirm opening hours for sights at local tourist information offices.

As a general rule any time of year, the climate north of the Alps is mild (like Seattle), while south of the Alps it's like Arizona. For specifics, see the Climate Chart in the appendix. If you wilt in the heat, avoid the Mediterranean in summer. If you want blue skies in the Alps, Britain, and Scandinavia, travel during the height of summer.

Plan your itinerary to meet your needs. To beat the heat, start in the south in the spring and work your way north. To moderate culture shock, start in Britain and travel south and east. You can minimize exposure to crowds by remembering that touristy places in the core of Europe—Germany, the Alps, France, and Italy—are the most crowded.

Sightseeing Priorities

Only have a week to "see" Europe? You can't, of course, but if you're organized and energetic, you can see the two art-filled cultural capitals of London and Paris plus Europe's most magnificent landscape—the Swiss Alps.

Whether you have a week or longer, here are my recommended priorities. These itineraries are fast-paced, but doable by car or train, and each allows about two nights in each spot (I've taken geographical proximity into account). Most work best if you fly "open jaw."

If you have...

5 days:	Paris, Swiss Alps
7 days, add:	London
10 days, add:	Rome
14 days, add:	Rhine, Amsterdam, Haarlem
17 days, add:	Venice, Florence
21 days, add:	Cinque Terre, Rothenburg, Bavaria
28 days, add:	Bath, Salzburg, Hallstatt, French Riviera
35 days, add:	Provence, Barcelona, Madrid
42 days, add:	Vienna, Prague, Berlin
50 days, add:	Bruges

Europe's Best Destinations

Travel Smart

Your trip to Europe is like a complex play—easier to follow and really appreciate on a second viewing. While no one does the same trip twice to gain that advantage, reading this book's chapters on your intended destinations before your trip accomplishes much the same thing.

As you read this book, note the days of markets and festivals and when sights are closed. When setting up your itinerary, anticipate problem days. On Mondays, many sights are closed in Florence; Tuesdays are bad in Paris. Museums and sights, especially large ones, usually stop admitting people 30–60 minutes before closing time.

Sundays have the same pros and cons as they do for travelers in the US. Sightseeing attractions are generally open, shops and banks are closed, and city traffic is light. Rowdy evenings are rare on Sundays. Saturdays in Europe are virtually weekdays with earlier closing hours. Hotels in tourist areas are most crowded on Fridays and Saturdays.

Be sure to mix intense and relaxed periods in your itinerary. Every trip (and every traveler) needs at least a few slack days. Plan ahead for laundry, picnics, and Internet stops. Pace yourself.

Assume you will return.

As you travel, reread this book, and when you arrive in a new town, visit the local tourist information office. Buy a phone card and use it for reservations, reconfirmations, and double-checking hours. Enjoy the friendliness of the local people. Slow down and ask questions—most locals are eager to point you in their idea of the right direction. Wear your money belt, and learn the local currency and how to estimate prices in dollars. Keep a notepad in your pocket for organizing your thoughts. Those who expect to travel smart, do.

RESOURCES

Tourist Offices in Europe

The local tourist information office (abbreviated as **TI** in this book) is your best first stop in any new city. Try to arrive, or at least telephone, before it closes. TIs throughout Europe are usually well-organized and English-speaking.

As national budgets tighten, many TIs have been privatized. This means they become sales agents for big tours and hotels, and their "information" becomes unavoidably biased. While the TI has listings of all the rooms and is eager to book you one, use their room-finding service only as a last resort. Across Europe, room-finding services are charging commissions from hotels, taking fees from travelers, and blacklisting establishments that resist their rules. They are also not allowed to give opinions on the relative value of one place over another. By using the listings in this book, you can avoid that kind of "help."

More Resources from Rick Steves

Guidebooks and Online Updates

This book is updated every year—but once you pin Europe down, it wiggles. For the latest, visit www.ricksteves.com/update (select the country instead of the book title). Also at my website, you'll find a valuable list of reports and experiences—good and bad—from fellow travelers (www.ricksteves.com/feedback).

This book is only one of a series of 30+ books on European travel that includes country guidebooks, city guidebooks (Paris, London, etc.), and my budget-travel skills handbook, *Rick Steves' Europe Through the Back Door;* all are annually updated. My phrase books—for Italian, French, German, Spanish, and Portuguese—are practical and budget-oriented. My other books are *Europe 101* (a crash course on art and history), *European Christmas* (on traditional and modern-day celebrations), and *Postcards from Europe* (a fun memoir of my travels over 25 years). For a complete list of my books, see the inside of the last page of this book.

Public Television and Radio Shows

My series, *Rick Steves' Europe,* covers European destinations. My weekly public radio show, *Travels with Rick Steves,* features interviews with travel experts from around the world. All the TV scripts and radio shows are at www.ricksteves.com. The radio shows for the countries covered in this book offer hours of practical discussion with local guides; you can listen to the shows at any time—or download them on your MP3 player to take along on your trip.

Other Guidebooks

You may want additional information, especially if you'll be traveling beyond my recommended destinations. When you consider the improvements they'll make in your $3,000 vacation, $25 or $35 for extra maps and books is money well-spent. The weight and expense are negligible, especially for several people traveling by car.

The following series of guidebooks are not updated annually; be sure to check the publication date before you buy. The Lonely Planet guides to various European countries are thorough, well-researched, and packed with good maps and hotel recommendations for low- to moderate-budget travelers. The hip, insightful Rough Guide series (by British researchers) and the highly opinionated Let's Go series (by Harvard students) are great for students and vagabonds. The skinny, green Michelin guides (covering most southern countries and French regions) are excellent, especially if you're driving. They're known for their city and sightseeing maps, dry but concise and helpful information on all major sights, and good cultural and historical background. You can buy English editions at tourist shops and gas stations.

Maps

The maps in this book are drawn by Dave Hoerlein, who is well-traveled in Europe. Dave's maps help you locate recommended places and get to the tourist offices, where you can pick up a more in-depth map (usually free) of the city or region. More detailed maps are also sold at newsstands and bookstores—look before you buy to be sure the map has the level of detail you want. For drivers, I'd recommend a 1:200,000- or 1:300,000-scale map for each country.

TRANSPORTATION

By Car or Train?

Each has pros and cons. Cars are an expensive headache in big cities, but let you delve deep into the countryside. Groups of three or more travel cheaper by car, and if you're packing heavy (with kids), go by car. Trains are best for city-to-city travel and give you the convenience of doing long stretches overnight. By train, I arrive relaxed and well rested—not so by car. A EurailDrive pass allows you to mix train and car travel. When thoughtfully used, this pass economically gives you the best of both transportation worlds.

Traveling by Train

A major mistake Americans make is relating public transportation in Europe to the pathetic public transportation they're used to at home. By rail, you'll have Europe by the tail. While many people simply buy tickets as they go ("point to point"), the various train passes give you the simplicity of ticket-free, unlimited travel, and depending on how many trips you do, often offer a tremendous savings over regular point-to-point tickets.

Europe by Rail: Dollars and Time

For a summary of railpass deals and point-to-point ticket options (available in the US and in Europe), check our free Railpass Guide at www.ricksteves.com/rail. The Eurailpass gives you several choices. If you decide to get a railpass, this guide will help you

Europe by Rail: Dollars and Hours

Connect the dots, add up the cost, and see if a railpass is right for your trip.

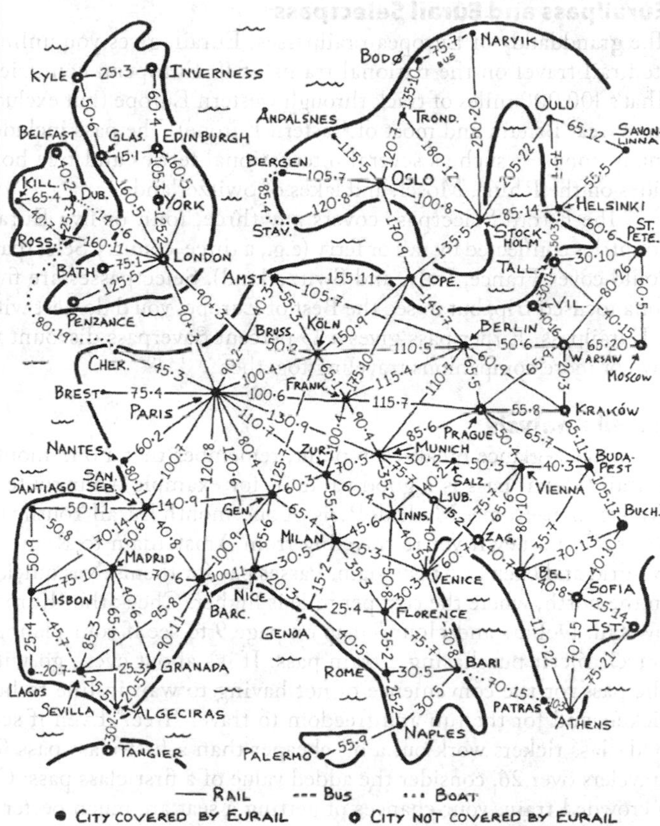

First number between cities = Approximate cost in US dollars for a one-way, second class ticket. **Second number** = Number of hours the trip takes.

Important: These fares and times are based on European web sources. Actual prices may vary due to currency fluctuations and local promotions. Local competition can cut the actual price of some boat crossings (from Italy to Greece, for example) by 50 percent or more. For approximate first-class rail prices, add 50 percent. Travel times and fares are for express trains where applicable.

know you're getting the right one for your trip. To study train schedules in advance on the Web, look up http://bahn.hafas.de/bin/query.exe/en (Germany's excellent all-Europe timetable).

Eurailpass and Eurail Selectpass

The granddaddy of European railpasses, Eurail, gives you unlimited rail travel on the national trains of 18 European countries. That's 100,000 miles of track through western Europe (but excluding Great Britain and most of Eastern Europe). The pass includes many bonuses, such as several international ferries and free boat rides on the Rhine, Mosel, and lakes of Switzerland.

The Eurail Selectpass covers any three, four, or five Eurail countries connected by rail or ferry (e.g., a three-country Selectpass could cover France, Italy, and Switzerland). Selectpasses are fine for a focused trip, but to see the Best of Europe, you'd do best with a Eurailpass. Either pass gives a 15 percent Saverpass discount to two or more companions traveling together.

Eurail Analysis

For an at-a-glance break-even point, remember that a one-month Eurail Global pass is a good value if, for example, your route is Amsterdam–Rome–Madrid–Paris. A one-month Eurail Youthpass saves you money if you're traveling from Amsterdam to Rome to Madrid and back to Amsterdam. Passes pay for themselves quicker in the north, where the cost per mile is higher. Check the "Europe by Rail: Dollars and Hours" map on page 9 to see if your planned travels merit purchasing a train pass. If it's about even, go with the pass for the convenience of not having to wait in line to buy tickets and for the fun and freedom to travel "free." Even if second-class tickets work out a bit cheaper than a first-class pass for travelers over 26, consider the added value of a first-class pass: On a crowded train, your chances of getting a seat are much better if your pass allows you to sit anywhere on the train.

Using one Eurailpass versus a series of country passes: While nearly every country has its own mini-version of the Eurailpass, trips covering several countries are usually cheapest with the budget whirlwind traveler's old standby, the Eurail Global Pass, or its cousin, the Eurail Selectpass. The reason is that the more rail days that are included in a pass, the cheaper your per-day cost. A group of country passes with a few rail days apiece will have a high per-day cost, while a Eurailpass with a longer life span offers a better deal overall. However, if you're traveling in a single country, an individual country railpass (such as the France or the Germany pass) is often a better value than any of the Eurail passes.

EurailDrive Pass: The EurailDrive Pass is for those who want to combine train travel with the freedom of having a car a day here and a day there. Great areas for a day of joyriding include the Dutch countryside, Germany's Rhine or Bavaria, France's Provence, Italy's Tuscany and Umbria, and the Alps (for "car hiking"). When comparing prices, remember that each day of car rental comes with about $30 of extra expenses (CDW insurance, gas, parking), which you can divide among the people in your party.

Renting a Car

Your American driver's license is all you need in most European countries. Confirm with your rental company if an international license is required in the countries you plan to visit. Those traveling in Austria, Germany, Italy, Spain, and Eastern Europe should probably get an international driver's license (available at your local AAA office—$15 plus the cost of two passport-type photos—see www.aaa.com).

I use the freeways whenever possible. They're free in the Netherlands and Germany; you'll pay for a road-fee decal to display in your window as you enter Switzerland (about $30), Austria (about $10), and the Czech Republic (about $8). The Italian autostradas and French autoroutes are punctuated by tollbooths (charging about $1 for every 10 minutes).

Parking is a costly headache in big cities. You'll pay about $20 a day to park safely. Ask at your hotel for advice. I keep a pile of coins in my ashtray for parking meters, public phones, launderettes, and wishing wells.

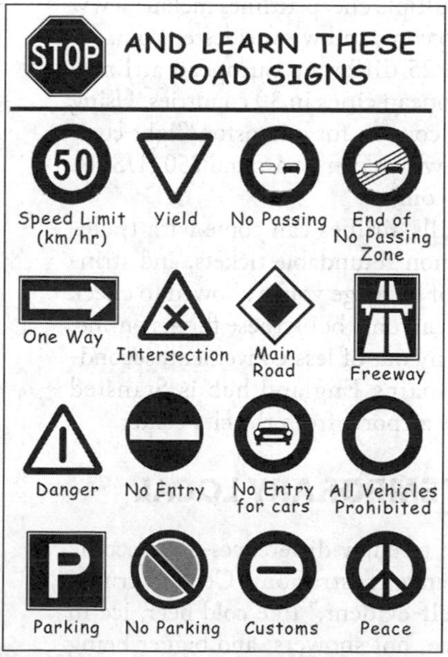

If you'll be traveling from Western to Eastern Europe—to Prague, for example—tell the rental company. Many companies have additional rules and required documentation for eastward excursions (for example, you can only take cheaper cars, and you may have to pay extra insurance fees). Ask your car-rental company.

When you rent a car, you are liable for a very high deductible, sometimes equal to the entire value of the car. There are various ways you can limit your financial risk in case of an accident. You have three main options: buy

STOP AND LEARN THESE ROAD SIGNS

50
Speed Limit (km/hr)
Yield
No Passing
End of No Passing Zone
One Way
Intersection
Main Road
Freeway
Danger
No Entry
No Entry for cars
All Vehicles Prohibited
P
Parking
No Parking
Customs
Peace

Collision Damage Waiver insurance from the car-rental company; get coverage through your credit card if your card automatically includes zero-deductible coverage; or buy protection from Travel Guard, which sells collision insurance at very affordable rates (tel. 800-826-4919, www.travelguard.com). Buying CDW insurance is the easiest but priciest option. Using the coverage that comes with your credit card is cheaper, but can involve more hassle. If you're taking a short trip (but not in Italy or Ireland), the cheapest solution is to buy Travel Guard's very affordable CDW. For more information on CDW insurance, see www.ricksteves.com/cdw. For trips of at least three weeks, leasing—which includes taxes and insurance—is the best way to go.

Note that if you'll be driving in Italy, theft insurance (separate from CDW insurance) is mandatory. The insurance usually costs about $10–15 a day, payable when you pick up the car.

Cheap Flights

Connecting your itinerary by air is cheaper than you might think. Thanks to Europe's new budget airlines, you can get between many European cities for significantly less than $100 one-way. Some amazing promotional deals can even bring fares down into the single digits. The best deals are from major hub cities.

New budget airlines are continually being launched, but a handful of them are more established, including easyJet (www.easyjet.com) and Ryanair (www.ryanair.com). Some good websites you can use to search routes on multiple cheap airlines include www.skyscanner.net, www.mobissimo.com, and www.sidestep.com.

Europe by Air works with 25 different European airlines, offering flights between 150 European cities in 30 countries. Using their "Flight Pass" system, each coupon for a nonstop flight costs $99 plus taxes and airport fees—which can be around $50 (US tel. 888-321-4737, www.europebyair.com).

Be warned that these no-frills airlines can come with trade-offs: minimal customer service, non-refundable tickets, and stringent restrictions on the amount of baggage you're allowed to check without paying extra. Often you can only book these flights online. Also note that you'll sometimes fly out of less convenient, secondary airports. For example, Ryanair's England hub is Stansted Airport, the farthest of London's airports from the city center.

TRAVELING AS A TEMPORARY LOCAL

We travel all the way to Europe to enjoy differences—to become temporary locals. You'll experience frustrations. Certain truths that we find "God-given" or "self-evident," like cold beer, ice in drinks, bottomless cups of coffee, hot showers, and bigger being better, are suddenly not so true. One of the benefits of travel is the eye-opening realization that there are logical, civil, and even better alternatives. A willingness to go local ensures that you'll enjoy a full dose of local hospitality.

If there is a negative aspect to the European image of Americans, we can appear aggressive, impolite, rich, loud, superficially friendly, and a bit naive. Americans tend to be noisy in public places, such as restaurants and trains. Our raised voices can demolish Europe's reserved ambience. Talk softly. While Europeans look bemusedly at some of our Yankee excesses—and worriedly at others—they nearly always afford us individual travelers all the warmth we deserve.

While updating this book, I heard over and over again that my readers are considerate and fun to have as guests. Thank you for traveling as temporary locals who are sensitive to the culture. It's fun to follow you in my travels.

Judging from all the positive comments I receive from travelers who have used this book, it's safe to assume you'll enjoy a great, affordable vacation—with the finesse of an experienced, independent traveler. Thanks, and happy travels!

BACK DOOR TRAVEL PHILOSOPHY

From *Rick Steves' Europe Through the Back Door*

Travel is intensified living—maximum thrills per minute and one of the last great sources of legal adventure. Travel is freedom. It's recess, and we need it.

Experiencing the real Europe requires catching it by surprise, going casual..."Through the Back Door."

Affording travel is a matter of priorities. (Make do with the old car.) You can travel—simply, safely, and comfortably—anywhere in Europe for $100 a day plus transportation costs. In many ways, spending more money only builds a thicker wall between you and what you came to see. Europe is a cultural carnival, and, time after time, you'll find that its best acts are free and the best seats are the cheap ones.

A tight budget forces you to travel close to the ground, meeting and communicating with the people, not relying on service with a purchased smile. Never sacrifice sleep, nutrition, safety, or cleanliness in the name of budget. Simply enjoy the local-style alternatives to expensive hotels and restaurants.

Extroverts have more fun. If your trip is low on magic moments, kick yourself and make things happen. If you don't enjoy a place, maybe you don't know enough about it. Seek the truth. Recognize tourist traps. Give a culture the benefit of your open mind. See things as different but not better or worse. Any culture has much to share.

Of course, travel, like the world, is a series of hills and valleys. Be fanatically positive and militantly optimistic. If something's not to your liking, change your liking. Travel is addictive. It can make you a happier American as well as a citizen of the world. Our Earth is home to six and a half billion equally important people. It's humbling to travel and find that people don't envy Americans. Europeans like us, but, with all due respect, they wouldn't trade passports.

Globe-trotting destroys ethnocentricity. It helps you understand and appreciate different cultures. Regrettably, there are forces in our society that want you dumbed down for their convenience. Don't let it happen. Thoughtful travel engages you with the world—more important than ever these days. Travel changes people. It broadens perspectives and teaches new ways to measure quality of life. Rather than fear the diversity on this planet, travelers celebrate it. Many travelers toss aside their hometown blinders. Their prized souvenirs are the strands of different cultures they decide to knit into their own character. The world is a cultural yarn shop, and Back Door travelers are weaving the ultimate tapestry. Join in!

AUSTRIA

VIENNA

(Wien)

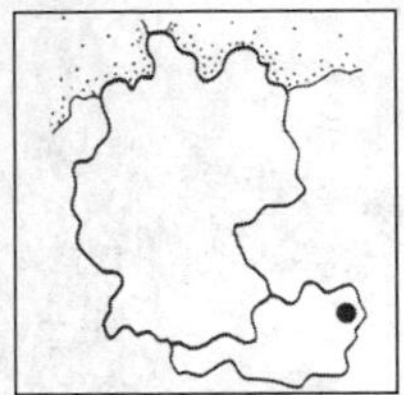

Vienna is a head without a body. For 640 years the capital of the once-grand Hapsburg Empire, she started and lost World War I, and with it her far-flung holdings. Today, you'll find a grand and elegant capital of 1.6 million people (one-fifth of Austria's population) ruling a small, relatively insignificant country. Culturally, historically, and from a sightseeing point of view, this city is the sum of its illustrious past. The city of Freud, Brahms, Maria Theresa's many children, a gaggle of Strausses, and a dynasty of Holy Roman Emperors ranks right up there with Paris, London, and Rome.

Vienna has always been the easternmost city of the West. In Roman times, it was Vindobona, on the Danube facing the Germanic barbarians. In the Middle Ages, Vienna was Europe's bastion against the Ottomans—a Christian breakwater against the riding tide of Islam (hordes of up to 200,000 Ottomans were repelled in 1529 and 1683). During this period, as the Ottomans dreamed of conquering what they called "the big apple" for their sultan, Vienna lived with a constant fear of invasion (and the Hapsburg court ruled from safer Prague). You'll notice none of Vienna's great palaces were built until after 1683, when the Turkish threat was finally over.

While Vienna's old walls held out the Ottomans, World War II bombs destroyed nearly a quarter of the city's buildings. In modern times, neutral Austria took a big bite out of the USSR's Warsaw Pact buffer zone. And today, Vienna is a springboard for newly popular destinations in Eastern Europe.

The truly Viennese person is not Austrian, but a second-generation Hapsburg cocktail, with grandparents from the distant corners of the old empire—Hungary, the Czech Republic, Slovakia, Poland, Slovenia, Croatia, Bosnia, Serbia, Romania, and Italy. Vienna is the melting-pot capital of a now-collapsed empire that, in its heyday, consisted of 60 million people—only eight million of whom were Austrian.

In 1900, Vienna's 2.2 million inhabitants made it the world's fifth-largest city (after New York, London, Paris, and Berlin). But these days—with dogs being the preferred "child" and the average Viennese mother having only 1.3 children—the population is down to around 1.6 million.

The Hapsburgs, who ruled the enormous Austrian Empire from 1273 to 1918, shaped Vienna. Some ad agency has convinced Vienna to make Elisabeth, wife of Emperor Franz Josef—with her narcissism and struggles with royal life—the darling of the local tourist scene. You'll see "Sisi" (SEE-see) all over town. But stay focused on the Hapsburgs who mattered: Maria Theresa (r. 1740–1780) and Franz Josef (r. 1848–1916).

After Napoleon's defeat and the Congress of Vienna in 1815 (which shaped 19th-century Europe), Vienna enjoyed its violin-filled belle époque, which shaped our romantic image of the city: fine wine, chocolates, cafés, and waltzes.

Planning Your Time

For a big city, Vienna is pleasant and laid-back. Packed with sights, it's worth two days and two nights on the speediest trip. To be grand-tour efficient, you could sleep in and sleep out on the train (Berlin, Kraków, Venice, Rome, the Swiss Alps, Paris, and the Rhine Valley are each handy night trains away).

I'd spend two days this way:

Day 1: 9:00–Circle the Ring by tram, following my self-guided tour (page 24); 10:00–Drop by the TI for any planning and ticket needs, then see the sights in Vienna's old center (using my self-guided commentary)—Monument Against War and Fascism, Kaisergruft crypt, Kärntner Strasse, St. Stephen's Cathedral, and Graben; 12:00–Finger sandwiches for lunch at Buffet Trzesniewski; 13:00–Tour the Hofburg and treasury; 16:00–Hit one more museum, or shop, browse, and people-watch; 19:30–Choose classical music (concert or opera), Haus der Musik, or *Heuriger* wine garden.

Day 2: Morning–choose between Schönbrunn Palace (redundant if you saw the Hofburg on Day 1; arrive at 9:00, return to central Vienna by noon) or the Lipizzaner stallions' morning practice (Tue–Sat 10:00–12:00, no practice Sun–Mon); 12:00–Have lunch at Naschmarkt; 13:00–Tour the Opera (check red sign on door for today's schedule); 14:00–Kunsthistorisches Museum; 16:00–Your choice of the many sights left to see in

Vienna; Evening–See Day 1 evening options.

For efficient sightseeing, drivers should note that Schönbrunn Palace is conveniently on the way out of town toward Salzburg.

ORIENTATION

(area code: 01)

Vienna—Wien in German (pronounced "veen")—sits between the Vienna Woods (Wienerwald) and the Danube (Donau). To the southeast is industrial sprawl. The Alps, which arc across Europe from Marseille, end at Vienna's wooded hills, providing a popular playground for walking and sipping new wine. This greenery's momentum carries on into the city. More than half of Vienna is parkland, filled with ponds, gardens, trees, and statue-maker memories of Austria's glory days.

Think of the city map as a target. The bull's-eye is St. Stephen's Cathedral, the first circle is the Ringstrasse, and the second is the Gürtel outerbelt. The old town—snuggling around a towering cathedral south of the Danube—is bound tightly by the Ringstrasse, marking what used to be the city wall. The Gürtel, a broader ring road, contains the rest of downtown.

Addresses start with the district, or *Bezirk,* followed by street and building number. The Ring circles the first *Bezirk.* Any address higher than the ninth *Bezirk* is beyond the Gürtel, far from the center. The middle two digits of Vienna's postal codes show the *Bezirk.* The address "7, Lindengasse 4" is in the seventh district, #4 on Linden street. Its postal code would be 1070.

Nearly all your sightseeing will be done in the core first district or along the Ringstrasse. As a tourist, concern yourself only with this compact old center. When you do, sprawling Vienna suddenly becomes manageable.

Tourist Information

Vienna's one real tourist office is a block behind the Opera at Albertinaplatz (daily 9:00–19:00, tel. 01/24555, press 2 for English info, www.vienna.info). Confirm your sightseeing plans and pick up the free and essential city map with a list of museums and hours (also available at most hotels), the monthly program of concerts (called *Wien-Programm*—details below), the biannual city guide *(Vienna Journal),* and the youth guide *(Vienna Hype).* The TI also books rooms for a €2.90 fee. While hotel and ticket-booking agencies at the train stations and airport can answer questions and give out maps and brochures, I'd rely on the official TI if possible.

The ***Wien-Programm*** monthly entertainment guide is particularly important in Europe's music capital. It includes a daily calendar and information on the contemporary cultural scene, including

Greater Vienna

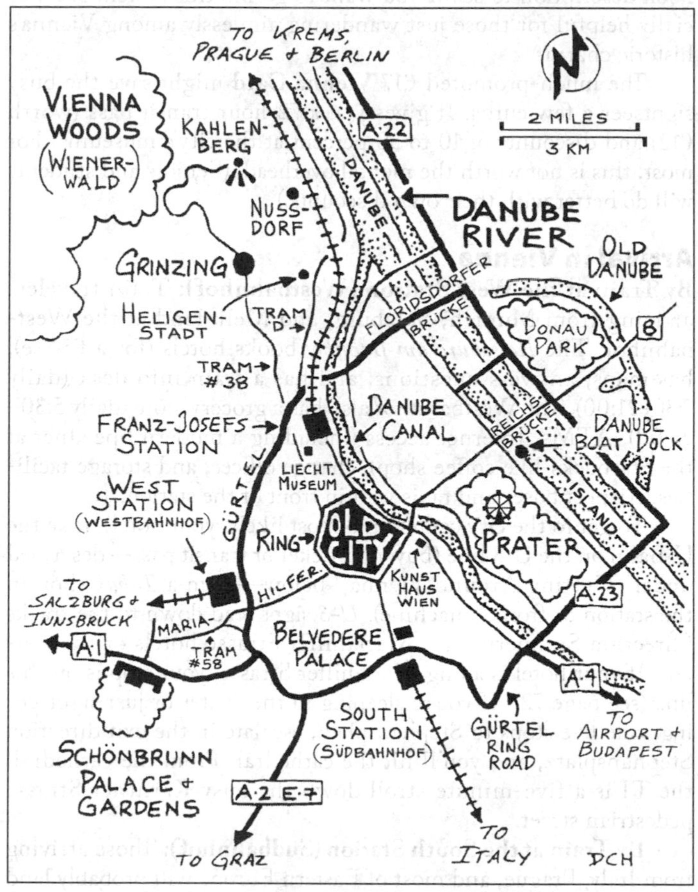

live music, jazz, walks, expositions, and evening museum options. First you see the month's events, then guided walks offered (*E* means in English), then the opera schedule, followed by other theaters and concert halls (with phone numbers to call direct to check seat availability, and to save the 20 percent booking fees you'll pay for buying tickets through an agency). Last is the calendar section (with codes for venues that are all listed—with their phone numbers—on the first page of the section).

Consider the TI's handy €3.60 ***Vienna from A to Z*** booklet. Every important building sports a numbered flag banner that keys into this guidebook. *A to Z* numbers are keyed into the TI's city map. When lost, find one of the "famous-building flags" and match its number to your map. If you're at a famous building, check the map to see what other key numbers are nearby, then check the *A to Z* book description to see if you want to go in. This system is especially helpful for those just wandering aimlessly among Vienna's historic charms.

The much-promoted €17 **Vienna Card** might save the busy sightseer a few euros. It gives you a 72-hour transit pass (worth €12) and discounts of 10 to 50 percent at the city's museums. For most, this is not worth the mental overhead. (Seniors and students will do better with their own discounts.)

Arrival in Vienna

By Train at the West Station (Westbahnhof): Train travelers arriving from Munich, Salzburg, and Melk land at the Westbahnhof. The *Reisebüro am Bahnhof* books hotels (for a €5 fee), has maps, answers questions, and has a train info desk (daily 7:30–21:00). The Westbahnhof also has a grocery store (daily 5:30–23:00), ATMs, Internet access (including a modern Speednet at the Starbucks-like coffee shop), change offices, and storage facilities. Airport buses and taxis wait in front of the station.

To get to the city center (and most likely, your hotel), take the U-Bahn on the U-3 line (buy your ticket or transit pass—described under "Getting Around Vienna," below—from a *Tabak* shop in the station or from a machine). *U-3* signs lead down to the tracks (direction Simmering for Mariahilfer Strasse hotels or the center). If your hotel is along Mariahilfer Strasse, your stop is on this line (see page 72). If you're sleeping in the center or just sightseeing, ride five stops to Stephansplatz, escalate in the exit direction Stephansplatz, and you'll hit the cathedral. From the cathedral, the TI is a five-minute stroll down the busy Kärntner Strasse pedestrian street.

By Train at the South Station (Südbahnhof): Those arriving from Italy, Prague, and most of Eastern Europe will probably land here. The Südbahnhof has all the services, including left luggage and a TI (daily 9:00–19:00). To reach Vienna's center, tram D goes to the Ring (departs every 5 minutes, stops right at the Opera). Bus #13A goes to Mariahilfer Strasse. (You can also take the S- or U-Bahn, but the tram or bus is much easier.)

By Train at Franz Josefs Station: If you're coming from Krems (in the Danube Valley), you'll arrive at Vienna's Franz Josefs station. From here, take tram D into town. Better yet, get off your train at Spittelau (the stop before Franz Josefs) and use its handy U-Bahn station.

By Plane: Vienna International Airport is 12 miles from the center (airport code: VIE, tel. 01/700-722-233, www.viennaairport.com). It's connected to the very central Wien-Mitte station by S-Bahn (S-7 yellow, €3, 2/hr, 24 min) and the newer City Airport Train (CAT, follow green signs, €9, 2/hr, usually departs at :05 and :35, 16 min, www.cityairporttrain.com). Express airport buses (parked immediately in front of the arrival hall, €6, 2/hr, 30 min, buy ticket from driver, note time to destination on curbside TV monitors) go conveniently to Schwedenplatz (for city-center hotels), Westbahnhof (for Mariahilfer Strasse hotels), and Südbahnhof, where it's easy to continue by taxi or public transportation (see above). Taxis into town cost about €35 (including the €11 airport surcharge); taxis also wait at the downtown terminus of each airport transit service. Hotels arrange for fixed-rate car service to the airport (€30, 30-min ride).

Bratislava Airport: Some budget carriers—especially SkyEurope—fly into Bratislava Airport (Letisko Bratislava, airport code: BTS, www.letiskobratislava.sk). This airport is marketed as "Vienna-Bratislava" thanks to its proximity to both capitals (it's six miles northeast of downtown Bratislava). To reach Vienna, there are several buses coordinated to meet SkyEurope flights (€10–15, trip takes about 90 min), or you can take a taxi (figure €60–90, depending on whether you use a Slovak or an Austrian cab). SkyEurope's website has more details (www.skyeurope.com).

Helpful Hints

Money: ATMs are everywhere. Banks are open weekdays roughly from 8:00 to 15:00 (until 17:30 on Thu). After hours, you can change money at train stations, the airport, post offices, or the American Express office (Mon–Fri 9:00–17:30, Sat 9:00–12:00, closed Sun, Kärntner Strasse 21–23, tel. 01/5124-0040).

Internet Access: The TI has a list of Internet cafés. **BigNet** is the dominant outfit (www.bignet.at), with lots of stations at Kärntner Strasse 61 (daily 10:00–24:00) and Hoher Markt 8–9 (daily 10:00–24:00). **Surfland Internet Café** is near the Opera (daily 10:00–23:00, Krugerstrasse 10, tel. 01/512-7701).

Post Offices: Choose from the main post office (Postgasse in center, daily 8:00–20:00, handy metered phones), Westbahnhof (Mon–Fri 7:00–22:00, Sat–Sun 9:00–20:00), Südbahnhof (daily 7:00–22:00), near the Opera (Mon–Fri 7:00–19:00, closed Sat–Sun, Krugerstrasse 13), and many other locations scattered around town.

English Bookstores: Consider the **British Bookshop** (Mon–Fri 9:30–19:30, Sat 9:30–18:00, closed Sun, at corner of Weihburggasse and Seilerstätte, tel. 01/512-1945; same hours at branch at Mariahilfer Strasse 4, tel. 01/522-6730) or **Shakespeare & Co.** (Mon–Sat 9:00–19:00, closed Sun, north of Hoher Markt square, Sterngasse 2, tel. 01/535-5053).

Keeping Up with the News: Don't buy newspapers. Read them for free in Vienna's marvelous coffee houses. It's much classier.

Travel Agency: Intropa is convenient, with good service for flights and train tickets (Mon–Fri 9:00–18:00, Sat 10:00–13:00, closed Sun, Neuer Markt 8, tel. 01/513-4000). Train tickets come with a €7 service charge when purchased from an agency rather than at the station—but, for many, the convenience is worth it.

Getting Around Vienna

By Public Transportation: Take full advantage of Vienna's simple, cheap, and super-efficient transit system, which includes trams, buses, subway (U-Bahn), and faster suburban trains (S-Bahn). I use the tram mostly to zip around the Ring (tram #1 or #2) and take the U-Bahn to outlying sights or hotels. Numbered lines (such as #38) are trams, and numbers followed by an *A* (such as #38A) are buses. The smooth, modern trams are Porsche-designed, with "backpack technology" locating the engines and mechanical hardware on the roofs for a lower ride and easier entry. Lines that begin with U (e.g., U-3) are U-Bahn lines (directions are designated by the end-of-the-line stops). Blue lines are the speedier S-Bahns. Take a moment to study the eye-friendly city-center map on station walls to internalize how the transit system can help you. The free tourist map has essentially all the lines marked, making the too-big €1.50 transit map unnecessary (information tel. 01/790-9105).

Trams, buses, the U-Bahn, and the S-Bahn all use the same tickets. Buy your tickets from *Tabak* shops, station machines, *Vorverkauf* offices in the station, or on board (just on trams, single tickets only, more expensive). You have lots of choices:

- Single tickets (€1.50, €2 if bought on tram, good for one journey with necessary transfers);
- 24-hour transit pass (€5);
- 72-hour transit pass (€12);
- 7-day transit pass (*Wochenkarte,* €12.50, pass always starts on Mon); or
- 8-day card *(Acht Tage Karte)*, covering eight full days of free transportation for €24 (can be shared—for example, 4 people for 2 days each). With a per-person cost of €3/day (compared to €5/day for a 24-hour pass), this can be a real saver for groups. Kids under 15 travel free on Sundays and holidays.

Stamp a time on your ticket as you enter the Metro system, tram, or bus (stamp it only the first time for a multiple-use pass). Cheaters pay a stiff €50 fine if caught—and then they make you buy a ticket. Rookies miss stops because they fail to open the door. Push buttons, pull latches—do whatever it takes. Study the excellent wall-mounted street map before you exit the U-Bahn station. Choosing the right exit—signposted from the moment you step off the train—saves lots of walking.

Cute little electric buses wind through the tangled old center (bus #1A is best for a joy ride—hop on and see where it takes you).

By Taxi: Vienna's comfortable, civilized, and easy-to-flag-down taxis start at €2.50. You'll pay about €8 to go from the Opera to the Westbahnhof. Pay only what's on the meter—any surcharges (other than the €2 fee added to fares when you telephone them, or €10 for the airport) are just crude cabbie rip-offs.

By Car with Driver: Consider the luxury of having your own car and driver. Johann (a.k.a. John) Lichtl is a kind, honest, English-speaking cabbie who can take up to four passengers in his car (€25/1 hr, €20/hr for 2 or more hours, mobile 0676-670-6750). Consider hiring gentle Johann to drive you to Salzburg with Wachau sightseeing en route (€300, up to 14 hrs; other trips by negotiation).

By Bike: Vienna is a great city for biking—*if* you own a bike. The bike path along the Ring is wonderfully entertaining. But bike rental is a hassle (get list at TI). Your best biking is likely up and down the traffic-free and people-filled Danube Island. Shops at two bridges—Floridsdörferbrücke (€3.60/hr, €18/day, near tram #31 stop, tel. 01/278-8698) and Reichsbrücke (tel. 01/263-5242)—each rent from about 9:30 until dusk, weather permitting, March through October. American Rick Watts runs Pedal Power, and will deliver your bike to your hotel, and pick it up when you're done (€32/day including delivery, Ausstellungsstrasse 3, tel. 01/729-7234, www.pedalpower.at). There are no other bike-rental options in the center, except for...

Citybikewien: The bikes you'll see parked in public racks all over town are part of a clever system that works fine for locals and technically works for tourists (but the complexity of the credit-card forms befuddled me). The bikes lock in their stalls (50 of which are scattered through the city center) and are released when you insert your credit card and log on. Figure it out, and you have a bike for €2 per hour (first hour free, fliers explain the process in English, www.citybikewien.at).

By Buggy: Rich romantics get around by traditional horse and buggy. These buggies, called *Fiakers,* clip-clop visitors on tours lasting 20 minutes (€40—old town), 40 minutes (€65—old town and the Ring), or one hour (€95—all of the above, but more thorough). You can share the ride and cost with up to five people. Because it's a kind of guided tour, before settling on a carriage, talk to a few drivers and pick one who's fun and speaks English.

TOURS

Walking Tours—The TI's *Walks in Vienna* brochure describes Vienna's many guided walks. The basic 90-minute "Vienna First Glance" introductory walk is offered daily throughout the summer

(€12, leaves at 14:00 from near the Opera, in English and German, tel. 01/894-5363, www.wienguide.at). Various specialized tours go once a week and are listed on their website.

Hop-On, Hop-Off Bus Tours—Vienna Sightseeing operates hop-on, hop-off tours (departures from Opera at top of each hour 10:00–17:00, recorded commentary). The schedule is posted curbside (three different routes, €13 for one, €16 for two). You could pay much more for 24 hours of hop-on and -off privileges, but given the city's excellent public transportation and this outfit's meager one-bus-per-hour frequency, I'd take this not to hop on and off, but only to get the narrated orientation drive through town.

City Bus Tour—Vienna Sightseeing offers a basic three-hour city tour including a tour of Schönbrunn Palace (€35; daily at 10:30 from the Opera, live guide speaks German and English). While they advertise several departures daily "starting from the Opera House," only the 10:30 tour really starts at the Opera (others shuttle you through various pick-ups to start elsewhere 30 minutes later; call 01/7124-6830 to reserve or get info on their many other tours).

Local Guides—The tourist board website (www.vienna.info) has a long list of local guides with their specialties and contact information. Lisa Zeiler is an excellent English-speaking guide (two-hour walks for €130—if she's booked up, she can set you up with another guide, tel. 01/402-3688, lisa.zeiler@gmx.at). Ursula Klaus, an art scholar specializing in turn-of-the-century Vienna, music, art, and architecture, also offers two-hour tours for €130 (tel. 01/522-8556, mobile 0676-421-4884, ursula.klaus@aon.at). Lisa and Ursula are both top-notch, bring art museums to life masterfully, and can tailor tours to your interests.

SELF-GUIDED TRAM TOUR

Around the Ringstrasse

In the 1860s, Emperor Franz Josef had the city's ingrown medieval wall torn down and replaced with a grand boulevard 190 feet wide. The road, arcing nearly three miles around the city's core, predates all the buildings that line it—so what you'll see is very "neo": Neoclassical, Neo-Gothic, and Neo-Renaissance. One of Europe's great streets, the Ringstrasse is lined with many of the city's top sights. Trams #1 and #2 and a great bike path circle the whole route—and so should you.

This self-guided tram tour, rated ▲▲, gives you a fun orientation and a ridiculously quick glimpse of the major sights as you glide by (€1.50, €2 if bought on tram, 30-min circular tour). Tram #1 goes clockwise; tram #2, counterclockwise. Most sights are on the outside, so use tram #2 (sit on the right, ideally in the front

Vienna

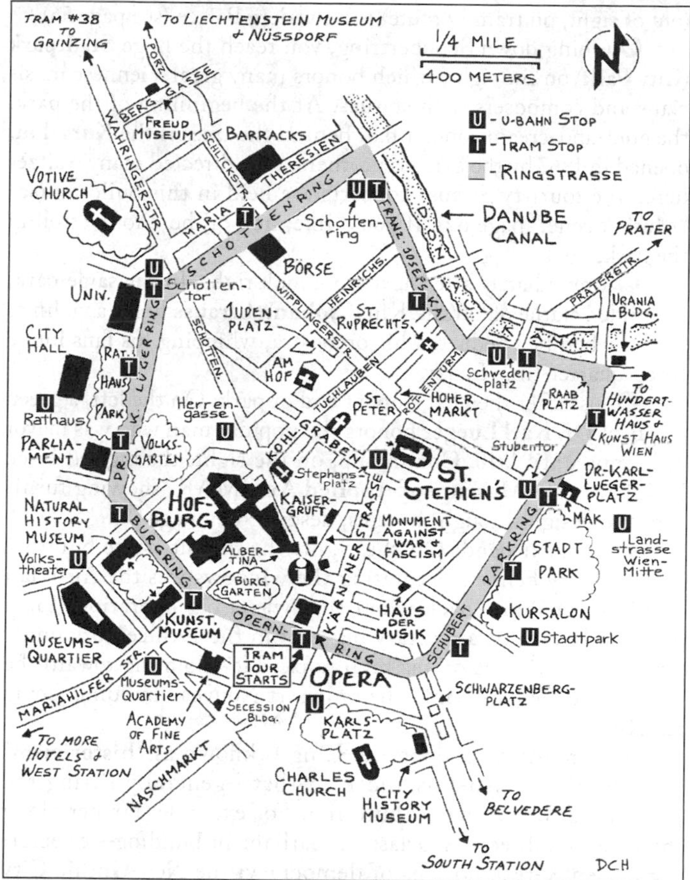

seat of the front car). Start immediately across the street from the Opera. You can (and should) jump on and off as you go (trams come every 5 min). Read ahead and pay attention—these sights can fly by. Let's go:

➔ Immediately on the left: The city's main pedestrian drag, Kärntner Strasse, leads to the zigzag-mosaic roof of **St. Stephen's Cathedral.** This tram tour makes a 360-degree circle around the cathedral, staying about this same distance from it.

➔ At first bend (before first stop): Look right, toward the tall fountain and the guy on a horse. Schwarzenberg Platz shows off its **equestrian statue** of Prince Charles Schwarzenberg, who fought Napoleon. Behind that is the Russian monument (behind the fountain with the Soviet soldier holding a flag), which was built in 1945 as a forced thanks to the Soviets for liberating Austria from the Nazis. Formerly a sore point, now it's just ignored. Beyond that (out of sight, on tram D route) is Belvedere Palace (see page 56).

➔ Going down Schubertring, you reach the huge **Stadtpark** (City Park) on the right, which honors many great Viennese musicians and composers with statues. At the beginning of the park, the gold-and-cream concert hall behind the trees is the **Kursalon,** opened in 1867 by the Strauss brothers, who directed many waltzes here. The touristy Strauss concerts are held in this building (see "Music Scene," page 62). If you'd like, hop off here for a stroll in the park.

➔ Immediately after next stop, look right: In the same park, the gilded statue of "Waltz King" **Johann Strauss** holds a violin as he did when he conducted his orchestra, whipping his fans into a three-quarter-time frenzy.

➔ Just after the next stop, at end of park: On the left, a green statue of **Dr. Karl Lueger** honors the popular man who was mayor of Vienna until 1910. Coming up, on the right, the big red-brick building is the **Museum of Applied Art** (MAK, showing furniture and design through the ages; described on page 59).

➔ At next bend: On the right, the quaint white building with military helmets decorating the windows was the **Austrian Ministry of War**—back when that was a big operation. Field Marshal Radetzky, a military big shot in the 19th century under Franz Josef, still sits on his high horse. He's pointing toward the Post Office Savings Bank, the only Art Nouveau building facing the Ring.

The architecture along the Ring is known as **"historicism"** because it's all Neo-this and Neo-that—generally fitting the purpose of the particular building. For example, farther along the Ring, we'll see a Neoclassical parliament building—celebrating ancient Greek notions of democracy; the Neo-Gothic City Hall—recalling when medieval burghers ran the city government in Gothic days; Neo-Renaissance museums—celebrating learning; and the Neo-Baroque National Theater—recalling the age when opera and theater flourished.

➔ At next corner: The white-domed building over your right shoulder as you turn is the Urania, Franz Josef's 1910 **observatory.** Lean forward and look behind it for a peek at the huge red cars of the giant 100-year-old Ferris wheel in Vienna's Prater Park (fun for families, described on page 60).

➔ Now you're rolling along the **Danube Canal.** This "Baby Danube" is one of the many small arms of the river that once made up the Danube at this location. The rest have been gathered together in a mightier modern-day Danube, farther away. This neighborhood was thoroughly bombed in World War II. The buildings across the canal are typical of postwar architecture

(1960s). They were built on the cheap, and are now being replaced by sleek, futuristic buildings. On your left was the site of the original Roman town, Vindobona.

In three long blocks, on the left (opposite the BP station, be ready—it passes fast), you'll see the ivy-covered walls and round Romanesque arches of St. Ruprecht's, the oldest church in Vienna (built in the 11th century on a bit of Roman ruins). Remember, medieval Vienna was defined by that long-gone wall that you're tracing on this tour. Across the river is an OPEC headquarters, where oil ministers often meet to set prices. Relax for a few stops (or marvel at the public-transit infrastructure Vienna enjoys) until the corner.

➔ Leaving the canal, turning left up Schottenring, at first corner: A block down on the right, you can see a huge red-brick **castle**—actually high-profile barracks built here at the command of a nervous Emperor Franz Josef (who found himself on the throne as an 18-year-old in 1848, the same year people's revolts against autocracy were sweeping across Europe).

➔ At next stop: On the left, the orange-and-white, Neo-Renaissance temple of money—the **Börse**—is Vienna's stock exchange.

➔ Next stop, at corner: The huge, frilly, Neo-Gothic church on the right is a **"votive church,"** built to thank God when an 1853 assassination attempt on Emperor Franz Josef failed. Ahead on the right (in front of tram stop) is the **Vienna University** building (established in 1365, it has no real campus as the buildings are scattered around town). It faces (on the left, behind a gilded angel across the Ring) a chunk of the old **city wall.** Beethoven lived and composed in the building just above the piece of wall.

➔ At next stop, on right: The Neo-Gothic **City Hall** (Rathaus), flying the flag of Europe, towers over Rathaus Platz. This square is a festive site in summer, with a huge screen showing outdoor movies, operas, and concerts and a thriving food circus. In the winter, the City Hall becomes a huge Advent calendar, with 24 windows opening—one each day—as Christmas approaches.

Immediately across the street (on left) is the **Burgtheater,** Austria's national theater. Behind that is the Landtmann Café (the only café built with the Ringstrasse buildings, and one of the city's finest).

➔ At next stop, on right: The Neo-Greek temple of democracy houses the **Austrian Parliament.** The lady with the golden helmet is Athena, goddess of wisdom. Across the street (on left) is the imperial park called the **Volksgarten,** with a fine rose garden (free and open to the public).

➔ After the next stop on the right is the **Natural History Museum,** the first of Vienna's huge twin museums. It faces the

Kunsthistorisches Museum, containing the city's greatest collection of paintings (see page 48). The **MuseumsQuartier** behind them completes the ensemble with a collection of mostly modern art museums (see page 50). A hefty statue of Empress Maria Theresa squats between the museums, facing the grand gate to the **Hofburg,** the emperor's palace (on left, across the Ring, described on page 37). Of the five arches, only the center one was used by the emperor. (Your tour is essentially finished. If you want to jump out here, you're near many of Vienna's top sights.)

➔ Fifty yards after the next stop, on the left through a gate in the black-iron fence, is a statue of Mozart. It's one of many charms in the **Burggarten,** which until 1918 was the private garden of the emperor. Vienna had more than its share of intellectual and creative geniuses. A hundred yards farther (on left, just out of the park), the German philosopher Goethe sits in a big, thought-provoking chair playing trivia with Schiller (across the street on your right). Behind the statue of Schiller is the **Academy of Fine Arts** (and next to it is the Burg Kino, which plays the movie *The Third Man* three times a week in English—see page 53).

➔ Hey, there's the **Opera** again. Jump off the tram and see the rest of the city.

SELF-GUIDED WALK

Welcome to Vienna

This walk connects the top three sights in Vienna's old center: the Opera, St. Stephen's Cathedral, and the Hofburg Palace. Along the way, you'll get a glimpse of Vienna past and present. The total trip takes about an hour, not counting sightseeing stops (which could be lengthy).

• *Begin by standing on the square in front of Vienna's landmark Opera.*

Opera: This is regarded by music-lovers as one of the planet's premier houses of music. If you're a fan, consider taking a guided tour of the Opera, or spring for a performance (standing-room tickets are surprisingly cheap; for information on all your Opera options, see page 33). The U-Bahn station in front of the Opera is actually a huge underground shopping mall with fast food, newsstands, lots of pickpockets, and even an Opera Toilet Vienna experience (€0.60, *mit Musik*).

• *Walk behind the Opera to find the famous...*

Sacher Café: This is the home of every chocoholic's fantasy, the *Sachertorte.* While locals complain that the cakes have gone downhill (and many tourists are surprised how dry they are), a coffee and slice of cake here can be €8 well invested. For maximum elegance, sit inside (daily 8:00–23:30, Philharmoniker Strasse 4, tel. 01/51456). While the café itself is grotesquely touristy, the adjacent

Vienna Self-Guided Walk

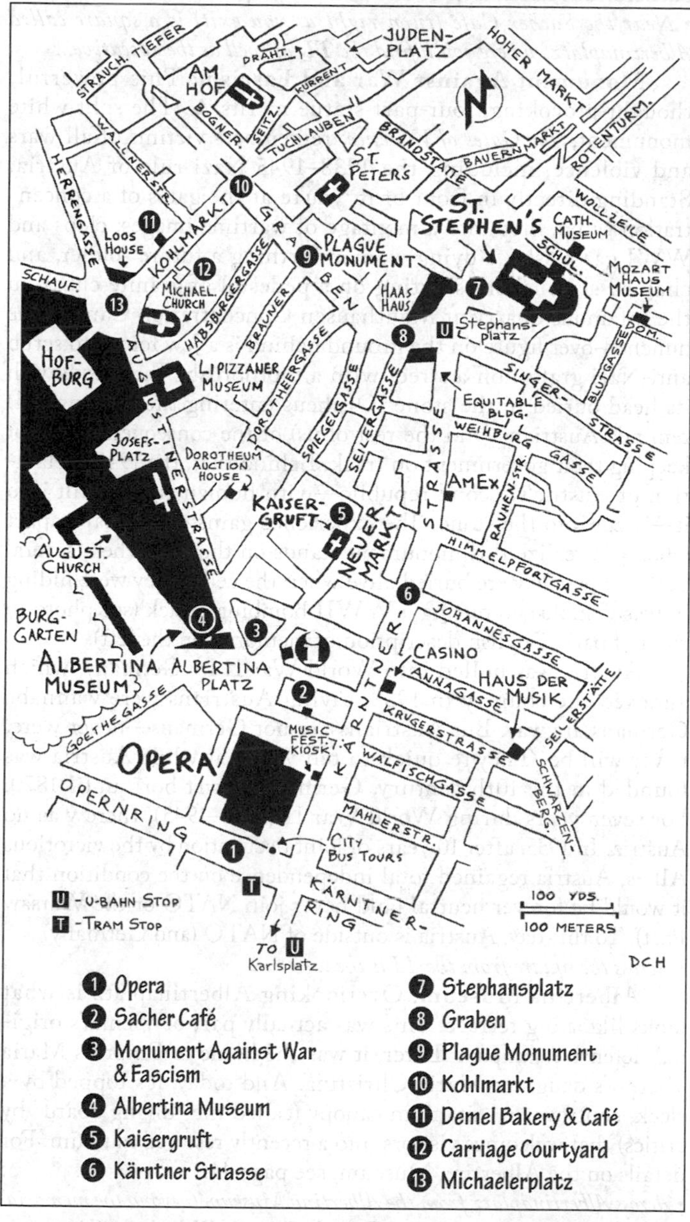

Sacher Stube has ambience and natives to spare.

• *Near the Sacher Café (turn right as you exit) is a square called Albertinaplatz, where you'll find the **TI**, as well as the evocative...*

Monument Against War and Fascism: This powerful, thought-provoking, four-part statue merits ▲. The split white monument, *The Gates of Violence,* remembers victims of all wars and violence, including the 1938–1945 Nazi rule of Austria. Standing directly in front of it, you're at the gates of a concentration camp. Step into a montage of wartime images: clubs and WWI gas masks, a dying woman birthing a future soldier, and chained slave laborers sitting on a pedestal of granite cut from the infamous quarry at Mauthausen Concentration Camp. The hunched-over figure on the ground behind is a Jew forced to scrub anti-Nazi graffiti off a street with a toothbrush. The statue with its head buried in the stone (Orpheus entering the underworld) reminds Austrians (and the rest of us) of the consequences of not keeping their government on track. Behind that, the 1945 declaration of Austria's second republic—with human rights built into it—is cut into the stone. The experience gains emotional impact when you realize this monument stands on the spot where several hundred people were buried alive when the cellar they were hiding in was demolished during a WWII bombing attack (see photo to right of park, English description of memorial on the left).

Austria was pulled into World War II by Germany, which annexed the country in 1938, saying Austrians were wannabe Germans anyway. But Austrians are not Germans—never were, never will be. They're quick to tell you that while Austria was founded in the 10th century, Germany wasn't born until 1870. For seven years during World War II (1938–1945), there was no Austria. In 1955, after 10 years of joint occupation by the victorious Allies, Austria regained total independence on the condition that it would be forever neutral (and never join NATO or the Warsaw Pact). To this day, Austria is outside of NATO (and Germany).

• *Across the square from the TI is the...*

Albertina Museum: Overlooking Albertinaplatz is what looks like a big terrace. This was actually part of Vienna's original defensive rampart. Later, it was the home to Empress Maria Theresa's daughter Maria Christina. And today, it's topped by a sleek, controversial titanium canopy (called the "diving board" by critics) that welcomes visitors into a recently restored museum. For details on the Albertina Museum, see page 46.

• *Across Albertinaplatz from the Albertina Museum (beyond the memorial photo plaque) is the street called Tegetthoffstrasse. Walk down this street a block to the square called Neuer Markt. Fronting the square is the...*

Kaisergruft: This church has a crypt filled with the fancy coffins of the Hapsburgs. Before moving on, consider paying your respects here (described on page 47).

• *After visiting the Kaisergruft, cross to the center of the square.*

The **fountain,** with the "four rivers" of the Hapsburg Empire (only the Danube is famous), dates from the mid-1700s. The original nude statues were replaced with more modest versions by Maria Teresa (originals are in the Lower Belvedere Palace). The buildings all around you were rebuilt after World War II, when half of the first district was intentionally destroyed by Churchill to demoralize the Viennese, who were disconcertingly enthusiastic about the Nazis.

• *Atop the fountain is a statue of Providence. Her one bare breast points to Kärntner Strasse (50 yards away). Go there and turn left.*

Kärntner Strasse: This grand, mall-like street (traffic-free since 1974) is the people-watching delight of this in-love-with-life city. While it's mostly a crass commercial pedestrian mall with its famed elegant shops now long gone, locals know it's the same road Crusaders marched down as they headed off for the Holy Land in the 12th century. Its name indicates that it points south, in the direction of the region of Kärnten (Carinthia, today divided between Austria and Slovenia).

Along this drag, you'll find lots of action: shops, street music, the city casino (at #41), the venerable Lobmeyr Crystal shop (#26—climb up the classic Old World interior to the glass museum), American Express (#21), the minimalism of the Loos American Bar (designed by Adolf Loos, Vienna's answer to Frank Lloyd Wright; dark, plush, small; great €8 cocktails, no shorts, Kärntnerdurchgang 10, tel. 01/512-3283), and then, finally, the cathedral. Where Kärntner Strasse hits Stephansplatz (at #3), the Equitable Building (filled with lawyers, bankers, and insurance men) is a fine example of historicism from the turn of the 20th century. Look up and imagine how slick Vienna must have felt in 1900.

Across the street on the corner, facing St. Stephen's, is the sleek concrete-and-glass **Haas Haus** by noted Austrian architect Hans Hollein (finished in 1990). The curved facade is supposed to echo the Roman fortress of Vindobona (whose ruins were found near here)...but the Viennese, who protested having this stark modern tower right next to their beloved cathedral, were not convinced. Since then, it's become a fixture of Vienna's main square. Notice the way the smooth, rounded glass reflects St. Stephen's pointy Gothic architecture, providing a great photo opportunity. The café and pricey restaurant inside offer a nice perch, complete with a view of Stephansplatz below.

• *At the end of Kärntner Strasse, you'll wander into...*

Stephansplatz: Vienna's fun and colorful main square is also home to its cathedral, St. Stephen's. Now's the time to visit this massive church (see page 35).

• *When you're finished on Stephansplatz, head for the Hofburg. At the bottom of the square (near the start of Kärntner Strasse) is the street called...*

Graben: This was once a *Graben,* or ditch—originally the moat for the Roman military camp. In the middle of this pedestrian zone (at the intersection with Bräuner Strasse), top-notch street entertainers dance around an extravagant **plague monument,** officially called the Trinity Column (step back to notice the wonderful gilded "Father, Son, and Holy Ghost" at its top). In the Middle Ages, people didn't understand the causes of plagues, and figured they were a punishment from God. It was common for survivors to bribe or thank God with a monument like this one (c. 1690). One-third of Vienna died—so this column is thanks from the other two-thirds. Find Emperor Leopold, who ruled during the plague and made this statue in gratitude. (Hint: The typical inbreeding of royal families left him with a gaping underbite.) Below Leopold, Faith (with the help of a disgusting little cupid) tosses an old naked woman—symbolizing the plague—into the abyss.

Just before the plague monument is Dorotheergasse, leading to the Dorotheum auction house (see page 51). Just beyond the monument, you'll pass a fine set of **public WCs.** Around 1900, a local chemical-maker needed a publicity stunt. He purchased two wine cellars under the Graben and had classy WCs built in the Modernist style (complete with chandeliers and finely crafted mahogany) to prove that his chemicals really got things clean. The restrooms remain clean to this day—in fact, they're so inviting that they're used for poetry readings. Locals and tourists happily pay €0.50 for a quick visit.

• *The Graben dead-ends at the aristocratic supermarket Julius Meinl am Graben (see "Eating," page 77). At the end of Graben, turn left onto...*

Kohlmarkt: This is Vienna's most elegant shopping street (except for "American Catalog Shopping" at #5, second floor), with the emperor's palace at the end. Strolling Kohlmarkt, daydream about the edible window displays at **Demel** (#14, daily 10:00–19:00). Demel is the ultimate Viennese chocolate shop. The room is filled with Art Nouveau boxes of Empress Sisi's choco-dreams come true: *Kandierte Veilchen* (candied violet petals), *Katzenzungen* (cats' tongues), and so on. The cakes here are moist (compared to the dry *Sachertortes*). The delectable window displays change about monthly, reflecting current happenings in Vienna. Inside, an impressive cancan of cakes is displayed to tempt visitors into springing for the €10 cake-and-coffee deal (point to the cake you want). You can sit inside, with a view of the cake-making, or outside, with the street action. (Upstairs is less crowded.) Shops like this boast "K. u. K."—good enough for the *König und Kaiser* (king and emperor—same guy).

Next to Demel, the Manz bookstore has a Loos-designed facade. Just beyond Demel and across the street, at #1152, you can pop into a charming little Baroque **carriage courtyard,** with the surviving original carriage garages.

• *Kohlmarkt ends at...*

Michaelerplatz: In the center of this square, a scant bit of Roman Vienna lies exposed. On the left are the fancy Loden Plankl shop, with traditional formal wear, and the stables of the Spanish Riding School. Study the grand entry facade to the Hofburg Palace—it's Neo-Baroque from around 1900. The four heroic giants illustrate Hercules wrestling with his great challenges (much like the Hapsburgs, I'm sure). Opposite the facade, notice the modern Loos House (now a bank), which was built at about the same time. It was nicknamed the "house without eyebrows" for the simplicity of its windows. An anti-Art Nouveau statement (inspired by Frank Lloyd Wright and considered Vienna's first "modern" building), this was actually shocking at the time. To quell some of the outrage, the architect added flower boxes (or, some would say, moustaches).

• *You've made it to the Hofburg Palace. To get to the sights inside, simply walk through the gate, under the dome, and into the first square (In der Burg). For details on all the sights here, see page 37.*

SIGHTS

For a self-guided walk connecting these first three landmark sights, see page 28.

Opera (Staatsoper)

The Opera, facing the Ring and near the TI, is a central point for any visitor—easily worth ▲▲▲. While the critical reception of the building 130 years ago led the architect to commit suicide, and though it's been rebuilt since being destroyed by WWII bombs, it's still a sumptuous place.

Tours: Unless you're attending a performance, you can enter the Opera only with a guided 35-minute tour, offered daily in English (€6.50, generally July–Aug at 11:00, 13:00, 14:00, 15:00, and often at 10:00 and 16:00; Sept–June fewer tours, afternoons only, tel. 01/514-442-606). Tour times are often changed or cancelled due to rehearsals and performances. The opera posts a monthly schedule (blue, on the wall), but the more accurate schedule is the daily listing (red, posted on the door on the Operngasse side of building, farthest from St. Stephen's Cathedral). Tour tickets include the tiny and disappointing Opera Museum (across the street toward the Hofburg), except on Monday, when the museum is closed.

Opera Museum: Included in your opera tour ticket (whether you like it or not), the Opera Museum is a let-down, with descriptions only in German and rotating six-month-long special exhibits (€3, or included in the €6.50 tour ticket, Tue–Sun 10:00–18:00, closed Mon, a block away from the Opera, near Albertina Museum).

Performances: The Vienna State Opera—with musicians provided by the Vienna Philharmonic Orchestra in the pit—is one of the world's top opera houses. There are 300 performances a year, but in July and August the singers rest their voices (or go on tour). Since there are different operas nearly nightly, you'll see big trucks out back and constant action backstage—all the sets need to be switched each day. Even though the expensive seats normally sell out long in advance, the opera is perpetually in the red and subsidized by the state.

Opera Tickets: To buy tickets in advance, call 01/513-1513 (phone answered daily 10:00–21:00, www.wiener-staatsoper.at). The theater's box office is open from 9:00 until two hours before each performance. Unless Placido Domingo is in town, it's easy to get one of 567 **standing-room tickets** (*Stehplätze*, €2 at the top or €3.50 downstairs). While the front doors open one hour before the show starts, a side door (middle of building, on the Operngasse side) opens 80 minutes before curtain time, giving those in the know an early grab at standing-room tickets. Just walk in straight, then head right until you see the ticket booth marked *Stehplätze* (tel. 01/514-442-419). If fewer than 567 people are in line, there's no need to line up early. If you're one of the first 160 in line, try for the "Parterre" section and you'll end up directly under the Emperor's Box. You can even buy standing-room tickets after the show has started—in case you want only a little taste of opera. Dress is casual (but do your best) at the standing-room bar. Locals save their spot along the rail by tying a scarf to it.

Rick's Crude Tips: For me, three hours is a lot of opera. But just to see and hear the Opera in action for half an hour is a treat. You can buy a standing-room spot and just drop in for part of the show. Ushers don't mind letting tourists with standing-room tickets in for a short look. Ending time is posted in the lobby—you could stop by for just the finale. If you go at the start or finish, you'll see Vienna dressed up. Of the 567 people with cheap standing-room tickets, invariably many will not stand through the entire performance. You can drop by at about 21:30, ask for standing-room tickets, and if none are available, just wait for tourists to leave and bum their tickets off them. Guards don't care. Even those with standing-room tickets are considered "ticket-holders," and are welcome to explore the building. As you leave, wander around the first floor (fun if leaving early, when halls are empty) to enjoy the sumptuous halls (with prints of famous stage sets and performers) and the grand entry staircase. The last resort (and worst option) is to drop into the Opera Café and watch the opera live on TV screens (reasonable menu and drinks).

St. Stephen's Cathedral (Stephansdom)

This massive church, worth ▲▲, is the Gothic needle around which Vienna spins. According to the medieval vision, it stands like a giant jeweled reliquary, offering praise to God from the center of the city. It has survived Vienna's many wars and today symbolizes the city's freedom.

Cost: Entering the church is free (except July–mid-Oct, when it's €3 to get past the rear of the nave). Going up the towers costs €3 (by stairs, south tower) or €4 (by elevator, north tower). For more information, see "Towers" below.

Hours: The church doors are open Mon–Sat 6:00–22:00, Sun 7:00–22:00, but the nave is only open for tourists Mon–Sat 8:30–11:30 & 13:00–16:30, Sun 13:00–16:30. During services, you can't enter the main nave (unless you're attending Mass), but you can go into the back of the church to reach the north tower elevator (daily April–Oct 8:30–17:30, Nov–March 8:30–16:30). The stairs up to the south tower (enter from outside) are open daily 9:00–17:30.

Tours: The €4 tours in English are entertaining (daily April–Oct at 15:45, check information board inside entry to confirm schedule). Audioguides may be available.

➲ **Self-Guided Tour:** This is the third church to stand on this spot. The church survived the bombs of World War II, but, in the last days of the war, fires from the ruins leapt to the rooftop. The original timbered Gothic rooftop burned, and the cathedral's huge bell crashed to the ground. With a financial outpouring of civic pride, the roof was rebuilt in its original splendor by 1952. The ceramic tiles are purely decorative (locals who contributed to the postwar reconstruction each "own" one for their donation). Dramatic photos show WWII damage (with bricks neatly stacked and ready).

The **grounds** around the church were a cemetery until Josef II emptied it as an "anti-plague" measure in 1780. All the tombs were removed, and the remains were dumped into mass graves outside of town (as was the case when Mozart died here in 1791). A few of the most important tombstones decorate the church walls (see west facade flanking entry). You can still see the footprint of the old cemetery church in the pavement, today ignored by the buskers and human statues. Remains of the earlier Virgil Chapel (dating from the 13th century) are immediately under this (actually on display underground, in the U-Bahn station).

Study the church's **main entrance** (west end). You can see the original Romanesque facade (c. 1240) with classical Roman statues embedded in it. Above are two stubby towers nicknamed "pagan towers" because they're built with a few Roman stones (flipped over to hide the inscriptions and expose the smooth sides). The two 30-foot-tall columns flank the main entry. If you stand back and look at the tops, you'll see that they symbolize creation (one's a penis, the other's a vagina).

Stepping inside, you'll find a Gothic nave with a Baroque overlay. While the columns support the roof, they also tell a story. Richly populated with statues, the columns make a saintly parade leading to the high altar. Near the church's right rear, find the "Madonna with the Protective Mantle"—showing people of all walks of life seeking and finding refuge in the holy mother. The Tupperware-colored glass windows date from 1950. Before World War II, the entire church was lit with windows like the richly colored ones behind the altar. Those, along with the city's top art treasures, were hidden safely from the Nazis in cellars and mines. The altar painting of the stoning of St. Stephen is early Baroque, painted on copper.

St. Stephen's is proud to be Austria's national church. A **plaque** (10 feet up, three pillars in front of the main altar) explains how each region contributed to the rebuilding after World War II: windows from Tirol, furniture from Vorarlberg, the floor from Lower Austria, and so on.

The Gothic sandstone pulpit in the rear of the nave (on left) is a realistic masterpiece carved from three separate blocks (find the seams). A spiral stairway winds up to the lectern, surrounded and supported by the four Latin Church fathers: Saints Ambrose, Jerome, Gregory, and Augustine. The railing leading up swarms with symbolism: lizards (animals of light) and toads (animals of darkness). The "Dog of the Lord" stands at the top, making sure none of those toads pollutes the sermon. Below the toads, wheels with three parts (the Trinity) roll up, while wheels with four parts (the four seasons, symbolizing mortal life) roll down. This work, attributed by most scholars to Anton Pilgram, has all the elements of the Flamboyant Gothic style—in miniature. Gothic art was done for the glory of God. Artists were anonymous. But this was around 1500, and the Renaissance was going strong in Italy. While Gothic persisted in the North, the Renaissance spirit had already arrived. In the more humanist Renaissance, man was allowed to shine—and artists became famous. So Pilgram included a rare self-portrait bust in his work (the guy with sculptor's tools, in the classic "artist observing the world from his window" pose under the stairs). A few steps farther ahead on the left wall, you'll see a similar self-portrait of Pilgram in color (symbolically supporting the heavy burden of being a master builder of this huge place).

Towers: You can ascend both towers—the south (outside right transept, by spiral staircase) and the north (via crowded elevator inside on the left). The 450-foot-high south tower, called St. Stephen's Tower, offers the far better view, but you'll earn it by hiking 343 tightly wound steps up the spiral staircase (€3, daily 9:00–17:30, this hike burns about 1 *Sachertorte* of calories). From the top, use your city map to locate the famous sights. The north tower elevator takes you to a mediocre view and a big bell: the 21-ton Pummerin, cast from the cannon captured from the Ottomans in 1683, and supposedly the second biggest bell in the world that rings by swinging (locals know it as the bell that rings in the Austrian New Year; elevator-€4, daily April–Oct 8:30–17:30, Nov–March 8:30–16:30).

Cathedral Museum (Dom Museum): This forlorn museum (outside left transept, past the horses) gives a close-up look at piles of religious paintings, statues, and a treasury (€5, Tue–Sat 10:00–17:00, closed Sun–Mon, Stephansplatz 6, tel. 01/515-523-560).

Hofburg Palace

The complex, confusing, and imposing Imperial Palace, with 640 years of architecture, demands your attention. This first Hapsburg residence grew with the family empire from the 13th century until 1913, when the last "new wing" opened. The winter residence of the Hapsburg rulers until 1918, it's still the home of the Spanish Riding School, the Vienna Boys' Choir, the Austrian president's office, 5,000 government workers, and several important museums.

Rather than lose yourself in its myriad halls and courtyards, focus on three sections: the Imperial Apartments, Treasury, and Neue Burg (New Palace). Note that Hapsburg sights not actually inside the Hofburg (including the Lipizzaner Stallions, the Augustinian Church, and the Albertina Museum) are covered on page 44.

Orientation from In der Burg: Begin at the square called In der Burg (enter through the gate from Michaelerplatz). The statue is of Emperor Franz II, grandson of Maria Theresa, grandfather of Franz Josef, and father-in-law of Napoleon. Behind him is a tower with three kinds of clocks (the yellow disk shows the stage of the moon tonight). On the right, a door leads to the Imperial Apartments. Franz faces the oldest part of the palace. The colorful gate (behind you), which used to have a drawbridge, leads to the 13th-century Swiss Court (named for the Swiss mercenary guards once stationed here), the Treasury (Schatzkammer), and the Imperial Chapel (Hofburgkapelle, where the Boys' Choir sings the Mass—see page 63). For the Heroes' Square and the New Palace, continue opposite the way you entered In der Burg, passing through the left-most tunnel.

Vienna's Hofburg Palace

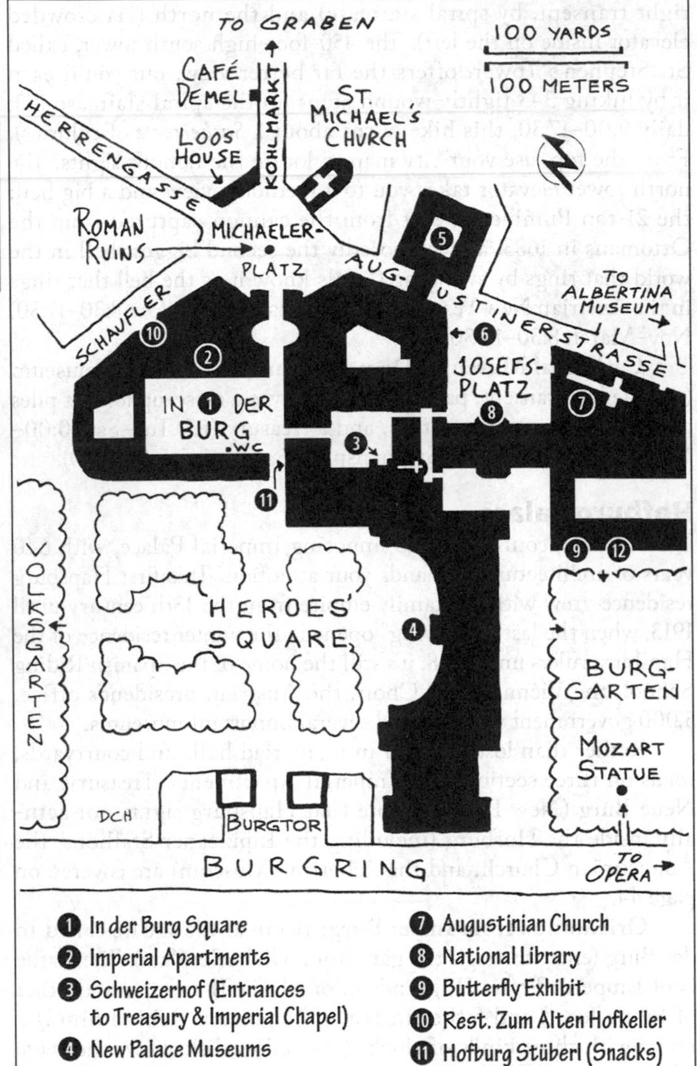

1. In der Burg Square
2. Imperial Apartments
3. Schweizerhof (Entrances to Treasury & Imperial Chapel)
4. New Palace Museums
5. Lipizzaner Museum
6. Lipizzaner Stallions Ticket Line
7. Augustinian Church
8. National Library
9. Butterfly Exhibit
10. Rest. Zum Alten Hofkeller
11. Hofburg Stüberl (Snacks)
12. Café Rest. Palmenhaus

Eating at the Hofburg: Down the tunnel to Heroes' Square (described below) is a tiny but handy sandwich bar called **Hofburg Stüberl** (same €2/sandwich price whether you sit or go, Mon–Fri 7:00–18:00, Sat–Sun 10:00–16:00). For a cheap, quick meal, duck into the **Restaurant zum Alten Hofkeller** in a cellar under the palace (€5 plates, Mon–Fri 11:00–13:30, closed Sat–Sun, breakfast from 7:30, cafeteria-style, mod and efficient, Schauflergasse 7).

▲▲▲Imperial Apartments (Kaiserappartements)—These lavish, Versailles-type, "wish-I-were-God" royal rooms are the downtown version of the grander Schönbrunn Palace. If you're rushed and have time for only one palace, do this (€9, daily 9:00–17:00, last entry 30 min before closing; from courtyard through St. Michael's Gate, just off Michaelerplatz; tel. 01/533-7570, www.hofburg-wien.at). Palace visits are a one-way romp through 20 rooms. You'll find some helpful posted English information, and the included audioguide brings the exhibit to life. With those tools and the following description, you won't need the €8 *Imperial Apartments and Sisi* museum guidebook. Your ticket also gets you into the royal silver and porcelain collection *(Silberkammer)* near the turnstile. If touring the silver and porcelain, do it first to save walking.

➲ **Self-Guided Tour:** Get your ticket, tour the silver and porcelain collection, climb the stairs, go through the turnstile, consider the WC, and use the big model of the palace complex to understand the complex lay of the imperial land. Then head into the...

Sisi Museum: The first six rooms tell the life story of Empress Elisabeth's fancy world—her luxury homes and fairy-tale existence. While Sisi's life story is the perfect stuff of legends, the exhibit tries to keep things from getting too giddy, and doesn't add to the sugary, kitschy image that's been created. The exhibit starts with her assassination (see her death mask) and traces the development of her legend, analyzing how her fabulous but tragic life could create a 19th-century Princess Diana from a rocky start (when she was disdained for abandoning Vienna and her husband, the venerable Emperor Franz Josef). You'll read bits of her poetic writing, see exact copies of her now-lost jewelry, and learn about her escapes, dieting mania, and chocolate bills. Admire Sisi's hard-earned thin waist (20 inches at age 16, 21 inches at age 50...after giving birth to four children). The black statue in the dark room represents the empress after the suicide of her son—aloof, thin, in black, with her back to the world. At the end, ponder the crude knife that killed Sisi.

A special exhibit opened in August 2006 to celebrate the 50th anniversary of the films that made Sisi a household name (at least in Austria): *Sisi* (1955); *Sisi: The Young Empress* (1956); *Sisi: Fateful*

Years of an Empress (1957); and the condensed English version, *Forever My Love* (1962). The exhibition showcases the furniture borrowed from the palace for the movies, along with photographs and props from the filming.

After the Sisi Museum, a one-way route takes you through a series of royal rooms. The first room—as if to make clear that there was more to the Hapsburgs than Sisi—shows a family tree tracing the Hapsburgs from 1273 to their messy WWI demise. From here you enter the private apartments of the royal family (Franz Josef's first, then Sisi's).

Waiting Room for the Audience Room: A map and mannequins from the many corners of the Hapsburg realm illustrate the multi-ethnicity of the vast empire. Every citizen had the right to meet privately with the emperor. Three huge paintings entertained guests while they waited. They were propaganda, showing crowds of commoners enthusiastic about their Hapsburg rulers. On the right: an 1809 scene of the emperor returning to Vienna, celebrating news that Napoleon had begun his retreat. Left: the return of the emperor from the 1814 Peace of Paris, the treaty that ended the Napoleonic wars. (The 1815 Congress of Vienna that followed was the greatest assembly of diplomats in European history. Its goal: to establish peace through a "balance of power" among nations. While rulers ignored nationalism in favor of continued dynastic rule, it worked for about a century, until a colossal war—World War I—wiped out the Hapsburgs and the rest of Europe's royal families.) Center: Less important, the emperor makes his first public appearance to adoring crowds after recovering from a life-threatening illness (1826). The chandelier—considered the best in the palace—is Baroque, made of Bohemian crystal.

Audience Room: Suddenly, you were face-to-face with the emp. The portrait on the easel shows Franz Josef in 1915, when he was over 80 years old. Famously energetic, he lived a spartan life dedicated to duty. He'd stand at the high table here to meet with commoners, who came to show gratitude or make a request. (Standing kept things moving.) On the table, you can read a partial list of 56 appointments he had on January 3, 1910 (three columns: family name, meeting topic, and *Anmerkung*—the emperor's "action log").

Conference Room: The emperor presided here over the equivalent of cabinet meetings. After 1867, he granted Hungary some authority over his sprawling and suddenly unruly lands (creating the "Austro-Hungarian Empire")—so Hungarians also attended these meetings. The paintings on the wall show the military defeat of a popular Hungarian uprising...subtle.

Emperor Franz Josef's Study: This room evokes how seriously the emperor took his responsibilities as the top official of a vast empire. The desk was originally between the windows. Franz Josef could look up from his work and see his lovely, long-haired, tiny-waisted Empress Elisabeth's reflection in the mirror. Notice the trompe l'oeil paintings above each door, giving the believable illusion of marble relief. Notice also all the family photos—the perfect gift for the dad/uncle/hubby who has it all.

The walls between the rooms are wide enough to hide servants' corridors (the hidden door to his valet's room is in the back left corner). The emperor lived with a personal staff of 14: "three valets, four lackeys, two doormen, two manservants, and three chambermaids."

Emperor's Bedroom: Franz Josef famously slept on this no-frills iron bed, and used the portable washstand until 1880 (when the palace got running water). While he had a typical emperor's share of mistresses, his dresser was always well-stocked with photos of Sisi. Franz Josef lived here after his estrangement from Sisi. An etching shows the empress—a fine rider and avid hunter—riding sidesaddle while jumping a hedge.

Large Salon: This room was for royal family gatherings, and went unused after Sisi's death. The big, ornate stove in the corner was fed from behind. Through the 19th century, this was a standard form of heating.

Small Salon: This is dedicated to the memory of the assassinated Emperor Maximilian of Mexico (bearded portrait, Franz Josef's brother, killed in 1867). This was also a smoking room—necessary in the early 19th century, when smoking was newly fashionable (but only for men—never in the presence of women). Left of the door is a small button the emperor had to buzz before entering his estranged wife's quarters. You, however, can go right in.

Empress' Bedroom and Drawing Room: This was Sisi's, refurbished Neo-Rococo in 1854. She lived here—the bed was rolled in and out daily—until her death in 1898.

Sisi's Dressing/Exercise Room: Servants worked two hours a day on Sisi's famous hair here. She'd exercise on the wooden structure. You can psychoanalyze Sisi from the people and photos she hung on her walls. It's mostly her favorite dogs, her Bavarian family, and several portraits of the romantic and anti-monarch poet Heinrich Heine. Her infatuation with the liberal Heine caused a stir in royal circles.

Sisi's Bathroom: Detour into the behind-the-scenes palace. In the narrow passageway, you'll walk by Sisi's hand-painted-porcelain, dolphin-head WC (on the right). In the main bathroom, you'll see her huge copper tub (with the original wall coverings behind it). Sisi was the first Hapsburg to have running water in her bathroom (notice the hot and cold faucets). You're walking on the first linoleum ever used in Vienna (c. 1880).

Servants' Quarters: Next, enter the servants' quarters, with tropical scenes painted by Bergl in 1766. Take time to enjoy Bergl's playful details. As you leave these rooms and re-enter the imperial world, look back to the room on the left.

Empress' Great Salon: The room is painted with Mediterranean escapes, the 19th-century equivalent of travel posters. The statue is of Elisa, Napoleon's oldest sister (by the Neoclassical master Canova). A print shows how the emperor and Sisi would share breakfast in this room. Turn the corner and pass through the anterooms of Alexander's apartments.

Small Salon: The portrait is of Crown Prince Rudolf, Franz Josef and Sisi's son, who supposedly committed suicide at age 30. The mysterious circumstances around his death at Mayerling hunting lodge have been dramatized in numerous movies, plays, opera—and even a ballet.

Red Salon: The Gobelin wall hangings were a 1776 gift from Marie-Antoinette and Louis XVI in Paris to their Viennese counterparts.

Dining Room: It's dinnertime, and Franz Josef has called his extended family together. The settings are modest...just silver. Gold was saved for formal state dinners. Next to each name card was a menu with the chef responsible for each dish. (Talk about pressure.) While the Hofburg had tableware for 4,000, feeding 3,000 was a typical day. The cellar was stocked with 60,000 bottles of wine. The kitchen was huge—50 birds could be roasted on the hand-driven spits at once. (Drop off your audioguide in this room.)

Zip through the shop, go down the stairs, and you're back on the street. Two quick lefts take you back to the palace square (In der Burg), where the treasury awaits just past the black, red, and gold gate on the far side.

▲▲▲Treasury (Weltliche und Geistliche Schatzkammer)—This "Secular and Religious Treasure Room" contains the best jewels on the Continent. Slip through the vault doors and reflect on the glitter of 21 rooms filled with scepters, swords, crowns, orbs, weighty robes, double-headed eagles, gowns, gem-studded bangles, and a unicorn horn (€8, Wed–Mon 10:00–18:00, closed Tue, follow *Schatzkammer* signs to the Schweizerhof, tel. 01/5252-4486, www.hofburg-wien.at).

➲ Self-Guided Tour: While no English descriptions are provided within the treasury, the well-produced, €2 audioguide provides a wealth of information and is worth renting. Here's an insufficient rundown of the highlights (the audioguide is much more complete).

Room 2: The personal crown of Rudolf II has survived since 1602—it was considered too well-crafted to cannibalize for other crowns. It's a big deal because it's the adopted crown of the Austrian Empire, established in 1806 after Napoleon dissolved the Holy Roman Empire (an alliance of Germanic kingdoms so named because it wanted to be considered the continuation of the Roman Empire). Pressured by Napoleon, the Austrian Francis II—who had been Holy Roman Emperor—became Francis I, Emperor of Austria. Francis I/II (the stern guy on the wall, near where you entered) ruled from 1792 to 1835. Look at the crown. Its design symbolically merges the typical medieval king's crown and a bishop's miter.

Rooms 3 and 4: These contain some of the coronation vestments and regalia needed for the new Austrian emperor.

Room 5: Ponder the Throne Cradle. Napoleon's son was born in 1811 and made king of Rome. The little eagle at the foot is symbolically not yet able to fly, but glory-bound. Glory is symbolized by the star, with dad's big *N* raised high.

Room 8: The eight-foot-tall, 500-year-old unicorn horn (possibly a narwhal tusk), was considered incredibly powerful in the old days, giving its owner the grace of God. This was owned by the Holy Roman Emperor—clearly a divine monarch.

Room 11: The collection's highlight is the 10th-century crown of the Holy Roman Emperor (HRE). The imperial crown swirls with symbolism "proving" that the emperor was both holy and Roman. The jeweled arch over the top is reminiscent of the parade helmet of ancient Roman emperors whose successors the HRE claimed to be. The cross on top says the HRE ruled as Christ's representative on earth. King Solomon's portrait (on the crown, right of cross) is Old Testament proof that kings can be wise and good. King David (next panel) is similar proof that they can be just. The crown's eight sides represent the celestial city of Jerusalem's eight gates. The jewels on the front panel symbolize the 12 apostles.

The nearby 11th-century Imperial Cross preceded the emperor in ceremonies. Encrusted with jewels, it carried a substantial chunk of *the* cross and *the* holy lance (supposedly used to pierce the side of Jesus while on the cross; both items displayed in the same glass case). This must be the actual holy lance, as Holy Roman Emperors actually carried this into battle in the 10th century. Look behind the cross to see how it was a box that could be clipped open and shut, used for holding holy relics. You can see bits of the "true cross" anywhere, but this is a prime piece—with the actual nail hole.

The other case has jewels from the reign of Karl der Grosse (Charlemagne), the greatest ruler of medieval Europe. Notice Charlemagne modeling the crown (which was made a hundred years after he died) in the tall painting adjacent.

Room 12: The painting shows the coronation of Maria Theresa's son Josef II in 1764. In a room filled with the literal big wigs of the day, Josef is wearing the same crown and royal garb you've just seen.

Room 16: Most tourists walk right by perhaps the most exquisite workmanship in the entire treasury, the royal vestments (15th century). Look closely—they're painted with gold and silver threads.

▲Heroes' Square (Heldenplatz) and the New Palace (Neue Burg)—This last grand addition to the palace, from the early 20th century, was built for the Hapsburg heir Franz Ferdinand (it was tradition for rulers not to move into their predecessor's quarters). But—while he was waiting politely for his long-lived uncle, Emperor Franz Josef, to die so he could move into his new digs—Franz Ferdinand was assassinated in Sarajevo in 1914, sparking the beginning of World War I.

The palace's grand facade arches around Heroes' Square. Notice statues of two great Austrian heroes on horseback: Prince Eugene of Savoy (who defeated the Ottomans that had earlier threatened Vienna) and Archduke Charles (first to beat Napoleon in a battle, breaking Nappy's image of invincibility and heralding the end of the Napoleonic age). The frilly spires of Vienna's Neo-Gothic City Hall break the horizon, and a line of horse-drawn carriages await their customers.

▲▲New Palace Museums: Armor, Music, and Ancient Greek Statues—The Neue Burg—technically part of the Kunsthistorisches Museum across the way—houses three fine museums (same ticket): an armory (with a killer collection of medieval weapons), historical musical instruments, and classical statuary from ancient Ephesus. The included audioguide brings the exhibits to life and lets you actually hear the collection's fascinating old instruments being played. An added bonus is the chance to wander all alone among those royal Hapsburg halls, stairways, and painted ceilings (€8; armor and music Tue–Sun 10:00–18:00, closed Mon; Greek Wed–Mon 10:00–18:00, closed Tue; almost no tourists, tel. 01/5252-4484).

More Hapsburg Sights near the Hofburg

Central Vienna has plenty more sights associated with the Hapsburgs. With the exception of the last one (on Mariahilfer Strasse), these are all near the Hofburg. Remember that the biggest Hapsburg sight of all, Schönbrunn Palace, makes a great half-day trip (four miles from the center—see page 57).

Palace Garden (Burggarten)—This greenbelt, once the backyard of the Hofburg and now a people's park, welcomes you to loiter on the grass. On nice days, it's lively with office workers enjoying a break. The statue of Mozart facing the Ringstrasse is popular. The iron-and-glass pavilion now houses the recommended Palmenhaus

Restaurant (see page 81) and a small but fluttery butterfly exhibit (€5; April–Oct Mon–Fri 10:00–16:45, Sat–Sun 10:00–18:15; Nov–March daily 10:00–15:45). The butterfly zone is delightfully muggy on a brisk off-season day, but trippy any time of year. If you tour it, notice the butterflies hanging out on the trays with rotting slices of banana. They lick the fermented banana juice as it beads, and then just hang out there in a stupor...or fly giddy loop-de-loops.

▲Lipizzaner Museum—While the famous court horses of the Hapsburg emperors were originally from Spain, by the 16th century they were moved closer to Vienna (to the Slovenian town of Lipica, then part of the Hapsburg Empire). For four centuries, the "Lipizzaner Stallions" have been bred, raised, and trained in Lipica. They actually have "surnames" that can be traced to the original six 16th-century stallions that made the trip from Spain. A must for horse-lovers, this tidy museum in the Renaissance Stallburg Palace shows (and tells in English) the 400-year history of the famous Spanish Riding School and the Lipizzaner Stallions (€5, €15 combo-ticket includes training session—see below, daily 9:00–18:00, between Josefsplatz and Michaelerplatz at Reitschulgasse 2, tel. 01/5252-4583, www.lipizzaner.at). Any time of day, you can see the horses prance on video in the museum's window.

➲ **Self-Guided Tour:** This commentary will make your visit more meaningful.

First Room: One horse's family tree—Conversano Toscana (born 1984)—is shown, tracing his father's line (Conversano) back to 1767. Paintings show how horses were bred for small heads and legs, but massive bodies. The three-minute video is quite graphic, starting with a horse worked up and ready to "joust," followed by a horse giving birth, then a wobbly baby—just minutes old—taking its first steps.

Second Room: Videos clearly illustrate how the traditional moves so appreciated today evolved. After horses were antiquated on the battlefield, dressage morphed from no-nonsense military moves to court entertainment. The "dancing" originated as battle moves: *pirouette* (quick turns for surviving in the thick of battle) and *courbette* (on hind legs, to make a living shield for the knight). The *capriole* is a strong back-kick that could floor any enemy.

Third Room: Each of the main movements is illustrated on video.

Basement Theater: A 45-minute movie with great horse footage runs constantly (showings alternate between German and English, ask upon arrival about the next English showing).

Upstairs: Here an exhibit retells the dramatic WWII Lipizzaner rescue story. Lipizzaner fans have a warm spot in their hearts for General Patton, who, at the end of World War II—knowing that the Soviets were about to take control of Vienna—ordered a raid on the stable to save the horses and ensure the survival of their fine old bloodlines.

If all this horse information gets you fired up for more, consider...

Seeing the Lipizzaner Stallions—Seats for performances by Vienna's prestigious Spanish Riding School book up months in advance, but standing room is often available the same day (tickets-€45–160, standing room-€28, Feb–June and Sept–Oct Sun at 11:00, sometimes also Fri at 18:00, no shows July–Aug, fewer Nov–Jan, tel. 01/533-9031, www.srs.at). Luckily for the masses, training sessions with music in a chandeliered Baroque hall are open to the public (€12 at the door, roughly Feb–June and Sept–Oct Tue–Sat 10:00–12:00—but only when the horses are in town).

Tourists line up early at Josefsplatz, gate 2. Save money and avoid the wait by buying the €15 combo-ticket that covers both the museum and the training session (and lets you avoid that ticket line). If you want to hang out with Japanese tour groups, get there early and wait for the doors to open at 10:00. Better yet, simply show up late. Almost no one stays for the full two hours—except for the horses. As people leave, new tickets are printed continuously, so you can just waltz in with no wait at all. Don't have high expectations, as the horses often do little more than trot and warm up.

With the riding school enduring financial problems, other ways to see the horses and their stables are now possible (pricey, but for some a good value, details on the Web—www.lipizzaner.at).

▲Augustinian Church (Augustinerkirche)—This is the Gothic and Neo-Gothic church where the Hapsburgs latched, then buried, their hearts (weddings took place here, and the royal hearts are in the vault). Don't miss the exquisite, tomb-like Canova memorial (Neoclassical, 1805) to Maria Theresa's favorite daughter, Maria Christina, with its incredibly sad white-marble procession. The church's 11:00 Sunday Mass is a hit with music-lovers—both a Mass and a concert, often with an orchestra accompanying the choir. To pay, contribute to the offering plate and buy a CD afterwards. Programs are available at the table by the entry all week (church open long hours daily, Augustinerstrasse 3).

The church faces Josefsplatz, with its statue of the great reform emperor Josef II. The **National Library** (€5, Tue–Sun 10:00–18:00, Thu until 21:00, closed Mon, next to the Augustinian Church) is impressive.

▲▲Albertina Museum—This building, at the southern tip of the Hofburg complex (near the Opera), was the residence of Maria Teresa's favorite daughter: Maria Christina, who was the only one allowed to marry for love rather than political strategy. Her many sisters were jealous. (Marie-Antoinette had to marry the French king...and lost her head over it.) Maria Christina's husband, Albert of Saxony, was a great collector of original drawings. He amassed an enormous assortment of works by Dürer, Rembrandt, Rubens, and others. Today the Albertina presents wonderful exhibitions of these fine works and allows visitors to tour its elegant state rooms and enjoy temporary exhibits of other artists (€9, price can vary based on special exhibits, €3.50 audioguide also available for both permanent and temporary exhibits, daily 10:00–18:00, Wed until 21:00, overlooking Albertinaplatz across from TI and Opera, tel. 01/534-830, www.albertina.at).

The Albertina consists of three components. First, stroll through the Hapsburg staterooms (French Classicism—lots of white marble). Top-quality facsimiles of the collection's greatest pieces hang in these rooms. Then browse the modern gallery, featuring special exhibitions. Finally, the Albertina also displays selections from its own spectacular collection of works by Michelangelo, Rubens, Rembrandt, and Raphael, plus a huge sampling of precise drawings by Albrecht Dürer. Of 400 original Dürer drawings that survived, Albert collected 300. Most were sold or stolen over the ages, and today the collection is down to about 100. Since these fragile sketches and exquisite drawings are very sensitive to light, they're kept mostly in darkness and shown only rarely, in rotation. The collection is vast, so you'll always see exciting originals, thoughtfully described in English.

▲▲Kaisergruft, the Remains of the Hapsburgs—Visiting the imperial remains is not as easy as you might imagine. These original organ donors left their bodies—about 150 in all—in the unassuming Kaisergruft (Capuchin Crypt), their hearts in the Augustinian Church (described above; church open long hours daily, but to see the goods you'll have to talk to a priest), and their entrails in the crypt below St. Stephen's Cathedral. Don't tripe.

Upon entering the Kaisergruft (€4, daily 9:30–16:00, last entry at 15:40, behind Opera on Neuer Markt), buy the €0.50 map with a Hapsburg family tree and a chart locating each coffin.

The double coffin of **Maria Theresa** (1717–1780) and her husband, **Franz I** (1708–1765), is worth a close look for its artwork. Maria Theresa outlived her husband by 15 years—which she spent in mourning. Old and fat, she installed a special lift enabling her to get down into the crypt to be with her dear, departed Franz (even though he had been far from faithful). The couple recline—Etruscan-style—atop their fancy lead coffin. At each corner are the crowns of the Hapsburgs—the Holy Roman Empire, Hungary, Bohemia, and Jerusalem. Notice the contrast between the Rococo splendor of Maria Theresa's tomb and the simple box holding her more modest son, **Josef II** (at his parents' feet).

Franz Josef (1830–1916) is nearby, in an appropriately austere military tomb. Flanking Franz Josef are the tombs of his son, the archduke **Rudolf,** and Empress Elisabeth. Rudolf and his teenage mistress supposedly committed suicide together in 1889 at Mayerling hunting lodge and—since the Church figured he forced her and was therefore a murderer—it took considerable legal hair-splitting to win Rudolf this spot (after examining his brain, it was determined that he was physically retarded and therefore incapable of knowingly killing himself and his girl). *Kaiserin* Elisabeth (1837–1898), a.k.a. **Sisi,** always gets the "Most Flowers" award.

In front of those three is the most recent Hapsburg tomb. **Empress Zita** was buried in 1989. Her burial procession was probably the last such Old Regime event in European history. The monarchy died hard in Austria.

While it's fun to chase down all these body parts, remember that the real legacy of the Hapsburgs is the magnificence of this city. Step outside. Pan up. Watch the clouds glide by the ornate gables of Vienna.

▲Imperial Furniture Collection (Kaiserliches Hofmobiliendepot)—Bizarre, sensuous, eccentric, or precious, this is your peek at the Hapsburgs' furniture—from grandma's wheelchair to the emperor's spittoon—all thoughtfully described in English. The Hapsburgs had many palaces, but only the Hofburg was permanently furnished. The rest were furnished on the fly—set up and taken down by a gang of royal roadies called the "Depot of Court Movables" (Hofmobiliendepot). When the monarchy was dissolved in 1918, the state of Austria took possession of the Hofmobiliendepot's inventory—165,000 items. Now this royal storehouse is open to the public in a fine and sprawling museum. Don't go here for the *Jugendstil* furnishings. The older Baroque, Rococo, and Biedermeier pieces are the most impressive and tied most intimately to the royals. Combine a visit to this museum with a stroll down the lively shopping boulevard, Mariahilfer Strasse (€7, Tue–Sun 10:00–18:00, closed Mon, Mariahilfer Strasse 88, U-3: Zieglergasse, tel. 01/5243-3570).

Kunsthistorisches Museum

This exciting museum, across the Ring from the Hofburg Palace, is worth ▲▲▲. It showcases the grandeur and opulence of the Hapsburgs' collected artwork in a grand building (built as a museum in 1888). There are European masterpieces galore, all well-hung on one glorious floor, plus a fine display of Egyptian, classical, and applied arts (€10, audioguide-€2, Tue–Sun 10:00–18:00, Thu until 21:00, closed Mon, on the Ringstrasse at Maria-Theresien-Platz, U-2 or U-3: Volkstheater/Museumsplatz, tel. 01/525-240, www.khm.at).

The Kunsthistorwhateveritis Museum—let's just say

Kunsthistorisches Museum

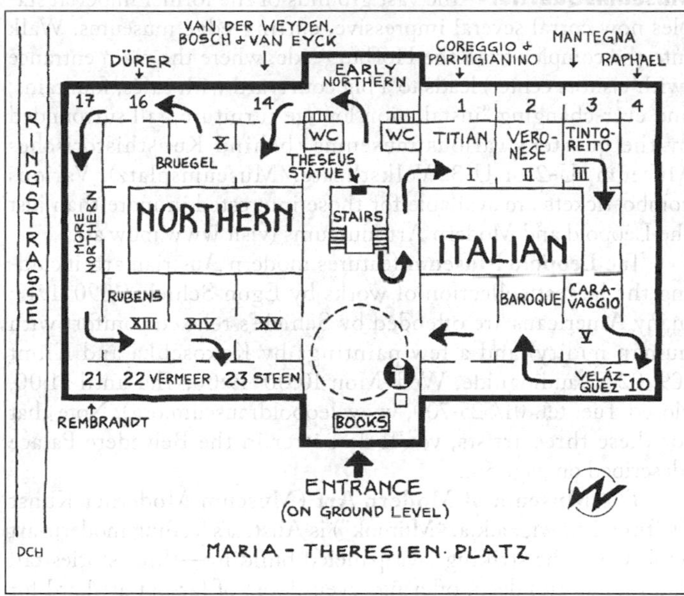

"Koonst"—houses some of the most beautiful, sexy, and fun-loving art from two centuries (c. 1450–1650). The collection reflects the joie de vivre of Austria's luxury-loving Hapsburg rulers. At their peak of power in the 1500s, the Hapsburgs ruled Austria, Germany, northern Italy, the Netherlands, and Spain—and you'll see a wide variety of art from all these places and beyond.

Of the museum's many exhibits, focus on the Painting Gallery (Gemäldegalerie) on the first floor. Climb the main staircase, featuring Antonio Canova's statue of *Theseus Clubbing the Centaur*. Italian Art is in the right half of the building (as you face Theseus), and Northern Art to the left. Notice that the museum labels the largest rooms with Roman numerals (Saal I, II, III), and the smaller rooms around the perimeter with Arabic (Rooms 1, 2, 3). Look for works by Titian, Veronese, Tintoretto, Raphael, Caravaggio, Bruegel, Dürer, Rembrandt, and Vermeer.

Near the Kunsthistorisches Museum

▲Natural History Museum—In the twin building facing the Kunsthistorisches Museum, you'll find moon rocks, dinosaur stuff, and a copy of the fist-sized *Venus of Willendorf*—at 30,000 years old, the world's oldest sex symbol, found in the Danube Valley (the original is in the museum's vault). This museum is a hit with children (€8, Wed–Mon 9:00–18:30, Wed until 21:00, closed Tue, tel. 01/521-770).

MuseumsQuartier—The vast grounds of the former imperial stables now corral several impressive, cutting-edge museums. Walk into the complex from the Hofburg side, where the main entrance (with visitors center) leads to a big courtyard with cafés, fountains, and ever-changing "installation lounge furniture," all surrounded by the quarter's various museums (behind Kunsthistorisches Museum, U-2 or U-3: Volkstheater/Museumsplatz). Various combo-tickets are available for those interested in more than just the Leopold and Modern Art museums (visit www.mqw.at).

The **Leopold Museum** features modern Austrian art, including the largest collection of works by Egon Schiele (1890–1918; many Americans are offended by Schiele's relaxed comfort with human nudity) and a few paintings by Kokoschka and Klimt (€9, €2.50 audioguide, Wed–Mon 10:00–19:00, Thu until 21:00, closed Tue, tel. 01/525-700, www.leopoldmuseum.org). Note that for these three artists, you'll do better in the Belvedere Palace (described on page 56).

The **Museum of Modern Art** (Museum Moderner Kunst Stiftung Ludwig, a.k.a. "Mumok") is Austria's leading modern-art gallery. It's the striking lava-paneled building—three stories tall and four stories deep, offering seven floors of far-out art hard for most to appreciate. This huge, state-of-the-art museum displays revolving exhibits showing off art of the last generation—including Klee, Picasso, and Pop (€8, Tue–Sun 10:00–18:00, Thu until 21:00, closed Mon, tel. 01/525-001-440, www.mumok.at).

Rounding out the sprawling MuseumsQuartier are an architecture museum, Transeuropa, Electronic Avenue, children's museum, and the Kunsthalle Wien—an exhibition center for contemporary art (€7.50, Thu–Tue 10:00–19:00, Thu until 22:00, closed Wed, tel. 01/521-8933, www.kunsthallewien.at).

Central Vienna, Inside the Ring

▲▲Haus der Musik—Vienna's "House of Music" has a small first-floor exhibit on the Vienna Philharmonic, and upstairs you'll enjoy fine audiovisual exhibits on each of the famous hometown boys (Haydn, Mozart, Beethoven, Strauss, and Mahler). But the museum is unique for its effective use of interactive touch-screen computers and headphones to actually explore the physics of sound. You can twist, dissect, and bend sounds to make your own musical language, merging your voice with a duck's quack or a city's traffic roar. Wander through the "sonosphere" and marvel at the amazing acoustics—I could actually hear what I thought only a piano tuner could hear. Pick up a virtual baton to conduct the Vienna Philharmonic Orchestra (each time you screw up, the musicians put their instruments down and ridicule you). Really experiencing the place takes time. It's open late and makes a good evening activity (€10, daily 10:00–22:00, last entry 1 hour before closing, 2 blocks from Opera at Seilerstätte 30, tel. 01/51648, www.hdm.at).

Mozart Haus Museum—Opened in 2006 for Wolfgang's 250th birthday, this museum is easy to get excited about, but disappoints. Exhibits fill the only surviving Mozart residence in Vienna (where he lived from 1784 to 1787, when he had lots of money). You'll learn his life story, with an emphasis on his most creative years...when he lived here. Included is a rundown on the Vienna music scene during the Mozart years, a quirky look at his gambling habits and his interest in crudely erotic peep shows, and a four-minute montage of his most famous arias in a mini-theater. Unfortunately, visiting the museum is like reading a book standing up—rather than turning pages, you climb stairs. There are almost no real artifacts. Wolfie would have found the audioguide dreadful. While the museum might be worth the time and money for Mozart enthusiasts, both Mozart sights in Salzburg (the Birthplace and the Residence—see Salzburg chapter) are more gratifying. In Vienna, I enjoy the Haus der Musik (described above) much more (€9, daily 10:00–20:00, a block behind the cathedral, go through arcade at #5 and walk 50 yards to Domgasse 5, tel. 01/512-1791, www.mozarthausvienna.at).

▲Vienna's Auction House, the Dorotheum—For an aristocrat's flea market, drop by Austria's answer to Sotheby's, the Dorotheum. Its five floors of antique furniture and fancy knickknacks have been put up either for immediate sale or auction, often by people who inherited old things they don't have room for. Wandering through here, you feel like you're touring a museum with exhibits you can buy (Mon–Fri 10:00–18:00, Sat 9:00–17:00, closed Sun, classy little café on second floor, between Graben and Hofburg at Dorotheergasse 17, tel. 01/515-600, www.dorotheum.com). The info desk at the ground floor has a building map and schedule of upcoming auctions. Labels on each item predict the auction value. Continue your hunt for the perfect curio on the streets around the Dorotheum, lined with many fine antique shops.

Judenplatz Memorial and Museum—The square called Judenplatz marks the location of Vienna's 15th-century Jewish community, one of Europe's largest at the time. The square, once filled with a long-gone synagogue, is now dominated by a blocky memorial to the 65,000 Austrian Jews killed by the Nazis. The memorial—a library turned inside out—symbolizes Jews as "people of the book" and causes viewers to ponder the huge loss of culture, knowledge, and humanity that took place between 1938 and 1945.

The Judenplatz Museum, while sparse, has displays on medieval Jewish life and a well-done video re-creating community scenes from five centuries ago. Wander the scant remains of the medieval synagogue below street level—discovered during the construction of the Holocaust memorial. This was the scene of a medieval massacre. Since Christians weren't allowed to lend money, Jews were Europe's moneylenders. As so often happened in Europe, when Viennese Christians fell too deeply into debt, they found a convenient excuse to wipe out the local ghetto—and their debts at the same time. In 1421, 200 of Vienna's Jews were burned at the stake. Others who refused a forced conversion committed mass suicide in the synagogue (€3, €7 combo-ticket includes synagogue and Jewish Museum of the City of Vienna—see page 60, Sun–Thu 10:00–18:00, Fri 10:00–14:00, closed Sat, Judenplatz 8, tel. 01/535-0431, www.jmw.at).

Near Karlsplatz

These sights cluster around Karlsplatz, just southeast of the Ringstrasse (U-1, U-2, or U-4: Karlsplatz).

Karlsplatz—This picnic-friendly square, with its Henry Moore sculpture in the pond, is ringed with sights. The Art Nouveau station pavilions—from the late 19th-century municipal train system *(Stadtbahn)*—are textbook *Jugendstil* by Otto Wagner, with iron frames, decorative marble slabs, and painted gold ornaments. One of Europe's first subway systems, this precursor to today's U-Bahn was built with a military purpose in mind: to move troops quickly in time of civil unrest—specifically, out to Schönbrunn Palace. One of the pavilions is open as an exhibit on Otto Wagner (€2, June–Oct Tue–Sun 9:00–18:00, closed Mon and Nov–May).

Charles Church (Karlskirche)—Charles Borromeo, a 16th-century bishop from Milan, was an inspiration during plague times. This "votive church" was dedicated to him in 1713, when an epidemic spared Vienna. The church offers the best Baroque in Vienna, with a unique combination of columns (showing scenes from the life of Charles Borromeo, à la Trajan's Column in Rome), a classic pediment, and an elliptical dome. The church underwent restoration work throughout much of 2007 (€6 includes audioguide and a skippable one-room museum; Mon–Sat 9:00–12:30 & 13:00–18:00, Sun 13:00–18:00, last entry 30 min before closing). The entry fee may seem steep, but remember that it helps fund the recent restoration.

Visitors ride the industrial lift to a platform at the base of the dome. (Consider that the church was built and decorated with a scaffolding system essentially the same as this one.) Once up there, you'll climb stairs to the steamy lantern at the extreme top of the church. At that dizzying height, you're in the clouds with cupids and angels. Many details that appear smooth and beautiful from ground level—such as gold leaf, rudimentary paintings, and fake marble—look rough and sloppy up close. It's surreal to observe the 3-D figures from an unintended angle. Faith, Hope, Charity, and Borromeo triumph and inspire—while Protestants and their stinkin' books are trashed. Borromeo lobbies heaven for plague relief. At the very top, you'll see the tiny dove representing the Holy Ghost, surrounded by a cheering squad of nipple-lipped cupids.

Historical Museum of the City of Vienna (Wien Museum Karlsplatz)—This under-appreciated museum walks you through the history of Vienna with fine historic artifacts. You'll work your way up, chronologically: The ground floor exhibits Roman artifacts and original statues from St. Stephen's Cathedral (c. 1350), with various Hapsburgs showing off the slinky hip-hugging fashion of the day. The first floor features old city maps, booty from a Turkish siege, and an 1850 city model showing the town just before the wall was replaced by the Ring. Finally, the second floor displays a city model from 1898 (with the new Ringstrasse), sentimental Biedermeier paintings and objets d'art, and early 20th-century paintings (including some by Gustav Klimt). The museum is worth the €4 admission (free Sun and Fri morning, open Tue–Sun 9:00–18:00, closed Mon, www.wienmuseum.at).

▲Academy of Fine Arts (Akademie der Bildenden Künste)—This small but exciting collection includes works by Bosch, Botticelli, and Rubens (quick, sketchy cartoons used to create his giant canvases); a Venice series by Guardi; and a self-portrait by a 15-year-old van Dyck. It's all magnificently lit and well-described by the €2 audioguide, and comes with comfy chairs (€5, Tue–Sun 10:00–18:00, closed Mon, 3 blocks from Opera at Schillerplatz 3, tel. 01/5881-6225, www.akademiegalerie.at). The fact that this is a working art academy gives it a certain realness. As you wander the halls of the academy, ponder how history might have been different if Hitler—who applied to study architecture here but was rejected—had been accepted as a student. Before leaving, peek into the ground floor's central hall—textbook historicism, the Ringstrasse style of the late 1800s.

▲The Secession—This little building, behind the Academy of Fine Arts, is nicknamed the "golden cabbage" today. It was created by the Vienna Secession movement, a group of non-conformist artists led by Gustav Klimt, Otto Wagner, and friends. The Secession, whose slogan was "To each age its art, and to art its liberty," first exhibited their "liberty-style" art here in 1897. The young trees carved into the walls and its bushy "cabbage" rooftop are symbolic of renewal cycle. Today, the Secession continues to showcase cutting-edge art, as well as one of Gustav Klimt's most famous works, the *Beethoven Frieze* (€6, Tue–Sun 10:00–18:00, Thu until 20:00, closed Mon, Friedrichstrasse 12, tel. 01/587-5307, www.secession.at).

While the staff hopes you take a look at the temporary exhibits (and the ticket includes this whether you like it or not), most tourists head directly for the basement, home to a small exhibit about the history of the building and the museum's highlight: Klimt's classic *Beethoven Frieze* (a.k.a. the "Searching Souls"). One of the masterpieces of Viennese Art Nouveau, this 105-foot-long fresco was a centerpiece of a 1902 "homage to Beethoven" exhibition. Sit down and read the free flier, which explains Klimt's still-powerful work. The theme, inspired by Beethoven's *Ninth Symphony*, features floating female figures "yearning for happiness." They drift and weave and search—like most of us do—through internal and external temptations and forces, falling victim to base and ungodly temptations, and losing their faith. Then, finally, they become fulfilled by poetry, music, and art as they reach the "Ideal Kingdom" where "True Happiness, Pure Bliss, and Absolute Love" are found in a climactic embrace.

Glass cases show sketches Klimt did in preparation for this work. The adjacent room tells the history of this masterpiece, and how the building was damaged in WWII.

▲Naschmarkt—In 1898, the city decided to cover up its Vienna River. The long, wide square they created was filled with a lively produce market that still bustles most days (closed Sun). It's long been known as *the* place to get exotic far-away foods. In fact, locals say, "From here start the Balkans."

From near the Opera, the Naschmarkt (roughly, "Munchies Market") stretches along Wienzeile Street. This "Belly of Vienna" comes with two parallel lanes—one lined with fun and reasonable eateries, and the other featuring the town's top-end produce and gourmet goodies. This is where top chefs like to get their ingredients. At the gourmet vinegar stall, you sample the vinegar like perfume—with a drop on your wrist (see photo). Farther from the center, the Naschmarkt becomes likeably seedy and surrounded by sausage stands, Turkish *Döner Kebab* stalls, cafés, and theaters. At the market's far end is a line of buildings with fine Art Nouveau facades. Each Saturday, the Naschmarkt is infested by a huge flea market where, in olden days, locals would come to hire a monkey to pick little critters out of their hair (Mon–Fri 6:00–18:30, Sat 6:00–17:00, closed Sun, closes earlier in winter, U-4: Kettenbruckengasse). For a picnic in the park, pick up your grub here and walk over to Karlsplatz (described above).

Beyond the Ring

▲Liechtenstein Museum—The noble Liechtenstein family (who own only a tiny country, but whose friendship with the Hapsburgs goes back generations) amassed an incredible private art collection. Their palace was long a treasure for Vienna art lovers. Then, in 1938—knowing Hitler was intent on plundering artwork to create an immense "Führer Museum"—the family fled to their tiny homeland with their best art. Since the museum reopened in 2004, attendance has been disappointing, and each year the museum cuts back its hours. The problem is its location...not its worthiness.

The Liechtensteins' "world of Baroque pleasures" includes the family's rare French Rococo carriage (which was used for their grand entry into Paris; it had to be carted to the edge of town and assembled, as nearly all such carriages were destroyed in the French Revolution), a plush Baroque library, an inviting English Garden, and an impressive collection of paintings including a complete cycle of early Rembrandts (€10, €4 audioguide, Fri–Mon 10:00–17:00, closed Tue–Thu, tram D to Bauernfeldplatz, Fürstengasse 1, tel. 01/319-5767-252, www.liechtensteinmuseum.at).

▲KunstHausWien: Hundertwasser Museum—This "make yourself at home" museum is a hit with lovers of modern art. It mixes the work and philosophy of local painter/environmentalist Friedensreich Hundertwasser (1928–2000). Stand in front of the colorful checkerboard building and consider Hundertwasser's style. He was against "window racism": Neighboring houses allow only one kind of window, but 100H_2O's windows are each different—and he encouraged residents to personalize them. He recognized "tree tenants" as well as human tenants. His buildings are spritzed with a forest and topped with dirt and grassy little parks—close to nature...good for the soul. Floors and sidewalks are irregular—to "stimulate the brain" (although current residents complain it just causes wobbly furniture and sprained ankles). Thus 100H_2O waged a one-man fight—during the 1950s and 1960s, when concrete and glass ruled—to save the human soul from the city. (Hundertwasser claimed that "straight lines are godless.") Inside the museum, start with his interesting biography. His fun-loving paintings are half *Jugendstil* ("youth style") and half just kids' stuff. Notice the photographs from his 1950s days as part of Vienna's bohemian scene. Throughout the museum, notice the fun philosophical quotes from an artist who believed, "If man is creative, he comes nearer to his creator" (€9 for Hundertwasser Museum, €12 combo-ticket includes special exhibitions, half-price on Mon, open daily 10:00–19:00, extremely fragrant and colorful garden café, Weissgerberstrasse 13, U-3: Landstrasse, tel. 01/712-0491, www.kunsthauswien.com).

Hundertwasserhaus: The KunstHausWien provides by far the best look at Hundertwasser. For an actual lived-in apartment complex by the green master, walk five minutes to the one-with-nature Hundertwasserhaus (free, at Löwengasse and Kegelgasse). This complex of 50 apartments, subsidized by the government to provide affordable housing, was built in the 1980s as a breath of architectural fresh air in a city of boring, blocky apartment complexes.

While not open to visitors, it's worth visiting for its fun-loving and colorful patchwork exterior and the Hundertwasser festival of shops across the street. Don't miss the view from Kegelgasse to see the "tree tenants" and the internal winter garden residents enjoy.

Hundertwasser detractors—of which there are many—remind visitors that 100H_2O was a painter, not an architect. They describe the Hundertwasserhaus as a "1950s house built in the 1980s," and colorfully painted with no real concern about the environment, communal living, or even practical comfort. Nearly all the original inhabitants got fed up with the novelty and moved out.

▲▲Belvedere Palace—This is the elegant palace of Prince Eugene of Savoy (1663–1736), the still-much-appreciated conqueror of the Ottomans. Eugene, a Frenchman considered too short and too ugly to be in the service of Louis XIV, offered his services to the Hapsburgs. While he was short and ugly indeed, he became the greatest military genius of his age. When you conquer cities, as Eugene did, you get really rich. He had no heirs, so the state got his property and Emperor Josef II established the Belvedere as Austria's first great public art gallery. Today, his palace boasts sweeping views and houses the Austrian gallery of 19th- and 20th-century art (€9, €3 audioguide, Tue–Sun 10:00–18:00, closed Mon, entrance at Prinz-Eugen-Strasse 27, tel. 01/7955-7134, www.belvedere.at). To get here from the center, catch tram D at the Opera (direction Südbahnhof, it stops at the palace gate).

The palace is actually two grand buildings separated by a fine garden. For our purposes, the **Upper Belvedere Palace** is what matters. The Upper Palace was Eugene's party house. Today, like the Louvre in Paris (but much easier to enjoy), this palace contains a fine collection of paintings. The collection is arranged chronologically: on the first floor, you'll find historicism, Romanticism, Impressionism, Realism, tired tourism, Expressionism, Art Nouveau, and early modernism. Each room tries to pair Austrian works from that period with much better-known European works. It's fun to see the original work of artists like van Gogh, Munch, and Monet hung with their lesser-known Austrian contemporaries. As Austria becomes a leader in art around 1900, the collection gets stronger, with fine works by Gustav Klimt, Oskar Kokoschka, and Egon Schiele. The Klimt room (facing the city center, on the far right) shows how even in his early work, the face was vivid and the rest dissolved into decor. During his "golden period," this background became his trademark gold leaf studded with stones. The highlight is Klimt's most famous (and often-replicated) work, *The Kiss*. (Some Klimt paintings formerly in this collection have been returned to their rightful owners.) The corner room shows a small exhibit on Prince Eugene, Archduke Franz Ferdinand, and the signing of the state treaty in 1955. Don't miss the poignant Schiele family portrait from 1918—his wife died while he was still working on it. (Schiele and his child were soon taken by the influenza epidemic that swept through Europe after WWI.)

The upper floor shows off early 19th-century Biedermeier paintings (hyper-sensitive, super-sweet, uniquely Viennese Romanticism—the poor are happy, things are lit impossibly well, and folk life is idealized). Your ticket also includes the Austrian Baroque and Gothic art in the Lower Belvedere Palace. Prince Eugene lived in that palace, but he's long gone and I wouldn't bother to visit.

View: *Belvedere* means "beautiful view." Sit at the top palace and look over the Baroque gardens, the mysterious sphinxes (which symbolized solving riddles and the finely educated mind of your host, Eugene), the lower palace, and the city. The spire of St. Stephen's Cathedral is 400 feet tall, and no other tall buildings are allowed inside the Ringstrasse. The hills—covered with vineyards—are where the Viennese love to go to sample the new wine. You can see Kahlenberg, from where you can walk down to several recommended *Heurigen* (wine gardens) beyond the spire (see page 66). These are the first of the Alps, which stretch from here all the way to Marseilles, France. The square you're overlooking was filled with people on May 15, 1955, as local leaders stood on the balcony of the Upper Palace (behind you) and proclaimed Austrian independence following a decade-long Allied occupation after World War II.

Schönbrunn Palace (Schloss Schönbrunn)

Among Europe's palaces, only Schönbrunn rivals Versailles. Worth ▲▲▲, this summer residence of the Hapsburgs is located four miles from the center. It's big (1,441 rooms), but don't worry—only 40 rooms are shown to the public. (Today the families of 260 civil servants rent simple apartments in the rest of the palace, enjoying rent control and governmental protections so they can't be evicted.)

Getting There: Take U-4 to Schönbrunn and walk 400 yards (just follow the crowds). The main entrance is in the left side of the palace as you face it.

Royal Apartments—While the exterior is Baroque, the interior was finished under Maria Theresa in let-them-eat-cake Rococo. The chandeliers are either of hand-carved wood with gold-leaf gilding or of Bohemian crystal. Thick walls hid the servants as they ran around stoking the ceramic stoves from the back, and attending to other behind-the-scenes matters. Most of the public rooms are decorated in Neo-Baroque, as they were under Franz Josef (r. 1848–1916). When WWII bombs rained on the city and the palace grounds, the palace itself took only one direct hit. Thankfully, that bomb, which crashed through three floors—including the sumptuous central ballroom—was a dud.

Cost: The admission price is based on which route you select (each one includes an audioguide): the **Imperial Tour** (22 rooms, €9, 45 min, Grand Palace rooms plus apartments of Franz Josef and Elisabeth—mostly 19th-century and therefore least interesting) or the **Grand Tour** (40 rooms, €11.50, 60 min, includes Imperial tour plus Maria Theresa's apartments—18th-century Rococo). A combo-ticket called the **Schönbrunn Pass Classic** includes the Grand Tour, as well as other sights on the grounds: the Gloriette viewing terrace, maze, privy garden, and court bakery—complete with *Apfelstrudel* demo and tasting (€15, available April–Oct only). I'd go for the Grand Tour.

Hours: Daily July–Aug 8:30–18:00, April–June and Sept–Oct 8:30–17:00, Nov–March 8:30–16:30. Information: www.schoenbrunn.at.

Crowd-Beating Tips: Schönbrunn suffers from crowds. It can be a jam-packed sauna in the summer. It's busiest from 9:30 to 11:30, especially on weekends and in July and August; it's least crowded from 12:00 to 14:00 and after 16:00, when there are no groups. To avoid the long delays in summer, make a reservation by telephone (tel. 01/8111-3239, answered daily 8:00–17:00, wait through the long message for the operator). You'll get an appointment time and a ticket number. Check in at least 30 minutes early. Upon arrival, go to the "Group and Reservations" desk (immediately inside the gate on the left at the gate house—long before the actual palace), give your number, pick up your ticket, and jump in ahead of the masses. If you show up in peak season without calling first, you deserve the frustration. (In this case, you'll have to wait in line, buy your ticket, and wait until the listed time to enter—which could be tomorrow.) If you have any time to kill, spend it exploring the gardens or Coach Museum.

Palace Gardens—After strolling by the Hapsburgs tucked neatly into their crypts, a walk through the emperor's garden with countless commoners is a celebration of the evolution of civilization from autocracy into real democracy. As a civilization, we're doing well.

Most of the park itself is free, as it has been since the 1700s (open daily sunrise to dusk, entrance on either side of the palace). The small side-gardens are the most elaborate. The Kammergarten on the left was a fancy private garden for the Hapsburgs (now restored and with a fee). The so-called Sisi Gardens on the right are free. Inside are several other sights, including a **palm house** (€3.50, daily May–Sept 9:30–18:00, Oct–April 9:30–17:00), Europe's oldest **zoo** (*Tiergarten*, built by Maria Theresa's husband for the entertainment and education of the court in 1752; €12, May–Sept daily 9:00–18:30, less off-season, tel. 01/877-9294), and—at the end of the gardens—the **Gloriette,** a purely decorative monument celebrating an obscure Austrian military victory and offering a fine city view (viewing terrace-€2, included in €15 Schönbrunn Pass Classic, daily April–Sept 9:00–18:00, July–Aug until 19:00, Oct 9:00–17:00, closed Nov–March). A touristy choo-choo train makes the rounds all day, connecting Schönbrunn's many attractions.

Coach Museum Wagenburg—The Schönbrunn coach museum is a 19th-century traffic jam of 50 impressive royal carriages and sleighs. Highlights include silly sedan chairs, the death-black hearse carriage (used for Franz Josef in 1916, and most recently for Empress Zita in 1989), and an extravagantly gilded imperial carriage pulled by eight Cinderella horses. This was rarely used other than for the coronation of Holy Roman Emperors, when it was disassembled and taken to Frankfurt for the big event (€4.50; April–Oct daily 9:00–18:00; Nov–March Tue–Sun 10:00–16:00, closed Mon; last entry 30 min before closing, 200 yards from palace, walk through right arch as you face palace, tel. 01/877-3244).

"Honorable Mentions": More Vienna Museums

These museums, scattered around the city, are worth a peek if you have a special interest.

Museum of Applied Art—The Österreichisches Museum für Angewandte Kunst, or MAK, is Vienna's answer to London's Victoria and Albert collection. It shows off the fancies of local aristocratic society, including a fine *Jugendstil* collection. The MAK is more than just another grand building on the Ringstrasse. It was built to provide models of historic design for Ringstrasse architects, and is a delightful space in itself (many locals stop in to enjoy a coffee on the plush couches in the main lobby). Each wing is dedicated to a different era. Exhibits, well-described in English, come with a playful modern flair—notable modern designers were assigned various spaces (€8, €10 includes a big English guidebook, free on Sat, open Tue–Sun 10:00–18:00, Tue until 24:00, closed Mon, Stubenring 5, tel. 01/711-360, www.mak.at).

The associated **Restaurant Österreicher im MAK** is named for a chef renowned for his classic and modern Viennese cuisine. Classy and mod, it's trendy for locals (daily, reserve for evening, €10–15 plates).

Sigmund Freud Museum—Freud enthusiasts travel to Vienna just to see this humble apartment and workplace of the man who fundamentally changed our understanding of the human psyche. Freud established his practice here in 1891, and it was here that he wrote his work on the interpretation of dreams. Freud, who was Jewish, fled with the rise of Nazism, and took most of his furniture with him. You won't see "the couch," but you will see his waiting room, along with three rooms packed with papers, photos, mementos, and documents. These, along with a family video from the 1930s, give an intimate peek at Freud's life. The old-fashioned exhibit is tediously described in a three-ring info binder loaned to visitors, which complements the more general audioguide (€6, daily 9:00–17:00, July–Sept until 18:00, cool shop, half a block from a tram D stop at Berggasse 19, tel. 01/319-1596, www.freud-museum.at).

More Museums—There's much, much more. The city map lists everything. If you're into Esperanto, undertakers, tobacco, clowns, firefighting, or the homes of dead composers, you'll find them all in Vienna.

These good museums try very hard but are submerged in the greatness of Vienna: **Jewish Museum of the City of Vienna** (€5, or €7 combo-ticket includes synagogue and Judenplatz Museum—described on page 51, Sun–Fri 10:00–18:00, Thu until 20:00, closed Sat, Dorotheergasse 11, tel. 01/535-0431, www.jmw.at), **Folkloric Museum of Austria** (Tue–Sun 10:00–17:00, closed Mon, Laudongasse 15, tel. 01/406-8905), and **Museum of Military History,** one of Europe's best if you like swords and shields (Heeresgeschichtliches Museum, €5.10, includes audioguide, Sat–Thu 9:00–17:00, closed Fri, Arsenal district, Objekt 18, tel. 01/795-610).

ACTIVITIES

People-Watching and Strolling

These activities allow you to take it easy and enjoy the Viennese good life.

▲City Park (Stadtpark)—Vienna's City Park is a waltzing world of gardens, memorials to local musicians, ponds, peacocks, music in bandstands, and Viennese escaping the city. Notice the *Jugendstil* entrance at the Stadtpark U-Bahn station. The Kursalon, where Strauss was the violin-toting master of waltzing ceremonies, hosts daily touristy concerts in three-quarter time.

▲Prater—Since the 1780s, when the reformist Emperor Josef II gave his hunting grounds to the people of Vienna as a public park, this place has been Vienna's playground. While tired and a bit run-down these days, Vienna's sprawling amusement park still tempts visitors with its huge 220-foot-tall, famous, and lazy Ferris wheel *(Riesenrad)*, roller coaster, bumper cars, Lilliputian railroad, and endless eateries. Especially if you're traveling with kids, this is a fun, goofy place to share the evening with thousands of Viennese (daily 9:00–24:00 in summer, but quiet after 22:00, U-1: Praterstern). For a local-style family dinner, eat at Schweizerhaus (good food, great Czech "Budweiser" beer, classic conviviality).

Danube Island (Donauinsel)—In the 1970s, the city dug a canal parallel to the mighty Danube River, creating both a flood barrier and a much-loved island escape from the city (easy U-Bahn access on U-1 to Donauinsel). This skinny, 12-mile long island provides a natural wonderland. All along the traffic-free, grassy park you'll find Viennese—especially immigrants and those who can't afford their own cabin or fancy vacation—at play. The swimming comes tough, though, with rocky entries rather than sand. The best activity here is a bike ride (see "Getting Around Vienna—By Bike," page 23). Be careful—if you venture too far from the crowds, you're likely to encounter nudists on rollerblades.

A Walk in the Vienna Woods (Wienerwald)—For a quick side-trip into the woods and out of the city, catch the U-4 to Heiligenstadt, then bus #38A to Kahlenberg, where you'll enjoy great views and a café overlooking the city. From there, it's a peaceful 45-minute downhill hike to the *Heurigen* of Nussdorf or Grinzing to enjoy some new wine (see "Vienna's Wine Gardens," page 66). Your free TI-produced city map can be helpful...just go downhill. For the very best views, stay on bus #38A to Leopoldsberg, where you'll find a lovely Baroque church, a breezy *Weinstube* (pub), and shady tables with expansive panoramas of the city and the Danube. While it seems like a long way to go for a big view, buses are cheap (or free with a transit pass) and go twice an hour until 22:00.

Naschmarkt—Vienna's busy produce market is a great place for people-watching (see page 54).

Shopping for Traditional Austrian Clothing—Two famous shops are fun to visit if you're interested in picking up a classy felt suit or dirndl. Most central is the fancy **Loden Plankl** shop (across from the Hofburg, at Michaelerplatz 6). But the **Tostmann Trachten** shop is the ultimate for serious shopping. Mrs. Tostmann powered the resurgence of this style. Her place is like a shrine to traditional Austrian and folk clothing—handmade and very expensive (Schottengasse 3A, 3-min walk from Am Hof, tel. 01/533-5331, www.tostmann.at).

Fast Boat to Bratislava—The generally overlooked (I've long thought for good reason) capital of Slovakia is suddenly on the radar screen for Vienna travelers for three reasons: its newly lively economy (thanks to its recent EU membership and intense foreign investment); its popular discount airport (see page 21); and the fast catamaran day trip. The DDSG line offers several daily boat trips from Schwedenplatz (where Vienna's old town hits the canal) to Bratislava in 75 minutes with good views (€23 each way, cheaper at less convenient times). For a fine day trip, you can depart at 8:30, arrive at 9:45 in Bratislava's Old Town, explore Bratislava (see below), and return to Vienna at 14:15 or 18:15 (departures daily June–Oct only, they also offer a guided day tour with guide and lunch for €60, tel. 01/58880, www.ddsg-blue-danube.at). The train makes the trip a bit faster and much cheaper (hourly, 1-hour trip).

If you visit Bratislava, you'll find a charming, increasingly rejuvenated Old Town (Staré Mesto) with cobbles upon cobbles of trendy cafés and restaurants. The Old Town is watched over by a drab hilltop fortress (worth climbing for the view, but not for the museums inside) and surrounded by ugly communist sprawl. The intensely dreary suburb of Petržalka, across the river, is an endless sea of concrete, communist-era apartment blocks. Bratislava has few worthwhile museums—especially compared to the world-class gems in Vienna—but the Old Town's relaxed café-culture ambience is nearly Mediterranean. Frankly, this trip isn't quite as exciting as it sounds. But Bratislava offers a Slavic flavor that's completely different from anything else in this book, and its much smaller size can be a nice break from the big-city intensity of Vienna. If you're not making the trek to Prague (or elsewhere in the East), this is your most convenient dip into Eastern Europe.

EXPERIENCES

Music Scene

As far back as the 12th century, Vienna was a mecca for musicians—both sacred and secular (troubadours). The Hapsburg emperors of the 17th and 18th centuries were not only generous supporters of music, but fine musicians and composers themselves. (Maria Theresa played a mean double bass.) Composers like Haydn, Mozart, Beethoven, Schubert, Brahms, and Mahler gravitated to this music-friendly environment. They taught each other, jammed together, and spent a lot of time in Hapsburg palaces. Beethoven was a famous figure, walking—lost in musical thought—through Vienna's woods. In the city's 19th-century belle époque, "Waltz King" Johann Strauss and his brothers kept Vienna's 300 ballrooms spinning.

This musical tradition continues into modern times, leaving some prestigious Viennese institutions for today's tourists to enjoy: the Opera (see page 33), the Boys' Choir, and the great Baroque halls and churches, all busy with classical and waltz concerts. As you poke into churches and palaces, you may hear groups practicing. You're welcome to sit and listen.

Vienna is Europe's music capital. It's music *con brio* from October through June, reaching a symphonic climax during the Vienna Festival each May and June. Sadly, in July and August, the Boys' Choir, the Opera, and many more music companies are—like you—on vacation. But Vienna hums year-round with live classical music. Except for the Boys' Choir, the musical events listed below are offered in summer.

Vienna Boys' Choir—The boys sing (from a high balcony, where they are heard but not seen) at the 9:15 Sunday Mass from September through March in the Hofburg's Imperial Chapel (Hofburgkapelle; entrance at Schweizerhof, from Josefsplatz go through tunnel). Reserved seats must be booked two months in advance (€5–29, reserve by fax, email, or mail: fax from the US 011-431-533-992-775, hmk@aon.at, or write Hofmusikkapelle, Hofburg-Schweizerhof, 1010 Wien; call 01/533-9927 for information only—they can't book tickets at this number). Much easier, standing room inside is free and open to the first 60 who line up. Even better, rather than line up early, you can simply swing by and stand in the narthex just outside, where you can hear the boys and see the Mass on a TV monitor. Boys' Choir concerts (on stage at the Musikverein) are also given Fridays at 16:00 in May, June, September, and October (€35–48, standing room goes on sale at 15:30 for €15, Karlsplatz 6, U-1, U-2, or U-4: Karlsplatz, tel. 01/5880-4141). They're nice kids, but, for my taste, not worth all the commotion. Remember, many churches have great music during Sunday Mass. Just 200 yards from the Boys' Choir chapel, Augustinian Church has a glorious 11:00 service each Sunday (see page 46).

Touristy Mozart and Strauss Concerts—If the music comes to you, it's touristy—designed for flash-in-the-pan Mozart fans. Powdered-wig orchestra performances are given almost nightly in grand traditional settings (€25–50). Pesky wigged-and-powdered Mozarts peddle tickets in the streets. They rave about the quality of the musicians, but you'll get second-rate chamber orchestras, clad in historic costumes, performing the greatest hits of Mozart and Strauss. These are casual, easygoing concerts with lots of tour groups. While there's not a Viennese person in the audience, the tourists generally enjoy the evening. To sort through all your options, check with the ticket office in the TI (same price as on the street, but with all venues to choose from). Savvy locals suggest getting the cheapest tickets, as no one seems to care if cheapskates move up to fill unsold pricier seats. Critics explain that the musicians are actually very good (often Hungarians, Poles, and Russians working a season here to fund an entire year of music studies back home), but that they haven't performed much together so aren't "tight." Of the many fine venues, the Mozarthaus is a small room richly decorated in Venetian Renaissance style with intimate chamber-music concerts (€35–42, almost nightly at 19:30, near St. Stephen's Cathedral at Singerstrasse 7, tel. 01-911-9077).

Strauss Concerts in the Kursalon—For years, Strauss concerts have been held in the Kursalon, where the "Waltz King" himself directed wildly popular concerts 100 years ago (€38–54, concerts nightly generally at 20:30, tel. 01/512-5790 to reserve). Shows last

1.75 hours and are a mix of ballet, waltzes, and a 15-piece orchestra. It's touristy—tour guides holding up banners with group numbers wait out front after the show. Even so, the performance is playful, visually fun, fine quality for most, and with a tried-and-tested, crowd-pleasing format. The conductor welcomes the crowd in German (with a wink) and English; after that...it's English only.

Serious Concerts—These events, including the Opera, are listed in the monthly *Wien-Programm* (available at TI, described on page 18). Tickets run from €36 to €75 (plus a stiff 22 percent booking fee when booked in advance or through a box office like the one at the TI). While it's easy to book tickets online long in advance, spontaneity is also workable, as there are invariably people with tickets they don't need selling them at face value or less outside the door before concert time. If you call a concert hall directly, they can advise you on the availability of (cheaper) tickets at the door. Vienna takes care of its starving artists (and tourists) by offering cheap standing-room tickets to top-notch music and opera (generally an hour before each performance).

Theater an der Wien—Considered the oldest theater in Vienna, this was designed in 1801 for Mozart operas—intimate, with just a thousand seats. Reopened in 2006 for Mozart's 250th birthday, it treats Vienna's music lovers to a different opera every month—generally Mozart with a contemporary setting and modern interpretation—with the top-notch Vienna Radio Orchestra in the pit. With the reopening of Theater an der Wien, Vienna now supports three opera companies. This one is the only company playing through the summer (facing the Naschmarkt at Linke Wienzeile 6, tel. 01/5818-1110 for information, tickets available at www.theater-wien.at).

Summer of Music Festival (a.k.a. "KlangBogen")—This annual festival assures that even from June through September, you'll find lots of great concerts, choirs, and symphonies (special *KlangBogen* brochure at TI; get tickets at Wien Ticket pavilion off Kärntner Strasse next to Opera, or go directly to location of particular event; Summer of Music tel. 01/42717, www.klangbogen.at).

Musicals—The Wien Ticket pavilion sells tickets to contemporary American and British musicals done in German language (€10–95, €2.50 standing room), and offers these tickets at half price from 14:00 until 17:00 the day of the show. Or you can reserve (full-price) tickets for the musicals by phone (call combined office for the three big theaters at tel. 01/58885).

Films of Concerts—To see free films of great concerts in a lively, outdoor setting near City Hall, check "Nightlife," page 68.

Dance Evening—If you'd like to actually dance (waltz and ballroom), or watch people who are really good at it, consider the Dance Evening at the Tanz Café in the Volksgarten (€5–10, May–Aug Fri–Sun from 19:00, www.volksgarten.at).

Classical Music to Go—To bring home Beethoven, Strauss, or the Wiener Philharmonic on a top-quality CD, shop at Gramola on the Graben, EMI on Kärntner Strasse, or Virgin Megastore on Mariahilfer Strasse.

Vienna's Cafés

In Vienna, the living room is down the street at the neighborhood coffee house. This tradition is just another example of Viennese expertise in good living. Each of Vienna's many long-established (and sometimes even legendary) coffee houses has its individual character (and characters). These classic cafés are a bit tired, with a shabby patina and famously grumpy waiters who treat you like an uninvited guest invading their living room. Still, it's a welcoming place. They offer newspapers, pastries, sofas, quick and light workers' lunches, elegance, smoky ambience, and "take all the time you want" charm for the price of a cup of coffee. Order it *melange* (like a cappuccino), *brauner* (strong coffee with a little milk), or *schwarzer* (black). Americans who ask for a latte are mistaken for Italians and given a cup of hot milk. Rather than buy the *Herald Tribune* ahead of time, spend the money on a cup of coffee and read the paper for free, Vienna-style, in a café.

These are my favorites:

Café Hawelka has a dark, "brooding Trotsky" atmosphere, paintings by struggling artists who couldn't pay for coffee, a saloon-wood flavor, chalkboard menu, smoked velvet couches, an international selection of newspapers, and a phone that rings for regulars. Mrs. Hawelka died just a couple weeks after Pope John Paul II. Locals suspect the pontiff wanted her much-loved *Buchteln* (marmalade-filled doughnuts) in heaven. Mr. Hawelka, now alone and understandably a bit forlorn, still oversees the action (Wed–Mon 8:00–2:00, Sun from 16:00, closed Tue, just off Graben, Dorotheergasse 6).

Café Sperl dates from 1880, and is still furnished identically to the day it opened—from the coat tree to the chairs (Mon–Sat 7:00–23:00, Sun 15:00–20:00 except closed Sun July–Aug, just off Naschmarkt near Mariahilfer Strasse, Gumpendorfer 11, tel. 01/586-4158).

Café Braunerhof, between the Hofburg and the Graben, offers a classic ambience with no tourists, live music on weekends (light classics, no cover, Sat–Sun 15:00–18:00), and a practical menu with daily specials (open long hours daily, Stallburgasse 2).

Other Classics in the Old Center: All of these places are open long hours daily: **Café Pruckel** (at Dr.-Karl-Lueger-Platz, across from the City Park at Stubenring 24); **Café Tirolerhof** (2 blocks from the Opera, behind the TI on Tegetthoffstrasse, at Führichgasse 8); and **Landtmann Café** (directly across from the

City Hall on the Ringstrasse at Dr.-Karl-Lueger-Ring 4). The Landtmann is unique, as it's the only grand café built along the Ring with all the other grand buildings.

Vienna's Wine Gardens *(Heurigen)*

The *Heuriger* (HOY-rih-gur; plural is *Heurigen*, HOY-rih-gehn) is a uniquely Viennese institution. When the Hapsburgs let Vienna's vintners sell their own new wine (called *Sturm*) tax-free, several hundred families opened *Heurigen* (wine-garden restaurants clustered around the edge of town)—and a tradition was born. Today they do their best to maintain the old-village atmosphere, serving the homemade new wine (the last vintage, until November 11, when a new vintage year begins) with light meals and strolling musicians. Most *Heurigen* are decorated with enormous antique presses from their vineyards. Wine gardens might be closed on any given day; always call ahead to confirm, if you have your heart set on a particular place. (For a near-*Heuriger* experience right downtown, drop by Gigerl Stadtheuriger—see page 77.)

At any *Heuriger*, fill your plate at a self-serve cold cut buffet (€6–9 for dinner). Food is sold by the *"10 dag"* unit. (A *dag* is a decigram, so *10 dag* is 100 grams...about a quarter-pound.) Dishes to look for...or look out for: *Stelze* (grilled knuckle of pork), *Fleischlaberln* (fried ground-meat patties), *Schinkenfleckerln* (pasta with cheese and ham), *Schmalz* (a spread made with pig fat), *Blunzen* (black pudding...sausage made from blood), *Presskopf* (jellied brains and innards), *Liptauer* (spicy cheese spread), *Kornspitz* (whole-meal bread roll), and *Kummelbraten* (crispy roast pork with caraway). Waitresses will then take your wine order (€2.20 per quarter-liter, about 8 oz). Many locals claim it takes several years of practice to distinguish between the *Sturm* wine and vinegar.

There are more than 1,700 acres of vineyards within Vienna's city limits, and countless *Heuriger* taverns. For a *Heuriger* evening, rather than go to a particular place, take a tram to the wine-garden district of your choice and wander around, choosing the place with the best ambience.

Getting to the *Heurigen*: You have three options: a 15-minute taxi ride, trams and buses, or a goofy tourist train.

Trams make a trip to the Vienna Woods quick and affordable. The fastest way is to ride U-4 to its last stop, Heiligenstadt, where trams and buses in front of the station fan out to the various neighborhoods. Ride tram D to its end point for Nussdorf. Ride bus #38A for Grinzing and on to the Kahlenberg viewpoint—#38A's end station. (Note that tram #38—different from bus #38A—starts at the Ring and finishes at Grinzing.) To get to Neustift am Walde, ride U-6 to Nussdorfer Strasse and catch bus

#35A. Connect Grinzing and Nussdorf with bus #38A and tram D (transfer at Grinzinger Strasse).

The **Heurigen Express** tourist train is tacky but handy and relaxing, chugging you on a hop-on, hop-off circle from Nussdorf through Grinzing and around the Vienna Woods with light narration (€7.30, buy ticket from driver, 1 hour, daily April–Oct 12:00–19:00, departs from end station of tram D in Nussdorf at the top of the hour, tel. 01/479-2808).

Here are a couple of good *Heuriger* neighborhoods:

Grinzing—Of the many *Heuriger* suburbs, Grinzing is the most famous, lively...and touristy. Many people precede their visit to Grinzing by riding tram #38 from Schottentor (on the Ring) to its end (up to Kahlenberg for a grand Vienna view), and then ride 20 minutes back into the *Heuriger* action. From the Grinzing tram stop, follow Himmelgasse uphill toward the onion-top dome. You'll pass plenty of wine gardens—and tour buses—on your way up. Just past the dome, you'll find the heart of the *Heurigen.*

Heiligenstadt (Pfarrplatz)—Between Grinzing and Nussdorf, this area features several decent spots, including the famous and touristy Mayer am Pfarrplatz (a.k.a **Beethovenhaus,** Mon–Sat 16:00–23:00, Sun 11:00–23:00, bus #38A stop: Fernsprechamt/Heiligenstadt, walk 5 min uphill on Dübling Nestelbachgasse to Pfarrplatz 2, tel. 01/370-1287). This place has a charming inner courtyard with an accordion player and a sprawling backyard with a big children's play zone. Beethoven lived—and composed his *Sixth Symphony*—here in 1817. He hoped the local spa would cure his worsening deafness. **Weingut and Heuriger Werner Welser,** a block uphill from Beethoven's place, is lots of fun, with music nightly from 19:00 (open daily 15:30–24:00, Probusgasse 12, tel. 01/318-9797).

Nussdorf—A less-touristy district, characteristic and popular with the Viennese, Nussdorf has plenty of *Heuriger* ambience. Right at the end station of tram D, you'll find three long and skinny places side by side: **Schübel-Auer Heuriger** (Tue–Sat 16:00–24:00, closed Sun–Mon, Kahlenberger Strasse 22, tel. 01/370-2222) is my favorite. Also consider **Heuriger Kierlinger** (daily 15:30–24:00, Kahlenberger Strasse 20, tel. 01/370-2264) and **Steinschaden** (daily 15:00–24:00, Kahlenberger Strasse 18, tel. 01/370-1375). Walk through any of these and you pop out on Kahlenberger Strasse, where a walk 20 yards uphill takes you to some more eating and drinking fun: **Bamkraxler** ("Tree Jumper"), the only beer garden amid all these vineyards. It's a fun-loving, youthful place with fine keg beer and a regular menu—traditional, ribs, veggie, kids' menu—rather than the *Heuriger* cafeteria line (€6–10 meals, kids' playground, Tue–Sat 16:00–24:00, Sun 11:00–24:00, closed Mon, Kahlenberger Strasse 17, tel. 01/318-8800).

Sirbu Weinbau Heuriger—This option is actually in the vineyards, high above Vienna with great city and countryside views, a top-notch buffet, a glass veranda, and a traditional interior for cool weather. It's a bit more touristy, since it's more upmarket and famous as "the ultimate setting" (April–Oct from 15:00, closed Sun, big children's play zone, Kahlenberger Strasse 210, tel. 01/320-5928). It's high above regular transit service, but fun to incorporate into a little walking. Ideally, ride bus #38A to the end at Kahlenberg, and ask directions to the *Heuriger* (a 20-min walk downhill).

NIGHTLIFE

If old music and new wine aren't your thing, Vienna has plenty of alternatives. For an up-to-date rundown on fun after dark, get the TI's free *Vienna Hype* booklet.

Open-Air Classical Music Cinema and Food Circus—A thriving people scene erupts each evening in July and August at the park in front of City Hall (Rathaus, on the Ringstrasse). Thousands of people keep a food circus of 24 simple stalls busy. There's not a paper plate or plastic cup anywhere, just real plates and glasses—Vienna wants the quality of eating to be as high as the music that's about to begin. About 3,000 folding chairs face a 60-foot-wide screen up against the City Hall's Neo-Gothic facade. When darkness falls, an announcer explains the program, and then the music starts. The program is different every night—mostly movies of opera and classical concerts, with some films. The schedule is at the TI (programs generally last around two hours, starting when it's dark—between 9:30 in July and 8:30 in August).

Since 1991, the city has paid for 60 of these summer event nights each year. Why? To promote culture. Officials know the City Hall Music Festival is mostly a "meat market" where young people come to hook up. But they believe many of these people will develop a little appreciation of classical music and high culture on the side.

English Cinema—Two great theaters offer three or four screens of English movies nightly (€6–9): **English Cinema Haydn,** near my recommended hotels on Mariahilfer Strasse (Mariahilfer Strasse 57, tel. 01/587-2262, www.haydnkino.at); and **Artis International Cinema,** right in the town center a few minutes from the cathedral (Schultergasse 5, tel. 01/535-6570).

***The Third Man* at Burg Kino**—This movie, voted the best British film ever by the British Film Institute, takes place in 1949 Vienna—when it was divided like Berlin between the four victorious Allies. With a dramatic Vienna cemetery scene, coffee-house culture surviving amid the rubble, and Orson Wells being chased through the sewers, the tale of a divided city about to fall under Soviet rule and rife with smuggling is an enjoyable two-hour experience while in Vienna (€8, in English with German subtitles; three showings weekly: Fri at 23:00, Tue and Sun around 15:30 depending on other film times; Opernring 19, tel. 01/587-8406, www.burgkino.at).

SLEEPING

As you move out from the center, hotel prices drop. My listings are in the old center (figure at least €100 for a decent double), along the likeable Mariahilfer Strasse (around €80), and near the Westbahnhof (around €60). While few accommodations in Vienna are air-conditioned (they are troubled by the fact that, per person, Las Vegas expends more energy keeping people cool than arctic Norway does keeping people warm), you can generally get fans on request. Places with elevators often have a few stairs to climb, too.

These hotels lose big and you pay more if you find a room through Internet booking sites. Book direct by phone, fax, or email and save. The city has deliberately created an expensive hell for cars in the center. Don't even try. If you must bring a car into Vienna, leave it at an expensive garage.

Within the Ring, in the Old City Center

You'll pay extra to sleep in the atmospheric old center, but if you can afford it, staying here gives you the best classy Vienna experience.

$$$ Hotel am Stephansplatz is a four-star business hotel with 56 rooms. It's plush but not over-the-top, and reasonably priced for its incredible location—literally facing the cathedral—and sleek comfort. Every detail is modern and quality, breakfast is superb

Sleep Code

(€1 = about $1.30, country code: 43, area code: 01)
S = Single, **D** = Double/Twin, **T** = Triple, **Q** = Quad, **b** = bathroom, **s** = shower only. English is spoken at each place. Unless otherwise noted, credit cards are accepted and breakfast is included.

To help you sort easily through these listings, I've divided the rooms into three categories, based on the price for a standard double room with bath:

$$$ Higher Priced—Most rooms €120 or more.
$$ Moderately Priced—Most rooms between €75–120.
$ Lower Priced—Most rooms €75 or less.

Hotels in Central Vienna

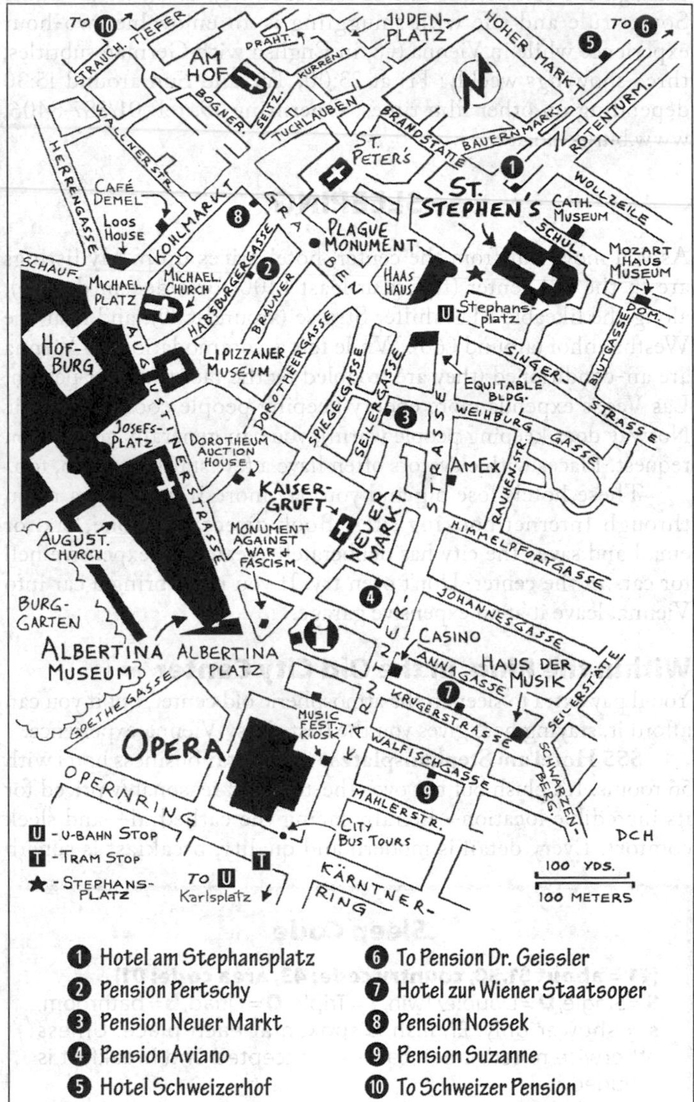

with a view of the city waking up around the cathedral, and the staff is always ready with a friendly welcome (Db-€205–245, Tb-€245, €20 less July–Aug and in winter, €15 less Fri–Sat, children free or very cheap, elevator, Stephansplatz 9, U-1 or U-3: Stephansplatz, tel. 01/534-050, fax 01/5340-5710, www.hotelamstephansplatz.at, office@hotelamstephansplatz.at).

$$$ Pension Pertschy, circling an old courtyard, is bigger and more hotelesque than the options below. Its 50 rooms are huge, but well-worn and a bit musty. Those on the courtyard are quietest (Sb-€90–105, small Db-€133, large Db-€151, cheaper off-season, extra bed-€32, non-smoking rooms, elevator, Habsburgergasse 5, U-1 or U-3: Stephansplatz, tel. 01/534-490, fax 01/534-4949, www.pertschy.com, pertschy@pertschy.com).

$$$ Pension Aviano is another peaceful place, with 17 comfortable rooms on the fourth floor above lots of old center action (Sb-€93, Db-€136–143 depending on size, 15 percent cheaper Nov–March, extra bed-€32, non-smoking rooms, fans, elevator, between Neuer Markt and Kärntner Strasse at Marco d'Avianogasse 1, tel. 01/512-8330, fax 01/5128-3306, www.secrethomes.at, aviano@secrethomes.at, new owners Sabina and Gerhard Kavka).

$$$ Hotel Schweizerhof is classy, with 55 big rooms, all the comforts, shiny public spaces, and a more formal ambience. It's centrally located midway between St. Stephen's Cathedral and the Danube Canal (Sb-€84–95, Db-€111–140, extra bed-€32, low prices are for July–Aug and slow times, elevator, Bauernmarkt 22, U-1 or U-3: Stephansplatz, tel. 01/533-1931, fax 01/533-0214, www.schweizerhof.at, office@schweizerhof.at). Since this is in the "Bermuda Triangle" nightclub area, it can be noisy on weekends. Ask for a quiet room when you reserve.

$$$ Hotel zur Wiener Staatsoper, the Schweizerhof's sister hotel, is quiet, with a more traditional elegance. Its 22 tidy rooms come with high ceilings, chandeliers, and fancy carpets on parquet floors (tiny Sb-€85, Db-€111–128, Tb-€133–150, extra bed-€22, cheaper prices are for July–Aug and Dec–March, fans on request, elevator, a block from Opera at Krugerstrasse 11, U-1, U-2, or U-4: Karlsplatz, tel. 01/513-1274, fax 01/513-127-415, www.zurwienerstaatsoper.at, office@zurwienerstaatsoper.at, manager Claudia).

$$ At **Pension Nossek,** an elevator takes you above any street noise into Frau Bernad's and Frau Gundolf's world, where the children seem to be placed among the lace and flowers by an interior designer. With 30 rooms right on the wonderful Graben, this is a particularly good value (S-€46–54, Ss-€58, Sb-€69–73, Db-€115, €28 extra for sprawling suites, extra bed-€35, cash only, elevator, Graben 17, U-1 or U-3: Stephansplatz, tel. 01/5337-0410, fax 01/535-3646, www.pension-nossek.at, reservation@pension-nossek.at).

$$ Pension Suzanne, as Baroque and doily as you'll find in this price range, is wonderfully located a few yards from the Opera. It's small, but run with the class of a bigger hotel. The 25 rooms are packed with properly Viennese antique furnishings (Sb-€77, Db-€96–117 depending on size, 4 percent discount if you pay cash, extra bed-€30, spacious apartment for up to 6 also available, discounts in winter, fans on request, elevator, Internet access, a block from Opera, Walfischgasse 4, U-1, U-2, or U-4: Karlsplatz and follow signs for Opera exit, tel. 01/513-2507, fax 01/513-2500, www.pension-suzanne.at, info@pension-suzanne.at, manager Michael).

$$ Pension Neuer Markt is family-run, with 37 quiet, comfy rooms in a perfectly central locale. Its hallways have the ambience of a cheap cruise ship (Ss-€85, Sb-€90–115, smaller Ds-€80–96, Db-€110–135, prices vary with season and room size, extra bed-€20, request a quiet room when you reserve, elevator, Seilergasse 9, tel. 01/512-2316, fax 01/513-9105, www.hotelpension.at/neuermarkt, neuermarkt@hotelpension.at).

$$ Schweizer Pension has been family-owned for three generations. The current owners, Anita and Gerhard, run an extremely tight ship, offering 11 homey rooms for a great price, with parquet floors and lots of tourist info (S-€40–45, big Sb-€55–65, D-€58–68, Db-€78–89, Tb-€102–112, Qb-€126–131, prices depend on season and room size, cash only, entirely non-smoking, elevator, laundry-€14/load, Heinrichsgasse 2, U-2 or U-4: Schottenring, tel. 01/533-8156, fax 01/535-6469, www.schweizerpension.com, schweizer.pension@chello.at).

$$ Pension Dr. Geissler has 23 comfortable rooms on the eighth floor of a modern, nondescript apartment building about 10 blocks northeast of St. Stephen's, near the canal (S-€48, Ss-€68, Sb-€76, D-€65, Ds-€77, Db-€95, 20 percent less in winter, elevator, Postgasse 14, U-1 or U-4: Schwedenplatz, tel. 01/533-2803, fax 01/533-2635, www.hotelpension.at/dr-geissler, dr.geissler@hotelpension.at).

Hotels and Pensions Along Mariahilfer Strasse

Lively Mariahilfer Strasse connects the Westbahnhof (West Train Station) and the city center. The U-3 line, starting at the Westbahnhof, goes down Mariahilfer Strasse to the cathedral. This very Viennese street is a tourist-friendly and vibrant area filled with shopping malls, simpler storefronts, and cafés. Its smaller hotels and private rooms are generally run by people from the non-German-speaking part of the former Hapsburg Empire (i.e., Eastern Europe). Most hotels are within a few steps of a U-Bahn stop, just one or two stops from the Westbahnhof (direction from the station: Simmering). The nearest place to do laundry is

Hotels and Restaurants Outside the Ring

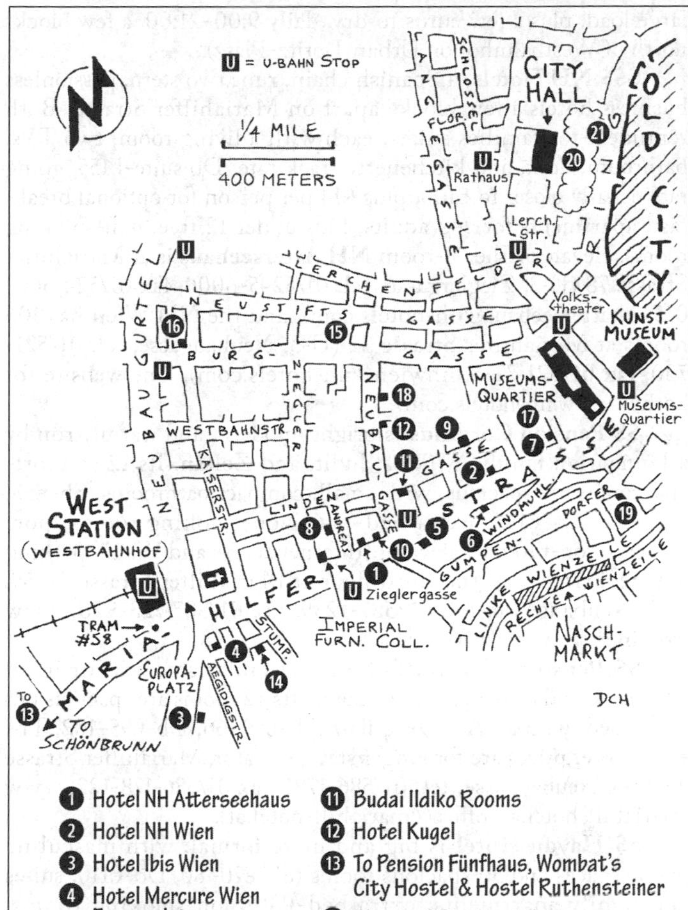

1 Hotel NH Atterseehaus
2 Hotel NH Wien
3 Hotel Ibis Wien
4 Hotel Mercure Wien Europaplatz
5 Pension Corvinus & Haydn Hotel
6 Pension Mariahilf
7 Hotel Admiral
8 Pension Hargita
9 Pension Lindenhof
10 K&T Boardinghouse
11 Budai Ildiko Rooms
12 Hotel Kugel
13 To Pension Fünfhaus, Wombat's City Hostel & Hostel Ruthensteiner
14 Westend City Hostel
15 Jugendherberge Myrthengasse
16 Lauria Rooms & Hostel
17 Spittelberg Quarter Restaurants
18 Schnitzelwirt
19 Café Sperl
20 City Hall Food Circus
21 Landtmann Café

Vienna

Schnell & Sauber Waschcenter (wash-€6 for small load or €9 for large load, plus a few euros to dry, daily 9:00–21:00, a few blocks north of Westbahnhof on Urban-Loritz-Platz).

$$$ NH Hotels, a Spanish chain, runs two stern, passionless business hotels a few blocks apart on Mariahilfer Strasse. Both rent ideal-for-families suites, each with a living room, two TVs, bathroom, desk, and kitchenette (rack rate: Db suite-€155, going rate usually closer to €100, plus €14 per person for optional breakfast, apartments for 2–3 adults, kids under 12 free, non-smoking rooms, elevator). The 78-room **NH Atterseehaus** is at Mariahilfer Strasse 78 (U-3: Zieglergasse, tel. 01/5245-6000, fax 01/524-560-015, nhatterseehaus@nh-hotels.com), and the **NH Wien** has 106 rooms at Mariahilfer Strasse 32 (U-3: Neubaugasse, tel. 01/521-720, fax 01/521-7215, nhwien@nh-hotels.com). The website for both is www.nh-hotels.com.

$$ Pension Corvinus is bright, modern, and warmly run by a Hungarian family: Miklós, Judit, and Zoltan. Its 12 comfortable rooms are spacious, with small, compact bathrooms (Sb-€58, Db-€91, Tb-€105, extra bed-€26, non-smoking rooms, portable air-con-€10/day, elevator, Internet access and Wi-Fi, parking garage-€11/day, on the third floor at Mariahilfer Strasse 57–59, U-3: Neubaugasse, tel. 01/587-7239, fax 01/587-723-920, www.corvinus.at, hotel@corvinus.at).

$$ Pension Mariahilf offers a clean, aristocratic air in an affordable and cozy pension package. Its 12 rooms are spacious but outmoded, with an Art Deco flair (Sb-€59–66, Db-€95–102, Tb-€124, lower prices are for longer stays, elevator, Mariahilfer Strasse 49, U-3: Neubaugasse, tel. 01/586-1781, fax 01/586-178-122, www.mariahilf-hotel.at, office@mariahilf-hotel.at).

$$ Haydn Hotel is big and more formal, with masculine public spaces and 50 spacious rooms (Sb-€70–80, Db-€110, suites and family apartments, extra bed-€30, non-smoking rooms, air-con, elevator, Internet access, Mariahilfer Strasse 57–59, U-3: Neubaugasse, tel. 01/587-44140, fax 01/586-1950, www.haydn-hotel.at, info@haydn-hotel.at, Nouri).

$$ Hotel Admiral is huge, quiet, and practical, with 80 large, comfortable rooms (Sb-€66, Db-€91, extra bed-€23, cheaper in winter, breakfast-€5 per person, free Internet access, limited free parking, a block off Mariahilfer Strasse at Karl-Schweighofer-Gasse 7, U-2 or U-3: Volkstheater, tel. 01/521-410, fax 01/521-4116, www.admiral.co.at, hotel@admiral.co.at).

$$ Hotel Kugel is run with pride and attitude. "Simple quality and good value" is the motto of the hands-on owner, Johannes Roller. It's a big 34-room hotel with simple Old World charm, offering a fine value (S-€35, Sb-€55, D-€48, Db-€83, supreme Db with canopy beds-€100, Siebensterngasse 43, at corner with

Neubaugasse, U-3: Neubaugasse, tel. 01/523-3355, fax 01/5233-3555, www.hotelkugel.at, office@hotelkugel.at). Herr Roller is happy to offer his cheaper rooms for backpackers.

$ Pension Hargita rents 24 generally small, bright, and tidy rooms (mostly twins) with Hungarian decor. This spick-and-span, well-located place is a good value (S-€38, Ss-€45, Sb-€55, D-€52, Ds-€58, Db-€66, Ts-€73, Tb-€80, Qb-€110, extra bed-€12, breakfast-€5, reserve with credit card but pay with cash to get these rates, corner of Mariahilfer Strasse and Andreasgasse, Andreasgasse 1, U-3: Zieglergasse, tel. 01/526-1928, fax 01/526-0492, www.hargita.at, pension@hargita.at, Erika and Tibor). As the pension has some street noise, request a room in the back.

$ K&T Boardinghouse is a top value, renting four big, bright, airy, and comfortable rooms facing the bustling Mariahilfer Strasse (Db-€65, Tb-€85, Qb-€105, 2-night minimum, no breakfast, air-con-€10/day, cash only, non-smoking, Internet access, coffee in rooms, 3 flights up, no elevator, Mariahilfer Strasse 72, U-3: Neubaugasse, tel. 01/523-2989, fax 01/522-0345, www.kaled.at, kaled@chello.at, Tina).

$ Pension Lindenhof rents 19 worn but clean rooms. It's a dark and mysteriously dated time-warp filled with plants (S-€30, Sb-€37, D-€51, Db-€67, cash only, elevator, Lindengasse 4, U-3: Neubaugasse, tel. 01/523-0498, fax 01/523-7362, pensionlindenhof@yahoo.com, Gebrael family, Keram and his father speak English).

$ ***Private Room:*** If you're on a tight budget and wish you had a grandmother to visit in Vienna, stay with English-speaking **Budai Ildiko.** She rents high-ceilinged rooms with Old World furnishings out of her dark and homey apartment. Two cavernous rooms, which sleep two to four, and a skinny twin room all share one bathroom (S-€32, D-€45, T-€64, Q-€79, no breakfast but free coffee, cash only, lots of tourist information, classic old elevator, laundry-€4, Lindengasse 39, apartment #5, U-3: Neubaugasse, tel. 01/523-1058, tel. & fax 01/526-2595, www.wienwien.at, budai@hotmail.com).

Near the Westbahnhof (West Station)

$$$ Hotel Mercure Wien Europaplatz offers high-rise modern efficiency and comfort in 210 air-conditioned rooms, directly across from the Westbahnhof (Db-€130–150 depending on season, online deals as cheap as Db-€80 if you book well in advance, breakfast-€13, elevator, Matrosengasse 6, U-3: Westbahnhof, tel. 01/599-010, fax 01/597-6900, www.mercure.com, h1707@accor.com).

$$ Hotel Ibis Wien, a modern high-rise hotel with American charm, is ideal for anyone tired of quaint old Europe. Its 340 cookie-cutter rooms are bright, comfortable, and modern, with all the conveniences (Sb-€71, Db-€86, Tb-€101, €5 cheaper in July, breakfast-€9, non-smoking rooms, air-con, elevator, parking garage-€11/day; exit Westbahnhof to the right and walk 400 yards, Mariahilfer Gürtel 22–24, U-3: Westbahnhof; tel. 01/59998, fax 01/597-9090, www.ibishotel.com, h0796@accor.com).

$ Pension Fünfhaus is big, clean, and stark—almost institutional. The neighborhood is run-down (with a few ladies loitering late at night) and the staff can be grouchy, but this 47-room pension offers the best doubles you'll find for around €50 (S-€32, Sb-€40, D-€44, Db-€54, T-€66, Tb-€78, 4-person apartment-€92, cash only, closed mid-Nov–Feb, Sperrgasse 12, U-3: Westbahnhof, tel. 01/892-3545 or 01/892-0286, fax 01/892-0460, www.pension5haus.at, pension5haus@tiscali.at, Frau Susi Tersch). Half the rooms are in the main building and half are in the annex, which has good rooms but is near the train tracks and a bit scary on the street at night. From the station, ride tram #52 or #58 two stops down Mariahilfer Strasse away from center, and ask for Sperrgasse.

Cheap Dorms and Hostels near Mariahilfer Strasse

$ Jugendherberge Myrthengasse is your classic huge and well-run youth hostel, with 260 beds (€15–19 per person in 4- to 6-bed rooms, includes sheets and breakfast, non-members pay €3.50 extra, always open, no curfew, lockers and lots of facilities, Myrthengasse 7, tel. 01/523-6316, fax 01/523-5849, hostel@chello.at).

$ Westend City Hostel, just a block from the Westbahnhof and Mariahilfer Strasse, is well-run and well-located, with 180 beds in 4- to 12-bed dorms (€17–25 per person, depending on how many in the room; includes sheets, breakfast, and locker; cash only, Internet access, laundry, Fügergasse 3, tel. 01/597-6729, fax 01/597-672-927, www.westendhostel.at, westendcityhostel@aon.at).

$ Lauria Rooms and Hostel is a creative little place run by friendly Gosha, with two 10-bed coed dorms with lockers for travelers ages 17 to 30 (€13.50/bed), plus several other rooms sleeping two to six each (any age, €24/bed, D-€48; Kaiserstrasse 77, tram #5 or a 10-min walk from Westbahnhof, tel. 01/522-2555, lauria_vienna@hotmail.com).

$ *More Hostels:* Other hostels with €16 beds and €40 doubles near Mariahilfer Strasse are **Wombat's City Hostel** (near tracks behind the station at Grangasse 6, tel. 01/897-2336, www.wombats-hostels.com, office@wombats-vienna.at) and **Hostel Ruthensteiner** (Robert-Hamerling-Gasse 24, tel. 01/893-4202, www.hostelruthensteiner.com, info@hostelruthensteiner.com).

EATING

The Viennese appreciate the fine points of life, and right up there with waltzing is eating. The city has many atmospheric restaurants. As you ponder the Eastern European specialties on menus, remember that Vienna's diverse empire may be gone, but its flavor lingers.

While cuisines are routinely named for countries, Vienna claims to be the only *city* with a cuisine of its own: Vienna soups come with fillings (semolina dumpling, liver dumpling, or pancake slices). *Gulasch* is a beef ragout of Hungarian origin (spiced with onion and paprika). Of course, Viennese schnitzel *(Wiener Schnitzel)* is traditionally a breaded and fried veal cutlet (though pork is more common these days). Another meat specialty is boiled beef *(Tafelspitz)*. While you're sure to have *Apfelstrudel,* try the sweet cheese strudel, too (*Topfenstrudel*—wafer-thin strudel pastry filled with sweet cheese and raisins). The *dag* you see in some prices stands for "decigram" (10 grams). Therefore, *10 dag* is 100 grams, or about a quarter-pound.

On nearly every corner, you can find a colorful *Beisl* (BYE-zul). These uniquely Viennese taverns are a characteristic cross between an English pub and a French brasserie—filled with poetry teachers and their students, couples loving without touching, housewives on their way home from cello lessons, and waiters who enjoy serving hearty food and good drink at an affordable price. Ask at your hotel for a good *Beisl.*

Near St. Stephen's Cathedral

Each of these eateries is within about a five-minute walk of the cathedral.

Gigerl Stadtheuriger offers a friendly near-*Heuriger* experience (à la Grinzing—see "Vienna's Wine Gardens," page 66), often with accordion or live music, without leaving the city center. Just point to what looks good. Food is sold by the weight; 100 grams *(10 dag)* is about a quarter-pound (cheese and cold meats cost about €3 per 100 grams, salads are about €2 per 100 grams; price sheet is posted on the wall to right of buffet line). The *Karree* pork with herbs is particularly tasty and tender. They also have menu entrées, spinach strudel (€2), quiche, *Apfelstrudel,* and, of course, casks of new and local wines (sold by the *Achtel*). Meals run €7 to €11 (daily 15:00–24:00, indoor/outdoor seating, behind cathedral, a block off Kärntner Strasse, a few cobbles off Rauhensteingasse on Blumenstock, tel. 01/513-4431).

Am Hof Eateries: The square called Am Hof (U-3: Herrengasse) is surrounded by a maze of atmospheric medieval lanes; the following eateries are all within a block of the square. **Restaurant**

Ofenloch serves good, old-fashioned Viennese cuisine with friendly service, both indoors and out. This 300-year-old eatery, with great traditional ambience, is dressy (with white tablecloths) but intimate and woodsy. It's central but not overrun with tourists (€12–18 main dishes, Tue–Sat 11:30–24:00, Mon 18:00–24:00, closed Sun, Kurrentgasse 8, tel. 01/533-8844). **Brezel-Gwölb,** a Tolkien-esque wine cellar with outdoor dining on a quiet square, serves delicious light meals, fine *Krautsuppe* (cabbage soup), and old-fashioned Viennese dishes. It's ideal for a romantic late-night glass of wine (daily 11:30–1:00; leave Am Hof on Drahtgasse, then take first left to Ledererhof 9; tel. 01/533-8811). Around the corner, **Beisl "Zum Scherer"** is untouristy and serves traditional plates for €10. Sitting outside, you'll face a stern Holocaust memorial. The interior offers a soothing woody atmosphere and intriguing decor (Mon–Sat 11:30–22:00, closed Sun, Judenplatz 7, tel. 01/533-5164). Just below Am Hof, the ancient and popular **Esterhazykeller** has traditional fare deep underground. For a cheap and sloppy buffet, climb down to the lowest cellar. For table service on a pleasant square, sit outside (Mon–Fri 11:00–23:00, Sat–Sun 16:00–23:00, Haarhof 1, tel. 01/533-3482).

Wine Cellars: These wine cellars are fun and touristy but typical, in the old center, with reasonable prices and plenty of smoke: **Melker Stiftskeller,** less touristy, is a *Stadtheuriger* in a deep and rustic cellar with hearty, inexpensive meals and new wine (Tue–Sat 17:00–24:00, closed Sun–Mon and most of July, between Am Hof and Schottentor U-Bahn stop at Schottengasse 3, tel. 01/533-5530). **Zu den Drei Hacken** is famous for its local specialties (€10 plates, Mon–Sat 11:00–23:00, closed Sun, indoor/outdoor seating, Singerstrasse 28, tel. 01/512-5895).

Zum Schwarzen Kameel ("The Black Camel") is popular for its two classy but very different scenes: a tiny, elegant restaurant and a trendy wine bar. The small, dark-wood, 12-table, Art Nouveau restaurant serves fine gourmet Viennese cuisine (three-course dinner-€43 plus pricey wine). The wine bar is filled with a professional local crowd enjoying small plates from the same kitchen at a better price. This is *the* place for horseradish and thin-sliced ham (*Beinschinken mit Kren,* €7 a plate). I'd order the *Vorspeisenteller* (a great *antipasti* dish that comes with ham and horseradish) and their *Tafelspitz* (boiled ham and vegetable, €15). Stand, grab a stool, or sit anywhere you can—it's customary to share tables in the wine-bar section. Fine Austrian wines are sold by the *Achtel* (eighth-liter glass) and listed on the board. They also have a buffet of tiny €1–2 sandwiches (daily 11:00–23:00, Bognergasse 5, tel. 01/533-8125).

Wrenkh Vegetarian Restaurant and Bar is well-liked for its high vegetarian cuisine. Chef Wrenkh offers daily €8 fixed-price lunches and €8 to €13 dinner plates in a bright, mod bar or in a

Restaurants in Central Vienna

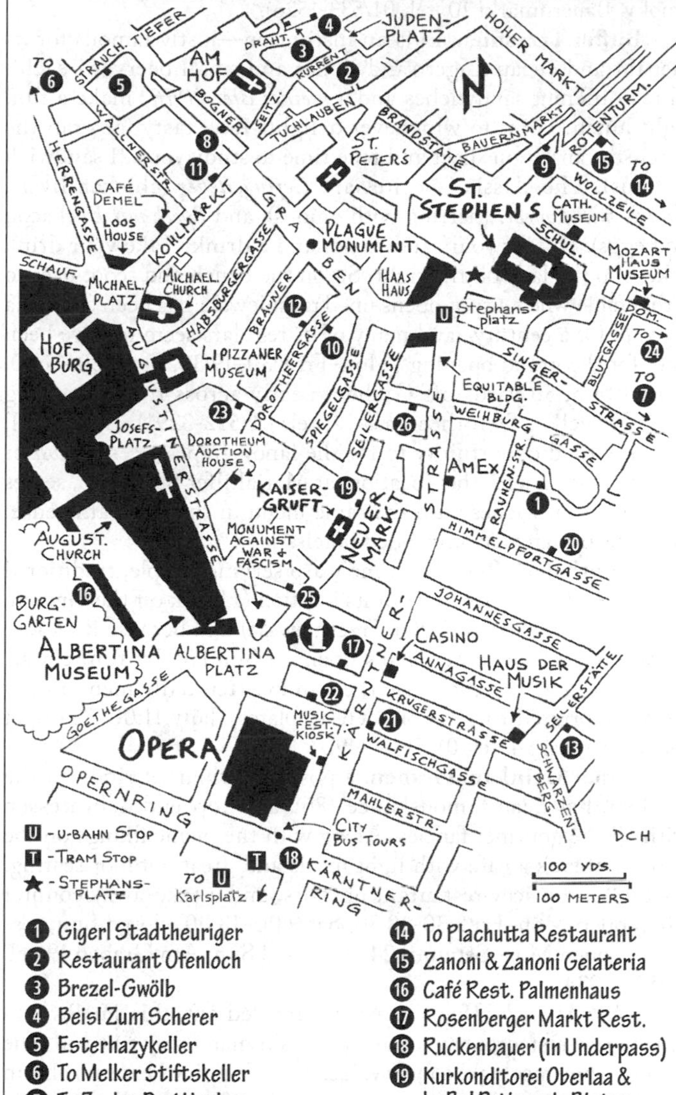

1. Gigerl Stadtheuriger
2. Restaurant Ofenloch
3. Brezel-Gwölb
4. Beisl Zum Scherer
5. Esterhazykeller
6. To Melker Stiftskeller
7. To Zu den Drei Hacken
8. Zum Schwarzen Kameel
9. Wrenkh Vegetarian Restaurant & Bar
10. Buffet Trzesniewski
11. Julius Meinl am Graben Deli
12. Café Hawelka & Reinthaler's Beisl
13. Gyros
14. To Plachutta Restaurant
15. Zanoni & Zanoni Gelateria
16. Café Rest. Palmenhaus
17. Rosenberger Markt Rest.
18. Ruckenbauer (in Underpass)
19. Kurkonditorei Oberlaa & Le Bol Patisserie Bistro
20. Danieli Ristorante
21. Starbucks
22. Sacher Café
23. Café Braunerhof
24. To Café Pruckel
25. Café Tirolerhof
26. Loos American Bar

dark, fancier restaurant (Mon–Sat 11:30–23:00, closed Sun, can be smoky, Bauernmarkt 10, tel. 01/533-1526).

Buffet Trzesniewski is an institution—justly famous for its elegant and cheap finger sandwiches and small beers (€1 each). Three different sandwiches and a *kleines Bier (Pfiff)* make a fun, light lunch. Point to whichever delights look tasty (or grab the English translation sheet and take time to study your 21 sandwich options). The classic favorites are *Geflügelleber* (chicken liver), *Matjes mit Zwiebel* (herring with onions), and *Speck mit Ei* (bacon and eggs). Pay for your sandwiches and a drink. Take your drink tokens to the lady on the right. Sit on the bench and scoot over to a tiny table when a spot opens up. Trzesniewski has been a Vienna favorite for a century...and many of its regulars seem to have been here for the grand opening (Mon–Fri 8:30–19:30, Sat 9:00–17:00, closed Sun; 50 yards off Graben, nearly across from brooding Café Hawelka, Dorotheergasse 2; tel. 01/512-3291). In the fall, this is a good opportunity to try the fancy grape juices—*Most* or *Traubenmost*. Their other location, at Mariahilfer Strasse 95, serves the same sandwiches with the same menu in the same ambience, and is near many recommended hotels.

Reinthaler's Beisl is a time warp serving simple, traditional *Beisl* fare all day. It's handy for its location (a block off the Graben, across the street from Buffet Trzesniewski) and because it's a rare restaurant in the center that's open on Sunday. Its fun, classic interior winds way back (use the handwritten daily menu rather than the printed English one, €6–10 plates, daily 11:00–23:00, at Dorotheergasse 4, tel. 01/513-1249).

Julius Meinl am Graben, a posh supermarket right on the Graben, has been famous since 1862 as a top-end delicatessen with all the gourmet fancies. Along with the picnic fixings on the shelves, there's a café with light meals and great outdoor seating, a stuffy and pricey restaurant upstairs, and a take-away counter (shop open Mon–Fri 8:30–19:30, Sat 9:00–18:00, closed Sun; restaurant open Mon–Sat until 24:00, closed Sun; Am Graben 19, tel. 01/532-3334).

Akakiko Sushi: If you're just schnitzeled out, this small chain of Japanese restaurants with an easy sushi menu may suit you. The €9 bento box meals are a tasty value. Three locations have no charm but are fast, reasonable, and convenient (€7–10 meals, all open daily 10:30–23:30): Singerstrasse 4 (a block off Kärntner Strasse near the cathedral), Heidenschuss 3 (near other recommended eateries just off Am Hof), and Mariahilfer Strasse 42–48 (fifth floor of Kaufhaus Gerngross, near many recommended hotels).

Gyros is a humble little Greek/Turkish joint run by Yilmaz, a fun-loving Turk from Izmir. He simply loves to feed people—the food is great, the price is cheap, and you almost feel like you took a quick trip to Turkey (daily 10:00–23:30, a long block off Kärntner Strasse at corner of Fichtegasse and Seilerstätte, tel. 01/228-9551).

Plachutta Restaurant, with a stylish green-and-crème, elegant-but-comfy interior and breezy covered terrace, is famous for the best beef in town. You'll find an enticing menu with all the classic Viennese beef dishes, fine deserts, attentive service, and an enthusiastic and sophisticated local clientele. They've developed the art of beef to the point of producing popular cookbooks. Their specialty is a page-long list of *Tafelspitz*—a traditional copper pot of boiled beef with broth and vegetables. Treat the broth as your soup course. A chart on the menu lets you choose your favorite cut. Make a reservation for this high-energy Vienna favorite (€16–21 per pot, daily 11:30–23:00; 10-min walk from St. Stephen's Cathedral, Wollzeile 38, U-3: Stubentor; tel. 01/512-1577).

***Ice Cream!:* Zanoni & Zanoni** is a very Italian *gelateria* run by an Italian family. They're mobbed by happy Viennese hungry for their huge €2 cones to go. Or, to relax and watch the thriving people scene, lick your gelato in their fun outdoor area (daily 7:00–24:00, 2 blocks up Rotenturmstrasse from cathedral at Lugeck 7, tel. 01/512-7979).

Near the Opera

Café Restaurant Palmenhaus overlooks the Palace Garden (Burggarten—see page 44). Tucked away in a green and peaceful corner two blocks behind the Opera in the Hofburg's back yard, this is a world apart. If you want to eat modern Austrian cuisine with palm trees rather than tourists, this is it. And, since it's at the edge of a huge park, it's great for families. Their fresh fish with generous vegetables specials are on the board (€8 two-course lunches available Mon–Fri, €15–18 entrées, open daily 10:00–24:00, serious vegetarian dishes, fish, extensive wine list, indoors in greenhouse or outdoors, tel. 01/533-1033).

Rosenberger Markt Restaurant is mobbed with tour groups. Still, if you don't mind a freeway cafeteria ambience in the center of the German-speaking world's classiest city, this self-service eatery is fast and easy. It's just a block toward the cathedral from the Opera. The best cheap meal here is a small salad or veggie plate stacked high (daily 10:30–23:00, lots of fruits, veggies, fresh-squeezed juices, addictive banana milk, ride the glass elevator downstairs, Maysedergasse 2, tel. 01/512-3458).

Ruckenbauer, a fast-food kiosk in a transit underpass (under the street in front of the Opera), is a favorite for a quick bite (daily 6:00–20:00). Their €1.50 *Tramezzini* sandwiches and fine pastries make a classy, quick picnic lunch or dinner before the opera (just 100 yards away).

Kurkonditorei Oberlaa may not have the royal and plush

fame of Demel (see page 32), but this is where Viennese connoisseurs serious about the quality of their pastries go to get fat. With outdoor seating on Neuer Markt, it's particularly nice on a hot summer day (€10 daily three-course lunches, great selection of cakes, daily 8:00–20:00, Neuer Markt 16, tel. 01/5132-9360). Next door, **Le Bol Patisserie Bistro** satisfies your need for something French. The staff speaks to you in French, serving fine €8 salads, baguette sandwiches, and fresh croissants (daily 8:00–22:00, Neuer Markt 14).

Danieli Ristorante is your best classy Italian bet in the old center. White-tablecloth dressy, but not at all stuffy, it has reasonable prices (€8–12 pizza and pastas, fresh fish, open daily, 30 yards off Kärntner Strasse opposite Neuer Markt at Himmelpfortgasse 3, tel. 01/513-7913).

City Hall (Rathaus) Food Circus: During the summer, scores of outdoor food stands and hundreds of picnic tables are set up in the park in front of the City Hall. Local mobs enjoy mostly ethnic meals on disposable plates for decent-but-not-cheap prices. The fun thing here is the energy of the crowd, and a feeling that you're truly eating as the Viennese do...not schnitzel and quaint traditions, but trendy "world food" with young people out having fun in a fine Vienna park setting (July–Aug daily from 11:00 until late, in front of City Hall on the Ringstrasse).

Spittelberg Quarter

A charming cobbled grid of traffic-free lanes and Biedermeier apartments has become a favorite neighborhood for Viennese wanting a little dining charm between the MuseumsQuartier and Mariahilfer Strasse (handy to many recommended hotels; take Stiftgasse from Mariahilfer Strasse, or wander over here after you close down the Kunsthistorisches Museum). Tables tumble down sidewalks and into breezy courtyards filled with appreciative natives enjoying dinner or a relaxing drink. It's only worth the trip on a balmy summer evening, as it's dead in bad weather. Stroll Spittelberggasse, Schrankgasse, and Gutenberggasse and pick your favorite. Don't miss the vine-strewn wine garden at Schrankgasse 1.

Amerlingbeisl, with a casual atmosphere both on the cobbled street and in its vine-covered courtyard, is a great value (€7 plates, €6–8 daily specials, salads, veggie dishes, traditional specialties, daily 9:00–24:00, Stiftgasse 8, tel. 01/526-1660).

Plutzer Bräu, next door, is also good (ribs, burgers, traditional dishes, Tirolean beer from the keg, daily 11:00–2:00, food until 22:30, Schrankgasse 4, tel. 01/526-1215).

Witwe Bolte is classier and a good choice for uninspired Viennese cuisine with tablecloths. Its tiny square has wonderful leafy ambience (daily 11:30–15:00 & 17:30–23:30, Gutenberggasse 13, tel. 01/523-1450).

Zu Ebener Erde and Erster Stock is a charming little restaurant with a near-gourmet menu. The upstairs is Biedermeier-style, with violet tablecloths and seating for about 20. The downstairs is more casual and woody. Reservations are smart (modern Viennese seasonal fixed-price meal-€40, traditional three-course fixed-price meal-€28, Tue–Sat from 18:00, closed Sun–Mon, Burggasse 13, tel. 01/523-6254).

Near Mariahilfer Strasse

Mariahilfer Strasse is filled with reasonable cafés serving all types of cuisine. For a quick yet traditional bite, consider the venerable **Buffet Trzesniewski** sandwich bar at Mariahilfer Strasse 95 (described above).

Schnitzelwirt is an old classic with a 1950s patina and a clientele to match. In this smoky, working-class place, no one finishes their schnitzel ("to go" for the dog is wrapped in newspaper, "to go" for you is wrapped in foil). You'll find no tourists, just cheap €6 schnitzel meals (Mon–Sat 11:00–22:00, closed Sun, Neubaugasse 52, tel. 01/523-3771).

Naschmarkt (described on page 54) is Vienna's best Old World market, with plenty of fresh produce, cheap local-style eateries, cafés, *Döner Kebab* and sausage stands, and the best-value sushi in town (Mon–Fri 6:00–18:30, Sat 6:00–17:00, closed Sun, closes earlier in winter, U-4: Kettenbrückengasse). Survey the lane of eateries at the end of the market nearest the Opera. The circa 1900 pub is inviting. Picnickers can buy supplies at the market and eat on nearby Karlsplatz (plenty of chairs facing the Charles Church).

TRANSPORTATION CONNECTIONS

Vienna has two main train stations: the Westbahnhof (West Station), serving Munich, Salzburg, Melk, and Budapest; and the Südbahnhof (South Station), serving Budapest, Prague, Poland, Slovenia, Croatia, and usually Italy (though some Italy-bound trains go from the Westbahnhof). A third station, Franz Josefs, serves Krems and the Danube Valley (but Melk is served by the Westbahnhof). There are exceptions, so always confirm which station your train leaves from. Metro line U-3 connects the Westbahnhof with the center, tram D takes you from the Südbahnhof and the Franz Josefs station to downtown, and tram #18 connects West and South stations. Train info: tel. 051-717 (to get an operator, dial 2, then 1).

From Vienna by Train to: Melk (2/hr, 1 hr, some with

change in St. Pölten), **Krems** (hourly, 1 hr), **Salzburg** (hourly, 3 hrs), **Innsbruck** (every 2 hrs, 5.5 hrs), **Bratislava** (about hourly, 1 hr; or try the boat trip described on page 61), **Budapest** (6/day, 3 hrs), **Prague** (6/day, 4.5 hrs), **Český Krumlov** (5/day, 6–7 hrs, up to 3 changes), **Munich** (3/day direct, 4 hrs; otherwise about hourly, 5 hrs, transfer in Salzburg), **Berlin** (5/day, 10 hrs, longer on night train), **Zurich** (3/day, 9 hrs), **Ljubljana** (7/day, 6–7 hrs, convenient early-morning direct train, others change in Villach or Maribor), **Zagreb** (8/day, 6–10 hrs, 3 direct, others with up to 3 changes including Villach and Ljubljana), **Kraków** (4/day, 6–9 hrs, 2 direct including a night train departing at about 22:00, arriving around 6:00), **Warsaw** (4/day, 7–10 hrs, 2 direct including a night train), **Rome** (1/day, 13 hrs), **Venice** (3/day, 7 hrs, longer on night train), **Frankfurt** (8/day, direct every 2 hours, 7 hrs, more with up to 2 changes, usually in Munich and Salzburg), **Amsterdam** (1/day, 14 hrs).

Excursions by Car with Driver: Those wishing they had wheels may consider hiring Johann (see page 23) for Danube excursions from Vienna or en route to Salzburg (particularly economic for groups of 3–4).

To Eastern Europe: Vienna is the springboard for a quick trip to Prague and Budapest—three hours by train from Budapest (€40 one-way; covered by any railpass that includes both Austria and Hungary) and four hours from Prague (€44 one-way, €88 round-trip; Eurailpass-holders need only a ticket from the Czech border into Prague: €28 one-way, €56 round-trip). Americans and Canadians do not need visas to enter the Czech Republic or Hungary. Purchase tickets at most travel agencies.

SALZBURG

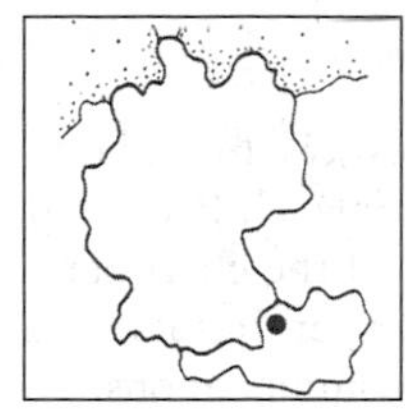

Salzburg is forever smiling to the tunes of Mozart and *The Sound of Music.* Thanks to its charmingly preserved old town, splendid gardens, Baroque churches, and Europe's largest intact medieval fortress, Salzburg feels made for tourism. It's a museum city with class. Vagabonds wish they had nicer clothes.

But even without Mozart and the von Trapps, Salzburg is steeped in history. In about A.D. 700, Bavaria gave Salzburg to Bishop Rupert for his promise to Christianize the area. Salzburg remained an independent state until Napoleon came (around 1800). Thanks in part to its formidable fortress, Salzburg managed to avoid the ravages of war for 1,200 years...until World War II. Much of the city was destroyed by WWII bombs (mostly around the train station), but the historic old town survived.

The year 2005 marked the 250th birthday of Salzburg's beloved and most marketable son, Mozart. While that particular money-maker may be history, you'll still notice how greedily the town exercises all its creative powers to milk the composer's legacy. Eight million tourists crawl Salzburg's cobbles each year. That's a lot of Mozart balls—and all that popularity has led to a glut of businesses hoping to catch the tourist dollar. Still, Salzburg is both a must and a joy.

Planning Your Time

While Vienna measures much higher on the Richter scale of sightseeing thrills, Salzburg is simply a touristy stroller's delight. If you're going into the nearby Salzkammergut lake country (see next chapter), skip the *Sound of Music* tour—if not, allow half a day for it. The *S.O.M.* tour kills a nest of sightseeing birds with one ticket (city overview, *S.O.M.* sights, and a fine drive through the lakes). You'll probably need two nights for Salzburg—nights are important for swilling beer in atmospheric local gardens and attending concerts in Baroque halls and chapels. Seriously consider one of Salzburg's many evening musical events (a few are free, some are as cheap as €12, and most average €30–40). While the sights are mediocre, the town itself is an enjoyable Baroque museum of cobbled streets and elegant buildings. And to get away from it all, bike down the river or hike across the Mönchsberg.

The town of Hallstatt provides the best glimpse at the nearby Salzkammergut lake district (see next chapter). A day trip from Salzburg to Hallstatt is doable, but involves about five hours of travel time and makes for a very long day (not worth the trouble in the winter, when Hallstatt is pretty dead).

ORIENTATION

(area code: 0662)

Salzburg, a city of 150,000 (Austria's fourth largest), is divided into old and new. The old town, sitting between the Salzach River and its mini-mountain (Mönchsberg), holds nearly all the charm and most of the tourists. The new town, across the river, has its own share of sights and museums, plus some good accommodations.

Tourist Information

Salzburg has three helpful TIs (main tel. 0662/889-870 or 0662/8898-7330, www.salzburg.info): at the **train station** (daily May–Sept 8:30–20:00, July–Aug until 21:00, Oct–April 8:30–19:30), on **Mozartplatz** in the old center (daily 9:00–18:00, July–Aug until 19:00), and at the **Salzburg Süd park-and-ride** (generally open 10:00–18:00, often closed Mon–Tue, closed in winter, tel. 0662/8898-7360).

At any TI, you can pick up a free city-center map (the €0.70 map has a broader coverage and more information on sights, but probably isn't necessary), the Salzburg Card brochure (listing sights with current hours and prices), and a bimonthly schedule of events. Book a concert upon arrival. The TIs also book rooms for a fee.

Salzburg Card: The TI sells the Salzburg Card, which covers all your public transportation (including elevator and funicular) and admission to all the city sights (including Hellbrunn Castle and the river cruise). The card is pricey (€23/24 hrs, €29/48 hrs, €34/72 hrs), but if you'd like to pop into all the sights without concern for the cost, this can save money and enhance your experience. To analyze your potential savings, here are the major sights and what you'd pay without the card: Hohensalzburg Fortress and funicular-€9.80, Mozart's Birthplace and Residence-€9.50,

Hellbrunn Castle-€9, Salzburg Panorama 1829-€2, Salzach River cruise-€12, 24-hour transit pass-€3.40. Busy sightseers can save plenty. Get this card, feel the financial pain once, and the city's all yours.

Arrival in Salzburg

By Train: The Salzburg station is user-friendly. The TI is at track 2A. Downstairs at street level, you'll find a place to store your luggage, buy tickets, and get train information. Bike rental is nearby (see "Getting Around Salzburg," below). City buses depart from the lot facing the station (monitors clearly show each bus's destination—any bus heading for "Zentrum" stops near the main bridge in the old town, including buses #1, #5, #6, #25, and #53; get off at the first stop after you cross the river for most sights and city-center hotels, or just before the bridge for Linzergasse hotels). Figure €7 for a taxi to the center. To walk downtown (15 min), leave the station ticket hall to the left, and walk straight down Rainerstrasse, which leads under the tracks past Mirabellplatz, turning into Dreitaltigkeitsgasse. From here, you can turn left onto Linzergasse for many of the recommended hotels, or cross the Staatsbrücke bridge for the old town (and more hotels). For a more dramatic approach, leave the station the same way but follow the tracks to the river, turn left, and walk the riverside path toward the fortress.

By Car: Follow *Zentrum* signs to the center, and park short-term on the street (3-hour limit, pay the meter) or longer in the various garages (best under Mönchsberg mountain, €14/day). Ask at your hotel for suggestions. (For more details, see "Transportation Connections," page 120)

Helpful Hints

Recommendations Skewed by Kickbacks: Salzburg is addicted to the tourist dollar, and it can never get enough. Virtually all hotels are on the take when it comes to concert and tour recommendations, influenced more by their potential kickback than by what's best for you. Take their advice with a grain of salt.

Internet Access: Internet access is rare and pricey in the old town (€2/10 min at the place two doors down from the TI). Across the river, it's no problem. **Gambler's Internet** is fast, and cheap (€1/20 min, daily 10:00–22:00, near recommended Linzergasse hotels at Wolf-Dietrich-Strasse 8). There's also a big, handy place on Theatergasse (near Mozart's Residence) and plenty of places near the station (including **Bubblepoint,** a modern launderette—see "Laundry," below). Readers of this book can get online free at the Panorama Tours terminal on Mirabellplatz (daily 8:00–18:00).

Post Office: A full-service post office is located in the heart of town, in the new Residenz (Mon–Fri 7:00–18:30, Sat 8:00–10:00, closed Sun).

Laundry: The launderette at the corner of Paris-Lodron-Strasse and Wolf-Dietrich-Strasse, near my recommended Linzergasse hotels, is handy (€10 self-service, €15 same-day full-service, Mon–Fri 7:30–18:00, Sat 8:00–12:00, closed Sun, tel. 0662/876-381). To do your laundry and email at the same time, head to **Bubblepoint** (wash and dry for €7, six Internet terminals, daily 7:00–23:00, in CityCenter Mall opposite train station, Karl-Wurmb-Strasse 2, tel. 0664/471-1484).

American Express: AmEx has travel-agency services, but doesn't sell train tickets (Mon–Fri 9:00–17:30, closed Sat–Sun, Mozartplatz 5, tel. 0662/843-8400).

Lockers in the Old Town: The TI generously provides lockers right on Mozartplatz (€1/day, pick up key at the desk).

Getting Around Salzburg

By Bus: Single-ride tickets for central Salzburg *(Einzelkarte-Kernzone)* are sold on the bus for €1.80. At machines and *Tabak/Trafik* shops, you can buy €1.60 single-ride tickets or a €3.40 day pass (*Tageskarte,* good for 24 hours, €4.20 if you buy it on the bus). To signal the driver that you want to get off, press the buzzer on the pole. Bus info: tel. 0662/4480-1500.

By Bike: Salzburg is fun for cyclists. The following two bike-rental shops offer 20 percent off with a valid train ticket or Eurailpass; ask for it. **Top Bike** rents bikes from two outlets—at the river side of the train station (exit to the left and walk 50 yards); and on the river next to the Staatsbrücke (€6/2 hrs, €10/4 hrs, €15/24 hrs, usually daily April–June and Sept–Oct 10:00–17:00, July–Aug 9:00–19:00, closed Nov–March, tel. 06272/4656, mobile 0676-476-7259, www.topbike.at, Sabine). **Velo-Active** rents bikes on Residenzplatz, across from the American Express office in the old town (€4/hr, €12/24 hrs; mountain bikes-€6/hr, €18/24 hrs; daily 9:00–18:00 but hours unreliable—you may have to call or let the Panorama Tours man nearby help you, shorter hours off-season and in bad weather, passport number for security deposit, tel. 0662/435-595, mobile 0676-435-5950).

By Funicular and Elevator: The old town is connected to the top of the Mönchsberg mountain (and great views) via funicular and elevator. The **funicular** *(Festungsbahn)* whisks you up to the imposing Hohensalzburg Fortress (included in castle admission, goes every few minutes). The **elevator** *(MönchsbergAufzug)* on the east side of the old town propels you to the recommended Gasthaus Stadtalm café and hostel, the Museum of Modern Art, wooded paths, and more great views (€2 one-way, €3 round-trip, daily 8:00–17:00, July–Aug until 24:00).

By Taxi: Meters start around €3 (from train station to your hotel, allow about €8). As always, small groups can taxi for about the same price as riding the bus.

By Buggy: The horse buggies *(Fiaker)* that congregate at Residenzplatz charge €35 for a 25-minute trot around the old town (www.fiaker-salzburg.at).

TOURS

Walking Tours—The tourist office offers two-language, one-hour guided walks of the old town. They are informative, but you'll be listening to a half-hour of German (€8, daily at 12:15, meet at TI on Mozartplatz, just show up and pay the guide, tel. 0662/8898-7330). To save money (and avoid all that German), you can easily do it on your own using my self-guided walk, below. An independent group of guides also offers one-hour city walks daily at 14:00 (€10, in several languages, departs from Mozartplatz TI; themes include Mozart and Salzburg's "Rome of the North" history).

Local Guides—Christiana Schneeweiss ("Snow White"), a hardworking young guide with a passion for fitting local history into the big picture, gives spirited private tours (€75/1 hr, €129/2 hrs, €150/3 hrs, tel. 0664/340-1757, www.kultur-tourismus.com, info@kultur-tourismus.com). Check her website for bike tours and more. **Bärbel Schalber,** one of Salzburg's senior guides, offers a two-hour walk packed with information and spicy opinions for €75 (tel. 0662/632-225, schalber.salzburg@aon.at). Salzburg has many other good guides (to book, call tel. 0662/840-406).

▲▲*Sound of Music* Tour—I took this tour skeptically (as part of my research chores) and liked it. It includes a quick but good general city tour, hits the *S.O.M.* spots (including the stately home, flirtatious gazebo, and grand wedding church), and shows you a lovely stretch of the Salzkammergut lake district. This is worthwhile for *S.O.M.* fans and those who won't otherwise be going into the Salzkammergut. Warning: Many think rolling through the Austrian countryside with 30 Americans singing "Doe, a Deer" is pretty schmaltzy. Local Austrians don't understand all the commotion, and the audience is mostly native English speakers.

Of the many companies doing the tour, consider Bob's Special Tours (usually uses a mini-bus) and Panorama Tours (more typical and professional, big 50-seat bus). Each one provides essentially the same tour (in English with a live guide, 4 hours, free hotel pick-up) for about the same price: €35 for Panorama, €38 for Bob's. Getting a spot is simple—just call and make a reservation.

Minibus Option: Ninety percent of **Bob's Special Tours** use an eight-seat mini-bus and therefore have good access to old-town

Salzburg

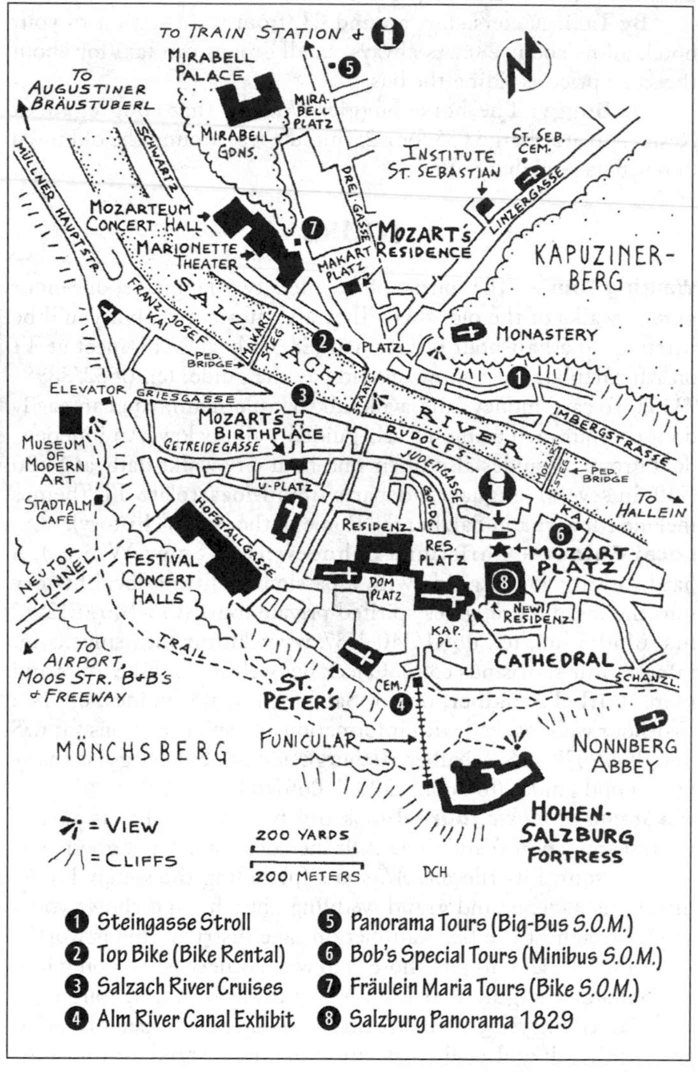

sights, promote a more casual feel, and spend less time waiting to load and unload (daily at 9:00 and 14:00 year-round, buses leave from Bob's office along the river just east of Mozartplatz at Rudolfskai 38—or they'll pick you up at your hotel for the morning tour, tel. 0662/849-511, mobile 0664-541-7492, www.bobstours.com). Nearly all of Bob's tours stop for the luge ride when the weather is dry (mountain bobsled-€4 extra, confirm beforehand). Some travelers looking for Bob's tours at Mozartplatz have been hijacked by other companies...have Bob's pick you up at your hotel (morning only) or meet the bus at their office.

Big-Bus Option: Salzburg Panorama Tours depart from their smart kiosk at Mirabellplatz daily at 9:30 and 14:00 year-round (book by calling 0662/874-029 or online at www.panoramatours.com). Many travelers appreciate their more businesslike feel, roomier buses, slightly higher vantage point, and better reliability.

Bike Option: Alternatively, you can meet **Fräulein Maria** at the Mirabell Gardens (behind Hotel Bristol) for a *S.O.M.* bike tour. Main attractions you'll pass during the seven-mile pedal include the Mirabell Gardens, the horse pond, St. Peter's Cemetery, Nonnberg Abbey, Leopoldskron Palace and, of course, the gazebo (€22 includes bike, kids under 15 pay €15, daily at 9:30, allow 3 hours, mid May–Aug only, family-friendly, tel. 0650/342-6297, www.mariasbicycletours.com).

More Tours—Both Bob's and Panorama Tours also offer an extensive array of other day trips from Salzburg (Berchtesgaden Eagle's Nest, salt mines, and Salzkammergut lakes and mountains are the most popular). The tours are all explained in their brochures, which litter hotel lobbies all over town.

Salzach River Cruises runs a basic 40-minute round-trip cruise with recorded commentary (€12, 8/day April–Sept). For a longer cruise, ride to Hellbrunn and return by bus (€15, 1–2/day April–Sept). Boats leave from the old-town side of the river just downstream of the Staatsbrücke (tel. 0662/8257-6912). While views can be cramped, passengers are treated to a fun finale just before docking, when the captain twirls a fun "waltz."

SELF-GUIDED WALK

Salzburg's Old Town

I've linked the best sights in the old town into this handy self-guided orientation walk, rated ▲▲▲.

• *Begin in the heart of town, just up from the river, near the TI on...*

Mozartplatz: All the happy tourists around you probably wouldn't be here if not for the man honored by this statue—Mozart (erected in 1842). Mozart spent much of his first 25 years (1756–1777) in Salzburg, the greatest Baroque city north of the Alps. But the city's much older. The Mozart statue actually sits on bits of Roman Salzburg. And the pink church of St. Michael overlooking the square dates from A.D. 800. The first Salzburgers settled right around here. Near you are the American Express office and the tourist information office (with a concert box office). Just around the downhill corner is a pedestrian bridge leading over the Salzach River to the quiet, most medieval street in town, Steingasse (described on page 104).

Salzburg's Old Town Walk
1 Mozartplatz
2 Residenzplatz
3 Old Residenz
4 New Residenz & Glockenspiel
5 Salzburg Panorama 1829
6 Salzburg Cathedral
7 Kapitelplatz
8 St. Peter's Cemetery
9 St. Peter's Church
10 Toscanini Hof
11 Universitätsplatz
12 Getreidegasse
13 Mozart's Birthplace
P - PARKING
- VIEW
KAPUZINERBERG
SALZACH RIVER
MOZART PLATZ
CATHEDRAL
MOZART'S BIRTHPLACE
MOZARTS RESIDENCE
FESTIVAL CONCERT HALLS
ST. PETERS
CEMETERY
FUNICULAR
HOHEN-SALZBURG FORTRESS
NONNBERG ABBEY
MÖNCHSBERG
TOSCANINI HOF
STADTALM CAFÉ
ELEVATOR
MUSEUM OF MODERN ART
TO AIRPORT, FREEWAY & MOOS STR.
TO P
TO HALLEIN
TO HELLBRUNN PALACE
LINZER GASSE
STEINGASSE
IMBERGSTRASSE
GISELAKAI
MOZART STEG
RUDOLFSKAI
JUDENGASSE
GOLD.
RESIDENZ PLATZ
POST
KAPITEL PLATZ
KAPITEL
DOM PLATZ
FRANZ.
MAX REIN. PLATZ
HOFSTALL
TUNNEL
GETREIDE-GASSE
GRIESGASSE
F. HANUSCH-PLATZ
FRANZ JOSEF-KAI
MULLNER
BURGERSPITAL GASSE
MAKART-STEG
ELISABETHKAI
PLATZL
STAATS BRÜCKE
PFEIFERGASSE
KALGASSE
HERRENGASSE
KAJETANER PLATZ
RUDOLFS PLATZ
NONNTALER BRÜCKE
NONNTALER HAUPTSTR.
PETERSBRUNNSTR.
NEUTOR
200 YARDS
200 METERS
DCH

• *Walk toward the cathedral and into the big square with the huge fountain.*

Residenzplatz: Important buildings ringed this square when it was the ancient Roman forum...and they still do. Salzburg's energetic Prince-Archbishop Wolf Dietrich (who ruled from 1587–1612) was raised in Rome, counted the Medicis as his buddies, and had grandiose Italian ambitions for Salzburg. After a convenient fire destroyed the cathedral, he set about building "the Rome of the North." This square, with his new cathedral and palace, was the centerpiece of his Baroque dream city. A series of interconnecting squares—like you'll see nowhere else—make a grand processional way, leading from here through the old town.

For centuries, Salzburg's leaders were both important church officials *and* princes of the Holy Roman Empire, hence the title "prince-archbishop"—mixing sacred and secular authority. But Wolf Dietrich misplayed his hand, losing power and spending his last five years imprisoned up in the Salzburg castle.

The fountain is as Italian as can be, with a Triton matching Bernini's famous Triton Fountain in Rome. Lying on a busy trade route to the south, Salzburg was well aware of the exciting things going on in Italy. Things Italian were respected (as in colonial America, when a bumpkin would "stick a feather in his cap and call it macaroni"). Local artists even Italianized their names in order to raise their rates.

Residenz: Dietrich's skippable palace is connected to the cathedral by a skyway. A series of ornately decorated rooms and an art gallery are open to visitors with time to kill (€8 includes both palace and gallery with audioguide for staterooms, Tue–Sun 10:00–17:00, closed Mon, tel. 0662/8042-2690).

Opposite the old Residenz is the new Residenz, which has long been a government administration building. Today it houses the central post office, the Heimatwerk (a fine shop showing off all the best local handicrafts, Mon–Fri 9:00–18:00, Sat 9:00–13:00, closed Sun) and the fascinating Salzburg Panorama 1829 exhibit (worth the €2 and described below). In 2007, the city's grand Salzburg Museum of history and art opened in this building (€8, daily 9:00–18:00, Thu until 20:00, tel. 0662/6208-08123, www.salzburgmuseum.at).

• *Atop the new Residenz rings the famous...*

Glockenspiel: This bell tower has a carillon of 35 17th-century bells (cast in Antwerp) that chimes throughout the day and plays tunes (appropriate to the month) at 7:00, 11:00, and 18:00. There was a time when Salzburg could afford to take tourists to the top of the tower to actually see the big barrel with adjustable tabs turn (like a giant music-box mechanism)...pulling the right bells in the right rhythm. Notice the ornamental top: an upside-down heart in flames surrounding the solar system (symbolizing that God loves all of creation).

Look back, past Mozart's statue, to the 4,220-foot-high Gaisberg—the forested hill with the television tower. A road leads to the top for a commanding view. Its summit is a favorite destination for local nature-lovers and kids learning to ski.

• *Before continuing our walk, drop into the...*

Salzburg Panorama 1829: This enjoyable sight is worth ▲. In the early 19th century, 360-degree "panorama" paintings of great cities or events were popular. These creations were even taken on extended road trips. Salzburg, at a stagnant stage in its development, had this circular view painted by Johann Michael Sattler: the city as seen from the top of its castle. When complete, it spent 10 years touring the great cities of Europe, showing off the city's breathtaking setting. Today the exquisitely restored painting offers a fascinating look at the city in 1829. The river was slower and had beaches. The old town looks essentially as it does today, and Moosstrasse still leads into idyllic farm country. Paintings from that era of other great cities around the world are hung around the outside wall with numbers but without labels, as a kind of quiz game. A flier gives the cities names on one side, and keys them to the numbers. See how many 19th-century cities you can identify (€2, daily 9:00–18:00, Thu until 21:00, Residenzplatz 9).

• *Back on Residenzplatz, walk under the prince-archbishop's skyway and step into Cathedral Square (Domplatz), where you'll find the...*

Salzburg Cathedral: This ▲▲ sight was one of the first Baroque buildings north of the Alps. It was consecrated in 1628, during the Thirty Years' War. (Pitting Roman Catholics against Protestants, this war devastated much of Europe and brought most grand construction projects to a halt.) Experts differ on what motivated the builders: to emphasize Salzburg's commitment to the Roman Catholic cause and the power of the Church here, or to show that there could be a peaceful alternative to the religious strife that was racking Europe at the time. Salzburg's archbishop was technically the top papal official north of the Alps, but the city managed to steer clear of the war. With its rich salt production, it had enough money to stay out of the conflict and carefully maintain its independence from the warring sides.

The dates on the iron gates refer to milestones in the church's history: In 774, the previous church (long since destroyed) was founded by St. Virgil, to be replaced in 1628 by the church you see today. In 1959, the reconstruction was completed after a WWII bomb blew through the dome.

Cathedral Square is surrounded by the prince-archbishop's secular administration buildings. The **statue of Mary** (1771) is looking away from the church, but if you stand in the rear of the square, immediately under the middle arch, you'll see that she's positioned to be crowned by the two angels on the church facade.

Step inside the cathedral (donation requested; May–Oct Mon–Sat 9:00–18:30, Sun 13:00–18:30; Nov–April Mon–Sat 10:00–17:00, Sun 13:00–17:00). Enter the cathedral as if part of a festival procession—drawn toward the resurrected Christ by the brightly lit area under the dome, and cheered on by ceiling paintings of the Passion. The stucco, by a Milanese artist, is exceptional. Sit under the dome—surrounded by the tombs of ten 17th-century archbishops—and imagine all four organs playing, each balcony filled with musicians...glorious surround-sound. Mozart, who was the organist here for two years, would advise you that the acoustics are best in pews immediately under the dome. Study the symbolism of the decor all around you—intellectual, complex, and cohesive. Think of the altar in Baroque terms, as the center of a stage, with sunrays as spotlights in this dramatic and sacred theater. In the left transept, stairs lead down into the crypt (Krypta), where you can see foundations of the earlier church, more tombs, and a tourist-free chapel (reserved for prayer) directly under the dome.

Built in just 14 years (1614–1628), the church boasts harmonious architecture. When Pope John Paul II visited in 1998, 5,000 people filled the cathedral (330 feet long and 230 feet tall). The baptismal font (dark bronze, left of the entry) is from the previous cathedral (basin from about 1320, although the lid is modern). Mozart was baptized here ("Amadeus" means "beloved by God"). Concert and Mass schedules are posted at the entrance; the Sunday Mass at 10:00 is famous for its music.

The **Cathedral Museum** (Dom Museum) has a rich collection of church art (entry at portico, €5, mid-May–Oct and Dec Mon–Sat 10:00–17:00, Sun 11:00–18:00, closed Nov and Jan–mid-May, tel. 0662/844-189).

From Cathedral Square to St. Peter's Cemetery: From the cathedral, exit left and walk toward the fortress into the next square (passing the free underground public WCs and the giant chessboard), and head for the pond. This was a **horse bath,** the 18th-century equivalent of a car wash. Notice the puzzle above it—the artist wove the date of the structure into a phrase. It says, "Leopold the Prince Built Me," using the letters LLDVICMXVXI, which total 1732 (add it up...it works)—the year it was built. A small road (back by the chessboard) leads uphill to the fortress (and fortress lift). The stage is set up for the many visiting choirs who are unable to line up a gig. They are welcome to sing here anytime at all. With your back to the cathedral, leave the square through a gate in the right corner that reads *St. Peter.* It leads to a waterfall and St. Peter's Cemetery.

The **waterfall** is part of a canal system that has brought water into Salzburg from Berchtesgaden, 16 miles away, since the 13th century. Climb uphill a few steps to feel the medieval water power. The stream, divided from here into smaller canals, was channeled through town to provide fire protection, to flush out the streets (Sat morning was flood-the-streets day), and to power factories (there were more than 100 watermill-powered firms as late as the 19th century). There's a good view of the funicular climbing up to the castle from here. Drop into the fragrant and traditional **bakery** at the waterfall. It's hard to beat their rocklike *Roggenbrot* (various fresh rolls for less than €1, Thu–Tue 7:00–17:30, Sat until 12:00, closed Wed). For more on the canal system, check out the free Alm River Canal exhibit nearby (described on page 102).

• *Now find the* Katakomben *sign and step into...*

St. Peter's Cemetery: This collection of lovingly tended mini-gardens abuts the Mönchberg's rock wall (free, silence is requested, daily April–Sept 6:30–19:00, Oct–March 6:30–18:00). Walk in about 50 yards to the intersection of lanes at the base of the cliff marked by a stone ball. (It's seemingly made-to-order for a little back-stretching break. Go ahead...I'll wait.) You're surrounded by three churches, each founded in the sixth century atop a pagan Celtic holy site. St. Peter's Church is closest to the stone ball. Notice the fine Romanesque stonework on the chapel nearest you, and the fancy rich guys' Renaissance-style tombs decorating its walls.

Wealthy as those guys were, they ran out of caring relatives. The graves surrounding you are tended by descendants of the deceased. In Austria, gravesites are rented, not owned. Rent bills are sent out every 10 years. If no one cares enough to make the payment, your remains are chucked. Iron crosses were much cheaper than stone tombstones. While the cemetery where the von Trapp family hid out in *The Sound of Music* was actually in Hollywood, it was inspired by this one.

Look up the cliff. Legendary medieval hermit monks are said to have lived in the hillside—but "catacombs" they're not. For €1, you can climb lots of steps to see a few old caves, a chapel, and some fine views (May–Sept Tue–Sun 10:30–17:00, closed Mon, shorter hours off-season).

• *Continue downhill through the cemetery and out the opposite end. Just outside, hook right and drop into...*

St. Peter's Church: Just inside, enjoy a carved Romanesque welcome. Over the inner doorway, a fine tympanum shows Jesus on a rainbow flanked by Peter and Paul over a stylized tree of life and under a Latin inscription reading, "I am the door to life, and only through me can you find eternal life." Enter the nave and notice how the once purely Romanesque vaulting has since been iced with a sugary Rococo finish. Salzburg's only Rococo interior feels Bavarian (because it is—the fancy stucco work was done by

Bavarian artists). Up the right side aisle is the tomb of St. Rupert, with a painting showing Salzburg in 1750 (one bridge, salt ships sailing the river, and angels hoisting barrels of salt to heaven as St. Rupert prays for his city). On pillars farther up the aisle are faded bits of 13th-century Romanesque frescos. Similar frescoes hide under Rococo whitewash throughout the church.

Leaving the church, notice the Stiftskeller St. Peter restaurant (on the left—described under "Eating," page 115, and for its "Mozart Dinner Concert," page 108). Charlemagne ate here in A.D. 803—allowing locals to claim it's the oldest restaurant in Europe. Opposite where you entered the square (look through the arch), you'll see St. Rupert waving you into the next square (early-20th-century Bauhaus-style dorms for student monks), with a modern crucifix (1926) on the far wall. To the right of the crucifix (at #8), press the red button on the bronze door, enter, and see an unforgettable Expressionist-carved crucifix (also from the 1920s, free, open until 11:30 only).

• *The next square is...*

Toscanini Hof: This square faces the 1925 Festival Hall. The hall's three theaters seat 5,000. This is where the nervous Captain von Trapp waited before walking onstage (in the movie, he sang "Edelweiss"), just before he escaped with his family. On the left is the city's 1,500-space, inside-the-mountain parking lot; ahead, behind the *Felsenkeller* sign, is a tunnel (generally closed) leading to the actual concert hall; and to the right is the backstage of a smaller hall where carpenters are often building stage sets (door open on hot days).

• *Walk downhill through Max-Reinhardt-Platz, to the right of the church and past the public WC into...*

Universitätsplatz: This square hosts an open-air produce market—Salzburg's liveliest (mornings Mon–Sat, best on Sat). Locals are happy to pay more here for the reliably fresh and top-quality produce. (These days, half of Austria's produce is grown organically.) The market really bustles on Saturday mornings, when the farmers are in town. Public marketplaces have fountains for washing fruit and vegetables. The fountain here—a part of the medieval water system—plummets down a hole and to the river. The sundial (over the water hole) is accurate (except for the daylight savings hour) and two-dimensional, showing both the time (obvious) and the date (less obvious). The fanciest facade overlooking the square (the yellow one) is the backside of Mozart's Birthplace (described below).

• *Continue past the fountain to the end of the square, passing several characteristic and nicely arcaded medieval tunnels (on right) that connect the square to Getreidegasse. Cross the big road for a look at the giant horse troughs, adjacent to the prince's stables. Paintings show the various breeds and temperaments of horses in his stable. Like Vienna, Salzburg had a passion for the equestrian arts. Take two right turns and you're at the start of...*

Getreidegasse: This street, worth ▲▲, was old Salzburg's busy, colorful main drag. It's lined with *Schmuck* (jewelry) shops. Famous for its old wrought-iron signs (best viewed from this end), the architecture on the street still looks much as it did in Mozart's day—though its former elegance is now mostly gone, replaced by chain outlets.

Schnapps Pit Stop: On the right at #39, Sporer serves up homemade spirits (€1.30 per shot). This has been a family-run show for a century—fun-loving, proud, and English-speaking. Nuss is nut, Marille is apricot (typical of this region), the Kletzen cocktail is like a super-thick Baileys with pear, and Edle Brande are the stronger schnapps. The many homemade firewaters are in jugs at the end of the bar. Austrian wines are sold by the Achtel (eighth of a liter).

Continue down Getreidegasse, noticing the old doorbells—one per floor. At #40, Eisgrotte serves good ice cream. Across from Eisgrotte, a tunnel leads to Bosna Stand, the local choice for the very best sausage in town (see page 118). Farther along, you'll pass McDonald's (while required to keep its arches Baroque and low-key, it just couldn't hang anything less than the biggest sign on the street).

• *The knot of excited tourists and salesmen hawking goofy gimmicks mark the home of Salzburg's most famous resident.*

Mozart's Birthplace (Geburtshaus): The house where Mozart was born, and where he composed many of his early works, is worth a visit for his true fans (rated ▲, described below). But for most, his Residence, across the river, is more interesting (described on page 104).

• *Our walk is finished. From here, you can head up to the Hohensalzburg Fortress on Mönchsberg mountain over the old town (see page 99); or continue to some of the sights across the river. To reach the across-the-river sights, head for the river, jog left (past the fast-fish restaurant and free WCs), climb to the top of the Makartsteg pedestrian bridge, and turn to page 102.*

SIGHTS AND ACTIVITIES

Mozart's Birthplace (Geburtshaus)

Mozart was born here in 1756. It was in this building—the most popular Mozart sight in town, and worth ▲—that he composed most of his boy-genius works. For fans, it's almost a pilgrimage. American artist Robert Wilson was recently hired to spiff up the exhibit, to make if feel more conceptual and less like a museum.

But I was unimpressed. If you're tackling just one Mozart sight, skip the birthplace; instead, walk 10 minutes from here to Mozart's Residence (described on page 104), which provides a more informative visit. But if you want to max out on Mozart, a visit here is worthwhile.

Cost, Hours, Location: €6, or €9.50 for combo-ticket that includes Mozart's Residence, daily 9:00–18:00, July–Aug until 19:00, last entry 30 min before closing, Getreidegasse 9, tel. 0662/844-313.

➲ **Self-Guided Tour:** Here's what you'll see as you shuffle through with the herd:

Room 1: Around a baby crib showing an infant both old and young (Mozart's music is timeless...get it?) are walls heavy with historic etchings, portraits, and documents. Most important: an engraving of the family (lower right) and a fine "portrait with a bird's nest" of Mozart, painted from life when he was nine years old (upper left).

Room 2: The living room shows off authentic family portraits: Wolfgang's mom, dad, sister, and wife. Wolfgang composed his first pieces as a child on a clavichord (like the one in this room). A predecessor of the piano, it hit the strings with simple teeter-totter keys that played very softly...ideal for composers living in tight apartment quarters.

Room 3: The nursery is decorated like Mozart's music: light and free as a bird (hence the flying birds). Embedded in the walls are Mozart's personal possessions—his ring, silk wallet, and violin. He was born in this room, and the entire family slept here until Wolfgang was 14.

Room 4: Exactly what Mozart looked like is a bit of a mystery. Various portraits in this room give us something to go on.

Corridor: The neon phrase shows his juvenile sense of humor. It's a rhyme: *Madame Mutter, ich esse gerne Butter.* (Dear mother, I love to eat butter.) The next room is wallpapered with reproductions of actual circa 1840 photos of Mozart's wife and son (as an old man). More strange Wilson-designed rooms follow: Mozart loved to turn things upside-down—so the Salzburg cityscapes are that way, with stars on the floor. Downstairs, just before the shop, rooms dedicated to Mozart's operas play various video clips continuously.

On Mönchsberg Mountain, Above the Old Town

The main "sight" on Mönchsberg is the Hohensalzburg Fortress. But if you just want to enjoy the sweeping views over Salzburg, you have a couple of options: take the elevator at the other end of Mönchsberg (explained under "Getting Around Salzburg," page 88); or visit the castle in the evening on a night when they're hosting a concert (after 18:30, about 300 nights a year). This is the only time you can buy a €3.20 funicular ticket without paying for the castle entrance—since the castle museum is closed, but the funicular is still running to bring up concert-goers.

▲▲Hohensalzburg Fortress (Festung)—Built on a rock 400 feet above the Salzach River, this fortress was never really used. That's the idea. It was a good investment—so foreboding, nobody attacked the town for a thousand years. The city was never taken by force, but when Napoleon stopped by, Salzburg wisely surrendered. After a stint as a military barracks, the fortress was opened to the public in the 1860s by Emperor Franz Josef. Today it remains one of Europe's mightiest castles, dominating Salzburg's skyline and offering incredible views.

Cost: Your ticket includes the price of the funicular up and down, as well as admission to the fortress grounds and all the museums inside—whether you want to see them or not (€9.80, €22.60 family ticket, €8.60 per person if you hike to the castle without using the funicular).

Hours: The complex is open daily year-round (May–Sept 9:00–18:00, July–Aug until 19:00, Oct–April 9:30–17:00, last entry 30 min before closing, tel. 0662/8424-3011). On nights when there's a concert, the castle grounds are free and open until 21:30.

Concerts: The fortress also serves as a venue for evening concerts (Festungskonzerte). For details, see the "Entertainment" section on page 106.

Orientation: The fortress visit has three parts: a relatively dull courtyard with some fine views from its various ramparts; the fortress itself (with a required and escorted 45-minute audio tour); and the palace museum (by far the best exhibit of the lot). At the bottom of the funicular, you'll pass through an interesting little exhibit on the town's canal system (free, described below).

➲ **Self-Guided Tour:** Climb from the top of the funicular to the inner courtyard. Immediately inside, circling to the left (clockwise), you'll encounter cannons (still poised to defend Salzburg against a Turkish invasion), the marionette exhibit, the palace museum, the Kuenburg bastion, scant ruins of a Romanesque church, the courtyard (with path down for those walking), toilets, shops, a restaurant, and the fortress tour.

• *Begin at the...*

Marionette Exhibit: Several fun rooms show off this local tradition, with three videos playing continuously: two with peeks at Salzburg's ever-enchanting Marionette Theater performances of Mozart classics, and one with a behind-the-scenes look at the action. Give the hands-on marionette a whirl.

• *Hiking through the former palace, you'll find the site's best exhibits by far at the...*

Palace Museum (Festungsmuseum Carolino Augusteum): The second floor has exhibits on castle life, from music to torture. The top floor shows off fancy royal apartments, a sneak preview of the room used for the nightly fortress concerts, and the Rainier military museum, dedicated to the Salzburg regiments that fought in both World Wars.

Castle Courtyard: The courtyard was the main square of the castle residents, a community of a thousand—which could be self-sufficient when necessary. The square was ringed by the shops of craftsmen, blacksmiths, bakers, and so on. The well dipped into a rain-fed cistern. The church is dedicated to St. George, the protector of horses (logical for an army church) and decorated by fine red marble reliefs (c. 1502). Behind the church is the top of the old lift that helped supply the fortress. (From near here, steps lead back into the city, or to the mountaintop "Mönchsberg Walk," described later in this chapter.) The scant remains of a Romanesque chapel are well-described.

• *Near the chapel, turn left into the Kuenburg Bastion (once a garden) for fine city and castle views.*

Kuenburg Bastion: Notice how the castle has three parts: the original castle inside the courtyard, the vast whitewashed walls (built when the castle was a residence), and the lower, beefed-up fortifications (added for extra defense against the expected Turkish invasion). Survey Salzburg from here and think about fortifying an important city using its natural surroundings. Mönchsberg (the little mountain you're on) naturally cradles the old town, with just a small gate between the mountain and the river needed to bottle up the place. The new town across the river needed a bit of a wall arcing from the river to its hill. Back then, only one bridge crossed the Salzach into town, and it had a fortified gate.

• *Back inside the castle courtyard, continue your circle. The Round Tower (1497) helps you visualize the inner original castle.*

Fortress Interior: Tourists are allowed in this part of the fortified palace only with an escort. (They say that's for security, though while touring it, you wonder what they're protecting.) A crowd assembles at the turnstile, and every 15 minutes 40 people are issued their audioguides and let in for the escorted walk. You'll go one room at a time, listening to a 45-minute commentary. While the interior furnishings are mostly gone—taken by Napoleon—the rooms survived as well as they did because no one wanted to live here after 1500, so the building was never modernized. Your tour includes a room dedicated to the art of "excruciating questioning" ("softening up" prisoners, in current American military jargon)—filled with tools of that gruesome trade. The highlight is the commanding city view from the top of a tower.

• *After seeing the fortress, consider hiking down to the old town, or along the top of Mönchsberg (both described below). If you take the funicular down, keep an eye out for the...*

Alm River Canal Exhibit: At the base of the funicular, below the castle, is this fine little exhibit on how the river was broken into five smaller streams—powering the city until steam took up the energy-supply baton. Pretend it's the year 1200 and follow (by video) the flow of the water from the river through the canals, into the mills, and finally being dumped into the Salzach River (free, access from the bottom of the lift as you're leaving, or through Amber shop next door if you're not riding the funicular).

▲Mönchsberg Walk—For a great 30-minute hike, exit the fortress by taking the steep lane down from the castle courtyard. At the first intersection, right leads into the old town, and left leads across the Mönchsberg. The lane leads 20 minutes through the woods high above the city (stick to the high lanes, or you'll end up back in town), taking you to the Gasthaus Stadtalm café (light meals, cheap beds—see page 112 of "Sleeping," and page 118 of "Eating"). From the Stadtalm, pass under the medieval wall and walk left along the wall to a tableau showing how it once looked. Take the switchback to the right and follow the lane downhill to the Museum of Modern Art (described below), where the elevator zips you back into town (€2 one-way, €3 round-trip, daily 8:00–17:00, July–Aug until 24:00). If you stay on the lane past the elevator, you eventually pass the Augustine church that marks the rollicking Augustiner Bräustübl (see page 119).

In 1669, a huge Mönchsberg landslide killed more than 200 townspeople. Since then the cliffs have been carefully checked each spring and fall. Even today, you might see crews on the cliffs, monitoring their stability.

Museum of Modern Art on Mönchsberg—The modern-art museum on top of Mönchsberg, built in 2004, houses Salzburg's Rupertinum Gallery, plus special exhibitions. While the collection is not worth climbing a mountain for, the restaurant has some of the best views in town (€8, Tue–Sun 10:00–18:00, Wed until 21:00, closed Mon, at top of Mönchsberg elevator, tel. 0662/842-220, www.museumdermoderne.at).

In the New Town, North of the River

The following sights are on the far (north) side of the river from the old town. I've connected them with walking instructions.

• *Begin at the Makartsteg pedestrian bridge, where you can survey the...*

Salzach River—Salzburg's river is called "salt river" not because it's salty, but because of the precious cargo it once carried—the salt mines of Hallein are just nine miles upstream. Salt could be transported from here all the way to the Danube, and on to the

Mediterranean via the Black Sea. The riverbanks and roads were built when the river was regulated in the 1850s. Before that, the Salzach was much wider and slower-moving. Houses opposite the old town fronted the river with docks and "garages" for boats. The grand buildings just past the bridge (with their elegant promenades and cafés) were built on reclaimed land in the late 19th century, in the historicist style of Vienna's Ringstrasse.

Scan the cityscape. Notice all the churches. Salzburg, nicknamed the "Rome of the North," has 38 Catholic churches (plus two Protestant churches and a synagogue). Find the five streams gushing into the river. These date from the 13th century, when the river was split into five canals running through the town to power its mills. Hotel Stein (upstream, just left of next bridge, has a popular roof-terrace café, described on page 105). Downstream, notice the Museum of Modern Art atop Mönchsberg, with a view café and a faux castle (actually a water reservoir). The Romanesque bell tower with the copper dome in the distance is the Augustine church, site of the best beer hall in town (the Augustiner Bräustübl—see page 119).

• *Cross the bridge, pass the Café Bazar (a fine place for a drink—see page 119), walk two blocks inland, and take a left past the heroic statues into...*

▲Mirabell Gardens and Palace (Schloss)—The bubbly gardens laid out in 1730 for the prince-archbishop have been open to the public since 1850 (thanks to Emperor Franz Josef, who was rattled by the popular revolutions of 1848). The gardens are free and open until dusk. The palace is only open as a concert venue (explained below). The statues and the arbor (far left) were featured in *The Sound of Music*. Walk through the gardens to the palace. Look back, enjoy the garden/cathedral/castle view, and imagine how the prince-archbishop must have reveled in a vista that reminded him of all his secular and religious power. Then go around to the river side of the palace and find the horse.

The rearing **Pegasus statue** (rare and very well-balanced) is the site of a famous *Sound of Music* scene where the kids all danced before lining up on the stairs (with Maria 30 yards farther along). The steps lead to a small mound in the park (made of WWII rubble, and today a rendezvous point for Salzburg's gay community).

Nearest the horse, stairs lead between two lions to a pair of tough dwarfs (early volleyball players with spiked mittens) welcoming you to Salzburg's **Dwarf Park.** Cross the elevated walk (noticing the city's fortified walls) to meet statues of a dozen actual dwarfs who served the prince-archbishop—modeled after real people with real fashions in about 1600. This was Mannerist art, from the hyper-realistic age that followed the Renaissance.

There's plenty of **music,** both in the park and in the palace.

A brass band plays free park concerts (May–Aug Sun at 10:30 and Wed at 20:30). To properly enjoy the lavish Mirabell Palace—once the prince-archbishop's summer palace, and now the seat of the mayor—get a ticket to a Schlosskonzerte (my favorite venue for a classical concert—see "Entertainment," page 106).

• *To visit Salzburg's best Mozart sight, go a long block southeast to Makartplatz, where you'll find...*

▲▲Mozart's Residence (Wohnhaus)—This reconstruction of Mozart's second home (his family moved here when he was 17) is the most informative Mozart sight in town. The English-language audioguide (included with admission, 90 min) provides a fascinating insight into Mozart's life and music, with the usual scores, old pianos, and an interesting 30-minute film (#17 on your audioguide for soundtrack) that runs continuously (€6, or €9.50 for combo-ticket that includes Mozart's Birthplace in the old town, daily 9:00–18:00, July–Aug until 19:00, last entry 1 hour before closing, allow at least 1 hour for visit, Makartplatz 8, tel. 0662/8742-2740).

In the main hall—used by the Mozarts to entertain Salzburg's high society—you can hear original instruments from Mozart's time. Mozart was proud to be the first in his family to compose a duet. Notice the family portrait (circa 1780) on the wall, showing Mozart with his sister Nannerl, their father, and their mother—who'd died two years earlier in Paris. Mozart also had silly crude bull's-eyes made for the pop-gun game popular at the time (licking an "arse," Wolfgang showed his disdain for the rigors of high society). Later rooms feature real artifacts that explore his loves, his intellectual pursuits, his travels, and more.

• *From here, you can walk a few blocks back to the main bridge (Staatsbrücke), where you'll find Platzl, a square once used as a hay market. Pause to enjoy the kid-pleasing little fountain. Near the fountain (with your back to the river), Steingasse leads darkly to the right.*

▲Steingasse—This street, a block in from the river, was the only street in the Middle Ages going south over the Alps to Venice (this was the first stop north of the Alps). Today, it's wonderfully tranquil and free of Salzburg's touristy crush.

At #9, a plaque (of questionable veracity) shows where Joseph Mohr, who wrote the words to "Silent Night," was born—poor and illegitimate—in 1792. There is no doubt, however, that the popular Christmas carol was composed and first sung in the village of Oberndorf, just outside of Salzburg, in 1818. Stairs lead from near here up to the monastery.

On the next corner, the wall is gouged out. This scar was left even after the building was restored, to remind locals of the American GI who tried to get a tank down this road during a visit to the town brothel—two blocks farther up Steingasse. Inviting cocktail bars along here come alive at night (described on page 120).

At #19, find the carvings on the old door. Some say these are notices from beggars to the begging community (more numerous after post-Reformation religious wars, which forced many people out of their homes and towns)—a kind of "hobo code" indicating whether the residents would give or not. Trace the wires of the old-fashioned doorbells to the highest floors.

Farther on, you'll find a commanding Salzburg view across the river. Notice the red dome marking the oldest nunnery in the German-speaking world (established in 712) under the fortress and to the left. The real Maria from *The Sound of Music* taught in this nunnery's school. In 1927, she and Captain von Trapp were married in the church you see here (not the church filmed in the movie). He was 47. She was 22. Hmmmm.

From here look back, above the arch you just passed through, at part of the town's medieval fortification. The coat of arms on the arch is of the prince-archbishop who paid Bavaria a huge ransom to stay out of the Thirty Years' War (smart move). He then built this fortification (in 1634) anticipating rampaging armies from both sides.

Today, this street is for making love, not war. The Maison de Plaisir (a few doors down, at #24) has for centuries been a Salzburg brothel. But the climax of this walk is more touristic.

• *For a grand view, head back to Platzl and the bridge, enter the Hotel Stein (left corner, overlooking the river), and ride the elevator to...*

Stein Terrasse—This café offers perhaps the best views in town (aside from the castle). Hidden from the tourist crush, it's a trendy, professional, local scene. You can discretely peek at the view, or enjoy a drink or light meal (€7 business lunch specials, indoor/outdoor seating, daily, 9:00–24:00).

• *Back at Platzl and the bridge, you can head straight up Linzergasse (away from the river) into a neighborhood packed with recommended accommodations, as well as our final new-town sight...*

▲St. Sebastian Cemetery—Wander through this quiet place, so Baroque and so Italian (free, daily April–Oct 9:00–19:00, Nov–March 9:00–16:00, entry usually at Linzergasse 43). Mozart is buried in Vienna, his mom's in Paris, and his sister is in Salzburg's old town (St. Peter's)—but Wolfgang's father Leopold and his wife Constantia are buried here (from the black iron gate entrance on Linzergasse, walk 17 paces and look left). When Prince-Archbishop Wolf Dietrich had the cemetery moved from around the cathedral and put here, across the river, people didn't like it. To help popularize it, he had his own mausoleum built as its centerpiece. Continue straight past the Mozart tomb to this circular building (English description at door).

▲Hellbrunn Castle—Around the year 1610, Prince-Archbishop Sittikus (after meditating on stewardship and Christ-like values) decided he needed a lavish palace with a vast and ornate garden purely for pleasure. He built this and just loved inviting his VIP guests out for a fun with his trick fountains. Today the visit is worthwhile for the garden full of clever fountains...and the sadistic joy the tour guide gets from soaking tourists. (Hint: When you see a wet place, cover your camera.) After buying your ticket, you wait for the English tour, laugh and scramble through the entertaining 40-minute trick-water toy tour, and are then free to tour the forgettable palace with an included audioguide (€8.50, daily May–Sept 9:00–17:30, July–Aug until 22:00, April and Oct 9:00–16:30, closed Nov–March, tel. 0662/820-372, www.hellbrunn.at).

Hellbrunn is nearly four miles south of Salzburg (bus #25 from station or from Staatsbrücke bridge, 2/hr, 20 min). While it can be fun—especially on a hot day or with kids—for many, it's a lot of trouble for a few water tricks. The Hellbrunn Baroque garden, one of the oldest in Europe, now features *S.O.M.*'s "Sixteen Going on Seventeen" gazebo.

Hellbrunn makes a good 30-minute bike excursion along riverbank from Salzburg (described below).

▲▲Riverside or Meadow Bike Ride—The Salzach River has smooth, flat, and scenic bike lanes along each side (thanks to medieval tow paths—cargo boats would float downstream and be dragged back up by horse). On a sunny day, I can think of no more shout-worthy escape from the city. The nearly four-mile path upstream to Hellbrunn Castle is easy, with a worthy destination (leave Salzburg on castle side). For a nine-mile ride, continue on to Hallein (the north, or new-town, side of river is most scenic). Perhaps the most pristine meadow farm-country route is the four-mile Hellbrunner Allee from Akademiestrasse. Even a quickie ride across town is a great Salzburg experience. In the evening, the riverbanks are a floodlit-spires world.

ENTERTAINMENT

Music Scene

▲▲Salzburg Festival (Salzburger Festspiele)—Each summer, from late July to the end of August, Salzburg hosts its famous Salzburg Festival, founded in 1920 to employ Vienna's musicians in the summer. This fun and festive time is crowded, but there are plenty of beds (except for a few August weekends). There are three big halls: the Opera and Orchestra venues in the Festival House, and the Landes Theater, where German-language plays are performed. Tickets for the big festival events are generally expensive (€50–200) and sold out well in advance (bookable from Jan). Most tourists think they're "going to the Salzburg Festival" by seeing smaller non-festival events that go on during the festival weeks.

For these lesser events, same-day tickets are normally available (the ticket office on Mozartplatz, in the TI, prints a daily list of concerts and charges a 30 percent fee to book them). For specifics on this year's festival schedule and tickets, visit www.salzburgfestival.at, or contact the Austrian National Tourist Office in the United States (P.O. Box 1142, New York, NY 10108-1142, tel. 212/944-6880, fax 212/730-4568, www.austria.info, travel@austria.info). While I've never planned in advance, I've enjoyed great concerts with every visit.

▲▲**Musical Events Year-Round**—Salzburg is busy throughout the year, with 2,000 classical performances in its palaces and churches annually. Pick up the events calendar at the TI (free, bimonthly). Whenever you visit, you'll have a number of concerts (generally small chamber groups) to choose from. Here are some of the more accessible events:

Concerts at Hohensalzburg Fortress (Festungskonzerte): Nearly nightly concerts—Mozart's greatest hits for beginners—are held atop Mönchsberg, in the "prince's chamber" of the fortress, featuring small chamber groups (open seating after the first five more expensive rows, €31 or €38 plus €3.20 for the funicular, at 19:30, 20:00, or 20:30, doors open 30 min early, tel. 0662/825-858 to reserve, pick up tickets at the door). The medieval-feeling chamber has windows overlooking the city, and the concert gives you a chance to enjoy the grand city view and a stroll through the castle courtyard. (The funicular ticket costs €3.20 within an hour of the show—ideal for people who just want to ascend for the view.) For €50, you can combine the concert with a four-course dinner (starts two hours before concert).

Concerts at the Mirabell Palace (Schlosskonzerte): The nearly nightly chamber music concerts at the Mirabell Palace are performed in a lavish Baroque setting. They come with more sophisticated programs and better musicians than the fortress concerts. Baroque music flying around a Baroque hall is a happy bird in the right cage (open seating after the first five pricier rows, €30–36, at 19:30, 20:00, or 20:30, doors open 30 min early, tel. 0662/848-5860, www.salzburger-schlosskonzerte.at).

"Five O'Clock Concerts" (5-Uhr-Konzerte): These concerts—next to St. Peter's in the old town—are cheaper, since they feature young artists (€12, July–Sept Thu–Tue at 17:00, no concerts Wed or Oct–June, 45 min, tel. 0662/8445-7619, www.5-uhr-konzerte.com). While the series is formally named after the brother of Joseph Haydn, it offers music from various masters.

Mozart Piano Sonatas: St. Peter's Abbey hosts these concerts each weekend (€18, €9 for children, €45 for a family of four, Fri and Sat at 19:00 year-round, tel. 0662/423-5645). This short and inexpensive concert is ideal for families.

Marionette Theater: Salzburg's much-loved marionette theater offers operas with spellbinding marionettes and recorded music. Music-lovers are mesmerized by the little people on stage (€18–35, nearly nightly at 19:30 June–Sept except Sun, also some in May, some matinees, tel. 0662/872-406, www.marionetten.at). For a sneak preview, check out the videos playing at the marionette exhibit up in the fortress.

Mozart Dinner Concert: For those who'd like some classical music but would rather not sit through a concert, Stiftskeller St. Peter offers a traditional candlelit meal with Mozart's greatest hits performed by a string quartet and singers in historic costumes gavotting among the tables. In this elegant Baroque setting, tourists clap between movements and get three courses of food (from Mozart-era recipes) mixed with three 20-minute courses of crowd-pleasing music (€45, almost nightly at 20:00, dress is "smart casual," call to reserve at 0662/828-6950, www.mozartdinnerconcert.com). When they run out of space, they book a second quartet to perform in the adjacent Haydn Zimmer. I find the ambience much nicer in the main Baroque Hall—when making the booking, get a promise that that's where you'll be seated. For more details, see page 115.

Sound of Salzburg Dinner Show: The show at the Sternbräu Inn (see page 117) is Broadway in a dirndl with tired food. But it's a good show, and *Sound of Music* fans leave with hands red from clapping. A piano player and a hardworking quartet of singers wearing historical costumes perform an entertaining mix of *S.O.M.* hits and traditional folk songs (€44 for dinner, begins at 19:30). You can also come by at 20:30, pay €29, skip the dinner, and get the show (nightly mid-May–mid-Oct, Griesgasse 23, tel. 0662/826-617, www.soundofsalzburgshow.com).

Music at Mass: Each Sunday morning, three great churches offer a Mass generally with glorious music. The Salzburg Cathedral is likely your best bet for fine music to worship by (10:00). The Franciscan church (9:00) and St. Peter's Church (10:30) are also enthusiastic about their musical Masses. See the Salzburg events guide for details.

Free Brass Band Concert: A traditional brass band plays in the Mirabell Gardens (May–Aug Sun at 10:30 and Wed at 20:30).

SLEEPING

Finding a room in Salzburg, even during its music festival (mid-July–Aug), is usually easy. Rates rise significantly (20–30 percent) during the music festival, and sometimes also around Easter and Christmas; these higher prices do not appear in the ranges I've listed below. You'll often be charged 10 percent extra for a one-night stay.

Sleep Code

(€1 = about $1.30, country code: 43, area code: 0662)
S = Single, **D** = Double/Twin, **T** = Triple, **Q** = Quad, **b** = bathroom, **s** = shower only. Unless otherwise noted, credit cards are accepted and breakfast is included. All of these places speak English.

To help you sort easily through these listings, I've divided the rooms into three categories, based on the price for a standard double room with bath:

$$$ Higher Priced—Most rooms €90 or more.
$$ Moderately Priced—Most rooms between €60–90.
$ Lower Priced—Most rooms €60 or less.

In the New Town, North of the River

These listings, clustering around Linzergasse, are in a pleasant neighborhood (with easy parking) a 15-minute walk from the train station (for directions, see "Arrival in Salzburg," earlier in this chapter) and a 10-minute walk to the old town. If you're coming from the old town, simply cross the main bridge (Staatsbrücke) to the mostly traffic-free Linzergasse. If driving, exit the highway at Salzburg-Nord, follow Vogelweiderstrasse straight to its end, and turn right.

$$$ Altstadthotel Wolf-Dietrich, around the corner from Linzergasse on pedestrians-only Wolf-Dietrich-Strasse, is well-located (with half its rooms overlooking St. Sebastian Cemetery). With 27 tastefully plush rooms, it's the best value I could find for a big, stylish hotel (Sb-€69–94, Db-€109–164, rates depend on room size, family deals, €40 more during festival time, elevator, pool with loaner suits, sauna, free DVD library, Wolf-Dietrich-Strasse 7, tel. 0662/871-275, fax 0662/882-320, www.salzburg-hotel.at, office@salzburg-hotel.at). Their annex across the street has 14 equally comfortable rooms (but no elevator, and therefore slightly cheaper prices).

$$$ Hotel Trumer Stube, three blocks from the river just off Linzergasse, has 20 clean, cozy rooms and a friendly, can-do owner (Sb-€65, Db-€103, Tb-€125, Qb-€140, top-floor rooms have lower ceilings and are €7 less expensive; entirely non-smoking, elevator, Internet access, Bergstrasse 6, tel. 0662/874-776, fax 0662/874-326, www.trumer-stube.at, info@trumer-stube.at, pleasant Silvia).

$$ Hotel Goldene Krone, about five blocks from the river, is an excellent value with 25 rooms. Big, quiet, and creaky-traditional but well-kept, it'll feel like home right away (Sb-€60, Db-€88, Tb-€128, dim lights, elevator, relaxing backyard garden, Linzergasse 48, tel.

Central Salzburg Hotels

1. Altstadthotel Wolf-Dietrich
2. Hotel Trumer Stube
3. Hotel Goldene Krone
4. To Bergland Hotel & Hotel-Pension Jedermann
5. Institute St. Sebastian
6. Hotel-Pension Chiemsee
7. Blaue Gans Arthotel
8. Hotel Weisse Taube
9. Gasthaus zur Goldenen Ente
10. Hotel am Dom
11. To Hotel Rosenvilla
12. Christkönig Pension
13. Gasthaus Stadtalm
14. To Haus Arenberg
15. To Moosstrasse Zimmer
16. Launderette

0662/872-300, fax 0662/8723-0066, www.hotel-goldenekrone.com, office@hotel-goldenekrone.com, Claudia and Günther Hausknost). Ask about Günther's tours.

$$ Institute St. Sebastian is in a somewhat sterile but very clean historic building next to St. Sebastian Cemetery. From October through June, the institute houses female students from various Salzburg colleges, and also rents 40 beds for travelers (men or women). From July through September, the students are gone and they rent all 100 beds (including 20 doubles) to travelers. The building has spacious public areas, a roof garden, a piano that guests are welcome to play, and some of the best rooms and dorm beds in town for the money. The immaculate doubles come with modern baths and head-to-toe twin beds (S-€31, Sb-€38, D-€50, Db-€62, T-€66, Tb-€75, Q-€80, Qb-€90, includes breakfast, elevator, self-service laundry-€4/load, reception open daily July–Sept 7:30–12:00 & 13:00–21:30, Oct–June 8:00–12:00 & 16:00–21:00, Linzergasse 41, enter through arch at #37, tel. 0662/871-386, fax 0662/8713-8685, www.st-sebastian-salzburg.at, office@st-sebastian-salzburg.at). Students like the €19 bunks in 4- to 10-bed dorms (€2 less if you have sheets, no lockout time, free lockers, free showers). You'll find self-service kitchens on each floor (fridge space is free; request a key).

Pensions on Rupertgasse: These two hotels are about five blocks farther from the river on Rupertgasse, a breeze for drivers but with more street noise than the places on Linzergasse. They're both modern and well-run—good values if you don't mind being a bit away from the old town. **$$$ Bergland Hotel** is charming and classy, with comfortable, neo-rustic rooms. It's a modern building, and therefore spacious and solid (Sb-€60, Db-€90, Tb-€107, Qb-€127, elevator, Internet access, English library, bike rental-€6/day, Rupertgasse 15, tel. 0662/872-318, fax 0662/872-3188, www.berglandhotel.at, kuhn@berglandhotel.at, Kuhn family). The similar, boutique-like **$$ Hotel-Pension Jedermann,** a few doors down, is also tastefully done and comfortable, with an artsy painted-concrete ambience and a backyard garden (Sb-€55, Db-€85, Tb-€100, Qb-€120, much more during music festival, 5 percent discount with cash and 2-night stay, Internet access, Rupertgasse 25, tel. 0662/873-241, fax 0662/873-2419, www.hotel-jedermann.com, office@hotel-jedermann.com, Herr und Frau Gmachl).

In or Above the Old Town

Most of these hotels are near Residenzplatz. While this area is car-restricted, you're allowed to drive your car in to unload, pick up a map and parking instructions, and head for the €14-per-day garage in the mountain.

$$$ Blaue Gans Arthotel is ultra-modern, giving you a break from charming old Salzburg with artsy public spaces and 40 sleek but nothing-special rooms. It's beautifully located at the far end of Getreidegasse (Sb-€105–115, standard Db-€145, bigger superior Db-€175, fancier suites, elevator, Getreidegasse 41, tel. 0662/842-4910, fax 0662/842-4919, www.blauegans.at, office@blauegans.at).

$$$ Gasthaus zur Goldenen Ente is in a 600-year-old building with medieval stone arches and narrow stairs. Located above a good restaurant, it's as central as you can be on a pedestrian street in old Salzburg. The 17 rooms are modern yet worn (most of the year: Sb-€68, Db-€90; late July–Aug and Dec: Sb-€78, Db-€125; extra person-€29, non-smoking, elevator, Internet access, Goldgasse 10, tel. 0662/845-622, fax 0662/845-6229, www.ente.at, hotel@ente.at). Ulrika, Franziska, and Anita run a tight ship for the absentee owners.

$$$ Hotel Weisse Taube is a big, quiet, old-feeling, 30-room place with more comfort than character, well-located about a block off Mozartplatz (Sb-€61, Db with shower-€96, bigger Db with bath-€106, elevator, Internet access, tel. 0662/842-404, fax 0662/841-783, Kaigasse 9, www.weissetaube.at, hotel@weissetaube.at).

$$ Hotel am Dom, while pretty forgettable, is perfectly located—on Goldgasse a few steps from the cathedral. Its 14 rooms are big, old, and basic, but well-maintained (Db-€88, extra bed-€33, non-smoking, Goldgasse 17, tel. 0662/842-765, fax 0662/8427-6555, www.amdom.at, bach@salzburg.co.at).

$$ Christkönig Pension makes you feel like a guest of the bishop because, in a sense...you are. With 20 rooms in a 14th-century church building just under the castle and behind the cathedral, this is where the bishop's visitors stay. It's a charming, quiet, and unique way to sleep well and cheaply in the old center (S-€36, Sb-€40, Db-€80, twin beds only, €6 extra for 1-night stays, cash only, Kapitelplatz 2a, tel. 0662/842627, www.christkoenig-kolleg.at, christkoenig-pension@salzburg.co.at). Heavenly Frau Anna Huemer will take excellent care of you.

$$ Hotel-Pension Chiemsee is a stony dollhouse nestled in a quiet lane just behind the cathedral. Hardworking Frau Holbacher rents six big, homey rooms and two apartments (Sb-€45, or €40 for 2 nights or more; Db-€76, or €70 for 2 nights or more; €95 for apartment for up to 4 people, Chiemseegasse 5, tel. 0662/844-208, fax 0662/8442-0870, www.hotel-ami.de/hotel/chiemsee, hotel-chiemsee@aon.at).

$ Gasthaus Stadtalm (a.k.a. the Naturfreundehaus) is a local version of a mountaineer's hut—renovated in 2007—and a great budget alternative. Snuggled in a forest on the remains of a 15th-century castle wall atop the little mountain overlooking Salzburg, it has magnificent town and mountain views. While the 26 beds are designed-for-backpackers rustic, the price and view are the best in town—with the right attitude, it's a fine experience (€15/person in 2-, 4-, and 6-bed dorms, includes breakfast and shower, cash only, lockers, open mid-April–Oct, 2 minutes from top of €2.60 round-trip Mönchsberg elevator, Mönchsberg 19C, tel. & fax 0662/841-729, www.diestadtalm.com, ng.esterer@utanet.at, Peter and Roland). Once again, be warned: This is a rustic hostel on the mountaintop in a forest, an elevator ride above the city.

Near the Train Station

$$ Pension Adlerhof, a plain and decent old pension, is two blocks in front of the train station (left off Kaiserschutzenstrasse), but a 15-minute walk from the sightseeing action. It has a quirky staff, a boring location, and 30 stodgy-but-spacious rooms (Sb-€55, D-€52, Db-€75–85, Tb-€87–105, Qb-€112–120, cash only, elevator, Elisabethstrasse 25, tel. 0662/875-236, fax 0662/873-663, www.gosalzburg.com, adlerhof@pension-adlerhof.at).

$ International Youth Hotel, a.k.a. the "Yo-Ho," is the most lively, handy, and American of Salzburg's hostels (€17 in 6- to 8-bed dorms, €20 in dorms with bathrooms, Q-€18/person, Qb-€21/person, includes sheets, cheap breakfast, 6 blocks from station toward Linzergasse and 6 blocks from river at Paracelsusstrasse 9, tel. 0662/879-649, fax 0662/878-810, www.yoho.at, office@yoho.at). This easygoing place speaks English first; has cheap meals, 160 beds, lockers, Internet access, laundry, tour discounts, and no curfew; plays *The Sound of Music* free daily at 10:30; runs a lively bar; and welcomes anyone of any age. The noisy atmosphere and lack of a curfew can make it hard to sleep.

Four-Star Hotels in Residential Neighborhoods away from the Center

Two plush, modern hotels in nondescript residential neighborhoods a 15-minute walk from the old town are a fine value for those wanting elegant, stylish furnishings, spacious public spaces, generous balconies, gardens, and free parking. While not ideal for train travelers, drivers in need of no-stress comfort for a home base should consider these: **$$$ Hotel Rosenvilla,** closer to the river, offers 14 rooms with modern art, bright minimalist furnishings, and an organic closeness to nature (Sb-€78, Db-€128, bigger Db-€142, Hofelgasse 4, tel. 0662/621-765, fax 0662/625-2308, www.rosenvilla.com, hotel@rosenvilla.com). **$$$ Haus Arenberg,** higher up opposite the old town, rents 17 big, breezy rooms—most with generous balconies—in a quiet garden setting (Db-€120, Blumensteinstrasse 8, tel. 0662/640-097, fax 0662/640-0973, www.arenberg-salzburg.at, info@arenberg-salzburg.at, family Leobacher).

Zimmer (Private Rooms)

These are generally roomy and comfortable, and come with a good breakfast, easy parking, and tourist information. Off-season, competition softens prices. While they are a bus ride from town, with a €3.40 transit day pass *(Tageskarte)* and the frequent service, this shouldn't keep you away. In fact, most will happily pick you up at the train station if you simply telephone them and ask. Most will also do laundry for a small fee for those staying at least two nights. I've listed prices for two nights or more. If staying only one night, expect a 10 percent surcharge. Some push tours and concerts to earn a commission—check to make sure you won't pay additional charges compared to booking direct.

Beyond the Train Station

$ Brigitte Lenglachner rents six basic rooms with no public spaces a 30-minute walk or easy bus ride away from the center in a quiet, suburban-feeling neighborhood (S-€24, D-€37, Db-€44, T-€51, Tb-€61, Qb-€88, bigger apartment Db-€56, easy and free parking, happy to pick you up from the station, Scheibenweg 8, tel. & fax 0662/438-044, bedandbreakfast4u@yahoo.de). It's a 10-minute walk from station: Head for the river, cross the pedestrian Pioneer Bridge (Pioniersteg), turn right, and walk along the river to the third street (Scheibenweg). Turn left, and it's halfway down on the right.

On Moosstrasse

The busy street called Moosstrasse, which runs southwest of Mönchsberg (behind the mountain and away from the old town center), is lined with *Zimmer*. Handy bus #21 connects Moosstrasse to the center frequently (Mon–Fri 4/hr until 17:00, evenings and weekends 2/hr). To get to these from the train station, take bus #1, #5, #6, or #25 to Makartplatz, where you'll change to #21. If you're coming from the old town, catch bus #21 from Hanuschplatz, just downstream of the Staatsbrücke bridge near the *Tabak* kiosk. Buy a €1.60 *Einzelkarte-Kernzone* ticket (for 1 trip) or a €3.40 *Tageskarte* (day pass, good for 24 hours) from the streetside machine and punch it when you board the bus. The bus stop you use for each *Zimmer* is listed below. If you're driving from the center, go through the tunnel, continue straight on Neutorstrasse, and take the fourth left onto Moosstrasse. Drivers exit autobahn at *Süd* and then head in the direction of *Grodig*.

$ Frau Ballwein offers four cozy, charming, and fresh rooms in two buildings, all with intoxicating view balconies (S-€25, D-€44, Db-€48–52, Tb-€65–75, family deals, cash only, farm-fresh breakfasts, non-smoking, small pool, Moosstrasse 69-A, bus stop: Gsengerweg, tel. & fax 0662/824-029, www.haus-ballwein.at, haus.ballwein@gmx.net).

$ Helga Bankhammer rents four nondescript rooms in a farmhouse, with a real dairy farm out back (D-€44, Db-€48, no surcharge for 1-night stays, family deals, non-smoking, laundry-about €5 per load, Moosstrasse 77, bus stop: Marienbad, tel. & fax 0662/830-067, www.privatzimmer.at/helga.bankhammer, bankhammer@aon.at).

$ Haus Reichl, with three good rooms at the end of a long lane, feels the most remote (Db-€55, Tb-€66, Qb-€88, doubles and triples have balcony and view, non-smoking, between Ballwein and Bankhammer B&Bs, 200 yards down Reiterweg to #52, bus stop: Gsengerweg, tel. & fax 0662/826-248, www.privatzimmer.at/haus-reichl, haus.reichl@telering.at). Elizabeth offers free loaner bikes for guests (20-min pedal to the center).

$ Pension Bloberger Hof, while more a hotel than a *Zimmer,* is comfortable and friendly, with a peaceful, rural location and 20 farmer-plush, good-value rooms. It's the farthest out, but reached by the same bus #21 from the center (Sb-€41–51, Db-€60, big newer Db with balcony-€85, extra bed-€15, family apartment, non-smoking, restaurant for guests, free loaner bikes, free station pick-up if staying 3 nights, Hammerauer Strasse 4, bus stop: Hammerauer Strasse, tel. 0662/830-227, fax 0662/827-061, www.blobergerhof.at, office@blobergerhof.at).

Salzburg

EATING

In the Old Town

Salzburg boasts many inexpensive, fun, and atmospheric eateries. I'm a sucker for big cellars with their smoky, Old World atmosphere, heavy medieval arches, time-darkened paintings, antlers, hearty meals, and plump patrons. Most of these restaurants are centrally located in the old town, famous with visitors, but also enjoyed by the locals.

Gasthaus zum Wilden Mann is *the* place if the weather's bad and you're in the mood for *Hofbräu* atmosphere and a hearty, cheap meal at a shared table in one small, smoky, well-antlered room. Notice the 1999 flood photo on the wall. For a quick lunch, get the *Bauernschmaus,* a mountain of dumplings, kraut, and peasant's meats (€9.50). Owner Robert—who runs the restaurant with Schwarzenegger-like energy—enjoys fostering a convivial ambience (you'll share tables with strangers) and serving fresh traditional cuisine at great prices. I simply love this place (€6–8 daily specials, Mon–Sat 11:00–21:00, Sun 11:00–17:00, 2 min from Mozart's Birthplace, enter from Getreidegasse 20 or Griesgasse 22, tel. 0662/841-787).

Stiftskeller St. Peter has been in business for more than 1,000 years—it was mentioned in the biography of Charlemagne.

Central Salzburg Restaurants

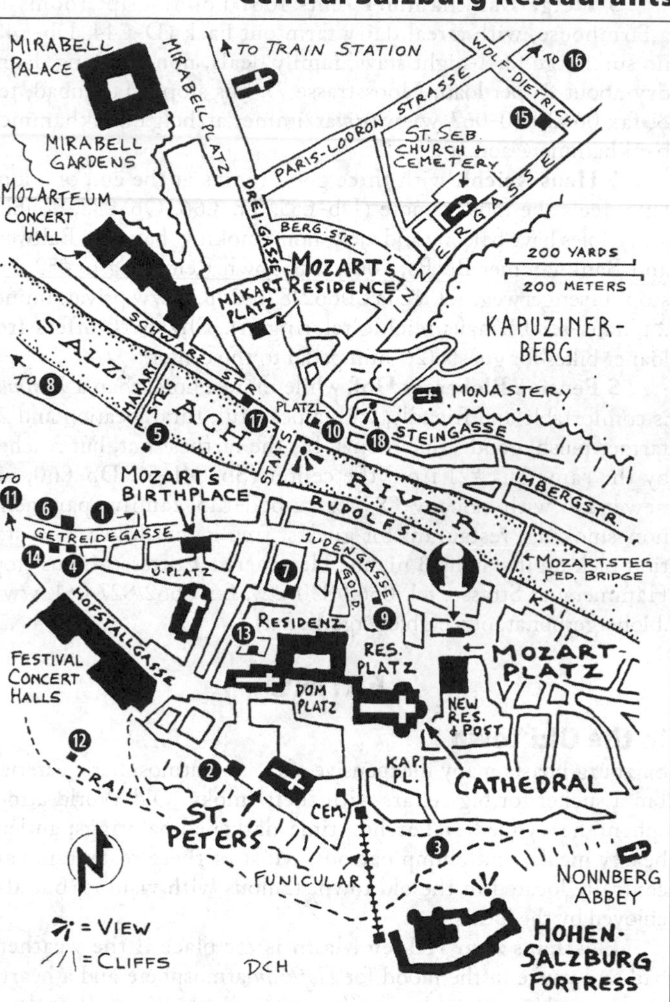

1. Gasthaus zum Wilden Mann
2. Stiftskeller St. Peter Rest.
3. St. Paul's Stub'n Beer Garden
4. Sporer Schnapps Pub
5. Fisch Krieg Rest.
6. Sternbräu Inn
7. Café Tomaselli
8. To Augustiner Bräustübl
9. Saran Essbar Rest.
10. Stein Terrasse
11. To Bar Club Café Republic
12. Gasthaus Stadtalm
13. Toskana Cafeteria Mensa
14. Bosna Sausage Stand
15. Spicy Spices Rest.
16. Biergarten die Weisse
17. Café Bazar
18. Steingasse Pub Crawl

It's classy and central as can be, serving uninspired traditional Austrian cuisine at high prices (€15–25 meals, daily 11:30–24:00, indoor/outdoor seating, next to St. Peter's Church at foot of Mönchsberg, restaurant tel. 0662/841-268). They host the Mozart Dinner Concert described in "Music Scene," on page 106 (€45, nearly nightly at 20:00, call 0662/828-6950 to reserve). Over the centuries, they've learned to charge for each piece of bread and not serve free tap water.

St. Paul's Stub'n Beer Garden is tucked secretly away under the castle with an ignore-the-tourists-attitude (menu in German only). The food is better than a beer hall, and a young, Bohemian-chic clientele fills its two smoky, troll-like rooms and its idyllic, tree-shaded garden. *Kasnock'n* is a tasty mountaineers' pasta with cheese served in an iron pan with a side salad for €8 (€10 daily specials, €10–15 plates, Mon–Sat 17:00–22:00, open later for drinks only, closed Sun, Herrengasse 16, tel. 0662/843-220).

Fisch Krieg Restaurant, on the river where the fishermen used to sell their catch, is a great value. They serve fast, fresh, and inexpensive fish in a casual dining room—where trees grow through the ceiling—as well as great riverside seating (€2 fishwiches to go, self-serve €7 meals, salad bar, Mon–Fri 8:30–18:30, Sat 8:30–13:00, closed Sun, Hanuschplatz 4, tel. 0662/843-732).

Sternbräu Inn, a sloppy, touristy Austrian food circus, is a sprawling complex of popular eateries (traditional, Italian, self-serve, and vegetarian) in a cheery garden setting. Explore both courtyards before choosing a seat (Bürgerstube is classic, most restaurants open daily 9:00–24:00). One fancy, air-conditioned room hosts the Sound of Salzburg dinner show (see description on page 108).

Café Tomaselli (with its Kiosk annex across the way) has long been Salzburg's top place to see and be seen. While overpriced and often over-crowded, it is good for lingering and people-watching. Tomaselli serves light meals and lots of drinks, keeps long hours daily, and has fine seating on the square, a view terrace upstairs, and indoor tables. Despite its fancy inlaid wood paneling, 19th-century portraits, and chandeliers, it is surprisingly low-key (€3–6 entrées, daily 7:00–21:00, until 24:00 during music festival, Alter Markt 9, tel. 0662/844-488).

Saran Essbar is the product of hardworking Mr. Saran (from the Punjab), who cooks and serves with his heart. This delightful little eatery is rich orange under medieval vaults. Its fun menu is small (Mr. Saran is committed to both freshness and value), mixing Austrian (great schnitzel and strudel), Italian, Asian vegetarian, and salads (€9–12 meals, daily 11:00–22:00, a block off Mozartplatz at Judengasse 10, tel. 0662/846-628).

Bar Club Café Republic, a hip hangout for local young people near the end of Getreidegasse, feels like a theater lobby during intermission. It serves good food with smoky indoor and outdoor seating. It's ideal if you want something mod, untouristy, and unwursty (trendy breakfasts 8:00–18:00, Asian and international menu, €6–12 plates, lots of hard drinks, daily until late, music with a DJ Fri and Sat from 23:00, salsa music on Tue night, no cover, Anton Neumayr Platz 2, tel. 0662/841-613).

Gasthaus Stadtalm, Salzburg's mountaineers' hut, sits high above the old town on the edge of the cliff with cheap prices, good food, and great views. If hiking across Mönchsberg, make this your goal (traditional food, salads, cliffside garden seating or cozy-mountain-hut indoor seating, an indoor view table booked for a decade of New Year's celebrations, 2 min from top of €3 round-trip Mönchsberg elevator, Mönchsberg 19C, tel. & fax 0662/841-729, Peter and Roland). While they're open daily in season from 6:00 to 24:00, they close at 18:00 in bad weather.

Eating Cheaply in the Old Town

Toskana Cafeteria Mensa is the students' lunch canteen, fast and cheap—with indoor seating and a great courtyard for sitting outside with students and teachers instead of tourists. They serve a daily soup-and-main course special for €3.50 (Mon–Fri 9:00–15:30, hot meals served 11:00–13:30 only, closed Sat–Sun, behind the Residenz, in the courtyard opposite Sigmund-Haffnergasse 16).

Sausage stands serve the town's favorite fast food. The best stands (like those on Universitätsplatz) use the same boiling water all day, which gives the weenies more flavor. Key words: *Weisswurst*—boiled white sausage, *Bosna*—with onions and curry, *Käsekrainer*—with melted cheese inside, *Debreziner*—spicy Hungarian, *Frankfurter*—our weenie, *frische*—fresh ("eat before the noon bells"), and *Senf*—mustard (ask for *süss*—sweet or *scharf*—sharp). Only a tourist puts the sausage in a bun like a hot dog. Munch alternately between the meat and the bread ("that's why you have two hands"), and you'll look like a native. Generally, the darker the weenie, the spicier it is. The Salzburgers' favorite spicy sausage is sold at the 55-year-old **Bosna Stand,** run by chatty Frau Ebner (€2.60—survey the four spicy options, described in English, and choose a number, take-away only, steady and sturdy local crowd, Mon–Fri 11:00–19:00, May–Dec also Sat 11:00–17:00, July–Dec also Sun 16:00–20:00, hiding down the tunnel marked #33 across from Getreidegasse 40).

Picnickers will appreciate the bustling morning **produce market** (daily except Sun) on Universitätsplatz, behind Mozart's house (see page 104).

Away from the Center

Augustiner Bräustübl, a monk-run brewery, is rustic and crude. It's closed for lunch, but on busy nights, it's like a Munich beer hall with no music but the volume turned up. When it's cool, you'll enjoy a historic setting with beer-sloshed and smoke-stained halls. On balmy evenings, it's a Monet painting with beer breath under chestnut trees in the garden. Local students mix with tourists eating hearty slabs of schnitzel with their fingers or cold meals from the self-serve picnic counter, while children frolic on the playground kegs. For your beer: Pick up a half-liter or full-liter mug (*schank* means self-serve price, *bedienung* is the price with waiter service), pay the lady, wash your mug, give Mr. Keg your receipt and empty mug, and you will be made happy. Waiters don't bring food—instead, go up the stairs, survey the hallway of deli counters, and assemble your own meal (or, as long as you buy a drink, you can bring in a picnic). Classic pretzels from the bakery and spiraled and salty radishes make great beer even better. For dessert—after a visit to the strudel kiosk—enjoy the incomparable floodlit view of old Salzburg from the nearby Müllnersteg pedestrian bridge and a riverside stroll home (open daily 15:00–23:00; about a 15-min walk along the river—with the river on your right—from the Staatsbrücke bridge, head up Müllner Hauptstrasse northwest along the river and ask for "Müllnerbräu," its nickname; Augustinergasse 4, tel. 0662/431-246). Don't be fooled by second-rate gardens serving the same beer nearby. Augustiner Bräustübl is a huge, 1,000-seat beer garden within the Augustiner brewery.

Salzburg

North of the River, near Recommended Linzergasse Hotels

Spicy Spices is a trippy vegetarian-Indian restaurant where Suresh Syad serves tasty take-out curry and rice, samosas, organic salads, vegan soups, and fresh juices (€6 specials, Mon–Sat 10:00–22:00, Sun 12:00–21:00, Wolf-Dietrich-Strasse 1, tel. 0662/870-712).

Biergarten die Weisse, close to the hotels on Rupertgasse and away from the tourists, is a longtime hit with the natives. If a beer hall can be happening, this one—modern yet with antlers—is it. Their famously good beer is made right there; favorites include their fizzy wheat beer *(Weisse)* and their seasonal beers (on request). Enjoy the beer with their good, cheap traditional food in the great garden seating, or in the wide variety of indoor rooms—sports bar, young and noisy, or older and more elegant (daily specials, Mon–Sat 10:00–24:00, closed Sun, Rupertgasse 10, east of Bayerhamerstrasse, tel. 0662/872-246).

Café Bazar, overlooking the river between Mirabell Gardens and the Staatsbrücke bridge, is as close as you'll get to a Vienna coffee house in Salzburg. It's *the* venerable spot for a classy drink with an old-town and castle view (daily €7 plate and light meals, Mon–Sat 7:30–23:00, closed Sun, Schwarzstrasse 3, tel. 0662/874-278).

Steingasse Pub Crawl

For a fun post-concert activity, crawl through medieval Steingasse's trendy pubs (all open until the wee hours). This is a local and hip scene, but accessible to older tourists: dark bars filled with well-dressed Salzburgers lazily smoking cigarettes and talking philosophy, with avant-garde Euro-pop throbbing on the soundtrack. Most of the pubs are in cellar-like caves...extremely atmospheric. (For more on Steingasse, see page 104.) These four pubs are all within about 100 yards of each other. Start at the Linzergasse end of Steingasse.

Pepe Cocktail Bar, with Mexican decor and Latin music, serves tostadas with fun toppings *con* cocktails (nightly 19:00–3:00 in the morning, live DJs Fri–Sat from 23:00, Steingasse 3, tel. 0662/873-662).

Shrimps, next door and less claustrophobic, is more a restaurant than a bar, serving creative international dishes (spicy shrimp sandwiches and salads, nightly 18:00–24:00, Steingasse 5, tel. 0662/874-484).

Saiten Sprung wins the "Best Atmosphere" award. The door is kept closed to keep out the crude and rowdy. Ring the bell and enter its hellish interior—lots of stone and red decor, with mountains of melted wax beneath age-old candlesticks and a classic soul music ambience. Stelios, who speaks English with Greek charm, serves cocktails, fine wine, and wine-friendly Italian antipasti (nightly 21:00–4:00 in the morning, Steingasse 11, tel. 0662/881-377).

Fridrich, a tiny place next door with lots of mirrors and a silver ceiling fan, specializes in wine. Bernd Fridrich is famous for his martinis, and passionate about Austrian wines and food (€5–12 small entrées, nightly from 17:00, Steingasse 15, tel. 0662/876-218).

TRANSPORTATION CONNECTIONS

By train, Salzburg is the first stop over the German–Austrian border. This means that if Salzburg is your only stop in Austria, and you're using a Eurail Selectpass that does not include Austria, you do not have to pay extra or add Austria to your pass to get here.

From Salzburg by Train to: Innsbruck (direct every 2 hrs, 2 hrs), **Vienna** (hourly, 3 hrs), **Hallstatt** (every 2 hrs: 50 min to Attnang Puchheim, 20-min wait, then 90 min to Hallstatt), **Mauthausen** (hourly, 2.5 hrs, change in St. Valentin), **Melk** (at least hourly, 2.5 hrs, transfer in Amstetten or St. Pölten), **Reutte** (every 2 hrs, 4 hrs, transfer to a bus in Innsbruck), **Munich** (hourly, 1.5–2 hrs), **Nürnberg** (hourly with change in Munich, 3.5 hrs).

Train info: tel. 051-717 (to get an operator, dial 2, then 1).

By Car: To leave town driving west, go through the Mönchsberg tunnel and follow blue *A-1* signs to Munich. It's 90 minutes from Salzburg to Innsbruck.

HALLSTATT

and the SALZKAMMERGUT

Commune with nature in Austria's lake district, the Salzkammergut. "The hills are alive," and you're surrounded by the loveliness that has turned on everyone from Emperor Franz Josef to Julie Andrews. This is *Sound of Music* country. Idyllic and majestic, but not rugged, it's a gentle land of lakes, forested mountains, and storybook villages, rich in hiking opportunities and inexpensive lodging. Settle down in the postcard-pretty, lake-cuddling town of Hallstatt.

Planning Your Time

While there are plenty of lakes and charming villages in the Salzkammergut, Hallstatt is really the only one that matters. One night and a few hours to browse are all you'll need to fall in love. To relax or take a hike in the surroundings, give it two nights and a day. It's a relaxing break between Salzburg and Vienna.

ORIENTATION

(area code: 06134)

Lovable Hallstatt is a tiny town bullied onto a ledge between a selfish mountain and a swan-ruled lake, with a waterfall ripping furiously through its middle. It can be toured on foot in about 15 minutes. The town is one of Europe's oldest, going back centuries before Christ. The symbol of Hallstatt, which you'll see all over town, is two adjacent spirals—a design based on jewelry found in Bronze Age Celtic graves high in the nearby mountains.

The charms of Hallstatt are the village and its lakeside setting. Go there to relax, nibble, wander, and paddle. While tourist crowds can trample much of Hallstatt's charm in August, the place is almost dead in the off-season. The lake is famous for its good fishing and pure water.

Tourist Information

At the helpful TI, on the main drag, Claudia and her staff can explain hikes and excursions, arrange private tours of Hallstatt (€65), and find you a room (July–Aug Mon–Sat 9:00–17:00, closed Sun; Sept–June 9:00–12:00 & 14:00–17:00, closed Sat–Sun; a block from Market Square toward lakefront parking, above post office, Seestrasse 169, tel. 06134/8208, www.inneres-salzkammergut.at, hallstatt@inneres-salzkammergut.at).

In the summer, the TI offers 90-minute **walking tours** of the town in English and German (€5, May–Sept Sat at 10:00, July–Aug also Wed at 10:00, confirm schedule at the TI).

Arrival in Hallstatt

By Train: Hallstatt's train station is a wide spot on the tracks across the lake. *Stefanie* (a boat) meets you at the station and glides scenically across the lake into town (€2, meets each train until about 18:30—don't arrive after that). The last departing boat-train connection leaves Hallstatt around 18:00, and the first boat goes in the morning at 6:50 (9:20 on Sun). Once in Hallstatt, walk left from the boat dock for the TI and most hotels. Since there's no train station in town, the TI can help you find schedule information, or check www.oebb.at.

By Car: The main road skirts Hallstatt via a long tunnel above the town. Parking is tight mid-June through mid-October. Hallstatt has several numbered parking areas outside the town center. Parking lot #1 is in the tunnel above the town (swing through to check for a spot, free with guest card, it's a laid-back system—just show your card later). Otherwise, several numbered lots are just after the tunnel. If you have a hotel reservation, the guard will let you drive into town to drop your bags (ask if your hotel has any in-town parking). It's a lovely 10- to 20-minute lakeside walk to the center of town from the lots. Without a guest card, you'll pay €4.20 per day for parking. Off-season (Nov–April), parking in town is easy and free.

Helpful Hints

Internet Access: Try **Hallstatt Umbrella Bar** (€4/hr, summers only, weather permitting—since it's literally under a big umbrella, halfway between Lahn boat dock and Museum Square at Seestrasse 145). You can get online all year at **Hotel Grüner Baum** (expensive at €10/hr).

Hallstatt

Laundry: A small full-service **launderette** is at the campground up from the town's man-made island, Bade-Insel, just off the main road (about €8/load, mid-April–mid-Oct daily 7:00–12:00 & 15:00–22:00, closed off-season, tel. 06134/83224). In the center, **Hotel Grüner Baum** does laundry for non-guests (€11/load, facing Market Square).

Parks and Swimming: Green and peaceful lakeside parks line the south end of Lake Hallstatt. If you walk 10 minutes south of town to Hallstatt-Lahn, you'll find a grassy public park, playground, mini-golf, and swimming area *(Badestrand)* with the fun Bade-Insel play-island.

Views: For a great view over Hallstatt, hike above Helga Lenz's *Zimmer* as far as you like (see page 135), or climb any path leading up the hill. The 40-minute steep hike down from the salt-mine tour gives the best views (see page 129). While most visitors stroll the lakeside drag between the old and new parts of town, make a point to do the trip once taking the more higgledy-piggledy high lane called Dr.-Morton-Weg.

Evening Events: As Hallstatt is very touristy in the summer, check at the TI for evening entertainment. In July and August, the town stages concerts on most Tuesday evenings, and candlelit boat rides on Friday evenings.

SELF-GUIDED WALK

Welcome to Hallstatt

This short walk starts at the dock.

Boat Landing: There was a Hallstatt before there was a Rome. In fact, because of the importance of salt mining here, an entire epoch—the Hallstatt Era, from 800 to 400 B.C.—is named for this important spot. Through the centuries, salt was traded and people came and went by boat. You'll still see the traditional *Fuhr* boats, designed to carry heavy loads in shallow water.

Towering above the town is the Catholic church. Its faded St. Christopher—patron saint of travelers, with his cane and baby Jesus on his shoulder—watched over those sailing in and out. Until 1875, the town was extremely remote...then came a real road and the train. The good ship *Stefanie* shuttles travelers back and forth from here to the Hallstatt train station, immediately across the lake. The *Bootverleih* sign advertises boat rentals. By the way, *Schmuck* is not an insult...it's jewelry.

Notice the one-lane road out of town (below the church). Until 1966, when a bigger tunnel was built above Hallstatt, all the traffic crept single-file right through the town.

Look down the shore at the huge homes. Several families lived in each of these houses back when Hallstatt's population was about double its present 1,000. Today the population continues to shrink, and many of these generally underused houses rent rooms to visitors.

Parking is tight here in the tourist season. Locals and hotels have cards getting them into the prime town-center lot. From November through April, the barricade is lifted and anyone can park here. Hallstatt gets about three months of snow each winter, but the lake hasn't frozen over since 1981.

See any swans? They've patrolled the lake like they own it since the 1860s, when Emperor Franz Josef and Empress Sisi—the Princess Diana of her day—made this region their annual holiday retreat. Sisi loved swans, so locals made sure she'd see them here. During this period, the Romantics discovered Hallstatt, many top painters worked here, and the town got its first hotel. Today that hotel (the big, derelict Haus Kranz facing the square), with an absentee owner and a floor plan so tangled it's too expensive to renovate, just sits, looking ugly in the heart of Hallstatt.

Tiny Hallstatt has two big churches—Protestant (bordering the square on the left, with a grassy lakeside playground) and Catholic (up above, with its fascinating bone chapel—described under "Sights," below).

• *Walk over the town's stream, and pop into the...*

Protestant Church: In 1860, Emperor Franz Josef allowed non-Catholic Christians to build churches. Before that, they were allowed only to worship in low-key "houses of prayer." Back then, the Catholic Church was the church of royalty and the wealthy. The working class was more likely to be Protestant. As this was a mining town, it was quite Protestant. In 1863, the miners pooled their humble resources and built this fine church. Step inside (free and often open). It's very plain, emphasizing the pulpit and organ rather than fancy art and saints. Check out the portraits: Martin Luther (left of altar), the town in about 1865 with its new church (left wall), and a century of pastors.

• *Continue past the church to the...*

Market Square (Marktplatz): In 1750, a fire leveled this part of town. The buildings you see now are all late 18th-century and built of stone rather than flammable wood. The three big buildings on the left are government-subsidized housing (mostly for seniors and people with health problems). Take a close look at the two-dimensional, up-against-the-wall pear tree (it likes the sun-warmed wall). The statue features the Holy Trinity.

• *Continue a block past Gasthof Simony. At the first corner, just before the Gemeindeamt (City Hall), jog left across the little square and then right down the tiny lane marked* Am Hof, *which leads through an intimate bit of domestic town architecture, boat houses, lots of firewood, and maybe a couple of swans hanging out. The lane circles back to the main drag and the...*

Museum Square: Because 20th-century Hallstatt was of no industrial importance, it was untouched by World War II. But once upon a time, its salt was worth defending. High above, peeking out of the trees, is Rudolfsturm (Rudolf's Tower). Originally a 13th-century watchtower protecting the salt mines, and later the mansion of a salt-mine boss, it's now a restaurant with a great view. A zigzag trail connects the town with Rudolfsturm and the salt mines just beyond. The big, white houses by the waterfall were water-powered mills that once ground Hallstatt's grain. (If you hike up a few blocks, you'll see the river raging through town.)

Around you are the town's TI, post office, museum, City Hall, and Dachstein Sport Shop (described below). A statue recalls the mine manager who excavated prehistoric graves around 1850. Much of the *Schmuck* sold locally is inspired by the jewelry found in the area's Bronze Age tombs.

The memorial wooden stairs in front of the museum are a copy of those found in Hallstatt's prehistoric mine—the original stairs are more than 2,500 years old. For thousands of years, people have been leaching salt out of this mountain. A brine spring sprung here, attracting Bronze Age people around 1600 B.C. Later, they dug tunnels to mine the rock (which was 70 percent salt), dissolved it into a brine, and distilled out the salt—precious for preserving meat. For a look at early salt-mining implements and the town's story, visit the museum (described under "Sights," below).

Across from the TI, Pension Hallberg has a quirky hallway full of Nazi paraphernalia and other stuff found on the lake bed (€1). Only recently did local divers realize that, for centuries, the lake had been Hallstatt's garbage can. If something was *kaput*, locals would just toss it into the lake. In 1945, Nazi medals decorating German and Austrian war heroes suddenly became dangerous to own. Throughout the former *Reich,* hard-earned medals floated to lonely lake beds such as Hallstatt's.

Under the TI is the "Post Partner"—a government-funded attempt to turn inefficient post offices into something more viable (selling souvenirs, renting bikes, and employing people with disabilities who would otherwise be unemployable). The *Fischerei* provides the town with its cherished fresh lake fish. The county allows two commercial fishermen on the lake. They spread their nets each morning and sell their catch here to town restaurants, or to any locals cooking up a special dinner (Mon–Fri 9:00–12:00, closed Sat–Sun).

• *Nearby, still on Museum Square, find the...*

Dachstein Sport Shop: During a renovation project, the builders dug down and hit a Celtic and ancient Roman settlement. Peek through the glass pavement on the covered porch to see where the Roman street level was. If the shop is open, pop in and go downstairs (free). You'll walk on Roman flagstones and see the small gutter that channeled water to power an ancient hammer mill (used to pound iron into usable shapes). In prehistoric times, people lived up by the mines. Romans were the first Hallstatt lakeside settlers. The store's owners are committed to sharing Hallstatt's fascinating history, and often display old town paintings and folk art.

• *From this square, the first right (after the bank) leads up a few stairs to...*

Dr.-Morton-Weg: House #26A dates from 1597. Follow the lane uphill to the left past more old houses. Until 1890, this was the town's main drag, and the lake lapped at the lower doors of these houses. Therefore, many main entrances were via the attic from this level. Enjoy this back-street view of town. Just after the arch, near #133, check out the old tools hanging outside the workshop, and the piece of wooden piping. It's a section taken from the 25-mile wooden pipeline that carried salt brine from Hallstatt to Ebensee. This was in place from 1595 until the last generation, when the last stretch of wood was replaced by plastic piping. At the pipe, enjoy the lake view and climb down the stairs. From lake level, look back up at the striking traditional architecture (the fine woodwork on the left was recently rebuilt after a fire; parts of the old house on the right date to medieval times).

• *Your tour is finished. From here, you have boat rentals, the salt mine tour, the town museum, and the Catholic church (with its bone chapel) all within a few minutes' walk.*

SIGHTS AND ACTIVITIES

▲▲Catholic Church and Bone Chapel—Hallstatt's Catholic church overlooks the town from above. From near the main boat dock, hike up the covered wooden stairway and follow the *Kath. Kirche* signs. The lovely church has twin altars. The one on the left was made by town artists in 1897. The one on the right is more historic—dedicated in 1515 to Mary, who's flanked by St. Barbara (on right, patron of miners) and St. Catherine (on left, patron of foresters—a lot of wood was needed to fortify the many miles of tunnels, and to boil the brine to distill out the salt).

Behind the church, in the well-tended graveyard, stands the 12th-century Chapel of St. Michael (even older than the church). Its bone chapel—or charnel house (Beinhaus)—contains more than 600 painted skulls. Each skull has been lovingly named, dated, and decorated (skulls with dark, thick garlands are oldest—18th century; those with flowers more recent—19th century). Space was so limited in this cemetery that bones had only 12 peaceful, buried years here before making way for the freshly dead. Many of the dug-up bones and skulls ended up in this chapel. They stopped this practice in the 1960s, about the same time the Catholic Church began permitting cremation. But one woman (who died in 1983) managed to sneak her skull in later (dated 1995, under the cross, with the gold tooth). The skulls on the books are priests (€1, free English flier, daily July–Aug 10:00–18:00, Easter–mid-May 11:00–16:00, mid-May–June and Sept 10:00–16:00, Oct 10:00–17:00—weather permitting, closed Nov–Easter).

▲Hallstatt Museum—This pricey little museum tells the story of Hallstatt. It focuses on the Hallstatt Era (800–400 B.C.), when this village was the salt-mining hub of a culture that spread from France to the Balkans. Back then, Celtic tribes dug for precious salt, and Hallstatt was, as its name means, the "place of salt." While its treasures are the countless artifacts excavated from prehistoric gravesites around the mine, you'll get the whole gamut—with displays on everything from the region's flora and fauna to local artists and the surge in Hallstatt tourism during the Romantic Age. Everything's in German, and the skimpy €2 English guide is worth borrowing, but not buying (€7.50, May–Sept 10:00–18:00, shorter hours off-season, Seestrasse 56, adjacent to TI, tel. 06134/828-015).

▲Lake Trip—For a quick boat trip, you can ride the *Stefanie* across the lake and back for €4. It stops at the tiny Hallstatt train station for 30 minutes (note return time in the boat's window), giving you time to walk to a hanging bridge (ask the captain to point you to the *Hängebrücke*—HENG-eh-brick-eh—a 10-minute lakeside stroll to the left). Longer lake tours are also available (€8/50 min, €9/75 min, sporadic schedules—especially off-season—so check chalkboards by boat docks for today's times). Those into relaxation can rent a sleepy electric motorboat to enjoy town views from the water. There are two rental places: **Riedler,** next to ferry dock or across from Bräugasthof (tel. 06134/8320); or **Hemetsberger,** near Gasthof Simony or past the bridge before Bade-Insel (tel. 06134/8228). Both are open daily until 19:00 in-season and in good weather. Boats have two speeds: slow and stop (€11/hr, spend an extra €3/hr for faster 500-watt boats).

▲Salt Mine Tour—If you have yet to tour a salt mine, consider Hallstatt's—which claims to be the oldest in the world. First you'll ride a steep funicular high above the town (€8.50 round-trip, €5.10 one-way, 4/hr, daily May–mid-Sept 9:00–18:00, mid-Sept–Oct 9:00–16:30, closed Nov–April). Then you'll hike 10 minutes to the mine (past excavation sites of many prehistoric tombs and a glass case with 2,500-year-old bones—but there's little to actually see). Report back 10 minutes before the tour time on your ticket, check your bag, and put on old miners' clothes. Then hike 200 yards higher in your funny outfit to meet your guide, who escorts your group down a tunnel dug in 1719. Inside the mountain, you'll watch a slide show, follow your guide through several caverns as you learn about mining techniques over the last 7,000 years, see a silly laser show on a glassy subterranean lake, peek at a few waxy cavemen with pickaxes, and ride the train out. The highlight for most is sliding down two banisters (the second one is longer and ends with a flash for an automatic souvenir photo that clocks your speed—see how you did compared to the rest of your group after the tour).

The presentation is very low-tech, as the mining company owns all three mine tours in the area and sees little reason to invest in the experience when they can simply mine the tourists. While the tour is mostly in German, the guide is required to speak English if you ask...so ask (salt mine tour-€15.50, €21 combo-ticket for mine and funicular round-trip saves €3, you can buy mine tickets at cable-car station—note the time and tour number on your ticket, daily May–mid-Sept 9:30–16:30, mid-Sept–Oct 9:30–15:00, closed Nov–April, the 16:00 funicular departure catches the last tour at 16:30, no children under age 4, arrive early or late to avoid summer crowds, dress for the constant 47-degree temperature, tel. 06132/200-2400). If you skip the funicular, the scenic 40-minute hike back into town is (with strong knees) a joy.

At the base of the funicular, notice train tracks leading to the Erbstollen tunnel entrance. This lowest of the salt tunnels goes many miles into the mountain, where a shaft connects it to the tunnels you just explored. Today, the salty brine from these tunnels flows 25 miles through the world's oldest pipeline—made of wood until quite recently—to the huge modern salt works (next to the highway) at Ebensee.

▲Local Hikes—Mountain-lovers, hikers, and spelunkers who use Hallstatt as their home base keep busy for days (ask the TI for ideas). Local hikes are well-described in the TI's *Dachstein Hiking Guide* (€6, in English). A good, short, and easy walk is the two-hour round-trip up the Echern Valley to the Waldbachstrub waterfall and back. From the parking lot, follow signs to the salt mines, then follow the little wooden signs marked *Echerntalweg*. With a car, consider hiking around nearby Altaussee (flat, 3-hour hike) or along Grundlsee to Toplitzsee. Regular buses connect Hallstatt with Gosausee for a pleasant hour-long walk around that lake. Or consider walking nine miles halfway around Lake Hallstatt via the town of Steeg (boat to train station, left along lake and past idyllic farmsteads, returning to Hallstatt along the old salt trail, *Soleleitungsweg*). The TI can also recommend a great two-day hike with an overnight in a nearby mountain hut.

Biking—Ask about the new lakeside bike path. The best two bike rides take nearly the same routes as the hikes listed above: up the Echern Valley, and around the lake (bikers do better going via Obertraun along the new bike path—start with a ride on the *Stefanie*). Two places in town rent bikes: **Post Partner** (the stamp-selling place formerly known as the post office; €5/2 hrs, €9/half-day, €12/day, Mon–Fri 8:00–16:00, closed Sat–Sun, on Museum Square, tel. 06134/8201) and **Hotel Grüner Baum** (€2.50/hr, €9/half-day, €16/day, on Market Square).

Near Hallstatt

▲▲Dachstein Mountain Cable Car and Caves—For a refreshing activity, ride a scenic cable car up a mountain to visit huge, chilly caves.

Dachstein Cable Car: From Obertraun, three miles beyond Hallstatt on the main road (or directly across the lake as the crow flies), a mighty gondola goes in three stages high up the Dachstein Plateau—crowned by Dachstein, the highest mountain in the Salzkammergut (over 9,000 feet). The first segment stops

Salzkammergut

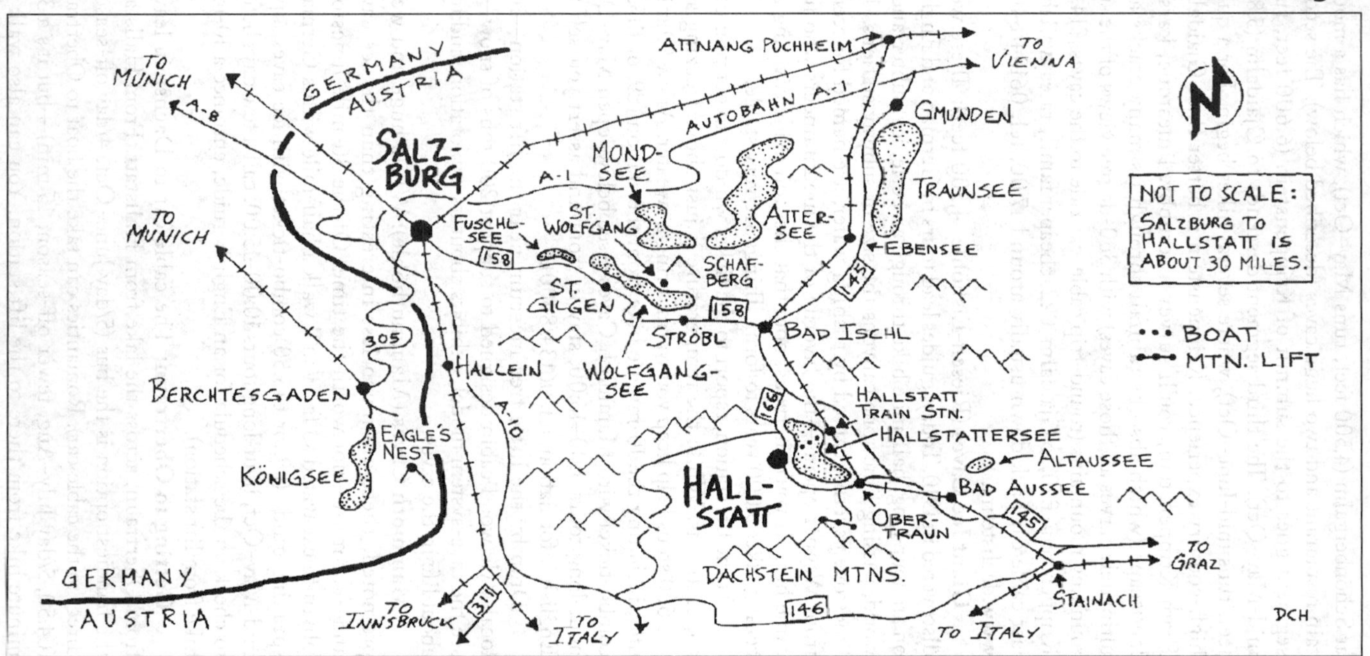

at Schönbergalm (4,500 feet, runs May–Oct), which has a mountain restaurant and two huge caves (described below). The second segment goes to the summit of Krippenstein (6,600 feet, runs mid-May–Oct). The third segment descends to Gjaidalm (5,800 feet, runs mid-June–Oct), where several hikes begin. For a quick high-country experience, Krippenstein is better than Gjaidalm. From Krippenstein, you'll survey a scrubby, limestone, karstic landscape (which absorbs rainfall through its many cracks and ultimately carves all those caves) with 360-degree views of the surrounding mountains (round-trip cable-car ride to the caves-€14, to Krippenstein-€20, to Gjaidalm-€22, cheaper family rates available, last cable car back down usually around 17:00, tel. 06134/8400, www.dachstein.at).

Giant Ice Caves (Riesen-Eishöhle, 4,500 feet): These were discovered in 1910. Today, guides lead tours in German and English on an hour-long, half-mile hike through an eerie, icy, subterranean world, passing limestone canyons the size of subway stations. The limestone caverns, carved by rushing water, are named for scenes from Wagner operas—the favorite of the mountaineers who first came here. If you're nervous, note that the iron oxide covering the ceiling takes 5,000 years to form. Things are very stable.

At the lift station, report to the ticket window to get your cave appointment. While the temperature is just above freezing and the 600 steps help keep you warm, bring a sweater. Allow 90 minutes, including the 10-minute hike from the station (€9, or €13.50 combo-ticket with Mammoth Caves—see below, open May–Oct, hour-long tours 9:00–16:00, stay in front and assert yourself for English information, tel. 06134/8400).

Drop by the little free museum near the lift station—in a local-style wood cabin designed to support 200 tons of snow—to see the cave-system model, exhibits about its exploration, and info about life in the caves.

Mammoth Caves (Mammuthöhle): While huge and well-promoted, these are much less interesting than the ice caves and—for most—not worth the time. Of the 30-mile limestone labyrinth excavated so far, you'll walk a half-mile with a German-speaking guide (€9, or €13.50 combo-ticket with ice caves, open mid-May–Oct, hour-long tours 10:00–15:00, call a few days before to check on the schedule for an English guide, entrance a 10-min hike from lift station).

Getting to Obertraun: The cable car to Dachstein leaves from Obertraun, across the lake from Hallstatt. From Hallstatt, the handiest option is the bus (5/day June–Oct, 4/day off-season, direct to the cable car). Romantics can take the boat to Obertraun (€4.50, 5/day July–Aug, fewer off-season, 15 min)—but it's a 30-minute hike from there to the lift station. You can also walk an hour from the Hallstatt train-station boat dock to the cable car. The impatient can consider hitching a ride—virtually all cars leaving Hallstatt to the south will pass through Obertraun in a few minutes.

Luge Rides (Sommerrodelbahn) on the Hallstatt–Salzburg Road—If you're driving between Salzburg and Hallstatt, you'll pass two luge rides. Each is a ski lift that drags you backward up the hill as you sit on your go-cart. At the top, you ride the cart down the winding metal course. It's easy: Push to go, pull to stop, take your hands off your stick and you get hurt.

Each course is just off the road with easy parking. The ride up and down takes about 15 minutes. The one near Fuschlsee (closest to Salzburg, look for *Sommerrodelbahn* sign) is half as long and cheaper (€4/ride, 1,970 feet, tel. 06235/7297). The one near Wolfgangsee (look for *Riesenschutzbahn* sign) is a double course, more scenic with grand lake views (€6/ride, €40/10 rides, 4,265 feet, each track is the same speed, tel. 06137/7085). Courses are open Easter through October from 10:00 to 18:00 (July–Aug 9:30–19:00)—but will generally close in bad weather. These are fun, but the concrete courses near Reutte are better.

NIGHTLIFE

Locals would laugh at the thought. But if you do want some action after dinner, you have two options: **Gasthaus zur Mühle** (youth hostel with a rustic sports-bar ambience in its restaurant when drinks replace the food, open late, closed Tue Sept–mid-May, run by Ferdinand). Or, for your late-night drink, savor the Market Square from the trendy little pub called **Ruth Zimmermann,** where locals congregate with soft music, a good selection of drinks, two small rooms, and tables on the square (daily June–Oct 9:00–2:00 in the morning, Nov–May 12:00–2:00, tel. 06134/8306).

SLEEPING

Hallstatt's TI can almost always find you a room (either in town or at B&Bs and small hotels outside of town—which are more likely to have rooms available and come with easy parking). Mid-July and August can be tight. Early August is worst. Hallstatt is not the place to splurge—some of the best rooms are in *Zimmer,* just as nice and modern as the bigger hotels, at half the cost. A bed in a private home costs about €20 with breakfast. It's hard to get a one-night advance reservation. But if you drop in and they have a spot, one-nighters are welcome. Prices include breakfast, lots of stairs, and a silent night. *"Zimmer mit Aussicht?"* (TSIM-mer mit OWS-zeekt) means "Room with view?"—worth asking for. Unlike many

Sleep Code

(€1 = about $1.30, country code: 43, area code: 06134)
S = Single, **D** = Double/Twin, **T** = Triple, **Q** = Quad, **b** = bathroom, **s** = shower only. Unless otherwise noted, credit cards are accepted, English is spoken, and breakfast is included.

To help you sort easily through these listings, I've divided the rooms into three categories, based on the price for a standard double room with bath:

$$$ Higher Priced—Most rooms €80 or more.
$$ Moderately Priced—Most rooms between €50–80.
$ Lower Priced—Most rooms €50 or less.

businesses in town, the cheaper places don't take credit cards.

$$$ Hotel Grüner Baum offers the priciest beds in town. Its 22 rooms are huge, each with a separate living area with modern furnishings on ancient hardwoods. The owner, Monika, moved in from Vienna and renovated this stately old hotel with urban taste (suite-like Db-€130–150, family rooms, Internet access, laundry service, rental bikes, 20 yards from boat dock over looking the lake and Market Square, tel. 06134/8263, fax 06134/826-344, www.gruenerbaum.cc, gruener.baum@magnet.at).

$$$ Gasthof Zauner is run by a friendly mountaineer, Herr Zauner, whose family has owned it since 1893. The 13 pricey, pine-flavored rooms on the inland side of the main square are decorated with sturdy alpine-inspired furniture. Lederhosen-clad Herr Zauner recounts tales of local mountaineering lore, including his own impressive ascents (Sb-€55, Db-€102, cheaper mid-Dec–April, closed mid-Nov–mid-Dec, Marktplatz 51, tel. 06134/8246, fax 06134/82468, www.zauner.hallstatt.net, zauner@hallstatt.at).

$$$ Pension Hallberg-Tauchergasthof (Diver's Inn), across from the TI, rents five big, modern rooms above their antique shop. The hallway is lined with a funky mini-museum of WWII artifacts found in the lake and a chorus line of mounted fish heads (Db-€70–120, rooms for up to 5 also available, price depends on size, €20 less off season, cash preferred, tel. 06134/8709, fax 06134/20621, www.pension-hallberg.at.tf, hallberg@aon.at, Gerda the "Salt Witch" and Eckbert Winkelmann).

$$$ Gasthof Simony is a well-worn, grandmotherly place on the square, with a lake view, balconies, ancient beds, creaky wood floors, slippery rag rugs, antique furniture, a lakefront garden for swimming, and a huge breakfast. Reserve in advance, ideally by phone or fax. For safety, reconfirm your room and price a day or two before you arrive and call again if arriving late

(S-€38, D-€55, Ds-€65, Db-€80, third person-€30 extra, cash only, kayaks for guests, Marktplatz 105, tel. & fax 06134/8231, www.hallstatt.net/gasthof/simony, Susanna Scheutz).

$$ Bräugasthof Hallstatt is like a museum, filled with antique furniture and ancient family portraits. This creaky old place—a former brewery with eight clean, cozy rooms—is run by Virena and her daughter, Virena. Six of the rooms have gorgeous little lakeview balconies (Sb-€45, Db-€76, Db with balcony-€84, Tb-€120, just past TI on the main drag at Seestrasse 120, tel. 06134/8221, fax 06134/82214, www.brauhaus-lobisser.com, info@brauhaus-lobisser.com, Lobisser family).

$$ Gasthof Pension Grüner Anger is practical and modern—your best value in town for comfort—but located away from the medieval town center (a few blocks from the base of the salt-mine lift, and a 15-minute walk from the Market Square). It's big and quiet, with 11 rooms and no creaks or squeaks (Sb-€36, Db-€63, €3 more per room July–Aug, third person-€15, non-smoking, Internet access and Wi-Fi, free loaner bikes, free parking, Lahn 10, tel. 06134/8397, fax 06134/83974, www.anger.hallstatt.net, anger@aon.at, Sulzbacher family). If arriving by train, have the boat captain call Herr Sulzbacher, who will pick you up at the dock. They run a good-value restaurant, too.

$$ Pension Sarstein, popular with students and other travelers, is a big, funky, flower-bedecked house heavy with lakeview balconies. You can swim from its plush and inviting lakeside garden (Db-€60, cash only, 200 yards to the right of boat dock at Gosaumühlstrasse 83, tel. 06134/8217, fax 06134/20635, www.pension-sarstein.at.tf, pension.sarstein@aon.at, Isabelle Fischer).

$$ Pension Seethaler is a dark, homey old lodge with 45 beds and a breakfast room mossy with antlers, perched above the lake. The confusing floor plan is like an M. C. Escher house with fire hazards. While overpriced, this place is a sleepable last resort (€22/person in S, D, T, or Q; €30/person in Db, Tb, or Qb; cash only, coin-op showers downstairs, closed Nov, Dr.-Morton-Weg 22, climb the stairs to the left of Seestrasse 116, tel. 06134/8421, pension-seethaler@aon.at).

$ Helga Lenz's Zimmer rents two fine rooms a steep five-minute climb above the Pension Seethaler (look for the green *Zimmer* sign). This large, sprawling, woodsy house has a nifty garden perch, wins the Best View award, and is ideal for those who sleep well in tree houses and don't mind the ascent from town (Db-€40, Tb-€54, 1-night stays-€1 per person extra, family room, cash only, closed Nov–March, Hallberg 17, tel. & fax 06134/8508, www.hallstatt.net/privatzimmer/helga.lenz, haus-lenz@aon.at).

$ Two ***Zimmer*** are a few minutes' stroll south of the center, just past the bus stop/parking lot and over the bridge. **Haus Trausner**

has four clean, bright, new-feeling rooms adjacent the Trausner family home (Ds-€36, Db-€40, 2-night minimum, cash only, breakfast comes to your room, Lahnstrasse 27, tel. 06134/8710, trausnerl@utanet.at, charming Maria Trausner makes you want to settle right in). **Herta Höll** rents out three spacious, modern rooms on the ground floor of her modern riverside house crawling with kids (Db-€44, apartment for up to five-€60, cash only, Malerweg 45, tel. 06134/8531, fax 06134/825-533, frank.hoell@aon.at).

$ ***Hostel:*** **Gasthaus zur Mühle Jugendherberge,** below the waterfall, has 46 of the cheapest good beds in town (bed in 3- to 14-bed coed dorms-€13, D-€26, family quads, sheets-€3 extra, breakfast-€3, big lockers with a €15 deposit, closed Nov, reception closed Tue Sept–mid-May—so arrange in advance if arriving on Tue, below tunnel car park, Kirchenweg 36, tel. & fax 06134/8318, toeroe.f@magnet.at, Ferdinand Törö). It's also popular for its great, inexpensive pizza—see below.

EATING

In this town, when someone is happy to see you, they'll often say, "Can I cook you a fish?" While everyone cooks the typical Austrian fare, your best bet here is trout. *Reinanke* trout is caught wild out of Lake Hallstatt and served the same day. You can enjoy good food inexpensively, with delightful lakeside settings. Restaurants in Hallstatt tend to have unreliable hours and close early on slow nights, so don't wait too long to get dinner. The first four eateries listed below are also recommended under "Sleeping," above.

Restaurant Bräugasthof has great lakeside tables. You can feed the swans while your trout is being cooked. Under new management, it hopes to offer good traditional plates. For now, the only certainty is that its lakeside dining, on a balmy evening, offers the best ambience in town (Seestrasse 120, tel. 06134/8221).

Hotel Grüner Baum is another lakefront option (daily May–Oct 11:30–22:00, closed Nov–April, at bottom of Market Square, tel. 06134/8263). Its **Restaurant zum Salzbaron** is a classy place with tables overlooking the lake inside and out (elegant service, €15–€20 plates). Its **Kaiserstüberl** is more casual and rustic, with a folksy feel, no lake views, and €10 meals.

Gasthof Zauner's classy restaurant lacks a lakeside setting, but it's well-respected for its grilled meat with "cracklings" and fish. The service comes in lederhosen, the ivy is real, and most agree that the food is worth the few extra euros (daily 11:30–14:30 & 17:30–22:00, closed Nov–mid Dec, at top of Market Square).

Gasthaus zur Mühle serves the best pizza in town. Chow down cheap and hearty here with fun-loving locals and the youth-hostel crowd (€7 pizza, lots of Italian, some Austrian, daily in summer 11:00–14:00 & 17:00–21:00, closed Tue and no lunch Sept–mid-May, Kirchenweg 36, Ferdinand).

Strand Café, a smoky local favorite, is a 10-minute lakeside hike away, near the town beach, or Bade-Insel (€8–12 plates, plenty of alcohol, April–Oct Tue–Sun 10:00–21:00, closed Mon and Nov–March, great garden setting on the lake, Seelande 102, tel. 06134/8234).

Picnics and Cheap Eats: The **Zauner** bakery/butcher/grocer, great for picnickers, makes fresh sandwiches to go (Mon–Fri 7:00–12:00 & 15:00–18:00, closed most of the weekend, uphill to the left from Market Square). The only **supermarket** is in Lahn at the bus stop (Konsum, Mon–Sat 7:30–12:00 & 15:00–18:00, closed Sun). The **hot-dog stand** on the Market Square sells *Döner Kebabs* and so on for €3 (tables and fine lakeside picnic options nearby).

TRANSPORTATION CONNECTIONS

For tips for drivers coming here from Salzburg, see the end of the Salzburg chapter.

From Hallstatt by Train: Most travelers leaving Hallstatt are going to Salzburg or Vienna. In either case, you need to catch the shuttle boat (€2, departs 15 minutes before every train) to the little station across the lake, and ride 90 minutes to **Attnang Puchheim** (hourly from about 7:00–18:00). Trains are synchronized, so after a short wait in Attnang Puchheim, you'll catch your connection to **Salzburg** (50 min) or **Vienna** (2.5 hrs). Day-trippers stopping by Hallstatt between Salzburg and Vienna can check their bags at the Attnang Puchheim station (follow signs for *Schliessfächer*, coin-op lockers are at the street, curbside near track 1, €2.50/24 hrs, a ticket serves as your key). Note: Connections can be fast—check the TV monitor. Hallstatt doesn't show up on schedules, but trains to Ebensee and Bad Ischl stop here. Train info: tel. 051-717 (to get an operator, dial 2, then 1).

By Bus: Some consider the bus ride from Hallstatt to **Salzburg** (with an easy change in Bad Ischl) more scenic than the train, and just as practical (9/day, allow 2 hrs, no bus in icy weather, www.ooevv.at or get details at Hallstatt TI).

BELGIUM

BRUGES

(Brugge)

With Renoir canals, pointy, gilded architecture, vivid time-tunnel art, and stay-a-while cafés, Bruges is a heavyweight sightseeing destination, as well as a joy. Where else can you ride a bike along a canal, munch mussels and wash them down with the world's best beer, savor heavenly chocolate, and see Flemish Primitives and a Michelangelo, all within 300 yards of a bell tower that jingles every 15 minutes? And there's no language barrier.

The town is Brugge (BROO-ghah) in Flemish, and Bruges (broozh) in French and English. Its name comes from the Viking word for wharf. Right from the start, Bruges was a trading center. In the 11th century, the city grew wealthy on the cloth trade.

By the 14th century, Bruges' population was 35,000, as large as London's. As the middleman in sea trade between northern and southern Europe, it was one of the biggest cities in the world and an economic powerhouse. In addition, Bruges had become the most important cloth market in northern Europe.

In the 15th century, while England and France were slugging it out in the Hundred Years' War, Bruges was the favored residence of the powerful Dukes of Burgundy—and at peace. Commerce and the arts boomed. The artists Jan van Eyck and Hans Memling had studios here.

But by the 16th century, the harbor had silted up and the economy had collapsed. The Burgundian court left, Belgium became a minor Hapsburg possession, and Bruges' Golden Age abruptly ended. For generations, Bruges was known as a mysterious and dead city. In the 19th century, a new port, Zeebrugge, brought renewed vitality to the area. And in the 20th century, tourists discovered the town.

Today, Bruges prospers because of tourism: It's a uniquely well-preserved Gothic city and a handy gateway to Europe. It's no secret, but even with the crowds, it's the kind of city where you don't mind being a tourist.

Bruges' ultimate sight is the town itself, and the best way to enjoy it is to get lost on the back streets, away from the lace shops and ice-cream stands.

Planning Your Time

Bruges needs at least two nights and a full, well-organized day. Even non-shoppers enjoy browsing here, and the Belgian love of life makes a hectic itinerary seem a little senseless. With one day—other than a Monday, when the three museums are closed—the speedy visitor could do the Bruges blitz described below:

9:30 Climb the bell tower on Market Square.
10:00 Tour the sights on Burg Square.
11:00 Tour the Groeninge Museum.
12:00 Tour the Gruuthuse Museum.
13:00 Eat lunch and buy chocolates.
14:00 Take a short canal cruise.
14:30 Visit the Church of Our Lady and see Michelangelo's *Madonna and Child*.
15:00 Tour the Memling Museum.
16:00 Catch the De Halve Maan Brewery tour (note that their last tour runs at 15:00 in winter).
17:00 Calm down in the Begijnhof courtyard.
18:00 Ride a bike around the quiet back streets of town or take a horse-and-buggy tour.
20:00 Lose the tourists and find dinner.

If this schedule seems insane, skip the bell tower and the brewery—or stay another day.

OVERVIEW

(area code: 050)

The tourist's Bruges—and you'll be sharing it—is less than one square mile, contained within a canal (the former moat). Nearly everything of interest and importance is within a convenient cobbled swath between the train station and Market Square (a 15-min walk). Many of my quiet, charming, recommended accommodations lie just beyond Market Square.

Tourist Information

The main tourist office, called **In&Uit** ("In and Out"), is in the big, red concert hall on the square called 't Zand (daily 10:00–18:00, Thu until 20:00, take a number from the touch-screen machines and wait, 't Zand 34, tel. 050/448-686, www.brugge.be). The other TI is at the train station (generally Tue–Sat 10:00–13:00 & 14:00–17:00, closed Sun–Mon).

The TIs sell a great €1 Bruges visitors guide with a map and listings of all of the sights and services. You can also pick up a monthly English-language program called *events@brugge*. The TIs have information on train schedules and on the many tours available (see "Tours," below). Bikers will want the *5X on the Bike Around Bruges* map/guide (€1.50) that shows five routes through the countryside. Many hotels give out free maps with more detail than the map the TIs sell.

Arrival in Bruges

By Train: Coming in by train, you'll see the square bell tower that marks the main square (Market Square, the center of town). Upon arrival, stop by the train station TI to pick up the €1 Bruges visitors guide (with map). The station lacks ATMs, but has lockers (€2–3.50, daily 6:00–24:00).

The best way to get to the town center is by **bus.** Buses #1, #3, #4, #6, #11, #13, #14, and #16 go directly to Market Square. Simply hop on, pay €1.50, and in four minutes, you're there. Buses #4 and #14 continue on to the northeast part of town (to the windmills and recommended accommodations on Carmersstraat). The **taxi** fare from the train station to most hotels is about €8.

It's a 20-minute **walk** from the station to the center—no fun with your luggage. If you want to walk to Market Square, cross the busy street and canal in front of the station, head up Oostmeers, and turn right on Zwidzandstraat. You can rent a **bike** at the station for the duration of your stay, but other bike rental shops are closer to the center (see "Helpful Hints," below).

By Car: Park at the train station for just €2.50 for 24 hours and take the bus into town. There are pricier underground parking garages at the square called 't Zand and around town (€10/day, all of them well-marked). Paid parking on the street in Bruges is limited to four hours. Driving in town is very complicated because of the one-way system.

Helpful Hints

Market Days: Bruges hosts markets on Wednesday morning (Market Square) and Saturday morning ('t Zand). On Saturday and Sunday, a flea market hops along Dijver in front of the Groeninge Museum.

Shopping: Shops are generally open from 10:00 to 18:00. Grocery stores are usually closed on Sunday. The main shopping street, Steenstraat, stretches from Market Square to 't Zand square. The Hema department store is at Steenstraat 73 (Mon–Sat

Bruges

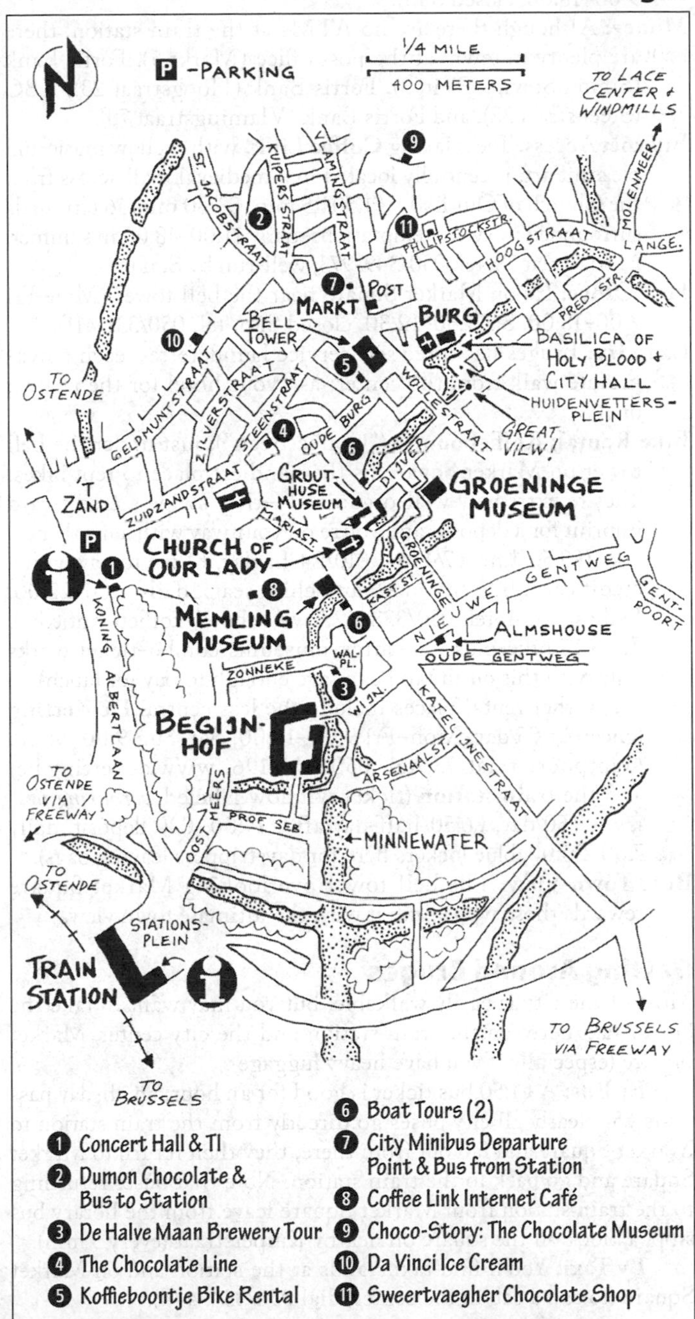

P -PARKING
1/4 MILE
400 METERS
TO LACE CENTER + WINDMILLS
ST. JACOBSSTRAAT
KUIPERSSTRAAT
VLAMINGSTRAAT
PHILIPSTOCKSTR.
HOOGSTRAAT
LANGE.
MOLENMEER
PRED. STR.
POST
MARKT
BURG
BELL TOWER
BASILICA OF HOLY BLOOD + CITY HALL
HUIDENVETTERS-PLEIN
GREAT VIEW!
WOLLESTRAAT
TO OSTENDE
GELDMUNTSTRAAT
ZILVERSTRAAT
STEENSTRAAT
OUDE BURG
DIJVER
ZUIDZANDSTRAAT
'T ZAND
GRUUTHUSE MUSEUM
GROENINGE MUSEUM
MARIAST.
CHURCH OF OUR LADY
GROENINGE
KAST. ST.
NIEUWE GENTWEG
GENTPOORT
KONING ALBERTLAAN
MEMLING MUSEUM
ALMSHOUSE
OUDE GENTWEG
ZONNEKE
WALPL.
WIJN.
KATELIJNESTRAAT
BEGIJNHOF
ARSENAALST.
TO OSTENDE VIA FREEWAY
OOSTMEERS
PROF. SEB.
MINNEWATER
TO OSTENDE
STATIONSPLEIN
TRAIN STATION
TO BRUSSELS VIA FREEWAY
TO BRUSSELS
1 Concert Hall & TI
2 Dumon Chocolate & Bus to Station
3 De Halve Maan Brewery Tour
4 The Chocolate Line
5 Koffieboontje Bike Rental
6 Boat Tours (2)
7 City Minibus Departure Point & Bus from Station
8 Coffee Link Internet Café
9 Choco-Story: The Chocolate Museum
10 Da Vinci Ice Cream
11 Sweertvaegher Chocolate Shop

9:00–18:00, closed Sun).

Money: Although there are no ATMs at the train station, there are plenty in town: at the post office (Markt 5), Fortis Bank (Simon Stevins Plein 3), Fortis Bank (Hoogstraat 23), KBC (Steenstraat 38), and Fortis Bank (Vlamingstraat 78).

Internet Access: The relaxing **Coffee Link,** with mellow music and pleasant art, is centrally located in a medieval mall across from the Church of Our Lady (€1.50/15 min, €3/30 min, 16 terminals surrounded by sweet temptations, daily 11:00–18:00 in summer, Mariastraat 38, tel. 050/349-973, well-run by Staf).

Post Office: It's on Market Square near the bell tower (Mon–Fri 9:00–18:00, Sat 9:30–12:30, closed Sun, tel. 050/331-411).

Laundry: Bruges has three self-service launderettes, each a five-minute walk from the center; ask your hotel for the nearest one.

Bike Rental: Koffieboontje ("Coffee Bean"), just under the bell tower on Market Square, is the handiest place to rent bikes. They're extremely well-organized—they swipe a credit-card imprint for a deposit, and you're on your way with a nearly new bike (€3.50/1 hr, €7/4 hrs, €10/24-hr day, €1 fee to pay with a credit card, free city maps and child seats, daily 9:00–22:00, Hallestraat 4, tel. 050/338-027, www.hotel-koffieboontje.be). The €15 bike-plus-any-three-museums combo-ticket works only with this outfit (and can save enough to pay for lunch).

Other rental places include the less central **De Ketting** (cheap at €5/day, Mon–Fri 9:00–19:00, Sat–Sun 9:00–14:00, Gentpoortstraat 23, tel. 050/344-196, www.deketting.be) and the **train station** (ticket window labeled *verhuring fietsen*, €9.50/day, €6.50/half-day after 14:00, €20 deposit, daily 7:00–20:00, blue lockers here for day-trippers leaving bags).

Best Town View: The bell tower overlooking Market Square rewards those who climb it with the ultimate town view.

Getting Around Bruges

Most of the city is easily walkable, but you may want to take the bus or taxi between the train station and the city center, Market Square (especially if you have heavy luggage).

By Bus: A €1.50 bus ticket is good for an hour; an all-day pass costs €5. Nearly all city buses go directly from the train station to Market Square and fan out from there; they then return to Market Square and go back to the train station. Note that buses returning to the train station from Market Square leave from the library bus stop, a block off the square on nearby Kuiperstraat (every 5 min).

By Taxi: You'll find taxi stands at the station and on Market Square (to call a cab in the center, dial 050/334-444).

TOURS

Of Bruges

Bruges by Boat—The most relaxing and scenic (though not informative) way to see this city of canals is by boat, with the captain narrating. (Always let them know you speak English to ensure you'll understand the spiel.) Several companies offer basically the same 30-minute tour (€5.70, 4/hr, daily 10:00–17:00). Try one of these two companies: Boten Stael (just over the canal from Memling Museum at Katelijnestraat 4, tel. 050/332-771) and Gruuthuse (Nieuwstraat 11, opposite Groeninge Museum, tel. 050/333-393).

City Minibus Tour—City Tour Bruges gives a rolling overview of the town in an 18-seat, two-skylight minibus with dial-a-language headsets and video support (€11.50, 50 min). The tour leaves hourly from Market Square (10:00–20:00 in summer, until 18:00 in spring, until 17:00 in fall, less in winter, tel. 050/355-024, www.citytour.be). The narration, while clear, is slow-moving and a bit boring. But the tour is a lazy way to cruise past virtually every sight in Bruges.

Walking Tour—Local guides walk small groups through the core of town (€6, €15 for a family, 2 hours, daily July–Aug, Sat–Sun only June and Sept, no tours Oct–May, depart from TI on 't Zand square at 14:30—just drop in a few minutes early and buy tickets at the TI desk). Though earnest, the tours are heavy on history and given in two languages, so they may be less than peppy. Still, to propel you beyond the pretty gables and canal swans of Bruges, they're good medicine.

Private Guide—A private two-hour guided tour costs €45 (reserve at least one week in advance through TI, tel. 050/448-686). Or contact Christian and Danielle Scharle, who give two-hour walks for €50 and three-hour guided drives for €100 (Christian's mobile 0475-659-507, Danielle's mobile 0476-493-203, tmb@skynet.be).

Horse-and-Buggy Tour—The buggies around town can take you on a clip-clop tour (€30, 35 min; price is per carriage, not per person). When divided among four or five people, this can be a good value.

From Bruges

Quasimodo Countryside Tours—This company offers those with extra time two entertaining, all-day, English-only bus tours through the rarely visited Flemish countryside.

The "In Flanders Fields" tour concentrates on WWI battlefields, trenches, memorials, and poppy-splattered fields (April–Oct Tue–Sun 9:15–17:00; Nov–March Sun, Tue, and Thu only; visit to In Flanders Fields Museum not included).

The other tour, "Triple Treat," focuses on Flanders' medieval past and rich culture, with tastes of chocolate, waffles, and beer (Mon, Wed, and Fri 9:15–17:00). Be ready for lots of walking.

Tours cost €50, or €40 if you're under 26 (includes a picnic lunch, 30-seat, non-smoking bus, reservations required—call tel. 050/370-470 or toll-free tel. 0800-97525, www.quasimodo.be). After making a few big-hotel pick-ups, the buses leave town at 9:15 from the Park Hotel on 't Zand square.

Daytours—Tour guide Frank loves leading small groups on fascinating "Flanders Fields Battlefield" day trips. This tour is like Quasimodo's (listed above), but more expensive. The differences: seven travelers on a minibus rather than a big busload; pick-up from any hotel or B&B (because the small bus is allowed in the town center); restaurant lunch included rather than a picnic; and a little more serious lecturing and a stricter focus on World War I. For instance, you actually visit the In Flanders Fields Museum in Ieper (Ypres in French). Tours cost €59 (Wed–Sun 9:00–17:00, no tours Mon–Tue, call 050/346-060 or toll-free 0800-99133 to reserve).

Bruges by Bike—QuasiMundo Biketours Brugge leads daily five-mile bike tours around the city (departs at 10:00, 2.5 hours). Their other tour, "Border by Bike," goes through the nearby countryside to Damme (departs at 13:00 March–Oct, 15 miles, 4 hours). Either tour costs €20 (tel. 050/330-775, www.quasimundo.com). Both tours include bike rental, a light raincoat (if necessary), water, and a drink in a local café. Meet on Burg Square. If you already have a bike, you're welcome to join either tour for €14.

Bus and Boat Tour—The Sightseeing Line offers a bus trip to Damme and a boat ride back (€16.50, April–Sept daily at 14:00, 2 hours, leaves from the post office at Market Square, tel. 050/355-024, www.citytour.be).

SIGHTS AND EXPERIENCES

These sights are listed in walking order from Market Square to Burg Square to the cluster of museums around the Church of our Lady to the Begijnhof (10-min walk from beginning to end, without stops).

▲Market Square (Markt)—Ringed by a bank, the post office, lots of restaurant terraces, great old gabled buildings, and the iconic bell tower, this is the modern heart of the city (most city buses run from near here to the train station—library bus stop, a block down Kuiperstraat). Under the bell tower are two great Belgian french-fry stands, a quadrilingual Braille description of the old town, and a metal model of the tower. In Bruges' heyday as a trading center, a canal came right up to this square.

Geldmuntstraat, just off the square, is a delightful street with many fun and practical shops and eateries.

▲▲**Bell Tower (Belfort)**—Most of this bell tower has presided over Market Square since 1300, serenading passersby with carillon music. The octagonal lantern was added in 1486, making it 290 feet high—that's 366 steps. The view is worth the climb and the €5 (daily 9:30–17:00, last entry 45 min before closing, €0.30 WC in courtyard).

▲▲**Burg Square**—This opulent square is Bruges' civic center, historically the birthplace of Bruges and the site of the ninth-century castle of the first Count of Flanders. Today, it's the scene of outdoor concerts and surrounded by six centuries of architecture.

▲**Basilica of the Holy Blood**—Originally the Chapel of Saint Basil, this church is famous for its relic of the blood of Christ, which, according to tradition, was brought to Bruges in 1150 after the Second Crusade. The lower chapel is dark and solid—a fine example of Romanesque style. The upper chapel (separate entrance, climb the stairs) is decorated Gothic. An interesting treasury museum is next to the upper chapel (treasury entry-€1.50; April–Sept Thu–Tue 9:30–11:45 & 14:00–17:45, Wed 9:30–11:45 only; Oct–March Thu–Tue 10:00–11:45 & 14:00–15:45, Wed 10:00–11:45 only; Burg Square, tel. 050/336-792, www.holyblood.org).

▲**City Hall**—This complex houses several interesting sights. Your €2.50 ticket includes an audioguide; access to a room full of old town maps and paintings; the grand, beautifully restored **Gothic Room** from 1400, starring a painted and carved wooden ceiling adorned with hanging arches (daily 9:30–17:00, Burg 12); and the less impressive **Renaissance Hall** (Brugse Vrije), basically just one ornate room with a Renaissance chimney (Tue–Sun 9:30–12:30 & 13:30–16:30, closed Mon, separate entrance—in corner of square at Burg 11a).

▲▲▲**Groeninge Museum**—This museum houses a world-class collection of mostly Flemish art, from Memling to Magritte. While there's plenty of worthwhile modern art, the highlights are the vivid and pristine Flemish Primitives. ("Primitive" here means before the Renaissance.) Flemish art is shaped by its love of detail, its merchant patrons' egos, and the power of the Church. Lose yourself in the halls of Groeninge: Gaze across 15th-century canals, into the eyes of reassuring Marys, and through town squares littered with leotards, lace, and lopped-off heads (€8, includes audioguide, Tue–Sun 9:30–17:00, closed Mon, Dijver 12, tel. 050/448-743).

▲**Gruuthuse Museum**—The 15th-century mansion of a wealthy Bruges merchant displays period furniture, tapestries, coins, and musical instruments. Nowhere in the city do you get such an intimate look at the materialistic revolution of Bruges' glory days. With the help of the excellent and included audioguide, just browse through rooms of secular objects that are both functional and beautiful (€6, includes audioguide and entry to apse in Church of Our Lady, Tue–Sun 9:30–17:00, closed Mon, Dijver 17, Bruges museums tel. 050/448-8711).

▲▲Church of Our Lady—The church stands as a memorial to the power and wealth of Bruges in its heyday. A delicate *Madonna and Child* by Michelangelo is near the apse (to the right if you're facing the altar). It's said to be the only Michelangelo statue to leave Italy in his lifetime (thanks to the wealth generated by Bruges' cloth trade). If you like tombs and church art, pay to wander through the apse (Michelangelo viewing is free, art-filled apse-€2.50, covered by €6 Gruuthuse admission, Mon–Fri 9:30–16:50, Sat 9:30–15:50, Sun 13:30–16:50 only, Mariastraat).

▲▲Memling Museum/St. John's Hospital (Sint Janshospitaal)—The former monastery/hospital complex has two entrances—one is to a welcoming visitors center (free), the other to the Memling Museum. The museum, in the monastery's former church, was once a medieval hospital and now contains six much-loved paintings by the greatest of the Flemish Primitives, Hans Memling. His *Mystical Wedding of St. Catherine* triptych is a highlight, as is the miniature gilded oak shrine to St. Ursula (€8, includes fine audioguide, Tue–Sun 9:30–17:00, closed Mon, across the street from the Church of Our Lady, Mariastraat 38, Bruges museums tel. 050/448-8711).

▲▲Begijnhof—*Begijnhofs* (pronounced gutturally: buh-HHHINE-hof) were built to house women of the lay order called beguines, who spent their lives in piety and service (without having to take the same vows a nun would). For military or other reasons, there were more women than men in the medieval Low Countries. The order of beguines offered women (often single or widowed) a dignified place to live and work. When the order died out, many *begihnhofs* were taken over by towns for subsidized housing, but some became homes for nuns.

Bruges' Begijnhof—now inhabited by Benedictine nuns—almost makes you want to don a habit and fold your hands as you walk under its wispy trees and whisper past its frugal little homes. For a good slice of Begijnhof life, walk through the simple museum, the Beguine's House museum (€2, daily 10:00–12:00 & 13:45–17:00, shorter hours off-season, English explanations, museum is left of entry gate).

Minnewater—Just south of the Begijnhof is Minnewater, an idyllic world of flower boxes, canals, and swans.

Almshouses—Walking from the Begijnhof back to the town center, you might detour along Nieuwe Gentweg to visit one of about 20 almshouses in the city. At #8, go through the door marked *Godshuis de Meulenaere 1613* into the peaceful courtyard (free). This was a medieval form of housing for the poor. The rich would pay for someone's tiny room here in return for lots of prayers.

The small **Diamond Museum** at the start of Nieuwe Gentweg is a little more interesting than reading an encyclopedia (€6, daily 10:30–17:30, Katelijnestraat 43, tel. 050/342-056, www.diamondhouse.net).

Bruges Experiences: Beer, Chocolate, Lace, and Biking

▲▲De Halve Maan Brewery Tour—Belgians are Europe's beer connoisseurs. This fun, handy tour is a great way to pay your respects. The "Brugse Zot" is the only beer actually brewed in Bruges, and the happy gang at this working family brewery gives entertaining and informative, 45-minute, three-language tours (often by friendly Inge, €4.50 tour includes a beer, lots of very steep steps, great rooftop panorama, daily on the hour 11:00–16:00, Oct–March at 11:00 and 15:00 only—more often on winter weekends if there's a crowd, take a right down skinny Stoofstraat to #26 on Walplein, tel. 050/332-697, www.halvemaan.be).

During your tour, you'll learn that "the components of the beer are vitally necessary and contribute to a well-balanced life pattern. Nerves, muscles, visual sentience, and a healthy skin are stimulated by these in a positive manner. For longevity and lifelong equilibrium, drink Brugse Zot in moderation!"

Their bistro, where you'll be given your included beer, serves quick, hearty lunch plates. You can eat indoors with the smell of hops, or outdoors with the smell of hops. This is a great place to wait for your tour or to linger afterward.

▲Chocolate Shops—Bruggians are connoisseurs of fine chocolate. You'll be tempted by chocolate-filled display windows all over town. While Godiva is the best big-factory/high-price/high-quality brand, there are plenty of smaller, family-run places in Bruges that offer exquisite handmade chocolates. Each of the following chocolatiers is proud of its creative varieties. They are all generous with samples and welcome you to pick any five or six chocolates to assemble a 100-gram assortment.

Dumon: Perhaps Bruges' smoothest and creamiest chocolates are at Dumon (€1.75/100 grams). Madame Dumon and her children (Stefaan and Christophe) make their top-notch chocolate daily and sell it fresh just off Market Square (Thu–Tue 10:00–18:00, closed Wed, old chocolate molds on display in basement, Eiermarkt 6, tel. 050/346-282). The Dumons don't provide English labels because they believe it's best to describe their chocolates in person—and they do it with an evangelical fervor. Try a small mix-and-match box to sample a few out-of-this-world flavors, and come back for more of your favorites.

The Chocolate Line: Locals and tourists alike flock to The Chocolate Line (€3.40/100 grams) to taste the *gastronomique* varieties concocted by Dominique Person—the mad scientist of chocolate. His unique creations include Havana cigar (marinated in rum, cognac, and Cuban tobacco leaves—so therefore technically illegal in the US), lemongrass, lavender, ginger (shaped like a Buddha), saffron curry, spicy chili, and a Moroccan mint that will take you to Marrakech. My fave: the sheets of chocolate with crunchy roasted cocoa beans. New combinations from Dominique's imagination are a Pop Rocks/cola chocolate, as well as "wine vinegar" chocolate (surprisingly good). The kitchen—busy whipping up 80 varieties—is on display in the back. Enjoy the window display, renewed monthly (daily 9:30–18:00, between Church of Our Lady and Market Square at Simon Stevinplein 19, tel. 050/341-090).

Sweertvaegher: This small shop, near Burg Square, features high-quality chocolate (€2.86/100 grams) that's darker rather than sweeter, made with fresh ingredients and no preservatives (Tue–Sat 9:30–18:00, closed Sun–Mon, Philipstockstraat 29, tel. 050/338-367).

Choco-Story: The Chocolate Museum—This museum, rated ▲ for chocoholics, explains why, in the ancient Mexican world of the Mayas and the Aztecs, chocolate was considered the drink of the gods, and cocoa beans were used as a means of payment. With lots of actual artifacts well-described in English, the museum fills you in on the production of truffles, chocolates, hollow figures, and bars of chocolate. Then you'll view a delicious little video (8 min long, repeating continuously, alternating Flemish, French, and then English; peek into the theater to check the schedule. If you have time before the next English showing, visit the exhibits in the top room). Your finale is in the "demonstration room," where—after a 10-minute cooking lesson—you get a taste (€6, daily 10:00–17:00, where Wijnzakstraat meets Sint Jansstraat at Sint Jansplein, 3-min walk from Market Square, tel. 050/612-237, www.choco-story.be). Notice how chocolaty the fine building looks from across the street.

Windmills and Lace by the Moat—A 15-minute walk from the center to the northeast end of town brings you to four windmills strung along a pleasant grassy setting on the "big moat" canal. If biking, don't miss the lovely park along the canal.

Windmill: The St. Janshuysmolen windmill is open to visitors (€2, May–Aug daily 9:30–12:30 & 13:30–17:00, closed Sept–April, at the end of Carmersstraat, between Kruispoort and Dampoort, on Bruges side of the moat).

Lace: To actually see lace being made, drop by the nearby **Lace Center** (Kant Centrum), where ladies toss bobbins madly while their eyes go bad (€2.50 includes afternoon demo and small lace museum, as well as adjacent Jerusalem Church, Mon–Fri 10:00–12:00 & 14:00–18:00, Sat until 17:00, closed Sun, Peperstraat 3, tel. 050/330-072). The **Folklore Museum,** in the same neighborhood, is cute but forgettable (€3, Tue–Sun 9:30–17:00, closed Mon, Balstraat 43, tel. 050/448-764). To find either place, ask for the Jerusalem Church (mentioned below, under "Damme Bike Ride").

▲▲Biking—The Flemish word for bike is *fiets* (pronounced "feets"). While Bruges' sights are close enough for easy walking, the town is a treat for bikers. And a bike quickly gets you into dreamy back lanes without a hint of tourism. Take a peaceful evening ride through the town's nooks and crannies and around the outer canal. Consider keeping a bike for the duration of your stay—it's the way the locals get around in Bruges.

Rental shops have maps and ideas (see "Bike Rental" on page 144 for more info). The TI sells a handy *5X on the Bike Around Bruges* map/guide (€1.50) describing five different bike routes (10–18 miles) through the idyllic countryside nearby. The best trip is 30 minutes along the canal out to Damme and back (described below). The Belgium/Netherlands border is a 40-minute pedal beyond Damme.

Near Bruges

In Flanders Fields Museum—This World War I museum, about 40 miles southwest of Bruges, provides a moving look at the battles fought near Ieper (Ypres in French). Use interactive computer displays to trace the wartime lives of individual soldiers and citizens. Powerful videos and ear-shattering audio complete the story (€7.50; April–Sept daily 10:00–18:00; Oct–March Tue–Sun 10:00–17:00, closed Mon; last entry one hour before closing, Grote Markt 34, Ieper, tel. 057/239-220, www.inflandersfields.be). From Bruges, catch a train to Ieper via Kortrijk (2 hrs), or take a tour (see "Tours," page 145). Drivers, take E-403 to Kortrijk, then A-19 to Ieper, following signs to *Bellewaerde*.

SLEEPING

Bruges is a great place to sleep, with Gothic spires out your window, no traffic noise, and the cheerily out-of-tune carillon heralding each new day at 8:00 sharp. (Thankfully, the bell tower is silent from 22:00 to 8:00.)

Most Bruges accommodations are located between the train station and the old center, with the most distant (and best) being a few blocks to the north and east of Market Square.

B&Bs offer the best value (listed after "Hotels," below). All are on quiet streets and (with a few exceptions) keep the same prices throughout the year.

Sleep Code

(€1 = about $1.30, country code: 32)
S = Single, **D** = Double/Twin, **T** = Triple, **Q** = Quad, **b** = bathroom, **s** = shower only. Everyone speaks English. Unless otherwise noted, credit cards are accepted and breakfast is included.

To help you easily sort through these listings, I've divided the rooms into three categories, based on the price for a standard double room with bath:

$$$ **Higher Priced**—Most rooms €120 or more.
$$ **Moderately Priced**—Most rooms between €80–120.
$ **Lower Priced**—Most rooms €80 or less.

Bruges is most crowded Friday and Saturday evenings from Easter through October, with July and August weekends being the worst. Many hotels charge a bit more on Friday and Saturday, and won't let you stay just one night if it's a Saturday.

Hotels

$$$ Hotel Heritage offers 24 rooms, with chandeliers that seem hung especially for you, in a solid and completely modernized old building. Tastefully decorated and offering all the amenities, it's one of those places that does everything just right yet still feels warm and inviting (Db-€182, superior Db-€228, deluxe Db-€275, singles take a double for nearly the same cost, suites available, includes breakfast, skipping their fine breakfast saves €15 per person, non-smoking, air-con, elevator, free Internet access in lobby and €2/hr Internet access in rooms, sauna, tanning bed, fitness room, bike rental for €6.50/half-day, Niklaas Desparsstraat 11, a block north of Market Square, tel. 050/444-444, fax 050/444-440, www.hotel-heritage.com, info@hotel-heritage.com, run by cheery and hardworking Johan and Isabelle).

$$$ Hotel Egmond is a creaky mansion quietly located in the middle of the idyllic Minnewater. Its eight 18th-century rooms are plain, with small modern baths shoehorned in, and the guests-only garden is just waiting for a tea party. This hotel is ideal for romantics who want a countryside setting—where you sleep in a park, not in the city (Sb-€92, small twin Db-€112, larger Db-€120–130, Tb-€150, cash only, parking-€10/day, Minnewater 15, tel. 050/341-445, fax 050/342-940, www.egmond.be, info@egmond.be).

$$$ Crowne Plaza Hotel Brugge is the most modern, comfortable, and central hotel option. With 96 air-conditioned rooms, it's just like a fancy American hotel (Db-€254–276, higher prices are for view rooms, prices drop as low as €200 on weekdays and

Bruges Hotels

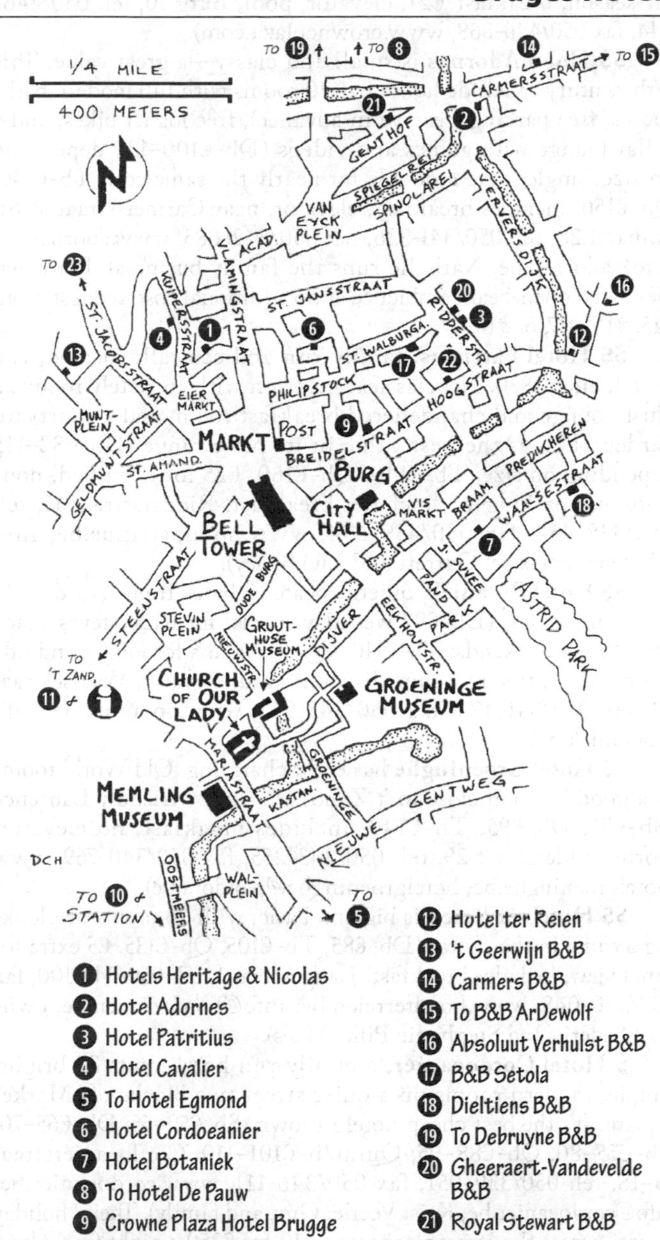

off-season, breakfast-€21, elevator, pool, Burg 10, tel. 050/446-844, fax 050/446-868, www.crowneplaza.com).

$$ Hotel Adornes is small and classy—a great value. This 17th-century canalside house has 20 rooms with full modern bathrooms, free parking (reserve in advance), free loaner bikes, and a cellar lounge with games and videos (Db-€100–130 depending on size, singles take a double for nearly the same cost, Tb-€140, Qb-€150, includes breakfast, elevator, near Carmersstraat at St. Annarei 26, tel. 050/341-336, fax 050/342-085, www.adornes.be, info@adornes.be, Nathalie runs the family business). For canal views and open-beam ambience at no additional cost, request room #15, #16, #17, or #18.

$$ Hotel Patritius, family-run and centrally located, is a grand, circa-1830, Neoclassical mansion with 16 stately rooms, a plush lounge and chandeliered breakfast room, and a courtyard garden. This is the best value in its price range (Db-€82–115 depending on size, Tb-€140, Qb-€160, €25 for extra bed, non-smoking, parking-€5, includes breakfast, Riddersstraat 11, tel. 050/338-454, fax 050/339-634, www.hotelpatritius.be, info@hotelpatritius.be, Garrett and Elvi Spaey).

$$ Hotel Botaniek, quietly located a block from Astrid Park, rents nine rooms (Db-€92 weekday special for Rick Steves' readers, €98 on weekends; Tb-€110, Qb-€120, less for longer and off-season stays, free museum-discount card, elevator, Waalsestraat 23, tel. 050/341-424, fax 050/345-939, www.botaniek.be, info@botaniek.be).

Bruges

$$ Hotel Groeninghe has eight charming, Old World rooms in a good location close to 't Zand. It's run by friendly Laurence (Sb-€75, Db-€95, Tb-€140, includes breakfast, no elevator, Korte Vulderstraat 29, tel. 050/343-255, fax 050/340-769, www.hotelgroeninghe.be, hotelgroeninghe@pandora.be).

$$ Hotel ter Reien is big and basic, with 26 rooms overlooking a canal in the center (Db-€85, Tb-€105, Qb-€135, €5 extra for canal view, includes breakfast, Langestraat 1, tel. 050/349-100, fax 050/340-048, www.hotelterreien.be, info@hotelterreien.be, owners Diederik and Stephanie Pille-Maes).

$ Hotel Cordoeanier, a family-run hotel, rents 22 bright, simple, modern rooms on a quiet street two blocks off Market Square. It's the best cheap hotel in town (Sb-€59–65, Db-€65–70, Tb-€75–80, Qb-€88–95, Quint/b-€101–110, Cordoeanierstraat 16–18, tel. 050/339-051, fax 050/346-111, www.cordoeanier.be, info@cordoeanier.be; Kris, Veerle, Guy, and family). Their "holiday house" across the street sleeps up to 10 for €250 a night (includes a kitchen; cheaper for longer stays).

$ Hotel Cavalier, with more stairs than character, rents eight decent rooms and serves a hearty buffet breakfast in a once-royal setting (Sb-€52, Db-€64, Tb-€78, Qb-€85, two lofty "backpackers' doubles" on fourth floor-€42 or €47, includes breakfast, Kuipersstraat 25, tel. 050/330-207, fax 050/347-199, www.hotelcavalier.be, run by friendly Viviane de Clerck).

$ Hotel de Pauw is tall, skinny, and family-run, with eight straightforward rooms, on a quiet street next to a church (Sb-€60, Db-€65–70, renovated Db-€75, free and easy street parking or pay garage, Sint Gilliskerkhof 8, tel. 050/337-118, fax 050/345-140, www.hoteldepauw.be, info@hoteldepauw.be, Philippe and Hilde).

$ Hotel Nicolas feels like an old-time boarding house that missed Bruges' affluence bandwagon. Its 14 big, plain rooms are a good value, and the location is ideal—on a quiet street a block off Market Square (Sb-€50, Db-€60–62, Tb-€73, includes breakfast, Niklaas Desparsstraat 9, tel. 050/335-502, hotel.nicolas@telenet.be).

Near the Train Station: **$ Hotel 't Keizershof** is a dollhouse of a hotel that lives by its motto, "Spend a night...not a fortune." It's simple and tidy, with seven small, cheery, old-time rooms split between two floors, with a shower and toilet on each (S-€25, D-€40, T-€62, Q-€72, includes breakfast, cash only, free and easy parking, laundry service-€7.50, Oostmeers 126, a block in front of station, tel. 050/338-728, www.hotelkeizershof.be, info@hotelkeizershof.be, Stefaan and Hilde).

Bed-and-Breakfasts

These B&Bs, run by people who enjoy their work, offer a better value than hotels. Most families rent out their entire top floor—generally three rooms and a small sitting area. And most are mod and stylish, in medieval shells. Each is central, with lots of stairs and €60 doubles you'd pay €100 for in a hotel. Most places charge extra for one-night stays. Parking is generally easy on the street (pay 9:00–19:00, free overnight).

$ Absoluut Verhulst is a great, modern-feeling B&B in a 400-year-old house, run by friendly Frieda and Benno (Sb-€50, Db-€80, huge and lofty suite-€110 for two, €130 for three, and €150 for four, one-night stays pay €10 more, cash only, five-minute walk east of Market Square at Verbrand Nieuwland 1, tel. & fax 050/334-515, www.b-bverhulst.com, b-b.verhulst@pandora.be).

$ B&B Setola, run by Lut and Bruno Setola, offers three modern rooms and a spacious breakfast/living room in their house (Sb-€50–65, Db-€60–75, Tb-€80–95, Qb-€100–115, one-night stays pay €10 more, cash only, non-smoking, five-minute walk from Market Square, Sint Walburgastraat 12, tel. 050/334-977, fax 050/332-551, www.bedandbreakfast-bruges.com, setola@bedandbreakfast-bruges.com).

$ Koen and Annemie Dieltiens are a friendly couple who enjoy getting to know their guests while sharing a wealth of information on Bruges. You'll eat a hearty breakfast around a big table in their comfortable house (Sb-€50–55, Db-€60–65, Tb-€80–85, cash only, non-smoking, Waalse Straat 40, three blocks southeast of Burg Square, tel. 050/334-294, fax 050/335-230, www.bedandbreakfastbruges.be, dieltiens@bedandbreakfastbruges.be).

$ Debruyne B&B, run by Marie-Rose and her architect husband, Ronny, offers artsy, original decor (check out the elephant-size white doors—Ronny's design) and genuine warmth. If Gothic is getting old, this is refreshingly modern (Sb-€55, Db-€60, Tb-€80, one-night stays pay €10 more, cash only, non-smoking, free Internet access in lobby, seven-minute walk north of Market Square, two blocks from the little church at Lange Raamstraat 18, tel. 050/347-606, fax 050/340-285, www.bedandbreakfastbruges.com, marie.debruyne@advalvas.be).

$ Paul and Roos Gheeraert-Vandevelde live in a Neoclassical mansion and rent three huge, bright, comfy rooms (Sb-€60, Db-€65, Tb-€85, €5 less off-season, two-night minimum stay required, cash only, strictly non-smoking, fridges in rooms, free Wi-Fi, free Internet access in lobby, Riddersstraat 9, five-minute walk east of Market Square, tel. 050/335-627, fax 050/345-201, www.bb-bruges.be, bb-bruges@skynet.be).

$ 't Geerwijn B&B, run by Chris de Loof, offers homey rooms in the old center. Check out the fun, lofty A-frame room upstairs (Ds/Db-€60, Tb-€75, pleasant breakfast room and a royal lounge, cash only, non-smoking, Geerwijnstraat 14, tel. 050/340-544, fax 050/343-721, www.geerwijn.be, chris.deloof@scarlet.be).

$ Carmers B&B, owned by the Van Nevel family, rents three attractive rooms with built-in beds on the top floor of a 16th-century house (D-€55, Db-€65, one-night stays pay €10 more, third person-€17, parking-€7, cash only, non-smoking, 10-minute walk from Market Square, or bus #4 or #14 from train station or Market Square to Carmersbridge, Carmersstraat 13, tel. 050/346-860, fax 050/347-616, www.brugesbb.com, robert.vannevel@advalvas.be). Affable Robert, who works at the Memling Museum, enthusiastically shares the culture and history of Bruges with his guests.

$ B&B ArDewolf is a family-friendly place with a boarding-house feel, run by Nicole and Arnold. It's in a stately, quiet neighborhood at the far edge of the old town, near the windmills and moat (S-€35, D-€40–45, T-€60, Q-€70, Quint/b-€80, cash only, two free parking spaces—but reserve ahead of time, Oostproosse 9, tel. 050/338-366, www.ardewolf.be, info@ardewolf.be). This is good for drivers, but a long walk from the center. From the train station, take bus #4 to Sasplein. Walk to the path behind the first windmill and turn left on Oostproosse.

$ Royal Stewart B&B, run by Scottish Maggie and her husband, Gilbert, has three thoughtfully decorated rooms in a quiet, almost cloistered 17th-century house that was inhabited by nuns until 1953 (S-€45, D/Db-€57, Tb-€80, cash only, non-smoking, pleasant breakfast rooms, Genthof 25–27, five-minute walk from Market Square, tel. & fax 050/337-918, www.royalstewart.be, r.stewart@pandora.be).

Hostels

Bruges has several good hostels offering beds for around €10–12 in two- to eight-bed rooms. Breakfast is about €3 extra. The American-style **Charlie Rockets** hostel and bar is the liveliest and most central. The ground floor feels like a 19th-century sports bar, with a foosball-and-movie-posters party ambience. Upstairs is an industrial-strength pile of hostel dorms (75 beds, €16 per bed with sheets, 4–6 beds per room, D-€45, lockers, Hoogstraat 19, tel. 050/330-660, fax 050/343-630, www.charlierockets.com). Other small, loose, and central places are **Snuffel Backpacker Hostel** (€14–18, sheets-€2, Ezelstraat 47, tel. 050/333-133, www.snuffel.be) and the funky **Passage** (€14, 4–7 beds per room, D-€45, Db-€60, prices include sheets and breakfast, Dweerstraat 26, tel. 050/340-232, www.passagebruges.com).

EATING

Bruges' specialties include mussels cooked a variety of ways (one order can feed two), fish dishes, grilled meats, and french fries. Don't eat before 19:30 unless you like eating alone. Tax and service are always included.

You'll find plenty of affordable, touristy restaurants on floodlit squares and along dreamy canals. Bruges feeds 3.5 million tourists a year, and most are seduced by a high-profile location. These can be fine experiences for the magical setting and views, but the quality of food and service is low. I wouldn't blame you for eating at one of these places, but I won't recommend any. I prefer the candle-cool bistros that flicker on back streets.

Rock Fort is a chic, eight-table spot with a modern, fresh coziness and a high-powered respect for good food. Two young chefs, Peter Laloo and Hermes Vanliefde, give their French cuisine a creative and gourmet twist. Reservations are required for dinner but not lunch. This place is a winner (€11 Mon–Fri lunch special with coffee, beautifully presented €15–20 dinner plates, open Mon–Fri 12:00–14:30 & 18:30–23:00, closed Sat–Sun, great pastas and salads, Langestraat 15, tel. 050/334-113). They also run the Barsalon restaurant next door (listed below).

Barsalon Tapas Bar, more than a tapas bar, is the brainchild of Peter Laloo from Rock Fort (listed above), allowing him to spread his creative cooking energy. This long, skinny slice of

Bruges Restaurants

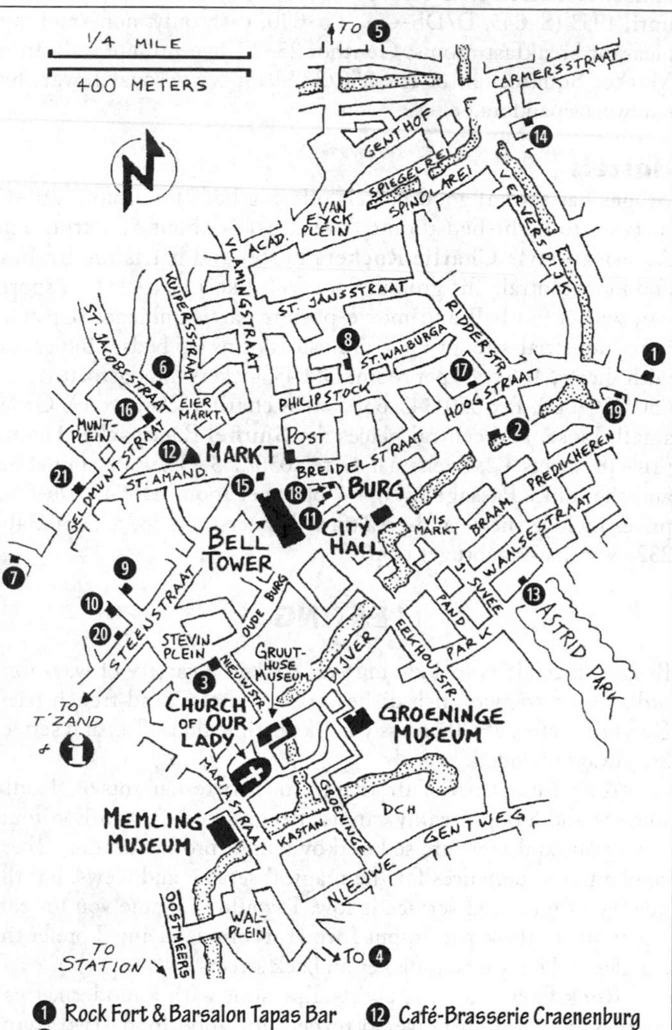

1. Rock Fort & Barsalon Tapas Bar
2. Rest. Chez Olivier
3. Rest. de Koetse
4. To Bistro de Bekoring
5. To Tom's Diner
6. Bistro in den Wittenkop
7. The Flemish Pot
8. Lotus Vegetarian Restaurant
9. The Hobbit
10. 't Brugs Beertje Pub
11. De Garre Pub
12. Café-Brasserie Craenenburg
13. L'Estaminet Restaurant
14. Herberg Vlissinghe Pub
15. Frituur Stands
16. Pickles Frituur
17. Pili Pili Restaurant
18. Restaurant Hennon
19. De Torre Tea Room & Rest.
20. Tea Room Laurent
21. Delhaize-Proxy Supermarket & Da Vinci Ice Cream

L.A. thrives late into the evening with Bruges' beautiful people. Choose between the long bar, comfy stools, and bigger tables in back. Come early for fewer crowds. The playful menu comes with €6 "tapas" dishes taking you from Spain to Japan (three dishes fill two hungry travelers) and more elaborate €14 plates—and don't overlook their daily "suggestions" board with some special wines by the glass and a "teaser" sampler plate of desserts. Barsalon shares the same kitchen, hours, and dressy local clientele as the adjacent Rock Fort.

Restaurant Chez Olivier, with 10 classy, white-tableclothed tables, is considered the best fancy French cuisine splurge in town. While delicate Anne serves, her French husband, Olivier, is busy cooking up whatever he found freshest that day. While you can order à la carte, it's wise to go with the recommended, daily fixed-price meals (€34 for three-course lunch, €50 for three-course dinner, €58 for four-course dinner, wine adds €15–20, Mon–Wed and Fri–Sat 12:00–13:30 & 19:00–21:30; closed Sat afternoon, Sun, and Thu; reserve for dinner, Meestraat 9, tel. 050/333-659).

De Torrc, a tea room and restaurant, has a fresh interior and a scenic, shady, canalside terrace. I'd eat here only to be along a canal (€10 three-course lunch, €22–35 fixed-price dinners, Thu–Tue 10:00–22:00, closed Wed, Langestraat 8, tel. 050/342-946).

Pili Pili is a mod and inviting pasta place, where Reinout and Tom prepare and serve 10 different pastas and great salads at very good prices. The place is clean, low-key, and brimming with quality (€9 lunch plate with wine, €12.50 pasta and wine dinner, Thu–Tue 12:00–14:30 & 18:00–22:30, closed Sun and Wed, Hoogstraat 17, tel. 050/491-149).

Restaurant de Koetse is a good bet for central, affordable, quality, local-style food. The feeling is traditional, yet fun and kid-friendly. The cuisine is Belgian and French, with an emphasis on grilled meat, seafood, and mussels (€28.50 three-course meals, €20 plates include vegetables and a salad, Fri–Wed 12:00–14:30 & 18:00–22:00, closed Thu, non-smoking section, Oude Burg 31, tel. 050/337-680).

Bistro de Bekoring, cute, candlelit, and Gothic, fills two almshouses with people thankful for good food. Rotund and friendly Chef Roland and his wife, Gerda, love to tempt people—as the name of their bistro implies. They serve traditional Flemish food (especially eel and beer-soaked stew) from a small menu to people who like holding hands as they dine (€12 weekday lunch, €32 dinners, Wed–Sat 12:00–13:30 and from 18:30, closed Sun evening, and Mon–Tue, out past the Begijnhof at Arsenaalstraat 53, tel. 050/344-157).

Bistro in den Wittenkop, very Flemish, is a cluttered, laid-back, old-time place specializing in the local favorites. While Lieve cooks, her husband Daniel serves in a cool-and-jazzy, candlelit Flemish ambience (€16–25 main courses, Tue–Sat 12:00–14:00 & 18:00–21:30, closed Sun–Mon, terrace in back in summer, Sint Jakobsstraat 14, tel. 050/332-059).

The Flemish Pot (a.k.a. The Little Pancake House) is a hard-working eatery serving up traditional peasant-style Flemish meals. They crank out pancake meals (savory and sweet) and homemade *wafels* for lunch. Then, at 18:00, enthusiastic chefs Mario and Rik stow their waffle irons and pull out a traditional menu of vintage Flemish plates (€25 fixed-price dinners, Fri–Wed 12:00–22:00, closed Thu, family-friendly, just off Geldmuntstraat at Helmstraat 3, tel. 050/340-086).

Lotus Vegetarian Restaurant serves serious lunch plates (€9 *plat du jour* offered daily), salads, and homemade chocolate cake in a smoke-free, bustling, and upscale setting without a trace of tie-dye (Mon–Sat 11:45–14:00, closed Sun, just off north of Burg at Wapenmakersstraat 5, tel. 050/331-078).

The Hobbit, featuring an entertaining menu, is always busy with happy eaters. For a swinging deal, try the all-you-can-eat spareribs with salad for €14. It's nothing fancy, just good, basic food in a fun, traditional grill house (daily 18:00–24:00, family-friendly, Kemelstraat 8–10, tel. 050/335-520).

Tom's Diner, a "bistro eetcafé," glows with a love of food in a quiet, cobbled residential area a 10-minute walk from the center. Young chef Tom gives traditional dishes a delightful modern twist, and your meal comes gorgeously presented in a "high food" style. The "diner" comes with Creedence Clearwater Revival soft rock, rusty 1960s kitsch knickknacks under 16th-century beams, and friendly and helpful service (hearty yet delicate €15 plates, Thu–Mon 18:00–24:00, closed Tue–Wed, reserve on weekends, north of Market Square near Sint-Gilliskerk at West-Gistelhof 23, tel. 050/333-382).

Market Square Restaurants: Most tourists seem to be eating on Market Square with the bell tower high overhead and horse carriages clip-clopping by. The square is ringed by tourist traps with aggressive waiters expert at getting you to consume more than you realized. Still, if you order smartly, you can have a memorable meal or drink here on one of the finest squares in Europe at a reasonable price. Consider **Café-Brasserie Craenenburg,** with a straightforward menu, where you can get pasta and beer for €10 or €12 and spend all the time you want ogling the magic of Bruges (daily 7:30–24:00, Markt 16, tel. 050/333-402).

Bars Offering Light Meals, Beer, and Ambience

Stop into one of the city's atmospheric bars for a light meal or a drink with great Bruges ambience.

The **'t Brugs Beertje** has a huge selection of Belgian beers, but it's smoky. While any pub or restaurant carries the basic beers, you'll find a selection here of more than 300 types, including brews to suit any season. They serve light meals, including pâté, spaghetti, and sandwiches, or a traditional cheese plate (five cheeses, bread, and salad for €9; Thu–Tue 16:00–24:00, closed Wed, Kemelstraat 5, tel. 050/339-616, run by fun-loving manager Daisy).

De Garre is another good place to gain an appreciation of the Belgian beer culture. Rather than a noisy pub scene, it has a dressy, sit-down-and-focus-on-your-friend-and-the-fine-beer vibe (great selection of 150 beers, daily 12:00–24:00, additional seating up tiny staircase, off Breidelstraat between Burg and Markt, on tiny Garre alley, tel. 050/341-029). Don't come here expecting to eat anything more than grilled cheese sandwiches...this is for beer and camaraderie.

L'Estaminet is a youthful, brown-café-feeling, jazz-filled eatery. Almost intimidating in its lack of tourists, it's popular with local students who come for the Tolkien-chic ambience and hearty €7 spaghetti and good salads. It has more beer than wine, a super-characteristic interior, and a relaxed patio facing the peaceful Astrid Park under an all-weather canopy (Tue–Wed and Fri–Sun 11:30–24:00, Thu 14:00–24:00, closed Mon, Park 5, tel. 050/330-916).

Herberg Vlissinghe is the oldest pub in town (1515), where Bruno keeps things simple and laid-back, serving just hot snacks (lasagna and grilled cheese sandwiches), but great beer in the best old-time tavern atmosphere in town. This must have been the Dutch Masters' rec room. The garden outside comes with a *boules* court—free for guests to watch or play (Wed–Sun open from 11:00 on, closed Mon–Tue, Blekersstraat 2, tel. 050/343-737).

Fries, Fast Food, and Picnics

Local french fries *(frites)* are a treat. Proud and traditional *frituurs* serve tubs of fries and various local-style shish kebabs. Belgians dip their *frites* in mayonnaise, but ketchup is there for the Yankees (along with spicier sauces). For a quick, cheap, and scenic meal, hit a *frituur* and sit on the steps or benches overlooking Market Square (convenience benches are about 50 yards past the post office).

***Market Square* Frituur:** Twin take-away french fries carts are on Market Square at the base of the bell tower (daily 10:00–24:00).

Pickles Frituur, a block off Market Square, is handy for sit-down fries. Its forte is greasy, fast, deep-fried Flemish corn dogs. The "menu 2" comes with three traditional gut bombs: shrimp, chicken, and "spicy gypsie" (daily 11:30–24:00, at the corner of Geldmuntstraat and Sint Jakobstraat, tel. 050/337-957).

Delhaize-Proxy Supermarket is ideal for picnics (push-button produce pricer lets you buy as little as one mushroom, Mon–Sat 9:00–19:00, closed Sun, 3 blocks off the Market Square on Geldmuntstraat). For midnight munchies, you'll find Indian-run corner grocery stores.

Belgian Waffles and Ice Cream

While Americans think of "Belgian" waffles for breakfast, the Belgians (who don't eat waffles or pancakes for breakfast) think of *wafels* as Liège-style (dense, sweet, eaten plain, and heated up) and Brussels-style (lighter, often with powdered sugar or whipped cream and strawberries, served in teahouses only in the afternoons 14:00–18:00). You'll see waffles sold at restaurants and take-away stands.

For good Liège-style *wafels* (€2), stop by **Restaurant Hennon**—their waffles and other dishes are made with fresh ingredients (€2.50–6 plates, Tue–Sun 9:00–18:30, closed Mon, cash only, between Market Square and Burg at Breidelstraat 16). You can also try **Tea Room Laurent** for waffles and pancakes (€5–10 plates, Steenstraat 79) and the **Flemish Pot** (listed above).

Da Vinci Ice Cream, the local favorite for good homemade ice cream, has creative flavors and a great, fun ambience. As you approach, you'll see a line of happy lickers. Before ordering, ask to sample the Ferrero Rocher (chocolate, nuts, and crunchy cookie) and Bacio Bianco—rice with white chocolate (daily 10:00–24:00, Geldmuntstraat 34, run by Sylvia from Austria).

Nightlife

Herberg Vlissinghe and **De Garre,** listed above, are great places to just nurse a beer.

Charlie Rockets is an American-style bar—lively and central—with foosball games, darts, and five pool tables in the inviting back room. It also runs a youth hostel upstairs and therefore is filled with a young, international crowd (a block off Market Square at Hoogstraat 19). Nearby is **De Versteende Nacht Jazzcafe,** another youthful, more local hangout devoted to music and drinking (Langestraat 11).

Nighttime Bike Ride: Great as these pubs are, my favorite way to spend a late summer twilight evening in Bruges is on a rental bike, savoring the cobbled wonders of its back streets, far from the touristic commotion.

Evening Carillon Concerts: The tiny courtyard behind the bell tower has a few benches where people can enjoy the free carillon concerts (generally Mon, Wed, and Sat at 21:00 in the summer; schedule posted on the wall).

TRANSPORTATION CONNECTIONS

Trains

From Bruges by Train to: Brussels (2/hr, usually at :31 and :57, 1 hr, €11.80), **Ghent** (2/hr, 40 min), **Ostende** (3/hr, 15 min), **Köln** (6/day, 3.5 hrs), **Paris** (hourly via Brussels, 2.5 hrs, must pay supplement of €14.50 second class, €22 first class—even with a railpass), **Amsterdam** (hourly, 3.5 hrs, transfer in Antwerp or Brussels), **Amsterdam's Schiphol Airport** (hourly, 3.5 hrs, transfer in Antwerp or Brussels, €38). Train info: tel. 050/302-424.

Trains from London: Bruges is an ideal "Welcome to Europe" stop after London. Take the Eurostar train from London to Brussels (9/day, 2.75 hrs), then transfer, backtracking to Bruges (2/hr, 1 hr, entire trip is covered by same Eurostar ticket).

Full-fare one-way tickets cost $277 for second class and $380 for first class (full-fare tickets are exchangeable and fully refundable, even after your departure date). Passholders, seniors, and youths have several different prices. For instance, second class ticket prices start at $81, $123, or $142 for travelers with a railpass, while $94, $124, or $149 are the best rates without a pass. For each train departure, the lowest prices in each category sell out first.

You can check and book fares by phone or online in the US (order online at www.ricksteves.com/rail/eurostar.htm, prices listed in dollars; or order by phone at US tel. 800-EUROSTAR) or in Belgium (www.eurostar.com, prices listed in euros; Belgian tel. 02/528-2828). While tickets are usually cheaper if purchased in the US, fares offered in Europe follow different discount rules—so it can be worth it to check www.eurostar.com before purchasing. If you buy from a US company, you'll pay for ticket delivery in the US. In Europe, you can buy your Eurostar ticket at any major train station in any country or at any travel agency that handles train tickets (expect a booking fee).

Trains to London leave from platforms #1 and #2 at Brussels Midi. Arrive 30 minutes early to get your ticket validated, and your luggage and passport checked by British authorities (similar to an airport check-in for an international flight).

By Bus to: London (cost can vary, but generally €50 one-way, €75 round-trip, about 9 hrs, Eurolines tel. 02/203-0707 in Brussels, www.eurolines.com).

THE CZECH REPUBLIC

PRAGUE

(Praha)

It's amazing what nearly two decades of freedom can do. Prague has always been historic. Now it's fun, too. No other place in Europe has become so popular so quickly. And for good reason: Prague—the only Central European capital to escape the bombs of the last century's wars—is one of Europe's best-preserved cities. It's filled with sumptuous Art Nouveau facades, offers tons of cheap Mozart and Vivaldi, and brews the best beer in Europe. Beyond its architecture and traditional culture, it's an explosion of pent-up entrepreneurial energy jumping for joy after 40 years of communist rule. Its low prices can cause you to jump for joy, too.

Planning Your Time

Prague demands a minimum of two full days (with 3 nights, or 2 nights and a night train). From Budapest, Warsaw, or Kraków, it's a handy night train. From Munich, Berlin, and Vienna, Prague is about a six-hour train ride by day (you also have the option of a longer night train from Munich).

With two days in Prague, I'd spend a morning seeing the castle and a morning in the Jewish Quarter. Use your afternoons for loitering around the Old Town, Charles Bridge, and the Little Quarter, and split your nights between beer halls and live music. Keep in mind that Jewish Quarter sights close on Saturday.

ORIENTATION

Locals call their town "Praha" (PRAH-hah). It's big, with 1.2 million people, but focus on its relatively compact old center during a quick visit. As you wander, take advantage of brown street signs

Prague

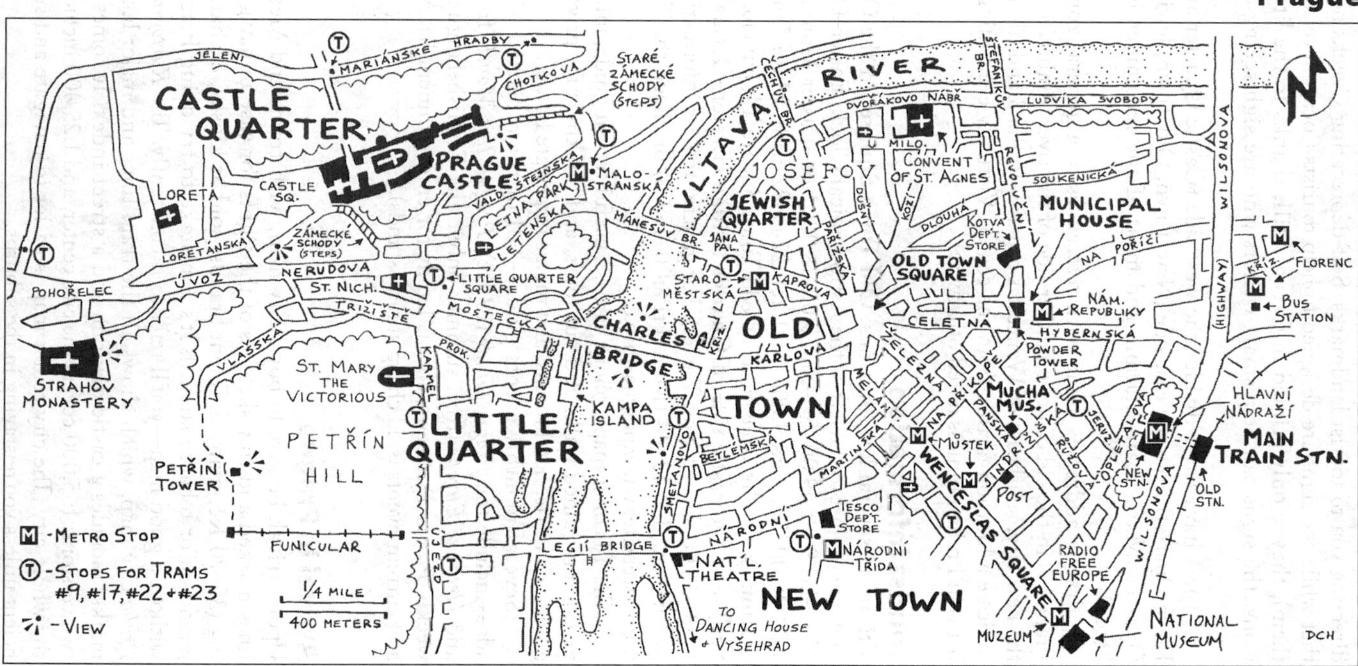

Castle Quarter
Prague Castle
Loreta
Castle Sq.
Strahov Monastery
Pohořelec
Úvoz
Loretánská
Jelení
Mariánské Hradby
Chotkova
Staré Zámecké Schody (Steps)
Zámecké Schody (Steps)
Nerudova
St. Nich.
Little Quarter Square
Tržiště
Mostecká
Vlašská
St. Mary the Victorious
Karmel
Prok.
Petřín Hill
Petřín Tower
Little Quarter
Kampa Island
Funicular
Újezd
Legií Bridge
Valdštejnská
Letná Park
Letenská
Malostranská
Mánesův Br.
Vltava River
Čechův Br.
Štefánikův Br.
Dvořákovo Nábř
Josefov
Jewish Quarter
Jana Pal.
Staroměstská
Kaprova
Pařížská
Dušní
Kozí
U Milo.
Convent of St. Agnes
Ludvíka Svobody
Revoluční
Soukenická
Municipal House
Dlouhá
Kotva Dep't. Store
Old Town Square
Na Poříčí
Nám. Republiky
Celetná
Hybernská
Powder Tower
Charles Bridge
Křiž.
Old Town
Karlova
Melant.
Železná
Na Příkopě
Mucha Mus.
Panská
Jindřišská
Jeruz.
Růžová
Opletalova
Smetanovo
Betlémská
Martinská
Můstek
Post
Wenceslas Square
Národní
Tesco Dep't. Store
Národní Třída
Nat'l. Theatre
To Dancing House + Vyšehrad
New Town
Radio Free Europe
Muzeum
National Museum
Wilsonova
(Highway)
Křiž.
Florenc
Bus Station
Hlavní Nádraží
Main Train Stn.
New Stn.
Old Stn.
M - Metro Stop
T - Stops for Trams #9, #17, #22 + #23
- View
1/4 mile
400 meters
DCH

directing you to tourist landmarks. Self-deprecating Czechs note that while the signs are designed to help tourists (locals never use them), they're only printed in Czech. Still, thanks to the little icons, the signs can help smart visitors who are sightseeing on foot.

The Vltava River divides the west side (Castle Quarter and Little Quarter) from the east side (New Town, Old Town, Jewish Quarter, Main Train Station, and most of the recommended hotels).

Prague addresses come with references to a general zone. Praha 1 is in the old center on either side of the river. Praha 2 is in the new city, southeast of Wenceslas Square. Praha 3 and higher indicate a location farther from the center. Virtually everything I list is in Praha 1 (unless noted otherwise).

Tourist Information

TIs are at several key locations: **Old Town Square** (in the Old Town Hall, just to the left of the Astronomical Clock; Easter–Oct Mon–Fri 9:00–19:00, Sat–Sun 9:00–18:00; Nov–Easter Mon–Fri 9:00–18:00, Sat–Sun 9:00–17:00; tel. 224-482-018), **Main Train Station** (generally same hours as Old Town Square TI, but closed Sun), and the castle side of **Charles Bridge** (Easter–Oct daily 10:00–18:00, closed Nov–Easter). For general tourist information in English, dial 12444 (Mon–Fri 8:00–19:00) or check the TIs' useful website: www.prague-info.cz.

The TIs offer maps, phone cards, a useful transit guide, information on guided walks and bus tours, and bookings for private guides, concerts, hotel rooms, and rooms in private homes.

Several monthly events guides—all of them packed with ads—include the *Prague Guide* (29 Kč), *Prague This Month* (free), and *Heart of Europe* (free, summer only). The English-language weekly *Prague Post* newspaper is handy for entertainment listings and current events (sold cheap at newsstands).

Arrival in Prague

Upon arrival, be sure to buy a city map, with trams and Metro lines marked and tiny sketches of the sights for ease in navigating (30–70 Kč, many different brands; sold at kiosks, exchange windows, or tobacco stands). It's a mistake to try doing Prague without a good map—you'll refer to it constantly. The *Kartografie Praha* city map, which shows all the tram lines and major landmarks, includes a castle diagram and a street index. It comes in two versions: 1:15,000 covers the city center, and 1:25,000 includes the whole city. The city center map is easier to navigate and sufficient unless you're staying in the suburbs.

By Train

Prague has two train stations. The Main Station (Hlavní Nádraží) serves all trains from Kraków, Frankfurt, Munich, and Salzburg; some trains from Budapest and Vienna; and most trains within the Czech Republic. The secondary station (Nádraží Holešovice) handles all trains from Berlin, some trains from Vienna and Budapest, and the high-speed SC Pendolino train to the eastern Czech Republic.

Upon arrival, get money. The stations have ATMs (best rates) and exchange bureaus (rates are generally bad, but can vary—compare by asking at two windows what you'll get for $100, but keep in mind that many of the windows are run by the same company). Then buy your map and confirm your departure plans. Those arriving on an international train may be met at the tracks by room hustlers, trying to snare tourists for cheap rooms. These can be a good value.

Main Station (Hlavní Nádraží): This station's low-ceilinged hall contains a fascinating mix of travelers, kiosks, gamblers, loitering teenagers, and older riffraff. The creepy station ambience is the work of communist architects, who expanded a classy building to make it just big, painting it the compulsory dreary gray with reddish trim. An ATM is near the subway entrance. The station's baggage-storage counter is reportedly safer than the lockers.

At the Wasteels travel office, Jaroslav and Jaromír offer a helpful and friendly service. You can drop by here upon arrival to get a transit ticket without using the ATM (they take euro coins) and confirm and buy your outbound train tickets. They can help you figure out train connections, and sell train tickets to anywhere in Europe—with domestic stopovers if you like—along with tickets for fast local trains and cheap phone cards (no commission; Mon–Fri 9:00–17:00 or later, Sat 9:00–16:00, closed Sun, tel. 972-241-954, www.wasteels.cz). You can even leave your bags here for a short time.

The information office for Czech Railways (downstairs on the left) is less helpful, and the ticket windows downstairs don't give schedule information. The windows marked *vnitrostátní* sell tickets within the Czech Republic.

The AVE office on the main floor books rooms in hotels and pensions, and sells taxi vouchers for trips into town at double the fair rate (daily 6:00–23:00; with your back to the tracks, walk down to the orange ceiling and past the "Meeting Point"—their office is in the left corner by the exit to the taxis; tel. 251-551-011, fax 251-555-156, www.avetravel.cz, ave@avetravel.cz).

If you're killing time at the station (or for a wistful glimpse of a more genteel age), go upstairs into the Art Nouveau hall. Here, under an elegant dome, you can sip coffee, enjoy music from the

1920s, watch boy prostitutes looking for work, and see new arrivals spilling into the city.

The station was originally named for Emperor Franz Josef. Later, it was renamed for President Woodrow Wilson (see the commemorative plaque in the main exit hall leading away from the tracks), because his promotion of self-determination led to the creation of the free state of Czechoslovakia in 1918. Under the communists (who weren't big fans of Wilson), it was bluntly renamed simply Hlavní Nádraží—"Main Station."

Even though the Main Station is basically downtown, it can be a little tricky to get to your hotel. The biggest challenge is that the **taxi** drivers at the train station are a gang of no-neck mafia thugs who wait around to charge an arriving tourist five times the regular rate. To get an honest cabbie, I'd walk a few blocks and hail one off the street; pay a premium for a voucher at the AVE office (see above); or call AAA Taxi (tel. 233-113-311). A taxi should get you to your hotel for no more than 200 Kč (see "Getting Around Prague," page 173). A better option may be to take the **Metro.** It's dirt-cheap and easy, with very frequent departures. Once you're on the Metro, you'll wonder why you'd bother with a taxi (inside the train station arrival hall, look for the red *M* with two directions: Háje or Ládví). To get to hotels in the Old Town, catch a Háje-bound train to the Muzeum stop, then transfer to the green line (direction: Dejvická) and get off at either Můstek or Staroměstská; these stops straddle the Old Town. Or, if your hotel is close enough, consider **walking** (Wenceslas Square, a downtown landmark, is less than a 10-minute walk away: Turn left out of the station and follow Wilsonova street to the huge National Museum).

Holešovice Station (Nádraží Holešovice): This station, slightly farther from the center, is suburban mellow. The main hall has all the services of the Main Station in a more compact area. On the left are international and local ticket windows (open 24 hours), an information office, and an AVE office for last-minute accommodations (daily 12:00–20:00, tel. 972-224-660). On the right is a little-frequented café with Internet access (1 Kč/min, daily 8:00–19:30). Two ATMs are immediately outside the first glass doors, and the Metro is 50 yards to the right (follow signs toward *Vstup,* which means "entrance"; it's three stops to Hlavní Nádraží—the Main Station—or four stops to the city-center Muzeum stop). Taxis and trams are outside to the right (allow 200 Kč for a cab to the center). The airport bus (45 Kč, 2/hr) is outside to the left.

By Plane

Prague's modern, tidy, low-key **Ruzyně Airport,** located 12 miles (about 30 min) west of the city center, is as user-friendly as any airport in Western Europe or the US. The airport has ATMs (avoid the change desks); desks promoting their transportation service (such as city transit and shuttle buses); kiosks selling city maps and phone cards; and a tourist service with few printed materials. Airport info: tel. 220-113-314, operator tel. 220-111-111.

Getting to and from the airport is easy. Leaving the airport, you have four options:

Dirt Cheap: Take bus #119 to the Dejvická Metro station, or #100 to the Zličín Metro station (20 min), then take the Metro into the center (20 Kč, info desk in airport arrival hall).

Cheap: Take the Čedaz minibus shuttle to Náměstí Republiky, across from Kotva department store (daily 5:30–21:30, 2/hr, pay 90 Kč directly to driver, info desk in arrival hall).

Moderate: Take a Čedaz minibus directly to your hotel, with a couple of stops likely en route (480 Kč for a group of up to 4 to the same hotel, tel. 220-114-286).

Expensive: Catch a taxi. Cabbies wait at the curb directly in front of the arrival hall. Airport taxi cabbies are honest but more expensive. Carefully confirm the complete price before getting in. It's a fixed rate of 600–700 Kč, with no meter.

Helpful Hints

Medical Help: A **24-hour pharmacy** is at Palackého 5 (a block from Wenceslas Square, tel. 224-946-982). There are two state **hospitals** in the center: the **General Hospital** (open daily 24 hours, right above Karlovo Náměstí at U Nemocnice 2, Praha 2, use entry G, tel. 224-962-564); and the **Na Františku Hospital** (on the embankment next to Hotel InterContinental, Na Františku 1, go to the main entrance, for English assistance call Mr. Hacker between 8:00–14:00, tel. 222-801-278 or tel. 222-801-371—serious problems only). The reception staff may not speak English, but doctors do. For better-than-standard assistance in English (including dental service), consider the top-quality **Hospital Na Homolce** (less than 1,000 Kč for an appointment, from 8:00–16:00 tel. 252-922-146; for after-hours emergencies tel. 257-211-111; bus #167 from Anděl Metro station, Roentgenova 2, Praha 5).

Internet Access: Internet cafés are well-advertised and scattered through the Old and New Towns. Consider **Bohemia Bagel** near the Jewish Quarter (see page 232). **Káva Káva Káva Coffee,** on the boundary between the Old and New Towns, is in the Platýz courtyard off Národní 37.

Bookstores: Prague has several enjoyable bookshops with English titles. **Anagram Bookshop,** in the Ungelt courtyard behind the Týn Church, sells books in English on a wide range of topics (Mon–Sat 10:00–20:00, Sun 10:00–19:00, Týn 4, tel.

Rip-Offs in Prague

Prague's new freedom comes with new scams. There's no particular risk of violent crime, but green, rich tourists do get taken by con artists. Simply be on guard, particularly when traveling on trains (thieves thrive on overnight trains), changing money (tellers with bad arithmetic and inexplicable pauses while counting back your change), dealing with taxis (see "By Taxi," page 176), paying in restaurants (see "Eating," page 226), and in seedy neighborhoods.

Anytime you pay for something, make a careful note of how much it costs, how much you're handing over, and how much you expect back. Count your change. Someone selling you a phone card marked 190 Kč might first tell you it's 790 Kč, hoping to pocket the difference. If you call her bluff, she'll pretend it never happened.

Plainclothes policemen "looking for counterfeit money" are con artists. Don't show them any cash or your wallet. If you're threatened with an inexplicable fine by a "policeman," conductor, or other official, you can walk away, scare him away by saying you'll need a receipt (which real officials are legally required to provide), or ask a passerby if the fine is legit. On the other hand, do not ignore the plainclothes inspectors on the Metro and trams who have shown you their badges.

Pickpockets can be little children, or adults dressed as professionals or even as tourists. They target Western visitors. Many thieves drape jackets over their arms to disguise busy fingers. Thieves work the crowded and touristy places in teams. They use mobile phones to coordinate their bumps and grinds. Be careful if anyone creates a commotion at the door of a Metro or tram car (especially around the Národní Třída and Vodičkova tram stops, or on the made-for-tourists trams #22 and #23)—it's a smokescreen for theft.

Car theft is also a big problem in Prague (many Western European car-rental companies don't allow their rentals to cross the Czech border). Never leave anything valuable in your car—not even in broad daylight on a busy street.

The sex clubs on Skořepka street, just south of Havelská Market, routinely rip off naive tourists and can be dangerous. They're filled mostly with Russian prostitutes and German and Asian guys. Lately this district has become the rage for British "stag" parties (happy to take cheap airline flights to get to cheap beer and cheap thrills).

This all sounds intimidating. But Prague is safe. It has its share of petty thieves and con artists, but very little violent crime. Don't be scared—just be alert.

224-895-737). **V Ráji,** next to Maisel Synagogue in the Jewish Quarter, is the flagship store of a small publishing house dedicated to books about Prague. They offer an assortment of photo publications, fairy tales, and maps (Maiselova 12, tel. 222-326-925). **Kiwi Map Store,** near Wenceslas Square, is one of Prague's best sources for maps (Mon–Fri 9:00–19:00, Sat 9:00–14:00, closed Sun, Jungmanova 23, tel. 224-948-455).

Laundry: A full-service laundry near most of the recommended hotels is at Karolíny Světlé 10 (200 Kč/8-pound load, wash and dry in 2 hours, Mon–Fri 7:30–19:00, closed Sat–Sun, 200 yards from Charles Bridge on Old Town side). Or surf the Internet while your undies tumble-dry at Korunní 14 (160 Kč/load wash and dry, Internet access-2 Kč/min, daily 8:00–20:00, near Náměstí Míru Metro stop, Praha 2).

Local Help: Magic Praha is a tiny travel service run by hardworking Lída Jánská. A charming Jill-of-all-trades who takes her clients' needs seriously, she's particularly helpful with accommodations and transfers throughout the Czech Republic, private tours, and side-trips to historic towns (tel. 235-325-170, mobile 604-207-225, www.magicpraha.cz, magicpraha@magicpraha.cz).

Car Rental: All of the biggies have offices in Prague (check each company's website, or ask at the TI). For a local alternative, consider **Alimex,** which features a wide variety of new vehicles (tel. 233-350-001, toll-free tel. 800-150-170, www.alimexcr.cz). The cheapest model, a Škoda Fabia, is a great value (450 Kč/day with basic insurance, plus 238 Kč/day for full theft and damage insurance; additional fees: 500-Kč tax for airport pickup, 357 Kč for delivery to your hotel; discounts if you book online, smart to reserve up to a week ahead in peak season). Note that the cheapest cars sometimes have giant ads pasted on the side. They have branches at the airport (daily 8:00–22:00) and near the Holešovice Station (daily 8:00–18:00).

Best Views: Enjoy the "Golden City of a Hundred Spires" during the early evening, when the light is warm and the colors are rich. Good viewpoints include the terrace at the Strahov Monastery (above the castle), the top of St. Vitus Cathedral (at the castle), the top of either tower on Charles Bridge, the Old Town Square clock tower (has an elevator), the Restaurant u Prince Terrace (see page 232), and the steps of the National Museum overlooking Wenceslas Square.

Getting Around Prague

You can walk nearly everywhere. But after you figure out the public transportation system, the Metro is slick, the trams fun, and the taxis quick and easy. For details, pick up the handy transit guide at the TI. City maps show the tram, bus, and Metro lines.

By Metro and Tram

Affordable and excellent public transit is perhaps the best legacy of the communist era (locals ride all month for 460 Kč). The three-line Metro system is handy and simple, but doesn't always get you right to the tourist sights (landmarks such as the Old Town Square and Prague Castle are several blocks from the nearest Metro stops). The trams rumble by every two or three minutes and take you just about anywhere.

Tickets: The trams and Metro work on the same cheap tickets:

- 20-minute basic ticket with limited transfer options *(základní s omezenou přestupností)*—14 Kč. With this ticket, no transfers are allowed on trams and buses, but on the Metro you can go up to five stops with one transfer (not valid for night trams or night buses).
- 75-minute transfer ticket with unlimited transfers *(základní přestupní)*—20 Kč.
- 24-hour pass *(jízdenka na 24 hodin)*—80 Kč.
- 3-day pass *(jízdenka na 3 dny)*—220 Kč.
- 7-day pass *(jízdenka na 7 dní)*—280 Kč.

Buy tickets from your hotel, at newsstand kiosks, or from automated machines (select ticket price, then insert coins). For convenience, buy all the tickets you think you'll need—but estimate conservatively. Remember, Prague is a great walking town, so unless you're commuting from a hotel far outside the center, you will likely find that individual tickets work best. Be sure to validate your ticket on the tram, bus, or Metro by sticking it in the machine (which stamps a time on it—watch locals and imitate). Inspectors routinely ambush ticketless riders (including tourists) and fine them 500 Kč on the spot.

Tips: Navigate by signs listing end stations. When you come to your stop, push the yellow button if the doors don't automatically open. Although it seems that all Metro doors lead to the neighborhood of Výstup, that's simply the Czech word for "exit." When a tram pulls up to a stop, two different names are announced: first, the name of the stop you're currently at, followed by the name of the stop that's coming up next. Confused tourists, thinking they've heard their stop, are notorious for rushing off the tram one stop too soon. Trams run every 5–10 minutes in the daytime (a schedule is posted at each stop). The Metro closes at midnight, and the nighttime tram routes (identified with white numbers on blue backgrounds at tram stops) run all night at 30-minute intervals. There's more information and a complete route planner at www.dp-praha.cz.

Prague Metro

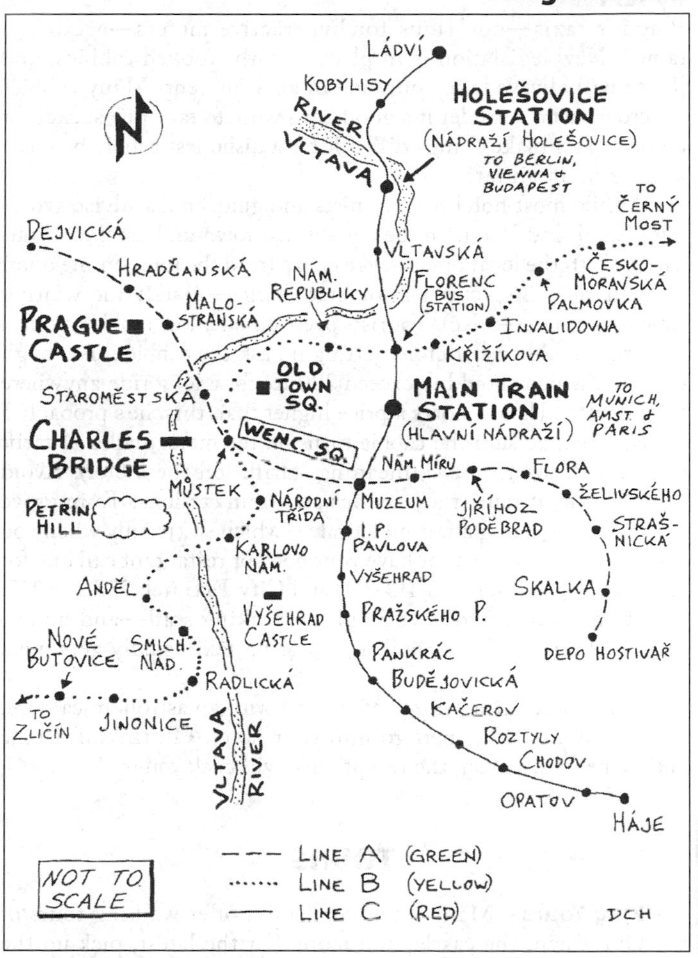

Handy Trams: Trams #22 and #23 are practically made for sightseeing, using the same route to connect the New Town with the Castle Quarter (find the line marked on the color map at beginning of this book). The trams use some of the same stops as the Metro (making it easy to get to—or travel on from—the tram route). Of the many stops these trams make, the most convenient are two in the New Town (Národní Třída Metro stop, between the bottom of Wenceslas Square and the river; and Národní Divadlo, at the National Theatre), one stop in the Little Quarter (Malostranská Metro station), and three stops above Prague Castle (Královský Letohrádek, Pražský Hrad, and Pohořelec; for details, see "Getting to Prague Castle—By Tram" on page 204).

By Taxi

Prague's taxis—notorious for hyperactive meters—are being tamed. New legislation is in place to curb crooked cabbies, and police will always take your side in an argument. Many cabbies are crooks who consider it a good day's work to take one sucker for a ride. You'll make things difficult for a dishonest cabbie by challenging an unfair fare.

While most hotel receptionists and guidebooks advise avoiding taxis, I find Prague to be a great taxi town and use them routinely. With the local rate, they're cheap (read the rates on the door: drop charge—36 Kč; per-kilometer charge—25 Kč; and waiting time per minute—5 Kč). Tourists overestimate how much a typical taxi trip should cost. Before getting in, ask the cabbie for a rough estimate, which shouldn't exceed 200 Kč for a long ride anywhere in the center. (If he quotes a price higher than this, he's probably a crook.) Then be sure the cabbie turns on the meter at the #1 tariff (look for the word *sazba,* meaning "tariff," on the meter). Avoid cabs waiting at tourist attractions and train stations. To improve your odds of getting a fair meter rate—which starts only when you take off—call for a cab (or have your hotel or restaurant call one for you). **AAA Taxi** (tel. 233-113-311) and **City Taxi** (tel. 257-257-257) are the most likely to have English-speaking staff—and honest cabbies. I also find that hailing a passing taxi usually gets me a decent price.

If a cabbie surprises you at the end with an astronomical fare, simply pay 200 Kč, then go into your hotel. On the miniscule chance he follows you, the receptionist will back you up.

TOURS

Walking Tours—Many small companies offer walking tours of the Old Town, the castle, and more. For the latest, pick up the walking tour fliers at the TI. Since guiding is a routine side-job for local university students, you'll generally get hardworking young guides at good prices. While I'd rather go with my own private guide (described below), public walking tours are cheaper, cover themes you might not otherwise consider, connect you with other English-speaking travelers, and allow for spontaneity. **Prague Walks** is as good as any (250–1,000 Kč, 1.5–6 hrs, tel. 222-322-309, fax 261-214-603, mobile 603-271-911, www.praguewalks.com, pwalks@comp.cz). Consider their clever Good Morning Walk, which starts at 8:00 (April–Aug only), before the crowds hit.

▲▲Private Guides—In Prague, hiring a local guide is particularly smart—they're twice as helpful for half the price compared to guides in Western Europe. Because prices are usually per hour (not per person), small groups can inexpensively use a guide for several days. Guides meet you wherever you like and tailor the tour to your interests. Visit their websites in advance for details on various walks, airport transfers, countryside excursions, and other services offered, and then make arrangements by email.

Katka Svobodová, an anthropologist and historian, is a hard-working guide who know her stuff, speaks excellent English, and enjoys showing individuals and small groups around (400 Kč/hr, 3-hour minimum, mobile 603-181-300, www.praguewalker.com, katerina@praguewalker.com). **Šárka Pelantová** and her team of guides get beyond the dates and famous buildings to provide insight into the culture, and are eager to build a walk around your interests (400 Kč/hr for 1 or 2 people, 600 Kč/hr for 3 or more, mobile 777-225-205, www.prague-guide.info, saraguide@volny.cz). My readers have also recommended **Renata Blažková** (tel. 222-716-870, mobile 602-353-186, blazer@volny.cz) and **Martin Bělohradský** (martinb@uochb.cas.cz).

The **TI** also has plenty of private guides (rates for a 3-hour tour: 1,200 Kč/1 person, 1,400 Kč/2 people, 1,600 Kč/3 people, 2,000 Kč/4 people; desk at Old Town Square TI, arrange and pay in person at least 2 hours in advance, tel. 224-482-562, guides@pis.cz). For a listing of more private guides, see www.guide-prague.cz.

Jewish-Themed Walks: Silvie Wittmann, a native Czech Jew, has developed a diverse group of knowledgeable guides who aspire to bring Jewish traditions back to life in Prague. Consider her three-hour walking tour of the Jewish Quarter (630 Kč includes entry to the Jewish Museum, May–Oct Sun–Fri at 10:30 and 14:30, Nov–April Sun–Fri at 10:30 only, no tours on Sat) or her six-hour trip to Terezín Concentration Camp (1,150 Kč includes transportation and all entries, departs May–Oct daily at 10:00; mid-March–April and Nov–Dec no Mon, Wed, or Fri tours; Jan–mid-March by appointment only). All tours require prior reservation and meet in front of Hotel InterContinental at the end of Pařížská Street (tel. & fax 222-252-472, mobile 603-168-427, www.wittmann-tours.com, sylvie@wittmann-tours.com).

Outside Prague: To get beyond Prague, call Thomas Zahn, who runs **Pathways Guided Travel.** Thomas, an American who married into the Czech Republic, specializes in helping Americans of Czech descent find their roots. He also organizes and leads creative, affordable (mostly one- and two-day) excursions from Prague. Hiking, biking, horseback riding, or canoeing, you'll explore the unknown charms of the region with a small group and a committed guide. Explore Thomas' website for ways to connect with the rural Czech countryside and experience more than Prague on your visit (tel. 257-940-113, mobile 603-758-983, www.pathfinders.cz).

Bus Tours—While I generally recommend cheap big-bus orientation tours for an efficient, once-over-lightly look at great cities, Prague just isn't built for bus tours. In fact, most bus tours of the city are walking tours that use buses for pick-ups and transfers. The sightseeing core (Castle Quarter, Charles Bridge, and the Old Town) is not accessible by bus. So if you insist on a bus, you're playing basketball with a catcher's mitt.

Bus tours make more sense for day trips out of Prague. Several companies have kiosks on Na Příkopě where you can comparison-shop. **Premiant City Tours** offers 20 different tours, including Terezín Concentration Camp, Karlštejn Castle, and Český Krumlov (1,750 Kč, 10 hrs), and a river cruise. The tours feature live guides and depart from near the bottom of Wenceslas Square at Na Příkopě 23. Get tickets at an AVE travel agency, your hotel, on the bus, or at Na Příkopě 23 (tel. 224-946-922, mobile 606-600-123, www.premiant.cz). Tour salespeople are notorious for telling you anything to sell a ticket. Some tours, especially those heading into the countryside, can be in as many as four different languages. Hiring a private guide, many of whom can drive you around in their car, can be a much better value (see above).

Cruises—Prague isn't ideal for a boat tour. Still, the hour-long Vltava River cruises, which leave from near the castle end of Charles Bridge about hourly, are scenic and relaxing, though not informative (100–150 Kč).

▲Paddleboat Cruises—Renting a rowboat or paddleboat on Slovanský Island (by the National Theatre) is a better way to enjoy the river. You'll float at your own pace among the swans and local lovers in their own paddleboats (about 80 Kč/hr, bring photo ID for deposit).

SIGHTS

I've arranged these sights according to which of Prague's four, historically distinct towns you'll find them in: Old Town, New Town, Little Quarter, or Castle Quarter.

The Old Town (Staré Město)

From Prague's dramatic centerpiece, the Old Town Square, sightseeing options fan out in all directions. Get oriented on the square before venturing onward. You can find out about Jewish heritage in the Jewish Quarter (Josefov), a few blocks from the Old Town Square. Closer to the square, you'll find the quaint and historic Ungelt courtyard and Celetná street, which leads to the Museum of Czech Cubism and the landmark Estates Theatre. Nearby, Karlova street funnels all the tourists to the famous Charles Bridge. All

Prague's Old Town

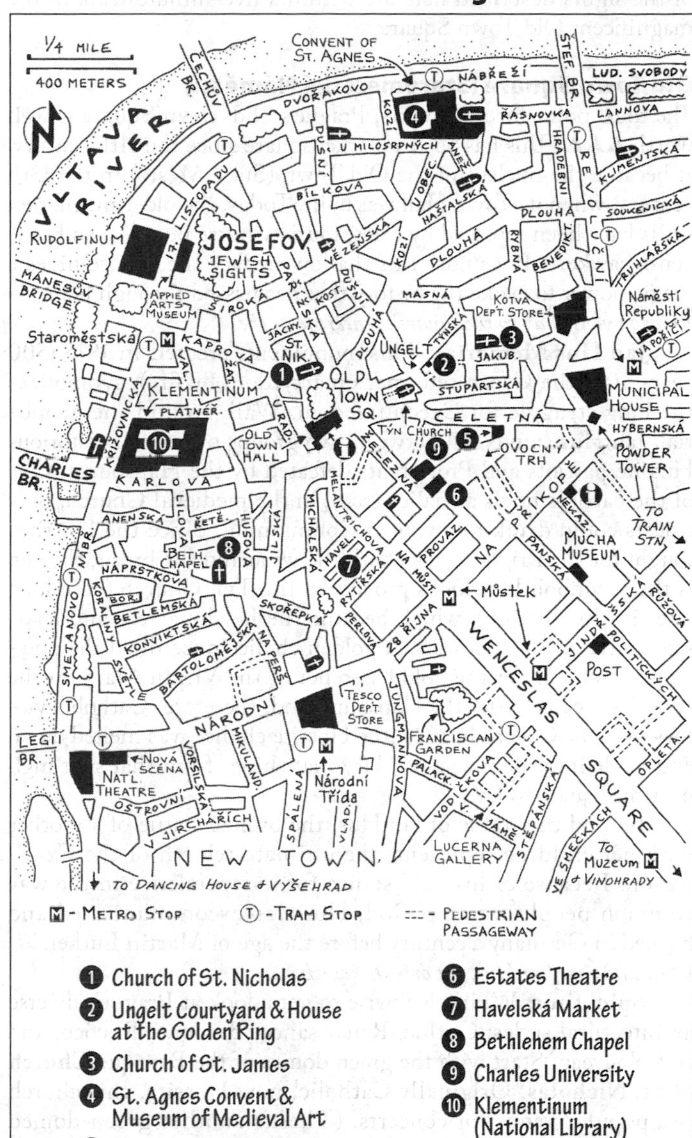

1/4 MILE
400 METERS
VLTAVA RIVER
CONVENT OF ST. AGNES
JOSEFOV
JEWISH SIGHTS
RUDOLFINUM
MÁNESŮV BRIDGE
APPLIED ARTS MUSEUM
Staroměstská
KLEMENTINUM
CHARLES BR.
OLD TOWN SQ.
OLD TOWN HALL
TÝN CHURCH
UNGELT
KOTVA DEPT. STORE
MUNICIPAL HOUSE
POWDER TOWER
Náměstí Republiky
MUCHA MUSEUM
Můstek
WENCESLAS SQUARE
POST
BETH. CHAPEL
TESCO DEPT. STORE
FRANCISCAN GARDEN
Národní Třída
NOVÁ SCÉNA
NATL. THEATRE
LUCERNA GALLERY
NEW TOWN
TO TRAIN STN.
TO DANCING HOUSE & VYŠEHRAD
TO Muzeum & VINOHRADY
M - METRO STOP
T - TRAM STOP
PEDESTRIAN PASSAGEWAY
1 Church of St. Nicholas
2 Ungelt Courtyard & House at the Golden Ring
3 Church of St. James
4 St. Agnes Convent & Museum of Medieval Art
5 Museum of Czech Cubism in the Black Madonna House
6 Estates Theatre
7 Havelská Market
8 Bethlehem Chapel
9 Charles University
10 Klementinum (National Library)

Prague

of the sights described here are within a five-minute walk of the magnificent Old Town Square.

Old Town Square (Staroměstské Náměstí)

The focal point for most visits, Prague's Old Town Square is well worth ▲▲▲. This has been a market square since the 11th century. It became the nucleus of the Old Town (Staré Město) in the 13th century, when its Town Hall was built. Today, the old-time market stalls have been replaced by cafés, touristy horse buggies, and souvenir hawkers. But under this shallow surface the square hides a magic power to evoke the history that has passed through here.

• *Gawk your way to the square's centerpiece, the...*

Jan Hus Memorial: This monument, erected in 1915 (500 years after the Czech reformer's martyrdom by fire), symbolizes the long struggle for Czech freedom. Walk around the memorial. Jan Hus stands tall between two groups of people: victorious Hussite patriots and Protestants defeated by the Hapsburgs. One of the patriots holds a chalice (cup); in the medieval Church, only priests could drink the wine at Communion. Since the Hussites fought for their right to take both the wine and the bread, the cup is their symbol. Hus looks proudly at the Týn Church (described later in this section), which became the headquarters and leading church of his followers. A golden chalice once filled the now-empty niche under the gold bas-relief of the Virgin Mary on the church's facade. After the Hapsburg (and, therefore, Catholic) victory over the Czechs in 1620, the Hussite chalice was melted down and made into the image of Mary that shines from that spot high over the square today.

Behind the statue of Jan Hus, the bronze statue of a mother with her children represents the ultimate rebirth of the Czech nation. Because of his bold stance for independence in the way common people worship God, Hus was excommunicated and burned in Germany a century before the age of Martin Luther.

• *Standing by Jan Hus, get oriented with a...*

Spin-Tour: Whirl clockwise to get a look at Prague's diverse architectural styles: Gothic, Renaissance, Baroque, Rococo, and Art Nouveau. Start with the green domes of the Baroque **Church of St. Nicholas.** Originally Catholic, now Hussite, this church is a popular venue for concerts. (There's another green-domed Church of St. Nicholas—also popular for concerts—by the same architect across the Charles Bridge in the Little Quarter.) The Jewish Quarter (Josefov) is a few blocks behind the church, down the uniquely tree-lined Pařížská—"Paris street." (For more on the Jewish Quarter, see page 188.) Pařížská, an eclectic cancan of mostly Art Nouveau facades, leads to a bluff that once sported a 100-foot-tall stone Stalin. Demolished in 1962 after Khrushchev

Prague's Old Town Square

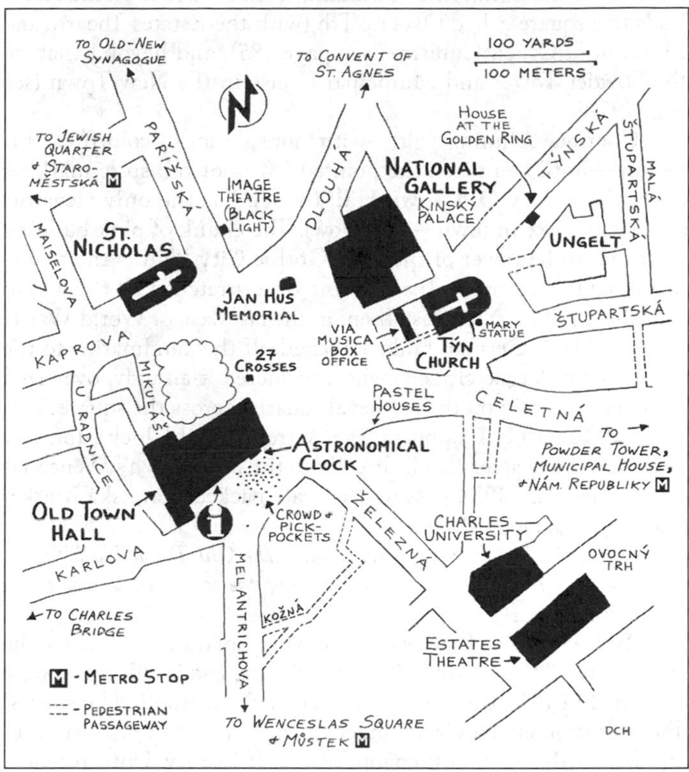

exposed Stalin's crimes, it was replaced in 1991 by a giant ticking **metronome**—partly to commemorate Prague's centennial exhibition (the 1891 exhibition is remembered by the Little Quarter's Eiffel-esque Petřín Tower), and partly to send the message that for every power, there's a time to go.

Spin to the right, past the Hus Memorial and the fine yellow Art Nouveau building. The large Rococo palace on the right is part of the **National Gallery;** the temporary exhibits here are often the best in town.

To the right, you can't miss the towering, Gothic **Týn Church** (pronounced "teen"), with its fanciful spires flanking the gold bas-relief of Mary. For 200 years after Hus' death, this was Prague's leading Hussite church (described in more detail later in this section). A narrow lane leading to the church's entrance passes the **Via Musica,** the most convenient ticket office in town (see page 214). Behind the Týn Church is a gorgeously restored medieval courtyard called **Ungelt** (see page 184). The row of pastel houses in front of Týn Church has a mixture of Gothic, Renaissance, and Baroque facades. To the right of these buildings, shop-lined **Celetná street** leads to a square called Ovocný Trh (with the Estates Theatre and Museum of Czech Cubism—see page 185), and beyond that, to the Powder Tower and Municipal House in the New Town (see page 197).

Continue spinning right—with more gloriously colorful architecture—until you reach the pointed 250-foot-tall spire marking the 14th-century **Old Town Hall** (which has the only elevator-accessible tower in town—see below). The chunk of pink building attached to the tower of the Neo-Gothic City Hall is the town's memorial to bad losers. The building once stretched all the way to the Church of St. Nicholas. Then, in the last days of World War II (May of 1945), German tanks knocked off this landmark—to the joy of many Prague citizens who considered it an ugly, oversized 19th-century stain on the medieval square. Across the square from the Old Town Hall (opposite the Astronomical Clock), touristy **Melantrichova street** leads directly to the New Town's Wenceslas Square (see page 192), passing the craft-packed Havelská Market (see page 186) along the way.

• *Now wander across the square, toward the Old Town Hall Tower. Embedded in the pavement at the base of the tower (near the snack stand), you'll see...*

Twenty-Seven Crosses: These white inlaid crosses mark the spot where 27 Protestant nobles, merchants, and intellectuals were beheaded in 1621 after rebelling against the Catholic Hapsburgs. The execution ended Czech independence for 300 years—and it's still one of the grimmest chapters in their history. Until recently, Czechs walked around this sacred spot, avoiding stepping on it, and many would stop to pay their respects. But today the sacred soil is home to a hot-dog vendor, and few notice the crosses in the pavement.

Prague

• *Looming behind the crosses is the Old Town Hall. Near the base of the tall tower, around the corner to the left, is Prague's famous...*

Astronomical Clock: Join the gang for the striking of the hour on the Old Town Hall clock, worth ▲▲ (daily 8:00–21:00, until 20:00 in winter). As you wait, see if you can figure out how the clock works.

With revolving disks, celestial symbols, and sweeping hands, this clock keeps several versions of time. Two outer rings show the hour: Bohemian time (gold Gothic numbers on black background, counts from sunset—find the zero, between 23 and 1...supposedly the time of tonight's sunset) and modern time (24 Roman numerals, XII at the top being noon, XII at the bottom being midnight). Five hundred years ago, everything revolved around the earth (the fixed middle background—with Prague marking the center, of course).

To indicate the times of sunrise and sunset, arcing lines and moving spheres combine with the big hand (a sweeping golden sun) and the little hand (a moon that spins to show various stages). Look for the orbits of the sun and moon as they rise through day (the blue zone) and night (the black zone).

If this seems complex to us, it must have been a marvel 500 years ago. Because the clock was heavily damaged during World War II, a lot of what you see today is a reconstruction. The circle below (added in the 19th century) shows the signs of the zodiac, scenes from the seasons of a rural peasant's life, and a ring of saints' names—one for each day of the year, with a marker showing today's special saint (at top).

Four statues flanking the clock represent the 15th-century outlook on time. A Turk with a mandolin symbolizes hedonism, a Jewish moneylender is greed, and the figure staring into a mirror stands for vanity. All these worldly goals are vain in the face of Death, whose hourglass reminds us that our time is unavoidably running out.

At the top of the hour (don't blink—the show is pretty quick): First, Death tips his hourglass and pulls the cord, ringing the bell; then the windows open and the 12 apostles parade by, acknowledging the gang of onlookers; then the rooster crows; and then the hour is rung. The hour is often off because of daylight saving time (completely senseless to 15th-century clockmakers). At the top of the next hour, stand under the tower—protected by a line of banner-wielding, powdered-wigged concert salespeople—and watch the tourists.

• *To the left of the clock is Prague's main TI, which has an information desk and sells tickets for a pair of activities...*

Tower Climb and Old Town Hall Tour: In good weather, zip up the Old Town Hall tower via elevator for some of Prague's best views (50 Kč, daily 9:00–18:00). Slightly less interesting is the 45-minute tour of the Old Town Hall, which includes a Gothic chapel and a close-up look at the inner workings of the Astronomical Clock (plus its statues of the 12 apostles; 50 Kč, 2/hr).

• *Now that you're oriented, you can use this delightful square as your launchpad for the rest of Prague's Old Town sights.*

Týn Church

While this church, rated ▲, has a long history, it's most notable for its 200-year-stint as the leading church of the Hussite movement (generally open daily 10:00–13:00 & 15:00–17:00). It was Catholic before the Hussites, and returned to Catholicism after the Hussites were defeated. As if to insult Hus and his doctrine of simplicity, the church's once elegant and pure Gothic columns are now encrusted with noisy Baroque altars. While Gothic, the church interior is uncharacteristically bright because of its Baroque-age clear windowpanes and whitewash. Read the church's story (posted in English, rear-left side) for a Catholic spin on the church's story—told with barely a mention of Hus. The fine 16th-century, carved John the Baptist altar (right aisle) is worth a look.

Outside, on the side of the church facing Celetná street, find a statue of St. Mary resting on a temporary column against the wall. The Catholics are still waiting for a chance to reinstall St. Mary in the middle of the Old Town Square, where she used to stand more than a century ago.

Behind Týn Church

▲Ungelt Courtyard (Týnský Dvůr)—Ever since the Old Town was established, the Ungelt courtyard—located directly behind the Old Town Square's Týn Church—has served as a hostel for foreign merchants, much like a Turkish caravanserai. Here the merchants (usually German) would store their goods and pay taxes before setting up stalls on the Old Town Square. Notice there are only two entrances into the complex—guaranteeing the safety of goods and merchants. After decades of disuse, the courtyard had fallen into such disrepair by the 1980s that authorities considered demolishing it. Marvelously restored a few years ago, the Ungelt courtyard is now the most pleasant area in the Old Town for an outdoor coffee (such as at Ebel Coffee House—see page 233), sorting through wooden crafts, and paging through English books (at Anagram Bookshop, described on page 171).

Church of St. James (Kostel Sv. Jakuba)—Perhaps the most beautiful church in the Old Town, the Church of St. James is just behind Ungelt courtyard. The Franciscan Order has occupied this church and the adjacent monastery nearly as long as merchants occupied Ungelt. A medieval city was a complex phenomenon: side-by-side, there existed commerce, brothels, and a life of contemplation. (I guess it's not that much different from today.) Artistically, St. James (along with the church at Strahov Monastery—see page 206) is a stunning example of how simple Gothic spaces could be transformed into sumptuous feasts of Baroque decoration. The blue light in the altar highlights one of Prague's most venerated treasures—the bejeweled Madonna Pietatis. Above the *pietà*, as if held aloft by hummingbird-like angels, is a painting of the martyrdom of St. James (free, daily 9:30–12:00 & 14:00–16:00).

As you leave, find the black and shriveled-up arm with clenched fingers (15 feet above and to the left of the door). According to legend, a thief attempted to rob the Madonna Pietatis from the altar, but his hand was frozen the moment he touched the statue. The monks had to cut off the arm in order for it to let go. The dried-up arm now hangs here as a warning—and the entire delightful story is posted nearby in English.

North of the Old Town Square, near the River

▲▲Museum of Medieval Art—The Museum of Medieval Art in Bohemia and Central Europe (1200–1550) is housed in the St. Agnes Convent. The 14th century was Prague's Golden Age, and the religious art displayed in this Gothic space is a testament to the rich cultural life of the period. Each exquisite piece is well-lit and thoughtfully described in English. Follow the arrows on a chronological sweep through Gothic art history. The various Madonnas and saints were gathered here from churches all over Central Europe (100 Kč, Tue–Sun 10:00–18:00, closed Mon, two blocks northeast of the Spanish Synagogue, along the river at Anežská 12).

On Celetná Street, Toward the New Town

Celetná, a pedestrian-only street, is a convenient and relatively untouristy way to get from the Old Town Square to the New Town (specifically the Powder Tower and Municipal House, described on page 197). Along the way, at the square called Ovocný Trh, you'll find these sights.

Museum of Czech Cubism—Cubism was a potent force in Prague in the early 20th century. The fascinating Museum of Czech Cubism in the Black Madonna House (Dům u Černé Matky Boží) offers the complete Cubist experience: Cubist architecture (stand back and see how masterfully it makes its statement while mixing with its neighbors...then get up close and study the details), a great café (upstairs), a ground-floor shop, and, of course, a museum. On three floors, you'll see paintings, furniture, graphics, and architectural drafts by Czech Cubists. This building is an example of what has long been considered the greatest virtue of Prague's architects: the ability to adapt their grandiose plans to the existing cityscape (museum entry-100 Kč, Tue–Sun 10:00–18:00, closed Mon, corner of Celetná and Ovocný Trh at Ovocný Trh 19, tel. 224-301-003). If you're not interested in touring the museum itself, consider a drink in the similarly decorated upstairs Grand Café Orient (see page 233).

Estates Theatre (Stavovské Divadlo)—Built by a nobleman in the 1770s, this classicist building—gently opening its greenish walls onto Ovocný Trh—was the prime opera venue in Prague at a time when an Austrian prodigy was changing the course of music. Wolfgang Amadeus Mozart premiered *Don Giovanni* in this building, and personally directed many of his works here. Prague's theater-goers would whistle arias from Mozart's works on the streets the morning after they premiered here. Today part of the National Theatre group, the Estates Theatre continues to produce *The Marriage of Figaro, Don Giovanni*, and occasionally *The Magic Flute*. For a more intimate encounter with Mozart, go to Villa Bertramka (see page 216).

On Melantrichova Street

▲Havelská Market—Skinny, tourist-clogged Melantrichova street leads directly from the Old Town Square's Astronomical Clock to the bottom of Wenceslas Square. But even along this most crowded of streets, a genuine bit of Prague remains: Havelská Market, offering crafts and produce. The open-air market was set up in the 13th century for the German trading community. Though heavy on souvenirs these days, the market still keeps hungry locals and vagabonds fed cheaply. It's ideal for a healthy snack; merchants are happy to sell a single vegetable or piece of fruit; and you'll find a washing fountain and plenty of inviting benches midway down the street. The market is also a fun place to browse for crafts. It's a homegrown, homemade kind of place; you'll often be dealing with the actual artist or farmer (market open daily 9:00–18:00, produce best on weekdays; more souvenirs, puppets, and toys on weekends). The many cafés and little eateries circling the market offer a fine and relaxing vantage point from which to view the action.

From Old Town Square to Charles Bridge

Karlova Street—Karlova street winds through medieval Prague from the Old Town Square to the Charles Bridge (it zigzags...just follow the crowds). This is a commercial gauntlet, and it's here that the touristy feeding-frenzy of Prague is most ugly. Street signs keep you on track, and *Karlův most* signs point to the bridge. Obviously, you'll find few good values on this drag. Two favorite places providing a quick break from the crowds are just a few steps off Karlova on Husova street: **Cream and Dream Ice Cream** (Husova 12) and **U Zlatého Tygra,** a colorful pub serving great, cheap beer in a classic and untouristy setting (Husova 17; see page 229).

Klementinum—The Czech Republic's massive National Library borders touristy Karlova street. The contrast could not be starker—step out of the most souvenir-packed stretch of Eastern Europe, into the meditative silence of Eastern Europe's biggest library. The Klementinum was built to house a college in the 1600s by the Jesuits, who had been invited to Prague by the Catholic Hapsburgs to offset the influence of the predominantly Protestant Charles University nearby. The building was transformed into a library in the early 1700s, when the Jesuits took firm control of the university. Their books, together with the collections of several noble families (written in all possible languages...except Czech), form the nucleus of what is now the six-million-volumes-strong National and University Library. (Note that the Klementinum's Chapel of Mirrors is a popular venue for evening concerts.)

Charles Bridge (Karlův Most)

Among Prague's defining landmarks, this much-loved bridge offers one of the most pleasant and entertaining quarter-mile strolls in Europe. It's well worth ▲▲▲. Enjoy the bridge at different times of day. The bridge is most memorable early—before the crowds—and late, during the "magic hour" prized by photographers, when the sun is low in the sky. The bridge may be partially closed for restoration at times.

At the Old Town end of the bridge, in a little square, is a statue of the bridge's namesake, **Charles IV.** This Holy Roman Emperor (*Karlo Quatro*—the guy on the 100-Kč bill) ruled his vast empire from Prague in the 14th century. He's holding a contract establishing Prague's university, the first in Northern Europe. This statue was erected in 1848 to celebrate the university's 500th birthday. The women around Charles' pedestal symbolize the university's four subjects: the arts, medicine, law, and theology. (From the corner by the busy street, many think the emperor's silhouette makes it appear that he's peeing on the tourists.)

Bridges had been built on this spot before, as the remnant tower from the Judith Bridge (the smaller of the two bridge towers at the far end) testifies. All were washed away by floods. After a major flood in 1342, Emperor Charles IV decided to commission an entirely new structure rather than repair the old one. Until the 19th century, this was Prague's only bridge crossing the river.

How do you make a bridge last seven centuries? Back in the 1300s, they believed in the magic of time and numbers. The founding stone was laid in 1357, on the 9th of July at 5:31 (it's a palindrome: 135797531). On the Old Town bank, a spot was chosen for the ending of the bridge that lined up perfectly with the tomb of St. Vitus (in the cathedral across the river) and the setting sun at summer solstice.

This magical spot is now occupied by the **bridge tower,** considered one of the finest Gothic gates anywhere. Contemplate the fine sculpture on the Old Town side of the tower, showing the 14th-century hierarchy of kings, bishops, and angels. Climbing the tower rewards you with wonderful views over the bridge (40 Kč, daily 10:00–19:00, as late as 22:00 in summer).

In the 17th century, there were no statues on the bridge—only a **cross,** which you can still see as part of the third sculpture on the right. The gilded Hebrew inscription celebrating Christ was paid by a fine imposed on a Jew for mocking the cross.

The bronze Baroque statue depicting **St. John of Nepomuk**—a saint of the Czech people—draws a crowd (look for the guy with the five golden stars around his head, near the Little Quarter end of the bridge on the right). John of Nepomuk was a 14th-century priest to whom the queen confessed all her sins. According to a 17th-century legend, the king wanted to know his wife's secrets, but Father John dutifully refused to tell. He was tortured and eventually killed by being tossed off the bridge. When he hit the water, five stars appeared. The shiny plaque at the base of the statue depicts the heave-ho. Devout pilgrims—from Mexico and Moravia alike—touch the engraving to make a wish come true. You get only one chance in life for this wish, so think carefully before you touch the saint. Notice the date on the inscription: This oldest statue on the bridge was unveiled in 1683, on the supposed 300th anniversary of the martyr's death. You'll find statues like this one on squares and bridges throughout the country. The actual spot of the much-talked about heave-ho is a few steps farther away from the castle—find the five points of the Orthodox cross between two statues on the bridge railing.

Most of the other Charles Bridge statues date from the late 1600s and early 1700s. Today half of them are replicas—the originals are in city museums, out of the polluted air.

At the far end of Charles Bridge, you reach the **Little Quarter.** For sights in this neighborhood, see page 200.

Jewish Quarter (Josefov)

Prague's Jewish Quarter neighborhood and its well-presented, profoundly moving museum tell the story of this region's Jews. For me, this is the most interesting collection of Jewish sights in Europe, well worth ▲▲▲. The Jewish Quarter is an easy walk from Old Town Square, up delightful Pařížská street (next to the green-domed Church of St. Nicholas).

As the Nazis decimated Jewish communities in the region, Prague's Jews were allowed to collect and archive their treasures here. While the archivists were ultimately killed in concentration camps, their work survives. Seven sights scattered over a three-block area make up the tourists' Jewish Quarter. Six of the sights—all except the Old-New Synagogue—are called "The Museum" and are covered by one admission ticket. Your ticket comes with a map locating the sights and listing admission appointments—the times you'll be let in if it's very busy. (Ignore the times unless it's really crowded.) You'll notice plenty of security (stepped up since 9/11).

Cost, Hours, Tours: To visit all seven sights, you'll pay 500 Kč (300 Kč for the six sights that make up The Museum, plus 200 Kč for the Old-New Synagogue; all sights open Sun–Fri April–Oct 9:00–18:00, Nov–March 9:00–16:30, closed Sat—the Jewish Sabbath—and on Jewish holidays). Each sight is thoroughly and thoughtfully described in English, making a guided tour unnecessary for most visitors. Occasional guided walks in English start at the Maisel Synagogue (50 Kč, 3 hours, tel. 222-317-191).

Cemetery: The Old Jewish Cemetery—with its tightly packed tombstones—is, for many, the most evocative part of the experience. Unfortunately, there's no ticket just to see the cemetery,

Prague's Jewish Quarter

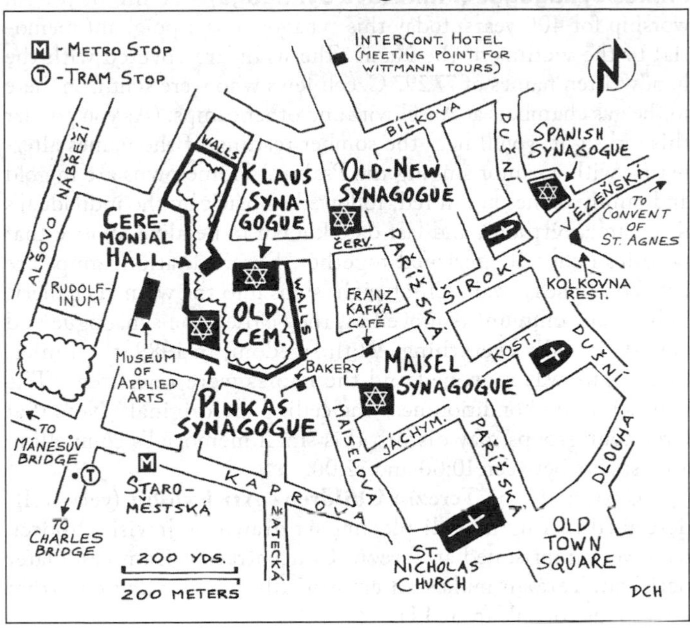

and they've closed off most free viewpoints into the cemetery. If the 300-Kč museum ticket is too steep for you and you just want a free peek at the famous cemetery, climb the steps to the covered porch of the Ceremonial Hall (but don't rest your chin on the treacherous railing).

Planning Your Time: The most logical start (if you'll be seeing everything) is to buy your ticket at Pinkas Synagogue and visit this most powerful memorial of the museum complex first. From there, walk through the Old Jewish Cemetery, which leads to the Ceremonial Hall and Klaus Synagogue. After visiting those, head over to the Old-New Synagogue, have a coffee break (Pekařství bakery or Franz Kafka Café, both described on page 232, are nearby). Next, visit the museum-like Maisel Synagogue, and finally the Spanish Synagogue. (Note that Prague's fine Museum of Medieval Art in Bohemia and Central Europe, described on page 185, is only a few blocks from the Spanish Synagogue.)

Art Nouveau and the New Josefov: Going from sight to sight in the Jewish Quarter, you'll walk through perhaps Europe's finest Art Nouveau neighborhood. Make a point to enjoy the circa-1900 buildings with their marvelous trimmings and oh-wow entryways. While today's modern grid plan has replaced the higgledy-piggledy medieval streets of old, Široká ("Wide Street") was and remains the main street of the ghetto.

Pinkas Synagogue (Pinkasova Synagóga)—A site of Jewish worship for 400 years, today this synagogue is a poignant memorial to the victims of the Nazis. The walls are covered with the handwritten names of 77,297 Czech Jews who were sent from here to the gas chambers at Auschwitz and other camps. (As you ponder this sad sight, you'll hear the somber reading of the names alternating with a cantor singing the Psalms.) Hometowns are in gold and family names are in red, followed in black by the individual's first name, birthday, and last date known to be alive. Notice that families generally perished together. Extermination camps are listed on the east wall. Climb eight steps into the women's gallery. When the communists moved in, they closed the synagogue and erased virtually everything. With freedom, in 1989, the Pinkas Synagogue was reopened and the names were rewritten. (The names in poor condition near the ceiling are original.) Note that large tour groups may disturb this small memorial's compelling atmosphere between 10:00 and 12:00.

Upstairs is the **Terezín Children's Art Exhibit** (very well-described in English), displaying art drawn by Jewish children who were imprisoned at Terezín Concentration Camp and later perished. Terezín makes an emotionally moving day trip from Prague (get details from TI).

Old Jewish Cemetery (Starý Židovský Hřbitov)—From the Pinkas Synagogue, you enter one of the most wistful scenes in Europe—Prague's Old Jewish Cemetery. As you wander among 12,000 evocative tombstones, remember that from 1439 until 1787, this was the only burial ground allowed for the Jews of Prague. Because of limited space, the Jewish belief that the body should not be moved once buried, and the sheer number of graves, tombs were piled atop each other. With its many layers, the cemetery became a small plateau. And as things settled over time, the tombstones got crooked. The Hebrew word for cemetery means "House of Life." Many Jews believe that death is the gateway into the next world. Pebbles on the tombstones are "flowers of the desert," reminiscent of the old days when rocks were placed upon the sand gravesite to keep the body covered. Wedged under some of the pebbles are scraps of paper containing prayers.

Ceremonial Hall (Obřadní Síň)—Leaving the cemetery, you'll find a Neo-Romanesque mortuary house built in 1911 for the purification of the dead (on left). It's filled with a worthwhile exhibition, described in English, on Jewish medicine, death, and burial traditions. A series of crude but instructive paintings (hanging on walls throughout the house) show how the "burial brotherhood" took care of the ill and buried the dead. As all are equal before God, the rich and poor alike were buried in embroidered linen shrouds similar to the one you'll see on display.

Klaus Synagogue (Klauzová Synagóga)—This 17th-century synagogue (also near the cemetery exit) is the final wing of a museum devoted to Jewish religious practices. Exhibits on the ground floor explain the Jewish calendar of festivals. The central case displays a Torah (the first five books of the Bible) and solid silver pointers used when reading—necessary since the Torah is not to be touched. Upstairs is an exhibit on the rituals of Jewish life (circumcision, bar and bat mitzvah, weddings, kosher eating, and so on).

Old-New Synagogue (Staronová Synagóga)—For more than 700 years, this has been the most important synagogue and the central building in Josefov. Standing like a bomb-hardened bunker, it feels like it has survived plenty of hard times. Stairs take you down to the street level of the 13th century and into the Gothic interior. Built in 1270, it's the oldest synagogue in Eastern Europe (separate 200-Kč admission includes worthwhile 10-minute tour—ask about it, Sun–Thu 9:30–18:00, Fri 9:30–17:00, closed Sat). Snare an attendant who likely loves to show visitors around. The steep admission keeps many away, but even if you decide not to pay, you can see the exterior and a bit of the interior. (Go ahead...pop in and crane your cheapskate neck.)

The lobby (down the stairs, where you show your ticket) has two fortified old lockers—in which the most heavily taxed community in medieval Prague stored its money in anticipation of the taxman's arrival. As 13th-century Jews were not allowed to build, the synagogue was erected by Christians (who also built the St. Agnes Convent nearby). The builders were good at four-ribbed vaulting, but since that resulted in a cross, it wouldn't work for a synagogue. Instead, they made the ceiling using clumsy five-ribbed vaulting.

The interior is pure 1300s. The Shrine of the Ark in front is the focus of worship. The holiest place in the synagogue, it holds the sacred scrolls of the Torah. The old rabbi's chair to the right remains empty (notice the thin black chain) out of respect. The red banner is a copy of the one the Jewish community carried through town during medieval parades. Notice the yellow-pointed hat within the Star of David (on the banner), which the pope ordered all Jewish men to wear in 1215. Twelve is a popular number (e.g., windows) because it symbolizes the 12 tribes of Israel. The horizontal slit-like windows are an 18th-century addition, allowing women to view the male-only services.

Maisel Synagogue (Maiselova Synagóga)—This synagogue was built as a private place of worship for the Maisel family during the 16th-century Golden Age of Prague's Jews. Maisel, the financier of the Hapsburg king, had lots of money. The synagogue's interior is decorated Neo-Gothic. In World War II, it served as a warehouse for the accumulated treasures of decimated Jewish communities that Hitler planned to use for his "Museum of the Extinct Jewish Race." The one-room exhibit shows a thousand years of Jewish history in Bohemia and Moravia. Well-explained in English, topics include the origin of the Star of David, Jewish mysticism, discrimination, and the creation of Prague's ghetto. Notice the eastern wall, with the holy ark containing the scroll of the Torah. The central case shows the silver ornamental Torah crowns that capped the scroll.

Spanish Synagogue (Španělská Synagóga)—Jewish history continues through the 18th, 19th, and tumultuous 20th centuries in this ornate, Moorish-style synagogue built in the 1800s. The upstairs is particularly intriguing, with circa-1900 photos of Josefov, an exhibit on the fascinating story of this museum and its relationship with the Nazi regime, and life in Terezín. The Winter Synagogue (also upstairs) shows a trove of silver worship aids gathered from depopulated Jewish neighborhoods in the countryside in the early 1940s, and gives a sense of what the Nazis stockpiled.

The New Town (Nové Město)

Enough of medieval Prague—let's leap into the modern era. The New Town, with Wenceslas Square as its focal point, is today's urban Prague. This part of the city offers bustling boulevards and interesting neighborhoods. The New Town is the best place to view Prague's remarkable Art Nouveau art and architecture and to learn more about its recent communist past.

Wenceslas Square (Václavské Náměstí)

More a broad boulevard than a square (until recently, trams rattled up and down its parklike median strip), this ▲▲ city landmark is named for King Wenceslas—featured both on the 20-Kč coin and the equestrian statue that stands at the top of the boulevard. Wenceslas Square (Václavské Náměstí) functions as a stage for modern Czech history: The creation of the Czechoslovak state was celebrated here in 1918; in 1968, the Soviets put down huge popular demonstrations here; and, in 1989, more than 300,000 Czechs and Slovaks converged here to claim their freedom.

• *Start near the Wenceslas statue at the top (Metro: Muzeum). Look to the building crowning the top of the square.*

National Museum (Národní Muzeum): While its collection is dull, this building offers a powerful view, and the interior is richly decorated in the Czech Revival Neo-Renaissance style that heralded the 19th-century rebirth of the Czech nation. The light-colored patches in the museum's columns fill holes where Soviet bullets hit during the crackdown against the 1968 "Prague Spring" uprising. Lowly masons—defying their communist bosses, who

Prague's New Town

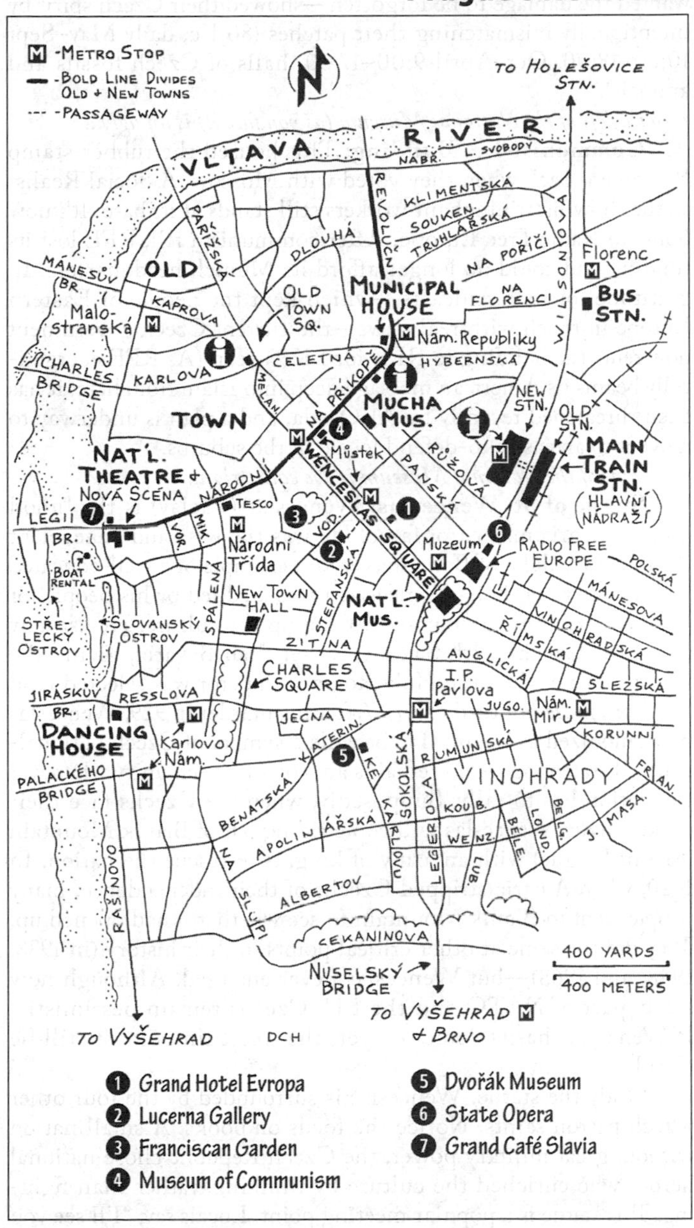

1. Grand Hotel Evropa
2. Lucerna Gallery
3. Franciscan Garden
4. Museum of Communism
5. Dvořák Museum
6. State Opera
7. Grand Café Slavia

wanted the damage to be forgotten—showed their Czech spirit by intentionally mismatching their patches (80 Kč, daily May–Sept 10:00–18:00, Oct–April 9:00–17:00, halls of Czech fossils and animals).

• *To the left of the National Museum (as you face it) is an ugly...*

Communist-Era Building: This housed the rubber-stamp Parliament back when they voted with Moscow. A Social Realist statue showing triumphant workers still stands at its base. It's now home to Radio Free Europe. After communism fell, RFE lost its funding and could no longer afford its Munich headquarters. In gratitude for its broadcasts—which kept the people of Eastern Europe in touch with real news—the current Czech government now rents the building to RFE for 1 Kč a year. (As RFE energetically beams its American message deep into Islam from here, it has been threatened recently by Al-Qaeda, and a plan is underway to move it to an easier-to-defend locale in the suburbs.)

• *In front of the National Museum is the equestrian...*

Statue of St. Wenceslas: Wenceslas (Václav) is the "good king" of Christmas-carol fame. He was the wise and benevolent 10th-century duke of Bohemia. A rare example of a well-educated and literate ruler, King Wenceslas I was credited by his people for Christianizing his nation and lifting up the culture. He astutely allied the Czechs with Saxony, rather than Bavaria, giving the Czechs a vote when the Holy Roman Emperor was selected (and therefore more political clout). After his murder in 929, Wenceslas was canonized as a saint. He became a symbol of Czech nationalism and statehood—and remains an icon of Czech unity whenever the nation has to rally. Supposedly, when the Czechs face their darkest hour, Wenceslas will come riding out of Blaník Mountain (east of Prague) with an army of knights to rescue the nation. In 1620, when Austria stripped Czechs of their independence, many people went to Blaník Mountain to see whether it had opened up. They did the same at other critical points in their history (in 1938, 1948, and 1968)—but Wenceslas never emerged. Although now safely part of NATO and the EU, Czechs remain pessimistic: If Wenceslas hasn't come out yet, the worst times must still lie ahead.

Study the statue. Wenceslas is surrounded by the four other Czech patron saints. Notice the focus on books. A small nation without great military power, the Czech Republic chose national heroes who enriched the culture by thinking, rather than fighting. This statue is a popular meeting point. Locals say, "I'll see you under the horse's...tail."

• *Thirty yards below the big horse is a small garden with a low-key...*

Memorial: This commemorates victims of communism, such as Jan Palach. In 1969, a group of patriots decided that an act of self-immolation would stoke the fires of independence. Jan Palach, a philosophy student who loved life, but wanted it with freedom, set himself on fire on the steps of the National Museum for the cause of Czech independence and died a few days later in a hospital ward. Czechs are keen on anniversaries. Huge demonstrations swept the city on the 20th anniversary of Palach's death. These led, 10 months later, to the overthrow of the Czech communist government in 1989.

This grand square is a gallery of modern **architectural styles.** As you wander downhill, notice the fun mix, all post-1850: Romantic Neo-Gothic, Neo-Renaissance, and Neo-Baroque from the 19th century; Art Nouveau from around 1900; ugly Functionalism from the mid-20th century (the "form follows function" and "ornamentation is a crime" answer to Art Nouveau); Stalin Gothic from the 1950s "communist epoch" (a good example is the Jalta building, halfway downhill on the right); and the glass-and-steel buildings of the 1970s.

• *Walk a couple of blocks downhill through the real people of Prague (not tourists) to* ***Grand Hotel Evropa,*** *with its hard-to-miss, dazzling Art Nouveau exterior and plush café interior full of tourists. Stop for a moment to ponder the events of...*

November of 1989: This huge square was filled every evening with more than 300,000 ecstatic Czechs and Slovaks, believing freedom was at hand. Assembled on the balcony of the building opposite Grand Hotel Evropa (look for the *Marks & Spencer* sign) were a priest, a rock star (famous for his unconventional style, which constantly unnerved the regime), Alexander Dubček (hero of the 1968 revolt), and Václav Havel (the charismatic playwright, newly released from prison, who was every freedom-loving Czech's Mandela). Through a sound system provided by the rock star, Havel's voice boomed over the gathered masses, announcing the resignation of the politburo and saying that the Republic of Czechoslovakia's freedom was imminent. Picture that cold November evening, with thousands of Czechs jingling their keychains in solidarity, chanting at the government, "It's time to go now!" (To quell this revolt, government tanks could have given it the Tiananmen Square treatment—which spilled lots of patriotic blood in China just six months earlier. Locals believe Gorbachev must have made a phone call recommending that blood not be shed over this.) The wave of peaceful demonstrations, known as the "Velvet Revolution," ended later that year with the election of Václav Havel as the president of a free Czechoslovakia.

• *Immediately opposite Grand Hotel Evropa is the Lucerna Gallery (use entry marked* Palác Rokoko *and walk straight in).*

Lucerna Gallery: This grand mall retains some of its Art Deco glamour from the 1930s, with shops, theaters, a ballroom in the basement, and the fine Lucerna Café upstairs. You'll see a sculpture—called *Wenceslas Riding an Upside-Down Horse*—hanging like a swing from a glass dome. David Černý, who created the statue in 1999, is the Czech Republic's most original contemporary artist. Always aspiring to provoke controversy, Černý has painted a menacing Russian tank pink, attached crawling babies to the rocket-like Žižkov TV tower, defecated inside the National Gallery to protest the policies of its director, and sunk a shark-like Saddam Hussein inside an aquarium for a 2005 exhibition. Inside are also a **Ticketpro box office** (with all available tickets, daily 9:30–18:00) and a lavish 1930s Prague cinema (under the upside-down horse, shows artsy films in Czech with English subtitles, or vice versa, 110 Kč).

Directly across busy Vodičkova street (with a handy tram stop) is the Světozor mall. Inside you'll find the **World of Fruit Bar Světozor;** it's every local's favorite ice-cream joint. True to its name, the bar tops its ice cream with every variety of fruit. They sell cakes and milkshakes, too. Ask at the counter for an English menu.

• *Farther down the mall on the left is the entrance to the peaceful...*

Franciscan Garden (Františkánská Zahrada): Its white benches and spreading rosebushes are a universe away from the fast beat of the city that throbs behind the buildings surrounding the garden.

Back on Wenceslas Square, if you're in the mood for a mellow hippie teahouse, consider a break at **Dobrá Čajovna** ("Good Teahouse") near the bottom of the square (#14—see page 234). Or, if you'd like an old-time wine bar, pop into the plain **Šenk Vrbovec** (nearby at #10); it comes with a whiff of the communist days, embracing the faintest bits of genteel culture from an age when refinement was sacrificed for the good of the working class. They serve traditional drinks, Czech keg wine, Moravian wines (listed on blackboard outside), *becherovka* (the 13-herb liqueur), and—only in autumn—*burčák* (young wine that tastes like grape juice halfway to wine).

The bottom of Wenceslas Square is called **Můstek,** which means "Bridge"; a bridge used to cross a moat here, allowing entrance into the Old Town (you can still see the original Old Town entrance down in the Metro station).

• *Running to the right from the bottom of Wenceslas Square is the street called...*

Na Příkopě: Meaning "On the Moat," this busy boulevard follows the line of the Old Town wall, leading to one of the wall's former gates, the Powder Tower. Along the way, it passes the Museum of Communism (see page 198) and a couple of Art Nouveau sights. City tour buses (see page 178) leave from along this street, which offers plenty of shopping temptations (such as these malls: Slovanský Dům at Na Příkopě 22, and Černá Růže at Na Příkopě 12, next door to Mosers, with a crystal showroom upstairs).

Na Příkopě: Art Nouveau Prague

Stroll up Na Příkopě to take in two of Prague's best Art Nouveau sights. The first one is on the street called Panská (turn right up the first street you reach as you walk up Na Příkopě from Wenceslas Square); the second is two blocks farther up Na Příkopě, next to the big, Gothic Powder Tower.

▲▲Mucha Museum—This is one of Europe's most enjoyable little museums. I find the art of Alfons Mucha (MOO-kah, 1860–1939) insistently likeable. See the crucifixion scene he painted as an eight-year-old boy. Read how this popular Czech artist's posters, filled with Czech symbols and expressing his people's ideals and aspirations, were patriotic banners that aroused the national spirit. And check out the photographs of his models. With the help of this abundant supply of slinky models, Mucha was a founding father of the Art Nouveau movement. Partly overseen by Mucha's grandson, the museum is two blocks off Wenceslas Square and wonderfully displayed on one comfortable floor (120 Kč, daily 10:00–18:00, well-described in English, Panská 7, tel. 224-233-355, www.mucha.cz). The included 30-minute video is definitely worthwhile (in English, generally at :15 and :45 past the hour—ask for the starting time); it describes the main project of Mucha's life—the *Slavic Epic,* now on display in Moravský Krumlov (a small town in the eastern Czech Republic).

• *Coming back to Na Příkopě and continuing toward the Powder Tower, notice the Neo-Renaissance* ***Živnostenská Banka*** *building on the corner of Nekázanka. It houses a modern bank with classy circa-1900 ambience (enter and peek into the main hall upstairs).*

At the end of Na Příkopě, you'll arrive at the...

▲▲Municipal House (Obecní Dům)—The Municipal House is the "pearl of Czech Art Nouveau." Financed by cultural and artistic leaders, it was built (1905–1911) as a ceremonial palace to reinforce the self-awareness of the Czech nation. It features Prague's largest concert hall, a recommended Art Nouveau café (Kavárna Obecní Dům, see page 234), and two other restaurants. Pop in and wander around the lobby of the concert hall. Walk through to the ticket office on the ground floor. For the best look, including impressive halls and murals you won't otherwise see, take one of the regular hour-long **tours** (open daily 10:00–18:00; tours—150 Kč, generally at 10:15, 12:00, 14:00, and 16:00, in English 2/day, buy ticket from ground-floor shop where tour departs; tel. 222-002-101).

Standing in front of the Municipal House, you can survey four different styles of architecture. First, enjoy the pure Art Nouveau of the Municipal House itself. Featuring a goddess-like Praha presiding over a land of peace and high culture, the *Homage to Prague* mosaic on the building's striking facade stoked cultural pride and nationalist sentiment. Across the street, the classical fixer-upper from 1815 was the customs house (currently being renovated). The stark national bank building (Česká Národní Banka) is textbook Functionalism from the 1930s. Across the square, former barracks are making way for Prague's biggest shopping mall, which promises none of its neighbors' elegance.

Powder Tower: The big, black Powder Tower (not worth touring inside) was the Gothic gate of the town wall, built to house the city's gunpowder. The decoration on the tower, portraying Czech kings, is the best 15th-century sculpture in town. If you go through the tower, you'll reach Celetná street, which leads past a few sights (described on page 178) to the Old Town Square.

Národní Třída: Communist Prague

From Můstek at the bottom of Wenceslas Square, you can head west on Národní Třída (in the opposite direction from Na Příkopě and the Art Nouveau sights) for an interesting stroll through urban Prague to the National Theatre and the Vltava River. But first, consider dropping into the Museum of Communism, a few steps down Na Příkopě (on the right).

▲▲Museum of Communism—This museum traces the story of communism in Prague: the origins, dream, reality, and nightmare; the cult of personality; and finally, the Velvet Revolution. Along the way it gives a fascinating review of the Czech Republic's 40-year stint with Soviet economics, "in all its dreariness and puffed-up glory." You'll find propaganda posters, busts of communist all-stars (Marx, Lenin, Stalin), and a photograph of the massive stone Stalin that overlooked Prague until 1962. Slices of communist life are re-created here, from a bland store counter to a typical classroom (with textbooks using Russia's Cyrillic alphabet—no longer studied here—and a poem on the chalkboard extolling the virtues of the tractor). Don't miss the Jan Palach exhibit and the 20-minute video (plays continuously, English subtitles) showing how the Czech people chafed under the big red yoke from the 1950s through 1989 (180 Kč, daily 9:00–21:00, Na Příkopě 10, above a McDonald's and next to a casino—Lenin is turning over in his grave, tel. 224-212-966, www.museumofcommunism.com).

• *Now head for the river (with your back to Wenceslas Square, go left down 28 Října to Národní Třída). Along the way, Národní Třída has a story to tell.*

Along the Vltava River

I've listed these sights from north to south, beginning at the grand, Neo-Renaissance National Theatre, which is five blocks south of Charles Bridge and stands along the riverbank at the end of Národní Třída.

National Theatre (Národní Divadlo)—Opened in 1883 with Smetana's opera *Libuše*, this theater was the first truly Czech venue in Prague. From the very start, it was nicknamed the "Cradle of Czech Culture." The building is a key symbol of the Czech national revival that began in the late 18th century. In 1800, "Prag" was predominantly German. The Industrial Revolution brought Czechs from the countryside into the city, their new urban identity defined by patriotic teachers and priests. By 1883, most of the city spoke Czech, and the opening of this theater represented the birth of the modern Czech nation. It remains an important national icon: The state annually pours more subsidies into this theater than into all of Czech film production. It's the most beautiful venue in town for opera or ballet, often with world-class singers (see page 215).

Next door (just inland, on Národní Třída) is the boxy, glassy facade of the **Nová Scéna.** This "New National Theatre" building, dating from 1983 (the 100th anniversary of the original National Theatre building), reflects the bold and stark communist aesthetic. The Nová Scéna hosts Laterna Magica Black Light Theater performances, among other events (see page 215).

Across the street from the National Theatre is the former haunt of Prague's intelligentsia, **Grand Café Slavia,** a Viennese-style coffeehouse that makes a fine stop for a meal or drink with a view of the river (see page 233).

•*Just south of the National Theatre in the Vltava are...*

Prague's Islands—From the National Theatre, the Legions' Bridge (Most Legií) leads across the island called **Střelecký Ostrov.** Covered with chestnut trees, this island boasts Prague's best beach (on the sandy tip that points north to Charles Bridge). You might see a fisherman pulling out trout from a river that's now much cleaner than it used to be. Bring a swimsuit and take a dip just a stone's throw from Europe's most beloved bridge. In summer, the island hosts open-air movies (most in English or with English subtitles, nightly mid-July–early Sept at around 21:00, www.strelak.cz).

In the mood for boating instead of swimming? On the next island down, **Slovanský Ostrov,** you can rent a paddleboat (40 Kč/hr for rowboats, 60 Kč/hr for paddleboats, bring a picture ID as deposit). A lazy hour paddling around Střelecky Ostrov, or just floating sleepily in the middle of the river surrounded by this great city's architectural splendor, is a delightful experience on a sunny day. It's cheap, easy, fun—and it's good for you.

• *A 10-minute walk (or one stop on tram #17) from the National Theatre, beyond the islands, is Jirásek Bridge (Jiráskův Most), where you'll find the...*

Dancing House (Tančící Dům)—If ever a building could get your toes tapping, it would be this one, nicknamed "Fred and Ginger" by American architecture buffs. This metallic samba is the work of Frank Gehry (who designed the equally striking Guggenheim Museum in Bilbao, Spain, and Seattle's Experience Music Project). Eight-legged Ginger's wispy dress and Fred's metal mesh head are easy to spot. The building's top-floor restaurant, La Perle de Prague, is a fine place for a fancy French meal (VIPs often eat and drink here, reservation needed even to get into the elevator, tel. 221-984-160).

The Little Quarter (Malá Strana)

This charming neighborhood, huddled under the castle on the west bank of the river, is low on blockbuster sights but high on ambience. The most enjoyable approach from the Old Town is across Charles Bridge. From the end of the bridge (TI in tower), Mostecká street leads two blocks up to Little Quarter Square (Malostranské Náměstí) and the huge Church of St. Nicholas.

On or near Little Quarter Square

The focal point of this neighborhood, Little Quarter Square (Malostranské Náměstí) is dominated by the huge Church of St. Nicholas. Note that there's a handy Via Musica ticket office across from the church.

Church of St. Nicholas (Kostel Sv. Mikuláše)—When the Jesuits came to Prague, they found the perfect piece of real estate for their church and its associated school—right on Little Quarter Square. The church (built 1703–1760) is the best example of High Baroque in town. It's giddy with curves and illusions. The altar features a lavish gold-plated Nicholas flanked by the two top Jesuits: the founder, St. Ignatius Loyola and his missionary follower, St. Francis Xavier. Climb up the **gallery** through the staircase in the left transept for a close-up look at a collection of large canvases and illusionary frescoes by Karel Škréta, the greatest Czech Baroque painter. Notice that at first glance, the canvases are utterly dark. But as sunbeams shine through the window, various parts of the painting brighten up. Like a looking glass, it reflects the light, creating a play of light and darkness. This painting technique reflects a central Baroque belief: The world is full of darkness, and the only hope that makes it come alive comes from God. The church walls seem to nearly fuse with the sky, suggesting that happenings on earth are closely connected to heaven. Find St. Nick with his bishop's miter in the center of the ceiling, on his way to heaven

Prague's Little Quarter

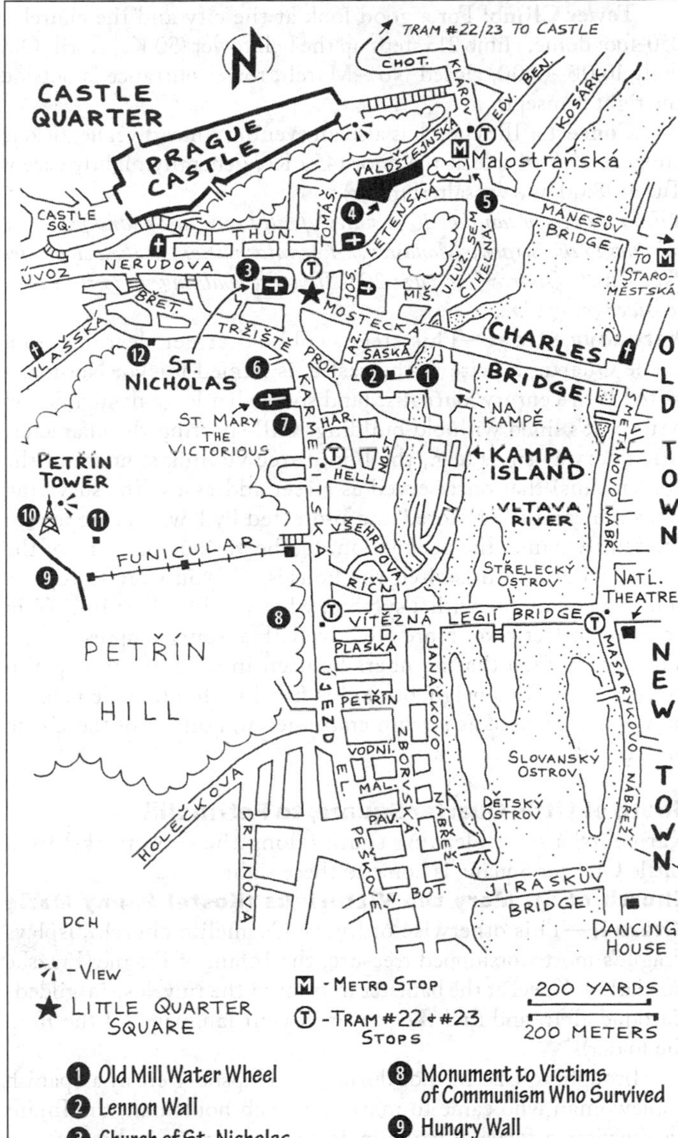

1. Old Mill Water Wheel
2. Lennon Wall
3. Church of St. Nicholas
4. Wallenstein Palace
5. Wallenstein Garden Entrance
6. Vrtba Garden
7. Church of St. Mary the Victorious
8. Monument to Victims of Communism Who Survived
9. Hungry Wall
10. Petřín Tower & Museum of Jára Cimrman
11. Mirror Maze
12. US Embassy

(60 Kč, church open daily 9:00–17:00, opens at 8:30 for prayer).

Tower Climb: For a good look at the city and the church's 250-foot dome, climb 215 steps up the bell tower (50 Kč, April–Oct daily 10:00–18:00, closed Nov–March, tower entrance is outside the right transept).

Concerts: The church is also an evening concert venue; tickets are generally on sale at the door (450 Kč, generally nightly except Tue at 18:00, www.psalterium.cz).

• *From here, you can hike 10 minutes uphill to the castle (and five more minutes to the Strahov Monastery). For information on these sights, see "The Castle Quarter" on page 203. If you're walking up to the castle, consider going via...*

Nerudova Street—This steep, cobbled street, leading from Little Quarter Square to the castle, is named for Jan Neruda, a gifted 19th-century journalist (and somewhat less talented fiction writer). It's lined with old buildings still sporting the characteristic doorway signs (e.g., the lion, three violinists, house of the golden suns) that once served as street addresses. The surviving signs are carefully restored and protected by law. They represent the family name, the occupation, or the various passions of the people who once inhabited the houses. (If you were to replace your house number with a symbol, what would it be?) In 1777, in order to collect taxes more effectively, Hapsburg empress Maria Theresa decreed that numbers be used instead of these quaint house names. This neighborhood is filled with old noble palaces, now generally used as foreign embassies and offices of the Czech parliament.

South of Little Quarter Square, to Petřín Hill

Karmelitská street, leading south (along the tram tracks) from Little Quarter Square, is home to these sights.

Church of St. Mary the Victorious (Kostel Panny Marie Vítězné)—This otherwise ordinary Carmelite church displays Prague's most worshipped treasure, the Infant of Prague (Pražské Jezulátko). Kneel at the banister in front of the tiny, lost-in-gilded-Baroque altar, and find the prayer in your language (of the 13 in the folder).

Brought to Czech lands during the Hapsburg era by a Spanish noblewoman who came to marry a Czech nobleman, the Infant has become a focus of worship and miracle tales in Prague and Spanish-speaking countries. South Americans come on pilgrimage to Prague just to see this one statue. An exhibit upstairs shows tiny embroidered robes given to the Infant, including ones from Maria Theresa of Austria (1754) and the government of Vietnam (1958), and a video showing a nun lovingly dressing the doll-like sculpture (free, Mon–Sat 9:30–17:30, Sun 13:00–17:00, English-language Mass Sun at 12:00, Karmelitská 9, www.pragjesu.com).

• *Continue a few more blocks down Karmelitská to the south end of the Little Quarter (where the street is called Újezd, roughly across the Legions' Bridge from the National Theatre). Here you find yourself at the base of...*

Petřín Hill—This hill, topped by a replica of the Eiffel Tower, features several unusual sights.

The figures walking down the steps in the hillside make up the **Monument to Victims of Communism Who Survived.** The monument's figures are gradually atrophied by the totalitarian regime. They do not die, but slowly disappear, one limb at a time. The statistics say it all: In Czechoslovakia alone, 205,486 people were imprisoned, 248 were executed, 4,500 died in prison, 327 were shot attempting to cross the border, and 170,938 left the country. To the left of the monument is the **Hungry Wall,** the 14th-century Charles IV's equivalent of FDR's work-for-food projects. On the right (50 yards away) is the base of a handy **funicular**—hop on to reach Petřín Tower (uses 20-Kč tram/Metro ticket, runs daily 8:00–22:00, every 10–15 min).

The summit of Petřín Hill is considered the best place in Prague to take your date for a romantic city view. Built for an exhibition in 1891, the 200-foot-tall **Petřín Tower** is a fifth the height of its Parisian big brother built two years earlier. Climbing the 400 steps rewards you with amazing views over the city. Local wives drag their men to Petřín Hill each May Day to reaffirm their love with a kiss under a blooming sour-cherry tree.

In the tower's basement is the funniest sight in Prague, the **Museum of Jára Cimrman, Genius Who Did Not Become Famous.** The museum traces the (fictional) life of the greatest Czech who never lived, including pictures and English descriptions of the thinker's overlooked inventions (50 Kč includes tower and Cimrman museum, daily 10:00–22:00).

The **mirror maze** next door is nothing special, but fun to quickly wander through since you're already here (50 Kč, daily 10:00–22:00).

The Castle Quarter (Hradčany)

Looming above Prague, dominating its skyline, is the Castle Quarter. Prague Castle and its surrounding sights are packed with Czech history as well as with tourists. In addition to the castle itself, I enjoy visiting the nearby Strahov Monastery—which has a fascinating old library and beautiful views over all of Prague.

Castle Square (Hradčanské Náměstí)—right in front of the castle gates—is at the center of this neighborhood. Stretching along the promontory away from the castle is a regal neighborhood that ends at the Strahov Monastery. Above the castle are the Royal

Gardens, and below the castle are more gardens and lanes leading down to the Little Quarter.

Getting to Prague Castle

If you're not up for a hike, the tram offers a sweat-free ride up to the castle. Taxis are expensive, as they have to go the long way around (200 Kč).

By Foot: Begin in the Little Quarter, just across Charles Bridge from the Old Town. Hikers can follow the main cobbled road (Mostecká) from Charles Bridge to Little Quarter Square, marked by the huge, green-domed Church of St. Nicholas. (The nearest Metro stop is Malostranská, from which Valdštejnská street leads down to Little Quarter Square.) From Little Quarter Square, hike uphill along Nerudova street (described on page 202). After about 10 minutes, a steep lane on the right leads to the castle. (If you continue straight, Nerudova becomes Úvoz and climbs to the Strahov Monastery.)

By Tram: Trams #22 and #23 take you up to the castle. While you can catch the tram in various places, these three stops are particularly convenient: at the Národní Třída Metro stop (between Wenceslas Square and the National Theatre in the New Town); in front of the National Theatre (Národní Divadlo, on the riverbank in the New Town); and at Malostranská (the Metro stop in the Little Quarter). After rattling up the hill, these trams make three stops near the castle: Get off at **Královský Letohrádek** for the scenic approach to the castle (through the Royal Gardens—free entry, open April–Oct daily 10:00–18:00, closed Nov–March); or stay on one more stop to get off at **Pražský Hrad** (most direct but least interesting—simply walk along U Prašného Mostu over the bridge into the castle); or go yet one more stop to **Pohořelec** to visit the Strahov Monastery before hiking down to the castle (to get to the monastery from this tram stop, follow tram tracks uphill for 50 yards, enter fancy gate on left near red-brick wall, you'll see twin spires of monastery).

Tram Tips: When you're choosing which of the castle's three tram stops to get off at, consider the time of day. The castle is plagued with crowds. If visiting in the morning, use the Pražský Hrad tram stop for the quickest commute to the castle. Be at the door of St. Vitus Cathedral when it opens at 9:00 (because just 10–15 minutes later, it'll be swamped with tour groups). See the castle sights quickly, then move on to the Strahov Monastery. I'd avoid the castle entirely mid-morning, but by mid-afternoon, the tour groups are napping and the grounds are (relatively) uncrowded. If going in the afternoon, take the tram to the Pohořelec stop, see the Strahov Monastery, then wander down to the castle.

Prague's Castle Quarter

1. Castle Square & Plague Column
2. Schwarzenberg Palace
3. Archbishop's Palace
4. Sternberg Palace
5. Castle Gate
6. Tickets & Information
7. St. Vitus Cathedral
8. Old Royal Palace
9. Basilica of St. George
10. Golden Lane
11. Toy & Barbie Museum
12. Steps to Terraced Gardens
13. Royal Gardens
14. Royal Summer Palace
15. Loreta Church
16. Strahov Monastery & Library
17. Museum of Miniatures
18. Černín Palace
19. Klášterní Pivovar (Brewery)
20. Restaurace Nad Úvozem
21. Hostinec u Černého Vola Pub
22. Malý Buddha Veggie Rest.
23. Espresso Kajetánka
24. Na Baště Café

Strahov Monastery and Library

Twin Baroque domes high above the castle mark the Strahov Monastery. Worth ▲, this complex is best reached from the Pohořelec stop on tram #22 or #23 (from the stop, go up the red-railed ramp and through the gate into the monastery grounds). If you're coming on foot from the Little Quarter, allow 15 minutes for the uphill hike. After seeing the monastery, hike down to the castle (a 5-min walk).

Monastery: The monastery (Strahovský Klášter Premonstrátů) had a booming economy of its own in its heyday, with vineyards and the biggest beer hall in town—still open. Its main church, dedicated to the Assumption of St. Mary, is an originally Romanesque structure decorated by the monks in textbook Baroque (usually closed, but look through the window inside the front door to see its interior).

Library: The adjacent library (Strahovská Knihovna) offers a peek at how enlightened thinkers in the 18th century influenced learning (80 Kč, daily 9:00–12:00 & 13:00–17:00). Cases in the library gift shop show off illuminated manuscripts (described in English). Some are in old Czech, but these are rare. Because the Enlightenment believed in the universality of knowledge, there was little place for vernaculars—therefore, few books here are in the Czech language. Two rooms (seen only from the door) are filled with 10th- to 17th-century books under elaborately painted ceilings. The theme of the first and bigger hall is philosophy, with the history of man's pursuit of knowledge painted on the ceiling. The other hall focuses on theology. Notice the gilded locked case containing the *libri prohibiti* (prohibited books) at the end of the room. Only the abbot had the key, and you had to have his blessing to read these books—by writers such as Nicolas Copernicus and Jan Hus, even including the French encyclopedia. As the Age of Enlightenment began to take hold in Europe at the end of the 18th century, monasteries still controlled the books. The hallway connecting these two library rooms was filled with cases illustrating the new practical approach to natural sciences. Find the baby dodo bird (which became extinct in the 17th century).

Nearby Views: Just downhill from the monastery, past the venerable linden trees (a symbol of the Czech people) and through the gate, the views from the **monastery garden** are among the best in Prague. From the public perch below the tables, you can see St. Vitus Cathedral (the heart of the castle complex), the green dome of the Church of St. Nicholas (marking the center of the Little Quarter), the two dark towers fortifying both ends of Charles Bridge, and the fanciful black spires of the Týn Church (marking the Old Town Square). On the horizon is the modern **Žižkov TV and radio tower** (conveniently marking the liveliest nightlife zone in town). Begun in the 1980s, it was meant to jam Radio Free Europe's broadcast from Munich. By the time it was finished, communism was dead and Radio Free Europe's headquarters had actually moved to Prague.

To reach the castle from Strahov Monastery, take Loretánská (the upper road, passing Loreta Square—see below); this is more interesting than going on the lower road, Úvoz, which takes you steeply downhill, below Castle Square (see map on page 205).

On Loreta Square, Between Strahov Monastery and Castle Square

From the monastery, take Loretánská street to Loreta Square (Loretánské Náměstí). As you wander this road, you'll pass several mansions and palaces, and an important pilgrimage church.

Loreta Church—This church has been a hit with pilgrims for centuries, thanks to its dazzling bell tower, peaceful yet plush cloister, sparkling treasury, and much-venerated "Holy House" (90 Kč, Tue–Sun 9:00–12:15 & 13:00–16:30, closed Mon).

Once inside the entry, follow the one-way clockwise route. Strolling along the cloister, notice that the ceiling is painted with the many places Mary has miraculously appeared to the faithful in Europe.

In the garden-like center of the cloister stands the ornate **Santa Casa** (Holy House), considered by some pilgrims to be part of Mary's home in Nazareth. Because many pilgrims returning from the Holy Land docked at the Italian port of Loreto, it's called the Loreta Shrine. The Santa Casa is the "little Bethlehem" of Prague. It is the traditional departure point for Czech pilgrims setting out on the long, arduous journey to Europe's most important pilgrimage site, Santiago de Compostela, in northwest Spain. Inside, on the left wall, hangs what some consider to be an original beam from the house of Mary. It's overseen by a beloved statue of the "Black Virgin." The Santa Casa itself might seem like a bit of a letdown, but consider that you're entering the holiest spot in the country for generations of believers.

The small Baroque church behind the Santa Casa is one of the most beautiful in Prague. The decor looks rich—but the marble and gold is all fake (tap the columns). From the window in the back, you can see a stucco relief on the Santa Casa showing angels rescuing the house from a pagan attack in Nazareth, and making a special delivery to Loreto in Italy.

Continue around the cloister. In the last corner is St. Bearded Woman (Svatá Starosta). This patron saint of unhappy marriages is a woman whose family arranged for her to marry a pagan man. She prayed for an escape, sprouted a beard...and the guy said, "No way." While she managed to avoid the marriage, it angered her father, who crucified her. The many candles here are from people suffering through unhappy marriages.

Take a left just before the exit and head upstairs, following signs to the treasury—a room full of jeweled worship aids (well-described in English). The highlight here is a monstrance (Communion wafer holder) from 1699, with over 6,000 diamonds.

Enjoy the short carillon concert at the top of the hour; from the lawn in front of the main entrance, you can see the racks of bells being clanged. (At the exit, you'll see a schedule of English Masses and upcoming *poutní*—pilgrimages—departing from here.)

Castle Square (Hradčanské Náměstí)

This is the central square of the Castle Quarter. Enjoy the awesome city view and the two entertaining bands that play regularly at the gate. (If the Prague Castle Orchestra is playing, say hello to friendly, mustachioed Josef, and consider getting the group's terrific CD.) A café with dramatic city views called Espresso Kajetánka hides a few steps down, immediately to the right as you face the castle (see page 236). From here, stairs lead into the Little Quarter.

Castle Square was a kind of medieval Pennsylvania Avenue—the king, the most powerful noblemen, and the archbishop lived here. Look uphill from the gate. The Renaissance **Schwarzenberg Palace** (on the left, with the big rectangles scratched on the wall, now under renovation) was where the Rožmberks "humbly" stayed when they were in town from their Český Krumlov estates. The Schwarzenberg family inherited the Krumlov estates and aristocratic prominence in Bohemia, and stayed in the palace until the 20th century.

The archbishop still lives in the yellow Rococo **palace** across the square (with the three white goose necks in the red field—the coat of arms of Prague's archbishops).

Through the portal on the left-hand side of the palace, a lane leads to the **Sternberg Palace** (Šternberský Palác), filled with the National Gallery's skippable collection of European paintings—including minor works by Albrecht Dürer, Peter Paul Rubens, Rembrandt, and El Greco (100 Kč, Tue–Sun 10:00–18:00, closed Mon).

The black Baroque sculpture in the middle of the square is a **plague column,** erected as a token of gratitude to the saints who saved the population from the epidemic, and an integral part of the main square of many Hapsburg towns.

The statue marked *TGM* honors **Tomáš Garrigue Masaryk** (1850–1937), a university professor and a pal of Woodrow Wilson. At the end of World War I, Masaryk united the Czechs and the Slovaks into one nation and became its first president.

Prague Castle (Pražský Hrad)

For more than a thousand years, Czech leaders have ruled from Prague Castle. Today Prague's Castle is, by some measures, the biggest on earth. A visit here is worth ▲▲. Four stops matter, and all are explained here: St. Vitus Cathedral, Old Royal Palace, Basilica of St. George, and the Golden Lane.

Hours: Castle sights are open daily April–Oct 9:00–17:00, Nov–March 9:00–16:00, last entry 15 minutes before closing; grounds are open daily 5:00–23:00. St. Vitus Cathedral is closed Sunday mornings for Mass. Be warned that the cathedral can be unexpectedly closed due to special services—consider calling ahead to confirm (tel. 224-373-368 or 224-372-434). If you're not interested in entering the museums, you could try a nighttime visit—the castle grounds are safe, peaceful, floodlit, and open late.

Tickets: The **cathedral** requires its own ticket (100 Kč, free for pilgrims accompanied by their priest). For the other castle sights, rather than the comprehensive long tour ticket (350 Kč), I recommend buying the short tour ticket (250 Kč, covers the Old Royal Palace, Basilica of St. George, and the Golden Lane at peak hours, buy in palace or in basilica). If you want to save time and money, skip the Golden Lane during the day and return at night for a romantic, crowd-free visit (free in the morning and evening).

Tours: Hour-long tours in English depart from the main ticket office about three times a day, but cover only the cathedral and Old Royal Palace (90 Kč plus ticket, tel. 224-373-368). Consider the worthwhile **audioguide** (250 Kč/2 hrs, 300 Kč/3 hrs, must leave ID).

Crowd-Beating Tips: Huge throngs of tourists turn the castle grounds into a sea of people during peak times (9:15–15:00). St. Vitus Cathedral is the most crowded part of the castle complex. If visiting in the morning, ideally be at the cathedral entrance promptly at 9:00, when the doors open. For 10 minutes, you'll have the sacred space for yourself (after about 9:15, tour guides jockeying unwieldy groups from tomb to tomb turn the church into a noisy human traffic jam). Late afternoon is least crowded.

Castle Gate and Courtyards—Begin at Castle Square. From here, survey the castle—the tip of a 1,500-foot-long series of courtyards, churches, and palaces. The guard changes on the hour (5:00–23:00), with the most ceremony and music at noon.

Walk under the fighting giants, under an arch, through the passageway, and into the courtyard. The modern green awning with the golden-winged cat (just past the ticket office) marks the offices of the Czech president. The current president, Václav Klaus, is popular with members of the older generation (who like consistency)—but is bitterly resented by younger people, many of whom see him as incapable of considering points of view other than his own. Outside the Czech Republic, Klaus is chiefly known for his unconstructive criticism of the European Union.

• *As you walk through another passageway, you'll find yourself facing...*

▲▲▲St. Vitus Cathedral (Katedrála Sv. Víta)—The Roman Catholic cathedral symbolizes the Czech spirit—it contains the tombs and relics of the most important local saints and kings, including the first three Hapsburg kings.

Cathedral Facade: Before entering, check out the facade. What's up with the guys in suits carved into the facade below the big round window? They're the architects and builders who finished the church. Started in 1344, construction was stalled by wars and plagues. But, fueled by the 19th-century rise of Czech nationalism, Prague's top church was finished in 1929 for the 1,000th anniversary of the death of St. Wenceslas. While it looks all Gothic, it's actually two distinct halves: the original 14th-century Gothic around the high altar, and the modern Neo-Gothic nave. For 400 years, a temporary wall sealed off the functional, yet unfinished, cathedral.

Mucha Stained-Glass Window: Go inside, buy your ticket, show your ticket at the fenced-off area, and find the third window on the left. This masterful 1931 Art Nouveau window is by Czech artist Alfons Mucha (if you like this, you'll love the Mucha Museum in the New Town—see page 197). Notice Mucha's stirring nationalism: Methodius and Cyril, widely considered the fathers of Slavic-style Christianity, are top and center. Cyril—the monk in black holding the Bible—brought the word of God to the Slavs. They had no written language in the ninth century—so he designed the necessary alphabet (Glagolitic, which later developed into Cyrillic). Methodius, the bishop, is shown baptizing a mythic, lanky, long-haired Czech man—a reminder of how he brought Christianity to the Czech people. Scenes from the life of Cyril on the left and scenes from the life of Methodius on the right bookend the stirring and epic Slavic scene. In the center are a kneeling boy and a prophesying elder—that's young St. Wenceslas and his grandmother, St. Ludmila. In addition to being specific historical figures, these characters are also symbolic: The old woman, with closed eyes, stands for the past and memory, while the young boy, with a penetrating stare, represents the hope and future of a nation. Notice how master designer Mucha draws your attention to these two figures through the use of colors—the dark blue on the outside gradually turns into green, then yellow, and finally the gold of the woman and the crimson of the boy in the center. In Mucha's color language, blue stands for the past, gold for the mythic, and red for the future. Besides all the meaning, Mucha's art is simply a joy to behold. (And on the bottom, the tasteful little ad for *Banka Slavie*, which paid for the work, is hardly noticeable.)

Relief of Prague: Continue circulating around the apse. As you walk around the high altar, study the fascinating carved-wood relief of Prague. It depicts the victorious Hapsburg armies entering the castle after the Battle of White Mountain, while the Protestant king Frederic escapes over the Charles Bridge (before it had any statues). Carved in 1630, 10 years after the famous event occurred, the relief also gives you a peek at Prague in 1620, stretching from the Týn Church to the cathedral (half-built at that time, up to where you are now). Notice that back then, the Týn Church was Hussite, so the centerpiece of its facade is not the Virgin Mary—but a chalice, symbol of Jan Hus' ideals. The old city walls—now replaced by the main streets of the city—stand strong. The Jewish Quarter (the slummy, muddy zone along the riverside below the bridge on the left) fills land no one else wanted.

Apse: Circling around the high altar, you pass graves of bishops, including the tomb of St. Vitus (behind the chair of the bishop). The stone sarcophagi are kings from the Přemysl dynasty (12th–14th centuries). Locals claim the gigantic, shiny tomb of St. John of Nepomuk has over a ton of silver (for more on St. John of Nepomuk, see page 187). After the silver tomb, look up at the royal box from where the king would attend Mass in his jammies (an elevated corridor connected his private apartment with his own altar-side box pew).

Look for the finely carved wood panel that gives a Counter-Reformation spin on the Wars of Religion. It shows the "barbaric" Protestant nobles destroying the Catholic icons in the cathedral after their short-lived victory.

Wenceslas Chapel: A fancy roped-off chapel (right transept) houses the tomb of St. Wenceslas, surrounded by precious 14th-century murals showing scenes of his life, and a locked door leading to the crown jewels. The Czech kings used to be crowned right here in front of the coffin, draped in red. The chapel is roped off because the wallpaper is encrusted with precious and semi-precious stones. (Lead us not into temptation.) You can view the chapel from either door (if the door facing the nave is crowded, duck around to the left to find a generally open door).

Spire: You can climb 287 steps up the spire for one of the best views of the whole city (included in cathedral ticket, April–Oct daily 9:00–17:00 except Sun morning, last entry 45 minutes before closing, closes at 16:00 Nov–March).

Back Outside the Cathedral: Leaving the cathedral, turn left (past the public WC). The **obelisk** was erected in 1928—a single piece of granite celebrating the 10th anniversary of the establishment of Czechoslovakia. It was originally much taller, but broke in transit—an inauspicious start for a nation destined to last only 70 years. Up in the fat, green tower of the cathedral is the Czech

Republic's biggest bell, nicknamed "Zikmund." In June of 2002, it cracked—and two months later, the worst flood in recorded history hit the city. As a nation sandwiched between great powers, Czechs are deeply superstitious. Often feeling unable to influence the course of their own history, they helplessly look at events as we might look at the weather and other natural phenomena—trying to figure out what fate has in store for them next.

Find the 14th-century **mosaic** of the Last Judgment outside on the right transept. It was commissioned Italian-style by King Charles IV, who was modern, cosmopolitan, and ahead of his time. Jesus oversees the action, as some go to heaven and some go to hell. The Czech king and queen kneel directly below Jesus and the six patron saints. On coronation day, they would walk under this arch, which would remind them (and their subjects) that even those holding great power are not above God's judgment. The royal crown and national jewels are kept in a chamber (see the grilled windows) above this entryway, which was the cathedral's main entry for centuries while the church remained uncompleted.

Across the square and 20 yards to the right, a door leads into the Old Royal Palace (in the lobby, there's a WC with a window shared by the men's and women's sections—meet your partner to enjoy the view).

Old Royal Palace (Starý Královský Palác)—This was the seat of the Bohemian princes starting in the 12th century. While extensively rebuilt, the **large hall** is late Gothic, designed as a multipurpose hall for the old nobility. It's big enough for jousts—even the staircase was designed to let a mounted soldier gallop in. It was filled with market stalls, giving nobles a chance to shop without actually going into town. In the 1400s, the nobility met here to elect their king. This tradition survived until modern times, as the parliament crowded into this room until the late 1990s to elect the Czechoslovak (and later Czech) president. (The last two elections happened in another, far more lavish hall in the castle.) Look up at the flower-shaped, vaulted ceiling.

On your immediate right, enter the two small Renaissance rooms known as the **"Czech Office."** From these rooms (empty today except for their 17th-century porcelain heaters), two governors used to oversee the Czech lands for the Hapsburgs in Vienna. In 1618, angry Czech Protestant nobles poured into these rooms and threw the two Catholic governors out of the window. An old law actually permits defenestration—throwing people (usually bad politicians) out of windows when necessary. Old prints on the wall show the second of Prague's many defenestrations. The two governors landed—fittingly—in a pile of horse manure. Even though they suffered only broken arms and bruised egos, this event kicked off the huge and lengthy Thirty Years' War.

As you exit through the side door, notice how the halls are big enough to accommodate knights on horseback. Before you gallop out, pause at the door to consider the subtle yet racy little Renaissance knocker. Go ahead—play with it for a little sex in the palace (be gentle).

• *Across from the palace exit is the...*

Basilica of St. George (Bazilika Sv. Jiří)—Step into the beautifully lit Basilica of St. George to see Prague's best-preserved Romanesque church. St. Wenceslas' mother, St. Ludmila, was reburied here in 973. The first Bohemian convent was established here near the palace.

Today, the **convent** next door houses the National Gallery's Collection of Old Masters, featuring the best Czech paintings from the Mannerist and Baroque periods (100 Kč, Tue–Sun 10:00–18:00, closed Mon).

• *Continue walking downhill through the castle grounds. Turn left on the first street, which leads into the...*

Golden Lane (Zlatá Ulička)—During the day, this street of old buildings, which originally housed goldsmiths, is jammed with tourists and lined with overpriced gift shops. Franz Kafka lived briefly at #22. There's a deli/bistro at the top. The tiny street is free, empty, and evocative in the morning (before 9:00) and at night (after 17:00 in summer, 16:00 in winter). Exit the lane through a corridor at the last house (#12).

Toy and Barbie Museum (Muzeum Hraček)—At the bottom of the castle complex, just after leaving the Golden Lane, a long, wooden staircase leads to two entertaining floors of old toys and dolls thoughtfully described in English. You'll see a century of teddy bears, 19th-century model train sets, and an incredible Barbie collection (the entire top floor). Find the buxom 1959 first edition, and you'll understand why these capitalistic sirens of material discontent weren't allowed here until 1989 (60 Kč, 120 Kč per family, not included in any castle tickets, daily 9:30–17:30, WC next to entrance).

After Your Castle Visit: Tourists squirt slowly through a fortified door at the bottom end of the castle. From there, you can follow the steep lane directly back to the riverbank (and the Malostranská Metro station).

Or you can take a hard right and stroll through the long, delightful park. Along the way, notice the modernist design of the **Na Valech Garden,** which was carried out by the "court architect" of the 1920s, Jože Plečnik of Slovenia.

Halfway through the long park is a viewpoint overlooking **terraced gardens;** you can zigzag down through these gardens into the Little Quarter (80 Kč, April–Oct daily 10:00–18:00, closed Nov–March).

If you continue through the park all the way to Castle Square, you'll find two more options: a staircase leading down into the Little Quarter, or a cobbled street taking you to historic Nerudova street (described on page 202).

Congratulations. You've conquered the castle.

ENTERTAINMENT

Prague booms with live and inexpensive theater, classical music, jazz, and pop entertainment. Everything's listed in several monthly cultural events programs (free at TI) and in the *Prague Post* newspaper.

You'll be tempted to gather fliers as you wander through the town. Don't bother. To really understand all your options (the street Mozarts are pushing only their concerts), drop by a **Via Musica** box office. There are two: One is next to Týn Church on the Old Town Square (daily 10:30–19:30, tel. 224-826-969), and the other is in the Little Quarter across from the Church of St. Nicholas (daily 10:30–18:00, tel. 257-535-568). The event schedule posted on their wall clearly shows everything that's playing today and tomorrow, including tourist concerts, Black Light Theater, and marionette shows, with photos of each venue and a map locating everything (www.viamusica.cz).

Ticketpro sells tickets for the serious concert venues and most music clubs (daily 8:00–12:00 & 12:30–16:30, Rytířská 31, between Havelská Market and Estates Theatre; also has a booth in Tourist Center at Rytířská 12, daily 9:00–20:00; English-language reservations tel. 296-329-999).

Consider buying concert tickets directly from the actual venues. You won't save money, but more of your money will go to the musicians.

Black Light Theater—A kind of mime/modern dance variety show, Black Light Theater has no language barrier and is, for many, more entertaining than a classical concert. Unique to Prague (though somewhat comparable to a very low-budget Cirque du Soleil), Black Light Theater originated in the 1960s as a playful and mystifying theater of the absurd. These days, some aficionados lament that it's becoming a cheesy variety show, while others are uncomfortable with the sexual flavor of some acts. Still, it's an unusual theater experience that most enjoy. Shows last about 90 minutes. Avoid the first four rows, which get you so close that it ruins the illusion. Each theater has its own personality: **Ta Fantastika** is traditional and poetic, with puppets and a little artistic nudity (*Aspects of Alice* nightly at 21:30, 620 Kč, reserved seating, near east end of Charles Bridge at Karlova 8, tel. 222-221-366, www.tafantastika.cz). **Image Theatre** has more mime and absurd, with shows including *Clonarium, Fiction,* and *The Best of Image: "It's precisely the fact that we are all so different that unites us"* (shows nightly at 18:00 and 20:00, 400 Kč, open seating—arrive early to grab a good spot, just off Old Town Square at Pařížská 4, tel. 222-314-448, www.imagetheatre.cz). **Laterna Magica,** in the big, glassy Nová Scéna building next to the National Theatre, mixes black-light techniques with film projection into a multimedia performance that draws Czech audiences (*Wonderful Circus, Rendezvous, Graffiti,* shows Mon–Sat at 20:00, no shows on Sun, 680 Kč, tel. 224-931-482, www.laterna.cz). The other Black Light Theaters advertising around town aren't as good.

Tourist Concerts—Each day, six to eight classical concerts designed for tourists fill delightful Old World halls and churches with music of the crowd-pleasing sort: Vivaldi, Best of Mozart, Most Famous Arias, and works by the famous Czech composer Antonín Dvořák. Concerts typically cost 400–1,000 Kč, start anywhere from 13:00 to 21:00, and last about an hour. Common venues are two buildings on Little Quarter Square (the Church of St. Nicholas and the Prague Academy of Music in Liechtenstein Palace); in the Klementinum's Chapel of Mirrors; at the Old Town Square (in a different Church of St. Nicholas); and in the stunning Smetana Hall in the Municipal House (see page 197). The artists vary from excellent to amateur.

A sure bet is the jam session held every Monday at 17:00 at **St. Martin in the Wall,** where Prague's best professional musicians gather to tune in and chat with each other (400 Kč, Martinská street, just north of the Tesco department store in the Old Town).

Serious Concerts—True music-lovers should consider Prague's top symphonic venue, the **Rudolfinum** (featuring the Czech Philharmonic, on Palachovo Náměstí, in Jewish Quarter on the Old Town side of Mánes Bridge). Concerts in the large Dvořák Hall or the small Suk Hall usually start at 19:30 (also afternoons on weekends). The ticket office is on the right side, under the stairs (250–1,000 Kč, open until just before the show starts, tel. 227-059-352).

The **National Theatre** (Národní Divadlo, on the New Town side of Legií Bridge)—with a must-see Neo-Renaissance interior (see page 199)—is best for opera and ballet (shows from 19:00, 300–1,000 Kč, tel. 224-912-673, www.nationaltheatre.cz). The **Estates Theatre** (Stavovské Divadlo) is where Mozart premiered and personally directed many of his most beloved works (see page 185). *Don Giovanni, The Marriage of Figaro,* and *The Magic Flute* are on the program a couple of times each month (shows from 20:00, 800–1,400 Kč, between the Old Town Square and the New Town on a square called Ovocný Trh, tel. 224-214-339, www.estatestheatre.cz). The ticket office for both of these theaters is in the little square (Ovocný Trh) behind the Estates Theatre.

The **State Opera** (Státní Opera) focuses on Verdi (shows at 19:00 or 20:00, 400–1,200 Kč, buy tickets at the theater, on 5 Května—the busy street between the Main Train Station and Wenceslas Square, see map on page 192, tel. 224-227-693, www.opera.cz).

During his frequent visits to Prague, Mozart stayed with his friends in the beautiful, small, Neoclassical **Villa Bertramka,** now the Mozart Museum. Surrounded by a peaceful garden, the villa preserves the time when the Salzburg prodigy felt more appreciated in Prague than in Austria. Intimate concerts are held some afternoons and evenings, either in the garden or the small concert hall (110 Kč, daily April–Oct 9:30–18:00, Nov–March 9:30–17:00, Mozartova 169, Praha 5; from Metro: Anděl, it's a 10-min walk—head to Hotel Mövenpick and then go up alley behind hotel; tel. 257-317-465, www.bertramka.cz).

World-class musicians are in town during these musical festivals: **Prague Spring** (mid-May–early June, www.festival.cz) and **Prague Autumn** (mid-Sept–mid-Oct, www.pragueautumn.cz).

For any of these concerts, locals dress up, but many tourists wear casual clothes—as long as you don't show up in sneakers and ripped jeans, you'll be fine.

SHOPPING

Prague's entire Old Town seems designed to bring out the shopper in visitors. Puppets, glass, and ceramics are traditional. Shop your way from the Old Town Square up Celetná to the Powder Tower, then along Na Příkopě to the bottom of Wenceslas Square (Václavské Náměstí). The city center is tourist-oriented—most locals do their serious shopping in the suburbs.

Celetná is lined with big stores selling all the traditional Czech goodies. Tourists wander endlessly here, mesmerized by the window displays. Celetná Crystal, about midway down the street, offers the largest selection of affordable crystal. You can have the glass safely shipped home directly from the shop (for purchases over 2,000 Kč, you can get a refund of the VAT tax).

Na Příkopě has a couple of good modern malls. The best is Slovanský Dům (daily 10:00–20:00, Na Příkopě 22), where you wander deep past a 10-screen multiplex into a world of classy restaurants and designer shops surrounding a peaceful, parklike inner courtyard. Another modern mall is Černá Růže (daily 10:00–20:00, Na Příkopě 12). Next door is Mosers, which has a museum-like crystal showroom upstairs.

Národní Třída (National Street) is less touristy and lined with some inviting stores. The big Tesco department store in the middle sells anything you might need, from a pin for a broken watchband to a swimsuit (generally daily 9:00–21:00, Národní Třída 26).

Crystal: Along with shops on Celetná and Na Příkopě, a small square just off the Old Town Square, Malé Náměstí, is ringed by three major crystal retailers (generally open daily 10:00–20:00): Mosers, Rott Crystal, and Crystalex (which claims to have "factory-direct" prices, at #6 on the square).

SLEEPING

Peak season for hotels in Prague is late April, May, June, September, and early October. Easter and Christmas are the most crowded times, when prices are jacked up a bit. I've listed peak-time prices—if you're traveling in July or August, you'll find rates generally 15 percent lower, and from November through March, about 30 percent lower.

Room-Booking Services

Prague is awash with fancy rooms on the push list; private, small-time operators with rooms to rent in their apartments; and roving agents eager to book you a bed and earn a commission. You can save about 30 percent by showing up in Prague without a reservation and finding accommodations upon arrival. It is, however, a hustle and you will not necessarily get your choice. If you're coming in by train or car, you'll encounter booking agencies. They can virtually always find you a reasonable place and, if it's a private guest house, your host can even come and lead you to the place.

Athos Travel has a line on 200 properties (ranging from hostels to five-star hotels), 90 percent of which are in the historical

Sleep Code

(20 Kč = about $1, country code: 420)

S = Single, **D** = Double/Twin, **T** = Triple, **Q** = Quad, **b** = bathroom, **s** = shower only. Unless otherwise noted, credit cards are accepted, and breakfast and tax are included. Everyone listed here speaks English.

To help you sort easily through these listings, I've divided the rooms into three categories based on the price for a standard double room with bath:

$$$ Higher Priced—Most rooms 4,000 Kč or more.

$$ Moderately Priced—Most rooms between 3,000–4,000 Kč.

$ Lower Priced—Most rooms 3,000 Kč or less.

center. To book a room, call them or use their handy website, which allows you to search for a room based on various criteria (best to arrange in advance during peak season, can also help with last-minute booking off-season, tel. 241-440-571, fax 241-441-697, www.a-prague.com, info@a-prague.com). Readers report that Athos is aggressive with its business policies—while there's no fee to cancel well in advance, they strictly enforce penalties on cancellations within 48 hours.

AVE, at the Main Train Station (Hlavní Nádraží), is another booking service (daily 6:00–23:00). With the tracks at your back, walk down to the orange ceiling and past the "Meeting Point" (don't go downstairs)—their office is in the left corner by the exit to the rip-off taxis. Their display board shows discounted hotels, and they have a slew of hotels and small pensions available (2,000-Kč pension doubles in old center, 1,500-Kč doubles a Metro ride away). You can reserve by email using your credit card as a deposit (tel. 251-551-011, fax 251-555-156, www.avetravel.cz, ave@avetravel.cz), or just show up at the office and request a room. Be clear on the location before you make your choice.

For a more personal touch, Lída Jánská's **Magic Praha** helps with accommodations (tel. 235-325-170, mobile 604-207-225, www.magicpraha.cz, magicpraha@magicpraha.cz; see "Helpful Hints," page 171). Lída rents a well-located apartment with a river view near the Jewish Quarter.

Web-booking services, such as Priceline.com and Biddingfortravel.com, enable budget travelers to snare fancy rooms on the push list for half the rack rate. It's not unusual to find a room in a four-star hotel for 1,300 Kč—but keep in mind that many of these international business-class hotels are far from the city center.

Old Town Hotels and Pensions

You'll pay higher prices to stay in the Old Town, but for many travelers, the convenience is worth the expense. These places are all within a 10-minute walk of the Old Town Square.

$$$ Hotel Maximilian is a sleek, mod, 70-room place with Art Deco black design, big, plush living rooms, and all the business services and comforts you'd expect in a four-star hotel. It faces a church on a perfect little square just a short walk from the action (Db-4,500 Kč, extra bed-1,500 Kč, their "preferred rate" gives you a 14 percent discount if you lock in a reservation with no cancellation option, check online for lower rates, Haštalská 14, tel. 225-303-111, fax 225-303-110, www.maximilianhotel.com, reservations@maximilianhotel.com).

$$$ Residence Řetězová is on a central but delightfully quiet cobbled lane. Its medieval shell has been remodeled into nine elegant,

Hotels in Prague's Old Town

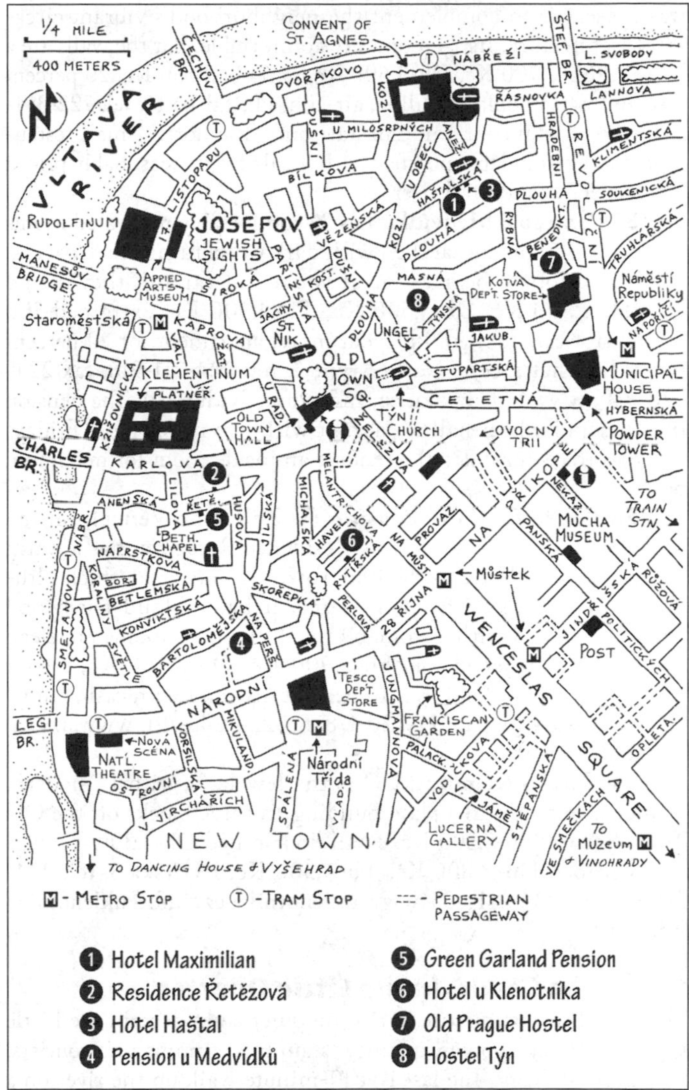

plush, and spacious apartments—each one is unique. You can enjoy the mystery and ambience of old Prague with all the modern comforts (Db-4,500–5,600 Kč, check online for lower rates and to choose your room, free Internet access, Řetězová 9, tel. & fax 222-221-800, www.residenceretezova.com, info@residenceretezova.com).

$$ Hotel Haštal, next to Hotel Maximilian (listed above) on the same quiet, hidden square in the Old Town, was a popular hotel back in the 1920s. Newly renovated, its Art Nouveau style was preserved to complement the neighborhood's vibrant circa-1900 architecture. Its 24 rooms are comfortable, but the walls are a bit thin (Sb-2,900 Kč, Db-3,600 Kč, extra bed-550 Kč, 20 percent discount when booking online, air-con, Haštalská 16, tel. 222-314-335, www.hastal.com, info@hastal.com). The hotel's small restaurant is understandably popular with locals for its reasonably priced lunch specials and draft beer.

$$ Pension u Medvídků has 31 comfortably renovated rooms in a big, rustic, medieval shell with dark wood furniture. Upstairs, you'll find lots of beams—or, if you're not careful, they'll find you (Sb-2,300 Kč, Db-3,500 Kč, Tb-4,500 Kč, extra bed-500 Kč, "historical" rooms 10 percent more, apartment for 20 percent more, Internet access, Na Perštýně 7, tel. 224-211-916, fax 224-220-930, www.umedvidku.cz, info@umedvidku.cz). The pension runs a popular beer-hall restaurant with live music most Fridays and Saturdays until 23:00—request an inside room for maximum peace.

$$ Green Garland Pension (U Zeleného Věnce), on the same quiet pedestrian street as Residence Řetězová, has a warm and personal feel rare in the Old Town. Located in a thick 14th-century building with open beams, it has a blond-hardwood charm decorated with a woman's touch. Its nine rooms are clean and simply furnished (big Sb-2,900 Kč, Db-3,400 Kč, bigger Db-3,700 Kč, Tb-4,400 Kč, 10 percent discount with cash, family suite, Řetězová 10, tel. 222-220-178, fax 224-248-791, www.uzv.cz, pension@uzv.cz).

$$ Hotel u Klenotníka ("At the Jeweler"), with 11 modern, comfortable rooms in a plain building, is three blocks off the Old Town Square (Sb-2,500 Kč, small double-bed Db-3,300 Kč, bigger twin-bed Db–3,800 Kč, Tb-4,500 Kč, Rytířská 3, tel. 224-211-699, fax 224-221-025, www.uklenotnika.cz, info@uklenotnika.cz).

Under the Castle, in the Little Quarter

The first three listings are buried on quiet lanes deep in the Little Quarter among cobbles, quaint restaurants, rummaging tourists, and embassy flags. The last is a 10-minute walk up the river on a quiet and stately street with none of the intense medieval cityscape of the others.

$$$ Dům u Velké Boty ("House at the Big Boot"), in front of the German Embassy, is the quintessential family hotel in Prague—homey, comfy, and extremely friendly. Charlotta, Jan, and their two sons treat every guest as a (thirsty) friend, and the wellspring of their stories never runs dry. Each of their 12 rooms is uniquely decorated, most in tasteful 19th-century Biedermeier style

Hotels and Restaurants in the Little Quarter

1. Dům u Velké Boty
2. Hotel Sax
3. Dům u Žluté Boty
4. Hostel Sokol
5. Hotel Julián
6. U Sedmi Švábů Rest. & U Osla v Kolébce Pub
7. U Hrocha Pub
8. Restaurace Rybářský Klub
9. Restaurace David & Baráčnická Rychta Club
10. Malostranská Beseda Club

(tiny S-2,100 Kč, two D rooms that share a bathroom-3,550 Kč each, Db-4,780 Kč, extra bed-725 Kč, prices can be soft when slow, cash only, free Internet access and Wi-Fi, Vlašská 30, tel. 257-532-088, www.bigboot.cz, info@bigboot.cz). While they don't include tax or breakfast in their rates, I've included them in the prices above for easy comparison. There's no hotel sign on the house—look for the splendid geraniums that Jan nurtures in the windows.

$$$ Hotel Sax will delight the artsy yuppie with its 22 business-style rooms, fruity atrium, and modern, stylish decor (Sb-4,100 Kč, Db-4,400 Kč, Db suite-5,100 Kč, extra bed-1,000 Kč, elevator, Jánský Vršek 3, tel. 257-531-268, fax 257-534-101, www.sax.cz, hotel@sax.cz).

$$$ Dům u Žluté Boty ("House at the Yellow Boot"), perhaps the most charming small hotel in Prague, is well-run by sisters Jana and Jiřina. Each of its seven rooms is unique: Some preserve the 16th-century wooden ceilings, some feel like mountain lodges, and others are a bit marred by an insensitive 1970s adaptation (Sb-3,800 Kč, Db-4,300 Kč, Tb-5,000 Kč, extra bed-900 Kč, some thin walls, Jánský Vršek 11, tel. 257-532-269, fax 257-534-134, www.zlutabota.cz, hotel@zlutabota.cz).

$$ Hotel Julián is an oasis of professional, predictable decency in a quiet, untouristy neighborhood. Its 32 spacious, fresh, well-furnished rooms and big, homey public spaces hide behind a noble Neoclassical facade (Sb-3,680 Kč, Db-3,980 Kč, Db suite-4,800 Kč, extra bed-900 Kč, 10 percent discount for Rick Steves' readers, free tea and coffee in room, air-con, elevator, plush and inviting lobby, parking lot; Metro: Andel, then an 8-min walk; or take tram #6, #9, #12, #20, or #58 for two stops; Elišky Peškové 11, Praha 5, reservation tel. 257-311-150, reception tel. 257-311-145, fax 257-311-149, www.julian.cz, casjul@vol.cz). Free lockers and a shower are available for those needing to check out early but stay until late (for example, for an overnight train). Mike's Chauffeur Service, based here, is reliable and affordable (see page 237).

Away from the Center

Moving just outside central Prague saves you money—and gets you away from the tourists and into some more workaday residential neighborhoods. The following listings (great values compared to the downtown hotels) are all within a five- to 15-minute tram or Metro ride from the center.

Beyond Wenceslas Square

These hotels are in urban neighborhoods on the outer fringe of the New Town, beyond Wenceslas Square. But they're still within several minutes' walk of the sightseeing zone, and are well-served by trams.

$$$ Sieber Hotel, with 20 rooms, is a quality, four-star, business-class hotel in an upscale residential neighborhood near the former royal vineyards (Vinohrady). They do a good job of being homey and welcoming (Sb-4,480 Kč, Db-4,780 Kč, extra bed-990 Kč, fourth night free, 30 percent discount for last-minute reservations, air-con, elevator, Internet access, 3-min walk to Metro: Jiřího z Poděbrad, or tram #11, Slezská 55, Praha 3, tel. 224-250-025, fax 224-250-027, www.sieber.cz, reservations@sieber.cz).

$$ Hotel Anna, with 24 bright, pastel, and classically charming rooms, is a bit closer in—just 10 minutes by foot east of Wenceslas Square (Sb-2,400 Kč, Db-3,300 Kč, Tb-4,000 Kč, non-smoking rooms, elevator, Budečská 17, Praha 2, Metro: Náměstí Míru, tel. 222-513-111, fax 222-515-158, www.hotelanna.cz, reception@hotelanna.cz). They run a similar hotel (same standards and prices) nearby.

$$ Hotel 16 is a sleek and modern business-class place with an intriguing Art Nouveau facade, polished cherry-wood elegance, high ceilings, and 14 fine rooms (Sb-2,800 Kč, Db-3,500 Kč, bigger Db-3,700 Kč, Tb-4,700 Kč, triple-paned windows, back rooms facing the garden are quieter, air-con, elevator, Internet access, 10-min walk south of Wenceslas Square, Metro: I. P. Pavlova, Kateřinská 16, Praha 2, tel. 224-920-636, fax 224-920-626, www.hotel16.cz, hotel16@hotel16.cz, Frantisek).

The Best Values, Farther from the Center

These accommodations are a 10- to 20-minute tram ride from the center, but once you make the trip, you'll see it's no problem—and you'll feel pretty smug saving $50–100 a night per double by not sleeping in the Old Town. These hotels are within a stone's throw of peaceful Vyšehrad park, with a legendary castle on a cliff overlooking the Vltava River.

$ Dům u Šemíka, a friendly hotel named for a heroic mythical horse, offers 25 rooms in a quiet residential neighborhood just below Vyšehrad Castle, a 10-minute tram ride south of the Old Town (Sb-1,900 Kč, Db-2,500 Kč, apartment-2,700–5,000 Kč for 2–4 people, extra bed-790 Kč, ask for the "direct booking" Rick Steves discount; from the center, take trams #3, #17, or #21 to Výtoň, go under rail bridge, and walk 3 blocks uphill to Vratislavova 36; Praha 2, tel. 224-920-736, fax 224-911-602, www.usemika.cz, usemika@usemika.cz).

$ Guest House Lída, with 12 homey and spacious rooms, fills a big house in a quiet residential area farther inland, a 15-minute tram ride from the center. Jan, Jiří, and Jitka Prouza, who run the place, are a wealth of information and know how to make people feel at home (Sb-1,380 Kč, small Db-1,440 Kč, Db-1,760 Kč, Tb-2,110 Kč, Qb-2,530 Kč, cash only, family rooms, top-floor

Hotels and Restaurants in the New Town and Beyond

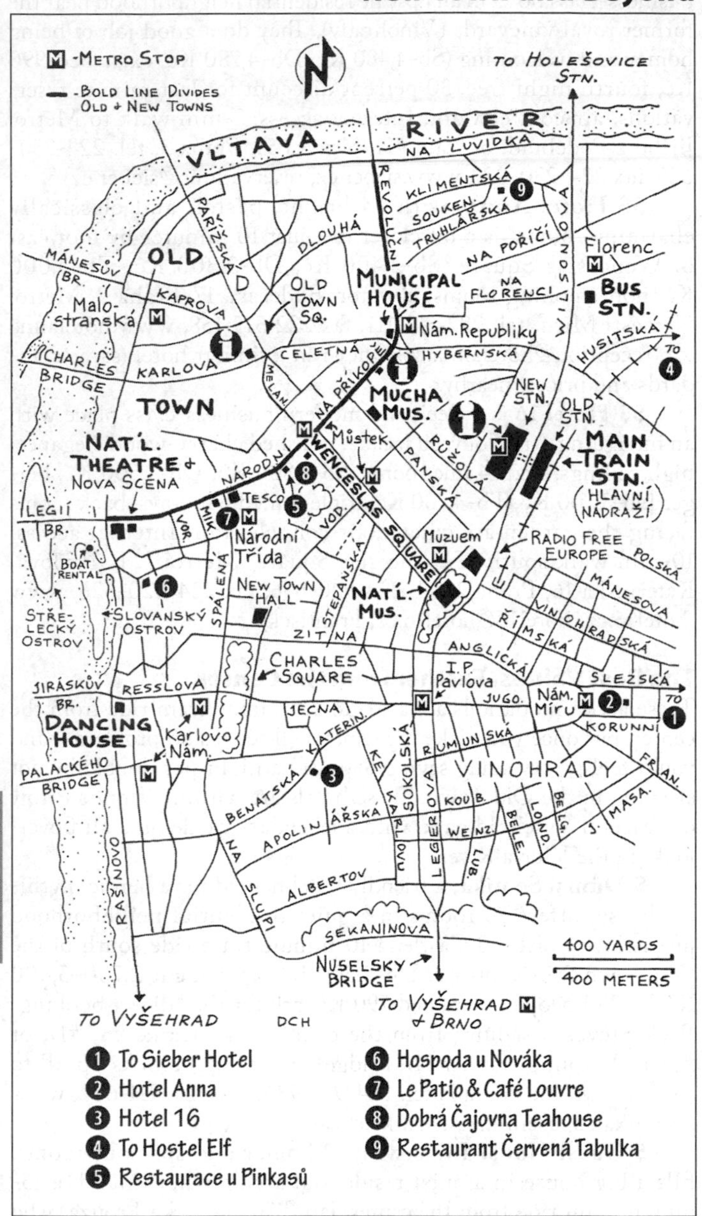

family suite with kitchenette, Internet access, parking garage-200 Kč/day, Metro: Pražského Povstání; exit Metro and turn left on Lomnického between the Metro station and big blue-glass ČSOB building, follow Lomnického for 500 yards, then turn left on Lopatecká, go uphill and ring bell at Lopatecká #26, no sign outside; Praha 4, tel. & fax 261-214-766, www.lidabb.eu, lidabb @seznam.cz). The Prouza brothers also rent four apartments across the river, an equal distance from the center (Db-1,500 Kč, Tb-1,920 Kč, Qb-2,100 Kč).

Hostels in the Center

It's tough to find a double for under 3,000 Kč in the old center. But Prague has an abundance of fine hostels—each with a distinct personality, and each excellent in its own way for anyone wanting a 400-Kč dorm bed or an extremely simple, twin-bedded room for around 1,300 Kč.

$ Old Prague Hostel is a small and very friendly place with 70 beds on the second and third floors of an apartment building on a back alley near the Powder Tower. The spacious rooms were once apartment bedrooms, so it feels less institutional than most hostels. Hanging out in the comfy TV lounge/breakfast room, you'll feel like part of an international family. Older travelers would feel comfortable in this mellow place (six D-1,360 Kč, bunk in 3–8-person room-450–530 Kč; includes breakfast, sheets, towels, lockers, and Internet access; reserve ahead, Benediktská 2, see map on page 219 for location, tel. 224-829-058, fax 224-829-060, www .oldpraguehostel.com, oldpraguehostel@seznam.cz).

$ Hostel Týn is hidden in a silent courtyard two blocks from the Old Town Square. Because the management is aware of its value, they don't bother being too friendly (D-1,200 Kč, T-1,350 Kč, bunk in 4–5-bed co-ed room-400 Kč, lockers, reserve ahead, Týnská 19, located on map on page 219, tel. 224-828-519, mobile 776-122-057, www.hostel-tyn.web2001.cz, backpacker@razdva.cz).

$ Hostel Elf, a 10-minute walk to both the Main Train Station and the Florenc bus station, is fun-loving, ramshackle, covered with noisy, self-inflicted graffiti, and the wildest of these hostels. They offer cheap, basic beds, a helpful staff, and lots of creative services—kitchen, free luggage room, laundry, no lockout, free tea, cheap beer, a terrace, and lockers (120 beds, D-900 Kč, bunk in 6–11-person room-320 Kč, includes sheets and breakfast, cash only, next to tracks heading into Main Train Station but noise isn't a problem, Husitská 11, Praha 3, tel. 222-540-963, www .hostelelf.com, info@hostelelf.com).

$ Hostel Sokol, plain and institutional with 100 beds, is peacefully located just off park-like Kampa Island in the Tyrš House buildings (the seat of the Czech Sokol Organization). Big

WWI hospital-style rooms are lined with single beds and lockers (bunk in 8–14-person room-350 Kč, cash only, no breakfast, easy to reserve without deposit by phone or email, open 24/7, kitchen, Nosticova 2, see map on page 221 for location, tel. 257-007-397, fax 257-007-340, www.sokol-cos.cz/index_en.htm, hostel@sokol-cos.cz). From the Main Train Station, ride tram #9 to Újezd. From the Holešovice station, take tram #12 to Hellichova. From either tram stop, walk 200 yards to the hostel.

EATING

A big part of Prague's charm is found in wandering aimlessly through the city's winding old quarters, marveling at the architecture, watching the people, and sniffing out fun restaurants. You can eat well here for very little money. What you'd pay for a basic meal in Vienna or Munich will get you a feast in Prague. In addition to meat-and-potatoes Czech cuisine, you'll find trendy, student-oriented bars and lots of fine ethnic eateries. For ambience, the options include traditional, dark Czech beer halls; elegant Art Nouveau dining rooms; and hip and modern cafés.

Watch out for scams. Many restaurants put more care into ripping off green tourists (and even locals) than in their cooking. Tourists are routinely served cheaper meals than what they ordered, given a menu with a "personalized" price list, charged extra for things they didn't get, or shortchanged. Speak Czech. Even saying "Hello" in Czech will get you better service. Avoid any menu without clear and explicit prices. Be careful of waiters padding the tab. Carefully examine your itemized bill and understand each line (a 10 percent service charge is sometimes added—in that case, there's no need to tip extra). Tax is always included in the price, so it shouldn't be tacked on later. Part with very large bills only if necessary, and deliberately count your change. Never let your credit card out of your sight. Make it a habit to get cash from an ATM to pay for your meals. (Credit cards can cost merchants as much as 10 percent.) Remember, there are two parallel worlds in Prague: the tourist town and the real city. Generally, if you walk two minutes away from the tourist flow, you'll find better value, ambience, and service.

I've listed these eating and drinking establishments by neighborhood. The most options—and highest prices—are in the Old Town. If you want a memorable splurge, see "Dining with Style" on page 236. For a light meal, consider one of Prague's many cafés (see "Cafés" on page 233). Many of the places listed here are handy for an efficient lunch, but may not offer fine evening dining. Others make less sense for lunch but are great for a slow, drawn-out dinner. Read the descriptions to judge which is which.

Fun, Touristy Neighborhoods: Several areas are pretty and well-situated for sightseeing, but lined only with touristy restaurants. While these places are not necessarily bad values, I've listed only a few of your many options—just survey the scene in these spots and choose whatever looks best. Kampa Square, just off the Charles Bridge, feels like a small-town square. Havelská Market is surrounded by colorful little eateries, any of which give a fine perch for viewing the market scene while you munch. The grand Old Town Square is *the* place to nurse a drink or enjoy a meal while watching the tide of people, both tourists and locals, sweep back and forth. There's often some event on the main square, and its many restaurants provide tasty and relaxing vantage points.

Dining with a View: For great views, consider these options: **U Prince** (rooftop dining above a fancy hotel, completely touristy but awesome views, recommended and described below); the **Bellavista Restaurant** at Strahov Monastery; **Petřínské Terasy** and **Nebozízek** next to the funicular stop halfway up Petřín Hill; and the many overpriced but elegant places serving scenic meals along the riverbanks. For the best cheap riverside dinner, have a picnic on a paddleboat (see page 178). There's nothing like drifting down the middle of the Vltava River as the sun sets while munching your picnic and sipping your beer with your favorite travel partner.

In or near the Old Town

While most of these eateries are in the Old Town proper, some are a few steps into the New Town.

Characteristically Czech Places

With the inevitable closing of cheap student pubs (replaced by shops and hotels that make more money), it's getting difficult to find a truly Czech pub in the historic city center. Most Czechs no longer go to "traditional" eateries, preferring the cosmopolitan taste of the world to the mundane taste of sauerkraut. As a result, ancient institutions with "authentic" Czech ambience have become touristy—but they're still great fun, a good value, and respected by Czechs. Expect wonderfully rustic spaces, smoke, surly service, and reasonably good, inexpensive food. Understand every line on your bill.

Plzeňská Restaurace u Dvou Koček ("By the Two Cats") is a typical Czech pub with cheap, no-nonsense, hearty Czech food and beer. Sandwiched between the two red-light-district streets, and filled now with tourists rather than Czechs, the restaurant somehow maintains its charm (200 Kč for three courses and beer, serving original Pilsner Urquell with accordion music nightly until

Prague Restaurants

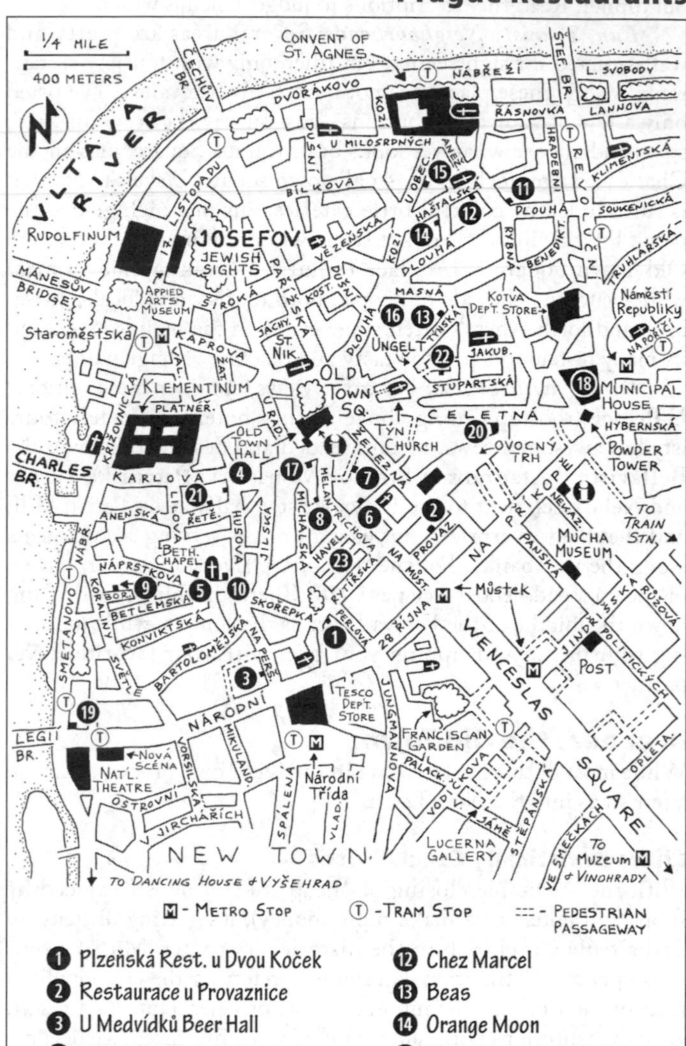

1. Plzeňská Rest. u Dvou Koček
2. Restaurace u Provaznice
3. U Medvídků Beer Hall
4. U Zlatého Tygra Pub
5. Restaurace u Betlémské Kaple
6. Česká Kuchyně
7. Restaurace Mlejnice
8. Country Life Veggie Restaurant
9. Lehká Hlava Veggie Restaurant
10. Klub Architektů
11. Dahab
12. Chez Marcel
13. Beas
14. Orange Moon
15. Molly Malone's Irish Pub
16. Bohemia Bagel
17. Rest. u Prince Terrace
18. Municipal House Eateries
19. Grand Café Slavia
20. Grand Café Orient
21. Café Montmartre
22. Ebel Coffee House
23. Havelská Market

23:00, under an arcade, facing a tiny square between Perlová and Skořepka streets).

Restaurace u Pinkasů, with a menu that reads like a 19th-century newspaper, is a Prague institution, founded in 1843. It's best in summer, when you sit in the garden behind the building in the shade of the Gothic buttresses of the St. Mary of the Snows Church. But beware—its waiters could win the award for the rudest service in town (daily 9:00–24:00, tucked in a courtyard near the bottom of Wenceslas Square, on the border between Old and New Towns, located on map on page 224, Jungmannovo Náměstí 16, tel. 221-111-150).

Restaurace u Provaznice ("By the Ropemaker's Wife") has all the Czech classics, peppered with the story of a once-upon-a-time-faithful wife. (Check the menu for details of the gory tale.) It's less touristed and less expensive than the other restaurants in this area. Natives congregate here for their famously good "pig leg" with horseradish and Czech mustard (daily 11:00–24:00, a block into the Old Town from the bottom of Wenceslas Square at Provaznická 3, tel. 224-232-528).

U Medvídků ("By the Bear Cubs"), which started out as a brewery in 1466, is now a flagship beer hall of the Czech Budweiser. The ambience of the one large room is bright, noisy, pretty touristy, and a bit smoky (daily 11:30–23:00, a block toward Wenceslas Square from Bethlehem Square at Na Perštýnì 7, tel. 224-211-916). The small beer bar next to the restaurant (daily 16:00–3:00 in the morning) is used by university students during emergencies—such as when most other pubs have closed.

U Zlatého Tygra ("By the Golden Tiger") has long embodied the proverbial Czech pub, where beer turns strangers into kindred spirits who cross the fuzzy line between memory and imagination as they tell their hilarious life stories to each other. Today "the Tiger" is a buzzing shrine to one of its longtime regulars, the writer Bohumil Hrabal, whose fictions immortalize many of the colorful characters that once warmed the wooden benches here (daily 15:00–23:00, often jam-packed, just south of Karlova at Husova 17).

Hospoda u Nováka, behind the National Theatre (i.e., not so central), is emphatically Czech, with few tourists. It takes good care of its regulars (you'll see the old monthly beer tabs in a rack just inside the door). Nostalgic communist-era signs are everywhere. During that time, pubs like this were close-knit communities where regulars escaped from the depression of daily life. Today the Nováka is a bright and smoky hangout where you can still happily curse whatever regime you happen to live under. While the English menu lists the well-executed Czech classics, it doesn't list the cheap daily specials (daily 10:00–23:00, V Jirchářích 2, tel. 224-930-639).

Restaurace u Betlémské Kaple, behind Bethlehem Chapel, is not "ye olde" Czech. It has light wooden decor, cheap lunch deals, and fish specialties that attract natives and visitors in search of a good Czech bite for Czech prices (daily 11:00–23:00, Betlémské Náměstí 2, tel. 222-221-639).

Česká Kuchyně ("Czech Kitchen") is a blue-collar cafeteria serving steamy old Czech cuisine to a local clientele. It's fast, practical, cheap, and traditional as can be. There's no English inside, so—if you want apple charlotte, but not tripe soup—be sure to review the small English menu in the window outside before entering. Note the numbers of your preferred dishes because they correspond to the Czech menu you'll see inside. Pick up your tally sheet as you enter, grab a tray, point liberally to whatever you'd like, and keep the paper to pay as you exit. It's extremely cheap... unless you lose your paper (daily 9:00–20:00, very central, across from Havelská Market at Havelská 23, tel. 224-235-574).

Restaurace Mlejnice ("The Mill") is a fun little pub strewn with farm implements and happy eaters, located just out of the tourist crush two blocks from the Old Town Square. They serve hearty traditional and modern Czech plates for 150–180 Kč (daily 11:00–24:00, reservations smart in evening, between Melantrichova and Železná at Kožná 14, tel. 224-228-635).

Hip Restaurants

Country Life Vegetarian Restaurant is a bright, easy, nonsmoking cafeteria with a well-displayed buffet of salads and hot veggie dishes. It's midway between the Old Town Square and the bottom of Wenceslas Square. They're serious about their vegetarianism, serving only plant-based, unprocessed, and unrefined food. Its dining area is quiet and elegantly woody for a cafeteria, with three tables and wicker chairs outside in the courtyard (Sun–Thu 9:00–20:30, Fri 9:00–17:00, closed Sat, through courtyard at Melantrichova 15/Michalská 18, tel. 224-213-366).

Lehká Hlava ("Clear Head") Vegetarian Restaurant, tucked away on a cul-de-sac, has a mission to provide a "clear atmosphere for enjoying food." Sitting as if in an enchanted forest, diners enjoy dishes from around the world (100–150-Kč plates, two-course 90-Kč daily special, no eggs, no smoke, lots of vegan dishes, daily 11:30–23:30, reservations smart in the evening, between Bethlehem Chapel and the river at Boršov 2, tel. 222-220-665).

Klub Architektů, next to Bethlehem Chapel, is a modern hangout in a medieval cellar serving excellent original dishes, hearty salads, Moravian wines, and Slovak beer. The friendly waiters make the atmospheric subterranean space into one of most welcoming places in the Old Town (daily, Betlémské Náměstí 169, tel. 224-401-214).

At **Le Patio,** on the big and busy Národní Třída, the first thing you'll notice are the many lanterns suspended from the ceiling—and the big ship moored out back (okay, just its hulking bow). Le Patio has a hip, continental feel to it, but for a place that also sells furniture (head straight back, and down the stairs), they definitely need comfier dining chairs. The atmosphere is as pleasant and carefully designed as the dishes, with international fare from India, France, and points in between. There's always a serious vegetarian option available (200–350-Kč plates, daily 8:00–23:00, Národní 22, tel. 224-934-375). Diners enjoy live music Friday and Saturday nights (19:30–22:30).

Ethnic Eateries on or near Dlouhá Street

Dlouhá, the wide street leading away from the Old Town Square behind the Jan Hus monument (left of Týn Church), is lined with ethnic restaurants catering mostly to cosmopolitan locals. Within a couple of blocks, you can eat your way around the world. From Dlouhá, wander the Rámová/Haštalská Masná area to survey a United Nations of eateries: You'll find Moroccan (**Dahab,** with some interesting hubbly-bubbly action at Dlouhá 33), Spanish, French (**Chez Marcel** at Haštalská 12 is understandably popular—with a fun-loving waitstaff), Afghan, Italian, and these four, which deserve special consideration:

Indian: **Beas** is a cheap vegetarian restaurant ruled by a Punjabi chef who concocts mild *thalis* (mixed platters) in the style of northern Indian plains and *dosas* of the southern Indian variety. Tucked away in a courtyard behind the Týn Church, this place is popular with university students (Mon–Sat 9:30–20:00, Sun 10:00–18:00, Týnská 19).

Thai: **Orange Moon** specializes in Thai curries, but you'll also find dishes from Myanmar (Burma) and India served in a space delightfully decorated with artwork from Southeast Asia. This restaurant attracts a mixture of locals, expats, and tourists (daily 11:30–23:30, reservations recommended, Rámová 5, tel. 222-325-119).

Irish: **Molly Malone's Irish Pub** may seem a strange recommendation in Prague—home of the world's best beer—but this is the kind of ambience locals (and not tourists) seek out. Having a drink here will likely put you in touch with a fun Czech crowd. This has been the expat and local favorite for Guinness ever since the Velvet Revolution enabled the Celts to return to one of their homelands. Worn wooden floors, dingy walls, and the Irish manager transport you right into the heart of blue-collar Dublin (which is, after all, a popular place for young Czechs to find jobs in the high-tech industry). Hidden in a forgotten corner of Josefov, Molly Malone's is a destination for those who have adopted Prague and aren't just passing through (Sun–Thu 11:00–1:00 in the morning, Fri–Sat 11:00–2:00 in the morning, U Obecního Dvora 4, tel. 224-818-851).

American: **Bohemia Bagel** is hardly authentic—exasperated Czechs insist that bagels have nothing to do with Bohemia. Owned by an American, this practical café caters mostly to youthful tourists, with good sandwiches (100–125 Kč), a little garden out back, and Internet access (1.50 Kč/min). If homesick, you'll love the menu, with everything from Philly cheesesteak to bacon and eggs (daily 7:00–24:00, Masná 2, tel. 224-812-560).

In the Jewish Quarter

These three eateries are well-located to break up a demanding tour of the Jewish Quarter—all within two blocks of each other on or near Široká (see the map on page 189).

Kolkovna is big and woody, yet modern, serving a fun mix of Czech and international cuisine—ribs, salads, cheese plates, and good beer (a bit overpriced but good energy, daily 11:00–24:00, across from Spanish Synagogue at V Kolkovně 8, tel. 224-819-701).

Franz Kafka Café, with a cool, dark, and woody interior strewn with historic photos of the ghetto and a few good sidewalk tables, is great for a relaxing salad, sandwich, snack, or drink (150-Kč salads, daily 10:00–21:00, a block from the cemetery at Široká 12).

Pekařství ("Bakery") is a little deli with fresh sandwiches, greasy microwavable meat pies, tempting cakes, yogurt, and a cooler full of drinks. It's self-serve and dirt-cheap, with plain circa-1960 linoleum loft seating upstairs (daily 7:00–22:30, Široká 10, near the Pinkas Synagogue). Head upstairs to see the insane director of the National Gallery throwing paint on a nude woman.

Dining with an Old Town Square View

Restaurant u Prince Terrace, in the five-star U Prince Hotel facing the Astronomical Clock, is designed for foreign tourists. A sleek elevator takes you to its rooftop, where every possible inch is used to serve good food (international fare with plenty of fish) from their open-air grill. The view is arguably the best in town—especially at sunset. The menu is a fun but overpriced mix, with photos to make ordering easy. Being in such a touristy spot, waiters are experts at nicking you with confusing menu charges; don't be afraid to confirm exact prices before ordering. This place is also great for just a drink at sunset or late at night (fine salads, 240–300-Kč plates, daily until 24:00, brusque staff, outdoor heaters when necessary, Staroměstské Náměstí 29, tel. 224-213-807—but no reservations possible).

Cafés

These places—dripping with history—are as much about the ambience as they are about the coffee. Most cafés also serve sweets and light meals.

Grand Café Slavia, across from the National Theatre (facing the Legions Bridge on Národní street), is a fixture in Prague, famous as a hangout for its literary elite. Today, it's tired and clearly past its prime, with an Art Deco interior, lousy piano entertainment, and celebrity photos on the wall. But its iconic status makes it a fun stop for a coffee—skip the food (daily 8:00–23:00, sit as near the river as possible). Notice the *Drinker of Absinthe* painting on the wall (and on the menu for 55 Kč)—with the iconic Czech writer struggling with reality.

Café Louvre is a longtime elegant favorite (opened in 1902) that still draws an energetic young crowd. From the big and busy Národní street, you walk upstairs into a venerable world of newspapers on sticks (including English) and waiters in vests and aprons. The back room has long been the place for billiard tables (100 Kč/hr). An English flier tells its history (200-Kč plates, 120-Kč two-course lunch offered 11:00–15:00, open daily 8:00–23:30, Národní 22, tel. 224-930-949).

Grand Café Orient is just two flights up off busy Celetná street, yet a world away from the crush of tourism below. Located in the Black Madonna House, the café is upstairs from the Museum of Czech Cubism (see page 185) and, fittingly, decorated with a Cubist flair. With its stylish old circa-1910 decor toned to dark green, this space is full of air and light—and a good value, to boot (salads, sandwiches, great balcony seating, Mon–Fri 9:00–22:00, Sat–Sun 10:00–22:00, Ovocný Trh 19, at the corner of Celetná near the Powder Tower, tel. 224-224-240).

Café Montmartre, on a small street parallel to Karlova, combines Parisian ambience with unbeatable Czech prices. Dreamy Czech minds have found their asylum here after Grand Café Slavia (see above) and other long-time favorites have either closed down or become stuck in their past. The main room is perfect for discussing art and politics, while the intimate room behind the courtyard is where you recite poetry to your date (Mon–Fri 10:00–23:00, Sat–Sun 12:00–23:00, Řetězová 7, tel. 222-221-244).

Ebel Coffee House, in the Ungelt courtyard behind the Týn Church, is the local Starbucks—priding itself on the wide assortment of fresh coffee grounds from every coffee-growing country in the world, inviting cakes, and a colorful setting that delights the mind as much as the caffeine does (daily 9:00–22:00, Týn 1, tel. 224-895-788).

Teahouses

Many Czech people are bohemian philosophers at heart and prefer the mellow, smoke-free environs of a teahouse to the smoky, traditional beer hall. Young Czechs are much more interested in traveling to exotic destinations like Southeast Asia, Africa, or Peru than to Western Europe, so the Oriental teahouses set their minds in vacation mode.

While there are teahouses all over town, a fine example in a handy locale is Prague's original one, established in 1991. **Dobrá Čajovna** ("Good Teahouse"), just a few steps off the bustle of Wenceslas Square, takes you into a very peaceful world that elevates tea to an almost religious ritual. At the desk you'll be given an English menu and a bell. Grab a seat and study the menu, which lovingly describes each tea. The menu lists a world of tea (very fresh, prices by the small pot), "accompaniments" (such as Exotic Miscellany), and light meals "for hungry tea drinkers." When you're ready to order, ring your bell to beckon a tea monk—likely a member of the "Lovers of Tea Society" (Mon–Sat 10:00–21:30, Sun 14:00–21:30, near the base of Wenceslas Square, opposite McDonald's at Václavské Náměstí 14, www.cajovna.com).

Art Nouveau Splendor

The **Municipal House** (Obecní Dům), the sumptuous Art Nouveau concert hall, has three restaurants: a café, a French restaurant, and a beer cellar (all at Náměstí Republiky 5). The dressy café, Kavárna Obecní Dům, is drenched in chandeliered, Art Nouveau elegance and offers the best value and experience here (light, pricey meals and drinks with great atmosphere and bad service, 250-Kč three-course special daily for lunch or dinner, open daily 7:30–23:00, live piano or jazz trio 16:00–20:00, tel. 222-002-763). The fine and formal French restaurant in the next wing oozes Mucha elegance (700–1,000-Kč meals, daily 12:00–16:00 and 18:00–23:00, tel. 222-002-777). For the location, see the map on page 228.

In the Little Quarter

These characteristic eateries are handy for a bite before or after your Prague Castle visit. For locations, see the map on page 221.

U Sedmi Švábů ("By the Seven Roaches") is a touristy den where even the cuisine is medieval. Since America was not yet discovered in the Middle Ages, you won't find any corn, potatoes, or tomatoes on the menu. The salty yellow things that come with the Krušovice beer are chickpeas. Carnivores thrive here: Try the skewered meats *(špíz u Sedmi Švábů)*, flaming beef *(flambák)*, or pork knuckle (daily 11:00–23:00, Janský Vršek 14, tel. 257-531-455).

U Osla v Kolébce ("By the Donkey in the Cradle") fills a peaceful courtyard just a minute off the touristy hubbub of

Nerudova. The laid-back scene consists of two restaurants with nearly identical simple menus, dominated by tasty sausages and salads (daily 10:00–22:00, Jánský Vršek 8, below Nerudova, next door to U Sedmi Švábů, tel. 731-407-036).

U Hrocha ("By the Hippo"), a very authentic little pub packed with beer-drinkers and smoke, serves simple, traditional meals—basically meat starters with bread. Just below the castle near Little Quarter Square (Malostranské Náměstí), it's actually the haunt of many members of Parliament, which is located just around the corner (daily 12:00–23:00, chalkboard lists daily meals in English, Thunovská 10).

Restaurace Rybářský Klub, on Kampa Island overlooking the river, is run by the Society of Czech Fishermen and serves one of the widest and tastiest selections of freshwater fish in Prague at reasonable prices. Dine on fish-cream soup, pike, trout, carp, or catfish under the imaginative artwork of Little Quarter painter Mr. Kuba. On warm evenings, late May through October, they fill their dock with tables and offer my choice for the best riverside dining in town (three-course meal for around 400 Kč, riverside menu not as extensive as indoor restaurant menu, daily 12:00–23:00, U Sovových Mlýnů 1, tel. 257-534-200).

In the Castle Quarter

To locate the following restaurants, see the map on page 205.

Klášterní Pivovar ("Monastery Brewery") was founded by an abbot in 1628. The brewery closed down in 1907, but it finally re-opened in 2004 after meticulous restoration in two large rooms and a pleasant courtyard. The wooden decor and circa-1900 newspaper clippings (including Hapsburg Emperor Franz Josef's "Proclamation to My Nations," announcing the beginning of World War I), bring you to the heart of the best in Czech pub dining. Beer-flavored cheese served on toasted black-yeast bread is a mandatory starter for any meal here. Both locally brewed beer and Czech Budweiser flow liberally (daily 10:00–22:00, Strahovské Nádvoří 301, tel. 233-353-155, www.klasterni-pivovar.cz). It's directly across from the entrance to the Strahov library (not to be confused with the enormous, group-oriented Klášterní Restaurace next door, to the right).

Restaurace Nad Úvozem is hidden in the middle of a staircase that connects Loretánská and Úvoz streets. This secret spot, which boasts superb views of Prague, offers excellent food for surprisingly low prices, given its location. Try the roast beef in plum sauce (170 Kč). The service is slower when the restaurant is full, as the kitchen has limited space (daily 12:00–21:00; as you go down Loretánská watch for pans, scoops, and spoons hanging on chains on your right at #15; tel. 220-511-532). To discourage pub-goers from mingling with diners, the beer here is terribly overpriced (69 Kč).

Hostinec u Černého Vola ("By the Black Ox") is a smoky, dingy old-time pub—its survival in the midst of all the castle splendor and tourism is a marvel. It feels like a kegger on the banks of the river Styx, with classic bartenders serving up Kozel beer (traditional "goat" brand with excellent darks) and beer-friendly light meals. The pub is located on Loretánská (no sign outside, sniff for cigarette smoke and look for the only house on the block without an arcade—or see map on page 205, daily 10:00–22:00, English menu on request).

Malý Buddha ("Little Buddha") serves delightful food—especially vegetarian—and takes its theme seriously. You'll step into a mellow, low-lit escape of bamboo and peace to be served by people with perfect complexions and almost no pulse (Tue–Sun 13:00–22:30, closed Mon, non-smoking, between the castle and Strahov Monastery at Úvoz 46, tel. 220-513-894).

Espresso Kajetánka, just off Castle Square, has magnificent city views. It's a good, if overpriced, place for a drink or snack as you start or end your castle visit (daily 10:00–20:00, Ke Hradu, tel. 257-533-735).

Na Baště, more convenient but not as scenic, is in a garden through the gate to the left of the main castle entry. The outdoor seating, among Jože Plečnik's ramparts and obelisks, is the castle at its most peaceful (Sun–Thu 11:00–23:00, Fri–Sat 11:00–24:00, tel. 281-933-010).

Dining with Style

In Prague, a fancy candlelit dinner with fine wines and connoisseur-approved dishes costs more than most locals can afford—but it's still a bargain in comparison to similar restaurants in Paris or Dallas. I list only two such splurges: one aristocratic, Old World, under the castle; one more modern, untouristy, and near the Old Town Square.

Restaurace David, with two little 18th-century rooms hiding on a small cobblestone street opposite the American Embassy in the Little Quarter, is my choice for a romantic splurge. The exquisite cuisine, a modern incarnation of traditional Czech, with French and European influences, ranges from game to roasted duck and liver. Your meal comes with the gourmet quotient of knives and fancy glasses, and graceful waiters serve you like an aristocrat—appropriately, considering the neighborhood (most meals 600–1,000 Kč, open daily, reservations recommended, Tržiště 21, tel. 257-533-109).

Restaurant Červená Tabulka ("Red Chalkboard") is in a low, nondescript townhouse in a quiet neighborhood outside of the tourist circus. Sit in the dressy candlelit interior or on the quiet and breezy cobbled courtyard. Either way, there's not a dumpling in sight. The menu features modern international dishes with a focus on fish (fine 300-Kč plates and gourmet presentation). The wines are excellent and a great value (daily 11:30–23:00, Lodecká 4, tel. 224-810-401). To get to the restaurant from the Municipal House, cross Náměstí Republiky and turn right onto Truhlářská; it's 200 yards down the street on the corner of quiet Petrské Náměstí square.

TRANSPORTATION CONNECTIONS

Getting to Prague: Centrally located Prague is a logical gateway between Western and Eastern Europe. If you're coming from the West and using a Eurailpass, you must purchase tickets to cover the portion of the journey from the Czech border into Prague (buy at the train station before you board the train for Prague—it's only about $12 from the border to Prague). From the East, Prague is connected by convenient night trains with Budapest, Kraków, and Warsaw.

You'll find handy Czech train and bus schedules at www.vlak-bus.cz (train info tel. 221-111-122, little English spoken). Remember that for all train connections, it's important to confirm which of Prague's stations to use.

From Prague by Train to: Český Krumlov (8/day, 1/day direct, 4 hrs), **Budapest** (every 2 hours, 7–8.5 hrs; 1 direct night train, 9 hrs), **Kraków** (3/day with changes, 7.5–8 hrs; 1 direct night train/day, 8.5 hrs), **Warsaw** (2/day direct including 1 night train, more with changes, 8.5–9.5 hrs), **Vienna** (7/day, 4–6 hrs), **Berlin** (7/day, 5 hrs), **Munich** (3/day with changes, 6 hrs; 1 direct night train), **Frankfurt** (4/day, 7 hrs).

By Bus to: Terezín (hourly, 1 hr), **Český Krumlov** (7/day, 3.5 hrs, from Florenc station; an easy direct 3-hr bus leaves at about 9:00).

By Car with a Driver: Mike's Chauffeur Service is a reliable family-run company with fair and fixed rates around town and beyond. Friendly Mike's motto is, "We go the extra mile for you" (round-trip fares with waiting time included: Český Krumlov-3,800 Kč, Terezín-1,700 Kč, Karlštejn-1,500 Kč, minivan with plenty of room for up to 4 people, minibus also available, tel. 241-768-231, mobile 602-224-893, www.mike-chauffeur.cz, mike.chauffeur@cmail.cz). On the way to Krumlov, Mike will stop at no extra charge at Hluboká Castle or České Budějovice, where the original Bud beer is made. Mike offers a "Panoramic Transfer to Vienna" for 7,000 Kč (depart Prague at 8:00, arrive Český Krumlov at 10:00, stay up to 6 hrs, 1-hr scenic Czech riverside-and-village drive, then a 2-hr autobahn ride to your Vienna hotel, maximum 4 people). Mike also offers a similar "Panoramic Transfer to Budapest" for 10,000 Kč (2 hrs to Český Krumlov, then 1-hr scenic drive to Linz, followed by 5–6 hrs on expressway to Budapest).

FRANCE

PARIS

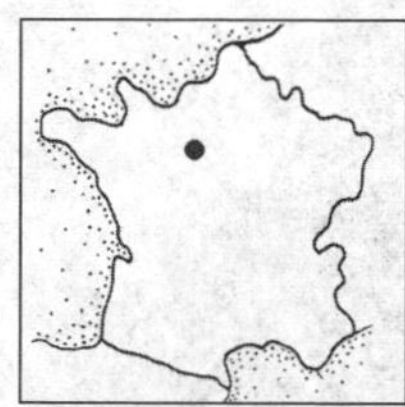

Paris—the City of Light—has been a beacon of culture for centuries. As a world capital of art, fashion, food, literature, and ideas, it stands as a symbol of all the fine things that human civilization can offer. Come prepared to celebrate, rather than judge, the cultural differences, and you'll capture the romance and joie de vivre that Paris exudes.

Paris offers sweeping boulevards, chatty crêpe stands, chic boutiques, and world-class art galleries. Sip decaf with deconstructionists at a sidewalk café, then step into an Impressionist painting in a tree-lined park. Climb Notre-Dame and rub shoulders with the gargoyles. Cruise the Seine, zip up the Eiffel Tower, and saunter down the avenue des Champs-Elysées. Master the Louvre and Orsay museums. Save some after-dark energy for one of the world's most romantic cities.

Planning Your Time

In the planning sections below for three very busy but doable days in Paris, I've listed sights in descending order of importance. Therefore, if you have only one day, just do Day 1; for two days, add Day 2; and so on. When planning where to plug in Versailles, remember that the palace is closed on Mondays and especially crowded on Sundays and Tuesdays—try to avoid these days if possible.

Day 1

Morning: Follow my self-guided "Historic Core of Paris Walk" (see page 254), featuring Ile de la Cité, Notre-Dame, the Latin Quarter, Sainte-Chapelle, and more.

Afternoon: Tour the Louvre, then stroll through the Tuileries Garden. (Hyperactive art lovers could include a quick visit to the Orangerie Museum, located in the garden.)
Evening: Go for a cruise on the Seine River or take the "Paris Illumination" nighttime bus tour.

Day 2

Morning: Wander the Champs-Elysées from the Arc de Triomphe down the grand avenue des Champs-Elysées to Tuileries Garden.
Midday: Cross the pedestrian bridge from the Tuileries Garden, then visit the Orsay Museum.
Afternoon: Tour the Rodin Museum or Napoleon's Tomb.
Evening: Enjoy the Trocadéro scene and a twilight ride up the Eiffel Tower.

Day 3

Morning: Explore the Marais, starting at place des Vosges, and tour your choice of sights: the Jewish Quarter (located along rue des Rosiers), the Picasso, Carnavalet, Pompidou Center, or Jewish Art and History museums.
Afternoon: See Versailles (take the RER suburban train).
Evening: Visit Montmartre and the Sacré-Cœur basilica.

ORIENTATION

Paris (population of city center: 2,150,000) is split in half by the Seine River, divided into 20 *arrondissements* (proud and independent governmental jurisdictions), circled by a ring-road freeway (the *périphérique*), and speckled with Métro stations. You'll find Paris easier to navigate if you know which side of the river you're on, which *arrondissement* you're in, and which Métro stop you're closest to. If you're north of the river (the top half of any city map), you're on the Right Bank (Rive Droite). If you're south of it, you're on the Left Bank (Rive Gauche). The bull's-eye of your Paris map is Notre-Dame, which sits on an island in the middle of the Seine. Most of your sightseeing will take place within five blocks of the river.

Paris *Arrondissements*

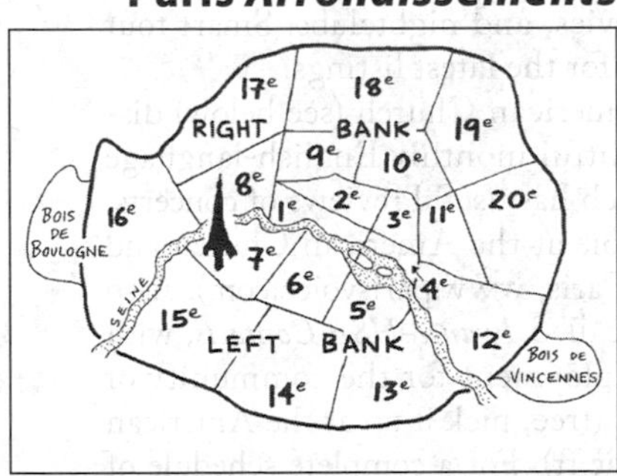

Arrondissements are numbered, starting at the Louvre and

moving in a clockwise spiral out to the ring road. The last two digits in a Parisian zip code are the *arrondissement* number. The abbreviation for "Métro stop" is "Mo." In Parisian jargon, Napoleon's tomb is on *la Rive Gauche* (the Left Bank) in the *7ème* (7th *arrondissement*), zip code 75007, Mo: Invalides.

Paris Métro stops are used as a standard aid in giving directions, even for those not using the Métro. As you're tracking down addresses, these words and pronunciations will help: Métro (may-troh), *place* (plahs—square), *rue* (roo—road), *avenue* (ah-vuh-noo), *boulevard* (boo-luh-var), and *pont* (pohn—bridge).

Tourist Information

Paris tourist offices, abbreviated **TI** in this book, have long lines, offer little information, and may charge for maps. This book, the *Pariscope* magazine (described below), and one of the freebie maps available at any hotel (or in the front of this book) are all you need. Paris' TIs share a single phone number: 08 92 68 30 00 (from the US, dial 011 33 8 92 68 30 00).

If you must visit a TI, there are several locations, including **Pyramides** (daily 9:00–19:00, at Pyramides Métro stop between the Louvre and Opéra), **Gare de Lyon** (Mon–Sat 8:00–18:00, closed Sun), and **Montmartre** (daily 10:00–19:00, place du Tertre). A fourth TI at **Grands Magasins** may have closed in 2007 (Mon–Sat 9:00–18:30, closed Sun, near Opéra Garnier at 11 rue Scribe); if so, use the Pyramides office, a five-minute walk away. The official website for Paris' TIs is www.parisinfo.com. Both **airports** have handy information offices (called ADP) with long hours and short lines (see "Airports," page 343).

Pariscope: The weekly €0.40 *Pariscope* magazine (or one of its clones, available at any newsstand) lists museum hours, art exhibits, concerts, festivals, plays, movies, and nightclubs. Smart tour guides and sightseers rely on this for the latest listings.

Other Publications: The American Church (see below) distributes a free, handy, and insightful monthly English-language newspaper called *Paris Voice,* which has useful reviews of concerts, plays, and current events (available at the American Church and about 200 locations throughout Paris, www.parisvoice.com). Also look for an advertisement paper called *France-USA Contacts*, with information on housing and employment for the community of 30,000 Americans living in Paris (free, pick it up at the American Church and elsewhere, www.fusac.fr). For a complete schedule of museum hours and English-language museum tours, get the free *Musées, Monuments Historiques, et Expositions* booklet from any museum.

American Church and Franco-American Center: This interdenominational church—in the rue Cler neighborhood, facing the river between the Eiffel Tower and Orsay Museum—is a nerve center for the American émigré community. The worship service at 11:00 on Sunday, the coffee hour after church, and the free Sunday concerts (generally Sept–May at 17:00 or 18:00—but not every week) are a great way to make some friends and get a taste of émigré life in Paris (reception open Mon–Sat 9:30–13:00 & 14:00–22:30, Sun 9:00–14:00 & 15:00–19:00, 65 quai d'Orsay, Mo: Invalides, tel. 01 40 62 05 00, www.acparis.org). It's also a good place to pick up copies of *Paris Voice* and *France-USA Contacts* (described above).

Arrival in Paris

For a comprehensive rundown on Paris' train stations and airports, see "Transportation Connections," page 340.

Helpful Hints

Heightened Security *(Plan Vigipirate):* You may notice an abundance of police at monuments, on streets, and on the Métro, as well as security cameras everywhere. You'll go through quick and reassuring airport-like security checks at many major attractions. This is all part of Paris' anti-terror plan. The police are helpful, the security lines move quickly, and there are fewer pickpocket problems than usual on the Métro.

Theft Alert: Although the greater police presence has scared off some pickpockets, these troublesome thieves still thrive—particularly on Métro and RER lines that serve high-profile tourist sights. Wear a money belt, put your wallet in your front pocket, loop your day bag over your shoulders, and keep a tight grip on your purse or shopping bag. Muggings are rare, but do occur. If you're out late, avoid the dark riverfront embankments and any place where the lighting is dim and pedestrian activity is minimal.

Street Safety: Parisian drivers are notorious for ignoring pedestrians. Look both ways (many streets are one-way) and be careful of seemingly quiet bus/taxi lanes. Don't assume you have the right of way, even in a crosswalk. When crossing a street, keep your pace constant and don't stop suddenly. By law, drivers must miss pedestrians by only one meter—a little more than three feet (1.5 meters in the countryside). Drivers carefully calculate your speed and won't hit you, provided you don't alter your route or pace.

Watch out for a lesser hazard: *merde.* Parisian dogs decorate the city's sidewalks with 16 tons of droppings per day. People get injured by slipping in it.

Paris Museum Pass: This worthwhile pass, covering most sights in Paris, is available at major Métro stations, TIs, and museums.

For detailed information, see page 246.

Museum Strategy: When possible, visit key museums first thing (when your energy is best) and save other activities for the afternoon. Remember, most museums require you to check daypacks and coats, and important museums have metal detectors that will slow your entry. The Louvre, Orsay, and Pompidou are open on selected nights, making for peaceful visits with fewer crowds.

Bookstores: There are many English-language bookstores in Paris where you can pick up guidebooks (at nearly double their American prices). Most carry this book. My favorite is the friendly **Red Wheelbarrow Bookstore** in the Marais neighborhood, run by charming Penelope and Abigail (Mon–Sat 10:00–19:00, Sun 14:00–18:00, 22 rue St. Paul, Mo: St. Paul, tel. 01 48 04 75 08). Others include **Shakespeare and Company** (some used travel books, daily 12:00–24:00, 37 rue de la Bûcherie, across the river from Notre-Dame, Mo: St. Michel, tel. 01 43 26 96 50), **W.H. Smith** (Mon–Sat 10:00–19:00, closed Sun, 248 rue de Rivoli, Mo: Concorde, tel. 01 44 77 88 99), **Brentanos** (Mon–Sat 10:00–19:00, closed Sun, 37 avenue de l'Opéra, Mo: Opéra, tel. 01 42 61 52 50), and **Village Voice** (near St. Sulpice Church at 6 rue Princesse, tel. 01 46 33 36 47).

Public WCs: Public toilets are free (though leaving a small tip if there's an attendant is appreciated). Modern, sanitary street-booth toilets provide both relief and a memory (don't leave small children inside unattended). The restrooms in museums are free and the best you'll find. Or walk into any sidewalk café like you own the place and find the toilet in the back. Keep toilet paper or tissues with you, as some toilets are poorly supplied.

Bike Rental: Fat Tire Bike Tours runs tours (see page 253) and also rents bikes (€2/hr, €15/24 hrs, includes helmets and locks, credit-card imprint required for deposit, ask for their suggested bike route map, daily 9:00–19:00, south of Eiffel Tower at 24 rue Edgar Faure, Mo: Dupleix, tel. 01 56 58 10 54, www.fattirebiketours.com).

Parking: Most of the time, drivers must pay to park curbside (buy parking card at tobacco shops), but not at night (19:00–9:00), all day Sunday, or anytime in August, when many Parisians are on vacation. There are parking garages under Ecole Militaire, St. Sulpice Church, Les Invalides, the Bastille, and the Panthéon for about €20–25 per day (it's cheaper the longer you stay). Some hotels offer parking for less—ask.

Tobacco Stands *(Tabacs)*: These little kiosks—usually just a counter inside a café—sell cards for parking meters, public-transit tickets, postage stamps, and...oh yeah, cigarettes. To find one anywhere in Paris, just look for a *Tabac* sign and the red, cylinder-shaped symbol above some (but not all) cafés.

Getting Around Paris

For such a sprawling city, Paris is easy to navigate. Your basic choices are Métro (in-city subway), RER (suburban rail tied into the Métro system), public bus, and taxi. (Also consider the hop-on, hop-off bus and boat tours, described under "Tours" on page 251.) You can buy tickets and passes at a *tabac* (tobacco stand—described above) and at most Métro stations. While the majority of Métro stations have staffed ticket windows, smaller stations might discontinue this service as the Métro system converts to automated machines.

Public-Transit Tickets: The Métro, RER, and buses all work on the same tickets. (Note that you can transfer between the Métro and RER on a single ticket, but combining a Métro or RER trip with a bus ride takes two tickets.) A **single ticket** costs €1.40. To save 30 percent, buy a ***carnet*** (kar-nay) of 10 tickets for €10.90 (that's €1.09 per ticket—€0.31 cheaper than single tickets). It's less expensive for kids (ages 4–10 pay €5.40 for a *carnet*).

If you're staying in Paris for even just a few days, consider the **Carte Orange** (kart oh-RAHNZH), which pays for itself in 15 rides. For about €16, you get free run of the bus and Métro system for one week, starting Monday and ending Sunday. Ask for the Carte Orange *hebdomadaire* (ehb-doh-mah-dair) and supply a passport-size photo. Larger Métro stations have photo booths. The month-long version costs about €51—request a Carte Orange *mensuelle* (mahn-soo-ehl, good from the first day of the month to the last, also requires photo). These passes cover only central Paris. You can pay more for passes covering regional destinations (such as Versailles), but for most visitors, this is a bad value (instead, buy individual tickets for longer-distance destinations). Despite what some Métro agents say, Carte Orange passes are definitely not limited to residents; if you're refused, simply go to another station or a *tabac* to buy your pass.

The overpriced **Paris Visite** passes were designed for tourists and offer minor reductions at minor sights (1 day/€9, 2 days/€14, 3 days/€19, 5 days/€28), but you'll get a better value with a cheaper *carnet* of 10 tickets or a Carte Orange.

By Métro

In Paris, you're never more than a 10-minute walk from a Métro station. Europe's best subway allows you to hop from sight to sight quickly and cheaply (runs daily 5:30–24:30). Learn to use it. Begin by studying the color Métro map (free at Métro stations and

The Paris Museum Pass

In Paris, there are two classes of sightseers—those with a Paris Museum Pass, and those who stand in line. Serious sightseers save time and money by getting this pass.

Most of the sights listed in this chapter are covered by the pass (see list below). Notable exceptions are: the Eiffel Tower, Montparnasse Tower, Marmottan Museum, Opéra Garnier, Notre-Dame treasury, Jacquemart-André Museum, Jewish Art and History Museum, Grand Palais, La Défense and La Grande Arche, Jeu de Paume, Catacombs, *Paris Story* film, Montmartre Museum, Sacré-Cœur's dome, Dalí Museum, Museum of Erotic Art, and the ladies of Pigalle.

The pass pays for itself with four admissions in two days, and lets you skip the ticket line at most sights (2 days/€30, 4 days/€45, 6 days/€60, no youth or senior discount). It's sold at the participating museums, monuments, and TIs (even at airports). Try to avoid buying the pass at a major museum (such as the Louvre), where supply can be spotty and lines long. For more info, call 01 44 61 96 60 or visit www.parismuseumpass.fr.

The pass isn't activated until the first time you use it (you write the starting date on the pass). Think and read ahead to make the most of your pass. You could spend a day or two at the beginning or end of your Paris visit seeing free sights (e.g., Carnavalet Museum and Victor Hugo's House) and sights that don't accept the pass (e.g., Eiffel Tower). Validate your pass only when you're ready to tackle the covered sights on consecutive days. The free directory that comes with your pass lists the current hours of sights, phone numbers, and the price that kids pay.

The pass isn't worth buying for children and teens, as most museums are free or discounted for those under 18 (teenagers may need to show ID as proof of age). Of the museums that charge for children, some allow kids in free if their parent has a Museum Pass, while others charge admission, depending on age (the cutoff age varies from 5 to 18). If a sight is free for kids, they can skip the line with their passholder parents.

Here's a list of included sights and their admission prices without the pass: Louvre (€8.50), Orsay Museum (€7.50),

included on freebie Paris maps at your hotel).

Pickpockets: Thieves dig the Métro. Be on guard. For example, if your pocket is picked as you pass through a turnstile, you end up stuck on the wrong side (after the turnstile bar has closed behind you) while the thief gets away. Stand away from Métro doors to avoid being a target for a theft-and-run just before the doors close. Any jostling or commotion—especially when boarding or leaving trains—is likely the sign of a thief or a team of thieves in

Orangerie Museum (€6.50), Sainte-Chapelle (€7.50), Arc de Triomphe (€8), Napoleon's Tomb/Army Museums (€7.50), Conciergerie (€7.50), Panthéon (€7.50), Sewer Tour (€4), Cluny Museum (€6.50), Pompidou Center (€7), Notre-Dame tower (€7.50), Paris Archaeological Crypt (€3.50), Picasso Museum (€6.50), Rodin Museum (€6), National Maritime Museum (€9), and the Delacroix Museum (€5). Outside Paris, the pass covers the Palace of Versailles (€13.50, does not cover Domaine de Marie-Antoinette), Château of Fontainebleau (€6.50), and Château of Chantilly (€8).

Tally up what you want to see—and remember, an advantage of the pass is that you skip to the front of most lines, which can save hours of waiting, especially in summer. Note that at a few sights (including the Louvre, Sainte-Chapelle, and Notre-Dame's tower), everyone has to shuffle through the slow-moving baggage-check lines for security.

To use your pass at sights, boldly walk to the front of the ticket line, hold up your pass, and ask the ticket-taker: *"Entrez, pass?"* (ahn-tray pahs). You'll either be allowed to enter at that point or you'll be directed to a special entrance. For major sights, such as the Louvre and Orsay, we've identified passholder entrances on the maps in this book.

With the pass, you'll pop freely into sights that you're walking by (even for a few minutes) that otherwise might not be worth the expense (e.g., the Conciergerie or Paris Archaeological Crypt).

Museum Tips: The Louvre and other museums are closed on Tuesday, and many others are closed on Monday. Some museums offer reduced prices on Sunday. Most sights stop admitting people 30–60 minutes before closing time, and many begin shutting down rooms 45 minutes before. For the fewest crowds, visit very early, at lunch, or very late. Most museums have slightly shorter hours October through March.

Before You Go: You can download free audio versions of my self-guided tours of Historic Paris, the Louvre, Orsay, and Versailles. All you need is an MP3 player and www.ricksteves.com.

action. Make any fare inspector show proof of identity (ask locals for help if you're not certain). Never show anyone your wallet.

How the Métro Works: To get to your destination, determine the closest "Mo" stop and which line or lines will get you there. The lines have numbers, but they're best known by their end-of-the-line stops. (For example, the La Défense/Château de Vincennes line, also known as line 1, runs between La Défense in the west and Vincennes in the east.) Once in the Métro station,

Paris

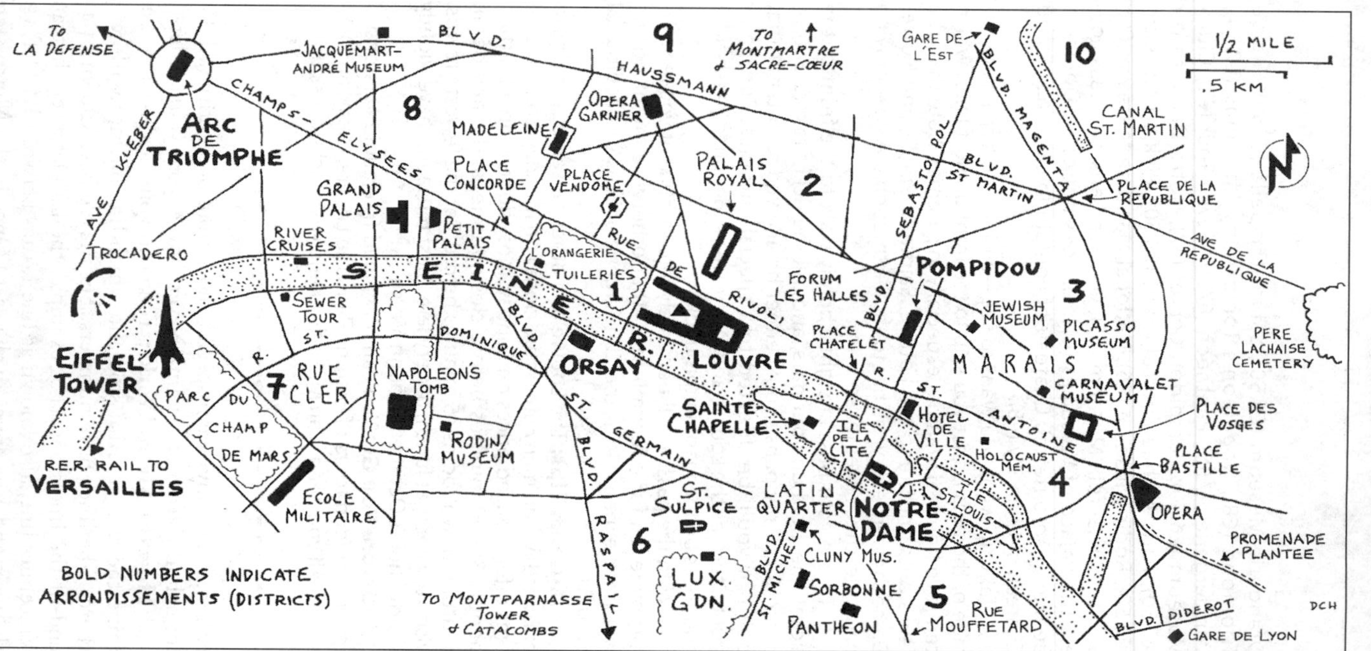
To LA DEFENSE
ARC DE TRIOMPHE
AVE KLEBER
CHAMPS-ELYSEES
JACQUEMART-ANDRÉ MUSEUM
BLVD.
HAUSSMANN
8
9
TO MONTMARTRE & SACRE-CŒUR
OPERA GARNIER
MADELEINE
PLACE CONCORDE
PLACE VENDOME
PALAIS ROYAL
2
GARE DE L'EST
BLVD. MAGENTA
10
CANAL ST. MARTIN
1/2 MILE
.5 KM
BLVD. ST MARTIN
PLACE DE LA REPUBLIQUE
AVE DE LA REPUBLIQUE
SEBASTOPOL
TROCADERO
GRAND PALAIS
PETIT PALAIS
RIVER CRUISES
L'ORANGERIE
TUILERIES
RUE DE RIVOLI
SEINE R.
1
FORUM LES HALLES
BLVD.
POMPIDOU
3
JEWISH MUSEUM
PICASSO MUSEUM
PERE LACHAISE CEMETERY
SEWER TOUR
ST. DOMINIQUE
R.
BLVD.
PLACE CHATELET
MARAIS
EIFFEL TOWER
7
RUE CLER
NAPOLEON'S TOMB
ORSAY
LOUVRE
R. ST. ANTOINE
CARNAVALET MUSEUM
PARC DU CHAMP DE MARS
SAINTE-CHAPELLE
ILE DE LA CITE
HOTEL DE VILLE
PLACE DES VOSGES
R.E.R. RAIL TO VERSAILLES
RODIN MUSEUM
BLVD. ST. GERMAIN
HOLOCAUST MEM.
PLACE BASTILLE
ECOLE MILITAIRE
ST. SULPICE
LATIN QUARTER
NOTRE-DAME
ILE ST. LOUIS
4
OPERA
6
BLVD. RASPAIL
BLVD. ST. MICHEL
CLUNY MUS.
PROMENADE PLANTEE
BOLD NUMBERS INDICATE ARRONDISSEMENTS (DISTRICTS)
TO MONTPARNASSE TOWER & CATACOMBS
LUX. GDN.
SORBONNE
PANTHEON
5
RUE MOUFFETARD
BLVD. DIDEROT
GARE DE LYON
DCH

you'll see blue-and-white signs directing you to the train going in your direction (e.g., *direction: La Défense*). Insert your ticket in the automatic turnstile, pass through, reclaim your ticket, and keep it until you exit the system (some stations require you to pass your ticket through a turnstile to exit). Fare inspectors regularly check for cheaters and accept absolutely no excuses.

Transfers are free and can be made wherever lines cross. When you transfer, look for the orange *correspondance* (connections) signs when you exit your first train, then follow the proper direction sign.

Even though the Métro whisks you quickly from one point to another, be prepared to walk significant distances within stations to reach your platform (most noticeable when you transfer). Escalators are common, but they're often out of order. To limit excessive walking, avoid transferring at these sprawling stations: Montparnasse-Bienvenüe, Chatelet-Les Halles, Charles de Gaulle-Etoile, Gare du Nord, and Bastille.

Before taking the *sortie* (exit) to leave the Métro, check the helpful *plan du quartier* (map of the neighborhood) to get your bearings, locate your destination, and decide which *sortie* you want. At stops with several *sorties,* you can save lots of walking by choosing the best exit.

After you exit the system, toss or tear your used ticket so you don't confuse it with your unused ticket—they look virtually identical.

By RER

The RER (Réseau Express Régionale; air-ay-air) is the suburban arm of the Métro, serving outlying destinations (such as Versailles, Disneyland Paris, and the airports). These routes are indicated by thick lines on your subway map and identified by the letters A, B, C, and so on. Some suburban routes are operated by France's railroad (SNCF) and are called **Transilien;** they function the same way and use the same tickets as the RER. On Transilien trains (but not RER trains), railpasses are accepted; show your pass at a ticket window to get a free ticket to get through the turnstiles.

Within the city center, the RER works like the Métro, but can be speedier (if it serves your destination directly) because it makes fewer stops. Métro tickets are good on the RER when traveling in the city center. (You can transfer between the Métro and RER systems with the same ticket.) But to travel outside the city (to Versailles or the airport, for example), you'll need to buy a separate, more expensive ticket at the station window before boarding. You need to insert your ticket in a turnstile to exit the RER lines. Also unlike the Métro, not every train stops at every station along the way; check the sign over the platform to see if your destination is listed as a stop (*"toutes les gares"* means it makes all stops along the way), or confirm with a local before you board.

By City Bus

Paris' excellent bus system is worth figuring out. Remember, even though buses use the same tickets as the Métro and RER, you can't use a single ticket to transfer between the systems—or even to transfer from one bus to another. One ticket buys you a bus ride anywhere in central Paris—but if you leave the city center (shown as zone 1 on the diagram on board the bus) or transfer to another bus, you must validate a second ticket.

Buses don't seem as romantic as the famous Métro and are subject to traffic jams, but savvy travelers know that buses can have you swinging through the city like Tarzan in an urban jungle. Bus stops are abundant, and offer all the information you need: a good city bus map, route maps showing exactly where each bus that uses this stop goes, a frequency chart and schedule, a *plan du quartier* map of the immediate neighborhood, and a *soirées* map explaining night service, if available. While the Métro shuts down at about 24:30, some buses continue much later (called *Noctilien* lines, www.noctilien.fr).

Enter buses through the front door. Punch your ticket in the machine behind the driver, or pay the higher cash fare. When you reach your destination, push the red button to signal you want a stop, then exit through the **rear door.** Even if you're not certain you've figured out the system, do some joyriding (outside of rush hour: Mon–Fri 8:00–9:30 & 17:30–19:30). Be warned: Not all of the city buses are air-conditioned, and can become rolling greenhouses on summer days. Handy bus-system maps *(plan des autobus)* are available in any Métro station (and in the €7 *Paris Pratique* map book sold at newsstands). Major stops are displayed on the side of each bus. The handiest bus routes are listed for each recommended hotel neighborhood (see "Sleeping," page 294).

By Taxi

Parisian taxis are reasonable, especially for couples and families. The meters are tamper-proof. Fares and supplements (described in English on the rear windows) are straightforward. There's a €5.20 minimum. A 10-minute ride (e.g., Bastille to Eiffel Tower) costs about €10 (versus €1.09 to get anywhere in town using a *carnet* ticket on the Métro or bus).

Higher rates are charged at night (19:00–7:00), all day Sunday, and to either airport. There's a €1 charge for each piece of baggage and for train station pickups. To tip, round up to the next euro (minimum €0.50).

You can try waving down a taxi, but it's often easier to ask for the nearest taxi stand (*"Où est une station de taxi?"*; oo ay oon stah-see-ohn duh taxi). Taxi stands are indicated by a circled T on good city maps, and on many maps in this book. A taxi can fit three people comfortably, and cabbies are legally required to take up to four for a small extra fee (though some might resist). Groups of up to five can use a *grand taxi,* which must be booked in advance—ask your hotel to call. If a taxi is summoned by phone, the meter starts as soon as the call is received, adding €3–6 to the bill.

Taxis are tough to find when it's raining and on Friday and Saturday nights, especially after the Métro closes (around 24:30). If you need to catch a train or flight early in the morning, book a taxi the day before.

TOURS

By Bus

Bus Tours—Paris Vision offers bus tours of Paris, day and night (advertised in hotel lobbies). I'd take a Paris Vision tour only at night (for more on the Paris Illumination tour, see page 294); during the day, the hop-on, hop-off bus tours (listed immediately below) and the Batobus (see "By Boat," below)—which both provide transportation between sights as well as commentary—are a better value.

Hop-on, Hop-off Bus Tours—Double-decker buses connect Paris' main sights while providing a basic running commentary, allowing you to hop on and hop off along the way. You get a disposable set of ear plugs (dial English and listen to the narration). You can get off at any stop, tour a sight, then catch a later bus. These are ideal in good weather, when you can sit up top. There are two nearly equal companies: L'Open Tours and Les Cars Rouges; pick up their brochures showing routes and stops from any TI or on their buses. You can start either tour at just about any of the major sights, such as the Eiffel Tower where both companies stop on avenue Joseph Bouvard.

L'Open Tours uses bright yellow buses and provides more extensive coverage (and slightly better commentary) on four different routes, rolling by most of the important sights in Paris. Their Paris Grand Tour (the green route) offers the best introduction. The same ticket gets you on any of their routes within the validity period. Buy your tickets from the driver (1 day-€25, 2 days-€28, kids 4–11 pay €12 for 1 or 2 days, allow 2 hours per tour). Two or three buses depart hourly from about 10:00 to 18:00; expect to wait 10–20 minutes at each stop (stops can be tricky to find—look for yellow signs; tel. 01 42 66 56 56, www.paris-opentour.com). A combo-ticket covers both the Batobus boats (described in "By Boat" below) and L'Open Tours buses (€35, kids under 12 pay €15, valid 2 days).

Les Cars Rouges' bright red buses offer largely the same service, with only one route and just nine stops, for a bit less money (adult-€22, kids 4–12 pay €11, good for 2 days, tel. 01 53 95 39 53, www.carsrouges.com).

By Boat

Seine Cruises—Several companies run one-hour boat cruises on the Seine (by far best at night).

Two companies are convenient to the rue Cler hotels: **Bateaux-Mouches,** which departs from pont de l'Alma's right bank, has the biggest, open-top, double-decker boats and tour groups by the dozens (€8, kids 4–12 pay €4, tel. 01 40 76 99 99, www.bateauxmouches.com). **Bateaux Parisiens** has smaller, covered boats with handheld audioguides and only one deck (€10, kids 4–11 pay €5, discounted half-price if you have a valid France or France–Switzerland railpass—does not use up a day of a flexipass, leaves from right in front of the Eiffel Tower, tel. 08 25 01 01 01, www.bateauxparisiens.com). Both companies run daily year-round (April–Oct 10:00–22:30, 2–3/hr; Nov–March shorter hours, runs hourly).

The smaller, more intimate **Vedettes du PontNeuf** are closer to the Marais and Luxembourg area hotels. During the day, they depart once an hour from the center of pont Neuf (2/hr after dark), but they come with a live guide giving explanations in French and English (€10, kids 4–12 pay €5, tip requested, tel. 01 46 33 98 38).

Hop-on, Hop-Off Boat Tour—**Batobus** allows you to get on and off as often you like at any of eight popular stops along the Seine: Eiffel Tower, Champs-Elysées, Orsay/place de la Concorde, the Louvre, Notre-Dame, St. Germain-des-Prés, Hôtel de Ville, and Jardin des Plantes. Safety-conscious glass enclosures turn the boats into virtual ovens on hot days (1 day-€11, 2 days-€13, boats run June–Aug 10:00–21:30, mid-March–May and Sept–Oct 10:00–19:00, Nov–Dec and Feb–mid-March 10:30–16:30, no boat last three weeks in Jan, every 15–20 minutes, 45 min one-way, 90 min round-trip, worthless narration). If you use this for getting around—sort of a scenic, floating alternative to the Métro—this can be worthwhile. But if you just want a guided boat tour, Batobus is not as good a value as the regular tour boats described above. A special combo-ticket covers L'Open Tours buses (described above) and Batobus boats (€35, kids under 12 pay €15, valid 2 days, www.batobus.com).

By Foot

Paris Walks—This company offers a variety of excellent two-hour walks, led by British or American guides. Tours are thoughtfully prepared, relaxing, and humorous. Don't hesitate to stand close to the guide to hear (€10 each, generally 2 tours/day, private tours available, tel. 01 48 09 21 40 for recorded schedule in English, also posted at www.paris-walks.com, paris@paris-walks.com). Tours focus on the Marais (4/week), Montmartre (3/week), medieval Latin Quarter (Mon), Ile de la Cité/Notre-Dame (Mon), the "Two Islands" (Ile de la Cité and Ile St. Louis, Wed), *Da Vinci Code* sights (Wed), and Hemingway's Paris (Fri). Ask about their family-friendly tours. Call a day or two ahead to learn their schedule and starting point. Most tours don't require reservations, but specialty tours (such as the *Da Vinci Code* tour) require advance reservations and prepayment with credit card (not refundable, even if you cancel months in advance).

Context Paris—These "intellectual by design" walking tours are led by docents (historians, architects, and academics) and cover both museums and neighborhoods, often with a fascinating theme (explained on their website). Try to book in advance, since groups are small and can fill up (limited to 6 participants, generally 3 hours long and €50 per person plus admissions, tel. 06 13 09 67 11, www.contextparis.com, info@contextparis.com). They also offer private tours.

Private Guides—For many, Paris merits hiring a Parisian as a personal guide. **Arnaud Servignat** is an excellent licensed local guide (€150/half-day, €250/day, also does car tours of the countryside around Paris for a little more, tel. 06 68 80 29 05, www.arnaud-servignat.com, arnaud.servignat@noos.fr). **Elizabeth Van Hest** is another highly likeable and capable guide (€170 maximum/half-day, €260/day, tel. 01 43 41 47 31, e.van.hest@noos.fr). **Paris Walks** or **Context Paris** can also set you up with one of their guides; some Paris Walks guides are trained to work with families (both companies are described above).

By Bike and Segway

Fat Tire Bike Tours—Hit the road with a younger crowd for frolicking four-hour guided rides in English through Paris. Daytime tours feature more history (€24, mid-Feb–Nov daily at 11:00, April–Oct also at 15:00), while nighttime tours are more lively and fun (€28, April–Oct nightly at 19:00). For all tours, meet at the south pillar of the Eiffel Tower, then go to the Fat Tire office to pick up bikes (cash only, up to 26 people per group, no bikes or reservations needed, helmets available upon request at no extra charge, office at 24 rue Edgar Faure, Mo: Dupleix, tel. 01 56 58 10 54, www.fattirebiketoursparis.com).

Fat Tire's pricey **Segway Tours**—on futuristic, stand-up motorized scooters—are novel in that you learn to ride a Segway while exploring Paris (€70, up to 8 per group, daily April–Oct at 9:30 and 18:30, plan on spending nearly an hour getting used to the machine, reservation required for this tour, www.parissegwaytours.com).

Excursions from Paris

Many companies offer bus tours to regional sights, including the day trips described in this book. **Paris Vision** offers mass-produced, full-size bus and minivan tours to several popular regional destinations, including the Loire Valley, Champagne region, D-Day beaches, and Mont St. Michel. Minivan tours are more expensive but more personal, given in English, and offer convenient pickup at your hotel (€130–200/person). Their full-size bus tours are multilingual and cost about half the price of a minivan tour—worthwhile for some travelers simply for the ease of transportation to the sights (about €60, destinations include Versailles and Giverny). Paris Vision's full-size buses depart from 214 rue de Rivoli (Mo: Tuileries, tel. 01 42 60 30 01, www.parisvision.com).

SELF-GUIDED WALK

Historic Core of Paris Walk

(This information is distilled from the Historic Paris Walk chapter in *Rick Steves' Paris,* by Rick Steves, Steve Smith, and Gene Openshaw.)

Allow four hours for this self-guided tour, including sightseeing. Start where the city did—on the Ile de la Cité. Face Notre-Dame and follow the dotted line on the "Historic Core of Paris" map (see page 255).

• *To get to Notre-Dame, ride the Métro to Cité, Hôtel de Ville, or St. Michel and walk to the big square facing the...*

Notre-Dame Cathedral

This 700-year-old cathedral, rated ▲▲, is packed with history and tourists. Study its sculpture and windows, take in a Mass, eavesdrop on guides, and walk all around the outside.

The **cathedral facade** is worth a close look. The church is dedicated to "Our Lady" (Notre-Dame). Mary is center stage—cradling Jesus, surrounded by the halo of the rose window. Adam is on the left and Eve is on the right.

Below Mary and above the arches is a row of 28 statues known as the Kings of Judah. During the French Revolution, these biblical kings were mistaken for the hated French kings. The citizens stormed the church, crying, "Off with their heads!" All were decapitated, but have since been recapitated.

Speaking of decapitation, look at the carving above the doorway on the left. The man with his head in his hands is St. Denis. Back when there was a Roman temple on this spot, Christianity

Historic Core of Paris

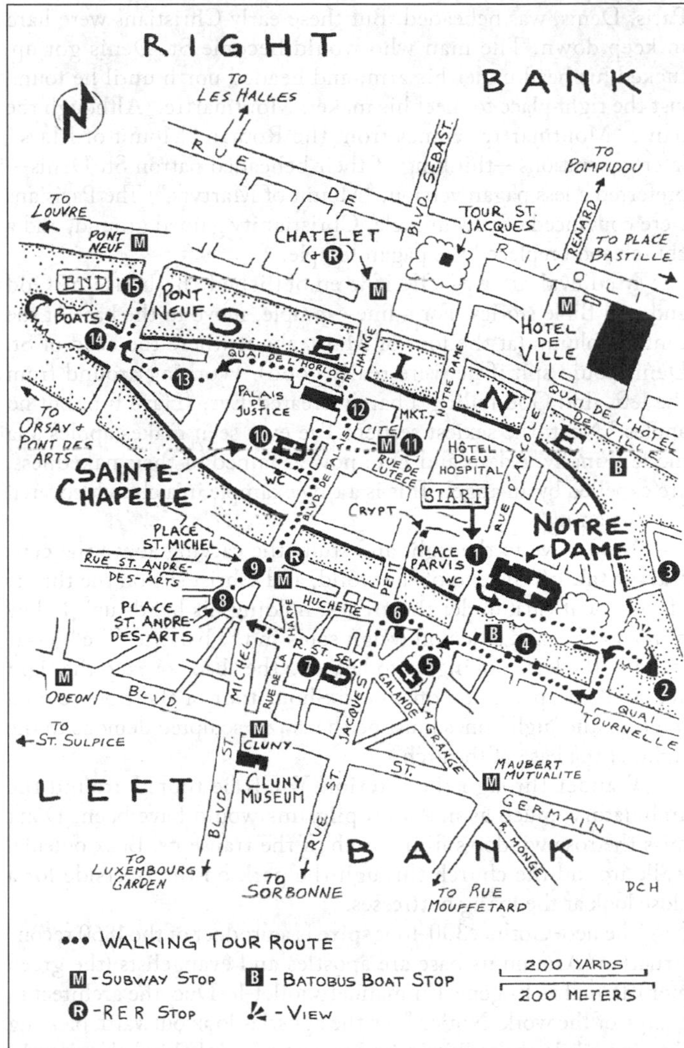

1. Point Zero
2. Deportation Memorial
3. Ile St. Louis
4. Left Bank Booksellers
5. Medieval Paris
6. Shakespeare & Co. Bookstore
7. St. Séverin
8. Place St. André-des-Arts
9. Place St. Michel
10. Sainte-Chapelle
11. Cité Métro Stop
12. Conciergerie
13. Place Dauphine
14. Statue of Henry IV
15. Pont Neuf

began making converts. The fourth-century bishop of Roman Paris, Denis, was beheaded. But these early Christians were hard to keep down. The man who would become St. Denis got up, tucked his head under his arm, and headed north until he found just the right place to meet his maker: Montmartre. (Although the name "Montmartre" comes from the Roman "Mount of Mars," later generations—thinking of their beheaded patron St. Denis—preferred a less pagan version, "Mount of Martyrs.") The Parisians were convinced of this miracle, Christianity gained ground, and a church soon replaced the pagan temple.

Medieval art was OK if it embellished the house of God and told Bible stories. For a fine example, move to the base of the central column (at the foot of Mary, about where the head of St. Denis could spit if he were really good). Working around from the left, find God telling a barely created Eve, "Have fun, but no apples." Next, the sexiest serpent I've ever seen makes apples à la mode. Finally, Adam and Eve, now ashamed of their nakedness, are expelled by an angel. This is a tiny example in a church covered with meaning.

Now move to the right and study the carving above the **central portal.** It's the end of the world, and Christ sits on the throne of Judgment (just under the arches, holding his hands up). Below him an angel and a demon weigh souls in the balance. The "good" stand to the left, looking up to heaven. The "bad" ones to the right are chained up and led off to a six-hour tour of the Louvre on a hot day. The "ugly" ones must be the crazy, sculpted demons to the right, at the base of the arch.

Wander through the interior. You'll be routed around the ambulatory, much as medieval pilgrims would have been. Don't miss the rose windows filling each of the transepts. Back outside, walk around the church through the park on the riverside for a close look at the flying buttresses.

The neo-Gothic, 300-foot **spire** is a product of the 1860 reconstruction. Around its base are apostles and evangelists (the green men) as well as Eugène-Emmanuel Viollet-le-Duc, the architect in charge of the work. Notice how the apostles look outward, blessing the city, while the architect (at top, seen from behind the church) looks up, admiring his spire.

The **archaeological crypt** is a worthwhile 15-minute stop with your Museum Pass (€3.50 without Museum Pass, Tue–Sun 10:00–18:00, closed Mon, enter 100 yards in front of cathedral). You'll see Roman ruins, trace the street plan of the medieval village, and see diagrams of how the earliest Paris grew and grew, all thoughtfully explained in English.

Cost, Hours, Location: Free, cathedral open daily 7:45–19:00; treasury-€2.50, not covered by Museum Pass, treasury open daily 9:30–17:30; audioguide-€5, ask about free English tours, normally Wed and Thu at 12:00, Sat at 14:30; Mo: Cité, Hôtel de Ville, or St. Michel; clean, free toilets in front of the cathedral near Charlemagne's statue; tel. 01 42 34 56 10, www.cathedraledeparis.com.

Tower: You can climb to the top of the facade between the towers, and then to the top of the south tower, 400 steps total, for a grand view (€7.50, covered by Museum Pass; July–Aug Mon–Fri 9:00–19:30, Sat–Sun 9:00–23:00; April–June and Sept daily 9:30–19:30, Oct–March daily 10:00–17:30, last entry 45 min before closing, arrive before 10:00 to avoid long lines).

• *Behind Notre-Dame, squeeze through the tourist buses, cross the street, and enter the iron gate into the park at the tip of the island. Look for the stairs and head down to reach the...*

Deportation Memorial

This memorial (Mémorial de la Déportation) to the 200,000 French victims of the Nazi concentration camps, rated ▲, draws you into their experience. As you descend the steps, the city around you disappears. Surrounded by walls, you become a prisoner. Your only freedom is your view of the sky and the tantalizing glimpse of the river below.

Enter the single-file chamber ahead. Inside, the circular plaque in the floor reads, "They went to the end of the earth and did not return." A hallway stretches in front of you, lined with 200,000 lighted crystals, one for each French citizen that died. Flickering at the far end is the eternal flame of hope. The tomb of the unknown deportee lies at your feet. Above, the inscription reads, "Dedicated to the living memory of the 200,000 French deportees sleeping in the night and the fog, exterminated in the Nazi concentration camps."

Above the exit as you leave is the message you'll find at all Holocaust sights: "Forgive, but never forget." (Free, daily April–Sept 10:00–12:00 & 14:00–19:00, Oct–March 10:00–12:00 & 14:00–17:00, at the east tip of the island named Ile de la Cité, behind Notre-Dame and near Ile St. Louis, Mo: Cité, tel. 01 49 74 34 00.)

• *Look across the river to the...*

Ile St. Louis

If the Ile de la Cité is a tug laden with the history of Paris, it's towing this classy little residential dinghy laden only with boutiques, famous sorbet shops, and restaurants (see "Eating," page 333). This island wasn't developed until much later (18th century). What was a swampy mess is now harmonious Parisian architecture. The pedestrian bridge, pont St. Louis, connects the two islands, leading right to rue St. Louis-en-l'Ile. This spine of the island is

Ile St. Louis

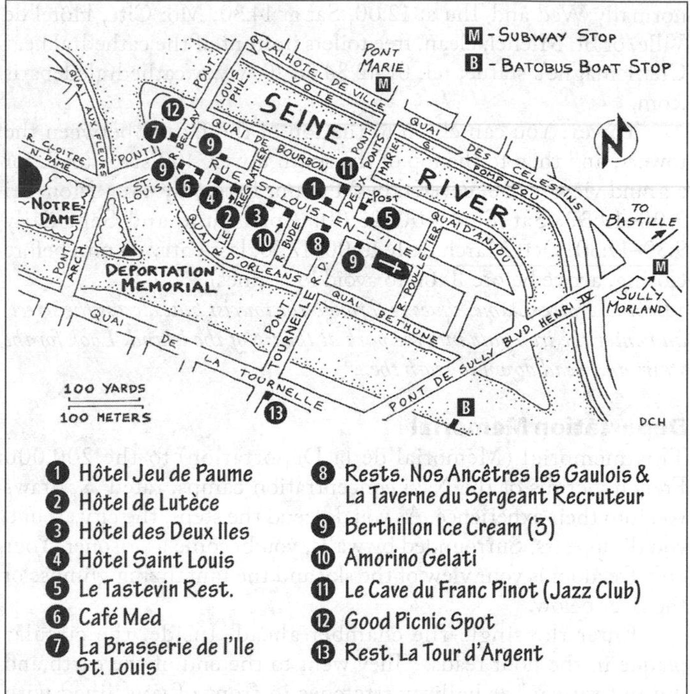

lined with interesting shops. A short stroll takes you to the famous Berthillon ice cream parlor (#31). Loop back to the pedestrian bridge along the parklike quays (walk north to the river and turn left). This walk is about as peaceful and romantic as Paris gets.

Before walking to the opposite end of the Ile de la Cité, loop through the Latin Quarter (as indicated on the map on page 276).

• *From the Deportation Memorial, cross the bridge onto the Left Bank and enjoy the riverside view of Notre-Dame, window-shopping among the green book stalls and browsing through used books, vintage posters, and souvenirs. At the little park and church (over the bridge from the front of Notre-Dame), venture inland a few blocks, basically arcing through the Latin Quarter and returning to the island two bridges down at place St. Michel.*

Latin Quarter

The touristic fame of this neighborhood, rated ▲, relates to its intriguingly artsy, bohemian character. This was perhaps Europe's leading university district in the Middle Ages—home, since the 13th century, to the prestigious Sorbonne University. Back then, Latin was the language of higher education. And, since students here came from all over Europe, Latin served as their linguistic common denominator. Locals referred to the quarter by its language: Latin.

The neighborhood's main boulevards (St. Michel and St. Germain) are lined with far-out bookshops, street singers, and jazz clubs. While still youthful and artsy, the area has become a tourist ghetto filled with cheap North African eateries. The cafés that were once the haunts of great poets and philosophers are now the hangout of tired tourists. For colorful wandering or café sitting, afternoons and evenings are best (Mo: St. Michel).

Walking along rue St. Séverin, you can still see the shadow of the medieval sewer system (the street slopes into a central channel of bricks). In the days before plumbing and toilets, when people still went to the river or neighborhood wells for their water, "flushing" meant throwing it out the window. Certain times of day were flushing times. Maids on the fourth floor would holler, *"Garde de l'eau!"* ("Watch out for the water!") and heave it into the streets, where it would eventually be washed down into the Seine.

Consider a visit to the Cluny Museum for its medieval art and unicorn tapestries (see page 275).

Place St. Michel (facing the St. Michel bridge) is the traditional core of the Left Bank's artsy, liberal, hippie district of poets, philosophers, winos, and tourists. In less commercial times, place St. Michel was a gathering point for the city's malcontents and misfits. Here, in 1871, the citizens took the streets from government troops, set up barricades *Les Miz*–style, and established the Paris Commune. During World War II, the locals rose up against their Nazi oppressors (read the plaques by St. Michel fountain). And in the spring of 1968, a time of social upheaval all over the world, young students—battling riot batons and tear gas—took over the square and demanded change.

• *From place St. Michel, look across the river and find the spire of Sainte-Chapelle church and its weathervane angel (below). Cross the river on pont St. Michel and continue along boulevard du Palais. On your left, you'll see the high-security doorway to the Sainte-Chapelle. You'll need to pass through a metal detector to get into the Sainte-Chapelle complex. Once past security, restrooms are ahead on the left. The line into the church may be long. (Museum Pass–holders can bypass this line; pick up an English info flier.) Enter the humble ground floor of...*

Sainte-Chapelle

This triumph of Gothic church architecture, rated ▲▲▲, is a cathedral of glass like no other. It was speedily built between 1242 and 1248 for Louis IX (the only French king who is now a saint) to house the supposed Crown of Thorns. Its architectural harmony is due to the fact that it was completed under the direction of one

Sainte-Chapelle

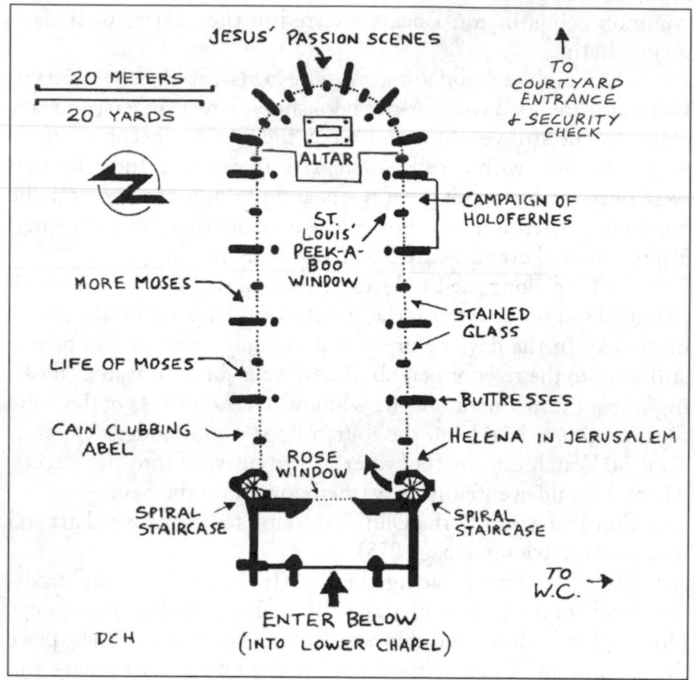

architect in only six years—unheard of in Gothic times. (Notre-Dame took more than 200 years to build.)

The design clearly shows an Old Regime approach to worship. The basement was for staff and other common folk. Royal Christians worshipped upstairs. The ground-floor paint job, a 19th-century restoration, is a reasonably accurate copy of the original.

Climb the spiral staircase to the **Chapelle Haute.** Fill the place with choral music, crank up the sunshine, face the top of the altar, and really believe that the Crown of Thorns is there, and this becomes one awesome space.

"Let there be light." In the Bible, it's clear: Light is divine. Light shining through stained glass was a symbol of God's grace shining down to earth. Gothic architects used their new technology to turn dark stone buildings into lanterns of light. The glory of Gothic shines brighter here than in any other church.

There are 15 separate panels of stained glass (6,500 square feet—two-thirds of it 13th-century original), with more than 1,100 different scenes, mostly from the Bible.

The altar was raised up high to better display the relic—the Crown of Thorns—around which this chapel was built. The supposed crown cost King Louis three times as much as this church. Today, it is kept in the Notre-Dame treasury and shown only on Fridays during Lent (€7.50, €11.50 combo-ticket covers Conciergerie—see below, both covered by Museum Pass; open daily March–Oct 9:30–18:00, Nov–Feb 9:00–17:00, last entry 30 min before closing, Mo: Cité).

• *Head back outside.*

Palais de Justice

As you walk around the church exterior, look down and notice how much Paris has risen in the 800 years since Sainte-Chapelle was built. You're in a huge complex of buildings that has housed the local government since ancient Roman times. It was the site of the original Gothic palace of the early kings of France. The only surviving medieval parts are the Sainte-Chapelle church and the Conciergerie prison.

Most of the site is now covered by the giant Palais de Justice, home of France's supreme court (built in 1776). *"Liberté, Egalité, Fraternité,"* emblazoned over the doors, is a reminder that this was also the headquarters of the Revolutionary government.

• *Now pass through the big iron gate to the noisy boulevard du Palais. Cross the street to the wide pedestrian-only rue de Lutèce and walk about halfway down.*

Cité "Métropolitain" Stop and Flower Market

Of the 141 original early-20th-century subway entrances, this is one of only a few survivors—now preserved as a national art treasure. The curvy, plantlike ironwork is a textbook example of Art Nouveau, the style that rebelled against the erector-set squareness of the Industrial Age (e.g., Mr. Eiffel's tower).

The flower and plant market on place Louis Lépine is a pleasant detour. On Sundays, this square is all aflutter with a busy bird market. And across the way is the Prefecture de Police, where Inspector Clouseau of *Pink Panther* fame used to work, and where the local resistance fighters took the first building from the Nazis in August of 1944, leading to the Allied liberation of Paris a week later.

• *Pause here to admire the view. Sainte-Chapelle is a pearl in an ugly architectural oyster. We'll double back to the Palais de Justice, turn right and enter the...*

Conciergerie

Though barren inside, this former prison echoes with history. It's a gloomy place. Kings used it to torture and execute failed assassins. The leaders of the Revolution put it to similar good use. A tower along the river, called "the babbler," was named for the painful sounds that leaked from it.

Marie-Antoinette was imprisoned here. During a busy eight-month period in the Revolution, she was one of 2,600 prisoners kept here on the way to the guillotine. You can see Marie-Antoinette's cell, which houses a collection of her mementos. In another room, a list of those made "a foot shorter at the top" by the "national razor" includes ex-King Louis XVI, Charlotte Corday (who murdered Jean-Paul Marat in his bathtub), and the chief revolutionary who got a taste of his own medicine, Maximilien de Robespierre (€7.50, €11.50 combo-ticket covers Sainte-Chapelle, both covered by Museum Pass, daily April–Sept 9:30–18:00, Oct–March 10:00–17:00, last entry 30 min before closing, 4 boulevard du Palais, tel. 01 53 40 60 80, www.monum.fr).

Back outside, turn left on boulevard du Palais and head toward the river (north). On the corner is the city's oldest public clock. The mechanism of the present clock is from 1334, and even though the case is Baroque, it keeps on ticking.

• *Turn left onto quai de l'Horloge and walk west along the river, past the round medieval tower called "the babbler." The bridge up ahead is the pont Neuf, where we'll end this walk. At the first corner, veer left into a sleepy triangular square called place Dauphine. Marvel at how such quaintness could be lodged in the midst of such greatness as you walk through the park to the end of the island (the departure point for Seine river cruises offered by Vedettes du Pont-Neuf; see page 252). At the equestrian statue of Henry IV, turn right onto the bridge and take refuge in one of the nooks on the Eiffel Tower side.*

Pont Neuf

This "new bridge" is now Paris' oldest. Built during Henry IV's reign (around 1600), its 12 arches span the widest part of the river. The fine view includes the park on the tip of the island (note Seine tour boats), the Orsay Museum, and the Louvre. These turrets were originally for vendors and street entertainers. In the days of Henry IV, who originated the promise of "a chicken in every pot," this would have been a lively scene.

• *As for now, you can tour the Seine by boat, continue to the Louvre, or head to the...*

Paris Plage (Beach)

The Riviera it's not, but this newly developed faux beach—assembled in summer along a two-mile stretch of the Seine on the Right Bank—is a fun place to stroll, play, and people-watch on a sunny day. Each summer since 2002, the Paris city government has shut down the embankment's highway and trucked in potted palm trees, hammocks, lounge chairs, and 2,000 tons of sand to create a colorful urban beach. You'll also find climbing walls, a swimming pool, trampolines, *boules*, a library, beach volleyball, badminton, and Frisbee areas in three zones: sandy, grassy, and wood-tiled. As you take in the playful atmosphere, imagine how much has changed here since the Middle Ages...when this was a grimy fishing community (free, mid-July–mid-Aug daily 7:00–24:00, no beach off-season; on Right Bank of Seine, just north of the Ile de la Cité, between pont des Arts and pont de Sully).

SIGHTS

Near the Tuileries Garden

Paris' grandest park, the Tuileries Garden, was once the private property of kings and queens. Today, it links the museums of the Louvre, Orangerie, Jeu de Paume, and the Orsay. And across from the Louvre are the tranquil, historic courtyards of the Palais Royal.

▲▲▲Louvre (Musée du Louvre)—This is Europe's oldest, biggest, greatest, and second-most-crowded museum (after the Vatican). Housed in a U-shaped, 16th-century palace (accentuated by a 20th-century glass pyramid), the Louvre is Paris' top museum and one of its key landmarks. It's home to the *Mona Lisa*, *Venus de Milo,* and hall after hall of Greek and Roman masterpieces, medieval jewels, Michelangelo statues, and paintings by the greatest artists from the Renaissance to the Romantics (mid-1800s).

Touring the Louvre can be overwhelming, so be selective. Focus on the **Denon Wing** (south, along the river), with Greek sculptures, Italian paintings (by Raphael and da Vinci), and—of course—French paintings (Neoclassical and Romantic). For extra credit, tackle the **Richelieu Wing** (north, away from the river), with works from ancient Mesopotamia (today's Iraq), as well as French, Dutch, and Northern art; or the **Sully Wing** (connecting the other two wings), with Egyptian artifacts and more French paintings.

Expcct changcs—thc sprawling Louvrc is constantly in flux. Rooms are periodically closed for renovation, and their paintings and sculpture are moved to a new place within the museum. To find the piece you're looking for, check with the nearest guard for its new location: say the title or point to a photo and ask, *"Où est, s'il vous plaît?"* (oo ay see voo play).

Cost: €8.50, €6 after 18:00 on Wed and Fri, free on first Sun of month, covered by Museum Pass.

Hours: Wed–Mon 9:00–18:00, closed Tue. Most wings open Wed and Fri until 21:45. Galleries start closing 30 minutes early. The last entry is 45 minutes before closing. Tel. 01 40 20 51 51, recorded info tel. 01 40 20 53 17, www.louvre.fr.

Location: At Palais Royal-Musée du Louvre Métro stop. (The old Louvre Métro stop, called Louvre-Rivoli, is farther from the entrance.)

Paris Museums near the Tuileries Garden

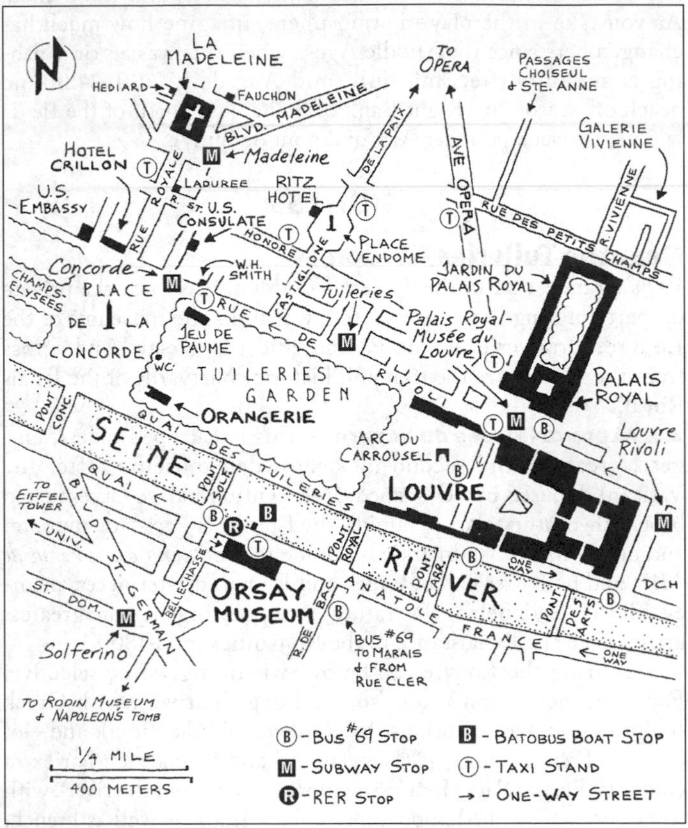

Buying Tickets: Inside the pyramid, self-serve ticket machines are faster than the ticket windows (they accept euro notes, coins, and Visa cards, but not MasterCard).

Crowd-Beating Tips: There is no grander entry than through the pyramid, but metal detectors (not ticket-buying lines) create a long line at times. There are several ways to avoid the line. Museum Pass–holders can use the group entrance in the pedestrian passageway between the pyramid and rue de Rivoli (under the arches, a few steps north of the pyramid, find the uniformed guard at the entrance, with the escalator down). Otherwise, you can enter the Louvre from its (usually less-crowded) underground entrance, accessed through the "Carrousel du Louvre" shopping mall. Enter the mall at 99 rue de Rivoli (the door with the red awning, daily 8:30–23:00) or directly from the Métro stop Palais Royal-Musée du Louvre (stepping off the train, exit to the left, following signs to *Carrousel du Louvre–Musée du Louvre*). The taxi stand is across rue de Rivoli next to the Métro station.

Tours: The 90-minute English-language tours leave three times daily except Sun (normally at 11:00, 14:00, and 15:45, €5 plus your entry ticket, tour tel. 01 40 20 52 63). Sign up for tours at the *Accueil des Groupes* area. Digital audioguides give you a directory of about 130 masterpieces, allowing you to dial a commentary on included works as you stumble upon them (available for €5 at entries to the 3 wings, at top of escalators). While I prefer the free, self-guided tour described below, the audioguide provides some interesting complementary information. Eager students should consider renting one as a supplement.

➲ **Self-Guided Tour:** Start in the Denon wing and visit the highlights, in the following order (thanks to Gene Openshaw for his help writing this).

Wander through the **ancient Greek and Roman works** to see the Parthenon frieze, Pompeii mosaics, Etruscan sarcophagi, and Roman portrait busts. Don't miss lovely *Venus de Milo (Aphrodite).* This goddess of love (c. 100 B.C., from the Greek island of Melos) created a sensation when she was discovered in 1820. Most "Greek" statues are actually later Roman copies, but Venus is a rare Greek original. She, like Golden Age Greeks, epitomizes stability, beauty, and balance. Later Greek art was Hellenistic, adding motion and drama. For a good example, see the exciting *Winged Victory of Samothrace* (*Victoire de Samothrace,* on the landing). This statue of a woman with wings, poised on the prow of a ship, once stood on a hilltop to commemorate a great naval victory. This is the *Venus de Milo* gone Hellenistic.

The **Italian collection** is on the other side of the *Winged Victory.* The key to Renaissance painting was realism, and for the Italians "realism" was spelled "3-D." Painters were inspired by the realism and balanced beauty of Greek sculpture. Painting a 3-D world on a 2-D surface is tough, and after a millennium of Dark Ages, artists were rusty. Living in a religious age, they painted mostly altarpieces full of saints, angels, Madonnas-and-bambinos, and crucifixes floating in an ethereal gold-leaf heaven. Gradually, though, they brought these otherworldly scenes down to earth. (The Italian collection—including the *Mona Lisa*—is scattered throughout the rooms of the long Grand Gallery.)

Two masters of the Italian High Renaissance (1500–1600) were Raphael (see his *La Belle Jardinière,* showing the Madonna, Child, and John the Baptist) and Leonardo da Vinci. The Louvre has the greatest collection of Leonardos in the world—five of them, including the exquisite *Virgin, Child, and St. Anne,* the neighboring *Madonna of the Rocks,* and the androgynous *John the Baptist.* The most famous, of course, is the *Mona Lisa.*

The ***Mona Lisa** (La Joconde)* is in the Salle des Etats, midway

The Louvre

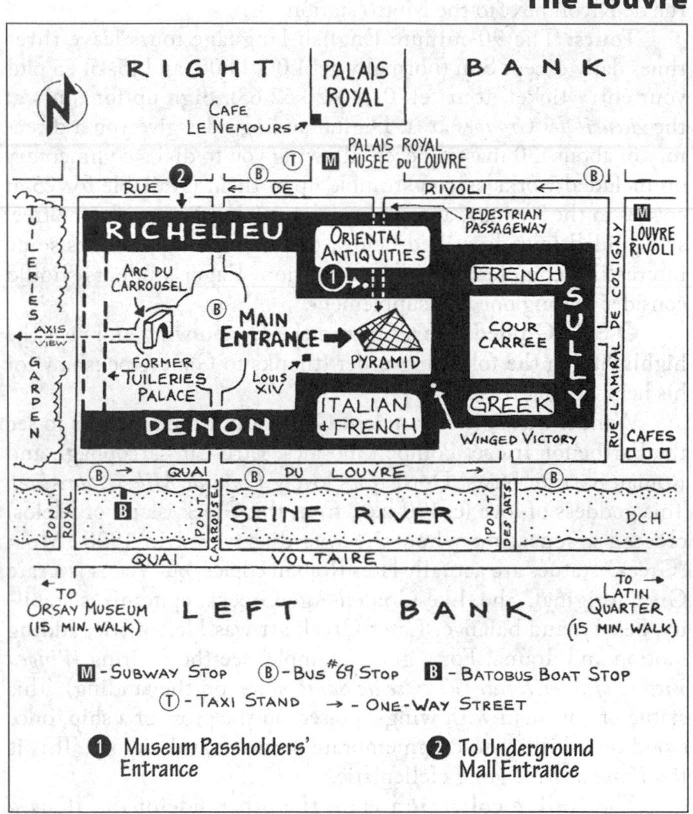

down the Grand Gallery, on the right. After a €5 million renovation, Mona is behind glass on her own false wall.

Leonardo was already an old man when François I invited him to France. Determined to pack light, he took only a few paintings. One was a portrait of Lisa del Giocondo, the wife of a wealthy Florentine merchant. When Leonardo arrived, François I immediately fell in love with the painting and made it the centerpiece of the small collection of Italian masterpieces that would, in three centuries, become the Louvre museum. He called it *La Gioconda*. We know it as a contraction of the Italian for "my lady Lisa"—*Mona Lisa*. Warning: François I was impressed, but *Mona* may disappoint you. She's smaller and darker than you'd expect, located in a huge room, behind a glaring pane of glass.

Mona's overall mood is one of balance and serenity, but there's also an element of mystery. Her smile and long-distance beauty are subtle and elusive, tempting but always just out of reach, like strands of a street singer's melody drifting through the Métro tunnel. *Mona* doesn't knock your socks off, but she winks at the patient viewer.

Now for something **Neoclassical.** Notice the fine work, such as *The Coronation of Napoleon* by Jacques-Louis David, near *Mona* in the Salle Daru. Neoclassicism, once the rage in France (1780–1850), usually features Greek subjects, patriotic sentiment, and a clean, simple style. After Napoleon quickly conquered most of Europe, he insisted on being made emperor (not merely king) of this "New Rome." He staged an elaborate coronation ceremony in Paris, and rather than let the pope crown him, he crowned himself. The setting is the Notre-Dame Cathedral, with Greek columns and Roman arches thrown in for effect. Napoleon's mom was also added, since she couldn't make it to the ceremony. A key on the frame describes who's who in the picture.

The **Romantic** collection, in an adjacent room (Salle Mollien), has works by Théodore Géricault *(The Raft of the Medusa)* and Eugène Delacroix *(Liberty Leading the People).* Romanticism, with an emphasis on motion and emotion, is the complete flip side of Neoclassicism, though they both flourished in the early 1800s. Delacroix's *Liberty,* commemorating the stirrings of democracy in France, is also a fitting tribute to the Louvre, the first museum opened to the common rabble of humanity. The good things in life don't belong only to a small wealthy part of society, but to all. The motto of France is *"Liberté, Egalité, Fraternité"*—liberty, equality, and brotherhood.

Exit the room at the far end (past the café) and go downstairs, where you'll bump into the bum of a large, twisting male nude who looks like he's just waking up after a thousand-year nap. The two *Slaves* (1513–1515) by Michelangelo are a fitting end to this museum—works that bridge the ancient and modern worlds. Michelangelo, like his fellow Renaissance artists, learned from the Greeks. The perfect anatomy, twisting poses, and idealized faces look like they could have been done 2,000 years earlier. Michelangelo said that his purpose was to carve away the marble to reveal the figures God had put inside. The *Rebellious Slave,* fighting against his bondage, shows the agony of that process and the ecstasy of the result.

Palais Royal Courtyards—Directly north of the Louvre on rue de Rivoli are the pleasant courtyards of the stately Palais Royal. Although the palace is closed to the public, the courtyards are open. As you enter, you'll pass through a whimsical courtyard filled with stubby, striped columns and playful fountains (with fun, reflective metal balls) into another, curiously peaceful courtyard. This is where in-the-know Parisians come to take a quiet break, walk their poodle, or enjoy a rendezvous—surrounded by a serene arcade and a handful of historic restaurants.

Exiting the courtyard at the side facing away from the Seine brings you to the Galeries Colbert and Vivienne, good examples of shopping arcades from the early 1900s (courtyards free, always open).

▲▲Orangerie Museum (Musée de l'Orangerie)—This Impressionist museum, lovely as a water lily, has recently reopened after years of renovation. Step out of the tree-lined, sun-dappled Impressionist painting that is the Tuileries Garden and into the Orangerie (oh-rahn-zheh-ree). You'll start with the museum's claim to fame: Monet's water lilies. Then head downstairs to enjoy a little *bijou* of select works by Utrillo, Cézanne, Renoir, Matisse, and Picasso (€6.50, covered by Museum Pass, audioguide-€4.50, Wed–Mon 12:30–19:00, until 21:00 Fri, closed Tue, located in Tuileries Garden near place de la Concorde, Mo: Concorde, tel. 01 44 77 80 07, www.musee-orangerie.fr).

Jeu de Paume (Galerie Nationale du Jeu de Paume)—The museum hosts rotating exhibits of top contemporary artists (€6, not covered by Museum Pass, Tue 12:00–21:30, Wed–Fri 12:00–19:00, Sat–Sun 10:00–19:00, closed Mon, on place de la Concorde, just inside Tuileries Garden on rue de Rivoli side, Mo: Concorde, tel. 01 47 03 12 50, www.jeudepaume.org).

▲▲▲Orsay Museum—The Musée d'Orsay (mew-zay dor-say) houses French art of the 1800s (specifically, art from 1848 to 1914), picking up where the Louvre leaves off. For us, that means Impressionism. The Orsay houses the best general collection anywhere of Edouard Manet, Claude Monet, Pierre-Auguste Renoir, Edgar Degas, Vincent van Gogh, Paul Cézanne, and Paul Gauguin.

The museum shows art that is also both old and new, conservative and revolutionary. You'll start on the ground floor with the Conservatives and the early rebels who paved the way for the Impressionists, then head upstairs to see how a few visionary young artists bucked the system, revolutionized the art world, and paved the way for the 20th century.

Cost: €7.50, €5.50 after 16:15 and on Sun, free first Sun of month, covered by Museum Pass. Tickets are good all day. Museum Pass–holders can enter on the right side of the building (Entrance C); ticket-buyers enter along the left (river) side (Entrance A).

Free Entry near Closing: Right when the ticket booth stops selling tickets (Tue–Wed and Fri–Sun at 17:00, Thu at 21:00), you're welcome to scoot in free of charge. (They won't let you in much after that, however.) You'll have the art mostly to yourself before the museum closes. The Impressionist galleries upstairs start shutting down first, so go there right away.

Hours: Tue–Sun 9:30–18:00, Thu until 21:45 year-round, last entry one hour before closing (45 min before on Thu), closed

Orsay Museum—Ground Floor

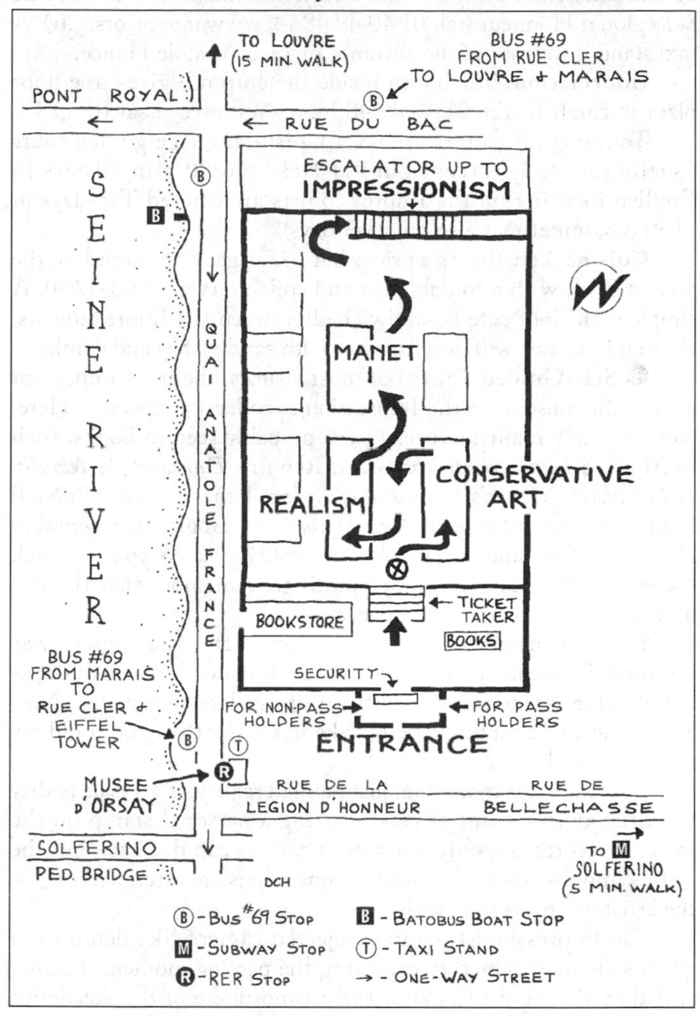

Mon. The Impressionist galleries begin closing at 17:15, frustrating unwary visitors. Note that the Orsay is crowded on Tuesday, when the Louvre is closed.

Location: The Orsay sits above the RER-C stop called Musée d'Orsay. The nearest Métro stop is Solférino, three blocks southeast of the Orsay. Bus #69 from the Marais neighborhood stops at the museum on the river side (quai Anatole France); from the rue Cler area, it stops behind the museum on the rue du Bac. From the Louvre, catch bus #69 along rue de Rivoli; otherwise, it's a lovely 15-minute walk through the Tuileries Garden and across the river on the pedestrian bridge to the Orsay. The museum is at 1 rue de la Légion d'Honneur (tel. 01 40 49 48 14, www.musee-orsay.fr). A taxi stand is in front of the entrance on quai Anatole France.

Information: The booth inside the entrance gives free floor plans in English. Tel. 01 40 49 48 14, www.musee-orsay.fr.

Tours: Audioguides are €5. English-language guided tours usually run daily (except Sun) at 11:30 (€6/90 min). Tours in English focusing on the Impressionists are offered Tuesdays at 14:30 (€6, sometimes also on other days).

Cuisine Art: There's a pricey but *très* elegant restaurant on the second floor, with affordable tea and coffee served 15:00–17:30. A simple fifth-floor café is sandwiched between the Impressionists; above it is an easy self-service place with sandwiches and drinks.

➲ **Self-Guided Tour:** For most visitors, the most important part of the museum is the Impressionist collection upstairs. Here, you can study many pictures you've probably seen in books, such as Manet's *Luncheon on the Grass*, Renoir's *Dance at the Moulin de la Galette,* Monet's *Cathedral of Rouen,* James Abbott McNeill Whistler's *Portrait of the Artist's Mother,* van Gogh's *The Church at Auvers-sur-Oise,* and Cézanne's *The Card Players.* As you approach these beautiful, easy-to-enjoy paintings, remember that there is more to this art than meets the eye.

Here's a primer on Impressionism: After the camera was invented, it threatened to make artists obsolete. A painter's original function was to record reality faithfully, like a journalist. Now a machine could capture a better likeness faster than you could say Etch-A-Sketch.

But true art is more than just painted reality. It gives us reality from the artist's point of view, putting a personal stamp on the work. It records not only a scene—a camera can do that—but the artist's impressions of that scene. Impressions are often fleeting, so the artist has to work quickly.

The Impressionist painters rejected camera-like detail for a quick style more suited to capturing the passing moment. Feeling stifled by the rigid rules and stuffy atmosphere of the Academy, the Impressionists took as their motto, "Out of the studio, into the open air." They grabbed their berets and scarves and took excursions to the country, where they set up their easels on riverbanks and hillsides, or sketched in cafés and dance halls. Gods, goddesses, nymphs, and fantasy scenes were out; common people and rural landscapes were in.

The quick style and simple subjects were ridiculed and called childish by the "experts." Rejected by the Salon, the Impressionists staged their own exhibition in 1874. They brashly took their name from an insult thrown at them by a critic, who laughed at one of Monet's impressions of a sunrise. During the next decade, they exhibited their own work independently. The public, opposed at first, was slowly drawn in by the simplicity, color, and vibrancy of Impressionist art.

Southwest Paris: The Eiffel Tower Neighborhood

▲▲▲Eiffel Tower (La Tour Eiffel)—It's crowded and expensive, but this 1,000-foot-tall ornament is worth the trouble. Visitors to Paris may find *Mona Lisa* to be less than expected, but the Eiffel Tower rarely disappoints, even in an era of skyscrapers.

Built a hundred years after the French Revolution (and in the midst of an industrial one), the tower served no function but to impress. Bridge-builder Gustave Eiffel won the contest for the 1889 Centennial World's Fair by beating out such rival proposals as a giant guillotine. To a generation hooked on technology, the tower was the marvel of the age, a symbol of progress and human ingenuity. Indeed, despite its 7,000 tons of metal and 50 tons of paint, the tower is so well-engineered that it weighs no more per square inch at its base than a linebacker on tiptoes. Not all were so impressed, however; many found it a monstrosity. The writer Guy de Maupassant routinely ate lunch in the tower just so he wouldn't have to look at it.

Delicate and graceful when seen from afar, the Eiffel Tower is massive—even a bit scary—from close up. You don't appreciate the size until you walk toward it; like a mountain, it seems so close but takes forever to reach. There are three observation platforms, at 200, 400, and 900 feet; the higher you go, the more you pay. One elevator will take you to the first or second level (just stay on after first stop), but the third level has a separate elevator and line. Plan on at least 90 minutes if you want to go to the top and back. While being on the windy top of the Eiffel Tower is a thrill you'll never forget, the view is actually better from the second level.

The stairs—yes, you can walk up to the second level—are next to the Jules Verne restaurant entrance (allow $300 per person for the restaurant, reserve three months in advance). As you ascend through the metal beams, imagine being a worker, perched high above nothing, riveting this giant erector set together.

The top level, called *le sommet* (900 feet), is tiny. (It can close temporarily without warning when it reaches capacity.) All you'll find here are wind and grand, sweeping views. The city lies before you, with a panorama guide. On a good day, you can see for 40 miles.

The second level (400 feet) has the best views because you're closer to the sights (walk up stairway to get above netting). There's also a cafeteria and WCs. While you'll save no money, consider taking the elevator up and the stairs down (five minutes from second level to first, five minutes more to ground) for good exercise and views.

Southwest Paris: The Eiffel Tower Neighborhood

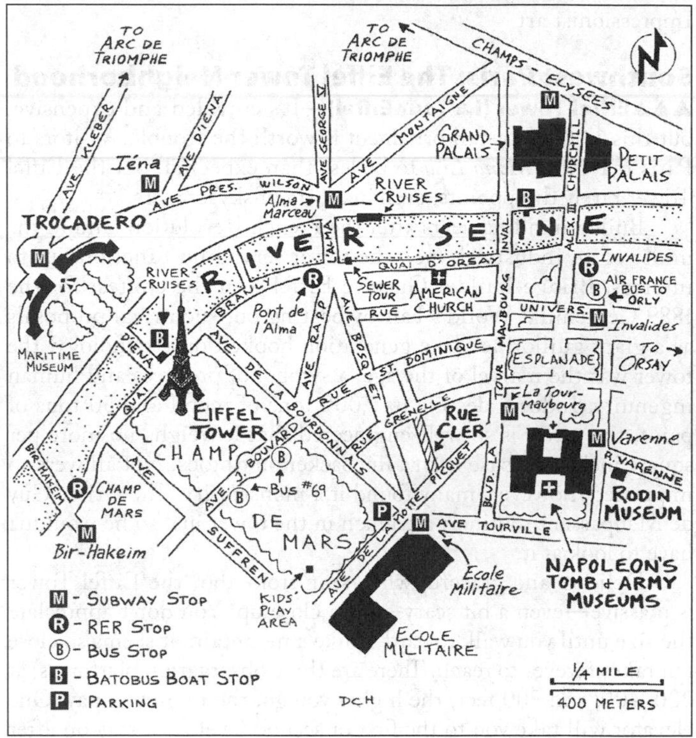

The first level (200 feet) has exhibits, a post office (daily 10:00–19:00, cancellation stamp will read Eiffel Tower), a snack bar, WCs, and souvenirs. Read the informative signs (in English) describing the major monuments, see the entertaining free movie on the history of the tower, and don't miss a century of fireworks—including the entire millennium blast—on video. Then consider a drink or a sandwich overlooking all of Paris at the snack café (outdoor tables in summer) or at the city's best view bar/restaurant, Altitude 95 (see page 325).

Seeing It All: If you don't want to miss a single level, here's a plan for getting the most out of your visit. Ride the lift to second level, then immediately line up and catch the next lift to the top. Enjoy the views on top, then ride back down to the second level. Frolic there for a while and take in some more views. When you're ready, hike down the stairs (no line) or line up for the lift to the first level. Explore the shops and exhibits on this level, have a snack, and take the stairs or lift back to earth.

Cost, Hours, Location: It costs €4.20 to go to the first level, €7.70 to the second, and €11 to go to the top (not covered by Museum Pass). You can skip the elevator line and climb the stairs to the first or second level for €4, or €3 if you're under 25 (daily mid-June–Aug 9:00–24:45 in the morning, last ascent to top level at 23:00, lower levels at 24:00; Sept–mid-June 9:30–23:45, last ascent to top level at 22:30, lower levels with elevator at 23:00 or by stairs at 18:00; shorter lines at night, Mo: Bir-Hakeim or Trocadéro, RER: Champ de Mars-Tour Eiffel, tel. 01 44 11 23 23, www.tour-eiffel.fr).

Tips: To avoid most crowds, go early (get in line by 8:45, before it opens) or late in the day (after 20:00 May–Aug, after 18:00 in off-season—see above for last ascent times); weekends and holidays are worst. Ideally, you should arrive with some light and stay as it gets dark.

To pass the time in line, pick up whatever free reading material is available at the tourist stands at ground level. I like the wonderful *Eiffel Tower Gazette,* a free newspaper featuring a century of Eiffel Tower headlines.

Before or after your tower visit, you can catch the Bateaux Parisiens boat for a Seine cruise (near the base of Eiffel Tower, see page 252 for details).

Best Views: The best place to view the tower is from Trocadéro Square to the north. It's a 10-minute walk across the river, a happening scene at night, and especially fun for kids. Consider arriving at the Trocadéro Métro stop for the view, then walking toward the tower. Another delightful viewpoint is the long, grassy field, Le Parc du Champ de Mars, to the south (great for dinner picnics). However impressive it may be by day, the tower is an awesome thing to see at twilight, when it becomes engorged with light, and virile Paris lies back and lets night be on top. When darkness fully envelops the city, the tower seems to climax at the top of each hour...for 10 minutes. (It's been doing this since the millennium festivities, when it was wired with thousands of special lights.)

National Maritime Museum (Musée National de la Marine)—This extensive museum houses an amazing collection of ship models, submarines, torpedoes, cannonballs, *beaucoup* bowsprits, and naval you-name-it—including a small boat made for Napoleon. You'll find limited English information on the walls, but kids like the museum either way (adults-€9, kids-€7, covered by Museum Pass, Wed–Mon 10:00–18:00, closed Tue, on left side of Trocadéro Square with your back to Eiffel Tower, www.musee-marine.fr, tel. 01 53 65 69 53).

▲Paris Sewer Tour (Les Egouts de Paris)—This quick and easy visit takes you along a few hundred yards of underground water tunnel lined with interesting displays, well-described in English, that explain the evolution of the world's longest sewer system.

(If you straightened out Paris' sewers, they would reach beyond Istanbul.) Don't miss the slideshow, the fine WCs just beyond the gift shop, and the occasional tour in English (€4, covered by Museum Pass, Sat–Wed May–Sept 11:00–17:00, Oct–April 11:00–16:00, closed Thu–Fri, located where pont de l'Alma greets the Left Bank, Mo: Alma-Marceau, RER: Pont de l'Alma, tel. 01 53 68 27 81).

▲▲Napoleon's Tomb and Army Museums (Les Invalides)—The emperor lies majestically dead inside several coffins under a grand dome glittering with 26 pounds of gold—a goose-bumping pilgrimage for historians. Napoleon is surrounded by the tombs of other French war heroes and fine military museums in Hôtel des Invalides. Follow signs to the "crypt" to find Roman Empire–style reliefs that list the accomplishments of Napoleon's administration. Check out the interesting World War II wing. The Army Museum's WWI exhibit is well-presented in English and complements the WWII rooms, while the East Wing will be closed for renovation (€7.50, covered by Museum Pass, free for all military personnel with ID, includes audioguide for tomb, daily April–Sept 10:00–18:00, mid-June–mid-Sept tomb stays open until 19:00, Oct–March 10:00–17:00, last entry 30 min before closing, Oct–May closed first Mon of every month, at Hôtel des Invalides at 129 rue de Grenelle; Mo: La Tour-Maubourg, Varenne, or Invalides; tel. 01 44 42 37 72, www.invalides.org).

▲▲Rodin Museum (Musée Rodin)—This user-friendly museum is filled with passionate works by the greatest sculptor since Michelangelo. Auguste Rodin (1840–1917) sculpted human figures on an epic scale, revealing through the body their deepest thoughts and feelings. Rodin's statues rise from the raw stone around them, driven by the life force. With missing limbs and scarred skin, these are prefab classics, making ugliness noble. Rodin's people are always moving restlessly. Even the famous *Thinker* is moving. Rodin worked with many materials—he chiseled marble (though not often), modeled clay, cast bronze, worked plaster, painted, and sketched. He often created different versions of the same subject in different media.

Paris

Rodin lived and worked in this mansion, renting rooms alongside Henri Matisse, the poet Rainer Maria Rilke (Rodin's secretary), and the dancer Isadora Duncan. Well-displayed exhibits trace Rodin's artistic development, explain how his bronze statues were cast, and show some of the studies he created to work up to his masterpiece (the unfinished *Gates of Hell*). Learn about Rodin's tumultuous relationship with his apprentice and lover, Camille Claudel. Mull over what makes his sculptures some of the most evocative since the Renaissance. For many, the gardens are the highlight of this museum. Here you'll find several of his greatest works, such as the *Thinker, Balzac,* the *Burghers of Calais,* and the *Gates of Hell.* The gardens are ideal for reflective strolling (but picnicking is no longer allowed).

Cost, Hours, Location: €6, €4 on Sun, free on the first Sun of the month, covered by Museum Pass. You'll pay €1 to get into the gardens only—which may be Paris' best deal, as many works are on display there (also covered by Museum Pass). April–Sept Tue–Sun 9:30–17:45, gardens close 18:45; Oct–March Tue–Sun 9:30–16:45, gardens close 17:00, last entry 30 minutes before closing, closed Mon. It's near Napoleon's Tomb, 77 rue de Varenne, Mo: Varenne, tel. 01 44 18 61 10, www.musee-rodin.fr.

▲▲Marmottan Museum (Musée Marmottan Monet)—In this private, intimate, untouristy museum, you'll find the best collection anywhere of works by Impressionist headliner Claude Monet. Follow Monet's life through over a hundred works, from simple sketches to the *Impression: Sunrise* painting that gave his artistic movement its start—and a name. You'll also enjoy classic Monet canvases featuring the water lilies from his garden at Giverny.

Cost, Hours, Location: €7, not covered by Museum Pass, Tue–Sun 10:00–18:00, last entry is 17:30, closed Mon, 2 rue Louis Boilly, Mo: La Muette, tel. 01 44 96 50 33, www.marmottan.com. To get to the museum from the Métro stop, follow the brown museum signs six blocks down chaussée de la Muette through the park; pause to watch kids play on the old time, crank-powered carousel.

Southeast Paris: The Left Bank

This Left Bank neighborhood, just opposite Notre-Dame, is the Latin Quarter. (For more information and a walking tour, see the "Historic Core of Paris Walk," page 254.)

▲▲Cluny Museum (Musée National du Moyen Age)—This treasure trove of Middle Age (Moyen Age) art fills old Roman baths, offering close-up looks at stained glass, Notre-Dame carvings, fine goldsmithing and jewelry, and rooms of tapestries. The star here is the exquisite *Lady and the Unicorn* tapestry series: In five panels, a delicate, as-medieval-as-can-be noble lady introduces a delighted unicorn to the senses of taste, hearing, sight, smell, and touch.

Cost, Hours, Location: €6.50, €4.50 on Sun, free first Sun of month, covered by Museum Pass, Wed–Mon 9:15–17:45, closed Tue, near corner of boulevards St. Michel and St. Germain at 6 place Paul Painlevé; Mo: Cluny-La Sorbonne, St. Michel, or Odéon; tel. 01 53 73 78 16, www.musee-moyenage.fr.

St. Germain-des-Prés—A church was first built on this site in A.D. 452. The church you see today was constructed in 1163 and is all that's left of a once sprawling and influential monastery. The colorful interior reminds us that medieval churches were originally

Southeast Paris: The Latin Quarter

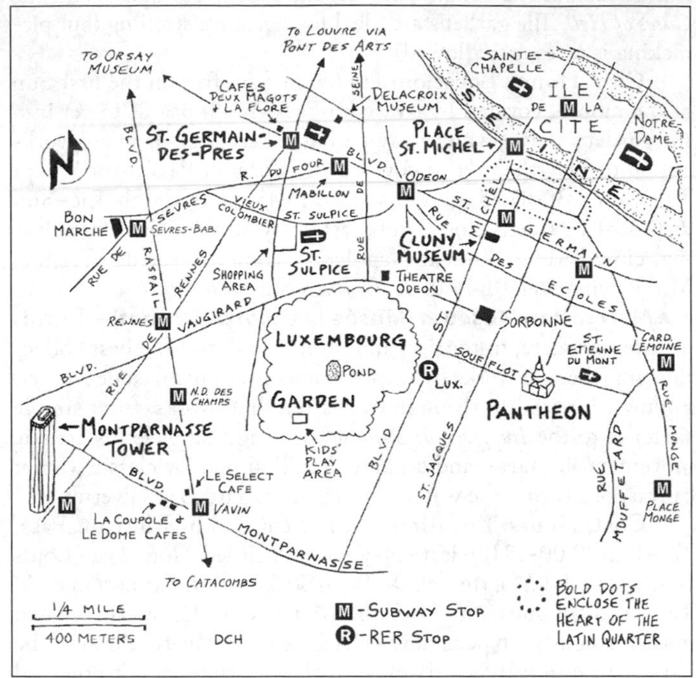

painted in bright colors. The surrounding area hops at night with venerable cafés, fire-eaters, mimes, and scads of artists (free, daily 8:00–20:00, Mo: St. Germain-des-Prés).

▲St. Sulpice Church and Organ Concert—Since it was featured in *The Da Vinci Code,* this grand church has become a trendy stop for the book's many fans. But the real reason to visit is to see and to hear its intimately accessible organ. For pipe-organ enthusiasts, this is one of Europe's great musical treats. The Grand Orgue at St. Sulpice Church has a rich history, with a succession of 12 world-class organists—including Charles-Marie Widor and Marcel Dupré—that goes back 300 years. Widor started the tradition of opening the loft to visitors after the 10:30 service on Sundays. Daniel Roth continues to welcome guests in three languages while playing five keyboards at once. (See www.danielrothsaintsulpice.org for his exact dates and concert plans.)

The 10:30–11:30 Sunday Mass is followed by a high-powered 25-minute recital. Then, just after noon, the small, unmarked door is opened (left of entry as you face the rear). Visitors scamper like sixteenth notes up spiral stairs, past the 19th-century Stairmasters that five men once pumped to fill the bellows, into a world of 7,000 pipes. You can see the organ and visit with Daniel. You'll generally have 30 minutes to kill (there's a plush lounge) before you can watch the master play during the next Mass; you can leave at any time. If you're late or rushed, show up around 12:30 and wait at the little door. As someone leaves, you can slip in, climb up, and catch the rest of the performance (church open daily 7:30–19:30, Mo: St. Sulpice or Mabillon).

Tempting boutiques surround the church, and nearby is the...

▲Luxembourg Garden (Jardin du Luxembourg)—Paris' most beautiful, interesting, and enjoyable garden/park/recreational area is a great place to watch Parisians at rest and play (open daily until dusk, Mo: Odéon, RER: Luxembourg). It's ideal for families. These private gardens are property of the French Senate (housed in the château) and have special rules governing their use (e.g., where cards can be played, where dogs can be walked, where joggers can run, when and where music can be played). The brilliant flower beds are completely changed three times a year, and the boxed trees are brought out of the orangery in May. Challenge the card and chess players to a game (near the tennis courts), rent a toy sailboat, or find a free chair near the main pond and take a breather. Notice any pigeons? The story goes that a poor Ernest Hemingway used to hand-hunt (read: strangle) them here.

The grand, Neoclassical-domed Panthéon, now a mausoleum housing the tombs of several great Frenchmen, is a block away and only worth entering if you have a Museum Pass.

If you enjoy the Luxembourg Garden and want to see more green spaces, you could visit the more elegant Parc Monceau (Mo: Monceau), the colorful Jardin des Plantes (Mo: Jussieu or Gare d'Austerlitz, RER: Gare d'Austerlitz), or the hilly and bigger Parc des Buttes-Chaumont (Mo: Buttes-Chaumont).

▲Panthéon—This dramatic Neoclassical monument celebrates France's illustrious history and people, balances Foucault's pendulum, and is the final home to many French VIPs. Step inside the vast building (360' by 280' by 270'), and you'll see an altar to liberty—the **Monument to the National Convention** (the political body that opposed the monarchy during the Revolution), inscribed with the familiar motto, "Live free or die." Working clockwise around the church-like space, you'll trace the celebrated struggles of the French people: a martyred St. Denis picking up his head, St. Genevieve saving Paris from the Franks, St. Louis as king and crusader, Joan of Arc and her exploits, and so on.

Foucault's pendulum swings gracefully at the end of a 220-foot cable suspended from the towering dome. It was here in 1851 that the scientist Léon Foucault first demonstrated the rotation of the Earth. Stand a few minutes and watch the pendulum's arc (appear to) shift as you and the earth rotate beneath it.

Stairs in the back lead down to the **crypt** where a pantheon of greats are buried, including famous French writers Victor Hugo *(Les Misérables, The Hunchback of Notre-Dame),* Alexandre Dumas *(The Three Musketeers, The Count of Monte Cristo)* and Emile Zola *(Les Rougon-Macquart).* You'll also find the discoverers of radium, Polish-born Marie Curie and her French husband, Pierre, along with many others. An **exhibit** explores the building's fascinating history (good English descriptions). And you can climb 206 steps to the **dome gallery** for fine views of the interior as well as the city (accessible only with an escort who leaves about every hour until 17:15—see schedule as you enter).

Cost, Hours, Location: €7.50, covered by Museum Pass, daily 10:00–18:30 in summer, until 18:00 in winter, last entry 45 minutes before closing (Mo: Cardinal Lemoine). Ask about occasional English tours or call ahead for schedule (tel. 01 44 32 18 00).

Montparnasse Tower (La Tour Montparnasse)—This 59-story superscraper is cheaper and easier to ascend than the Eiffel Tower, with the added bonus of one of Paris' best views. (The Eiffel Tower is in sight, and Montparnasse Tower isn't.) Buy the €3 photo guide to the city, then go to the rooftop and orient yourself. As you zip up 56 floors in 38 seconds, watch the altitude meter above the door. At the top, enjoy the surreal scene with a man in a box and a helipad surrounded by the window-cleaner track. Then scan the city with the wind in your hair, noticing the lush courtyards hiding behind grand street fronts. Back inside and downstairs, you'll find a small, overpriced café, fascinating historic black-and-white photos, and a plush little theater playing *Paris Like Never Seen* (free, 12 min, shows continuously). You'll float past unseen visual delights, spiraling down the Eiffel Tower as the French narration explains, "Paris is radiant and confident, like a lover who finally took her blouse off."

Cost, Hours, Location: €9, not covered by Museum Pass, daily April–Sept 9:30–23:30, Oct–March 9:30–22:30, last entry 30 minutes before closing, disappointing after dark, entrance on rue de l'Arrivée, Mo: Montparnasse-Bienvenüe, tel. 01 45 38 52 56, www.tourmontparnasse56.com. The tower is an efficient stop when combined with a day trip to Chartres, which begins at the Montparnasse train station.

▲Catacombs—These underground tunnels contain the anonymous bones of six million permanent Parisians. In 1785, the citizens of Paris decided to relieve congestion and improve sanitary conditions by emptying the city cemeteries (which traditionally surrounded churches) into an official ossuary. The perfect locale was the many miles of underground tunnels from limestone quarries, which were, at that time, just outside the city. For decades, priests led ceremonial processions of black-veiled, bone-laden carts into the quarries, where the bones were stacked into piles five feet high and as much as 80 feet deep behind neat walls of skull-studded tibiae. Each transfer was completed with the placement of a plaque indicating the church and district from which that stack of bones came and the date they arrived. Note to wannabe Hamlets: An attendant checks your bag at the exit for stolen souvenirs. A flashlight is handy. Being under 6'2" is helpful.

Cost, Hours, Location: €5, not covered by Museum Pass, Tue–Sun 10:00–17:00, ticket booth closes at 16:00, closed Mon, 1 place Denfert-Rochereau, tel. 01 43 22 47 63. Take the Métro to Denfert-Rochereau, then find the lion in the big traffic circle; if he looked left rather than right, he'd stare right at the green entrance to the Catacombs. You'll exit at 36 rue Remy Dumoncel, far from where you started. If you walk to the right, to avenue du Général Leclerc, you'll be equidistant from Métro stops Alésia (walk left) and Mouton Duvernet (walk right).

Northwest Paris: Champs-Elysées, Arc de Triomphe, and Beyond

▲▲Place de la Concorde and the Champs-Elysées—This famous boulevard is Paris' backbone, and has the greatest concentration of traffic. All of France seems to converge on the place de la Concorde, the city's largest square. The Tour de France bicycle race ends here, as do all parades (French or foe) of any significance. While the boulevard has become a bit hamburgerized, a walk here is a must.

In 1667, Louis XIV opened the first section of the street as a short extension of the Tuileries Garden. This date is considered the birth of Paris as a grand city. The Champs-Elysées soon became *the* place to cruise in your carriage. (It still is today—traffic can be jammed up even at midnight.) One hundred years later, the café scene arrived. It was here that the guillotine took the lives of thousands—including King Louis XVI and Marie-Antoinette. Back then it was called the place de la Revolution.

From the 1920s until the 1960s, this boulevard was pure elegance. Locals actually dressed up to come here. It was mainly residences, rich hotels, and cafés. Then, in 1963, the government pumped up the neighborhood's commercial metabolism by bringing in the RER (commuter underground). Suburbanites had easy access, and bam—there went the neighborhood.

The *nouveau* Champs-Elysées, revitalized in 1994, has new benches and lamps, broader sidewalks, and a fleet of green-suited workers armed with high-tech pooper-scoopers. Blink away the modern elements, and it's not hard to imagine the boulevard pre-1963, with only the finest structures lining both sides all the way to the palace gardens.

Northwest Paris: Champs-Elysées, Arc de Triomphe, and Beyond

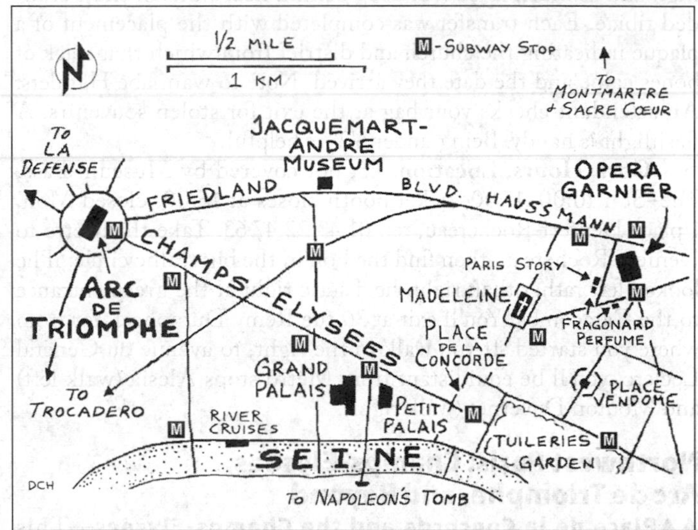

To saunter down the Champs-Elysées, take the Métro to the Arc de Triomphe (Mo: Charles de Gaulle-Etoile; Métro stops every few blocks: Franklin D. Roosevelt, George V, and Charles de Gaulle-Etoile).

Inspect the fancy car dealerships—**Peugeot** at #136 (showing off its futuristic concept cars next to the classic models) and **Mercedes-Benz,** a block down at #118 (like an English-language car show). In the 19th century, this was an area for horse stables; today, it's the district of garages, limo companies, and car dealerships.

Next to Mercedes is the famous **Lido,** Paris' largest cabaret (and a multiplex cinema). Check out the perky photos, R-rated videos, and shocking prices. Paris still offers the kind of burlesque-type spectacles combining music, comedy, and scantily clad women that have been performed here since the 19th century. Movie-going on the Champs-Elysées is also popular, at theaters that show the very latest releases. Check to see if there are films you recognize, then look for the showings *(séances)*. A "v.o." *(version originale)* next to the time indicates the film will be in its original language.

Fouquet's café-restaurant (#99), under the red awning, is a popular spot among French celebrities and charges accordingly (€4.90 for espresso). Opened in 1899 as a coachman's bistro, Fouquet's gained fame as the hangout of France's WWI biplane fighter pilots—those who weren't shot down by Germany's infamous "Red Baron." It also served as James Joyce's dining room.

Since the early 1900s, Fouquet's has been a favorite of French actors and actresses. The golden plaques by the entrance honor winners of France's Oscar-like film awards, the Césars—see plaques to Gérard Depardieu, Catherine Deneuve, and more.

Ladurée (two blocks downhill at #75, with green and purple awning) is a classic 19th-century tea salon/restaurant/*pâtisserie.* Its interior is right out of the 1860s. Wander in...even peeking into the cozy rooms upstairs. A coffee here is *très élégant* (only €3.30). The bakery sells traditional macaroons, cute little cakes, and gift-wrapped finger sandwiches to go (your choice of four mini-macaroons for €6).

▲▲▲Arc de Triomphe—Napoleon had the magnificent Arc de Triomphe commissioned to commemorate his victory at the battle of Austerlitz. There's no triumphal arch bigger (165 feet high, 130 feet wide). And, with 12 converging boulevards, there's no traffic circle more thrilling to experience—either from behind the wheel or on foot (take the underpass).

The foot of the arch is a stage on which the last two centuries of Parisian history have played out—from the funeral of Napoleon, to the goose-stepping arrival of the Nazis, to the triumphant return of Charles de Gaulle after the Allied liberation. Ponder the Tomb of the Unknown Soldier (from World War I, at base of arch), where the flame is rekindled daily at 18:30. Find François Rude's famous relief, "La Marseillaise" (on the right pillar), showing a shouting Lady Liberty rallying weary troops.

The 284 steps lead to a cute museum about the arch, sweeping skyline panoramas, and a mesmerizing view down onto the traffic that swirls around the arch.

Cost, Hours, Location: Outside—free, always open. Interior—€8, free on first Sun of month and for kids under 18, covered by Museum Pass, daily April–Sept 10:00–23:00, Oct–March 10:00–22:00, last entry 30 minutes before closing, place Charles De Gaulle, use underpass to reach arch, Mo: Charles de Gaulle-Etoile, tel. 01 55 37 73 77, www.momum.fr.

▲Opéra Garnier—This grand theater of the belle époque was built for Napoleon III and finished in 1875. From the avenue de l'Opéra, once lined with Paris' most fashionable haunts, the newly restored facade suggests "all power to the wealthy." And Apollo, holding his lyre high above the building, seems to declare, "This is a temple of the highest arts."

While the building is huge, the actual auditorium seats only 2,000. The real show was before and after the performance, when the elite of Paris—out to see and be seen—strutted their elegant stuff in the extravagant lobbies. Think of the grand marble stairway as a theater itself. As you wander the halls and gawk at the decor, imagine the place filled with the beautiful people of its day.

The massive foundations straddle an underground lake (inspiring the mysterious world of the *Phantom of the Opera*). Visitors can peek from two boxes into the actual red-velvet performance hall to view Marc Chagall's colorful ceiling (1964) playfully dancing around the eight-ton chandelier (guided tours take you into the performance hall). Note the box seats next to the stage—the most expensive in the house, with an obstructed view of the stage...but just right if you're here only to be seen.

The elitism of this place prompted President François Mitterrand to have a people's opera house built in the 1980s, symbolically on place de la Bastille, where the French Revolution started in 1789. This left the Opéra Garnier home only to ballet and occasional concerts. While the library/museum is of interest to opera buffs, anyone will enjoy the second-floor grand foyer and Salon du Glacier, iced with decor typical of 1900.

Cost, Hours, Location: €7, not covered by Museum Pass, daily 10:00–17:00, July–Aug until 18:00, closed during performances, 8 rue Scribe, Mo: Opéra, RER: Auber.

Tours: There are English tours of the building during summer and off-season weekends (€11, includes entry, 90 min, call for schedule, tel. 01 40 01 17 89).

Ballet and Concert Tickets: Check the performance schedule at the information booth (inside entry), in *Pariscope* magazine (sold at newsstands), or on their website to see the upcoming schedule (www.opera-de-paris.fr). To buy tickets by phone, call 08 92 89 90 90 (toll call, office closed Sun). There are usually no performances mid-July–mid-Sept.

Nearby: American Express, a TI, and the *Paris Story* film (see below) are on the left side of the Opéra, and the venerable Galeries Lafayette department store (top-floor café with marvelous views) is just behind. Across the street, the illustrious Café de la Paix has been a meeting spot for the local glitterati for generations. If you can afford the coffee, this offers a delightful break.

***Paris Story* Film**—This entertaining film offers a painless overview of the city's turbulent and brilliant past, covering 2,000 years in 45 fast-moving minutes. The theater's wide-screen projection and cushy chairs provide a break from bad weather and sore feet, and the movie's a fun activity with kids. It makes a good first-day orientation, but don't go out of your way to get here.

Cost, Hours, Location: €10, kids-€6, family of four-€21, not covered by Museum Pass. The film shows on the hour daily 9:00–19:00. Next to Opéra Garnier at 11 rue Scribe, Mo: Opéra, tel. 01 42 66 62 06.

Fragonard Perfume Museum—Near Opéra Garnier, two perfume shops masquerade as museums. Either location will teach you a little about how perfume is made (ask for the English handout), but the one on rue Scribe smells even sweeter—and it's in a beautiful 19th-century mansion (both free, daily 9:00–18:00, at 9 rue Scribe and 30 rue des Capucines, tel. 01 47 42 04 56, www.fragonard.com).

▲▲Jacquemart-André Museum (Musée Jacquemart-André)—This thoroughly enjoyable museum showcases the lavish home of a wealthy, art-loving, 19th-century Parisian couple. After wandering the grand boulevards, get inside for an intimate look at the lifestyles of the Parisian rich and fabulous. Edouard André and his wife Nélie Jacquemart—who had no children—spent their lives and fortunes designing, building, and then decorating this sumptuous mansion. What makes the visit so rewarding is the excellent audioguide tour (in English, free with admission, plan on spending an hour with the audioguide). The place is strewn with paintings by Rembrandt, Botticelli, Uccello, Mantegna, Bellini, Boucher, and Fragonard—enough to make a painting gallery famous.

Cost, Hours, Location: €10, not covered by Museum Pass, daily 10:00–18:00, elegant café, at 158 boulevard Haussmann, Mo: Miromesnil or Saint-Philippe de Roule, bus #80 makes a convenient connection to Ecole Militaire, tel. 01 45 62 11 59, www.musee-jacquemart-andre.com/jandre.

After Your Visit: Consider a break in the sumptuous museum tearoom, with delicious cakes and tea (daily 11:45–17:45). From here, walk north on rue de Courcelles to see Paris' most beautiful park, Parc Monceau.

Petit Palais (and its Musée des Beaux-Arts)—In this free museum, renovated in 2006, you'll find a broad collection of paintings and sculpture from the 1600s to the 1900s. To some, it feels like a museum of second-choice art, as the more famous museums in Paris have better collections from the same periods. Some even find the beautifully restored building more interesting than its art collection. Others find a few diamonds in the rough from Monet, Renoir, Boudin, and other Impressionists; some interesting Art Nouveau pieces; and a smattering of works from Dutch, Italian, and Flemish Renaissance artists (Tue 10:00–20:00, Wed–Sun 10:00–18:00, closed Mon, across from Grand Palais on avenue Winston Churchill, just west of place de la Concorde, tel. 01 53 43 40 00, www.petitpalais.paris.fr).

Grand Palais—This grand exhibition hall, built for the 1900 World's Fair, is busy with generally worthwhile temporary exhibits. Get details on the current schedule from the TIs, in *Pariscope*, or from www.rmn.fr (usually €10, not covered by Museum Pass, Mon and Thu–Sun 10:00–20:00, Wed 10:00–22:00, last entry 45 min before closing, closed Tue and between exhibitions, avenue Winston Churchill, Mo: Rond Point or Champs-Elysées, tel. 01 44 13 17 17, www.rmn.fr).

▲View from Hôtel Concorde-Lafayette—For a remarkable Parisian panorama and the perfect location for your next affair, take the Métro to the pedestrian-unfriendly Porte Maillot stop, then follow the *Palais de Congrés* signs to the glass-and-steel tower. (If you're strapped for time, the skies are clear, and the sun's about to set, spring for a taxi.) Take the free elevator in the rear of the lobby to the 33rd floor, walk up one flight, and enter a sky-high world of semicircular vinyl booths (complete with amorous couples), glass walls, pricey drinks (€6 espresso, €9 beer and wine, €14 cocktails), and jaw-dropping views (best before dark, not worth it in poor weather, bar open 17:30–2:00 in the morning, rooms start at €400, 3 place du General Koenig, tel. 01 40 68 50 68, www.concorde-lafayette.com).

▲La Défense and La Grande Arche—On the outskirts of Paris, the centerpiece of Paris' ambitious skyscraper complex (La Défense) is the Grande Arche. Inaugurated in 1989 on the 200th anniversary of the French Revolution, it was dedicated to human rights and brotherhood. The place is big—38 floors holding offices for 30,000 people on more than 200 acres. Notre-Dame Cathedral could fit under its arch. The complex at La Défense is an interesting study in 1960s land-use planning. More than 150,000 workers commute here daily, directing lots of business and development away from downtown and allowing central Paris to retain its more elegant feel. This makes sense to most Parisians, regardless of whatever else they feel about this controversial complex.

For an interesting visit, take the Métro to the La Défense stop, explore La Grande Arche (take the elevator to the top for great city views and displays on the arch's construction), then stroll among the glass buildings to the Esplanade de la Défense Métro station, and return home from there. After enjoying the elegance of downtown Paris' historic, glorious monuments, it's clear that man can build bigger, but not more beautiful.

Cost, Hours, Location: La Grande Arche elevator-€7.50, kids-€6, family deals, not covered by Museum Pass, daily April–Sept 10:00–20:00, Oct–May until 19:00, RER or Mo: La Défense, follow signs to *La Grande Arche,* tel. 01 49 07 27 57, www.grandearche.com. The entry price includes art exhibits and a film on the Arche's construction.

Northeast Paris: Marais Neighborhood and More

The Marais neighborhood extends along the Right Bank of the Seine from the Pompidou Center to the Bastille. It contains more pre-revolutionary lanes and buildings than anywhere else in town and is more atmospheric than touristy. It's medieval Paris. This is how much of the city looked until, in the mid-1800s, Napoleon III had Baron Haussmann blast out the narrow streets to construct

Northeast Paris: Marais Neighborhood and More

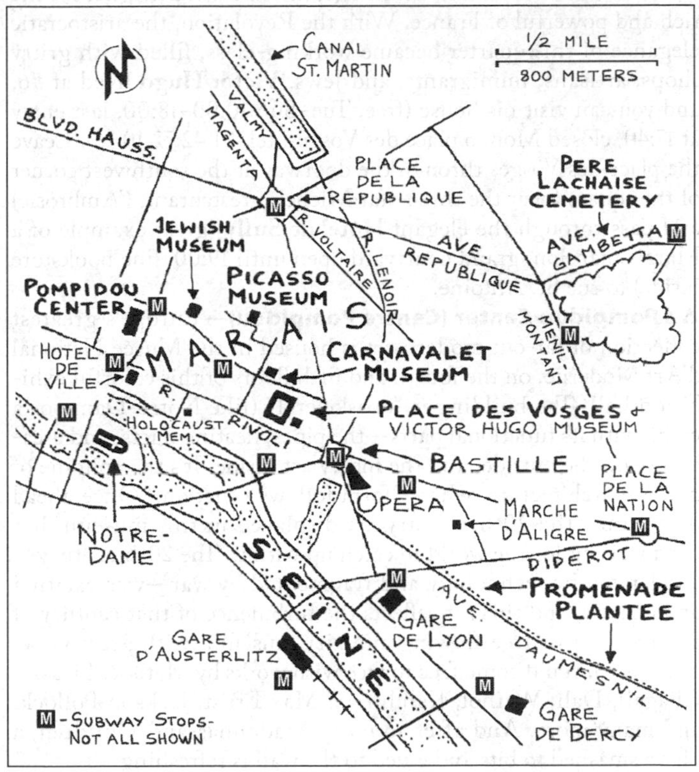

broad boulevards (wide enough for the guns and ranks of the army, too wide for revolutionary barricades), thus creating modern Paris. Originally a swamp *(marais)* during the reign of Henry IV, this area became the hometown of the French aristocracy. In the 17th century, big shots built their private mansions *(hôtels),* close to Henry IV's place des Vosges. When strolling the Marais, stick to the west–east axis formed by rue Sainte-Croix de la Bretonnerie, rue des Rosiers (heart of Paris' Jewish community), and rue St. Antoine. On Sunday afternoons, this trendy area pulses with shoppers and café crowds.

▲Place des Vosges—Study the architecture in this grand square: nine pavilions per side. Some of the brickwork is real, some is fake. Walk to the center, where Louis XIII sits on a horse surrounded by locals enjoying their community park. Children frolic in the sandbox, lovers warm benches, and pigeons guard their fountains while trees shade this retreat from the glare of the big city. Henry IV built this centerpiece of the Marais in 1605. As hoped, this turned the Marais into Paris' most exclusive neighborhood. As the nobility flocked to Versailles in a later age, this too was a magnet for the rich and powerful of France. With the Revolution, the aristocratic elegance of this quarter became working-class, filled with gritty shops, artisans, immigrants, and Jews. **Victor Hugo** lived at #6, and you can visit his house (free, Tue–Sun 10:00–18:00, last entry at 17:40, closed Mon, 6 place des Vosges, tel. 01 42 72 10 16). Leave the place des Vosges through the doorway at the southwest corner of the square (near the three-star Michelin restaurant, l'Ambrosie) and pass through the elegant **Hôtel de Sully** (great example of a Marais mansion, grand courtyard open until 19:00, fine bookstore inside) to rue St. Antoine.

▲▲Pompidou Center (Centre Pompidou)—Europe's greatest collection of far-out modern art is housed in the Musée National d'Art Moderne, on the fourth and fifth floors of this colorful exhibition hall. The building is "exoskeletal" (like Notre-Dame or a crab), with its functional parts—the pipes, heating ducts, and escalator—on the outside, and the meaty art inside. It's the epitome of modern architecture, where "form follows function." Once ahead of its time, the 20th-century art displayed in this museum has been waiting for the world to catch up with it. The 20th century—accelerated by technology and fragmented by war—was exciting and chaotic, and this art reflects the turbulence of that century of change. In this free-flowing and airy museum (with great views over Paris), you'll come face to face with works by Matisse, Picasso, Chagall, Dalí, Warhol, Kandinsky, Max Ernst, Jackson Pollock, and many more. And after so many Madonnas-and-Children, a piano smashed to bits and glued to the wall is refreshing.

The Pompidou Center and its square are lively, with lots of people, street theater, and activity inside and out—a perpetual street fair. Kids of any age enjoy the fun, colorful fountain called *Homage to Stravinsky*, next to the Pompidou Center. If you need a light meal or snack, try the places lining the Stravinsky fountain: Dame Tartine and Crêperie Beaubourg (to the right as you face the museum entrance; both have reasonable prices).

Cost, Hours, Location: €7, covered by Museum Pass, free on first Sun of month, Wed–Mon 11:00–21:00, ticket counters close at 20:00, closed Tue, Mo: Rambuteau or farther-away Hôtel de Ville, tel. 01 44 78 12 33, www.centrepompidou.fr.

▲▲Jewish Art and History Museum (Musée d'Art et Histoire du Judaïsme)—This fascinating museum, located in a beautifully restored Marais mansion, tells the story of Judaism throughout Europe, from the Roman destruction of Jerusalem to the theft of famous artworks during World War II. Displays illustrate the cultural unity maintained by this continually dispersed population. You'll learn about the history of Jewish traditions from bar

The Marais Neighborhood

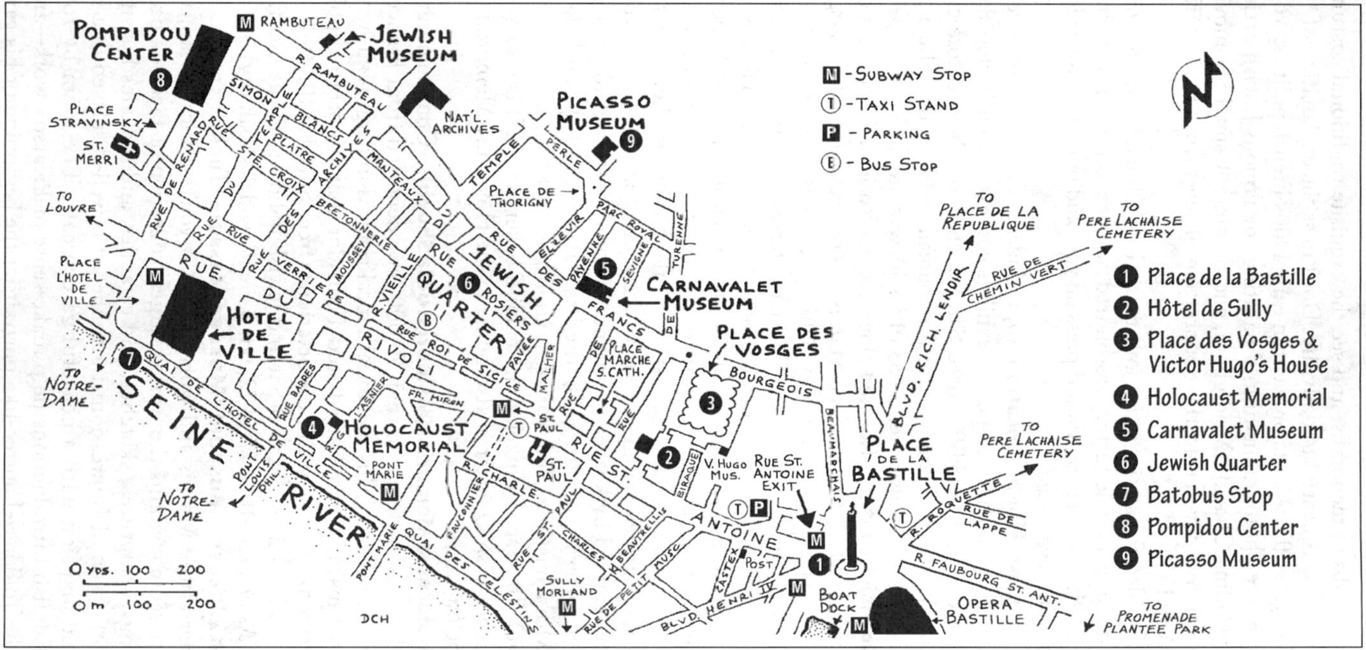

- M - Subway Stop
- T - Taxi Stand
- P - Parking
- B - Bus Stop

1. Place de la Bastille
2. Hôtel de Sully
3. Place des Vosges & Victor Hugo's House
4. Holocaust Memorial
5. Carnavalet Museum
6. Jewish Quarter
7. Batobus Stop
8. Pompidou Center
9. Picasso Museum

mitzvahs to menorahs, and see the exquisite traditional costumes and objects central to daily life. Don't miss the explanation of "the Dreyfus affair," a major event in early 1900s French politics. You'll also see photographs of and paintings by famous Jewish artists, including Chagall, Modigliani, and Soutine. A small but moving section is devoted to the deportation of Jews from Paris during World War II.

Helpful audioguides and many English explanations make this an enjoyable history lesson (red numbers on small signs indicate the number you should press on your audioguide). Move along at your own speed.

Cost, Hours, Location: €7, includes audioguide, not covered by Museum Pass, temporary exhibits cost extra, Sun 10:00–18:00, Mon–Fri 11:00–18:00, closed Sat, last entry one hour before closing, 71 rue du Temple, Mo: Rambuteau or Hôtel de Ville a few blocks farther away, tel. 01 53 01 86 60, www.mahj.org.

Jewish Quarter—Located along rue des Rosiers, the tiny yet colorful Jewish district of the Marais was once considered the largest in Western Europe. Today, while rue des Rosiers is lined with colorful Jewish shops and kosher eateries, the district is being squeezed by the trendy boutiques of modern Paris (visit any day but Saturday, when most businesses are closed, best on Sunday). Still, the area retains its historic character in several delicatessens and restaurants serving typical—but not kosher—Eastern European Jewish cuisine. If you're visiting at lunch time, you'll be tempted by kosher pizza and plenty of €4-falafel-to-go joints (*emporter* means "to go"). The best falafel is at L'As du Falafel, with a bustling New York deli atmosphere (at #34, sit-down or to go). The Sacha Finkelsztajn Yiddish bakery (at #27) is also good. The Jewish Quarter is also home to the Holocaust Memorial (see below).

Holocaust Memorial (Mémorial de la Shoah)—Commemorating the lives of the more than 76,000 Jews deported from France in World War II, this memorial's focal point is underground, where victims' ashes are buried, and a corridor contains original police records of arrests and deportations (free, Sun–Fri 10:00–18:00, Thu until 22:00, closed Sat and Jewish holidays, 17 rue Geoffroy l'Asnier, tel. 01 42 77 44 72, www.memorialdelashoah.org).

▲▲Picasso Museum (Musée Picasso)—Tucked into a corner of the Marais and worth ▲▲▲ if you're a Picasso fan, this museum contains the world's largest collection of Picasso's paintings, sculptures, sketches, and ceramics, and includes his small collection of Impressionist art. The art is well-displayed in a fine old mansion with a peaceful garden café. The room-by-room English introductions help make sense of Picasso's work—from the Toulouse-Lautrec-like portraits at the beginning of his career

to his gray-brown Cubist period to his return-to-childhood, Salvador Dalí–like finish. The well-done €3 English guidebook helps Picassophiles appreciate the context of his art and learn more about his interesting life. Most will be happy reading the posted English explanations while moving at a steady pace through the museum—the ground and first floors satisfied my curiosity.

Cost, Hours, Location: €6.50, covered by Museum Pass, additional fees for temporary exhibits, free on first Sun of month and for kids under 18 with ID, Wed–Mon April–Sept 9:30–18:00, Oct–March 9:30–17:30, last entry 45 minutes before closing, closed Tue, 5 rue de Thorigny, Mo: St. Paul or Chemin Vert, tel. 01 42 71 25 21, www.musee-picasso.fr.

▲▲Carnavalet Museum (Musée Carnavalet)—The tumultuous history of Paris is well-portrayed in this museum, offering a good overview of everything from Louis XIV period rooms, to Napoleon, to the belle époque. The Carnavalet, which opened in 1880, is housed in two Marais mansions connected by a corridor. The first half of the museum (pre-Revolution) dates from a period when people generally accepted the notion that some were born to rule, and most were born to be ruled. This section is difficult to follow (rooms numbered out of order, no English descriptions, and sections closed due to understaffing) so see it quickly, then concentrate your energy on the Revolution and beyond.

The Revolution is the museum's highlight. Fascinating exhibits cover this bloody period of French history, when atrocious acts were committed in the name of government "by, for, and of the people." The exhibits take you from events that led up to the Revolution, to the storming of the 100-foot-high walls of the Bastille, to the royal beheadings, and through the reigns of terror that followed. They then trace the rise and fall of Napoleon, and end with the Paris Commune uprisings. While explanations are in French only, many displays are fairly self-explanatory.

Cost, Hours, Location: Free, Tue–Sun 10:00–18:00, closed Mon; avoid lunchtime (12:00–14:00), when many rooms close; 23 rue de Sévigné, Mo: St. Paul, tel. 01 44 59 58 58, www.carnavalet.paris.fr.

▲Promenade Plantée Park—This two-mile-long, narrow garden walk on a viaduct was once used for train tracks and is now a joy. Part of the park is elevated. At times, you'll walk along the street until you pick up the next segment. The shops below the viaduct's arches (a creative use of once-wasted urban space) make for entertaining window-shopping.

Cost, Hours, Location: Free, opens Mon–Fri at 8:00, Sat–Sun at 9:00, closes at sunset. It runs from place de la Bastille (Mo: Bastille) along avenue Daumesnil to Saint-Mandé (Mo: Michel Bizot). From place de la Bastille (follow signs for *Sortie Opéra* or

Sortie rue de Lyon from Bastille Métro station), walk down rue de Lyon with the Opéra immediately on your left. Find the steps up the red brick wall a block after the Opéra.

▲Père Lachaise Cemetery (Cimetière du Père Lachaise)—Littered with the tombstones of many of the city's most illustrious dead, this is your best one-stop look at Paris' fascinating, romantic past residents. More like a small city, the cemetery is confusing, but maps will direct you to the graves of Frédéric Chopin, Molière, Edith Piaf, Oscar Wilde, Gertrude Stein, Jim Morrison, Héloïse and Abélard, and many more. Buy the helpful €2 map at the flower stores located near either entry.

Cost, Hours, Location: Free, Mon–Sat 8:00–18:00, Sun 9:00–18:00, actually closes at dusk. It's down rue Père Lachaise from Mo: Gambetta (also across the street from the less-convenient Père Lachaise Métro stop and reachable via bus #69). Tel. 01 55 25 82 10.

North Paris: Montmartre

▲▲Sacré-Cœur and Montmartre—Stroll along Paris' highest hilltop (420 feet) for a different perspective on the City of Light. Walk in the footsteps of the people who've lived here—monks stomping grapes (1200s), farmers grinding grain in windmills (1600s), dust-coated gypsum miners (1700s), Parisian liberals (1800s), modernist painters (1900s), and all the struggling artists, poets, dreamers, and drunkards who came here for cheap rent, untaxed booze, rustic landscapes, and cabaret nightlife. With vineyards, wheat fields, windmills, animals, and a village tempo of life, it was the perfect escape from grimy Paris.

The five-domed, Roman-Byzantine basilica of **Sacré-Cœur** took 44 years to build (1875–1919). It stands on a foundation of 83 pillars sunk 130 feet deep, necessary because the ground beneath was honeycombed with gypsum mines. The exterior is laced with gypsum, which whitens with age.

For an unobstructed panoramic view of Paris, climb 260 feet up the tight and claustrophobic spiral stairs to the top of the **dome** (church free, open daily 7:00–23:00; €5 to climb dome, ticket machine requires coins or Visa card, not covered by Museum Pass, daily June–Sept 9:00–19:00, Oct–May 10:00–18:00).

One block from the church, the **place du Tertre** was the haunt of Henri de Toulouse-Lautrec and the original bohemians. Today, it's mobbed with tourists and unoriginal bohemians, but it's still fun (go early in the morning to beat the crowds).

To get to Montmartre, take the Métro to the Anvers stop (one more Métro ticket buys your way up the funicular and avoids the stairs). Other nearby Métro stops are Abbesses and Pigalle. A taxi to the top of the hill saves time and avoids sweat (figure about €10

from the Seine or the Bastille to Sacré-Cœur, €20 at night). For restaurant recommendations, see "Eating," page 339.

Dalí Museum (L'Espace Dalí)—This beautifully lit black gallery (well-described in English) offers a walk through statues, etchings, and paintings by the master of surrealism. Don't miss the printed interview on the exit stairs (€8, not covered by Museum Pass, daily 10:00–18:00, 11 rue Poulbot, tel. 01 42 64 40 10, www.daliparis .com).

Montmartre Museum—This 17th-century home recreates the traditional cancan and cabaret Montmartre scene, with paintings, posters, photos, music, and memorabilia (€5.50, not covered by Museum Pass, Tue–Sun 10:00–18:00, closed Mon, 12 rue Cortot, tel. 01 49 25 89 37, www.museedemontmartre.fr).

Pigalle—Paris' red light district, the infamous "Pig Alley," is at the foot of butte Montmartre. *Ooh la la.* It's more shocking than dangerous. Walk from place Pigalle to place Blanche, teasing desperate barkers and fast-talking temptresses. In bars, a €150 bottle of cheap champagne comes with a friend. Stick to the bigger streets, hang onto your wallet, and exercise good judgment. Cancan can cost a fortune, as can con artists in topless bars. After dark, countless tour buses line the streets, reminding us that tour guides make big bucks by bringing their groups to touristy nightclubs like the famous Moulin Rouge (Mo: Pigalle or Abbesses).

Museum of Erotic Art (Musée de l'Erotisme)—Paris' sexy museum has five floors of risqué displays—mostly paintings and drawings—ranging from artistic to erotic to disgusting, with a few circa-1920 porn videos and a fascinating history of local brothels tossed in. It's in the center of the Pigalle red light district (€7, no... it's not covered by Museum Pass, daily 10:00–2:00 in the morning, 72 boulevard de Clichy, Mo: Blanche, tel. 01 42 58 28 73, www .musee-erotisme.com).

NIGHTLIFE

Paris is brilliant after dark. Save energy from your day's sightseeing and get out at night. Whether it's a concert at Sainte-Chapelle, an elevator up the Arc de Triomphe, or a late-night café, experience the City of Light when it's lit up. If a **Seine River cruise** sounds appealing, check out "Tours," on page 252.

The *Pariscope* magazine (€0.40 at any newsstand, in French) offers a complete weekly listing of music, cinema, theater, opera, and other special events—I decipher this useful periodical for you below. The *Paris Voice* newspaper, in English, has a monthly review of Paris entertainment (available at any English-language bookstore, French-American establishments, or the American Church, www.parisvoice.com).

Music

Jazz Clubs—With a lively mix of American, French, and international musicians, Paris has been an internationally acclaimed jazz capital since World War II. Unfortunately, many clubs are smoky, some wedge too many customers into too few tables, others are downright expensive, and some are guilty of all of the above. You'll pay €10–25 to enter a jazz club (one drink may be included; if not, expect to pay €5–10 per drink; beer is cheapest). See *Pariscope* magazine under "Musique" for listings, or, even better, the American Church's *Paris Voice* paper for a good monthly review, or drop by the clubs to check out the calendars posted on their front doors. Music starts after 21:00 in most clubs. Some offer dinner concerts from about 20:30 on. Here are several good bets:

Caveau de la Huchette, a characteristic old jazz club, fills an ancient Latin Quarter cellar with live jazz and frenzied dancing every night (about €10 admission on weekdays, €14 on weekends, €6 drinks, Tue–Sun 21:30–2:30 in the morning or later, closed Mon, 5 rue de la Huchette, Mo: St. Michel, recorded info tel. 01 43 26 65 05, www.caveaudelahuchette.fr).

For a hotbed of late-night activity and jazz, go to the two-block-long rue des Lombards, at boulevard Sébastopol, midway between the river and the Pompidou Center (Mo: Châtelet). **Au Duc des Lombards,** right at the corner, is one of the most popular and respected jazz clubs in Paris, with concerts generally at 21:00 (42 rue des Lombards, tel. 01 42 33 22 88). **Le Sunside** offers more traditional jazz—Dixieland and big band—and fewer crowds, with concerts generally at 21:00 (60 rue des Lombards, tel. 01 40 26 21 25).

At the more down-to-earth and mellow **La Cave du Franc Pinot,** you can enjoy a glass of chardonnay at the main-floor wine bar, then drop downstairs for a cool jazz scene. They have good dinner-and-jazz values as well—allow about €50 per person (closed Sun–Mon, located on Ile St. Louis where pont Marie meets the island, 1 quai de Bourbon, Mo: Pont Marie, tel. 01 46 33 60 64).

Old-Time Parisian Cabaret on Montmartre: Au Lapin Agile—This historic cabaret maintains the atmosphere of the heady days when bohemians would gather here to enjoy wine, song, and sexy jokes. For €24, you gather with about 25 French people in a dark room for a drink and as many as 10 different performers—mostly singers with a piano. Performers range from sweet and innocent Amélie types to naughty Maurice Chevalier types. While tourists are welcome, it's exclusively French, with no accommodation for English-speakers (and non-French-speakers will be lost). You sit at carved wooden tables in a dimly lit room, taste the traditional drink, and are immersed in a true Parisian ambience. The soirée covers traditional French standards, love ballads, sea chanteys, and more. The crowd sings along, as it has here for a century (Tue–Sun 21:00–2:00 in the morning, closed Mon, 22 rue des Saules, tel. 01 46 06 85 87, www.au-lapin-agile.com).

A Modern Cabaret near Canal St. Martin: Chez Raymonde—This proves the art of dinner cabaret is still alive in Paris. Your evening begins with a good three-course dinner (including apéritif, wine, and coffee) in an intimate dining room, where you get to know your neighbors. Around 22:00, the maître d'hôtel and the chef himself kick off the performance with a waltz together. Then it's feather boas, song, and dance—audience participation is encouraged (€55–60/person, Fri–Sun evenings only, dinner starts at 20:00 and performance usually finishes about 23:00, reservations necessary, 119 avenue Parmentier, Mo: Goncourt, Parmentier, or République, tel. 01 43 55 26 27, www.chez-raymonde.com).

Classical Concerts—For classical music on any night, consult *Pariscope* magazine; the "Musique" section under "Concerts Classiques" lists concerts (both free and for a fee). Look for posters at tourist-oriented churches. From March through November, these churches regularly host concerts: St. Sulpice, St. Germain-des-Prés, Ste. Madeleine, St. Eustache, St. Julien-le-Pauvre, and Sainte-Chapelle. It's well worth the €25 entry for the pleasure of hearing Mozart or Vivaldi while surrounded by the stained glass of the tiny **Sainte-Chapelle** (unheated—bring a sweater). Pick up concert schedules and tickets during the day at the small ticket booth to the left of the chapel entrance. Or call 01 42 77 65 65 to reserve ahead; you can leave your message in English (just speak clearly and spell your name). Seats are unassigned, so arrive 30 minutes early to snare a good view. There are often two concerts per evening at 19:00 and 20:30; specify which one you want when you buy or reserve your ticket. Look also for daytime concerts in parks, such as the Luxembourg Garden. Even the Galeries Lafayette department store offers concerts. Many concerts are free *(entrée libre)*, such as the Sunday atelier concert sponsored by the American Church (Sept–May at 17:00 or 18:00 but not every week, 65 quai d'Orsay, Mo: Invalides, RER: Pont de l'Alma, tel. 01 40 62 05 00).

Opera—Paris is home to two well-respected opera venues. The **Opéra Bastille** is the massive modern opera house that dominates place de la Bastille. Come here for state-of-the-art special effects and modern interpretations of classic ballets and operas. In the spirit of this everyman's opera, unsold seats are available at a big discount to seniors and students 15 minutes before the show. Standing-room-only tickets for €15 are also sold for some performances (Mo: Bastille, tel. 01 43 43 96 96). The **Opéra Garnier,** Paris' first opera house, hosts opera and ballet performances. Come here for less-expensive tickets and grand belle époque decor (Mo: Opéra, tel. 01 44 73 13 99). For tickets, call 01 44 73 13 00, go to the opera ticket offices (open 11:00–18:00), or—best—reserve on the Web at www.opera-de-paris.fr (for both opera houses).

After-Dark Bus Tour

Several companies offer evening tours of Paris. I've described the company offering the most tours below. These trips are sold through your hotel (brochures in lobby) or directly at the offices listed below. You save no money by buying direct.

Paris Illumination Tours, run by Paris Vision, connect all the great illuminated sights of Paris with a 100-minute bus tour in 12 languages. The double-decker buses have huge windows, but the most desirable front seats are sometimes reserved for customers who've bought tickets for the overrated Moulin Rouge. Left-side seats are better. Visibility is fine in the rain.

You'll stampede on with a United Nations of tourists, get a set of headphones, dial up your language, and listen to a tape-recorded spiel (which is interesting, but includes an annoyingly bright TV screen and a pitch for the other, more-expensive excursions). Uninspired as it is, the ride provides an entertaining first-night overview of the city at its floodlit and scenic best. Bring your city map to stay oriented as you go. You're always on the bus, but the driver slows for photos at viewpoints (adults-€25, kids under 11 ride free, departures 19:00–22:00 depending on time of year, usually April–Oct only, reserve 1 day in advance, arrive 30 min early to wait in line for best seats, departs from Paris Vision office at 214 rue de Rivoli, across the street from Mo: Tuileries, tel. 01 42 60 30 01, fax 01 42 86 95 36, www.parisvision.com). Skip their pricier minivan night tours.

SLEEPING

I've focused most of my recommendations on four safe, handy, and colorful neighborhoods: the village-like rue Cler (near the Eiffel Tower), the artsy and trendy Marais (near place de la Bastille), the lively and Latin yet classy Luxembourg (on the Left Bank), and a less central but up-and-coming neighborhood near Canal St. Martin (just north of the Marais). Before reserving, read the descriptions of the neighborhoods. Each offers different pros and cons, and your neighborhood is as important as your hotel for the success of your trip.

Reserve ahead for Paris—the sooner, the better. Conventions clog Paris in September (worst), October, May, and June (very tough). Holidays are busy. In August, when Paris is quiet, some hotels offer lower rates to fill their rooms (if you're planning to visit Paris in the summer, the extra expense of an air-conditioned room can be money well spent).

Sleep Code

(€1 = about $1.30, country code: 33)
To help you easily sort through these listings, I've divided the rooms into three categories based on the price for a standard double room with bath:

$$$ Higher Priced: Most rooms €150 or more.
$$ Moderately Priced: Most rooms between €100–150.
$ Lower Priced: Most rooms €100 or less.

Old, characteristic, budget Parisian hotels have always been cramped. Retrofitted with elevators, toilets, and private showers (as most are today), they are even more cramped. Even three-star hotel rooms are small and often not worth the extra expense in Paris. Some hotels include the hotel tax (*taxe du séjour*, about €1 per person per day), though most will add this to your bill.

Recommended hotels have an elevator unless otherwise noted. Quad rooms usually have two double beds. Because rooms with double beds and showers are cheaper than rooms with twin beds and baths, room prices vary within each hotel.

Continental breakfasts run about €8–10, buffet breakfasts (baked goods, cereal, yogurt, and fruit) cost about €10–15. Café or picnic breakfasts are cheaper, but hotels usually give unlimited coffee.

Get advice from your hotel for safe parking (consider long-term parking at either airport—Orly is closer—and a taxi in). Garages are plentiful (€20–25/day, with special rates through some hotels). Meters are free in August. Self-serve launderettes are common; ask your hotelier for the nearest one (*"Où est un laverie automatique?"* ooh ay uh lah-vay-ree auto-mah-teek).

Rue Cler

Lined with open-air produce stands six days a week, rue Cler is a safe, tidy, village-like pedestrian street. It's so French that when I step out of my hotel in the morning, I feel like I must have been a poodle in a previous life. How such coziness lodged itself between the high-powered government district and the wealthy Eiffel Tower and Invalides areas, I'll never know. This is a neighborhood of wide, tree-lined boulevards, stately apartment buildings, and lots of Americans. The American Church, American Library, American University, and many of my readers call this area home. Hotels here are relatively spacious and a good value, considering the elegance of the neighborhood and the higher prices of the more cramped hotels in other central areas. And for sightseeing, you're within walking distance of the Eiffel Tower, Napoleon's Tomb, the Seine River, and the Orsay and Rodin Museums.

Become a local at a rue Cler café for breakfast, or join the afternoon crowd for *une bière pression* (a draft beer). On rue Cler, you can eat and browse your way through a street full of pastry shops, delis, cheese shops, and colorful outdoor produce stalls. Afternoon *boules* (outdoor bowling) on the Esplanade des Invalides is a relaxing spectator sport (look for the dirt area to the upper right as you face Les Invalides). The manicured gardens behind the golden dome of Napoleon's Tomb are free, peaceful, and filled with flowers (at southwest corner of grounds, closes at about 19:00).

While hardly a happening nightlife spot, rue Cler offers many low-impact after-dark activities. Take an evening stroll above the river through the parkway between pont de l'Alma and pont des Invalides. For an after-dinner cruise on the Seine, it's a 15-minute walk to the river and the Bateaux-Mouches (see page 252). For a post-dinner cruise on foot, saunter into Champ de Mars park to admire the glowing Eiffel Tower. For more ideas on Paris after hours, see "Nightlife" on page 333.

American Church: The American Church and Franco-American Center is the community center for Americans living in Paris. They offer interdenominational worship services (every Sun at 11:00) and occasional concerts, and distribute the useful *Paris Voice* and *France-USA Contacts*. See page 242 for more info.

Services: There's a large post office at the end of rue Cler on avenue de la Motte-Picquet, and a handy SNCF train office at 78 rue St. Dominique (Mon–Sat 8:30–19:30, closed Sun). At both of these offices, take a ticket with a number and wait your turn. A smaller post office is closer to the Eiffel Tower on avenue Rapp, one block past rue St. Dominique towards the river.

Markets: Cross Champ de Mars park to mix it up with bargain-hunters at the twice-weekly open-air market, Marché Boulevard de Grenelle, under the Métro a few blocks southwest of Champ de Mars park (Wed and Sun until 12:30, between Mo: Dupleix and Mo: La Motte-Picquet-Grenelle). The Epicerie de la Tour grocery is open until midnight (197 rue de Grenelle). Rue St. Dominique is the area's boutique-browsing street.

Internet Access: Two Internet cafés compete in this neighborhood: Com Avenue is best (€5/hr, shareable and multi-use accounts, Mon–Sat 10:00–20:00, closed Sun, 24 rue du Champ de Mars, tel. 01 45 55 00 07); Cyber World Café is more expensive, but open later (€7/hr, Mon–Sat 12:00–22:00, Sun 12:00–20:00, 20 rue de l'Exposition, tel. 01 53 59 96 54).

Laundry: Three launderettes are close by, on rue Augereau (between rue St. Dominique and rue de Grenelle), on rue Amélie (also between rue St. Dominique and rue de Grenelle), and at the southeast corner of rue Valadon and rue de Grenelle.

Métro Connections: Key Métro stops are Ecole Militaire, La Tour-Maubourg, and Invalides. The RER-C line runs from the pont de l'Alma and Invalides stations, serving Versailles to the west; Auvers-sur-Oise to the north; and the Orsay Museum, Latin Quarter (St. Michel stop), and Austerlitz train station to the east.

Bus Routes: Smart travelers take advantage of these helpful bus routes (see map on page 298 for stop locations): Line **#69** runs east-west along rue St. Dominique and serves Les Invalides, Orsay, Louvre, Marais, and Père Lachaise Cemetery (Mon–Sat only—no Sun service). Line **#63** runs along the river (the quai d'Orsay), serving the Latin Quarter along boulevard St. Germain to the east (ending at Gare de Lyon), and Trocadéro and the Marmottan Museum to the west. Line **#92** runs along avenue Bosquet, north to the Champs-Elysées and Arc de Triomphe (far better than the Métro) and south to the Montparnasse Tower. Line **#87** runs on avenue de la Bourdonnais and serves St. Sulpice, Luxembourg Garden, the Sèvres-Babylone shopping area, and Gare de Lyon (also more convenient than Métro for these destinations). Line **#28** runs on boulevard de la Tour-Maubourg and serves Gare St. Lazare.

Sleeping in the Rue Cler Neighborhood

(7th *arrondissement,* Mo: Ecole Militaire, La Tour-Maubourg, or Invalides)

Rue Cler is the glue that holds this handsome neighborhood together. From here you can walk to the Eiffel Tower, Napoleon's Tomb, the Seine River, and the Orsay and Rodin museums.

In the Heart of Rue Cler

Many of my readers stay in the rue Cler neighborhood. If you want to disappear into Paris, choose a hotel elsewhere. The first five hotels listed below are within Camembert-smelling distance of rue Cler; the others are within a five- to 10-minute stroll.

$$$ Hôtel Relais Bosquet*** is modern, spacious, and a bit upscale, with snazzy, air-conditioned rooms, electric darkness blinds, and big beds. The friendly staff are politely formal and offer free breakfasts to anyone booking direct with this book (standard Db-€150, spacious Db-€170, ask about occasional promotional rates and off-season discounts, extra bed-€20, free Wi-Fi and Internet access, parking-€14, 19 rue du Champ de Mars, tel. 01 47 05 25 45, fax 01 45 55 08 24, www.relaisbosquet.com, hotel@relaisbosquet.com).

$$$ Hôtel la Motte Picquet*,** at the end of rue Cler, is elaborately decorated and feminine-feeling. Most of its 18 adorable,

Rue Cler Hotels

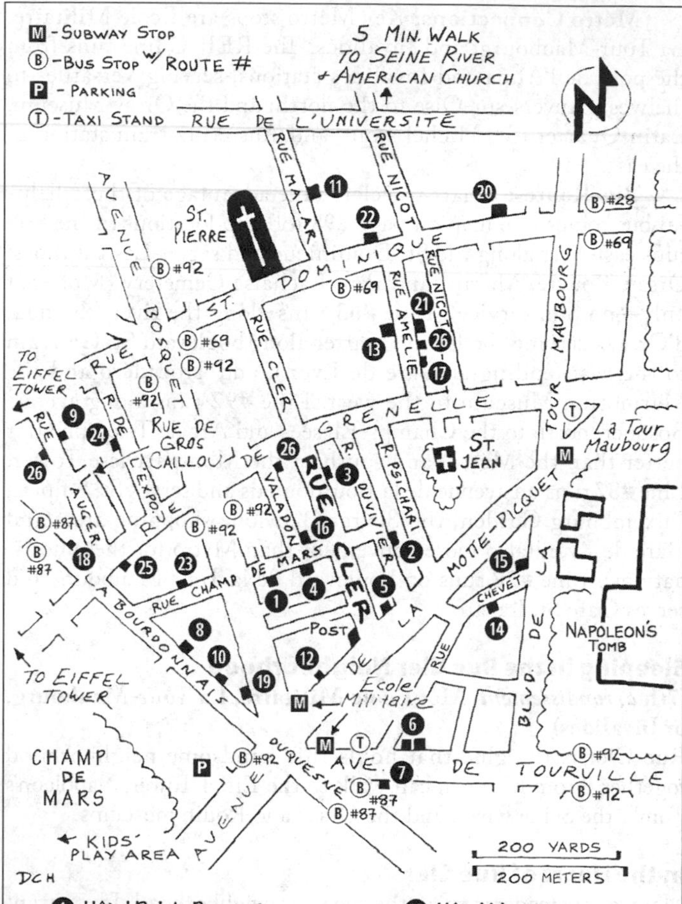

1. Hôtel Relais Bosquet
2. Hôtel Beaugency
3. Grand Hôtel Lévêque
4. Hôtel du Champ de Mars
5. Hôtel la Motte Picquet
6. Hôtels le Tourville & de Turenne
7. Hôtel Splendid
8. Hôtel de la Bourdonnais
9. Hôtel Londres Eiffel
10. Eber-Mars Hôtel
11. Hôtel de la Tulipe
12. Hôtel Royal Phare
13. Hôtel les Jardins Eiffel
14. Hôtel Muguet
15. Hôtel de l'Empereur
16. Hôtel du Cadran
17. Best Western Eiffel Park
18. Hôtel Kensington
19. Hôtel Prince
20. Hôtel le Pavillon
21. Hôtel Amélie
22. SNCF Office
23. Com Avenue Internet Café
24. Cyber World Internet Café
25. Epicerie de la Tour Grocery
26. Launderette (3)

tiny and spendy rooms face a busy street, but the twins are on the quieter side (Sb-€120–130, standard Db-€150, bigger Db with air-con-€180, 30 avenue de la Motte-Picquet, tel. 01 47 05 09 57, fax 01 47 05 74 36, www.hotelmottepicquetparis.com, book@hotelmottepicquetparis.com).

$$ Hôtel Beaugency*,** a particularly good value on a quieter street a short block off rue Cler, has 30 small cookie-cutter rooms, a helpful staff, and a lobby you can stretch out in (Sb-€105, Db-€110–120, Tb-€155, air-con, 21 rue Duvivier, tel. 01 47 05 01 63, fax 01 45 51 04 96, www.hotel-beaugency.com, infos@hotel-beaugency.com, Christelle).

Warning: The next two hotels are super values, but very busy with my readers (reserve long in advance).

$$ Grand Hôtel Lévêque** is ideally located, with a helpful staff (Christophe and Pascale), a singing maid, and a slow-dance elevator. The simple but well-designed rooms have all the comforts, including air-conditioning and ceiling fans (S-€60, Db-€90–115 depending on views and beds, Tb-€130 for two adults and one child only, first breakfast free with this book, additional breakfasts aren't worth the €8 price, 29 rue Cler, tel. 01 47 05 49 15, fax 01 45 50 49 36, www.hotel-leveque.com, info@hotel-leveque.com).

$ Hôtel du Champ de Mars,** with charming pastel rooms and helpful owners Françoise and Stephane, is a homier rue Cler option. This plush little hotel has a Provence-style, small-town feel from top to bottom. Rooms are little but comfortable, and an excellent value. Single rooms can work as tiny doubles (Sb-€78, Db-€86–90, Tb-€107, 30 yards off rue Cler at 7 rue du Champ de Mars, tel. 01 45 51 52 30, fax 01 45 51 64 36, www.hotelduchampdemars.com, reservation@hotelduchampdemars.com).

Near Rue Cler, Close to Ecole Militaire Métro Stop

The following listings are a five-minute walk from rue Cler, near Métro stop Ecole Militaire or RER: Pont de l'Alma.

$$$ Hôtel le Tourville**** is the classiest and most expensive of my rue Cler listings. It's surprisingly intimate for its four stars—from its homey lobby and vaulted breakfast area to its pretty but small pastel rooms (small standard Db-€170, superior Db-€220, Db with private terrace-€250, junior suite for 3–4 people-€310–330, air-con, 16 avenue de Tourville, tel. 01 47 05 62 62, fax 01 47 05 43 90, www.hoteltourville.com, hotel@tourville.com).

$$$ Hôtel de la Bourdonnais*** is a *très* Parisian place, mixing an Old World feel with comfortable and generous public spaces. Its mostly spacious rooms are traditionally decorated (Sb-€125, Db-€170, Tb-€180, Qb-€200–220, air-con, Internet access, 111 avenue de la Bourdonnais, tel. 01 47 05 45 42, fax 01 45 55 75 54, www.hotellabourdonnais.fr, hlb@hotellabourdonnais.fr).

$$ Hôtel Prince,** across avenue Bosquet from the Ecole Militaire Métro stop, has a spartan lobby and comfortable rooms at reasonable rates, considering they're air-conditioned (Sb-€79, Db with shower-€99, Db with tub-€117, Tb-€125, 66 avenue Bosquet, tel. 01 47 05 40 90, fax 01 47 53 06 62, www.hotel-paris-prince.com, paris@hotelprince.com).

$$ Eber-Mars Hôtel,** on a busy street, has larger-than-most rooms with weathered furnishings. The hotel features oak-paneled public spaces and a beam-me-up-Jacques, coffin-sized elevator. There's no air-conditioning and absolutely no eating in your room (Db-€105–125, Tb-€155, Qb-€175, 20 percent cheaper Nov–March and July–Aug, first breakfast free with this book, 117 avenue de la Bourdonnais, tel. 01 47 05 42 30, fax 01 47 05 45 91, www.hotelebermars.com, reservation@hotelebermars.com, manager Mr. Eber is a wealth of information for travelers).

$ Hôtel Royal Phare** is a simple yet solid value—ideal for backpackers—facing the busy Ecole Militaire Métro stop. The 34 basic rooms are unimaginative, but pink-pastel comfortable; those on the courtyard are quietest with peek-a-boo views of the Eiffel Tower from the fifth floor up (Sb-€65, Db with shower-€70–79, Db with tub-€85, Tb-€105, fridges in rooms, claustrophobic hallways, 40 avenue de la Motte-Picquet, tel. 01 47 05 57 30, fax 01 45 51 64 41, www.hotel-royalphare-paris.com, royalphare-hotel@wanadoo.fr).

$ Hôtel de Turenne** is simple and well-located, with the cheapest air-conditioned rooms I found. Even though the halls are frumpy and the rooms could use some work, the price is right. The bright, open lobby has a pleasant bar and sitting area. There are five truly single rooms and several connecting rooms good for families (Sb-€65, Db-€75–88, Tb-€106, extra bed-€10, 20 avenue de Tourville, tel. 01 47 05 99 92, fax 01 45 56 06 04, hotel.turenne.paris7@wanadoo.fr).

Near Rue Cler, Closer to Rue St. Dominique (and the Seine)

Paris

$$ Hôtel Londres Eiffel*** is my closest listing to the Eiffel Tower and Champ de Mars park. A particularly good value, it offers immaculate, warmly decorated rooms, cozy public spaces, Internet access, and air-conditioning. The helpful staff takes good care of their guests. It's less convenient to the Métro (10-min walk); handy bus #69 and RER: Pont de l'Alma are better options (Sb-€99–130, Db-€110–155, deluxe Db-€175, Tb-€165–195, check their website for occasional special discounts, 1 rue Augerau, tel. 01 45 51 63 02, fax 01 47 05 28 96, www.londres-eiffel.com, info@londres-eiffel.com).

$$ Hôtel de la Tulipe***,** three blocks from rue Cler toward the river, is unique. The 20 smallish but artistically decorated rooms—each one different—come with little, stylish bathrooms and surround a seductive wood-beamed lounge and a peaceful, leafy courtyard (Db-€140, Tb-€160, two-room suite for up to five people-€250, no elevator or air-con, 33 rue Malar, tel. 01 45 51 67 21, fax 01 47 53 96 37, www.paris-hotel-tulipe.com, friendly Jean-Louis, Daniel, and Bernhard behind the desk).

$ Hôtel Kensington** has tight and worn rooms and less personality, but it's a fair value (Sb-€55, Db-€70, big Db on back side-€85, extra bed-€12, Eiffel Tower views for those who ask, 79 avenue de la Bourdonnais, tel. 01 47 05 74 00, fax 01 47 05 25 81, www.hotel-kensington.com, hk@hotel-kensington.com, Daniele).

Near La Tour-Maubourg Métro Stop

The next three listings are within two blocks of the intersection of avenue de la Motte-Picquet and boulevard de la Tour-Maubourg.

$$$ Hôtel les Jardins Eiffel***, on a quiet street, feels like the modern motel it is, with professional service, its own parking garage (€23/day), and a spacious lobby. The 81 rooms—some with tiny balconies (ask for a room *avec petit balcon*)—are sufficiently comfortable, if unimaginative (Sb or Db-€155–175, Tb-€205, extra bed-€30 or free for a child up to 10, check their website for occasional better deals; air-con, Internet access, 8 rue Amélie, tel. 01 47 05 46 21, fax 01 45 55 28 08, www.hoteljardinseiffel.com, paris@hoteljardinseiffel.com).

$$ Hôtel Muguet**, a peaceful, stylish, and immaculate refuge, gives you three-star comfort for a two-star price. This delightful place offers 43 tasteful, air-conditioned rooms, a greenhouse lounge, and a small garden courtyard. The hands-on owner, Catherine, gives her guests a restful and secure home in Paris (Sb-€100, Db with one big bed-€120, twin Db-€130, small Db with view-€145, big Db with view and balcony-€175, Tb-€170, 11 rue Chevert, tel. 01 47 05 05 93, fax 01 45 50 25 37, www.hotelmuguet.com, muguet@wanadoo.fr, gentle Jacqueline runs reception).

$ Hôtel de l'Empereur** lacks intimacy, but it's roomy and a fair value. Its 38 pleasant rooms come with real wood furniture and all the comforts except air-conditioning. Streetside rooms have views, but some noise; fifth-floor rooms have small balconies and Napoleonic views (Db-€98, Tb-€120, Qb-€140, 2 rue Chevert, tel. 01 45 55 88 02, fax 01 45 51 88 54, www.hotelempereur.com, contact@hotelempereur.com).

Lesser Values in the Rue Cler Area

Given how fine this area is, these are acceptable last choices.

$$$ Hôtel du Cadran***, while perfectly located and with a nice lobby, lacks charm in its tight, narrow, and way overpriced rooms (Db-€170–185; Carol offers free breakfasts with this book, but you may find cheaper deals on their website in low season; bathtubs, air-con, 10 rue du Champ de Mars, tel. 01 40 62 67 00, fax 01 40 62 67 13, www.hotelducadran.com, info@cadranhotel.com).

$$$ Hôtel Splendid* ** is Art Deco modern, professional, and pricey, considering there's no air-conditioning and rooms are small. This hotel plays up its Eiffel Tower views: All rooms are street-side; sixth-floor rooms have small balconies with sideways tower views; and three small "suites" directly face the tower. Ask about their occasional promotional rates (Db-€170, Db with balcony and view-€190, Db suite-€230, 29 avenue de Tourville, tel. 01 45 51 24 77, fax 01 44 18 94 60, www.hotel-splendid-paris.com, reservation@hotel-splendid-paris.com).

$$$ Best Western Eiffel Park* ** is a dead quiet, concrete business hotel with all the comforts, a friendly staff, 36 pleasant if unexceptional rooms, and a rooftop terrace (Db-€185, bigger "luxe" Db-€195, check online for promotional rates, 17 bis rue Amélie, tel. 01 45 55 10 01, fax 01 47 05 28 68, www.eiffelpark.com, reservation@eiffelpark.com).

$$ Hôtel Amélie,** in a skinny building, has no lobby, no elevator, shabby halls, and rooms that could use a coat of paint but are decent (Sb-€90, Db-€100–120, 5 rue Amélie, tel. 01 45 51 74 75, fax 01 45 56 93 55, www.hotelamelie.fr, hotelamelie@wanadoo.fr).

$ Hôtel le Pavillon ** is quiet, with no-frills rooms, creaky floors, no elevator, and cramped halls in a charming location (Sb-€80, Db-€85; Tb, Qb, or Quint/b-€135; 54 rue St. Dominique, tel. 01 45 51 42 87, fax 01 45 51 32 79, patrickpavillon@aol.com).

Marais

Those interested in a more Soho/Greenwich Village locale should make the Marais their Parisian home. Not long ago, it was a forgotten Parisian backwater, but now the Marais is one of Paris' most popular residential, tourist, and shopping areas. This is jumbled, medieval Paris at its finest, where classy stone mansions sit alongside trendy bars, antique shops, and fashion-conscious boutiques. The streets are a fascinating parade of artists, students, tourists, immigrants, and babies in strollers munching baguettes. The Marais is also known as a hub of the Parisian gay and lesbian scene. This area is *sans doute* livelier (and louder) than the rue Cler area.

In the Marais, you have these sights close at hand: Picasso Museum, Carnavalet Museum, Victor Hugo's House, the Jewish Art and History Museum, and the Pompidou Center. You're also a manageable walk from Paris' two islands (Ile St. Louis and Ile de la Cité), home to Notre-Dame and the Sainte-Chapelle. The Opéra Bastille, Promenade Plantée park, place des Vosges (Paris' oldest square), Jewish Quarter (rue des Rosiers), and nightlife-packed rue de Lappe are also walkable. (For sight descriptions, see "Northeast Paris," page 284; for the Opéra, see page 293.)

Most of my recommended hotels are located a few blocks north of the Marais' main east–west drag, the rue St. Antoine/rue de Rivoli.

Tourist Information: The nearest TI is in Gare de Lyon (Mon–Sat 8:00–18:00, closed Sun, all-Paris TI tel. 08 92 68 30 00).

Services: Most banks and other services are on the main street, rue de Rivoli, which becomes rue St. Antoine. Marais **post offices** are on rue Castex and at the corner of rue Pavée and rue des Francs Bourgeois. There's an **SNCF Boutique** where you can take care of all train needs on rue St. Antoine at rue de Turenne (Mon–Sat 8:30–20:00, closed Sun). A quieter SNCF Boutique is nearer Gare de Lyon at 5 rue de Lyon (Mon–Sat 8:30–18:00, closed Sun).

Markets: The Marais has two good open-air markets: the sprawling **Marché de la Bastille,** around place de la Bastille (Thu and Sun until 12:30); and the more intimate, untouristy **Marché de la place d'Aligre** (Tue–Sun 9:00–12:00, cross place de la Bastille and walk about 10 blocks down rue du Faubourg St. Antoine, turn right at rue de Cotte to place d'Aligre; or, easier, take Métro line 8 from Bastille toward Créteil-Préfecture to the Ledru-Rollin stop and walk a few blocks southeast from there). Two little **grocery shops** are open until 23:00 on rue St. Antoine (near intersection with rue Castex). For your Parisian Sears, find the **BHV** next to Hôtel de Ville.

Bookstore: The Marais is home to the friendliest English-language bookstore in Paris, **Red Wheelbarrow** (Mon–Sat 10:00–19:00, Sun 14:00–18:00, 22 rue St. Paul, Mo: St. Paul, tel. 01 48 04 75 08). Abigail and Penelope sell most of my guidebooks and carry a great collection of other books about Paris and France for both adults and children.

Internet Access: Try **@aron** (3 rue des Ecouffes, Mo: St. Paul, tel. 01 42 71 05 07), **Paris CY** (8 rue de Jouy, Mo: St. Paul, tel. 01 42 71 37 37), or **Cyber Cube** (12 rue Daval, Mo: Bastille, tel. 01 49 29 67 67).

Laundry: Three launderettes are nearby—on impasse Guéménée (north of rue St. Antoine), on rue du Platre (just west of rue du Temple), and on rue Daval (near Cyber Cube).

Métro Connections: Key Métro stops in the Marais are, from east to west: Bastille, St. Paul, and Hôtel de Ville (Sully-Morland, Pont Marie, and Rambuteau stops are also handy). Métro service to the Marais neighborhood is excellent, with direct service to the Louvre, Champs-Elysées, Arc de Triomphe, and La Défense (all on line 1); the rue Cler area and Opéra Garnier (line 8 from Bastille stop); and four major train stations: Gare de Lyon, Gare du Nord, Gare de l'Est, and Gare d'Austerlitz (all accessible from Bastille stop).

Bus Routes: Line **#69** on rue St. Antoine takes you eastbound to Père Lachaise Cemetery and westbound to the Louvre, Orsay, and Rodin Museums, plus Napoleon's Tomb, ending at the Eiffel Tower (Mon–Sat only—no Sun service). Line **#86** runs down boulevard Henri IV, crossing Ile St. Louis and serving the Latin Quarter along boulevard St. Germain. Line **#87** follows a similar route, but also serves Gare de Lyon to the east and the Eiffel Tower and rue Cler neighborhood to the west. Line **#96** runs on rues Turenne and François Miron and serves the Louvre and boulevard St. Germain (near Luxembourg Garden), ending at the Gare Montparnasse. Line **#65** runs from Gare de Lyon up rue de Lyon, around place de la Bastille, and then up boulevard Beaumarchais to the Gare de l'Est and Gare du Nord.

Taxis: You'll find taxi stands on place de la Bastille (where boulevard Richard Lenoir meets the square), on the south side of rue St. Antoine (in front of St. Paul Church), and a quieter one on the north side of rue St. Antoine (where it meets rue Castex).

Sleeping in the Marais Neighborhood

(4th *arrondissement*, Mo: Bastille, St. Paul, and Hôtel de Ville)

The Marais runs from the Pompidou Center to the Bastille (a 15-min walk), with most hotels located a few blocks north of the main east–west drag, the rue de Rivoli/rue St. Antoine. It's about 15 minutes on foot from any hotel in this area to Notre-Dame, Ile St. Louis, and the Latin Quarter. Strolling home (day or night) from Notre-Dame along the Ile St. Louis is marvelous.

Near Place des Vosges

$$ Hôtel Castex*** feels Spanish, from the formal entry to the red-tiled floors and dark wood accents, and is well-situated on a quiet street near place de la Bastille. A clever system of connecting rooms allows families total privacy between two rooms, each with its own bathroom. The 30 rooms are narrow but tasteful and air-conditioned, and the elevator is big by Parisian standards. A good value year-round, your fourth night is free in August and from November through February, except around New Year's (Sb-€95–118, Db-€120–148, Tb-€190–220, free buffet breakfasts with this book, Wi-Fi, just off place de la Bastille and rue St. Antoine at 5 rue Castex, Mo: Bastille, tel. 01 42 72 31 52, fax 01 42 72 57 91, www.castexhotel.com, info@castexhotel.com).

$$ Hôtel Bastille Spéria***, a short block off place de la Bastille, offers business-type service. The 42 well-configured rooms are modern and comfortable, with big beds and air-conditioning. Walls are thin, and the elevator operates at glacial speed, but it's

Marais Hotels

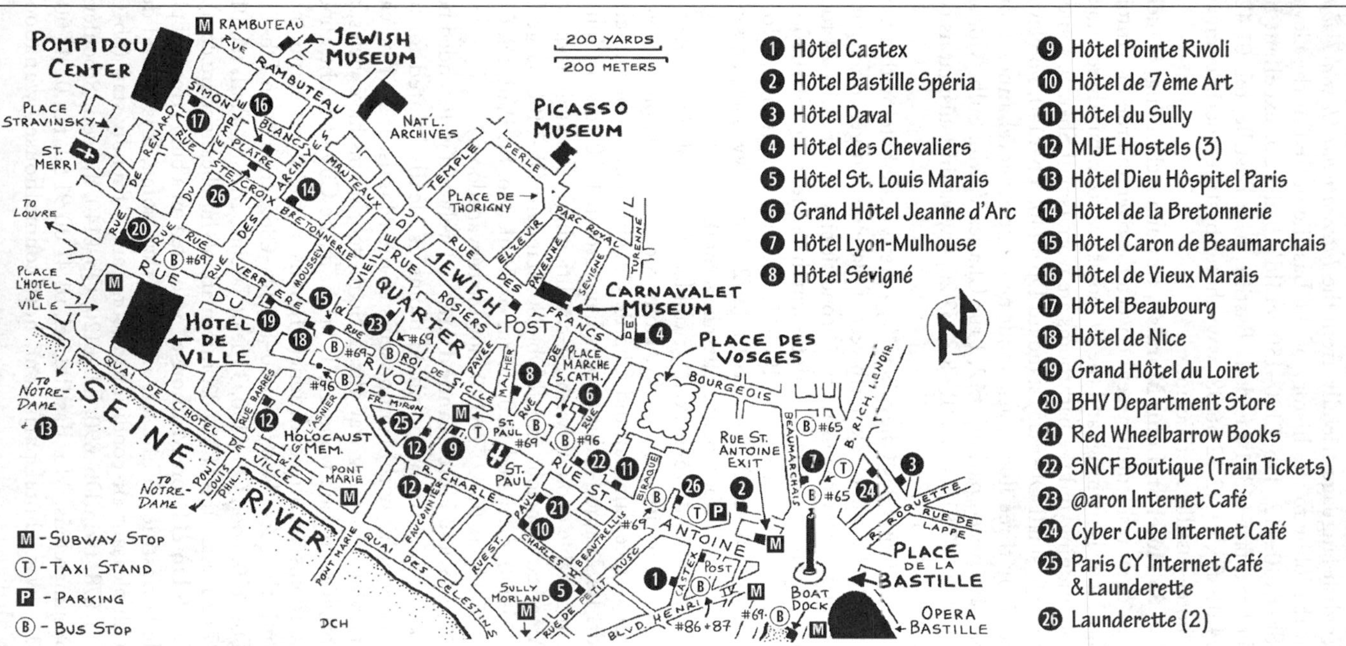

English-language-friendly, from the *International Herald Tribunes* in the lobby to the history of the Bastille posted in the elevator (Sb-€100–112, Db-€130–150, child's bed-€20, excellent buffet breakfast-€13, 1 rue de la Bastille, Mo: Bastille, tel. 01 42 72 04 01, fax 01 42 72 56 38, www.hotel-bastille-speria.com, info@hotel-bastille-speria.com).

$$ Hôtel St. Louis Marais,** tiny and welcoming, is tucked on a quiet residential street between the river and rue St. Antoine. The lobby is inviting, and the 19 rooms are cozy, but there's no air-conditioning and the bathrooms are worn (small Sb-€59, standard Sb-€99, small Db-€115, standard Db-€140, Tb-€140, no elevator but only three floors, ask about newer street-level annex rooms, bargain-priced parking-€12, 1 rue Charles V, Mo: Sully Morland, tel. 01 48 87 87 04, fax 01 48 87 33 26, www.saintlouismarais.com, slmarais@noos.fr).

$$ Hôtel des Chevaliers*,** a pretty little hotel with a handsome lobby one block northwest of place des Vosges, offers small, delicate, pricey rooms with air-conditioning. Four of its 24 rooms are off the street and quiet—worth requesting (Sb-€80–130, Db-€90–150, twin Db-€100–150, 30 rue de Turenne, Mo: St. Paul, tel. 01 42 72 73 47, fax 01 42 72 54 10, www.chevaliers-paris-hotel.com, info@hoteldeschevaliers.com).

$ Hôtel de 7ème Art,** two blocks south of rue St. Antoine toward the river, is a funky, Hollywood-nostalgia place. It has a full-service café-bar and Charlie Chaplin murals, but no elevator. Its 23 good-value rooms have brown 1970s decor, but are comfortable enough (with air-conditioning). The large rooms are American-spacious (small Db-€80, standard Db-€100, large Db-€115–140, extra bed-€20, 20 rue St. Paul, Mo: St. Paul, tel. 01 44 54 85 00, fax 01 42 77 69 10, hotel7art@wanadoo.fr).

$ Grand Hôtel Jeanne d'Arc,** a lovely and well-tended hotel with thoughtfully appointed rooms, is ideally located for (and very popular with) connoisseurs of the Marais. It's a fine value and worth booking way ahead. Sixth-floor rooms have views, and corner rooms are wonderfully bright in the City of Light, though no rooms are air-conditioned. Rooms on the street can be noisy until the bars close (Sb-€60–86, Db-€86, larger twin Db-€100, Tb-€120, good Qb-€150, 3 rue de Jarente, Mo: St. Paul, tel. 01 48 87 62 11, fax 01 48 87 37 31, information@hoteljeannedarc.com).

$ Hôtel Lyon-Mulhouse** is located on a busy street off place de la Bastille. While less intimate than some, it is a solid deal, with pleasant air-conditioned rooms and a friendly staff (Sb-€65, Db-€78, twin Db-€90, Tb-€120, Qb-€140, air-con, 8 boulevard Beaumarchais, Mo: Bastille, tel. 01 47 00 91 50, fax 01 47 00 06 31, www.1-hotel-paris.com, hotelyonmulhouse@wanadoo.fr, Nathalia).

$ Hôtel Daval**, an unassuming place with good rates on the lively side of place de la Bastille, is ideal for night owls. Ask for a quieter room on the courtyard side (Sb-€67, Db-€72, Tb-€85, Qb-€98, Wi-Fi, 21 rue Daval, Mo: Bastille, tel. 01 47 00 51 23, fax 01 40 21 80 26, www.hoteldaval.com, hoteldaval@wanadoo.fr, Didier).

$ Hôtel Sévigné** is a sharp little air-conditioned hotel with lavender halls, 30 tidy and comfortable rooms at good prices, and an unsmiling owner (M. Mercier) of few words (Sb-€64, Db-€74–86, Tb-€100, Qb-€120, 2 rue Malher, Mo: St. Paul, tel. 01 42 72 76 17, fax 01 42 78 68 26, www.le-sevigne.com, contact @le-sevigne.com).

$ Hôtel Pointe Rivoli*, across from the St. Paul Métro stop, is a jumbled treehouse in the thick of the Marais, with Paris' steepest stairs (no elevator), dark halls, and modest, air-conditioned rooms at reasonable rates (Sb-€65, Db-€78, four triple rooms can be used as huge doubles-€84, Tb-€115, 125 rue St. Antoine, Mo: St. Paul, tel. 01 42 72 14 23, fax 01 42 72 51 11, pointerivoli@libertysurf.fr).

$ Hôtel du Sully, sitting right on rue St. Antoine, is nothing fancy, but it is cheap. The entry is long and narrow, the rooms are dimly lit but sleepable, and friendly M. Zeroual is in charge (Db-€55, Tb-€72, no elevator, 48 rue St. Antoine, Mo: St. Paul, tel. 01 42 78 49 32, fax 01 44 61 76 50).

$ *MIJE Youth Hostels:* The Maison Internationale de la Jeunesse et des Etudiants (MIJE) runs three classy old residences clustered a few blocks south of rue St. Antoine. Each is well-maintained, with simple, clean, single-sex, one- to four-bed rooms for travelers of any age. None has an elevator or double beds, each has Internet access, and all rooms have showers. You can stay seven days maximum, and the rates favor single travelers (two people can find a double in a very simple hotel for a similar price). You can pay more to have your own room, or pay less and room with as many as three others (all prices per person: Sb-€45, Db-€33, Tb-€29, Qb-€28, cash only, includes breakfast but not towels; required membership card-€2.50 extra/person; rooms locked 12:00–15:00, curfew at 1:00 in the morning). The hostels are **MIJE Fourcy** (€11 dinners available with a membership card, 6 rue de Fourcy, just south of rue de Rivoli), **MIJE Fauconnier** (11 rue du Fauconnier), and the best, **MIJE Maubisson** (12 rue des Barres). They all share the same contact information (tel. 01 42 74 23 45, fax 01 40 27 81 64, www.mije.com, info@mije.com) and Métro stop (St. Paul). Reservations are accepted (two months ahead by email, one month ahead by phone), though you must show up by noon or call the morning of arrival to confirm a later arrival time.

Near the Pompidou Center

These hotels are farther west, closer to the Pompidou Center than to place de la Bastille. The Hôtel de Ville Métro stop works well for all of these hotels, unless a closer stop is noted.

$$$ Hôtel Caron de Beaumarchais*** feels like a folk museum, with its 20 sweet little rooms and a lobby cluttered with bits from an elegant 18th-century Marais house. Short antique collectors love this place (small back-side Db-€142, larger Db facing the front-€162, air-con, Wi-Fi, 12 rue Vieille du Temple, tel. 01 42 72 34 12, fax 01 42 72 34 63, www.carondebeaumarchais.com, hotel@carondebeaumarchais.com).

$$ Hôtel de la Bretonnerie*,** three blocks from the Hôtel de Ville, makes a fine Marais home. It has a big, welcoming lobby, classy decor, and 29 tastefully appointed rooms with an antique, open-beam warmth (perfectly good standard "classic" Db-€116, bigger "charming" Db-€149, Db suite-€180, Tb/Qb-€174, Tb/Qb suite-€205, no air-con, free Wi-Fi and Internet access, between rue Vieille du Temple and rue des Archives at 22 rue Ste. Croix de la Bretonnerie, tel. 01 48 87 77 63, fax 01 42 77 26 78, www.bretonnerie.com, hotel@bretonnerie.com).

$$ Hôtel de Vieux Marais,** with a quirky owner, is tucked away on a quiet street two blocks east of the Pompidou Center. The hallways are frumpy, but the rooms are a good value except in high season. Many have newer beds (Db-€115, increases to €145 March–mid-July, extra bed-€24, air-con, just off rue des Archives at 8 rue du Plâtre, Mo: Rambuteau or Hôtel de Ville, tel. 01 42 78 47 22, fax 01 42 78 34 32, www.vieuxmarais.com, hotel@vieuxmarais.com).

$$ Hôtel Beaubourg*** is a fine three-star value on a quiet street in the shadow of the Pompidou Center. Its 28 rooms are wood-beam comfy and air-conditioned, and the inviting lounge is warm and pleasant (standard Db-€110, bigger twin Db-€125, free Wi-Fi and Internet access, 11 rue Simon Le Franc, Mo: Rambuteau, tel. 01 42 74 34 24, fax 01 42 78 68 11, www.hotelbeaubourg.com, htlbeaubourg@hotellerie.net).

$$ Hôtel de Nice,** on the Marais' busy main drag, is a turquoise-and-fuschia, "Marie-Antoinette does tie-dye" place. Its narrow halls are littered with paintings and covered with carpets, and its 23 air-conditioned rooms are filled with thoughtful touches and include tight bathrooms. Twin rooms, which cost the same as doubles, are larger and on the street side—but have effective double-paned windows (Sb-€80, Db-€110, Tb-€135, Qb-€150, extra bed-€20, 42 bis rue de Rivoli, tel. 01 42 78 55 29, fax 01 42 78 36 07, www.hoteldenice.com, contact@hoteldenice.com).

$ Grand Hôtel du Loiret** is a centrally located backpacker hotel, though the rooms are better than you might think (S-€48,

Db-€64–84, Tb-€95, 8 rue des Mauvais Garçons, tel. 01 48 87 77 00, fax 01 48 04 96 56, www.hotel-loiret.fr, hotelduloiret@hotmail.com).

Near the Marais, on Ile St. Louis

The peaceful, residential character of this river-wrapped island, its brilliant location, and homemade ice cream have drawn Americans for decades, allowing hotels to charge dearly for their rooms. There are no budget values here, but the island's coziness and proximity to the Marais, Notre-Dame, and the Latin Quarter help compensate for higher rates. All are on the island's main drag, the rue St. Louis-en-l'Ile, where I list several restaurants (see page 333). Use Mo: Pont Marie or Sully-Morland.

$$$ Hôtel du Jeu de Paume****, located in a 17th-century tennis center, is the most expensive hotel I list in Paris. When you enter its magnificent lobby, you'll understand why. Greet Scoop, the hotel dog, then ride the glass elevator for a half-timbered-tree-house experience, and marvel at the cozy lounges. The 30 quite comfortable rooms are carefully designed and *très* tasteful, though small for the price (you're paying for the location and public spaces—check for special offers on their website). Most rooms face a small garden, and all are pin-drop peaceful (Sb-€165, standard Db-€230, larger Db-€280, deluxe Db-€310, 54 rue St. Louis-en-l'Ile, tel. 01 43 26 14 18, fax 01 40 46 02 76, www.jeudepaumehotel.com, info@jeudepaumehotel.com).

The following two hotels are owned by the same person. For both, if you must cancel, do so a week in advance or pay fees:

$$$ Hôtel de Lutèce*** charges top euro for its island address but comes with a sit-a-while, wood-paneled lobby, a fireplace, warmly designed rooms, and friendly Nathalie and Thierry at the reception. Twin rooms are larger and the same price as double rooms (Db-€185, Tb-€205, air-con, 65 rue St. Louis-en-l'Ile, tel. 01 43 26 23 52, fax 01 43 29 60 25, www.hotel-ile-saintlouis.com, lutece@hotel-ile-saintlouis.com).

$$$ Hôtel des Deux Iles*** is brighter and more colorful, with marginally smaller rooms (Db-€170, 59 rue St. Louis-en-l'Ile, tel. 01 43 26 13 35, fax 01 43 29 60 25, www.hotel-ile-saintlouis.com, 2isles@hotel-ile-saintlouis.com).

$$$ Hôtel Saint Louis*** has less personality but good rooms with parquet floors, air-conditioning, and comparatively good rates (Db-€142–160, 75 rue St. Louis-en-l'Ile, tel. 01 46 34 04 80, fax 01 46 34 02 13, slouis@noos.fr).

Near the Marais, on Ile de la Cité

$$ Hôtel Dieu Hôspitel Paris is the only Paris hotel with an Ile de la Cité address. It's located in the oldest city hospital of Paris.

Originally intended to receive families of patients, they now have rooms for tourists too. With a prime location in front of Notre-Dame, but only 14 rooms, you'll need to book well in advance. You'll be surprised by the modern, comfortable decor and may even forget you're in a hospital (Sb-€93, Db-€104, air-con, some rooms have peek-a-boo views of Notre-Dame, 1 place du Parvis, tel. 01 44 32 01 00, www.hotel-hospitel.com, hospitelhoteldieu@wanadoo.fr). Enter the Hôtel Dieu's main entrance, walk to the right, follow signs to wing B2, and take the elevator to the sixth floor.

Luxembourg Garden

This neighborhood revolves around Paris' loveliest park and offers quick access to the city's best shopping streets and grandest café-hopping. Sleeping in the Luxembourg area offers a true Left Bank experience without a hint of the low-end commotion of the nearby Latin Quarter tourist ghetto. The Luxembourg Garden, boulevard St. Germain, Cluny Museum, and Latin Quarter are all at your doorstep. Here you get the best of both worlds: youthful Left Bank energy and the classy trappings that surround the monumental Panthéon and St. Sulpice Church. Hotels in this central area are generally more expensive than in other areas I list.

Having the Luxembourg Garden at your back door allows strolls through meticulously cared-for flowers, a great kids' play area, and a purifying escape from city traffic. Place St. Sulpice offers an elegant, pedestrian-friendly square and some of Paris' best boutiques. Sleeping in the Luxembourg area also puts several movie theaters at your fingertips (Mo: Odéon), as well as lively cafés on the boulevard St. Germain, rue de Buci, rue des Canettes, place de la Sorbonne, and place de la Contrescarpe, all of which buzz with action until late.

Tourist Information: The nearest TI is across the river in Gare de Lyon (Mon–Sat 8:00–18:00, closed Sun, all-Paris TI tel. 08 92 68 30 00).

Markets: The colorful **street market** at the south end of rue Mouffetard is a worthwhile 10- to 15-minute walk down from these hotels (Tue–Sat 8:00–12:00 & 15:30–19:00, Sun 8:00–12:00, closed Mon, five blocks south of place de la Contrescarpe, Mo: Place Monge).

Bookstore: The **Village Voice** bookstore carries a full selection of English-language books (including mine) and is near St. Sulpice (Tue–Sat 10:00–19:30, Sun 13:00–18:00, Mon 14:00–19:30, 6 rue Princesse, tel. 01 46 33 36 47, www.villagevoicebookshop.com).

Internet Access: You'll find it at **XS Arena** (always open, between the Luxembourg Garden and Panthéon at 17 rue Soufflot) and at **Cyber Cube** (some English keyboards, daily 10:00–22:00,

5 rue Mignon, near the Odéon Métro stop, tel. 01 53 10 30 50).

Métro Connections: Métro lines 10 and 4 serve this area (10 connects to the Austerlitz train station, and 4 goes to the Montparnasse, Est, and Nord train stations). Neighborhood stops are Cluny La Sorbonne, Mabillon, Odéon, and St. Sulpice. RER-B (Luxembourg station is handiest) provides direct service to Charles de Gaulle airport and Gare du Nord trains, and access to Orly airport via the Orlybus (transfer at Denfert-Rochereau).

Bus Routes: Buses **#63, #86,** and **#87** run eastbound through this area on boulevard St. Germain, and westbound along rue des Ecoles, stopping on place St. Sulpice. Lines #63 and #87 provide direct connections to the rue Cler area. Line #63 also serves the Orsay, Invalides, Rodin, and Marmottan Museums and Gare de Lyon. Lines #86 and #87 run to the Marais, and #87 continues east to Gare de Lyon.

Sleeping in the Luxembourg Garden Area

(5th and 6th *arrondissements,* Mo: St. Sulpice, Mabillon, Odéon, and Cluny La Sorbonne; RER: Luxembourg)

While it takes only 15 minutes to walk from one end of this neighborhood to the other, I've located the hotels by the key monument they are close to (St. Sulpice Church, the Odéon Theater, and the Panthéon). No hotel is further than a five-minute walk from the Luxembourg Garden.

Hotels near St. Sulpice Church

These hotels are all within a block of St. Sulpice Church, and two blocks from the famous boulevard St. Germain. This is nirvana for boutique-minded shoppers—and you'll pay extra for the location. Métro stops St. Sulpice and Mabillon are equally close.

$$$ Hôtel de l'Abbaye*** feels hidden on a quiet street just west of Luxembourg Garden. It's a find for well-heeled connoisseurs of this appealing area. This luxury refuge, well-run by friendly manager Lionel and his helpful team, offers refined lounges and 44 plush rooms with every amenity (Db-€214, bigger Db-€320, suites and apartments available, 10 rue Cassette, tel. 01 45 44 38 11, fax 01 45 48 07 86, www.hotel-abbaye.com, hotel.abbaye@wanadoo.fr).

$$$ Hôtel Relais St. Sulpice*,** on the small street just behind St. Sulpice Church, feels like a cozy bar, with a melt-in-your-chair lounge and 26 pricey, carefully designed, air-conditioned rooms, most surrounding a leafy glass atrium. Top-floor rooms get more light (Db-€180–215 depending on size, most Db-€185–200, sauna free for guests, 3 rue Garancière, tel. 01 46 33 99 00, fax 01 46 33 00 10, www.relais-saint-sulpice.com, relaisstsulpice@wanadoo.fr).

$$$ Hôtel la Perle*** is a spendy pearl in the thick of the lively rue des Canettes, a block off place St. Sulpice. At this

Hotels and Restaurants near St. Sulpice and the Odéon Theater

1. Hôtel Relais St. Sulpice
2. Hôtel la Perle
3. Hôtel Bonaparte
4. Hôtel le Récamier
5. Hôtel Michelet Odéon
6. Grand Hôtel des Balcons & Hôtel Delavigne
7. Hôtel de l'Abbaye
8. Hôtel le Relais Médicis
9. Hôtel Stella
10. La Crêpe Rit du Clown
11. Chez Georges
12. Cyber Cube Internet Café
13. Village Voice Books
14. Launderette

snappy, modern, business-class hotel, sliding glass doors open onto the traffic-free street and a fun lobby built around a central bar and atrium greets you (standard Db-€175, bigger Db-€195, luxury Db-€235, air-con, check their website or call for last-minute deals within five days of your stay, 14 rue des Canettes, tel. 01 43 29 10 10, fax 01 46 34 51 04, www.hotellaperle.com, booking@hotellaperle.com).

$$ Hôtel Bonaparte** sits between boutiques, a few steps from place St. Sulpice on the smart rue Bonaparte. While the 29 humdrum rooms don't live up to the handsome entry, they're adequately comfortable and generally spacious, with air-conditioning, big bathrooms, molded ceilings, and clashing bedspreads (Sb-€95–117, Db-€124–147, big Db-€158, Tb-€167, includes breakfast, 61 rue Bonaparte, tel. 01 43 26 97 37, fax 01 46 33 57 67, www.hotelbonaparte.fr).

$$ Hôtel le Récamier**, romantically tucked in the corner of place St. Sulpice, feels like grandma's house. Flowery wallpaper, dark halls, and clean, simple rooms—some with views of the square—make this a good, if high-priced, Paris retreat (S-€90, Sb-€110, D-€90, Db-€110, bigger Db-€130, Tb-€155, Qb-€190, 3 bis place St. Sulpice, tel. 01 43 26 04 89, fax 01 46 33 27 73).

Near the Odéon Theater

These hotels are between the Odéon Métro stop and Luxembourg Garden (five blocks east of St. Sulpice), and may have rooms when others don't. Rooms in this area—both handy and elegant—are a particularly good value. In addition to the Odéon Métro stop, the RER-B Luxembourg stop is a short walk away.

$$$ Hôtel le Relais Médicis*** is perfect in every way—if you've always wanted to live in a Monet painting and can afford it. Its 16 rooms surround a fragrant little garden courtyard and fountain, giving you a countryside break fit for a Médici in the heart of Paris. This delightful place—tastefully decorated with a floral Old World charm, hues of Provence, and permeated with thoughtfulness and quality provides four-star comfort (Sb-€168, Db-€198–€228, €30 cheaper mid-July–Aug and Nov–March, sumptuous €10 continental breakfast required, faces the Odéon Theater at 23 rue Racine, tel. 01 43 26 00 60, fax 01 40 46 83 39, www.relaismedicis.com, reservation@relaismedicis.com, Isabelle). Don't confuse it with the similarly named but far less swanky Hôtel des Médicis, described below.

$$ Grand Hôtel des Balcons** has an inviting lobby with Art Nouveau flair and 50 spick-and-span rooms with interesting colors and generous space. Some rooms have narrow balconies, hence the name (Sb-€85, Db-€110–120, big corner Db-€140, big Tb or Qb-€200, look for summer discounts online, fans in rooms, Internet access, a block below the Odéon Theater, 3 Casimir-Delavigne, tel. 01 46 34 78 50, fax 01 46 34 06 27, www.balcons.com, resa @balcons.com).

$$ Hôtel Delavigne*** has a warm lobby, but a cold reception. While the beds may be a bit soft for some, the 34 rooms are adequate (Db-€120, bigger twin Db-€135, Tb-€150, €15 cheaper mid-July–Aug, 1 rue Casimir-Delavigne, tel. 01 43 29 31 50, fax 01 43 29 78 56, www.hoteldelavigne.com, resa@hoteldelavigne.com).

$$ Hôtel Michelet Odéon** sits shyly in a corner of place de l'Odéon, a mere block from the Luxembourg Garden. It's a good value for this pricey area. Most of the 24 spacious, simple rooms have modern decor and views of the square (Db-€100–120, Tb-€150, Qb-€170, 6 place de l'Odéon, tel. 01 53 10 05 60, fax 01 46 34 55 35, www.hotelmicheletodeon.com, hotel@micheletodeon.com).

$ Hôtel Stella* has been in the family for 100 years, but this time-warp place has just about run out of steam. Its well-worn wooden staircase, honky-tonk pianos, cartoon fuse boxes, ramshackle rooms, and rough, exposed timbers make it too basic for most—but a delight for cheapskate backpackers with a poem to write (Sb-€45, Db-€55, Tb-€75, Qb-€85, cash only, no public spaces, no complaining, some of its 24 rooms are huge, great location next to Polidor Restaurant at 41 rue Mr. le Prince, tel. 01 40 51 00 25, hotelstella@hotmail.com).

Near the Panthéon and Rue Mouffetard

The last three listings are cheap dives, but in a great area.

$$ Hôtel des Grandes Ecoles*** is idyllic. A short cobbled lane leads to three buildings protecting a flower-filled garden courtyard, preserving a sense of tranquility rare in downtown Paris. Its 51 rooms are reasonably spacious and comfortable, many with large beds. This romantic spot is deservedly popular, so call well in advance (Db-€110–135 depending on size, extra bed-€20, parking-€30, 75 rue du Cardinal Lemoine, Mo: Cardinal Lemoine, tel. 01 43 26 79 23, fax 01 43 25 28 15, www.hotel-grandes-ecoles.com, hotel.grandes.ecoles@wanadoo.fr, mellow Marie speaks English, Mama does not).

$$ Hôtel des 3 Collèges** is bright and well-run, with generous public spaces, claustrophobic hallways, and tight yet comfy rooms (small Sb-€75, Db-€97–105, bigger Db-€120–140, Tb-€130–160, 16 rue Cujas, tel. 01 43 54 67 30, fax 01 46 34 02 99, www.3colleges.com, hotel@3colleges.com).

$ Hôtel Cluny Sorbonne** is smartly managed, a good deal, and conveniently located across from the famous university, just below the Panthéon. Rooms are clean and comfortable, with wood furnishings. Its public spaces are spacious, plain, and bright (standard Db-€85, big Db-€100, really big Db-€140, 8 rue Victor

Hotels and Restaurants near the Panthéon

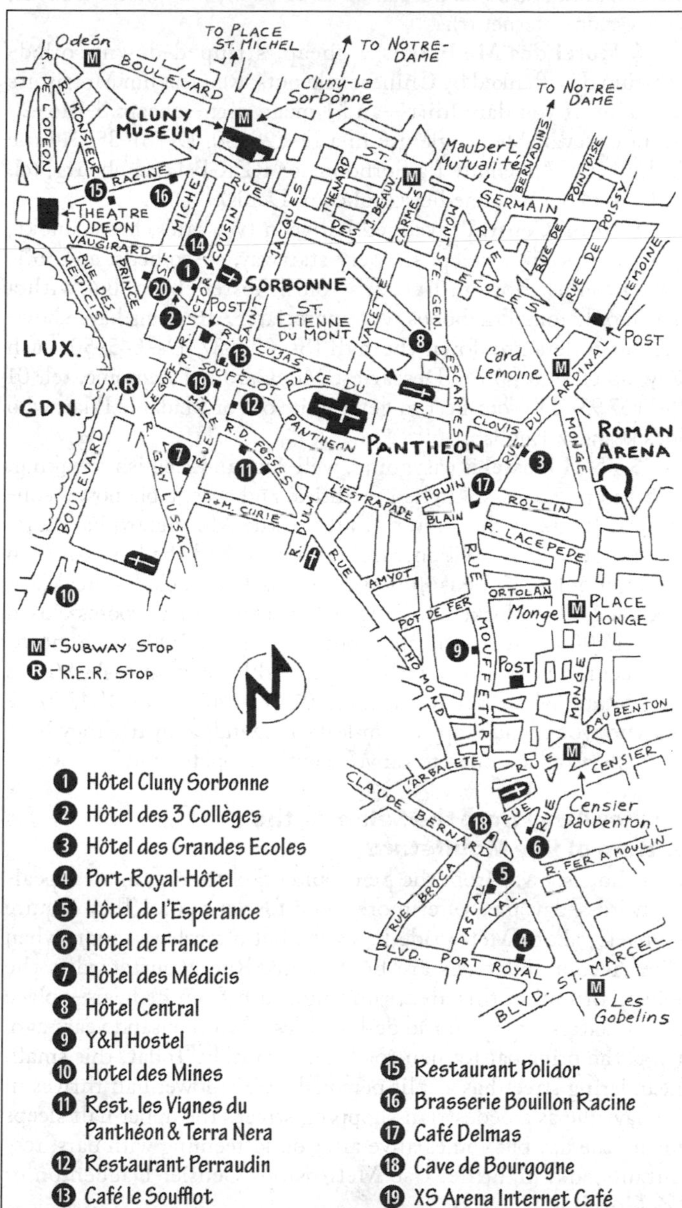

Cousin, tel. 01 43 54 66 66, fax 01 43 29 68 07, www.hotel-cluny.fr, cluny@club-internet.fr).

$ Hôtel des Médicis is a cheap, stripped-down, soiled-linoleum dive flanked by Chinese takeouts. Request Jim Morrison's old room, if you dare (dirt—and I mean dirt—cheap: S-€16–20 but rarely available, single use in a D-€28–30, D-€31–35, 214 rue St. Jacques, Mo: Cluny La Sorbonne or RER-B Luxembourg, tel. 01 43 54 14 66, hotelmedicis@aol.com, Denis).

$ Hôtel Central*, wedged between two cafés, has a smoky, dingy reception, a steep, slippery stairway, so-so beds, and mildewed rooms. Bottom line: It's youth-hostel cheap, but with a charm only romantic hobos will appreciate. All rooms have showers, but toilets are down the hall (Ss-€32–37, Ds-€45–50, cash only, no elevator, 6 rue Descartes, Mo: Cardinal Lemoine, tel. 01 46 33 57 93). Do your best to get a smile out of Madame Pilar, who doesn't speak English.

$ Y&H Hostel is easygoing, well-run, and English-speaking, with Internet access, kitchen facilities, and acceptable hostel conditions. It sits in the center of all the rue Mouffetard bar, café, and people action...which can be good or bad (beds in four- to 10-bed rooms-€23, beds in double rooms-€26, includes breakfast, sheets-€2.50, no lockers but safety box at reception, rooms closed 11:00–16:00 but reception stays open, curfew at 2:00 in the morning, secure reservations with credit card but pay in cash, 80 rue Mouffetard, Mo: Place Monge, tel. 01 47 07 47 07, fax 01 47 07 22 24, www.youngandhappy.fr, smile@youngandhappy.fr). They have 10 doubles and are open to "anyone with an open mind."

Farther Away from the Seine, at the Bottom of Rue Mouffetard

These hotels, away from the Seine and other tourists in an appealing work-a-day area, offer more room for your euro. They require a longer walk or Métro ride to sights, but often have rooms when other accommodations are booked up. Rue Mouffetard is the bohemian soul of this area, running south from its heart—place de la Contrescarpe—to rue de Bazeilles. Two thousand years ago, it was the principal Roman road south to Italy. Today, this small, meandering street has a split personality. The lower half thrives in the daytime as a pedestrian shopping street. The upper half sleeps during the day but comes alive after dark, teeming with bars, restaurants, and nightlife. Use Métro stops Censier-Daubenton or Les Gobelins.

$ Port-Royal-Hôtel* has only one star, but don't let that fool you. Its 46 rooms are polished top-to-bottom and have been well-run by the same proud family for 67 years. You could eat off the floors of its spotless, comfy rooms. Ask for a room away from the street (S-€41–55, D-€55, big shower down the hall-€3, Db-€79–89 depending on size, Tb-€99, cash only, cash deposit only, no refunds, on busy boulevard de Port-Royal at #8, Mo: Les Gobelins, tel. 01 43 31 70 06, fax 01 43 31 33 67, portroyalhotel@wanadoo.fr).

$ Hôtel de l'Espérance** is a solid two-star value. It's quiet, pink, fluffy, and comfortable, with thoughtfully appointed rooms, canopy beds and flamboyant and friendly owners Helen and André Aymard (Sb-€71–79, Db-€79–87, Tb-€105, 15 rue Pascal, Mo: Censier-Daubenton, tel. 01 47 07 10 99, fax 01 43 37 56 19, www.hoteldelesperance.fr, hotel.esperance@wanadoo.fr).

$ Hôtel de France** is set on a busy street, with adequately comfortable rooms, fair prices, and a charming owner, Madame Margo. The best and quietest rooms are *sur la cour* (on the courtyard), though streetside rooms are OK (Sb-€70, Db-€84, Tb-€88, 108 rue Monge, Mo: Censier Daubenton, tel. 01 47 07 19 04, fax 01 43 36 62 34, hotel.de.fce@wanadoo.fr).

On the South Side of Luxembourg Garden

$$ Hotel des Mines** has a less-central location, but is worth the walk. Its 50 well-appointed rooms come with air-conditioning, updated bathrooms, and helpful staff (standard Db-€89, bigger Db-€96–105, check for Web deals, between Luxembourg and Port-Royal stations on the RER-B line, a 10-min walk from **Panthéon,** one block past Luxembourg Garden at 125 boulevard St. Michel; tel. 01 43 54 32 78, fax 01 46 33 72 52, www.hotel-desmines-paris.com, hoteldesmines@wanadoo.fr).

Near Canal St. Martin

This up-and-coming neighborhood is just north of the Marais, between place de la République and Canal St. Martin. It feels real and reminds me of how many other neighborhoods looked 20 years ago. This area is the least touristy of those I list, and its hotels and restaurants tend to be great values (for restaurant suggestions, see page 337; for nighttime fun, head over to rue Oberkampf and join the crowd). This neighborhood is less polished and more remote—but if you can put up with some rough edges and don't mind using the Métro and buses for all of your sightseeing, you'll save plenty (hotels are €20–40 less for comparable rooms than in other areas I list).

The murky canal is the central feature of this unpretentious area, with pleasing walkways, arching footbridges, and occasional boats plying its water. A flowery parkway covers the canal where it goes underground toward place de la Bastille. When the weather agrees, the entire neighborhood seems to descend on the canal in late afternoon, filling the cafés, parkway, and benches.

Market: The parkway plays host to an open-air market on Tuesdays and Fridays until 14:00.

Métro Connections: The hotels listed are easily accessed from the République and Oberkampf Métro stations. Oberkampf is the smaller and closer station, but walking to the bigger République station—an important hub that serves five different train lines—can save you a Métro transfer. To connect directly to much of Paris, go through République to get to: the Marais (Mo: Bastille, line 8, and Hôtel de Ville, line 11), rue Cler (Mo: Ecole Militaire, line 8), Pompidou Center (Mo: Rambuteau, line 11), the Opéra Garnier (line 8), the Champs-Elysées (Mo: F. Roosevelt, line 9), the Eiffel Tower (Mo: Trocadéro, line 9), Père Lachaise Cemetery (line 3), and the Austerlitz, Est, and Nord train stations (all three on line 10).

Internet Access: Cyber Malte is convenient (Mon–Sat 10:30–22:00, closed Sun, across from Hôtel de Nevers at 38 rue de Malte).

Bus Routes: Bus **#65** connects place de la République with the Marais and Gare de Lyon via the rue du Temple, and the Nord and Est train stations along boulevard de Magenta.

Sleeping near Canal St. Martin

(10th and 11th *arrondissements*, Mo: République, Oberkampf)

This neighborhood is convenient to the Nord and Est train stations (about 15 minutes by foot to either) and is also a 15-minute walk from the Pompidou Center and the place des Vosges in the Marais.

Near Oberkampf Métro Station

These hotels cluster near each other. The best budget values are on rue Malte between avenue de la République and boulevard Voltaire. The Oberkampf Métro station is a bit closer than the République one.

$$ Hôtel Saint-Louis Bastille*** is a sharp hotel with a welcoming, wood-beamed lobby, light stone floors throughout, good firm beds, carefully selected furnishings, and air-conditioning. It's situated across from the canal parkway (Sb-€89–99, "superior" Sb-€99, Db-€109–129, 114 boulevard Richard Lenoir, Mo: Oberkampf, tel. 01 43 38 29 29, fax 01 43 38 03 18, www.saintlouisbastille.com, slbastille@noos.fr).

$ Hôtel Residence Alhambra** is well-run by two friendly brothers and a good value, with a big (by Paris standards) leafy courtyard with tables. The 58 rooms are simple and plain, while the lobby is spacious (Sb-€67, Db-€75–84, Tb-€91–112, Qb-€125, free breakfasts for Rick Steves readers July–Aug, no air-con, free Internet access, 13 rue de Malte, tel. 01 47 00 35 52, fax 01 43 57 98 75, www.hotelalhambra.fr, info@hotelalhambra.fr).

Hotels and Restaurants near Canal St. Martin

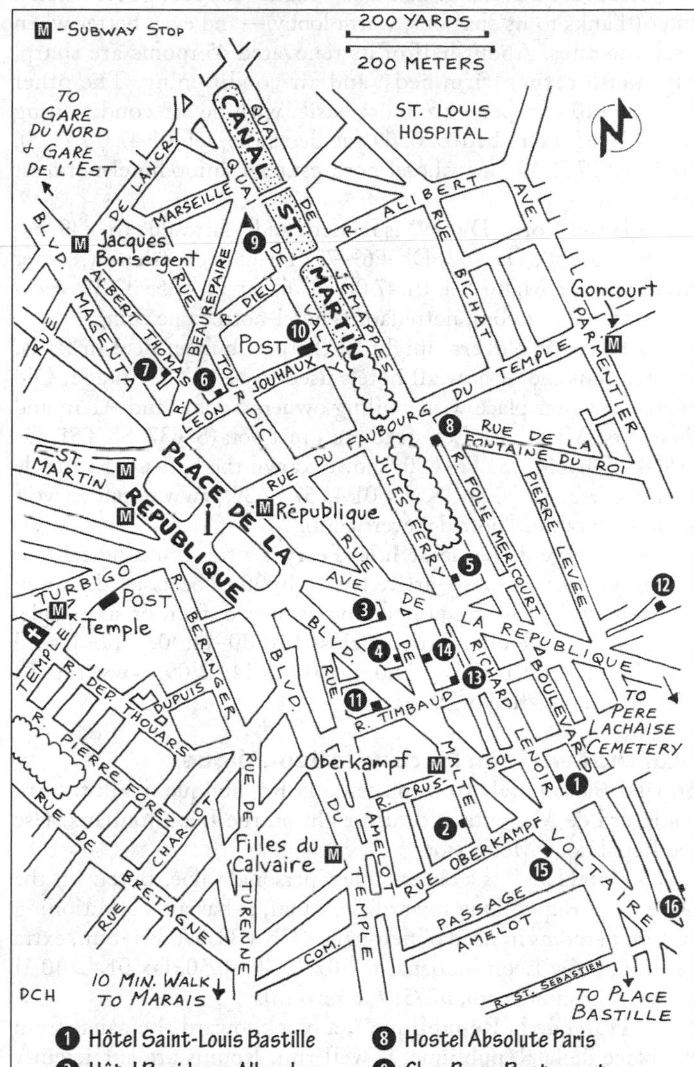

1. Hôtel Saint-Louis Bastille
2. Hôtel Residence Alhambra
3. Hôtel du Nord et de l'Est
4. Hôtel Notre-Dame & Hôtel de Nevers
5. Auberge de Jeunesse Jules Ferry (Hostel)
6. Hôtel Ibis
7. Hôtel de la République
8. Hostel Absolute Paris
9. Chez Prune Restaurant
10. La Marine Restaurant
11. Au Trou Normand Rest.
12. Les Tables de la Fontaine
13. Chez Imogene
14. Cyber Malte Internet Café
15. Launderette
16. Le Grand Méricourt Rest.

$ Hôtel du Nord et de l'Est** makes me feel good when I enter (thanks to its spacious, warm lobby)—and even better when I see the rates. About half of its renovated 45 rooms are sharp, with plush carpet, firm beds, and air-conditioning. The other rooms—€10 cheaper—are more basic, with no air-conditioning (Db-€75–85, extra bed-€20, 49 rue de Malte, tel. 01 47 00 71 70, fax 01 43 57 51 16, www.hotel-nord-est.com, info@hotel-nord-est .com).

$ Hôtel Notre-Dame** is modern and a fair value (S-€39, Ss-€47–57, Sb-€60, Ds-€62, Db-€69–75, Tb-€84–89, friendly owner Eva, 51 rue de Malte, tel. 01 47 00 78 76, fax 01 43 55 32 31, www .hotel-notredame.com, notredame@hotel-notredame.com).

$ Hôtel de Nevers* might be the best budget deal in Paris, and reminds me of how all hotels used to be. It's a vintage, Old World, one-star place with smiling owners Sophie and Alain and their cats, Misty and Lea, ready to greet you (S-€37, Sb-€51, D-€35–45, Db-€51–55, Tb-€80, shower down the hall-€4, 53 rue de Malte, tel. 01 47 00 56 18, fax 01 43 57 77 39, www.hoteldenevers .com, reservation@hoteldenevers.com).

$ Auberge de Jeunesse Jules Ferry is a fun youth hostel that accepts no reservations—arrive before 10:00 to be assured a room (€20 per bunk in sink-equipped rooms of two, four, or six people; more for non-members, rooms closed 10:00–14:00, 8 boulevard Jules Ferry, tel. 01 43 57 55 60, fax 01 43 14 82 09, www.fuaj.fr, paris.julesferry@fuaj.org).

Near the Canal and Place de la République

To find these hotels from place de la République, walk toward boulevard de Magenta and turn right on rue Léon Jouhaux. Use the République Métro stop.

$ Hôtel Ibis** is a cheery if less personal value. Barely off the place de la République toward the canal, it has air-conditioning and white rooms in need of new paint (Db-€88, €76 Fri–Sun, extra bed-€10, 9 rue Léon Jouhaux, tel. 01 42 40 40 50, fax 01 42 40 11 12, www.ibishotel.com, h0751@accor.com).

$ Hôtel de la République**, a block toward the canal from the place de la République, is well-run. Rooms are sufficiently comfortable, with good natural light, showers instead of baths, and small balconies on the fifth floor (Sb-€61–65, Db-€71–80, Tb-€81–85, includes buffet breakfast with this book, 31 rue Albert Thomas, Mo: République, tel. 01 42 39 19 03, fax 01 42 39 22 66, www.republiquehotel.com).

$ Hostel Absolute Paris is part two-star hotel, part four-beds-per-room hostel. It's in the thick of this lively area, facing the canal and filled with backpackers. The rooms are industrial-strength clean and adequate—only worth considering for dorm-style accommodations (€24 each in four-bed room with private bathroom, Db-€85, Tb-€100, includes breakfast, 1 rue de la Fontaine du Roi, tel. 01 47 00 47 00, fax 01 47 00 47 02, www.absolute-paris.com).

EATING

The Parisian eating scene is kept at a rolling boil. Entire books (and lives) are dedicated to the subject. Paris is France's wine-and-cuisine melting pot. While it lacks a style of its own (only French onion soup is truly Parisian), it draws from the best of France. Paris could hold a gourmets' Olympics and import nothing.

Picnic or go to bakeries for quick take-out lunches, or stop at a café for a lunch salad or *plat du jour,* but linger longer over dinner. Cafés are happy to serve a *plat du jour* (garnished plate of the day, about €10–16) or a chef-like salad (about €9) day or night, while restaurants expect you to enjoy a full dinner. Restaurants open for dinner around 19:00, and small local favorites get crowded after 21:00. Most of the restaurants listed below accept credit cards.

To save piles of euros, review the budget eating tips in this book's Introduction and consider dinner picnics (great take-out dishes available at charcuteries).

Good Picnic Spots: For great people-watching, try the Pompidou Center (by the *Homage to Stravinsky* fountains), the elegant place des Vosges (closes at dusk), and Luxembourg Garden. The Palais Royal (across the street from the Louvre) is a good spot for a peaceful, royal picnic.

For a romantic picnic place, try the pedestrian bridge (pont des Arts) across from the Louvre, with its unmatched views and plentiful benches; the Champ de Mars park under the Eiffel Tower; and the western tip of Ile St. Louis, overlooking Ile de la Cité. Bring your own dinner feast, and then watch the riverboats and the Eiffel Tower light up the city for you.

Restaurants

My recommendations are centered around the same great neighborhoods for which I list accommodations (above); you can come home exhausted after a busy day of sightseeing and have a good selection of restaurants right around the corner. And evening is a fine time to explore any of these delightful neighborhoods, even if you're sleeping elsewhere. Most restaurants I've listed in these areas offer fixed-price meals (called *menus*) between €15 and €30. In most cases, the few extra euros you pay are well-spent, and open up a variety of better choices. You decide.

If you are traveling outside of Paris, save your splurges for the countryside, where you'll enjoy regional cooking for less money.

Restaurant Price Code

To help you choose among these listings, I've divided the restaurants into three categories, based on the price for a typical meal without wine.

$$$ Higher Priced—Most meals €35 or more.
$$ Moderately Priced—Most meals between €20–35.
$ Lower Priced—Most meals under €20.

Many Parisian department stores have huge supermarkets hiding in the basement and top-floor cafeterias that offer affordable, low-risk, low-stress, what-you-see-is-what-you-get meals.

Rue Cler Neighborhood

The rue Cler neighborhood caters to its residents. Its eateries, while not destination places, have an intimate charm. My favorites are small mom-and-pop eateries that love to serve traditional French food at good prices to a local clientele. You'll generally find great dinner *menus* for €20–30 and *plats du jour* for around €12–16. Eat early with tourists or late with locals. For all restaurants listed in this area, use the Ecole Militaire Métro stop (unless another station is listed).

Close to Ecole Militaire, Between Rue de la Motte Picquet and Rue de Grenelle

$$$ Café de l'Esplanade is your opportunity to be surrounded by chic, yet older and sophisticated Parisians enjoying top-notch traditional cuisine as foreplay. It has a sprawling floor plan: Half its tables (with well-stuffed chairs) fill a plush, living-room-like interior, and the other half are lined up outside under its elegant awning facing the grand Esplanade des Invalides in front of Napoleon's Tomb. Notice the cannons that decorate the walls and the cannonballs used for chandeliers. Dress competitively, as this is *the* place to be seen in the 7th *arrondissement,* and consider a stylish drink if not dinner (€20 *plats du jour,* €45 plus wine for dinner, open daily, reserve ahead—especially if you want a curbside table, non-smoking room in the back, 52 rue Fabert, Mo: La Tour-Maubourg, tel. 01 47 05 38 80). This is the only actual business on the entire esplanade that stretches all the way to the Champs-Elysées.

$$$ Le Florimond is good for a special occasion. The ambience, while spacious and quiet, is also intimate and welcoming. Locals come for classic French cuisine with elegant indoor or breezy streetside seating. Friendly English-speaking Laurent—with his playful ties changing daily—will take good care of you

Rue Cler Restaurants

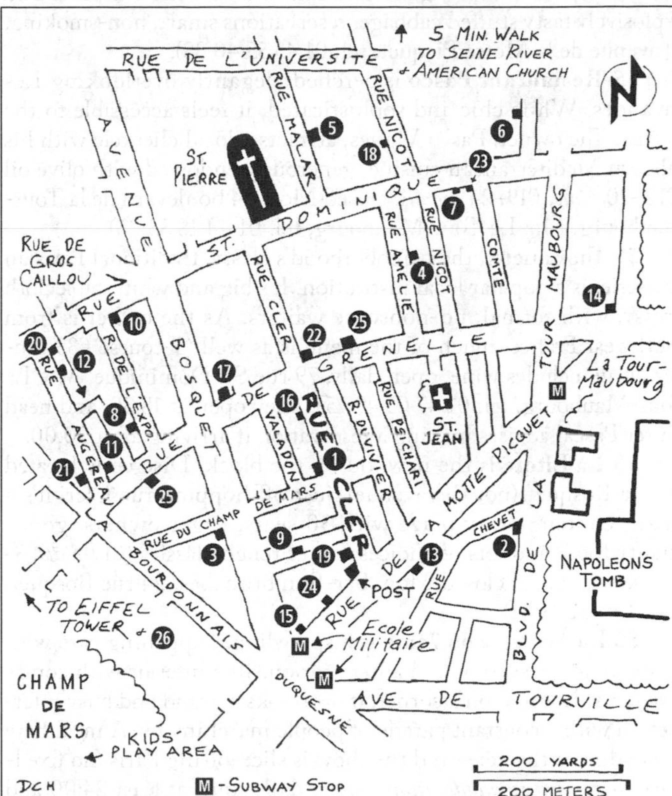

1. Café du Marché & Tribeca Rest.
2. Restaurant Pasco
3. Café le Bosquet
4. Chez Pierrot
5. L'Affriolé & L'Ami Jean
6. Au Petit Tonneau
7. Thoumieux Brasserie
8. Le P'tit Troquet
9. La Litote
10. La Fontaine de Mars
11. La Varangue
12. Chez Agnès
13. Le Florimond
14. Café de l'Esplanade
15. La Terrasse du 7ème
16. Ulysée en Gaule
17. Real McCoy
18. Pourjauran Bakery
19. Petite Brasserie PTT
20. Café Constant
21. La Gourmandise Pizzeria
22. Café la Roussillon
23. O'Brien's Pub
24. Lenôtre Deli
25. Late-Night Groceries (2)
26. To Altitude 95 Rest.

(€35 *menu*, closed Sun, good and reasonable wine selection and explosively tasty stuffed cabbage, reservations smart, non-smoking, 19 avenue de la Motte Picquet, tel. 01 45 55 40 38).

$$ Restaurant Pasco is perched elegantly overlooking Les Invalides. While chic and sophisticated, it feels accessible to the tourist. The owner, Pasco Vignes, attracts a local clientele with his modern Mediterranean cuisine, generously endowed with olive oil (€12–20 *plats*, €19–24 *menus*, closed Mon, 74 boulevard de la Tour-Maubourg, Mo: La Tour-Maubourg, tel. 01 44 18 33 26).

$$ Thoumieux, the neighborhood's classy, traditional Parisian brasserie, is a popular local institution. It's big and white-tablecloth dressy, with formal, no-nonsense waiters. As the owner is from southwest France, much of the menu is as well (3-course €33 dinner *menu* includes wine, open daily, 79 rue St. Dominique, Mo: La Tour-Maubourg, tel. 01 47 05 49 75). They open at 18:30, and head waiter Pascal advises making a reservation if arriving after 20:00.

$$ La Litote is the new kid on the block. Discreetly located on rue Bosquet (not the avenue), just off hopping rue Cler, it's a small, contemporary place with 30 seats, eager owners, good-quality food, and lots of choices from French classics (€19 *plats*, 3-course €33 *menu*, closed Mon, Sat–Sun brunches, 24 rue Bosquet, tel. 01 45 51 78 82).

$$ La Terrasse du 7ème is a sprawling, happening café with classic outdoor seating and a living-room-like interior with comfy love seats. Located on a corner, it overlooks a grand and busy intersection with a constant parade of people marching by. A meal here is like dinner theater—and the show is slice-of-life Paris (no fixed-price *menu*, great *salade niçoise*, open daily until at least 24:00 and sometimes until 2:00 in the morning, at Ecole Militaire Métro stop, tel. 01 45 55 00 02).

$$ Café le Bosquet is a modern, chic Parisian brasserie with dressy waiters and your choice of a slick interior or sidewalk tables on a busy street. Come here for a bowl of French onion soup, or a *plat du jour* with good fish and meat choices, and mix it up with waiters Daniel, Nina, and Antoine (closed Sun, many choices—including vegetarian options—from a fun menu, escargots are great here, the house red wine is plenty good, reservations smart on weekends, corner of rue du Champ de Mars and avenue Bosquet, at 46 avenue Bosquet, tel. 01 45 51 38 13).

$ Café du Marché boasts the best seats, coffee, and prices on rue Cler. The owner's philosophy: Brasserie on speed—crank out great food at great prices to trendy locals and savvy tourists. It's high-energy, with waiters who barely have time to smile...*très* Parisian. This place is ideal if you want a light lunch or dinner (good, hearty €11 salads) or a more substantial but simple meal (filling €11 *plats du jour*, listed on chalkboard; open Mon–Sat

11:00–23:00, Sun 11:00–17:00, arrive before 19:30 for dinner—it's packed at 21:00, can be smoky and service can be slow, at the corner of rue Cler and rue du Champ de Mars, at 38 rue Cler, tel. 01 47 05 51 27). Their **Tribeca Restaurant,** next door, offers similar (if not even better) value but more space, a calmer ambience, more patient service, and a menu focusing on pizza and Italian cuisine.

$ Ulysée en Gaule, in a prime location right on rue Cler, offers good, cheap, front-row seats for the people-watching fun. The Ulysée family—Stephanos, Chrysa, Katerina, and their English-speaking son, Vassilis—seem to make friends with all who drop by for a bite. The family loves to serve Greek dishes, and their excellent crêpes (to go or sit down for €2 extra) are your cheapest rue Cler hot meal (daily, 28 rue Cler, tel. 01 47 05 61 82).

$ Petite Brasserie PTT is a classic time warp, popular with postal workers and offering traditional café fare at reasonable prices next to the PTT (post office) on rue Cler. They offer a great *deux pour douze* breakfast deal for Rick Steves readers: two American breakfasts (normally €8 each) for €12 total (closed Sun, opposite 53 rue Cler).

Between Rue de Grenelle and the River

$$$ Altitude 95 is in the Eiffel Tower, 95 meters (about 300 feet) above the ground (€21–31 lunches, €50 dinners, dinner seatings nightly at 19:00 and 21:00, reserve well ahead for a view table; before you ascend to dine, drop by the booth between the north/*nord* and east/*est* pillars to buy your Eiffel Tower ticket and pick up a pass that enables you to skip the line; Mo: Bir-Hakeim or Trocadéro, RER: Champ de Mars-Tour Eiffel, tel. 01 45 55 20 04, fax 01 47 05 94 40).

$$$ L'Affriolé is a small, trendy eatery where you'll compete with young professionals to get a table. Stepping into this elegant but rollicking dining hall, you immediately feel you're eating at a restaurant well-deserving of its rave reviews. Menu selections change daily, and the wine list is extensive, with some good bargains (€35–45 *menu* based on your main course, closed Sun–Mon, 17 rue Malar, Mo: La Tour-Maubourg, tel. 01 44 18 31 33).

$$$ Au Petit Tonneau is a souvenir of old Paris. Fun-loving owner-chef Madame Boyer prepares everything herself, wearing her tall chef's hat like a crown as she rules from her family-style kitchen. The small, plain dining room doesn't look like it's changed in the 25 years she's been in charge. Her steaks and lamb are excellent (€30 for 2-course *menu,* open daily, can get smoky—come early, 20 rue Surcouf, Mo: La Tour-Maubourg, tel. 01 47 05 09 01).

$$$ La Fontaine de Mars is a longtime favorite for locals, charmingly situated on a classic, tiny Parisian street and jumbled square. It's a happening scene, with tables jammed together for the serious business of good eating. Reserve a table on the ground floor in advance (or in summer on the square), or risk eating in the non-smoking room upstairs without the fun street-level ambience (€25 *plats,* superb foie gras, open nightly, where rue de l'Exposition and rue St. Dominique meet, at #129 rue St. Dominique, tel. 01 47 05 46 44).

$$ Le P'tit Troquet, a petite eatery taking you back to the Paris of the 1920s, is gracefully and earnestly run by Dominique. She's particularly proud of her foie gras and lamb. The delicious, 3-course €30 *menu* comes with traditional choices. Its delicate charm and gourmet flair make this a favorite of connoisseurs (closed Sun, reservations smart, 28 rue de l'Exposition, tel. 01 47 05 80 39).

$$Chez Agnès, the smallest of my recommended Paris restaurants, is not for everyone. It's tiny, flowery, family-style, and filled with kisses on the cheek. Eccentric but sincere Agnès (a French-Tahitian Roseanne Barr) does it all—cooking in her minuscule kitchen and serving, too. Agnès, who cooks "French with an exotic twist" and clearly loves her work, makes children feel right at home. Don't come for a quick dinner (€23 *menu,* closed Mon, 1 rue Augereau, tel. 01 45 51 06 04).

$$ L'Ami Jean offers excellent Basque specialties at fair prices. The chef has made his reputation on the quality of his cuisine, not on the dark, simple decor. Arrive by 19:30 or call ahead—by 20:00, there's a line out the door of people waiting to join the shared tables and lively commotion of happy eaters (€25 for a plate of mixed Basque tapas, €28 *menu,* closed Sun–Mon, 27 rue Malar, Mo: La Tour-Maubourg, tel. 01 47 05 86 89).

$$ Chez Pierrot is a classic bistro with friendly and helpful owners who love to help you decipher the menu. Portions are large and the salads are, too—all at reasonable prices (open daily, count on €30 with wine, 9 rue Amélie, tel. 01 45 51 50 08).

$ Café Constant is a tiny, mod, two-level place that feels more like a small bistro–wine bar than a café. They serve delicious and reasonably priced dishes (€12 *plats*) in a fun setting to a well-established clientele (closed Sun–Mon, corner of rue Augereau and rue St. Dominique, next to recommended Hotel Londres Eiffel).

$ La Varangue is an entertaining one-man show featuring English-speaking Phillipe (who ran a French catering shop in Pennsylvania for three years). The restaurant may close—call before going there. If it's open, you'll join a mostly American clientele, who are all on a first-name basis. The food is cheap and basic (don't come here for high cuisine), the tables are few, and he opens early (at 17:30). Norman Rockwell would dig his tiny dining room. Try his snails and chocolate cake...but not together (€10 *plats,* €16 *menu,* always a vegetarian option, non-smoking, closed

Sun, 27 rue Augereau, tel. 01 47 05 51 22).

$ La Gourmandise is a tiny, friendly pizzeria across the street from La Varangue. Its good, cheap pizza is ideal for kids (closed Sun, eat-in or take-out, 28 rue Augereau, tel. 01 45 55 45 16).

Picnicking in Rue Cler

Rue Cler is a moveable feast that gives "fast food" a good name. The entire street is clogged with connoisseurs of good eating. Only the health-food store goes unnoticed. A festival of food, the street is lined with people whose lives seem to be devoted to their specialty: polished produce, rotisserie chicken, crêpes, or cheese.

For a magical picnic dinner at the Eiffel Tower, assemble it in no fewer than five shops on rue Cler. Then lounge on the best grass in Paris, with the dogs, Frisbees, a floodlit tower, and a cool breeze in the parc du Champ de Mars.

Asian delis (generically called *Traiteur Asie*) provide tasty, low-stress, low-price take-out treats (€6 dinner plates, the one on rue Cler near rue du Champ de Mars has tables). **Ulysée en Gaule,** the Greek restaurant on rue Cler across from Grand Hôtel Lévêque, sells take-away crêpes (described above). The elegant **Lenôtre charcuterie** offers mouthwatering meals to go (open daily until 23:00, at Ecole Militaire Métro stop). **Real McCoy** is a little shop selling American food and sandwiches (closed Sun, 194 rue de Grenelle). There are small **late-night groceries** at 186 and 197 rue de Grenelle (open nightly until midnight). For excellent baguettes and sandwiches, try **Julien's** bakery at 85 rue St. Dominique.

Breakfast in Rue Cler

Hotel breakfasts, while convenient, are generally not a good value. For a great rue Cler start to your day, drop by the **Petite Brasserie PTT** (a two-minute walk from most area hotels, described above), where managers Jerome and Eric promise Rick Steves readers a *deux pour douze* breakfast special (2 "American" breakfasts—juice, coffee, croissant, ham, and eggs—for €12). **Café la Roussillon** serves a good American-style breakfast for €9 (open daily, at corner of rue de Grenelle and rue Cler, tel. 01 45 51 47 53). To eat breakfast while watching Paris go to work, stop by **La Terrasse du 7ème** (described above). The **Pourjauran** bakery, offering great baguettes, hasn't changed in 70 years (closed Sun–Mon, 20 rue Jean Nicot).

Nightlife in Rue Cler

This sleepy neighborhood is not ideal for night owls, but there are a few notable exceptions. **Café du Marché** and **La Terrasse du 7ème** (both listed above) are busy with a Franco-American crowd until at least midnight, as is the flashier **Café la Roussillon** (nightly, corner of rue de Grenelle and rue Cler). **O'Brien's Pub** is a relaxed Parisian rendition of an Irish pub, full of anglophones (77 avenue St. Dominique, Mo: La Tour-Maubourg).

In the Marais Neighborhood

The trendy Marais is filled with locals enjoying good food in colorful and atmospheric eateries. The scene is competitive and changes all the time. I've listed an assortment of eateries—all handy to recommended hotels—that offer good food at reasonable prices, plus a memorable experience. For maximum ambience, go to place des Vosges or place du Marché Ste. Catherine (several restaurants listed below on each of these squares).

Dining on Romantic Place des Vosges

On this square, which offers Old World Marais elegance, you'll find four very different eateries. Enjoy a square stroll around the entire arcade—fun art galleries alternate with enticing restaurants. Choose the restaurant that best fits your mood and budget; each one has perfect arcade seating and provides big space heaters to make outdoor dining during colder months an option. Also consider a drink or dessert on the square at Café Hugo or Nectarine after eating elsewhere. To reach place des Vosges, use the St. Paul or Bastille Métro station.

$$$ Restaurant Coconnas is the dressiest option, with classic French cuisine, refined ambience, black-suited waiters, and artfully presented gourmet dishes. Check out the paintings of the former place Royal (€30 *plats,* €15 *entrées* and desserts, closed Mon, on the river side of the square at #2, tel. 01 42 78 58 16).

$$$ Ma Bourgogne is a classic old eatery where you'll sit under arcades in a whirlpool of Frenchness, as bow-tied and black-aproned waiters serve you traditional Burgundian specialties: steak, coq au vin, lots of French fries, escargot, and great red wine. Service at this institution comes with food but few smiles (€32 *menu,* open daily, dinner reservations smart, cash only, at northwest corner at #19, tel. 01 42 78 44 64).

$ Nectarine is small and demure—with a wicker, pastel, and feminine ambience. This peaceful teahouse serves healthy €10 salads, quiches, and €12 *plats du jour* both day and night. Its menu lets you mix and match omelets and crêpes. Its huge desserts are splittable, and dropping by here late for sweets and a drink is a peaceful way to end your day (open daily, at #16, tel. 01 42 77 23 78).

$ Café Hugo, named for the square's most famous resident, is best for drinks only, as the cuisine does not live up to its setting (open daily, at #22).

Marais Restaurants

1. Place du Marché Ste. Catherine Eateries
2. Vins des Pyrénées
3. Nectarine & Café Hugo
4. Ma Bourgogne
5. L'Impasse
6. Chez Janou
7. Brasserie Bofinger
8. Restaurant Coconnas
9. L'Enoteca
10. L'As du Falafel
11. Au Bourguignon du Marais
12. Bistrot les Sans Culottes
13. Restaurante Sant Antonio
14. Camille Brasserie
15. Le Pick-Clops Bar Rest.
16. Chez Marianne
17. Au Temps des Cerises
18. La Perla Bar
19. The Quiet Man Irish Pub
20. BHV Cafeteria
21. Le Rouge Gorge
22. La Bastoche Rest. & Hilaire Bakery

M - Subway Stop
T - Taxi Stand
P - Parking

Near the Bastille

The nearest Métro stop to the following restaurants is Bastille.

$$ Brasserie Bofinger, an institution for over a century, is famous for fish and traditional cuisine with Alsatian flair. You're surrounded by brisk, black-and-white-attired waiters. The sprawling interior features elaborately decorated rooms reminiscent of the Roaring 20s. Eating under the grand 1919 *coupole* is a memorable treat (as is using the "historic" 1919 WC downstairs). Check out the boys shucking and stacking seafood platters out front before you enter. Their €30 three-course *menu,* while not top cuisine, includes wine and is a good value. The kids' menu makes this restaurant family-friendly (open daily and nightly, reserve online and receive a 15 percent discount—print out your confirmation and bring it with you, mostly non-smoking, 5 rue de la Bastille, don't be confused by the lesser "Petite" Bofinger across the street, tel. 01 42 72 87 82).

$$ Chez Janou, a Provençal bistro, tumbles out of its corner building and fills its broad sidewalk with happy eaters. At first glance, you know this is a find. Don't let the trendy and youthful crowd intimidate you—it's relaxed and charming, with helpful and patient service. While the curbside tables are inviting, I'd sit inside to immerse myself in the happy commotion. The style is French Mediterranean, with an emphasis on vegetables (€15 *plats du jour* that change with the season, open daily, 2 blocks beyond place des Vosges at 2 rue Roger Verlomme, tel. 01 42 72 28 41). They're proud of their 81 different varieties of *pastis* (licorice-flavored liqueur; €3.50 each, browse the list).

$$ L'Impasse, a relaxed bistro on a quiet alley, serves an enthusiastically French three-course *menu* for €28. Françoise, a former dancer and artist, runs the place *con brio* (closed Sun, 4 impasse de Guéménée, tel. 01 42 72 08 45). Françoise promises anyone with this book a free glass of *byrrh*—it's pronounced "beer," but it's a French port-like drink. The restaurant is next to a self-serve launderette (open nightly until 21:30—clean your clothes while you dine).

$$ La Bastoche, which is Parisian slang for "the Bastille," is cozy and simple. In an 18th-century building with exposed timbers and a great mural of the storming of the old prison, choose from a nice selection of traditional French fare at reasonable prices. Caring owners Sylvie and Lise aim to please (3-course €22 *menu,* open daily, 7 rue St. Antoine, one block away from the Bastille, tel. 01 48 04 84 34).

$$ Bistrot les Sans Culottes, a zinc-bar classic on lively rue de Lappe, serves traditional French cuisine with a proper respect for fine wine (3-course €24 *menu,* closed Mon, 27 rue de Lappe, tel. 01 48 05 42 92). Stay out past your bedtime. Eat here. Then join the rue de Lappe party.

$$ Vins des Pyrénées draws a young, lively crowd with its fun ambience, varying menus with lots of choices, and a reasonable wine list (€15–20 *plats,* open daily, some smoke, 25 rue Beautreillis, tel. 01 42 72 64 94).

$ Au Temps des Cerises is a *très* local wine bar, with tight seating and wads of character. While they serve good, three-course, €13.50 lunch *menus,* it's also good for an early dinner or a pre-dinner glass of wine. "Dinner" is limited to bread, dry sausage, cheese, and wine served by goateed Yves and his wife, Michele. A mixed plate of cheese (€3.50), meat (€3.50), and a carafe of good wine (€3–6) surrounded by the intimate and woody, Old World ambience can be a good light meal (Mon–Fri until 20:00, closed Sat–Sun, at rue du Petit-Musc and rue de la Cerisaie).

Closer to Hôtel de Ville

These eateries, near the Pompidou Center, appear on the map on page 329. To reach them, use the Hôtel de Ville Métro stop.

$$$ Au Bourguignon du Marais is a small wine bar–bistro south of rue de Rivoli. Wine-lovers won't want to miss it. The excellent Burgundy wines blend well with a fine, though limited, selection of *plats du jour.* The escargots are delicious, and the dessert was...*délicieux* (€35–45 with wine, closed Sat–Sun, call by 19:00 to reserve, 52 rue Francois Miron, tel. 01 48 87 15 40).

$ Restaurante Sant Antonio is bustling and cheap, serving up pizza, salads, and Italian, on a fun square where rue de Bourg-Tibourg meets rue de Rivoli.

$ BHV Department Store's fifth-floor cafeteria provides nice views, an escape from the busy streets below, and no-brainer, point-and-shoot cafeteria cuisine (Mon–Sat 11:30–18:00, closed Sun, at intersection of rue du Temple and rue de la Verrerie, one block from Hôtel de Ville).

In the Heart of the Marais

These are closest to the St. Paul Métro stop.

$$ *On place du Marché Ste. Catherine:* This small, romantic square, just off rue St. Antoine, is an international food festival cloaked in extremely Parisian, leafy-square ambience. On a balmy evening, this is clearly a neighborhood favorite, with five popular restaurants offering €20–30 meals. Study the square, and you'll find a popular French bistro **(Le Marché)** and inviting eateries serving Italian, Korean, Russian, and Greek. You'll eat under the trees, surrounded by a futuristic-in-1800 planned residential quarter.

$$ L'Enoteca is a high-spirited, half-timbered wine bar–restaurant serving reasonably priced Italian cuisine (no pizza) with a tempting *antipasti* bar. It's a relaxed, open setting with busy, blue-aproned waiters serving two floors of local eaters (€13 pastas,

€15 *plats,* open daily, across from L'Excuse at rue St. Paul and rue Charles V, 25 rue Charles V, tel. 01 42 78 91 44).

$ **Camille,** a traditional corner brasserie, is a neighborhood favorite with great indoor and sidewalk seating. White-aproned waiters serve €12 salads and very French *plats du jour* (from €16) to a down-to-earth but sophisticated clientele (open daily, 24 rue des Francs Bourgeois at corner of rue Elzévir, tel. 01 42 72 20 50).

$ **Le Rouge Gorge** wine bar and bistro is small but cozy. Come for a meal (€10 lunch *plats,* €16 dinner *plats*), a coffee, or a glass of wine. Friendly François, the owner, will send you downstairs to the cave to choose your wine; there are different prices for take-away wine (closed Sun, 8 rue St. Paul, tel. 01 48 04 75 89).

$ Several hardworking **Chinese fast-food eateries,** great for a €6 meal, line rue St. Antoine.

On Rue des Rosiers in the Jewish Quarter

To reach the Jewish Quarter, use the St. Paul Métro stop.

$ **Chez Marianne,** a neighborhood fixture, offers classic Jewish meals and Parisian ambience. Choose from several indoor zones with a cluttered wine shop/deli ambience, or sit outside. You'll select from two dozen "Zakouski" elements to assemble your €15 plate (great vegetarian options, eat cheap with a €6 falafel sandwich, or even cheaper with take-out, long hours daily, corner of rue des Rosiers and rue des Hospitalieres St. Gervais, tel. 01 42 72 18 86). For take-out, pay inside first and get a ticket before you order outside.

$ **L'As du Falafel** seems to dominate the falafel scene in the Jewish quarter. Monsieur Isaac, the "Ace of Falafel" here since 1979, brags he's got "the biggest pita on the street...and he fills it up." Apparently it's Lenny Kravitz's favorite, too. Your inexpensive Jewish cuisine comes on plastic plates and a bustling ambience that seems to prove he's earned his success. While the €6 "special falafel" is the big hit, many Americans enjoy his lighter chicken version *(medaillon de poulet grillé).* Their take-out service draws a constant crowd (day and night until late, 34 rue des Rosiers).

Picnicking

Picnic at peaceful place des Vosges (closes at dusk) or on the Ile St. Louis *quais* (see below). Stretch your euros at the basement supermarket of the **Monoprix** department store (closed Sun, near place des Vosges on rue St. Antoine). Two small **grocery shops** are open until 23:00 on rue St. Antoine (near intersection with rue Castex).

Breakfast

For an incredibly cheap breakfast, try **Hilaire *boulangerie-pâtisserie,*** where the hotels buy their croissants (coffee machine-

€0.70, cheap baby quiches, 1 block off place de la Bastille, corner of rue St. Antoine and rue de Lesdiguières).

Nightlife

The best scene is the dizzying array of wacky eateries, bars, and dance halls on **rue de Lappe.** This street is what the Latin Quarter aspires to be. Just east of the stately place de la Bastille, it's one of the wildest nightspots in Paris. Sitting amid the chaos like a van Gogh painting is the popular, old-time **Bistrot les Sans Culottes** (see above).

Trendy cafés and bars—popular with gay men—also cluster on rue Vieille du Temple, rue des Archives, and rue Ste. Croix de la Bretonnerie (close at about 2:00 in the morning). You'll find a line of bars and cafés providing front-row seats for the buff parade on rue Vieille du Temple, a block north of rue de Rivoli. Nearby, rue des Rosiers bustles with youthful energy, but there are no cafés to observe from. **Vins des Pyrénées** is young and fun—find the small bar in the back (see above). **La Perla** is full of Parisian yuppies in search of the perfect margarita (26 rue François Miron). **The Quiet Man** is a traditional Irish pub with happy hour from 16:00 to 20:00 (5 rue des Haudriettes).

$ Le Pick-Clops Bar Restaurant is a happy peanuts-and-lots-of-cocktails diner with bright neon, loud colors, and a garish local crowd. It's perfect for immersing yourself in today's Marais world—a little boisterous, a little edgy, a little gay, fun-loving, easygoing...and no tourists. Sit inside, on old-fashioned diner stools, or streetside to watch the constant Marais parade. The name means "Steal the Cigarettes"—but you'll pay €10 for your big salad (daily 7:00–24:00, 16 rue Vieille du Temple, tel. 01 40 29 0218).

The most enjoyable peaceful evening may be simply donning your floppy "three musketeers" hat and slowly strolling around the place des Vosges, window-shopping the art galleries.

Ile St. Louis

The Ile St. Louis is a romantic and peaceful neighborhood to window-shop for plenty of promising dinner possibilities. Cruise the island's main street for a variety of options, from cozy *crêperies* to Italian eateries (intimate pizzerias and upscale) to typical brasseries (a few with fine outdoor seating facing the bridge to Ile de la Cité). After dinner, sample Paris' best sorbet and stroll across to the Ile de la Cité to see an illuminated Notre-Dame, or enjoy a scenic drink on the deck of a floating café moored under the Notre-Dame's right transept. All of these listings line the island's main drag, the rue St. Louis-en-l'Ile (see map on page 258; to get here, use the Pont Marie Métro stop). Consider skipping dessert to enjoy a stroll licking the best ice cream in Paris (described under

"Ice-Cream Dessert," on the next page).

$$$ Le Tastevin is an eight-table, mother-and-son-run restaurant serving top-notch traditional French cuisine with white-tablecloth, candlelit, gourmet elegance under heavy wooden beams. The three-course *menus* start at about €34 and offer plenty of classic choices that change with the season to ensure freshness (open daily, good wine list, reserve for late-evening eating, 46 rue St. Louis-en-l'Ile, tel. 01 43 54 17 31; owner Madame Puisieux speaks just enough English, while her son, Jean-Philippe, tends the kitchen).

$$$ ***Medieval Theme Restaurants:*** **Nos Ancêtres les Gaulois** on rue St. Louis-en-l'Ile is famous for its rowdy, medieval-cellar atmosphere. Ideal for barbarians—as the name ("Our Ancestors the Gauls") implies—they serve all-you-can-eat buffets with straw baskets of raw veggies (cut whatever you like with your dagger), massive plates of pâté, a meat course, and all the wine you can stomach for €37. The food is just food; burping is encouraged. If you want to eat a lot, drink a lot of wine, be surrounded with tourists, and holler at your friends while receiving smart-aleck buccaneer service, this food fest can be fun (open daily from 19:00, at #39, tel. 01 46 33 66 07). **La Taverne du Sergeant Recruteur,** next door, serves up the same formula for €39 with a different historic twist: The "Sergeant Recruiter" used to get young Parisians drunk and stuffed here, then sign them into the army. You might swing by both and choose the..."ambience" is not quite the right word... that fits your mood (tel. 01 43 54 75 42).

$$ La Brasserie de l'Ile St. Louis is situated at the prow of the island's ship as it faces Ile de la Cité, offering purely Alsatian cuisine (try the *choucroute garni* for €18), served in Franco-Germanic ambience with no-nonsense brasserie service. This is your perfect balmy-evening perch for watching the Ile St. Louis promenade—or, if it's chilly, the interior is plenty characteristic for a memorable night out (closed Wed, no reservations, 55 quai de Bourbon, tel. 01 43 54 02 59).

$ Café Med, near Notre-Dame at #77, is best for inexpensive salads, crêpes, and light €12 *menus* in a tight but cheery setting (limited wine list, open daily, tel. 01 43 29 73 17, charming Eva). There are two similar *crêperies* just across the street: **Le Sarrasin et Le Froment** and **Au Lys d'Argent.**

Riverside Picnic

On sunny lunchtimes and balmy evenings, the *quai* on the Left Bank side of Ile St. Louis is lined with locals who have more class than money, spreading out tablecloths and even lighting candles for elegant picnics. Otherwise, it's a great walk for people-watching.

Ice-Cream Dessert

Half the people strolling Ile St. Louis are licking an ice-cream cone, because this is the home of *les glaces Berthillon*. The original **Berthillon** shop, at 31 rue St. Louis-en-l'Ile, is marked by the line of salivating customers (closed Mon–Tue). Another Berthillon shop is across the street, and there's one more around the corner on rue Bellay. The three shops are so popular that the wealthy people who can afford to live on this fancy island complain about the congestion they cause. For a less famous but at-least-as-tasty treat, the homemade Italian gelato a block away at **Amorino Gelati** is giving Berthillon competition (no line, bigger portions, easier to see what you want, and they offer little tastes—Berthillon doesn't need to, 47 rue St. Louis-en-l'Ile, tel. 01 44 07 48 08). Having some of each is not a bad thing.

Luxembourg Neighborhood

Sleeping in the Luxembourg neighborhood puts you near many appealing dining and after-hours options. Because my hotels in this area cluster around the Panthéon and St. Sulpice Church (see page 311), I've organized restaurant listings the same way. Restaurants near the Panthéon tend to be calm, those around St. Sulpice more boisterous; it's a short walk from one area to the other. Anyone sleeping in this area is close to the inexpensive eateries that line the always-bustling rue Mouffetard.

Near the Panthéon

For locations, see the map on page 315.

These eateries are served by the Cluny-La Sorbonne Métro stop and the RER-B Luxembourg station.

$$ Les Vignes du Panthéon, on a quiet street a block from the Panthéon, is homey, formal, and traditional. It specializes in fish and southwestern French cuisine, and features a zinc bar, original flooring, white tablecloths, and whispering ambience. The mostly local clientele will make you feel you're truly in Paris (€17–20 *plats,* closed Sat–Sun, 4 rue des Fossés St. Jacques, tel. 01 43 54 80 81).

$$ Terra Nera is a small Italian restaurant with a privileged position on a broad sidewalk overlooking a peaceful square just a block from the Panthéon. Its noisy red facade gives it a fun and casual feel. Two can easily split the big *antipasti* (€13, ask for mozzarella with it) and each get a pasta main course for a total of about €22 per person (closed Sun, limited and pricey wine list, 18 rue des Fossés St. Jacques, tel. 01 43 54 83 09). That *other* Italian restaurant across the street serves more basic, cheaper pizzas and pastas.

$$ Restaurant Perraudin is a welcoming, family-run, red-checkered-tablecloth eatery understandably popular with tourists. Gentle M. Rameau serves classic *cuisine bourgeoise* with an emphasis on Burgundian dishes. The decor is classic turn-of-the-20th-century, with big mirrors and old wood paneling, and the volume is rollicking (*bœuf bourguignon* is a specialty here, €28 dinner *menus,* €18 lunch *menus,* closed Sat–Sun, between the Panthéon and Luxembourg Garden at 157 rue St. Jacques, tel. 01 46 33 15 75).

$ Le Soufflot is my favorite café between the Panthéon and Luxembourg Garden, with a nifty, library-like interior and outdoor tables on a wide sidewalk with point-blank views of the Panthéon. The cuisine is café-classic: great €10 salads, omelets, and *plats du jour* (open daily, a block below the Panthéon on the right side of rue Soufflot as you walk toward Luxembourg Garden, tel. 01 43 26 57 56).

$ *Place de la Sorbonne:* This cobbled-and-leafy square, with a small fountain facing the Sorbonne University just a block from the Cluny Museum, offers several decent opportunities for a quick outdoor lunch or light dinner. At the tiny **Baker's Dozen,** you'll pay take-away prices for salads and sandwiches you can sit down to eat (daily €5 salad and quiche special, open daily until 19:00). **Café de l'Ecritoire** is a typical, lively brasserie with happy diners enjoying €9 salads, €13 *plats,* and fine square seating (daily, 3 place de la Sorbonne, tel. 01 43 54 60 02).

Near the Odéon Theater

To reach these, use the Odéon Métro stop.

$$ Brasserie Bouillon Racine takes you back to 1906 with an Art Nouveau carnival of carved wood, stained glass, and old-time lights reflected in beveled mirrors. The over-the-top decor, energetic waiters, and affordable menu combine to give it an inviting conviviality. Check upstairs before choosing a table (€18 *plats,* traditional French with lots of fish and meat, daily 12:00–2:00 & 7:00–23:00, 3 rue Racine, tel. 01 44 32 15 60).

$ Restaurant Polidor, a bare-bones neighborhood fixture since the 19th century, is much-loved for its unpretentious quality cooking, fun old Paris ambience, and fair value. Their menu features *plats* from every corner of France, and their *menu fraicheur* is designed for lighter summer eating (3-course €20 *menu,* €10–13 *plats du jours,* daily 12:00–14:30 & 19:00–23:00, cash only, no reservations, 41 rue Monsieur-Le-Prince, tel. 01 43 26 95 34, Amelia).

On Rue Mouffetard

Lying several blocks behind the Panthéon, rue Mouffetard is a conveyer belt of comparison-shopping eaters with wall-to-wall budget options (fondue, crêpes, Italian, falafel, and Greek). Come here to join the fun parade of diners and eat a less-expensive meal (you get what you pay for). This street stays up late and likes to party (particularly place de la Contrescarpe). The gauntlet starts and finishes with fun squares, each with a fine café (recommended below) to eat, drink, and watch the action. The top square is pedestrian and touristic. The bottom square is more real and Parisian. And anywhere between is no-man's land for consistent quality. Still, strolling with so many fun-seekers is enjoyable, whether you eat here or not. To get here, use the Censier-Daubenton Métro stop.

$ Café Delmas, at the top of rue Mouffetard on picturesque place de la Contrescarpe, is *the* place to see and be seen. Come here for a before- or after-dinner drink on the broad outdoor terrace, or for typical café cuisine (€12 salads, €15 *plats,* great chocolate ice cream, open daily).

$ Cave de Bourgogne serves reasonably priced café fare at the bottom of rue Mouffetard, with picture-perfect tables on a raised terrace, and a warm interior (€12–16 *plats,* specials listed on chalkboards, open daily, 144 rue Mouffetard).

Near St. Sulpice Church

Rue des Canettes and Rue Guisarde: For an entirely different experience, roam the streets between the St. Sulpice Church and boulevard St. Germain, abounding with restaurants, *crêperies,* wine bars, and jazz haunts (use Mo: St. Sulpice). Find rue des Canettes and rue Guisarde, and window-shop the many French and Italian eateries—most with similar prices, but each with a slightly different feel. For excellent crêpes, try **La Crêpe Rit du Clown** (Mon–Sat 12:00–23:00, closed Sun, 6 rue des Canettes, tel. 01 46 34 01 02). And for a bohemian pub with a cigarette-rolling gang surrounded by black-and-white photos of the artsy and revolutionary French '60s, have a drink at **Chez Georges.** Sit in a cool little streetside table nook, or venture downstairs to find a smoky, drippy-candle, traditionally French world in the Edith Piaf–style dance cellar (cheap drinks from old-fashioned menu, Tue–Sat 14:00–2:00 in the morning, closed Sun–Mon and in Aug, 11 rue des Canettes).

Near Canal St. Martin

Along the Canal, North of République

Escape the crowded tourist areas and enjoy a cool canalside experience. Take the Métro to place de la République and walk down rue Beaurepaire to Canal St. Martin. There you'll find two worthwhile cafés. They're both lively, with similarly reasonable prices; you decide: **$ Chez Prune** (canal ambience inside and out, well-prepared food, €10 salads, €15 *plats,* open daily, 71 quai de Valmy, tel. 01 42 41 30 47) or **$ La Marine** (closed Sun, 2 blocks to the right as you leave Chez Prune, 55 bis quai de Valmy, tel. 01 42 39 69 81).

In the summertime, most bars and cafés offer beer and wine

to go *(à emporter),* so you can take it to the canal's edge and picnic there with the young locals.

Near Rue Oberkampf, South of République

$$ Le Grand Méricourt is a cool find. Grégory, the 22-year-old chef, inspires with his original flavor combinations and beautiful presentation. It's traditional French—but with a twist. Marie-Elizabeth (his mom) serves gently, while Greg's team of two cook everything fresh in a tiny kitchen. Don't come for a quick meal; this is a good place for special occasions (*menus* start at €29, reservations smart, 22 rue de la Folie Méricourt, tel. 01 43 38 94 04).

$$ Les Tables de la Fontaine, on a pleasant, leafy square, is a popular neighborhood place, with lots of windows and outdoor seating. Come for the seafood specialties, salads, or traditional bistro fare (*menus* from €23, open daily, 33 rue Jean-Pierre Timbaud, tel. 01 43 57 26 00).

$ Au Trou Normand, near the recommended hotels on rue Malte, is a small, red-checkered-tablecloth eatery with reasonable prices (€12–16 *plats,* open daily, just off boulevard Voltaire at 9 rue Jean-Pierre Timbaud, tel. 01 48 05 80 23).

$ Chez Imogene is a brightly colored corner *crêperie,* with fresh products, friendly service, and nothing but locals around you (3-course €14 dinner *menu,* closed Sun–Mon, 25 rue Jean-Pierre Timbaud, tel. 01 48 07 14 59).

Eating Elsewhere in Paris

Near the Louvre

$ Café le Nemours, a staunchly Parisian fixture serving pricey but good light lunches, is tucked into the corner of the Palais Royal adjacent to the Comédie Française (leaving the Louvre, cross rue de Rivoli and veer left). Elegant with brass and Art Deco, and with outdoor tables under an arcade two minutes from the pyramid, this spot makes a great post-Louvre retreat (fun and filling €11 salads, open daily, 2 place Colette, Mo: Palais Royal, tel. 01 42 61 34 14).

Near Opéra Garnier

$ Bouillon Chartier is a noisy, old, classic eatery. It's named for the bouillon it served the neighborhood's poor workers back in 1896, when its calling was to provide an affordable warm meal for those folks. Workers used to eat *à la gamelle* (from a tin lunch box). That same spirit—complete with surly waiters and a cheap menu—survives today. With over 300 simple seats and 15 frantic waiters, you can still see the napkin drawers for its early regulars (€15 *menus,* open daily 11:30–15:00 & 18:00–22:00, east of the Opéra Garnier near boulevard Poissonniere, 7 rue de Faubourg-Montmartre, Mo: Bonne-Nouvelle, tel. 01 47 70 86 29).

Montmartre

Montmartre is extremely touristy, with many mindless mobs following guides to cancan shows. But the ambience is undeniably fun, and an evening up here overlooking Paris is a quintessential experience in the City of Light. The steps in front of Sacré-Cœur are perfect for a picnic with a view. Along the touristy main drag (near place du Tertre and just off it), several fun piano bars serve reasonable crêpes with great people-watching. To reach this area, use the Anvers Métro stop.

$$ Restaurant Chez Plumeau, just off the jam-packed place du Tertre, is touristy yet moderately priced, with indifferent service and great seating on a tiny, characteristic square (€16 lunch *menu,* €28 dinner *menu,* elaborate €16 salads, closed Wed, place du Calvaire, tel. 01 46 06 26 29).

$ L'Eté en Pente Douce hides under generous branches below the crowds on a classic neighborhood corner. It features fine indoor and outdoor seating, €10 *plats du jour* and salads, vegetarian options, and good wines (open daily, 23 rue Muller, many steps below Sacré-Cœur to the left as you leave, down the stairs below the WC, tel. 01 42 64 02 67).

Dinner Cruises

The following companies all offer dinner cruises (reservations required). **Bateaux Mouches** and **Bateaux Parisiens** have the best reputations and the highest prices. They offer multi-course meals and music on enormous floating dining rooms with glass tops and good views. For both, proper dress is required—no denim, shorts, or sport shoes, and Bateaux Mouches requires a jacket and tie for men. The main difference between these companies is the ambience: Bateaux Mouches offers violin and piano to entertain your romantic evening, while Bateaux Parisiens boasts a lively atmosphere with a singer, band, and dance floor.

Bateaux Mouches, started in 1949, is hands-down the most famous. You can't miss its sparkling port on the north side of the river at Pont de l'Alma. Board from 19:30 to 20:15, depart at 20:30, and return at 22:45 (€125/person, tel. 01 42 25 96 10, www.bateauxmouches.com).

Bateaux Parisiens leaves from Port de la Bourdonnais, just east from the bridge under the Eiffel Tower. Begin boarding at 19:45, leave at 20:30, and return at 23:00 (€92–135/person, 3 price tiers, depends on seating—the middle level is best, tel. 08 25 62 75 13, www.bateauxparisiens.com). Pay the few extra euros to get seats on the lower level next to the windows—it's more romantic and private, with sensational views.

Le Capitaine Fracasse offers the blue-collar option (€45/person, tables are first-come, first-served so get there early, boarding times vary by season and day of week, usually at 19:45, 21:15 in summer, closed Mon, walk down stairs in the middle of Bir Hakeim bridge near the Eiffel Tower to Iles aux Cygne, tel. 01 46 21 48 15, www.lecapitainefracasse.com).

TRANSPORTATION CONNECTIONS

Trains

Paris is Europe's rail hub, with six major train stations, each serving different regions: Gare de l'Est (eastbound trains), Gare du Nord (northern France and Europe), Gare St. Lazare (northwestern France), Gare d'Austerlitz (southwestern France and Europe), Gare de Lyon (southeastern France and Italy), and Gare Montparnasse (northwestern France and TGV service to France's southwest). A smaller station, Gare de Bercy, is the departure point for most night trains to Italy. Any train station has schedule information, can make reservations, and sell tickets for any destination. Buying tickets is handier from an SNCF neighborhood office—including those at Louvre, Invalides, Orsay, Versailles, and airports—or at your neighborhood travel agency. It's worth the small fee. Look for *SNCF* signs in their window that indicate they sell train tickets.

All six train stations have banks or change offices, ATMs, information desks, telephones, cafés, newsstands, and clever pickpockets. Because of security concerns, note that not all have baggage check.

Métro and RER trains, as well as buses and taxis, are well-marked at every station. When arriving by Métro, follow signs for *Grandes Lignes*–SNCF to find the main tracks.

Each station offers two types of rail service: long distance to other cities, called *Grandes Lignes* (major lines); and suburban service to outlying areas, called *banlieue* or RER. Both *banlieue* and RER trains serve outlying areas and the airports; the only difference is that *banlieue* lines are operated by SNCF (France's train system, called Transilien) and RER lines are operated by RATP (Paris' Métro and bus system). You may also see ticket windows identified as *Ile de France*. This is for Transilien (SNCF) trains serving destinations outside Paris in the Ile de France region (usually no more than an hour from Paris).

Paris train stations can be intimidating, but if you slow down, avoid peak times, take a deep breath, and ask for help, you'll find them manageable and efficient. Bring a pad of paper for clear communication at ticket/info windows. All stations have helpful *accueil* (information) booths; the bigger stations have roving helpers, usually in red vests. They're capable of answering rail questions more quickly than the information or ticket windows.

To make your trip go more smoothly, be sure to review the many train tips in "Transportation," on page 8 in this book's Introduction.

Station Overview

Here's an overview of Paris' major train stations. Métro and RER trains, as well as buses and taxis, are well marked at every station. When arriving by Métro, follow signs for *Grandes Lignes*–SNCF to find the main tracks.

Gare du Nord

Key Destinations Served by Gare du Nord *Grandes Lignes:* Chantilly-Gouvieux (nearly hourly, fewer on weekends, 25 min, also served by RER lines), **Brussels** (about 2/hr, 1.5 hrs), **Bruges** (about 2/hr, 2.5 hrs, change in Brussels), **Amsterdam** (hourly, 4.5 hrs), **Copenhagen** (7/day, 14–18 hrs, two night trains), **Koblenz** (9/day, 5 hrs, most change in Köln), and **London** via Eurostar Chunnel train (14/day, 3 hrs, tel. 08 36 35 35 39, www.eurostar.com).

By *Banlieue*/RER Lines: Chantilly-Gouvieux (3/day, 45 min), **Charles de Gaulle Airport** (5/hr, 30 min, runs 5:00–24:00, track 4), **Auvers-sur-Oise** (2/hr, 1 hr, transfer at Pontoise or St. Ouen).

Gare Montparnasse

Key Destinations Served by Gare Montparnasse: Chartres (at least hourly, 1 hr, *banlieue* lines), **Pontorson/Mont St. Michel** (7/day, 4 hrs, via Rennes or Lison, some with bus from Rennes), **Dinan** (6/day, 4 hrs, change in Rennes and Dol), **Bordeaux** (20/day, 3.5 hrs), **Sarlat** (7/day, 6 hrs, change in Bordeaux, Libourne, or Souillac), **Toulouse** (13/day, 5–7 hrs, most require change, usually in Bordeaux or Montpellier), **Albi** (6/day, 6–7.5 hrs, change in Toulouse, also night train), **Carcassonne** (14/day, 6.5 hrs, most require changes in Toulouse or Montpellier, direct trains take 8 hrs, night train also available), **Tours** (18/day, 1 hr), **Madrid** (3/day, 13–16 hrs, one overnight via Irun, more night trains from Gare d'Austerlitz), and **Lisbon** (2/day, 21 hrs, or 27 hrs via Madrid).

Gare de Lyon

Key Destinations Served by Gare de Lyon: Vaux-le-Vicomte (train to Melun, 2/hr by train and RER, 30 min), **Fontainebleau** (nearly hourly, 40 min), **Disneyland** (RER line A-4 to Marne-la-Vallée-Chessy, at least 3/hr, 45 min), **Beaune** (nearly hourly, 2.5 hrs, most require change in Dijon), **Dijon** (nearly hourly, 1.5 hrs), **Chamonix** (9/day, 6–8 hrs, night train possible), **Annecy** (14/day,

4–5 hrs), **Lyon** (at least hourly, 2 hrs), **Avignon** (11/day in 2.5 hrs, 7/day in 3–4 hrs with change), **Arles** (14/day, 3.5–5 hrs, most with change in Marseille, Avignon, or Nîmes), **Nice** (10/day, 5.5–7 hrs, many with change in Marseille, night train possible out of Gare d'Austerlitz), ***Venice** (3/day, 4/night, 10–16 hrs, 1 direct overnight, important to reserve ahead), ***Rome** (2/day, 6/night, 15–18 hrs, 1 direct overnight, important to reserve ahead), **Bern** (9/day, 5–7 hrs, most require changes, night train possible), **Interlaken** (9/day, 7 hrs, night train possible via Basel out of Gare de l'Est), and **Barcelona** (3/day, 9 hrs, 1–2 changes; night trains from Gare d'Austerlitz).

Gare de Bercy

This smaller station handles some night train service to Italy (specifically, destinations marked with an *, above) during renovation work at the Gare de Lyon (Mo: Bercy, one stop east of Gare de Lyon on line 14).

Gare de l'Est

Key Destinations Served by Gare de l'Est: Colmar (12/day, 5.5 hrs, change in Strasbourg, Dijon, or Mulhouse, with TGV 3 hrs), **Strasbourg** (13/day, 4 hrs, with TGV 2.5 hrs, night train available), **Reims** (12/day, 1.5 hrs, with TGV 45 min), **Verdun** (5/day, 3–5 hrs, change in Metz or Chalon, with TGV 65 min), **Munich** (7/day, 9 hrs, some require changes, night train possible), **Vienna** (2/day, 13–18 hrs, 1–7 changes, also 1 direct night train), **Zürich** (14/day, 7 hrs, most require changes, night train), and **Prague** (5/day, 14–18 hrs, night train possible via Frankfurt).

Gare St. Lazare

Key Destinations Served by Gare St. Lazare: Giverny (train to Vernon, 6/day get there in time to visit the gardens, 45 min, then bus or taxi 15 min to Giverny), **Rouen** (20/day, 1–1.5 hrs), **Honfleur** (13/day, 3 hrs, via Lisieux, then bus), **Bayeux** (9/day, 2.5 hrs, some with change in Caen), **Caen** (14/day, 2 hrs), and **Pontorson/Mont St. Michel** (2/day, 4–5.5 hrs, via Caen; more trains from Gare Montparnasse).

Key Destinations Served by Gare d'Austerlitz: Versailles (via RER line C, 4/hr, 40 min), **Amboise** (11/day in 1.5 hrs with change in St. Pierre-des-Corps, requires TGV reservation; 10/day direct in 2 hrs, no reservation needed), **Cahors** (5/day, 5 hrs, also 1 direct night train; other slower trains from Gare Montparnasse), **Barcelona** (3/night, 12–14 hrs, 1 direct; day trains from Gare de Lyon), and **Madrid** (2/night, 13 hrs direct, 16 hrs via Irun; day trains from Gare Montparnasse).

Airports

Charles de Gaulle Airport

Paris' primary airport has two main terminals, T-1 and T-2, and one lesser terminal, T-3. Most flights from the US serve T-1 or T-2. Due to construction at T-1, it's impossible to predict which airlines will serve this terminal in 2008—call ahead or check the airport's Web site (tel. 01 48 62 22 80, www.adp.fr). In 2006, SAS, United, US Airways, and Lufthansa served T-1. Air France, British Airways, Continental, American, Alitalia, Northwest, and KLM served T-2. Smaller airlines and charter flights use T-3 (though some major airlines are expected to use this terminal during T-1's construction). Terminals are connected every few minutes by a free *navette* (shuttle bus), though a new train should be completed by mid-2007 that will zip travelers between the terminals effortlessly. Baggage storage in T-1 is on the arrival level at doors labeled "12-14" (open daily, drop-off 10:00–16:00, pick up 8:30–19:30, tel. 01 48 16 34 90). Baggage storage in T-2 is at both 2A (door 3, daily 8:00–20:00, tel. 01 48 16 20 61) and 2F (arrival level, door 4, daily 7:00–19:00, tel. 01 48 16 20 64). Be especially aware of pickpockets on *navettes* between terminals, and on RER trains. Do not take an unauthorized taxi from the men greeting you on arrival. Official taxi stands are well-signed.

Transportation Between Charles de Gaulle Airport and Paris: Efficient public-transportation routes, taxis, and airport shuttle vans link the airport's terminals with central Paris. All are well-marked, and stops are centrally located at all terminals. If you're carrying lots of baggage—or are just plain tired—taxis are well worth the extra cost.

Roissy-Buses run every 15–20 minutes to Paris' Opéra Garnier 6:30–21:00 (€8.50, 40–60 min, buy ticket on bus, driver can change small bills). You'll arrive at a bus stop on rue Scribe at the American Express office, on the left side of the Opéra building. To get to the Métro entrance, turn left out of the bus and walk counterclockwise around the Opéra to the front. The Métro station entrance is on the island in the middle of the square. For rue Cler hotels, take Métro line 8 (direction: Balard) to La Tour Maubourg or Ecole Militaire. For hotels in the Marais neighborhood, take the same line 8 (direction: Créteil Préfecture) to the Bastille stop. You can also take a taxi (€12–15) to any of my listed hotels from behind the Opéra (the stand is in front of Galeries Lafayette department store).

Air France buses serve central Paris and continue to Orly Airport about every 30 minutes from 5:45 to 23:00 on three different routes. Allow 45 minutes to the Arc de Triomphe and Porte Maillot, 45 minutes to the Gare de Lyon train station, and 60 minutes to Montparnasse Tower/train station. To reach Marais hotels from the Gare de Lyon, take Métro line 1 (direction: La Défense) to the Bastille, St. Paul, or Hôtel de Ville stops. A ticket costs €12 one-way, €18 round-trip (pay driver).

Taxis with luggage run about €50 with bags, more if traffic is bad. Your hotel can call for a taxi to the airport. Usually 20 minutes ahead is enough time, unless your flight is very early (always ask ahead at your hotel). Specify that you want a real taxi *(un taxi normal),* and not a limo service that costs €20 more. Remember, you pay a bit more on Sundays, before 7:00, and after 19:00. If you're happy with your driver, tip €2–3.

Airport shuttles also go straight to and from your hotel, and—since they're cheaper than taxis and have more space than cabs—are a good budget option for single travelers or families of four or more (too many for a cab). Shuttles work well for getting out to the airport, but taxis work better for airport pickup, since arrival times of international flights are fairly unpredictable, and shuttles must be booked ahead (plan on a 30-min wait at the airport and be clear on where and how you are to meet your driver). If your hotel does not work with a shuttle service, reserve directly (book at least a day in advance—most hoteliers will make the call for you). Airport shuttles cost about €20–30 for one person, €30–40 for two, and €40–52 for three. Some offer deals if you do a round trip, and most are more expensive at night (20:00–6:00 in the morning).

Golden Air is the most reliable of the many shuttles (from Paris to Charles de Gaulle: €27 for one person, €17 per person for two; from Charles de Gaulle to Paris: €35 for one person, €20 per person for two; these special prices possible only for readers of this book in 2007, tel. 01 34 10 12 92, fax 01 34 10 93 89, www.paris-airport-shuttle-limousine.com, goldenair@goldenair.net).

Orly Airport

This airport feels small. It's good for rental-car pickup and drop-off, as it's closer to Paris and far easier to navigate than Charles de Gaulle Airport.

Transportation Between Orly Airport and Paris: Several efficient public-transportation routes, taxis, and a couple of airport shuttle services link Orly with central Paris. The gate locations listed below apply to Orly Sud, but the same transportation services are available from both terminals.

Air France buses (outside Gate K) run to Montparnasse train station (with many Métro lines) and to Invalides Métro stop (€8 one-way, €12 round-trip, 4/hr, 40 min to Invalides). These buses are handy for those staying in or near the rue Cler neighborhood (from Invalides bus stop, take the Métro to La Tour Maubourg or Ecole Militaire to reach recommended hotels). Remember that to continue on the Métro, you'll need to buy a separate ticket (for ticket types and prices, see "Getting Around Paris," page 245).

Jetbus (outside Gate H, €5.50, 4/hr) is the quickest way to the Paris subway and a good way to the Marais and Luxembourg Garden neighborhoods. Take Jetbus to the Villejuif-Louis Aragon Métro stop. To reach the Marais neighborhood, take the Métro to the Sully Morland stop. For the Luxembourg area, take the same train to the Censier Daubenton or Place Monge stops. If taking the Jetbus from the Marais to the airport, make sure before you board the Métro that your train is going to Villejuif-Louis Aragon (not Mairie d'Ivry), as the route splits at the end of the line.

The **Orlybus** (outside Gate H, €6, 3/hr) takes you to the Denfert-Rochereau RER-B line and the Métro, offering Métro access to central Paris, including the Luxembourg Area and Notre-Dame Cathedral, as well as the Gare du Nord train station.

Taxis are to the far right as you leave the terminal, at Gate M. Allow €25–35 with bags for a taxi into central Paris.

Airport shuttles are good for single travelers or families of four or more, but better from Paris to the airport (see page 344 for a company to contact; from Orly, figure about €23/1 person, €30/2 people, less per person for larger groups and kids).

Beauvais Airport

Budget airlines such as Ryanair use this airport, offering dirt-cheap airfares, but leaving you 50 miles north of Paris. Still, this small airport has direct buses to Paris (see below). It's ideal for drivers who want to rent a car here and head to Normandy or north to Belgium (airport tel. 08 92 68 20 66, www.aeroportbeauvais.com; Ryanair tel. 08 92 68 20 73, www.ryanair.com).

Transportation Between Beauvais Airport and Paris: Buses depart from the airport about 20 minutes after flights arrive, and take 90 minutes to reach Paris. Buy your ticket at the little kiosk to the right as you exit the airport (€13). Buses wait nearby and depart once they are full (baggage goes underneath), and arrive at Porte Maillot on the west edge of Paris, which has a Métro and RER stop. The closest taxi stand is across the street at Hôtel Concorde LaFayette.

Buses depart Paris for Beauvais Airport three hours before scheduled flight departures (catch bus at Porte Maillot in parking lot on boulevard Pershing next to Hôtel Concorde LaFayette). Bus tickets must be booked 24 hours in advance; call Beauvais Airport for details or buy tickets on their Web site (see contact info above).

Trains connect Beauvais and Paris Gare du Nord (20/day, 80 min).

Taxis run from Beauvais Airport to Paris: €120 to central Paris, €11 to Beauvais' train station or city center.

Palace of Versailles

Every king's dream palace, the powerful court of Louis XIV at Versailles (vehr-"sigh") set the standard of culture for all of Europe, right up to modern times. Today, if you're planning to visit just one palace in all of Europe, make it Versailles. Versailles is undergoing a complete reorganization to better accommodate the hordes of visitors it welcomes every year. Expect some changes from the following information in entry fees and entry points.

Visiting Versailles can seem daunting because of its size. Fortunately the new changes are making it easier. There are two areas with separate entries: the all-important Château (the main palace) and the less-important Domaine de Marie-Antoinette (Marie-Antoinette's Estate).

At the château, the main palace at Versailles, the most significant change for visitors is a new color-coded entry system. Stand in the courtyard directly in front of the Château and get oriented to the various entrances. Note that red, blue, and yellow itineraries all start at the main entrance.

Red Itinerary: State and Private Apartments
Blue Itinerary: Chapel and Opera House
Yellow Itinerary: History of France Gallery
Purple Itinerary: Mesdames Apartments
Green Itinerary: Dauphin's Apartments

Ticketholders and passholders (visitors with a Versailles One-Day Pass or Paris Museum Pass) will find a specially marked line at the main entrance, allowing for quick entry. Note that tickets are not sold at the entrances of the Mesdames Apartments (open weekends only) or Dauphin's Apartments.

Cost: The **Château,** the main palace, costs €13.50 (€10 after 16:00, under 18 always free, covered by Paris Museum Pass and the Versailles One-Day Pass, below). The Château contains the **State Apartments** (with the famous Hall of Mirrors), the **Private Apartments,** the **Chapel** and **Opera House** (may be closed for renovation), the new **French History Gallery,** the **Dauphin's Apartments** (heirs to the throne), and the **Mesdames Apartments** (Louis XV's daughters); all are included with your Château ticket.

Entry to the **Domaine de Marie-Antoinette,** the estate of the queen, costs €9 (€5 after 17:00, under 18 always free, also covered by Versailles One-Day Pass, but not the Paris Museum Pass). With this ticket, you'll see the queen's Hamlet, the Grand and Petit Trianons (though the Petit Trianon may be closed for renovation), and a smattering of other nearby buildings.

The **gardens** are free, except on weekends April–Sept, when the fountains blast and the price shoots up to €7 (see "Fountain

Versailles

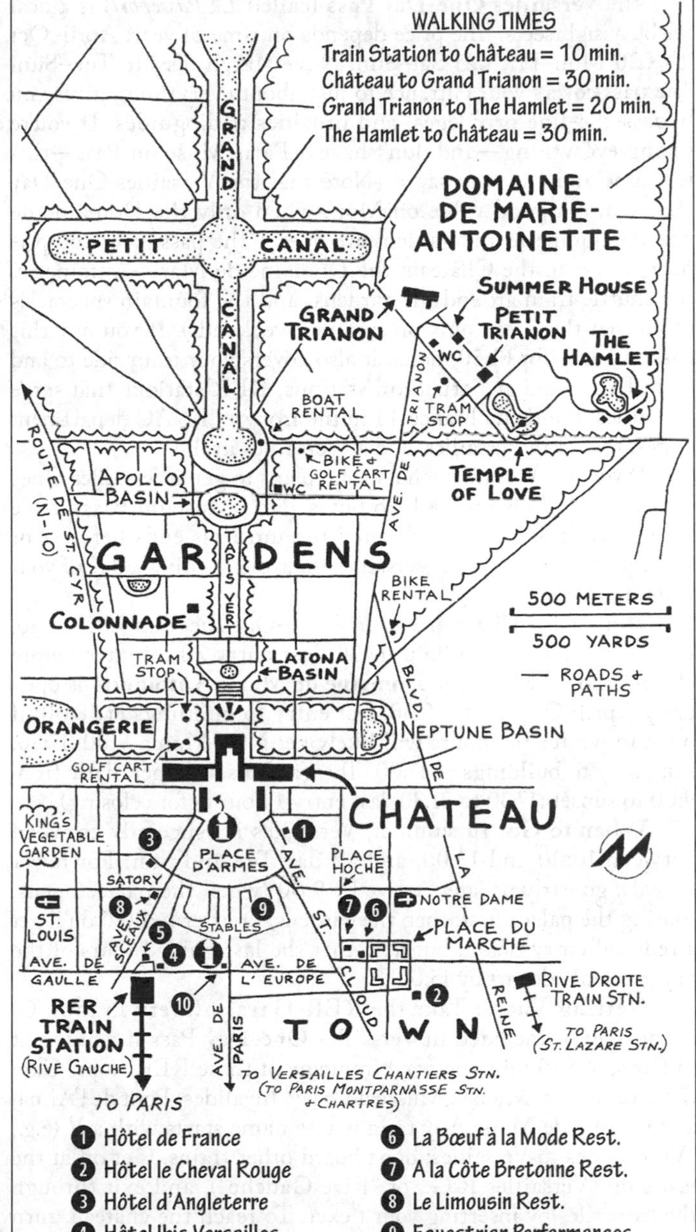
WALKING TIMES
Train Station to Château = 10 min.
Château to Grand Trianon = 30 min.
Grand Trianon to The Hamlet = 20 min.
The Hamlet to Château = 30 min.
DOMAINE DE MARIE-ANTOINETTE
GRAND CANAL
PETIT CANAL
SUMMER HOUSE
PETIT TRIANON
GRAND TRIANON
THE HAMLET
WC
BOAT RENTAL
TRAM STOP
AVE. DE TRIANON
BIKE + GOLF CART RENTAL
TEMPLE OF LOVE
ROUTE DE ST. CYR (N-10)
APOLLO BASIN
GARDENS
TAPIS VERT
BIKE RENTAL
500 METERS
500 YARDS
COLONNADE
TRAM STOP
LATONA BASIN
— ROADS + PATHS
ORANGERIE
NEPTUNE BASIN
BLVD. DE LA REINE
GOLF CART RENTAL
CHATEAU
KING'S VEGETABLE GARDEN
PLACE D'ARMES
PLACE HOCHE
AVE. ST. CLOUD
SATORY
ST. LOUIS
NOTRE DAME
AVE. SCEAUX
STABLES
PLACE DU MARCHE
AVE. DE GAULLE
AVE. DE L'EUROPE
RIVE DROITE TRAIN STN.
RER TRAIN STATION (RIVE GAUCHE)
AVE. DE PARIS
TOWN
TO PARIS (ST. LAZARE STN.)
TO VERSAILLES CHANTIERS STN. (TO PARIS MONTPARNASSE STN. + CHARTRES)
TO PARIS
1 Hôtel de France
2 Hôtel le Cheval Rouge
3 Hôtel d'Angleterre
4 Hôtel Ibis Versailles
5 Hôtel du Palais
6 La Bœuf à la Mode Rest.
7 A la Côte Bretonne Rest.
8 Le Limousin Rest.
9 Equestrian Performances
10 City of Versailles TI: Ticket Sales, Hotel Info, etc.

Spectacles," page 350).

The **Versailles One-Day Pass** (called *Le Passeport*) is a deal for busy sightseers. The price depends on time of year: April–Oct it's €20 Mon–Fri, €25 Sat–Sun; Nov–March it's €16 Tue–Sun. The pass covers your entrance to just about everything, gives you bypass-the-line privileges, and provides audioguides. If you're seeing everything—and don't have a Paris Museum Pass—this is a time and a money-saver. (Note that the Versailles One-Day Pass is not a good value on Mon, when only the Domaine de Marie-Antoinette and gardens are open.) The pass gives you priority access to the Château, the Domaine de Marie-Antoinette, the shuttle train around the gardens, and the fountain spectacles (note that these run only on summer weekends). If you buy this pass in Paris (for €1.50 more), it also covers your train ride to and from Paris (sold at Paris train stations, RER stations that serve Versailles, the Ile de France TI in the Louvre, FNAC department stores, the TI in Versailles, and at Versailles itself).

If you're a Versailles-aholic who plans to get a Versailles One-Day Pass, and also intends to buy a Paris Museum Pass, make sure the validity period of your Museum Pass ends before—or starts after—your visit to Versailles (to avoid wasting a day of your Museum Pass).

Hours: The **Château** is open April–Oct Tue–Sun 9:00–18:30, Nov–March Tue–Sun 9:00–17:30, last entry 30 minutes before closing, closed Mon. The **Domaine de Marie Antoinette** is open daily April–Oct 12:00–19:30, last entry to buildings at 18:00; if open in winter the hours will likely be: Nov–March 9:00–17:30, last entry to buildings at 17:00. The **gardens** are open daily from 9:00 to sunset (17:30 to 21:30, last entry 1 hour before closing).

When to Go: In summer, Versailles is especially crowded between 10:00 and 13:00, and all day Tue and Sun. For fewer crowds, go early or late: Arrive by 9:00 (when the palace opens, touring the palace first, then the gardens) or after 16:00 (you'll get a reduced entry ticket, but note that the last guided tours of the day generally depart by 15:00).

Getting There: Take the **RER-C train** (every 15 min, €6 round-trip or included in Versailles One-Day Pass if you buy it in Paris, 30–40 min one-way) from any of these RER stops: Gare d'Austerlitz, St. Michel, Musée d'Orsay, Invalides, Pont de l'Alma, and Champ de Mars. Any train whose name starts with a V (e.g., "Vick") goes to Versailles; don't board other trains. Get off at the last stop (Versailles R.G., or "Rive Gauche"), and exit through the turnstiles by inserting your ticket. To reach the château, turn right out of the train station, then left at the first boulevard. It's a 10-minute walk to the palace.

Your Eurailpass covers this inexpensive trip, but it uses up a valuable "flexi" day. To get free passage, show your railpass at an SCNF ticket window and get a *contremarque de passage.* Keep this ticket to exit the system.

When returning to Paris from Versailles, look through the windows past the turnstiles for the departure board. Any train leaving Versailles serves all downtown Paris RER stops on the C line (they're marked on the schedule as stopping at *"toutes les gares jusqu'à Austerlitz,"* meaning "all stations up to Austerlitz").

Taxis for the 30-minute ride between Versailles and Paris cost about €50.

It's a 30-minute drive to reach Versailles from Paris by **car,** if the traffic's not bad. Get on the *périphérique* freeway that circles Paris, and take the toll-free A13 autoroute toward Rouen. Follow signs into Versailles, then look for *château* signs and park in the huge pay lot.

Information: To plan your visit before you go, visit Versailles' good Web site at www.chateauversailles.fr (tel 01 30 83 78 00). It's easy to buy a Versailles One-Day pass at the uncrowded, helpful TI, just past the Sofitel Hôtel on your walk from the RER station to the palace (daily April–Sept 9:00–19:00, Oct–March 9:00–18:00, tel. 01 39 24 88 88, www.versailles-tourisme.com). You'll also find an information office on the left side of the Château courtyard (as you face the Château), where you can buy tickets and passes and book tours (see below). The useful *Versailles Orientation Guide* brochure explains your sightseeing options.

Guided Tours: The most popular guided tour of Versailles in English covers the Private Apartments of Louis XV and XVI (in the Château) and the Opera House (€7.50 not including palace admission—see above, 90 min). Guided visits of the Domaine de Marie-Antoinette are expected to be added in 2007 (€7.50 not including admission to Marie's estate—see above, 90 min). To take a guided tour, make reservations upon arrival at the information office in the Château courtyard, as tours can sell out by 13:00 (first tours generally begin at 10:00; last tours usually depart by 15:00). The tours can be long, but those with an appetite for palace history will enjoy them. It's smart to keep your ticket as proof you've paid for the palace entry—in case you decide to take a guided tour after you've wandered through Versailles by yourself. For a basic visit, this chapter's self-guided tour (below) works great.

Audioguide Tours: Audioguides are available for the State Apartments and the King's Private Apartments (€10 weekends, €6 weekdays, included in Versailles One-Day Pass, also covered if you pay €13.50 Château admission, but not included with Paris Museum Pass). A free audioguide version of this tour is available for users of iPods and MP3 players at www.ricksteves.com.

Length of This Tour: Allow two to three hours for the palace and two for the Domaine de Marie-Antoinette and the gardens. Add another two hours to cover your round-trip transit time, and it's a 5–10-hour day trip from Paris.

Baggage Check: There are two free checkrooms—one at the main entrance, and the other at the green entrance (Dauphin's Apartments). These do not offer "coat service," but a place to check forbidden items (food, big bags, baby carriages, and so on). If you qualify, it's free, easy, and leaves you unencumbered and better able to enjoy your time here.

WCs: Reminiscent of the days when dukes urinated behind the potted palm trees, WCs are few and far between, and come with long lines. Make a point to use the public WC just before the palace gates.

Cuisine Art: In the **palace,** the cafeteria and WCs are at the main entrance (red, blue, and yellow itineraries). There's a sandwich kiosk and a restaurant at the canal in the gardens.

In the **town,** you'll find restaurants on the street to the right of the parking lot (as you face the Château), though the best eateries line the pleasant market square, place du Marché, in the town center. A handy McDonald's is immediately across from the train station (WC without crowds, Internet café next door), and a fun assortment of appealing restaurants line rue de Satory between the station and the palace.

Photography: Allowed indoors without a flash.

Fountain Spectacles: On spring and summer weekends, classical music fills the king's backyard, and the garden's fountains are in full squirt (April–Sept Sat–Sun 10:30–12:00 & 15:00–16:30, finale 16:50–17:00). On these "spray days," the gardens cost €7 (not covered by Paris Museum Pass, ask for a map of fountains). Louis had his engineers literally reroute a river to fuel these fountains. Even by today's standards, they are impressive. Pick up the helpful *Les Grandes Eaux Musicales* brochure at any information booth. Also ask about the various impressive evening spectacles (Sat in July–Aug).

Equestrian Performances: The Equestrian Performance Academy (Academie du Spectacle Equestre) has brought the art of horseback riding back to Versailles. You can watch its rigorous training sessions, including "equestrian fencing," performed to classical music inside the main area of Versailles (€7, 60 min, shows at 10:00 and 11:00 on Thu–Sun only). The stables (Grande Ecurie)—where you can buy tickets—are across the square from the château, next to the post office. Information: tel. 01 39 02 07 14, www.acadequestre.fr.

PROVENCE

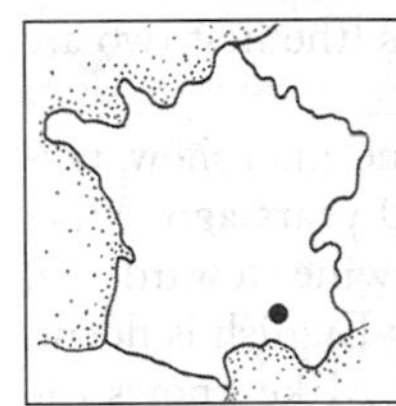

This magnificent region is shaped like a giant wedge of quiche. From its sunburned crust, fanning out along the Mediterranean coast from Nîmes to Nice, it stretches north along the Rhône Valley to Orange. The Romans were here in force and left many ruins—some of the best anywhere. Seven popes; great artists such as van Gogh, Cézanne, and Picasso; and author Peter Mayle all enjoyed their years in Provence. The region offers a splendid recipe of arid climate (except for occasional vicious winds, known as the mistral), captivating cities, exciting hill towns, dramatic scenery, and oceans of vineyards.

Explore France's greatest Roman ruin, Pont du Gard. Spend your starry, starry nights where van Gogh did, in Arles. Uncover its Roman past, then find the linger-longer squares and café corners that inspired Vincent. Youthful but classy Avignon bustles in the shadow of its brooding pope's palace. It's a short hop from Arles or Avignon into the splendid scenery and villages of the Côtes du Rhône and Luberon regions that make Provence so popular today.

Planning Your Time

Make Arles or Avignon your sightseeing base, particularly if you have no car. Arles has a blue-collar quality and good-value hotels, while Avignon (three times larger than Arles) feels sophisticated and offers more nightlife and shopping. Italophiles prefer smaller Arles, while poodles pick urban Avignon.

You'll want a full day for sightseeing in Arles (best on Wed or Sat, when the morning market rages), a half-day for Avignon, and a day or two for the villages and sights in the countryside.

Getting Around Provence

By Car: The Michelin map #528 is good for drivers and covers the Riviera as well as Provence (map #332 also works, but covers only Provence). Avignon (pop. 100,000) is a headache for drivers; Arles (pop. 35,000) is easier, though it still requires go-cart driving skills. Park only in well-watched spaces, and leave nothing in your car.

By Train or Bus: Travelers relying on public transportation might find their choices limited. Public transit is good between cities and decent to some towns, but marginal at best to the villages. Frequent trains link Avignon and Arles (about 30 min between each). The Pont du Gard—and, to a lesser extent, Vaison la Romaine and some Côtes du Rhône villages—are also connected by bus from Avignon.

Tours of Provence

Local TIs have brochures on all of these excursions and can help you make a reservation. Here are several options (the first two are best):

Wine Safari—Dutchman Mike Rijken runs a one-man show, taking travelers through the region he adopted 20 years ago. Mike came to France to train as a chef, later became a wine steward, and has now found his calling as a driver/guide. His English is fluent, and while his focus is wine and wine villages, Mike knows the region thoroughly and is a good teacher of its history (€45/half-day, €90/day, priced per person, tel. 04 90 35 59 21, mobile 06 19 29 50 81, www.winesafari.net, mikeswinesafari@wanadoo.fr).

Taxi des Oliviers—Friendly Roland Vanove offers tours with English commentary. His air-conditioned minivan has room for up to eight people (same price regardless of how many). He'll take you wherever you like in his native Provence, or to the Riviera (no pre-set itineraries). Roland's services are a boon for car-less visitors wanting to explore the Luberon and the Côtes du Rhône villages near Vaison la Romaine (€150/half-day, €250/day, best to contact by phone, tel. 06 80 75 40 90, taxidesoliviers@wanadoo.fr).

Visit Provence—This tour company, based in Avignon, offers a good variety of guided tours in eight-seat minivans with English commentary (about €50/half-day, €100/day; they'll pick you up at your hotel in Avignon). For example, a half-day tour to both the Châteauneuf-du-Pape vineyards (with wine-tasting) and Orange (including Triumphal Arch, Roman Theater, and audioguide for theater) costs €50. Other day trips include Les Baux and Arles; and St. Rémy, Les Baux, and Pont du Gard. Not all tours include entry fees for sights, but reservations are required for all (tel. 04 90 14 70 00, www.provence-reservation.com).

Lieutaud—This company operates cheap, unguided big-bus excursions from Avignon to many hard-to-reach places at a fraction

Provence

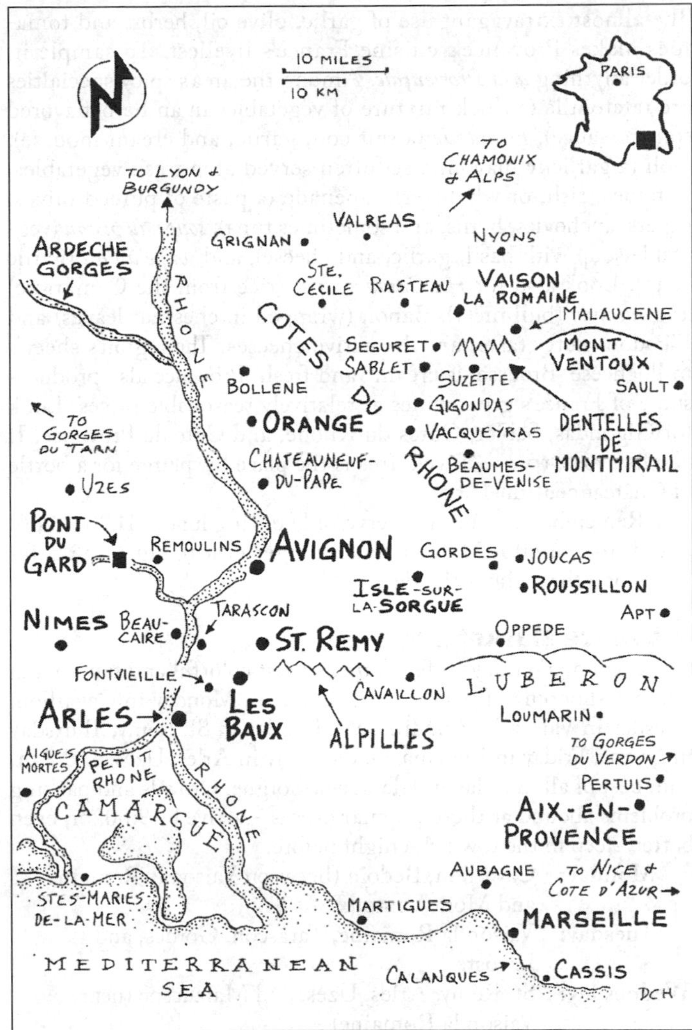

of the price you'd pay for a taxi (admission fees not included). Different itineraries are available each day, and can change with the season. Trips often include Pont du Gard (€15/half-day, 3/week); Châteauneuf-du-Pape and Orange (€22/half-day, 1/week, usually Mon); and Les Baux and the Alpilles Mountains (€22/half-day, 1/week). The departure point is outside Lieutaud's offices in Avignon, between the train station and the Grand Hôtel (tel. 04 90 86 36 75, www.cars-lieutaud.fr).

Cuisine Scene in Provence

The almost extravagant use of garlic, olive oil, herbs, and tomatoes makes Provence's cuisine France's liveliest. To sample it, order anything *à la Provençale.* Among the area's spicy specialties are ratatouille (a thick mixture of vegetables in an herb-flavored tomato sauce), *brandade* (a salt cod, garlic, and cream mousse), aioli (a garlicky mayonnaise, often served atop fresh vegetables, potatoes, fish, or whatever), tapenade (a paste of pureed olives, capers, anchovies, herbs, and sometimes tuna), *soupe au pistou* (vegetable soup with basil, garlic, and cheese), and *soupe à l'ail* (garlic soup). Look also for *riz Camarguaise* (rice from the Camargue) and *taureau* (bull meat). Banon (wrapped in chestnut leaves) and Picodon (nutty taste) are the native cheeses. The region's sheep's milk cheese, Brousse, is creamy and fresh. Provence also produces some of France's great wines at relatively reasonable prices. Look for Gigondas, Sablet, Côtes du Rhône, and Côte de Provence. If you like rosé, try the Tavel. This is the place to splurge for a bottle of Châteauneuf-du-Pape.

Remember, restaurants serve only during lunch (11:30–14:00) and dinner (19:00–21:00, later in bigger cities), but some cafés serve food throughout the day.

Provence Market Days

Provençal market days offer France's most colorful and tantalizing outdoor shopping. The best markets are on Monday in Cavaillon, Tuesday in Vaison la Romaine, Wednesday in St. Rémy, Thursday in Nyons, Friday in Lourmarin, Saturday in Arles, Uzès, and Apt, and, best of all, Sunday in Isle-sur-la-Sorgue. Crowds and parking problems abound at these popular events—arrive by 9:00, or, even better, sleep in the town the night before.

Monday: Cavaillon, Bedoin (between Vaison la Romaine and Mont Ventoux)

Tuesday: Vaison la Romaine, Tarascon, Gordes, and Lacoste

Wednesday: St. Rémy, Arles, Uzès, and Malaucène (near Vaison la Romaine)

Thursday: Nyons, Beaucaire, Vacqueyras, Roussillon, and Isle-sur-la-Sorgue

Friday: Lourmarin, Remoulins (near Pont du Gard), Bonnieux, and Châteauneuf-du-Pape

Saturday: Arles, Uzès, Apt, and Valréas (north of Vaison la Romaine)

Sunday: Isle-sur-la-Sorgue, Coustellet, Mausanne (near Les Baux), and Beaucaire

Arles

By helping Julius Caesar defeat Marseille, Arles (pronounced "arl") earned the imperial nod and was made an important port city. With the first bridge over the Rhône River, Arles was a key stop on the Roman road from Italy to Spain, the Via Domitia. After reigning as the seat of an important archbishop and a trading center for centuries, the city became a sleepy backwater of little importance in the 1700s. Vincent van Gogh settled here a hundred years ago, but left only a chunk of his ear (now gone). American bombers destroyed much of Arles in World War II as the townsfolk hid out in its underground Roman galleries. But today Arles thrives again, with its evocative Roman ruins, an eclectic assortment of museums, made-for-ice-cream pedestrian zones, and squares that play hide-and-seek with visitors. It's an understandably popular home base from which to explore Provence.

ORIENTATION

Arles faces the Mediterranean and turns its back on Paris. While the town is built along the Rhône, it completely ignores the river (it was the part of Arles most damaged by Allied bombers in World War II, and therefore the least appealing today).

Landmarks hide in Arles' medieval tangle of narrow, winding streets. Virtually everything is close—but first-time visitors can walk forever to get there. Hotels have good, free city maps, and Arles provides helpful street-corner signs that point you toward sights and hotels. Racing cars enjoy Arles' medieval lanes, turning sidewalks into tightropes and pedestrians into leaping targets.

Tourist Information

The main TI is on the ring road, boulevard des Lices, at esplanade Charles de Gaulle (April–Sept daily 9:00–18:45; Oct–March Mon–Sat 9:00–16:45, Sun 10:00–12:45; tel. 04 90 18 41 20, www.tourisme.ville-arles.fr). There's also a TI at the train station (Mon–Sat 9:00–13:00, closed Sun). Pick up the city map with current museum prices and hours, note the bus schedules, and get English information on nearby destinations. Ask about bullgames (Provence's more humane version of bullfights—see page 364) and walking tours of Arles. If you're a van Gogh fan, buy the €1 brochure locating his "easels". Both TIs charge €1 to reserve hotel rooms (you'll pay a small fraction of the room price here, and the rest at the hotel).

Arrival in Arles

By Train and Bus: The train station is on the river, a 10-minute walk from the town center (baggage storage not available). Next door is one of Arles' two bus stations, called Gare Routière. Before heading into town, get what you need at the train station TI (see above). To reach the town center, turn left out of the train station, or take bus #3 from the shelter directly across from the station (2/hr, €0.80, buy ticket from driver). There's no taxi stand, ask at the TI or call 04 90 96 90 03 (rates are fixed, allow about €9 to any of my recommended hotels). Arles' other bus station, called Centre-Ville, is at 16 boulevard Clemenceau, two blocks below the main TI on boulevard des Lices (next to Café le Wilson).

By Car: Most hotels have nearby parking—ask for detailed directions. Arles' only parking structure is Parking des Lices, near the TI on boulevard des Lices (€7/24 hours). Otherwise, follow signs to *Centre-Ville*, then *Gare SNCF* (train station). You'll come to a huge roundabout (place Lamartine) with a Monoprix department store to the right. You can park along the city wall or in nearby lots; pay attention to *No Parking* signs on Wednesday and Saturday until 13:00 (violators will be towed to make way for Arles' huge outdoor produce markets). Theft is a big problem; leave nothing in your car, and trust your hotelier's advice on where to park. From place Lamartine, walk into the city between the two stumpy towers. From here, the hotels I list are no more than a 10-minute walk away.

Helpful Hints

Market Days: The big markets are on Wednesdays and Saturdays. For all the details, see page 364.

Supermarket: A big, handy **Monoprix** supermarket/department store is on place Lamartine (Mon–Sat 8:30–19:25, closed Sun).

Internet Access: Arles has many Internet cafés—ask at the TI. **Cyber City** is central (open daily, 41 rue du 4 Septembre, tel. 04 90 96 87 76), but **Cyber Espace** has longer hours (daily 8:00–23:00, 10 boulevard Gambetta, tel. 04 90 52 51 30).

Laundry: There's a launderette at 12 rue Portagnel (daily 7:00–21:00, you can stay later to finish if you're already inside, English instructions).

Bike Rental: Try the **Peugeot store** (15 rue du Pont, tel. 04 90 96 03 77).

Car Rental: Avis is at the train station (tel. 04 90 96 82 42), **Europcar** and **Hertz** are downtown (2 bis avenue Victor Hugo, Europcar tel. 04 90 93 23 24, Hertz tel. 04 90 96 75 23), and **Sixt** is just off place Lamartine toward the station (4 avenue Paulin Talabot, tel. 04 90 93 02 17).

Local Guide: Charming Jacqueline Neujean, an excellent guide, knows Arles and nearby sights intimately, and loves her work (€90/2 hrs, tel. 04 90 98 47 51).

Language and Cooking Courses: Food- or language-lovers might enjoy a class offered by outgoing American (and Arles resident) Madeleine Vedel and her French husband, Eric. In addition to renting out rooms (see Maison d'Hôtes en Provence under "Sleeping," page 365), they present a wide range of cooking and language-learning experiences (www.cuisineprovencale.com).

Public Pools: Arles has three public pools (indoor and outdoor). Ask at the TI or your hotel.

Boules: The local "*boul*ing alley" is by the river on place Lamartine. After their afternoon naps, the old boys congregate here for a game of *pétanque*—it's fun to watch this popular local pastime.

Getting Around Arles

In this flat city, everything's within walking distance. Only the Ancient History Museum requires a long walk (take a taxi for €9, or a public bus for €0.80—details in listing on page 359). The elevated riverside promenade provides Rhône views and a direct (if odorous) route to the Ancient History Museum (to the southwest) and the train and bus stations (to the northeast). Keep your head up for *Starry Night* memories, but eyes down for decorations by dogs with poorly trained owners.

Arles' **taxis** charge a set fee of about €9, but nothing except the Ancient History Museum is worth a taxi ride. To call a cab, dial 04 90 96 90 03.

SIGHTS AND ACTIVITIES

The worthwhile **Monument Pass** *(le pass monuments)* covers almost all of Arles' sights (adults-€13.50, under 18-€12, sold at each sight except the Arlaten Folk Museum; Fondation Van Gogh discounted, but not fully covered). The less-tempting €9 ***Circuit Romain*** ticket covers Arles' four Roman sights, but not the Ancient History Museum. With no pass, you'll pay €3–5.50 per sight. While any sight is worth a few minutes, many aren't worth the individual admission.

Start at the Ancient History Museum for a helpful overview (drivers should try to do this museum on their way into Arles), then dive into the city-center sights. Remember, many sights stop selling tickets 30–60 minutes before closing (both before lunch and at the end of the day).

Arles

Van Gogh Sights
1 Place Lamartine
2 Hôtel Terminus et Van Gogh
3 Starry Night Over the Rhône View
4 Fondation Van Gogh
5 Place du Forum (Café Van Gogh)
6 Espace Van Gogh
Other
7 Europcar & Hertz Car Rentals
8 Launderette
9 Internet Café (2)
10 Sixt Car Rental
11 Avis Car Rental
100 YARDS
100 METERS
N
FORUM SQUARE
P - PARKING
B - BUS STOP
- VIEW
TO LES BAUX, FONTVIEILLE & AVIGNON
TO TRAIN & BUS STATIONS & 11
AVE. STALIN
MONOPRIX
PLACE LAM.
PETANQUE
GATE
RHONE
RUE JULES FERRY
QUAI LAMARTINE
RUE JOUVEAU
CAVALERIE
R. L. BLUM
REATTU MUSEUM
TO ANCIENT HISTORY MUSEUM
QUAI MARX DORMOY
PLACE VOLTAIRE
R. CONDOR.
RUE DU GRAND PRIEURE
RUE QUATRE SEPT.
R. AMPH.
VOLTAIRE
RUE PORTAGNEL
R. TARDIEU
RUE
RUE DU SUISSES
SAUVAGE
RUE DE HOTEL DE VILLE
DR. FANTON
RUE REFUGE
ROMAN ARENA
RUE DES ARENES
R. LIBERTE
R. DIDEROT
FOND. V.G.
TO 9
R. BALZE
RUE CALADE
WC
ST. TROPHIME
PLACE REPUB.
RUE DE CLOITRE
RUE DE LA REPUBLIQUE
PORTE DE LAURE
ANCIENT CITY WALLS
CLASSICAL THEATER
ARLATEN FOLK MUSEUM
JARDIN D'ETE
CLOISTER
BD. E. COMBES
VAN GOGH HOSPITAL
MONTEE VAUBAN
BLVD. DES LICES
POST & TAXIS
PLAYGROUND
V. HUGO
TO ANCIENT HISTORY MUSEUM
R. E. FASSIN
TO LES AYLSCAMPS CEMETERY
DCH

Provence

Ancient History Museum (Musée de l'Arles et de la Provence Antiques)

Begin your Arles tour here—it's Roman Arles 101, worth ▲▲. On the site of the Roman chariot racecourse (the arc of which is built into the parking lot), this air-conditioned, all-on-one-floor museum is just west of central Arles along the river. Models and original sculptures (with almost no English translations) re-create the Roman city, making work-a-day life and culture easier to imagine.

You're greeted by an impressive row of pagan and early-Christian sarcophagi (from the second to fifth centuries). These would have lined the Via Aurelia outside the town wall. In the early days of the Church, Jesus was often portrayed beardless and as the good shepherd, with a lamb over his shoulder (see relief at end of ramp, #41).

Next, you'll find models of every Roman structure in (and near) Arles. These are the highlight for me, as they breathe a little life into buildings as they looked 2,000 years ago. Find the Forum (still the center of town, though only two columns survive today); the pontoon bridge (over the widest, and therefore slowest, part of the river); the Arena (with its moveable stadium cover, which sheltered spectators from sun or rain); and the Circus, or chariot racecourse (while long gone, it must have been like Rome's Circus Maximus in its day—its obelisk is now the centerpiece of Arles' place de la République).

The model of the Roman city shows that an emphasis on sports—with the Arena and huge stadium—is not unique to modern America. It also illustrates how little Arles seems to have changed over two millennia—warehouses still on the opposite side of the river and houses clustered around the city center.

All of the museum's statues are original, except for the greatest—the *Venus of Arles*, which Louis XIV took a liking to and had moved to Versailles. It's now in the Louvre (and, as locals say, "When it's in Paris...bye-bye"). Jewelry, fine metal and glass artifacts, and well-crafted mosaic floors make it clear that Roman Arles was a city of art and culture.

Cost, Hours, Location: €5.50, covered by Monument Pass, daily April–Oct 9:00–19:00, Nov–March 10:00–17:00, presqu'île du Cirque Romain.

Information: There's no English information because "there's never been any English information." But there are free 90-minute English tours July–Sept daily at 17:00. Tel. 04 90 18 88 88, www.arles-antique.org.

Getting There: To reach the museum by **foot** from the city center (a 25-min walk), turn left at the river and take the riverside path to the big, modern building just past the new bridge. The

taxi ride costs €9 (museum can call a taxi for your return). **Bus** #1 gets you within a five-minute walk (€0.80, 3/hr, daily except Sun). Catch the bus in Arles on boulevard des Lices, then get off at the Musée de l'Arles Antique stop and follow the signs (to your left as you step off the bus).

In Central Arles

Ideally, visit these sights in the order listed below. I've included some walking directions to connect the dots.

▲▲Forum Square (Place du Forum)—Named for the Roman forum that once stood here, this was the political and religious center of Roman Arles. Still lively, this café-crammed square is a local watering hole and popular for a *pastis* (see "Eating," page 368). The bistros on the square, while no place for a fine dinner, can put together a good-enough salad or *plat du jour*—and when you sprinkle on the ambience, that's €10 well spent.

At the corner of Grand Hôtel Nord-Pinus, a plaque shows how the Romans built a foundation of galleries to make the main square level. The two columns are all that survive of a temple. Steps leading to the entrance are buried (the Roman street level was about 20 feet below you).

The statue on the square is of **Frédéric Mistral** (1830–1914). This popular poet, who wrote in the local dialect rather than French, was a champion of Provençal culture. After receiving the Nobel Prize in Literature in 1904, Mistral used his prize money to preserve and display the folk identity of Provence. He founded the regional folk museum (see "Arlaten Folk Museum," page 363) at a time when France was rapidly centralizing. (The local mistral wind—literally, "master"—has nothing to do with his name.)

The **bright yellow café** is famous as the subject of one of Vincent van Gogh's most famous works in Arles. While his painting showed the café in a brilliant yellow from the glow of gas lamps, the facade was bare limestone, just like the other cafés on this square. The café's current owners have painted it to match van Gogh's version...and to cash in on the Vincent-crazed hordes who pay too much to eat or drink here.

• *A few blocks up rue du Hôtel de Ville (away from the river), you'll find the big...*

Republic Square (Place de la République)—This square used to be called "place Royale"...until the French Revolution. The obelisk was the centerpiece of Arles' Roman Circus. The lions at its base are the symbol of the city, whose slogan is (roughly) "the gentle lion." Find a seat and watch the peasants—pilgrims, locals, and street musicians. There's nothing new about this scene.

• *Overlooking this square is...*

St. Trophime Church—Named after a third-century bishop of Arles and located on a large square, this church sports the finest Romanesque main entrance (west portal) I've seen anywhere.

Like a Roman triumphal arch, the church facade trumpets the promise of Judgment Day. The tympanum (the semicircular area above the door) is filled with Christian symbolism. Christ sits in majesty, surrounded by symbols of the four evangelists: Matthew—the winged man, Mark—the winged lion, Luke—the ox, and John—the eagle. The 12 apostles are lined up below Jesus. It's Judgment Day...some are saved and others aren't. Notice the condemned (on the right)—a chain gang doing a sad bunny-hop over the fires of hell. For them, the tune trumpeted by the three angels above Christ is not a happy one. Below the chain gang, St. Stephen is being stoned to death, with his soul leaving through his mouth and instantly being welcomed by angels. Ride the exquisite detail back to a simpler age. In an illiterate medieval world, long before the vivid images of our Technicolor time, this was a neon billboard over the town square.

There's no charge to enter the church (daily April–Sept 9:00–12:00 & 14:00–18:30, Oct–March 9:00–12:00 & 14:00–17:00). A handy chart just inside the door on the right locates the interior highlights and helps explain the carvings you just saw on the tympanum.

The tall, 12th-century Romanesque nave is decorated by a set of tapestries showing scenes from the life of Mary (17th century, from French town of Aubusson). Immediately to the left of the entry is a chapel built on an early-Christian sarcophagus from Roman Arles (from around A.D. 300). The heads were lopped off during the French Revolution. On its right side (a dark niche, cut into the wall), the three Magi give gifts to the Baby Jesus, and a frieze below shows the flight to Egypt. Amble around the Gothic apse. Just to the left of the high altar, check out the relic chapel—with its fine golden boxes that hold long-venerated bones of obscure saints. This church is a stop on the ancient pilgrimage route to Santiago de Compostela in northwest Spain. For 800 years, pilgrims on their way to Santiago have paused here...and they still do today. As you leave, notice the modern-day pilgrimages advertised on the far right near the church's entry.

• *Leaving the church, turn left, then left again through a courtyard to enter the cloisters.*

The adjacent **cloisters** are interesting, with many small columns that were scavenged from the ancient Roman theater. Enjoy the sculpted capitals, the rounded 12th-century Romanesque arches, and the pointed 14th-century Gothic ones. On the second floor, you'll walk an angled rooftop designed to catch rainwater—

notice the slanted gutter that channeled the water into a cistern (€3.50, same hours as church).

• *To get to the next sight (the Classical Theater), face the church, walk left, then take the first right on rue de la Calade.*

Classical Theater (Théâtre Antique)—This first-century B.C. Roman theater once seated 10,000. In the Middle Ages, it served as a convenient town quarry—precious little of the original theater survives. Walk to a center aisle and pull up a stone seat. To appreciate its original size, look to the upper-left side of the tower and find the protrusion that supported the highest of three seating levels. Today, 3,000 can attend events here. Two lonely Corinthian columns look out from the stage over the audience. The orchestra section is defined by a semicircular pattern in the stone. Stepping up onto the left side of the stage, look down to the slender channel that allowed the curtain to disappear below, like magic. Go backstage and browse through broken bits of Rome, and loop back to the entry behind the grass (€3, covered by Monument Pass, daily May–Sept 9:00–18:00, March–April and Oct 9:00–13:00 & 14:00–17:30, Nov–Feb 10:00–11:30 & 14:00–16:30). Before paying the €3, consider peeking in over the fence from rue du Cloître, from which you can see just about everything for free.

• *A block uphill is the...*

▲▲▲Roman Arena (Amphithéâtre)—Nearly 2,000 years ago, gladiators fought wild animals here to the delight of 20,000 screaming fans. Today, local daredevils still fight wild animals here—bullgame posters around the Arena advertise upcoming spectacles (see "Bullgames," below). A lengthy restoration process is well underway, giving the amphitheater an almost bleached-teeth whiteness.

In Roman times, games were free (sponsored by city bigwigs) and fans were seated by social class. The many exits allowed for rapid dispersal after the games—fights would break out among frenzied fans if they couldn't leave quickly. Through medieval times and until the early 1800s, the arches were bricked up and the stadium became a fortified town—with 200 humble homes crammed within its circular defenses. Three of the medieval towers survive (the one above the ticket booth is open and rewards those who climb it with a good view). To see two still-sealed arches—complete with cute medieval window frames—turn right as you leave, walk to the Andaluz restaurant, and look back (€5.50, covered by Monument Pass, daily May–Sept 9:00–18:00, March–April and Oct 9:00–17:30, Nov–Feb 9:00–16:30, tel. 08 91 70 03 70, www.arenes-arles.com).

• *Turn left out of the Arena and walk uphill to find the...*

▲▲Fondation Van Gogh—Refreshing to any art lover, and especially interesting to van Gogh fans, this small gallery features works by contemporary artists who pay homage to Vincent through thought-provoking interpretations of his works. Many pieces are explained in English by the artists. The black-and-white photographs (both art and shots of places Vincent painted) complement the paintings. Unfortunately, this collection is often on the road July through September, when non–van Gogh material is shown (€7, €5 with Monument Pass, great collection of van Gogh prints and postcards for sale in free entry area; June daily 10:00–18:00; July–Sept daily 10:00–19:00; Oct–May Tue–Sun 10:00–18:00, closed Mon; facing Arena at 24 bis rond-point des Arènes, tel. 04 90 49 94 04, www.fondationvangogh-arles.org).

▲Arlaten Folk Museum (Musée Arlaten/Museon Arlaten)—Built on the remains of the Roman Forum (first century A.D., see the courtyard), this museum houses the treasures of daily Provençal life.

A one-way route takes you through 30 rooms and past guards in traditional dress. The first few rooms display folk costumes chronologically until about 1900, when the traditional garb was replaced by the modern, nondescript norm. Portraits of people are matched with glass cases of artifacts that may have been part of their lives. You'll then see free-standing wedding armoires, which were given to brides by parents and filled with essentials to begin a new home. Finely crafted wooden cages—called *panetières*—hung from walls and kept bread away from mice. *Santons* were popular figurines giving local nativity scenes a Provençal look.

The second floor shows local history, and a large room covers lifestyles of residents of the marshy Camargue. A round thatched hut demonstrates how life was tailored to survive the constant mistral wind. A fascinating case shows antique bullfighting memorabilia, including this region's unique hooks and ribbons used in *courses camarguaises* (see page 364) and a stuffed champion bull named Lion, who died of old age.

The last rooms display two dioramas, the museum's pride and joy. In one, a wealthy mom is shown with her newborn. Her friends visit with gifts representing four physical and moral qualities hoped for in a new baby—good as bread, full as an egg, wise as salt, and straight as a match. The cradle is fully stocked with everything needed to raise an infant in 1888.

The next room shows "the great supper"—a traditional feast served on Christmas Eve before midnight Mass. It's 1860, and everything on the table is locally produced. Traditionally, 13 sweets—for Jesus and the 12 apostles—were served. Grandma and grandpa warm themselves in front of the fireplace; grandpa pours wine on a log for good luck in the coming year (€4, covered by Monument Pass, free first Sun and last Wed of the month; open July–Sept daily 9:00–13:00 & 14:00–18:30; Oct–June Tue–Sun

9:30–12:30 & 14:00–17:00, sometimes until 18:00, closed Mon; last entry 1 hour before closing, enjoyable audioguide-€2, 29 rue de la République, tel. 04 90 96 08 23, www.cg13.fr).

Réattu Museum (Musée Réattu)—Housed in a beautiful 15th-century mansion, this mildly interesting, mostly modern art collection includes 57 Picasso drawings (some two-sided and all done in a flurry of creativity—I liked the bullfights best), a room of Henri Rousseau's Camargue watercolors, and an unfinished painting by the Neoclassical artist Jacques Réattu...but none with English explanations (€5.50, covered by Monument Pass, extra for special exhibits, daily July–Aug 10:00–19:00, March–June and Sept–Nov 10:00–12:30 & 14:00–18:30, Dec–Feb 13:00–18:00, last entry 30 min before closing for lunch or at end of day, 10 rue du Grand Prieuré, tel. 04 90 96 37 68).

▲▲Wednesday and Saturday Markets—Twice a week in the morning, Arles' ring road erupts into an open-air market of fish, flowers, produce, and you-name-its. The Wednesday market runs along boulevard Emile Combes, between place Lamartine and avenue Victor Hugo; the segment nearest place Lamartine is all about food, and the upper half is about clothing, tablecloths, purses, and so on. On the first Wednesday of the month, it's a flea market, with less produce. The Saturday market is along boulevard des Lices near the TI. Join in, buy flowers, try the olives, sample some wine, and swat a pickpocket. Both markets are open until 12:00.

▲▲Bullgames (Courses Camarguaises)—Occupy the same seats fans have used for nearly 2,000 years, and take in Arles' most memorable experience—the *courses camarguaise* in the ancient Arena. These non-violent "bullgames" are more sporting than bloody Spanish bullfights. The bulls of Arles (who, locals stress, "die of old age") are promoted in posters even more boldly than their human foes. In the bullgame, a ribbon *(cocarde)* is laced between the bull's horns. The *razeteur*, with a special hook, has 15 minutes to snare the ribbon. Local businessmen encourage a *razeteur* (dressed in white with a red cummerbund) by shouting out how much money they'll pay for the *cocarde*. If the bull pulls a good stunt, the band plays the famous "Toreador" song from *Carmen*. The following day, newspapers report on the games, including how many *Carmen*s the bull earned.

Three classes of bullgames—determined by the experience of the *razeteurs*—are advertised in posters: The *course de protection* is for rookies. The *trophée de l'Avenir* comes with more experience. And the *trophée des As* features top professionals. During Easter and the fall rice harvest festival (Féria du Riz), the Arena hosts actual Spanish bullfights (look for *corrida*) with outfits, swords, spikes, and the whole gory shebang. Bullgame tickets run €5–15, while bloody bullfights *(corrida)* are pricier (€12–80). Schedules change every year—ask at the TI or check online at www.arenes-arles.com (in 2006, the bullgames were every Wed at 17:00 in June–Aug).

Don't pass on a chance to see *Toro Piscine,* a silly spectacle for warm summer evenings where the bull ends up in a swimming pool (uh-huh...get more details at TI). Nearby villages stage *courses camarguaises* in small wooden bullrings nearly every weekend; the TI has the latest schedule.

SLEEPING

In Arles

Hotels are a great value here; many are air-conditioned, though few have elevators. The Calendal, Musée, and Régence hotels offer exceptional value.

$$$ Hôtel Calendal,** located between the Arena and Classical Theater, is Provençal chic and does everything right. Its comfortable rooms, in all shapes and sizes, surround a large, palm-shaded courtyard. Enjoy the great €8 buffet breakfast, the €14 salad-and-pasta lunch buffet, the children's play area, and the seductive ambience. They even have my Provence video on DVD in the lobby (smallest Db-€47, standard Db-€72–85, Db with balcony-€90–100, price depends on room size, air-con, free Internet access, reserve ahead for parking-€10, just above Arena at 5 rue Porte de Laure, tel. 04 90 96 11 89, fax 04 90 96 05 84, www.lecalendal.com, contact@lecalendal.com).

$$$ Hôtel d'Arlatan*,** built over the site of a Roman basilica, is classy in every sense of the word. It has sumptuous public spaces, a tranquil terrace, a designer pool, a turtle pond, and antique-filled rooms, most with high, wood-beamed ceilings and stone walls. In

Sleep Code

(€1 = about $1.30, country code: 33)
S = Single, **D** = Double/Twin, **T** = Triple, **Q** = Quad, **b** = bathroom, **s** = shower only, ***** = French hotel rating system (0–4 stars). Unless otherwise noted, credit cards are accepted and English is spoken.

To help you sort easily through these listings, I've divided the rooms into three categories based on the price for a standard double room with bath:

$$$ Higher Priced—Most rooms €80 or more.
$$ Moderately Priced—Most rooms between €55–80.
$ Lower Priced—Most rooms €55 or less.

the lobby of this 15th-century building, a glass floor looks down into Roman ruins (smallest Db-€90, standard Db-€105–120, bigger Db-€120–155, Db/Qb suites-€180–250, excellent buffet breakfast-€11, air-con, bathrobes, ice machines, elevator, parking-€11, 1 block below place du Forum at 26 rue Sauvage, tel. 04 90 93 56 66, fax 04 90 49 68 45, www.hotel-arlatan.fr, hotel-arlatan@wanadoo.fr, contact@hotel-arlatan.fr).

$$ Hôtel du Musée** is a quiet and affordable manor-home hideaway tucked deep in Arles. This delightful refuge comes with 28 air-conditioned rooms, a flowery two-tiered courtyard, and a snazzy art-gallery lounge. The rooms in the new section are worth the few extra euros and steps. Claude and English-speaking Laurence, the gracious owners, are eager to help (Sb-€43–50, Db-€55–65, Tb-€70–80, Qb-€85, higher prices are for new section, buffet breakfast-€7, parking-€7, follow signs to Réattu Museum, 11 rue du Grand Prieuré, tel. 04 90 93 88 88, fax 04 90 49 98 15, www.hoteldumusee.com, contact@hoteldumusee.com).

$$ Hôtel de la Muette**, with on-the-ball owners Brigitte and Alain, is a good choice. Located in a quiet corner of Arles, this low-key hotel is well-kept, with stone walls, wood beams, and air-conditioning (Db-€48–65, Tb-€65–70, Qb-€80, buffet breakfast with eggs-€8, no elevator, Internet access, Wi-Fi likely, parking-€7, 15 rue des Suisses, tel. 04 90 96 15 39, fax 04 90 49 73 16, www.hotel-muette.com, hotel.muette@wanadoo.fr).

$$ Maison d'Hôtes en Provence, run by engaging American Madeleine and her soft-spoken French husband Eric, combines an interesting B&B experience—four spacious and funky-but-comfy rooms—with optional Provençal cooking workshops. Foodies should check out their website for its affordable range of gourmet classes (Db-€65, extra person-€15, good family room, across from launderette at 11 rue Portagnel, tel. & fax 04 90 49 69 20, www.cuisineprovencale.com, actvedel@wanadoo.fr).

$$ Hôtel le Cloître** was originally the cloister provost's residence. Caring owners Jean-François and Agnes run a warm, ramshackle place with 30 worn but character-filled rooms (no air-conditioning or elevator). The best rooms are on the first floor (Ss or Ds-€40, Sb or Db-€49, bigger Db-€60–65, Tb-€65, Qb-€75, breakfast-€6, parking-€5, closed Nov–mid-March, 16 rue du Cloître, tel. 04 90 96 29 50, fax 04 90 96 02 88, www.hotelcloitre.com, hotel_cloitre@hotmail.com).

$ Hôtel Régence**, about the best deal in Arles, has a riverfront location, immaculate, comfortable Provençal rooms, good beds, safe parking, and easy access to the train station (Db-€40–50, Tb-€50–60, Qb-€60–70, good buffet breakfast-€5, choose river view or quieter courtyard rooms, most rooms have showers, air-con, no elevator but only 2 floors, Internet and Wi-Fi access,

Arles Hotels and Restaurants

1 Hôtel d'Arlatan
2 Bistrot à Vins Restaurant
3 Hôtel du Musée
4 Hôtel Calendal
5 Hôtel Régence
6 Hôtel Acacias
7 Hôtel Voltaire
8 Hôtel de la Muette
9 Maison d'Hôtes en Provence
10 Hôtel le Cloître
11 Restaurants le 16, Au Bryn du Thym & la Paillotte
12 La Bohème Rest.
13 La Cuisine de Comptoir Rest.
14 Le Grillon Rest.
15 Soleilei Ice Cream
16 Café de la Major (Coffee/Tea)
17 L'Atelier Restaurant
100 YARDS
100 METERS
FORUM SQUARE
B - BUS STOP
P - PARKING
- VIEW
TO LES BAUX, FONTVIEILLE & AVIGNON
TO TRAIN + BUS STATIONS
AVE. STALIN.
MONOPRIX
PLACE LAM.
PETANQUE
GATE
RHONE
RUE JULES FERRY
RUE JOUVEAU
CAVALERIE
QUAI LAMARTINE
RUE R.L. BLUM
PLACE VOLTAIRE
R. CONDOR.
REATTU MUSEUM
TO ANCIENT HISTORY MUSEUM
QUAI MARX DORMOY
RUE DU GRAND PRIEURE
RUE DU QUATRE SEPT.
R. AMPH.
VOLTAIRE
R. TARDIEU
RUE PORTAGNEL
RUE DU SUISSES
SAUVAGE
HOTEL DE VILLE
RUE REFUGE
DR. FANTON
R. LIBERTE
RUE DES ARENES
ROMAN ARENA
CRYPTO-PORTIQUES DU FORUM
R. DIDEROT
RUE DE
FOND. V.G.
R. BALZE
WC
RUE CALADE
ST. TROPHIME
RUE DE CLOITRE
LAURE
ANCIENT CITY WALLS
PLACE REPUB.
RUE REPUBLIQUE
PORTE DE
CLASSICAL THEATER
ARLATEN FOLK MUSEUM
RUE
JARDIN D'ETE
CLOISTER
MONTEE VAUBAN
BD. E. COMBES
VAN GOGH HOSPITAL
BLVD. DES LICES
POST + TAXIS
V. HUGO
TO ANCIENT HISTORY MUSEUM
PLAYGROUND
R. E. FASSIN
TO LES AYLSCAMPS CEMETERY
DCH

Provence

from place Lamartine turn right immediately after passing between towers to reach 5 rue Marius Jouveau, tel. 04 90 96 39 85, fax 04 90 96 67 64, www.hotel-regence.com, contact@hotel-regence.com). The gentle Nouvions speak some English.

$ Hôtel Acacias,** just off place Lamartine and inside the old city walls, is a modern, pastel paradise. Its smallish, well-maintained, reasonably priced rooms have all the comforts (Sb or Db-€46–55, larger Db-€62–71, extra bed-€15, buffet breakfast-€6, air-con, elevator, 1 rue Marius Jouveau, tel. 04 90 96 37 88, fax 04 90 96 32 51, www.hotel-acacias.com, contact@hotel-acacias.com, Christophe and Sylvie).

$ Hôtel Voltaire* rents 12 small and spartan rooms with ceiling fans and nifty balconies overlooking a caffeine-stained square. A block below the Arena, it's perfect for starving artists. Smiling owner Mr. Ferran (fur-ran) loves the States (his dream is to travel there), and hopes you'll add to his postcard collection (D-€28, Ds-€30, Db-€38, 1 place Voltaire, tel. 04 90 96 49 18, fax 04 90 96 45 49, levoltaire@aol.com). They also serve lunch and dinner (see "Eating," below).

EATING

You can dine well in Arles on a modest budget—in fact, it's hard to blow a lot on dinner here (most of my listings have fixed-price meals called *menus* for €22 or less). The bad news is that restaurants here change regularly, so double-check my suggestions. All restaurants I list (except Bistrot à Vins and La Bohème) have outdoor seating. Before dinner, go local on place du Forum and enjoy a *pastis.* This anise-based apéritif is served straight in a glass with ice, plus a carafe of water—dilute to taste.

On or near Place du Forum

Great atmosphere and mediocre food at fair prices await on place du Forum. By all accounts, the garish yellow Café la Nuit is worth avoiding. A half-block below the Forum, on rue du Dr. Fanton, lies a lineup of more tempting restaurants (including the first three listed below).

Le 16, with warm ambience inside and out, is an affordable place to enjoy a fresh salad (€8–10, bright and creative) or a one-course dinner (their "bull and red rice" is popular). They also offer a daily *plat du jour,* a two-course €14 *formula*, and a seasonal *menu* (closed Sat–Sun, 16 rue du Dr. Fanton, tel. 04 90 93 77 36).

La Paillotte, a few doors down, features soft tablecloths under wood-beamed comfort inside, a nice terrace outside, and fine regional cuisine at affordable prices. It's quite popular with tourists (€17–28 *menus*, closed Wed, 28 rue du Dr. Fanton, tel. 04 90 96 33 15).

Au Bryn du Thym, almost next door, has long been reliable and specializes in traditional Provençal cuisine. Arrive early for an outdoor table (€19 *menu*, closed Tue, 22 rue du Dr. Fanton, tel. 04 90 49 95 96).

Bistrot à Vins is for wine addicts who love matching food and wine. This comfortable *bistrot* is run by affable Ariane. She speaks English and offers simple, tasty dishes designed to highlight her reasonably priced wines (many available by the glass; closed Mon, 2 rue du Dr. Fanton, tel. 04 90 52 00 65).

La Bohème seems lost a block above the Forum. Here you'll be greeted by gentle Nicholas and dine under a long, vaulted ceiling with good budget options (€15 vegetarian *menu*, €19 Provençal *menu*, closed Sun–Mon, 6 rue Balze, tel. 04 90 18 58 92). The occasional tour group usually leaves by 19:30.

At **La Cuisine de Comptoir,** locals leave behind Provençal decor and pretend they're urbanites in Paris. This cool little bistro serves light €8 *tartine* dinners—a cross between pizza and bruschetta served with soup or salad (closed Sun, just off place du Forum's lower end at 10 rue de la Liberté, tel. 04 90 96 86 28). While there is a non-smoking room, tables with the best ambience come with smoke.

Recharge at **Café de la Major** with some serious coffee or tea (closed Sun, 7 bis rue Réattu, tel. 04 90 96 14 15).

Near the Roman Arena

For about the same price as on place du Forum, you can enjoy regional cuisine with a point-blank view of the Arena. Of several passable eateries overlooking the Arena, my favorite is the relaxed **Le Grillon,** with good salads, crêpes, and *plats du jour* for €12 or less (closed Wed, next to Le Pistou at the top of the Arena, on rond point des Arènes, tel. 04 90 96 70 97).

The recommended **Hôtel Calendal** (see "Sleeping," above) hosts an all-you-can-eat salad-and-pasta bar (€14, daily 12:00–15:00); the selection is as good as the quality. Retreat from the city and enjoy a healthy lunch in the hotel's palm-shaded garden (just above the Arena at 5 rue Porte de Laure, tel. 04 90 96 11 89).

The recommended **Hôtel Voltaire** (see "Sleeping," above) serves a nothing-fancy three-course dinner (or lunch) for €11 and hearty salads for €8–10—try the *salade Fermière* (open daily, 1 place Voltaire, tel. 04 90 96 49 18).

A Gastronomic Dining Experience

L'Atelier is so intriguing that people travel great distances just for the experience of dining here. Diners fork over €50 and trust Chef Jean-Luc Rabanel to create a memorable evening (which he does). There is no menu, just an onslaught of about 20 delicious taste sensations served on sleek white dishes. Don't plan on a quick dinner and don't come for the setting—it's a contemporary shoebox-shaped dining room with a get-to-know-your-neighbor atmosphere where you can't help but join the party (closed Mon, best to book ahead, friendly server Sebastian will hold your hand through this palate-widening experience, 50 yards downhill from place de la République at 7 rue des Carmes, tel. 04 90 91 07 69, www.rabanel.com).

And for Dessert...

Soleilei has Arles' best ice cream, with all-natural ingredients and unusual flavors such as *fadoli*—olive oil (open daily, across from recommended Le 16 restaurant at 9 rue du Dr. Fanton).

TRANSPORTATION CONNECTIONS

From Arles by Train to: Paris (17/day, 2 direct TGVs in 4 hrs, 15 with transfer in Avignon in 5 hrs), **Avignon Centre-Ville** (11/day, 20 min, less frequent in the afternoon), **Nîmes** (9/day, 30 min), **Orange** (4/day direct, 35 min, more with transfer in Avignon), **Aix-en-Provence Centre-Ville** (10/day, 2 hrs, requires at least 1 transfer, in Marseille), **Marseille** (20/day, 1–2 hrs), **Cassis** (7/day, 2 hrs), **Carcassonne** (6/day, 3 hrs, 3 with transfer in Narbonne), **Beaune** (10/day, 4.5 hrs, 9 with transfer in Nîmes or Avignon and Lyon), **Nice** (11/day, 3.5 hrs, most require transfer in Marseille), **Barcelona** (2/day, 6 hrs, transfer in Montpellier), **Italy** (3/day, transfer in Marseille and Nice; from Arles, it's 4.5 hrs to Ventimiglia on the border, 8 hrs to Milan, 9.5 hrs to Cinque Terre, 11 hrs to Florence, and 13 hrs to Venice or Rome).

By Bus to: Avignon TGV (11/day, 1 hr, take SNCF bus), **Nîmes** (6/day, 1 hr), **St. Rémy** (3/day Mon–Sat only, 50 min), **Fontvieille** (6/day, 10 min), **Camargue/Stes-Maries-de-la-Mer** (6/day Mon–Sat, 3/day Sun, 1 hr). There are two bus stops in Arles: the Centre-Ville stop is at 16 boulevard Clemenceau (2 blocks below main TI, next to Café le Wilson); the other, called Gare Routière, is at the train station. Bus info: tel. 04 90 49 38 01 (unlikely to speak English).

Avignon

Famous for its nursery rhyme, medieval bridge, and brooding Palace of the Popes, contemporary Avignon (ah-veen-yohn) bustles and prospers behind its mighty walls. During the 68 years (1309–1377) that Avignon starred as the *Franco Vaticano*, it grew from a quiet village into the thriving city it remains today. With its large student population and fashionable shops, today's Avignon is an intriguing blend of youthful energy and urban sophistication. Street performers entertain the international crowds who fill Avignon's ubiquitous cafés and trendy boutiques. If you're here in July, be prepared for the rollicking theater festival. (Reserve your hotel months in advance.) Clean, sharp, and popular with tourists, Avignon is more impressive for its outdoor ambience than for its museums and monuments. See the Palace of the Popes, and then explore the city's thriving streets and beautiful vistas from the parc des Rochers des Doms.

ORIENTATION

The cours Jean Jaurès, which turns into rue de la République, runs straight from the train station to place de l'Horloge and the Palace of the Popes, splitting Avignon in two. The larger eastern half is where the action is. Climb to the parc des Rochers des Doms for a fine view, enjoy the people scene on place de l'Horloge, meander the back streets, and lose yourself in a quiet square. Avignon's shopping district fills the traffic-free streets where rue de la République meets place de l'Horloge.

Tourist Information

The main TI is between the Centre-Ville train station and the old town, at 41 cours Jean Jaurès (April–Oct Mon–Sat 9:00–18:00, or until 19:00 in July, Sun 9:00–17:00; Nov–March Mon–Fri 9:00–18:00, Sat 9:00–17:00, Sun 10:00–12:00; tel. 04 32 74 32 74, www.avignon-tourisme.com). From April to September, a branch TI office, called Espace Ferruce, is usually open at the St. Bénezet Bridge (but is slow, with just one person working).

At either TI, get the good tear-off map and pick up the free and handy *Guide Pratique* (info on car and bike rental, hotels, and museums). Also pick up the free **Avignon Passion Pass** (valid 15 days). Get the pass stamped when you pay full price at your first sight, and then receive reductions at the others; for example, €2 less at Palace of the Popes and €3 less at Petit Palais. The pass comes with the Avignon "Passion" map and guide, which includes several good (but tricky-to-follow) walking tours.

The TI offers informative, two-hour English **walking tours** of Avignon (€10–15, €8–10 with Avignon Passion Pass; April–Oct Mon–Sat at 10:00, no Sun tours, Nov–March on Sat only; depart from main TI, themes vary daily). The TI also offers information and bookings for bus excursions to popular regional sights, including the wine route, Luberon, and the Camargue (see "Tours of Provence" on page 352).

Arrival in Avignon

By Train

Avignon has two train stations, the TGV and Centre-Ville (connected by frequent shuttle bus—see details below, under "Arrival at the TGV Station"). Avignon's space-age TGV train station—located away from the center—is big news. While it makes Paris a zippy three-hour ride away, locals say it benefits rich Parisians the most. Now that Provence is within easy weekend striking distance of the French capital, rural homes are being gobbled up by urbanites at inflated prices that Avignon natives can't afford.

Arrival at the TGV Station (Gare TGV): There is no baggage check here, though you can check your bags at the Centre-Ville station (see below). For the city shuttle bus *(navette)*, go out the north exit *(sortie nord)*, down the stairs, and to the left. Look for the shuttle bus or the stop marked *Avignon Centre* (€1.20, 3/hr, 15 min, buy tickets at info booth or from the driver). It drops you close to the other station (Centre-Ville), just off cours Jean Jaurès. The TI is three blocks down, at #41.

A taxi ride between from the station and downtown Avignon costs about €13. For car rentals, take the south exit *(sortie sud)* to find the *location de voitures.*

From Downtown Avignon to the TGV Station: The bus stop for the shuttle bus to the TGV station is in front of the main post office (*poste principale*, across from the Centre-Ville station on cours Président Kennedy). When a market fills that street, the bus waits on the east side of cours Jean Jaurès (shown on map).

Arrival at Centre-Ville Station (Gare Avignon Centre-Ville): All non-TGV trains serve the central station. You can check bags here (exit the station to the left, look for *consignes* sign, daily May–Sept 6:00–22:00, Oct–April 7:00–19:00). The bus station *(gare routière)* is 100 yards to the right of the Centre-Ville station as you leave (beyond and below Ibis Hôtel). To reach the town center, walk out of the train station and through the city walls onto cours Jean Jaurès. The TI is three blocks down, at #41.

By Bus

The dingy bus station is located just east of the Centre-Ville train station; to get to Avignon's sights, follow the walking directions explained above.

By Car

Drivers entering Avignon should follow *Centre-Ville* and *Gare SNCF* (train station) signs. Park in the parking structure next to the Centre-Ville train station (€5/half-day, €10/day). Free parking is available near the city walls (on boulevard Saint-Roch near Porte

Avignon

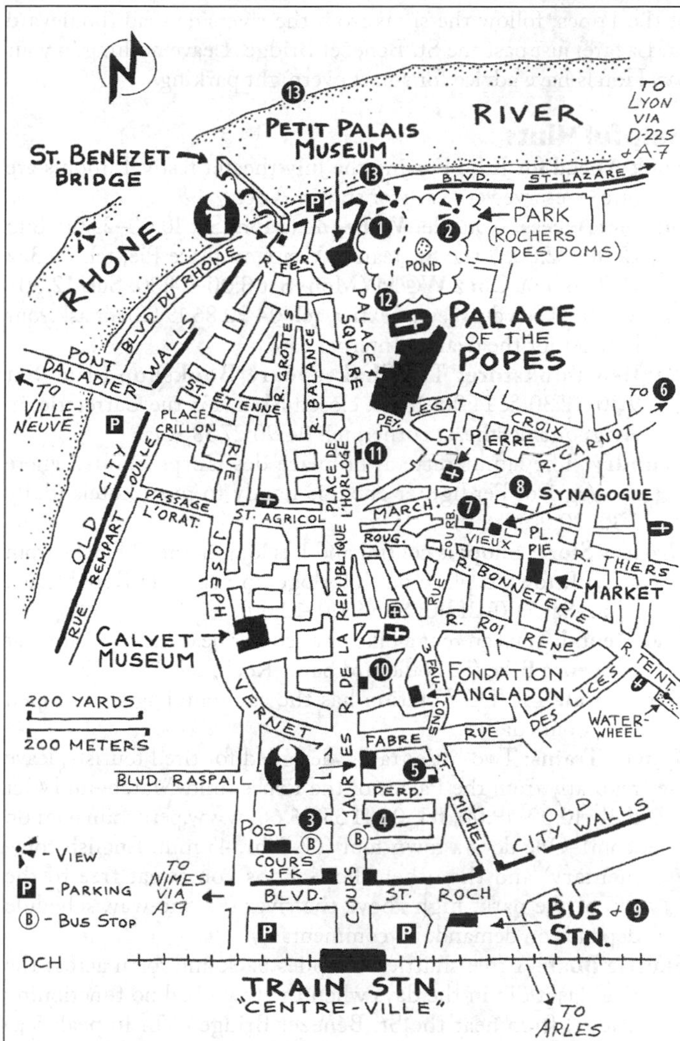
RIVER
RHONE
TO LYON VIA D-225 & A-7
PETIT PALAIS MUSEUM
ST. BENEZET BRIDGE
BLVD. ST-LAZARE
PARK (ROCHERS DES DOMS)
POND
BLVD. DU RHONE
R. FER.
PALACE SQUARE
PALACE OF THE POPES
PONT DALADIER
TO VILLE-NEUVE
WALLS
ST. ETIENNE
R. GROTTES
R. BALANCE
PLACE CRILLON
RUE LOULLE
OLD CITY
REMPART
LEGAT
PEY.
CROIX
R. CARNOT
TO 6
ST. PIERRE
SYNAGOGUE
PASSAGE L'ORAT.
ST. AGRICOL
PLACE DE L'HORLOGE
MARCH.
ROUG.
FOUR RB.
VIEUX
PL. PIE
R. THIERS
R. BONNETERIE
MARKET
JOSEPH
RUE
R. DE LA REPUBLIQUE
RUE
R. ROI RENE
CALVET MUSEUM
3 FAU. CONS
FONDATION ANGLADON
R. TEINT.
RUE DES LICES
WATER-WHEEL
200 YARDS
200 METERS
VERNET
FABRE
BLVD. RASPAIL
JAURES
PERD.
ST. MICHEL
OLD CITY WALLS
POST
COURS JFK
COURS
BLVD. ST. ROCH
TO NIMES VIA A-9
BUS & 9 STN.
- VIEW
P - PARKING
B - BUS STOP
DCH
TRAIN STN. "CENTRE-VILLE"
TO ARLES
1 Best View of Bridge & Stairs to Ramparts
2 More Views & Orientation Table
3 TGV Shuttle Stop
4 TGV Shuttle Stop on Market Days
5 Launderette
6 To Shakespeare Bookshop
7 Chez W@M Internet Café
8 Webzone Internet Café
9 Provence Bike Rental
10 Shopi Grocery
11 City Hall
12 Tourist Train Stop
13 Shuttle Boat Stops

de la République). To park in an underground garage at the Palace of the Popes, follow the signs from the riverside road (boulevard St. Lazare) just past the St. Bénezet Bridge. Leave nothing in your car. Hotels have advice for smart overnight parking.

Helpful Hints

Book Ahead for July: During the July theater festival, rooms are rare—reserve very early or stay in Arles.

Internet Access: Consider **Webzone** (Mon–Sat 10:00–23:00, Sun 12:00–22:00, 3 rue St. Jean le Vieux on place Pie, tel. 04 322 76 29 47) or **Chez W@M** (Mon–Sat 8:00–24:00, Sun 12:00–24:00, 41 rue du Vieux Sextier, tel. 04 90 86 19 03), or ask your hotelier for the nearest Internet café.

English Bookstore: Try **Shakespeare Bookshop** (Tue–Sat 9:30–12:30 & 14:00–18:30, closed Mon, 155 rue Carreterie, in Avignon's northeast corner, tel. 04 90 27 38 50).

Laundry: The launderette at 66 place des Corps-Saints, where rue Agricol Perdiguier ends, is handy to most hotels (daily 7:30–20:00).

Grocery Store: Shopi is central and has long hours (2 blocks from the TI, toward place de l'Horloge on rue de la République, Mon–Sat 7:00–21:00, Sun 9:00–12:00).

Bike Rental: You can rent a bike or a scooter near the bus station at **Provence Bike** (52 boulevard Saint-Roch, tel. 04 90 27 92 61).

Car Rental: The TGV station has the car-rental agencies (open long hours daily).

Tourist Trains: Two little trains, designed for tired tourists, leave regularly from the Palace of the Popes (mid-March–mid-Oct daily 10:00–19:00, tel. 06 11 35 06 66, www.petittrainavignon.com). One does a town tour (€7, 3/hr, 45 min, English commentary) and the other choo-choos you sweat-free to the top of the park, high above the river (€1 one-way, schedule depends on demand, no commentary).

Shuttle Boat: A free shuttle boat plies back and forth across the river (as it did in the days when the town had no functioning bridge) from near the St. Bénezet Bridge (3/hr in peak season). It drops you on the peaceful Ile de la Barthelasse, with its riverside restaurant and grassy walks with city views.

Commanding City Views: Walk or drive across the Daladier Bridge (pont Daladier) for a great view of Avignon and the Rhône River. You can enjoy other impressive vistas from the top of parc des Rochers des Doms and from the end of the famous, broken St. Bénezet Bridge.

SELF-GUIDED WALK

Welcome to Avignon

This walk, worth ▲▲, connects Avignon's best sights.

• *Start your tour where the Romans did, on place de l'Horloge, and find a seat on a stone bench in front of City Hall (Hôtel de Ville).*

Place de l'Horloge

This café square was the town forum during Roman times and the market square through the Middle Ages. (Restaurants here come with *beaucoup* ambience, but they also have high prices and low-quality meals.) Named for a medieval clock tower that the City Hall now hides, this square's present popularity arrived with the trains in 1854.

• *Walk past the merry-go-round (public WCs behind), veer right, and continue into...*

Palace Square (Place du Palais)

This grand square is surrounded by the forbidding Palace of the Popes, the Petit Palais, and the cathedral. In the 1300s, the Vatican moved the headquarters of the Catholic Church to Avignon. The Church bought Avignon and gave it a complete makeover. Along with clearing out vast spaces like this square and building this three-acre palace, the Church erected more than three miles of protective wall, with 39 towers, "appropriate" housing for cardinals (read: mansions), and residences for the entire Vatican bureaucracy. The city was Europe's largest construction zone. Avignon's population grew from 6,000 to 25,000 in short order. (Today, 13,000 people live within the walls.) The limits of pre-pope Avignon are outlined on city maps: Rues Joseph Vernet, Henri Fabre, des Lices, and Philonarde all follow the route of the city's earlier defensive wall.

The Petit Palais (Little Palace) seals the uphill end of the square and was built for a cardinal; today, it houses medieval paintings (museum described below). The church to the left of the Palace of the Popes is Avignon's cathedral. It predates the Church's purchase of Avignon by 200 years. Its small size reflects Avignon's modest, pre-pope population. The gilded Mary was added in 1854, when the Vatican established the doctrine of her Immaculate Conception. Mary is purposefully taller than the Palace of the Popes. The Vatican never accepted what it called the "Babylonian Captivity," and had a bad attitude about Avignon long after the pope was definitively back in Rome.

Directly across the square from the palace's main entry stands a cardinal's residence built in 1619. Its fancy Baroque facade was a visual counterpoint to the stripped-down Huguenot aesthetic of the age. During this time, Provence was a hotbed of Protestantism—but, buried within this region, Avignon was a Catholic stronghold.

Notice the stumps in front of the Conservatoire National de Musique. Nicknamed *bites*, slang for the male anatomy, they effectively keep cars from double-parking in areas designed for people. Many of the metal ones slide up and down by remote control to let privileged cars come and go.

• *You can visit the massive Palace of the Popes (described on page 378) now, but it works better to visit that palace at the end of this walk. But now is a good time to take in the...*

Petit Palace Museum (Musée du Petit Palais)

This palace displays the Church's collection of mostly medieval Italian painting (including one delightful Botticelli) and sculpture. All 350 paintings deal with Christian themes. A visit here before going to the Palace of the Popes helps furnish and populate that otherwise barren building (€6, €3 with Avignon Passion Pass; June–Sept Wed–Mon 10:00–13:00 & 14:00–18:00, closed Tue; Oct–May Wed–Mon 9:30–13:00 & 14:00–17:30, closed Tue; at north end of Palace Square, tel. 04 90 86 44 58).

• *From Palace Square, we'll head up to the rocky hilltop where Avignon was first settled, then down to the river. With this short loop, you can enjoy a park, hike to a grand river view, walk a bit of the wall, and visit Avignon's beloved broken bridge—an experience worth* ▲▲. *Begin by hiking (or taking the tourist train—see "Helpful Hints," above) up to the...*

Parc des Rochers des Doms

While the park itself is a delight, don't miss the climax—a panoramic view of the Rhône River Valley and the broken bridge. To find the highest view (and the spot where teenage lovers hang out), climb the rocky stairs behind the fountain on the north side of the park.

On the largest terrace in the north side of the park, an orientation table explains the view; all around the terrace, several tableaus provide a little history in English. On a clear day, the tallest peak you see, with its white limestone cap, is Mont Ventoux ("Windy Mountain"). St. André Fortress (across the river) was built by the French in 1360, shortly after the pope moved to Avignon, to counter the papal incursion into this part of Europe. The castle was in the kingdom of France. Avignon's famous bridge was a key border crossing, with towers on either end—one French and one Vatican.

• *From the viewpoint closest to the river, take the stairs (closed at night) down to the tower and bridge. As the stairs spiral down, just before the St. Bénezet Bridge, catch a glimpse of the...*

Ramparts

The only bit of the rampart you can walk on is just beyond the tower (we'll walk this on our visit to the St. Bénezet Bridge). When the pope came in the 1360s, small Avignon had no town wall...so he built one (restored in the 19th century).

• *When you come out of the tower on street level, exit towards the river and walk left to find the bridge's entrance (it's outside the walls on boulevard du Rhône).*

St. Bénezet Bridge (Pont St. Bénezet)

This bridge, whose construction and location were inspired by a shepherd's religious vision, is the "pont d'Avignon" of nursery-rhyme fame. The ditty (which you've probably been humming all day) dates back to the 15th century: *Sur le pont d'Avignon, on y danse, on y danse, sur le pont d'Avignon, on y danse tout en rond* ("On the bridge of Avignon, we will dance, we will dance, on the bridge of Avignon, we will dance all in a circle").

But the bridge was a big deal even outside of its kiddie-tune fame. Built between 1171 and 1185, it was the only bridge crossing the mighty Rhône in the Middle Ages. It was damaged several times by floods and subsequently rebuilt, until 1668, when most of it was knocked down by a disastrous icy flood. The townsfolk decided not to rebuild this time, and for over a century, Avignon had no bridge across the Rhône. While only four arches survive today, the original bridge was huge: Imagine a 22-arch, 3,000-foot-long bridge extending from Vatican territory to the lonely Tower of Philip the Fair, which marked the beginning of France. A Romanesque chapel on the bridge is dedicated to St. Bénezet. While there's not much to see on the bridge, the audioguide included with your ticket tells a good story. It's also fun to be in the breezy middle of the river with a fine city view.

Cost and Hours: €4, €3 with Avignon Passion Pass, €12 combo-ticket includes Palace of the Popes, daily July 9:00–21:00, Aug–Sept 9:00–20:00, April–June and Oct 9:00–19:00, Nov–March 9:30–17:45, last entry 1 hour before closing, tel. 04 90 27 51 16). The ticket booth is housed in what was a medieval hospital for the poor (funded by bridge tolls). Admission includes a small museum about the song of Avignon's bridge *(Musée de la Chanson d'Avignon)* and your only chance to walk a bit of the ramparts (both keep same hours as bridge and are entered from the tower).

• *Step off the bridge and turn left out of the tower to walk on the rampart wall (called* chemin de ronde*). To cross the river on the free shuttle boat (a good restaurant on the opposite side is described on page* 387*), look for the small boat near the base of the bridge. To get to the Palace of the Popes from here, exit left, turn left again back into the walls (following signs to* Palais des Papes*), then go right onto rue Ferruce. After* *a block, look for the brown signs leading you left under the passageway, and up the stairs to Palace Square and the Palace of the Popes.*

SIGHTS

Palace of the Popes (Palais des Papes)

In 1309, a French pope was elected (Pope Clement V). At the urging of the French king, His Holiness decided he'd had enough of unholy (and dangerous) Italy. So he loaded up his carts and moved to Avignon for a secure rule under a supportive king. The Catholic Church literally bought Avignon (then a two-bit town), and popes resided here until 1403. From 1378 on, there were twin popes, one in Rome and one in Avignon, causing a schism in the Catholic Church that wasn't fully resolved until 1417.

The mighty yet barren papal palace visit—worth ▲▲—comes with an audioguide that leads you along a one-way route and does a credible job of overcoming the lack of furnishings. It teaches the basic history while allowing you to tour at your own pace.

As you wander, ponder that this palace—the biggest surviving Gothic palace in Europe—was built to accommodate 500 people as the administrative center of the Vatican and home of the pope. This was the most fortified palace of the age (remember, the pope left Rome to be more secure). You'll walk through the pope's personal quarters (frescoed with happy hunting scenes), see models of how the various popes added to the building, and learn about its state-of-the-art plumbing. The rooms are huge. The "pope's chapel" is twice the size of the adjacent Avignon cathedral.

While the last pope checked out in 1417, the Vatican owned Avignon until the French Revolution in 1789. During this interim period, the pope's "legate" (official representative...normally a nephew) ruled Avignon from this palace. Avignon residents spoke Italian for a century after the pope left, making it a linguistic island within France. In the Napoleonic age, the palace was a barracks, housing 1,800 soldiers. Climb the tower (Tour de la Gâche) for a grand view and windswept café.

A room at the end of the tour is dedicated to the region's wines, of which they claim the pope was a fan. Sniff "Le Nez du Vin"—a black box with 54 tiny bottles designed to develop your "nose." (Blind test your travel partner.) The nearby village of Châteauneuf-du-Pape is where the pope summered in the 1320s. Its famous wine is a direct descendant of his wine. You're welcome to taste here (free, or split the €6 tasters deal, which comes with a souvenir tasting cup).

Cost and Hours: €10, €8 with Avignon Passion Pass, €12 combo-ticket includes St. Bénezet Bridge, daily July 9:00–21:00, Aug–Sept 9:00–20:00, April–June and Oct 9:00–19:00, Nov–

March 9:30–17:45, last entry 1 hour before closing, tel. 04 90 27 50 74, www.palais-des-papes.com.

• *After you finish, you'll exit at the rear of the palace. To return to Palace Square, make two rights after exiting the palace.*

More Sights

Avignon's Synagogue—Jews first arrived in Avignon with the Diaspora (exile) of the first century. Avignon's Jews were nicknamed "the Pope's Jews" because of the protection that the Pope offered to Jews expelled from France. While this synagogue dates from 1220s, in the mid-19th century it was completely rebuilt in a Neoclassical Greek-temple style by a non-Jewish architect. This is the only synagogue under a rotunda that you'll see anywhere. The ark holding the Torah is in the east—next to a list of Jews deported from here to Auschwitz in 1942, after Vichy France was overtaken by the Nazis. To visit the synagogue, press the buzzer and friendly Rabbi Moshe Amar will be your guide (Mon–Fri 10:00–12:00 & 15:00–17:00, closed Sat–Sun, 2 place Jerusalem).

Rue des Teinturiers—This "Street of the Dyers" is Avignon's headquarters for all that's hip. You'll pass the Grey Penitents chapel. The facade shows the GPs, who dressed up in robes and pointy hoods to do their anonymous good deeds back in the 13th century (long before the KKK dressed this way).

As you stroll, you'll see the work of amateur sculptors, who have carved whimsical car barriers out of limestone. Earthy cafés, galleries, and a small stream (a branch of the Sorgue River) with waterwheels line this tie-dyed street. This was the cloth industry's dyeing and textile center in the 1800s. Those stylish Provençal fabrics and patterns you see for sale everywhere started here, after a pattern imported from India.

For trendy restaurants on this atmospheric street, see page 384.

• *Farther down rue des Teinturiers, you'll come to the...*

Waterwheel—Standing here, imagine the Sorgue River—which hits the mighty Rhône in Avignon—being broken into several canals in order to turn 23 such wheels. Around 1800, waterwheels powered the town's industries. The little cogwheel above the big one could be shoved into place, kicking another machine into gear behind the wall. Across from the wheel at #41 is **La Cave Breysse,** offering regional wines by the glass and good lunch fare (see page 384).

Fondation Angladon-Dubrujeaud—Visiting this museum is like being invited into the elegant home of a rich and passionate art collector. It mixes a small but enjoyable collection of art from Post-Impressionists (including Paul Cézanne, Vincent van Gogh, Honoré Daumier, Edgar Degas, and Pablo Picasso) with re-created art studios and furnishings from many periods. It's a quiet place with a few superb paintings (€6, €4 with Avignon Passion Pass; May–Nov Tue–Sun 13:00–18:00, closed Mon; Dec–April Wed–Sun 13:00–18:00, closed Mon–Tue; 5 rue Laboureur, tel. 04 90 82 29 03, www.angladon.com).

Calvet Museum (Musée Calvet)—This fine-arts museum impressively displays its good collection without a word of English explanation (€6, €3 with Avignon Passion Pass, Wed–Mon 10:00–13:00 & 14:00–18:00, closed Tue, on quieter west half of town at 65 rue Joseph Vernet, its antiquities collection is a few blocks away at 27 rue de la République—same hours and ticket, tel. 04 90 86 33 84).

Near Avignon, in Villeneuve-lès-Avignon

▲Tower of Philip the Fair (Tour Philippe-le-Bel)—Built to protect access to St. Bénezet Bridge in 1307, this bulky tower offers the finest view over Avignon and the Rhône basin. It's best late in the day (€2, €1 with Avignon Passion Pass, April–Sept daily 10:00–12:30 & 14:00–18:30; March and Oct–Nov Tue–Sun 10:00–12:00 & 14:00–17:00, closed Mon and Dec–Feb; tel. 04 32 70 08 57). To reach the tower from Avignon, you can drive (5 min, cross Daladier Bridge, follow signs to *Villeneuve-lès-Avignon*); take a boat (Bateau-Bus departs from Mireio Embarcadère near Daladier Bridge); or take bus #11 (2/hr, catch bus across from Centre-Ville train station, in front of post office, on cours Président Kennedy).

SLEEPING

Hotel values are better in Arles. Avignon is particularly popular during its July festival, when you must book ahead (expect inflated prices). Also note that only a few hotels have elevators—specifically, the first three listed near place de l'Horloge.

Near Avignon's Centre-Ville Station

The first three listings are a 10-minute walk from the main train station; turn right off cours Jean Jaurès on rue Agricol Perdiguier.

$$ Hôtel Colbert** is a safe mid-range bet with a variety of rooms in many sizes. Your hosts—Patrice, Annie, and *le chien* Brittany—care for this restored manor house and its cozy public spaces (Sb-€45–55, Db-€51–72, Tb-€75–83, air-con, parking-€9, 7 rue Agricol Perdiguier, tel. 04 90 86 20 20, fax 04 90 85 97 00, www.lecolbert-hotel.com, contact@avignon-hotel-colbert.com).

$ Hôtel du Parc* is a spotless value with white walls, tiny bathrooms, and stone accents. It's scrupulously managed by entertaining Avignon native Madame Rous, who bakes her own bread and pastries for breakfast—and even made the bedspreads by hand (S-€28, Ss-€36, D-€39, Ds-€46, Db-€50, Tb-€65, no TVs or phones, tel.

Avignon Hotels

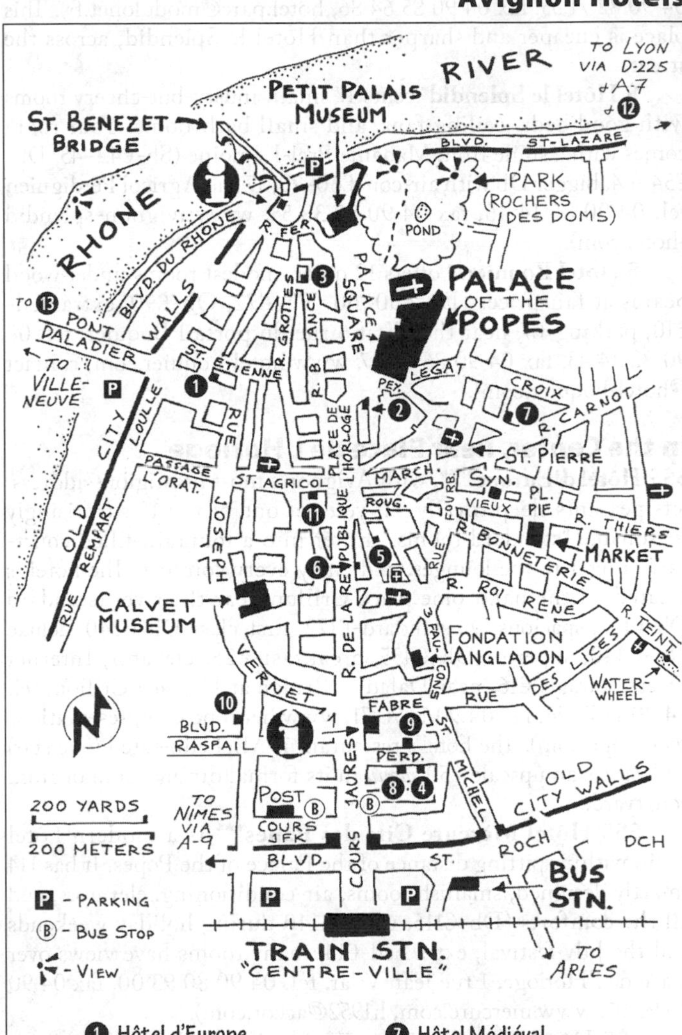

1. Hôtel d'Europe
2. Hôtel Mercure Cité des Papes
3. Hôtel Pont d'Avignon
4. Hôtel Colbert
5. Hôtel de Blauvac
6. Hôtel Danieli
7. Hôtel Médiéval
8. Hôtel le Splendid
9. Hôtel du Parc
10. Hôtel Boquier
11. Villa Agapè
12. To Le Clos du Rempart Rooms
13. To Auberge Bagatelle

04 90 82 71 55, fax 04 90 85 64 86, hotel.parc@modulonet.fr). This place is cheaper and sharper than Hôtel le Splendid, across the street.

$ Hôtel le Splendid* rents 17 small, musty-but-cheery rooms with good beds, ceiling fans, and small bathrooms. Your room comes with a smile from Madame Prel-Lemoine (Sb-€42–45, Db-€54–64, bigger Db with air-con-€60–70, 17 rue Agricol Perdiguier, tel. 04 90 86 14 46, fax 04 90 85 38 55, www.avignon-splendid-hotel.com).

$ Hôtel Boquier** offers 12 quiet, modest rooms under wood beams at fair prices (Db-€50–60, Tb-€72, Qb-€90, extra bed-€10, parking-€7, near the TI at 6 rue du portail Boquier, tel. 04 90 82 34 43, fax 04 90 86 14 07, www.hotel-boquier.com, contact@hotel-boquier.com).

In the Center, near Place de l'Horloge

$$$ Hôtel d'Europe****, with Avignon's most prestigious address, lets peasants sleep royally—if you get one of the 15 surprisingly reasonable "standard rooms." Enter into a fountain-filled courtyard, linger in the lounges, and enjoy every comfort. The hotel is located on the handsome place Crillon near the river (standard Db-€142, spacious Db standard-€172, first-class Db-€240, deluxe Db-€340, superior Db-€455, breakfast-€25, elevator, Internet access, garage-€16, near Daladier Bridge at 12 place Crillon, tel. 04 90 14 76 76, fax 04 90 14 76 71, www.heurope.com, reservations@heurope.com). The hotel's restaurant is Michelin-rated (one star) and serves an upscale €50 *menu* in its formal dining room or front courtyard.

$$$ Hôtel Mercure Cité des Papes*** is a modern hotel chain within spitting distance of the Palace of the Popes. It has 114 smartly designed, smallish rooms, air-conditioning, elevators, and all the comforts (Db-€115, up to €140 during holiday weekends and the July festival, extra bed-€14, many rooms have views over place de l'Horloge, 1 rue Jean Vilar, tel. 04 90 80 93 00, fax 04 90 80 93 01, www.mercure.com, h1952@accor.com).

$$$ Hôtel Pont d'Avignon***, just inside the walls near St. Bénezet Bridge, is part of the same chain as the Hôtel Mercure Cité des Papes, with the same prices for its 90 rooms (direct access to a garage makes parking easier than at the Mercure, elevator, on rue Ferruce, tel. 04 90 80 93 93, fax 04 90 80 93 94, www.mercure.com, h0549@accor.com).

$$$ Hôtel Danieli** is a *Hello Dolly* fluffball of a place that rents 29 colorful and simple rooms on the main drag and has lots of tour groups (Sb-€70, Db-€80, Tb-€95, Qb-€110, 17 rue de la République, tel. 04 90 86 46 82, fax 04 90 27 09 24, www.hotel-danieli-avignon.com, contact@hotel-danieli-avignon.com, kind owner Madame Shogol).

$$ At **Hôtel de Blauvac**,** friendly owner Veronica offers 16 mostly spacious, high-ceilinged rooms (many with an additional upstairs loft) and a sky-high atrium. It's a faded old manor home near the pedestrian zone with reliable noise at night (Sb-€65–75, Db-€70–80, Tb-€85–95, Qb-€100, €10 less off-season, 1 block off rue de la République at 11 rue de la Bancasse, tel. 04 90 86 34 11, fax 04 90 86 27 41, www.hotel-blauvac.com, blauvac@aol.com).

$$ Hôtel Médiéval** is burrowed deep a few blocks from the Church of St. Pierre. Built as a cardinal's home, this massive stone mansion has a small garden, friendly managers, and 35 wood-paneled, unimaginative-but-adequate rooms (Sb-€45, Db-€55–70, larger Db-€78–84, Tb-€84, kitchenettes available but require 3-night minimum stay, 5 blocks east of place de l'Horloge, behind Church of St. Pierre at 15 rue Petite Saunerie, tel. 04 90 86 11 06, fax 04 90 82 08 64, www.hotelmedieval.com, hotel.medieval@wanadoo.fr, Mike).

Chambres d'Hôte

$$$ Villa Agapè, just off busy place de l'Horloge right in the center of town, is an oasis of calm and good taste. Run by friendly Madame de La Pommeraye, the villa has three handsomely decorated rooms, a peaceful courtyard, lovely public spaces, and a soaking pool to boot (Db-€100–150, extra person-€30, includes breakfast, 2-night minimum in high season, Internet access and Wi-Fi; from place de l'Horloge it's one block down on left above the pharmacy at 13 rue St. Agricol—ring buzzer; tel. & fax 04 90 85 21 92, mobile 06 07 98 71 30, www.villa-agape.com, michele@villa-agape.com). For a week-long stay, ask about renting her entire house, where you get Madame's room, study, and kitchen.

$$$ Le Clos du Rempart, while less central, is still within the walls and worth considering. Madame Assad, another Parisian refugee, rents two rooms and one apartment on a pleasant courtyard decorated in a Middle Eastern theme, complete with a hammock (Db-€90–120 depending on season and room size, 2-bedroom apartment for 4 with kitchen-€150–230, apartment cheaper by the week, includes breakfast, air-con, 1 parking spot in garage, a 20-min walk from the Centre-Ville station at 35–37 rue Crémade, call for directions, tel. & fax 04 90 86 39 14, www.closdurempart.com, aida@closderempart.com).

Sleeping Cheaply near Avignon

$ Auberge Bagatelle's hostel offers dirt-cheap beds, a lively atmosphere, café, grocery store, launderette, great views of Avignon, and campers for neighbors (D-€26–29, dorm bed-€12, across Daladier Bridge on l'Ile de la Barthelasse, bus #10 from main post office, tel. 04 90 86 71 31, fax 04 90 27 16 23, www.aubergebagatelle.fr, auberge.bagatelle@wanadoo.fr).

EATING

Skip the overpriced places on place de l'Horloge (Les Domaines and La Civette near the carousel are the least of evils here) and find a more intimate location for your dinner. Avignon has many delightful squares filled with tables ready to seat you.

Near the Church of St. Pierre

The church has enclosed squares on both sides, offering outdoor yet intimate ambience.

L'Epicerie, located on a small, unpretentious square, serves the highest-quality cuisine around the Church of St. Pierre (€20 main dishes, closed Sun, cozy interior good in bad weather, 10 place St. Pierre, tel. 04 90 82 74 22).

Pass under the arch by L'Epicerie restaurant and enter enchanting place des Châtaignes, a tasty commotion of tables from four restaurants: **Crêperie du Cloître** (big salad and main-course crêpe for about €13, closed Sun–Mon); **Restaurant la Goulette** (Tunisian specialties, *tagine* or couscous-€19, closed Mon); **Restaurant Nem** tucked in the corner (Vietnamese, family-run, *menus* from €10); and **Pause Gourmande** (lunch only, *plats du jour*-€7, always a veggie option).

Place Crillon

This large and trendy open square just off the river provides more atmosphere than quality. Several cafés offer inexpensive bistro fare with *menus* from €15, *plats* from €12, and many tables to choose from. **Restaurant les Artistes** is most popular (daily, 21 place Crillon, tel. 04 90 82 23 54).

Rue des Teinturiers

While a bit of a walk from the center, this street has a wonderful concentration of eateries popular with the natives. It's a youthful and trendy area, recently spiffed up with a canalside ambience and little hint of tourism. I'd survey the four eateries listed here before choosing.

La Cave Breysse is a fun and colorful stop for a lunch salad, or a good pause before dinner. Mid-day or evening, Christine and Tim would love to serve you a fragrant €2.50 glass of regional wine. Choose from the blackboard by the bar that lists all the bottles open today. You're welcome to take yours out and sit by the canal. In the evening, this place is a hit with the young local crowd for its wine (flexible hours, usually Tue–Sat 11:00–15:00 & 18:00–22:30,

Avignon Restaurants

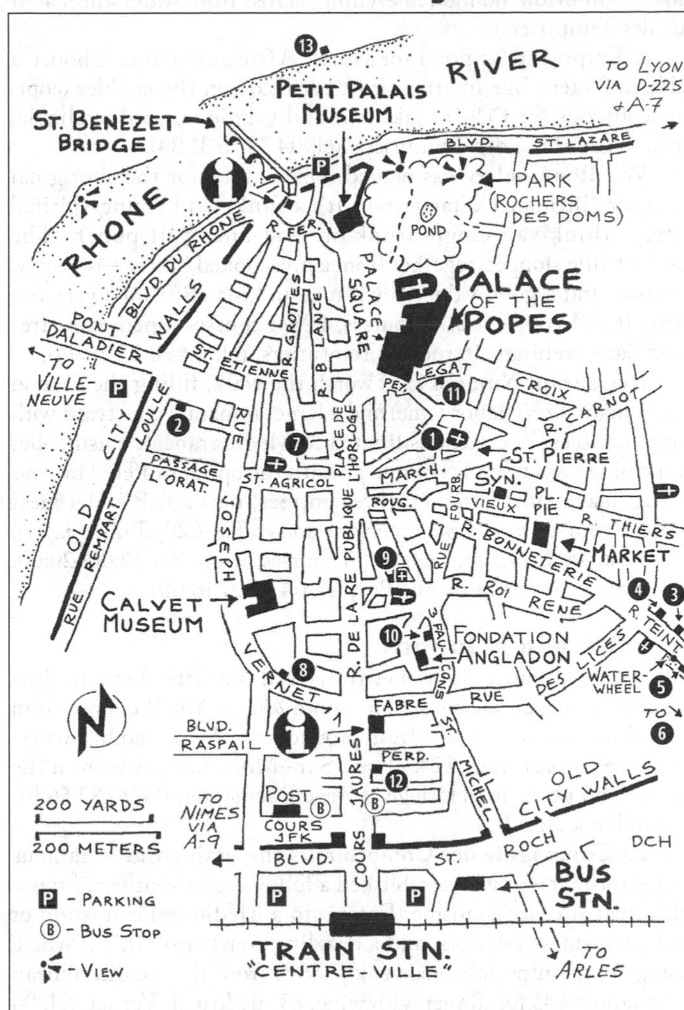

1. L'Epicerie, Crêperie du Cloître, Rest. la Goulette, Rest. Nem, & Pause Gourmande
2. Restaurant les Artistes & Other Place Crillon Eateries
3. La Cave Breysse Wine Bar
4. Restaurant l'Empreinte
5. Woolloomooloo Rest.
6. To Restaurant Numéro 75
7. L'Isle Sonnante Rest.
8. La Compagnie des Comptoirs Rest.
9. La Crêperie du Figuier
10. Le Caveau du Théâtre Rest.
11. Hôtel la Mirande Restaurant
12. Bakery Eric Convert
13. Le Bercail Rest.

closed Sun–Mon, no food in evening; across from waterwheel at 41 rue des Teinturiers).

L'Empreinte is good for North African cuisine. Choose a table in its tent-like interior, or sit canalside on the cobbles (copious couscous for €11–16, take-out and veggie options available, open daily, 33 rue des Teinturiers, tel. 04 32 76 31 84).

Woolloomooloo was named, Dada-style, for the aboriginal term for "little black kangaroo." It's a funky and young-spirited eatery...think van Gogh drunk on rum-and-fruit punch. The food—while slopped together from a pre-cooked buffet—is hearty, creative, and a good value. You'll mix and match from a very fun menu (€15/1 course, €21/2 courses, €28/3 courses, open daily, frequent jazz evenings, 16 rue des Teinturiers, tel. 04 90 85 28 44).

Restaurant Numéro 75 is worth the walk, filling the Pernod mansion (of *pastis* liquor fame) and a large, romantic courtyard with outdoor tables. The menu is limited to Mediterranean cuisine, but everything's *très* tasty. It's best to go with the options offered by your young, black-shirted server (three entrées, plus a fish and a meat main; 2-course lunch *menu* with wine and coffee-€20; dinner *menus:* €22/1 course, €26/2 courses, €30/3 courses; Mon–Sat 12:00–20:00, closed Sun, 75 rue Guillaume Puy, tel. 04 90 27 16 00).

Elsewhere in Avignon

At **L'Isle Sonnante,** join chef Boris and his wife Anne to dine intimately in their charming one-room *bistrot.* You'll choose from a small menu offering only fresh products and be served by owners who care (*menus* from €24, closed Sun–Mon, 100 yards from the carousel on place de l'Horloge at 7 rue Racine, tel. 04 90 82 56 01, best to book ahead).

La Compagnie des Comptoirs is the brainchild of famous twin-brother chefs who established a following in southern France with their inventive cuisine. Enter into a Mediterranean world of cool bars, smart interiors, and a dazzling courtyard. This is where young Avignon professionals enjoy foods from the Mediterranean basin (allow €45 for dinner with wine, 83 rue Joseph Vernet, tel. 04 90 85 99 04).

La Crêperie du Figuier has good crêpes and salads that won't break the bank (dinner crêpe or salad for €11, closed Sun, 3 rue du Figuier, tel. 04 90 82 60 67).

Le Caveau du Théâtre invites relaxed diners to share a glass of wine or dinner at one of a few sidewalk tables. Its wild posters decorate a carefree interior (€13 *plats*, €19 *menus*, fun ambience for free, closed Sun, 16 rue des Trois Faucons, tel. 04 90 82 60 91).

Hôtel la Mirande is the ultimate Avignon splurge. Reserve ahead here for understated elegance and Avignon's top cuisine (€33 lunch *menu*, €105 dinner tasting *menu*, closed Tue–Wed, behind

Palace of the Popes, 4 place de la Mirande, tel. 04 90 86 93 93, fax 04 90 86 26 85).

Bakery Eric Convert has excellent bread and sandwiches for lunch. Here you'll find a great selection of breads, including olive, Roquefort, orange chocolate, and dark Russian, and all varieties of baguettes and mouthwatering pastries (closed Sun, 45 cours Jean Jaurès, tel. 04 90 85 80 62).

Across the River

Le Bercail offers a fun opportunity to get out of town and take in *le* fresh air with a great view of Avignon, all while enjoying traditional cooking served in big portions. Book ahead, as this restaurant is popular (*menu*s from €16, serves late, daily April–Oct, take the small shuttle boat near St. Bénezet Bridge to l'Ile de la Barthelasse, tel. 04 90 82 20 22).

TRANSPORTATION CONNECTIONS

Trains

Remember, there are two train stations in Avignon: the suburban TGV station and the Centre-Ville station in the city center (€1.20 shuttle buses connect to both stations, 3/hr, 15 min). Only the Centre-Ville station has baggage check (see "Arrival in Avignon," page 372). Car rental is available at the TGV station. Some cities are served both by slower local trains from the Centre-Ville station and by faster TGV trains from the TGV station; I've listed the most convenient stations for each trip.

From Avignon's Centre-Ville Station by Train to: Arles (11/day, 20 min, less frequent in the afternoon), **Orange** (10/day, 15 min), **Nîmes** (14/day, 30 min), **Isle-sur-la-Sorgue** (10/day on weekdays, 5/day on weekends, 30 min), **Lyon** (10/day, 2 hrs, also from TGV station—see below), **Carcassonne** (8/day, 7 with transfer in Narbonne, 3 hrs), **Barcelona** (2/day, 6 hrs, transfer in Montpellier).

From Avignon's TGV Station to: Arles (11/day, 1 hr, by SNCF bus—take the faster train from the Centre-Ville station instead), **Nice** (20/day, 13 of which are via TGV, 4 hrs, most require transfer in Marseille), **Marseille** (10/day, 1 hr), **Aix-en-Provence TGV** (10/day, 25 min), **Lyon** (12/day, 1.5 hrs, also from Centre-Ville station—see above), **Paris**' Gare de Lyon (9/day in 2.5 hrs, 6/day in 4 hrs with change), **Paris**' Charles de Gaulle airport (7/day, 3 hrs).

Buses

The bus station *(gare routière)* is just past and below the Ibis Hôtel to the right as you exit the train station (information desk open

Mon–Fri 10:15–13:00 & 14:00–18:00, Sat 8:00–12:00, closed Sun, tel. 04 90 82 07 35). Nearly all buses leave from this station. The biggest exception is the SNCF bus service from the Avignon TGV station to Arles (see above). The Avignon TI has schedules. Service is reduced or nonexistent on Sundays and holidays.

From Avignon by Bus to: Pont du Gard (8/day in summer, 4/day Sun and off-season, 45 min). Consider visiting Pont du Gard, continuing on to Nîmes or Uzès, and returning to Avignon from there. (To catch the bus from Pont du Gard to Nîmes and Uzès, stand at the same Pont du Gard bus stop where you arrived.) Try these plans: Take the 12:05 bus from Avignon, arriving at Pont du Gard at 12:50. Then take either the 14:45 bus from there to the Roman ruins-packed city of **Nîmes** (where trains run hourly back to Avignon), or a 16:00 bus (Mon–Fri only) on to enchanting **Uzès,** arriving at 16:35, with a return bus to Avignon at 18:00. This is the last bus back to Avignon—verify times with the TI.

By Bus to Other Regional Destinations: Orange (hourly, 55 min); **Vaison la Romaine** and other Côtes du Rhône villages—**Nyons, Sablet,** and **Séguret** (2–3/day during school year, called *période scolaire*, 1/day otherwise and 1/day from TGV station, 75–90 min); **Isle-sur-la-Sorgue** (6/day, 45 min), **Gordes** (via Cavaillon, 1/day, not on Wed or Sun, 2 hrs, spend the night or taxi back to Cavaillon), **Lourmarin** (3/day, 90 min), **Uzès** (3/day Mon–Sat, none Sun, 1 hr), **St. Rémy** (6/day, 50 min, handy way to visit its Wed market).

Pont du Gard

The Pont du Gard is a short hop west of Avignon and on the way to/from Languedoc for drivers. Travelers relying on public transportation will find their choices very limited.

Throughout the ancient world, aqueducts were like flags of stone that heralded the greatness of Rome. A visit to this sight still works to proclaim the wonders of that age. This perfectly preserved Roman aqueduct was built as the critical link of a 30-mile canal that, by dropping one inch for every 350 feet, supplied nine million gallons of water per day (about 100 gallons per second) to Nîmes—one of ancient Europe's largest cities. Though most of the aqueduct is on or below the ground, at the Pont du Gard it spans a canyon on a massive bridge—one of the most remarkable surviving Roman ruins anywhere.

Getting to the Pont du Gard

The famous aqueduct is between Remoulins and Vers-Pont du Gard on D-981, 17 miles from Nîmes and 13 miles from Avignon.

Pont du Gard

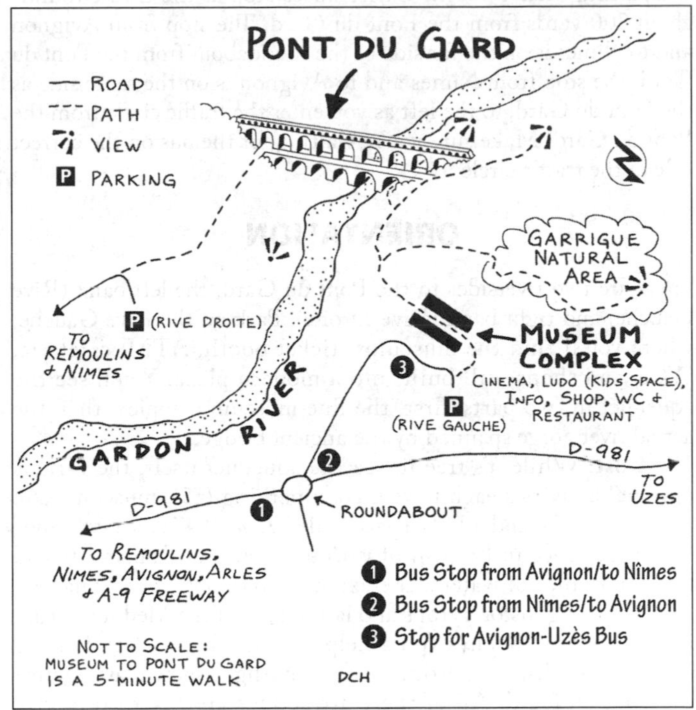

By Car: The Pont du Gard is an easy 25-minute drive due west of Avignon on N-100 and D-981 (follow signs to *Nîmes*, then *Pont du Gard*) and 45 minutes northwest of Arles (via Tarascon). The handy Rive Gauche parking is off D-981 (the road from Remoulins to Uzès). (Parking is also available on the Rive Droite side, but it's farther away from the museum.) If going to Arles from the Pont du Gard, follow signs to *Nîmes* (not Avignon), then follow D-986.

By Bus: Buses run to Pont du Gard (on the Rive Gauche side) from Nîmes, Uzès, and Avignon. Combining Pont du Gard with Nîmes or Uzès makes a good day-trip excursion from Avignon. Line #169 runs from Avignon to Nîmes via the Pont du Gard, and line #205 runs from Avignon to Uzès via the Pont du Gard. Together these two lines provide eight buses each day from **Avignon** Monday through Saturday in summer (4/day Sun and off-season; 45 min). From **Nîmes,** take line #168 (direction: Collias) or #169 (direction: Avignon) to Pont du Gard (€10-round-trip, Mon–Sat 9 trips/day both buses combined, 3/day Sun and off-season, 45 min; check return times before you leave, tel. 04 66 29 27 29, www.stdgard.com).

Buses from Avignon enter the Pont du Gard site and stop at

the parking ticket booth. Other buses stop at the traffic roundabout 300 yards from the Pont du Gard. The stop from Avignon and to Nîmes is on the far side of the roundabout from the Pont du Gard; the stop from Nîmes and to Avignon is on the same side as the Pont du Gard, to the left as you enter the traffic circle from the Pont du Gard. Make sure you're waiting for the bus on the correct side of the traffic circle.

ORIENTATION

There are two riversides to the Pont du Gard: the left bank (Rive Gauche) and right bank (Rive Droite). Park on the Rive Gauche, where you'll find the museums, ticket booth, ATM, cafeteria, WCs, and shops—all built into a modern plaza. You'll see the aqueduct in two parts: first, the fine museum complex, then the actual river gorge spanned by the ancient bridge.

Cost: While it's free to see the aqueduct itself, the various optional activities each have a cost: parking (€5), museum (€6), corny film (€3), and a kids' space called *Ludo* (€4.50, scratch-and-sniff experience in English of various aspects of Roman life and the importance of water). The extensive outdoor *garrigue* natural area, featuring historic crops and landscapes of the Mediterranean, is free (though €4 buys you a helpful English booklet). During summer months, a nighttime sound-and-light show plays against the Pont du Gard. All of these attractions are designed to give the sight more meaning—and they do—but for most visitors, only the museum is worth paying for. The **€10 combo-ticket**—which covers all sights, plus parking—is a no-brainer for drivers, and the best bet for most visitors. Families save even more money with the **€20 family ticket** (covers two parents and up to four kids). If you get a combo-ticket, check the movie schedule; the romancing-the-aqueduct 25-minute film is silly, but it offers good information in a flirtatious French style...and a cool, entertaining, and cushy break.

Hours: The museum is open May–Sept Tue–Sun 9:30–19:00, Mon 13:00–19:00; Oct–April 9:30–17:00, Mon 13:00–17:00; closed two weeks in Jan. The aqueduct itself is free and open until 1:00 in the morning, as is the parking lot.

Information: Tel. 08 20 90 33 30, www.pontdugard.fr.

Canoe Rental: Consider seeing the Pont du Gard by canoe. Collias Canoes will pick you up at the Pont du Gard (or elsewhere, if prearranged) and shuttle you to the town of Collias. You'll float down the river to the nearby town of Remoulins, where they'll pick you up and take you back to the Pont du Gard (€18 per person, €9 for kids under 12, usually 2 hours, though you can take as long as you like, good idea to reserve the day before in July–Aug, tel. 04 66 22 85 54).

SIGHTS

▲Museum—The state-of-the-art museum's multimedia approach (well-presented in English) shows how water was an essential part of the Roman "art of living." You'll see examples of lead pipes, faucets, and siphons; walk through a rock quarry; and learn how they moved those huge rocks into place and how those massive arches were made. While actual artifacts from the aqueduct are few, the exhibit shows the immensity of the undertaking as well as the payoff. Imagine the excitement as this extravagant supply of water finally tumbled into Nîmes. A relaxing highlight is the scenic video helicopter ride along the entire 30-mile course of the structure, from its start at Uzès all the way to Nîmes.

▲▲▲Viewing the Aqueduct—A park-like path leads to the aqueduct. Until a few years ago, this was an actual road—adjacent to the aqueduct—that had spanned the river since 1743. Before you cross the bridge, pass under it and hike about 300 feet along the riverbank for a grand viewpoint from which to study the second-highest standing Roman structure. (Rome's Colosseum is only six feet taller.)

This was the biggest bridge in the whole 30-mile-long aqueduct. It seems exceptional because it is: The arches are twice the width of standard aqueducts, and the main arch is the largest the Romans ever built—80 feet (so it wouldn't get its feet wet). The bridge is about 160 feet high, and was originally about 1,100 feet long. Today, 12 arches are missing, reducing the length to 790 feet.

While the distance from the source (in Uzès) to Nîmes was only 12 miles as the eagle flew, engineers chose the most economical route, winding and zigzagging 30 miles. The water made the trip in 24 hours with a drop of only 40 feet. Ninety percent of the aqueduct is on or under the ground, but a few river canyons like this required bridges. A stone lid hides a four-foot-wide, six-foot-tall chamber lined with waterproof mortar that carried a stream for over 400 years. For 150 years, this system provided Nîmes with good drinking water. Expert as the Romans were, they miscalculated the backup caused by a downstream corner, and had to add the thin extra layer you can see just under the lid to make the channel deeper.

The bridge and the river below provide great fun for holiday-goers. While parents suntan on rocks, kids splash into the gorge from under the aqueduct. Some daredevils actually jump from the aqueduct's lower bridge—not knowing that crazy winds scrambled by the structure cause painful belly flops and sometimes even accidental deaths. For the most refreshing view, float flat on your back underneath the structure. (Bring a swimsuit and sandals for the rocks.)

The appearance of the entire gorge changed in 2002, when a huge flood flushed lots of greenery downstream. Those floodwaters put Roman provisions to the test. Notice the triangular-shaped buttresses at the lower level—designed to split and divert the force of any flood *around* the feet of the arches rather than *into* them. The 2002 floodwaters reached the top of those buttresses. Anxious park rangers winced at the sounds of trees crashing onto the ancient stones...but the arches stood strong.

The stones that jut out—giving the aqueduct a rough, unfinished appearance—supported the original scaffolding. The protuberances were left, rather than cut off, in anticipation of future repair needs. The lips under the arches supported wooden templates that allowed the stones in the round arches to rest on something until the all-important keystone was dropped into place. Each stone weighs four to six tons. The structure stands with no mortar—taking full advantage of the innovative Roman arch, made strong by gravity.

Hike over the bridge for a closer look. Across the river, a high trail (marked *panorama*) leads upstream and offers commanding views. On the exhibit side of the structure, a trail marked *Accès l'Aqueduc* leads up to surviving stretches of the aqueduct. For a peaceful walk alongside the top of the aqueduct (where it's on land and no longer a bridge), follow the red-and-yellow markings. Remains of this part are scant because of medieval cannibalization—frugal builders couldn't resist the pre-cut stones as they constructed local churches. The ancient quarry (about a third of a mile downstream on the exhibit side) may open to the public soon.

Museum Pass: The **Riviera Carte Musées pass,** a good value only for serious museum-goers, includes admission to many major Riviera museums such as Nice's Chagall and Matisse museums, Antibes' Picasso Museum (closed for much of 2007), La Trophée des Alpes, and the Exotic Gardens in Eze-le-Village. This pass will save you money only if you're planning to visit more than two museums in a day, or several museums over a few days (€10/1 day, €17/3 days, €27/7 days, buy at any participating sight).

Events: The Riviera is famous for staging major events. Unless you're actually taking part in the festivities, these events give you only room shortages and traffic jams. Here are the three biggies: Nice Carnival, Grand Prix of Monaco, and Festival de Cannes, better known as the Cannes Film Festival.

Getting Around the Riviera

Nice is well-located for exploring the Riviera by public transport. Eze-le-Village, Villefranche-sur-Mer, Antibes, and St-Paul-de-Vence are all within a 50-minute bus or train ride of Nice (details are provided under each destination). Boats go from Nice to Monaco and St-Tropez.

By Bus and Train: Many key Riviera destinations are connected by direct service from Nice. As the fare for any bus ride is just €1.30, the pricier train is only a better choice when it saves you time. You make the call—both modes of transportation work well.

Destination	Bus from Nice	Train from Nice
Villefranche	4/hr, 20 min	2/hr, 10 min, €1.70
Cap Ferrat	every 40 min, 30 min	none
Monaco	4/hr, 45 min	2/hr, 20 min, €3.30
Antibes	3/hr, 60 min	2/hr, 15–30 min, €3.80
Cannes	3/hr, 75 min	2/hr, 30–40 min, €5.80
St-Paul	every 40 min, 45 min	none
Vence	every 40 min, 50 min	none
Grasse	every 40 min, 65 min	1/hr, 75 min, €7
Eze-le-Village	7/day, 25 min	none
La Turbie	4/day, 45 min	none

By Minivan Excursion: Local TIs and most hotels have information on minivan excursions from Nice (€50–60/half-day, €80–110/day). **Med-Tour** is one of many (tel. 04 93 82 92 58 or 06 73 82 04 10, www.med-tour.com); **Tour Azur** is a bit pricier (tel. 04 93 44 88 77 or 06 71 90 76 70, www.tourazur.com); and **Revelation Tours** specializes in English tours (tel. 04 93 53 69 85 or 06 60 02 98 42, www.revelation-tours.com). All companies also offer private

THE FRENCH RIVIERA

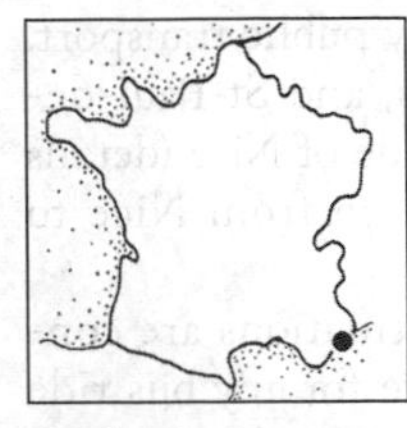

A hundred years ago, celebrities from London to Moscow flocked here to socialize, gamble, and escape the dreary weather at home. The belle époque is today's tourist craze, as this most sought-after, fun-in-the-sun destination now caters to budget travelers as well. Some of the Continent's most stunning scenery and intriguing museums lie along this strip of land—as do millions of heat-seeking tourists.

My favorite home base is Nice, the region's capital and France's fifth-largest city. With convenient train and bus connections to most regional sights, it's practical for train travelers. Urban Nice has a full palette of world-class museums, a grand beachfront promenade, a seductive old town, and all the drawbacks of a major city (traffic, crime, pollution, etc.). Evenings on the Riviera, a.k.a. the Côte d'Azur, were made for a stroll and outdoor dining. Nice also has the best selection of hotels in all price ranges, and good nightlife options. A car is a headache in Nice, though it's easily stored at one of the many pricey parking garages.

Helpful Hints

Medical Help: Riviera Medical Services has a list of English-speaking physicians for anywhere along the Riviera. They can help you make an appointment or call an ambulance (tel. 04 93 26 12 70, www.rivieramedical.com).

Sightseeing Reminder: On Monday, the Modern and Contemporary Art Museum, Fine Arts Museum, and cours Saleya market in Nice, along with Antibes' Marché Provençal, are closed; on Tuesday, the Chagall, Matisse, and Archaeological Museums in Nice are closed.

The French Riviera

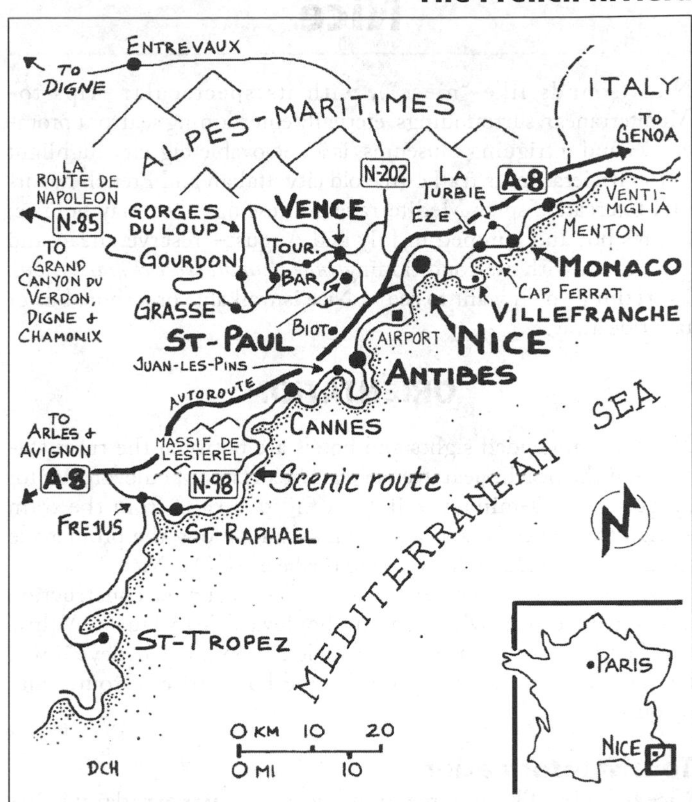

tours by the day or half day (check with them for their outrageous prices, about €90/hour).

By Boat: Trans Côte d'Azur offers scenic trips from Nice to Monaco and St-Tropez in the summer. Boats leave in the morning and return in the evening, giving you all day to explore your destination. Drinks and WCs are available on board. Boats to **Monaco** depart at 9:30 and return at 18:00 (€28 round-trip, 50 min each way; July–Aug daily; June and Sept Tue, Thu, and Sat only). Boats to **St-Tropez** depart at 9:00 and return at 19:00 (€55 round-trip, 2.5 hrs each way; July–Aug Tue–Sun, no boats Mon; late June and early Sept Tue, Thu, and Sun only). Tickets for St-Tropez boats often sell out—book a few days ahead (tel. 04 92 00 42 30, fax 04 92 00 42 31, www.trans-cote-azur.com). The boats leave from Nice's port, bassin des Amiraux, just below Castle Hill, with a blue ticket booth *(billeterie)* on quai de Lunel (see map on page 397). The same company also runs one-hour round-trip cruises along the coast to Cap Ferrat (see "Tours" for Nice, page 400).

Nice

Nice (sounds like "niece"), with its spectacular Alps-to-Mediterranean surroundings, eternally entertaining seafront promenade, and intriguing museums, is an enjoyable big-city highlight of the Riviera. In its traffic-free old city, Italian and French flavors mix to create a spicy Mediterranean dressing. Nice may be nice, but it's hot and jammed in July and August—reserve ahead and get a room with air-conditioning *(une chambre avec climatisation)*. Everything you'll want to see in Nice is walkable or a short bus or taxi ride away.

ORIENTATION

Most recommended sights and hotels are between the train station and the beach, near avenue Jean Médecin or boulevard Victor Hugo. It's a 20-minute walk (or a €10 taxi ride) from the train station to the beach, and a 20-minute walk along the promenade from the fancy Hôtel Negresco to the heart of Old Nice.

The first of three new tramway lines is under construction along avenue Jean Médecin and boulevard Jean Jaurès. While this first line is supposed to be completed soon, few believe it will be done on time. Be ready for car and bus traffic re-routes and detours.

Tourist Information

Nice's helpful TI has three locations: at the **airport** (daily 8:00–21:00), next to the **train station** (Mon–Sat 8:00–19:00, Sun 10:00–17:00, 1 hour later in summer), and facing the **beach** at 5 promenade des Anglais (same hours as train station TI except closed Sun, tel. 08 92 70 74 07 costs €0.34/min, www.nicetourisme.com). Pick up the thorough *Practical Guide to Nice,* information on day trips (such as city maps and details on boat excursions), and a free Nice map (or find a better one at your hotel).

Only art-lovers should consider buying a **museum pass** for sights in Nice or throughout the Riviera (sold at any participating sight). The Riviera Carte Musées pass covers many regional sights, including four museums in Nice (Chagall, Matisse, Fine Arts, and Modern/Contemporary Art; €10/1 day, €17/3 days, €27/7 days; for more information, see page 394). A seven-day Nice-only museum pass, called Carte Passe-Musées 7 Jours, is also available (€6, does not include Chagall Museum).

Nice

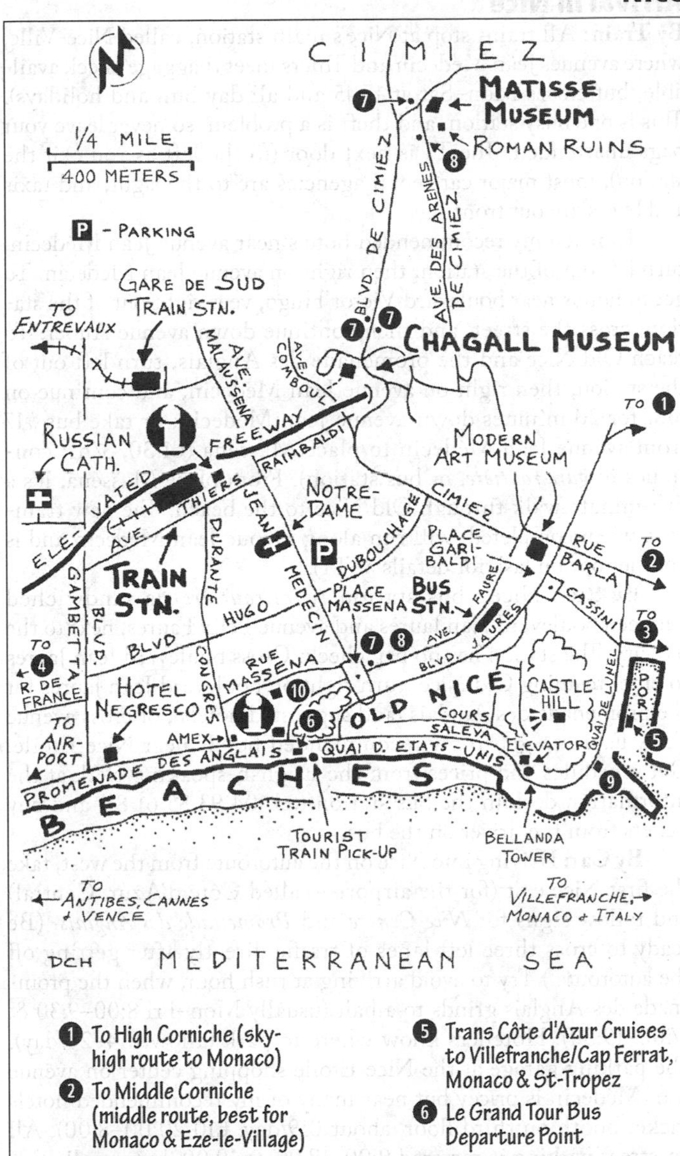

CIMIEZ
MATISSE MUSEUM
ROMAN RUINS
1/4 MILE
400 METERS
P - PARKING
BLVD. DE CIMIEZ
AVE. DES ARENES DE CIMIEZ
GARE DE SUD TRAIN STN.
TO ENTREVAUX
AVE. MALAUSSENA
AVE. COMBOUL
CHAGALL MUSEUM
TO 1
FREEWAY
RUSSIAN CATH.
RAIMBALDI
MODERN ART MUSEUM
ELEVATED
AVE. THIERS
JEAN
NOTRE-DAME
CIMIEZ
DUBOUCHAGE
PLACE GARIBALDI
RUE BARLA
TO 2
TRAIN STN.
DURANTE
MEDECIN
BUS STN.
AVE. FAURE
CASSINI
GAMBETTA BLVD.
HUGO
PLACE MASSENA
TO 3
TO 4 R. DE FRANCE
BLVD
RUE MASSENA
BLVD. JAURES
QUAI DE LUNEL
PORT
HOTEL NEGRESCO
CONGRES
OLD NICE
CASTLE HILL
TO AIRPORT
AMEX
COURS SALEYA
ELEVATOR
PROMENADE DES ANGLAIS
QUAI D. ETATS-UNIS
BEACHES
TOURIST TRAIN PICK-UP
BELLANDA TOWER
TO ANTIBES, CANNES & VENCE
TO VILLEFRANCHE, MONACO & ITALY
DCH
MEDITERRANEAN SEA
1 To High Corniche (sky-high route to Monaco)
2 To Middle Corniche (middle route, best for Monaco & Eze-le-Village)
3 To Low Corniche (low route to Villefranche-sur-Mer)
4 To Fine Arts Museum
5 Trans Côte d'Azur Cruises to Villefranche/Cap Ferrat, Monaco & St-Tropez
6 Le Grand Tour Bus Departure Point
7 Bus #15 Stop
8 Bus #17 Stop
9 World War II Monument
10 US Embassy

Arrival in Nice

By Train: All trains stop at Nice's main station, called Nice-Ville, where avenues Jean Médecin and Thiers meet (baggage check available, but closes Mon–Sat at 17:45 and all day Sun and holidays). This is one busy station, and theft is a problem, so never leave your bags unattended. The TI is next door (to the left as you exit the station), most major car-rental agencies are to the right, and taxis and buses are out front.

To reach my recommended hotels near avenue Jean Médecin, turn left out of the station, then right on avenue Jean Médecin. To get to hotels near boulevard Victor Hugo, veer right out of the station, cross the street, and then continue down avenue Auber. To reach Old Nice and the promenade des Anglais, turn left out of the station, then right on avenue Jean Médecin, and continue on foot for 20 minutes down avenue Jean Médecin; or take bus #17 from avenue Jean Médecin to place Masséna (€1.30, 3/hr; continues to *gare routière,* or bus station). From place Masséna, it's a five-minute walk through Old Nice to the beach. The new tramway, when completed, will run along avenue Jean Médecin and is another option (ask for details at TI).

By Bus: Nice's bus station *(gare routière)* is sandwiched between boulevard Jean Jaurès and avenue Felix Faures, next to the old city. The station has no bag check. Cross boulevard Jean Jaurès to enter teeming Old Nice, turn right on boulevard Jean Jaurès for the promenade des Anglais (and suggested hotels), or cross avenue Félix Faure to get to my recommended hotels near Nice Etoile. Get schedules and prices from the English-speaking clerk at the information desk in the bus station (tel. 04 93 85 61 81) and buy tickets from the driver on the bus.

By Car: Driving into Nice on the autoroute from the west, take the first Nice exit (for the airport—called Côte d'Azur, Central) and follow signs for *Nice Centre* and *Promenade des Anglais.* (Be ready to cross three left lanes of traffic directly after getting off the autoroute.) Try to avoid arriving at rush hour, when the promenade des Anglais grinds to a halt (usually Mon–Fri 8:00–9:30 & 17:00–19:30). Hoteliers know where to park (allow €14–20/day). The parking garage at the Nice Etoile shopping center on avenue Jean Médecin is pricey but near many of my recommended hotels (ticket booth on third floor, about €19/day, €10 20:00–8:00). All on-street parking is metered 9:00–18:00 or 19:00, but usually free all day on Sunday.

By Plane: For information on Nice's airport, see "Transportation Connections," page 420.

Helpful Hints

Theft Alert: Nice has more than its share of pickpockets. Have nothing important on or around your waist, unless it's in a money belt tucked out of sight (thieves target fanny packs); don't leave anything visible in your car; be wary of scooters when standing at intersections; don't leave things unattended on the beach while swimming; and stick to main streets in Old Nice after dark.

US Consulate: You'll find it at 7 avenue Gustave V (tel. 04 93 88 89 55, fax 04 93 87 07 38).

Canadian Consulate: It's at 10 rue Lamartine (tel. 04 93 92 93 22, fax 04 93 92 55 51).

Museums: Some Nice museums (Chagall, Matisse, Archaeological) are closed Tuesdays, while others (Modern and Contemporary Art, Fine Arts) close on Mondays. Most are free (and crowded) the first Sunday of the month.

Grocery Store: The big **Monoprix** on avenue Jean Médecin and rue Biscarra has a wide selection and cold drinks (closed Sun). You'll also find many small grocery stores (some open Sun and late hours) near my recommended hotels.

Internet Access: Places to get online are everywhere in Nice. Ask at your hotel, or just look up as you walk.

English Bookstore: The **Cat's Whiskers** has an eclectic selection of novels and regional travel books, including mine. Say *bonjour* to mellow owner Linda (Mon–Sat 9:30–12:00 & 14:00–19:00, closed Sun, 26–30 rue Lamartine, near recommended Hôtel du Petit Louvre, tel. 04 93 80 02 66).

Laundry: You'll find launderettes everywhere in Nice—ask your hotelier for the nearest one. The self-service **Point Laverie** at the corner of rue Alberti and rue Pastorelli, next to Hôtel Vendôme, is central (daily 8:00–20:00).

Renting a Bike (and Other Wheels): Roller Station rents bikes (*vélos,* €5/hr, €10/half-day, €15/day), rollerblades (*rollers,* €6/day), Razor-type scooters (*trotinettes,* €6/half-day, €9/day), and skateboards (€6/half-day, €9/day). You'll need to leave your ID as a deposit (daily 10:00–19:00, across from seaside promenade at 49 quai des Etats-Unis—see map on page 411, another location at 10 rue Cassini near place Garibaldi, tel. 04 93 62 99 05).

Car Rental: Renting a car is easiest at Nice's airport, which has offices for all of the major companies. You'll also find these companies represented at Nice's main train station: **Budget** (tel. 04 93 21 42 51), **Europcar** (tel. 04 93 82 17 34), and **Hertz** (tel. 04 97 03 01 20).

American Express: A small office is at the airport.

English Radio: Tune into Riviera-Radio at FM 106.5.

Views: For panoramic views, climb Castle Hill (see page 405), or take a one-hour boat trip (under "Tours," below).

Rocky Beaches: To make life tolerable on the rocks, swimmers should buy a pair of the cheap plastic beach shoes sold at many shops (flip-flops fall off in the water).

Getting Around Nice

While you can easily walk to most attractions in Nice, you'll want to ride the **bus** to the Chagall and Matisse museums. A single ride costs €1.30 (ticket good for 74 min in one direction—can't be used for a round-trip), and an all-day pass is €4. Remember that because of construction on the new tramway, bus routes may change—confirm at the TI or as you board.

Taxis are handy for the Chagall and Matisse museums and the Russian Cathedral (figure €10–12 from promenade des Anglais, 10 percent more at night and on Sundays). They normally pick up only at taxi stands *(tête de station)*, or you can call (tel. 04 93 13 78 78).

The first line of the brand-new **tramway**—which might be up and running in 2007—will run along avenue Jean Médecin and boulevard Jean Jaurès. Get the latest from the TI.

The hokey **tourist train** is handy for getting to Castle Hill (see "Tours," below).

TOURS

Bus Tour—Le Grand Tour Bus provides a hop-on, hop-off option on an open-deck bus with headphone commentary. The full route (about 90 min) includes the promenade des Anglais, old port, Cap de Nice, and the Chagall and Matisse museums on Cimiez Hill (€19/1-day pass, €22/2-day pass, cheaper for seniors and students, €10 for last tour of the day at about 18:45, departures 2/hr, buy tickets on bus, main stop is near where promenade des Anglais and quai des Etats-Unis meet, across from plage Beau Rivage—look for signs, tel. 04 92 29 17 00). This tour is a pricey way to get to the Chagall and Matisse museums, but it's a good option if you also want a city overview tour.

Tourist Train—For €6, you can spend 40 embarrassing minutes on the *petit train* tooting along the promenade, through the old city, and up to Castle Hill. This is a sweat-free way to get to Castle Hill (every 30 min, recorded English commentary, meet train near Le Grand Tour Bus stop on quai des Etats-Unis, tel. 04 93 62 85 48).

▲Boat Cruise—On this one-hour, star-studded tour offered by Trans Côte d'Azur, you'll cruise in a comfortable, yacht-sized vessel to Cap Ferrat and past Villefranche-sur-Mer, then return to Nice with a run along the promenade des Anglais. French (and sometimes English-speaking) guides point out mansions owned by some pretty rich people, including Elton John (just as you leave Nice, soft-yellow square-shaped place right on the water), Sean Connery (on the hill above Elton, with rounded arches and tower), Microsoft mogul Paul Allen (in saddle of Cap Ferrat hill, above yellow-umbrella beach with sloping red-tile roof), and Mick Jagger (between Cap Ferrat and Villefranche, pink place hidden by trees). The best views are from the seats on top (€13, June–Oct 2/day, fewer departures in off-season, arrive 30 min early to get best seats, drinks and WCs available). For directions to the dock and contact information, see "Getting Around the Riviera—By Boat" on page 394.

Walking Tour—The TI on the promenade des Anglais organizes guided walking tours of Old Nice from May through October (€12, 2.5 hours, 1/week, usually Sat mornings, reservations necessary, tel. 08 92 70 74 07). Nice's cultural association (Centre du Patrimoine) offers €3 walks on varying themes in English—call to get their schedule (tel. 04 92 00 41 90, most tours start at their office at 75 quai des Etats-Unis).

Local Guide—Lovely Pascale Rucker tailors excellent tours to your interests in and around Nice. Book in advance or on short notice (€110/half-day, €180/day, tel. & fax 04 93 87 77 89, mobile 06 16 24 29 52).

SELF-GUIDED WALK

A Scratch-and-Sniff Walk Through Old Nice

• *See the map on page 416, and start at Nice's main market square, the...*

Cours Saleya: Named for its broad exposure to the sun *(soleil)*, this commotion of color, sights, smells, and people has been Nice's market square since the Middle Ages (produce market held daily until 13:00—except on Monday, when an antique market takes over the square). Amazingly, part of this square was a parking lot until 1980, when an underground parking garage was finally built.

Stroll down the center of the cours. The first section is devoted to freshly cut flowers that seem to grow effortlessly and everywhere in this ideal climate. Carnations, roses, and jasmine are local favorites in what has been the Riviera's biggest flower market since the 19th century. The boisterous produce section trumpets the season with mushrooms, strawberries, white asparagus, zucchini flowers—whatever's fresh gets top billing.

Place Pierre Gautier (also called Plassa dou Gouvernou—bilingual street signs include the old Niçoise language, an Italian dialect) is where the actual farmers set up stalls to sell their produce and herbs directly.

Resume your stroll down the center of cours Saleya, stopping when you see La Cambuse restaurant on your left. In front, hovering over the black barrel fire with the paella-like pan on top, is the self-proclaimed Queen of the Market, Thérèse (tehr-ehz). When she's not looking for a husband, Thérèse is cooking *socca,* Nice's chickpea crêpe specialty. Spend €2 for a wad of *socca* (careful—it's hot, but good). If she doesn't have a pan out, that means it's on its way (watch for the frequent scooter deliveries). Wait in line...or else it'll be all gone when you return.

• *Continue down cours Saleya. The fine golden building at the end is where Henri Matisse lived for 17 years. Turn left at the Café des Ponchettes, and head down...*

Rue de la Poissonnerie: Look up at the first building on your right. Adam and Eve are squaring off, each holding a zucchini-like gourd. This scene (post-apple) represents the annual rapprochement in Nice to make up for the sins of a too-much-fun Carnival (Mardi Gras). Nice residents have partied hard during Carnival for more than 700 years. A few doors down, on the left, find the small church dedicated to St. Rita, the patron saint of desperate causes. She holds a special place in locals' hearts.

• *Turn right on the next street, then left on Right Street...*

Rue Droite: In the Middle Ages, this straight, skinny street provided the most direct route from wall to wall, or river to sea. Stop at Esipuno's bakery (at place du Jésus). Thirty years ago, this baker was voted the best in France, and his son now runs the place. Notice the firewood stacked by the oven and his trophies (earned for best breads). Farther along, at #28, Thérèse (whom you met earlier) cooks her *socca* in the wood-fired oven before she carts it to her barrel on cours Saleya. The balconies of the mansion in the next block mark the Palais Lascaris (1647), a rare souvenir from one of Nice's most prestigious families (free, Wed–Mon 10:00–18:00, closed Tue, worth touring for a peek at 1700s Baroque Italy high life, look up and make faces back at the guys under the balconies).

• *Turn left on the rue de la Loge, then left again on rue Centrale, to reach...*

Place Rossetti: The most Italian of Nice's piazzas, place Rossetti feels more like Rome than Nice. This square comes alive after dark. Fenocchio is popular for its many gelato flavors. Walk to the fountain and stare back at the church. This is the Cathedral of St. Réparate—an unassuming building for a major city's cathedral. The cathedral was relocated here in the 1500s, when Castle Hill was temporarily converted to military-only. The name comes from Nice's patron saint, a teenage virgin named Réparate whose martyred body floated to Nice in the fourth century, accompanied by angels. The interior is overwhelmingly Baroque. Remember that Baroque was a response to the Protestant Reformation. With the Catholic Church's "Counter-Reformation," the theatrical energy of churches was cranked up—with reenergized, high-powered saints and eye-popping decor.

• *Our walk is over. Castle Hill is straight up the stepped lane opposite the cathedral (see page 405).*

ACTIVITIES

▲Wheeling the Promenade—Get a bike and ride along the coast in both directions along Nice's waterfront boulevard (described below). Allow 30 minutes each way. Roller Station rents bikes, inline skates, and mini-scooters (see "Helpful Hints," above). Both of the following paths start along the promenade des Anglais.

The path to the west stops just before the airport at perhaps the most scenic *boules* courts in France. Stop and watch the old-timers while away their afternoon tossing those shiny metal balls.

Heading east, you'll round the hill—passing a scenic cape and the town's memorial to both World Wars—to the harbor of Nice, with a chance to survey some fancy yachts. Pedal around the harbor and follow the coast past the Corsica ferry terminal (you'll need to carry your bike up a flight of steps). From there, the path leads to an appealing tree-lined residential district.

Relaxing at the Beaches— Nice is where the masses relax on the rocks. After settling into the smooth pebbles, you can play beach volleyball, table tennis, or *boules;* rent paddleboats, personal watercraft, or windsurfing equipment; explore ways to use your zoom lens as a telescope; or snooze on comfy beach beds with end tables. To rent a spot on the beach, compare rates, as prices vary—beaches on the east end of the bay are usually cheaper (mattress and chaise lounge-€12–18, umbrella-€5, towel-€3). Many hotels have special deals with certain beaches for discounted rental (check with your hotel for details). Consider lunch in your bathing suit (€10–12 salads and pizzas in bars and restaurants all along the beach). For a peaceful cup of coffee on the beach, stop here first thing in the morning before the crowds hit. Several beach bars offer drinks with a view (ideal before dinner). *Plage Publique* signs explain the 15 beach no-nos (translated into English).

While Nice's beaches are traditionally rocky, a small sandy area appeared toward the Italy end of the bay in 2006.

SIGHTS

Along the Promenade des Anglais

There's something for everyone along this four-mile-long seafront circus, worth ▲▲▲. Watch the Europeans at play, admire the azure Mediterranean, anchor yourself on a blue bench, and prop your feet up on the made-to-order guardrail. Later in the day, come back to join the evening parade of tans along the promenade.

The broad sidewalks of the promenade des Anglais ("walkway of the English") were financed by wealthy English tourists who wanted a safe place to stroll and admire the view. In 1822, the walk was paved in marble for aristocrats who didn't want to dirty their shoes or smell the fishy gravel. For now, stroll like the belle époque English aristocrats for whom the promenade was built.

Start at the Hotel Negresco, then cross to the sea and end your promenade at Castle Hill. The following sights are listed in the order you'll pass them. This walk is ideally done at sunset (as a pre-dinner stroll).

Hôtel Negresco—Nice's finest hotel (also a historic monument) offers the city's most expensive beds and a free "museum" interior (always open—provided you're dressed decently, absolutely no beach attire). March straight through the lobby (as if you're staying there) into the exquisite Salon Royal. The chandelier hanging from the Eiffel-built dome is made of 16,000 pieces of crystal. It was built in France for the Russian czar's Moscow palace...but because of the Bolshevik Revolution in 1917, he couldn't take delivery. Read the explanation of the dome and saunter around counterclockwise: The bucolic scene, painted in 1913 for the hotel, sets the tone. Nip into the toilets for either a turn-of-the-century powder room or a Battle of Waterloo experience. The chairs nearby were typical of the age (cones of silence for an afternoon nap sitting up).

Bay of Angels (Baie des Anges)—Stand facing the sea. The body of Nice's patron saint, Réparate, was supposedly escorted into this bay by angels in the fourth century. To your right is where you might have been escorted into France—Nice's airport, built on a massive landfill. On that tip of land way beyond the runway is Cap d'Antibes. Until 1860, Antibes and Nice were in different countries—Antibes was French, but Nice was a protectorate of the Italian kingdom of Savoy-Piedmont, a.k.a. the Kingdom of Sardinia. (During that period, the Var River—just west of Nice—was the geographic border between these two peoples.) In 1850, the people here spoke Italian and ate pasta. As Italy was uniting, the region was given a choice: Join the new country of Italy or join France (which was enjoying good times under the rule of Napoleon III). The vast majority voted in 1860 to go French...and *voilà!*

To the far left lies Villefranche-sur-Mer (marked by the tower at land's end—and home to lots of millionaires), then Monaco (with more millionaires), then Italy (with millions of Italians). Behind you are the foothills of the Alps (Alpes Maritimes), which gather threatening clouds, ensuring that the Côte d'Azur enjoys sunshine more than 300 days each year. While half a million people live here, pollution is carefully treated—the water is routinely tested and very clean. Stroll the promenade with the sea starboard, and read about "Relaxing on the Beaches" (under "Activities," above).

Albert I Park—The park was named for the Belgian king who enjoyed wintering here. While the English came first, the Belgians and Russians were also huge fans of 19th-century Nice. The 1960 statue in the park commemorates Nice's being part of France for 100 years. If you detour from the promenade into the park and continue down the center of the grassy strip, you'll be walking over Nice's river, the Paillon (covered since the 1800s). For centuries, this river was Nice's natural defense. A fortified wall ran along its length to the sea. With the arrival of tourism in the 1800s, Nice expanded over and beyond the river.

Castle Hill (Colline du Château)—The hill, in an otherwise flat city center, offers good views over Nice, the port (to the east), the foothills of the Alps, and the Mediterranean. The views are best at sunset or if it's really clear (park closes at 20:00 in summer, earlier off-season). You can get to the top by foot, by elevator (€0.70 one-way, €1 round-trip, runs daily 10:00–19:00, until 20:00 in summer, next to beachfront Hôtel Suisse), or by tourist train (described under "Tours" on page 400).

The city of Nice was first settled here by Greeks circa 400 B.C. In the Middle Ages, there was a massive castle with turrets, high walls, and soldiers at the ready. With the river guarding one side and the sea the other, this mountain fortress seemed strong—until Louis XIV leveled it in 1706. Nice's medieval seawall ran along the lineup of two-story buildings below. Today, you'll find a waterfall, a playground, two cafés (fair prices), and a cemetery—but no castle—on Castle Hill. Nice's port, where you'll find Trans Côte d'Azur's boat cruises (described on page 395), is just below on the east edge of Castle Hill.

Museums

Remember that all Nice museums are free (and more crowded) the first Sunday of the month. The first two museums (Chagall and Matisse) are northeast of Nice's city center. Because they're both relatively difficult to reach and on the same bus line (in the same direction), it makes most sense to visit them on the same trip. The Chagall Museum is much closer to the center, while Matisse is a 30-minute walk (or quick bus ride) farther out.

▲▲▲Chagall Museum (Musée National Marc Chagall)—Even if you're suspicious of modern art, this museum—with the largest collection of Chagall's work in captivity anywhere—is a delight. After World War II, Chagall returned from the US to settle in nearby Vence. Between 1954 and 1967, he painted a cycle of 17 large murals designed for, and donated to, this museum. These paintings, inspired by the biblical books of Genesis, Exodus, and the Song of Songs, make up the "nave," or core, of what Chagall called the "House of Brotherhood."

Each painting is a lighter-than-air collage of images that draw from Chagall's Russian-folk-village youth, his Jewish heritage, biblical themes, and his feeling that he existed somewhere between heaven and earth. He believed that the Bible was a synonym for nature, and that color and biblical themes were key ingredients for understanding God's love for his creation. Chagall's brilliant blues and reds celebrate nature, as do his spiritual and folk themes.

On your way out, be sure to visit the three Chagall stained-glass windows in the auditorium (depicting God's creation of the universe). An idyllic garden café with fair prices awaits by the entrance to the museum grounds. A spick-and-span WC is to the far left in the garden as you face the museum (there's one inside, too).

Cost and Hours: €6.50, can cost a little more during special exhibits, covered by Riviera Carte Musées pass, Wed–Mon 10:00–17:00, July–Sept until 18:00, closed Tue, avenue Docteur Ménard, tel. 04 93 53 87 20, www.musee-chagall.fr.

Getting to the Chagall Museum: You can get there by bus or on foot. **Bus** #15 serves the Chagall Museum from place Masséna (stop faces eastbound on rue Gioffredo, a block east of Galleries Lafayette; €1.30, Mon–Sat 6/hr, Sun 3/hr). The museum's bus stop (called Musée Chagall) is on avenue de Cimiez. To **walk** from central Nice to the Chagall Museum, go to the train-station end of avenue Jean Médecin and turn right onto boulevard Raimbaldi. Walk four long blocks along the elevated road, then turn left onto avenue Raymond Comboul and follow *Musée Chagall* signs.

Leaving the Museum: Turn right out of the museum, then head left up boulevard de Cimiez to find the #15 bus stop. To catch the bus up to the Matisse Museum, use the stop across the street, heading uphill. For buses headed back to the city center, stay on the Chagall side of the street.

▲▲Matisse Museum (Musée Matisse)—This museum, worth ▲▲▲ for his fans, will be closed until sometime in 2007. It contains the world's largest collection of Henri Matisse paintings (though it's still not that big). It offers a painless introduction to the artist, whose style was shaped by Mediterranean light and by fellow Côte d'Azur artists Pablo Picasso and Pierre-Auguste Renoir. The collection is scattered through several rooms with a few worthwhile works, though it lacks a certain *je ne sais quoi* when compared to the Chagall Museum.

Henri Matisse, the master of leaving things out, could suggest a woman's body with a single curvy line—leaving it to the viewer's mind to fill in the rest. Ignoring traditional 3-D perspective, he used simple dark outlines saturated with bright blocks of color to create recognizable but simplified scenes composed into a decorative pattern to express nature's serene beauty. You don't look "through" a Matisse canvas, like a window; you look "at" it, like wallpaper.

Matisse understood how colors and shapes affect us emotionally. He could create either shocking, clashing works (Fauvism) or geometrical, balanced, harmonious ones (later works). While other modern artists reveled in purely abstract design, Matisse (almost) always kept the subject matter at least vaguely recognizable. He used unreal colors and distorted lines not just to portray what an object looks like, but to express the object's inner nature (even inanimate objects). Meditating on his paintings helps you connect with nature—or so Matisse hoped.

Touring the Museum: The entrance is on the middle floor. After entering (miniscule-print English handout available), go down one flight of stairs and find a timeline of Matisse's life (on a wall plaque, in English), a WC, and temporary exhibits of his work. A wildly colorful paper cutout *(Flowers and Fruits)*, hanging below, screams "Riviera."

Go back upstairs to the entry level and find the two rooms at the far right (Rooms 9 and 10) that house paintings from his formative years as a student. Other rooms on this floor highlight Matisse's fascination with dance, and display pencil drawings and bronze busts. Head up one flight of stairs, following the smaller steps halfway up to the right, and see sketches and models of his famous Chapel of the Rosary in nearby Vence, and related religious works. On the same floor, find paper cutouts from his *Jazz* series, more bronze sculptures, and linen embroideries inspired by his travels to Polynesia.

Cost, Hours, Location: €4, covered by Riviera Carte Musées pass, closed until sometime in 2007, Wed–Mon 10:00–18:00, closed Tue, tel. 04 93 81 08 08, www.musee-matisse-nice.org. The museum, at 164 avenue des Arènes de Cimiez, is set in an olive grove amid the ruins of the Roman city of Cemenelum.

Getting to the Matisse Museum: It's a long uphill walk from the city center. Take the bus (details below) or a cab (about €12 from the promenade des Anglais). Once here, walk into the park to find the pink villa.

Buses #15 and #17 offer frequent service to the Matisse Museum from just off place Masséna on rue Gioffredo, a block east of Galleries Lafayette department store (€1.30). The bus stop for the museum is called Arènes-Matisse. When leaving the museum, find the stop for bus #15 (with the most frequent service downtown, stopping en route at the Chagall Museum) by exiting the park and crossing boulevard de Cimiez, where the two roads meet (the stop is on boulevard de Cimiez, not avenue des Arènes de Cimiez; see map on page 411). The stop for bus #17 (less frequent, no Chagall stop) also faces downhill, but it's on avenue des Arènes de Cimiez. Confusing, I know.

Modern and Contemporary Art Museum (Musée d'Art Moderne et d'Art Contemporain)—This ultramodern museum features an explosively colorful, far-out, yet manageable permanent collection (on the second floor) of mostly American and European art from the 1960s and 1970s. The exhibits include a few works by Andy Warhol, Roy Lichtenstein, and Jean Tinguely, and small models of Christo's famous wrappings. Several of Niki de Saint Phalle's works are almost huggable. The temporary exhibits can be as appealing to modern-art-lovers as the permanent collection—ask the TI what's playing.

Cost, Hours, Location: €4, covered by Riviera Carte Musées pass, Tue–Sun 10:00–18:00, closed Mon, about a 15-minute walk from place Masséna, near bus station on promenade des Arts, tel. 04 93 62 61 62, www.mamac-nice.org.

Molinard Perfume Museum—The Molinard family has been making perfume in Grasse (about an hour's drive or train ride from Nice) since 1849. Their Nice store has a small museum in the back illustrating the story of their industry. Back when people believed water spread the plague (Louis XIV supposedly bathed less than once a year), doctors advised people to rub fragrances into their skin and then powder their body. Back then, perfume was a necessity of everyday life.

Room 1 shows photos of the local flowers used in perfume production. Room 2 shows the earliest (18th-century) production method. Petals would be laid on a bed of animal fat. After baking in the sun, the fat would absorb the essence of the flowers. Petals would be replaced daily for two months until the fat was saturated. Models and old photos show the later distillation process (660 pounds of lavender would produce only a quarter-gallon of essence). Perfume is "distilled like cognac and then aged like wine." Room 3 shows the desk of a "nose" (top perfume creator). Of the 150 real "noses" in the world, more than 100 are French. You are welcome to enjoy the testing bottles before heading into the shop.

Cost, Hours, Location: Free, daily 10:00–19:00, sometimes closed Mon off-season, just between beach and place Masséna at 20 rue St. François de Paule, tel. 04 93 62 90 50, www.molinard.com.

Other Nice Museums—These museums are acceptable rainy-day options.

The **Fine Arts Museum** (Musée des Beaux-Arts), located in a sumptuous villa with lovely gardens, houses 6,000 works from the 17th to 20th centuries, and will satisfy your need for a fine-arts fix

(€4, covered by Riviera Carte Musées pass, Tue–Sun 10:00–18:00, closed Mon, 3 avenue des Baumettes, western end of Nice, take bus #38 from the bus station, tel. 04 92 15 28 28).

The **Archaeological Museum** (Musée Archeologique) displays various objects from the Romans' occupation of this region. It's convenient—just below the Matisse Museum—but has little of interest to anyone but Ancient Roman aficionados. You also get access to the Roman bath ruins...which are, sadly, overgrown with weeds (€4, very limited information in English, Wed–Mon 10:00–18:00, closed Tue, near Matisse Museum at 160 avenue des Arènes de Cimiez, tel. 04 93 81 59 57).

Nice's city history museum, **Museum Masséna** (Musée Masséna), is closed, likely through 2007 (but may re-open earlier than expected—check with the TI for the latest).

Russian Cathedral

Nice's Russian Orthodox church (Cathédrale Russe)—claimed to be the finest outside Russia—is worth ▲ and a visit. Five hundred rich Russian families wintered in Nice in the late 19th century. Since they couldn't pray in a Catholic church, the community needed a worthy Orthodox house of worship. Czar Nicholas I's widow saw the need and provided the land (which required tearing down her house). Czar Nicholas II gave this church to the Russian community in 1912. (A few years later, Russian comrades—who didn't winter on the Riviera—assassinated him.) Here in the land of olives and anchovies, these proud onion domes seem odd. But, I imagine, so did those old Russians.

Cost, Hours, Location: €2.50, daily 9:00–12:00 & 14:30–18:00, until 17:00 off-season, chanted services Sat at 17:30 or 18:00, Sun at 10:00, no tourist visits during services, no shorts, 10-minute walk behind station at 17 boulevard du Tzarewitch, tel. 04 93 96 88 02.

NIGHTLIFE

The promenade des Anglais, cours Saleya, and rue Masséna are all worth an evening walk. Nice's bars play host to one of the Riviera's most happening late-night scenes, full of jazz and rock 'n' roll. Most activity focuses on Old Nice, near place Rossetti and along rue Droite. Plan on a cover charge or expensive drinks. If you're out very late, avoid walking alone. The plush bar at Hôtel Negresco is fancy-cigar old-English. Nice is well-known for its lively after-dark action; for more relaxed and accessible nightlife, consider nearby Antibes.

SLEEPING

Don't look for charm in Nice. Go for modern and clean, with a central location and, from June to September, air-conditioning. Reserve early for summer visits. The rates listed here are for April through October. Prices generally drop €10–20 from November through March, and go sky-high during the Nice Carnival, Monaco's Grand Prix, and the Cannes film festival. June is convention month, and Nice is one of Europe's top convention cities—so book ahead and be ready for higher prices at some hotels. For parking, ask your hotelier (several have limited private parking), or see "Arrival in Nice—By Car," page 398.

I've divided my sleeping recommendations into three areas: between the train station and Nice Etoile shopping center (with easy access to the train station and a 15-min walk to Old Nice, or a 20-min walk to the promenade des Anglais); between Nice Etoile and Old Nice (east of avenue Jean Médecin, with better access to Old Nice and the sea at quai des Etats-Unis); and between boulevard Victor Hugo and the promenade des Anglais (a somewhat classier area, offering better access to the promenade but longer walks to the train station and Old Nice). I've also listed two hotels near the airport.

Between the Train Station and Nice Etoile

Most hotels near the station ghetto are overrun, overpriced, and loud. These are the pleasant exceptions (most are near avenue Jean Médecin).

$$$ Hôtel Excelsior***, one block below the station, is an appealing place with turn-of-the-century decor, a pleasing garden courtyard, and 40 top-notch rooms (standard Db-€120, bigger

Sleep Code

(€1 = about $1.30, country code: 33)
S = Single, **D** = Double/Twin, **T** = Triple, **Q** = Quad, **b** = bathroom, **s** = shower only, * = French hotel rating (0–4 stars). Hotels speak English, have elevators, and accept credit cards unless otherwise noted.

To help you sort easily through these listings, I've divided the rooms into three categories based on the price for a standard double room with bath:

$$$ Higher Priced—Most rooms €100 or more.
$$ Moderately Priced—Most rooms between €70–100.
$ Lower Priced—Most rooms €70 or less.

Nice Hotels

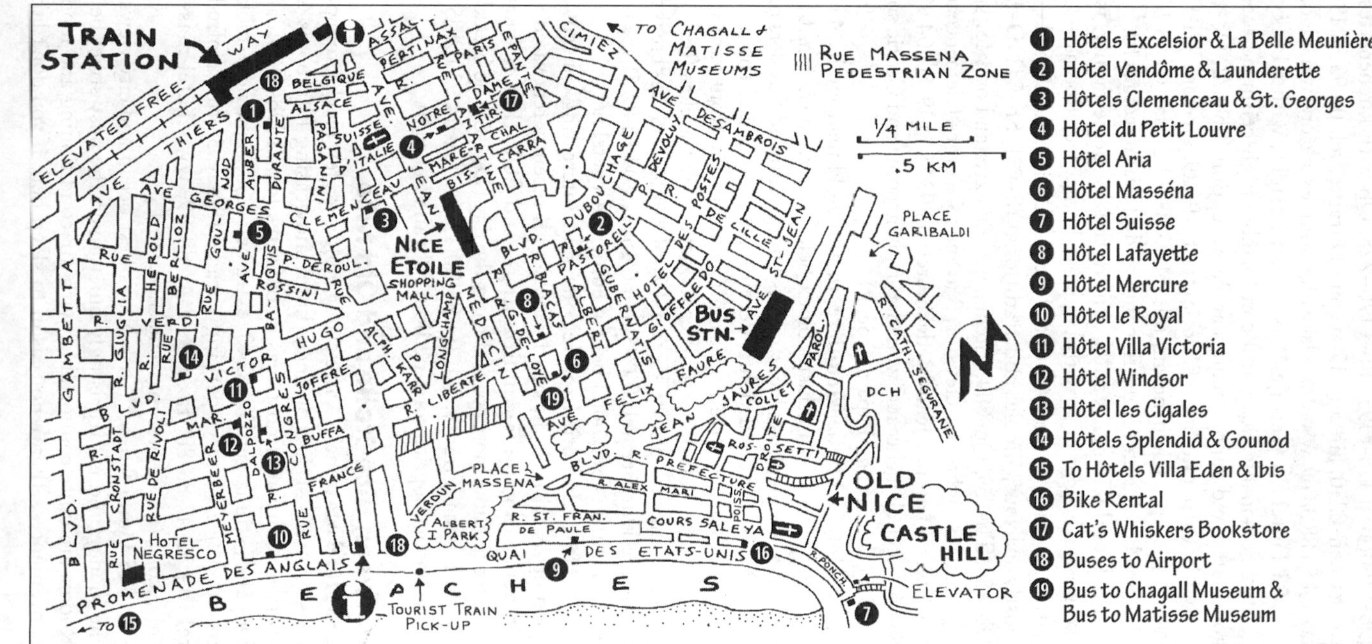
Train Station
To Chagall & Matisse Museums
Rue Massena Pedestrian Zone
1/4 Mile
.5 KM
Nice Etoile Shopping Mall
Bus Stn.
Place Garibaldi
Place Massena
Albert I Park
Old Nice
Castle Hill
Elevator
Hotel Negresco
Tourist Train Pick-up
Promenade des Anglais
Quai des Etats-Unis
Cours Saleya
Beaches
To 15
1 Hôtels Excelsior & La Belle Meunière
2 Hôtel Vendôme & Launderette
3 Hôtels Clemenceau & St. Georges
4 Hôtel du Petit Louvre
5 Hôtel Aria
6 Hôtel Masséna
7 Hôtel Suisse
8 Hôtel Lafayette
9 Hôtel Mercure
10 Hôtel le Royal
11 Hôtel Villa Victoria
12 Hôtel Windsor
13 Hôtel les Cigales
14 Hôtels Splendid & Gounod
15 To Hôtels Villa Eden & Ibis
16 Bike Rental
17 Cat's Whiskers Bookstore
18 Buses to Airport
19 Bus to Chagall Museum & Bus to Matisse Museum

Db-€160, best Db-€195, Tb-€190–225, Qb with kitchenettes on the garden-€250, air-con, 19 avenue Durante, tel. 04 93 88 18 05, fax 04 93 88 38 69, www.excelsiornice.com, excelsior@wanadoo.fr).

$$ Hôtel St. Georges** is big and bright, with a backyard garden, reasonably clean and comfortable high-ceilinged rooms, good rates, and happy Jacques at the reception (Sb-€72, Db-€85, Tb with 3 separate beds-€106, extra bed-€19, air-con, Wi-Fi, 7 avenue Georges Clemenceau, tel. 04 93 88 79 21, fax 04 93 16 22 85, www.hotelsaintgeorges.fr, contact@hotelsaintgeorges.fr).

$ Hôtel Clemenceau**, run by the La Serre family, is an exceptional budget value with a modest, homey feel. Rooms—some with balconies, some without closets, all air-conditioned—are mostly spacious, simple, and traditional (S-€31, Sb-€43, D-€46, Db-€58, Tb-€69, Qb-€84, kitchenette-€8 extra and only for stays of at least 3 nights, no elevator, 3 avenue Georges Clemenceau, 1 block west of avenue Jean Médecin, tel. 04 93 88 61 19, fax 04 93 16 88 96, hotel-clemenceau@wanadoo.fr, Marianne and Cedric speak English, Mama and Papa no speak).

$ Hôtel La Belle Meunière, in a fine old mansion has cheap beds and private rooms just a block below the train station. Lively and hostel-esque, this place attracts budget-minded travelers of all ages with basic-but-adequate, decent-value rooms and charismatic Madame Marie-Pierre presiding. Tables in the front yard greet guests and provide opportunities to meet other travelers (bed in 4-person dorm with private shower-€20, Db-€55, includes breakfast, 21 avenue Durante, tel. 04 93 88 66 15, fax 04 93 82 51 76, www.bellemeuniere.com, hotel.belle.meuniere@cegetel.net).

$ Hôtel du Petit Louvre* offers an interesting concept at a good price, with clean, small rooms—all recently renovated with kitchenettes and air-conditioning—and beds that convert to couches to allow more space during the day (Db-€58, no breakfast, 10 rue Emma Tiranty, tel. 04 93 80 15 54, fax 04 93 62 45 08, www.hotelgoodprice.com, petilouvr@wanadoo.com).

Between Nice Etoile and Old Nice

$$$ Hôtel Masséna****, in a classy building a few blocks from place Masséna, is a stylish business hotel showcasing 100 rooms with every amenity at almost-reasonable rates (small Db-€130, larger Db-€165, still larger Db-€240, extra bed-€30, some non-smoking rooms, Wi-Fi, reserve parking ahead-€18/day, 58 rue Giofreddo, tel. 04 92 47 88 88, fax 04 92 47 88 89, www.hotel-massena-nice.com, info@hotel-massena-nice.com).

$$$ Hôtel Suisse*** has Nice's best ocean and city views for the money, and is surprisingly quiet given the busy street below. Rooms are quite comfortable, with air-conditioning and modern conveniences. There's no reason to sleep here if you don't land a view, so I've listed prices only for view rooms—many of which have balconies (Db-€145–175, extra bed-€36, breakfast-€15, 15 quai Rauba Capeu, tel. 04 92 17 39 00, fax 04 93 85 30 70, www.hotels-ocre-azur.com, hotel.suisse@hotels-ocre-azur.com).

$$$ Hôtel Mercure*,** a chain hotel brilliantly situated across from the sea and behind cours Saleya, offers smallish yet tastefully designed rooms (some with beds in a loft). The rates are good, considering the terrific location (Sb-€97–121, Db-€112–125, Tb-€137–150, sea view-€30 extra, air-con, 91 quai des Etats-Unis, tel. 04 93 85 74 19, fax 04 93 13 90 94, h0962@accor.com).

$$$ Hôtel Vendôme*** gives you a whiff of the belle époque, with pink pastels, high ceilings, and grand staircases in a mansion set off the street with limited parking (book ahead, €11/day). It could be sharper (many tour groups stay here), but the location is good, prices are fair, and rooms are modern and come in all sizes. The best have balconies—request *une chambre avec balcon* (Sb-€95–110, Db-€115–140, Tb-€135–160, air-con, Internet access, 26 rue Pastorelli, tel. 04 93 62 00 77, fax 04 93 13 40 78, www.vendome-hotel-nice.com, contact@vendome-hotel-nice.com).

$$ Hôtel Lafayette*,** well-located a block behind Galleries Lafayette department store, looks average from the outside. But inside, it's homey and a good value, with 18 well-designed, mostly spacious rooms, all one floor up from the street. Sweet Sandrine and relaxed Scotsman George take darned good care of you (standard Db-€85–105, spacious Db-€95–115, extra bed-€22, central air-con, no elevator, 32 rue de l'Hôtel des Postes, tel. 04 93 85 17 84, fax 04 93 80 47 56, www.hotellafayettenice.com, info@hotellafayettenice.com).

Between Boulevard Victor Hugo and the Promenade des Anglais

$$$ Hôtel Windsor*** is a snazzy garden retreat that feels like a mix between a modern art museum and a health spa. The contemporary rooms include some designed by modern artists that defy explanation (ask for a traditional room). It has a swimming pool and gym (both free for guests), a €10 sauna, €55 massages, and light, well-priced meals in the garden (standard Db-€115, bigger Db-€145, big Db with balcony-€170, extra bed-€20, rooms over garden worth the higher price, air-con, Internet access, 11 rue Dalpozzo, tel. 04 93 88 59 35, fax 04 93 88 94 57, www.hotelwindsornice.com, reservation@hotelwindsornice.com).

$$$ Hôtel Les Cigales*** is a smart little pastel place with tasteful decor, 19 plush rooms (most with tub-showers), air-conditioning, and a nifty upstairs terrace, all well-managed by friendly Mr. Valentino with Veronique and Elaine (standard Db-€90–115, big Db-€110–135, Tb-€150, €30 more during major events, extra bed-€20, 16 rue Dalpozzo, tel. 04 97 03 10 70, fax 04 97 03 10 71, www.hotel-lescigales.com, info@hotel-lescigales.com).

$$$ Hôtel Splendid**** is a worthwhile splurge if you miss your Marriott. The panoramic rooftop pool, Jacuzzi, bar, restaurant, and breakfast room alone almost justify the cost...but throw in good rooms (4 of 6 floors are non-smoking), a free gym, Internet access, Wi-Fi, and air-conditioning, and you're as good as home (Db-€225, deluxe Db with terrace-€250, suites-€335–360, free breakfast if you stay at least 3 nights, parking-€20/day, 50 boulevard Victor Hugo, tel. 04 93 16 41 00, fax 04 93 16 42 70, www.splendid-nice.com, info@splendid-nice.com).

$$$ Hôtel Gounod*** is behind Hôtel Splendid and shares the same owners, who allow its clients free access to Hôtel Splendid's pool, Jacuzzi, and other amenities. Don't let the lackluster lobby fool you. Rooms are richly decorated, with high ceilings and air-conditioning—though the quality can vary (Db-€145, palatial 4-person suites-€225, parking-€14/day, 3 rue Gounod, tel. 04 93 16 42 00, fax 04 93 88 23 84, www.gounod-nice.com, info@gounod-nice.com).

$$$ Hôtel le Royal*** stands shoulder-to-shoulder on the promenade des Anglais with the big boys (Hôtels Negresco, Concorde, and Westminster). With 140 rooms, big old lounges, and hallways that stretch forever, it feels a bit like a retirement home–turned-hotel. But considering the solid, air-conditioned comfort and terrific location, this is a fine value. They sometimes have rooms when others don't (seaview rooms: Sb-€115, Db-€140, mini-suites-€160 and well worth the extra euros; non-seaview rooms: Sb-€70, Db-€95; 23 promenade des Anglais, tel. 04 93 16 43 00, fax 04 93 16 43 02, www.hotel-royal-nice.cote.azur.fr, royal@vacancesbleues.com).

$$$ Hôtel Villa Victoria*** is well-managed by cheery Marlena, who welcomes travelers in a classy old building with a green awning and an attractive lobby overlooking a generous garden. Rooms are traditional and well-kept, with space to stretch out (Db-€113–133, Tb-€125–150, pricier rooms face the garden, air-con, some parking spaces, 33 boulevard Victor Hugo, tel. 04 93 88 39 60, fax 04 93 88 07 98, www.villa-victoria.com).

$$ Hôtel Aria*** is a soft-yellow refuge with 30 comfortable rooms, half of which overlook a small park. It's well-run and a good value (Sb-€85, Db-€95–119, Tb-€139, junior suite-€179, extra bed-€20, good buffet breakfast-€9, air-con, handy parking garage, 15 avenue Auber, tel. 04 93 88 30 69, fax 04 93 88 11 35, www.aria-nice.com, reservation@aria-nice.com).

Closer to the Airport

$$ Hôtel Villa Eden** is a little belle époque time-warp place among the sprawling waterfront hotels lining the promenade des Anglais. This former mansion of a Russian aristocrat now rents 13 rooms with a faded family-run ambience. It's set back enough to lose the street noise and much of the sea view, but if you want to be close to the beach and the airport (though far from Old Nice), this is a good budget option (seaside Db-€65–80, garden-side Db-€55–75, extra bed-€15, 10-min walk beyond Hôtel Negresco, bus #12 or #23 from station, 99 promenade des Anglais, tel. 04 93 86 53 70, fax 04 93 97 67 97, www.hotel-villaeden.com, booking @hotel-villaeden.com).

$$ Hôtel Ibis** offers a handy port-in-the-storm outlet for those with early flights or single nights (Db-€75, 359 promenade des Anglais, tel. 04 89 88 30 30, fax 04 93 21 19 43, h0749@accor.com).

EATING

Remember, you're in a resort...go for ambience and fun, and lower your palette's standards. Italian is a low-risk and local cuisine. My recommended restaurants are concentrated in neighborhoods close to my favorite hotels. Several offer fixed-price, multi-course meals called *menus*. The promenade des Anglais is ideal for picnic dinners on warm, languid evenings. Old Nice has the best and busiest dining atmosphere, while the Nice Etoile area is central and offers the best range of choice. To eat cheaply, explore the area around the train station. For a more peaceful meal, dine in nearby Villefranche-sur-Mer. For terribly touristy trolling, wander the wall-to-wall places lining rue Masséna. Yuck.

In Old Nice

Nice's dinner scene converges on cours Saleya (koor sah-lay-yuh)—entertaining enough in itself to make its restaurants' generally mediocre food a good value. It's a fun, festive place to compare tans and mussels. Even if you're eating elsewhere, wander through here in the evening. For locations, see the map on page 416.

La Cambuse, a small island of refinement for those who want to dine on cours Saleya, is the one place along here that doesn't try to reel in passers-by. Split a starter like the filling *petit farcis niçois* (stuffed vegetables), then order your own *plat* (€13 starters, €18–24 *plats*, open daily, 5 cours Saleya, tel. 04 93 80 82 40).

Le Safari has just average food but the best "dining energy" on cours Saleya, and serves all afternoon (open daily, at Castle Hill end of cours Saleya at #1, tel. 04 93 80 18 44).

Nissa Socca offers good, cheap Italian cuisine and a lively atmosphere in a small room a few blocks from cours Saleya. Inside

Old Nice Hotels and Restaurants

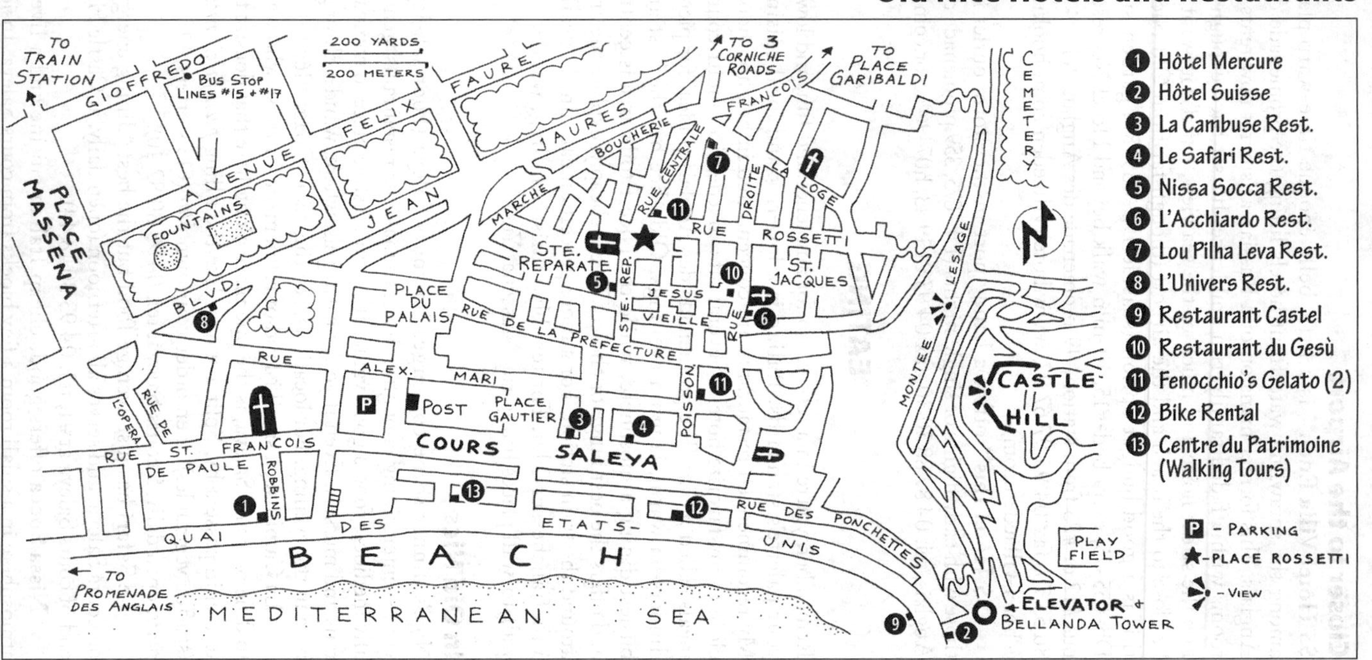

tables are usually steamy—arrive early to land a table outside (Mon–Sat from 19:00, closed Sun, a block off place Rossetti on rue Ste. Réparate, tel. 04 93 80 18 35).

Restaurant du Gesù, a happy-go-lucky budget eatery, squeezes plastic tables into a slanting square deep in the old city. It's a good, fun value. Arrive early or join the mobs waiting for an outside table, or have fun in the soccer banner–draped interior (closed Sun, 1 place du Jésus, tel. 04 943 62 26 46).

L'Acchiardo, deeper in the old city, is a budget traveler's friend, with simple, hearty, traditional cuisine at fair prices in a dark, homey setting (€13 dinner *plats,* closed Sat–Sun, 38 rue Droite, tel. 04 93 85 51 16).

Lou Pilha Leva offers a fun, *très* cheap dinner option with *niçoise* specialties and outdoor-only benches. Order your food from one side and drinks from the other (open daily, located where rue de la Loge and Centrale meet in Old Nice).

L'Univers, a block off place Masséna, earned a Michelin star while maintaining a warm ambience. This elegant place is as relaxed as a "top" restaurant can be, from its casual decor to the tasteful dinnerware. When the artfully presented food arrives, you know this is high cuisine (*menus* from €42, closed Sun, 53 boulevard Jean Jaurès, tel. 04 93 62 32 22, plumailunivers@aol.com).

Restaurant Castel is your best eat-on-the-beach option. You're right on the beach below Castle Hill, perfectly positioned to watch evening swimmers get in their last laps as the sky turns pink and city lights flicker on. Lunch views are unforgettable; you can even have lunch at your beach chair if you've rented one. Dinner here is best, so arrive before sunset and linger long enough to merit the few extra euros the place charges (open daily, €13–15 salads and pastas, €20–24 main courses, 8 quai des Etats-Unis, tel. 04 93 85 22 66).

And for Dessert: Gelato-lovers should save room for the tempting ice cream stands in Old Nice—such as **Fenocchio,** which serves up 86 flavors, from tomato to lavender (daily until 23:30, 2 locations in Old Nice: on place Rossetti and on rue de la Poissonnerie).

Eating near Nice Etoile

On Rue Biscarra: Laid-back cafés line up along the broad sidewalk on rue Biscarra (just east of avenue Jean Médecin behind Nice Etoile, all closed Sun). **L'Authentic, Le Vin sur Vin, Marre'n,** and **Le Cenac** are all reasonable enough. **L'Authentic** is best, with owners (burly Philippe and sleek Laurent) who use fresh products and offer tasty *plats*. I'd go with their suggestions (closed Sun, 18 bis rue Biscarra, tel. 04 93 62 48 88).

More Nice Restaurants

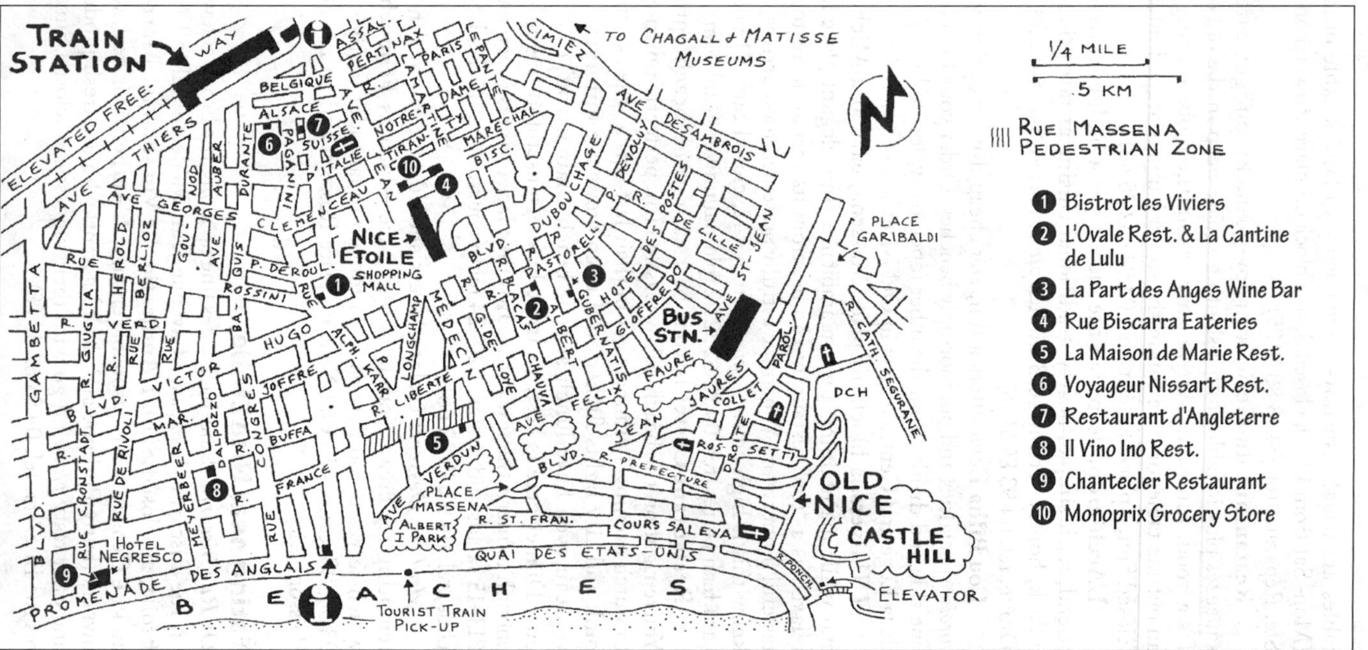

Bistrot les Viviers appeals to those who require attentive service, silver warming covers, and authentic *niçoise* cuisine. It's a cozy splurge—allow €60 per person for wine and 3 courses. Fish is the chef's forte (closed Sun, 22 rue Alphonse Karr, 5-min walk west of avenue Jean Médecin, tel. 04 93 16 00 48). Make sure to reserve for the *bistrot,* not their formal restaurant next door (prices are the same, but ambience is different).

L'Ovale is a find. How this ever-so-local and relaxed, rugby-loving café survives in a tourist mecca, I'll never know. It's run by Nice's friendliest couple, Jean-Marie and Jacqueline, whose goal is to serve quality food at a good price. It's popular with locals, and the ambience is lively. I prefer eating inside, though it can be smoky; it's quieter outside (€10 *plats*, good €14 3-course *menu*, meat-eaters enjoy *la planche de charcuterie* as a first course, closed Sun, 29 rue Pastorelli, tel. 04 93 80 31 65).

La Maison de Marie is a surprisingly high-quality refuge off touristy rue Masséna, where most other places serve mediocre food to tired tourists. Enter through a deep-red arch to a bougainvillea-draped courtyard, and enjoy the fair prices and good food that draw locals and travelers alike. The interior tables are as appealing as those in the courtyard (*menus* from €20, open daily, look for the square red flag at 5 rue Masséna, tel. 04 93 82 15 93).

La Cantine de Lulu is small, charming, and Czech-owned, with homemade recipes from Nice and Prague (closed Sat–Mon, 26 rue Alberti, tel. 04 93 62 15 33).

La Part des Anges, an atmospheric wine shop with a few tables in the back, serves a limited, good menu with a large selection of wines (open daily for lunch, Fri–Sat only for dinner, reserve ahead, 17 rue Gubernatis, tel. 04 93 62 69 80).

Near the Promenade des Anglais

Il Vino Ino, near several recommended hotels a block from promenade des Anglais, has street appeal. This lively, reasonably priced eatery serves only Italian food amid cheery decor inside or out (closed Sun, 33 rue de la Buffa, tel. 04 93 87 94 25).

Chantecler has Nice's most prestigious address—inside the Hôtel Negresco. This is everything a luxury restaurant should be: elegant, soft, and top-quality. If your trip is ending in Nice, you've earned this splurge (*menus* from €70, open daily, 37 promenade des Anglais, tel. 04 93 16 64 00, negresco@nicematin.fr).

Near the Train Station

Restaurant d'Angleterre is ideal for hungry travelers on a tight budget. For €13 you get a filling three-course dinner with tasty choices and great service (indoor and outdoor tables, closed Sun–Mon, 25 rue d'Angleterre, tel. 04 03 88 64 48).

Voyageur Nissart blends budget cuisine with cool Mediterranean ambience and friendly service (€15 *menus*, closed Mon, 19 rue d'Alsace-Lorraine, tel. 04 93 82 19 60).

TRANSPORTATION CONNECTIONS

For train, bus, and boat schedules from Nice to nearby towns, see "Getting Around the Riviera" on page 394. Note that most long-distance train connections to other French cities require a change in Marseille.

From Nice by Train to: Arles (11/day, 3.5 hrs, most change in Marseille or Avignon), **Avignon** (20/day, 13 of which are by TGV, 4 hrs, a few direct, most require transfer in Marseille), **Marseille** (18/day, 2.5 hrs), **Paris**' Gare de Lyon (11/day, 6 hrs, may require change), **Aix-en-Provence** TGV station (10/day, 3.5 hrs, may require transfer in Marseille or Toulon), **Chamonix** (4/day, 11 hrs, 3 transfers), **Beaune** (7/day, 7 hrs, 1–2 changes), **Munich** (4/day, 12–13 hrs with 2–4 transfers, night trains possible via Italy), **Interlaken** (6/day, 9–11 hrs, 2–5 transfers), **Florence** (6/day, 7–9 hrs, 1–3 transfers), **Milan** (7/day, 5 hrs, 3 with transfers), **Venice** (5/day, 2/night, 8–9 hrs, all require transfers except one direct night train), **Barcelona** (3/day, 11.5 hrs, night train possible).

Nice's Airport

Nice's easy-to-navigate airport (Aéroport de Nice Côte d'Azur) is on the Mediterranean, a 20–30-minute drive west of the city center. Planes leave about hourly to Paris (1-hour flight, about the same price as a train ticket). The two terminals (Terminal 1 and Terminal 2) are connected by frequent shuttle buses. Both terminals have TIs, banks, ATMs, taxis, and buses to Nice (www.nice.aeroport.fr, tel. 08 20 42 33 33 or 04 89 88 98 28).

Taxis into the center are expensive, charging €30 to Nice hotels and €50 to Villefranche-sur-Mer (10 percent more at night—that's 19:00–7:00—and all day Sunday). Taxis stop outside door *(Porte)* A-1 at Terminal 1 and outside *Porte* A-3 at Terminal 2. Nice taxis are not always so nice, and are notorious for overcharging. If your fare for a ride into Nice is much higher than €30 (or €33 at night or on Sun), refuse to pay more. If this doesn't work, tell the cabbie to call a *gendarme* (police officer).

Airport shuttle vans work with some of my recommended hotels. These only make sense when going *to* the airport, not when arriving. Unlike taxis, shuttle vans offer a fixed price that doesn't rise on Sundays, early mornings, or evenings. Prices are best for groups (figure €25 for one person, and only a little more for additional people—ask at your hotel).

Three bus lines connect the airport with the city center,

offering good alternatives to high-priced taxis and shuttles. **Bus #99** runs from both terminals to Nice's main train station (€4, 2/hr, 8:00–21:00, 30 min, drops you within a 10-min walk of many recommended hotels). To take this bus *to* the airport, catch it right in front of the train station (departs on the half-hour). If you're sleeping within walking distance of the station, this bus is a €4 breeze. The **yellow "NICE" bus #98** serves both terminals, and runs along the promenade des Anglais to Nice's main bus station *(gare routière)*, near Old Nice (€4, 3/hr, 30 min). The slower, cheaper local **bus #23** serves only Terminal 1, and makes every stop between the airport and train station (€1.30, 4/hr, 40 min, direction: St. Maurice). Buy tickets in the bus information office just outside either terminal, or from the driver. To reach the bus information office and bus stops at Terminal 1, turn left after passing customs and exit the doors at the far end. Buses serving Terminal 2 stop across the street from the exit. If you take bus #98 or #99, keep your ticket, which is good all day on any public bus in Nice, and for busing between Nice and nearby towns (see page 394 for details).

To get to **Villefranche-sur-Mer** from the airport, take the yellow "NICE" bus #98 to Nice's bus station *(gare routière)*, then transfer to the Villefranche-sur-Mer bus (bus #100, use same ticket).

To reach **Antibes,** take line #200 from either terminal (€1.30, hourly, 45–70 min to Antibes depending on traffic; continues on to Cannes in an additional 30 min). Express buses (line #110) run directly to **Monaco** from the airport (€15, hourly, 50 min).

GERMANY

BAVARIA AND TIROL

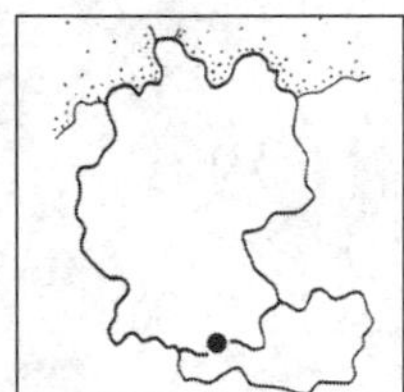

Two hours south of Munich, between Germany's Bavaria and Austria's Tirol, is a timeless land of fairy-tale castles, painted buildings shared by cows and farmers, and locals who still yodel when they're happy.

In Germany's Bavaria, tour "Mad" King Ludwig II's ornate Neuschwanstein Castle, Europe's most spectacular. In Austria's Tirol, hike to the ruined Ehrenberg castle, scream down a ski slope on an oversized skateboard, and then catch your breath for an evening of yodeling and slap dancing.

Tirol is easier and cheaper than touristy Bavaria. My favorite home base for exploring Bavaria's castles is actually in Austria, in the town of Reutte. Füssen, in Germany, is a handier home base for train travelers.

Planning Your Time

While Germans and Austrians vacation here for a week or two at a time, the typical speedy American traveler will find two days' worth of sightseeing. With a car and more time, you could enjoy three or four days. If the weather's good and you're not going to Switzerland, be sure to ride a lift to an alpine peak.

By Public Transportation: Train travelers can use Füssen as a base and bus or bike the three miles to Neuschwanstein. Reutte is connected by bus with Füssen (except Sat–Sun; taxi €30 one-way). If you're based in Reutte, you can bike to the Ehrenberg ruins (just outside Reutte) and to Neuschwanstein Castle (90 min). A one-way taxi from Reutte to Neuschwanstein costs about €35. Or, if you stay at the recommended Gutshof zum Schluxen hotel, it's a one-hour hike through the woods to Neuschwanstein.

Highlights of Bavaria and Tirol

Getting Around Bavaria and Tirol

By Car: This region is ideal by car. All the sights are within an easy 60-mile loop from Reutte or Füssen. Even if you're doing the rest of your trip by train, consider renting a car in Füssen for the day here (as cheap as €50/day; see "Car Rental," page 427).

By Public Transportation: It can be frustrating. Local bus service in the region is spotty for sightseeing. If you're rushed and without wheels, Reutte and most of the luge rides are probably not worth the trouble.

Füssen, with hourly train connections to and from Munich

(2-hour trip, some with transfer in Buchloe), is three miles from Neuschwanstein Castle, easily reachable by bus or bike (see below).

Reutte is a 35-minute bus ride from Füssen (Mon–Fri 6/day, none Sat–Sun, less off-season, €3.40; taxis from Reutte to the castles are €35 one-way; to Füssen, €30). Ask your hotel to help you find the most up-to-date schedule.

Confirm all bus schedules in Füssen: Check the big board at the bus stop across from the train station, buy the indispensable bus timetable (€0.30, *OVG Fahrpläne der Linienbusse*) at the TI or train station, check online at www.rva-bus.de, or call 08362/939-0505. For longer-distance bus trips (such as to Garmisch), you'll save money if you buy a *Tagesticket* (day pass).

If you'll be taking a lot of trains in Bavaria (for example, day-tripping from Munich to the castles), consider the **Bayern-Ticket** (covers up to four people from Munich to anywhere in Bavaria and back for only €27/day, valid Mon–Fri from 9:00).

By Tour: If you're interested only in Bavarian castles, consider an all-day organized bus tour of the Bavarian biggies as a side-trip from Munich.

By Bike: This is great biking country. Shops in or near train stations rent bikes for €8–15 per day. The ride from Reutte to Neuschwanstein is great for those with the time and energy.

By Thumb: Hitchhiking, always risky, is a slow-but-possible way to connect the public-transportation gaps.

Füssen

Füssen has been a strategic stop since ancient times. Its main street sits on the Via Claudia Augusta, which crossed the Alps (over the Brenner Pass) in Roman times. The town was the southern terminus of a medieval trade route now known among modern tourists as the "Romantic Road." Dramatically situated under a renovated castle on the lively Lech River, Füssen recently celebrated its 700th birthday.

Unfortunately, Füssen is overrun by tourists in the summer. Traffic can be exasperating. Apart from Füssen's cobbled and arcaded town center, there's little real sightseeing here. The striking-from-a-distance **Castle** (Hohes Schloss) houses a boring picture gallery. The mediocre **City Museum** (Kloster St. Mang) in the monastery below the castle exhibits lifestyles of 200 years ago and the story of the monastery, and offers displays on the development of the violin, for which Füssen is famous (€2.50, €3 includes castle gallery; April–Oct Tue–Sun 11:00–16:00, closed Mon; Nov–March Tue–Sun 14:00–16:00, closed Mon; English descriptions, tel. 08362/903-146).

Halfway between Füssen and the border (as you drive, or a woodsy walk from the town) is the **Lechfall,** a thunderous waterfall (with a handy WC).

ORIENTATION

(area code: 08362)

Füssen's train station is a few blocks from the TI, the town center (a cobbled shopping mall), and all my hotel listings (see "Sleeping," below). If necessary, the **TI** can help you find a room (June–mid-Sept Mon–Fri 9:00–18:00, Sat 10:00–14:00, Sun 10:00–12:00, less off-season, 3 blocks down Bahnhofstrasse from station, tel. 08362/93850, fax 08362/938-520, www.fuessen.de). After hours, the little self-service info pavilion (7:00–24:30) near the front of the TI features an automated room-finding service.

Arrival in Füssen: Exit left as you leave the train station (lockers available, €1–2) and walk a few straight blocks to the center of town and the TI. To get to Neuschwanstein or Reutte, catch a bus from in front of the station.

Helpful Hints

Internet Access: Try **Videoland** (€2/30 min, €3/hr, Mon–Sat 14:00–22:00, Sun 14:00–20:00, Luitpoldstrasse 11, tel. 08362/38300).

Bike Rental: Friendly Christian runs **Preisschranke** next to the train station (€8/24 hrs, May–Sept Mon–Fri 9:00–19:00, Sat 9:00–14:00, closed Sun and Oct–April, mobile 0176-2205-3080). **Rad Zacherl** has a bigger selection, but a less convenient location (€8/24 hrs, mountain bikes-€15/24 hrs, passport number for deposit; May–Sept Mon–Fri 9:00–18:00, Sat 9:00–13:00, closed Sun; Oct–April Mon–Fri 9:00–12:00 & 14:00–18:00, Sat 9:00–13:00, closed Sun; three-quarters of a mile out of town at Kemptener Strasse 26, tel. 08362/3292).

Car Rental: Peter Schlichtling is more central and cheaper (€50/day, includes insurance, Mon–Fri 8:00–18:00, Sat 9:00–12:00, closed Sun, Kemptener Strasse 26, tel. 08362/922-122, www.schlichtling.de) than **National** (Mon–Fri 9:00–12:00 & 13:00–18:00, Sat 9:00–12:00, closed Sun, Füssener Strasse 112, tel. 08362/986-580).

SLEEPING

Though I prefer sleeping in Reutte (see page 437), convenient Füssen is just three miles from Ludwig's castles and offers a cobbled, riverside retreat. It's very touristy, but it has plenty of rooms.

Füssen

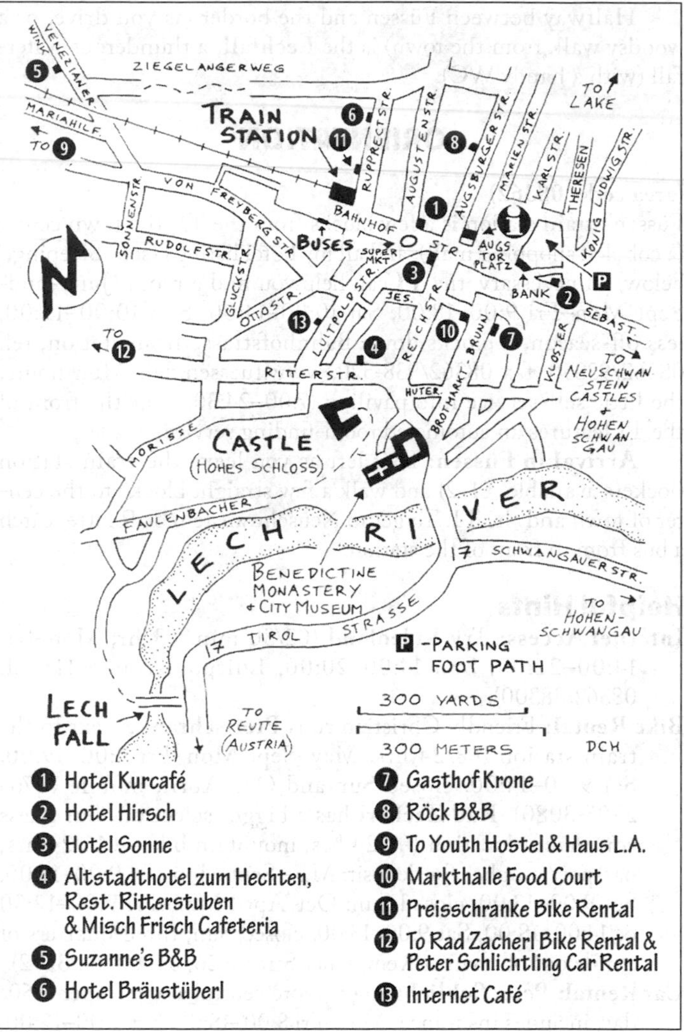

All recommended accommodations are within a few blocks of the train station and the town center. Parking is easy at the station. Prices listed are for one-night stays. Most hotels give about 5 to 10 percent off for two-night stays—always request this discount. Competition is fierce, and off-season prices are soft. High season is mid-June through September. Rooms are generally about 12 percent less in shoulder season and much cheaper in off-season. To locate these hotels, see the map above.

Sleep Code

(€1 = about $1.30, country code: 49, area code: 08362)
S = Single, **D** = Double/Twin, **T** = Triple, **Q** = Quad, **b** = bathroom, **s** = shower only. Unless otherwise noted, credit cards are accepted, English is spoken, and breakfast is included. The €1.35 per person, per night "tourist tax" is not included in these rates.

To help you sort easily through these listings, I've divided the rooms into three categories, based on the price for a standard double room with bath:

$$$ **Higher Priced**—Most rooms €100 or more.
$$ **Moderately Priced**—Most rooms between €60–100.
$ **Lower Priced**—Most rooms €60 or less.

$$$ Hotel Kurcafé is deluxe, with 30 spacious rooms and all of the amenities. The standard rooms are comfortable, and the newer, bigger rooms have elegant touches and fun decor—like canopy drapes and cherubic frescoes over the bed (Sb-€85, standard Db-€105–119, bigger Db-€129–145 depending on size, Tb-€129, Qb-€145, 4-person suite-€169–199, €10 more for weekends and holidays, ask about package deals, cheaper off-season, non-smoking rooms, elevator, parking-€5/day, carries some US newspapers, on tiny traffic circle a block in front of station at Bahnhofstrasse 4, tel. 08362/930-180, fax 08362/930-1850, www.kurcafe.com, info@kurcafe.com, Schöll family).

$$$ Hotel Hirsch is a big, romantic, old tour-class hotel with 53 rooms on the main street in the center of town. Their standard rooms are fine, and their theme rooms are a fun splurge (Sb-€56–82, standard Db-€87–133, theme Db-€118–162, prices depend on room size and demand, cheaper Nov–March and during slow times, only the expensive theme rooms are non-smoking, family rooms, elevator, free parking, Kaiser-Maximilian-Platz 7, tel. 08362/93980, fax 08362/939-877, www.hotelhirsch.de, info@hotelhirsch.de).

$$$ Hotel Sonne, in the heart of town, rents 32 stylish and spacious rooms (Sb-€90–107, Db-€115–132, Tb-€130–147, higher prices are for huge rooms in the new wing, cheaper Oct–mid-June, non-smoking rooms, elevator, parking-€2.50–4.50/day, kitty-corner from TI at Prinzregentenplatz 1, tel. 08362/9080, fax 08362/908-100, www.hotel-sonne.de, info@hotel-sonne.de).

$$ Altstadthotel zum Hechten, with 35 rooms, offers all the modern comforts in a friendly, traditional shell right under Füssen Castle in the old-town pedestrian zone (S-€32, Sb-€47,

D-€60, Db-€80, Tb-€105, Qb-€120, cheaper off-season and for longer stays, beds can be short, non-smoking rooms, fun miniature bowling alley in basement, free parking, nearby church bells ring hourly at night; from TI, walk down pedestrian street and take second right to Ritterstrasse 6; tel. 08362/91600, fax 08362/916-099, www.hotel-hechten.com, hotel.hechten@t-online.de, Pfeiffer and Tramp families).

$$ Suzanne's B&B is run by a plainspoken, no-nonsense American woman who strikes some travelers as brusque. Suzanne runs a tight ship, offering lots of local travel advice, backyard-fresh eggs, local cheese, a children's yard, laundry (€25/load), and bright, woody, spacious rooms (Db-€85, Tb-€120, Qb-€150, suite from €120 can hold up to 10—ask for details; attic special: €70 for 2 people, €100 for 3, €120 for 4; cash only, non-smoking, Internet access-€5/hr; exit station right and backtrack 2 blocks along tracks, cross tracks at Venetianerwinkel to #3; tel. 08362/38485, fax 08362/921-396, www.suzannes.de, svorbrugg@t-online.de). Her kid-friendly attic loft has very low ceilings (you'll crouch), a private bathroom (you'll crouch), and up to six beds.

$$ Hotel Bräustüberl has 16 decent rooms at fair rates attached to a gruff, musty, old beer hall–type place. Don't expect much service (Sb-€45, Db-€78, cash only, Rupprechtstrasse 5, 1 block from station, tel. 08362/7843, fax 08362/923-951, brauereigasthof-fuessen@t-online.de).

$ Gasthof Krone, a rare bit of pre-glitz Füssen in the pedestrian zone, has dumpy halls and stairs and 12 big, time-warp rooms at good prices (S-€28, D/Ds-€52, extra bed-€26, extra bed for kids under 12-€20, €3 more per person for 1-night stays, reception in medieval-themed restaurant, closed Nov–June; from TI, head down pedestrian street and take first left to Schrannengasse 17; tel. 08362/7824, fax 08362/37505, www.krone-fuessen.de, info@krone-fuessen.de).

$ Wilhelm and Elisabeth Röck, a sweet old couple, rent out two rooms in their home a block from the TI (D-€51, Db-€55, Tb-€75, cash only, non-smoking, Augsburgerstrasse 7, tel. 08362/6353, just enough English spoken).

$ Füssen Youth Hostel, a fine, German-run place, welcomes travelers (€18 dorm beds in 2- to 6-bed rooms, D-€42, €3 more for non-members, includes breakfast and sheets, guests over age 26 allowed only if there's room, non-smoking, laundry-€3.20/load, dinner for a few euros, bike rental, office open 7:00–12:00 & 17:00–23:00, until 22:00 off-season, from station backtrack 10 min along tracks, Mariahilfer Strasse 5, tel. 08362/7754, fax 08362/2770, www.fuessen.jugendherberge.de, jhfuessen@djh-bayern.de).

$ Haus L.A. has three very basic but clean rooms at youth-hostel prices. If you don't mind the 20-minute walk from the station, it works just fine (D-€40, light breakfast served in room; from station, follow Von Freybergstrasse until it turns into Welfenstrasse, #39 is on the left, tel. 08362/38534, mobile 0170-6248610, swirinoyo@lycos.de).

EATING

Füssen's old town and main pedestrian drag are lined with a variety of eateries. The first three listings cluster on Ritterstrasse, just under the castle, off the top of the main street.

Ritterstuben offers delicious, reasonably priced fish, salads, veggie plates, and a fun kids' menu (€6–12 plates, Tue–Sun 11:30–14:30 & 17:30–23:00, closed Mon, Ritterstrasse 4, tel. 08362/7759). Demure Gabi serves while her husband cooks.

Zum Hechten Restaurant serves hearty, traditional Bavarian fare and specializes in pike *(Hecht)* pulled from the Lech River (€8–13 plates, Thu–Tue 11:00–14:00 & 17:00–20:30, Wed 17:00–20:30, tel. 0836/91600, Ritterstrasse 6).

Misch Frisch is a clever and modern self-service eatery that sells its hot meals and salad bar by weight and offers English newspapers (about €3 for a filling salad, €5 meals, Mon–Fri 11:00–18:00, Sat 10:30–15:00, closed Sun, Ritterstrasse 6).

Hotel Kurcafé's fine restaurant, right on Füssen's main traffic circle, has good weekly specials, plus a tempting bakery (daily 11:30–14:30 & 17:30–21:30, choose between a traditional dining room and a pastel winter garden, €11 Bavarian BBQ on Fri nights, live Bavarian zither music most Fri–Sat during dinner, Bahnhofstrasse 4, tel. 08362/930-180).

The **Markthalle** food court, just across the street from Gasthof Krone, offers a wide selection of reasonably priced, non-wurst items. Located in an old corn warehouse from 1483, it's now home to a fishmonger; Chinese, Turkish, and Italian delis; a fruit stand; a bakery; and a wine bar. Buy your food from one of the vendors, park yourself at any one of the tables, then look up and admire the Renaissance ceiling (Mon–Fri 7:30–18:30, Sat 7:30–14:00, closed Sun, corner of Schrannengasse and Brunnengasse).

Picnic Supplies: Bakeries and *Metzger*s (butcher shops) abound and frequently have ready-made sandwiches. For groceries, try **Plus** supermarket at the roundabout on your way into town from the train station (Mon–Sat 8:00–20:00, closed Sun).

TRANSPORTATION CONNECTIONS

From Füssen to: Neuschwanstein (hourly buses, 10 min, €1.55 one-way, €3.10 round-trip; taxis cost €9 one-way), **Oberammergau** (4–5 buses/day, fewer off-season, 1.5 hrs, some with transfer in

Echelsbacher Brücke; bus often marked *Garmisch,* confirm with driver that bus will stop in Oberammergau); **Reutte** (Mon–Fri 6 buses/day, none Sat–Sun, 35 min, €3.40 one-way; taxis cost €30 one-way), **Munich** (hourly trains, 2 hrs, some change in Buchloe). Train info: tel. 11861 (€0.50/min).

Romantic Road Buses: I don't recommend this bus (which has declined in value and service over the years), but here's the scoop if you want to take it. The northbound Romantic Road bus departs Füssen at 10:00; the southbound bus arrives Füssen at 19:10 (bus stops at train station). A railpass gets you a 60 percent discount on the Romantic Road bus (without using up a day of a flexipass).

Neuschwanstein and Hohenschwangau Castles

The most popular tourist destinations in Bavaria are the "King's Castles" *(Königsschlösser).* With fairy-tale turrets in a fairy-tale alpine setting built by a fairy-tale king, they are understandably beloved.

Planning Your Time

The well-organized visitor can have a great four-hour visit. Others will just stand in line and possibly not even see the castles. The key: Phone ahead for a reservation (details below) or arrive by 8:00 to wait in line for tickets (you'll have time to see both castles, consider fun options nearby—mountain lift, luge course, Füssen town—and get out by early afternoon). Off-season (Oct–June), you have a little more flexibility, but it's still a good idea to get an early start (try to arrive by 9:00).

Getting There

If arriving by **car,** note that road signs in the region refer to the sight as *Königsschlösser,* not Neuschwanstein. There's plenty of parking (all lots-€4). Get there early, and you'll park where you like. Lot E—past the ticket center and next to the lake—is my favorite (it's called Lot 5 until you reach the tollbooth).

From **Füssen,** those without cars can catch the roughly hourly **bus** (€1.55 one-way, €3.10 round-trip, 10 min, note times carefully on the meager schedule, catch bus at train station), take a **taxi** (€9 one-way), or ride a rental **bike** (2 miles).

From **Reutte,** take the bus to Füssen (Mon–Fri 4/day, none Sat–Sun, €3.40, 35 min), then hop a city bus to the castle.

For a romantic twist, hike or mountain-bike from the trailhead at the recommended hotel **Gutshof zum Schluxen** in Pinswang (see page 446). When the dirt road forks at the top of the hill, go right (downhill), cross the Austria–Germany border (marked by a sign and deserted hut), and follow the narrow paved road to the castles. It's a 60- to 90-minute hike or a great circular bike trip (allow 30 min; cyclists can return to Schluxen from the castles on a different 30-min bike route via Füssen).

SIGHTS

The King's Castles

▲▲▲Neuschwanstein Castle—Imagine "Mad" King Ludwig as a boy, climbing the hills above his dad's castle, Hohenschwangau (see below), dreaming up the ultimate fairy-tale castle. He had the power to make his dream concrete and stucco. Neuschwanstein (noy-SHVAHN-shtine) was designed by a painter first...then an architect. It looks medieval, but it's only about as old as the Eiffel Tower. It feels like something you'd see at a home show for 19th-century royalty. Built from 1869 to 1886, it's the epitome of the Romanticism popular in 19th-century Europe. Construction stopped with Ludwig's death (only a third of the interior was finished), and within six weeks, tourists were paying to go through it.

Today, guides herd groups of 60 through the castle, giving an interesting—if rushed—30-minute tour. You'll go up and down more than 300 steps, through lavish Wagnerian dream rooms, a royal state-of-the-19th-century-art kitchen, the king's gilded-lily bedroom, and his extravagant throne room. You'll visit 15 rooms with their original furnishings and fanciful wall paintings. After the tour, you'll see a room lined with fascinating drawings (described in English) of the castle plans, construction, and drawings from 1883 of Falkenstein—a whimsical, over-the-top, never-built castle that makes Neuschwanstein look stubby. Falkenstein occupied Ludwig's fantasies the year he died. Following the tour, a 20-minute slide show (alternating German and English) plays continuously. If English is on, pop in. If not, it's not worth waiting for.

Mary's Bridge (Marienbrücke)—Before or after the Neuschwanstein tour, climb up to Mary's Bridge to marvel at Ludwig's castle, just as Ludwig did. This bridge was quite an engineering accomplishment 100 years ago. From the bridge, the frisky can hike even higher to the *Beware—Danger of Death* signs and an even more glorious castle view. (Access to the bridge is closed in bad winter weather, but many travelers walk around the barriers to get there—at their own risk, of course.) For the most interesting descent from Neuschwanstein (15 min longer and extremely slippery when wet), follow signs to the Pöllat Gorge.

Neuschwanstein and Hohenschwangau Castles

▲▲Hohenschwangau Castle—Standing quietly below Neuschwanstein, the big, yellow Hohenschwangau (hoh-en-SHVAHN-gow) Castle was Ludwig's boyhood home. Originally built in the 12th century, it was ruined by Napoleon. Ludwig's father, Maximilian, rebuilt it, and you'll see it as it looked in 1836. It's more lived-in and historic, and excellent 30-minute tours actually give a better glimpse of Ludwig's life than the more-visited and famous Neuschwanstein Castle tour.

Visiting the Castles

Cost and Hours: Each castle costs €9, a *Königsticket* for both castles costs €17, and children under 18 (accompanied by an adult) are admitted free (castles open April–Sept daily from 9:00 with last tour departing at 18:00, Oct–March daily from 10:00 with last tour at 16:00).

Getting Tickets for the Castles: Every tour bus in Bavaria converges on Neuschwanstein, and tourists flush in each morning from Munich. A handy reservation system (described below) sorts out the chaos for smart travelers. Tickets come with admission times. To tour both castles, you must do Hohenschwangau first (logical, since this gives a better introduction to Ludwig's short life). You'll get two tour times: Hohenschwangau and then, two hours later, Neuschwanstein. If you miss your appointed tour time, you can't get in.

If you arrive late and without a reservation, you'll spend two hours in the ticket line and may find all tours for the day booked. A **ticket center** for both Neuschwanstein and Hohenschwangau is located at street level between the two castles (daily April–Sept 8:00–17:00, Oct–March 9:00–15:00, last tickets sold for Neuschwanstein 1 hour before closing, for Hohenschwangau 30 min before closing). Tickets purchased at the ticket center are for that day only. First tours start around 9:00 (or 10:00 Oct–March). Arrive by 8:00 in summer, and you'll likely be touring by 9:00. Warning: During the summer, tickets for English tours can run out by 16:00.

It's best to **reserve ahead** in peak season (July–Sept, especially Aug). You can make reservations a minimum of 24 hours in advance by contacting the ticket office by phone (tel. 08362/930-830), email (info@ticket-center-hohenschwangau.de), or booking online (www.ticket-center-hohenschwangau.de). Tickets reserved in advance cost €1.80 extra (per person, per castle), and ticket holders must be at the ticket office well before the appointed entry time (30 min before for Hohenschwangau, 60 min before for Neuschwanstein—this allows you sufficient time to make your way up to the castle). Remember that many of the businesses are owned by the old royal family, so they encourage you to space the two tours longer than necessary in hopes that you'll spend a little more money. Insist on the tightest schedule—with no lunch break—if you don't want too much down time.

Services: The helpful TI, bus stop, ATM, stamp machine, WC (€0.50, handy change machine outside), and telephones cluster around the main intersection (**TI** hours are sporadic, but generally open daily May–Sept 11:00–19:00, Oct–April 11:00–17:00, tel. 08362/819-765, www.schwangau.de). The "village" at the foot of Europe's Disney castle feeds off the droves of hungry, shop-happy tourists. The Bräustüberl cafeteria serves the cheapest grub (often with live folk music). The Alpsee lake is ideal for a picnic, but there are no grocery shops nearby. Your best bet is to get food to go from one of the many bratwurst stands (between the ticket center and TI) for a lazy lunch at the lakeside park or in one of the old-fashioned rowboats (rented by the hour in summer).

Getting to the Castles: From the ticket booth, Hohenschwangau is an easy 10-minute climb. Neuschwanstein is a steep 30-minute hike. To minimize hiking to Neuschwanstein, you can take a shuttle bus (from in front of Hotel Lisl, just above ticket office and to the left) or horse-drawn carriage (from in front of Hotel Müller, just above ticket office and to the right), but neither gets you to the castle doorstep. The frequent shuttle buses drop you off at Mary's Bridge, leaving you a steep 10-minute downhill walk from the castle—be sure to see the view from Mary's Bridge before hiking down (€1.80 up, €2.60 round-trip not worth it since you have to hike up to bus stop for return trip). Carriages (€5 up, €2.50 down) are slower than walking and stop below Neuschwanstein, leaving you a five-minute uphill hike. Note: If it's less than an hour until your Neuschwanstein tour time, you'll need to hike, and even at a brisk pace, it still takes 30 minutes. For a lazy, varied, and economical plan, ride the bus to Mary's Bridge for the view, hike down to the castle, and then catch the carriage from there back down.

SLEEPING

In Hohenschwangau, near Neuschwanstein Castle

(€1 = about $1.30, country code: 49, area code: 08362)

Inexpensive farmhouse *Zimmer* (B&Bs) abound in the Bavarian countryside around Neuschwanstein, offering drivers a decent value. Look for *Zimmer Frei* signs ("room free," or vacancy). The going rate is about €50 to €65 for a double, including breakfast.

$$ Alpenhotel Meier is a small, family-run hotel with 15 rooms in a bucolic setting within walking distance of the castles, just beyond the lower parking lot (Sb-€46, Db-€77, Tb-€105, cheaper for longer stays, non-smoking rooms, all rooms have porches or balconies, family rooms, sauna, easy parking, just before tennis courts at Schwangauer Strasse 37, tel. 08362/81152, fax 08362/987-028, www.alpenhotel-allgaeu.de, info@alpenhotel-allgaeu.de, Frau Meier).

$$ Romantic Pension Albrecht, in the shadow of Neuschwanstein, offers seven rooms in a historic home. Just a three-minute walk from the ticket booth, you enjoy proximity to the castle without all the hustle and bustle. This charming house is a little tired—but at 102 years old, you would be, too. Many of the rooms have balconies, and friendly Frau Strauss—who welcomes her guests as her mother did before her—is happy to share her garden with you (S-€29–35, Sb-€39, Db-€68, more for 1-night stays, cash only, free parking, Pfleger Rothut Weg 2, tel. & fax 08362/81102, www.albrecht-neuschwanstein.de, info@albrecht-neuschwanstein.de).

$ Beim "Landhannes" is a 200-year-old working dairy farm run by Johann and Traudl Mayr. They rent six creaky but fresh and sunny rooms, and keep flowers on the balconies, big bells and antlers in the halls, and cows in the yard (Sb-€30, Db-€60, 20 percent discount for 3 or more nights, cash only, poorly signed in the village of Horn on the Füssen side of Schwangau, look for the farm 100 yards in front of Hotel Kleiner König, Am Lechrain 22, tel. & fax 08362/8349, www.landhannes.de, mayr@landhannes.de).

$ Sonnenhof is a big, woody, old house with four spacious, traditionally decorated rooms (all with balconies) and a cheery garden. It's a 15-minute walk through the fields to the castles (S-€35, D-€50, Db-€60, cash only; at Pension Schwansee on the Füssen–Neuschwanstein road, follow the small lane 100 yards to Sonnenweg 11; tel. 08362/8420, Frau Görlich).

Reutte

Reutte (ROY-teh, with a rolled *r*), a relaxed Austrian town of 5,700, is located 20 minutes across the border from Füssen. It's far from the international tourist crowd, but popular with Germans and Austrians for its climate. Doctors recommend its "grade 1" air. Reutte's one claim to fame with Americans: As Nazi Germany was falling in 1945, Hitler's top rocket scientist, Werner von Braun, joined the Americans (rather than the Russians) in Reutte. You could say the American space program began here.

Reutte isn't featured in any other American guidebook. While its generous sidewalks are filled with smart boutiques and lazy coffeehouses, its charms are subtle. It was never rich or important. Its castle is ruined, its buildings have painted-on "carvings," and its churches are full. Here men yodel for each other on birthdays, and energy is spent soaking Austrian and German guests in *Gemütlichkeit.* Most guests stay for a week, so the town's attractions are more time-consuming than thrilling. If the weather's good, hike to the mysterious Ehrenberg ruins, ride the luge, or rent a bike. For a slap-dancing bang, enjoy a Tirolean folk evening. For accommodations, see page 443.

ORIENTATION

(€1 = about $1.30, country code: 43, area code: 05672)

Tourist Information

Reutte's TI is a block in front of the train station (Mon–Fri 8:00–12:00 & 14:00–17:00, Sat 8:30–12:00, closed Sun, tel. 05672/62336, from Germany dial 00-43-5672/62336, www.reutte.com). Go over your sightseeing plans, ask about a folk evening, pick up city and biking maps and the *Sommerprogramm* events schedule (in German only), and ask about discounts with the hotel guest cards. Their free informational booklet has a good self-guided town walk.

Helpful Hints

Laundry: There isn't an actual launderette in town, but the recommended hotels Maximilian and Ernberg let even nonguests use their self-service machines (see page 444). Or stay at the recommended Gutshof zum Schluxen or the local campground, which both have washing machines and dryers.

Bike Rental: Try Intersport (€15/day, €10 after 14:00, open Mon–Fri 9:00–18:00, Sat 9:00–17:00, closed Sun, Lindenstrasse 25, tel. 05672/62352), or check at Hotel Maximilian.

SIGHTS AND ACTIVITIES

Ehrenberg Castle Ensemble (Festungsensemble Ehrenberg)

Just a mile outside of Reutte are the brooding ruins of four castles that once made up the largest fort in Tirol (built for defense against the Bavarians). Today, these castles are gradually being turned into one expansive European Castle Museum, showing off 500 years of military architecture in one swoop. The European Union is helping fund the project because it promotes the heritage of a multinational region—Tirol—rather than a country (the EU's vision includes a zone of regions rather than nations).

Three of the castles cluster together; the fourth (Fort Claudia) is across the valley (an hour by foot on the *Wanderweg*). All four were once connected by walls. The first three—the easiest and most interesting to visit—are described below, from lowest to highest. Signs throughout the castle complex help you find your way and explain some background on the region's history, geology, geography, culture, flora, and fauna.

Getting to the Castle Ensemble: The Klause, Ehrenberg, and Schlosskopf castles are on the road to Lermoos and Innsbruck. These are a pleasant walk or a short bike ride from Reutte; bikers can use the *Radwanderweg* along the Lech River (the TI has a good map).

▲Klause Valley Fort—At the parking lot at the base of the ruin-topped hill, you'll find the recently modernized remains of a Gothic fortification. It was located on the medieval salt road (which used to be the ancient Roman road, Via Claudia Augusta). Beginning in the 14th century, the fort controlled traffic and levied tolls on all who passed through this strategic valley. Today it houses a 60-minute

Reutte

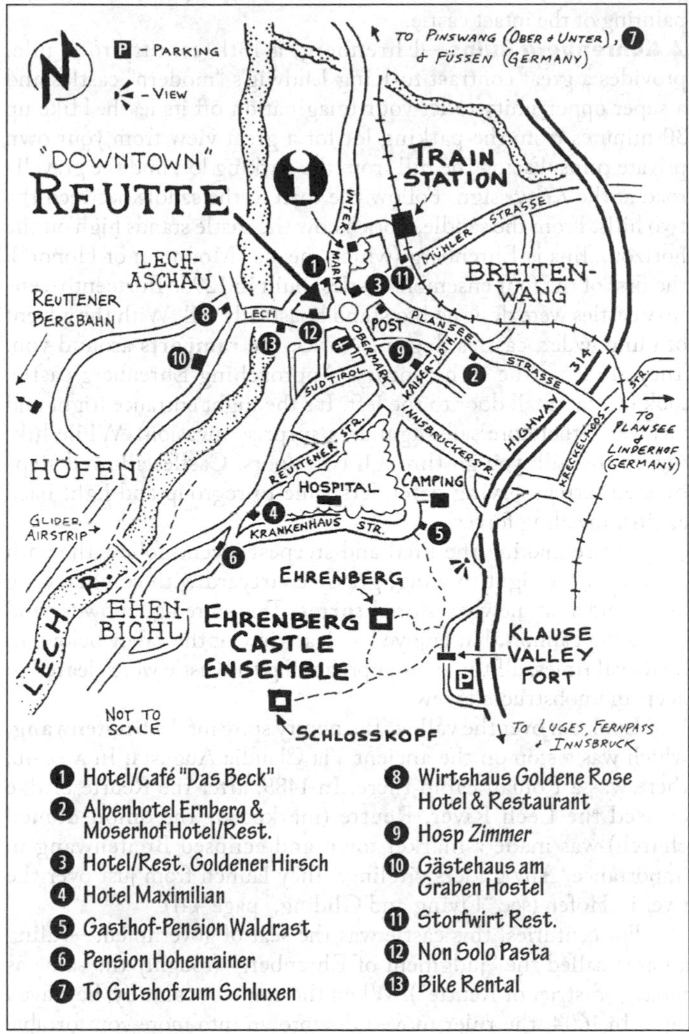

multimedia **Sound and Vision Show** about the castles (€10, Tue and Thu at 16:00, in English at 17:00 if you ask, tel. 05672/62007). You'll sit inside the shell of the old castle while the 2,000-year history of this valley's fortresses is projected on the old stone walls and modern screens around you. There's also an extensive family-friendly **museum** about the castle ensemble (€6.80, €15 family pass for 2 adults and unlimited kids, plentiful English signage, Tue–Sun 10:00–17:00, closed Mon, tel. 05672/62007, www.ehrenberg.at). If you're hungry, drop by the nearby café/guest house, Gasthof Klause (closed Mon), which offers a German-language flier and a wall painting of the intact castle.

▲▲Ehrenberg Ruins—Ehrenberg, a 13th-century rock pile, provides a great contrast to King Ludwig's "modern" castles and a super opportunity to let your imagination off its leash. Hike up 30 minutes from the parking lot for a great view from your own private ruins. Facing the hill from the parking lot, find the gravelly road at the *Klause* sign. Follow the road to the saddle between the two hills. From the saddle, notice how the castle stands high on the horizon. This is Ehrenberg (which means "Mountain of Honor"), the first of the four ensemble castles, built in 1296. Thirteenth-century castles were designed to stand boastfully tall. With the advent of gunpowder, castles dug in. Notice the **ramparts** around you. They are from the 18th century. Approaching Ehrenberg castle, look for the small door to the left. It's the night entrance (tight and awkward, therefore safer against a surprise invasion). While hiking up the hill, you go through two doors. Castles allowed step-by-step retreat, giving defenders time to regroup and fight back against invading forces.

Before making the final and steepest ascent, follow the path around to the right to a big, grassy courtyard with commanding views and a fat, newly restored **turret.** This stored gunpowder and held a big cannon that enjoyed a clear view of the valley below. In medieval times, all the trees approaching the castle were cleared to keep an unobstructed view.

Look out over the valley. The pointy spire marks **Breitenwang,** which was a stop on the ancient Via Claudia Augusta. In A.D. 46, there was a Roman camp there. In 1489, after the Reutte bridge crossed the Lech River, Reutte (marked by the onion-domed church) was made a market town and eclipsed Breitenwang in importance. Any gliders circling? They launch from just over the river in Höfen (see "Flying and Gliding," page 441).

For centuries, this castle was the seat of government—ruling an area called the "judgment of Ehrenberg" (roughly the same as today's "district of Reutte"). When the emperor came by, he stayed here. In 1604, the ruler moved downtown into more comfortable quarters, and the castle was no longer a palace.

Now climb the steep hill to the top of the castle. Take the high ground. There was no water supply here—just kegs of wine, beer, and a cistern to collect rain.

Ehrenberg repelled 16,000 Swedish soldiers in the defense of Catholicism in 1632. Ehrenberg saw three or four other battles, but its end was not glorious. In the 1780s, a local businessman bought the castle in order to sell off its parts. Later, when vagabonds moved in, the roof was removed to make squatting miserable. With the roof gone, deterioration quickened, leaving this evocative shell and a whiff of history.

▲Schlosskopf—If you have energy left after conquering Ehrenberg, hike up another 30 minutes to the mighty Schlosskopf ("Castle Head"). When the Bavarians captured Ehrenberg in 1703, the Tiroleans climbed up to the bluff above it to rain cannonballs down on their former fortress. In 1740, a mighty new castle—designed to defend against modern artillery—was built on this same sky-high strategic location. By the end of the 20th century, the castle was completely overgrown with trees—you couldn't see it from Reutte. But today the trees are shaved away, and the castle has been excavated. In 2005, the Castle Ensemble project reconstructed the original equipment used to build this fortress (such as wooden cranes)—and then began using those same means to restore parts of it. By 2007, Schlosskopf will be partially rebuilt, and the 18th-century construction equipment will retire and become part of the exhibit.

In Reutte

Folk Museum (Heimatsmuseum)—Reutte's Heimatmuseum, offering a quick look at the local folk culture and the story of the castles, is more cute than impressive. Ask to borrow the packet of information in English (€2, May–Oct Tue–Sun 10:00–17:00, closed Mon and Nov–April, in the bright-green building on Untermarkt, around corner from Hotel Goldener Hirsch, tel. 05672/72304).

▲▲Tirolean Folk Evening—Ask the TI or your hotel if there's a Tirolean folk evening scheduled. During the summer (July–mid-Sept), Reutte and nearby towns sometimes put on an evening of yodeling, slap dancing, and Tirolean frolic worth the €8 to €10 and short drive. Off-season, you'll have to do your own yodeling. There are also weekly folk concerts featuring the local brass band in Reutte's park (free, July–Aug only, ask at TI). For listings of these and other local events, pick up a copy of the German-only *Sommerprogramm* schedule at the TI.

▲Flying and Gliding—For a major thrill on a sunny day, drop by the tiny airport in Höfen across the river, and fly. A small single-prop plane can buzz the Zugspitze summit (at 9,700 feet, the highest point in Germany) and Ludwig's castles, and give you a bird's-eye peek at Reutte's Ehrenberg ruins (2 people for 30 min-€110, 1 hour-€220, tel. 05672/62827, phone rarely answered and then not in English, so your best bet is to show up at the Höfen airport on good-weather afternoons). Or, for something more angelic, how about *Segelfliegen*? For €40, you get 30 minutes in a glider for two (you and the pilot). Just watching the towrope launch the graceful glider like a giant, slow-motion rubber-band gun is exhilarating (May–mid-Sept 12:00–19:00, in good but breezy weather only, find someone in the know at the "Thermic

Ranch," tel. 05672/64010, or mobile 0676-711-0100).

Reuttener Bergbahn—This mountain lift swoops you high above the tree line to a starting point for several hikes and an alpine flower park, with special paths leading you past countless varieties of local flora. Unique to this lift is a barefoot hiking trail *(Barfusswanderweg)*, designed to be walked without shoes—no joke (€9 one-way, €13 round-trip, flowers best in late July, lift usually mid-May–Oct daily 9:00–11:50 & 13:00–16:30, tel. 05672/62420, www.reuttener-seilbahnen.at).

Near Reutte

▲▲Luge Courses *(Sommerrodelbahn)*—Near Lermoos, on the road from Reutte to Innsbruck, you'll find two exciting luge courses. Both luges charge the same price (€6 per run, 5- and 10-trip discount cards) and shut down at the slightest bit of rain (call ahead to make sure they're open; you're more likely to get luge info in English if you call the regional TI, tel. 05673/20000). If you're without a car, these are not worth the trouble.

The short and steep luge: Bichlbach, the first course (330-foot drop over a 2,600-foot course), is four miles beyond Reutte's castle ruins. Look for a chairlift on the right, and exit on the tiny road at the *Almkopfbahn Rosthof* sign (June–Sept daily 10:00–17:00, sometimes opens in spring and fall—especially weekends—depending on weather, closed in winter, tel. 05674/5350).

The longest luge: The Biberwier *Sommerrodelbahn* is a better luge and, at 4,250 feet, the longest in Austria (15 min farther from Reutte than Bichlbach, just past Lermoos in Biberwier—the first exit after a long tunnel). The only drawbacks are its short season and hours (late May–June Sat–Sun 9:00–16:30 only, closed Mon–Fri; July–Sept daily 9:00–16:30; closed Oct–April; tel. 05673/2323 or 05673/2111).

▲Fallerschein—Easy for drivers and a special treat for those who may have been Kit Carson in a previous life, this extremely remote log-cabin village is a 4,000-foot-high, flower-speckled world of serene slopes and cowbells. Thunderstorms roll down the valley like it's God's bowling alley, but the pint-size church on the high ground, blissfully simple in a land of Baroque, seems to promise that this huddle of houses will survive, and the river and breeze will just keep flowing. The couples sitting on benches are mostly Austrian vacationers who've rented cabins here. Many of them, appreciating the remoteness of Fallerschein, are having affairs.

Getting to Fallerschein: The village, at the end of the 1.25-mile Berwang Road, is near Namlos and about 45 minutes southwest of Reutte. You'll find a parking lot at the end of the road, leaving you with a two-mile walk down a drivable but technically closed one-lane road.

SLEEPING

In and near Reutte

(€1 = about $1.30, country code: 43, area code: 05672)

Reutte is a mellow Füssen with fewer crowds and easygoing locals with a contagious love of life. Come here for a good dose of Austrian ambience and lower prices. Those with a car should make their home base here; those without should consider it but plan very carefully. (To call Reutte from Germany, dial 00-43-5672, then the local number.) You'll drive across the border without stopping. Reutte is popular with Austrians and Germans, who come here year after year for one- or two-week vacations. The hotels are big, elegant, and full of comfy, carved furnishings and creative ways to spend lots of time in one spot. They take great pride in their restaurants, and the owners send their children away to hotel-management schools. All include a great breakfast, but few accept credit cards. Most hotels give about a 5 percent discount for stays of two nights or longer.

The Reutte TI has a list of 50 private homes that rent out generally good rooms *(Zimmer)* with facilities down the hall, pleasant communal living rooms, and breakfast. Most charge €20 per person per night and speak little or no English. Reservations are nearly impossible for one- or two-night stays, but short stops are welcome if you just drop in and fill available gaps. Most *Zimmer* charge around €1.50 extra for heat in winter (worth it). I've listed a few favorites below, but the TI can always find you a room when you arrive.

Reutte is surrounded by several distinct "villages" that basically feel like suburbs—many of them, such as Breitenwang (described below), within easy walking distance of the Reutte town center. While there are some good hotels in central Reutte itself, these nearby communities are also worth considering. If you want to hike through the woods to Neuschwanstein Castle, stay at Gutshof zum Schluxen (listed on page 446). To locate the recommended accommodations, see the map on page 439.

In Central Reutte

$$ Hotel "Das Beck" offers 16 clean, sunny, modern rooms (many with balconies) in the heart of town. It's a great value, and guests are personally taken care of by Hans, Inge, and Pipi. Enjoy their homemade marmalade at breakfast in the open kitchen/coffee bar or on the sunny patio. Their small café offers tasty snacks and specializes in Austrian and Italian wines (Sb-€42, Db-€64–68, Tb-€83, Qb-€98, non-smoking rooms, free parking, they'll pick you up from the station, Untermarkt 11, tel. 05672/62522, fax 05672/625-2235, www.welcome.to/hotel-das-beck, hotel-das-beck@eunet.at).

$$ Hotel Goldener Hirsch, located in the center of Reutte just two blocks from the station, is a grand old hotel renovated with Tirolean *Jugendstil* flair. It boasts 56 rooms and one lonely set of antlers (Sb-€60, Db-€85, Tb-€125, Qb-€140, 2-night discounts, family rooms, elevator, restaurant—see "Eating," later in this section, tel. 05672/62508, fax 05672/625-087, www.goldener-hirsch.at, info@goldener-hirsch.at; Monika, Helmut, and daughters Vanessa and Nina).

In Breitenwang

Right next door to Reutte is the older and quieter village of Breitenwang (with good *Zimmer* and a fine bakery). It's a 20-minute walk from the Reutte train station (at post office roundabout, follow Planseestrasse past onion dome to pointy straight dome, near the two hotels; the Hosps—as well as other *Zimmers*—are along unmarked Kaiser-Lothar-Strasse, the first right past this church).

$$ Alpenhotel Ernberg is run with great care by friendly Hermann, who combines Old World elegance with modern touches. Nestle in for some serious coziness among the carved-wood eating nooks and tiled stoves (Sb-€39, Db-€78, less for longer stays, self-service laundry for €7—also available for non-guests, restaurant, Planseestrasse 50, tel. 05672/71912, fax 05672/191-240, www.ernberg.at, info@ernberg.at).

$$ Moserhof Hotel has 30 new-feeling rooms plus an elegant dining room (Sb-€54, Db-€84, extra bed-€35, most rooms have balconies, elevator, Internet access-€3/hr, restaurant, free parking, Planseestrasse 44, tel. 05672/62020, fax 05672/620-2040, www.hotel-moserhof.at, info@hotel-moserhof.at, Hosp family).

Zimmer: **$ Walter and Emilie Hosp** rent three rooms in a comfortable, quiet, and modern house two blocks from the Breitenwang church steeple (D-€40, D-€36 for 2 nights or more, T-€60, Q-€80, cash only, Kaiser-Lothar-Strasse 29, tel. 05672/65377).

In Ehenbichl, near the Ehrenberg Ruins

The next three listings are a bit farther from central Reutte, a couple miles upriver in the village of Ehenbichl (under the Ehrenberg ruins). From central Reutte, go south on Obermarkt and turn right on Reuttener Strasse, following signs to Ehenbichl.

$$ Hotel Maximilian is a great value. It includes free bicycles, table tennis, a children's playroom, and the friendly service of the Koch family. They host many special events, and their hotel has lots of wonderful extras such as a sauna, a masseuse, and a beauty salon (Sb-€40–45, Db-€74–84, family deals, Internet access, laundry service for €12—also available for non-guests, good restaurant, tel. 05672/62585, fax 05672/625-8554, www.maxihotel.com, maxhotel@netway.at). They rent cars to guests only (1 Renault, 1 VW van, book in advance) and bikes to anyone (€6/half-day, €10/day).

$ Gasthof-Pension Waldrast, separating a forest and a meadow, is run by the farming Huter family and their huge, friendly dog, Bari. The place feels hauntingly quiet and has no restaurant, but it does offer 10 nice rooms with sitting areas and castle-view balconies (Sb-€35, Db-€58, Tb-€69, Qb-€92, cash only, non-smoking; less than 1 mile from Reutte, just off main drag toward Innsbruck, past campground and under castle ruins on Ehrenbergstrasse; tel. & fax 05672/62443, www.waldrasttirol.com, info@waldrasttirol.com).

$ Pension Hohenrainer is a big, no-frills alternative to Hotel Maximilian—a quiet, good value with 12 modern rooms and some castle-view balconies (Sb-€23–29, Db-€46–52, €3 per person extra for 1-night stays, cheaper for longer stays, cash only, family rooms, Internet access, restaurant across the street, follow signs up the road behind Hotel Maximilian into village of Ehenbichl, tel. 05672/62544 or 05672/63262, fax 05672/62052, www.hohenrainer.at, hohenrainer@aon.at).

In Other Villages near Reutte

$$ Wirtshaus Goldene Rose, while officially in the village of Lechaschau, is only about a 15-minute walk from the center of Reutte. This no-nonsense, sprawling, traditional hotel—complete with antlers and portraits of the *Kaiser*—makes a good home base for those spending several days in the area and who want amenities like easy parking, a restaurant, and a sauna (Sb-€40, Db-€74, from downtown Reutte cross bridge and take the first right, Dorfstrasse 2, tel. 05672/62411, fax 05672/624-117, www.hotel-goldene-rose.at, info@hotel-goldene-rose.at, Klotz family).

$ The homey **Gästehaus am Graben** hostel has two to six beds per room and includes breakfast and sheets. Frau Reyman and her son Rudy keep the place traditional, clean, and friendly, and serve a great €6.50 dinner for guests only. This is a super value. If you've never hosteled and are curious (and have a car or don't mind a bus ride), try it. They accept non-members of any age (dorm bed-€20, Db-€50, cash only, non-smoking rooms, Internet access, laundry service, no curfew, closed April and Nov–mid-Dec, less than 2 miles from Reutte, bus connection to Neuschwanstein via Reutte; from downtown Reutte cross bridge and follow main road left along river, or take the bus—hourly until 19:30, ask for Graben stop, no buses Sun; Graben 1, tel. 05672/626-440, fax 05672/626-444, www.hoefen.at, info@hoefen.at).

In Pinswang

The village of Pinswang is closer to Füssen (and Ludwig's castles), but still in Austria.

$$ Gutshof zum Schluxen, run by helpful Hermann, gets the "Remote Old Hotel in an Idyllic Setting" award. This family-friendly working farm offers modern rustic elegance draped in goose down and pastels, and a chance to pet a rabbit and feed the deer. "Mad" King Ludwig himself is said to have slept here. Its picturesque meadow setting will turn you into a dandelion picker, and its proximity to Neuschwanstein will turn you into a hiker; the castle is just an hour's hike away—see page 432 (Sb-€41, Db-€82, extra person-€22, 10 percent discount for 4 nights or more, Internet access, self-service laundry, mountain-bike rental, good restaurant, fun bar, between Reutte and Füssen in village of Pinswang, free pickup from Reutte or Füssen, tel. 05677/8903, fax 05677/890-323, www.schluxen.com, welcome@schluxen.com).

EATING

In Reutte

The hotels here take great pride in serving local cuisine at reasonable prices to their guests and the public. Rather than go to a cheap restaurant, try a hotel. Most offer €8 to €14 dinners from 18:00 to 21:00 and are closed one night a week. Reutte itself has plenty of inviting eateries, including traditional, ethnic, fast food, grocery stores, and delis.

Restaurant Goldener Hirsch, located in the hotel of the same name (recommended under "Sleeping," above), offers local specialties in a traditional setting. If you need a break from Tirolean food, try the tasty vegetable plate, or *Gemüseplatte* (€8–12 entrées, Tue–Sun 11:00–14:00 & 17:30–22:30, closed Mon, Mühlerstasse 1, tel. 05672/62508).

Wirtshaus Goldene Rose is known for its grill and game specialties. Go here for a fancy dinner of regionally inspired dishes featuring fresh asparagus, mushrooms, or whatever's in season. Families will feel comfortable here, too (€9–18 plates, daily 12:00–14:00 & 17:30–21:30, Dorfstrasse 2, tel. 05672/62411, fax 05672/624-117, www.hotel-goldene-rose.at, info@hotel-goldene-rose.at).

Alpenhotel Ernberg, Moserhof Hotel, and **Hotel Maximilian** also offer fine restaurants (see "Sleeping," above).

Storfwirt is *the* place for a quick lunch or light dinner. You can get the usual sausages here, as well as baked potatoes, salads, and pizza. Check for daily lunch or dinner specials (€3–7 meals, Tue–Fri 7:00–18:00, Sat–Sun 8:00–12:00, closed Mon, Schrettergasse 15, tel. 05672/62640).

Non Solo Pasta, just off the traffic circle, is a local favorite for Italian food (€7–10 entrées, Mon–Fri 11:30–14:00 & 18:00–23:00, Sat 18:00–23:00, closed Sun, Lindenstrasse 1, tel. 05672/72714).

Picnic Supplies: **Billa** supermarket has everything you'll need (across from TI, Mon–Fri 8:00–19:00, Sat 8:00–17:00, closed Sun).

TRANSPORTATION CONNECTIONS

From Reutte by Train to: Garmisch (every 2 hrs, 1 hr), **Innsbruck** (every 2 hrs, 2.5 hrs, change in Garmisch), **Munich** (hourly, 2.5–3 hrs, change in Garmisch, Pfronten-Steinach, or Kempten).

By Bus to: Füssen (Mon–Fri 4/day, none Sat–Sun, 35 min, €3.40, buses depart from in front of the train station, pay driver). Taxis cost €30 one-way.

By Car from Germany into Reutte: Skip the north *(Nord)* exit and take the south *(Süd)* exit into town. While Austria requires a toll sticker for driving on its highways (€8/10 days, buy at the border, gas stations, car-rental agencies, or Tabak shops), those just dipping into Tirol from Bavaria do not need one.

ROTHENBURG

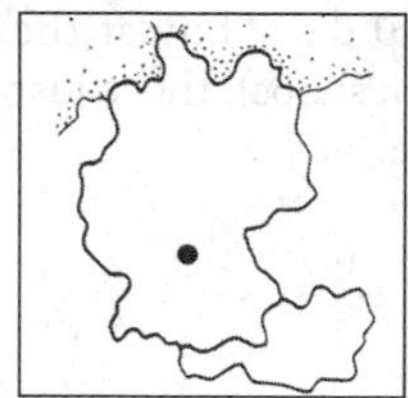

In the Middle Ages, when Frankfurt and Munich were just wide spots on the road, Rothenburg ob der Tauber was Germany's second-largest free imperial city, with a whopping population of 6,000. Today, it's her best-preserved medieval walled town, enjoying tremendous tourist popularity without losing its charm.

During Rothenburg's heyday, from 1150 to 1400, it was a strategic stop on the trade route between northern and southern Europe. That route is now Germany's "Romantic Road," linking Frankfurt to Munich through a medieval heartland strewn with picturesque villages, farmhouses, onion-domed churches, and walled cities. Rothenburg is the cream of the crop.

Today, Rothenburg's great trade is tourism: Two-thirds of the townspeople are employed to serve you. While 2.5 million people visit each year, a mere 500,000 spend the night. Rothenburg is yours after dark, when the tour groups vacate and the town's flood-lit cobbles wring some romance out of any travel partner.

Too often, Rothenburg brings out the shopper in visitors before they've had a chance to see the historic town. True, this is a fine place to do your German shopping, but appreciate Rothenburg's great history and sights, too.

Planning Your Time

If time is short, you can make just a two- to three-hour midday stop in Rothenburg, but the town is really best appreciated after the day-trippers have gone home. Spend at least one night in Rothenburg. With two nights and a day, you'll be able to see more than the essentials and actually relax a little.

Rothenburg in one day is easy, with four essential experiences: the Medieval Crime and Punishment Museum, Tilman Riemenschneider's wood carving in St. Jakob's Church, a walk along the city wall, and the entertaining Night Watchman's Tour (the first two sights are covered in my self-guided tour, below). With more time, there are several mediocre but entertaining museums, hikes, and bike rides in the nearby countryside, and lots of cafés and shops.

Rothenburg is very busy through the summer and in the Christmas Market month of December. Spring and fall are a joy, but it's pretty bleak from January through March—when most locals are hibernating or on vacation. Many shops stay open on Sundays during the tourist season, but close on Sundays in November and from Christmas to Easter.

ORIENTATION

(area code: 09861)

To orient yourself in Rothenburg, think of the town map as a human head. Its nose—the castle garden—sticks out to the left, and the skinny lower part forms a wide-open mouth, with the hostel and some of the best hotels in the chin. The town is a delight on foot. No sights or hotels are more than a 15-minute walk from the train station or each other.

Most of the buildings you'll see were in place by 1400. The city was born around its long-gone castle—built in 1142, destroyed in 1356—which was located where the castle garden is now. You can see the shadow of the first town wall, which defines the oldest part of Rothenburg, in its contemporary street plan. A few gates from this wall still survive. The richest and biggest houses were in this central part. The commoners built higgledy-piggledy (read: picturesque) houses farther from the center, but still inside the present walls.

Tourist Information

The TI is on Market Square (May–Oct Mon–Fri 9:00–12:00 & 13:00–18:00, Sat–Sun 10:00–15:00; Nov–April Mon–Fri 9:00–12:00 & 13:00–17:00, Sat 10:00–13:00, closed Sun; Marktplatz 2, tel. 09861/404800, www.rothenburg.de). If there's a long line, just raid the rack where they keep all the free pamphlets. The free *Map & Guide* comes with a walking guide to the town. The *RoTour* monthly guide lists all the events and entertainment (also look for current concert listing posters here and at your hotel). Ask about the daily English walking tour at 14:00 (€6, April–Oct and Dec; see "Tours," page 452). The TI has a free Internet terminal (15-min maximum). Visitors who arrive after closing can check the

Rothenburg

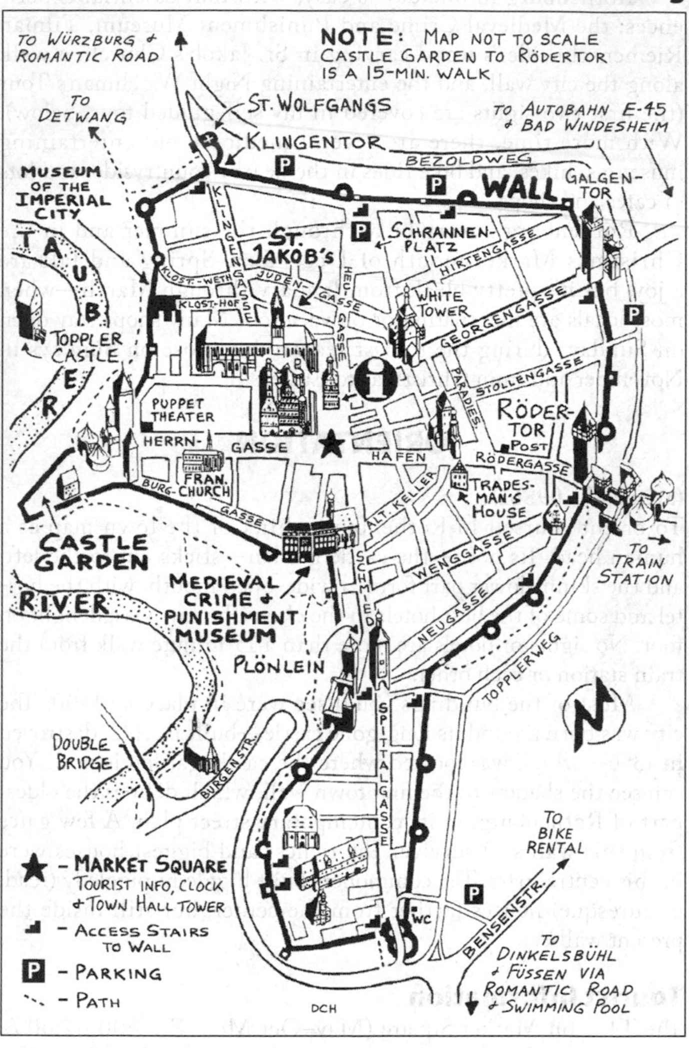

handy map highlighting which hotels have rooms available, with a free direct phone connection to them; it's just outside the door. A better town map is available free with this book at the Friese shop, two doors west from the TI (toward St. Jakob's Church; see "Shopping," page 462).

Arrival in Rothenburg

By Train: It's a 10-minute walk from the station to Rothenburg's Market Square (following the brown *Altstadt* signs, exit left from station, turn right on Ansbacher Strasse, and head straight into the Middle Ages). Day-trippers can leave luggage in station lockers (€2, on platform) or at the Friese shop on Market Square. Arrange train and couchette/sleeper reservations at the combined ticket office and travel agency in the station (Mon–Fri 9:00–18:00, Sat 9:00–13:00, closed Sun, tel. 09861/7711). Free WCs are behind the snack bar next door to the station. Taxis wait at the station (€5 to any hotel).

By Car: While much of the town is closed to traffic, anyone with a hotel reservation can drive in and through pedestrian zones to get to their hotel. But driving in town can be a nightmare, with many narrow, one-way streets. If you're packing light, just park outside the walls and walk five minutes to the center. Parking lots line the town walls, and are generally free (the P1 parking lot, on the south end of town near Spitaltor, and P5 parking lot just outside Klingentor, on the north end of town, are each handy, depending on where you're staying). Only those with a hotel reservation can park within the walls after hours (but not during festivals). The easiest way to enter and leave Rothenburg is generally via Spitalgasse and the Spitaltor (south end).

Helpful Hints

Festivals: Rothenburgers dress up in medieval costumes, and beer gardens spill out into the street to celebrate Mayor Nusch's Meistertrunk victory (see story of the draught that saved the town under "Meistertrunk Show" on page 453, more info at www.meistertrunk.de) and 700 years of history in the Imperial City Festival (late August, with fireworks).

Christmas Market: Rothenburg is dead in November, January, and February, but December is its busiest month—the entire town cranks up the medieval cuteness with concerts and costumes, shops with schnapps, stalls filling squares, hot spiced wine, giddy nutcrackers, and mobs of earmuffed Germans. Christmas markets are big all over Germany, and Rothenburg's is considered one of the best. The festival takes place each year during Advent, the four weeks leading up to the last Sunday before Christmas. Virtually all sights listed in this chapter are open longer hours during these four weeks. Try to avoid Saturdays and Sundays, when big-city day-trippers really clog the grog.

Internet Access: When it comes to getting online, Rothenburg is still pretty medieval. Few hotels have phones in the rooms or offer Internet access. The **TI** has a free terminal for brief use (maximum 15 min). **Inter@Play,** the only Internet café in town, has eight fast terminals and kids playing video games (€3/hr, daily 8:00–24:00, 2 blocks down Hafengasse from Market Square and around the corner to the left at Milchmarkt 3, see map on page 454, tel. 09861/935-599).

Laundry: A handy launderette is near the station, off Ansbacher Strasse (€5.50/load, includes soap, English instructions, opens at 8:00, last load in Mon–Fri at 18:00, Sat at 14:00, closed Sun, Johannitergasse 9, tel. 09861/2775).

Swimming: Rothenburg has a fine modern recreation center with an indoor/outdoor pool *(Hallenbad)* and sauna. It's just a few minutes' walk south of town down the road towards Dinkelsbühl (adults-€3.50, kids-€2, swimsuit and towel rental-€2 each, Mon 14:00–21:00, Tue–Thu 9:00–21:00, Fri–Sun 9:00–18:00, Nördlinger Strasse 20, tel. 09861/4565).

Bike Rental: You can rent bikes at **Rad & Tat,** and follow the suggested route on page 462 (€2.50/hr, €7.50/half-day, €10/day, Mon–Fri 9:00–18:00, Sat 9:00–13:00, closed Sun, Bensenstrasse 17, on other side of Sportplatz from train station near corner of Bensenstrasse and Erlbacher Strasse, passport number required, tel. 09861/87984, www.mietraeder.de, Daniel Lorenz).

TOURS

▲▲Night Watchman's Tour—This tour is flat-out the most entertaining hour of medieval wonder anywhere in Germany. The Night Watchman (a.k.a. Hans-Georg Baumgartner) jokes like a medieval Jerry Seinfeld as he lights his lamp and takes tourists on his rounds, telling slice-of-gritty-life tales of medieval Rothenburg (€6, free for kids, mid-March–Dec nightly at 20:00 in English, meet at Market Square, www.nightwatchman.de). This is the best evening activity in town.

Old Town Historic Walk—The TI offers 90-minute guided walking tours in English (€6, April–Oct and Dec daily at 14:00, departs from Market Square). While the Night Watchman's Tour is fun, take this tour for the serious side of Rothenburg's history, and to make sense of the town's architecture. The tours are completely different, and it would be a shame not to take advantage of this informative tour just because you took the other.

Private Guides—A local historian can really bring the ramparts alive. Prices are standardized (€53/90 min, €70/2 hrs). Gisela Vogl (tel. 09861/4957, werner.vogl@t-online.de) and Anita Weinzierl (tel. 09868/7993, anitaweinzierl@aol.com) are both good. Martin Kamphans, a potter, also works as a guide (tel. 09861/7941, kamphans@t-online.de). Other guides are also available—just send an email to the TI (info@rothenburg.de) to reserve.

Horse-and-Buggy Rides—These farm boys, who are generally about as charming as their horses, give a relaxing 30-minute clip-clop through the old town, starting from Market Square or Schrannenplatz. Good luck negotiating a fair price (private buggy for €30–50, or wait for one to fill up for €6 per person).

SELF-GUIDED WALK

Welcome to Rothenburg

This one-hour circular walk weaves Rothenburg's top sights together.

• *Start the walk on Market Square.*

Market Square Spin Tour: Stand at the bottom of Market Square (10 feet below the wooden post on the corner) and—ignoring the little white arrow—spin 360 degrees clockwise, starting with the Town Hall tower. Now do it again, this time more slowly, following these notes:

Town Hall and Tower: Rothenburg's tallest spire is the **Town Hall tower** (Rathausturm). At 200 feet, it stands atop the old Town Hall, a white, Gothic, 13th-century building. Notice the tourists enjoying the best view in town from the black top of the tower (€1 and a rigorous but interesting climb, 214 steps, narrow and steep near the top—watch your head, April–Oct daily 9:30–12:30 & 13:00–17:00, closed Nov–March, enter on Market Square through middle arch of new Town Hall). After a fire burned down part of the original building, a **new Town Hall** was built alongside what survived of the old one (fronting the square). This half of the rebuilt complex is in the Renaissance style from 1570.

Meistertrunk ("Master Draught") Show: At the top of Market Square stands the proud **Councillors' Tavern** (clock tower from 1466). In its day, the city council—the rich guys who ran the town government—drank here. Today, it's the TI and the focus of most tourists' attention when the little doors on either side of the clock flip open and the wooden figures (from 1910) do their thing. Be on Market Square at 11:00, 12:00, 13:00, 14:00, 15:00, 20:00, 21:00, or 22:00 for the ritual gathering of the tourists to see the less-than-breathtaking reenactment of the Meistertrunk story:

In 1631, the Catholic army took the Protestant town, and was about to do its rape, pillage, and plunder thing. As was the etiquette, the mayor had to give the conquering general a welcoming drink. The general enjoyed a huge tankard of local wine. Feeling really good, he told the mayor, "Hey, if you can drink this entire three-liter tankard of wine in one gulp, I'll spare your town." The mayor amazed everyone by drinking the entire thing, and Rothenburg was saved.

While this is a nice story, it was dreamed up in the late 1800s for a theatrical play designed (effectively) to promote a romantic image of the town. In actuality, if Rothenburg was spared, it

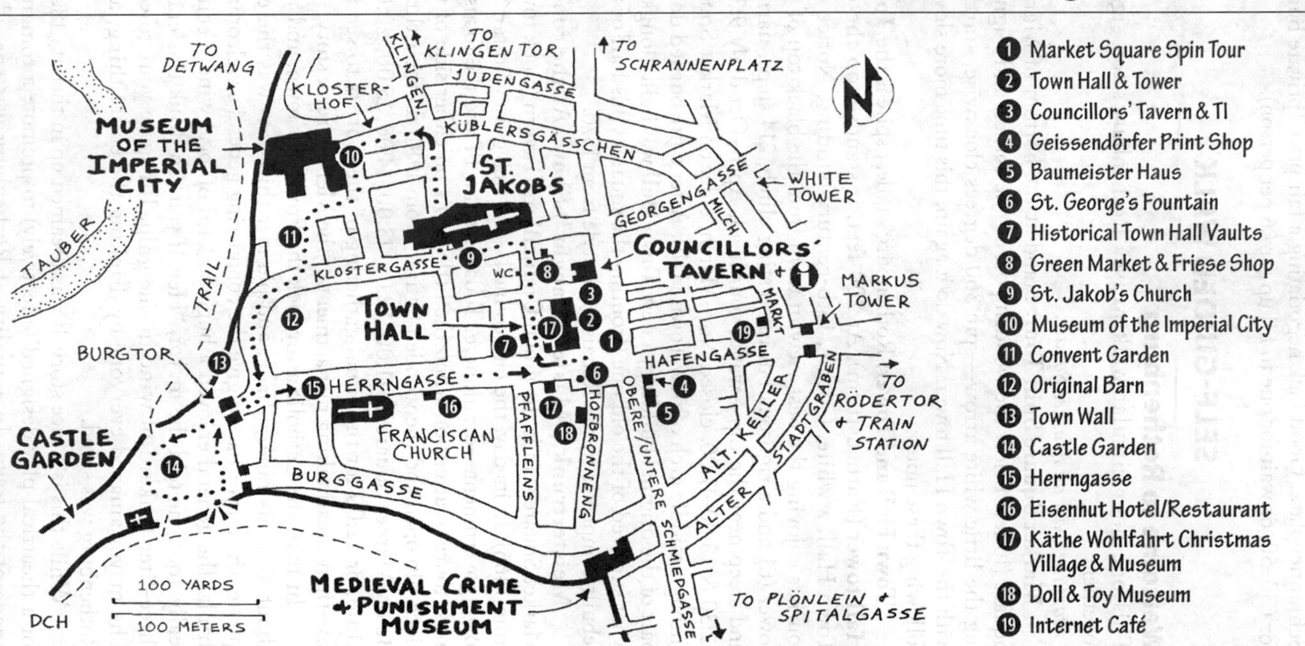
Rothenburg Self-Guided Walk
1 Market Square Spin Tour
2 Town Hall & Tower
3 Councillors' Tavern & TI
4 Geissendörfer Print Shop
5 Baumeister Haus
6 St. George's Fountain
7 Historical Town Hall Vaults
8 Green Market & Friese Shop
9 St. Jakob's Church
10 Museum of the Imperial City
11 Convent Garden
12 Original Barn
13 Town Wall
14 Castle Garden
15 Herrngasse
16 Eisenhut Hotel/Restaurant
17 Käthe Wohlfahrt Christmas
Village & Museum
18 Doll & Toy Museum
19 Internet Café
TO DETWANG
TO KLINGENTOR
TO SCHRANNENPLATZ
KLOSTER-HOF
KLINGEN.
JUDENGASSE
KÜBLERSGÄSSCHEN
MUSEUM OF THE IMPERIAL CITY
ST. JAKOB'S
WHITE TOWER
GEORGENGASSE
MILCH
TAUBER R.
TRAIL
KLOSTERGASSE
WC
COUNCILLORS' TAVERN + i
MARKUS TOWER
MARKT
TOWN HALL
BURGTOR
HAFENGASSE
HERRNGASSE
TO RÖDERTOR + TRAIN STATION
FRANCISCAN CHURCH
PFAFFLEINS
HOFBRONNENG
OBERE / UNTERE SCHMIEDGASSE
ALT. KELLER
STADTGRABEN
ALTER
CASTLE GARDEN
BURGGASSE
100 YARDS
100 METERS
DCH
MEDIEVAL CRIME + PUNISHMENT MUSEUM
TO PLÖNLEIN + SPITALGASSE

happened because it bribed its way out of a jam. It was occupied and ransacked several times in the Thirty Years' War, and it never recovered—which is why it's such a well-preserved time capsule today. Hint: For the best show, don't watch the clock; watch the open-mouthed tourists gasp as the old windows flip open. At the late shows, the square flickers with camera flashes.

Bottom of Market Square: On the bottom end of the square, the cream-colored building has a fine **print shop** (upstairs—see "Shopping," page 462). Adjoining that is the **Baumeister Haus,** featuring a famous Renaissance facade with statues of the seven virtues and the seven vices—the former supporting the latter. The statues are copies; the originals are in the Museum of the Imperial City (listed below). The green house below that is the former home of the 15th-century Mayor Toppler (it's now the recommended Gasthof Goldener Greifen).

Keep circling to the big 17th-century **St. George's fountain.** The long metal gutters slid, routing the water into the villagers' buckets. Rothenburg had an ingenious water system. Built on a rock, it had onc real source above the town which was plumbed to serve a series of fountains; water flowed from high to low through Rothenburg. Its many fountains had practical functions beyond providing drinking water (some were stocked with fish on market days and during times of siege). Water was used for fighting fires, and because of its plentiful water supply—and its policy of requiring relatively wide lanes as fire breaks—the town never burned entirely, as so many neighboring villages did.

Two fine buildings behind the fountain show the old-time lofts with warehouse doors and pulleys on top for hoisting. All over town, lofts were filled with grain and corn. A year's supply was required by the city so they could survive any siege. The building behind the fountain is an art gallery showing off the work of local profcssional artists (free, Tue–Fri 13:00–17:00, Sat–Sun 11:00–17:00, closed Mon). To the right is an old-time pharmacy mixing old and new in typical Rothenburg style.

The broad street running under the Town Hall tower is **Herrngasse** (also see end of tour, below). The town originated with its castle (built in 1142 but now long gone; only the castle garden remains). Herrngasse connected the castle to Market Square. The last leg of this circular walking tour will take you from the castle garden up Herrngasse to where you now stand. For now, walk a few steps down Herrngasse and stand by the arch under the Town Hall tower (between the new and old town halls). On the left wall are the town's measuring rods—a reminder that medieval Germany was made of 300 independent little countries, each with its own weights and measures. Merchants and shoppers knew that these were the local standards: the rod (4.3 yards), the *Schuh* (or shoe, roughly a foot), and the *Ell* (from elbow to fingertip—four inches longer than mine...try it). Notice the protruding cornerstone. These are all over town—originally to protect buildings from reckless horse carts (and vice versa).

• *Under the arch, you'll find the...*

Historical Town Hall Vaults (Historiengewölbe): This grade-schoolish little museum, worth ▲, gives a waxy but interesting look at Rothenburg during the Catholics-vs.-Protestants Thirty Years' War. With helpful English descriptions, it offers a look at "the fateful year 1631," a replica of the mythical Meistertrunk tankard, and a dungeon complete with three dank cells and some torture lore (€2, April–Oct daily 10:00–17:00, closed Nov–March, tel. 09861/86751).

• *Leaving the museum, turn left, and walk through the courtyard to a square called...*

Green Market (Grüner Markt): Once a produce market, it's now a parking lot that fills with Christmas shops during December. Notice the clay tiled roofs. These "beaver tail" tiles became standard after thatched roofs were outlawed to prevent fires. Today, all of the town's roofs are made of these. The little fences keep the snow from falling, and catch tiles that blow off during storms. The free public WC is on your left, the recommended **Friese shop** (see "Shopping," page 462) is on your right, and straight ahead is St. Jakob's Church.

Outside the church, you'll see 14th-century statues (mostly original) showing Jesus praying at Gethsemane, a common feature of Gothic churches. The artist is anonymous, because in the Gothic age (pre-Albrecht Dürer) artists were just nameless craftspeople working only for the glory of God. Five yards to the left (on the wall), notice the nub of a sandstone statue—a rare original, looking pretty bad after 500 years of weather and, more recently, pollution. Original statues are now in the city museum. Better-preserved statues you see on the church are copies.

• *If it's your wedding day, take the first entrance. Otherwise, use the second (downhill) door to enter...*

St. Jakob's Church: Built in the 14th century, this ▲▲ church has been Lutheran since 1544. The interior was "purified" by Romantics in the 19th century—cleaned of everything Baroque or not original, and refitted in the Neo-Gothic style. (For example, the baptismal font and the pulpit above the second pew *look* Gothic, but are actually Neo-Gothic.) The stained-glass windows behind the altar (most colorful in the morning light) are originals from the 1330s. Entrance costs €2 (April–Oct and Dec Mon–Sat 9:00–17:30, Sun 10:45–17:30; Nov and Christmas–March daily 10:00–12:00 & 14:00–16:00; free helpful English info sheet).

Stay in the back of the church. Take the back stairs that lead up behind the pipe organ to the artistic highlight of Rothenburg, and perhaps the most wonderful wood carving in all of Germany: the glorious 500-year-old, 35-foot-high ***Altar of the Holy Blood.*** Tilman Riemenschneider, the Michelangelo of German woodcarvers, carved this from 1499 to 1504 to hold a precious rock-crystal capsule, set in a cross that contains a scrap of tablecloth miraculously stained in the shape of a cross by a drop of communion wine. It's a realistic commotion, showing that Riemenschneider—while a High Gothic artist—was ahead of his time. Below, in the scene of the Last Supper, Jesus gives Judas a piece of bread, marking him as the traitor, while John lays his head on Christ's lap. Everything is portrayed exactly as described in the Bible. On the left: Jesus enters Jericho with the shy tax collector Zacchaeus looking on from his tree. Notice the fun attention to detail—down to the nails on the horseshoe. On the right: Jesus prays in the Garden of Gethsemane. Notice how Judas, with his big bag of cash, could be removed from the scene—illustrated by photos on the wall nearby—as was the tradition for the four days leading up to Easter.

Head back down the stairs to the church's main hall. Go up front to take a close look at the main altar (from 1466, by Friedrich Herlin). Below Christ are statues of six saints; St. James (Jakob in German, pronounced "YAH-kohp") is the one with the shell. He's the saint of pilgrims, and this church was a stop on the medieval pilgrimage route to Santiago ("St. James" in Spanish) de Compostela in Spain. Study the painted panels—ever see Peter with spectacles? Around the back of the altarpiece (upper left) is a painting of Rothenburg's Market Square in the 15th century—looking much like it does today, with the exception of the full-Gothic Town Hall (as it was before the big fire of 1501). Notice Christ's face on the veil of Veronica (center of back side). It follows you as you walk from side to side—it must have given the faithful the religious heebie-jeebies four centuries ago.

The small altar to the left is also worth a look. It's a century older than the main altar. Notice the unusual Trinity: the Father and Son are literally bridged by a dove representing the Holy Spirit. Stepping back, you can see that Jesus is standing on a skull—clearly "overcoming death."

Before leaving the front of the church, notice the old medallions above the carved choir stalls. They feature the coats of arms of Rothenburg's leading families and portraits of city and church leaders.

• *Leave the church and, from its outside steps, walk around the corner to the right and under the chapel (built over the road). Go two blocks down Klingengasse and stop at the corner of Klosterhof street. Looking down Klingengasse, you see the...*

Klingentor: This cliff tower was Rothenburg's water reservoir.

From 1595 until 1910, a copper tank high in the tower provided clean spring water (pumped up by river-power) to the privileged. To the right of Klingentor is a good stretch of wall rampart to walk. To the left, the wall is low and simple, lacking a rampart because it guards only a cliff. Now find the shell decorating a building on the street corner next to you. That's the symbol of St. James (pilgrims commemorated their visit to Santiago de Compostela with a shell), indicating that this building is associated with the church.

• *Turn left down Klosterhof, passing the shell and, on your right, the colorful Altfränkische Weinstube (see "Eating," page 471), to reach the...*

Museum of the Imperial City (Reichsstadt-Museum): You'll get a scholarly sweep through Rothenburg's history at this ▲▲ sight. The museum is housed in the former Dominican convent. Cloistered nuns used the lazy Susan embedded in the wall (to the right of museum door) to give food to the poor without being seen.

Highlights include *The Rothenburg Passion,* a 12-panel series of paintings from 1492 showing scenes leading up to Christ's crucifixion (in the *Konventsaal*); an exhibit of Jewish culture through the ages in Rothenburg *(Judaika);* a 14th-century convent kitchen *(Klosterküche)* with a working model of the lazy Susan and a massive chimney; romantic paintings of the town *(Gemäldegalerie);* the fine Baumann collection of weapons and armor; and sandstone statues from the church and Baumeister Haus (the seven vices and seven virtues). Follow the *Rundgang Tour* signs (€3, €6 combo-ticket that includes Medieval Crime and Punishment Museum saves a whopping €0.50, daily April–Oct 9:30–17:30, Nov–March 13:00–16:00, English info sheet and descriptions, Klosterhof 5, tel. 09861/939-043, www.reichsstadtmuseum.rothenburg.de).

• *Leaving the museum, go around to the right and into the...*

Convent Garden: This spot is a peaceful place to work on your tan...or mix a poisoned potion (free, same hours as museum). Enjoy the herb garden. Monks and nuns, who were responsible for concocting herbal cures in the olden days, often tended herb gardens. Smell (but don't pick) the *Pfefferminze, Juniper* (gin), *Chamomilla* (disinfectant), and *Origanum.* Don't smell the plants in the poison corner (potency indicated by the number of crosses... like the stars that indicate spiciness in a Chinese restaurant).

• *Exit opposite from where you entered, angling left through the nuns' garden (site of the now-gone Dominican church), eventually leaving via an arch at the far end. Looking to your left, you'll see the back end of an...*

Original Barn: This is the back side of a complex that fronts Herrngasse. Medieval Germans often lived in large structures like this that were like small villages in themselves, with a grouping of buildings and open spaces. The typical design included a house, a courtyard, a stable, a garden, and, finally, a barn.

• *Now go downhill to the...*

Town Wall: This part of the wall (view through bars, look to far right) takes advantage of the natural fortification provided by the cliff, and is therefore much smaller than the ramparts. Angle left along the wall to the big street (Herrngasse), then right under the Burgtor tower. Notice the tiny "eye of the needle" door cut into the big door. If trying to get into town after curfew, you could bribe the guard to let you through this door (which was small enough to keep out any fully armed attackers).

• *Step through the gate and outside the wall. Look around and imagine being locked out in the year 1400. This was a wooden drawbridge (see the chain slits above). Notice the "pitch nose" mask—designed to pour boiling Nutella on anyone attacking. High above is the town coat of arms: a red castle* (roten Burg).

Castle Garden (Burggarten): The garden before you was once that red castle (destroyed in the 14th century). Today, it's a picnic-friendly park. The chapel (50 yards into the park on the left) is the only bit of the original castle to survive. It's now a memorial to local Jews killed in a 1298 slaughter. A few steps beyond that is a grapevine trellis that provides a fine picnic spot. If you walk all the way out to the garden's far end, you'll find a great viewpoint (well past the tourists, and considered the best place to kiss by romantic local teenagers). But the views of the lush Tauber River Valley below are just as good from the top end of the park. Facing the town, on the left, a path leads down to the village of Detwang (you can see the church spire below)—a town even older than Rothenburg (for a walk to Detwang, see "A Walk in the Countryside," page 461). To the right is a fine view of the fortified Rothenburg and the "Tauber Riviera" below.

• *Return to the tower, cross carefully under the pitch nose, and hike back up Herrngasse to your starting point.*

Herrngasse: Many towns have a Herrngasse, where the richest patricians and merchants (the *Herren*) lived. Predictably, it's your best chance to see the town's finest old mansions. Strolling back to Market Square, you'll pass the old-time puppet theater (German only, on left), the Franciscan church (from 1285, oldest in town, on right), and the hippie Sawasdee shop (where the Night Watchman spends his days dreaming of his next trip to Thailand while his girlfriend sells the things they've imported, Herrngasse 23). To see the traditional house-courtyard-stables-garden-barn layout, pop into either #14 (now an apartment block) or—if that's closed—the shop next door, at #11. The Eisenhut Hotel, Rothenburg's fanciest, is worth a peek inside (see "Eating," page 469). The Käthe Wohlfahrt Christmas shops (at Herrngasse 1 and 2, see "Shopping," page 462) are your last, and perhaps greatest, temptation before reaching your starting and ending point: Market Square.

SIGHTS AND ACTIVITIES

Museums Within a Block of Market Square

▲▲Medieval Crime and Punishment Museum (Mittelalterliches Kriminalmuseum)—This museum is the best of its kind, specializing in everything connected to medieval criminal justice. Learn about medieval police, medieval criminal law, and above all, instruments of punishment and torture—even a special cage complete with a metal gag for nags. The museum is more eclectic than its name, and includes exhibits on general history, superstition, biblical art, and temporary exhibits in a second building. Follow the yellow arrows—the one-way traffic system makes it hard to double back. Exhibits are tenderly described in English (€3.50, €6 combo-ticket includes the €3 Museum of the Imperial City, daily April–Oct 9:30–18:00, Nov and Jan–Feb 14:00–16:00, Dec and March 10:00–16:00, last entry 45 min before closing, fun cards and posters, Burggasse 3–5, tel. 09861/5359, www.kriminalmuseum.rothenburg.de).

▲Doll and Toy Museum (Puppen- und Spielzeugmuseum)—Two floors of historic *Kinder* cuteness is a hit with many. Pick up the free English binder (just past the entry curtain) for an extensive description of the exhibits (€4, family ticket-€10, daily March–Dec 9:30–18:00, Jan–Feb 11:00–17:00, just off Market Square, downhill from the fountain at Hofbronnengasse 11–13, tel. 09861/7330, kath.engels@web.de).

▲German Christmas Museum (Deutsches Weihnachtsmuseum)—This excellent museum, upstairs in the giant Käthe Wohlfahrt Christmas Village shop, tells the history of Christmas decorations. There's a unique and thoughtfully described collection of Christmas-tree stands, mini-trees sent in boxes to WWI soldiers at the front, early Advent calendars, old-time Christmas cards, 450 clever ways to crack a nut, and a look at tree decorations through the ages—including the Nazi era and when you were a kid. The museum is not just a ploy to get shoppers to spend more money, but a serious collection managed by professional curator Felicitas Höptner (€4, April–Dec daily 10:00–17:30, Jan–March Sat–Sun 10:00–17:30 and irregularly on weekdays, Herrngasse 1, 09861/409-365, www.germanchristmasmuseum.com).

More Sights and Activities in Rothenburg

▲▲Walk the Wall—Just over a mile and a half around, providing great views and a good orientation, this walk can be done by those under six feet tall and without a camera in less than an hour. The hike requires no special sense of balance. This covered walk is a great option in the rain. Photographers go through lots of film, especially before breakfast or at sunset, when the lighting is best and the crowds are fewest. The best fortifications are in the Spitaltor (south end). Walk from there counterclockwise to the "forehead" (note on the Rothenburg map how the town outline looks like a head). Climb the Rödertor en route. The names you see along the way are people who donated money to rebuild the wall after World War II, and those who've recently donated €1,000 per meter for the maintenance of Rothenburg's heritage. You can enter or exit the ramparts at nearly every tower.

▲Rödertor—The wall tower nearest the train station is the only one you can climb. It's worth the 135 steps for the view and a short but fascinating rundown on the bombing of Rothenburg in the last weeks of World War II, when the east part of the city was destroyed (€1, pay at top, unreliable hours, usually open April–Oct daily 10:00–16:00, closed Nov–March, WWII photos have English translations). If you climb this, you can skip the Town Hall tower.

▲▲The Allergic-to-Tourists Wall and Moat Walk—For a quiet and scenic break from the tourist crowds and a chance to appreciate the marvelous fortifications of Rothenburg, consider this hike: From the Castle Garden, walk outside the wall to Klingentor. At Klingentor, climb up to the ramparts and walk on the wall past Rödertor to Galgentor. Then descend, leave the old town, and hike through the park (once the moat) down to Spitaltor. Explore the fortifications here before hiking a block up Spitalgasse, turning left to pass the youth hostel, popping back outside the wall, and heading along the upper scenic reaches of the "Tauber Riviera" back to the Castle Garden.

▲Tradesman's House (Alt-Rothenburger Handwerkerhaus)—See the everyday life of a Rothenburger in the town's heyday in this restored 700-year-old home (€2.20; Easter–Oct Mon–Fri 11:00–17:00, Sat–Sun 10:00–17:00; Nov–Dec daily 14:00–16:00; closed Jan–Easter; Alter Stadtgraben 26, near Markus Tower, tel. 09861/94280).

St. Wolfgang's Church—This fortified Gothic church is built into the medieval wall at Klingentor. Its dungeon-like passages and shepherd's-dance exhibit are pretty lame (€1.50, April–Sept Wed–Mon 10:00–13:00 & 14:30–17:00, Oct until 16:00, closed Tue and Nov–March).

Near Rothenburg

▲A Walk in the Countryside—From the *Burggarten* (castle garden), head down the path into the Tauber Valley. Bear north (with Rothenburg on your right), cross the wooden covered bridge, and then turn left to reach the **Toppler Castle** (Topplerschlösschen), the cute, skinny, 600-year-old castle/summer home of the medieval Mayor Toppler. The tower's top looks like a house—a sort of tree fort for grownups. It's in a farmer's garden and is open whenever he's around and willing to let you in (€1.50, normally Fri–Sun 13:00–16:00, closed Mon–Thu and Nov, 1 mile from town center at Taubertalweg 100, tel. 09861/7358). People say the mayor had this valley-floor escape to get people to relax about leaving the fortified town...or to hide a mistress.

To extend your stroll, walk back along the river—past the wooden covered bridge and huge trout—to the peaceful village of **Detwang.** One of the oldest villages in Franconia, Detwang dates from 968. Like Rothenburg, it has a Riemenschneider altarpiece in its church.

Franconian Bike Ride—To get a fun, breezy look at the countryside around Rothenburg, rent a bike from Rad & Tat (see "Helpful Hints," page 452). For a pleasant half-day pedal, bike along Topplerweg to Spitaltor and down into the Tauber Riviera, over the double-arcaded bridge, and along the small riverside road to Detwang, passing the cute Topplerschlösschen (described above). From Detwang, follow Liebliches Taubertal bike path signs as far up the Tauber River (direction: Bettwar) as you like.

Franconian Open-Air Museum (Fränkisches Freilandmuseum)—A 20-minute drive from Rothenburg in the undiscovered "Rothenburgy" town of Bad Windsheim is an open-air folk museum that, compared with others in Europe, is a bit humble. But it tries very hard and gives you the best look around at traditional rural Franconia (€5, daily March–Sept 9:00–18:00, Oct–Dec 10:00–16:00, closed Jan–Feb, last entry 1 hour before closing, tel. 09841/66800, www.freilandmuseum.de).

SHOPPING

Be warned...Rothenburg is one of Germany's best shopping towns. Do it here and be done with it. Lovely prints, carvings, wineglasses, Christmas-tree ornaments, and beer steins are popular. Rödergasse is the old town's everyday shopping street. There is also a modern shopping center across the street from the train station.

Christmas Souvenirs

Rothenburg is the headquarters of the **Käthe Wohlfahrt** Christmas trinkets empire, which is spreading across the half-timbered reaches of Europe. In Rothenburg, tourists flock to two Käthe Wohlfahrt stores (at Herrngasse 1 and 2, just off Market Square). Start with the **Christmas Village** (Weihnachtsdorf) at Herrngasse 1. This Christmas wonderland is filled with enough twinkling lights to require a special electrical hookup. You're greeted by instant

Christmas mood music (best appreciated on a hot day in July) and American and Japanese tourists hungrily filling little woven shopping baskets with €5 to €8 goodies to hang on their trees. Let the spinning flocked tree whisk you in, but pause at the wall of Steiffs, jerking uncontrollably and mesmerizing little kids. (OK, I admit it, my Christmas tree sports a few KW ornaments.) The **Christmas Museum** upstairs is described under "Sights and Activites" (page 460). The smaller **Christmas Market** (Weihnachtsmarkt), across the street at Herrngasse 2, specializes in finely crafted wooden ornaments. A third, much smaller store is at Untere Schmiedgasse 19. Note: Prices are padded with tour-guide incentives (all stores open Mon–Sat 9:00–18:00, May–Dec also most Sun 10:00–18:00, Jan–April generally closed Sun, tel. 09861/4090, www.wohlfahrt.com). Käthe started the business in Stuttgart in 1963, and it's now run by her son Harald Wohlfahrt, who lives in Rothenburg.

Traditional German Souvenirs

The **Friese shop** has been welcoming readers of this book for over 20 years (on the smaller square just off Market Square, west of TI, on corner across from free public WC). Cuckoo with friendliness, trinkets, and souvenirs, it gives shoppers with this book tremendous service: a 10 percent discount, 16 percent tax deducted if you have it mailed, and a free map (normally €1.50). Anneliese Friese, who runs the place with her sons Frankie and Berni and grandson Rene, charges only her cost for shipping, and lets tired travelers leave their bags in her back room for free. If he's not busy, ask Rene to show you pictures of the local American football team he played on. For fewer crowds and more attentive service, visit after 14:00 (Mon–Sat 8:30–17:00, Sun 9:30–17:00, Grüner Markt 8, tel. 09861/7166, fax 09861/936-619, friese-kabalo@gmx.de).

Passage 12, a huge, more commercial souvenir shop with a vast selection of steins, knives, and noisy clocks, is just a block below Market Square at Obere Schmiedgasse 12 (April–Dec Mon–Sat 9:00–19:00, Sun 10:00–19:00; Jan–March Mon–Sat 10:00–18:00, closed Sun; tel. 09861/8196).

Werkstattladen Lebenshilfe sells tasteful, original, unconventional souvenirs made in sheltered workshops by disabled Germans. It's a tiny shop down the side street behind Herrngasse 10 (Mon–Fri 10:30–17:30, Sat–Sun 13:00–17:00, Jan–April closed Sun, Kirchgasse 1, tel. 09861/938-401).

Romantic Prints: The Ernst Geissendörfer print shop sells fine prints, etchings, and paintings (May–Dec Mon–Sat 10:00–18:00, Sun 10:00–17:00; Jan–April Mon–Sat 10:00–18:00, closed Sun; enter through teddy bear shop on corner of Market Square, Hafengasse, and Obere Schmiedgasse; Obere Schmiedgasse 1, go up one floor, tel. 09861/2005, www.geissendoerfer.de).

Wine Stuff: For characteristic wineglasses, winemaking gear, and the real thing from the town's oldest winemakers, drop by the **Weinladen am Plönlein** (daily 9:00–18:00, Untere Schmiedgasse 27—see "Wine-Drinking in the Old Center," page 473, for info on wine-tasting). Although Rothenburg is technically in Bavaria, the region around Rothenburg is called *Franken* (Franconia). You'll recognize Franconian wines by the shape of the bottle—short, stubby, and round.

Books: A good bookstore is at Rödergasse 3, on the corner of Alter Stadtgraben (Mon–Sat 9:00–18:30, Sun 11:00–18:30, Jan–April closed Sun).

Mailing Your Goodies Home: You can get handy yellow €2.50 boxes at the old town **post office** (Mon–Fri 9:00–13:00 & 14:00–17:30, Sat 9:00–12:00, closed Sun, inside photo shop at Rödergasse 11). The main post office is in shopping center across from train station.

Pastries: Those who prefer to eat their souvenirs shop the ***Bäckereien*** (bakeries). Their succulent pastries, pies, and cakes are pleasantly distracting...but skip the bad-tasting Rothenburger *Schneeballen*. Unworthy of the heavy promotion they receive, *Schneeballen* are bland pie crusts crumpled into a ball and dusted with powdered sugar or frosted with sticky-sweet glop. There's little reason to waste your pleasure on a *Schneeball* when you can enjoy a curvy *Mandelhörnchen* (almond crescent), a triangular *Nussecke* (nut bar), a round *Florentiner* cookie, a couple of fresh *Krapfen* (like jelly donuts), or even just a soft, warm German pretzel.

SLEEPING

Rothenburg is crowded with visitors, but most are day-trippers. Except for the rare Saturday night and festivals (see "Festivals," page 451), finding a room is easy throughout the year. If you want to splurge, you'll snare the best value by paying extra for the biggest and best rooms at the hotels I recommend.

Many hotels and guesthouses will pick up tired heavy-packers at the station. If you're driving and unable to find where you're sleeping, stop and give them a call. They will likely come rescue you. Keep your key when out late. Rothenburg's hotels are small, and often lock the front entrance around 22:00, asking you to let yourself in through a side door.

You may be greeted at the station by *Zimmer* skimmers who have rooms to rent. If you have reservations, resist them and honor your reservation. But if you haven't booked ahead, you could try talking one of these eager beavers into giving you a bed-and-breakfast room for a youth-hostel price. Be warned: These people are notorious for taking you to distant hotels and then charging

Sleep Code

(€1 = about $1.30, country code: 49, area code: 09861)
S = Single, **D** = Double/Twin, **T** = Triple, **Q** = Quad, **b** = bathroom, **s** = shower only. Unless otherwise noted, credit cards are accepted, English is spoken, and breakfast is included.

To help you sort easily through these listings, I've divided the rooms into three categories, based on the price for a standard double room with bath:

$$$ Higher Priced—Most rooms €65 or more.
$$ Moderately Priced—Most rooms between €40–65.
$ Lower Priced—Most rooms €40 or less.

you for the ride back if you decline a room. The automated hotel vacancy board at the TI (described on page 449) is another option for those without reservations.

In the Old Town

$$$ Gasthof Goldener Greifen, once Mayor Toppler's home, is a big, traditional, 600-year-old place with 17 large rooms and all the comforts. It's run by a helpful family staff and creaks with rustic splendor (small Sb-€38, Sb-€48, small Db-€60, big Db-€82, Tb-€97–102, Qb-€117–122, 10 percent off for 3-night stays, full-service laundry-€8, free and easy parking, half a block downhill from Market Square at Obere Schmiedgasse 5, tel. 09861/2281, fax 09861/86374, www.gasthof-greifen.rothenburg.de, info@gasthof-greifen.rothenburg.de, Brigitte and Klingler family). The family also has a couple of loaner bikes free for guests, and runs a good restaurant, serving meals in the back garden or dining room.

$$$ Hotel Gerberhaus, a classy and stylish hotel in an old building, is warmly run by Inge and Kurt, who mix modern comforts into 20 bright and airy rooms while maintaining a sense of half-timbered elegance. Enjoy the pleasant garden in back (Sb-€50–60, Db-€62–84, Tb-€99–109, Qb-€114–130, prices depend on room size; 2-room apartment with kitchen-€89/2 people, €145/4 people; 10 percent off and a free *Schneeball* if you stay 2 nights and pay cash, no smoking, 4 rooms have canopied 4-poster *Himmel* beds, Internet access, laundry-€5, Spitalgasse 25, tel. 09861/94900, fax 09861/86555, www.gerberhaus.rothenburg.de, gerberhaus@t-online.de). The downstairs café and beer garden serve good soups, salads, and light lunches.

$$$ Hotel Kloster-Stüble, deep in the old town near the castle garden, is my classiest listing. Rudolf does the cooking, while Erika—his fun and energetic first mate—welcomes guests. Twenty-one

Rothenburg Hotels

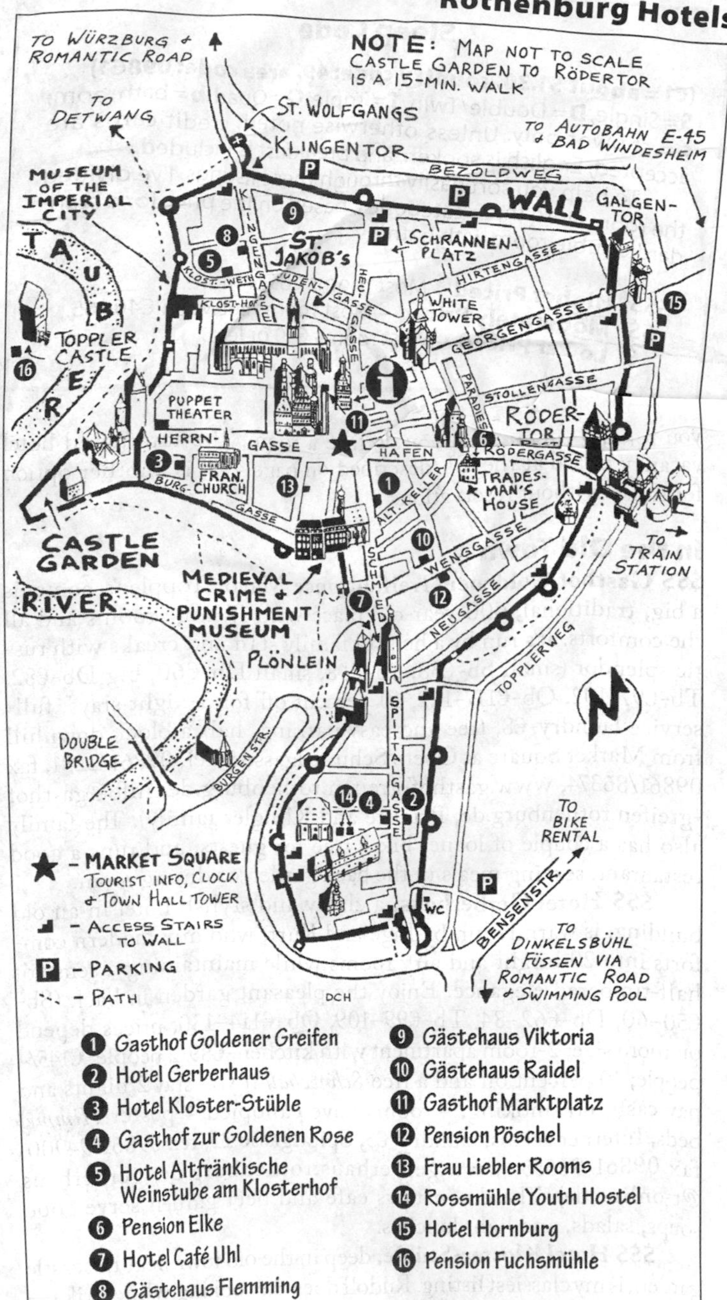

NOTE: MAP NOT TO SCALE
CASTLE GARDEN TO RÖDERTOR IS A 15-MIN. WALK
TO WÜRZBURG & ROMANTIC ROAD
TO DETWANG
ST. WOLFGANGS
KLINGENTOR
TO AUTOBAHN E-45 & BAD WINDESHEIM
BEZOLDWEG
WALL
GALGENTOR
MUSEUM OF THE IMPERIAL CITY
TAUBER
KLINGENGASSE
ST. JAKOB'S
SCHRANNENPLATZ
KLOST.-WETH
KLOST.-HOF
JUDENGASSE
HEUGASSE
HIRTENGASSE
WHITE TOWER
GEORGENGASSE
TOPPLER CASTLE
PUPPET THEATER
STOLLENGASSE
PARADIES
RÖDERTOR
HERRNGASSE
HAFEN
RÖDERGASSE
FRAN. CHURCH
BURGGASSE
ALT. KELLER
TRADESMAN'S HOUSE
CASTLE GARDEN
SCHMIEDGASSE
WENGGASSE
TO TRAIN STATION
MEDIEVAL CRIME & PUNISHMENT MUSEUM
RIVER
NEUGASSE
TOPPLERWEG
PLÖNLEIN
SPITTALGASSE
DOUBLE BRIDGE
BURGENSTR.
TO BIKE RENTAL
BENSENSTR.
WC
TO DINKELSBÜHL & FÜSSEN VIA ROMANTIC ROAD & SWIMMING POOL
★ - MARKET SQUARE
TOURIST INFO, CLOCK & TOWN HALL TOWER
- ACCESS STAIRS TO WALL
P - PARKING
- PATH
DCH
1 Gasthof Goldener Greifen
2 Hotel Gerberhaus
3 Hotel Kloster-Stüble
4 Gasthof zur Goldenen Rose
5 Hotel Altfränkische Weinstube am Klosterhof
6 Pension Elke
7 Hotel Café Uhl
8 Gästehaus Flemming
9 Gästehaus Viktoria
10 Gästehaus Raidel
11 Gasthof Marktplatz
12 Pension Pöschel
13 Frau Liebler Rooms
14 Rossmühle Youth Hostel
15 Hotel Hornburg
16 Pension Fuchsmühle

rooms fill two medieval buildings, connected by a modern atrium. The hotel is just off Herrngasse on a tiny side street (Sb-€48–68, traditional Db-€78–98, bigger and more modern Db-€108, Tb-€108–118, family rooms-€118–155, apartment with balcony or suites-€118 for 2 or up to €215 for 6, family deals, kids under age 5 free, Internet access, Heringsbronnengasse 5, tel. 09861/938-890, fax 09861/6474, www.klosterstueble.de, hotel@klosterstueble.de).

$$ Gasthof zur Goldenen Rose is a classic, 12-room, family-run place—simple, traditional, comfortable, and a great value—where scurrying Karin serves breakfast and stately Henni keeps everything in good order. Flowers spill out of the window boxes, and there's a peaceful back garden. A few cheaper rooms share a bath (S-€22, D-€38, Ds-€48, Db-€50–55, some triples; spacious family apartment-€107/4 people, €128/5 people, €148/6 people; kid-friendly, streetside rooms can be noisy, closed Jan–Feb, Spitalgasse 28, tel. 09861/4638, fax 09861/86417, www.thegoldenrose.de, info@thegoldenrose.de). The family also serves good, reasonably priced meals (restaurant closed Wed).

$$ Hotel Altfränkische Weinstube am Klosterhof is the place for well-heeled bohemians. Mario, Hanne, and their lovely daughter Viktoria rent six cozy rooms above their dark and smoky pub in a 600-year-old building. It's an upscale, *Lord of the Rings* atmosphere, with TVs, modern showers, open-beam ceilings, and canopied four-poster beds (Sb-€48, Db-€55, bigger Db-€68, Db suite-€75, Tb-€75, prefer cash, kid-friendly, off Klingengasse at Klosterhof 7, tel. 09861/6404, fax 09861/6410, www.romanticroad.com/altfraenkische-weinstube). Their pub is a candlelit classic, serving hot food to Hobbits until 22:30, and closing at 1:00 in the morning. Drop by on Wednesday evening (19:00–24:00) for the English Conversation Club (see "Meet the Locals," page 473).

$$ Pension Elke, run by the spry Erich Endress and his son Klaus, rents 12 bright, airy, and comfy rooms above the family grocery store. Guests who jog are welcome to join Klaus on his half-hour run around the city every evening at 19:30 (S-€28, Sb-€38, D-€42–48, Db-€60–65, prices depend on size, extra bed-€15, cash only; reception in grocery store until 19:00, otherwise go around corner to back of building and ring bell at top of stairs; near Markus Tower at Rödergasse 6, tel. 09861/2331, fax 09861/935-355, www.pension-elke-rothenburg.de, info@pension-elke-rothenburg.de).

$$ Hotel Café Uhl offers 12 fine rooms over a bakery (Sb-€30–45, Db-€50–68, prices depend on room size, third person-€18, fourth person-€13, non-smoking rooms, reception in café, parking-€4/day, closed Jan, Plönlein 8, tel. 09861/4895, fax 09861/92820, www.hotel-uhl.de, info@hotel-uhl.de, Paul and Robert the baker).

$$ Gästehaus Flemming has seven tastefully modern, fresh, and comfortable rooms and a peaceful garden behind St. Jakob's Church (Sb-€45, Db-€57, Tb-€79, cash only, non-smoking rooms, Klingengasse 21, tel. 09861/92380, fax 09861/976-384, www.gaestehaus-flemming.de, gaestehaus-flemming@t-online.de, Regina).

$$ Gästehaus Viktoria is a cheery little place right next to the town wall. Its three rooms overflow with furniture, ribbons, and silk flowers, and lovely gardens surround the house (Db-€48–58, larger Db suite-€68, Tb-€56–66, cash preferred, a block from Klingentor at Klingenschutt 4, tel. 09861/87682, www.romanticroad.com/gaestehaus-viktoria, Hanne).

$$ Gästehaus Raidel rents 14 large rooms in a 500-year-old house filled with beds and furniture, all handmade by friendly Norry Raidel himself. The ramshackle ambience makes me want to sing the *Addams Family* theme song—but the place has a rare, time-passed family charm (S-€19, Sb-€29, D-€39, Db-€49, Tb-€70, cash only, Wenggasse 3, tel. 09861/3115, Norry asks you to use the reservations form at www.romanticroad.com/raidel). Norry plays in a Dixieland Band, and invented a fascinating hybrid saxophone/trombone called the Norryphone.

$$ Gasthof Marktplatz, right on Market Square, rents nine tidy rooms with 1970s-era wallpaper and unenthusiastic staff. Most of the rooms have their own sink but share a hall shower and toilet (S-€21, D-€38, Ds-€43, Db-€48, T-€50, Ts-€57, Tb-€62, cash only, Grüner Markt 10, tel. & fax 09861/6722, www.gasthof-marktplatz.de, Herr Rosner). The maddening Town Hall bells ring throughout the night.

$$ Pension Pöschel is simple and friendly, with six plain rooms in a concrete but pleasant building, and an inviting garden out back. Only one room has a private shower and toilet (S-€20, D-€35, Db-€45, T-€45, Tb-€55, small kids free, cash only, Wenggasse 22, tel. 09861/3430, pension.poeschel@t-online.de, Bettina).

$ Frau Liebler rents two large, modern, ground-floor rooms with kitchenettes. They're great for those looking for real privacy—you'll have your own room fronting a quiet cobbled lane just below Market Square (Db-€40, extra bed-€10, no breakfast, cash only, laundry-€5, behind Christmas shop at Pfaffleinsgässchen 10, tel. 09861/709-215, fax 09861/709-216).

$ Rossmühle Youth Hostel—This charming hostel, run since 1981 by Eduard Schmitz, rents 186 beds in two buildings. While it's mostly four- to six-bed dorms, they also have 15 doubles. Reception is in the droopy-eyed building—formerly a horse mill, it was used when the old town was under siege and the river-powered mill was inaccessible (dorm bed-€19, bunk-bed Db-€43, includes breakfast and sheets, all-you-can-eat dinner-€5.40, self-serve laundry including soap-€5, entrance on Rossmühlgasse, tel. 09861/94160, fax 09861/941-620, www.rothenburg.jugendherberge.de, book through www.djh-ris.de, jhrothenburg@djh-bayern.de).

Outside the Wall

$$$ Hotel Hornburg, a grand 1903 mansion, is close to the train station, a two-minute walk outside the wall. With groomed grounds, gracious sitting areas, and 10 spacious, tastefully decorated rooms, it's a super value (Sb-€51–69, Db-€71–98, Tb-€95–120, ground-floor rooms, non-smoking rooms, family-friendly, avoid if you're allergic to dogs, Wi-Fi, parking-€3/day; if walking, exit station and go straight on Ludwig-Siebert-Strasse, then turn left on Mannstrasse until you're 100 yards from town wall; if driving, the hotel is across from parking lot P4; Hornburgweg 28, at intersection with Mannstrasse, tel. 09861/8480, fax 09861/5570, www.hotel-hornburg.de, info@hotel-hornburg.de, friendly Gabriele and Martin).

$$ Pension Fuchsmühle is a guest house in a renovated old mill on the river below the castle end of Rothenburg, across from the Toppler Castle. It feels rural, but is a pleasant (though steep) 15-minute hike to Market Square. Alex and Heidi Molitor, a young couple, offer free tours of the mill (in use until 1989) and run a used-book business on the side. Eight bright, modern, light-wood rooms fill the building's three floors (Sb-€40, Db-€60, Tb-€80, Qb-€100, 6-bed apartment-€140, extra bed-€18, €5 less if you stay 3 nights, non-smoking, healthy farm-fresh breakfasts, piano, parking, free pickup at station, flashlights provided for your walk back after dark, Taubertalweg 103, tel. 09861/92633, www.fuchsmuehle.de, fuchsmuehle@t-online.de).

EATING

Many restaurants take a mid-afternoon break, and stop serving lunch at 14:00 and dinner as early as 20:00. My recommendations are all within a five-minute walk of Market Square. While all survive on tourism, many still feel like local hangouts. Your choices are typical German or ethnic. A good dish to try is *Maultaschen*. This Swabian ravioli smuggles meat in a big piece of pasta—a custom that some say started as a culinary trick used by Catholics to eat meat when it wasn't allowed. Any bakery will sell you a sandwich for a couple euros.

Traditional German Restaurants

Eisenhut Restaurant, in Hotel Eisenhut, is a fine place for a dress-up splurge with a surprisingly reasonable price. You'll enjoy

Rothenburg Restaurants

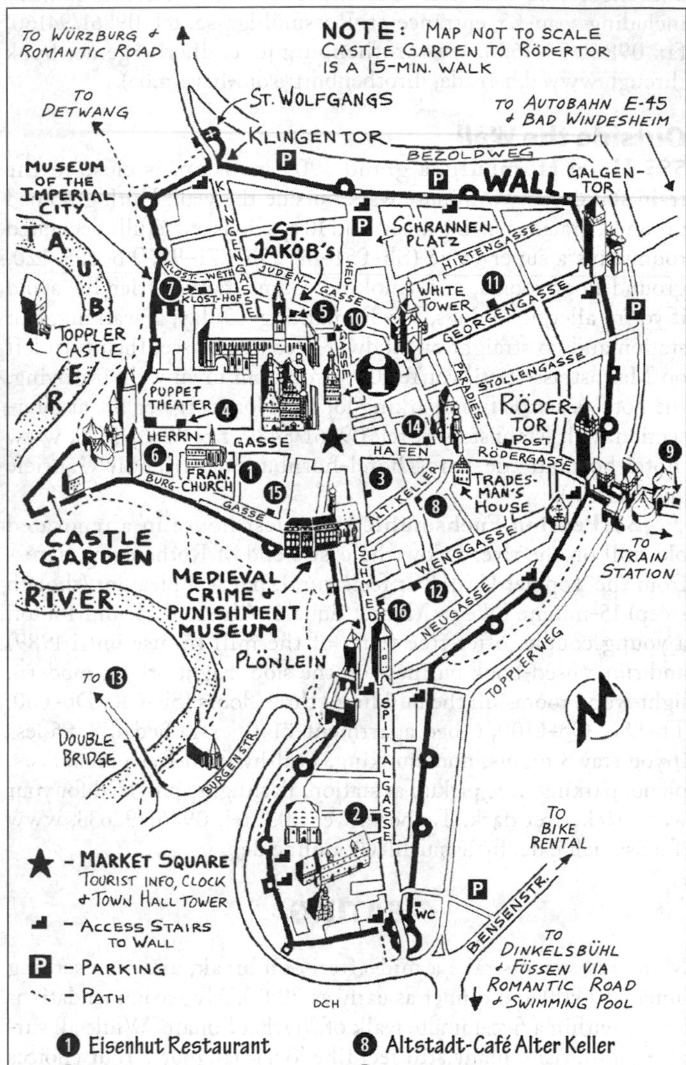

1. Eisenhut Restaurant
2. Zur Goldenen Rose
3. Gasthof Goldener Greifen
4. Bürgerkeller
5. Reichs-Küchenmeister
6. Hotel Restaurant Klosterstüble
7. Altfränkische Weinstube am Klosterhof
8. Altstadt-Café Alter Keller
9. Gasthof Rödertor & Beer Garden
10. Lotus China
11. Pizzeria Roma
12. Döner Kebap Shop
13. To Unter den Linden Beer Garden
14. Eis Café D' Isep (Ice Cream)
15. Trinkstube zur Hölle ("Hell")
16. Restaurant Glocke

elegantly presented, traditional dishes with formal service. Sit in their royal dining room or on their garden terrace (€17–22 main dishes, Herrngasse 3, tel. 09861/7050).

Zur Goldenen Rose is a hardworking eatery in a small hotel at the south end of the old town. Reno cooks up traditional German fare at great prices as Henni stokes your appetite (Tue 11:00–14:00, Thu–Mon 11:00–14:00 & 17:30–20:30, closed Wed, leafy garden terrace out back open in sunny weather, Spitalgasse 28, tel. 09861/4638).

Gasthof Goldener Greifen is in a historic building just off the main square. The Klingler family serves quality Franconian food to in-the-know locals at a good price...and with a smile. The wood is ancient and polished from generations of happy use, and the ambience is practical rather than posh—and that's just fine with me (€7–13 entrées, €10 three-course daily specials, super-cheap kids' meals, Mon–Sat 11:30–21:30, Sun 11:30–15:00, Obere Schmiedgasse 5, tel. 09861/2281).

Bürgerkeller is a typical European cellar restaurant with a quiet, calming atmosphere, medieval murals, and pointy pikes. Without a burger in sight (*Bürger* means "townsman"), Harry Terian and his family pride themselves on quality local cuisine, offering a small but inviting menu and reasonable prices. Harry likes oldies, and you're welcome to look over his impressive playlist and request your favorite music (€6–12 entrées, Thu–Tue 11:30–14:00 & 18:00–21:00, closed Wed, a few sidewalk tables, near bottom of Herrngasse at #24, tel. 09861/2126).

Reichs-Küchenmeister is a typical big-hotel restaurant, but on a balmy evening, its pleasant, tree-shaded terrace overlooking St. Jakob's Church is hard to beat. Their *Vesperbrett* plate is a fine selection of cold cuts (€8–17 entrées, daily 11:00–22:00, Kirchplatz 8, tel. 09861/9700).

Hotel Restaurant Klosterstüble, on a small street off Herrngasse near the castle garden, is a classy place for delicious and beautifully presented traditional cuisine. Chef Rudy's food is better than his English, so head waitress Erika makes sure communication goes smoothly. The shady terrace is nice on a warm summer evening. I prefer their traditional dining room to the stony, sleek, non-smoking room (€10 entrées, daily 11:00–14:00 & 18:00–21:00, Heringsbronnengasse 5, tel. 09861/938-890).

Altfränkische Weinstube am Klosterhof seems designed for gnomes to celebrate their anniversaries. At this very dark and smoky pub, classically candlelit in a 600-year-old building, Mario whips up gourmet pub grub (€6–12 entrées, hot food served 18:00–22:30, closes at 1:00 in the morning, off Klingengasse at Klosterhof 7, tel. 09861/6404). If you'd like dinner company, drop by on Wednesday evening, when the English Conversation Club has a big table reserved from 19:00 on (see "Meet the Locals," page 473). You'll eat well and with new friends—both travelers and locals.

Altstadt-Café Alter Keller is just right for a light meal near the center. Eat indoors under walls festooned with old pots and jugs, or outdoors on a quiet little square. Herr Hufnagel, a baker and pastry chef, whips up a tempting array of cakes, pies, and giant meringue cookies, while gracious Christine makes sure you understand your options (€3 soup with bread, €5–7 main dishes, Sat–Thu 11:00–20:00, Sun 11:00–18:00, closed Fri, Alter Keller 8, tel. 09861/2268).

Gasthof Rödertor, just outside the wall through the Rödertor gate, is a lively place where Rothenburgers go for a hearty meal at a good price. Their passion is potatoes—the menu is dedicated to spud cuisine (€6–11 entrées, daily 11:30–14:00 & 17:30–22:30, Ansbacher Strasse 7, tel. 09861/2022). They also run a popular beer garden (see below).

Breaks from Pork and Potatoes

Lotus China is a peaceful world apart, serving good Chinese food (€8–10 entrées, €6 two-course lunch specials, daily 11:30–14:30 & 17:30–23:00, 2 blocks behind TI near church, Eckele 2, tel. 09861/86886).

Pizzeria Roma is smoky because it's the locals' favorite for €6.50 pizza and pastas with good Italian wine. The Magrini family moved here from Tuscany in 1970 (many Italians immigrated to Germany in those years) and they've been cooking pasta for Rothenburg ever since (Thu–Tue 11:30–24:00, closed Wed and mid-Aug–mid-Sept, Galgengasse 19, tel. 09861/4540, Ricardo).

The **Döner Kebap** shop at Wenggasse 4, just off Untere Schmiedgasse, serves cheap and tasty food to go. This tiny place offers what must be the best €3 hot meal in Rothenburg (daily 11:00–21:00, tel. 09861/92417).

There's a small **grocery store** in the center of town at Rödergasse 6 (Mon–Fri 7:30–19:00, Sat 7:30–18:00, April–Dec also Sun 10:00–18:00, closed Sun Jan–March). **Supermarkets** are outside the wall. Exit the town through Rödertor, turn left through the cobbled gate, and cross the parking lot to reach the Comet supermarket, or head to the even bigger one in the shopping center across from the train station (Mon–Fri 8:00–20:00, Sat 8:00–18:00, closed Sun).

Beer Gardens

Rothenburg's beer gardens can be great fun, but they're only open when the weather is balmy.

Unter den Linden, a beer garden in the valley along the river, is worth the 20-minute hike on a pleasant evening (daily in season with decent weather, 10:00–22:00 and sometimes later, self-service food and good beer, call first to confirm it's open, tel. 09861/5909). As it's in the valley on the river, it's cooler than Rothenburg; bring a sweater.

Gasthof Rödertor, just outside the wall through the Rödertor gate, runs a backyard beer garden that's great for a rowdy crowd, cheap food, and good beer (May–Sept daily 17:00–24:00, look for wood gate, tel. 09861/2022). If the beer garden is closed, their indoor restaurant (described above) is a good value.

Dessert

Eis Café D' Isep, with a pleasant interior, is the town's ice-cream parlor, serving up cakes, drinks, and fancy sundaes (daily 9:30–22:00, closed mid-Oct–mid-Feb, 1 block off Market Square at Hafengasse 17).

Wine-Drinking in the Old Center

Trinkstube zur Hölle ("Hell") is dark and foreboding, offering a thick wine-drinking atmosphere, pub food, and a few main dishes. It's small and can get painfully touristy in summer (daily 17:00–24:00, closed Sun Jan–March, a block past Medieval Crime and Punishment Museum on Burggasse, with devil hanging out front, tel. 09861/4229).

Mario's **Altfränkische Weinstube am Klosterhof** (see "Traditional German Restaurants," above) is the liveliest place, and the clear favorite with locals for an atmospheric drink or late meal. When every other place is asleep, you're likely to find good food, drink, and energy here.

Eisenhut, behind the fancy hotel of the same name on Herrngasse, is a good bet for gentle and casual beer-garden ambience within the old center (also listed under "Traditional German Restaurants," above).

Restaurant Glocke, a *Weinstube* (wine bar) popular with locals, is run by Rothenburg's oldest wine-makers, the Thürauf family. The menu, which has a very extensive wine list, is in German only because the friendly staff wants to explain your options in person. Their €4.20 deal, which lets you sample five Franconian wines, is popular (€10–15 entrées, Mon–Sat 10:30–23:00, Sun 10:30–14:00, Plönlein 1, tel. 09861/958-990).

Meet the Locals

For a rare chance to mix it up with locals who aren't selling anything, bring your favorite slang and tongue twisters to the **English Conversation Club** at Mario's Altfränkische Weinstube am Klosterhof (Wed 19:00–24:00, Anneliese from the Friese shop and

Hermann the German are regulars; see restaurant listing under "Traditional German Restaurants," above). This group of intrepid linguists has met more than 1,000 times. Consider arriving early for dinner, or after 21:00, when the beer starts to sink in, the crowd grows, and everyone seems to speak that second language a bit more easily.

TRANSPORTATION CONNECTIONS

From Rothenburg ob der Tauber by Train: A tiny branch train line connects Rothenburg to the outside world via **Steinach** (generally 1/hr from Rothenburg at :05 and from Steinach at :36, 14 min). If you plan to arrive in Rothenburg in the evening, note that the last train from Steinach to Rothenburg departs at around 20:30. All is not lost if you arrive in Steinach after 20:30. The German government believes in providing public transport to its visitors, as well as its citizens—it subsidizes the taxi fare to Rothenburg. If you make an appointment with a participating taxi service (such as tel. 09861/2000) at least an hour in advance, they'll drive you from Steinach to Rothenburg for the train fare (€3.60/person) rather than the regular €22 taxi fare. Other taxi companies: tel. 09861/7227 and 09861/95100.

From Steinach by Train to: Würzburg (hourly, 45 min), **Nürnberg** (hourly, 1–1.5 hr, most change in Ansbach or Neustadt an der Aisch), **Munich** (hourly, 3–4 hrs, 1–2 changes), **Frankfurt** (hourly, 3 hrs, change in Würzburg), **Berlin** (hourly, 5 hrs, 2 changes).

Train connections in Steinach are usually quick and efficient (trains to and from Rothenburg generally use track 5). The station at Steinach is not staffed, but has touch-screen terminals for fare and schedule information and ticket sales. Visit the ticket office in Rothenburg, or as a last resort call for train info at tel. 11861 (€0.50/min).

From Rothenburg by Bus: The Romantic Road bus stops at Schrannenplatz in Rothenburg each afternoon (April–Oct) on its way between Frankfurt and Munich (and vice versa).

RHINE VALLEY

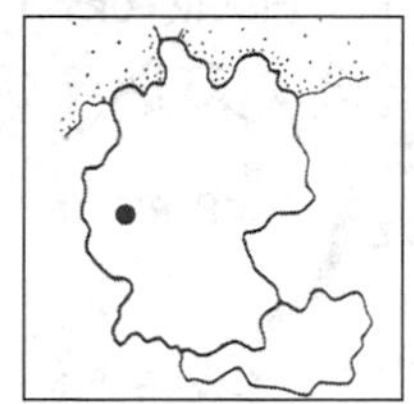

The Rhine Valley is storybook Germany, a fairy-tale world of legends and robber-baron castles. Cruise the most castle-studded stretch of the romantic Rhine as you listen for the song of the treacherous Loreley. For hands-on thrills, climb through the Rhineland's greatest castle, Rheinfels, above the town of St. Goar. Spend your nights in a castle-crowned village, either Bacharach or St. Goar.

Planning Your Time

For a good look, cruise in, tour a castle or two, sleep in a medieval town, and take the train out. If you have limited time, cruise less and explore Rheinfels Castle. Both Bacharach and St. Goar are an easy 90-minute train ride from Frankfurt Airport, and make a good first or last stop for air travelers.

Ideally, spend two nights here, sleep in Bacharach, cruise the best hour of the river (from Bacharach to St. Goar), and tour the Rheinfels Castle. Those with more time can ride the riverside bike path.

The Best of the Rhine

Ever since Roman times, when this was the empire's northern boundary, the Rhine has been one of the world's busiest shipping rivers. You'll see a steady flow of barges with 1,000- to 2,000-ton loads. Tourist-packed buses, hot train tracks, and highways line both banks.

Many of the castles were "robber-baron" castles, put there by

Rhine Overview

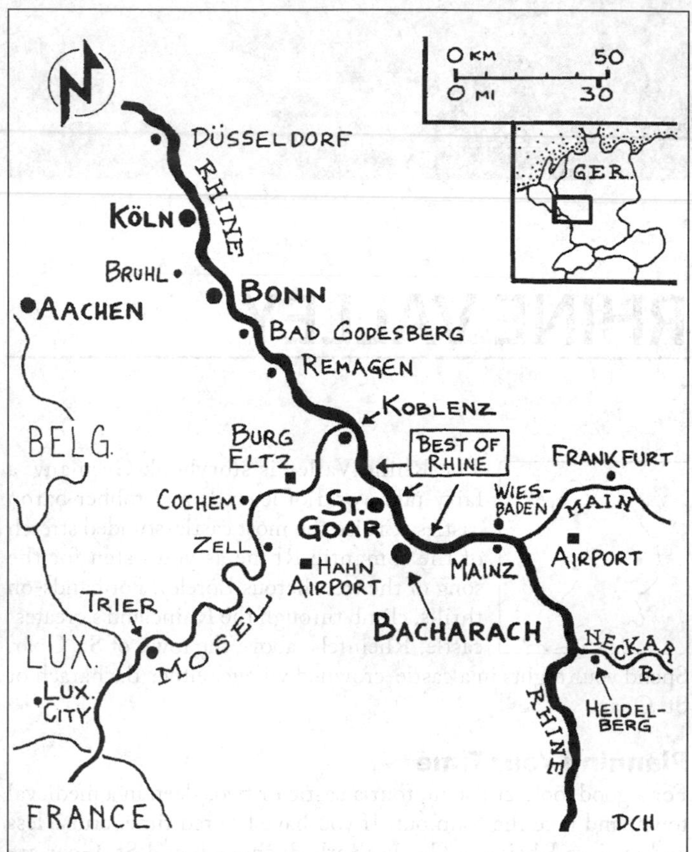

petty rulers (there were 300 independent little countries in medieval Germany, a region about the size of Montana) to levy tolls on passing river traffic. A robber baron would put his castle on, or even in, the river. Then, often with the help of chains and a tower on the opposite bank, he'd stop each ship and get his toll. There were 10 customs stops in the 60-mile stretch between Mainz and Koblenz alone (no wonder merchants were early proponents of the creation of larger nation-states).

Some castles were built to control and protect settlements, and others were the residences of kings. As times changed, so did the lifestyles of the rich and feudal. Many castles were abandoned for more comfortable mansions in the towns.

Most Rhine castles date from the 11th, 12th, and 13th centuries. When the pope successfully asserted his power over the German emperor in 1076, local princes ran wild over the rule of their emperor. The castles saw military action in the 1300s and 1400s, as emperors began reasserting their control over Germany's many silly kingdoms.

The castles were also involved in the Reformation wars, in which Europe's Catholic and Protestant dynasties fought it out using a fragmented Germany as their battleground. The Thirty Years' War (1618–1648) devastated Germany. The outcome: Each ruler got the freedom to decide if his people would be Catholic or Protestant, and one-third of Germany was dead. (Production of Gummi bears ceased entirely.)

The French—who feared a strong Germany and felt the Rhine was the logical border between them and Germany—destroyed most of the castles prophylactically (Louis XIV in the 1680s, the Revolutionary army in the 1790s, and Napoleon in 1806). Many were rebuilt in Neo-Gothic style in the Romantic Age—the late 1800s—and today are enjoyed as restaurants, hotels, hostels, and museums. These days, the Rhine Valley is in a bit of a rut. After the US military pulled out of the region, tourism took a hit, and jobs became scarce.

Getting Around the Rhine

While the Rhine flows north from Switzerland to Holland, the scenic stretch from Mainz to Koblenz hoards all the touristic charm. Studded with the crenellated cream of Germany's castles, it bustles with boats, trains, and highway traffic. Have fun exploring with a mix of big steamers, tiny ferries *(Fähre)*, trains, and bikes.

By Boat: While some travelers do the whole Mainz-to-Koblenz trip by boat (5.5 hours downstream, 8.5 hours up), I'd just focus on the most scenic hour—from St. Goar to Bacharach. Sit on the top deck with your handy Rhine map-guide (or the kilometer-keyed tour in this chapter) and enjoy the parade of castles, towns, boats, and vineyards.

Two boat companies take travelers along this stretch of the Rhine. Most travelers sail on the bigger, more expensive, and romantic Köln-Düsseldorfer (K-D) line (free with a German railpass or any Eurailpass that covers Germany, but uses up a day of any flexipass; otherwise about €9 for the first hour, then progressively cheaper per hour; the recommended Bacharach–St. Goar trip costs €9.20 one-way, €11.30 round-trip; bikes cost €1.50; half-price days: Tue for bicyclists, Mon and Fri for seniors over 60; tel. 06741/1634 in St. Goar, tel. 06743/1322 in Bacharach, www.k-d.com). Boats run daily in both directions April through October, with no boats off-season. Complete, up-to-date schedules are posted in any Rhineland station, hotel, or TI; at www.k-d.com; and at www.euraide.de/ricksteves. Purchase tickets at the dock up to five minutes before departure. (Confirm times at your hotel the night before.) The boat is never full. Romantics will enjoy the old-time paddle-wheel *Goethe*, which sails each direction once a day (€1.50 extra, confirm time locally).

The smaller Bingen-Rüdesheimer line is slightly cheaper than K-D (railpasses not valid, buy tickets on boat, tel. 06721/14140, www.bingen-ruedesheimer.com), with three two-hour round-trip St. Goar–Bacharach trips daily from mid-April to October (€9 one-way, €11 round-trip; departing St. Goar at 11:00, 14:10, and 16:10; departing Bacharach at 10:10, 12:00, and 15:00).

By Car: Drivers have these options: 1) skip the boat; 2) take a round-trip cruise from St. Goar or Bacharach; 3) draw pretzels and let the loser drive, prepare the picnic, and meet the boat; 4) rent a bike, bring it on the boat for free, and bike back; or 5) take the boat one-way and return by train. When exploring by car, don't hesitate to pop onto one of the many little ferries that shuttle across the bridgeless-around-here river (see below).

By Ferry: While there are no bridges between Koblenz and Mainz, you'll see car-and-passenger ferries (usually family-run for generations) about every three miles (pay on the boat). Bingen–Rüdesheim, Lorch–Niederheimbach, Engelsburg–Kaub, and St. Goar–St. Goarshausen are some of the most useful routes (times vary; St. Goar–St. Goarshausen ferry departs each side every 20 min, Mon–Sat 6:00–21:00, Sun 8:00–21:00, May–Sept until 23:00, adult-€1.30, car and driver-€3, www.faehre-loreley.de). For a fun little jaunt, take a quick round-trip with some time to explore the other side.

By Bike: You can bike on either side of the Rhine, but for a designated bike path, stay on the west side, where a 35-mile path runs between Koblenz and Bingen. The six-mile stretch between St. Goar and Bacharach is smooth and scenic, but mostly along the highway. The bit from Bacharach to Bingen hugs the riverside and is road-free. Either way, biking is a great way to explore the valley. Many hotels provide free or cheap bikes to guests; in St. Goar, Hotel am Markt rents bikes to guests for €5 per day. In Bacharach, anyone can rent bikes at Hotel Hillen (see below, €10/day for non-guests).

Consider biking one way and taking the bike on the riverboat back (free with ticket), or designing a circular trip using the fun and frequent shuttle ferries. A good target might be Kaub (where a tiny boat shuttles sightseers to the better-from-a-distance castle on the island) or Rheinstein Castle.

By Train: Hourly milk-run trains down the Rhine hit every town (St. Goar–Bacharach, 12 min; Bacharach–Mainz, 60 min; Koblenz–Mainz, 90 min). Some train schedules list St. Goar but not Bacharach as a stop, but any schedule listing St. Goar also stops at Bacharach. Tiny stations are not staffed—buy tickets at the platform machines (user-friendly, takes paper money). Prices are cheap (for example, €2.80 between St. Goar and Bacharach). Express trains speed past the small towns, taking only 50 minutes between Koblenz and Mainz.

SELF-GUIDED TOUR

Rhine Blitz Tour by Train or Boat

One of Europe's great train thrills is zipping along the Rhine enjoying this blitz tour, rated ▲▲▲. Or, even better, do it relaxing on the deck of a Rhine steamer, surrounded by the wonders of this romantic and historic gorge. Here's a quick and easy tour (you can cut in anywhere) that skips the syrupy myths filling normal Rhine guides. You can follow along on a train, bike, car, or boat. By train or boat, sit on the left (river) side going south from Koblenz. While nearly all the castles listed are viewed from this side, train travelers need to clear a path to the right window for the times I yell, "Cross over!"

You'll notice large black-and-white kilometer markers along the riverbank. I erected these years ago to make this tour easier to follow. They tell the distance from the Rhinefalls, where the Rhine leaves Switzerland and becomes navigable. Now the river-barge pilots have accepted these as navigational aids as well. We're tackling just 36 miles (58 kilometers) of the 820-mile-long (1,320-kilometer) Rhine. Your Rhine Blitz Tour starts at Koblenz and heads upstream to Bingen. If you're going the other direction, it still works. Just hold the book upside-down.

Km 590—Koblenz: This Rhine blitz starts with Romantic Rhine thrills—at Koblenz. Koblenz is not a nice city (it was really hit hard in World War II), but its place as the historic *Deutsche Eck* (German corner)—the tip of land where the Mosel joins the Rhine—gives it a certain historic charm. Koblenz, from the Latin for "confluence," has Roman origins. Walk through the park, noticing the reconstructed memorial to the *Kaiser.* Across the river, the yellow Ehrenbreitstein Castle now houses a hostel. It's a 30-minute hike from the station to the Koblenz boat dock.

Km 585—Lahneck Castle (Burg Lahneck): Above the modern autobahn bridge over the Lahn River, this castle *(Burg)* was built in 1240 to defend local silver mines; the castle was ruined by the French in 1688 and rebuilt in the 1850s in Neo-Gothic style. Burg Lahneck faces another Romantic rebuild, the yellow Schloss Stolzenfels (out of view above the train, a 10-min climb from tiny parking lot, open for touring, closed Mon). Note that a *Burg* is a defensive fortress, while a *Schloss* is mainly a showy palace.

Km 580—Marksburg Castle: This castle (black and white, with the 3 modern chimneys behind it, just before town of Spay)

Best of the Rhine

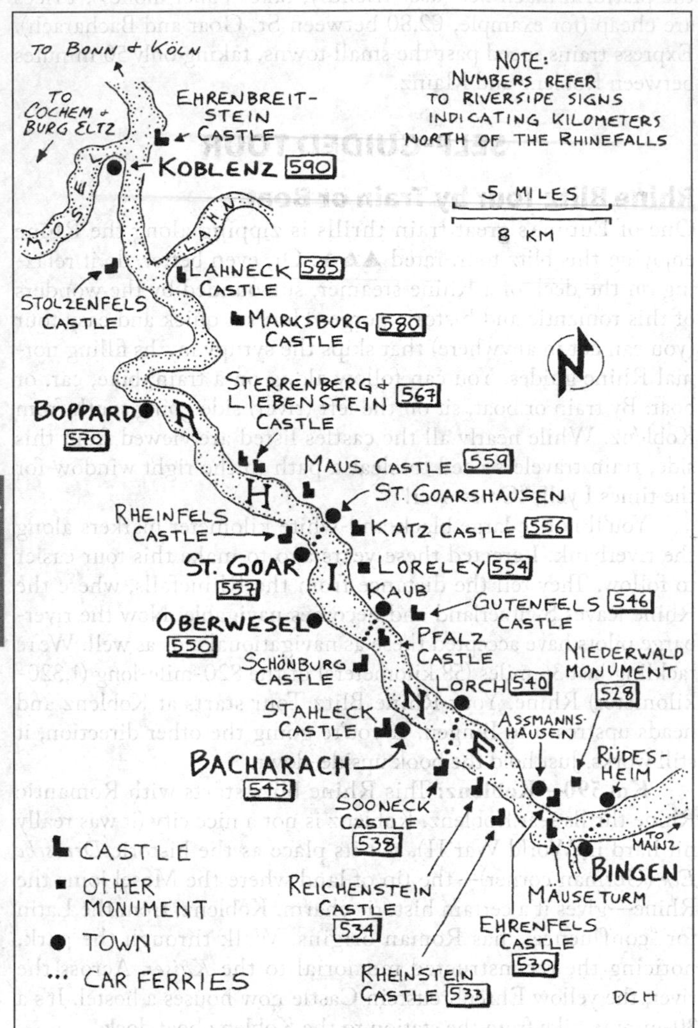

is the best-looking of all the Rhine castles and the only surviving medieval castle on the Rhine. Because of its commanding position, it was never attacked. It's now open as a museum with a medieval interior second only to the Mosel's Burg Eltz. The three modern smokestacks vent Europe's biggest car-battery recycling plant just up the valley.

Km 570—Boppard: Once a Roman town, Boppard has some impressive remains of fourth-century walls. Notice the Roman towers and the substantial chunk of Roman wall near the train station, just above the main square.

If you visit Boppard, head to the fascinating church below the main square. Find the carved Romanesque crazies at the doorway. Inside, to the right of the entrance, you'll see Christian symbols from Roman times. Also notice the painted arches and vaults. Originally most Romanesque churches were painted this way. Down by the river, look for the high-water *(Hochwasser)* marks on the arches from various flood years. (You'll find these flood marks throughout the Rhine and Mosel Valleys.)

Km 567—Sterrenberg Castle and Liebenstein Castle: These are the "Hostile Brothers" castles across from Bad Salzig. Take the wall between the castles (actually designed to improve the defenses of both castles), add two greedy and jealous brothers and a fair maiden, and create your own legend. Burg Liebenstein is now a fun, friendly, and affordable family-run hotel (9 rooms, Db-€98, suite-€120, giant king-and-the-family room-€195, easy parking, tel. 06773/308 or 06773/251, www.castle-liebenstein.com, hotel-burg-liebenstein@rhinecastles.com, Nickenig family).

Km 560: While you can see nothing from here, a 19th-century lead mine functioned on both sides of the river, with a shaft actually tunneling completely under the Rhine.

Km 559—Maus Castle (Burg Maus): The Maus (mouse) got its name because the next castle was owned by the Katzenelnbogen family. (*Katz* means "cat.") In the 1300s, it was considered a state-of-the-art fortification...until Napoleon had it blown up in 1806 with state-of-the-art explosives. It was rebuilt true to its original plans around 1900. Today, the castle hosts a falconry show (€6.50, Tue–Sun at 11:00 and 14:30, closed Mon, 20-min walk up, tel. 06771/7669, www.burg-maus.de).

Km 557—St. Goar and Rheinfels Castle: Cross to the other side of the train. The pleasant town of St. Goar was named for a sixth-century hometown monk. It originated in Celtic times (really old) as a place where sailors would stop, catch their breath, send home a postcard, and give thanks after surviving the seductive and treacherous Loreley crossing. St. Goar is worth a stop to explore its mighty Rheinfels Castle. (For information, a guided castle tour, and accommodations, see page 494.)

Km 556—Katz Castle (Burg Katz): Burg Katz (Katzenelnbogen) faces St. Goar from across the river. Together, Burg Katz (built in 1371) and Rheinfels Castle had a clear view up and down the river, effectively controlling traffic. There was absolutely no duty-free shopping on the medieval Rhine. Katz got Napoleoned in 1806 and rebuilt around 1900.

Today, the castle is shrouded by intrigue and controversy. In 1995, a wealthy and eccentric Japanese man bought it for about $4 million. His vision: to make the castle—so close to the Loreley that Japanese tourists are wild about—an exotic escape for his countrymen. But the town wouldn't allow his planned renovation of the historic (and therefore protected) building. Stymied, the frustrated investor just abandoned his plans. Today Burg Katz sits empty...the Japanese ghost castle.

Below the castle, notice the derelict grape terraces—worked since the eighth century, but abandoned only in the last generation. The Rhine wine is particularly good because the slate absorbs the heat of the sun and stays warm all night, resulting in sweeter grapes. Wine from the flat fields above the Rhine gorge is cheaper and good only as table wine. The wine from the steep side of the Rhine gorge—harder to grow and harvest—is tastier and more expensive.

About Km 555: A statue of the Loreley, the beautiful-but-deadly nymph (see next listing for legend), combs her hair at the end of a long spit—built to give barges protection from vicious icebergs that until recent years would rage down the river in the winter. The actual Loreley, a cliff (marked by the flags), is just ahead.

Km 554—The Loreley: Steep a big slate rock in centuries of legend and it becomes a tourist attraction—the ultimate Rhinestone. The Loreley (flags on top, name painted near shoreline), rising 450 feet over the narrowest and deepest point of the Rhine, has long been important. It was a holy site in pre-Roman days. The fine echoes here—thought to be ghostly voices—fertilized legend-tellers' imaginations.

Because of the reefs just upstream (at kilometer 552), many ships never made it to St. Goar. Sailors (after days on the river) blamed their misfortune on a *wunderbares Fräulein* whose long blonde hair almost covered her body. Heinrich Heine's *Song of Loreley* (the *Cliffs Notes* version is on local postcards) tells the story of a count who sent his men to kill or capture this siren after she distracted his horny son, causing him to drown. When the soldiers cornered the nymph in her cave, she called her father (Father Rhine) for help. Huge waves, the likes of which you'll never see today, rose from the river and carried Loreley to safety. And she has never been seen since.

But alas, when the moon shines brightly and the tour buses are parked, a soft, playful Rhine whine can still be heard from the Loreley. As you pass, listen carefully ("Sailors...sailors...over my bounding mane").

Km 552: Killer reefs, marked by red-and-green buoys, are called the "Seven Maidens." Okay, one more goofy legend: The prince of Schönburg Castle (*ober* Oberwesel) had seven spoiled daughters who always dumped men because of their shortcomings. Fed up, he invited seven of his knights up to the castle and demanded that his daughters each choose one to marry. But they complained that each man had too big a nose, was too fat, too stupid, and so on. The rude and teasing girls escaped into a riverboat. Just downstream, God turned them into the seven rocks that form this reef. While this story probably isn't entirely true, there's a lesson in it for medieval children: Don't be hard-hearted.

Km 550—Oberwesel: Cross to the other side of the train. Oberwesel was a Celtic town in 400 B.C., then a Roman military station. It now boasts some of the best Roman-wall and medieval-tower remains on the Rhine, and the commanding Schönburg Castle. Notice how many of the train tunnels have entrances designed like medieval turrets—they were actually built in the Romantic 19th century. Okay, back to the river side.

Km 546—Gutenfels Castle and Pfalz Castle, the Classic Rhine View: Burg Gutenfels (see white-painted *Hotel* sign) and the shipshape Pfalz Castle (built in the river in the 1300s) worked very effectively to tax medieval river traffic. The town of Kaub grew rich as Pfalz raised its chains when boats came and lowered them only when the merchants had paid their duty. Those who didn't pay spent time touring its prison, on a raft at the bottom of its well. In 1504, a pope called for the destruction of Pfalz, but the locals withstood a six-week siege, and the castle still stands. Notice the overhanging outhouse (tiny white room—with faded medieval stains—between two wooden ones). Pfalz (also known as Pfalzgrafenstein) is tourable but bare and dull (€2 ferry from Kaub, €2.10 entry; April–Oct Tue–Sun 10:00–18:00, closed Mon; Nov and Feb–March Sat–Sun 10:00–17:00, closed Mon–Fri; closed Dec–Jan; last entry 60 min before closing, tel. 0172/262-2800).

In Kaub, on the riverfront directly below the castles, a green statue honors the German general Blücher. He was Napoleon's nemesis. In 1813, as Napoleon fought his way back to Paris after his disastrous Russian campaign, he stopped at Mainz—hoping to fend off the Germans and Russians pursuing him by controlling that strategic bridge. Blücher tricked Napoleon. By building the first major pontoon bridge of its kind here at the Pfalz Castle, he crossed the Rhine and outflanked the French. Two years later, Blücher and Wellington teamed up to defeat Napoleon once and for all at Waterloo.

Km 544—"The Raft Busters": Immediately before Bacharach, at the top of the island, buoys mark a gang of rocks notorious for busting up rafts. The Black Forest, upstream from here, was once poor, and wood was its best export. Black Foresters would ride log booms down the Rhine to the Ruhr (where their timber fortified coal-mine shafts) or to Holland (where logs were sold to shipbuilders). If they could navigate the sweeping bend just before Bacharach and then survive these "raft busters," they'd come home reckless and likely horny—the German folkloric equivalent of American cowboys after payday.

Km 543—Bacharach and Stahleck Castle (Burg Stahleck): Cross to the other side of the train. The town of Bacharach is a great stop (see details and accommodations below). Some of the Rhine's best wine is from this town, whose name likely derives from "altar to Bacchus." Local vintners brag that the medieval Pope Pius II ordered Bacharach wine by the cartload. Perched above the town, the 13th-century Burg Stahleck is now a hostel.

Km 540—Lorch: This pathetic stub of a castle is barely visible from the road. Check out the hillside vineyards. These vineyards once blanketed four times as land as they do today, but modern economics have driven most of them out of business. The vineyards that do survive require government subsidies. Notice the small car ferry (3/hr, 10 min), one of several along the bridgeless stretch between Mainz and Koblenz.

Km 538—Sooneck Castle: Cross back to the other side of the train. Built in the 11th century, this castle was twice destroyed by people sick and tired of robber barons.

Km 534—Reichenstein Castle and **Km 533—Rheinstein Castle:** Stay on the other side of the train to see two of the first castles to be rebuilt in the Romantic era. Both are privately owned, tourable, and connected by a pleasant trail.

Km 530—Ehrenfels Castle: Opposite Bingerbrück and the Bingen station, you'll see the ghostly Ehrenfels Castle (clobbered by the Swedes in 1636 and by the French in 1689). Since it had no view of the river traffic to the north, the owner built the cute little *Mäuseturm* (mouse tower) on an island (the yellow tower you'll see near the train station today). Rebuilt in the 1800s in Neo-Gothic style, it's now used as a Rhine navigation signal station.

Km 528—Niederwald Monument: Across from the Bingen station on a hilltop is the 120-foot-high Niederwald monument, a memorial built with 32 tons of bronze in 1877 to commemorate "the reestablishment of the German Empire." A lift takes tourists to this statue from the famous and extremely touristy wine town of Rüdesheim.

From here, the Romantic Rhine becomes the industrial Rhine, and our tour is over.

Bacharach

Once prosperous from the wine and wood trade, Bacharach (BAHKH-ah-rahkh, with a guttural *kh* sound) is now just a pleasant half-timbered village of a thousand people working hard to keep its tourists happy.

ORIENTATION

Tourist Information

The TI is on the main street in the Posthof courtyard next to the church (April–Oct Mon–Fri 9:00–17:00, Sat–Sun 10:00–13:00; Nov–March Mon–Fri 9:00–12:00, closed Sat–Sun; one coin-op Internet terminal-€2/hr, Oberstrasse 45, from train station turn right and walk 5 blocks down main street with castle high on your left, tel. 06743/919-303, www.bacharach.de or www.rhein-nahe-touristik.de, Herr Kuhn and his team). The TI stores bags for day-trippers and provides ferry schedules.

Helpful Hints

Shopping: The Jost German gift stores carry most everything a shopper could want (from beer steins to cuckoo clocks). The main shop is across the main square from the church (Blücherstrasse 4), while another branch (which may have closed in 2007) is a block away at Rosenstrasse 16. The Josts offer a 10 percent discount to readers of this book who pay cash. They can also ship things to the US—even if you don't buy it at their shop (both shops open March–Oct Mon–Fri 8:30–18:30, Sat 8:30–17:00, Sun 10:00–17:00, shorter hours in winter and closed Sun, tel. 06743/1224, www.phil-jost-germany.com, phil.jost@t-online.de).

Post Office: It's inside a shop, at Oberstrasse 37 between the train station and the TI (Mon–Fri 9:00–12:00 & 15:00–18:00, Sat 9:00–12:00, closed Sun).

Bike Rental: While many hotels loan bikes to guests, the only real bike-rental business in the town center is run by Erich at Hotel Hillen (see listing on page 492). He rents 25 new bikes daily from 9:00 until dark (€10/day for non-guests, €5/day for guests, Langstrasse 18, tel. 06743/1287).

Local Guides and Walking Tours: Get acquainted with Bacharach by taking a walking tour. Charming Herr Rolf Jung, retired headmaster of the Bacharach school, is a superb English-speaking guide who loves sharing his town's story with Americans (€30, 90 min, call to reserve, tel. 06743/1519). Manuela Maddes also gives good tours (tel. 06743/2759). If Herr Jung or Manuela is not available, call the TI for advice, or take my self-guided walk (below). On Saturdays at 11:00 from May to October, the TI offers a walking tour (€4) primarily in German—but if you ask for English, you'll get it as well.

SELF-GUIDED WALK

Welcome to Bacharach

• *Start at the Köln-Düsseldorfer ferry dock (next to a fine picnic park).*

View the town from the parking lot—a modern landfill. The Rhine used to lap against Bacharach's town wall, just over the present-day highway. Every few years the river floods, covering the highway with several feet of water. The **castle** on the hill is now a youth hostel. Two of the town's original 16 towers are visible from here (up to five if you look really hard). The huge roadside wine keg declares this town was built on the wine trade.

Reefs up the river forced boats to unload upriver and reload here. Consequently, Bacharach became the biggest wine trader on the Rhine. A riverfront crane hoisted huge kegs of prestigious "Bacharach" wine (which, in practice, was from anywhere in the region). The tour buses next to the dock and the flags of the biggest spenders along the highway remind you that today's economy is basically founded on tourism.

• *Before entering the town, walk upstream through the riverside park.*

This park was laid out in 1910 in the English style. Notice how the trees were planted to frame fine town views, highlighting the most picturesque bits of architecture. Until recently, stepping on the grass was *verboten*. The dark, sad-looking monument—its eternal flame long snuffed-out—is a war memorial. The German psyche is permanently scarred with memories of wars. Today, many Germans would rather avoid monuments like this, which revisit the dark periods before Germany became a nation of pacifists. Take a close look at the monument. Each panel honors sons of Bacharach who died for the Kaiser: in 1864 against Russia, in 1870 against France, in 1914 during World War I. The military Maltese Cross—flanked by classic German helmets—comes with a W, for Kaiser Wilhelm.

• *Continue to where the park meets the playground, and then cross the highway to the fortified riverside wall of the Catholic church—decorated with high-water marks recalling various floods.*

Check out the metal ring on the medieval slate wall. Before the 1910 reclamation project, the river extended out to here, and boats would use the ring to tie up. Upstream from here, there's a trailer park, and beyond that there's a campground. In Germany, trailer vacationers and campers are two distinct subcultures. Folks who travel in trailers, like many retirees in the US, are a nomadic bunch, hauling around the countryside in their mobile homes and paying about €6 a night to park. Campers, on the other hand, tend to set up camp—complete with comfortable lounge chairs and even TVs—and stay put for weeks, even months. They often come back to the same plot year after year, treating it like their own private

Bacharach

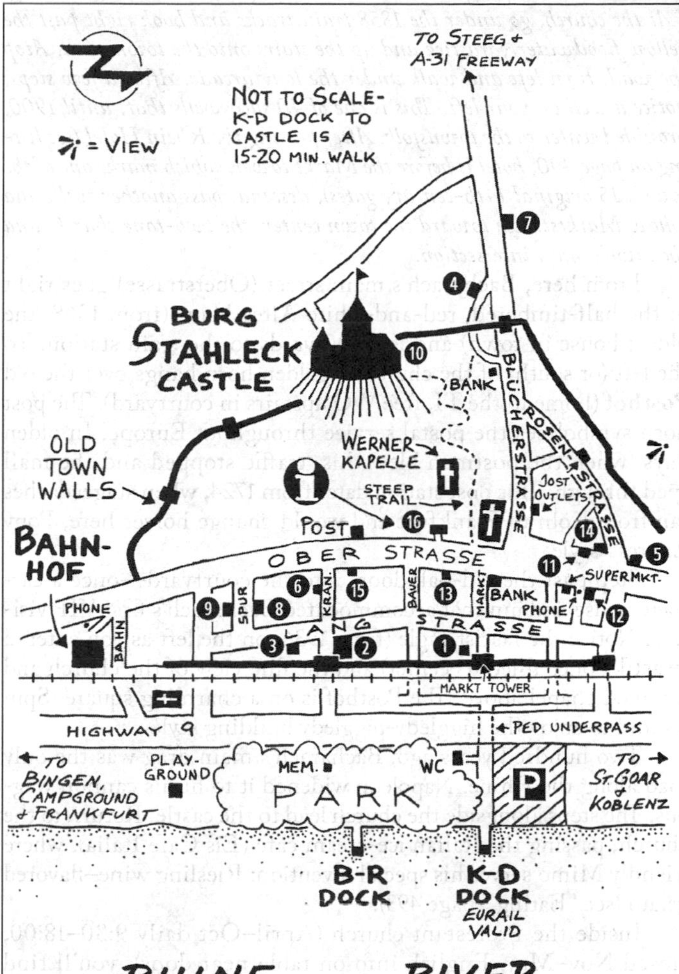

1. Rhein Hotel & Stüber Rest.
2. Hotel/Rest. Kranenturm
3. Hotel Hillen & Bike Rental
4. Pension im Malerwinkel
5. Pension Binz
6. Pension Lettie
7. Pension Winzerhaus
8. Ursula Orth B & B
9. Irmgard Orth B & B
10. Jugendherberge Stahleck Hostel
11. Altes Haus Restaurant
12. Kurpfälzische Münze Restaurant
13. Eis Café Italia
14. Bastian's Weingut zum Grüner Baum
15. Weingut Karl Heidrich
16. Old Posthof

estate. These camping devotees have made a science out of relaxing.

• *At the church, go under the 1858 train tracks and hook right past the yellow floodwater yardstick and up the stairs onto the town wall. Atop the wall, turn left and walk under the long arcade. After a few steps, notice a well on your left. This is one of 40 such wells that, until 1900, provided water to the townsfolk. After passing the Rhein Hotel (see listing on page 490; hotel is before the Markt tower, which marks one of the town's 15 original 14th-century gates), descend, pass another well, and follow Marktstrasse toward the town center, the two-tone church, and the town's main intersection.*

From here, Bacharach's main street (Oberstrasse) goes right to the half-timbered, red-and-white Altes Haus (from 1368, the oldest house in town) and left 400 yards to the train station. To the left (or south) of the church, a golden horn hangs over the old **Posthof** (home to the TI, free WC upstairs in courtyard). The post horn symbolizes the postal service throughout Europe. In olden days, when the postman blew this, traffic stopped and the mail sped through. This post station dates from 1724, when stagecoaches ran from Köln to Frankfurt and would change horses here, Pony Express-style.

Step past the old-oak doors into the courtyard—once a carriage house and inn that accommodated Bacharach's first VIP visitors. Notice the fascist eagle (from 1936, on the left as you enter; a swastika once filled its center) and the fine view of the church and a ruined chapel above. The Posthof is on a charming square. Spin around to enjoy the higgledy-piggledy building style.

Two hundred years ago, Bacharach's main drag was the only road along the Rhine. Napoleon widened it to fit his cannon wagons. The steps alongside the church lead to the castle. Return to the church, passing the Italian ice-cream café (Eis Café Italia), where friendly Mimo serves his special invention: Riesling wine–flavored gelato (see "Eating," page 493).

Inside the Protestant church (April–Oct daily 9:30–18:00, closed Nov–May, English info on table near door), you'll find Grotesque capitals, brightly painted in medieval style, and a mix of round Romanesque and pointed Gothic arches. Left of the altar, some medieval frescoes survive where an older Romanesque arch was cut by a pointed Gothic one.

• *Continue down Oberstrasse to the* ***Altes Haus.***

Notice the 14th-century building style—the first floor is made of stone, while upper floors are half-timbered (in the ornate style common in the Rhine Valley). Some of its windows still look medieval, with small flattened circles as panes (small because that's all that glass-blowing technology of the time would allow), pieced together with molten lead. Frau Weber welcomes visitors to enjoy the fascinating ground floor of her Altes Haus, with its evocative old photos and etchings (consider eating here later—see "Eating," page 493).

• *Keep going down Oberstrasse to the* **old mint** *(Münze), marked by a crude coin in its sign.*

Across from the mint, the Bastian family's wine garden is the liveliest place in town after dark (see page 494). Above you in the vineyards stands a lonely white-and-red tower—your destination.

At the next street, look right and see the mint tower, painted in the medieval style (illustrating that the Dark Ages weren't really *that* dark), and then turn left. Wander 30 yards up Rosenstrasse to the **well.** Notice the sundial and the wall painting of 1632 Bacharach with its walls intact. Climb the tiny-stepped lane behind the well up into the vineyard and to the tall, lonely tower. The slate steps lead to a small path through the vineyard that deposits you at a viewpoint atop the stubby remains of the old town wall. If the tower's open, hike to its top floor for the best view.

A grand medieval town spreads before you. For 300 years (1300–1600), Bacharach was big (population 4,000), rich, and politically powerful.

From this perch you can see the chapel ruins and six surviving **city towers.** Visually trace the wall to the castle. The castle was actually the capital of Germany for a couple of years in the 1200s. When Holy Roman Emperor Frederick Barbarossa went away to fight the Crusades, he left his brother (who lived here) in charge of his vast realm. Bacharach was home of one of seven electors who voted for the Holy Roman Emperor in 1275. To protect their own power, these elector-princes did their best to choose the weakest guy on the ballot. The elector from Bacharach helped select a two-bit prince named Rudolf von Hapsburg (from a no-name castle in Switzerland). The underestimated Rudolf brutally silenced the robber barons along the Rhine and established the mightiest dynasty in European history. His family line, the Hapsburgs, ruled much of Central Europe until 1918.

Plagues, fires, and the Thirty Years' War (1618–1648) finally did Bacharach in. The town, with a population of about a thousand, has slumbered for several centuries. Today, the castle houses commoners—40,000 overnights annually by youth hostelers.

In the mid-19th century, painters such as J. M. W. Turner and writers such as Victor Hugo were charmed by the Rhineland's romantic mix of past glory, present poverty, and rich legend. They put this part of the Rhine on the old "grand tour" map as the "Romantic Rhine." Victor Hugo pondered the ruined 15th-century chapel that you see under the castle. In his 1842 travel book, *Rhein Reise (Rhine Travels),* he wrote, "No doors, no roof or windows, a magnificent skeleton puts its silhouette against the sky. Above it, the ivy-covered castle ruins provide a fitting crown. This is

Bacharach, land of fairy tales, covered with legends and sagas." If you're enjoying the Romantic Rhine, thank Victor Hugo and company.

• *To get back into town, take the level path away from the river that leads along the once-mighty wall up the valley past the next tower. Then cross the street into the parking lot. Pass Pension Malerwinkel on your right, being careful not to damage the old arch with your head. Follow the creek past a delightful little series of half-timbered homes and cheery gardens known as "Painters' Corner"* (Malerwinkel). *Resist looking into some pervert's peep show (on the right) and continue downhill back to the village center. Nice work.*

SLEEPING

(country code: 49, area code: 06743)

Ignore guest houses and restaurants posting *Recommended by Rick Steves* signs. If they're not listed in the current edition of this book, I do not recommend them. The only hotel in Bacharach with Internet access is the Kranenturm. For locations, see the map on page 487.

$$$ Rhein Hotel, with 14 spacious and comfortable rooms, is classy, well-run, decorated with a modern flair, and overlooks the river. Since it's right on the train tracks, its river- and train-side rooms come with four-paned windows and air-conditioning (Sb-€53, Db-€86, cheaper for 2 nights, weekly deals, half-board option, free loaner bikes for guests, directly inland from the K-D boat dock at Langstrasse 50, tel. 06743/1243, fax 06743/1413, info@rhein-hotel-bacharach.de, www.rhein-hotel-bacharach.de). This place has been in the Stüber family for six generations. For a culinary splurge, consider dining here (see "Eating," page 493).

$$ Hotel Kranenturm, offering castle ambience without the climb, combines hotel comfort with *Zimmer* coziness right downtown. Run by hardworking Kurt Engel and his intense but friendly wife, Fatima, this hotel is actually part of the medieval fortification. Its former *Kran* (crane) towers are now round rooms. When the riverbank was higher, cranes on this tower loaded barrels of wine onto Rhine boats. While just 15 feet from the train tracks, a combination of medieval sturdiness, triple-paned windows, and included earplugs makes the riverside rooms sleepable (Sb-€40–44, Db-€55–62, bigger Db-€58–65, Db in huge tower rooms with castle and river views-€70–80, Tb-€80–95, honeymoon special-€90–105, the lower price is for off-season or stays of at least 3 nights in high season, family deals, cash preferred, Rhine views come with ripping train noise, back rooms are quieter, kid-friendly, good breakfast, Internet access-€2/hr, laundry service-€12.50, Langstrasse 30, tel. 06743/1308, fax 06743/1021,

Sleep Code

(€1 = about $1.30)
S = Single, **D** = Double/Twin, **T** = Triple, **Q** = Quad, **b** = bathroom, **s** = shower only. All hotels speak some English. Breakfast is included and credit cards are accepted unless otherwise noted.

To help you sort easily through these listings, I've divided the rooms into three categories, based on the price for a standard double room with bath:

$$$ Higher Priced—Most rooms €70 or more.
$$ Moderately Priced—Most rooms between €50–70.
$ Lower Priced—Most rooms €50 or less.

The Rhine is an easy place for cheap sleeps. *Zimmer* and *Gasthäuser* with €25 beds abound (and *Zimmer* normally discount their prices for longer stays). Rhine-area hostels offer €17 beds to travelers of any age. Each town's TI is eager to set you up, and finding a room should be easy any time of year (except for winefest weekends in Sept and Oct). Bacharach and St. Goar, the best towns for an overnight stop, are 10 miles apart, connected by milk-run trains, riverboats, and a riverside bike path. Bacharach is a much more interesting town, but St. Goar has the famous castle (see "St. Goar," page 494). Parking in Bacharach is simple along the highway next to the tracks (3-hour daytime limit is generally not enforced) or in the boat parking lot. Parking in St. Goar is tighter; ask at your hotel.

www.kranenturm.com, hotel-kranenturm@t-online.de). Kurt, a good cook, serves €6–18 dinners.

$$ Pension im Malerwinkel sits like a grand gingerbread house just outside the wall at the top end of town in a quiet little neighborhood so charming it's called "Painters' Corner" *(Malerwinkel)*. The Vollmer family's 20-room place is super-quiet and comes with a sunny garden on a brook and easy parking (Sb-€35, Db-€55–59 for 1 night, €53 for 2 nights, €50 for 3 nights or more, cash only, some rooms have balconies, no train noise, bike rental-€6/day, from town center go uphill until you pass the old town gate and look left to Blücherstrasse 41, tel. 06743/1239, fax 06743/93407, www.im-malerwinkel.de, pension@im-malerwinkel.de).

$$ Pension Binz offers four large, bright, plainly furnished rooms in a good location with no train noise (Sb-€33, Db-€55, third person-€18, apartment with kitchen but no breakfast and 2-night minimum-€65, Koblenzer Strasse 1, tel. 06743/1604, fax 06743/937-9916, pension.binz@freenet.de, Carla speaks a little English).

$ Hotel Hillen, a block south of the Hotel Kranenturm, has a little less charm and similar train noise, with spacious rooms, good food, and friendly owners. They just installed new windows to minimize train noise—but to get a room on the quiet side, ask for *ruhige Seite* (S-€25, Sb-€30, D-€35, Ds-€40, Db-€45, Tb-€60, Qb-€75, prices are for a 2-night minimum, €5 more for 1-night stays, closed mid-Nov–March, family rooms, Langstrasse 18, tel. 06743/1287, fax 06743/1037, hotel-hillen@web.de, kind Iris speaks some English). The Hillen also rents bikes (see page 485).

$ At **Pension Lettie,** effervescent and eager-to-please Lettie offers four bright rooms. Lettie speaks English (she worked for the US Army before they withdrew) and does laundry—€10.50 per load (Sb-€34, Db-€48, Tb-€65, Qb-€85, 5b-€100, discount for 2-night stays, 10 percent more if paying with credit card, strictly non-smoking, buffet breakfast with waffles and eggs, no train noise, a few doors inland from Hotel Kranenturm, Kranenstrasse 6, tel. 06743/2115, fax 06743/947564, pension.lettie@t-online.de).

$ Pension Winzerhaus, a 10-room place run by friendly Sybille and Stefan, is outside the town walls, 200 yards up the side-valley road from the town gate, directly under the vineyards. Though there's no train noise, the front rooms have a bit of street noise (ask for the back side). The rooms are simple, clean, and modern, and parking is easy (Sb-€30, Db-€49, Tb-€60, Qb-€69, cash only, non-smoking, free loaner bikes for guests, Blücherstrasse 60, tel. 06743/1294, winzerhaus@compuserve.de).

$ Orth Zimmer: Delightful sisters-in-law run two fine little B&Bs across the lane from each other (from station walk down Oberstrasse, turn right on Spurgasse, look for *Orth* sign). **Ursula Orth** rents five rooms and speaks a smidge of English (Sb-€22, Db-€35, Tb-€45, cash only, rooms 4 and 5 on ground floor, Spurgasse 3, tel. 06743/1557). **Irmgard Orth** rents two fresh rooms, one of which has a bathroom in the hall. She speaks even less English but is exuberantly cheery and serves homemade honey with breakfast (S-€20, D-€33, Db-€35, cash only, Spurgasse 2, look for beehive signs, tel. 06743/1553). Their excellent prices assume you're booking direct, instead of through the TI.

$ Jugendherberge Stahleck hostel is a 12th-century castle on the hilltop—500 steps above Bacharach—with a royal Rhine view. Open to travelers of any age, this is a gem with eight beds and a private modern shower and WC in most rooms. A steep 20-minute climb on the trail from the town church, the hostel is warmly run by Evelyn and Bernhard Falke (FALL-keh), who serve hearty €6.20 all-you-can-eat buffet dinners. The hostel pub serves cheap local wine until midnight. To reach the hostel with luggage from the train station, call an €8 taxi at 06743/1653 or 06743/1418 (€17 dorm beds with breakfast and sheets, €3.10 extra for non-members, couples can share one of five €45 Db, no smoking in rooms, open all day but 22:00 curfew, laundry-€4.70, dorm beds normally available but call and leave your name—they'll hold a bed until 18:00, tel. 06743/1266, fax 06743/2684, bacharach@diejugendherbergen.de). If driving, don't go in the driveway; park on the street and walk 200 yards.

EATING

Restaurants

You can easily find inexpensive (€10–15), atmospheric restaurants offering indoor and outdoor dining. There's also a cozy pizzeria and a *Döner Kebab* joint on the main street.

The Rhein Hotel's **Stüber Restaurant** is Bacharach's best top-end choice. Chef Andreas Stüber is the sixth generation to prepare regional, seasonal plates, served on river- and track-side seating or indoors with a spacious wood-and-white-tablecloth elegance. Consider their William Turner pâté sampler plate, named after the British painter who liked Bacharach (€11–17 entrées, March–mid-Dec Wed–Mon 12:00–14:00 & 17:30–21:30, closed Tue and mid-Dec–Feb, call to reserve an outdoor table, facing the K-D boat dock just below the center of town, Langstrasse 50, tel. 06743/1243).

Altes Haus, the oldest building in town (see page 488), serves reliably good food with Bacharach's most romantic atmosphere (€9–15 entrées, Thu–Tue 12:00–15:30 & 18:00–23:00, last orders at 21:30, closed Wed and Dec–Easter, dead center by the church, tel. 06743/1209). Find the cozy little dining room with photos of the opera singer who sang about Bacharach, adding to its fame.

Kurpfälzische Münze, while more expensive than Altes Haus, is a popular standby for lunch or a drink on its sunny terrace or in its pubby candlelit interior (€7–19 entrées, daily 10:00–22:00, in the old mint, a half-block down from Altes Haus, tel. 06743/1375).

Hotel Kranenturm is another good value, with hearty dinners and good main-course salads. If you like trains, sit on their track-side terrace and trade travel stories with new friends over dinner, letting screaming trains punctuate your conversation. If you prefer charming old German decor, sit inside (see hotel listing on page 490; restaurant open daily 17:00–21:00).

Eis Café Italia, on the main street and run by friendly Mimo Calabrese, is known for its Riesling-flavored gelato. Notice the big sundae bowls on the shelves. To enjoy your *Eis* German-style, sit down and order ice cream off the menu, or just stop by for a cone before an evening stroll (€0.60/scoop, no tastes offered, April–mid-Oct daily 10:00–22:00, closed off-season, opposite Posthof at Oberstrasse 48).

Wine-Tasting

Bacharach is proud of its wine. Two places in town—Bastian's rowdy and rustic Grüner Baum, and sophisticated Weingut Heidrich—offer visitors an inexpensive chance to join in on the fun. Each place samples many varieties of wines in small glasses on spinning wine carousels.

At **Bastian's Weingut zum Grüner Baum,** groups of two to six people pay €13.50 for a wine carousel of 15 glasses—14 different white wines and one lonely rosé—and a basket of bread. Your mission: Team up with others who have this book to rendezvous here after dinner. Spin the Lazy Susan, share a common cup, and discuss the taste. Doris Bastian insists: "After each wine, you must talk to each other." They offer soup and cold cuts, and good ambience indoors and out (Mon–Wed and Fri from 13:00, Sat–Sun from 12:00, closed Thu and Feb–mid-March, just past Altes Haus, tel. 06743/1208). To make a meal of a carousel, consider the *Käse Teller* (7 different cheeses, including *Spundekäse,* the local soft cheese).

For a fun, family-run wine shop and *Stube* in the town center, visit **Weingut Karl Heidrich** (at Oberstrasse 18, near Hotel Kranenturm), where Markus proudly shares his family's wine while passionately explaining its fine points to travelers. They offer a variety of wine carousels with six wines (€10), which are ideal for the more sophisticated wine-taster (April–Oct Thu–Tue 11:00–22:00, closed Wed and Nov–March, tel. 06743/93060).

St. Goar

St. Goar is a classic Rhine town. Its hulk of a castle overlooks a half-timbered shopping street and leafy riverside park, busy with sightseeing ships and contented strollers. Rheinfels Castle, once the mightiest on the Rhine, is the single best Rhineland ruin to explore. From the riverboat docks, the main drag—a dull pedestrian mall without history—cuts through town before ending at the road up to the castle.

While the town of St. Goar itself isn't much more than a few hotels and restaurants—and is less interesting than Bacharach—it still makes a good base for hiking or biking the region. A tiny car ferry will shuttle you back and forth across the busy Rhine from here. (One of my favorite pastimes in St. Goar is chatting with friendly Heike at the K-D boat kiosk.)

Tourist Information

The helpful St. Goar TI, which books rooms and offers a free baggage-check service, is on the pedestrian street, three blocks from the K-D boat dock and train station (May–Sept Mon–Fri

9:00–12:30 & 13:30–18:00, Sat 10:00–12:00, closed Sun; Oct–April Mon–Fri until 16:30, closed Sat–Sun; from train station, go downhill around church and turn left, Heerstrasse 86, tel. 06741/383, www.st-goar.de).

Helpful Hints

Picnics: St. Goar's waterfront park is hungry for a picnic. The small **Edeka supermarket** on the pedestrian street is great for picnic fixings. You can buy any quantity of produce—just push the photo or number on the scales (July–Sept Mon–Fri 8:00–18:00, Sat 8:00–13:00, closed Sun, shorter hours off-season, Heerstrasse 108).

Shopping: The friendly and helpful Montag family runs three **shops** (steins—Misha, Steiffs—Maria, and cuckoo clocks—Marion) and a hotel, all at the base of the castle hill road. The stein shop under the hotel has Rhine guides, fine steins, and copies of this year's *Rick Steves' Germany & Austria* guidebook. All three shops offer 10 percent off any of their souvenirs (including Hummels) for travelers with this book (€5 minimum purchase). On-the-spot VAT refunds cover about half your shipping costs (if you're not shipping, they'll give you VAT form to claim refund at airport).

Internet Access: Hotel Montag offers expensive coin-op access (€8/hr, 5 terminals, disk-burning service, Heerstrasse 128, tel. 06741/1629).

Bike Rental: Try **Hotel zur Loreley,** and call ahead if possible (€6.50/day, Heerstrasse 87, tel. 06741/1614).

SIGHTS

St. Goar's Rheinfels Castle

Sitting like a dead pit bull above St. Goar, this mightiest of Rhine castles rumbles with ghosts from its hard-fought past. Burg Rheinfels *was* huge—once the biggest castle on the Rhine (built in 1245). It withstood a siege of 28,000 French troops in 1692. But in 1797, the French Revolutionary army destroyed it. The castle was used for ages as a source of building stone, and today—while still mighty—it's only a small fraction of its original size. This hollow but interesting shell offers your single best hands-on ruined-castle experience on the river.

Cost and Hours: €4, family card-€10; mid-March–Nov daily 9:00–18:00, last entry at 17:00; Dec–mid-March only open Sat–Sun 11:00–17:00, last entry at 16:00—weather permitting.

Tours and Information: Call in advance or gather 10 English-speaking tourists and beg to get an English tour—perhaps from Günther, the "last knight of Rheinfels" (tel. 06741/7753,

St. Goar

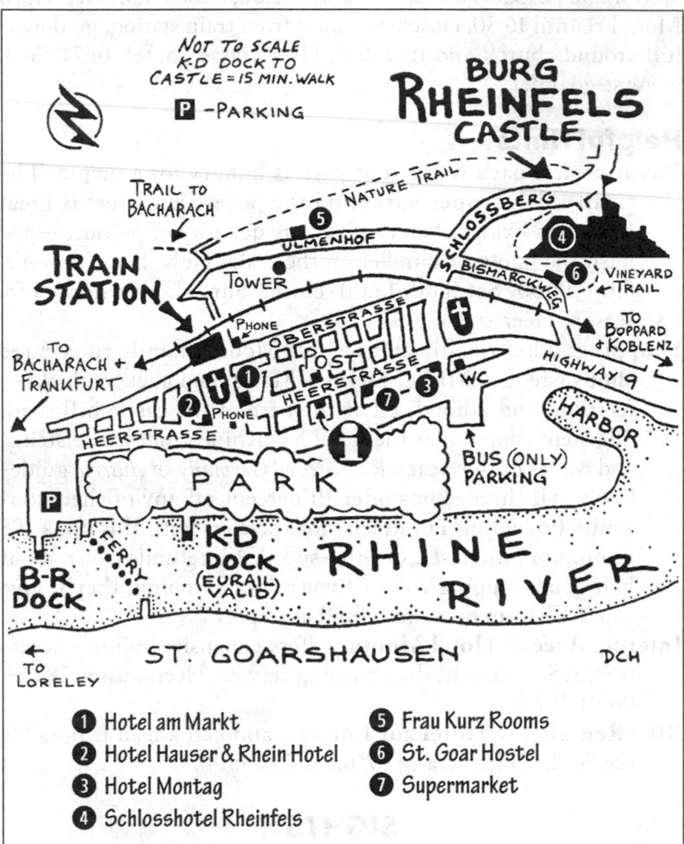

www.burg-rheinfels.com). Otherwise, follow my self-guided tour (below). The castle map is mediocre; the €2 English booklet is better, with history and illustrations. If it's damp, be careful of slippery stones. A handy WC is immediately across from the ticket booth (check out the guillotine urinals—stand back when you pull to flush).

Let There Be Light: If planning to explore the mine tunnels, bring a flashlight, or do it by candlelight (museum sells candles with matches, €0.50).

Getting to the Castle by Taxi or Mini-Train: A taxi up from town costs €5 (tel. 06741/7011). Or take the kitschy "tschu-tschu" tourist train (€2 one-way, €3 round-trip, 7 min to the top, daily 10:00–17:00 but sometimes unpredictable, 3/hr, runs from square between station and dock, also stops by beer-stein shop, complete with lusty music, mobile 0171-496-3762).

Hiking Up to the Castle: Two steep but scenic paths take you up to the castle from the town (allow 15–20 minutes up). You can also simply follow the main road up through the railroad underpass at the top end of the pedestrian street, but it's not as much fun.

To take the **vineyard trail,** start at the beer-stein shop at the end of the pedestrian street, walk uphill through the underpass, make an immediate right on Bismarcksweg along the railroad tracks following the *Fussweg Burg Rheinfels* and yellow *Zur Burg* signs, pass the youth hostel, and then follow the yellow *Zur Burg* signs up the hill through the vineyard. The last couple hundred yards are along the road.

To take the **nature trail,** start at the St. Goar train station. Take the underpass under the tracks at the north end of the station, climb the stairs uphill, and turn right (following *Burg Rheinfels* signs) along the path just above the old city wall, which takes you to the castle in 10 minutes.

➲ **Self-Guided Tour:** Rather than wander aimlessly, visit the castle by following this tour: From the ticket gate, walk straight. Pass *Grosser Keller* on the left (where we'll end this tour) and walk through an internal gate past the *zu den gedeckten Wehrgängen* sign on the right (where we'll pass later) uphill to the museum (daily 10:00–12:30 & 13:00–17:30, included in castle entry) in the only finished room of the castle. The museum is pleasant, with good English descriptions, but it's not as important as seeing the castle itself—skip the museum if you're short on time.

❶ **Museum and Castle Model:** The seven-foot-tall carved stone immediately inside the door (marked *Keltische Säule von Pfalzfeld*)—a tombstone from a nearby Celtic grave—is from 400 years before Christ. There were people here long before the Romans...and this castle. Find the old wooden library chair near the tombstone. If you smile sweetly, the man behind the desk may demonstrate—pull the chair's back forward and it becomes stairs for accessing the highest shelves.

The sweeping castle history exhibit in the center of the room is well-described in English. The massive fortification was the only Rhineland castle to withstand Louis XIV's assault during the 17th century. At the far end of the room is a model reconstruction of the castle (not the one with the toy soldiers) showing how much bigger it was before French Revolutionary troops destroyed it in the 18th century. Study this. Find where you are (hint: look for the tall tower). This was the living quarters of the original castle, which was only the smallest ring of buildings around the tiny central courtyard (13th century). The ramparts were added in the 14th century. By 1650, the fortress was largely complete. Ever since its destruction by the French in the late 18th century, it's had no military value. While no WWII bombs were wasted on this ruin, it

St. Goar's Rheinfels Castle

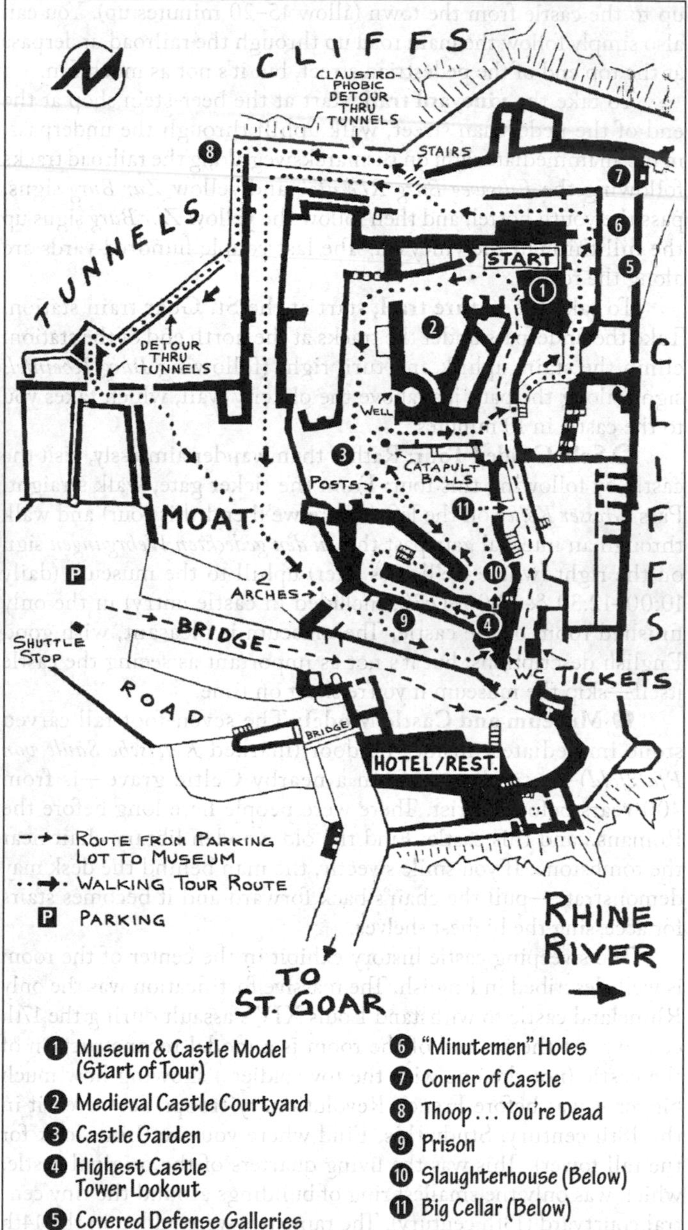

CLIFFS
CLAUSTRO-PHOBIC DETOUR THRU TUNNELS
STAIRS
TUNNELS
START
DETOUR THRU TUNNELS
WELL
CATAPULT BALLS
POSTS
MOAT
2 ARCHES
BRIDGE
SHUTTLE STOP
ROAD
WC
TICKETS
CLIFFS
BRIDGE
HOTEL/REST.
Route from Parking Lot to Museum
Walking Tour Route
Parking
RHINE RIVER
TO ST. GOAR
1 Museum & Castle Model (Start of Tour)
2 Medieval Castle Courtyard
3 Castle Garden
4 Highest Castle Tower Lookout
5 Covered Defense Galleries
6 "Minutemen" Holes
7 Corner of Castle
8 Thoop . . . You're Dead
9 Prison
10 Slaughterhouse (Below)
11 Big Cellar (Below)

Rhine Valley

served St. Goar as a stone quarry for generations. The basement of the museum shows the castle pharmacy and an exhibit of Rhine-region odds and ends, including tools and an 1830 loom. Don't miss the photos of ice-breaking on the Rhine. While once routine, ice-breaking hasn't been necessary here since 1963.

• *Exit the museum and walk 30 yards directly out, slightly uphill into the castle courtyard.*

❷ **Medieval Castle Courtyard:** Five hundred years ago, the entire castle circled this courtyard. The place was self-sufficient and ready for a siege with a bakery, pharmacy, herb garden, brewery, well (top of yard), and livestock. During peacetime, 300 to 600 people lived here; during a siege, there would be as many as 4,000. The walls were plastered and painted white. Bits of the original 13th-century plaster survive.

• *Continue through the courtyard and out Erste Schildmauer, turn left into the next courtyard, and walk straight to the two old, wooden, upright posts. Find the pyramid of stone catapult balls on your left.*

❸ **Castle Garden:** Catapult balls like these were too expensive not to recycle—they'd be retrieved after any battle. Across from the balls is a well—essential for any castle during the age of sieging. Look in. Spit. The old posts are for the ceremonial baptizing of new members of the local trading league. While this guild goes back centuries, it's now a social club that fills this court with a huge wine party the third weekend of each September.

• *If weary, skip to #5; otherwise, climb the cobbled path up to the castle's best viewpoint—up where the German flag waves.*

❹ **Highest Castle Tower Lookout:** Enjoy a great view of the river, the castle, and the forest. Remember, the fortress once covered five times the land it does today. Notice how the other castles (across the river) don't poke above the top of the Rhine canyon. That would make them easy for invading armies to see.

• *Return to the catapult balls, walk down the road, go through the tunnel, veer left through the arch marked* zu den gedeckten Wehrgängen *("to the covered defense galleries"), go down two flights of stairs, and turn left into the dark, covered passageway. From here, we will begin a rectangular walk taking us completely around (counterclockwise) the perimeter of the castle.*

❺ & ❻ **Covered Defense Galleries with "Minutemen" Holes:** Soldiers—the castle's "minutemen"—had a short commute: defensive positions on the outside, home in the holes below on the left. Even though these living quarters were padded with straw, life was unpleasant. A peasant was lucky to live beyond age 45.

• *Continue straight through the dark gallery and to the corner of the castle, where you'll see a white painted arrow at eye level. Stand with your back to the arrow on the wall.*

❼ **Corner of Castle:** Look up. A three-story, half-timbered building originally rose beyond the highest stone fortification. The two stone tongues near the top just around the corner supported the toilet. (Insert your own joke here.) Turn around and face the wall. The crossbow slits below the white arrow were once steeper. The bigger hole on the riverside was for hot pitch.

• *Follow that white arrow along the outside to the next corner. Midway you'll pass stairs on the right leading down* zu den Minengängen *(sign on upper left). Adventurers with flashlights can detour here (see "Optional Detour—Into the Mine Tunnels," below). You may come out around the next corner. Otherwise, stay with me, walking level to the corner. At the corner, turn left.*

❽ **Thoop...You're Dead:** Look ahead at the smartly placed crossbow slit. While you're lying there, notice the stonework. The little round holes were for scaffolds used as they built up. They indicate this stonework is original. Notice also the fine stonework on the chutes. More boiling pitch...now you're toast, too.

• *Continue along the castle wall around the corner. At the grey railing, look up the valley and uphill where the sprawling fort stretched. Below, just outside the wall, is land where attackers would gather. The mine tunnels are under there, waiting to blow up any attackers (read below).*

Keep going along the perimeter, jog left, go down five steps and into an open field, and walk toward the wooden bridge. You may detour here into the passageway (on right) marked 13 Halsgraben. *The "old" wooden bridge is actually modern. Angle left through two arches (before the bridge) and through the rough entry to the* Verliess *(prison) on the left.*

❾ **Prison:** This is one of six dungeons. You just walked through an entrance prisoners only dreamed of 400 years ago. They came and went through the little square hole in the ceiling. The holes in the walls supported timbers that thoughtfully gave as many as 15 residents something to sit on to keep them out of the filthy slop that gathered on the floor. Twice a day, they were given bread and water. Some prisoners actually survived longer than two years in here. While the town could torture and execute, the castle only had permission to imprison criminals in these dungeons. Consider this: According to town records, the two men who spent the most time down here—2.5 years each—died within three weeks of regaining their freedom. Perhaps after a diet of bread and water, feasting on meat and wine was simply too much.

• *Continue through the next arch, under the white arrow, then turn left and walk 30 yards to the* Schlachthaus.

❿ **Slaughterhouse:** Any proper castle was prepared to survive a six-month siege. With 4,000 people, that's a lot of provisions. The cattle that lived within the walls were slaughtered in this room. The castle's mortar was congealed here (by packing all the organic waste from the kitchen into kegs and sealing it). Notice the drainage gutters. "Running water" came through from drains built into the walls (to keep the mortar dry and therefore strong... and less smelly).

• *Back outside, climb the modern stairs to the left. A skinny, dark passage (yes, that's the one) leads you into the...*

⓫ **Big Cellar:** This *Grosser Keller* was a big pantry. When the castle was smaller, this was the original moat—you can see the rough lower parts of the wall. The original floor was 13 feet deeper. The drawbridge rested upon the stone nubs on the left. When the castle expanded, the moat became this cellar. Halfway up the walls on the entrance side of the room, square holes mark spots where timbers made a storage loft, perhaps filled with grain. In the back, an arch leads to the wine cellar (sometimes blocked off) where finer wine was kept. Part of a soldier's pay was wine... table wine. This wine was kept in a single 180,000-liter stone barrel (that's 47,550 gallons), which generally lasted about 18 months.

The count owned the surrounding farmland. Farmers got to keep 20 percent of their production. Later, in more liberal feudal times, the nobility let them keep 40 percent. Today, the German government leaves the workers with 60 percent...and provides a few more services.

• *You're free. Climb out, turn right, and leave. For coffee on a terrace with a great view, visit Schlosshotel Rheinfels, opposite the entrance (WC at base of steps).*

Optional Detour—Into the Mine Tunnels: Around 1600, to protect their castle, the Rheinfellers cleverly booby-trapped the land just outside their walls by building tunnels topped with thin slate roofs and packed with explosives. By detonating the explosives when under attack, they could kill hundreds of invaders. In 1626, a handful of underground Protestant Germans blew 300 Catholic Spaniards to—they figured—hell. You're welcome to wander through a set of never-blown-up tunnels. But be warned: It's 600 feet long, assuming you make no wrong turns; it's pitch-dark, muddy, and claustrophobic, with confusing dead-ends; and you'll never get higher than a deep crouch. It cannot be done without a light (candles available at entrance—see above). At stop #6 of the above tour, follow the stairs on the right leading down *zu den Minengängen* (sign on upper left).

The *Fuchsloch* sign welcomes you to the foxhole. Walk level (take no stairs) past the first steel railing (where you hope to emerge later) to the second steel railing. Climb down. The "highway" in this foxhole is three feet high. The ceiling may be painted with a white line indicating the correct path. Don't venture into the narrower side aisles. These were once filled with the gunpowder. After a small decline, take the second right. At the T-intersection, go right (uphill). After about 10 feet, go left. Take the next right and look for a light at the end of the tunnel. Head up a rocky incline under the narrowest part of the tunnel and you'll emerge at that first steel railing. The stairs on the right lead to freedom. Cross the field, walk under the bigger archway, and continue uphill toward the old wooden bridge. Angle left through two arches (before the bridge) and through the rough entry to the *Verliess* (prison) on the left. Rejoin the tour here at stop #8.

SLEEPING

(country code: 49, area code: 06741)

$$$ Schlosshotel Rheinfels ("Rheinfels Castle Hotel") is the town splurge. Part of the castle, but in a purpose-built new building, this luxurious 60-room place is good for those with money and a car (Db-€145–185 depending on river views and balconies, extra adult bed-€37, extra bed for kids ages 7–11—€25, kids under age 7 free, elevator, indoor pool and sauna, dress-up restaurant, free parking, Schlossberg 47, tel. 06741/8020, fax 06741/802-802, www.schlosshotel-rheinfels.de, info@burgrheinfels.de).

$$$ Hotel Montag, with 28 rooms, is on the castle end of the pedestrian street just across the street from the world's largest free-hanging cuckoo clock. Manfred and Maria Montag and their son Mike speak New Yorkish. As this place is overpriced and packed with tour groups, I'd consider it a last resort (Sb-€35–45, Db-€70–80, Tb-€90–100, pricey coin-op Internet access-€8/hr, disk-burning service, Heerstrasse 128, tel. 06741/1629, fax 06741/2086, hotelmontag@freenet.de). Check out their adjacent crafts shop (heavy on beer steins).

$$ Hotel am Markt, well-run by Herr and Frau Velich, is rustic and a good deal, with all the modern comforts. It features a hint of antler with a pastel flair, 18 bright rooms, Wi-Fi, and a good restaurant where the son, Gil, is a fine chef (see "Eating," below). It's a good value and a stone's throw from the boat dock and train station (S-€35, Sb-€43, standard Db-€59, bigger river-view Db-€69, cheaper March–mid-April and Oct–mid-Nov, closed mid-Nov–Feb, Am Markt 1, tel. 06741/1689, fax 06741/1721, www.hotelammarkt1.de, hotel.am.markt@gmx.de). Rental bikes are available to guests (€5/day). They also rent 10 rooms of equal quality (for the same price) in the smaller riverside Rhein Hotel a block away (www.rheinhotel-stgoar.de).

$ Hotel Hauser, facing the boat dock, is another good deal, warmly run by another Frau Velich. Its 12 simple rooms sit over a fine restaurant (S-€22, D-€45, Db-€50, great Db with Rhine-view balconies-€56, costs more with credit card, à-la-carte half-pension-€12, Wi-Fi, Heerstrasse 77, tel. 06741/333, fax 06741/1464, www.hotelhauser.de, hotelhauser@t-online.de).

$ Frau Kurz offers St. Goar's best *Zimmer* deal, renting three delightful rooms with a breakfast terrace, garden, fine view, and homemade marmalade (S-€23, D-€43, Db with private bathroom down the hall-€44, 2-night minimum, cash only, no smoking, free and easy parking, honor your reservation or call to cancel, Ulmenhof 11, tel. & fax 06741/459, www.gaestehaus-kurz.de, jeanette.kurz@t-online.de). It's a memorably steep five-minute hike from the train station (exit left from station, take immediate left at the yellow phone booth, pass under tracks to paved path, go up stairs and follow zigzag path, turning right through archway onto Ulmenhof; #11 is just past tower).

$ St. Goar Hostel, the big beige building down the hill from the castle, rents two singles, 14 doubles, and piles of beds in 4- to 10-bed dorms. It has a well-run, strong, institutional atmosphere with a 22:00 curfew (but you can borrow the key) and hearty €5 dinners (dorm beds-€14, S-€14, D-€27, includes breakfast, non-members pay €3.10 extra, all ages welcome, open all day, Bismarckweg 17, tel. 06741/388, fax 06741/2869, st-goar@diejugendherbergen.de). It's a fairly level 10-minute walk from the train station: Veer left and go all the way down narrow red-brick Oberstrasse, then turn left through the underpass and make an immediate right on Bismarcksweg, following the red *Jugendherberge* signs.

Rhine Valley

EATING

Hotel am Markt serves tasty traditional meals with plenty of game and fish (try Chef Gil's specialties: roast wild boar and homemade cheesecake) at fair prices with good atmosphere and service (€8–16 daily specials, daily 11:00–21:00, closed mid-Nov–Feb, Am Markt 1, tel. 06741/1689). For your Rhine splurge, walk, taxi, or drive up to **Schlosshotel Rheinfels** for its incredible view terrace in an elegant, dressy setting (€17–25 main dishes, daily 12:00–21:15, reserve a table by the window, cheaper €7–12 main dishes without view in downstairs cellar restaurant, tel. 06741/8020, see hotel listing above). There are a couple of Italian places in town and plenty of ways to gather a picnic to enjoy on the riverside park. For plenty more options, take the quick train to Bacharach, leaving and returning hourly until very late (see below).

TRANSPORTATION CONNECTIONS

Milk-run trains stop at Rhine towns each hour starting as early as 6:00, connecting at Mainz and Koblenz to trains farther afield. Trains between St. Goar and Bacharach depart at about :20 after the hour in each direction (€2.80, buy tickets from the machine in the unstaffed stations). The timings listed below are calculated from Bacharach; for St. Goar, the difference is only 12 minutes. Train info: tel. 11861 (€0.50/min).

From Bacharach by Train to: St. Goar (hourly, 12 min), **Cochem** (hourly, 1.5 hrs, change in Koblenz), **Trier** (hourly, 2.5 hrs, change in Koblenz), **Köln** (hourly, 1.75 hrs, change in Koblenz), **Frankfurt Airport** (hourly, 1.5 hrs, most change in Mainz or Bingen, first train Mon–Fri at 5:30, Sat at 6:30, Sun at 7:30), **Frankfurt** (hourly, 1.5 hrs, change in Mainz), **Rothenburg ob der Tauber** (hourly, 4.5 hrs, 3–4 changes), **Munich** (hourly, 5 hrs, change in Mainz and Mannheim), **Berlin** (hourly, 7 hrs, 2 changes), **Amsterdam** (7/day, 4.5 hrs, change in Koblenz and Köln).

BERLIN

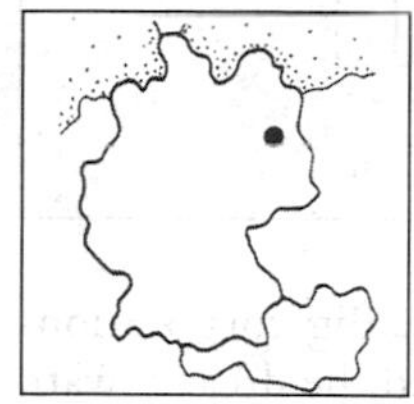

No tour of Germany is complete without a look at its historic and reunited capital. Over the last decade, Berlin has been a construction zone. Standing over ripped-up tracks and under a canopy of cranes, visitors witnessed the rebirth of a great European capital. Today, as we enjoy the thrill of walking over what was the Wall and through the well-patched Brandenburg Gate, it's clear that history is not contained in some book, but an exciting story that we are a part of. Historians find Berlin exhilarating.

Berlin had a tumultuous 20th century. After the city was devastated in World War II, it was divided by the Allied powers: The American, British, and French sectors became West Berlin, and the Soviet sector, East Berlin. That division was set in stone in 1961 when the Soviets boxed in the East by building the Berlin Wall. The Wall lasted 28 years. In 1990, less than a year after the Wall fell, the two Germanys officially became one. When the dust settled, Berliners from both sides of the once-divided city faced the monumental challenge of reunification.

While the work is far from over, a new Berlin has emerged. Berliners joke they don't need to go anywhere because their city's always changing. Spin a postcard rack to see what's new. A five-year-old guidebook on Berlin covers a different city.

Reunification has had its negative side, and locals are fond of saying, "The Wall survives in the minds of some people." Some "Ossies" (impolite slang for Easterners) miss their security. Some "Wessies" miss their easy ride (military deferrals, subsidized rent, and tax breaks). For free spirits, walled-in West Berlin was a citadel of freedom within the East.

The city government has been eager to charge forward with

Berlin Sightseeing Modules

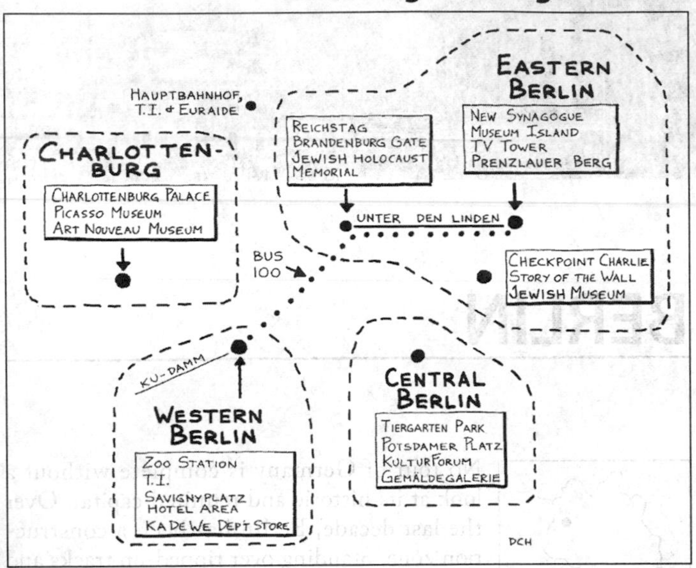

little nostalgia for anything that was Eastern. Big corporations and the national government have moved in, and the dreary swath of land that was the Wall and its notorious "death strip" has been transformed. City planners are boldly taking Berlin's reunification and the return of the national government as an opportunity to make Berlin a great capital once again.

Today Berlin feels like the nuclear fuel rod of a great nation. It's so vibrant with youth, energy, and an anything-goes-and-anything's-possible buzz that Munich feels spent in comparison. Berlin is both extremely popular and surprisingly affordable, and as a tourist attraction, it's booming.

Berlin

Planning Your Time

Because of Berlin's inconvenient location, try to enter and/or leave by either night train or plane. I'd give Berlin at least two days and spend them this way:

Day 1: Begin your day getting oriented to this huge city: Either take the 10:00 "Discover Berlin" guided walking tour offered by Original Berlin Walks (see page 515); or follow my "Do-It-Yourself Orientation Tour" by bus to the Reichstag (page 517), then continue by foot down Unter den Linden (page 526). Focus on sights along Unter den Linden, including the Reichstag dome (most crowded 10:00–16:00; best to visit 8:00–9:00 or 21:00–22:00) and Museum Island (with the Pergamon and Egyptian museums).

Day 2: Today concentrate on the sights in central Berlin, and in eastern Berlin south of Unter den Linden. Spend the morning lost in the paintings at the Gemäldegalerie. After lunch, hike via Potsdamer Platz to the Topography of Terror exhibit and along the surviving Zimmerstrasse stretch of Wall to the Museum of the Wall at Checkpoint Charlie. If you're not museum-ed out yet, swing by the magnificent Jewish Museum. Finish your day in the lively East—particularly the once glum, then edgy, now fun-loving and trendy Prenzlauer Berg district.

If you're maximizing your sightseeing, you could squeeze a hop-off, hop-on bus tour into Day 1. Remember that the Reichstag dome and the Museum of the Wall are open late.

ORIENTATION

(area code: 030)

Berlin is huge, with 3.4 million people. But the tourist's Berlin can be broken into three digestible chunks:

1. Eastern Berlin: The former East Berlin has the highest concentration of worthwhile sights and colorful neighborhoods, plus the Hauptbahnhof (Main Train Station). Near the famous Brandenburg Gate, you'll find the Reichstag building, Pariser Platz, and the new Holocaust Memorial. From the Brandenburg Gate, the famous Unter den Linden boulevard runs east through eastern Berlin, passing Museum Island (Pergamon Museum, Egyptian Museum, and Berlin Cathedral) on the way to Alexanderplatz (TV Tower). The intersection of Unter den Linden and Friedrichstrasse is emerging as the new center of the city. South of Unter den Linden, you'll find the delightful Gendarmenmarkt square, most Nazi sites (including the Topography of Terror exhibit), the Jewish Museum, the best Wall-related sights (Museum of the Wall at Checkpoint Charlie and East Side Gallery), and the colorful Turkish neighborhood of Kreuzberg. North of Unter den Linden are these worth-a-wander neighborhoods: around Oranienburger Strasse (Jewish Quarter and New Synagogue), Hackescher Markt, and Prenzlauer Berg (called Prenzl'berg by locals; several recommended hotels and a very lively restaurant/nightlife zone).

2. Central Berlin: Potsdamer Platz, the Kulturforum museum cluster (Gemäldegalerie, New National Gallery, Museum of Arts and Crafts, Musical Instruments Museum, and Philharmonic Concert Hall), and the giant Tiergarten park.

3. Western Berlin: This is the area around the Bahnhof Zoo (Zoo Train Station) and the grand Kurfürstendamm Boulevard, nicknamed "Ku'damm" (transportation hub, tours, information, shopping, and recommended hotels). The East is all the rage. But the West, while staid, is still vibrant, with lots of big-name stores and destination restaurants that keep Berliners coming back.

During the Cold War, this "Western Sector" was the hub for Western visitors. Capitalists visited the West, with a nervous side-trip behind the Wall into the grim and foreboding East. (Cubans, Russians, Poles, and Angolans stayed in and did their sightseeing in the East.) Remnants of this Iron Curtain–era Western focus have left today's visitors with a stronger focus on the Ku'damm and Bahnhof Zoo than the district really deserves.

Tourist Information

Berlin's TIs are run by a for-profit agency working for the city's big hotels, which colors the information they provide. TI branches are appropriately called "infostores" (tel. 030/250-025, www.berlin-tourist-information.com). Berlin's largest TI is at the **Hauptbahnhof** train station (daily 8:00–22:00, by main entrance); another is just five minutes from Bahnhof Zoo, in the once-impressive **Europa Center** (with Mercedes symbol on top, enter outside to left at Budapester Strasse 45, Mon–Sat 10:00–19:00, Sun 10:00–18:00). Smaller TIs are on the **Ku'damm** (in the Neues Kranzler Eck Passage at Kurfürstendamm 21, April–Oct Mon–Sat 10:00–20:00, Sun 10:00–18:00; Nov–March daily 10:00–18:00), in a pavilion near the **Reichstag** (on Scheidemannstrasse, daily April–Oct 8:00–20:00, Nov–March 10:00–18:00), in the **Brandenburg Gate** (daily April–Oct 9:30–18:00, Nov–March 10:00–18:00), and at the base of the TV Tower at **Alexanderplatz** (same hours as Brandenburg Gate TI).

The TIs sell a good city map (€1), the *Schaulust* Museumspass and WelcomeCard Culture (both described below), and various local publications, including the *Berlin Calendar* (see below). They also offer a €3 room-finding service (but only to hotels that give them kickbacks—many don't). Most hotels have free city maps.

Alternative Tourist Information: EurAide's information office, located in the *Reisezentrum* of the Hauptbahnhof, or Main Train Station (on the lower level, *Untergeschoss* or *UG 1* on station maps—follow signs to tracks 5–6), provides an excellent service. They have answers to all your questions about Berlin or train travel around Europe. It's staffed by Americans (so communication is simple), and they have a knack for predicting your needs, then publishing free fliers to serve you (April–Sept daily 9:00–19:00; Oct–March Mon–Fri 9:00–19:00, closed Sat–Sun; great opportunity to get future train and *couchette* reservations nailed down ahead of time, www.euraide.com). To get the most out of EurAide, have your questions ready before your visit. EurAide also gives out a good, free city map and sells all public-transit tickets (including the €5.80 day pass) and the WelcomeCard (see "Getting Around Berlin," page 512)—making a trip to the TI probably unnecessary. Finally, they've researched and printed a *Get Me Outta Here* flier describing good day trips to small towns, and another flier on the nearby Sachsenhausen Concentration Camp (which many consider as interesting as Dachau; a Sachsenhausen day trip is also offered by Original Berlin Walks—see "Tours," page 515).

Museum Passes: The ***Schaulust Museumspass*** is a €15, three-day combo-ticket covering many of Berlin's national museums (including the Pergamon, Egyptian Museum, and Gemäldegalerie) as well as several others (such as the Jewish Museum). Entry to most of these museums costs €5–8, so the Museumspass pays for itself if you visit at least three of the included museums (not valid for special exhibitions, purchase at TI or participating museums). Note that if a museum is closed on one of the days of your Museumspass, you have access to that museum on the fourth day to make up for lost time. Also be aware that the national museums covered by this pass are different from the private attractions and sights covered by the transit-and-discount WelcomeCard (see "Getting Around Berlin," page 512). The **WelcomeCard Culture** combines a *Schaulust* Museumspass with the three-day transportation pass (€35), saving you a total of €3. Finally, various different ***Standort* day passes** cover entry to all the museums in a specific cluster (such as Museum Island or Kulturforum). For example, if you only have one day to hit all the museums on Museum Island, get a *Standortkarte Museumsinsel* (€12, available at any of the museums in that cluster) rather than paying €8 for each one.

Local Publications: Various magazines can help make your time in Berlin more productive (all available at the TI and most newsstands). ***Berlin Programm*** is a comprehensive German-language monthly that lists upcoming events and museum hours (€1.60, www.berlin-programm.de). The German-English, bimonthly, TI-produced ***Berlin Calendar*** magazine offers timely features on Berlin and a partial calendar of events (also €1.60). ***Exberliner Magazine*** is the only real English-language monthly (mostly for expat Americans, but also helpful for curious travelers). It has an edgy, youthful focus and gives a fascinating insider's look at this fast-changing city (€2, www.exberliner.com). Or pick up the free, informative magazines that promote the upstart tour companies **New Berlin Walks** and **Insider Tours** (described on page 516).

Arrival in Berlin

By Train at the Hauptbahnhof: Berlin's newest and grandest train station, Berlin Hauptbahnhof (literally, "Main Train Station"; sometimes called by its former name, Berlin Lehrter Bahnhof), opened amid fireworks and much fanfare in 2006. Virtually all long-distance trains now arrive at Europe's biggest, mostly underground train station. Berliners have dubbed it the "transfer station," where the national train system meets the city train system (S-Bahn). My recommended hotels are nowhere near this station, so transfer is exactly what you'll do here. If, on the other hand, you're just passing through (for example, sleeping in and out on night trains), you can check your bag at this station and head right into town—you're just a few minutes' walk from the Reichstag and Unter den Linden.

The Hauptbahnhof, a huge four-story shopping and transportation hub, can be a disorientating place. Some of the tracks (with single digits, tracks 1–8) are underground, while others (double digits, tracks 11–16, including the S-Bahn and some major national and international trains) are above ground. It can be time-consuming to find the right track in this huge, multi-level station, so be patient.

To reach the **S-Bahn** to transfer to another part of town, make your way to tracks 15–16 (take the escalator to the uppermost floor, following signs to *2. Obergeschoss or OG 2*). Trains from track 15 go east (toward Ostbahnhof), and trains from track 16 go west (toward Bahnhof Zoo). So, to get to Bahnhof Zoo station (near many of my recommended hotels), simply catch any S-Bahn from track 16 west for three stops (that station is explained under "By Train at Bahnhof Zoo," below). If you're sleeping in the Prenzlauer Berg neighborhood, take the S-Bahn east from track 15 for two stops to Hackescher Markt, then catch the M1 tram north (or take the bus out front—see below). If you have a train ticket or valid railpass, it covers any S-Bahn routes also covered by the big trains (for example, between the Hauptbahnhof and Bahnhof Zoo), but it does not cover other U-Bahn or S-Bahn routes.

To exit to **taxis** and **buses,** follow signs to *Europaplatz* on the "ground floor" (level *Erdgeschoss* or *EG*). Here you can catch the TXL airport bus or bus #240 to Rosenthalerplatz in the Prenzlauer Berg district.

For **train information,** there are two branches of the Deutsche-Bahn *Reisezentrum* (one is on *1. Obergeschoss* or *OG 1;* the other is on *1. Untergeschoss* or *UG 1*—follow signs to tracks 5–6; both open daily 6:00–22:00). Better yet, visit EurAide (at the *Reisezentrum* on UG 1; described under "Tourist Information," above).

Because of heightened security concerns, there are no luggage lockers. Instead, you can **check your bags** at the Gepäck Center on level EG by track 14, across from the Virgin Megastore (€3/day per bag, daily 6:00–22:00). The WC Center (public **toilets**) is next to the Virgin Megastore.

By Train at Bahnhof Zoo: Since the Hauptbahnhof opened, Bahnhof Zoo (rhymes with "toe," a.k.a. Bahnhof Zoologischer Garten) has gone from being a grand train hub to just an oversized subway station. No long-distance trains stop here anymore, so you'll have to transfer here on the city's transit system (S-Bahn). It is small, well-organized, and handy (lockers and baggage check available in back of station).

Upon arrival by train at Bahnhof Zoo, orient yourself like this: Inside the station, follow signs to *Hardenbergplatz*. Step into this busy square filled with city buses, taxis, the transit office, and derelicts. The Original Berlin Walks start from the curb immediately outside the station, at the top of the taxi stand (see "Tours," page 515). Between you and the McDonald's across the street is the stop for bus #100 (departing to the right for my "Do-It-Yourself Orientation Tour," page 517). Turn right and tiptoe through the riffraff to the eight-lane highway, Hardenbergstrasse. Walk to the median strip and stand with your back to the tracks. Ahead you'll see the black, bombed-out hulk of the Kaiser Wilhelm Memorial Church and the Europa Center (Mercedes symbol spinning on roof), which houses the TI. Just ahead on the left, amid the traffic, is the BVG transport information kiosk (where you can buy a €5.80 day pass covering the subway and buses, and pick up a free subway map). If you're facing the church, my recommended western Berlin hotels are behind you to your right (see page 550).

By Plane: For information on Berlin's airports, see "Transportation Connections," at the end of this chapter.

Helpful Hints

Medical Help: If you need to see a doctor, dial "Call a Doc" at tel. 01804-2255-2362 (www.calladoc.com). This non-profit referral service is designed for tourists. Payment is arranged between you and the doctor, and is likely far more affordable than similar care in the US.

Museum Hours: Many major Berlin museums are closed on Monday. All national museums, including the Pergamon and Gemäldegalerie (plus others as noted in "Sights," page 519), are free for the last four hours on Thursdays (that is, if it closes at 18:00, it's free from 14:00 on; www.museen-berlin.de).

Monday Activities: Since many museums are closed on Monday, save the day for Berlin Wall sights, the Reichstag dome, my "Do-It-Yourself Orientation Tour" and strolling Unter den Linden, walking/bus tours, the Jewish Museum, churches, the zoo, or shopping along Kurfürstendamm (Ku'damm) Boulevard or at the Kaufhaus des Westens (KaDeWe) department store. Be aware that when Monday is a holiday—as it is several times a year—museums are open then and closed Tuesday.

Addresses: Many Berlin streets are numbered with odd and even numbers on the same side of the street, often with no connection to the other side (for example, Ku'damm #212 can be across the street from #14). To save steps, check the white street signs on curb corners; many list the street numbers covered on that side of the block.

Internet Access: You'll find cheap, fast Internet access in most hostels and hotels, as well as at small Internet cafés all over the city. Try the **easyInternetcafé** outlets (generally open daily 6:00–23:00). Handy locations include Hardenbergplatz 2 (across from Bahnhof Zoo, next to McDonald's), Ku'damm 224 (10-min walk from Bahnhof Zoo, near several recommended hotels), and Rathaus-Passagen (on Alexanderplatz). Buy a ticket at the self-service machines and follow the English instructions. Unused time can be used at any locale for up to a week.

Bookstore: Berlin Story, a big, fun-loving bookshop, has the best selection anywhere in town of English-language books on Berlin. They also have a fascinating and free little museum in the back with a model of Unter den Linden from 1930 and a room showing a good 25-minute Berlin history video (in English). The shop has a knowledgeable staff and stocks an amusing mix of knickknacks and East Berlin nostalgia souvenirs (daily 10:00–19:00, Unter den Linden 40, tel. 030/2045-3842, www.berlinstory.de).

Laundry: Schnell und Sauber Waschcenter is a handy launderette near my recommended western Berlin hotels (€5–9 wash and dry, daily 6:00–23:00, Leibnizstrasse 72, 4 blocks west of Savignyplatz, near intersection with Kantstrasse). Near my recommended hotels in Prenzlauer Berg, try **Holly's Wasch-Theke** (€5–9 wash and dry, includes detergent, daily 9:00–23:00, last load in at 21:30, attached café, Kollwitzstrasse 93, tel. 030/443-9210).

Travel Agency: Last Minute Flugbörse can help you find a flight in a hurry (next to TI in Europa Center, Mon–Sat 10:00–20:00, closed Sun, tel. 030/2655-1050, www.lastminuteflugboerse.de). **American Express** is near Unter den Linden at Friedrichstrasse 172 (Mon–Fri 9:00–19:00, Sat 10:00–14:00, closed Sun, travel agency tel. 030/201-7400; for lost traveler's checks, call tel. 0800-101-2362).

Getting Around Berlin

Berlin's sights spread far and wide. Right from the start, commit yourself to the fine public-transit system.

By Subway and Bus: The U-Bahn (*Untergrund-Bahn,* Berlin's subway), S-Bahn (*Schnell-Bahn,* or "fast train," mostly above ground and with fewer stops), *Strassenbahn* (streetcars), and all buses are consolidated into one "BVG" system that uses the same tickets. *Erwachsener* means "adult"—anyone 14 or older. Here are your options:

• A basic ticket *(Einzelfahrschein)* for two hours of travel in one direction on buses or subways—€2.10. It's easy to make this ticket stretch to cover several rides...as long as they're all in the same direction.

• A cheap short-ride ticket *(Kurzstrecke)* for a single short ride of six bus stops or three subway stations, with one transfer—€1.20.

• A day pass *(Tageskarte)* covering zones A and B, the city proper—€5.80 (good until 3:00 the morning after). To get out to Potsdam, you need a ticket covering zone C—€6. (For longer stays, a 7-day *Tageskarte* is also available—€25.40, or €31.30 including zone C; or buy 2 WelcomeCards, described below.)

• The Berlin/Potsdam **WelcomeCard** gives you transportation in zones A, B, and C, and 25-percent discounts on lots of minor and a few major museums (including Checkpoint Charlie), sightseeing tours (including 25 percent off the recommended Original Berlin Walks), and music and theater events (€16/48 hrs, €22/72 hrs; valid for an adult and up to three kids younger than 14). If you plan to cover a lot of ground during a two- or three-day visit, this is usually the best transit deal.

Buy your U- or S-Bahn tickets from machines at stations. (They are also sold at BVG pavilions at train stations and airports, the TI, and EurAide.) Don't be afraid of the automated machines: First select the type of ticket you want, then load in the coins or paper bills. As you board the bus or tram, or enter the subway system, punch your ticket in a red or yellow clock machine to validate it (or risk a €40 fine; for an all-day or multi-day pass, only validate it the first time you ride). The double-decker buses are a joy (can buy ticket on bus), and the subway is a snap. S-Bahn lines between major train stations (but not other S-Bahn or U-Bahn lines) are free with a validated Eurailpass (but it starts use of a flexi-day).

Sections of the U- or S-Bahn sometimes close temporarily for repairs. In this situation, a bus route often replaces the train (*Ersatzverk*[illegible] placement transportation"). Bus schedules are [illegible] the helpful BVG website, www.bvg.de.

By Taxi: Taxis are easy to flag down, and taxi stands are common. A typical ride within town costs €10–16, and a cross-town trip (for example, Bahnhof Zoo to Alexanderplatz) will run you around €25. A local law designed to help people get safely and affordably home from their subway station late at night is handy for tourists any time of day: A short ride of no more than two kilometers (1.25 miles) is a flat €3. (Ask for *"Kurzstrecke, drei euro, bitte."*) To get this cheap price, you must hail a cabbie on the street rather than go to a taxi stand (from a stand, it's a minimum €5 charge). Cabbies aren't crazy about the law, so insist on the price and be sure to keep the ride short.

Berlin

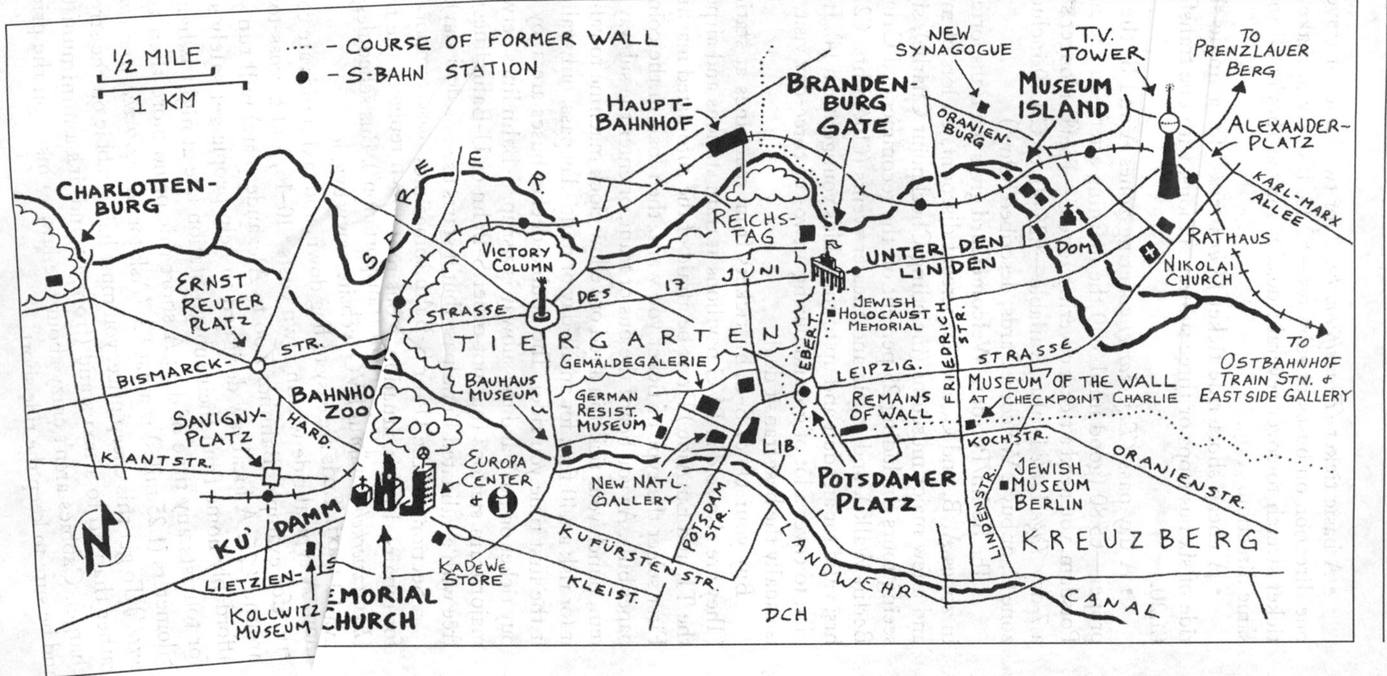
Berlin
1/2 MILE
1 KM
- COURSE OF FORMER WALL
- S-BAHN STATION
NEW SYNAGOGUE
T.V. TOWER
TO PRENZLAUER BERG
HAUPT-BAHNHOF
BRANDEN-BURG GATE
MUSEUM ISLAND
ORANIEN-BURG
ALEXANDER-PLATZ
KARL-MARX ALLEE
CHARLOTTEN-BURG
SPREE R.
REICHS-TAG
DOM
RATHAUS
NIKOLAI CHURCH
VICTORY COLUMN
UNTER DEN LINDEN
JUNI
17
DES
STRASSE
ERNST REUTER PLATZ
JEWISH HOLOCAUST MEMORIAL
TIERGARTEN
FRIEDRICH STR.
STRASSE
TO OSTBAHNHOF TRAIN STN. & EAST SIDE GALLERY
STR.
BISMARCK-
GEMÄLDEGALERIE
EBERT.
LEIPZIG.
MUSEUM OF THE WALL AT CHECKPOINT CHARLIE
BAUHAUS MUSEUM
GERMAN RESIST. MUSEUM
REMAINS OF WALL
BAHNHO ZOO
SAVIGNY-PLATZ
HARD.
ZOO
LIB.
KOCHSTR.
K ANTSTR.
EUROPA CENTER
POTSDAMER PLATZ
JEWISH MUSEUM BERLIN
ORANIENSTR.
NEW NAT'L GALLERY
POTSDAM STR.
LINDENSTR.
KU' DAMM
KUFÜRSTEN STR.
KREUZBERG
LANDWEHR
KADEWE STORE
LIETZEN-
KLEIST.
CANAL
KOLLWITZ MUSEUM
MEMORIAL CHURCH
DCH

By Bike: Be careful—in Berlin, motorists don't brake for bicyclists (and bicyclists don't brake for pedestrians). Fortunately, some roads and sidewalks have special red-painted bike lanes. Just don't ride on the regular sidewalk—it's *nicht erlaubt* (not allowed).

In western Berlin, you can rent good bikes at the **Bahnhof Zoo** left-luggage counter, next to the lockers at the back of the station (€10/day, €23/3 days, €35/7 days, requires passport and €50 cash deposit; bikes come with lock, air pump, and mounted basket; daily 7:00–21:00, there's a limited supply of bikes and they've been known to run out). In the east, **Fahrradstation** near the Friedrichstrasse S-Bahn station has a huge number of bikes (€15/day, passport required; April–Oct daily 8:00–20:00; Nov–March Mon–Fri 10:00–19:00, Sat 10:00–15:00, closed Sun; leave the S-Bahn station via Friedrichstrasse exit, turn left on Dorotheenstrasse, and you'll find it at the entrance to the parking garage at Dorotheenstrasse 30; tel. 030/2045-4500).

TOURS

Walking Tours

Berlin is an ideal city to get to know with a walking tour—it's a ▲▲▲ experience. The city is a battle zone of extremely competitive and creative walking tour companies, all offering employment to American and British expats and students and cheap, informative tours to visiting travelers. The Original Berlin Walks was, as its name implies, the original. Smelling a business opportunity, some of its former guides and others spliced guerilla business tactics into O.B.W.'s established model and started their own walking tour companies. All give variations on the same themes: general introductory walk, Hitler and Nazi sites walk, communism walk, and day trips to Potsdam and the Sachsenhausen Concentration Camp. The youth-oriented outfits also do nightly pub crawls. By next year, there will likely be other companies with guides on street corners handing out fliers to promote their tours (for which they are not paid, but rely on tips). For details, see the various websites. Here's my take on the current situation.

The Original Berlin Walks—This is the most established operation, with the most serious tours aiming at a clientele with a longer attention span. They don't offer "free tours" or pub crawls. I've enjoyed the help of O.B.W.'s high-quality, high-energy guides for many years, and routinely hire them when my tour groups are in town. I've always been impressed with the caliber of the guides that founder Nick Gay has assembled. Tours generally cost €12 (€9 with the WelcomeCard, or €10 if you're under 26). For any of these tours, just show up at the taxi stand in front of Bahnhof Zoo. Many tours have a second departure point 30 minutes later in eastern Berlin's Hackescher Markt S-Bahn station, outside Häagen-Dazs.

The Original Berlin Walks' itineraries include the following: **Discover Berlin** introductory walk (daily year-round at 10:00, April–Oct also daily at 14:30); **Infamous Third Reich Sites** (May–Sept Wed at 10:00, Sat at 14:30, Sun at 10:00; also available Oct–April—check their website or pick up a flier for the schedule; departs from Bahnhof Zoo meeting point only); **Jewish Life in Berlin** (May–Sept Mon at 10:00); and the newest itinerary, **Nest of Spies** (May–Sept only, check website or flier for tour times). Many of the Third Reich and Jewish history sights are difficult to pin down without these excellent walks. Also consider their six-hour trip to **Sachsenhausen Concentration Camp,** intended "to provide a challenging history lesson with universal applications" (€15; May–Sept Tue and Thu–Sun at 10:15; check website or flier for Oct–April schedule; departs from Bahnhof Zoo meeting point only, requires transit day ticket with zone C—or buy from guide, call office for specifics). Confirm this schedule at EurAide or by phone with Nick or his wife and partner, Serena (tel. 030/301-9194, www.berlinwalks.de, info@berlinwalks.de). As you pay for Original Berlin Walks up front, tipping is not expected. Nick can also arrange private guides (€150/3 hrs, email him for details).

Insider Tours and New Berlin Walks—Unlike in other European cities, there are no regulations controlling who can give tours in Berlin. Lots of upstart companies come and go, but these two feisty and aggressive newcomers are well-established. They target a younger crowd and offer free intro tours. Their guides make their money off of tips, cross-selling their specialty tours, and the hugely successful pub crawls (with profit supplemented by featured bars). Each company publishes a wonderful, free Berlin guide magazine (distributed all over town and worth grabbing for the sightseeing information even if you're not taking their walks). They offer essentially the same itineraries as Original Berlin Walks and roughly this formula: You take their introductory walk for free, then choose—if you wish—to take any of their other walks (€10–12 each). For all the details, see their magazines or visit www.insidertour.com or www.newberlintours.com.

Insider Tours and New Berlin Walks each offer €10 pub crawls (or, some would say, "pub brawls"). Insider Tours leaves at 20:30 from Hackescher Markt, New Berlin Walks at 21:00 from the Oranienburger Strasse S-Bahn station. Both generally visit four bars and two clubs, and are a great way to get drunk with new English-speaking friends from around the world while getting a peek at the Berlin bar scene...invaded by 50 loud tourists.

Brewer's Berlin Tours—For a more exhaustive (or, for some, exhausting) walking tour of Berlin, consider Brewer's Berlin Tours.

These are run by Terry, a former British embassy worker in East Berlin, and his well-trained staff. Their All-Day Berlin tours are legendary for their length, and best for those with a long attention span and a serious interest in Berlin (€12, tour lasts 8 hrs or more, departs daily at 10:00 from Kaiser Wilhelm Memorial Church near Bahnhof Zoo, or 30 min later from Australian Ice Cream Shop at Friedrichstrasse U- and S-Bahn station, tel. 030/2248-7435, mobile 0177-388-1537, www.brewersberlintours.com).

Bus and Bike Tours

City Bus Tours—For bus tours, the old, sedate Severin & Kühn company dominates (their office on Karl-Liebknecht-Strasse is across from the TV Tower in eastern Berlin, tel. 030/880-4190, www.severin-kuehn-berlin.de). You have two options.

1. Full-blown Bus Tours: Severin & Kühn offers a long list of bus tours in and around Berlin; their three-hour "Big Berlin Tour" is a good introduction (€21.50, daily at 10:00 and 14:00, live guides in two languages, departs from Ku'damm 216).

2. Hop-on, Hop-off Circle Tours: Several companies make a circuit of the city (City-Circle Sightseeing is good, offered by Severin & Kühn). The TI has all the brochures. The tours offer unlimited hop-on, hop-off privileges for their routes (about 14 stops) with a recorded commentary (€20, daily 10:00–18:00, last bus leaves from Ku'damm at 16:00, Nov–March last boarding at 15:00, 2–4/hr, 2-hour loop). Just hop on where you like and pay the driver. On a sunny day when some double-decker buses go topless, these are a photographer's delight, cruising slowly by just about every major sight in town.

Bike Tours—Berlin is a flat, bike-friendly city. **Fat Tire Bike Tours** offers three different four-hour, six-mile tours (€20; City Tour—daily March–Nov at 11:00, June–Aug also at 16:00; Berlin Wall Tour—mid-May–Sept Mon, Thu, and Sat at 10:30; Third Reich Tour—mid-May–Sept Wed, Fri, and Sun at 10:30; meet at TV Tower at Alexanderplatz, no need to reserve, tel. 030/2404-7991, fax 030/2404-8837, www.fattirebiketoursberlin.com, info@fattirebiketoursberlin.com).

SELF-GUIDED TOUR

Do-It-Yourself Orientation Tour: Bus #100 from Bahnhof Zoo to the Reichstag

This tour narrates the route of convenient bus #100, which connects my recommended hotel neighborhood in western Berlin with the sights in eastern Berlin. If you have the €20 and two hours for a hop-on, hop-off bus tour (described above), take that instead. But this short €2.10 bus ride is a fine city introduction. Bus #100 is a sightseer's dream, stopping at Bahnhof Zoo, Europa Center/Hotel Palace, Victory Column (Siegessäule), Reichstag, Brandenburg Gate, Unter den Linden, Pergamon Museum, and ending at Alexanderplatz. While you could ride it to the end, it's more fun to get out at the Reichstag and walk down Unter den Linden at your own pace (using my commentary on page 526). When combined with the self-guided walk down Unter den Linden, this tour merits ▲▲▲. Before you take this bus into eastern Berlin, consider checking out the sights in western Berlin (see page 546). Note that as Berlin adjusts itself around its new mega-station, the Hauptbahnhof, bus #100 may swing farther north to this station before reaching the Reichstag.

The Tour Begins: Buses start from Hardenbergplatz in front of Bahnhof Zoo. Buses come every 10 minutes, and single tickets are good for two hours—so take advantage of hop-on-and-off privileges. To ensure the best seat, you can board one stop earlier, at Hertzallee (exit out the back of the station, go right, and walk one block to Hertzallee—the bus stop is on the left). Climb aboard, stamp your ticket (giving it a time), and grab a seat on top. This is about a 10-minute ride. The upcoming stop will light up on the reader board inside the bus.

➔ On your left and then straight ahead, before descending into the tunnel, you'll see the bombed-out hulk of the **Kaiser Wilhelm Memorial Church,** with its postwar sister church (described on page 546) and the **Europa Center.** This is the "West End" shopping district, a bustling people zone with big department stores nearby. When the Wall came down, East Berliners flocked to this area's department stores (especially KaDeWe, described on page 547). Soon after, the biggest, swankiest new stores were built in the East. Now the West is trying to win those shoppers back by building even bigger and better shopping centers around Europa Center. Across from the Zoo station, the under-construction Zoofenster tower will be taller than all the buildings you see here.

Emerging from the tunnel, on your immediate right you'll see the Berlin tourist information office.

➔ At the stop in front of Hotel Palace: On the left, the elephant gates mark the entrance to the **Berlin Zoo** and its aquarium (described on page 548).

➔ Driving down Kurfürstenstrasse, you'll pass several Asian restaurants—a reminder that, for most, the best food in Berlin is not German. Turning left, with the huge Tiergarten park in the distance ahead, you'll cross a canal and see the famous **Bauhaus Archive** (an off-white, blocky building) behind the trees on the right. The Bauhaus movement ushered in a new age of modern architecture that emphasized function over beauty, giving rise to blocky steel-and-glass skyscrapers in big cities around the world. On the left is Berlin's new embassy row. The big turquoise wall marks the communal home of all five Nordic embassies. This building is perfectly "green," run entirely by solar power.

➲ The bus enters a 400-acre park called the **Tiergarten,** packed with cycling paths, joggers, and—on hot days—nude sunbathers. Straight ahead, the **Victory Column** (Siegessäule, with the gilded angel, described on page 522) towers above this vast city park that was once a royal hunting grounds, now nicknamed the "green lungs of Berlin."

➲ On the left, a block after leaving the Victory Column: The 18th-century, late-Rococo **Bellevue Palace** is the German White House. Formerly a Nazi VIP guest house, it's now the residence of the federal president (whose power is mostly ceremonial). If the flag's out, he's in.

➲ Driving along the Spree River: This park area was a residential district before World War II. Now, on the left-hand side, it's filled with the buildings of the **national government.** The huge brick "brown snake" complex was built to house government workers—but it didn't sell, so now its apartments are available to anyone. A metal Henry Moore sculpture entitled *Butterfly* floats in front of the slope-roofed House of World Cultures (Berliners have nicknamed this building "the pregnant oyster"). The modern tower (next on left) is a carillon with 68 bells (1987).

Somewhere around here, the bus may detour north to the **Hauptbahnhof.** Stick with it, and you'll veer back south towards the Reichstag.

➲ Leap out at the Platz der Republik stop. (While you could continue on bus #100, it's better on foot from here.) Through the trees on the left you'll see Germany's new and sprawling **Chancellory.** Started during the more imperial rule of Helmut Kohl, it's now considered overly grand. The big park is the **Platz der Republik,** where the Victory Column stood until Hitler moved it. The gardens were recently dug up to build underground train tracks serving the Hauptbahnhof (across the field between the Chancellory and the Reichstag). Watch your step—excavators found a 250-pound, undetonated American bomb.

➲ Just down the street stands an old building with a new dome...the **Reichstag.**

SIGHTS

Eastern Berlin

I've arranged the following sights in the order of a convenient self-guided orientation walk, picking up where my "Do-It-Yourself Orientation Tour" (above) leaves off. Allow a comfortable hour for this walk from the Reichstag to Alexanderplatz, including time for lingering (but not museum stops).

Near the Brandenburg Gate

▲▲▲Reichstag Building—The parliament building—the heart of German democracy—has a short but complicated and emotional history. When it was inaugurated in the 1890s, the last emperor, Kaiser Wilhelm II, disdainfully called it the "house for chatting." It was from here that the German Republic was proclaimed in 1918. In 1933, this symbol of democracy nearly burned down. While the Nazis blamed a Communist plot, some believe that Hitler himself (who needed what we'd call today a "new Pearl Harbor") planned the fire, using it as a handy excuse to frame the Communists and grab power. As World War II drew to a close, Stalin ordered his troops to take the Reichstag from the Nazis by May 1 (the workers' holiday). More than 1,500 Nazis made their last stand here—extending World War II by two days. On April 30, 1945, it fell to the Allies. It was hardly used from 1933 to 1999. For the building's 101st birthday in 1995, the Bulgarian-American artist Christo wrapped it in silvery-gold cloth. It was then wrapped again in scaffolding, rebuilt by British architect Lord Norman Foster, and turned into the new parliamentary home of the Bundestag (Germany's lower house). To many Germans, the proud resurrection of the Reichstag symbolizes the end of a terrible chapter in the country's history.

The **glass cupola** rises 155 feet above the ground. Its two sloped ramps spiral 755 feet to the top for a grand view. Inside the dome, a cone of 360 mirrors reflects natural light into the legislative chamber below. Lit from inside at night, this gives Berlin a memorable nightlight. The environmentally friendly cone also helps with air circulation, drawing hot air out of the legislative chamber and pulling in cool air from below.

Cost, Hours, Location: Free, daily 8:00–24:00, last entry at 22:00, most crowded 10:00–16:00 (wait in line to go up—good street musicians, metal detectors, no big luggage allowed, some hour-long English tours when parliament is not sitting). Platz der Republik 1, S- or U-Bahn: Friedrichstrasse or Unter den Linden, tel. 030/2273-2152, www.bundestag.de.

Crowd-Beating Tips: Berlin is now Germany's biggest tourist attraction. Lines at the Reichstag can be terrible. If possible, visit before 9:00 or after 21:00. Pick up the English-language flier just before the security checkpoint to have something to read as you wait. Those with table reservations at the Dachgarten rooftop restaurant don't wait in the long lines—go straight to the front and tell them you have a reservation (reserve your table in the restaurant by phone or email; €15–26 entrées with a view, daily 9:30–16:30

Eastern Berlin

& 18:30–24:00, tel. 030/2262-9933, kaeferreservierung.berlin @feinkost-kaefer.de).

➲ **Self-Guided Tour:** As you approach the building, look above the door, surrounded by stone patches from WWII bomb damage, to see the motto and promise: *Dem Deutschen Volke* ("To the German People"). The open, airy lobby towers 100 feet high, with 65-foot-tall colors of the German flag. See-through glass doors show the **central legislative chamber.** The message: There will be no secrets in government. Look inside. The seats are

"Reichstag blue," a lilac-blue color designed by the architect to brighten the otherwise gray interior. The German eagle (a.k.a. the "fat hen") spreads his wings behind the podium. Notice the doors marked "Yes," "No," and "Abstain"...the Bundestag's traditional "sheep jump" way of counting votes (for critical and close votes, all 669 members leave and vote by walking through the door of their choice).

Ride the elevator to the base of the glass **dome.** Take time to study the photos and read the circle of captions—an excellent exhibit telling the Reichstag story. Then study the surrounding architecture: a broken collage of new on old, like Germany's history. Notice the dome's giant and unobtrusive sunscreen that moves as necessary with the sun. Peer down through the skylight to look over the shoulders of the elected representatives at work. For Germans, the best view from here is down—keeping a close eye on their government.

Start at the ramp nearest the elevator and wind up to the top of the **double ramp.** Take a 360-degree survey of the city as you hike: First, the big park is the **Tiergarten,** the "green lungs of Berlin." Beyond that is the **Teufelsberg,** or "Devil's Hill" (built of rubble from the destroyed city in the late 1940s, and famous during the Cold War as a powerful ear of the West—notice the telecommunications tower on top). Knowing the bombed-out and bulldozed story of their city, locals say, "You have to be suspicious when you see the nice, green park." Find the **Victory Column** (Seigessäule, moved by Hitler in the 1930s from in front of the Reichstag to its present position in the Tiergarten). Next, scenes of the new Berlin spiral into your view—**Potsdamer Platz,** marked by the conical glass tower that houses Sony's European headquarters. The yellow building to the right is the Berlin Philharmonic Concert Hall, marking the museums at the Kulturforum. Continue circling left, and find the green chariot atop the **Brandenburg Gate.** A monument to Roma (Gypsy) victims of the Holocaust will be built between the Reichstag and Brandenburg Gate. (The Roma, as disdained by the Nazis as were the Jews, lost the same percentage of their population to Hitler.) The new **Jewish Holocaust Memorial** stretches south of Brandenburg Gate. Next, you'll see **former East Berlin** and the city's next huge construction zone, with a forest of 300-foot-tall skyscrapers in the works. Notice the TV Tower (with the Pope's Revenge—explained on page 534), the Berlin Cathedral's massive dome, the red tower of the City Hall, the golden dome of the New Synagogue, and the Reichstag's **Dachgarten Restaurant** (see "Crowd-Beating Tips," above).

Follow the train tracks in the distance to the left toward Berlin's huge, central train station, the **Hauptbahnhof.** Just in front of it, alone in a field, is the Swiss Embassy. It used to be surrounded by buildings, but now it's the only one left. Complete your spin-tour with the blocky **Chancellory,** nicknamed by Berliners "the washing machine." It may look like a pharaoh's tomb, but it's the office and home of Germany's most powerful person, the chancellor (currently Angela Merkel).

Memorial to Politicians Who Opposed Hitler—As you leave the Reichstag, look for the row of slate slabs imbedded in the ground by the park across from the main entry (looks like a fancy slate bicycle rack). This is a memorial to the 96 politicians (the equivalent of our congressmen) who were murdered and persecuted because their politics didn't agree with Chancellor Hitler's. They were part of the weak and ill-fated attempt at post-WWI democracy in Germany, the Weimar Republic. These were the people who could have stopped Hitler...so they became his first victims. Each slate slab remembers one man—his name, party (mostly KPD, or Communists, and SPD, or Socialists), and date and location of death—generally in concentration camps. (*KZ* means "concentration camp.") They are honored here because it's in front of the building in which they worked.

To the Brandenburg Gate: Let's continue our walk and cross what was the Berlin Wall, the 100-mile long barrier erected by the communist government to "protect" East Berlin from the Western world. Leaving the Reichstag, follow the busy road to the left, around the building. At the rear of the building (across the street, at the edge of the park) is a small **memorial to East Berliners** who died trying to cross the Wall. Look at the faces of these exceptionally free spirits. The Wall was built on August 13, 1961. These people died within months—mostly by trying to swim the river.

The Brandenburg Gate is ahead. Stay on the park side of the street for a better view of the gate. The road construction is an American taxpayer-funded project. Because the US Embassy needs a buffer zone from traffic for security concerns, the road is being moved back, and will be replaced by a bigger pedestrian zone.

As you cross at the light, notice the double row of **cobblestones**—it goes all around the city, marking where the Wall used to stand. (You could go directly to the Jewish Holocaust Memorial from here, but we'll go through the Brandenburg Gate first, then reach the memorial through Pariser Platz.)

▲▲Brandenburg Gate (Brandenburger Tor)—The historic Brandenburg Gate (1791) was the grandest, and is the last survivor, of 14 gates in Berlin's old city wall (this one led to the neighboring city of Brandenburg). The gate was the symbol of Prussian Berlin... and later the symbol of a divided Berlin. It's crowned by a majestic four-horse chariot with the Goddess of Peace at the reins. Napoleon took this statue to the Louvre in Paris in 1806. After the Prussians defeated Napoleon and got it back (1813), she was renamed the Goddess of Victory.

The gate sat unused, part of a sad circle dance called the Wall, for more than 25 years. Now postcards all over town show the ecstatic day—November 9, 1989—when the world enjoyed the sight of happy Berliners jamming the gate like flowers on a parade float. Pause a minute and think about struggles for freedom—past and present. (There's actually a special room built into the gate for this purpose.) Around the gate, look at the information boards with pictures of how much this area changed throughout the 20th century. The latest chapter: The shiny white gate was completely restored in 2002 (but you can still see faint patches marking war damage). The TI within the gate is open daily (April–Oct 9:30–18:00, Nov–March 10:00–18:00, S-Bahn: Unter den Linden).

The Brandenburg Gate, the center of old Berlin, sits on a major boulevard running east to west through Berlin. The western segment, called Strasse des 17 Juni (named for a workers' uprising against the DDR government in the 1950s), stretches for four miles from the Brandenburg Gate and Victory Column to the Olympic Stadium. But we'll follow this city axis in the opposite direction, east, walking along what is known as Unter den Linden—into the core of old imperial Berlin and past what was once the palace of the Hohenzollern family who ruled Prussia and then Germany. The palace—the reason for just about all you'll see—is a phantom sight, long gone (though some Berliners hope to rebuild it). Alexanderplatz, which marks the end of this walk, is near the base of the giant TV Tower hovering in the distance.

Ponder the fact that you're standing in what was the so-called "death strip." Now cross through the gate, into...

▲Pariser Platz—"Paris Square," so named after the Prussians defeated Napoleon in 1813, was once filled with important government buildings—all bombed to smithereens in World War II. For decades, it was an unrecognizable, deserted no-man's-land. But now, sparkling new banks, embassies (the French Embassy rebuilt where it was before WWII), a palace of coffee (Starbucks), and a swanky hotel have filled in the void. The winners of World War II got prime real estate: The American, French, British, and Soviet (now Russian) embassies are all on or near this square.

Face the gate and look to your left. The **US Embassy** once stood here, and a new one will stand in the same spot (due to be completed in 2008). This new embassy has been controversial; for safety's sake, Uncle Sam wanted it away from other buildings, but the Germans preferred it in its original location. A compromise was reached, building the embassy by the gate—but rerouting several major roads (at the expense of American taxpayers) to reduce the security risk. And, for good measure, there will be no front door to protect. Throughout the world, American embassies are the most fortified buildings in town. Taking security one step further, the US Embassy in Berlin will be reached by a tunnel that visitors will enter from the park across the big street opposite the Brandenburg Gate.

Just to the left, the **DZ Bank building** is by Frank Gehry, the unconventional American architect famous for Bilbao's organic Guggenheim Museum, Prague's Dancing House, Seattle's EMP, Chicago's Millennium Park, and Los Angeles' Walt Disney Concert Hall. Gehry fans might be surprised at the DZ Bank building's low profile. Structures on Pariser Platz are expected to be bland so as not to draw attention away from the Brandenburg Gate. (The glassy facade of the Academy of Arts, next to Gehry's building, is controversial for that very reason.) For your fix of the good old Gehry, step into the lobby and check out its undulating interior. It's a fish—and you feel like you're both inside and outside of it. Gehry's vision is explained on a nearby plaque.

The **Academy of Arts** (Akademie der Kunst), with its notorious glass facade, is next door. Its doors lead to a mall (daily 10:00–22:00), which leads directly to the vast...

▲▲Memorial to the Murdered Jews of Europe (Denkmal für die Ermordeten Juden Europas)—The new Holocaust memorial, consisting of 2,711 gravestone-like pillars and completed in 2005, is an essential stop for any visit to Berlin. This is the first formal German government-sponsored Holocaust memorial. Jewish-American architect Peter Eisenman won the competition for the commission (and built it on time and on budget—€27 million). It's controversial for its focus—just Jews. The government promises to make memorials to the other groups targeted by Hitler.

The pillars are made of hollow concrete, each chemically coated for easy removal of graffiti. The number of pillars, symbolic of nothing, is simply how many fit on the provided land.

Is it a labyrinth...symbolic cemetery...intentionally disorienting? The meaning is entirely up to the visitor to derive. The idea is for you to spend time pondering this horrible chapter in human history.

The pondering takes place under the sky. For the learning, you go under the field of concrete pillars to the state-of-the-art exhibition area. This studies the Nazi system of extermination, humanizes the victims, traces stories of individual families and collects vivid personal accounts, and lists 200 different places of genocide (all well-explained in English, free, Tue–Sun 10:00–20:00, closed Mon, last entry 45 min before closing, S-Bahn: Unter den Linden or Potsdamer Platz, tel. 030/2639-4336, www.stiftung-denkmal.de).

The location—where the Wall once stood—is coincidental.

It's just a place where lots of people will experience it. Nazi propagandist Joseph Goebbels' bunker was discovered during the work and left buried under the northeast corner of the memorial. Hitler's bunker is just 200 yard away, under a nondescript parking lot. Such Nazi sites are intentionally left hidden to discourage neo-Nazi's from creating a shrine.

Now backtrack to Pariser Platz, and begin strolling...

Along Unter den Linden

Unter den Linden, worth ▲▲, is the heart of former East Berlin. In Berlin's good old days, Unter den Linden was one of Europe's grand boulevards. In the 15th century, this carriageway led from the palace to the hunting grounds (today's big Tiergarten). In the 17th century, Hohenzollern princes and princesses moved in and built their palaces here so they could be near the Prussian emperor.

Named centuries ago for its thousand linden trees, this was the most elegant street of Prussian Berlin before Hitler's time, and the main drag of East Berlin after his reign. Hitler replaced the venerable trees—many 250 years old—with Nazi flags. Popular discontent actually drove him to replant linden trees. Today, Unter den Linden is no longer a depressing Cold War cul-de-sac, and its pre-Hitler strolling café ambience is returning.

➔ **Self-Guided Walk:** As you walk toward the giant TV Tower, the big building you see jutting out into the street on your right is the **Hotel Adlon.** It hosted such notables as Charlie Chaplin, Albert Einstein, and Greta Garbo. This was where Garbo said, "I want to be alone," during the filming of *Grand Hotel.* And, perhaps fresher in your memory, this is where Michael Jackson shocked millions by dangling his little baby over the railing (second balcony up, center of facade). Destroyed by Russians just after World War II, the grand Adlon was rebuilt in 1996. See how far you can get inside.

The Unter den Linden S-Bahn station ahead of you is one of Berlin's former **ghost subway stations.** During the Cold War, most underground train tunnels were simply blocked at the border. But a few Western lines looped through the East. To make a little hard Western cash, the Eastern government rented the use of these tracks to the West, but the stations (which happened to be in East Berlin) were strictly off-limits. For 28 years, the stations were unused, as Western trains slowly passed through, seeing only eerie DDR (East German) guards and lots of cobwebs. Literally within days of the fall of the Wall, these stations were reopened, and today they are a time warp (looking essentially as they did when built in 1931, with dreary old green tiles and original signage). Go down into the station, walk along the track (the walls

Unter den Linden

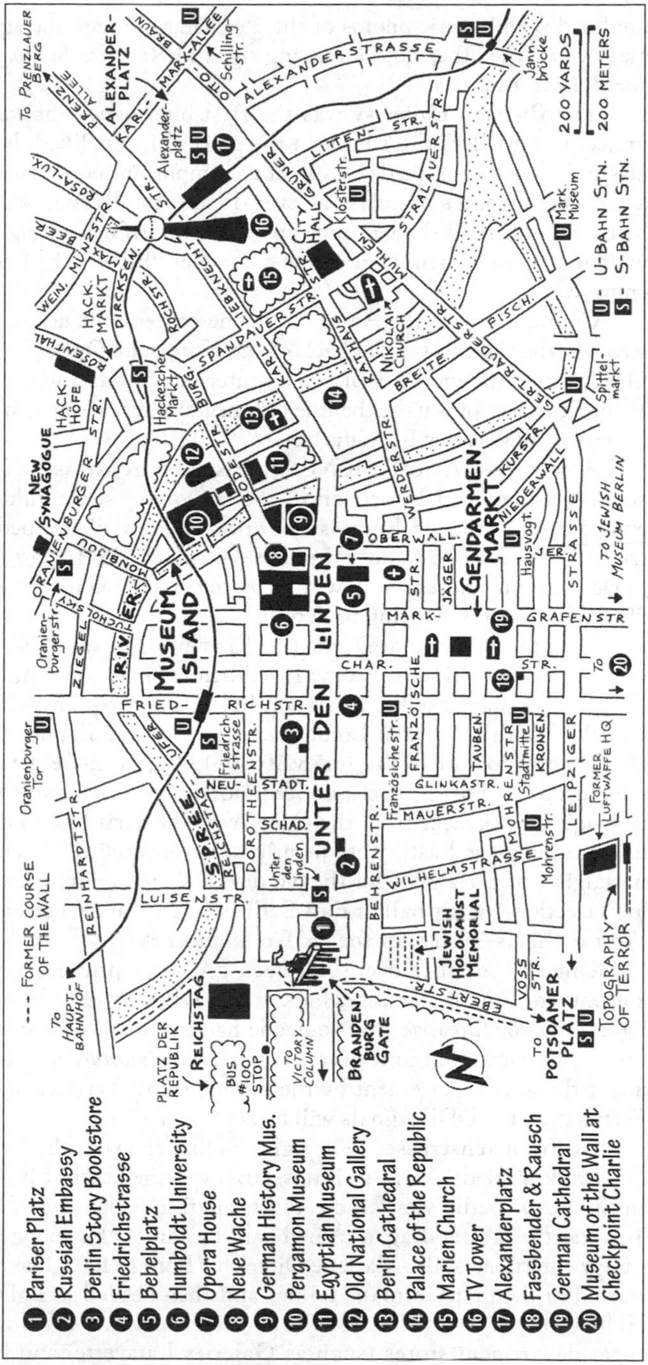

1 Pariser Platz
2 Russian Embassy
3 Berlin Story Bookstore
4 Friedrichstrasse
5 Bebelplatz
6 Humboldt University
7 Opera House
8 Neue Wache
9 German History Mus.
10 Pergamon Museum
11 Egyptian Museum
12 Old National Gallery
13 Berlin Cathedral
14 Palace of the Republic
15 Marien Church
16 TV Tower
17 Alexanderplatz
18 Fassbender & Rausch
19 German Cathedral
20 Museum of the Wall at Checkpoint Charlie
--- FORMER COURSE OF THE WALL
U- U-BAHN STN.
S- S-BAHN STN.
200 YARDS
200 METERS
UNTER DEN LINDEN
MUSEUM ISLAND
GENDARMENMARKT
ALEXANDERPLATZ
REICHSTAG
BRANDENBURG GATE
NEW SYNAGOGUE
JEWISH HOLOCAUST MEMORIAL
TOPOGRAPHY OF TERROR
FORMER LUFTWAFFE HQ
TO POTSDAMER PLATZ
TO VICTORY COLUMN
TO HAUPTBAHNHOF
TO PRENZLAUER BERG
TO JEWISH MUSEUM BERLIN
BUS #100 STOP
PLATZ DER REPUBLIK
SPREE RIVER
CITY HALL
NIKOLAI CHURCH
HACK. HÖFE
HACK. MARKT

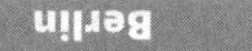

are lined with historic photos of the Reichstag through the ages), and exit on the other side, following signs to *Russische Botschaft...* the Russian Embassy.

The **Russian Embassy** was the first big postwar building project in East Berlin. It's built in the powerful, simplified, Neoclassical style Stalin liked. While not as important now as it was a few years ago, it's immense as ever. It flies the Russian white, blue, and red. Find the hammer-and-sickle motif decorating the window frames—a reminder of the days when this was the USSR embassy.

Continuing past the Aeroflot Airline offices, look across the street to the right to see the back of the **Komische Oper** (Comic Opera; program and view of ornate interior posted in window). While the exterior is ugly, the fine old theater interior—amazingly missed by WWII bombs—survives.

Across from Aeroflot is **Neustadtische Kirchstrasse.** This street is a commercial wasteland—the fate of any street unlucky enough to host the US Embassy. While cars are *verboten,* pedestrians are welcome to wander through. When the US Ambassador moves into his impressive new digs by the Brandenburg Gate in 2008, this street will spring back to life.

Back on the main drag, next to Einstein Café (at #40), is a great bookstore, **Berlin Story.** In addition to a wide range of English-language books, this shop has a free museum (with a model of 1930s Unter den Linden) and a 25-minute English film about the history of Berlin (daily 10:00–19:00; for more details, see page 512). This is also a good opportunity to pick up some nostalgic knickknacks from the Cold War. The West lost no time in consuming the East; consequently, some are feeling a wave of nostalgia—or *Ost*-algia—for the old days of East Berlin. In recent local elections, nearly half of East Berlin's voters—and 6 percent of West Berliners—voted for the old Communist Party.

One symbol of that era has been given a reprieve. As you continue to Friedrichstrasse, look at the DDR-style pedestrian lights, and you'll realize that someone had a sense of humor back then. The perky red and green men—***Ampelmännchen***—were under threat of replacement by the far less jaunty Western signs. Fortunately, the DDR signals will be kept after all.

At **Friedrichstrasse,** look right. Before the war, the Unter den Linden/Friedrichstrasse intersection was the heart of Berlin. In the 1920s, Berlin was famous for its anything-goes love of life. This was the cabaret drag, a springboard to stardom for young and vampy entertainers like Marlene Dietrich. (Born in 1901, Dietrich starred in the first German "talkie" and then headed straight to Hollywood.) Over the last few years, this boulevard—lined with super department stores (such as Galeries Lafayette) and big-time hotels (such as the Hilton and Regent)—has slowly begun to replace Ku'damm as the grand commerce and café boulevard of Berlin. (More recently, the West is retaliating with some new stores of its own.) Across from Galeries Lafayette is American Express (handy for any train-ticket needs—see page 512). Consider dropping into the Galeries Lafayette, with its cool marble and glass waste-of-space interior (Mon–Sat 9:30–20:00, closed Sun; belly up to its amazing ground-floor viewpoint, or have lunch in its cafeteria—see page 559).

If you continued down Friedrichstrasse, you'd wind up at the sights listed in "South of Unter den Linden," below—including the Museum of the Wall at Checkpoint Charlie (a 10-min walk from here). But for now, continue along Unter den Linden. You'll notice big, colorful **water pipes** around here, and throughout Berlin. As long as the city remains a big construction zone, it will be laced with these drainage pipes—key to any building project. Berlin's high water table means any new basement comes with lots of pumping out.

Continue down Unter den Linden a few more blocks, past the large equestrian statue of Frederick III ("the Great"), and turn right into the square called **Bebelplatz.** Stand on the glass window in the center.

Frederick the Great—who ruled from 1740 to 1786—established Prussia as a military power. This square was the center of the "new Rome" Frederick envisioned. His grand palace was just down the street (long since destroyed, but there's talk of rebuilding it—explained below).

Look down through the glass you're standing on (center of Bebelplatz): The room of empty bookshelves is a memorial to the notorious Nazi **book burning.** It was on this square in 1933 that staff and students from the university threw 20,000 newly forbidden books (like Einstein's) into a huge bonfire on the orders of the Nazi propaganda minister Joseph Goebbels. A memorial plaque nearby reminds us of the prophetic quote by the German Jewish philosopher Heinrich Heine. In 1820, he said, "When you start by burning books, you'll end by burning people." A century later, his books were among those that went up in flames on this spot.

Bebelplatz is bounded by great buildings. The **German State Opera** was bombed in 1941, rebuilt to bolster morale and to celebrate its centennial in 1943, and bombed again in 1945. The former **state library** is where Vladimir Lenin studied much of his exile away. If you climb to the second floor of the library and go through the door opposite the stairs, you can see a stained-glass window depicting Lenin's life's work with almost biblical reverence. On the ground floor is a great little student café with light food, Tim's Canadian Deli (student prices—€2 plates, garden seating, Mon–Sat 7:00–20:00, closed

Sun). The round, Catholic **St. Hedwig's Church**—nicknamed the "upside-down teacup"—was built to placate the subjects of Catholic lands Frederick added to his empire. (Step inside to see the cheesy DDR government renovation.)

Humboldt University, across Unter den Linden, was one of Europe's greatest. Marx and Lenin (not the brothers or the sisters) studied here, as did Grimm (both brothers) and more than two dozen Nobel Prize winners. Einstein, who was Jewish, taught here until taking a spot at Princeton in 1932 (smart guy).

Continue down Unter den Linden. The next square on your right holds the **Opera House.** The Opernpalais, preening with fancy prewar elegance, hosts a number of pricey restaurants. Its Operncafé, with the best desserts and the longest dessert bar in Europe, is popular with Berliners for their *Kaffee und Kuchen* (see page 558).

On the university side, the Greek temple-like building set in the small, chestnut tree–filled park is the **Neue Wache** (the emperor's "New Guardhouse," from 1816). When the Wall fell, this memorial to the victims of fascism was transformed into a new national memorial. Look inside, where a replica of the Käthe Kollwitz statue, *Mother with Her Dead Son,* is surrounded by thought-provoking silence. This marks the tombs of Germany's unknown soldier and the unknown concentration camp victim. The inscription in front reads, "To the victims of war and tyranny." Read the entire statement in English (on wall, left of entrance). The memorial, open to the sky, incorporates the elements—sunshine, rain, snow—falling on this modern-day *pietà.*

After the Neue Wache, the next building you'll see is Berlin's pink-yet-formidable Zeughaus, or arsenal. Dating from 1695, it's considered the oldest building on the boulevard. It houses the **German History Museum** (Deutsches Historisches Museum, €4, daily 10:00–13:00, €2.50 audioguide, tel. 030/2030-4751, www.dhm.de). It's a two-part affair: the pink former Prussian arsenal building (reopened in June 2006 following a major renovation), and the I. M. Pei–designed annex (opened in 2004 to house temporary exhibits).

The main building houses the permanent collection. Two huge rectangular floors are packed with more than 8,000 artifacts telling the story of Berlin—making this the top history museum in town. Historical objects, photographs, and models are intermingled with multimedia stations to help put everything in context. The first floor traces German history from 1 B.C. to 1918, with exhibits on early cultures, the Middle Ages, Reformation, Thirty Years' War, German Empire, and First World War. Exhibits on the second floor continue with the Weimar Republic, Nazism, World War II, Allied occupation, and divided Germany, wrapping up with reunification and a quick look at Germany today.

During the main building's multi-year renovation, the big attraction was the far-out architecture in the *Pei-Bau* (Pei Building). From the old building (with the Pei glass canopy over its courtyard), take a tunnel to the new wing, emerging under a striking glass spiral staircase that unites four floors with surprising views and lots of light. It's here that you'll experience why Pei—famous for his glass pyramid at Paris' Louvre—is called the "perfector of classical modernism," "master of light," and a magician of uniting historical buildings with new ones. (If you can't get in through the arsenal, venture down the street—Hinter dem Giesshaus—to the left of the museum to see the Pei annex.)

Next, Unter den Linden crosses the **Spree River.** Just before the bridge, wander left along the canal through a tiny but colorful arts-and-crafts market (weekends only; a larger flea market is just outside the Pergamon Museum—see below). Canal tour boats leave from here (€7, 1 hour, departures on the half-hour, tour in German only but so lame it hardly matters). Then go back out to the main road and cross the bridge to...

Museum Island (Museumsinsel)

This island, home of Germany's first museums, is gradually being renovated to consolidate the art collections of East and West Berlin. Today it plays host to three great museums: the Pergamon (classical antiquities), the Altes Museum (housing the Egyptian Museum, with the bust of Queen Nefertiti), and the Old National Gallery (19th-century German Romantic painting). Closed for repairs since 1997, a fourth museum—the **Bode Museum,** with its collection of sculptures, coins, and Byzantine art—was scheduled to reopen here in late fall of 2006 (daily 10:00–18:00, confirm at the TI, or check www.smb.museum.de). The nearest S-Bahn station is Hackescher Markt.

All of these museums are covered by the €15 Museumspass (see page 509) or a single €12 Museum Island ticket *(Standortkarte Museumsinsel)*. Individual admissions are €8 each. Visit any of these museums, and other Museum Island attractions, before continuing our walk. Once you're finished, skip down to "Museum Island to Alexanderplatz," page 533, to resume the self-guided tour.

For 300 years, the island's big central square, the **Lustgarten,** has flip-flopped between being a military parade ground and a people-friendly park, depending upon the political tenor of the time. In 1999, it was made into a park again (read the history posted in corner opposite church). On a sunny day, it's packed with relaxing locals and is one of Berlin's most enjoyable public spaces.

▲▲Pergamon Museum—This world-class museum, part of Berlin's Collection of Classical Antiquities (Antikensammlung), stars the fantastic Pergamon Altar. From a second-century B.C. Greek temple, the altar shows the Greeks under Zeus and Athena beating the giants in a dramatic pig pile of mythological mayhem. Check out the action spilling onto the stairs. The Babylonian Ishtar Gate (glazed blue tiles from the sixth century B.C.) and many ancient Greek and Mesopotamian treasures are also impressive (€8, also covered by €12 Museum Island ticket or €15 Museumspass, free Thu after 18:00, open Tue–Sun 10:00–18:00, Thu until 22:00, closed Mon, courtyard café, Am Kupfergraben, tel. 030/2090-5577). The excellent audioguide (free with admission, but €4 during free Thu extended hours) covers the museum's highlights. Don't mind the scaffolding. Renovation projects (due to last until 2008) may cause small sections of the museum to close temporarily, but the museum will remain open.

▲▲Egyptian Museum (Ägyptisches Museum)—Showing off one of the world's top collections of Egyptian art, this wonderfully presented new museum fills the second floor of Berlin's Altes Museum (Old Museum), facing the grassy Lustgarten park (€8, also covered by €12 Museum Island ticket or €15 Museumspass, free Thu after 18:00, open daily 10:00–18:00, Thu until 22:00, Am Lustgarten, tel. 030/343-5730).

The curator welcomes you on the included audioguide and encourages a broader approach to the museum than just seeing its claim to fame, the bust of Queen Nefertiti (described below). The fine audioguide celebrates new knowledge about ancient Egyptian civilization and offers fascinating insights into workaday Egyptian life as it describes the vivid papyrus collection, slice-of-life artifacts, and dreamy wax portraits decorating mummy cases.

But let's face it: The main reason to visit is to enjoy one of the great thrills in art appreciation—gazing into the still-young-and-beautiful face of 3,000-year-old Queen Nefertiti, the wife of King Akhenaton. This bust of Queen Nefertiti (c. 1340 B.C.) is the most famous piece of Egyptian art in Europe. Discovered in 1912, Nefertiti—with all the right beauty marks: long neck, symmetrical face, and just the right makeup—is called "Berlin's most beautiful woman." The bust never left its studio, but served as a master model for all other portraits of the queen. (That's probably why the left eye was never inlaid.) Buried for over 3,000 years, she was found in the early 1900s by a German team who, by agreement with the Egyptian government, got to take home any workshop models they found. Although this bust is not particularly representative of Egyptian art in general, it has become a symbol for Egyptian art by popular acclaim.

Old National Gallery (Alte Nationalgalerie)—This gallery, behind the Egyptian Museum/Altes Museum, shows 19th-century German Romantic art: man against nature, Greek ruins dwarfed in enchanted forests, medieval churches, and powerful mountains (€8, also covered by €12 Museum Island ticket or €15 Museumspass, free Thu after 18:00, open Tue–Sun 10:00–18:00, Thu until 20:00, closed Mon, Bodestrasse 1–3, tel. 030/2090-5801).

Berlin Cathedral (Berliner Dom)—This century-old church towers over Museum Island (€5 includes access to dome gallery, not covered by Museum Island ticket, Mon–Sat 9:00–20:00, Sun 12:00–20:00, until 19:00 in winter, www.berliner-dom.de; many organ concerts offered each week, ticket office on Lustgarten side, daily 10:00–18:00, tel. 030/2026-9136). Inside, the great reformers (Luther, Calvin, and company) stand around the brilliantly restored dome like stern saints guarding their theology. Frederick I rests in an ornate tomb (right transept, near entrance to dome). The 270-step climb to the outdoor dome gallery is tough, but offers pleasant, breezy views of the city at the finish line (last entry 45 min before closing). The crypt downstairs is not worth a look.

Across Unter den Linden is a construction site that once held the decrepit **Palace of the Republic**—formerly East Berlin's parliament building/futuristic entertainment complex, and a symbol of the communist days. Much of Frederick the Great's earlier palace actually survived World War II, but was replaced by the communists with a blocky Soviet-style building. The landmark building fell into disrepair after reunification, and was eventually torn down in 2006. After long debate, the German Parliament has decided to rebuild the old palace...when funding becomes available. In the meantime, the area will be turned into a park.

Museum Island to Alexanderplatz

Continue walking down Unter den Linden. Before crossing the bridge (and leaving Museum Island), look right. The pointy twin spires of the 13th-century Nikolai Church mark the center of medieval Berlin. This Nikolai-Viertel (district) was restored by the DDR and was trendy in the last years of socialism. Today it's a lively-at-night riverside restaurant district.

As you cross the bridge, look left in the distance to see the gilded **New Synagogue dome,** rebuilt after WWII bombing (see page 539). Across the river to the left of the bridge is the giant SAS Radisson Hotel and shopping center, with a huge aquarium in the center. The elevator goes right through the middle of an undersea world (you can see it from the Radisson lobby). Here in the center of the old communist capital, it seems capitalism has settled in with a spirited vengeance.

Across the street, in the park, are grandfatherly statues of Marx and Engels (nicknamed by locals "the old pensioners"). Surrounding them are stainless-steel monoliths depicting the struggles of the workers of the world. Walk toward

Marien Church (from 1270, interesting but very faded old *Dance of Death* mural inside door) at the base of the TV Tower. The big, red-brick building past the trees on the right is the **City Hall,** built after the revolution of 1848 and arguably the first democratic building in the city.

The 1,200-foot-tall **TV Tower** (Fernsehturm) offers a fine view from halfway up (€7.50, daily March–Oct 9:00–1:00 in the morning, Nov–Feb 10:00–24:00). The tower offers a handy city orientation and an interesting view of the flat, red-roofed sprawl of Berlin—including a peek inside the city's many courtyards *(Höfe).* Consider a kitschy trip to the observation deck for the view and lunch in its revolving restaurant (mediocre food, €12 plates, horrible lounge music, reservations smart for dinner, tel. 030/242-3333). It's very retro and somewhat trendy these days, so expect a line if you ascend. Built (with Swedish know-how) in 1969, the tower was meant to show the power of the atheistic state at a time when DDR leaders were having the crosses removed from church domes and spires. But when the sun shined on their tower—the greatest spire in East Berlin—a huge cross was reflected on the mirrored ball. Cynics called it "The Pope's Revenge." East Berliners dubbed the tower the "Big Asparagus." They joked that if it fell over, they'd have an elevator to the West.

Farther east, pass under the train tracks into **Alexanderplatz.** This area—especially the Kaufhof department store—was the commercial pride and joy of East Berlin. Today, it's still a landmark, with a major U- and S-Bahn station.

Our orientation stroll is finished. For a ride through workaday eastern Berlin, with its Lego-hell apartments (dreary even with their new face-lifts), hop back on bus #100 from here. It loops five minutes to the end of the line and then, after a couple minutes' break, heads on back. (This bus retraces your route, finishing at Bahnhof Zoo.) Or consider extending this foray into eastern Berlin to...

Karl-Marx-Allee

The buildings along Karl-Marx-Allee in East Berlin (just beyond Alexanderplatz) were completely leveled by the Red Army in 1945. When Stalin decided this main drag should be a showcase street, he had it rebuilt with lavish Soviet aid, and named it Stalin Allee. Today this street, done in the bold "Stalin Gothic" style so common in Moscow in the 1950s, has been restored, re-named after Karl Marx, and lined with "workers' palaces"—providing a rare look at Berlin's communist days. Distances are a bit long for convenient walking, but you can cruise Karl-Marx-Allee by taxi, or ride the U-Bahn to Strausberger Platz and walk to Frankfurter Tor. Notice the Social Realist reliefs on the buildings and the lampposts, which incorporate the wings of a phoenix (rising from the ashes) in their design.

The **Café Sibylle,** just beyond the Strausberger Platz U-Bahn station, is a fun spot for a coffee, traditional DDR ice-cream treats, and a look at its free, informal museum that tells the story of the most destroyed street in Berlin. While the humble exhibit is nearly all in German, it's fun to see the ear and half a moustache from what was the largest statue of Stalin in Germany (the centerpiece of the street until 1961) and a few intimate insights into apartment life in a DDR flat. The café is known for its good coffee and *Schwedeneisbecher mit Eierlikor*—an ice-cream sundae with a shot of liquor, popular among those nostalgic for communism (daily 10:00–20:00, Karl-Marx-Allee 72, at intersection with Koppenstrasse, a block from U-Bahn: Strausberger Platz, tel. 030/2935-2203).

Heading out to Karl-Marx-Allee (just beyond the TV Tower), you're likely to notice a giant colorful **mural** decorating a blocky communist-era skyscraper. This was the Ministry of Education, and the mural is a tile mosaic trumpeting the accomplishments of the DDR's version of "No Child Left Behind."

South of Unter den Linden

The following sights—heavy on Nazi and Wall history—are listed roughly north to south (as you reach them from Unter den Linden).

▲▲Gendarmenmarkt—This delightful and historic square is bounded by twin churches, a tasty chocolate shop, and the Berlin Symphony's concert hall (designed by Schinkel, the man who put the Neoclassical stamp on Berlin). In summer, it hosts a few outdoor cafés, *Biergarten*s, and sometimes concerts. The name of the square—part French and part German—reminds us that in the 17th century, a fifth of all Berliners were French émigrés, Protestant Huguenots fleeing Catholic France. Back then, tolerant Berlin was a magnet for the persecuted. The émigrés vitalized the city with new ideas and know-how.

The German Cathedral (described below) on the square has an exhibit worthwhile for history buffs. The French Cathedral (Französischer Dom) offers a humble museum on the Huguenots and a chance to climb 254 steps to the top for a grand city view (€2, Tue–Sat 12:00–17:00, Sun 11:00–17:00, closed Mon, U-Bahn: Französische Strasse or Stadtmitte).

Fassbender & Rausch, on the corner near the German Cathedral, claims to be Europe's biggest chocolate store. After 150 years of chocolate-making, this family-owned business proudly displays its sweet delights—250 different kinds—on a 55-foot-long buffet. Truffles are sold for about €0.50 each (Mon–Fri 10:00–20:00, Sat 10:00–18:00, Sun 12:00–20:00, corner of Mohrenstrasse at Charlottenstrasse 60, tel. 030/2045-8440).

Gendarmenmarkt is buried in what has recently emerged as Berlin's new "Fifth Avenue" shopping district. For the ultimate in top-end shops, find the corner of Jägerstrasse and Französische Strasse and wander through the Quartier 206 (Mon–Fri 10:30–19:30, Sat 10:00–18:00, closed Sun, www.quartier206.com).

German Cathedral (Deutscher Dom)—This cathedral, bombed flat in the war and rebuilt only in the 1980s, houses the thought-provoking *Milestones, Setbacks, Sidetracks (Wege, Irrwege, Umwege)* exhibit, which traces the history of the German parliamentary system. The exhibit—while light on actual historical artifacts—is well done and more interesting than it sounds. It takes you quickly from the revolutionary days of 1848 to the 1920s, and then more deeply through the tumultuous 20th century. There are no English descriptions, but you can follow the essential, excellent, and free 90-minute English-language audioguide or buy the wonderfully detailed €10 guidebook. If this museum seems to be an attempt by the German government to develop a more sophisticated and educated electorate in the interest of stronger democracy, it is. Germany knows (from its own troubled history) that a dumbed-down electorate, manipulated by clever spin-meisters and sound-bite media blitzes, is a dangerous thing (free; May–Sept Tue–Sun 10:00–19:00, Tue until 22:00, closed Mon; Oct–April Tue–Sun 10:00–18:00, Tue until 22:00, closed Mon; on Gendarmenmarkt just off Friedrichstrasse, tel. 030/2273-0431).

▲▲▲Museum of the Wall at Checkpoint Charlie (Mauermuseum Haus am Checkpoint Charlie)—While the famous border checkpoint between the American and Soviet sectors is long gone, its memory is preserved by one of Europe's most interesting, though cluttered, museums. During the Cold War, the House at Checkpoint Charlie stood defiantly—spitting distance from the border guards—showing off all the clever escapes over, under, and through the Wall. Today, while the drama is over and hunks of the Wall stand like victory scalps at its door, the museum still tells a gripping history of the Wall, recounts the many ingenious escape attempts (early years—with a cruder wall—saw more escapes), and includes plenty of video coverage of those heady days when people-power tore down the Wall (€9.50, assemble 10 tourists and get in for €5.50 each, €3 audioguide, discount with WelcomeCard but not covered by Museumspass, cash only, daily 9:00–22:00, U-6 to Kochstrasse or—better from Zoo—U-2 to Stadtmitte, Friedrichstrasse 43–45, tel. 030/253-7250, www.mauermuseum.de). If you're pressed for time, this is a good after-dinner sight. With extra time, consider the "Hear We Go" audioguide about the Wall that takes you outside the museum (€7.50, 80 min, leave ID as deposit).

Where Checkpoint Charlie once stood, notice the thought-provoking post with larger-than-life posters of a young American soldier facing east and a young Soviet soldier facing west. Around you are reconstructions of the old checkpoint. It's not named for a person, but because it was checkpoint number three—as in Alpha (at the East–West German border, a hundred miles west of here), Bravo (as you enter Berlin proper), and Charlie (the most famous because it was the only one where foreigners could pass). A few yards away (on Zimmerstrasse), a glass panel describes the former checkpoint. From there, a double row of cobbles in Zimmerstrasse traces the former path of the Wall. These innocuous cobbles run throughout the city, even through some modern buildings. Follow the cobbles one very long block to Wilhelmstrasse, a surviving stretch of Wall, and the...

Topography of Terror (Topographie des Terrors)—The park behind the Zimmerstrasse/Wilhelmstrasse bit of Wall marks the site of the command center of Hitler's Gestapo and SS. Because of the horrible things planned here, the rubble of these buildings will always be left as rubble. The SS, Hitler's personal bodyguards, grew to become a state-within-a-state, with its talons in every corner of German society. Along an excavated foundation of the building, an exhibit tells the story of National Socialism and its victims in Berlin (free, info booth open daily May–Sept 10:00–20:00, Oct–April 10:00–18:00 or until dark, tel. 030/2548-6703, www.topographie.de). All of the posted information is in German, so the free English-language audioguide is essential (available only until 18:45 in summer).

Across the street (facing the Wall) is the **German Finance Ministry** (Bundesministerium der Finanzen). Formerly the headquarters of the Nazi Luftwaffe (Air Force), this is the only major Hitler-era government building that survived the war's bombs. The communists used it to house their—no joke—Ministry of Ministries. Walk up Wilhelmstrasse (to the north) to see an entry gate (on your left) that looks much like it did when Germany occupied nearly all of Europe. On the north side of the building (farther up Wilhelmstrasse, at corner with Leipziger Strasse) is a wonderful example of communist art. The mural, from the 1950s, is classic Social Realism, showing the entire society—industrial laborers, farm workers, women, and children—all happily singing the same patriotic song. This was the communist ideal. For the reality, look at the ground in the courtyard in front of the mural to see an enlarged photograph from a 1953 uprising here against the communists—quite a contrast.

▲▲▲Jewish Museum Berlin (Jüdisches Museum Berlin)—This museum is one of Europe's best Jewish sights. The highly conceptual building is a sight in itself, and the museum inside—an overview of the rich culture and history of Europe's Jewish community—is excellent. The Holocaust is appropriately remembered, but it doesn't overwhelm this celebration of Jewish life.

Designed by American architect Daniel Libeskind (who is re-developing New York City's World Trade Center site), the zinc-walled building's zigzag shape is pierced by voids symbolic of the irreplaceable cultural loss caused by the Holocaust. Enter through the 18th-century Baroque building next door, then go through an underground tunnel to reach the museum interior.

Before you get to the exhibit, your visit starts with three memorial spaces. Underground, follow the Axis of Exile to a disorienting slanted garden with 49 pillars. Then the Axis of Holocaust leads to an eerily empty tower shut off from the outside world. A detour near the bottom of the long stairway leads to the "Memory Void," a thought-provoking space of "fallen leaves": heavy metal faces that you walk on, making un-human noises with each step.

Finally, climb the stairs to the top of the museum, from where you stroll chronologically through the 2,000-year story of Judaism in Germany. The exhibit, on two floors, is engaging. Interactive bits (for example, spell your name in Hebrew) make it lively for kids. English explanations interpret both the exhibits and the design of the very symbolic building. Even though the museum is in a nondescript residential neighborhood (a 10-min walk from the Hallesches Tor U-Bahn station or the Checkpoint Charlie museum), it's well worth the trip (€5, covered by Museumspass, discount with WelcomeCard, daily 10:00–20:00, Mon until 22:00, last entry 1 hour before closing, closed on Jewish holidays, tight security includes bag check and metal detectors; U-Bahn line 1, 6, or 15 to Hallesches Tor, take exit marked *Jüdisches Museum,* exit straight ahead, then turn right on Franz-Klühs-Strasse, museum is 5 min ahead on your left at Lindenstrasse 9; tel. 030/2599-3300, www.juedisches-museum-berlin.de). The museum has a good café/restaurant (€9 daily specials, lunch 12:00–16:00, snacks at other times, tel. 030/2593-9760).

East Side Gallery—The biggest remaining stretch of the Wall is now "the world's longest outdoor art gallery." It stretches for nearly a mile and is covered with murals painted by artists from around the world. The murals are routinely whitewashed so new ones can be painted. This segment of the Wall makes a poignant walk. For a quick look, take the S-Bahn to the Ostbahnhof station (follow signs to *Stralauerplatz* exit; once outside, TV Tower will be to your right; go left and at next corner look to your right—the Wall is across the busy street). The gallery only survives until a land-ownership dispute can be solved, when it will likely be developed like the rest of the city. (Given the recent history, imagine the complexity of finding rightful owners of all this suddenly-very-valuable land.) If you walk the entire length of the East Side Gallery, you'll find a small Wall souvenir shop at the end and a bridge crossing the river to a subway station at Schlesisches Tor (in Kreuzberg).

Kreuzberg—This district—once abutting the dreary Wall and inhabited mostly by poor Turkish guest laborers and their families—is still run-down, with graffiti-riddled buildings and plenty of student and Turkish street life. It offers a gritty look at melting-pot Berlin, in a city where original Berliners are as rare as old buildings. Berlin is the fourth-largest Turkish city in the world, and Kreuzberg is its "downtown." But to call it a "little Istanbul" insults the big one. You'll see *Döner Kebab* stands, shops decorated with spray paint, and mothers wrapped in colorful scarves looking like they just got off a donkey in Anatolia. But lately, an influx of immigrants from many other countries has diluted the Turkishness of Kreuzberg. Berliners come here for fun ethnic eateries. For a dose of Kreuzberg without getting your fingers dirty, joyride on bus #129 (catch it near Jewish Museum). For a colorful stroll, take the U-Bahn to Kottbusser Tor and wander—ideally on Tuesday and Friday between 12:00 and 18:00, when the Turkish Market sprawls along the Maybachufer riverbank.

North of Unter den Linden

While there are few major sights to the north of Unter den Linden, this area has some of Berlin's trendiest, most interesting neighborhoods.

▲▲New Synagogue (Neue Synagogue)—A shiny gilded dome marks the New Synagogue, now a museum and cultural center on Oranienburger Strasse. Only the dome and facade have been restored—a window overlooks the vacant field marking what used to be the synagogue. The largest and finest synagogue in Berlin before World War II, it was desecrated by Nazis on "Crystal Night" (Kristallnacht) in 1938, bombed in 1943, and partially rebuilt in 1990. Inside, past tight security, there's a small but moving exhibit on the Berlin Jewish community through the centuries with some good English descriptions (ground floor and first floor). On its facade, the *Vergesst es nie* message—added by East Berlin Jews in 1966—means "Never forget." East Berlin had only a few hundred Jews, but now that the city is united, the Jewish community numbers about 12,000 (€3; April–Sept Sun–Mon 10:00–20:00, Tue–Thu 10:00–18:00, Fri 10:00–17:00, closed Sat; March and Oct Sun–Mon 10:00–20:00, Tue–Thu 10:00–18:00, Fri 10:00–14:00, closed Sat; Nov–Feb Sun–Thu 10:00–18:00, Fri 10:00–14:00, closed Sat; last entry 30 min before closing, Oranienburger Strasse 28/30, U-Bahn: Oranienburger Tor, tel. 030/8802-8300 and press 1, www.cjudaicum.de).

A block from the synagogue, walk 50 yards down Grosse Hamburger Strasse to a little park. This street was known for 200 years as the "street of tolerance" because the Jewish community donated land to Protestants so that they could build a church. Hitler turned it into the "street of death" *(Todes Strasse)*, bulldozing 12,000 graves of the city's oldest Jewish cemetery and turning a Jewish nursing home into a deportation center. Note the two memorials—one erected by the former East Berlin government, the other built later by the city's unified government. With the small but persistent neo-Nazi element still a problem in Berlin, a plainclothes police officer keeps watch over this park somewhere nearby.

▲Oranienburger Strasse—Berlin is developing so fast, it's impossible to predict what will be "in" next year. The area around Oranienburger Strasse is definitely trendy (but is being challenged by hip Friedrichshain, farther east, and Prenzlauer Berg, described below). While the area immediately around the synagogue is dull, 100 yards away things get colorful. The streets behind Grosse Hamburger Strasse flicker with atmospheric cafés, *Kneipen* (pubs), and art galleries. At night (from about 20:00), techno-prostitutes line Oranienburger Strasse. Prostitution is legal here, but there's a big debate about taxation. Since they don't get unemployment insurance, why should they pay taxes?

Hackescher Markt—This neighborhood, near Oranienburger Strasse, is worth exploring. A block in front of the Hackescher Markt S-Bahn station is **Hackesche Höfe,** with eight courtyards bunny-hopping through a wonderfully restored 1907 *Jugendstil* building (www.hackesche-hoefe.com). Berlin's apartments are organized like this—courtyard after courtyard leading off the main roads. This complex is full of trendy restaurants (including a good Turkish place, Hasir—see page 559), theaters, and cinema (playing movies in their original languages). This is a wonderful example of how to make huge city blocks livable.

▲Prenzlauer Berg—Young, in-the-know locals agree that "Prenzl'berg" is one of Berlin's most colorful neighborhoods (roughly between Helmholtzplatz and Kollwitzplatz and along Kastanienallee, U-Bahn: Senefelderplatz and Eberswalder Strasse; or take the S-Bahn to Hackescher Markt and catch the M1 tram north). This part of the city was largely untouched during World War II, but its buildings slowly rotted away under the communists. Since the Wall fell, it's been overrun with laid-back hipsters, energetic young families, and clever entrepreneurs who are breathing life back into its classic old apartment blocks, deserted factories, and long-forgotten breweries. While no longer "up-and-coming," and on the road to gentrification, Prenzlauer Berg is a celebration of life and a joy to stroll through. The area feels strangely wholesome and family-friendly, as former ruffians with tattoos, piercings, and an appetite for the cutting-edge life are now responsible young parents. Though it's a few blocks farther out than the neighborhoods described above, it's a fun area to explore and have a meal (see page 559) or spend the night (see page 553).

Natural History Museum (Museum für Naturkunde)—This museum is worth a visit just to see the largest dinosaur skeleton ever assembled. While you're there, meet "Bobby" the stuffed ape (€3.50, Tue–Fri 9:30–17:00, Sat–Sun 10:00–18:00, closed Mon, last entry 30 min before closing, U-Bahn line 6 to Zinnowitzer Strasse, Invalidenstrasse 43, tel. 030/2093-8591, www.museum.hu-berlin.de).

Berlin Wall Documentation Center (Dokumentationszentrum Berliner Mauer)—The last surviving complete "Wall system" (with both sides of its Wall and its no-man's-land, or "death strip," all still intact) is now part of a sober little memorial and "Doku-Center." While it's really directed at German-speakers and far from other sights, it's handy enough to the S-Bahn that any Wall aficionado will find it worth a quick visit. The Documentation Center has a photo gallery and rooftop viewpoint (accessible by elevator), from which you can view the "Wall system." It's poignantly located where a church was destroyed to make way for the Wall; today a memorial chapel has been built where the church once stood (free, April–Oct Tue–Sun 10:00–18:00, Nov–March until 17:00, closed Mon year-round, Bernauer Strasse 111, tel. 030/464-1030, www.berliner-mauer-dokumentationszentrum.de). Take the S-Bahn to Nordbahnhof and walk 200 yards along Bernauer Strasse, which is still lined with a long chunk of Wall.

Central Berlin

Tiergarten Park

Berlin's "Central Park" stretches two miles from Bahnhof Zoo to the Brandenburg Gate.

Victory Column (Siegessäule)—The Tiergarten's centerpiece, the Victory Column, was built to commemorate the Prussian defeat of France in 1870. The pointy-helmeted Germans rubbed it in, decorating the tower with French cannons and paying for it all with francs received as war reparations. The three lower rings commemorate Bismarck's victories. I imagine the statues of Moltke and other German military greats—which lurk in the trees nearby—goose-stepping around the floodlit angel at night. Originally standing at the Reichstag, the immense tower was moved to this position by Hitler in 1938 to complement his anticipated victory parades. Streets leading to the circle are flanked by surviving Nazi guardhouses—built in the bold style that fascists loved. At the memorial's first level, notice how WWII bullets

Central Berlin

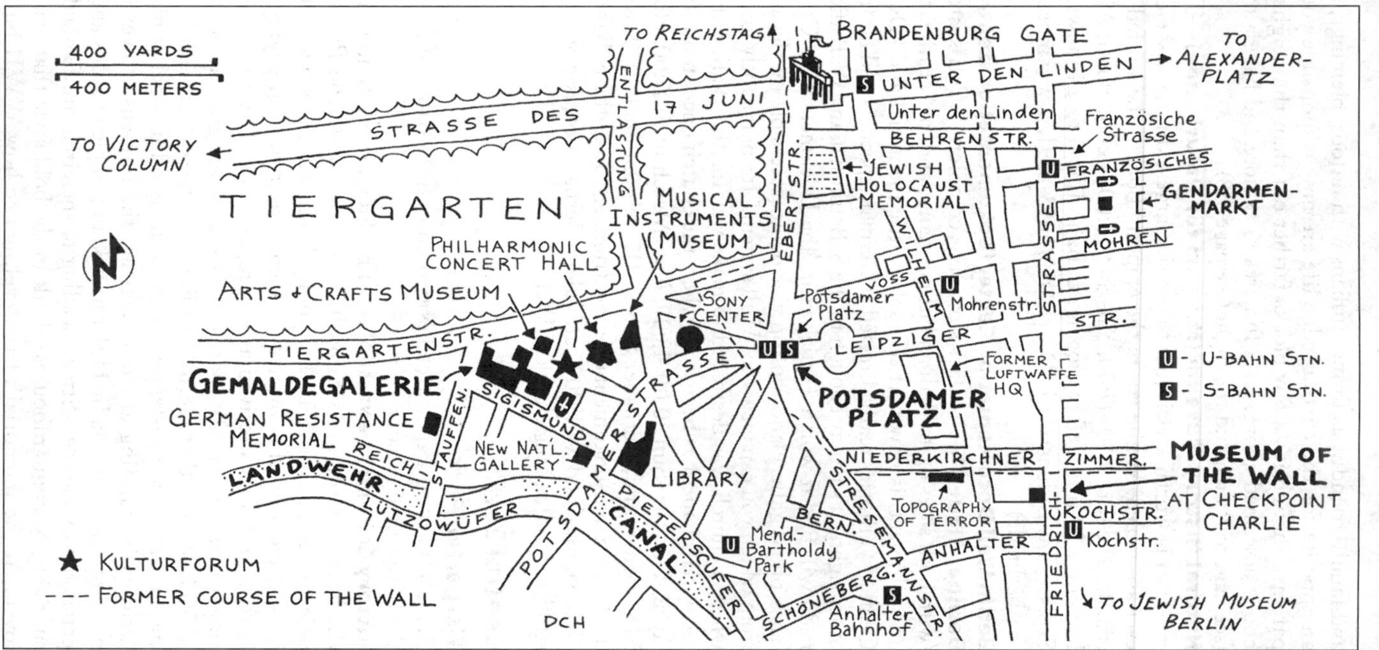

chipped the fine marble columns. Climbing its 285 steps earns you a breathtaking Berlin-wide view and a close-up look at the gilded angel that starred in the 1993 U2 video for their song "Stay (Faraway, so Close)" (€2.20; April–Sept Mon–Thu 9:30–18:30, Fri–Sun 9:30–19:00; Oct–March daily 9:30–17:30; closes in the rain, WCs for paying guests only, no elevator, bus #100, tel. 030/8639-8560). From the tower, the grand Strasse des 17 Juni leads east to the Brandenburg Gate.

Flea Market—A colorful flea market with great antiques, more than 200 stalls, collector-savvy merchants, and fun German fast-food stands thrives weekends beyond the Victory Column on Strasse des 17 Juni (Sat–Sun 6:00–16:00, S-Bahn: Tiergarten).

German Resistance Memorial (Gedenkstätte Deutscher Widerstand)—This memorial and museum, just south of the Tiergarten, tells the story of the German resistance to Hitler. The Bendlerblock was a military headquarters where an ill-fated attempt to assassinate Hitler was plotted (the actual attempt occurred in Rastenburg, eastern Prussia). Stauffenberg and his co-conspirators were shot here in the courtyard. While posted explanations are in German only, the spirit that haunts the place is multilingual (free, Mon–Fri 9:00–18:00, Thu until 20:00, Sat–Sun 10:00–18:00, free and good English audioguide with passport, €3 printed English translation, no crowds, near Kulturforum at Stauffenbergstrasse 13, enter in courtyard, door on left, main exhibit is on third floor, bus #M29, tel. 030/2699-5000).

Potsdamer Platz

The "Times Square" of Berlin, and possibly the busiest square in Europe before World War II, Potsdamer Platz was cut in two by the Wall and left a deserted no-man's-land for 40 years. Today, this immense commercial/residential/entertainment center, sitting on a futuristic transportation hub, is home to the European corporate headquarters of several big-league companies.

The new Potsdamer Platz was a vision begun in 1991, when it was announced that Berlin would resume its position as capital of Germany. Sony, Daimler-Chrysler, and other major corporations have turned the square once again into a center of Berlin. Like great Christian churches were built upon pagan holy grounds, Potsdamer Platz—with its corporate logos flying high and shiny above what was the Wall—trumpets the triumph of capitalism.

While Potsdamer Platz tries to give Berlin a common center, the city has always been—and remains—a collection of towns. Locals recognize 28 distinct neighborhoods that may have grown together but still maintain their historic orientation. While Munich has the single dominant Marienplatz, Berlin will always have Charlottenburg, Savignyplatz, Kreuzberg, Prenzlauer Berg, and so on. In general, Berliners prefer these characteristic neighborhoods. They're unimpressed by the grandeur of Potsdamer Platz, and consider it simply a good place for movies, with overpriced, touristy restaurants.

While most of the complex just feels big (the arcade is like any huge, modern, American mall), the entrance to the complex and Sony Center Platz are worth a visit.

For an overview of the new construction, and a scenic route to Sony Center Platz, start at the Bahnhof Potsdamer Platz (east end of Potsdamer Strasse, S- and U-Bahn: Potsdamer Platz). Find the green hexagonal clock tower with the traffic lights on top. This is a replica of the first automatic **traffic light** in Europe, which once stood at the six-street intersection of Potsdamer Platz. On either side of Potsdamer Strasse, you'll see enormous cubical entrances to the new underground Potsdamer Platz train station. Near these entrances, notice the slanted **glass cylinders** sticking out of the ground. The mirrors on the tops of the tubes move with the sun to collect light and send it underground. Notice the slabs of the Wall re-erected where the Wall once stood. The single slab marks the spot where the first piece was cut out (see photo and history on nearby panel). Now go in one of the train station entrances and follow signs to *Sony Center*. (While you're down there, look for the other ends of the big glass tubes.)

You'll come up the escalator into **Sony Center** under a grand canopy. At night, multicolored floodlights play on the underside of this tent. Office workers and tourists eat here by the fountain, enjoying the parade of people. The modern Bavarian Lindenbräu beer hall—the Sony boss wanted a *Bräuhalle*—serves traditional food (€5–16, daily 11:00–24:00, big salads, three-foot-long taster boards of eight different beers, tel. 030/2575-1280). The adjacent Josty Bar is built around a surviving bit of a venerable hotel that was a meeting place for Berlin's rich and famous before the bombs (€13–25 plates, daily 10:00–24:00, tel. 030/2575-9702). You can browse the futuristic Sony Style Store, visit the Filmhaus (Film Museum Berlin, with an exhibit on Marlene Dietrich and a rare cinema that plays movies in their original language—without German dubbing), and pop into the Zoon Center (where the VW "my first car" exhibit prepares kids for the exciting day that they get their license and they, too, can enjoy Germany's beloved autobahns).

Across Potsdamer Strasse, you can ride what's billed as "the fastest elevator in Europe" to skyscraping rooftop views at the **Panaromapunkt.** You'll travel at nearly 30 feet per second to the top of the 300-foot-tall Kollhoff tower. Its sheltered but open-air view deck provides a fun opportunity to survey Berlin's ongoing construction from above (€3.50, daily 11:00–20:00, last lift 19:30, closed Mon in winter, in red-brick building at Potsdamer Platz 1, tel. 030/2529-4372, www.panoramapunkt.de).

Kulturforum

Just west of Potsdamer Platz, with several top museums and Berlin's concert hall, is the city's cultural heart (admission to all Kulturforum sights covered by a single €8 combo-ticket *(Standortkarte Kulturforum)* or the €15 Museumspass; phone number for all museums: tel. 030/266-2951). Of its sprawling museums, only the Gemäldegalerie is a must. To reach the Kulturforum, take the S- or U-Bahn to Potsdamer Platz, then walk along Potsdamer Platz and Potsdamer Strasse with the Sony Center on your right. Cross Ben-Gurion-Strasse and pass the yellow Philharmonie; the Gemäldegalerie is another 200 yards straight ahead. From the Zoo station, you can also take bus #200 to Philharmonie. Across Potsdamer Strasse from the Kulturforum is the huge National Library (free English periodicals).

▲▲▲Gemäldegalerie—Germany's top collection of 13th- through 18th-century European paintings (more than 1,400 canvases) is beautifully displayed in a building that's a work of art in itself. Follow the excellent free audioguide. The North Wing starts with German paintings of the 13th to 16th centuries, including eight by Dürer. Then come the Dutch and Flemish—Jan van Eyck, Brueghel, Rubens, van Dyck, Hals, and Vermeer. The wing finishes with German, English, and French 18th-century art, such as Gainsborough and Watteau. An octagonal hall at the end features an impressive stash of Rembrandts. The South Wing is saved for the Italians—Giotto, Botticelli, Titian, Raphael, and Caravaggio (€8 Kulturforum ticket or €15 Museumspass, free Thu after 18:00, open Tue–Sun 10:00–18:00, Thu until 22:00, closed Mon, clever little loaner stools, great salad bar in cafeteria upstairs, Matthäikirchplatz 4).

New National Gallery (Neue Nationalgalerie)—This features 20th-century art, with ever-changing special exhibits (€8 Kulturforum ticket or €15 Museumspass, open Tue–Fri 10:00–18:00, Thu until 22:00, Sat–Sun 11:00–18:00, closed Mon, café downstairs, Potsdamer Strasse 50).

Museum of Arts and Crafts (Kunstgewerbemuseum)—Wander through a thousand years of applied arts—porcelain, fine *Jugendstil* furniture, Art Deco, and reliquaries. There are no crowds and no English descriptions (€8 Kulturforum ticket or €15 Museumspass, free Thu after 14:00, open Tue–Fri 10:00–18:00, Sat–Sun 11:00–18:00, closed Mon, Herbert-von-Karajan-Strasse 10).

▲Musical Instruments Museum (Musikinstrumenten Museum)—This impressive hall is filled with 600 exhibits from the 16th century to modern times. Wander among old keyboard instruments and funny-looking tubas. There's no English, aside from a €0.10 info sheet, but it's fascinating if you're into pianos (€8 Kulturforum ticket or €15 Museumspass, Tue–Fri 9:00–17:00, Thu until 22:00, Sat–Sun 10:00–17:00, closed Mon, low-profile white building east of the big, yellow Philharmonic Concert Hall, tel. 030/254-810).

Poke into the lobby of Berlin's **Philharmonic Concert Hall** and see if there are tickets available during your stay (ticket office open Mon–Fri 15:00–18:00, Sat–Sun 11:00–14:00, must purchase tickets in person, box office tel. 030/2548-8132).

Western Berlin

Throughout the Cold War, Western travelers learned to think of Berlin's "West End" as the heart of the city. But it no longer is. With the huge changes the city has undergone since 1989, the real "city center" is now, once again, Berlin's historic center (around Unter den Linden and Friedrichstrasse). While the West End has long had the best infrastructure to support your visit, and still works well as a home base, it's no longer the obvious base from which to explore Berlin. And after the Hauptbahnhof essentially put the Bahnhof Zoo out of business in 2006, this change became even more pronounced. Having said all that, there still are a few interesting sights within an easy walk of the recommended West End hotels and Bahnhof Zoo.

For a detailed map of this area, see page 551.

▲Kurfürstendamm—West Berlin's main drag, Kurfürstendamm boulevard (nicknamed "Ku'damm"), starts at Kaiser Wilhelm Memorial Church and does a commercial cancan for two miles. In the 1850s, when Berlin became a wealthy and important capital, her new rich chose Kurfürstendamm as their street. Bismarck made it Berlin's Champs-Elysées. In the 1920s, it became a chic and fashionable drag of cafés and boutiques. During the Third Reich, as home to an international community of diplomats and journalists, it enjoyed more freedom than the rest of Berlin. Throughout the Cold War, economic subsidies from the West made sure that capitalism thrived on Ku'damm. And today, while much of the old charm has been hamburgerized, Ku'damm is still a fine place to enjoy elegant shops (around Fasanenstrasse), department stores, and people-watching.

▲Kaiser Wilhelm Memorial Church (Gedächtniskirche)—This church was originally a memorial to the first emperor of Germany. Reliefs and mosaics show great events in the life of Germany's favorite *Kaiser,* from his coronation in 1871 to his death in 1888. The church's bombed-out ruins have been left standing as a memorial to the destruction of Berlin in World War II. Under a Neo-Romanesque mosaic ceiling, a small exhibit features interesting photos about the bombing and before-and-after models of the church (free, Mon–Sat 10:00–16:00, closed Sun, Breitscheidplatz, S-Bahn: Zoologischer Garten or U-Bahn: Wittenbergplatz, www.gedaechtniskirche.com).

After the war, some Berliners wanted to tear the church down and build it anew. Instead, it was decided to keep the ruin as a memorial, and stage a competition to design a modern add-on section. The winning selection—the short, modern building (1961) next to the church—offers a world of 11,000 little blue windows (free, daily 9:00–19:00). The blue glass was given to the church by the French as a reconciliation gift. For more information on both churches, pick up the English booklet (€2.60).

The lively square between the churches and the Europa Center (a once-impressive, shiny high-rise shopping center built as a showcase of Western capitalism during the Cold War) usually attracts street musicians.

The Story of Berlin—Filling most of what seems like a department store right on Ku'damm, this sprawling history exhibit is a business venture making money by telling the stormy 800-year story of Berlin in a creative way. While there are almost no real historic artifacts, the exhibit does a good job of cobbling together many dimensions of the life and tumultuous times of this great city. The highlight is the included 30-minute tour of a circa 1972 radiation-proof bomb shelter—designed to house 3,500 people for 14 days (€9.80, daily 10:00–20:00, last entry at 18:00, well-described in English, upon arrival confirm time of next English-language bunker tour, Kurfürstendamm 207, at corner of Uhlandstrasse, in the Ku'damm Karree Mall, tel. 030/8872-0100, www.story-of-berlin.com).

▲Käthe Kollwitz Museum—This local artist (1867–1945), who experienced much of Berlin's stormiest century, conveys some powerful and mostly sad feelings about motherhood, war, and suffering through the stark faces of her art (€5, €1 pamphlet has English explanations of a few major works, Wed–Mon 11:00–18:00, closed Tue, a block off Ku'damm at Fasanenstrasse 24, U-Bahn: Uhlandstrasse, tel. 030/882-5210, www.kaethe-kollwitz.de).

▲Kaufhaus des Westens (KaDeWe)—The "Department Store of the West" celebrated its 100th birthday in 2007. With a staff of 2,100 to help you sort through its vast selection of 380,000 items, KaDeWe claims to be the biggest department store on the Continent. You can get everything from a haircut and train ticket (basement) to souvenirs (third floor). The theater and concert box office on the sixth floor charges an 18 percent booking fee, but they know all your options (cash only). The sixth floor is a world of gourmet taste treats. The biggest selection of deli and exotic food in Germany offers plenty of classy opportunities to sit down and eat. Ride the glass elevator to the seventh floor's glass-domed Winter Garden self-service cafeteria—fun but pricey (Mon–Fri 10:00–20:00, Sat 9:30–20:00, closed Sun, S-Bahn: Zoologischer Garten or U-Bahn: Wittenbergplatz, tel. 030/21210, www.kadewe.de). The Wittenbergplatz U-Bahn station (in front of KaDeWe) is a unique opportunity to see an old-time station. Enjoy its interior.

Berlin Zoo (Zoologischer Garten Berlin)—More than 1,400 different kinds of animals call Berlin's famous zoo home—or so the zookeepers like to think. Germans enjoy seeing the pandas at play (straight in from the entrance). I enjoy seeing the Germans at play (€11 for zoo or world-class aquarium, €16.50 for both, children half-price, daily 9:00–18:30, Nov–Feb until 17:00, aquarium closes 30 min earlier; feeding times—*Fütterungszeiten*—posted on map just inside entrance, the best feeding show is the sea lions—generally at 11:00, 13:30, and 15:15; enter near Europa Center in front of Hotel Palace or opposite Bahnhof Zoo on Hardenbergplatz, Budapester Strasse 34, tel. 030/254-010, www.zoo-berlin.de).

Erotic Art Museum—This offers two floors of graphic art (especially Oriental), old-time sex toy knickknacks, and a special exhibit on the queen of German pornography, the late Beate Uhse. This amazing woman, a former test pilot for the Third Reich and groundbreaking purveyor of condoms and sex ed in the 1950s, was the female Hugh Hefner of Germany and CEO of a huge chain of porn shops (€5, Mon–Sat 9:00–24:00, Sun 13:00–24:00, last entry at 23:00, hard-to-beat gift shop, at corner of Kantstrasse and Joachimstalerstrasse, a block from Bahnhof Zoo, tel. 030/8862-6613). If you just want to see sex, you'll see much more for half the price in a private video booth next door.

NIGHTLIFE

Berlin is a happening place for nightlife—whether it's nightclubs, pubs, jazz music, cabaret, hokey-but-fun German variety shows, theater, or concerts. Tourists stroll the Ku'damm after dark.

Sources of Entertainment Info: *Berlin Programm* lists a nonstop parade of concerts, plays, exhibits, and cultural events (€1.60, in German, www.berlin-programm.de); *Exberliner Magazine* (€2, www.exberliner.com) and the TI-produced *Berlin Calendar* (€1.60) have less information, but are in English (all sold at kiosks and TIs). For the young and determined sophisticate, *Zitty* and *Tip* are the top guides to alternative culture (in German, sold at kiosks). Also pick up the free schedules *Flyer* and *030* in bars and clubs. The free magazines by walking-tour companies such as New Berlin Walks (www.newberlintours.com) and Insider Tour (www.insidertour.com) are also good, providing the English-language inside scoop on nightlife, cheap eats, and pub crawls (available all over town).

Visit KaDeWe's ticket office for your music and theater options (sixth floor, 18 percent fee but access to all tickets; see page 547). Ask about "competitive improvisation" and variety shows.

West End Jazz—To enjoy live music near my recommended Savignyplatz hotels in western Berlin, consider **A Trane Jazz Club** (all jazz, €7–18 cover depending on act, nightly 21:00–2:00 in the morning, Bleibtreustrasse 1, tel. 030/313-2550) and **Quasimodo Live** (mix of jazz, rock, and blues, €5–12 cover, Tue–Sat from 22:00, closed Sun–Mon, Kantstrasse 12A, under Delphi Cinema, tel. 030/312-8086, www.quasimodo.de).

Cabaret—Bar Jeder Vernunft offers modern-day cabaret a short walk from the recommended hotels in western Berlin. This variety show—under a classic old tent perched atop a modern parking lot—is a hit with German speakers, but can still be worthwhile for those who don't speak the language (as some of the music shows are in a sort of "Dinglish"). Even some Americans perform here periodically. Tickets are generally around €19, and shows change regularly (performances start Mon–Sat at 20:30, Sun at 20:00, Wed is non-smoking, seating can be a bit cramped, south of Ku'damm at Schaperstrasse 24, tel. 030/883-1582, www.bar-jeder-vernunft.de).

German Variety Show—To spend an evening enjoying Europe's largest revue theater, consider Revue Berlin at the Friedrichstadt Palast. The show basically depicts the history of Berlin, and is choreographed in a funny and musical way that's popular with the Lawrence Welk–type German crowd. It's entertaining for your entire English-speaking family (€17–61, Tue–Sat 20:00, Sat–Sun also at 16:00, no shows Mon, U-Bahn: Oranienburger Tor, tel. 030/2326-2326, www.friedrichstadtpalast.de).

Nightclubs and Pubs—Oranienburger Strasse's trendy scene (page 540) is being eclipsed by the action at Friedrichshain (farther east). To the north, you'll find the hip Prenzlauer Berg neighborhood, packed with everything from smoky pubs to small art bars and dance clubs (best scene is around Helmholtsplatz, U-Bahn: Eberswalder Strasse; see page 540).

Pub Crawls—Various walking-tour companies offer €10 pub crawls providing an opportunity to drink heavily in a series of bars and clubs with several dozen new English-speaking friends. For details, see page 516.

SLEEPING

When in Berlin, I sleep in the former West, on or near Savignyplatz. While Bahnhof Zoo and Ku'damm are no longer the center of Berlin, the trains, TI, and walking tours are all still handy to Zoo. And the streets around the tree-lined Savignyplatz (a 10-min walk

Sleep Code

(€1 = about $1.30, country code: 49, area code: 030)
S = Single, **D** = Double/Twin, **T** = Triple, **Q** = Quad, **b** = bathroom, **s** = shower only. Unless otherwise noted, credit cards are accepted, English is spoken, and breakfast is included.

To help you sort easily through these listings, I've divided the rooms into three categories, based on the price for a standard double room with bath:

$$$ Higher Priced—Most rooms €125 or more.
$$ Moderately Priced—Most rooms between €85–125.
$ Lower Priced—Most rooms €85 or less.

behind the station) have a neighborhood charm. While towering new hotels are being built in the new center, simple, small, friendly, good-value places abound here. My listings are generally located a couple of flights up in big, run-down buildings. Inside, they're clean, quiet, and spacious enough so that their well-worn character is actually charming. Rooms in back are on quiet courtyards.

As an alternative, I've also listed some suggestions in eastern Berlin's youthful and increasingly popular Prenzlauer Berg neighborhood, as well as a couple other possibilities elsewhere.

Berlin is packed and hotel prices go up on holidays, including Green Week in mid-January, Easter weekend, the first weekend in May, Ascension weekend in May, the Love Parade (mid-July), German Unity Day (Oct 3), Christmas, and New Year's.

Western Berlin

Near Savignyplatz and Bahnhof Zoo

These hotels and pensions are a 5- to 15-minute walk from Bahnhof Zoo (or take the S-Bahn to Savignyplatz). Asking for a quieter room in back gets you away from any street noise. The area has an artsy charm going back to the cabaret days in the 1920s, when it was the center of Berlin's gay scene. Of the accommodations listed in this area, Pension Peters offers the best value for budget travelers.

$$$ Hotel Askanischerhof is the oldest *Zimmer* in Berlin, posh as can be with 16 sprawling, antique-furnished living rooms you can call home. Photos on the walls brag of famous movie-star guests. Frau Glinicke offers Old World service and classic Berlin atmosphere (Sb-€95–110, Db-€117–145, extra bed-€25, non-smoking rooms, elevator, free parking, Ku'damm 53, tel. 030/881-8033, fax 030/881-7206, www.askanischer-hof.de, info@askanischer-hof.de).

Western Berlin

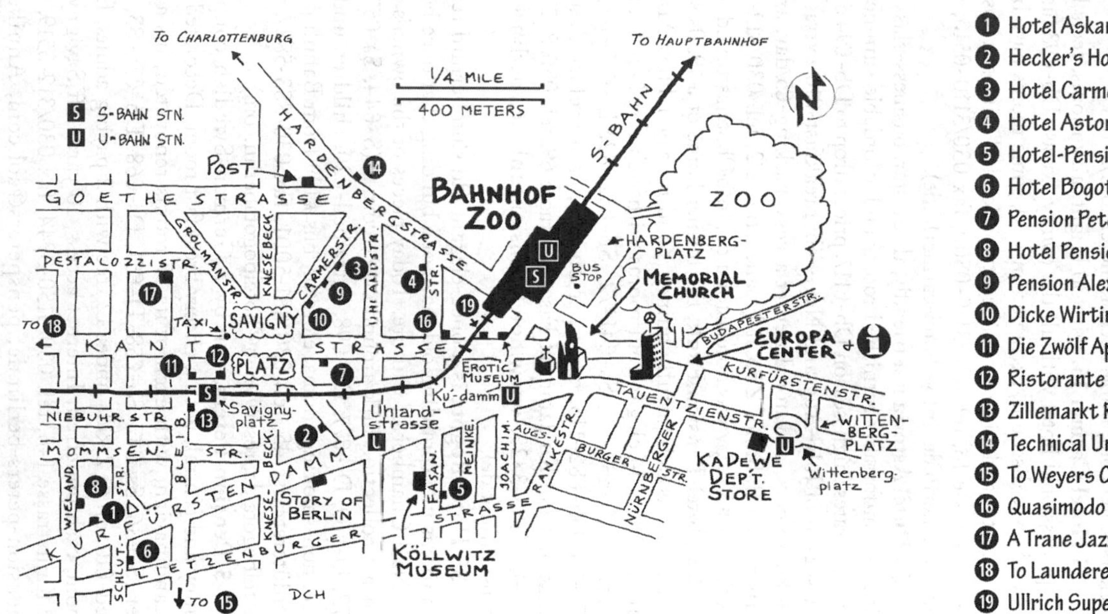

$$$ Hecker's Hotel is an ultramodern, four-star business hotel with 69 rooms and all the sterile Euro-comforts (Sb-€125, Db-€150, all rooms €200 during conferences but generally only €100 July–Aug, breakfast-€15, non-smoking rooms, elevator, parking-€9–12/day, between Savignyplatz and Ku'damm at Grolmanstrasse 35, tel. 030/88900, fax 030/889-0260, www.heckers-hotel.com, info@heckers-hotel.com).

$$ Hotel Carmer 16, with 30 bright, airy rooms, feels like a big, professional hotel with all the comfy extras (Db-€93, ask for a Rick Steves discount, extra person-€20, some rooms have balconies, elevator and a few stairs, beauty parlor and mini-spa upstairs, Carmerstrasse 16, tel. 030/3110-0500, fax 030/3110-0510, www.hotel-carmer16.de, info@hotel-carmer16.de).

$$ Hotel Astoria is a friendly, three-star, business-class hotel with 32 comfortably furnished rooms and affordable summer and weekend rates (high-season Db-€117; prices drop to Db-€94 during low season of July–Aug and Nov–Feb; breakfast-€10 extra, non-smoking floors, elevator, Internet access, parking-€5/day, around corner from Bahnhof Zoo at Fasanenstrasse 2, tel. 030/312-4067, fax 030/312-5027, www.hotelastoria.de, info@hotelastoria.de).

$$ Hotel-Pension Funk, the former home of a 1920s silent-movie star, is delightfully quirky. Kind manager Herr Michael Pfundt offers 14 elegant old rooms with rich Art Nouveau furnishings (S-€34–57, Ss-€41–72, Sb-€52–82, D-€52–82, Ds-€72–93, Db-€82–113, extra person-€23, cash preferred, a long block south of Ku'damm at Fasanenstrasse 69, tel. 030/882-7193, fax 030/883-3329, www.hotel-pensionfunk.de, berlin@hotel-pensionfunk.de).

$$ Hotel Bogota is a once-elegant old slumbermill renting 125 rooms in a sprawling old maze of a building that once housed the Nazi Chamber of Culture. Today pieces of the owner's modern-art collection lurk around every corner (S-€44, Ss-€57, Sb-€72, D-€69, Ds-€77, Db-€98, extra bed-€20, children under 12 free, non-smoking rooms, elevator, bus #109 from Bahnhof Zoo, Schlüterstrasse 45, tel. 030/881-5001, fax 030/883-5887, www.hotelbogota.de, reservieren@hotelbogotaberlin.com).

$ Pension Peters, run by a German-Swedish couple, is sunny and central, with a cheery breakfast room. Decorated sleek Scandinavian, with each of its 37 rooms renovated, it's a winner (S-€36, Ss-€47, Sb-€58, D-€51, Ds-€68, Db-€75–83, extra bed-€10, up to 2 kids under 12 free with 2 paying adults, family room, cash preferred, Internet access, 10 yards off Savignyplatz at Kantstrasse 146, tel. 030/3150-3944, fax 030/312-3519, www.pension-peters-berlin.de, penspeters@aol.com, Annika and Christoph). The same family also rents apartments in Prenzlauer Berg (ideal for small groups and longer stays).

$ Hotel Pension Alexandra has 11 pleasant rooms on a tree-lined street between Savignyplatz and Ku'damm. Expect the usual high ceilings and marble entryway found in these turn-of-the-century buildings, but with added touches—most rooms and the elegant breakfast room are decorated with original antique furniture (Ss-€45, Sb-€59, Ds-€65, Db with small bed-€70, standard Db-€85, extra bed-€30, Wielandstrasse 32, tel. 030/881-2107, fax 030/885-77818, www.hotelalexandra.de, info@hotelalexandra.de, Frau Kuhn).

$ Pension Alexis is a classic Old World four-room pension in a stately 19th-century apartment run by Frau and Herr Schwarzer (who speak just enough English). The shower and toilet facilities are old and cramped, but this, more than any other Berlin listing, has you feeling at home with a faraway aunt (S-€43, D-€65, T-€97, Q-€128, €5 extra for 1-night stay, cash only, big rooms, Carmerstrasse 15, tel. 030/312-5144).

Eastern Berlin

Prenzlauer Berg

If you want to sleep in the former East Berlin, set your sights on the youthful, colorful, fun Prenzlauer Berg district (or "Prenzl'berg" for short). After decades of neglect, this corner of the East has quickly come back to life. Gentrification has brought Prenzlauer Berg great hotels, tasty ethnic and German eateries (see page 559), and a happening nightlife scene. All the graffiti is just some people's way of saying they care. The huge and impersonal concrete buildings are now enlivened with a street fair of fun little shops and eateries. Prenzlauer Berg is about a mile and a half north of Alexanderplatz, roughly between Kollwitzplatz and Helmholtzplatz, and to the west, along Kastanienallee (known affectionately as "Casting Alley" for its extra share of beautiful people). The closest U-Bahn stops are Senefelderplatz at the south end of the neighborhood and Eberswalder Strasse at the north end. Or, for less walking, take the S-Bahn to Hackescher Markt, then catch the M1 tram north.

$$$ Myer's Hotel is a boutique-hotel splurge renting 41 simple, small, but elegant rooms. The gorgeous public spaces include a patio and garden. Details done right and impeccable service set this place apart. This peaceful hub—off a quiet courtyard and tree-lined street, just a 10-minute walk from Kollwitzplatz or the nearest U-Bahn stop (Senefelderplatz)—makes it hard to believe you're in a capital city (Sb-€85–135, Db-€110–175, price depends on size of room, Metzer Strasse 26, tel. 030/440-140, fax 030/4401-4104, www.myershotel.de, info@myershotel.de).

$$ Hotel Jurine (yoo-REEN) is a pleasant 53-room business-style hotel whose friendly staff aims to please. Enjoy the breakfast

Prenzlauer Berg Neighborhood

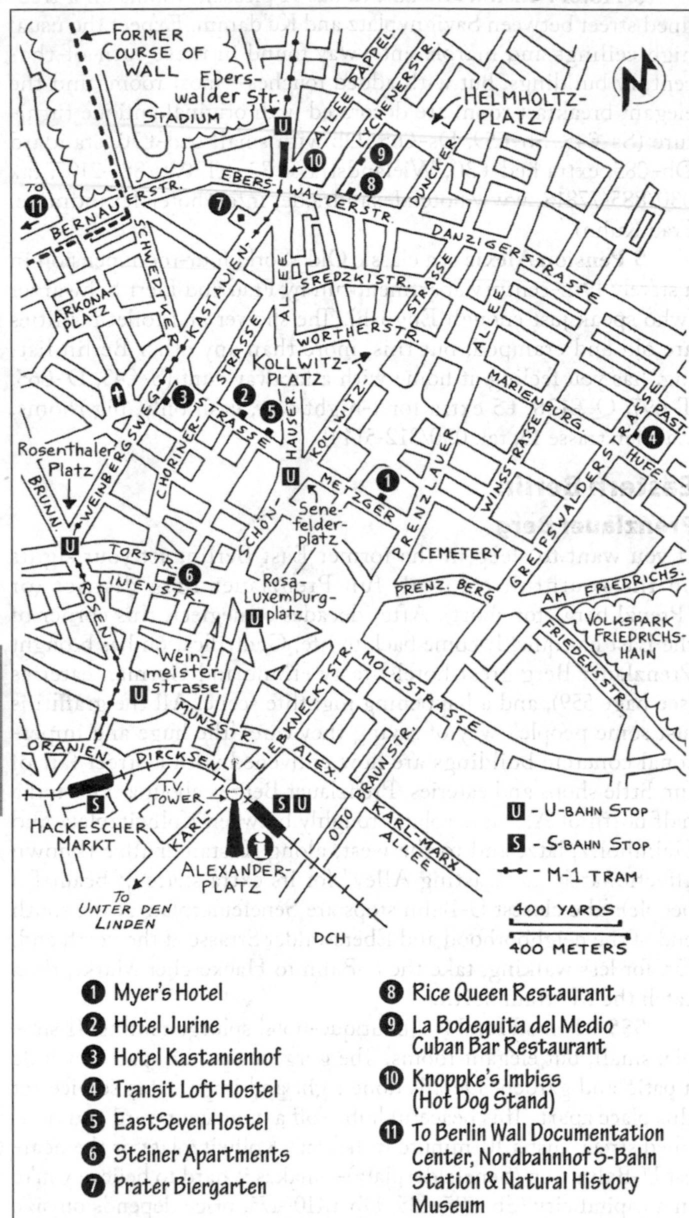

buffet surrounded by modern art, or relax in the lush backyard (Sb-€75, Db-€100, Tb-€130, extra bed-€35, prices can double during conventions, breakfast-€13, parking garage-€12/day, Schwedter Strasse 15, 10-min walk to U-Bahn: Senefelderplatz, tel. 030/443-2990, fax 030/4432-9999, www.hotel-jurine.de, mail@hotel-jurine.de).

$$ Hotel Kastanienhof is a simple, less-classy hotel offering 35 fine but slightly overpriced rooms. It's centrally located, making getting around Berlin a cinch, and it's near the hip Eberswalder Strasse bar scene (Sb-€78, Db-€103, just 40 yards from the M1 tram stop at Kastanienallee 65, tel. 030/443-050, fax 030/4430-5111, www.kastanienhof.biz, info@kastanienhof.biz).

$ Transit Loft is technically a hostel, but feels more like an upscale budget hotel. Located in a refurbished factory, it offers clean, bright, modern, new-feeling, mostly-blue rooms with an industrial touch. The reception—staffed by friendly, hip Berliners—is open 24 hours, with a bar serving drinks all night long (4- to 6-bed dorms-€19/bed, Sb-€60, Db-€71, Tb-€93, includes sheets and breakfast, no age limit, cheap Internet access, fully wheelchair-accessible, Emmanuelkirchstrasse 14A, U-Bahn: Alexanderplatz then tram M4 to Hufelandstrasse, tel. 030/4849-3773, fax 030/4405-1074, www.transit-loft.de, loft@hotel-transit.de).

$ EastSeven Hostel rents the best cheap beds in Prenzlauer Berg. It's sleek and modern, with all the hostel services and more: 24-hour reception, inviting lounge, fully equipped guests' kitchen, lockers, garden, and bike rental. Children are welcome. While most hostels—especially in Prenzlauer Berg—are annoyingly youthful to anyone over 30, easygoing people of any age are comfortable here (S-€30, D-€44, T-€57, €16 for a bed in a 4-, 5-, or 6-bed dorm, bathrooms always down the hall, one-time €3 fee for sheets, 100 yards from U-Bahn: Senefelderplatz at Schwedter Strasse 7, tel. 030/9362-2240, www.eastseven.de, info@eastseven.de).

$ Steiner Apartments, run by Annika and Christoph from Pension Peters, are nine well-located, modern, and comfortable apartments near Hackescher Markt (Sb-€50, Db-€70, Tb-€75, Qb-€80, cash only, up to 2 children under 12 sleep free with 2 paying adults, fully equipped as if you live there, Linienstrasse 60, near intersection with Gormannstrasse, 350 yards from S-Bahn: Hackescher Markt, even closer to U-Bahn: Rosenthaler Platz, www.pension-peters-berlin.de, penspeters@aol.com; to book, contact Pension Peters, described on page 552).

Hostels

Berlin is known among budget travelers for its fun, hip hostels. Here are three good bets: **$ Studentenhotel Meininger 10** (€14 dorm beds, D-€46, includes sheets and breakfast, cash only, no curfew, elevator, free parking, near City Hall on JFK Platz, Meiningerstrasse 10, U-Bahn: Rathaus Schöneberg, tel. 030/7871-7414, www.meininger-hostels.de), **$ Mitte's Backpacker Hostel** (€15 dorm beds, S-€30–35, D-€46–56, T-€63, Q-€80, sheets-€2.50, no breakfast, could be cleaner, no curfew, Internet access, English newspapers, laundry, bike rental, U-Bahn: Zinnowitzerstrasse, Chauseestrasse 102, tel. 030/2839-0965, fax 030/2839-0935, www.backpacker.de, info@backpacker.de), or **$ Circus** (€17–19 dorm beds, S-€33, Sb-€46, D-€50, Db-€62, T-€63, Q-€76, 2-person apartment with kitchen-€77, 4-person apartment-€134, sheets-€2, breakfast-€5, cash only, no curfew, Internet access; 2 locations—U-Bahn: Rosa-Luxemburg Platz, Rosa-Luxemburg Strasse 39, or U-Bahn: Rosenthaler Platz, Weinbergsweg 1a; both tel. 030/2839-1433, fax 030/2839-1484, www.circus-berlin.de, info@circus-berlin.de).

EATING

Don't be too determined to eat "Berlin-style." The city is known only for its mildly spicy sausage. Still, there is a world of restaurants in this ever-changing city to choose from. Your best approach may be to select a neighborhood rather than a particular restaurant.

For quick and easy meals, colorful pubs—called *Kneipen*—offer light meals and the fizzy local beer, *Berliner Weiss*. Ask for it *mit Schuss* for a shot of fruity syrup in your suds. If the kraut is getting wurst, try one of the many Turkish, Italian, or Balkan restaurants. Eat cheap at *Imbiss* snack stands, bakeries (sandwiches), and falafel/kebab counters. Train stations have grocery stores, as well as bright and modern fruit-and-sandwich bars.

Western Berlin

Near Savignyplatz

Several good restaurants are on or within 100 yards of Savignyplatz, near my recommended western Berlin hotels. Take a walk and survey these; continue your stroll along Bleibtreustrasse to discover many trendier, more creative little eateries.

Dicke Wirtin is a smoky pub with traditional old-Berlin *Kneipe* atmosphere and good, solid home cooking at reasonable prices—such as their famously cheap *Gulaschsuppe*. While their interior is fun and pubby, their streetside tables are also inviting (€6–10 daily specials, open daily from 12:00 with dinner served from 18:00, just off Savignyplatz at Carmerstrasse 9, tel. 030/312-4952).

Die Zwölf Apostel ("The Twelve Apostles") is trendy for good Italian food. Choose between indoors with candlelit ambience, on a sun-dappled patio, or overlooking the parade on its pedestrian street. A dressy local crowd packs this restaurant for €10 pizzas and €15–30 meals (open 24 hours daily, cash only, outside seating in summer until 22:00, immediately across from Savignyplatz S-Bahn entrance, Bleibtreustrasse 49, tel. 030/312-1433).

Ristorante San Marino, on the square, is another good Italian eatery, serving cheaper pasta and pizza. It's more kid-friendly (€7–12 plates, daily 11:00–1:00 in the morning, Savignyplatz 12, tel. 030/313-6086).

Zillemarkt Restaurant, which feels like an old-time Berlin beer garden, serves traditional Berlin specialties in the garden or in the rustic candlelit interior. Their *Berliner Allerlei* is a fun way to sample a bit of nearly everything (€10 meals, daily 10:00–24:00, near the S-Bahn tracks at Bleibtreustrasse 48A, tel. 030/881-7040).

Technical University Mensa, a student cafeteria with impossibly cheap prices, puts you in a modern university scene with fine food and good indoor or streetside seating (€5 meals, Mon–Fri 11:00–15:30, closed Sat–Sun, general public entirely welcome, cheap coffee bar downstairs with Internet access, just north of Uhlandstrasse at Hardenbergstrasse 34).

Weyers Café Restaurant, serving quality international and German cuisine, is a great value and worth the 15-minute walk from Savignyplatz. It's sharp, with white tablecloths, but not stuffy. On a sunny day, its patio is packed with natives (€10 dinner plates, daily 8:00–2:00 in the morning, seating indoors or outside on the leafy square called Ludwigkirchplatz, Pariser Strasse 16, reservations smart after 20:00, tel. 030/881-9378). Even though this restaurant is farther away, it gets you into a real neighborhood scene without a tourist in sight.

Ullrich Supermarkt is the neighborhood grocery store (Mon–Sat 9:00–22:00, Sun 11:00–22:00, Kantstrasse 7, under the tracks near Bahnhof Zoo). There's plenty of fast food near Bahnhof Zoo and on Ku'damm.

Near Bahnhof Zoo

Self-Service Cafeterias: The top floor of the famous department store, **KaDeWe,** holds the Winter Garden Buffet view cafeteria, and its sixth-floor deli/food department is a picnicker's nirvana. Its arterials are clogged with more than 1,000 kinds of sausage and 1,500 types of cheese (Mon–Fri 10:00–20:00, Sat 9:30–20:00, closed Sun, U-Bahn: Wittenbergplatz). **Wertheim** department store, a half-block from Kaiser Wilhelm Memorial Church, has cheap food counters in the basement and a city view from its self-service cafeteria, Le Buffet, located up six banks of escalators (Mon–Sat 9:30–20:00, closed Sun, U-Bahn: Ku'damm). **Marche,** a chain that's popped up in big cities all over Germany, is another inexpensive, self-service cafeteria within a half-block of Kaiser

Wilhelm Memorial Church (Mon–Thu 8:00–22:00, Fri–Sat 8:00–24:00, Sun 10:00–22:00, plenty of salads, fruit, made-to-order omelets, Ku'damm 14, tel. 030/882-7578).

Eastern Berlin

Along Unter den Linden

These eateries are listed as you'll reach them as you walk along Unter den Linden from west to east.

At the Opera House (Opernpalais): The **Operncafé** is perhaps the classiest coffee stop in Berlin, with a wide selection of decadent desserts (daily 8:00–24:00, across from university and war memorial at Unter den Linden 5, tel. 030/202-683). The beer and tea garden in front has a cheap food counter (from 10:00, depending on weather).

Near the Pergamon Museum: **Deponie3** is a trendy Berlin *Kneipe* usually filled with students from nearby Humboldt University. Garden seating in the back is nice if you don't mind the noise of the S-Bahn passing directly above you. The interior is a cozy, wooden wonderland of a bar with several inviting spaces. They serve basic sandwiches, salads, traditional Berlin dishes, and hearty daily specials (€3–7 breakfasts, €5–11 lunches and dinners, open daily from 9:00, sometimes live music, Georgenstrasse 5, 1 block from Pergamon under S-Bahn tracks, tel. 030/2016-5740). **Georgenstrasse** is home to other good restaurants, including a branch of Die Zwölf Apostel (daily until 24:00, described under "Near Savignyplatz," above).

Berlin

In the Heart of Old Berlin's Nikolai Quarter: During the Cold War, the Nikolai Quarter was the cute, cobbled, and characteristic old town of East Berlin. Today the district feels pretty soulless but is a popular restaurant zone at night. **Bräuhaus Georgbrau** is a thriving beer hall sitting on a picturesque courtyard overlooking the Spree River. Eat in the lively and woody but mod-feeling interior, or outdoors with fun riverside seating (cheap plates, three-foot-long sampler board with a dozen small glasses of beer, daily 10:00–24:00, 2 blocks south of Berlin Cathedral and across the river at Spreeufer 4, tel. 030/242-4244).

South of Unter den Linden, near Gendarmenmarkt

The twin churches of Gendarmenmarkt seem to be surrounded by people in love with food. The lunch and dinner scene is thriving with upscale restaurants serving good cuisine at highly competitive prices to local professionals. If in need of a quick-yet-classy lunch, stroll around the square and along Charlottenstrasse. Consider **Lutter & Wegner Restaurant,** well-known for its Austrian cuisine (*Schnitzel* and *Sauerbraten*) and popular with businesspeople. It's dressy, with fun sidewalk seating or a dark and elegant interior (two-course lunch with wine-€15, fixed-price gourmet dinner-€34, daily 11:00–22:00, Charlottenstrasse 56, tel. 030/202-9540). **Galeries Lafayette Food Circus** is a festival of fun eateries in the basement of the landmark department store (Mon–Sat 10:00–20:00, closed Sun, U-Bahn: Französische Strasse).

Turkish Cuisine North of Unter den Linden, near Hackescher Markt

As Berlin is one of the world's largest Turkish cities, it's no wonder you can find some good Turkish restaurants here. While most think of Turkish food as fast and cheap, **Hasir Turkish Restaurant** is your chance to dine with candles, hardwood floors, and happy Berliners as snappy Turkish waiters bring plates piled high with meaty Anatolian specialties. The restaurant, in a courtyard next to the Hackesche Höfe shopping complex (see page 540), offers indoor and outdoor tables filled with an enthusiastic local crowd (€13 plates, huge and splittable portions, daily from 11:30 until late, a block from the Hackescher Markt S-Bahn station at Oranienburger Strasse 4, tel. 030/2804-1616).

In Prenzlauer Berg

Prenzlauer Berg is packed with fine restaurants—German, ethnic, and everything in between. (For more on this district, see page 553.) Before making a choice, I'd spend half an hour strolling and browsing through this bohemian wonderland of creative eateries. Ideally, ride the U-Bahn to Rosenthaler Platz, check out that zone, then hike up Kastanienallee, which takes you past the recommended Prater Biergarten and side streets lined with impromptu outdoor tables. Kastanienallee dead-ends at Eberswalder Strasse, where you'll find Knoppke's Imbiss and, within a half-block, Rice Queen and La Bodeguita del Medio.

Prater Biergarten offers a mellow outdoor ambience. Berlin's oldest beer garden is a family-friendly delight. It has two zones: the restaurant (serious traditional *Biergarten* cuisine, huge indoor area, and a few tables outside) and the vast self-service beer garden under the trees (with a much simpler menu and an intriguing selection of munchies). This isn't the typical yodeling-and-lederhosen Bavarian beer garden—in addition to the wurst and beer are fine wine and snacks like olives, nuts, and pickles (Mon–Sat 18:00–24:00, Sun 12:00–24:00, cash only, Kastanienallee 7, tel. 030/448-5688).

Rice Queen Restaurant is crisp and casual, with a fruity minimalist decor. They serve cheap yet delicious South Asian dishes from a fun menu that makes you glad you're hungry (€6 plates, daily 17:00–24:00, 1 block from U-Bahn: Eberswalder Strasse at Danziger Strasse 13, tel. 030/4404-5800).

La Bodeguita del Medio Cuban Bar Restaurant is purely

fun-loving Cuba—Christmas lights, graffiti-caked walls, Che Guevara posters, animated staff, and an ambience that makes you want to dance. Come early to eat or late to drink. It seems the waiters know the regulars' drinks (€4–10 tapas, daily from 17:00, 1 block from U-Bahn: Eberswalder Strasse at Lychener Strasse 6, tel. 030/4171-4276). This restaurant has been here for over a decade—and in fast-changing Prenzlauer Berg, that's an eternity.

Knoppke's Imbiss, a super-cheap German-style hot-dog stand, has been a Berlin institution for over 70 years—it was family-owned even during DDR times. Berliners say Knoppke's cooks up the best *Currywurst* (grilled hot dog with curry-infused ketchup) in town. There are a few tables under a nearby tent for sit-down wurst-munching (Mon–Fri 6:00–20:00, Sat 12:00–19:00, closed Sun; Kastanienallee dead-ends at the elevated train tracks, and under them you'll find Knoppke's at Schönhauser Allee 44A). Don't be fooled by the Currystation at the foot of the stairs coming out of the station; Knoppke's is actually across the street, under the tracks.

TRANSPORTATION CONNECTIONS

Berlin used to have several major train stations. But now, with the Hauptbahnhof (Main Train Station, a.k.a. Berlin Lehrter Bahnhof) emerging as the single, massive central station, all the others are wilting into glorified subway stations. Virtually every long-distance train passes through the Hauptbahnhof.

From Berlin by Train to: Dresden (every 2 hrs, 2.25 hrs, more with a transfer in Leipzig), **Frankfurt** (hourly, 4 hrs, more with a transfer in Hannover), **Munich** (hourly, 6 hrs, 8 hrs overnight), **Köln** (hourly, 6 hrs), **Amsterdam** (3/day direct, 6 hrs, more with changes), **Budapest** (3/day, 13 hrs; these go via Czech Republic and Slovakia, where Eurailpass is not valid), **Copenhagen** (5/day, 6.5 hrs, change in Hamburg; also consider the direct overnight train-plus-ferry route to Malmö, Sweden, which is just 20 min from Copenhagen—covered by a railpass that includes Germany and Sweden), **London** (8/day, 11 hrs, but you're generally better off flying cheap on easyJet or Air Berlin—see below), **Paris** (6/day, 9 hrs, change in Köln, 1 direct 12-hr night train, all go via Belgium), **Zürich** (11/day, 8–9 hrs, 1 direct 12-hr night train), **Prague** (7/day, 5 hrs, no overnight trains), **Warsaw** (4/day, 6 hrs, 1 night train from Lichtenberg station; reservations required on all Warsaw-bound trains), **Kraków** (2/day, 10 hrs, more via Warsaw), **Vienna** (6/day, 10 hrs, most via Czech Republic—for second-class ticket, Eurailers pay an extra €40; the Berlin–Vienna via Passau train avoids Czech Republic—nightly at 20:00). It's wise but not required to reserve in advance for trains to or from Amsterdam or Prague. Train info:

tel. 11861 (€0.50/min).

Eurailpasses don't cover the Czech Republic, so you need to buy a ticket for the Czech portion of the trip before boarding a train. The **Prague Excursion pass** is no longer a good value. The staff at EurAide can help you figure out the most economical and effective route and ticket options.

There are **night trains** from Berlin to these cities: Munich, Frankfurt, Köln, Brussels, Paris, Vienna, Budapest, Kraków, Warsaw, Malmö, Basel, and Zürich. There are no night trains from Berlin to anywhere in Italy or Spain. A *Liegeplatz,* or berth (€13–36), is a great deal; inquire at EurAide at the Hauptbahnhof for details. Beds cost the same whether you have a first- or second-class ticket or railpass. Trains are often full, so reserve your bed a few days in advance from any travel agency or major train station in Europe.

The **Berlin–Paris night train** goes through Belgium. If you're using a railpass, either the pass must include Benelux, or you'll have to pay extra for the Belgian segment of the trip.

Berlin's Two Airports

Allow €25 for a taxi ride to or from either of Berlin's airports. **Tegel Airport** handles most flights from the United States and Western Europe (4 miles from center, catch the faster bus #X9 to Bahnhof Zoo, or bus #109 to Ku'damm and Bahnhof Zoo for €2.10; bus TXL goes to the Hauptbahnhof and Alexanderplatz in eastern Berlin). Flights from the east and discount airlines usually arrive at **Schönefeld Airport** (12.5 miles from center, short walk to S-Bahn station where you catch the regional express into the city, railpass valid). The central telephone number for both airports is 01805-000-186. For British Air, tel. 01805-266-522; Delta, tel. 01803-337-880; SAS, tel. 01803-234-023; or Lufthansa, tel. 01803-803-803.

Berlin, the New Discount Airline Hub: Berlin's Schönefeld Airport is now the Continental European hub for discount airlines such as easyJet (with lots of flights to Spain, Italy, Eastern Europe, the Baltics, and more—book long in advance to get the incredible €30-and-less fares, www.easyjet.com). Ryanair (www.ryanair.com) and Air Berlin (www.airberlin.com) are also making the London–Berlin trip (and other routes) dirt cheap. Consequently, in the last year, British visits to Berlin are up over 50 percent.

GREAT BRITAIN

LONDON

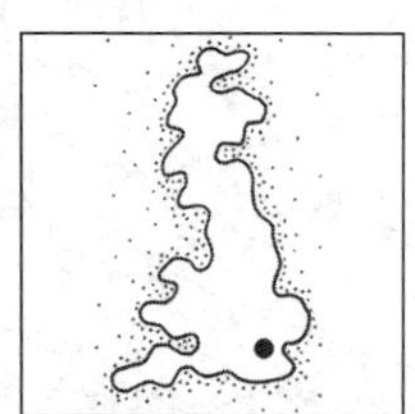

London is more than 600 square miles of urban jungle. With nine million people—who don't all speak English—it's a world in itself and a barrage on all the senses. On my first visit I felt very, very small.

London is more than its museums and landmarks. It's a living, breathing, thriving organism...a coral reef of humanity. The city has changed dramatically in recent years, and many visitors are surprised to find how "un-English" it is. Whites are now a minority in major parts of the city that once symbolized white imperialism. Arabs have nearly bought out the area north of Hyde Park. Chinese take-outs outnumber fish-and-chips shops. Eastern Europeans pull pints in British pubs. Many hotels are run by people with foreign accents (who hire English chambermaids), while outlying suburbs are home to huge communities of Indians and Pakistanis. With the English Channel Tunnel making travel between Britain and the Continent easier than ever, many locals see even more holes in their bastion of Britishness. London is learning—sometimes fitfully—to live as a microcosm of its formerly vast empire.

With just a few days here, you'll get no more than a quick splash in this teeming human tidal pool. But with a good orientation, you'll find London manageable and fun. You'll get a sampling of the city's top sights, history, and cultural entertainment, and a good look at its ever-changing human face.

Blow through the city on the open deck of a double-decker orientation tour bus, and take a pinch-me-I'm-in-London walk through the West End. Ogle the crown jewels at the Tower of London, hear the chimes of Big Ben, and see the Houses of

Parliament in action. Cruise the Thames River, and take a spin on the London Eye Ferris Wheel. Hobnob with the tombstones in Westminster Abbey, enjoy Shakespeare in a replica of the Globe Theatre, and stand in awe over the original Magna Carta at the British Library. Visit with Leonardo, Botticelli, and Rembrandt in the National Gallery. Whisper across the dome of St. Paul's Cathedral, and rummage through our civilization's attic at the British Museum. And sip your tea with pinky raised and clotted cream dribbling down your scone. Spend one evening at a theater and the others catching your breath.

Planning Your Time

The sights of London alone could easily fill a trip to England. It's worth at least four busy days. If you're flying in, consider starting your trip in Bath and making London your English finale. Especially if you hope to enjoy a play or concert, a night or two of jet lag is bad news.

Here's a suggested schedule:

Day 1: 9:00–Tower of London (crown jewels first, then Beefeater tour, then White Tower); 12:00–Munch a sandwich on the Thames while cruising from the Tower to Westminster Bridge; 13:00–Follow the self-guided Westminster Walk (see page 581) with a quick visit to the Churchill Museum and Cabinet War Rooms; 15:30–Trafalgar Square and National Gallery; 17:30–Visit the Britain and London Visitors Centre near Piccadilly, planning ahead for your trip; 18:30–Dinner in Soho. Take in a play or 19:30 concert at St. Martin-in-the-Fields.

Day 2: 9:00–Take a hop-on, hop-off bus tour (consider hopping off near the end for the 11:30 Changing of the Guard at Buckingham Palace); 12:30–Covent Garden for lunch and people-watching; 14:00–Tour the British Museum. Have a pub dinner before a play, concert, or evening walking tour.

Days 3 and 4: Choose among these remaining London highlights: Tour Westminster Abbey, British Library, Imperial War Museum, the two Tates (Tate Modern on the South Bank for modern art, Tate Britain on the North Bank for British art), St. Paul's Cathedral, or the Museum of London; take a spin on the London Eye Ferris Wheel or a cruise to Kew or Greenwich; do some serious shopping at one of London's elegant department stores or open-air markets; or take another historic walking tour.

After considering nearly all of London's tourist sights, I have pruned them down to just the most important (or fun) for a first visit of up to four days. You won't be able to see all of these, so don't try. You'll keep coming back to London. After dozens of visits myself, I still enjoy a healthy list of excuses to return.

London's Neighborhoods

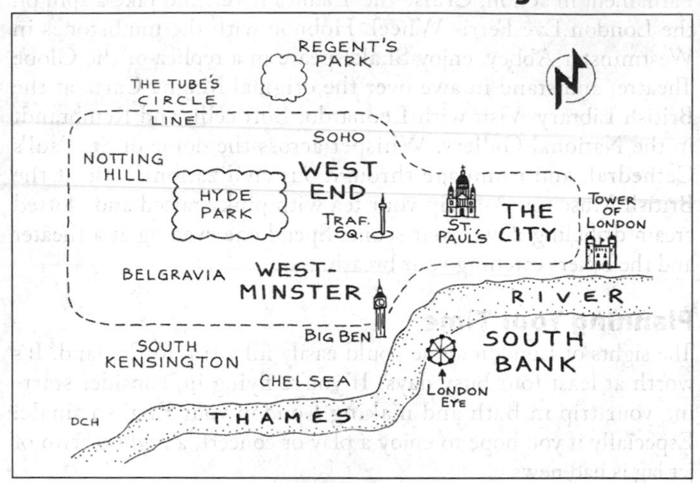

ORIENTATION

(area code: 020)

To grasp London more comfortably, see it as the old town in the city center without the modern, congested sprawl. The Thames River runs roughly west to east through the city, with most of the visitor's sights on the north bank. Mentally, maybe even physically, trim down your map to include only the area between the Tower of London (to the east), Hyde Park (west), Regent's Park (north), and the South Bank (south). This is roughly the area bordered by the Tube's Circle Line. This three-mile stretch between the Tower and Hyde Park (about a 90-min walk) looks like a milk bottle on its side (see above map), and holds 80 percent of the sights mentioned in this book.

London is a collection of neighborhoods:

The City: Shakespeare's London was a walled town clustered around St. Paul's Cathedral. Today, "The City" is the modern financial district.

Westminster: This neighborhood includes Big Ben, Parliament, the Churchill Museum and Cabinet War Rooms, Westminster Abbey, and Buckingham Palace, the grand government buildings from which Britain is ruled.

The West End: Lying between Westminster and The City (that is, at the "west end" of the original walled town), this is the center of London's cultural life. Trafalgar Square has major museums. Piccadilly Circus and Leicester Square host tourist traps, cinemas, and nighttime glitz. Soho and Covent Garden are thriving people-zones housing theaters, restaurants, pubs, and boutiques.

The South Bank: Until recently, the entire south bank of the Thames River was a run-down, generally ignored area, but now it's the hottest real estate in town, with upscale restaurants, major new sightseeing attractions, and pedestrian bridges allowing easy access from the rest of London.

Residential Neighborhoods to the West: Though they lack major tourist sights, the neighborhoods of Mayfair, South Kensington, Notting Hill, Chelsea, and Belgravia are home to the city's wealthy and trendy, as well as many shopping streets and enticing restaurants.

Tourist Information

The Britain and London Visitors Centre, just a block off Piccadilly Circus, is the best tourist information service in town (Mon–Fri 9:00–18:30, Sat–Sun 10:00–17:00, phone not answered after 17:00 Mon–Fri and not at all Sat–Sun, 1 Lower Regent Street, tel. 020/8846-9000, www.visitbritain.com, www.visitlondon.com). This TI has many different departments, all with their own sales desks (theater tickets, sightseeing passes, etc.). Bring your itinerary and a checklist of questions.

At the London desk, pick up these free publications: *London Map and Guide*, *London Planner* (a great free monthly that lists all the sights, events, and hours), walking-tour schedule fliers, a theater guide, *London Buses: Central London* map, and the Thames River Services brochure. After you've grazed through the great leaflet racks, head upstairs for the inviting tables and Internet access (small fee, with disk-burning service).

The "pink desk" sells long-distance bus tickets and passes, train tickets (convenient for reservations), and **Fast Track tickets** to some of London's attractions (at no extra cost), allowing you to skip the queue at the sights. These are worthwhile for places that sometimes have long ticket lines, such as the Tower of London, London Eye Ferris Wheel, and Madame Tussaud's Waxworks. (If you'll be going to the Waxworks, buy tickets here, since they're cheaper than at the sight itself.)

While the Visitors Centre books rooms, you can avoid their £5 booking fee by calling hotels direct (see "Sleeping," page 616). The entertainment desk to the left of the pink desk sells tickets to plays (20 percent booking fee).

The Britain tourism desk, located at the back of the TI, sells the various sightseeing deals, including the London Pass (skip it; remember that many of London's big attractions are free to enter). Busy sightseers taking far-flung trips could consider the British Heritage Pass, or English Heritage or National Trust memberships.

Nearby you'll find the **Scottish Tourist Centre** (Mon–Fri

8:00–20:00, Sat 9:00–17:30, Sun 10:00–16:00, Cockspur Street, tel. 0845-225-5121, www.visitscotland.com) and the slick **French National Tourist Office** (Mon–Fri 10:00–18:00, Sat until 17:00, closed Sun, 178 Piccadilly Street, tel. 0906-824-4123).

Unfortunately, **London's Tourist Information Centres** (which represent themselves as TIs at major train and bus stations and airports) are now simply businesses selling advertising space to companies with fliers to distribute. For solid information, visit the Britain and London Visitors Centre, mentioned above.

Arrival in London

By Train: London has eight train stations, all connected by the Tube (subway) and all with exchange offices and luggage storage. From any station, ride the Tube or taxi to your hotel.

By Bus: The bus ("coach") station is one block southwest of Victoria Station (which has a TI and a Tube entrance).

By Plane: For detailed information on getting from London's airports to downtown London, see "Transportation Connections," page 640.

Helpful Hints

Theft Alert: The Artful Dodger is alive and well in London. Be on guard, particularly on public transportation and in places crowded with tourists. Tourists, considered naive and rich, are targeted. More than 7,500 handbags are stolen annually at Covent Garden alone. Wear your money belt.

US Embassy: It's at 24 Grosvenor Square, just east of Hyde Park (for passport concerns, open Mon–Fri 8:30–17:30, closed Sat–Sun and for American and British holidays, Tube: Bond Street, tel. 020/7499-9000, www.usembassy.org.uk).

Pedestrian Safety: Cars drive on the left side of the road, so before crossing a street, I always look right, look left, then look right again just to be sure. Many crosswalks are even painted with instructions, reminding their foreign guests to "Look right" or "Look left."

Medical Problems: Local hospitals have 24-hour-a-day emergency care centers where any tourist who needs help can drop in and, after a wait, be seen by a doctor. The quality is good and the price is right (free). Your hotel has details. St. Thomas' Hospital, immediately across the river from Big Ben, has a fine reputation.

Changing Money: ATMs are the way to go. While regular banks charge several pounds to change traveler's checks, American Express offices offer a fair rate, and will change any brand of traveler's checks for no fee. Handy AmEx offices are at

Heathrow's Terminal 4 Tube station (daily 7:00–19:00) and near Piccadilly (Mon–Sat 9:00–18:00, Sun 10:00–17:00, 30 Haymarket, tel. 020/7484-9610; refund office 24-hour tel. 0800-521-313). Marks & Spencer department stores give good rates with no fees.

Avoid changing money at exchange bureaus. Their latest scam: They advertise very good rates with a same-as-the-banks fee of 2 percent. But the fine print explains that the fee of 2 percent is for buying pounds. The fee for selling pounds is 9.5 percent. Ouch!

Internet Access: The **easyInternetcafé** chain offers up to 500 computers per store, and is open long hours daily. Depending on the time of day, a £2 ticket buys anywhere from 80 minutes to six hours of computer time. The ticket is valid for four weeks and multiple visits at any of their branches, including: Trafalgar Square (456 Strand), Tottenham Court Road (#9–16), Oxford Street (#358, opposite Bond Street Tube station), and Kensington High Street (#160–166). They also sell 24-hour, seven-day, and 30-day passes (www.easyinternetcafe.com). **Access Printers,** across the street from Victoria Station (next to the Apollo Victoria Theatre), has plenty of terminals (£1/30 min, open long hours daily). You'll find an Internet café in the **Whiteleys Mall Food Court** in the Notting Hill neighborhood (see page 639).

Travel Bookstores: Located in Covent Garden, **Stanfords Travel Bookstore** is good, and stocks current editions of my books (Mon, Wed, and Fri 9:00–19:30, Tue 9:30–19:30, Thu 9:00–20:00, Sat 10:00–19:00, Sun 12:00–18:00, 12–14 Long Acre, Tube: Covent Garden, tel. 020/7836-1321, www.stanfords.co.uk). Two impressive **Waterstone's** bookstores have the biggest collection of travel guides in town: on Piccadilly (Mon–Sat 10:00–22:00, Sun 12:00–18:00, 203 Piccadilly, tel. 020/7851-2400) and on Trafalgar Square (Mon–Sat 9:30–21:00, Sun 12:00–18:00, with Costa Café on second floor, tel. 020/7839-4411).

Left Luggage: As security concerns heighten, train stations have replaced their lockers with left-luggage counters. Each bag must go through a scanner (just like at the airport), so lines can be long. Expect a wait to pick up your bags, too (each item-£6/24 hrs, daily 7:00–24:00). You can also check bags at the airports (£5/day). If leaving London and returning later, you may be able to leave a box or bag at your hotel for free—assuming you'll be staying there again.

Time Zone Difference: Remember that Britain is one hour earlier than most of continental Europe.

London

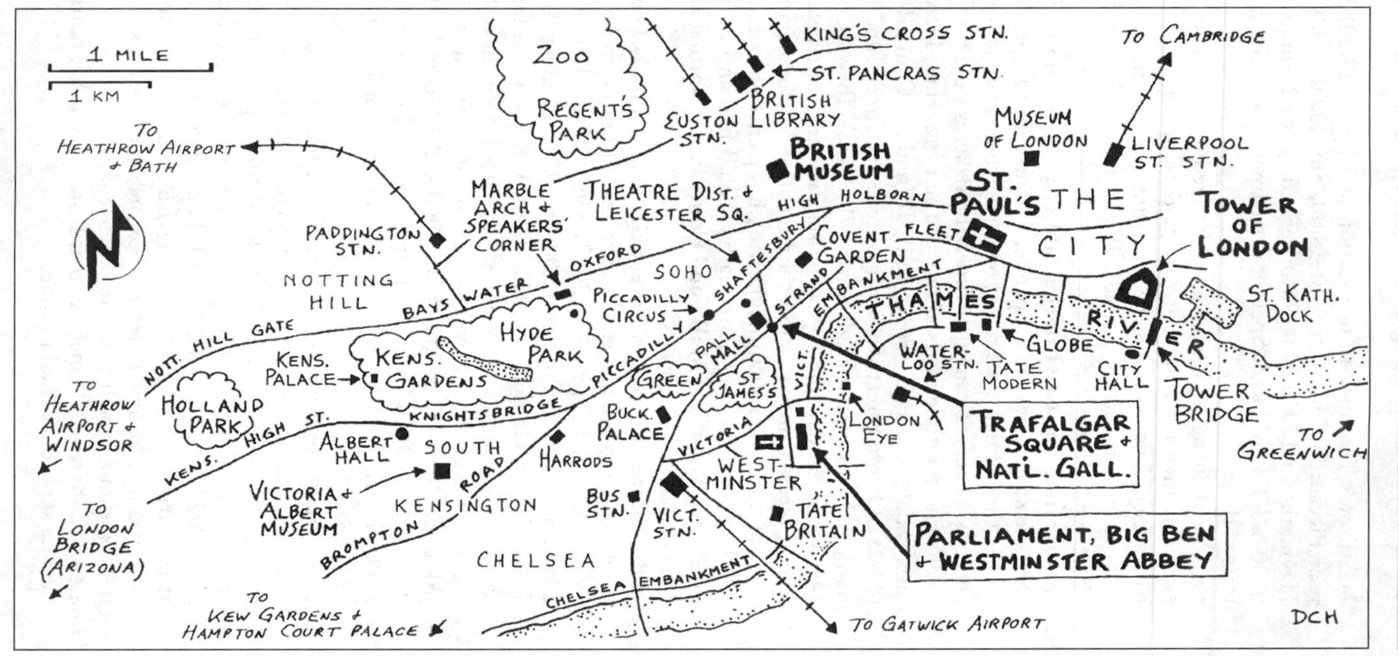

London

Getting Around London

To travel smart in a city this size, you must get comfortable with public transportation. London's excellent taxis, buses, and subway (Tube) system make a private car unnecessary. In fact, the "congestion charge" of £8 levied on any private car entering the city center has been effective in cutting down traffic jam delays and bolstering London's public transit. The revenue raised subsidizes the buses, which are now cheaper, more frequent, and even more user-friendly than before. Today, the vast majority of vehicles in the city center are buses, taxis, and service trucks. (Drivers, for all the details on the congestion charge, see www.cclondon.com.)

By Tube

London's subway system (called the Tube or Underground, but never "subway," which refers to a pedestrian underpass) is one of this planet's great people-movers, and often the fastest long-distance transport in town (runs Mon–Sat about 5:00–24:00, Sun about 7:00–23:00).

Start by studying a Tube map. You can pick one up at any station (and a Tube map is included as a part of most London maps). Each line has a name (such as Circle, Northern, or Bakerloo) and two directions (indicated by the end-of-the-line stop). Find the line that will take you to your destination, and figure out roughly what direction (north, south, east, or west) you'll need to go to get there.

You can use paper tickets, Travelcards, or an Oyster card to pay for your journey (see sidebar). At the Tube station, feed your paper ticket or Travelcard into the turnstile, reclaim it, and hang onto it—you'll need it to get through the turnstile at the end of your journey. Try not to crease paper tickets or cards, or they may become unreadable by the machines. If you are using a plastic Oyster card, touch the card to the yellow card reader both when you enter and exit the station. Find your train by following signs to your line and the (general) direction it's headed (such as Central Line: east).

Since some tracks are shared by several lines, you'll need to double-check before boarding a train: First, make sure your destination is one of the stops listed on the sign at the platform. Also, check the electronic signboards that announce which train is next, and make sure the destination (the end-of-the-line stop) is the one you want. Some trains, particularly on the Circle and District lines, split off for other directions, but each train has its final destination marked above its windshield. When in doubt, ask a local or a blue-vested staff person for help.

Trains run roughly every three to 10 minutes. If one train is absolutely packed and you notice another to the same destination is coming in three minutes, you can wait to avoid the sardine

Oyster Cards and Travelcards

You will definitely save money if you pay for your Tube and bus rides using a pass. There are two similar but distinct options: Oyster cards and Travelcards (details online at www.tfl.gov.uk, click "Tickets and Oyster").

Oyster Cards

Oyster cards—hard plastic transit cards embedded with computerized information—are popular. Tube fares are heavily discounted with Oyster cards (£1.50–2 per ride in Zones 1–6 off-peak, instead of £4 per ride if you pay cash). Bus fares are also discounted with an Oyster card (£1 in Zones 1–6 at any time, instead of £2 if you pay cash). They're worth considering if you'll be in London for longer than a few days.

You can buy Oyster cards at Tube stations that have ticket offices, at TIs, as well as at some newspaper stands and stores (look for *Oyster Card Sold Here* signs). They can be used on the Tube, buses, and Docklands Light Railway (DLR). On each type of transport, you touch the card to the yellow card reader, it flashes green, and you're good to go. Two kinds of Oyster cards work well for travelers:

With **pay-as-you-go Oyster cards,** you load up your Oyster with credit (paying for £10 at a time), and fares are then deducted as you ride. A price cap guarantees you'll never pay more than the One-Day Travelcard price within a 24-hour period (see "One-Day Travelcard," below). You'll also pay an additional £3 deposit to get the card, but this deposit (along with a cash refund of any remaining balance) is refundable at any Tube station ticket office if you return the card. Pay-as-you-go Oyster balances never expire, and you can use the card whenever you're in London (or lend it to someone else). When your balance gets low, add another £10 to keep riding.

For those in London four to seven consecutive days, the **Seven-Day Oyster card** is a good deal. The least expensive version is £23.20, and covers unlimited, peak-time travel through Zones 1 and 2 (cards covering more zones are also available). You can start the card on any day, with no deposit needed, and it will expire at 4:30 in the morning on the eighth consecutive day of use.

Travelcards

A paper Travelcard works like a traditional ticket: You buy it at any Tube station ticket window or machine, then feed it into a turnstile (and retrieve it) to enter and exit the Tube. On a bus, just show it to the driver when you get on. If you take at least two rides a day, a Travelcard is a better deal than buying individual tickets. Like the Oyster card, Travelcards are valid on the Tube, buses, and Docklands Light Railway. The following fares are for Zones 1 and 2; pricier versions covering more zones are also available. Note that you can use any Travelcard to get a 33 percent discount on most Thames cruises.

The **One-Day Travelcard** gives you unlimited travel for a day. The regular price is £6.60, but an "off-peak" version is £5.10 (good for travel starting after 9:30 on weekdays and anytime on weekends). A One-Day Travelcard for Zones 1–6, which includes Heathrow Airport, costs £13.20; the restricted off-peak version costs £6.70.

The **Three-Day Travelcard** for £16.40 costs almost 20 percent less than three One-Day "peak" Travelcards, and is also good any time of day. Most travelers staying three days will easily take enough Tube and bus rides to make this worthwhile. Buying three separate One-Day "off-peak" Travelcards will save you £1.10, but you'll only be able to travel after 9:30 on weekdays. Three-Day Travelcards are not available in an "off-peak" version.

Which Pass to Buy?

Trying to decide between an Oyster and a Travelcard? Here's what I recommend: For a one- or two-day trip, get a One-Day Travelcard each day. For three consecutive days, buy a Three-Day Travelcard. For four or more days in a row, a Seven-Day Oyster card is your best bet. If you won't be riding public transport every day, get the pay-as-you-go rechargeable Oyster card listed above.

Other Discounts

Groups of 10 or more adults can travel all day on the Tube for £3.50 each (but not on buses). Kids 12-17 pay £1 when part of a group of 10.

Families: A paying adult can take up to four kids (aged 10 and under) for free on the Tube all day, every day. In the Tube, use the manual gate, rather than the turnstiles, to be waved in. Families with children 11–15 also save with the "Kids for a Quid" promotion: Any adult with a Travelcard can buy an off-peak One-Day Travelcard for up to four kids 15 or younger for only £1 (a "quid") each.

experience. The system can be fraught with construction delays and breakdowns, so pay attention to signs and announcements explaining necessary detours. The Circle Line is notorious for problems. Rush hours (8:00–10:00 and 16:00–19:00) can be packed and sweaty. Bring something to do to make your waiting time productive. If you get confused, ask for advice at the information window located before the turnstile entry.

Remember that you can't leave the system without feeding your ticket or Travelcard to the turnstile or touching your Oyster card to an electronic reader. If you have a single-trip paper ticket, the turnstile will eat your now-expired ticket; if it's a Travelcard, it will spit your still-valid card back out. Save walking time by choosing the best street exit—check the maps on the walls or ask any station personnel. For Tube and bus information, visit www.tfl.gov.uk (and check out the journey planner).

Any ride in Zones 1–6 (the center of town out to Heathrow Airport) costs a steep £4 for adults paying cash. If you plan to ride the Tube more than once a day, you'll save money by getting an Oyster card or Travelcard.

If you do buy a single Tube ticket, you may be able to avoid ticket-window lines in stations by using the coin-op or credit-card machines; practice on the punchboard to see how the system works (hit "Adult Single" and your destination). These tickets are valid only on the day of purchase. Also, if your credit or debit card does not have a "smart chip," you may not be able to use these machines.

By Bus

Riding city buses doesn't come naturally to many travelers, but if you figure out the system you'll swing like Tarzan through the urban jungle of London. Pick up the free *London Buses: Central London* at a transport office, TI, or some major museums for a fine map listing all the bus routes best for sightseeing.

The first step in mastering the bus system is learning how to decipher the bus-stop signs. Find a bus stop and study the signs mounted on the pole next to the stop. You'll see a chart listing (alphabetically) the destinations served by buses that pick up at this spot or nearby; the names of the buses; and alphabet letters that identify exactly where the buses pick up. After locating your destination, remember or write down the bus name and bus stop letter. Next, refer to the neighborhood map (also on the pole) to find your bus stop. Just match your letter with a stop on the map. Make your way to that stop—you'll know it's yours because it will have the same letter on its pole—and wait for the bus with the right name to arrive. Some fancy stops have electric boards indicating the minutes until the next bus arrives; but remember to

Handy Bus Routes

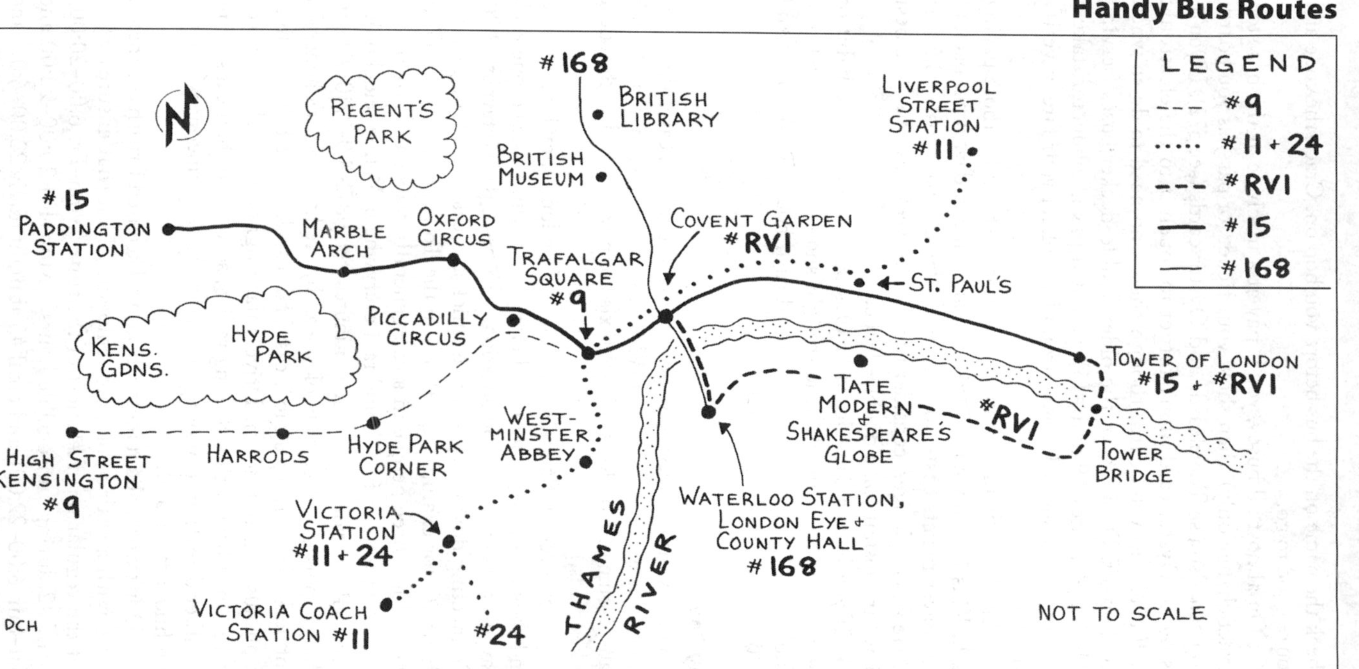
LEGEND
#9
#11 + 24
#RV1
#15
#168
#168
British Library
British Museum
Liverpool Street Station #11
Regent's Park
#15
Paddington Station
Marble Arch
Oxford Circus
Trafalgar Square #9
Covent Garden #RV1
St. Paul's
Piccadilly Circus
Kens. Gdns.
Hyde Park
Tower of London #15 + #RV1
Tate Modern + Shakespeare's Globe
#RV1
West-minster Abbey
Hyde Park Corner
Harrods
High Street Kensington #9
Tower Bridge
Victoria Station #11 + 24
Waterloo Station, London Eye + County Hall #168
Thames River
Victoria Coach Station #11
#24
DCH
Not to scale

check the name on the bus before you hop on. Crack the code and you're good to go.

On almost all buses, you'll pay at a machine at the bus stop (exact change only), then show your ticket (or pass) as you board. You can also use Travelcards and Oyster cards (see 572). If you're using an Oyster card, don't forget to touch it to the electronic card reader as you board, though there's no need to do so when you hop off. On a few of the older double-decker buses (serving "Heritage" routes #9 and #15), you still pay a conductor; take a seat and he or she will come around to collect your fare or verify your pass.

Any bus ride in downtown London costs £2 for those paying cash. Kids 13 and younger ride free any time of day. A six-pack of Bus Saver tickets costs £6 and an all-day bus pass costs £3.50. If you're staying longer, consider the £14 all-week bus pass. The best views are upstairs on a double-decker.

If you have a Travelcard or Oyster card, get in the habit of hopping buses for quick little straight shots, even just to get to a Tube stop. During bump-and-grind rush hours (8:00–10:00 and 16:00–19:00), you'll go faster by Tube.

By Taxi

London is the best taxi town in Europe. Big, black, carefully regulated cabs are everywhere. (While historically known as "black cabs," some of London's official taxis are now covered with wildly colored ads.)

I've never met a crabby cabbie in London. They love to talk, and they know every nook and cranny in town. I ride in one each day just to get my London questions answered. Rides start at £2.20. Connecting downtown sights is quick and easy, and will cost you about £6 (for example, St. Paul's to the Tower of London). For a short ride, three people in a cab generally travel at Tube prices. Groups of four or five should taxi everywhere. While telephoning a cab will get you one in a few minutes (tel. 0871-871-8710; £2 surcharge, plus extra fee to book ahead by credit card), it's generally not necessary; hailing a cab is easy and costs less. If a cab's top light is on, just wave it down. Drivers flash lights when they see you wave. They have a tiny turning radius, so you can hail cabs going in either direction. If waving doesn't work, ask someone where you can find a taxi stand.

Don't worry about meter cheating. Licensed British cab meters come with a sealed computer chip and clock that ensures you'll get the regular tariff #1 most of the time (Mon–Fri 6:00–20:00), tariff #2 during "unsociable hours" (Mon–Fri 20:00–22:00 and Sat–Sun 6:00–22:00), and tariff #3 at night (daily 22:00–6:00) and on holidays. (Rates go up about 15-20 percent with each higher tariff.) All extra charges are explained in writing on the cab wall. The only way a cabbie can cheat you is by taking a needlessly long route. Another pitfall is taking a cab when traffic is bad to a destination efficiently served by the Tube. On a recent trip to London, I hopped in a taxi at South Kensington for Waterloo Station and hit bad traffic. Rather than spending 20 minutes and £2 on the Tube, I spent 40 minutes and £16 in a taxi.

Tip a cabbie by rounding up (maximum 10 percent). If you over-drink and ride in a taxi, be warned: Taxis charge £40 for "soiling" (a.k.a., pub puke).

TOURS

▲▲▲Hop-on, Hop-off Double-Decker Bus Tours—Two competitive companies (Original and Big Bus) offer essentially the same two tours of the city's sightseeing highlights, with nearly 30 stops on each route. One tour has buses with live (English-only) guides, and a second (sometimes slightly different route) comes with tape-recorded, dial-a-language narration. These two-hour, once-over-lightly bus tours drive by all the famous sights, providing a stress-free way to get your bearings and see the biggies. With a good guide and nice weather, sit back and enjoy the entire two hours. Narration is important—and both companies have entertaining and boring guides—so hop on and hop off to see the sights or to change guides.

Buses run about every 10–15 minutes in summer, every 20 minutes in winter, and operate daily (from about 9:00 until early evening in summer, until late afternoon in winter). It's an inexpensive form of transport, stopping at a core group of sights regardless of which overview tour you're on: Victoria Station, Marble Arch, Piccadilly Circus, Trafalgar Square, the Tower of London, and elsewhere.

In addition to the overview tours, both Original and Big Bus include a narrated Thames boat tour covered by the same ticket (buy ticket from driver, credit cards accepted at major stops such as Victoria Station, ticket good for 24 hours, bring a sweater and a camera). Big Bus tours are a little better but more expensive (£20), while Original tours are cheaper (£16 with this book) and nearly as good. Pick up a map from any flier rack or from one of the countless salespeople, and study the complex system. Note: If you start at Victoria Station at 9:00, you'll finish near Buckingham Palace in time to see the Changing of the Guard at 11:30; ask your driver for the best place to hop off. Sunday morning—when the traffic is light and many museums are closed—is a fine time for a tour. The last full loop leaves Victoria at 17:00. Unless you're using the bus tour mainly for hop-on, hop-off transportation, consider saving money by taking a night tour (described below).

Original London Sightseeing Bus Tour: For a live guide on the city highlights tour, look for a yellow triangle on the front of the bus. A red triangle means a longer, tape-recorded multilingual tour that includes Madame Tussauds—avoid it, unless you have kids who'd enjoy the entertaining recorded kids' tour. A green triangle on the front denotes a short *Da Vinci Code* tour, while a blue triangle connects far-flung museums. All routes are covered by the same ticket. Keep it simple and just take the main, introductory tour (£19, £3 discount with this book, limit two discounts per book, they'll rip off the corner of this page—raise bloody hell if they don't honor this discount, also online deals, ticket good for 24 hours, tel. 020/8877-1722, www.theoriginaltour.com). Your ticket includes a 50-minute round-trip boat tour from Westminster Pier (departs hourly, tape-recorded narration) or a point-to-point boat trip from Embankment Pier to Greenwich, with stops in between (14 departures per day).

Big Bus Hop-on, Hop-off London Tours: For £20 (£18 if you book online), you get the same basic overview tours: Red buses come with a live guide, while the blue route has a recorded narration and a longer path around Hyde Park. Your ticket includes coupons for several silly one-hour London walks, as well as the scenic and usually entertainingly guided Thames boat ride between Westminster Pier and the Tower of London (normally £6). The pass and extras are valid for 24 hours. These pricier tours tend to have better, more dynamic guides than Original (daily 8:30–18:00, winter until 16:30, from Victoria Station, tel. 020/7233-9533, www.bigbus.co.uk).

At Night: The London by Night Sightseeing Tour operates two routes, but after hours, with none of the extras (e.g., walks, boat tours), and for half the price. While the narration can be pretty lame, the views at twilight are grand (though note that summer nights are light late). Their West End Tour drives by more biggies than their City Tour. Each tour costs £9 and lasts 60 minutes. You can pay the driver when you board (at any of the stops on their route, such as the London Eye, where the two routes intersect); or buy tickets at the Victoria Station or Paddington Station TIs; or save £2 by booking on their website (April–Dec only, West End Tour normally departs 19:30, 20:30, and 21:30 from Victoria Station, no 20:30 tour in winter; Taxi Road, at front of station near end of Wilton Road, tel. 020/8646-1747, www.london-by-night.net). For a memorable and economical evening, munch a scenic picnic dinner on the top deck. There are plenty of take-away options within the train stations and near the various stops.

▲▲Walking Tours—Several times a day, top-notch local guides lead (often big) groups through specific slices of London's past.

Schedule fliers litter the desks of TIs, hotels, and pubs. *Time Out* lists many, but not all, scheduled walks. Simply show up at the announced location, pay £6, and enjoy two chatty hours of Dickens, the Plague, Shakespeare, Legal London, the Beatles, Jack the Ripper, or whatever is on the agenda. **London Walks,** the dominant company, lists its extensive daily schedule in a beefy, plain, black-and-white *London Walks* brochure and on their website, where you can plan an itinerary online (walks offered year-round—even Christmas, private tours for groups-£100, tel. 020/7624-3978, for a recorded listing of today's walks call 020/7624-9255, www.walks.com). They also run **Explorer day trips,** a good option for those with limited time and transportation (different trip daily: Stonehenge/Salisbury, Oxford/Cotswolds, York, Bath, and so on).

The Beatles: Fans of the still-Fabulous Four can take one of two Beatles walks (Original London Walks, above, has 5/week; Big Bus, above, has a daily walk included with their bus tour). For a photo op, go to Abbey Road and walk the famous crosswalk (at intersection with Grove End, Tube: St. John's Wood). The Beatles Store is at 231 Baker Street (daily 10:00–18:30, next to Sherlock Holmes Museum, Tube: Baker Street, tel. 020/7935-4464, www.beatlesstorelondon.co.uk).

Private Guides—Standard rates for London's registered guides are £110 for four hours, £170 for eight hours (tel. 020/7780-4060, www.touristguides.org.uk, www.blue-badge.org.uk). Consider energetic Britt Lonsdale (tel. 020/7386-9907, mobile 07812/278-077, brittl@ntlworld.com).

Drivers: Robina Brown leads tours of small groups in her Toyota Previa (£250/half-day, £350–540/day, prices vary by destination, tel. 020/7228-2238, www.driverguidetours.com, robina@driverguidetours.com). Janine Barton provides a similar driver-and-guide tour and similar prices (£225–245/half-day for up to six people, £340–500/full-day, prices vary by destination, entrance fees extra, tel. 020/7402-4600, jbsiis@aol.com), and offers a 15 percent discount to readers of this book. Robina and Janine's services are particularly helpful for wheelchair-bound travelers who want to see more of London.

London Duck Tours—A bright-yellow amphibious WWII-vintage vehicle (the model that landed troops on Normandy's beaches on D-Day) takes a gang of 30 tourists past some famous sights on land—Big Ben, Trafalgar Square, Piccadilly Circus—then splashes into the Thames for a cruise (£17.50, 2/hr, daily 10:00–17:30, 75 min—45 min on land and 30 min in the river, these book up in advance, departs from Chicheley Street—you'll see the big ugly vehicle parked 100 yards behind London Eye Ferris Wheel, Tube: Waterloo or Westminster, tel. 020/7928-3132, www.londonducktours.co.uk). All in all, it's good fun at a rather steep price; the live guide works hard and it's kid-friendly to the point of goofiness.

▲▲**Cruises**—Boat tours with entertaining commentaries sail regularly from many points along the Thames. It's confusing, since there are several companies offering essentially the same thing. Your basic options are downstream (to the Tower and Greenwich), upstream (to Kew Gardens and Hampton Court), and round-trip scenic tour cruises. Most people depart from the Westminster Pier (at the base of Westminster Bridge under Big Ben). You can catch most of the same boats (with less waiting) from Waterloo Pier at the London Eye Ferris Wheel across the river. For pleasure and efficiency, consider combining a one-way cruise (to Kew, Greenwich, or wherever) with a Tube ride back. While Tube and bus tickets don't work on the boats, a Travelcard can snare you a 33 percent discount on most cruises (just show the card when you pay for the cruise). Children and seniors get discounts. You can purchase drinks and scant, pricey snacks on board. Buy boat tickets at the small ticket offices on the docks. Clever budget travelers pack a small picnic and munch while they cruise.

Here are some of the most popular cruise options:

To the Tower of London: City Cruises boats sail 30 minutes to the Tower from Westminster Pier (£6 one-way, £7 round-trip, one-way included with Big Bus London tour; covered by £9.50 "River Red Rover" ticket that includes Greenwich—see next paragraph; daily April–Oct roughly 10:00–21:00, until 18:00 in winter, every 40 min).

To Greenwich: Two companies head to Greenwich from Westminster Pier. Choose between **City Cruises** (£7 one-way, £9.50 round-trip; or get their £9.50 all-day, hop-on, hop-off "River Red Rover" ticket to have option of getting off at London Eye and Tower of London; daily April–Oct generally 10:00–17:00, less off-season, every 40 min, 70 min to Greenwich, usually narrated only downstream—to Greenwich, tel. 020/7930-9033 or 020/7740-0400, www.citycruises.com) and **Thames River Services** (£7 one-way, £9 round-trip, daily April–Oct 10:00–16:00, July–Aug until 17:00, has shorter hours and runs every 40 min rest of year, 2/hr, 50 min, usually narrated only to Greenwich, tel. 020/7930-4097, www.westminsterpier.co.uk).

Round-Trip Cruises: Fifty-minute round-trip cruises of the Thames go hourly from Westminster Pier to the Tower of London (£9, included with Original London Sightseeing Bus tour—listed above, tape-recorded narration, Catamaran Circular Cruises, tel. 020/7987-1185). The London Eye Ferris Wheel operates its own "River Cruise Experience," offering a similar 40-minute live-guided circular tour from Waterloo Pier (£10, £21 with London Eye, reservations recommended, departures generally :45 past hour, tel. 0870-443-9185, www.ba-londoneye.com).

From Tate to Tate: The Tate Boat service for art-lovers connects the Tate Modern and Tate Britain in 18 scenic minutes, stopping at the London Eye Ferris Wheel en route (£4.30 one-way or £7.30 for a day ticket; with a Travelcard it's £2.85-one-way/£4.90-day ticket; buy ticket at gallery desk or on board, departing every 40 min from 10:00–17:00, 18-min trip, tel. 020/7887-8008).

On Regent's Canal: Consider exploring London's canals by taking a cruise on historic Regent's Canal in north London. The good ship *Jenny Wren* offers 90-minute guided canal boat cruises from Walker's Quay in Camden Town through scenic Regent's Park to Little Venice (£7, March–Oct daily 12:30 and 14:30, Sat–Sun also at 16:30, Walker's Quay, 250 Camden High Street, 3-min walk from Tube: Camden Town, tel. 020/7485-6210, www.walkersquay.com). While in Camden Town, stop by the popular, punky Camden Lock Market to browse through trendy arts and crafts (daily 10:00–18:00, busiest on weekends, a block from Walker's Quay).

SELF-GUIDED WALK

Westminster Walk

Just about every visitor to London strolls the historic Whitehall boulevard from Big Ben to Trafalgar Square. Beneath London's moderqn traffic and big-city bustle lie 2,000 fascinating years of history. This three-quarter-mile, self-guided orientation walk (see map on next page) gives you a whirlwind tour and connects the sights listed in this section.

Start halfway across **Westminster Bridge** (❶) for that "Wow, I'm really in London!" feeling. Get a close-up view of the **Houses of Parliament** and **Big Ben** (floodlit at night). Downstream you'll see the **London Eye Ferris Wheel.** Down the stairs to Westminster Pier are boats to the Tower of London and Greenwich.

En route to Parliament Square, you'll pass a **statue of Boadicea** (❷), the Celtic queen defeated by Roman invaders in A.D. 60.

To thrill your loved ones (or bug the envious), call home from a pay phone near Big Ben at about three minutes before the hour. You'll find a phone on Great George Street, across from **Parliament Square** (❸). As Big Ben chimes, stick the receiver outside the booth and prove you're in London: Ding dong ding dong...dong ding ding dong.

Wave hello to Churchill in Parliament Square. To his right is **Westminster Abbey** with its two stubby, elegant towers.

Head north up Parliament Street, which turns into Whitehall, and walk toward Trafalgar Square (❹). You'll see the thought-provoking **Cenotaph** (❺) in the middle of the street, reminding

Westminster Walk

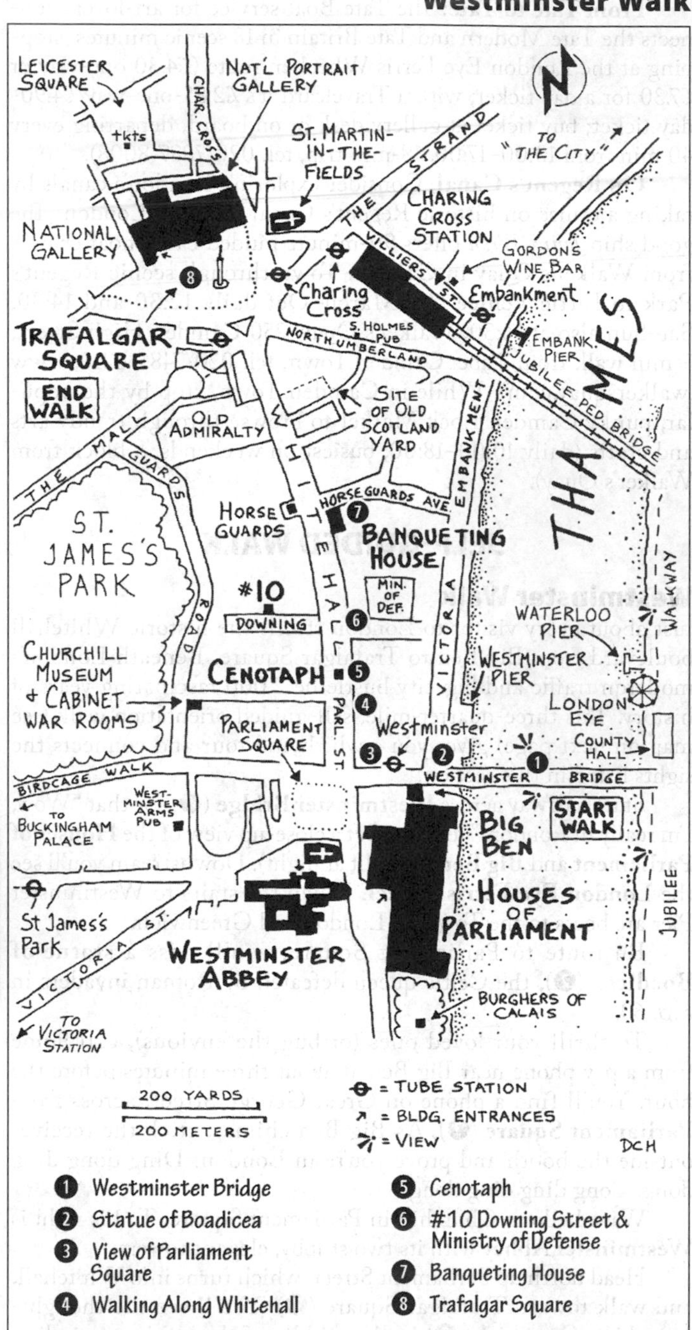

LEICESTER SQUARE
tkts
CHAR. CROSS
NAT'L PORTRAIT GALLERY
ST. MARTIN-IN-THE-FIELDS
THE STRAND
TO "THE CITY"
CHARING CROSS STATION
NATIONAL GALLERY
VILLIERS ST.
GORDON'S WINE BAR
Embankment
Charing Cross
TRAFALGAR SQUARE
S. HOLMES PUB
NORTHUMBERLAND
EMBANK. PIER
JUBILEE PED BRIDGE
THAMES
END WALK
SITE OF OLD SCOTLAND YARD
OLD ADMIRALTY
THE MALL
GUARDS ROAD
EMBANKMENT
WHITEHALL
HORSE GUARDS AVE.
HORSE GUARDS
BANQUETING HOUSE
ST. JAMES'S PARK
MIN. OF DEF.
#10
DOWNING
VICTORIA
WATERLOO PIER
WALKWAY
CHURCHILL MUSEUM + CABINET WAR ROOMS
CENOTAPH
WESTMINSTER PIER
LONDON EYE
PARLIAMENT SQUARE
PARL. ST
Westminster
COUNTY HALL
BIRDCAGE WALK
WESTMINSTER BRIDGE
WEST-MINSTER ARMS PUB
START WALK
TO BUCKINGHAM PALACE
BIG BEN
St James's Park
HOUSES OF PARLIAMENT
JUBILEE
VICTORIA ST.
WESTMINSTER ABBEY
BURGHERS OF CALAIS
TO VICTORIA STATION
200 YARDS
200 METERS
= TUBE STATION
= BLDG. ENTRANCES
= VIEW
DCH
1 Westminster Bridge
2 Statue of Boadicea
3 View of Parliament Square
4 Walking Along Whitehall
5 Cenotaph
6 #10 Downing Street & Ministry of Defense
7 Banqueting House
8 Trafalgar Square

passersby of Britain's many war dead. To visit the Churchill Museum and Cabinet War Rooms (see page 585), take a left before the Cenotaph, on King Charles Street.

Continuing on Whitehall, stop at the barricaded and guarded **#10 Downing Street** to see the British "White House" (❻), home of the prime minister. Break the bobby's boredom and ask him a question.

Nearing Trafalgar Square, look for the **Horse Guards** behind the gated fence (Changing of the Horse Guards Mon–Sat 11:00, Sun at 10:00, dismounting ceremony daily at 16:00) and the 17th-century **Banqueting House** across the street (❼); described on page 586.

The column topped by Lord Nelson marks **Trafalgar Square** (❽). The stately domed building on the far side of the square is the **National Gallery** (free), which has a classy café upstairs in the Sainsbury wing. To the right of the National Gallery is **St. Martin-in-the-Fields Church** and its Café in the Crypt (café reopens in fall 2007).

To get to Piccadilly from Trafalgar Square, walk up Cockspur Street to Haymarket, then take a short left on Coventry Street to colorful **Piccadilly Circus.**

Near Piccadilly you'll find the **Britain and London Visitors Centre** (on Lower Regent Street) and piles of theaters. **Leicester Square** (with its half-price "tkts" booth for plays, see page 612) thrives just a few blocks away. Walk through seedy **Soho** (north of Shaftesbury Avenue) for its fun pubs (see page 636 for the "Food is Fun" Dinner Crawl). From Piccadilly or Oxford Circus, you can take a taxi, bus, or the Tube home.

SIGHTS

Westminster Abbey

As the greatest church in the English-speaking world (worth ▲▲▲), Westminster Abbey has been the place where England's kings and queens have been crowned and buried since 1066. A thousand years of English history—3,000 tombs, the remains of 29 kings and queens, and hundreds of memorials—lie within its walls and under its stone slabs. Like a stony refugee camp huddled outside St. Peter's Pearly Gates, this place has a story to tell. You can take a tour (live or audioguide, see below), experience evensong or an organ concert (see below), visit several small museums, and even have coffee in the cloister...but you can't take photos.

Three tiny **museums** ring the cloisters: the Chapter House (where the monks held their daily meetings, notable for its fine architecture and well-described but faded medieval art), the Pyx Chamber (containing an exhibit on the king's treasury), and the

Abbey Museum (which tells of the abbey's history, royal coronations, and burials). Look into the impressively realistic eyes of Henry VII's funeral effigy (one of a fascinating series of wax-and-wood statues that, for three centuries, graced royal coffins during funeral processions).

The church hosts **evensong** performances every night but Wednesday (Mon–Tue and Thu–Fri at 17:00; Sat–Sun at 15:00) and a free 30-minute **organ recital** on Sunday (at 17:45).

Cost, Hours, Location: £10, £22 family ticket, includes cloisters and Abbey Museum, free for prayer, Mon–Fri 9:30–16:45, Wed until 19:00, Sat 9:30–14:45, last admission 60 min before closing, closed Sun to sightseers but open for services, Abbey Museum open daily 10:30–16:00, cloisters open daily 8:00–18:00, £4 guided tours—up to 6/day in summer, £3 audioguide tours, Tube: Westminster or St. James's Park, info desk tel. 020/7654-4900, www.westminster-abbey.org.

The main entrance, on the Parliament Square side, often has a sizable line; visit early or late to avoid tourist hordes. Midmornings are most crowded. On weekdays after 15:00 it's less crowded; come then and stay for the 17:00 evensong (except Wed). Since the church is often closed to the public for special services, it's wise to call first.

For a free peek inside and a quiet sit in the nave, you can tell a marshal at the west end (where the tourists exit) that you'd like to pay your respects to Britain's Unknown Soldier. If the marshal is nice, he might let you slip in.

Between the Abbey and Trafalgar Square

London

▲▲Houses of Parliament (Palace of Westminster)—This neo-Gothic icon of London, the royal residence from 1042 to 1547, is now the meeting place of the legislative branch of government. Tourists are welcome to view debates in either the bickering House of Commons or the genteel House of Lords (in session when a flag flies atop the Victoria Tower). While the actual debates are generally quite dull, it is a thrill to be inside and see the British government inaction (both Houses usually open Mon–Tue 14:30–22:30, Wed–Thu 11:30–17:50, Fri 9:30–15:00, closed Sat–Sun, generally less action and no lines after 18:00, Tube: Westminster, tel. 020/7219-4272; see www.parliament.uk for schedule). The House of Lords has more pageantry, shorter lines, and less interesting debates (tel. 020/7219-3107 for schedule, and visit www.parliamentlive.tv for a preview).

Houses of Parliament Tours: In August and September, you can get a behind-the-scenes peek at the royal chambers of both houses with a tour led by a Blue Badge guide (£7, 75 min, roughly Mon and Fri–Sat 9:15–16:30, Tue–Thu 1:15–16:30, confirm times when you book, first tours begin 15 min before the Houses open, to book a spot in advance—avoiding waits and guaranteeing a spot—use Keith Prowse ticket service, tel. 0870-906-3773, www.keithprowse.com, no booking fee).

Visiting the Houses of Parliament: In 2007, the Houses of Parliament underwent major changes, including the addition of a new Visitors Centre. To enter the venerable HOP, look for the new entrance on the west side of the building (across from Westminster Abbey); it'll be slightly north of the St. Stephen's entrance, which was the previous entry for tourists. You'll likely see construction in process; follow the people and signs, or ask a guard. If there's only one line outside, it's for the House of Commons. Go to the gate and tell the guard you want the House of Lords (it just takes a few minutes and both Houses are worth seeing). You may pop right in—that is, after you've cleared the security gauntlet. Once you've seen the Lords (hide your HOL flier), you can often slip directly over to the House of Commons and join the gang waiting in the lobby. Inside the lobby, you'll find an announcement board with the day's lineup for both houses.

Just past security to the left, study the big dark **Westminster Hall,** which survived the 1834 fire. The hall was built in the 11th century, and its famous self-supporting hammer-beam roof was added in 1397. The Houses of Parliament are located in what was once the Palace of Westminster, long the palace of England's medieval kings, until it was largely destroyed by fire in 1834. The palace was rebuilt in the Victorian Gothic style (a move away from Neoclassicism back to England's Christian and medieval heritage, true to the Romantic age). It was completed in 1860.

The **Jewel Tower** is the only other part of the old Palace of Westminster to survive (besides Westminster Hall). It contains a fine little exhibit on Parliament (first floor—history, second floor—Parliament today) with a 25-minute video and lonely, picnic-friendly benches (£2.70, daily April–Oct 10:00–17:00, Nov–March 10:00–16:00, across street from St. Stephen's Gate, tel. 020/7222-2219).

Big Ben, the clock tower (315 feet high), is named for its 13-ton bell, Ben. The light above the clock is lit when the House of Commons is sitting. The face of the clock is huge—you can actually see the minute hand moving. For a good view of it, walk halfway over Westminster Bridge.

▲▲▲Churchill Museum and Cabinet War Rooms—This is a fascinating walk through the underground headquarters of the British government's fight against the Nazis in the darkest days of the Battle for Britain. The 27-room nerve center of the British war effort was used from 1939 to 1945. Churchill's room, the map room, and other rooms are just as they were in 1945. For all the blood, sweat, toil, and tears details, pick up the excellent, essential, and included audioguide at the entry and follow the 60-minute tour; be patient—it's well worth it. Don't bypass the Churchill Museum (entrance is a half-dozen rooms into the exhibit), which shows the humanity behind the famous cigar, bowler hat, and V-for-victory sign—allow an hour for that museum alone. It shows his wit, irascibility, work ethic, American ties, writing talents, and drinking habits. A long touch-the-screen timeline lets you zero in on events in his life from birth (November 30, 1874) to his election as Prime Minister in 1940. It's all the more amazing considering that, in the 1930s, the man who became my vote for greatest statesman of the 20th century was considered a washed-up loony ranting about the growing threat of fascism (£12, daily 9:30–18:00, last entry 60 min before closing, on King Charles Street, 200 yards off Whitehall, follow the signs, Tube: Westminster, tel. 020/7930-6961, www.iwm.org.uk). The museum's gift shop is great for anyone nostalgic for the 1940s.

If you're hungry, get your rations at the Switch Room café (in the museum, daily 10:00–17:00) or, for a nearby pub lunch, try the Westminster Arms (food served downstairs, 9 Storey's Gate, a couple of blocks south of War Rooms).

Horse Guards—The Horse Guards change daily at 11:00 (10:00 on Sun), and there's a colorful dismounting ceremony daily at 16:00. The rest of the day, they just stand there—terrible for camcorders (on Whitehall, between Trafalgar Square and #10 Downing Street, Tube: Westminster). While Buckingham Palace pageantry is canceled when it rains, the horse guards change regardless of the weather.

▲Banqueting House—England's first Renaissance building was designed by Inigo Jones around 1620. It's one of the few London landmarks spared by the 1698 fire and the only surviving part of the original Palace of Whitehall. Don't miss its Rubens ceiling, which, at Charles I's request, drove home the doctrine of the legitimacy of the divine right of kings. In 1649—divine right ignored—Charles I was beheaded on the balcony of this building by a Cromwellian Parliament. Admission includes a restful 20-minute audiovisual history, which shows the place in banqueting action; a 30-minute audio tour—interesting only to history buffs; and a look at the exquisite banqueting hall (£4.50, Mon–Sat 10:00–17:00, closed Sun, last entry at 16:30, subject to closure for government functions, aristocratic WC, immediately across Whitehall from the Horse Guards, Tube: Westminster, tel. 020/7930-4179, www.hrp.org.uk). Just up the street is Trafalgar Square.

Trafalgar Square

▲▲Trafalgar Square—London's recently renovated central square, the climax of most marches and demonstrations, is a thrilling

Trafalgar Square

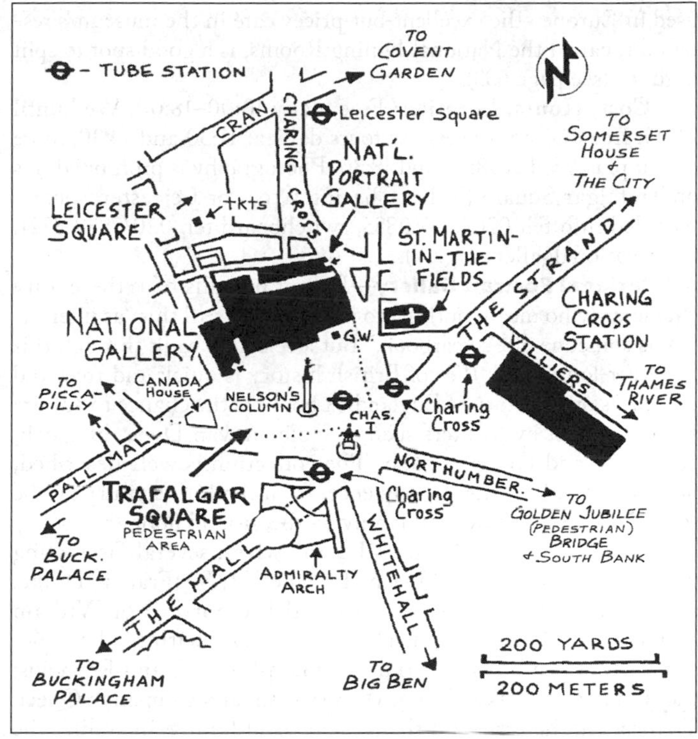

place to simply hang out. Lord Nelson stands atop his 185-foot-tall fluted granite column, gazing out to Trafalgar, where he lost his life but defeated the French fleet. Part of this 1842 memorial is made from his victims' melted-down cannons. He's surrounded by giant lions, splashing fountains, hordes of people, and—until recently—even more pigeons. London's mayor, Ken Livingstone, nicknamed "Red Ken" for his passion for an activist government, decided that London's "flying rats" were a public nuisance and evicted the venerable seed salesmen (Tube: Charing Cross).

▲▲▲National Gallery—Displaying Britain's top collection of European paintings from 1250 to 1900—including works by Leonardo, Botticelli, Velázquez, Rembrandt, Turner, van Gogh, and the Impressionists—this is one of Europe's great galleries. The huge collection traces European art history through medieval holiness, Renaissance realism, Dutch detail, Baroque excess, British restraint, and colorful French Impressionism. Cruise like an eagle with wide eyes for the big picture, seeing how each style progresses into the next. The main entrance offers visitors a grand first impression of Britain's greatest collection of paintings. The audioguide tour (suggested £3 donation) is one of the finest I've used in Europe. The excellent-but-pricey café in the museum's restaurant, called the National Dining Rooms, is a good spot to split high tea (see page 633).

Cost, Hours, Location: Free, daily 10:00–18:00, Wed until 21:00; free one-hour overview tours daily at 11:30 and 14:30, more on Sat plus Wed at 18:00 and 18:30. Photography is prohibited. It's on Trafalgar Square (Tube: Charing Cross or Leicester Square, recorded info tel. 020/7747-2885, switchboard tel. 020/7839-3321, www.nationalgallery.org.uk).

▲▲National Portrait Gallery—Put off by halls of 19th-century characters who meant nothing to me, I used to call this "as interesting as someone else's yearbook." But a selective walk through this 500-year-long *Who's Who* of British history is quick and free, and puts faces on the story of England. A bonus is the chance to admire some great art by painters such as Holbein, van Dyck, Hogarth, Reynolds, and Gainsborough. The collection is well-described, not huge, and in historical sequence, from the 16th century on the second floor to today's royal family on the ground floor.

Some highlights: Henry VIII and wives; several fascinating portraits of the "Virgin Queen" Elizabeth I, Sir Francis Drake, and Sir Walter Raleigh; the only real-life portrait of William Shakespeare; Oliver Cromwell and Charles I with his head on; self-portraits and other portraits by Gainsborough and Reynolds; the Romantics (Blake, Byron, Wordsworth, and company); Queen Victoria and her era; and the present royal family, including the late Princess Diana.

The excellent audioguide tours (free, but £2 donation requested) describe each room (or era in British history) and more than 300 paintings. You'll learn more about British history than art and actually hear interviews with 20th-century subjects as you stare at their faces.

London

Cost, Hours, Location: Free, daily 10:00–18:00, Thu–Fri until 21:00. It's 100 yards off Trafalgar Square (around corner from National Gallery, opposite Church of St. Martin-in-the-Fields, Tube: Charing Cross or Leicester Square, tel. 020/7306-0055, recorded info tel. 020/7312-2463, www.npg.org.uk). The elegant Portrait Restaurant on the top floor comes with views and high prices; the cheaper Portrait Café is in the basement.

▲St. Martin-in-the-Fields—This church, built in the 1720s with a Gothic spire atop a Greek-type temple, is an oasis of peace on the wild and noisy Trafalgar Square (free, donations welcome, open daily, Tube: Charing Cross, www.smitf.com). St. Martin cared for the poor. "In the fields" was where the first church stood on this spot (in the 13th century), between Westminster and the City. Stepping inside, you still feel a compassion for the needs

London's Top Squares

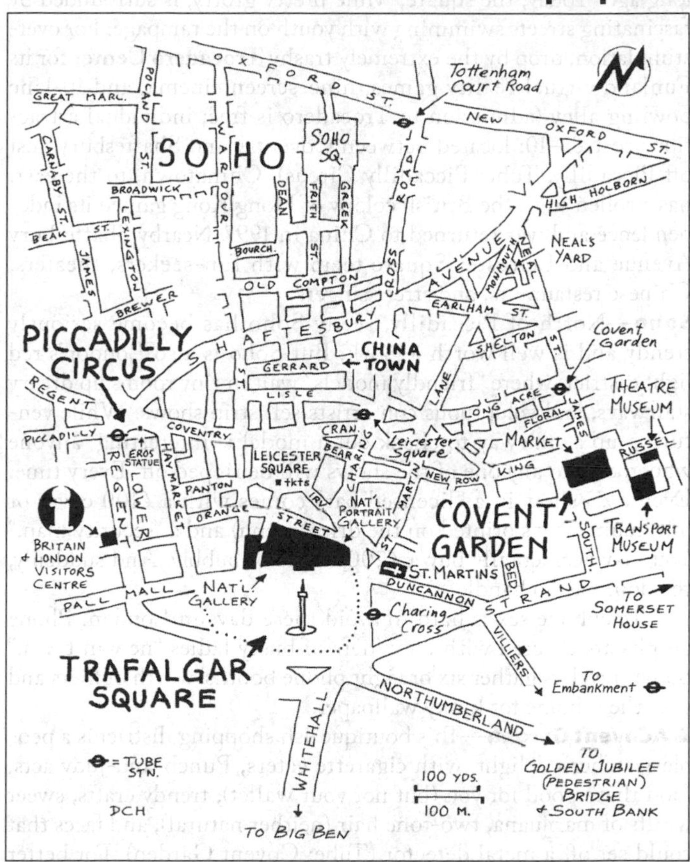

of the people in this community. A free flier provides a brief yet worthwhile self-guided tour. The church is famous for its concerts. Consider a free lunchtime concert (Mon, Tue, and Fri at 13:00) or an evening concert (£8–18, at 19:30 Thu–Sat and on some Tue and Wed, box office tel. 020/7839-8362, church tel. 020/7766-1100). Downstairs, you'll find a ticket office for concerts, and, reopening in fall 2007, a gift shop, brass-rubbing center, and fine support-the-church cafeteria (see page 632).

More Top Squares: Piccadilly, Soho, and Covent Garden

For a "Food is Fun" dinner crawl from Covent Garden to Soho, see "Eating," page 636.

▲▲Piccadilly Circus—London's most touristy square got its name from the fancy ruffled shirts—*picadils*—made in the neighborhood long ago. Today, the square, while pretty grotty, is surrounded by fascinating streets swimming with youth on the rampage. For over-stimulation, drop by the extremely trashy **Trocadero Center** for its Funland virtual-reality games, nine-screen cinema, and 10-lane bowling alley (admission to Trocadero is free; individual attractions cost £2–10; located between Coventry and Shaftesbury, just off Piccadilly, Tube: Piccadilly Circus). Chinatown, to the east, has swollen since the British colony of Hong Kong gained its independence and was returned to China in 1997. Nearby Shaftesbury Avenue and Leicester Square teem with fun-seekers, theaters, Chinese restaurants, and street singers.

Soho—North of Piccadilly, seedy Soho has become seriously trendy and is well worth a gawk. But Soho is also London's red light district, where "friendly models" wait in tiny rooms up dreary stairways, and voluptuous con artists sell strip shows. While venturing up a stairway to check out a model is interesting, anyone who goes into any one of the shows will be ripped off. Every time. Even a £5 show in a "licensed bar" comes with a £100 cover or minimum (as it's printed on the drink menu) and a "security man." You may accidentally buy a £200 bottle of bubbly. And suddenly, the door has no handle.

Telephone sex is hard to avoid these days in London. Phone booths are littered with racy fliers of busty ladies "new in town." Some travelers gather six or eight phone booths' worth of fliers and take them home for kinky wallpaper.

▲▲Covent Garden—This boutique-ish shopping district is a people-watcher's delight, with cigarette eaters, Punch-and-Judy acts, food that's good for you (but not your wallet), trendy crafts, sweet whiffs of marijuana, two-tone hair (neither natural), and faces that could set off a metal detector (Tube: Covent Garden). For better Covent Garden lunch deals, walk a block or two away from the eye of this touristic hurricane (check out the places north of the Tube station along Endell and Neal Streets).

Museums near Covent Garden

▲▲Somerset House—This grand 18th-century civic palace offers a marvelous public space, three fine art collections, and a riverside terrace (between the Strand and the Thames). The palace once housed the national registry that records Britain's births, marriages, and deaths: "...where they hatch 'em, match 'em, and dispatch 'em." Step into the courtyard to enjoy the fountain. Go ahead...walk through it. The 55 jets get playful twice an hour. (In the winter, this becomes a popular ice-skating rink with a toasty café for viewing.)

Surrounding you are three small and sumptuous sights: the Courtauld Gallery (paintings), the Gilbert Collection (fine arts), and the Hermitage Rooms (the art of czarist Russia). All three are open the same hours (daily 10:00–18:00, last entry 17:15, £5 per sight, £8 for any two sights, £12 for all three; easy bus #6, #9, #11, #13, #15, or #23 from Trafalgar Square; Tube: Temple or Covent Garden, tel. 020/7845-4600, www.somerset-house.org.uk). The website lists a busy schedule of tours, kids' events, and concerts. The riverside terrace is picnic-friendly (deli inside lobby).

The **Courtauld Gallery** is less impressive than the National Gallery, but its wonderful collection of paintings is still a joy. The gallery is part of the Courtauld Institute of Art, and the thoughtful description of each piece of art reminds visitors that the gallery is still used for teaching. You'll see medieval European paintings and works by Rubens, the Impressionists (Manet, Monet, and Degas), Post-Impressionists (such as Cézanne), and more (£5, free Mon until 14:00, downstairs cafeteria, lockers, and WC).

The **Hermitage Rooms** offer a taste of Romanov imperial splendor. As Russia struggles and tourists are staying away, someone had the bright idea of sending the best of its art to London to raise some hard cash. These five rooms host a different collection every six months, with a standard intro to the czar's winter palace in St. Petersburg (£5, tel. 020/7420-9410). To see what's on, visit www.somerset-house.org.uk/attractions/hermitage.

The **Gilbert Collection** displays 800 pieces of the finest in European decorative arts, from diamond-studded gold snuffboxes to intricate Italian mosaics. Maybe you've seen Raphael paintings and Botticelli frescoes...but this lush collection is refreshingly different (£5, includes free audioguide with a highlights tour and a helpful loaner magnifying glass).

▲London's Transport Museum—This wonderful museum, renovated in 2007, delights kids. Whether you're cursing or marveling at the buses and Tube, the growth of Europe's biggest city has been made possible by its public transit system. Watch the growth of the Tube, then sit in the simulator to "drive" a train (daily 10:00–18:00, in southeast corner of Covent Garden courtyard, Tube: Covent Garden, tel. 020/7379-6344 or recorded info tel. 020/7565-7299, www.ltmuseum.co.uk).

North London

▲▲▲British Museum, Great Court, and Reading Room—Simply put, this is the greatest chronicle of civilization...anywhere. A visit here is like taking a long hike through Encyclopedia Britannica National Park. Entering on Great Russell Street, you'll step into the Great Court, the glass-domed hub of a two-acre cultural complex, containing restaurants, shops, and lecture halls plus the Round Reading Room.

The most popular sections of the museum fill the ground

North London

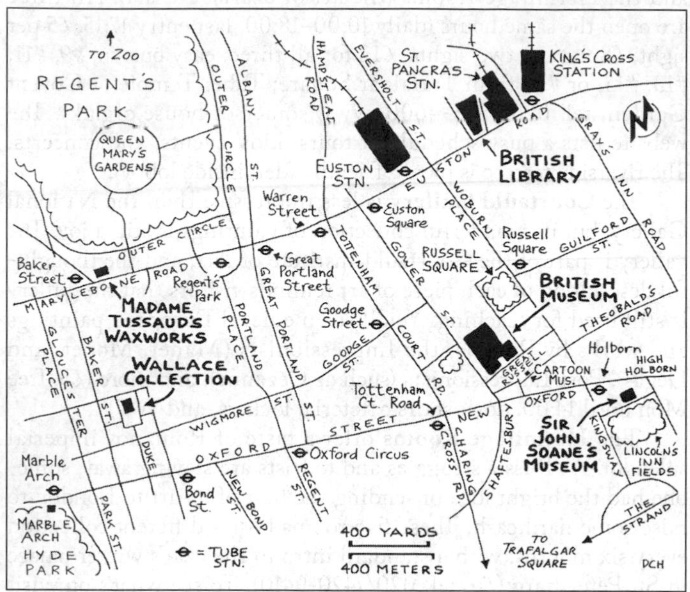

floor: Egyptian, Mesopotamian, and ancient Greek—with the famous Elgin Marbles from the Athenian Parthenon. Huge winged lions (which guarded Assyrian palaces 800 years before Christ) guard these great ancient galleries. For a brief tour, connect these ancient dots:

Start with the **Egyptian.** Wander from the Rosetta Stone past the many statues. At the end of the hall, climb the stairs to mummy land.

Back at the winged lions, explore the dark, violent, and mysterious **Assyrian** rooms. The Nimrud Gallery is lined with royal propaganda reliefs and wounded lions (from the ninth century B.C.).

The most modern of the ancient art fills the **Greek** section. Find Room 11, behind the winged lions, and start your walk through Greek art history with the simple and primitive Cycladic fertility figures. Later, painted vases show a culture really into partying. The finale is the Elgin Marbles. The much-wrangled-over bits of the Athenian Parthenon (from about 450 B.C.) are even more impressive than they look. To best appreciate these ancient carvings, take the audioguide tour (available in this gallery).

Be sure to venture upstairs to see artifacts from **Roman Britain** (Room 50) that surpass anything you'll see at Hadrian's Wall or elsewhere in Britain. Nearby, the Dark Age Britain exhibits offer a worthwhile peek at that bleak era; look for the Sutton

British Museum Overview

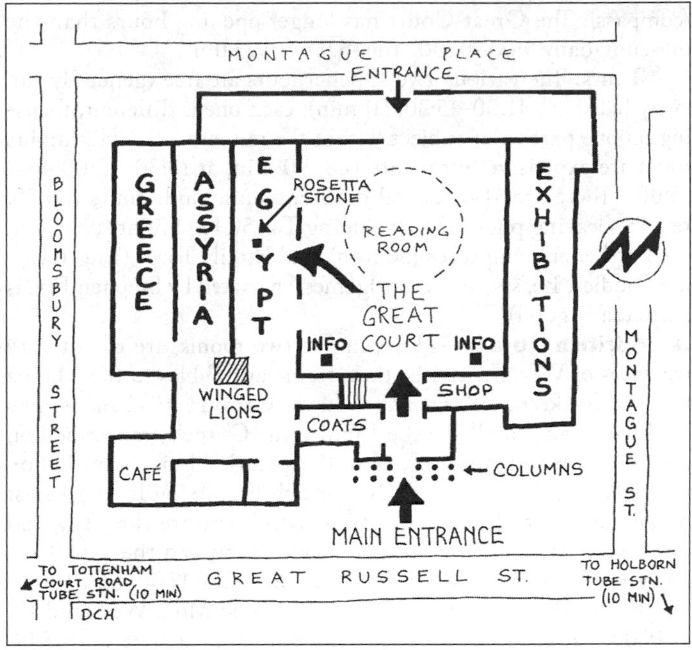

Hoo Burial Ship artifacts from a seventh-century royal burial on the east coast of England (Room 41). A rare Michelangelo cartoon (preliminary sketch) is in Room 90.

The **Great Court** is Europe's largest covered square—bigger than a football field. This people-friendly court—delightfully out of the London rain—was for 150 years one of London's great lost spaces...closed off and gathering dust. While the vast British Museum wraps around the court, its centerpiece is the stately **Reading Room,** famous as the place Karl Marx hung out while formulating his ideas on communism and writing *Das Kapital.* The Reading Room—one of the fine cast-iron buildings of the 19th century—is open to the public, but there's little to see that you can't see from the doorway.

Cost, Hours, Location: The British Museum is free (£3 donation requested, temporary exhibits extra, daily 10:00–17:30, plus Thu–Fri until 20:30—but from 17:30 only a few galleries are open, least crowded weekday late afternoons, Great Russell Street, Tube: Tottenham Court Road, tel. 020/7323-8000, recorded info tel. 020/7388-2227, www.thebritishmuseum.ac.uk).

The Reading Room is free and open daily 10:00–17:30. Computer terminals within the Reading Room allow you to take a virtual tour of the British Museum, delving deeply into whatever interests you (study ahead at www.thebritishmuseum.ac.uk/compass). The Great Court has longer opening hours than the museum (daily 9:00–18:00, Thu–Sat until 23:00).

Tours: The various Eye-Opener tours are free (generally run every half hour 11:00–15:30, 50 min); each one is different, focusing on one particular subject within the museum. The Highlights tours are expensive but meaty (£8, 90 min, at 10:30, 13:00, and 15:00). There are also several different audioguide tours (£3.50, requires leaving photo ID), including Top 50 Highlights (90 min), the Parthenon Sculptures (60 min), and Family Tours (length varies; "Bodies, Beasts, and Boardgames," narrated by Stephen Fry, is particularly good).

▲▲▲British Library—Here, in just two rooms, are the literary treasures of Western civilization, from early Bibles to the Magna Carta to Shakespeare's *Hamlet* to Lewis Carroll's *Alice's Adventures in Wonderland*. You'll see the Lindisfarne Gospels transcribed on an illuminated manuscript, as well as Beatles' lyrics scrawled on the back of a greeting card. The British Empire built its greatest monuments out of paper. And it's with literature that England made her lasting contribution to civilization and the arts (free, Mon–Fri 9:30–18:00, Tue until 20:00, Sat 9:30–17:00, Sun 11:00–17:00; 60-min tours for £6 are usually offered Mon, Wed, and Fri at 15:00; Sat at 10:30 and 15:00; the Sun tours at 11:30 and 15:00 cost a little more—£7; call 020/7412-7332 to confirm schedule and reserve; £3.50 audioguide—leave photo ID or £20 deposit; helpful free computers also give you extra info; Tube: King's Cross, from the station walk a block west to 96 Euston Road, library tel. 020/7412-7000, www.bl.uk). The ground-floor café is next to a vast and fun pull-out stamp collection, and the cafeteria upstairs serves good hot meals.

▲Wallace Collection—Sir Richard Wallace's fine collection of 17th-century Dutch Masters, 18th-century French Rococo, medieval armor, and assorted aristocratic fancies fills the sumptuously furnished Hertford House on Manchester Square. From the rough and intimate Dutch life-scapes of Jan Steen to the pink-cheeked Rococo fantasies of François Boucher, a wander through this little-visited mansion makes you nostalgic for the days of empire (free, daily 10:00–17:00, audioguide-£3; guided tours available—but call to confirm times; just north of Oxford Street on Manchester Square, Tube: Bond Street, tel. 020/7563-9500, www.wallacecollection.org).

▲Madame Tussauds Waxworks—This is gimmicky and expensive but dang good. The original Madame Tussaud did wax casts of heads lopped off during the French Revolution (such as Marie-Antoinette's). She took her show on the road and ended up in London. And now it's much easier to be featured. The gallery is one big photo-op—a huge hit with the kind of travelers who skip the British Museum. After looking a hundred famous people in their glassy eyes and surviving a silly hall of horror, you'll board a Disney-type ride and cruise through a kid-pleasing "Spirit of London" time trip. Your last stop is the auditorium for a 12-minute stage show (runs every 15 min). They've dumped anything really historical (except for what they claim is the blade that beheaded Marie-Antoinette) because "there's no money in it and we're a business." Now, it's all about squeezing Brad Pitt's bum, wining and dining with George Clooney, and partying with Beyoncé, Kylie, Britney, and Posh (admission-£24, kids-£20; after 17:00 it's £15, kids-£10; children under 5 always free; daily 9:30–18:30, last entry 60 min before closing, Marylebone Road, Tube: Baker Street).

Saving Money and/or Time: The Waxworks are popular. You can avoid a wait by booking ahead to get a ticket with an entry time (by calling 0870-400-3000, booking online at www.madame-tussauds.com for a £2 fee, or actually saving money by getting a Fast Track ticket at the Britain and London Visitors Centre or the TIs at Victoria and Waterloo train stations). Hotels can often get a good rate—so ask. Or you can buy the £32 London Eye combo-ticket (saving £5) if you're planning on seeing both sights. This is the cheapest way to get in: Arrive at the Waxworks at 17:00 to save £9 on admission and avoid any lines; 90 minutes is plenty of time for the exhibit.

Sir John Soane's Museum—Architects and fans of eclectic knickknacks love this quirky place, as do Martha Stewarts and lovers of Back Door sights. Tour this furnished home on a bird-chirping square and see 19th-century chairs, lamps, and carpets, wood-paneled nooks and crannies, and stained-glass skylights. The townhouse is cluttered with Soane's (and his wife's) collection of ancient relics, curios, and famous paintings, including Hogarth's series on *The Rake's Progress* (read the fun plot) and several excellent Canalettos. In 1833, just before his death, Soane established his house as a museum, stipulating that it be kept as nearly as possible in the state he left it. If he visited today, he'd be entirely satisfied. You'll leave wishing you'd known the man (free, Tue–Sat 10:00–17:00, first Tue of the month also 18:00–21:00, closed Sun–Mon, good £1 brochure, £3 guided tours Sat at 14:30, 13 Lincoln's Inn Fields, quarter-mile southeast of British Museum, Tube: Holborn, tel. 020/7405-2107).

Cartoon Museum—This humble but interesting museum, located in the shadow of the British Museum, opened in 2006 with three rooms of exhibition space. While it's filled with British cartoons unknown to most Americans, the satire of famous big wigs and politicians—from Napoleon to Margaret Thatcher, the Queen, and Tony Blair—shows the power of parody to deliver social commentary. Upstairs, you'll see pages spanning from *Tarzan* to *Tank Girl*—interesting only to comic-book diehards (£3, Tue–Sat 10:30–17:30, Sun 12:00–17:30, closed Mon, 35 Little Russell Street—go one block south of the British Museum on Coptic Street and make a left, Tube: Tottenham Court Road, tel. 020/7580-8155, www.cartoonmuseum.org).

Buckingham Palace

▲Buckingham Palace—This lavish home has been Britain's royal residence since 1837. When the queen's at home, the royal standard flies (a red, yellow, and blue flag); otherwise the Union Jack flaps in the wind. Recently, the queen has opened her palace to the public—but only in August and September, when she's out of town (£14 for state apartments and throne room, Aug–Sept only, daily 9:45–18:00, last admission 15:45, only 8,000 visitors a day—to get an entry time, come early or for £1.25 extra you can book ahead by phone or online, Tube: Victoria, tel. 020/7766-7300, www.royalcollection.org.uk).

▲Queen's Gallery at Buckingham Palace—Queen Elizabeth's 7,000 paintings make up the finest private art collection in the world, rivaling Europe's biggest national art galleries. It's actually a collection of collections, built on by each successive monarch since the 16th century. She rotates her paintings, enjoying some privately in her many palatial residences while sharing others with her subjects in public galleries in Edinburgh and London. Small, thoughtfully presented, and always exquisite displays fill the handful of rooms open to the public in a wing of Buckingham Palace. As you're in "the most important building in London," security is tight. You'll see a temporary exhibit and the permanent "treasures"—which come with a room full of "antique and personal jewelry." Compared to the crown jewels at the Tower, it may be Her Majesty's bottom drawer—but it's still a dazzling pile of diamonds. Temporary exhibits change about twice a year, and are always lovingly described by the £2 audioguide. While the admissions come with an entry time, this is only enforced during rare days when crowds are a problem (£7.50, £12 with Royal Mews, daily 10:00–17:30, last entry 60 min before closing, Tube: Victoria, tel. 020/7766-7301 but Her Majesty rarely answers). Men shouldn't miss the mahogany-trimmed urinals.

Royal Mews—The queen's working stables, or "mews," are open to visitors. The visit is likely to be disappointing (you'll see four horses out of the queen's 30, a fancy car, and a bunch of old carriages) unless you follow the included guided tour, in which case it's thoroughly entertaining—especially if you're interested in horses and/or royalty. The 40-minute tours go twice an hour and finish with the Gold State Coach (c. 1760, 4 tons, 4 mph). Queen

Buckingham Palace Area

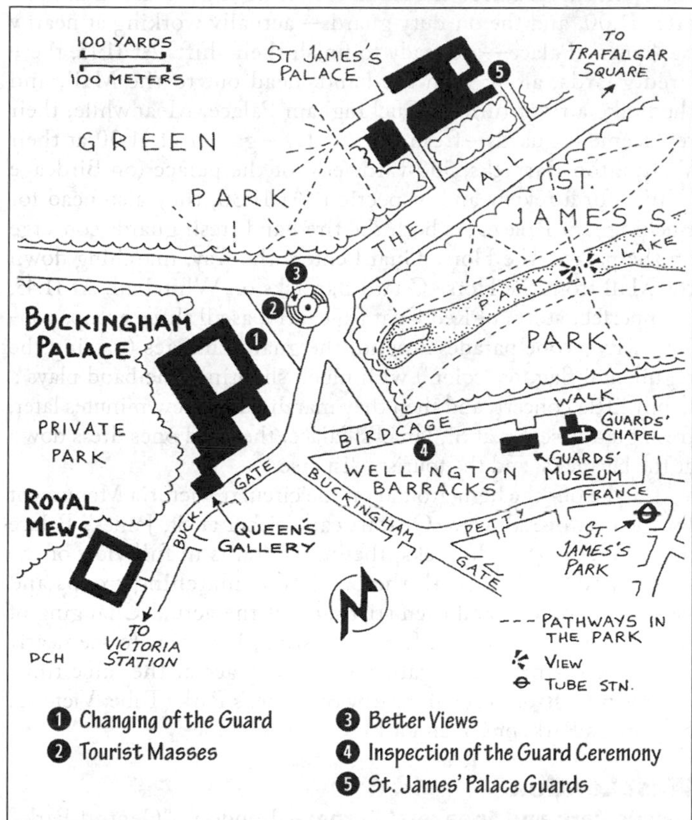

Victoria said absolutely no cars. When she died, in 1901, the mews got its first Daimler. Today, along with the hay-eating transport, the stable is home to five Rolls-Royce Phantoms, with one on display (£6.50, £12 with Queen's Gallery, Aug–Sept Sat–Thu 10:00–17:00, March–July and Oct Sat–Thu 11:00–16:00, closed Fri and Nov–Feb, Buckingham Palace Road, Tube: Victoria, tel. 020/7766-7302).

▲▲Changing of the Guard at Buckingham Palace—The guards change with much fanfare at around 11:30 almost daily in the summer and, at a minimum, every other day all year long (no band when wet). Each month it's either daily or on odd or even days. Call 020/7321-2233 for the day's plan, or check www.royalresidences.com. Then hop into a big black taxi and say, "Buck House, please" (a.k.a. Buckingham Palace).

Most tourists just mob the palace gates for a peek at the Changing of the Guard, but those who know the drill will enjoy the event more. Here's the lowdown on what goes down: It's just after 11:00, and the on-duty guards—actually working at nearby St. James's Palace—are ready to finish their shift. At 11:15, these tired guards, along with the band, head out to the Mall, and then take a right turn for Buckingham Palace. Meanwhile, their replacement guards—fresh for the day—gather at 11:00 at their Wellington Barracks, 500 yards east of the palace (on Birdcage Walk), for a review and inspection. At 11:30, they also head for Buckingham Palace. As both the tired and fresh guards converge on the palace, the Horse Guard enters the fray, marching down the Mall from the Horse Guard Barracks on Whitehall. At 11:45, it's a perfect storm of Red Coat pageantry, as all three groups converge. Everyone parades around, the guard changes (passing the regimental flag, or "color") with much shouting, the band plays a happy little concert, and then they march out. A few minutes later, fresh guards set up at St. James's Palace, the tired ones dress down at the barracks, and the tourists disperse.

Stake out the high ground on the circular Victoria Monument for the best overall view. Or start early either at St. James's Palace or the Wellington Barracks (the inspection is in full view of the street) and stride in with the band. The marching troops and bands are colorful and even stirring, but the actual Changing of the Guard is a nonevent. It is interesting, however, to see nearly every tourist in London gathered in one place at the same time. Afterwards, stroll through nearby St. James's Park (Tube: Victoria, St. James's Park, or Green Park).

West London

▲Hyde Park and Speakers' Corner—London's "Central Park," originally Henry VIII's hunting grounds, has more than 600 acres of lush greenery, a huge man-made lake, the royal Kensington Palace and Orangery, and the ornate neo-Gothic Albert Memorial across from the Royal Albert Hall. Early afternoons on Sunday (until early evening), Speakers' Corner offers soapbox oratory at its best (Tube: Marble Arch). "The grass roots of democracy" is actually a holdover from when the gallows stood here and the criminal was allowed to say just about anything he wanted to before he swung. I dare you to raise your voice and gather a crowd—it's easy to do.

The **Princess Diana Memorial Fountain** honors the "People's Princess" who once lived in nearby Kensington Palace. The low-key circular stream is in the eastern part of the park, near the Serpentine Gallery. (Don't be confused by signs to the Diana Princess of Wales Children's Playground, also found within the park.)

▲Apsley House (Wellington Museum)—Having beaten Napoleon at Waterloo, the Duke of Wellington was once the most

West London

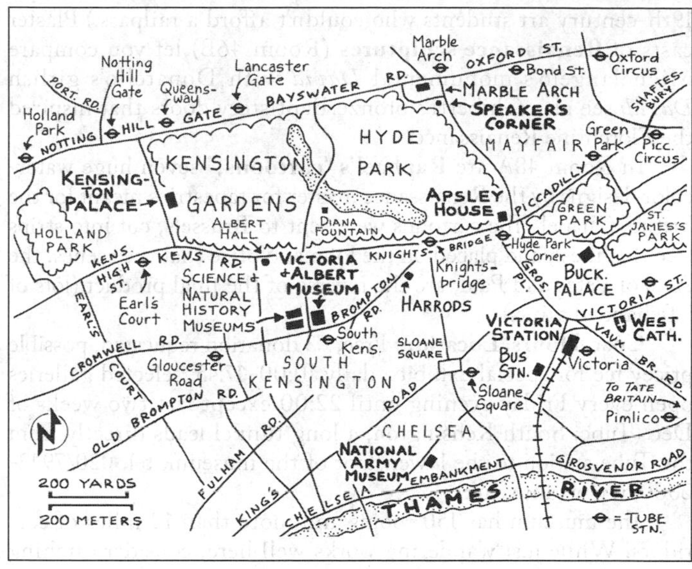

famous man in Europe. He was given London's ultimate address, #1 London. His newly refurbished mansion offers one of London's best palace experiences. An 11-foot-tall marble statue (by Canova) of Napoleon, clad only in a fig leaf, greets you. Downstairs is a small gallery of Wellington memorabilia (including a pair of Wellington boots). The lavish upstairs shows off the duke's fine collection of paintings, including works by Velázquez and Steen (£5.10, Tue–Sun 10:00–17:00 in summer, until 16:00 in winter, closed Mon, well-described by included audioguide, 20 yards from Hyde Park Corner Tube station, tel. 020/7499-5676, www.english-heritage.org.uk). Hyde Park's pleasant and picnic-wonderful rose garden is nearby.

▲▲**Victoria and Albert Museum**—The world's top collection of decorative arts (vases, stained glass, fine furniture, clothing, jewelry, carpets, and more) is a surprisingly interesting assortment of crafts from the West as well as Asian and Islamic cultures.

The V&A grew out of the Great Exhibition of 1851—that ultimate festival celebrating the greatness of Britain. After much support from Queen Victoria and Prince Albert, it was renamed after the royal couple.

Many visitors start with the **British Galleries** (upstairs)—a one-way tour stretching through 400 years of British lifestyles, almost a museum in itself.

In Room 46 are the plaster casts of **Trajan's Column,** a copy of Rome's 140-foot spiral relief telling the story of the conquest of Romania. (The V&A's casts are copies made for the benefit of 19th-century art students who couldn't afford a railpass.) Plaster casts of **Renaissance sculptures** (Room 46B) let you compare Michelangelo's monumental *David* with Donatello's girlish *David;* see also Ghiberti's bronze Baptistery doors that inspired the Florentine Renaissance.

In Room 48A are **Raphael's "cartoons,"** seven huge watercolor designs by the Renaissance master for tapestries meant for the Sistine Chapel. The cartoons were sent to Brussels, cut into strips (see the lines), and placed on the looms. Notice that the scenes, the Acts of Peter and Paul, are the reverse of the final product (lots of left-handed saints).

Cost, Hours, Location: Free, £3 donation requested, possible pricey fee for special exhibits, daily 10:00–17:45, selected galleries open every Friday evening until 22:00 except last two weeks of Dec (Tube: South Kensington, a long tunnel leads directly from the Tube station to the lower floor of the museum, tel. 020/7942-2000, www.vam.ac.uk).

The museum has 150 rooms and more than 12 miles of corridors. While just wandering works well here, consider catching one of the free 60-minute orientation **tours** (daily, usually on the half-hour from 10:30–15:30, also daily at 13:00, Wed at 16:30, and a half-hour version Wed at 18:30) or buying the fine £5 *V&A Guide Book*. The V&A's helpful website lists its current exhibitions and offers interesting mix-and-match podcasts that allow you to create your own audio tour.

▲Natural History Museum—Across the street from Victoria and Albert, this mammoth museum is housed in a giant and wonderful Victorian, Neo-Romanesque building. Built in the 1870s specifically for the huge collection (50 million specimens), it has two halves: the Life Galleries (creepy-crawlies, human biology, "our place in evolution," and awesome dinosaurs) and the Earth Galleries (meteors, volcanoes, earthquakes, and so on). Exhibits are wonderfully explained, with lots of creative, interactive displays. Pop in, if only for the wild collection of dinosaurs and the roaring *Tyrannosaurus rex* (free, possible fee for special exhibits, Mon–Sat 10:00–18:00, Sun 11:00–18:00, last entrance 17:30, a long tunnel leads directly from South Kensington Tube station to museum, tel. 020/7942-5000, exhibit info and reservations tel. 020/7942-5011, www.nhm.ac.uk). Parts of the museum were remodeled in 2007; the final goal is to display by 2008 every insect specimen the museum has ever collected.

▲Science Museum—Next door to the Natural History Museum, this sprawling wonderland for curious minds is kid-perfect. It offers hands-on fun, from moonwalks to deep-sea exploration, with trendy technology exhibits, an IMAX theater (£7–10 tickets for grownups, kids less), cool rotating themed exhibits, and a kids' zone in the basement, which may have moved to the third floor in 2007 (free, daily 10:00–18:00, Exhibition Road, Tube: South Kensington, tel. 0870-870-4868, www.sciencemuseum.org.uk).

▲▲Kensington Palace—In 1689, King William and Queen Mary moved their primary residence from Whitehall in central London to the more pristine and peaceful village of Kensington (now engulfed by London). With a little renovation help from Sir Christopher Wren, they turned the existing house into Kensington Palace, which was the center of English court life until 1760, when the royal family moved into Buckingham Palace. Since then, lesser royals have bedded down in Kensington Palace (as Princess Diana did from her 1981 marriage to Prince Charles until her death in 1997). The palace, while still functioning as a royal residence, also welcomes visitors with an impressive string of historic royal apartments and a few rooms of queens' dresses and ceremonial clothing (late 19th and 20th centuries). Enjoy a recreated royal tailor and dressmaker's workshop, the 17th-century splendor of the apartments of William and Mary, and the bed where Queen Victoria was born (fully clothed). The displays are wonderfully described by the included audioguide. The empty, unfurnished Apartment 1A, the former home of Princess Margaret, is skippable (£11.50, daily 10:00–18:00, until 17:00 in winter, last admission 1 hour before closing, a 10-min hike through Kensington Gardens from either Queensway or High Street Kensington Tube station, tel. 0870-751-5170). Garden enthusiasts enjoy popping into the secluded Sunken Garden, 50 yards from the exit.

Consider high tea at the nearby Orangery, built as a greenhouse for Queen Anne in 1704.

Victoria Station—From underneath this station's iron-and-glass canopy, trains depart for the south of England and Gatwick Airport. While Victoria Station is famous and a major Tube stop, few tourists actually take trains from here—most just come to take in the exciting bustle. It's a fun place to just be a "rock in a river" teeming with commuters and services. The station is surrounded by big red buses and taxis, travel agencies, and lousy eateries. It's next to the main bus station (National Express) and the best inexpensive B&Bs in town.

Westminster Cathedral—This largest Catholic church in England, just a block from Victoria Station, is striking but not very historic or important to visit. It opened in 1903 and has a brick neo-Byzantine flavor (surrounded by glassy office blocks). While it's definitely not Westminster Abbey, half the tourists wandering around inside seem to think it is. The highlight is the lift to the viewing gallery atop its bell tower (fine view, £3 for the lift, tower open daily 9:30–12:30 & 13:00–17:00, cathedral sometimes open longer hours for Mass; 5-min walk from Victoria Station or take bus #11, #24, #148, #211, or #507 to museum's door; just off Victoria Street, Tube: Victoria).

National Army Museum—This museum is not as awe-inspiring as the Imperial War Museum, but it's still fun, especially for kids into soldiers, armor, and guns. And while the Imperial War Museum is limited to wars of the 20th century, this tells the story of the British Army from 1415 through the Gulf War and Bosnian conflict, with lots of Red Coat lore and a good look at Waterloo. Kids enjoy trying on a Cromwellian helmet, seeing the skeleton of Napoleon's horse, and peering out from a WWI trench through a working periscope (free, daily 10:00–17:30, follow arrows in carpet to stay on track, bus #239 from Victoria Station stops at museum's door, Royal Hospital Road, Chelsea, Tube: Sloane Square, tel. 020-7730-0717, www.national-army-museum.ac.uk).

East London: The City

▲▲The City of London—When Londoners say "The City," they mean the one-square-mile business, banking, and journalism center that 2,000 years ago was Roman Londinium. The outline of the Roman city walls can still be seen in the arc of roads from Blackfriars Bridge to Tower Bridge. Within the City are 23 churches designed by Sir Christopher Wren, mostly just ornamentation around St. Paul's Cathedral. Today, while home to only 5,000 residents, the City thrives with more than 500,000 office workers coming and going daily. It's a fascinating district to wander on weekdays, but since almost nobody actually lives there, it's dull in the evenings and on Saturday and Sunday.

▲Old Bailey—To view the British legal system in action—lawyers in little blond wigs speaking legalese with a British accent—spend a few minutes in the visitors' gallery at the Old Bailey, called the "Central Criminal Court." Don't enter under the dome; signs point you to the two visitors' entrances (free, generally Mon–Fri 10:00–13:00 & 14:00–17:00 depending on caseload, closed Sat–Sun, reduced hours in Aug; no kids under 14; no bags, mobile phones, or cameras, but small purses OK; ask at one of the deli-type shops across the street about leaving your bag there for about £2; 2 blocks northwest of St. Paul's on Old Bailey Street, follow signs to public entrance, Tube: St. Paul's, tel. 020/7248-3277).

▲▲▲St. Paul's Cathedral—Wren's most famous church is the great St. Paul's, its elaborate interior capped by a 365-foot dome. The crypt (included with admission) is a world of historic bones and memorials, including Admiral Nelson's tomb and interesting cathedral models. The great West Door is opened only for great occasions, such as the wedding of Prince Charles and the late Princess Diana in 1981. Stand in the back of the church and

The City

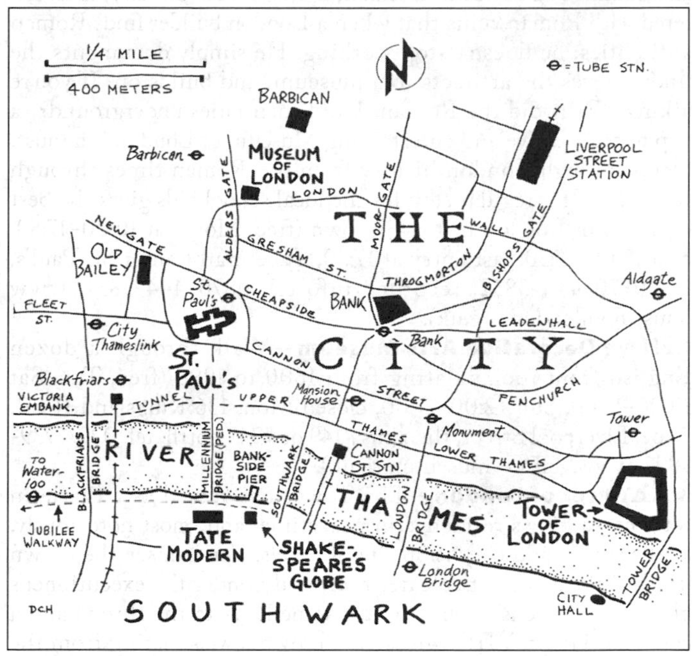

imagine how Diana felt before making the hike to the altar with the world watching. Sit under the second-largest dome in the world and eavesdrop on guided tours.

Since World War II, St. Paul's has been Britain's symbol of resistance. Despite 57 nights of bombing, the Nazis failed to destroy the cathedral, thanks to the St. Paul's volunteer fire watch, who stayed on the dome. Climb the dome for a great city view and some fun in the Whispering Gallery—where the precisely designed barrel of the dome lets sweet nothings circle audibly around to the opposite side.

The **evensong** services are free, but nonpaying visitors are not allowed to linger afterward (Mon–Sat at 17:00, Sun at 15:15, 40 min). On Sunday, there's a free **organ recital** at 17:00.

Cost, Hours, Location: £9, includes church entry and dome climb, Mon–Sat 8:30–16:30, last entry 16:00, last dome entry 16:15, closed Sun except for worship. No photography is allowed. Ninety-minute "super tours" of the cathedral and crypt cost £2.50 (Mon–Sat at 11:00, 11:30, 13:30, and 14:00—confirm schedule at church or call tel. 020/7236-4128; £3.50 for 1-hour audioguide which covers 17 stops, available Mon–Sat 9:15–15:30). There's a cheery café in the crypt of the cathedral (Tube: St. Paul's, tel. 020/7236-4128, www.stpauls.co.uk).

▲Museum of London—London, a 2,000-year-old city, is so littered with Roman ruins that when a London builder finds Roman antiquities, he doesn't stop working. He simply documents the finds, moves the artifacts to a museum, and builds on. If you're asking, "Why did the Romans build their cities underground?" a trip to the creative and entertaining Museum of London is a must. Stroll through London history from pre-Roman times through the 1920s. This regular stop for the local school kids gives the best overview of London history in town (free, Mon–Sat 10:00–17:50, Sun 12:00–17:50, last entry at 17:30, Tube: Barbican or St. Paul's, tel. 0870-444-3852, recorded info tel. 0870-444-3851, www.museumoflondon.org.uk).

Geffrye Decorative Arts Museum—Walk through a dozen English front rooms dating from 1600 to 1990 (free, Tue–Sat 10:00–17:00, Sun 12:00–17:00, closed Mon, 136 Kingsland Road, Tube: Liverpool Street, then bus #149 or #242 north, tel. 020/7739-9893, www.geffrye-museum.org.uk).

▲▲▲Tower of London—The Tower has served as a castle in wartime, a king's residence in peacetime, and, most notoriously, as the prison and execution site of rebels. You can see the crown jewels, take a witty Beefeater tour, and ponder the executioner's block that dispensed with troublesome heirs to the throne and a couple of Henry VIII's wives. The crown jewels, dating from the Restoration, are the best on Earth—and come with hour-long lines for most of the day. To avoid the crowds, arrive when the Tower opens and go straight for the jewels, doing the Beefeater tour and White Tower later—or do the jewels after 16:30.

Cost, Hours, Location: £15, family-£43, March–Oct Tue–Sat 9:00–18:00, Sun–Mon 10:00–18:00; Nov–Feb Tue–Sat 9:00–17:00, Sun–Mon 10:00–17:00; last entry 60 min before closing. The long but fast-moving ticket line is worst on Sunday. No photography is allowed of the jewels or in chapels. (Tube: Tower Hill, tel. 0870-751-5177, recorded info tel. 0870-756-6060, booking tel. 0870-756-7070, www.hrp.org.uk.) You can avoid the long lines by picking up your ticket at any London TI or the Tower Hill Tube station ticket office, or by buying online for an extra £3 fee. After your visit, consider taking the boat to Greenwich from here (see cruise info on page 580).

Ceremony of the Keys: Every night at precisely 21:30, with pageantry-filled ceremony, the Tower of London is locked up (as it has been for the last 700 years). To attend this free 30-minute event, you need to request an invitation at least two months before your visit. Write to Ceremony of the Keys, H.M. Tower of London, London EC3N 4AB. Include your name; the addresses, names, and ages of all people attending (up to 6 people, nontransferable, no kids under 8 allowed); requested date; alternative dates; and

London

two international reply coupons (buy at US post office—if your post office doesn't have the $1.85 coupons in stock, they can order them; the turnaround time is a few days).

More Sights near the Tower—The best remaining bit of London's **Roman Wall** is just north of the tower (at the Tower Hill Tube station). The impressive Tower Bridge is freshly painted and restored; for more information on this neo-Gothic maritime gateway to London, you can visit the **Tower Bridge Experience** for its 1894–1994 history exhibit and a peek at its Victorian engine room (£5.50, family-£10 and up, daily 10:00–18:30, last entry at 17:30, good view, poor value, enter at the northwest tower, tel. 020/7403-3761, www.towerbridge.org.uk). The chic **St. Katharine Dock,** just east of Tower Bridge, has mod shops and the classic old Dickens Inn, fun for a drink or pub lunch. Across the bridge is the South Bank, with the upscale Butlers Wharf area, City Hall, museums, and Jubilee Walkway.

South London, on the South Bank

The South Bank is a thriving arts and cultural center tied together by a riverside path. This popular, pub-crawling pedestrian promenade—called the Jubilee Walkway—stretches from Tower Bridge past Westminster Bridge, where it offers grand views of the Houses of Parliament. (The Walkway hugs the river except just east of London Bridge, where it cuts inland for a couple of blocks.)

City Hall—Opened in 2002, the glassy, egg-shaped building near the south end of Tower Bridge is London's City Hall, designed by Sir Norman Foster, the architect who worked on London's Millennium Bridge and Berlin's Reichstag. An interior spiral ramp allows visitors to watch and hear the action below in the Assembly Chamber; ride the lift to the second floor (the highest visitors can go) and spiral down. The Visitors Centre on the lower ground floor has a handy cafeteria. A top-floor observation deck known as "London's Living Room" is open for tours, usually on Monday morning (phone-in reservation required), and on occasional weekends from 10:00–16:30 (Visitors Centre open Mon–Fri 8:00–20:00, generally closed Sat–Sun but open occasional weekends—check website below, Tube: London Bridge station plus 10-min walk, or Tower Hill station plus 15-min walk; the Hall occasionally opens up for public tours—call or check website to confirm tour times and opening hours, tel. 020/7983-4100, www.london.gov.uk/gla/city_hall).

▲▲▲London Eye Ferris Wheel—Built by British Airways, the wheel towers above London opposite Big Ben. This is the world's highest observational wheel, giving you a chance to fly British Airways without leaving London. Designed like a giant bicycle wheel, it's a pan-European undertaking: British steel and Dutch

The South Bank

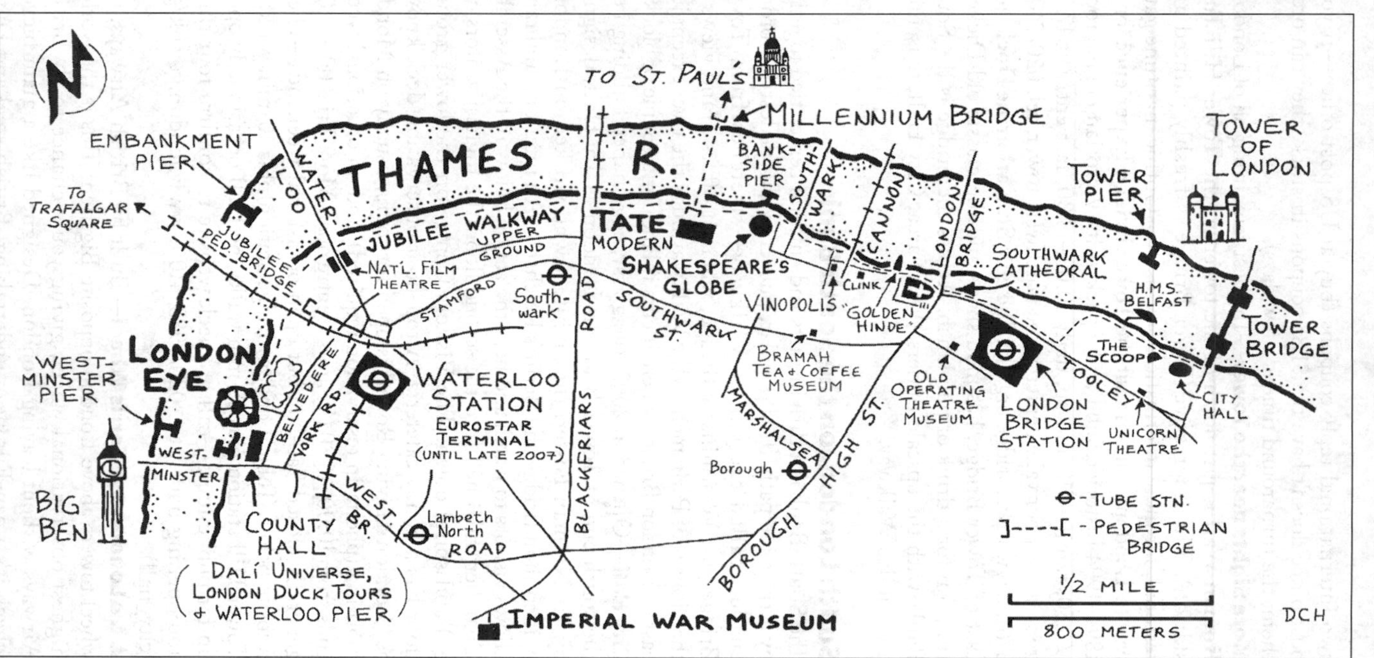

TO ST. PAUL'S
MILLENNIUM BRIDGE
TOWER OF LONDON
TOWER PIER
EMBANKMENT PIER
To TRAFALGAR SQUARE
THAMES R.
WATER-LOO
JUBILEE PED. BRIDGE
JUBILEE WALKWAY
UPPER GROUND
NAT'L. FILM THEATRE
TATE MODERN
BANK-SIDE PIER
SOUTH-WARK
CANNON
LONDON BRIDGE
SOUTHWARK CATHEDRAL
SHAKESPEARE'S GLOBE
CLINK
"GOLDEN HINDE"
VINOPOLIS
H.M.S. BELFAST
TOWER BRIDGE
STAMFORD
South-wark
ROAD
SOUTHWARK ST.
THE SCOOP
LONDON EYE
WEST-MINSTER PIER
BELVEDERE
YORK RD.
WATERLOO STATION
EUROSTAR TERMINAL
(UNTIL LATE 2007)
BRAMAH TEA + COFFEE MUSEUM
OLD OPERATING THEATRE MUSEUM
LONDON BRIDGE STATION
TOOLEY
CITY HALL
UNICORN THEATRE
WEST-MINSTER
BLACKFRIARS
MARSHALSEA
HIGH ST.
Borough
BIG BEN
COUNTY HALL
WEST. BR.
Lambeth North
ROAD
BOROUGH
(DALÍ UNIVERSE, LONDON DUCK TOURS + WATERLOO PIER)
IMPERIAL WAR MUSEUM
⊖ - TUBE STN.
]----[- PEDESTRIAN BRIDGE
1/2 MILE
800 METERS
DCH

engineering, with Czech, German, French, and Italian mechanical parts. It's also very "green," running extremely efficiently and virtually silently. Twenty-five people ride in each of its 32 air-conditioned capsules for the 30-minute rotation (each capsule has a bench, but most people stand). From the top of this 450-foot-high wheel—the highest public viewpoint in the city—Big Ben looks small. You go around only once; save a shot on top for the glass capsule next to yours. The London Eye's original five-year lease has been extended to 25 years, and it looks like it will become a permanent fixture on the London skyline. Thames boats come and go from here using the Waterloo Pier at the foot of the wheel.

Cost, Hours, Location: £13, daily June–Sept 10:00–21:00, until 22:00 in July–Aug, Oct–Christmas and mid-Jan–May 10:00–20:00, closed Christmas–mid-Jan for annual maintenance, Tube: Waterloo or Westminster, www.ba-londoneye.com.

Visitors face two lines: one to get your ticket, and the other to board. You can generally just buy your ticket at the wheel (never more than a 30-min wait, worst on weekends and school holidays). If you want to book a ticket (with an assigned time) in advance, call 0870-500-0600, or save 10 percent by booking online at www.ba-londoneye.com. Upon arrival, you either pick up your pre-booked ticket (if you've reserved ahead; use the ATM-type machines to save time—just type in your confirmation number) or wait in the line inside to buy tickets. Then you join the ticket-holders' line at the wheel (starting 10 min before your assigned half-hour time slot).

Dalí Universe—Cleverly located next to the hugely popular London Eye Ferris Wheel, this exhibit features 500 works of mind-bending art by Salvador Dalí. While pricey, it's entertaining if you like Surrealism and want to learn about Dalí (£12, audioguide-£2.50, daily 10:00–18:30, generally summer evenings until 20:00, last entry 30 min before closing, Tube: Waterloo or Westminster, tel. 020/7620-2720, www.countyhallgallery.com). The Dalí Universe currently also has a secondary show, "Picasso: Art of a Genius."

▲▲Imperial War Museum—This impressive museum covers the wars of the last century, from heavy weaponry to love notes and Vargas Girls, from Monty's Africa campaign tank to Schwartzkopf's Desert Storm uniform. You can trace the development of the machine gun, watch footage of the first tank battles, see one of more than a thousand V2 rockets Hitler rained on Britain in 1944 (each with more than a ton of explosives), hold your breath through the gruesome WWI trench experience, and buy WWII-era toys in the fun museum shop. The "Secret War" section gives a fascinating peek into the intrigues of espionage in World Wars I and II. The section on the Holocaust is one of the best on the subject anywhere. Rather than glorify war, the museum does its best to shine a light on the powerful human side of one of mankind's most persistent traits (free, sometimes small fees for special exhibitions, daily 10:00–18:00, 2 hours is enough time for most visitors, often guided tours on weekends—ask at info desk, interesting bookshop, Tube: Lambeth North or bus #12 from Westminster, tel. 020/7416-5320 or 020/7416-5321, www.iwm.org.uk). Don't miss the excellent temporary exhibition "The Children's War," showing how children had to flee London during the Blitz, and how they coped with World War II (free, through 2008).

The museum is housed in what was the Royal Bethlam Hospital. Also known as "the Bedlam asylum," the place was so wild it gave the world a new word for chaos: "bedlam." Back in Victorian times, locals—without trash-talk shows and cable TV—came here for their entertainment. The asylum was actually open to the paying public on weekends.

▲▲▲Tate Modern—Dedicated in the spring of 2000, the striking museum across the river from St. Paul's opened the new century with art from the old one. Its powerhouse collection of Monet, Matisse, Dalí, Picasso, Warhol, and much more is displayed in a converted powerhouse. Each year, the main hall features a different monumental installation by a prominent artist (free, fee for special exhibitions, daily 10:00–18:00, Fri–Sat until 22:00—a good time to visit, audioguide-£2; free guided tours at 11:00, 12:00, 14:00, and 15:00—confirm at info desk; view café on top floor; cross the Millennium Bridge from St. Paul's, or Tube: Southwark or Blackfriars plus a 10-min walk; or connect by Tate Boat ferry from Tate Britain for £4.30 one-way, discounted with Travelcard; switchboard tel. 020/7887-8888, recorded info tel. 020/7887-8008, www.tate.org.uk).

▲Millennium Bridge—The pedestrian bridge links St. Paul's Cathedral and the Tate Modern across the Thames. This is London's first new bridge in a century. When it first opened, the $25 million bridge wiggled when people walked on it, so it promptly closed for a $7 million, 20-month stabilization; now it's stable and open again (free). Nicknamed "a blade of light" for its sleek minimalist design—370 yards long, four yards wide, stainless steel with teak planks—it includes clever aerodynamic handrails to deflect wind over the heads of pedestrians.

▲▲Shakespeare's Globe—The original Globe Theater has been rebuilt, half-timbered and thatched, as it was in Shakespeare's time. (This is the first thatched roof in London since they were outlawed after the Great Fire of 1666.) The Globe originally accommodated 2,000 seated and another 1,000 standing. Today, slightly smaller and leaving space for reasonable aisles, the theater holds 900 seated and 600 groundlings. Its promoters brag that the theater melds "the three A's"—actors, audience, and architecture—with each contributing to the play.

Open as a museum and a working theater, it hosts authentic old-time performances of Shakespeare's plays (generally 14:00 and 19:30—but confirm). The Globe's exhibition on Shakespeare is the world's largest, with interactive displays and film presentations, a sound lab, a script factory, and costumes.

You can tour the theater when there are no plays going on—it's worth planning ahead for these excellent, actor-led guided tours.

Cost, Hours, Location: £9 includes exhibition and tour; theater complex open daily 9:00–17:00; exhibition and tours May–Sept daily 9:00–12:00 & 12:30–17:00—tours offered only in morning in summer, Oct–April daily 10:00–17:00—tours run all day in winter; tours go every 15–30 min, fewer tours in summer because of afternoon matinees (on the South Bank directly across Thames over Southwark Bridge from St. Paul's, Tube: London Bridge plus a 10-min walk, tel. 020/7902-1500, www.shakespeares-globe.org). For details on seeing a play, see page 613. The Globe Café is open daily (10:00–17:30, tel. 020/7902-1433).

Bramah Tea and Coffee Museum—Aficionados of tea or coffee will find this small museum fascinating. It tells the story of each drink almost passionately. The owner, Mr. Bramah, comes from a big tea family, and wants the world to know how the advent of commercial television, with breaks too short to brew a proper pot of tea, required a faster hot drink. In came the horrible English instant coffee. Tea countered with finely chopped leaves in tea bags, and it's gone downhill ever since (£4, daily 10:00–18:00, 40 Southwark Street, Tube: London Bridge plus 3-min walk, tel. 020/7403-5650, www.bramahmuseum.co.uk). Its café, which serves more kinds of coffees and teas than cakes, is open to the public (same hours as museum). The #RV1 bus zips you to the museum easily and scenically from Covent Garden.

▲▲Old Operating Theatre Museum and Herb Garret—Climb a tight and creaky wooden spiral staircase to a church attic where you'll find a garret used to dry medicinal herbs, a fascinating exhibit on Victorian surgery, cases of well-described 19th-century medical paraphernalia, and a special look at "anesthesia, the defeat of pain." Then you stumble upon Britain's oldest operating theater, where limbs were sawed off way back in 1821 (£4.95, daily 10:30–17:00, closed Dec 15–Jan 5, 9a St. Thomas Street, Tube: London Bridge, tel. 020/7188-2679, www.thegarret.org.uk).

▲▲Vinopolis: City of Wine—While it seems illogical to have a huge wine museum in London, Vinopolis makes a good case. Built over a Roman wine store and filling the massive vaults of an old wine warehouse, the museum offers an excellent audioguide with a light yet earnest history of wine. Sipping various reds and whites, ports, and champagnes—immersed in your headset as you stroll—you learn about the libation from its Georgian origins to Chile, including a Vespa ride through Chianti country in Tuscany. Allow some time, as the included audioguide takes 90 minutes—the sipping can slow things down wonderfully (Classic ticket-£15 for five wine tastes; Explorer ticket-£20 for five wine tastes plus tastes of whiskey, beer, and absinthe; daily 12:00–18:00, Mon and Fri–Sat until 21:00, last entry two hours before closing, between the Globe and Southwark Cathedral at 1 Bank End, Tube: London Bridge, tel. 0870-241-4040 or 020/7940-8322, www.vinopolis.co.uk).

South London, on the North Bank

▲▲Tate Britain—One of Europe's great art houses, Tate Britain specializes in British painting from the 16th century through modern times. The museum has a good representation of William Blake's religious sketches, the Pre-Raphaelites' realistic art, and J. M. W. Turner's swirling works (free, £2 donation requested, daily 10:00–17:50, last entry 17:00, fine free and necessary audioguide; free tours: normally Mon–Fri at 11:00—on 16th, 17th, and 18th centuries; at noon—19th century; at 14:00—Turner; at 15:00—20th century; Sat–Sun at 12:00 and 15:00—highlights; call to confirm schedule; kids' activities on weekends, no photography allowed, Tube: Pimlico, then 7-min walk; or arrive directly at museum by taking the Tate Boat ferry from Tate Modern or bus #88 from Oxford Circus or #77A from National Gallery, recorded info tel. 020/7887-8008, office tel. 020/7887-8888, www.tate.org.uk).

ENTERTAINMENT

Theater (a.k.a. "Theatre")

London's theater rivals Broadway's in quality and beats it in price. Choose from Shakespeare, musicals, comedy, thrillers, sex farces, cutting-edge fringe, revivals starring movie celebs, and more. London does it all well. I prefer big, glitzy—even bombastic—musicals over serious chamber dramas, simply because London can deliver the lights, sound, dancers, and multimedia spectacle I rarely get back home.

Most theaters, marked on tourist maps (also see map above), are found in the West End between Piccadilly and Covent Garden. Box offices, hotels, and TIs offer a handy free *London Theatre Guide* (also at www.londontheatre.co.uk) and *Entertainment Guide*. Performances are nightly except Sunday, usually with one or two matinees a week (Shakespeare's Globe is the rare theater that does offer performances on Sun, mid-May–Sept). Tickets range from about £11 to £55. Matinees are generally cheaper and rarely sell out.

To book a seat, simply call the theater box office directly, ask

London's Major Theaters

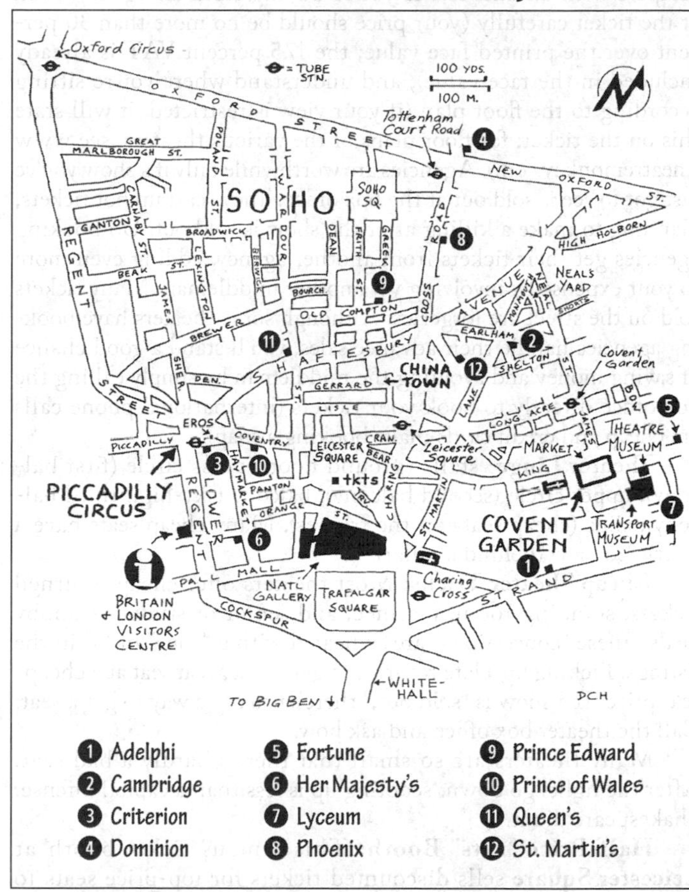

about seats and available dates, and buy a ticket with your credit card. You can call from the US as easily as from England (check www.officiallondontheatre.co.uk, the American magazine *Variety,* or photocopy your hometown library's London newspaper theater section). Arrive about 30 minutes before the show starts to pick up your ticket and to avoid lines.

For a booking fee, you can reserve online. Most theater websites link you to a preferred ticket vendor, usually www.ticketmaster.co.uk or www.seetickets.com. Keith Prowse Ticketing is also handy by phone or online (US tel. 800-223-6108, London tel. 020/7808-3871, www.keithprowse.com).

While booking through an agency is quick and easy, prices are inflated by a standard 25 percent fee. Ticket agencies (whether in the US, at London's TIs, or scattered throughout the city) are scalpers with an address. If you're buying from an agency, look at the ticket carefully (your price should be no more than 30 percent over the printed face value; the 17.5 percent VAT is already included in the face value), and understand where you're sitting according to the floor plan (if your view is restricted, it will state this on the ticket; for floor plans of the various theaters, see www.theatremonkey.com). Agencies are worthwhile only if a show you've just got to see is sold out at the box office. They scarf up hot tickets, planning to make a killing after the show is sold out. US booking agencies get their tickets from another agency, adding even more to your expense by involving yet another middleman. Many tickets sold on the street are forgeries. Although some theaters have booking agencies handle their advance sales, you'll stand a good chance of saving money and avoiding the middleman by simply calling the box office directly to book your tickets (international phone calls are cheap and credit cards make booking a snap).

Theater Lingo: stalls (ground floor), dress circle (first balcony), upper circle (second balcony), balcony (sky-high third balcony), slips (cheap seats on the fringes). Many cheap seats have a restricted view (behind a pillar).

Cheap Theater Tricks: Most theaters offer cheap returned tickets, standing-room, matinee, and senior or student standby deals. These "concessions" are indicated with a "conc" or "s" in the listings. Picking up a late return can get you a great seat at a cheap-seat price. If a show is "sold out," there's usually a way to get a seat. Call the theater box office and ask how.

Many theaters are so small that there's hardly a bad seat. After the lights go down, scooting up is less than a capital offense. Shakespeare did it.

Half-Price "tkts" Booth: This famous ticket booth at **Leicester Square** sells discounted tickets for top-price seats to shows on the push list the day of the show only (£2.50 service charge per ticket, Mon–Sat 10:00–19:00, Sun 12:00–15:00, matinee tickets from noon, lines often form early, list of shows available online, www.tkts.co.uk). Most tickets are half-price; other shows are discounted 25 percent.

Here are some sample prices: A top-notch seat to *Chicago* costs £49 bought directly from the theater, but only £27 at Leicester (LESS-ter) Square. The cheapest balcony seat (bought from the theater) is £17.50. Half-price tickets can be a good deal, unless you want the cheapest seats or the hottest shows. But check the board; occasionally they sell cheap tickets to good shows. For example, a first-class seat to the long-running *Les Misérables* (which rarely sells out) costs £50 when bought from the theater ticket office, but you'll pay £27.50 at the tkts booth. Note that the real half-price booth (with its "tkts" name) is a freestanding kiosk at the edge of the garden in Leicester Square. Several dishonest outfits nearby advertise "official half-price tickets"; avoid these.

A second tkts booth is at the Canary Wharf Docklands Light Railway (DLR) Station. The freestanding kiosk is located near platforms 4 and 5 above the DLR concourse (Mon–Sat 10:00–15:30, closed Sun, Tube: Canary Wharf).

West End Theaters: The commercial (non-subsidized) theaters cluster around Soho (especially along Shaftesbury Avenue) and Covent Garden. With a centuries-old tradition of pleasing the masses, these present London theater at its glitziest.

Royal Shakespeare Company: If you'll ever enjoy Shakespeare, it'll be in Britain. The RSC performs at various theaters around London and in Stratford year-round. To get a schedule, contact the RSC (Royal Shakespeare Theatre, Stratford-upon-Avon, tel. 01789/403-444, www.rsc.org.uk).

Shakespeare's Globe: To see Shakespeare in a replica of the theater for which he wrote his plays, attend a play at the Globe. This round, thatch-roofed, open-air theater performs the plays much as Shakespeare intended (with no amplification). The play's the thing from mid-May through October (usually Tue–Sat 14:00 and 19:30, Sun either 13:00 and 18:30 or 16:00 only, Mon 19:30, tickets can be sold out months in advance). You'll pay £5 to stand and £15–31 to sit (usually on a backless bench; only a few rows and the pricier Gentlemen's Rooms have seats with backs; £2 cushions and £2 add-on back rests are considered a good investment by many). The £5 "groundling" tickets—while open to rain—are most fun. Scurry in early to stake out a spot on the stage's edge leaning rail, where the most interaction with the actors occurs. You're a crude peasant. You can lean your elbows on the stage, munch a picnic dinner, or walk around. I've never enjoyed Shakespeare as much as here, performed as it was meant to be in the "wooden O." Plays can be long. Many groundlings leave before the end. If you like, hang out an hour before the finish and beg or buy a ticket from someone leaving early (groundlings are allowed to come and go).

For information on plays or £9 tours (see page 608), contact the theater at tel. 020/7902-1500 (or see www.shakespeares-globe.org). To reserve tickets for plays, call or drop by the box office (Mon–Sat 10:00–18:00, until 20:00 on day of show, at Shakespeare's Globe at New Globe Walk entrance, tel. 020/7401-9919). If you reserve online (www.seetickets.com/shakespeares-globe), be warned: Your ticket price will have an added booking fee (generally £1–2.20 per ticket).

The theater is on the South Bank, directly across the Thames over the Millennium Bridge from St. Paul's Cathedral (Tube: Mansion House or London Bridge). The Globe is inconvenient for public transport, but the courtesy phone in the lobby gets a minicab in minutes. (These minicabs have set fees—e.g., £8 to South Kensington—but generally cost less than a metered cab and provide fine and honest service.) During theater season, there's a regular supply of black cabs outside the main foyer on New Globe Walk.

Fringe Theatre: London's rougher evening-entertainment scene is thriving, filling pages in *Time Out*. Choose from a wide range of fringe theater and comedy acts (generally £5).

Classical Music

Concerts at Churches

For easy, cheap, or free concerts in historic churches, check TI listings for **lunch concerts,** especially:

- Wren's St. Bride's Church, with free lunch concerts twice a week at 13:15 (generally Tue, Wed, or Fri—confirm by phone or online, church tel. 020/7427-0133, www.stbrides.com).
- St. James at Piccadilly, with 50-minute concerts on Monday, Wednesday, and Friday at 13:10 (suggested donation £3, info tel. 020/7381-0441, www.st-james-piccadilly.org).
- St. Martin-in-the-Fields, offering free concerts on Monday, Tuesday, and Friday at 13:00 (church tel. 020/7766-1100, www.smitf.com).

St. Martin-in-the-Fields also hosts fine **evening concerts** by candlelight (£6–22, Thu–Sat at 19:30, sometimes also Tue or Wed, box office tel. 020/7839-8362).

Evensong and Organ Recitals at Churches

Evensong services are held at several churches, including:

- St. Paul's Cathedral (Mon–Sat at 17:00, Sun at 15:15).
- Westminster Abbey (Mon–Tue and Thu–Fri at 17:00, Sat–Sun at 15:00, no service on Wed).
- St. Bride's Church (Sun at 18:30, tel. 020/7427-0133, www.stbrides.com).

Free **organ recitals** are held on Sunday at Westminster Abbey (17:45, 30 min, tel. 020/7222-7110) and at St. Paul's (17:00, 30 min, tel. 020/7236-4128).

Prom Concerts and Opera

For a fun classical event (mid-July–early Sept), attend a **Prom Concert** (shortened from "Promenade Concert") during the annual festival at the Royal Albert Hall. Nightly concerts are offered at give-a-peasant-some-culture prices to "Promenaders"—those willing to stand throughout the performance (£4 standing-room spots sold at the door, £7 restricted-view seats, most £22–29 but depends on performance, Tube: South Kensington, tel. 020/7589-8212, www.royalalberthall.com).

Some of the world's best **opera** is belted out at the prestigious Royal Opera House, near Covent Garden (box office tel. 020/7304-4000, www.royalopera.org), and at the less-formal Sadler's Wells Theatre (Rosebery Avenue, Islington, Tube: Angel, info tel. 020/7863-8198, box office tel. 0870-737-7737, www.sadlerswells.com).

Walks, Bus Tours, and Cruises

Guided **walks** are offered several times a day. London Walks is the most established company (see page 578). Daytime walks vary: ancient London, museums, legal London, Dickens, Beatles, Jewish quarter, Christopher Wren, and so on. In the evening, expect a more limited choice: ghosts, Jack the Ripper, pubs, or a literary theme. Get the latest from a TI, fliers, or *Time Out*. Show up at the listed time and place, pay £6, and enjoy the two-hour tour.

To see the city illuminated at night, consider a **bus** tour. A one-hour London by Night Sightseeing Tour leaves every evening from Victoria Station and other points (see page 578).

During the summer, boats sail as late as 21:00 between Westminster Pier (near Big Ben) and the Tower of London. (For details, see page 580.)

A handful of outfits run Thames River evening **cruises** with four-course meals and dancing. London Showboat offers the best value (£62, April–Oct Wed–Sun, Nov–March Thu–Sat, 3 hours, departs at 19:00 from Westminster Pier and returns by 22:30, reservations necessary, tel. 020/7740-0400, www.citycruises.com). For more on cruising, get the *Thames River Services* brochure from a London TI.

Summer Evenings Along the South Bank

If you're visiting London in summer, consider the South Bank.

Take a trip around the **London Eye** while the sun sets over the city (rides go until 22:00 in July–Aug—see page 605). Then cap your night with an evening walk along the pedestrian-only **Jubilee Walkway,** which runs east–west along the river. It's where Londoners go to escape the heat. This pleasant stretch of the walkway—lined with pubs and casual eateries—goes from the London Eye past Shakespeare's Globe to London Bridge (you can walk in either direction, see www.jubileewalkway.com for maps and Tube stops).

If you're in the mood for a movie, take in a flick at the brand-new **National Film Theatre,** located just across from Waterloo Bridge on the South Bank. Run by the British Film Institute, the state-of-the-art theater shows Hollywood films (both new and classic), as well as art cinema (£8.60, Tube: Waterloo or Embankment, box office tel. 020/7928-3232, check www.bfi.org.uk/incinemas/nft for schedules).

Farther east along the South Bank is **The Scoop**—an outdoor amphitheater next to City Hall. It's a good spot for outdoor movies, concerts, and theater productions throughout the summer—with Tower Bridge as a scenic backdrop. These events are free, nearly nightly, and family-friendly. For a 2008 event schedule, see www.morelondon.com/thescoop (next to City Hall, Riverside, The Queen's Walkway, Tube: London Bridge).

SLEEPING

London is expensive. Cheaper rooms are relatively dumpy. Don't expect £90 cheeriness in a £60 room. For £70 ($125), you'll get a double with breakfast in a safe, cramped, and dreary place with minimal service and the bathroom down the hall. For £90 ($160), you'll get a basic, clean, reasonably cheery double in a usually cramped, cracked-plaster building with a private bath, or a soulless but comfortable room without breakfast in a huge Motel 6–type place. My London splurges, at £100–255 ($180–460), are spacious, thoughtfully appointed places good for entertaining or romancing. Off-season, it's possible to save money by arriving late without a reservation and looking around. Competition softens prices, especially for multi-night stays.

Hearty English or generous buffet breakfasts are included unless otherwise noted, and TVs are standard in rooms, but may come with only the traditional four British channels (no cable).

Reserve your London room with a phone call or email as soon as you can commit to a date. To call a London hotel from the United States or Canada, dial 011-44-20 (London's area code without the initial zero), then the local eight-digit number. Some hotels will hold a room until 16:00 without a deposit, although most places will ask you for a credit-card number. The pricier ones

Sleep Code

(£1 = about $2, country code: 44, area code: 020)
S = Single, **D** = Double/Twin, **T** = Triple, **Q** = Quad, **b** = bathroom, **s** = shower only. Unless otherwise noted, credit cards are accepted and prices include a generous breakfast.

To help you easily sort through these listings, I've divided the rooms into three categories, based on the price for a double room with bath:

$$$ **Higher Priced**—Most rooms £100 or more.
$$ **Moderately Priced**—Most rooms between £70–100.
$ **Lower Priced**—Most rooms £70 or less.

have expensive cancellation policies (such as no refund if you cancel with less than two weeks' notice). Some fancy £120 rooms rent for a third off if you arrive late on a slow day and ask for a deal.

Looking for Hotel Deals Online

Given the high hotel prices and relatively weak dollar, consider turning to the Internet to help score a hotel deal. Various websites list rooms in high-rise, three- and four-star business hotels. You'll give up the charm and warmth of a family-run establishment, and breakfast will probably not be included, but you might find the price is right.

Start by checking the websites of several big hotel chains to get an idea of typical rates and to check for online-only deals. Big London hotel chains include: Millennium/Copthorne (www.millenniumhotels.com), Thistle (www.thistlehotels.com), Intercontinental/Holiday Inn (www.ichotelsgroup.com), Radisson (www.radisson.com), and Red Carnation (www.redcarnationhotels.com). For information on the no-frills, more Motel 6–type chains, see "Big, Cheap, Modern Hotels," below.

Auction-type sites (such as www.priceline.com) can be great for matching flexible travelers with empty hotel rooms, often at prices well below the hotel's own rates. Don't feel you have to start as high as the site's suggested opening bid. (For more about the complicated world of online bidding strategies and success stories from other travelers, see www.biddingfortravel.com or www.betterbidding.com.) Warning: Scoring a deal this way may require more patience and flexibility than you have, but if you enjoy shopping for cars, you'll probably like this, too.

Other favorite hotel discount sites mentioned by my readers include www.londontown.com (an info site with a discount booking service), www.lastminute.com, www.visitlondon.com, www.findlondonrooms.com, and www.eurocheapo.com. Check the "Graffiti Wall" at www.ricksteves.com for the latest tips and discoveries.

For a good overview on finding London hotel deals, go to www.smartertravel.com and click on "Hotel."

Big, Cheap, Modern Hotels

These places—popular with budget tour groups—are well-run and offer elevators and all the modern comforts in a no-frills, practical package. With the notable exception of my second listing, they are often located on busy streets in dreary train-station neighborhoods, so use common sense after dark and wear your money belt. The doubles for £75–100 are a great value for London. Mid-week prices are generally higher than weekend rates. Online bookings are often the easiest way to make reservations, and will get you a

London's Hotel Neighborhoods

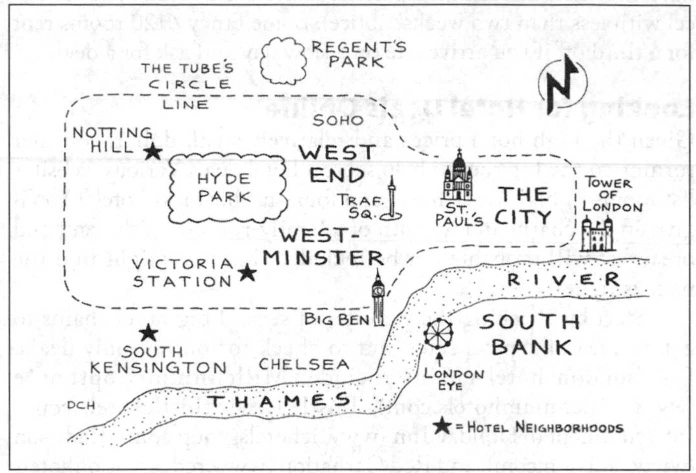

discount if you're staying at a Jurys or a Travelodge.

$$$ Jurys Inn Islington rents 200 compact, comfy rooms near King's Cross Station (Db/Tb-£100–110, some discounted rooms available online, 2 adults and 2 kids under age 12 can share 1 room, breakfast extra, non-smoking floors, 60 Pentonville Road, Tube: Angel, tel. 020/7282-5500, fax 020/7282-5511, www.jurysdoyle.com).

$$ Premier Travel Inn London County Hall, literally down the hall from a $400-a-night Marriott Hotel, fills one end of London's massive former County Hall building. This place is wonderfully located near the base of the London Eye Ferris Wheel and across the Thames from Big Ben. Its 300 slick rooms come with all the necessary comforts (Db-£92 for 2 adults and up to 2 kids under age 16, couples can request a bigger family room—same price, breakfast extra, book in advance, no-show rooms are released at 15:00, some non-smoking and easy-access rooms, elevator, 500 yards from Westminster Tube stop and Waterloo Station, Belvedere Road, central reservations tel. 0870-242-8000 or 0870-238-3300, you can fax 020/7902-1619 but you might not get a response, easiest to book online at www.premiertravelinn.com).

$$ Premier Travel Inn London Southwark, with 55 rooms, is near Shakespeare's Globe on the South Bank (Db for up to 2 adults and 2 kids-£84–88, Bankside, 34 Park Street, tel. 0870-990-6402, www.premiertravelinn.com).

$$ Premier Travel Inn King's Cross, with 276 rooms, is just east of King's Cross Station (Db-£75–85, breakfast extra, non-smoking rooms available, 24-hour reception, elevator, 26–30 York Way, tel.

0870-990-6414, fax 0870-990-6415, www.premiertravelinn.com).

Other **$$ Premier Travel Inns** charging £75–85 per room include **London Euston** (big, blue, Lego-type building packed with families on vacation on handy but noisy street, 141 Euston Road, Tube: Euston, tel. 0870-238-3301), **London Kensington** (11 Knaresboro Place, Tube: Earl's Court or Gloucester Road, tel. 0870-238-3304), and **London Putney Bridge** (farther out, 3 Putney Bridge Approach, Tube: Putney Bridge, tel. 0870-238-3302). Avoid the **Tower Bridge** location, which is an inconvenient, 15-minute walk from the nearest Tube stop. For any of these, call 0870-242-8000, fax 0870-241-9000, or the best option, book online at www.premiertravelinn.com.

$$ Hotel Ibis London Euston, which feels a bit classier than a Premier Travel Inn, is located on a quiet street a block behind and west of Euston Station (380 rooms, Db-£70–95, breakfast extra, no family rooms, non-smoking floor, 3 Cardington Street, tel. 020/7388-7777, fax 020/7388-0001, www.ibishotel.com, h0921@accor-hotels.com).

$ Travelodge London Kings Cross Royal Scot is another typical chain hotel with lots of cookie-cutter rooms just south of King's Cross Station (Db-£66–85, some £26 rooms available online only for scattered dates, breakfast extra, family rooms, non-smoking rooms available, 100 Kings Cross Road, tel. 0870-191-1773, fax 020/7833-8261, www.travelodge.co.uk). Other Travelodge London locations are at **Covent Garden, Liverpool Street,** and **Farringdon.** For all the details on each, see www.travelodge.co.uk.

Victoria Station Neighborhood (Belgravia)

The streets behind Victoria Station teem with budget B&Bs. It's a safe, surprisingly tidy, and decent area without a hint of the trashy, touristy glitz of the streets in front of the station. West of the tracks is Belgravia, where the prices are a bit higher and your neighbors include Andrew Lloyd Webber and Margaret Thatcher (her policeman stands outside 73 Chester Square). East of the tracks is Pimlico—cheaper and just as handy, but the rooms can be a bit dowdier. Decent eateries abound (see page 636).

All the recommended hotels are within a five-minute walk of the Victoria Tube, bus, and train stations. On hot summer nights, request a quiet back room. Nearby is the 400-space Semley Place NCP **garage** (£30/day, possible discounts with hotel voucher, just west of the Victoria Coach Station at Buckingham Palace Road and Semley Place, tel. 0870-242-7144, www.ncp.co.uk). The handy **Pimlico Launderette** is about five blocks southwest of Warwick Square (daily 8:00–20:00, self-service or full service, south of

Victoria Station Neighborhood

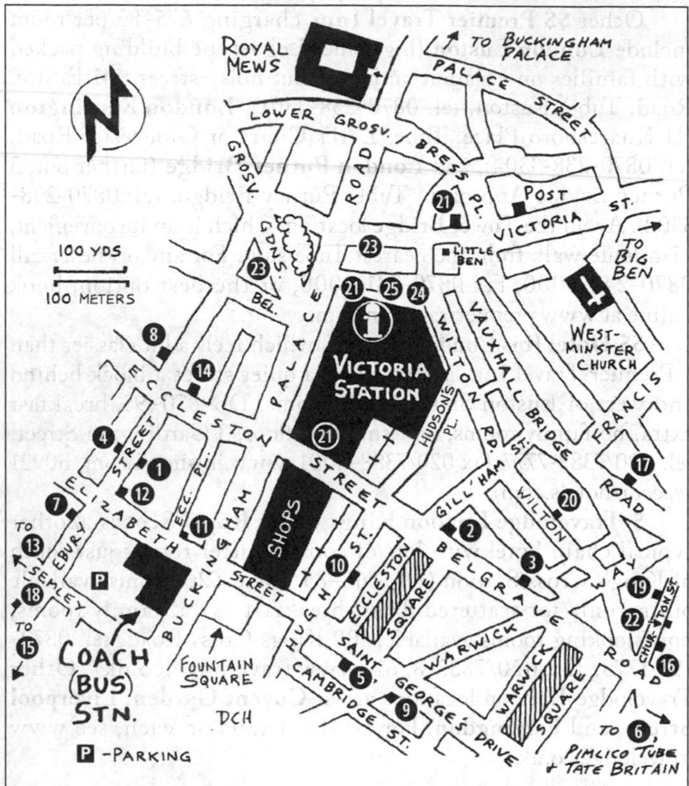

1. Lime Tree Hotel
2. Quality Hotel Westminster
3. Winchester Hotel
4. James House & Cartref House Hotels
5. Elizabeth Hotel & Jubilee Hotel
6. To Holiday Inn Express
7. Morgan House
8. Harcourt House
9. Elizabeth House & Bakers Hotel
10. Cherry Court Hotel
11. Goya Spanish Rest. & Tapas Bar
12. Ebury Wine Bar
13. To The Duke of Wellington Pub
14. Jenny Lo's Tea House
15. To La Poule au Pot Rest.
16. Grumbles Restaurant
17. The Jugged Hare Pub
18. The Belgravia Pub
19. Chimes English Rest. & Cider Bar
20. Seafresh Fish Rest.
21. Grocery Stores (3)
22. Launderette
23. Bus Tours - Day (2)
24. Bus Tours - Night
25. TI, Tube, Taxis, City Buses

Sutherland Street at 3 Westmoreland Terrace, tel. 020/7821-8692). **Launderette Centre** is a block north of Warwick Square (Mon–Fri 8:00–22:00, Sat–Sun until 19:30, £7 wash and dry, £9 with service, 31 Churton Street, tel. 020/7828-6039).

$$$ Lime Tree Hotel, enthusiastically run by David and Marilyn Davies and their daughter Charlotte, comes with 30 spacious and thoughtfully decorated rooms and a fun-loving breakfast room (Sb-£75–85, Db-£105–135 depending on room size, Tb-£140–165, family room-£150–180, £10 discount per night with cash, all non-smoking rooms, Internet access, £5 Wi-Fi, quiet garden, David deals in slow times and is creative at helping travelers in a bind, 135 Ebury Street, tel. 020/7730-8191, fax 020/7730-7865, www.limetreehotel.co.uk, info@limetreehotel.co.uk, trusty Alan covers the night shift).

$$$ Quality Hotel Westminster is big, modern (but with tired carpets), well-located, and a good bet for no-nonsense comfort (Db-£135–155, check for various Web specials, drop-ins can ask for "saver prices" on slow days, breakfast extra or bargained in, non-smoking floor, elevator, 82 Eccleston Square, tel. 020/7834-8042, fax 020/7630-8942, www.hotels-westminster.com, enquiries@hotels-westminster.com).

$$$ Holiday Inn Express fills an old building with 52 fresh, modern, and efficient rooms (Db-£114 rack rate, often £80—especially Sun or if booked online; up to 2 kids free, family rooms, non-smoking floor, elevator, 106 Belgrave Road, Tube: Pimlico, tel. 020/7630-8888, fax 020/7828-0441, www.hiexpressvictoria.co.uk, info@hiexpressvictoria.co.uk).

$$ Winchester Hotel, family-run, has 18 small rooms that are a fine value for the price (Db-£85, Tb-£110, Qb-£140, no groups, no infants, Internet access, 17 Belgrave Road, tel. 020/7828-2972, fax 020/7828-5191, www.winchester-hotel.net, enquiry@winchester-hotel.net, commanded by no-nonsense Jimmy plus his crew: Juanita and Shelina). The Winchester also rents apartments—with kitchenettes, sitting rooms, and beds on the quiet back side—around the corner (£125–230).

$$ James House and **Cartref House** are two nearly identical, well-run, 10-room places on either side of Ebury Street (S-£52, Sb-£62, D-£70, Db-£85, T-£95, Tb-£110, family bunk-bed Qb-£135, 5 percent discount with cash, all rooms with fans, all non-smoking, James House at 108 Ebury Street, tel. 020/7730-7338; Cartref House at 129 Ebury Street, tel. 020/7730-6176, www.jamesandcartref.co.uk, info@jamesandcartref.co.uk, Derek and Sharon).

$$ Elizabeth Hotel is a stately old place overlooking Eccleston Square, with fine public spaces and 40 well-worn, slightly overpriced, but spacious and decent rooms (S-£55, Sb-£77, D-£77, small Db-£93, big Db-£105, Tb-£118, Qb-£130, Quint/b-£135, air-con-£9, 37 Eccleston Square, tel. 020/7828-6812, fax 020/7828-6814, www.elizabethhotel.com, info@elizabethhotel.com). Be careful not to confuse this hotel with the nearby (cheaper but also recommended) Elizabeth House. Elizabeth Hotel also rents apartments that sleep up to six (£195/night, includes breakfast).

$$ Harcourt House rents 10 newly refurbished, neo-Victorian, non-smoking rooms (Sb-£60, Db-£85, Tb-£120, less off-season, 50 Ebury Street, tel. 020/7730-2722, www.harcourthousehotel.co.uk, harcourthouse@talk21.com, helpful David and Glesni Wood and cute dog Suki).

$$ Morgan House rents 11 good rooms and is entertainingly run, with lots of travel tips and friendly chat—especially about the local rich and famous—from owner Rachel Joplin and manager Fernanda (S-£52, D-£72, Db-£92, T-£92, family suites-£110–130 for 3–4 people, 120 Ebury Street, tel. 020/7730-2384, fax 020/7730-8442, www.morganhouse.co.uk, morganhouse@btclick.com).

$ Cherry Court Hotel, run by the friendly and industrious Patel family, rents 12 very small, basic, incense-scented rooms in a central location (Sb-£45, Db-£55, Tb-£75, Qb-£90, Quint/b-£105, paying with credit card costs 5 percent extra, fruit-basket breakfast in room, air-con, all non-smoking, free Internet access with free disk burning, peaceful garden patio, 23 Hugh Street, tel. 020/7828-2840, fax 020/7828-0393, www.cherrycourthotel.co.uk, bookings@cherrycourthotel.co.uk).

$ Jubilee Hotel is a well-run slumber mill with 26 tiny rooms and many tiny beds—but good prices for London (S-£35, Db-£50, tiny D-£50, tiny Db-£60, Db-£65, Tb-£75, Qb-£95, 31 Eccleston Square, tel. 020/7834-0845, www.jubileehotel.co.uk, reservations@jubileehotel.co.uk, Bob Patel).

$ Elizabeth House offers 40 of some of the best cheap—albeit spartan—rooms in town, with a professional reception and a guests' kitchen where you can do your own cooking (S-£35, D-£50, Db-£60, Tb-£70, Q-£80, Qb-£85, Quint/b-£90, includes continental breakfast, avoid some street noise by requesting quiet room in the back, 118 Warwick Way, tel. 020/7630-0741, fax 020/7630-0740, www.elizabethhouse.co.uk, elizabethhouselondon@yahoo.co.uk).

$ Bakers Hotel is a cheapie, with 10 small, tight, and very simple rooms, but it's well-located and offers youth hostel prices and a full breakfast (S-£30, D-£46, T-£55–60, family room-£65–70, 126 Warwick Way, tel. 020/7834-0729, www.bakershotel.co.uk, reservations@bakershotel.co.uk, Amin Jamani).

South Kensington Neighborhood

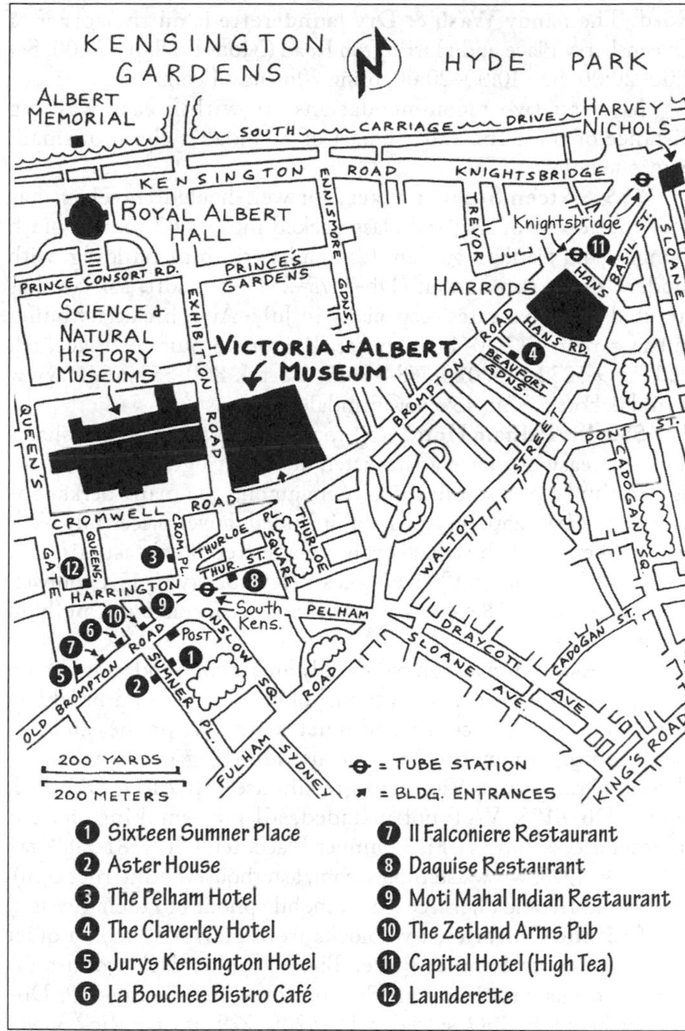

"South Kensington," She Said, Loosening His Cummerbund

To stay on a quiet street so classy it doesn't allow hotel signs, surrounded by trendy shops and colorful restaurants, call "South Ken" your London home. Shoppers like being a short walk from Harrods and the designer shops of King's Road and Chelsea. When I splurge, I splurge here. Sumner Place is just off Old Brompton Road, 200 yards from the handy South Kensington Tube station (on Circle Line, two stops from Victoria Station, direct Heathrow connection).

There's a taxi rank in the median strip at the end of Harrington Road. The handy **Wash & Dry launderette** is on the corner of Queensberry Place and Harrington Road (Mon–Fri 8:00–21:00, Sat 9:00–20:00, Sun 10:00–20:00, bring 20p and £1 coins).

My first two recommendations are within easy walking distance of the Tube and are part of Firmdale's chain of small, boutique hotels.

$$$ Sixteen Sumner Place, for well-heeled travelers, has over-the-top formality and class packed into its 42 rooms, plush lounges, and tranquil garden. It's in a labyrinthine building, with modern decor throughout (Db-£175–255—but soft, ask for discounted "seasonal rates" especially in July–Aug, breakfast buffet in the garden-£12.50–14.50 extra, elevator, 16 Sumner Place, tel. 020/7589-5232, fax 020/7584-8615, US tel. 800-553-6674, www.firmdalehotels.com, sixteen@firmdale.com).

$$$ The Pelham Hotel, a 52-room business-class hotel, shares the same easy elegance as its sister, above. It's genteel, with low lighting and a pleasant drawing room among the many perks (Sb-£160, Db-£180–250, breakfast not included, lower prices July–Aug and weekends, Web specials can include free breakfast, air-con, expensive Internet and Wi-Fi access, elevator, gym, 15 Cromwell Place, tel. 020/7287-4434, www.firmdalehotels.com, pelham@firmdale.com).

$$$ Aster House, run by friendly and accommodating Simon and Leonie Tan, has a sumptuous lobby, lounge, and breakfast room. Its rooms are comfy and quiet, with TV, phone, and air-conditioning. Enjoy breakfast or just lounging in the whisper-elegant Orangery, a Victorian greenhouse (Sb-£109, Db-£155, bigger Db-£185, VAT not included, all non-smoking, fee for Internet access and Wi-Fi, 3 Sumner Place, tel. 020/7581-5888, fax 020/7584-4925, www.asterhouse.com, asterhouse@btinternet.com). Simon and Leonie offer free loaner mobile phones to their guests.

$$$ The Claverley, two blocks from Harrods, is on a quiet street similar to Sumner Place. The 30 fancy, dark-wood-and-marble rooms come with all the comforts (S-£79, Sb-£99, Db-£149, deluxe Db-£199, sofa-bed Tb-£209–229, ask for Rick Steves discount, all non-smoking, some rooms with air-con, elevator, plush lounge, 13–14 Beaufort Gardens, Tube: Knightsbridge, tel. 020/7589-8541, fax 020/7584-3410, US tel. 800/747-0398, www.claverleyhotel.co.uk, reservations@claverleyhotel.co.uk).

$$$ Jurys Kensington Hotel is big, stately, and impersonal, with a greedy pricing scheme (Db-£100–140 depending on "availability," ask for a deal, drop-ins on slow nights sometimes luck into £50–90 discount rates, breakfast-£8, non-smoking floors, elevator, piano lounge, 109–113 Queen's Gate, tel. 020/7589-6300, fax 020/7581-1492, www.jurysdoyle.com, kensington@jurysdoyle.com).

Notting Hill and Bayswater Neighborhoods

Residential Notting Hill has quick bus and Tube access to downtown, and, for London, is very "homely" (Brit-speak for cozy). It's also peppered with trendy bars and restaurants, and is home to the historic Coronet movie theater, as well as the famous Portobello Road Market.

Popular with young international travelers, Bayswater's Queensway street is a multicultural festival of commerce and eateries (see "Eating," page 638). The neighborhood does its dirty clothes at **Galaxy Launderette** (£4 self-serve, £8 full-serve, daily 8:00–20:00, 65 Moscow Road, at corner of St. Petersburgh Place and Moscow Road, tel. 020/7229-7771). For **Internet access,** you'll find several stops along busy Queensway and a self-serve bank of easyInternetcafé computer terminals at the food circus level of the Whiteleys Shopping Centre (daily 8:30–24:00, corner of Queensway and Porchester Gardens).

Near Kensington Gardens Square

Several big old hotels line the quiet Kensington Gardens Square (not to be confused with the much bigger Kensington Gardens), a block west of bustling Queensway, north of Bayswater Tube station. These hotels are quiet for central London.

$$$ Phoenix Hotel, a Best Western modernization of a 125-room hotel, offers American business-class comforts; spacious, plush public spaces; and big, fresh, modern-feeling rooms. Its prices—which range from fine value to rip-off—are determined by a greedy computer program, with huge variations according to expected demand. See their website and book online to save money (Db-£90–150, elevator, impersonal staff, 1–8 Kensington Gardens Square, tel. 020/7229-2494, fax 020/7727-1419, US tel. 800/528-1234, www.phoenixhotel.co.uk, info@phoenixhotel.co.uk).

$$ Garden Court Hotel rents 34 comfortable, non-smoking rooms in what may be the best value for your hotel dollar in London. It's newly refurbished, with basic but bigger-than-average rooms, caring management, and a pleasant little garden out back (S-£42, Sb-£64, D-£66, Db-£92, T-£90, Tb-£120, Q-£100, Qb-£140, elevator, 30 Kensington Gardens Square, tel. 020/7229-2553, fax 020/7727-2749, www.gardencourthotel.co.uk, info@gardencourthotel.co.uk, well-run by Edward and his helpful staff).

$$ Kensington Gardens Hotel laces 16 decent rooms together in a tall, skinny place with lots of stairs and no elevator (S-£45–50, Sb-£50–55, Db-£75, Tb-£95, book by phone or email rather than through the pricier website, 9 Kensington Gardens Square, tel. 020/7221-7790, fax 020/7792-8612, www.kensingtongardenshotel.co.uk, info@kensingtongardenshotel.co.uk, charming Rowshanak).

Notting Hill and Bayswater Neighborhoods

1 Phoenix Hotel
2 Garden Court Hotel
3 Kensington Gardens Hotel
4 Vancouver Studios
5 London House Budget Hotel
6 Westland Hotel
7 Vicarage Private Hotel
8 To Norwegian YWCA
9 Maggie Jones Restaurant
10 The Churchill Arms Pub & Thai Kitchens
11 The Prince Edward Pub
12 Café Diana
13 Black & Blue Restaurant
14 Royal China Restaurant
15 The Orangery (High Tea)
16 Whiteleys Mall Food Court
17 Spar Market
18 Launderette

$$ Vancouver Studios offers 45 modern rooms with fully equipped kitchenettes (utensils, stove, microwave, and fridge) rather than breakfast (small Sb-£60, small Db-£99, big Db-£120, Tb-£140, extra bed-£18, 10 percent discount with week-long stay or more, call to confirm reservation a night or two before, welcoming lounge and garden, can be noisy, no elevator, near Kensington Gardens Square at 30 Prince's Square, tel. 020/7243-1270, fax 020/7221-8678, www.vancouverstudios.co.uk, info@vancouverstudios.co.uk).

$ London House Budget Hotel is a threadbare, chaotic, nose-ringed place renting more than 200 beds in about 80 stark rooms. While their rack rates are high (to hide Web booking commissions for those who don't go direct), their own website offers much better prices such as doubles for £43 (S-£40–50, Sb-£45–56, twin-£54, Db-£48–60, dorm bed-£16, prices flex downward with demand, includes continental breakfast, Internet access, lots of school groups, 81 Kensington Gardens Square, tel. 020/7243-1810, fax 020/7243-1723, www.londonhousehotel.co.uk, londonhousehotel@yahoo.co.uk).

Near Kensington Gardens

$$$ Westland Hotel is comfortable, convenient (5-min walk from Notting Hill neighborhood), and hotelesque, with a fine lounge. The rooms are spacious, recently refurbished, and quite plush. Their £105 doubles are the best value (Sb-£88–99, Db-£105, deluxe Db-£121, cavernous deluxe Db-£138, sprawling Tb-£132–154, gargantuan Qb-£150–175, Quint/b-£165–187, elevator, free garage with 6 spaces; between Notting Hill Gate and Queensway Tube stations, 154 Bayswater Road; tel. 020/7229-9191, fax 020/7727-1054, www.westlandhotel.co.uk, reservations@westlandhotel.co.uk, Nora ably staffs the front desk).

$$$ Vicarage Private Hotel, understandably popular, is family-run and elegantly British in a quiet, classy neighborhood. It has 17 rooms furnished with taste and quality, a TV lounge, and facilities on each floor. Mandy, Richard, and Francisca maintain a homey and caring atmosphere (S-£46, Sb-£75, D-£78, Db-£102, T-£95, Tb-£130, Q-£102, Qb-£140, 20 percent less in winter—check website, cash only, 6-min walk from Notting Hill Gate and High Street Kensington Tube stations, near Kensington Palace at 10 Vicarage Gate, tel. 020/7229-4030, fax 020/7792-5989, www.londonvicaragehotel.com, reception@londonvicaragehotel.com).

Near Holland Park

$ Norwegian YWCA (Norsk K.F.U.K.)—where English is definitely a second language—is for women under 30 only (and men under 30 with Norwegian passports). Located on a quiet, stately street, it offers non-smoking rooms, a study, TV room, piano lounge, and an open-face Norwegian ambience (goat cheese on Sundays!). They have mostly quads, so those willing to share with strangers are most likely to get a bed (July–Aug: Ss-£34, shared double-£32/bed, shared triple-£27/bed, shared quad-£24/bed, includes breakfast and sack lunch; includes dinner Sept–June; 52 Holland Park, tel. 020/7727-9346, fax 020/7727-8718, www.kfukhjemmet.org.uk, kontor@kfukhjemmet.org.uk). With each visit, I wonder which is easier to get—a sex change or a Norwegian passport?

Other Neighborhoods

North of Marble Arch: **$$$ The 22 York Street B&B** offers a casual alternative in the city center, renting 18 stark, hardwood, comfortable rooms (Sb-£89, Db-£100, Tb-£141, two-night minimum, strictly non-smoking, social breakfast, inviting lounge; from Baker Street Tube station, walk 2 blocks down Baker Street and take a right, 22 York Street; tel. 020/7224-3990, fax 020/7224-1990, www.22yorkstreet.co.uk, mc@22yorkstreet.co.uk, energetically run by Liz and Michael Callis).

$$$ The Sumner Hotel, housed in a 19th-century Georgian townhouse, is located a few blocks north of Hyde Park and Oxford Street, a busy shopping destination. Decorated with fancy modern Italian furniture, this place packs in all the extras (Db-£125–140, extra bed-£30, free Wi-Fi, 53–54 Upper Berkeley Street just off Edgware Road, Tube: Marble Arch, tel. 020/7584-7586, fax 020/7823-9962, www.sumnerdale.co.uk, manager Tom).

Near Covent Garden: **$$$ Fielding Hotel,** located on a charming, quiet pedestrian street just two blocks east of Covent Garden, offers 24 no-frills rooms, a fine location, and lots of stairs (Db-£100–120, Db with sitting room-£140, pricier rooms are bigger with better bathrooms, no breakfast, all non-smoking, no kids under 13, 4 Broad Court, Bow Street, tel. 020/7836-8305, fax 020/7497-0064, www.the-fielding-hotel.co.uk, reservations@the-fielding-hotel.co.uk, manager Graham Chapman).

Near Buckingham Palace: **$$ Vandon House Hotel,** run by the Central College in Iowa, is packed with students most of the year, but its 33 rooms are rented to travelers from late May through August at great prices. The rooms, while institutional, are comfy, and the location is excellent (S-£43, D-£68, Db-£84, Tb-£99, Qb-£118, only single beds, all non-smoking, elevator, on a tiny road 3-min walk west of St. James's Park Tube station or 7-min walk from Victoria Station, near east end of Petty France Street at 1 Vandon Street, tel. 020/7799-6780, fax 020/7799-1464, www.vandonhouse.com, info@vandonhouse.com).

Near Euston Station and the British Library: The **$$ Methodist International Centre,** a modern, youthful, Christian residence, fills its lower floors with international students and its top floor with travelers. Rooms are modern and simple yet comfortable, with fine bathrooms, phones, and desks. The atmosphere is friendly, safe, clean, and controlled; it also has a spacious lounge and game room (Db-£85, two-course buffet dinner-£13, non-smoking rooms, elevator, on a quiet street a block west of Euston Station, 81–103 Euston Street—not Euston Road, Tube: Euston Station, tel. 020/7380-0001, fax 020/7387-5300, www.micentre.com, acc@micentre.com). In June, July, and August, when the students are gone, they also rent simpler rooms (S-£45, D-£68).

Hostels and Dorms

$ A cluster of three **St. Christopher's Inn** hostels, south of the Thames near London Bridge, have cheap dorm beds (£19–22, 161–165 Borough High Street, Tube: Borough or London Bridge, tel. 020/7407-1856, www.st-christophers.co.uk).

$ The **City of London Youth Hostel,** near St. Paul's, is clean, modern, friendly, and well-run. Most of the 152 beds are in shared, single-sex bunk rooms (bed-£24.60, drops to £17 off-season, twin-bed D-£56, bunk-bed Q-£86, £2 extra without hostel card, includes breakfast, cheap meals, open 24 hours, 36 Carter Lane, Tube: St. Paul's, tel. 020/7236-4965, fax 020/7236-7681, www.yha.org.uk, city@yha.org.uk).

$ The **University of Westminster** opens up its dorm rooms to travelers during summer break, from mid-June through mid-September. Located in several high-rise buildings scattered around central London, the rooms—some with private bathrooms, others with shared bathrooms nearby—come with access to well-equipped kitchens and big lounges (S-£28–35, Sb-£28–37, "studio flat" Db-£60–65, tel. 020/7911-5181, www.wmin.ac.uk/comserv, comserv@wmin.ac.uk). University College London also has rooms for travelers from mid-June until mid-September; for details see www.ucl.ac.uk/residences.

Near Heathrow and Gatwick Airports

At the Airports: Innovative **$ Yotel** opened locations inside both airports in 2007. Based on Japanese capsule hotels, these small sleep dens offer a place to catch a quick nap (four hours for £25), or to stay overnight (tiny "standard cabin" starts at £40, "premium cabin" starts at £70), all with private bathrooms, free Internet and Wi-Fi, and rooms the size of a double bed (in Heathrow Terminal 4 and Gatwick South Terminal, www.yotel.com).

Near Heathrow Airport: It's so easy to get to Heathrow from central London, I see no reason to sleep there. But for budget beds near the airport, consider **$ Heathrow Ibis** (Db-£70, Db-£45–50 on Fri–Sun nights, Web specials as low as £35, breakfast extra;

£4 shuttle bus to/from terminals except T-4, look for "Hopabus" run by National Express; 112 Bath Road, tel. 020/8759-4888, fax 020/8564-7894, www.ibishotel.com, h0794@accor-hotels.com).

Near Gatwick Airport: **$ London Gatwick Airport Premier Travel Inn** rents cheap rooms at the airport (Db-£60, £2.50 shuttle bus from airport—must reserve in advance, tel. 0870-238-3305, www.premiertravelinn.com).

$ Gatwick Travelodge has budget rooms two miles from the airport (Db-£56, £3 shuttle from airport, breakfast extra, Church Road, Lowfield Heath, Crawley, tel. 0870-191-1531, www.travelodge.co.uk).

$ Barn Cottage, a converted 16th-century barn, sits in the peaceful countryside, with a tennis court, small swimming pool, and a good pub within walking distance. It has two wood-beamed rooms, antique furniture, and a large garden that makes you forget Gatwick is 10 minutes away (S-£50, D-£60, cash only, can drive you to airport or train station for £8, Church Road, Leigh, Reigate, Surrey, tel. 01306/611-347, warmly run by Pat and Mike Comer). Do not confuse this place with others of the same name; this Barn Cottage has no website.

$ Wayside Manor Farm is another rural alternative to a bland airport hotel. This four-bedroom countryside place is a 10-minute drive from Gatwick (Db-£65, Tb-£80, Norwood Hill, near Charlwood, tel. 01293/862-692, www.wayside-manor.com, info@wayside-manor.com).

EATING

If you want to dine (as opposed to eat), check out the extensive listings in the weekly entertainment guides sold at London newsstands (or catch a train for Paris). The thought of a £40 meal in Britain generally ruins my appetite, so my London dining is limited mostly to easygoing, fun, but inexpensive alternatives. I've listed places by neighborhood—handy to your sightseeing or hotel.

Pub grub is the most atmospheric budget option. Many of London's 7,000 pubs serve fresh, tasty buffets under ancient timbers, with hearty lunches and dinners for £6–8.

Ethnic restaurants—especially Indian and Chinese—are popular, plentiful, and cheap. Most large museums (and many churches) have inexpensive, cheery cafeterias. Of course, picnicking is the fastest and cheapest way to go. Good grocery stores and sandwich shops, fine park benches, and polite pigeons abound in Britain's most expensive city.

Central London Eateries

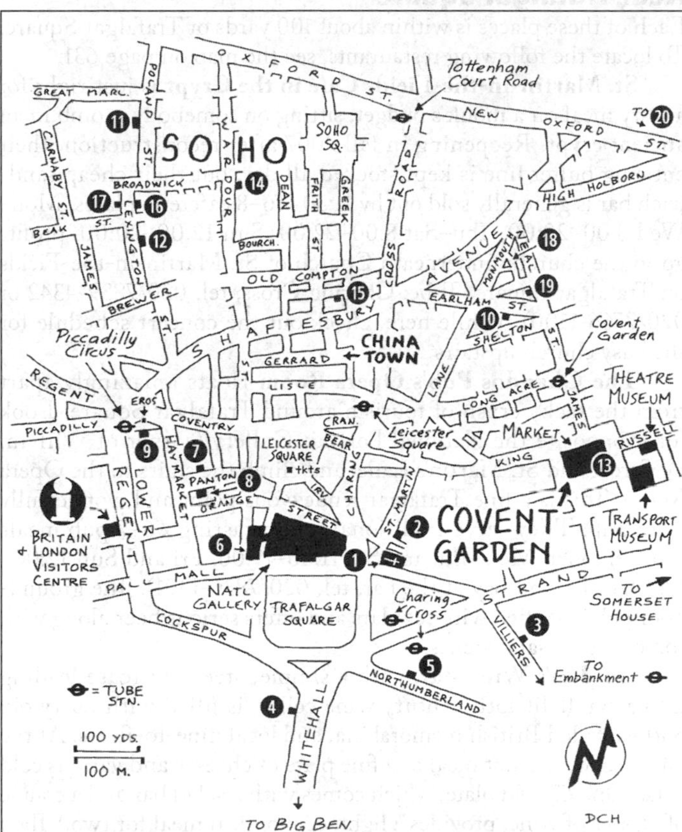

1. St. Martin-in-the-Fields Café in the Crypt
2. The Chandos Pub's Opera Room
3. Gordon's Wine Bar
4. The Lord Moon of the Mall Pub
5. The Sherlock Holmes Pub
6. The National Dining Rooms
7. Stockpot & West End Kitchen
8. Woodland South Indian Vegetarian Rest.
9. Criterion Restaurant
10. Belgo Centraal
11. Yo! Sushi
12. Wagamama Noodle Bar
13. Just Falafs
14. Soho Spice Indian & Busaba Eathai Thai Rest.
15. Y Ming Chinese Rest.
16. Andrew Edmunds Rest.
17. Mildred's Vegetarian Rest.
18. Neal's Yard Eateries
19. Food for Thought Café
20. To The Princess Louise Pub

Near Trafalgar Square

Each of these places is within about 100 yards of Trafalgar Square. To locate the following restaurants, see the map on page 631.

St. Martin-in-the-Fields Café in the Crypt is just right for a tasty meal on a monk's budget, sitting on somebody's tomb in an ancient crypt. Reopening in fall 2007 after reconstruction, their enticing buffet line is kept stocked all day, but their cheap sandwich bar is generally sold out by 11:30 (£6–8 cafeteria plates, Mon–Wed 8:00–20:00, Thu–Sat 8:00–22:00, Sun 12:00–20:00, profits go to the church; underneath Church of St. Martin-in-the-Fields on Trafalgar Square, Tube: Charing Cross; tel. 020/7839-4342 or 020/7766-1100). While here, check out the concert schedule for the busy church upstairs.

The Chandos Pub's Opera Room floats amazingly apart from the tacky crush of tourism around Trafalgar Square. Look for it opposite the National Portrait Gallery (corner of William IV Street and St. Martin's Lane) and climb the stairs to the Opera Room. This is a fine Trafalgar rendezvous point and wonderfully local pub. They serve traditional, plain-tasting £6–7 pub meals (kitchen open Mon–Thu and Sat 11:00–19:00, Fri and Sun 12:00–18:00, order and pay at the bar, tel. 020/7836-1401). The ground-floor pub is stuffed with regulars and offers serious beer along with some toasted sandwiches.

Gordon's Wine Bar, with a simple, steep staircase leading into a candlelit 15th-century wine cellar, is filled with dusty old bottles, faded British memorabilia, and local nine-to-fivers. At the buffet, choose a hot meal or a fine plate of cheeses and various cold cuts. (One £7 cold plate, which comes with a salad bar and a couple of glasses of wine, provides a light, economical meal for two.) Then step up to the wine bar and consider the many varieties of wine and port available by the glass. This place is passionate about port. The low, carbon-crusted vaulting deeper in the back seems to intensify the Hogarth-painting atmosphere. While it's crowded, you can normally corral two chairs and grab the corner of a table (arrive before 17:30 to get a seat, Mon–Sat 11:00–23:00, Sun 12:00–22:00, 2 blocks from Trafalgar Square, bottom of Villiars Street at #47, Tube: Embankment, tel. 020/7930-1408, manager Gerard Menan). On hot days, the crowd spills out into a leafy back patio.

The Lord Moon of the Mall pub has real ales on tap and good, cheap pub grub, including a two-meals-for-the-price-of-one deal (£7.50, offer valid Mon–Fri 14:00–22:00 and all day Sat–Sun). This kid-friendly pub fills a great old former Barclays Bank building a block down Whitehall from Trafalgar Square (daily 9:00–23:00, 18 Whitehall, tel. 020/7839-7701). Nearby are several cheap cafeterias and pizza joints.

The Sherlock Holmes pub has a casual ground-floor section serving cheap grub and a stodgier upstairs restaurant with a spy-theme menu (£10 main courses). Fans of the fictional detective will appreciate sitting next to a wonderful replica of Holmes' 221-B Baker Street home. The pub is located in the former Northumberland Hotel (featured in Holmes stories). The former Old Scotland Yard was just across the street (daily 11:00–22:00, 10 Northumberland Street, Tube: Charing Cross/Embankment, tel. 020/7930-2644).

The National Dining Rooms serves classy meals within the National Gallery, and is a good place to treat your palate to pricey cuisine (including high tea). While tables in the main dining room are often reserved for dinner, you can usually grab a seat in the bistro-like café anytime (£15 lunches, daily 10:00–17:00, later on Wed—when the museum stays open late, Tube: Charing Cross or Leicester Square, tel. 020/7747-2525).

Cheap Eating near Piccadilly

Hungry and broke in the theater district? Head for Panton Street (off Haymarket, 2 blocks southeast of Piccadilly Circus) where several hard-working little places compete, all seeming to offer a three-course meal for about £7. Peruse the entire block (vegetarian, Japanese, Pizza Express, Moroccan, Thai, Chinese, and two famous eateries) before making your choice. **Stockpot** is a mushy-peas kind of place, famous and rightly popular for its edible, cheap meals (daily 7:00–22:00, 38 Panton Street, cash only). The **West End Kitchen** (across the street at #5, same hours and menu) is a direct competitor that's also well-known and just as good. Vegetarians prefer the **Woodland South Indian Vegetarian Restaurant.**

The palatial **Criterion** serves a special £15 two-course Italian meal (or £18 for three courses) under gilded tiles and chandeliers in a dreamy Byzantine church setting from 1880. It's right on Piccadilly Circus but a world away from the punk junk. The house wine is great and so is the food (Mon–Sat 12:00–23:00, Sun 12:00–22:00, tel. 020/7930-0488). After 19:00, the menu becomes really expensive. Anyone can drop in for coffee or a drink.

Hip Eating from Covent Garden to Soho

London has a trendy, Generation X scene that most Beefeater-seekers miss entirely. These restaurants are scattered throughout the hipster, gay, and strip-club district, teeming each evening with fun-seekers and theater-goers. Even if you plan to have dinner elsewhere, it's a treat to just wander around this lively area.

Beware the extremely welcoming women standing outside the strip clubs (especially on Great Windmill Street). Enjoy the sales pitch—but only fools fall for the "£5 drink and show" lure. They don't get back out without emptying their wallet.

Belgo Centraal serves hearty Belgian specialties in a vast, 400-seat underground lair. It's a seafood, chips, and beer emporium dressed up as a mod-monastic refectory—with noisy acoustics and waiters garbed as Trappist monks. The classy restaurant section is more comfortable and less rowdy, but usually requires reservations (the wait can be up to two hours Fri–Sat without a reservation). It's often more fun to just grab a spot in the boisterous beer hall, with its tight, communal benches (no reservations accepted). The same menu and specials work on both sides. Belgians claim they eat as well as the French and as heartily as the Germans. Specialties include mussels, great fries, and a stunning array of dark, blond, and fruity Belgian beers (even beer ice cream). Belgo actually makes Belgian things trendy—a formidable feat (£10–14 meals; open Mon–Sat 12:00–23:30, Sun 12:00–22:30; Mon–Fri £5–6.30 "beat the clock" meal specials from 17:00–18:30—the time you order is the price you pay—include mussels, fries, and beer; no meal-splitting after 18:30, and you must buy food with beer; daily £6 lunch special 12:00–17:00; 2 kids eat free for each parent ordering a regular entrée; 1 block north of Covent Garden Tube station at intersection of Neal and Shelton streets, 50 Earlham Street, tel. 020/7813-2233).

Yo! Sushi is a futuristic Japanese-food-extravaganza. It's not cheap, but it's sure to be a memorable experience, complete with thumping rock, Japanese cable TV, a 195-foot-long conveyor belt—the world's longest sushi bar—and automated sushi machines. For £1 each you get unlimited tea or water (from spigot at bar, with or without gas). Snag a bar stool and grab dishes as they rattle by (priced by color of dish; check the chart: £1.50–5 per dish, £1.50 for miso soup, Mon–Sat 12:00–23:00, Sun 12:00–22:30, 2 blocks south of Oxford Street, where Lexington Street becomes Poland Street, 52 Poland Street, tel. 020/7287-0443). If you like Yo!, there are several locations around town, including a handy branch a block from the London Eye on Belvedere Road, as well as outlets within Selfridges, Harvey Nichols department stores, and Whiteleys Mall on Queensway—see below.

Wagamama Noodle Bar is a noisy, pan-Asian, organic slurpathon. As you enter, check out the kitchen and listen to the roar of the basement, where benches rock with happy eaters. Everybody sucks. Stand against the wall to feel the energy of all this "positive eating" (£7–12 meals, Mon–Sat 12:00–23:00, Sun 12:00–22:00, crowded after 20:00, 10-A Lexington Street, tel. 020/7292-0990 but no reservations taken). If you like this place, handy branches are all over town, including one near the British Museum (Streatham Street), High Street Kensington (#26), in

Harvey Nichols (109 Knightsbridge), Covent Garden (Tavistock Street), Leicester Square (Irving Street), Piccadilly Circus (Norris Street), Fleet Street (#109), and between St. Paul's and the Tower of London (22 Old Broad Street). You'll find Wagamamas in many other UK cities, as well.

Just Falafs is a healthy fast-food option in the chaos of Covent Garden. Located in the southeast corner, where rows of outdoor café tables line the tiny shop, they offer falafel sandwiches with yummy vegetarian-friendly extras (£6 sandwiches, Mon–Fri 8:00–21:00, Sat 10:00–21:00, Sun 10:00–18:00, closes earlier when it's raining, 27b Covent Gardens Square, tel. 020/7622-6262).

Soho Spice Indian is where modern Britain meets Indian tradition—fine cuisine in a trendy, jewel-tone ambience. Unlike many Indian restaurants, when you order an entrée here (£11), it comes with side dishes—nan, dal, rice, and vegetables (£7 lunch special, daily 12:00–23:00, 5 blocks north of Piccadilly Circus at 124 Wardour Street, tel. 020/7434-0808).

Busaba Eathai Thai Restaurant is a hit with locals for its snappy service, casual-yet-high-energy ambience and good, inexpensive Thai cuisine. You'll sit communally around big, square 16-person hardwood tables or in two-person tables by the window—with everyone in the queue staring at your noodles. They don't take reservations, so arrive by 19:00 or line up (£10–14 meals, daily 12:00–23:00, 106 Wardour Street, tel. 020/7255-8686).

Y Ming Chinese Restaurant—across Shaftesbury Avenue from the ornate gates, clatter, and dim sum of Chinatown—has dressy European decor, serious but helpful service, and authentic Northern Chinese cooking (Mon–Sat 12:00–23:45, closed Sun, good £10 meal deal offered 12:00–18:00—last order at 18:00, 35 Greek Street, tel. 020/7734-2721).

Andrew Edmunds Restaurant is a tiny, candlelit place where you'll want to hide your camera and guidebook and act as local as possible. This great little place—with a jealous and loyal clientele—is the closest I've found to Parisian quality in a cozy restaurant in London. The modern European cooking and creative seasonal menu are worth the splurge (£25 meals, daily 12:30–15:00 & 18:00–22:45, come early or call ahead, request ground floor rather than basement, 46 Lexington Street in Soho, tel. 020/7437-5708).

Mildred's Vegetarian Restaurant, across from Andrew Edmunds, has cheap prices, an enjoyable menu, and a plain-yet-pleasant interior filled with happy eaters (£7 meals, Mon–Sat 12:00–23:00, closed Sun, vegan options, 45 Lexington Street, tel. 020/7494-1634).

Neal's Yard is *the* place for cheap, hip, and healthy eateries near Covent Garden. The neighborhood is a tabouli of fun, hippie-type cafés. One of the best is **Food for Thought,** packed with local health nuts (good £5 vegetarian meals, £7 dinner plates, Mon–Sat 12:00–20:30, Sun 12:00–17:00, 2 blocks north of Covent Garden Tube station, 31 Neal Street, near Neal's Yard, tel. 020/7836-0239).

The Soho "Food is Fun" Three-Course Dinner Crawl: For a multicultural, movable feast, consider eating (or splitting) one course and enjoying a drink at each of these places. Start around 18:00 to avoid lines, get in on early specials, and find waiters willing to let you split a meal. Prices, while reasonable by London standards, add up. Servings are large enough to share. All are open nightly. Arrive before 18:00 at **Belgo Centraal** and split the early-bird dinner special: a kilo of mussels, fries, and dark Belgian beer. At **Yo! Sushi,** have beer or sake and a few dishes. Slurp your last course at **Wagamama Noodle Bar.** For dessert, people-watch at Leicester Square.

Near Recommended Victoria Station Accommodations

Here are places a few blocks southwest of Victoria Station where I've enjoyed eating (see map on page 620).

Ebury Wine Bar, filled with young professionals, provides a cut-above atmosphere, delicious £15–18 meals, and a £14 two-course special from 18:00–19:30. In the delightful back room, the fancy menu features modern European cuisine with an accent on French; at the wine bar, find cheaper food that's better than pub grub. This is emphatically a "traditional wine bar" with only a few beers on tap (Mon–Fri 11:00–23:00, Sat 12:00–23:00, Sun 18:00–22:00, reserve after 20:00, at intersection of Ebury and Elizabeth Streets, near bus station, 139 Ebury Street, tel. 020/7730-5447).

Goya Spanish Restaurant and Tapas Bar is popular for its old-church-library ambience and tasty, reasonably priced food (£12–15 meals, good Spanish wine by the glass, daily 11:30–23:00, 2 Eccleston Place, tel. 020/7730-4299). Several cheap places are around the corner on Elizabeth Street (#23 for take-out or eat-in, super-absorbent fish-and-chips).

The Duke of Wellington pub is dominated by local drinkers. It's the neighborhood place for a good dinner, with woody sidewalk seating and an inviting interior (£6–7 meals, daily specials, Mon–Sat 11:00–15:00 & 18:00–21:00, closed Sun, 63 Eaton Terrace, at intersection with Chester Row, tel. 020/7730-1782).

The Belgravia pub is a hardworking sports bar with less character than The Duke of Wellington, serving snacks and pub food under a set of big-screen TVs (£4–6 meals, beer garden seating or plush interior, daily 10:00–23:00, 11:00–23:00 in winter, corner of Ebury Street and South Eaton Place at 152 Ebury Street, tel. 020/7730-6040).

Jenny Lo's Tea House is a simple, budget place serving up reliably tasty £5–8 eclectic Chinese-style meals to locals in the know. While the menu is small, everything is high quality. Jenny clearly learned from her father, Ken Lo, one of the most famous Cantonese chefs in Britain, whose fancy place is just around the corner (Mon–Fri 12:00–15:00 & 18:00–22:00, Sat 18:00–22:00, closed Sun, cash only, 14 Eccleston Street, tel. 020/7259-0399).

La Poule au Pot, ideal for a romantic splurge, offers a classy, candlelit ambience with well-dressed patrons and expensive but fine country-style French cuisine (£18 lunch specials, £25 dinner plates, daily 12:30–14:30 & 18:45–23:00, Sun until 22:00, £50 for dinner with wine, leafy patio dining, reservations smart, end of Ebury Street at intersection with Pimlico Road, 231 Ebury Street, tel. 020/7730-7763).

Grumbles brags it's been serving "good food and wine at non-scary prices since 1964." Offering a delicious mix of "modern eclectic French and traditional English," this hip and cozy little place with four nice sidewalk tables is *the* spot to eat well in this otherwise workaday neighborhood (£8–16 plates, £10 early-bird special, daily 12:00–14:30 & 18:00–23:00, reservations wise, half a block north of Belgrave Road at 35 Churton Street, tel. 020/7834-0149). While they have seating downstairs, I'd avoid it; call ahead to reserve a spot outside or on the appealing and cozy ground floor. The self-serve launderette across the street is open evenings.

Chimes English Restaurant and Cider Bar comes with a fresh country farm ambience, serious ciders (rare in London), and very good, traditional English food (2-course meals £13, hearty salads, daily 12:00–14:30 & 17:30–22:15, 26 Churton Street, tel. 020/7821-7456). Experiment with the cider—it's legal here...just barely.

The Jugged Hare, a 10-minute walk from Victoria Station, is a pub in a lavish old bank building, its vaults replaced by tankards of beer and a fine kitchen. They have a fun, traditional menu with more fresh veggies than fries, and a plush and vivid pub scene good for a meal or just a drink (£7 meals, daily 12:00–21:30, 172 Vauxhall Bridge Road, tel. 020/7828-1543).

Seafresh Fish Restaurant is the neighborhood place for plaice—either take-out on the cheap or eat-in, enjoying a chrome-and-wood mod ambience with classic and creative fish-and-chips cuisine. It feels like the chippie of the 21st century (meals £5 to go, £8–13 to sit, Mon–Fri 12:00–15:00 & 17:00–22:30, Sat 12:00–17:00, closed Sun, 80 Wilton Road, tel. 020/7828-0747).

If you miss America, there's a mall-type **food court** at Victoria Place, upstairs in Victoria Station; **Café Rouge** seems to be the most popular here (£8–11 dinners, daily 9:30–22:30).

Groceries in and near Victoria Station: A handy **Marks & Spencer Simply Food** is inside Victoria Station (Mon–Sat 7:00–24:00, Sun 8:00–22:00, tel. 020/7828-9502), along with a small **Sainsbury's** (at rear entrance, on Eccleston Street) and a few other late-hours mini-markets. A large **Sainsbury's Local** is on Victoria Street in front of the station, just past the buses (daily 6:00–24:00).

Near Recommended Notting Hill B&Bs and Bayswater Hotels

The road called Queensway is a multi-ethnic food circus, lined with lively and inexpensive eateries. See the map on page 626.

Maggie Jones, exuberantly rustic and very English, serves my favorite £30 London dinner. You'll get fun-loving if brash service, and solid English cuisine, including huge plates of crunchy vegetables—by candlelight. Avoid the stuffy basement on hot summer nights, and request upstairs seating for the noisy but less cramped section. If you eat well once in London, eat here—and do it quick, before it burns down (daily 12:30–14:30 & 18:30–23:00, less expensive lunch menu, reservations recommended, friendly staff, 6 Old Court Place, just east of Kensington Church Street, near High Street Kensington Tube stop, tel. 020/7937-6462).

The Churchill Arms pub and **Thai Kitchens** (same location) is a local hangout, with good beer and old-English ambience in front, and hearty £6 Thai plates in an enclosed patio in the back. You can eat the Thai food in the tropical hideaway or in the atmospheric pub section. Arrive by 18:00 to avoid a line. During busy times, diners are limited to an hour at the table (Mon–Sat 12:00–22:00, Sun 12:00–21:30, 119 Kensington Church Street, tel. 020/7792-1246).

The Prince Edward pub serves good grub in a quintessential pub setting (£7–10 meals, Mon–Sat 12:00–15:00 & 18:00–22:00, Sun 12:00–21:00, plush-pubby indoor seating or sidewalk tables, 2 blocks north of Bayswater Road at the corner of Dawson Place and Hereford Road, 73 Prince's Square, tel. 020/7727-2221).

Café Diana is a healthy little eatery serving sandwiches, salads, and Middle Eastern food. It's decorated—almost shrine-like—with photos of Princess Diana, who used to drop by for pita sandwiches (daily 8:00–22:30, 5 Wellington Terrace, on Bayswater Road, opposite Kensington Palace Garden Gates—where Di once lived, tel. 020/7792-9606).

Black and Blue is a trendy bistro serving steaks and burgers to local hipsters. Follow the crowds to the gas torches and patio seating (£9–12 meals, daily 12:00–23:00, 215 Kensington Church Street, tel. 020/7727-0004).

Royal China Restaurant is filled with London's Chinese, who consider this one of the city's best eateries. It's dressy in black, white, and chrome, with candles, brisk waiters, and fine food (£7–11 dishes, Mon–Sat 12:00–23:00, Sun 11:00–22:00, dim sum until 16:45, 13 Queensway, tel. 020/7221-2535).

Whiteleys Mall Food Court offers a fun selection of ethnic and fast-food eateries among Corinthian columns in a delightful mall (Mon–Sat 10:00–20:00, Sun 12:00–18:00; options include Yo! Sushi, good salads at Café Rouge, pizza, Starbucks, and an Internet café; second floor, corner of Porchester Gardens and Queensway).

Supermarket: **Europa** is a half-block from the Notting Hill Gate Tube stop (Mon–Sat 8:00–23:00, Sun 12:00–18:00, near intersection with Pembridge Road, 112 Notting Hill Gate). The smaller **Spar Market** is at 18 Queensway (Mon–Sat 7:00–24:00, Sun 9:00–24:00).

Near Recommended Accommodations in South Kensington

Popular eateries line Old Brompton Road and Thurloe Street (Tube: South Kensington). See the map on page 623. The **Tesco Express** grocery store is handy for picnics (daily 7:00–24:00, 54 Old Brompton Road).

La Bouchee Bistro Café is a classy, hole-in-the-wall touch of France—candlelit and woody—serving an early-bird, two-course £10 dinner weekdays from 17:30–19:00 and £15 *plats du jour* all *jour* (daily 12:00–15:00 & 17:30–23:00, 56 Old Brompton Road, tel. 020/7589-1929).

Il Falconiere Restaurant, just down the street, is popular for its Italian cuisine (£8 pastas, £10 plates, £19 three-course dinner special, closed Sun, 84 Old Brompton Road, tel. 020/7589 2401).

Daquise, an authentic-feeling 1930s Polish time-warp, is ideal if you're in the mood for kielbasa and kraut. It's likeably dreary—fast, cheap, family-run—and a much-appreciated part of the neighborhood (£10 meals, £8 lunch special includes wine, daily 11:30–23:00, 20 Thurloe Street, tel. 020/7589-6117).

Moti Mahal Indian Restaurant is a favorite for value. Find minimalist-yet-classy mod ambience and attentive service (daily 12:00–23:00, 3 Glendower Place, tel. 020/7584-8428).

The Zetland Arms serves good pub meals in a classic pub atmosphere on the ground floor and a club-chair lounge upstairs (same menu throughout, £6–10 meals, food served Mon–Fri 12:00–20:30, Sat 11:00–21:00, Sun 12:00–20:30, 2 Bute Street, tel. 020/7589-3813).

Elsewhere in London

Between St. Paul's and the Tower: **The Counting House,** formerly an elegant old bank, offers great £7.50–8 meals, nice homemade meat pies, fish, and fresh vegetables (Mon–Fri 12:00–21:00, closed Sat–Sun, gets really busy with the buttoned-down 9-to-5 crowd after 12:15, near Mansion House in the City, 50 Cornhill, tel. 020/7283-7123).

Near St. Paul's: **De Gustibus Sandwiches** is where a top-notch artisan bakery meets the public, offering fresh, you-design-it sandwiches, salads, and soups with simple seating or take-out picnic sacks (great parks nearby), just a block below St. Paul's (Mon–Fri 7:00–17:00, closed Sat–Sun, from church steps follow signs to youth hostel a block downhill, 53-55 Carter Lane, tel. 020/7236-0056).

Near the British Library: Drummond Street (running just west of Euston Station) is famous in London for very cheap and good Indian vegetarian food. Consider **Chutneys** (124 Drummond, tel. 020/7388-0604) and **Ravi Shankar** (133 Drummond, tel. 020/7388-6458) for a good *thali* (both generally open daily until 21:30, later Fri–Sat).

TRANSPORTATION CONNECTIONS

Heathrow Airport

Heathrow Airport is the world's third busiest, after Atlanta and Chicago. Think about it: 68 million passengers a year on 470,000 flights from 185 destinations riding 90 airlines, like some kind of global maypole dance. While many complain about Heathrow, I think it's a great and user-friendly airport. Read signs, ask questions. For Heathrow's airport, flight, and transfers information, call the switchboard at 0870-000-0123 (www.baa.com). It has four terminals: T-1 (mostly domestic flights, with some European), T-2 (mainly European flights), T-3 (mostly flights from the US), T-4 (British Airways transatlantic flights and BA flights to Paris, Amsterdam, and Athens). Taxis know which terminal you'll need. Note that a fifth terminal (T-5) is due to be completed in 2008.

Each terminal has an airport information desk, car-rental agencies, exchange bureaus, ATMs, a pharmacy, a **VAT refund desk** (tel. 020/8910-3682; you must present the VAT claim form from the retailer here to get your tax rebate on items purchased in Britain), and a **baggage-check desk** (£6/day, daily 6:00–23:00 at each terminal). Get online 24 hours a day at Heathrow's **Internet cafés** (T-4, mezzanine level) and with a laptop at pay-as-you-go wireless "hotspots"—including many hosted by T-Mobile—in its departure lounges (T-1, T-3, and T-4). There are **post offices** in T-2 and T-4. Each terminal has cheap **eateries** (such as the cheery Food

Village self-service cafeteria in T-3). The **American Express** desk, in the Tube station at Terminal 4 (daily 7:00–19:00), has rates similar to the exchange bureaus upstairs, but doesn't charge a commission (typically 1.5 percent) for cashing any type of traveler's check.

Heathrow's small **TI** (tourist info shop), even though it's a for-profit business, is worth a visit to pick up free information: a simple map, the *London Planner*, and brochures (daily 8:30–18:00, 5-min walk from T-3 in Tube station, follow signs to Underground; bypass queue for transit info to reach window for London questions). Have your partner stay with the bags at the terminal while you head over to the TI. There are also info desks in each of the terminals in their arrivals concourse (generally open daily 7:00–21:30).

If you're taking the Tube into London, buy a one-day Travelcard or Oyster card to cover the ride (see below).

Getting to London from Heathrow Airport

By Tube (Subway): For £4, the Tube takes you the 14 miles to downtown London in 50–60 minutes on the Piccadilly Line, with stops (among others) at South Kensington, Leicester Square, and King's Cross Station (6/hr; depending on your destination, may require a change). Even better, buy a One-Day Travelcard that covers your trip into London and all your Tube travel for the day (£12.40 covers peak times, £6.30 "off-peak" card starts at 9:30, less-expensive Travelcards cover the city center only). Or consider an Oyster card if you're staying in London for five or more days. For information on both types of cards, see "Oyster Cards and Travelcards" on page 572. Buy tickets or cards at the Tube station ticket window. You can hop on the Tube at any terminal.

If taking the Tube to the airport, note that Piccadilly Line subway cars post which airlines are served by which terminals.

By Airport Shuttle Bus: Hotelink offers door-to-door service (Heathrow-£17 per person, Gatwick-£22 per person, book the day before departure, buy online and save £1–2, tel. 01293/532-244, www.hotelink.co.uk, reservations@hotelink.co.uk). The famous Airbus (which shuttled a generation of travelers between the airport and downtown) has gone extinct—replaced by the train link and minibus shuttles.

By Taxi: Taxis from the airport cost about £45–50 to west and central London (one hour). For four people traveling together, this can be a deal. Hotels can often line up a cab back to the airport for about £30. For the cheapest taxi to the airport, don't order one from your hotel. Simply flag down a few and ask them for their best "off-meter" rate.

By Heathrow Express Train: This slick train service zips you between Heathrow Airport and London's Paddington Station. At

Paddington Station, you're in the thick of the Tube system, with easy access to any of my recommended neighborhoods—Notting Hill Gate is just two stops away. It's only 15 minutes to downtown from Terminals 1, 2, and 3, and 20 minutes from Terminal 4 (at the airport, you can use the Express as a free transfer between terminals). Buy your ticket to London before you board, or pay a £2 surcharge to buy it on the train (£14.50 "express class" one-way, £13.50 from ticket machine or online, £27 round-trip, ask about discount promos at Heathrow ticket desk, kids under 16 ride half-price, under 5 ride free, covered by BritRail pass, 4/hr, daily 5:10–23:30, tel. 0845-600-1515, www.heathrowexpress.co.uk). For one person on a budget, combining the Heathrow Express with either a Tube or taxi ride (between your hotel and Paddington Station) is nearly as fast and half the cost of taking a cab directly to (or from) the airport. For groups of three or more, a taxi is faster and easier, as well as cheaper.

Getting to Bath from Heathrow Airport

By Bus: Direct buses run daily from Heathrow to Bath (£15, 11/day direct, 2.5 hours direct, more frequent with connection in London, tel. 0870-575-7747, www.nationalexpress.com). BritRail passholders may prefer the 2.5-hour Heathrow–Bath bus/train connection via Reading (£10 for bus, rail portion free with pass, otherwise £33 total, payable at desk in terminal): first catch the twice-hourly RailAir Link shuttle bus to Reading (RED-ding), then hop on the hourly express train to Bath. Factoring in the connection in Reading—which can add at least an hour to the trip—the train is a less convenient option than the direct bus to Bath.

Most Heathrow buses depart from the common area serving Terminals 1, 2, and 3 (a 5-min walk from any of these terminals), although some depart from T-4 (bus tel. 0870-574-7777).

Gatwick Airport

More and more flights, especially charters, land at Gatwick Airport, halfway between London and the southern coast (recorded airport info tel. 0870-000-2468).

Getting to London: Express trains—clearly the best way into London from here—shuttle conveniently between Gatwick and London's Victoria Station (£14, £25 round-trip, 4/hr during day, 1–2/hr at night, 30 min, runs 5:00–24:00 daily, can purchase tickets on train at no extra charge, tel. 0845-850-1530, www.gatwickexpress.co.uk). If you're traveling with three others, buy your tickets at the station before boarding, and you'll travel for the price of two. The only restriction on this impressive deal is that you have to travel together. So if you see another couple in line, get organized and save 50 percent.

You can save a few pounds by taking South Central rail line's slower and less frequent shuttle between Victoria Station and Gatwick (£9, 4/hr, hourly from midnight to 4:00, 45 min, tel. 08457-484-950, www.southcentraltrains.co.uk).

Getting to Bath: To get to Bath from Gatwick, you can catch a bus to Heathrow and the bus to Bath from there. By train, the best Gatwick–Bath connection involves a transfer in Reading (2.5 hrs, irregular schedule; avoid transfer in London, where you'll have to change stations).

Connecting London's Airports

The **National Express Airport** service offers direct Jetlink bus connections from **Heathrow** to **Gatwick Airport** (2/hr, 70 min or more, depending on traffic), departing just outside arrivals at all terminals (£18 one-way, £35.50 round-trip). To make a flight connection between Heathrow and Gatwick, allow three hours between flights.

More and more travelers are taking advantage of cheap flights out of London's smaller airports. A handy National Express bus runs between Heathrow, Gatwick, Stansted, and Luton airports—easier than having to cut through the center of London. Buses are frequent (less so between Stansted and Luton): Heathrow–Luton is 1.5 hours direct and costs £20.50 (£31 round-trip). Check schedules at www.nxairport.com.

To get from Luton Airport to the city center, take the easyJet bus to the Baker Street Tube stop. The online price varies from £2–8, depending on demand for individual departures. The walk-up price is at least £7 and is on a space-available, stand-by basis (their bright-orange minibuses have 16 seats). Ticket prices include space for one "medium-size" suitcase and one piece of hand luggage. If you have more, you need to pay for an extra seat or seats. For details, see www.easybus.co.uk.

Discounted Flights from London

Although bmi british midland has been around the longest, the other small airlines generally offer cheaper flights. A visit to www.skyscanner.net or www.mobissimo.com sorts the numerous options offered by the many discount airlines, enabling you to see the best schedules for your trip and come up with the best deal.

With **bmi british midland,** you can fly inexpensively to destinations in the UK and beyond (fares start at about £30 one-way to Edinburgh, Paris, Brussels, or Amsterdam; or about £50 one-way to Dublin; prices can be higher, but there can also be much cheaper mid-week or via Internet specials—check online). For the latest, call British tel. 0870-607-0555 or US tel. 800-788-0555 (check www.flybmi.com and their subsidiary, bmi baby, at www.bmibaby.com).

Book in advance. Although you can book right up until the flight departs, the cheap seats will have sold out long before, leaving the most expensive seats for latecomers.

With no frills and cheap fares, **easyJet** flies from Luton, Stansted, and Gatwick. Prices are based on demand, so the least popular routes make for the cheapest fares, especially if you book early (tel. 0905-821-0905 to book by phone, 10p per minute, or do it free online at www.easyjet.com).

Ryanair is a creative Irish airline that prides itself on offering the lowest fares. It flies from London (mostly Stansted airport) to often obscure airports in Dublin, Glasgow, Frankfurt, Stockholm, Oslo, Venice, Turin, and many others. Sample fares: London–Dublin—£60 round-trip (sometimes as low as £15), London–Frankfurt—£50 round-trip (Irish tel. 0818-303-030, British tel. 0871-246-0000, www.ryanair.com). Because they offer promotional deals any time of year, you can get great prices on short notice. There is a cost of £5 per checked bag, and you can carry on only a small daybag. Each checked bag can weigh up to 15 kilograms—about 33 pounds (up to five bags per passenger allowed). If you're traveling with lots of bags, a cheap Ryanair flight can quickly become a bad deal because of these £5-a-pop fees.

Virgin Express is a British-owned company with good rates (book by phone and pick up ticket at airport an hour before your flight, www.virgin-express.com). Virgin Express flies from London Heathrow and Brussels. From its hub in Brussels, you can connect cheaply to Barcelona, Madrid, Nice, Málaga, Copenhagen, Rome, or Milan (round-trip from Brussels to Rome for about £160). Their prices stay the same whether or not you book in advance.

Trains and Buses

London, Britain's major transportation hub, has a different train station for each region. Waterloo handles the Eurostar to Paris or Brussels. King's Cross and Euston stations cover northeast England, North Wales, and Scotland. Paddington covers west and southwest England (including Bath) and South Wales. For information, call 0845-748-4950 (or visit www.nationalrail.co.uk or www.eurostar.com; £5 booking fee for telephone reservations). Note that for security reasons, stations offer a left-luggage service (£6/day) rather than lockers.

By Train

To Points West from Paddington Station

To Bath: Trains leave London's Paddington Station twice every hour between 7:00 and 19:00 (at :15 and :45 after each hour) for the 90-minute ride to Bath (about £44, one-way after 9:30). Also consider a guided Evan Evans' tour by bus (see below).

Other Destinations: Oxford (2–4/hr, 1 hr, possible transfer in Didcot or Reading), **Penzance** (about hourly, 5–7 hrs, possible change in Plymouth), **Cardiff** (2/hr, 2 hrs).

To Points North

From King's Cross Station: Trains run at least hourly, stopping in **York** (2 hrs), **Durham** (3 hrs), and **Edinburgh** (4.5 hrs). Trains to **Cambridge** also leave from here (every 10–15 min, 1–1.5 hrs).

From Euston Station: Conwy (1/hr, 3.5–4 hrs, transfer in Crewe), **Liverpool** (1–2/hr, 2.5–3 hrs direct; possible transfer in Birmingham, Crewe, and/or Manchester), **Blackpool** (2/hr, 3 hrs, possible transfer at Preston), **Keswick** (10/day, 4–5 hrs, transfer at Penrith), **Glasgow** (1–2 hr, 4.5–5 hrs direct).

From London's Other Stations

Trains run between London and **Canterbury,** leaving from Charing Cross Station and arriving in Canterbury West, as well as from London's Victoria Station and arriving in Canterbury East (2/hr, 1.5 hrs).

Direct trains leave about for **Stratford-upon-Avon** from Marylebone Station, located near the southwest corner of Regents Park (every 2 hrs, 2–2.5 hrs).

Other Destinations: Dover (3–4/hr, 2 hrs, some require transfer, departs from Victoria Station), **Portsmouth** (4/hr, 1.5–2 hrs, almost all Portsmouth-bound trains depart from Waterloo Station, and a few a day from Victoria Station).

By Bus

National Express' excellent bus service is considerably cheaper than the train, and a fine option for destinations within England (call 0870-575-7747, or visit www.nationalexpress.com or the bus station a block southwest of Victoria Station).

To Bath: The National Express bus leaves from Victoria Station nearly hourly (a little over 3 hrs, one-way-£17.50, round trip-£23.50).

To get to Bath via Stonehenge, consider taking a guided bus tour from London to Stonehenge and Bath and abandoning the tour in Bath. **Evan Evans'** tour costs £65 (includes admissions). The tour leaves from the Victoria Coach station every morning at 8:30 (you can stow your bag under the bus), stops in Stonehenge (45 min), and then stops in Bath for lunch and a city tour before returning to London (offered year-round). You can book the tour at the Victoria Coach station, the Evan Evans' office (258 Vauxhall Bridge Road, near Victoria Coach station, tel. 020/7950-1777, US tel. 866-382-6868, www.evanevans.co.uk, reservations @evanevanstours.co.uk), or at the Green Line Travel Office (4a

Fountain Square, across from Victoria Coach station, tel. 0870-608-7261, www.greenline.co.uk). Golden Tours also runs a fully guided Stonehenge–Bath tour for the same price (departs from Fountain Square, located across from Victoria Coach Station, tel. 020/7233-7036, US tel. 800/548-7083, www.goldentours.co.uk, reservations@goldentours.co.uk). Another similarly priced day trip hits Oxford, Stratford, and Warwick.

To Other Destinations: Oxford (3/hr, 1.5 hrs), **Cambridge** (hourly direct, 2 hrs), **Canterbury** (hourly, 2–2.5 hrs), **Dover** (hourly, 2.75–3 hrs), **Penzance** (every 2 hrs direct, 9 hrs), **Cardiff** (every 2–3 hrs direct, 3 hrs), **Liverpool** (every 3 hrs direct, 4.5–6 hrs), **Blackpool** (2/day direct, 6–6.5 hrs), **York** (hourly, 6 hrs), **Durham** (5/day, 6–8 hrs, possible transfer in Leeds), **Glasgow** (2/day direct, 8.5 hrs, train is a much better option), **Edinburgh** (2/day direct, 8.5–9 hrs, go via train instead).

BATH

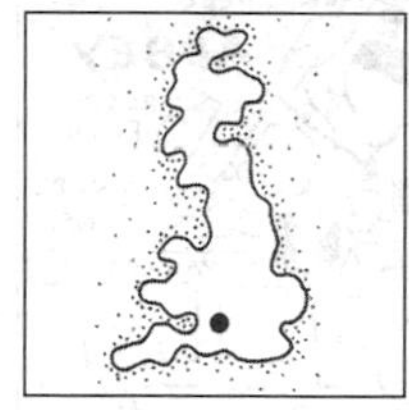

The best city to visit within easy striking distance of London is Bath—just a 90-minute train ride away. Two hundred years ago, this city of 85,000 was the trendsetting Hollywood of Britain. If ever a city enjoyed looking in the mirror, Bath's the one. It has more "government-listed" or protected historic buildings per capita than any other town in England. The entire city, built of the creamy warm-tone limestone called "Bath stone," beams in its cover-girl complexion. An architectural chorus line, it's a triumph of the Georgian style. Proud locals remind visitors that the town is routinely banned from the Britain in Bloom contest to give other towns a chance to win. Bath's narcissism is justified. Even with its mobs of tourists (2 million per year), Bath is a joy to visit.

Long before the Romans arrived in the first century, Bath was known for its mineral hot springs. The importance of Bath has always been shaped by the healing allure of its 116° F hot springs. Romans called the popular spa town Aquae Sulis. The town's importance continued through Saxon times, when it had a huge church on the site of the present-day abbey and was considered the religious capital of Britain. Its influence peaked in 973 with King Edgar's sumptuous coronation in the abbey. Later Bath prospered as a wool town.

Bath then declined until the mid-1600s, when it was just a huddle of huts around the abbey, with hot, smelly mud and 3,000 residents, oblivious to the Roman ruins 18 feet below their dirt floors. Then, in 1687, Queen Mary, fighting infertility, bathed here. Within 10 months she gave birth to a son...and a new age of popularity for Bath.

The revitalized town boomed as a spa resort. Ninety percent

Bath

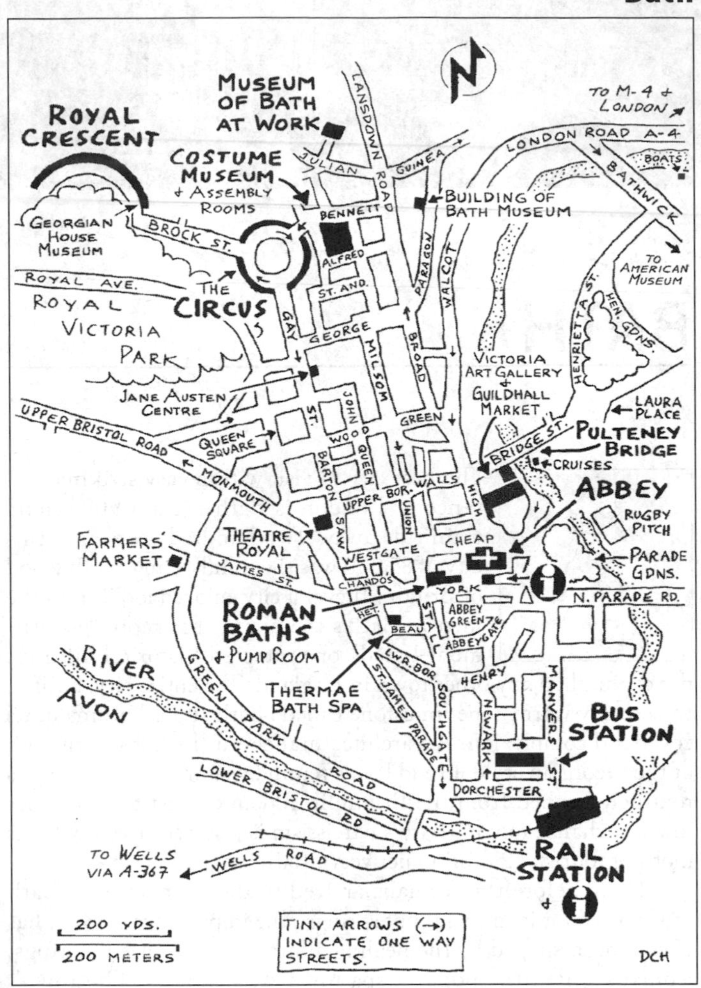

Bath

of the buildings you'll see today are from the 18th century. Local architect John Wood was inspired by the Italian architect Andrea Palladio to build a "new Rome." The town bloomed in the Neoclassical style, and streets were lined not with scrawny sidewalks but with wide "parades," upon which the women in their stylishly wide dresses could spread their fashionable tails.

Beau Nash (1673–1762) was Bath's "master of ceremonies." He organized both the daily regimen of the aristocratic visitors and the city, lighting and improving street security, banning swords, and opening the Pump Room. Under his fashionable baton, Bath became a city of balls, gaming, and concerts—the place to see and be seen in England. This most civilized place became even more so with the great Neoclassical building spree that followed.

The buzz in the early 21st century is that the venerable baths are in the spotlight again. The new Thermae Bath Spa—which finally opened in 2006 after years of delays—taps Bath's soothing hot springs, once again attracting visitors in need of a cure or a soak.

Planning Your Time

Bath deserves two nights even on a quick trip. Here's how I'd spend a day in Bath: 9:00–Tour the Roman Baths; 10:30–Catch the free city walking tour; 12:30–Picnic on the open deck of a Bath tour bus; 14:00–Free time in the shopping center of old Bath; 15:30–Tour the Costume Museum; 20:00–Bizarre Bath comedy walk.

ORIENTATION

(area code: 01225)

Bath's town square, three blocks in front of the bus and train station, is a bouquet of tourist landmarks, including the abbey, Roman and medieval baths, and the royal Pump Room.

Tourist Information

The TI is in the abbey churchyard (Mon–Sat 9:30–17:00, Sun 10:00–16:00, tel. 0870-420-1278, www.visitbath.co.uk). Pick up the £1.25 city map and—if you're interested in music, movies, and other nighttime listings—the free *This Month in Bath* booklet (be aware that its included map doesn't include sight information). Browse through scads of fliers, books, and maps. Skip their room-finding service (£5 fee and your host is nicked 10 percent) and book direct.

Arrival in Bath

The Bath **train station** has small-town charm, a national and international tickets desk, and a privately run tourism office masquerading as a TI. The **bus station** is immediately in front of the train station. To get to the TI from either station, walk two blocks up Manvers Street and turn left at the triangular "square," by following the small TI arrow on a signpost. My recommended B&Bs are all within a 10- to 15-minute walk or a £4–5 taxi ride from the station.

Helpful Hints

Festivals: Bath hosts book, music, and theater festivals in the spring, including the **Bath Literature Festival** (www.bathlitfest.org.uk), the **Bath International Music Festival** (classical, folk, jazz, contemporary; www.bathmusicfest.org.uk), and the eclectic **Bath Fringe Festival** (theater, walks, talks, bus trips; www.bathfringe.co.uk). The **Jane Austen Festival** unfolds genteelly in September (www.janeaustenfestival.co.uk). Bath's festival box office sells tickets for most events, and can tell you exactly what's on tonight (2 Church Street, tel. 01225/463-362, www.bathfestivals.org.uk). Bath's local paper, the *Bath Chronicle*, publishes a "What's On" event listing on Fridays (www.thisisbath.com).

Internet Access: Try **@Internet** a block in front of the train station (£1/20 min, daily 9:00–22:00, 12 Manvers Street, tel. 01225/443-181).

Laundry: The **Spruce Goose Launderette** is around the corner from the recommended Brock's Guest House, on the pedestrian lane called Margaret's Buildings (self-service daily 8:00–21:00, full-service Mon–Fri—but book ahead, tel. 01225/483-309). Anywhere in town, **Speedy Wash** can pick up your laundry for same-day service (£10/bag, Mon–Fri 7:30–17:30, most hotels work with them, tel. 01225/427-616). East of Pulteney Bridge, the humble **Lovely Wash** is on Daniel Street (daily 9:00–21:00, self-service only).

Car Rental: Enterprise and **Thrifty** are each handy to central Bath, and have roughly the same rates: £40/day, £80/weekend, and £130–160/week. Enterprise provides a pickup service for customers to and from their hotels, but doesn't do one-way rentals (at Lower Bristol Road in Bath, tel. 01225/443-311). **Thrifty** is just outside the Bath train station (tel. 01225/442-911). **National/Alamo** is a £7 taxi ride from the train station, but will do one-way rentals (at Brass Mill Lane—go west on Upper Bristol Road, tel. 01225/481-898). **Europcar** advertises that it's in Bath but it's relatively far outside of town. **Avis** is a mile from the Bristol train station; you'd need to rent a car to get there. Most offices close Saturday afternoon and all day Sunday, which complicates weekend pickups. Ideally, take the train or bus from downtown London to Bath, and rent a car as you leave Bath, rather than from within London.

TOURS

Of Bath

▲▲▲Walking Tours—Free two-hour tours are offered by **The Mayor's Corps of Honorary Guides,** led by volunteers who want to share their love of Bath with its many visitors. Their chatty, historical, and gossip-filled walks are essential for your understanding of this town's amazing Georgian social scene. How else will you learn that the old "chair ho" call for your sedan chair evolved into today's "cheerio" farewell? Tours leave from in front of the Pump Room (free, no tips, year-round Sun–Fri at 10:30 and 14:00, Sat at 10:30 only; evening walks offered May–Sept at 19:00 on Tue, Fri, and Sat). Advice for theatergoers: Guides stop to talk outside the Theatre Royal. You can skip out a moment, pop into the box office, and snare a great deal on a play for tonight (see "Nightlife" on page 657 for details).

For a **private tour,** call the local guides' bureau (£52/2 hrs, tel. 01225/337-111). For **Ghost Walks, Pub Crawls,** and **Bizarre Bath** tours, see "Nightlife," page 657. Bath's Jane Austen Centre offers a **Jane Austen** tour on weekends (see listing under "Sights," page 655).

▲▲City Bus Tours—City Sightseeing's hop-on, hop-off bus tours zip through Bath. Jump on a bus anytime at one of 17 signposted pick-up points, pay the driver, climb upstairs, and hear taped commentary about Bath (£9.50, ticket valid for 24 hours, generally 4/hr daily from 9:30–17:00, more frequent and with longer hours in summer). On a sunny day, this is a multitasking tourist's dream-come-true: You can munch a sandwich, work on a tan, snap great photos, and learn a lot all at the same time. Save money by doing the bus tour first—ticket stubs get you minor discounts at many sights. City Sightseeing has two routes: a 50-minute downtown tour, and a 45-minute "Skyline" route outside of town, handy for those wanting to visit the American Museum on the outskirts.

Taxi Tours—Local taxis, driven by good talkers, go where big buses can't. A group of up to four can rent a cab for an hour (about £20) and enjoy a fine, informative, and—with the right cabbie—entertaining private joyride. It's probably cheaper to let the meter run than to pay for an hourly rate, but ask the cabbie for advice.

SIGHTS

▲▲▲Roman and Medieval Baths—In ancient Roman times, high society enjoyed the mineral springs at Bath. From Londinium, Romans traveled so often to Aquae Sulis, as the city was called, to "take a bath" that finally it became known simply as Bath. Today, a fine museum surrounds the ancient bath. It's a one-way system leading you past well-documented displays, Roman artifacts, mosaics, a temple pediment, and the actual mouth of the spring, piled high with Roman pennies. Enjoy some quality time looking into the eyes of Minerva, goddess of the hot springs. The included self-guided tour audioguide makes the visit easy and plenty informative. For those with a big appetite for Roman history, in-depth 40-minute tours leave from the end of the museum at the edge of the actual bath (included with ticket, on the hour, a poolside clock is set for the next departure time). The water is greenish because of the lead—don't drink it. You can revisit the museum after the tour (£10, £13 combo-ticket includes Costume Museum—a £3.50 savings, family combo-£36, combo-tickets good for 1 week, daily July–Aug 9:00–22:00, March–June and Sept–Oct 9:00–18:00, Nov–Feb 9:30–17:30, last entry 1 hour before closing, tel. 01225/477-784, www.romanbaths.co.uk). The museum and baths are fun to visit in the evening in summer—romantic, gas-lit, and all yours. After touring the Roman Baths, stop by the attached Pump Room for a spot of tea, or to gag on the water.

▲Pump Room—For centuries, Bath was forgotten as a spa. Then, in 1687, the previously barren Queen Mary bathed here, became pregnant, and bore a male heir to the throne. A few years later Queen Anne found the water eased her painful gout. Word of its wonder waters spread, and Bath earned its way back on the aristocratic map. High society soon turned the place into one big pleasure palace. The Pump Room, an elegant Georgian hall just above the Roman Baths, offers the visitor's best chance to raise a pinky in this Chippendale grandeur. Drop by to sip coffee or tea or to enjoy a light meal (daily 9:30–12:00 for coffee and £6 breakfast; 12:00–14:30 for £12 lunches; 14:30–17:00 for £13 traditional high tea; £7 tea/coffee and pastry available in the afternoons; open for dinner July–Aug only; live music daily—string trio 10:00–12:00, piano 12:45–14:30, string trio in high season or piano in winter 15:00–17:00; tel. 01225/444-477). Above the newspaper table and sedan chairs, a statue of Beau Nash himself sniffles down at you.

The Spa Water: This is your chance to eat a famous (but forgettable) "Bath bun" and split (and spit) a 50p drink of the awful curative water. The water is served from the King's Spring by appropriately attired Martin, who's ready to minuet (but refuses to gavotte). He explains that the water is 10,000 years old, pumped from nearly 100 yards deep, and marinated in wonderful minerals. Convenient public WCs are in the entry hallway that connects the Pump Room with the baths (but are not associated with the spa water).

Thermae Bath Spa—After simmering unused for a quarter-century, Bath's natural thermal springs once again offer R&R for the masses. The state-of-the-art leisure and curative spa—housed in a complex combining old buildings with controversial new, blocky architecture—opened in 2006. The only natural thermal spa in the United Kingdom, it has an open-air rooftop thermal pool and all the "pamper thyself" extras: aromatherapy steam rooms, mud wraps, and various healing-type treatments and classes. Swimwear is required (£19/2 hrs, £29/4 hrs, £45/full day; baths generally open daily 9:00–22:00, last entry 20:00; visitors center open daily 9:30–17:00; treatments, massage, and solarium cost extra—ranging from £38–70; 100 yards from Roman and medieval baths on Beau Street, tel. 01225/331-234, book treatments at www.thermaebathspa.com).

▲Abbey—The town of Bath wasn't much in the Middle Ages, but an important church has stood on this spot since Anglo-Saxon times. In 973, Edgar was crowned here. Dominating the town center, the present church—the last great medieval church of England—is 500 years old and a fine example of Late Perpendicular Gothic, with breezy fan vaulting and enough stained glass to earn it the nickname "Lantern of the West." The glass, red-iron gas-powered lamps, and heating grates on the floor are all remnants of the 19th century. The window behind the altar shows 52 scenes from the life of Christ. A window to the left of the altar shows Edgar's coronation (worth the £2.50 donation, Mon–Sat 9:00–18:00, Sun usually 13:00–14:30 & 15:30–17:30, closes at 16:30 in winter, handy flier narrates a self-guided 19-stop tour, www.bathabbey.org).

Posted on the door is the schedule for concerts, services, and **evensong** (Sun at 15:30 year-round, plus most Sat in Aug at 17:00). The facade (c. 1500, but mostly restored) is interesting for some of its carvings. Look for the angels going down the ladder. The statue of Peter (to the left of the door) lost his head to mean iconoclasts; it was re-carved out of his once super-sized beard. Take a moment to appreciate the abbey's architecture from the Abbey Green square.

A small but worthwhile exhibit, the abbey's **Heritage Vaults** tell the story of Christianity in Bath since Roman times (free, Mon–Sat 10:00–16:00, last entry 15:30, closed Sun, entrance just outside church, south side).

▲Pulteney Bridge, Parade Gardens, and Cruises—Bath is inclined to compare its shop-lined Pulteney Bridge to Florence's Ponte Vecchio. That's pushing it. But to best enjoy a sunny day, pay about £1 to enter the Parade Gardens below the bridge (April–Sept daily 10:00–19:00, May–Aug until 20:00, shorter hours off-season, includes deck chairs, ask about concerts held some Sun at 15:00 in summer, tel. 01225/394-041). Taking a siesta to relax peacefully at the riverside provides a wonderful break (and memory).

Across the bridge at Pulteney Weir, tour boat companies run **cruises** (£7, up to 7/day if the weather's good, 50 min to Bathampton and back, WCs on board). Just take whatever boat is running. Avon Cruisers actually stop in Bathampton (allowing you to hop off and walk back); Pulteney Cruisers come with a sundeck ideal for picnics.

Guildhall Market—The little shopping mall, located across from Pulteney Bridge, is a frumpy time warp in this affluent town, but it's fun for browsing and picnic shopping. Its cheap Market Café is recommended under "Eating," page 664.

Victoria Art Gallery—The one-room gallery, next to Guildhall Market, is filled with paintings from the 18th and 19th centuries (free, includes audioguide, daily 10:00–17:00, WC, www.victoriagal .org.uk).

▲▲Royal Crescent and the Circus—If Bath is an architectural cancan, these are the knickers. These first Georgian "condos" by John Wood (the Elder and the Younger) are well-explained in the city walking tours. "Georgian" is British for "Neoclassical," or dating from the 1770s. As you cruise the Crescent, pretend you're rich. Pretend you're poor. Notice the "ha ha fence," a drop-off in the front yard that acted as a barrier, invisible from the windows, for keeping out sheep and peasants. The refined and stylish Royal Crescent Hotel sits unmarked in the center of the crescent. You're welcome to (politely) drop in to explore its fine ground floor public spaces. A gracious and traditional cream tea is served in the garden out back (£11 cream tea, £15.40 high tea, daily 15:30–17:00, reserve a day in advance in summer, tel. 01225/823-333).

Picture the round Circus as a coliseum turned inside out. Its Doric, Ionic, and Corinthian capital decorations pay homage to its Greco-Roman origin, and are a reminder that Bath (with its seven hills) aspired to be "the Rome of England." The frieze above the first row of columns has hundreds of different panels, each representing the arts, sciences, and crafts. The first floor was high off the ground, to accommodate aristocrats on sedan chairs and women with Cher-like hairdos. The tiny round windows on the top floors were the servants' quarters. While the building fronts are uniform, the backs are higgledy-piggledy, infamous for their "hanging loos." Stand in the middle of the Crescent among the grand plane trees, on the capped old well. Imagine the days when there was no indoor plumbing, and the servant girls gathered here to fetch water—this was gossip central. Standing on the well, your clap echoes three times around the circle (try it).

▲▲Georgian House at No. 1 Royal Crescent—This museum (corner of Brock Street and Royal Crescent) offers your best look into a period house. It's worth the £4 admission to get behind one of those classy exteriors. The volunteers in each room are determined to fill you in on all the fascinating details of Georgian life... like how high-class women shaved their eyebrows and pasted on carefully trimmed strips of furry mouse skin in their place. On the bedroom dresser sits a bowl of black beauty marks and a head scratcher from those pre-shampoo days. Fido spent his days in the kitchen treadmill powering the rotisserie (mid-Feb–Oct Tue–Sun 10:30–17:00, Nov Tue–Sun 10:30–16:00, last entry 30 min before closing, closed Mon and Dec–mid-Feb, "no stiletto heels, please," tel. 01225/428-126, www.bath-preservation-trust.org.uk).

▲▲▲Costume Museum—One of Europe's great museums, it displays 400 years of fashion—one frilly decade at a time—and is housed within Bath's Assembly Rooms. Follow the excellent included audioguide tour and allow two hours (£6.50, £13.00 combo-ticket covers Roman Baths—saving you £3.50, family combo-£36, daily March–Oct 11:00–18:00, Nov–Feb 11:00–17:00, last entry 1 hour before closing, on-site self-service café, tel. 01225/477-789, www.museumofcostume.co.uk).

The **Assembly Rooms,** which you can see for free en route to the museum, are big, grand, empty rooms. Card games, concerts, tea, and dances were held here in the 18th century, before the advent of fancy hotels with grand public spaces made them obsolete. Note the extreme symmetry (pleasing to the aristocratic eye) and the high windows (which assured their privacy). After the Allies bombed the historical and well-preserved German city of Lübeck, the Germans picked up a Baedeker guide and chose a similarly lovely city to bomb: Bath. The Assembly Rooms—gutted in this war time tit-for-tat by WWII bombs—have since been restored to their original splendor. (Only the chandeliers are original.)

Below the Costume Museum (to the left as you leave, 20 yards away) is one of the few surviving sets of iron house hardware. "Link boys" carried torches through the dark streets, lighting the way for big shots in their sedan chairs as they traveled from one affair to the next. The link boys extinguished their torches in the black conical "snuffers." The lamp above was once gas-lit. The crank on the left was used to hoist bulky things to various windows (see the hooks). Few of these sets survived the dark days of the WWII Blitz, when most were collected, melted down, and turned into weapons to power the British war machine. (Recent headlines have revealed to the Brits that all this patriotic extra commitment to the national struggle was for naught, since the metal ended up on junk heaps.)

▲▲▲Museum of Bath at Work—This is the official title for Mr. Bowler's Business, a 1900s engineer's shop, brass foundry, and fizzy-drink factory with a Dickensian office. It's just a pile of meaningless old gadgets until a volunteer guide lovingly resurrects Mr. Bowler's creative genius. Also featured are various Bath creations through the years, including a 1914 car and the versatile plasticine (proto-Play-Doh, handy for claymation and more). Don't miss the fine "Story of Bath Stone" in the basement. While there are included audioguides, the live tours are the key (wonderful 45-min tours go regularly). If rushed, join one already in session (£4, April–Oct daily 10:30–17:00, Nov–March weekends only, last entry at 16:00, 2 steep blocks up Russell Street from Assembly Rooms, tel. 01225/318-348, www.bath-at-work.org.uk).

Jane Austen Centre—This exhibition focuses on Jane Austen's tumultuous, sometimes-troubled five years in Bath (circa 1800, during which time her father died), and the influence Bath had on her writing. While the exhibit is thoughtfully done and a hit with "Jane-ites," there is little of historic substance here. You'll walk through a Georgian townhouse that she didn't live in (one of her real addresses in Bath was a few houses up the road, at 25 Gay Street), and see mostly enlarged reproductions of things associated with her writing. The museum describes various places from two novels set in Bath (*Persuasion* and *Northanger Abbey*). After a live intro (15 min, 3/hr) explaining how this romantic but down-to-earth woman dealt with the silly, shallow, and arrogant aristocrats' world where "the doing of nothings all day prevents one from doing anything," you see a 15-minute video and wander through the rest of the exhibit (£5.95; March–Oct Mon–Sat 10:00–17:30, Sun 10:30–17:30; Nov–Feb daily 11:00–16:30, 40 Gay Street between Queen's Square and the Circus, tel. 01225/443-000, www.janeausten.co.uk). Jane Austen–themed walking tours of the city begin across from the Roman Baths and end at the Centre (£4.50, 90 min, Sat–Sun at 11:00, ask at the Centre for more information—no reservation necessary). Avid fans gather for the annual Jane Austen Festival (see "Festivals," page 649).

Recently, the Centre opened a Jane-themed **café** on the top floor, where they offer so-so light lunches, snacks, and desserts with goofy names like Darcy's Chocolate Delight and Wetherby's Hot Cross Buns (same hours as Centre, above).

If you're male and feeling left out, head one door downhill from the museum and look through the window. You'll see a fine delftware-decorated powder bowl designed for men to touch up their wigs.

Building of Bath Museum—This offers an intriguing look behind the scenes at how the Georgian city was actually built. It's just a couple rooms of exhibits, but those interested in construction—inside and out—find it worth the £4 (Tue–Sun 10:30–17:00, closed Mon, last entry 45 min before closing, above the Circus on a street called "The Paragon," tel. 01225/333-895, www.bath-preservation-trust.org.uk).

▲American Museum—I know, you need this in Bath like you need a Big Mac. But this museum offers a compelling look at colonial and early-American lifestyles. Each of 18 completely furnished rooms (from the 1600s to the 1800s) is hosted by an eager guide waiting to fill you in on the candles, maps, bedpans, and various religious sects that make domestic Yankee history surprisingly interesting. One room is a quilter's nirvana (£6.50, April–Oct Tue–Sun 12:00–17:00, last entry 1 hour before closing, closed Mon and Nov–March, nice arboretum, at Claverton Manor, tel. 01225/460-503, www.americanmuseum.org). The museum is outside of town and a headache to reach if you don't have a car (10-min walk from bus #18).

ACTIVITIES

Walking—The Bath Skyline Walk is a six-mile wander around the hills surrounding Bath (leaflet at TI). Plenty of other scenic paths are described in the TI's literature. For additional options, get *Country Walks around Bath,* by Tim Mowls (£4.50 at TI or bookstores).

Hiking the Canal to Bathampton—An idyllic towpath leads from the Bath train station along an old canal to the sleepy village of Bathampton. Immediately behind the station, cross the footbridge and see where the canal hits the river. Turn left, noticing the series of industrial-age locks, and walk along the towpath, giving thanks that you're not a horse pulling a barge. You'll be in Bathampton in less than an hour, where a classic pub awaits with a nice lunch and cellar-temp beer.

Boating—The Bath Boating Station, in an old Victorian boathouse, rents boats and punts (£6 per person/first hour, then £2/additional hour, April–Sept daily 10:00–18:00, closed off-season, Forester Road, 1 mile northeast of center, tel. 01225/312-900, www.bathboating.co.uk).

Swimming—The Bath Sports and Leisure Centre has a fine pool for laps as well as lots of water slides and entertaining gadgets for kids (£3, daily 8:00–22:00 but kids' hours are limited, call for open swim times, just across North Parade Bridge, tel. 01225/462-565).

Shopping—There's great browsing between the abbey and the Assembly Rooms (Costume Museum). Shops close at 17:30, some have longer hours on Thursday, and many are open on Sunday (11:00–17:00). Explore the antique shops lining Bartlett Street just below the Assembly Rooms.

NIGHTLIFE

Events are listed in *This Month in Bath* (free, available at TI) and "What's On," appearing Fridays in the local newspaper, the *Bath Chronicle* (www.thisisbath.com). Younger travelers may enjoy the party-ready bar, club, and nightlife recommendations on www.itchybath.co.uk.

▲▲▲Bizarre Bath Street Theater—For an immensely entertaining walking-tour comedy act "with absolutely no history or culture," follow J. J. or Noel Britten on their creative and entertaining Bizarre Bath walk. This 90-minute "tour," which plays off local passersby as well as tour members, is a belly laugh a minute (£7, April–Sept nightly at 20:00, smaller groups Mon–Thu, heavy on magic, careful to insult all minorities and sensitivities, just racy enough but still good family fun, leave from The Huntsman pub near the abbey, confirm at TI or call 01225/335-124, www.bizarrebath.co.uk).

▲Plays—The 18th-century Theatre Royal, newly restored and one of England's loveliest, offers a busy schedule of London West End–type plays, including many "pre-London" dress-rehearsal runs (£11–25, generally start at 19:30 or 20:00, box office open Mon–Sat 10:00–20:00, Sun 12:00–20:00, tel. 01225/448-844, www.theatreroyal.org.uk). Forty nosebleed spots on a bench (misnamed "standby seats") go on sale at noon on the day of each performance (£5, pay cash at box office or call and book with credit card, 2 tickets maximum). Or, you can snatch up any unsold seat in the house for £10–15 a half hour before "curtain up."

A handy cheap sightseers' tip: During the free Bath walking tour, your guide stops here. Pop into the box office, ask what's playing tonight, and see if there are many seats left. If the play sounds good and if plenty of seats remain unsold, you're fairly safe to come back 30 minutes before curtain time to buy a ticket at that £10 price. Oh...and if you smell jasmine, it's the ghost of Lady Grey, a mistress of Beau Nash.

Evening Walks—Take your choice: comedy (Bizarre Bath, described above), history, ghost, or pub crawl. The free city history walks (a daily standard described on page 650) are now offered summer evenings (2 hours; May–Sept Tue, Fri, and Sat at 19:00; leave from Pump Room). Ghost Walks are a popular way to pass the after-dark hours (£6, 2 hours, unreliably April–Oct Mon–Sat at 20:00, Fri only in winter, leave from The Garrick's Head pub near Theatre Royal, tel. 01225/350-512, www.ghostwalksofbath.co.uk). York and Edinburgh—which have houses thought to be actually haunted—are better for these walks.

The **Great Bath Pub Crawl,** a relaxed stroll through the town, gives an insight into pubs: "the busy man's recreation, the idle man's business, the melancholy man's sanctuary, and the stranger's welcome" (£5, tours May–Sept nightly at 20:00, depart from outside the centrally located Parade Park Hotel, 10 North Parade, tel. 01225/310-364, www.greatbathpubcrawl.com, info@greatbathpubcrawl.com).

Pubs—Most pubs in the center are very noisy, catering to a rowdy twentysomething crowd. But on the top end of town you can still find some classic, old places with inviting ambience and live music (generally open nightly until 23:00, Sun until 22:30).

The Bell has a jazzy, pierced-and-tattooed, bohemian feel, but with a mellow older crowd. They serve pizza in the garden out back (live music Mon and Wed evenings and Sun lunch, 103 Walcot Street, tel. 01225/460-426).

The Farmhouse fills its spacious and laid-back interior with live jazz nightly from 21:00 (1 Landsdown Road, tel. 01225/316-162).

The Star Inn is smaller and less inviting, but it's much appreciated by local beer lovers for its fine ale and "no machines or music to distract from the chat." It's called a "spit 'n' sawdust" place. And its long bench, nicknamed "death row," still comes with a complimentary pinch of snuff from tins on the ledge (23 The Vineyards, top of The Paragon/A4 Roman Road, tel. 01225/425-072).

The Old Green Tree is a rare traditional pub right in the town center (locally brewed real ales, non-smoking back room, no children, Green Street, tel. 01225/448-259; also recommended under "Eating," page 664, for lunch).

Summer Nights at the Baths—In July and August, you can stretch your sightseeing day at the Roman Baths, open nightly until 22:00 (last entry 21:00), when the gas lamps flame and the baths are far less crowded and more atmospheric.

SLEEPING

Bath is a busy tourist town. To get a good B&B, make a telephone reservation in advance. Competition is stiff, and it's worth asking any of these places for a weekday, three-nights-in-a-row, or off-season deal. Friday and Saturday nights are tightest, especially if you're staying only one night, since B&Bs favor those staying longer. If staying only Saturday night, you're very bad news to a B&B hostess. At B&Bs (and cheaper hotels), expect lots of stairs and no elevators.

B&Bs near the Royal Crescent

These listings are all a 15-minute uphill walk or an easy £4–4.50 taxi ride from the train station. Or take any hop-on, hop-off bus tour from the station, and get off at the stop nearest your B&B (for Brock's, Assembly Rooms, and Marlborough Lane listings hop off at Royal Avenue; confirm with driver), check in, then finish the tour later in the day. All of these B&Bs are non-smoking.

Sleep Code

(£1 = about $2, country code: 44, area code: 01225)
S = Single, **D** = Double/Twin, **T** = Triple, **Q** = Quad, **b** = bathroom, **s** = shower only. Unless otherwise noted, credit cards are accepted.

To help you sort easily through these listings, I've divided the rooms into three categories based on the price for a standard double room with bath:

$$$ Higher Priced—Most rooms £80 or more.
$$ Moderately Priced—Most rooms between £50–80.
$ Lower Priced—Most rooms £50 or less.

Bath Accommodations

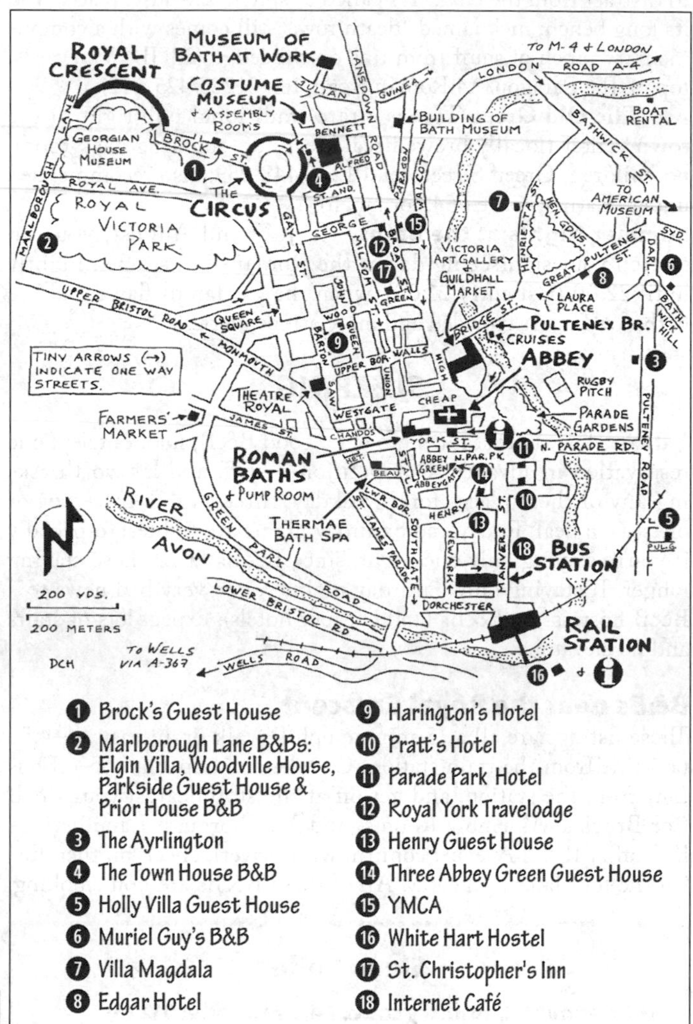

Marlborough Lane places have easier parking, but are less centrally located.

$$$ The Town House, overlooking the Assembly Rooms, is genteel, deluxe, and homey, with three fresh, mod rooms that have hardwood stylishness. In true B&B style, you'll enjoy a gourmet breakfast at a big family table with the other guests (Db-£85–89, Fri and Sat Db-£90–110, 7 Bennett Street, tel. & fax 01225/422-505, www.thetownhousebath.co.uk, stay@thetownhousebath.co.uk, Alan and Brenda Willey).

$$ Elgin Villa rents five comfy, well-maintained rooms (Ss-£38, Sb-£50, Ds-£50, Db-£75–80, Tb-£92, Qb-£112, more expensive for 1 night, discount for 3 nights, Wi-Fi access, special-diet breakfasts available, parking, 6 Marlborough Lane, tel. 01225/424-557, www.elginvilla.co.uk, stay@elginvilla.co.uk, friendly Anna Rutherford).

$$ Brock's Guest House, with six rooms, puts the bubbles in your Bath experience. This Georgian town house, built by John Wood in 1765, was redone in a way that would make the great architect proud. It's located between the prestigious Royal Crescent and thc courtly Circus (Db-£72–84, deluxe Db-£94, Tb-£101, reserve with credit card far in advance, little library on top floor, 32 Brock Street, tel. 01225/338-374, fax 01225/334-245, www.brocksguesthouse.co.uk, marion@brocksguesthouse.co.uk, Debbie and Mike Cavell).

$$ Parkside Guest House has five thoughtfully appointed Edwardian rooms and a spacious back garden (Db-£69, 11 Marlborough Lane, tel. & fax 01225/429-444, www.parksidebandb.co.uk, post@parksidebandb.co.uk, Erica and Inge Lynall).

$$ Prior House B&B, with four well-kept rooms, is run by hardworking Lynn Shearn (D-£55, Db-£60, serve-yourself breakfast at a common table, 3 Marlborough Lane, tel. 01225/313-587, www.greatplaces.co.uk/priorhouse, priorhouse@greatplaces.co.uk).

$ Woodville House, warmly run by Anne Toalster, is a grandmotherly little house with three tidy, charming rooms sharing two WCs and a TV lounge. Breakfast is served at a big, family-style table (D-£45, 2-night minimum, cash only, shared shower, some parking, below the Royal Crescent at 4 Marlborough Lane, tel. 01225/319-335, matoalster@freenet.co.uk).

B&Bs East of the River

These smoke-free listings are a 10-minute walk from the city center. While generally a better value, they are less conveniently located.

$$$ The Ayrlington, next door to a lawn-bowling green, has 14 attractive rooms with Asian decor, and hints of a more genteel time. Though this well-maintained hotel fronts a busy street, it's quiet and tranquil. Rooms in the back have pleasant views of sports greens and Bath beyond. For the best value, request a standard double with a view of Bath (huge price range due to varying sizes of rooms and policy of charging 30 percent more on Fri–Sun, Db-£75–175—see website for specifics; fine garden, easy parking, 24–25 Pulteney Road, tel. 01225/425-495, fax 01225/469-029, www.ayrlington.com, mail@ayrlington.com).

$$ Holly Villa Guest House, with a cheery garden, six bright rooms, and a cozy TV lounge, is enthusiastically and thoughtfully run by chatty, friendly Jill and Keith McGarrigle (Ds-£55, small Db-£60, big Db-£65, Tb-£90, cash only, easy parking; 8-min walk from station and city center—walk over North Parade Bridge, take the first right, and then take the second left to 14 Pulteney Gardens; tel. 01225/310-331, www.hollyvilla.com, jill@hollyvilla.com).

$$ Muriel Guy's B&B is another good value, mixing Georgian glamour with homey warmth and modern, artistic taste within its five rooms. Muriel is a fun and endearing live wire who serves organic food for breakfast (S-£35, Db-£65, Tb-£75, cash only; go over bridge on North Parade Road, left on Pulteney Road, cross to church, Raby Place is first row of houses on hill; 14 Raby Place, tel. 01225/465-120).

B&Bs East of Pulteney Bridge

These B&Bs are a five-minute walk from the city center.

$$$ Villa Magdala rents 18 stately, hotelesque rooms in a freestanding Victorian town house opposite a park (Db-£95–160; price varies depending on day of week, size of room, view, and type of bed—less off-season; in quiet residential area, inviting lounge, smoke-free, parking, Henrietta Street, tel. 01225/466-329, fax 01225/483-207, www.villamagdala.co.uk, enquiries@villamagdala.co.uk, Roy and Lois).

$$ Edgar Hotel, with 18 simple rooms and lots of stairs, gives you a budget-hotel option in this smart Georgian neighborhood (Sb-£45–55, Db-£60–85 depending on room, Tb-£100, Qb-£120, less in winter, smaller rooms on top, avoid #18 on ground level, smoke-free; pleasant sitting room with old organ, gramophones, and free Wi-Fi; 64 Great Pulteney Street, tel. 01225/420-619, fax 01225/466-916, www.edgar-hotel.co.uk, edgar-hotel@breatheconnect.com).

In the City Center

$$$ Three Abbey Green Guest House is newly renovated, bright, fresh, and located in a quiet courtyard only 50 yards from the abbey and the Roman Baths. Its spacious rooms are a fine value (Sb-£77, Db-£85–110, four-poster Db-£155, family rooms-£125–155, families welcome, tel. 01225/428-558, www.threeabbeygreen.com, stay@threeabbeygreen.com, Sue and Derek).

$$$ Harington's Hotel rents 13 fresh, modern, and newly refurbished rooms on a quiet street in the town center (Sb-£68–114, standard Db-£88–118, superior Db-£98–128, large Db-£108–138, family-room Qb-£118–148—higher prices are for Fri–Sat; smoke-free, lots of stairs, attached restaurant-bar open all day, 10 Queen Street, tel. 01225/461-728, fax 01225/444-804, www.haringtonshotel.co.uk, post@haringtonshotel.co.uk). Melissa and Peter offer a 5 percent discount with this book for two-night stays except on Fridays, Saturdays, and holidays. They also rent a self-catering apartment down the street that sleeps five (£300–360/night, £500–600/week).

$$$ Pratt's Hotel is as proper and old English as you'll find in Bath. Its creaks and frays are aristocratic. Even its public places make you want to sip a brandy, and its 46 rooms are bright and spacious (Sb-£90, Db-£135, advance reservations get highest rate, drop-ins after 16:00 often snare Db for £75, dogs-£7.50 but children free, attached restaurant-bar, elevator, 4 blocks from station on South Parade, tel. 01225/460-441, fax 01225/448-807, www.forestdale.com, pratts@forestdale.com).

$$ Parade Park Hotel rents 35 modern, basic rooms in a very central location (S-£38, D-£55, small Db-£65, large Db-£90, Tb-£95, Qb-£120, smoke-free, lots of stairs, lively bar downstairs and noisy seagulls, 10 North Parade, tel. 01225/463-384, fax 01225/442-322, www.paradepark.co.uk, info@paradepark.co.uk).

$$ Royal York Travelodge—which offers 66 American-style, characterless yet comfortable rooms—worries B&Bs with its reasonable prices (Db-£70–80, Tb-same price, as low as £26 if you book online in advance, up to 2 kids sleep free, breakfast extra, non-smoking rooms available, 1 York Building, George Street, tel. 01225/448-999, central reservation tel. 08700-850-950, www.travelodge.co.uk). This is especially economic for families of four (who enjoy the Db price).

$$ Henry Guest House is a bare-bone, vertical place, offering eight clean rooms. It's in a central location with some street noise, two blocks in front of the train station (S-£35, D-£50–65, T-£75–85, family deals, lots of narrow stairs, 3 showers and 3 WCs for everybody, 6 Henry Street, tel. 01225/424-052, fax 01225/316-669, www.thehenry.com, stay@thehenry.com, owners Steve and Liz).

Dorms

$ The **YMCA,** central on a leafy square, has 200 beds in industrial-strength rooms (S-£24–28, twin-£36, beds in big dorms-£13, £2 more per person on Fri and Sat, includes continental breakfast, cheap lunches, lockers, Internet access, dorms closed 10:00–14:00, down a tiny alley off Broad Street on Broad Street Place, tel. 01225/325-900, fax 01225/462-065, www.bathymca.co.uk, reservations@bathymca.co.uk).

$ White Hart Hostel is a simple place offering adults and families good, cheap beds in two- to six-bed dorms (£14/bed, D-£40, Db-£60, family rooms, smoke-free, kitchen, 5-min walk behind train station at Widcombe—where Widcombe Hill hits Claverton Street, tel. 01225/313-985, www.whitehartbath.co.uk, run by Jo).

$ St. Christopher's Inn, in a prime, central location, is part of a chain of low-priced, high-energy hubs for backpackers looking for beds and brews (60 beds in 4- to 12-bed rooms-£16–19.50, deals available online; lively and affordable pub and bar downstairs—20 percent off if you're a guest, non-smoking bedrooms, Internet access, laundry, lounge with video, 9 Green Street, tel. 01225/481-444, www.st-christophers.co.uk). Their beds are so cheap because they know you'll spend money on their beer.

EATING

Bath is bursting with quaint and stylish eateries. There's something for every appetite and budget—just stroll around the center of town. A picnic dinner of deli food or take-out fish-and-chips in the Royal Crescent Park is ideal for aristocratic hoboes. Reserve a table on Friday and Saturday evenings. Save money by eating before 19:00.

Near the Abbey

Three fine and popular places share North Parade Passage, a block south of the abbey:

Tilley's Bistro, popular with locals, serves healthy French, English, and vegetarian meals with candlelit ambience. Their fun menu lets you build your own meal, choosing from an interesting array of £7 starters (Mon–Sat 12:00–14:30 & 18:00–23:30, closed Sun, reservations smart, non-smoking, 3 North Parade Passage, tel. 01225/484-200).

Sally Lunn's House is a cutesy, quasi-historic place for traditional English meals, tea, pink pillows, and lots of lace (£15–20 meals, £10 early-bird two-course special 17:00–19:00, nightly, smoke-free, 4 North Parade Passage, tel. 01225/461-634). Their forte is a variety of cream teas and buns (£7, until 18:00). Lunch customers get a free peek at the basement Kitchen Museum (otherwise 30p).

The Crystal Palace, with typical pub grub under rustic timbers or in the sunny courtyard, is a handy standby (£7–9 meals served Mon–Sat 11:00–21:00, Sun 12:00–20:00, smoke-free, children welcome until 16:30, 11 Abbey Green, tel. 01225/482-666).

Near the Train Station

These two places are two blocks up from the train station on Pierrepont Street.

Bath Restaurants

1. Tilley's Bistro & Sally Lunn's House
2. The Crystal Palace
3. Mai Thai Restaurant
4. The Wife of Bath
5. Loch Fyne Restaurant
6. Martini Restaurant
7. Chandos Deli
8. The Eastern Eye
9. The Old Green Tree
10. Browns Restaurant
11. Ask Restaurant
12. The Moon and Sixpence
13. Guildhall Market
14. Cornish Bakehouse
15. No. 5 Restaurant & Rajpoot Tandoori
16. Yak Yeti Yak, The Boater & Pastiche Bistro
17. Circus Restaurant
18. Bistro Papillon
19. Royal Crescent Hotel (Cream Teas)
20. The Bell
21. To The Farmhouse
22. The Star Inn
23. Waitrose Supermarket
24. Marks & Spencer

Mai Thai Restaurant is a favorite with locals. It's cheap and crowded, serves good curry, and also does take-out food (£6–7 meals, daily 12:00–14:00 & 18:00–22:30, 6 Pierrepont Street, tel. 01225/445-557).

The Wife of Bath serves hearty English and French cuisine in a creaky, wood-beamed restaurant. They have an extensive wine selection, good banoffee (very sweet banana/toffee) pie, and a friendly waitstaff (£12–15 meals, £11 lunch and early-bird dinner specials, Tue–Sat 12:00–14:00 & 17:30–22:00, Sun–Mon 17:30–22:00 only, down the stairs across the street from the Mai Thai at 12 Pierrepont Street, tel. 01225/461-745).

Between the Abbey and the Circus

George Street is lined with cheery eateries: Thai, Italian, wine bars, and so on.

Loch Fyne Restaurant, a Scottish fish place with a bright, airy, and youthful atmosphere, fills a former bank. The fish is fresh, prices are reasonable (£8–14 meals, £10 early-bird dinner until 19:00), the energy is high, and it doesn't feel like a chain (daily 12:00–22:00, 24 Milsom Street, tel. 01225/750-120).

Martini Restaurant, a hopping, purely Italian place, has class and jovial waiters (£12–13 entrées, £7 pizzas, daily 12:00–14:30 & 18:00–22:30, plenty of veggie options, daily fish specials, extensive wine list, smoke-free section, reservations smart, 9 George Street, tel. 01225/460-818, Nunzio, Franco, and chef Luigi).

Chandos Deli has good coffee and tasty £6–7 sandwiches made on artisan breads. This upscale but casual eight-table place serves breakfast and lunch to dedicated foodies who don't want to pay too much (Mon–Sat 9:00–17:00, closed Sun, 12 George Street, tel. 01225/314-418).

The Eastern Eye is unique, serving decent Indian cuisine in an exquisite Georgian room under a triple-domed ceiling. The architecture almost overwhelms the food—and that's not a bad thing (£7 lunches, daily 12:00–14:30 & 18:00–23:00, 8 Quiet Street, tel. 01225/422-323).

The Old Green Tree, in the old town center, serves good lunches to locals in a characteristic pub setting (real ales on tap, lunch 12:00–15:00 only, no children, non-smoking back room, can be crowded on weekend nights, 12 Green Street, tel. 01225/448-259). As Bath is not a good pub-grub town, this is likely the best you'll do in the center.

Two big, noisy chain restaurants offer decent, inexpensive food to a loyal local following: **Browns** fills an old police station just across from the abbey, serving English food throughout the day (daily 12:00–23:00, kid-friendly, nice terrace, half-block east of the abbey, Orange Grove, tel. 01225/461-199). Family-friendly

Ask is a similar place up the street (pizza and pasta for £7, good salads, George Street, tel. 01225/789-997).

The Moon and Sixpence, prized by locals for its quality international cuisine, is tucked away on a quiet lane. It's dressy and a bit smoky, with well-presented food (£9 two-course lunch, £29 three-course dinner, daily 12:00–14:30 & 17:30–22:30, ground floor is preferable to upstairs, fine garden seating, 6a Broad Street, tel. 01225/460-962).

Guildhall Market, across from Pulteney Bridge, has produce stalls with food for picnickers. At its inexpensive Market Café, you can slurp a curry or sip a tea while surrounded by stacks of used books, bananas on the push list, and honest-to-goodness old-time locals (£4 meals, Mon–Sat 8:00–17:00, closed Sun, a block north of the abbey, on High Street).

The **Cornish Bakehouse,** near the Guildhall Market, has good take-away pasties (open until 17:30, off High Street at 11a The Corridor, tel. 01225/426-635).

Supermarkets: **Waitrose,** at the Podium shopping center, is great for picnics, with a good salad bar (Mon–Fri 8:30–20:00, Sat 8:30–19:00, Sun 11:00–17:00, just west of Pulteney Bridge and across from post office on High Street). **Marks & Spencer,** near the train station, has a grocery at the back of its department store (Mon–Sat 9:00–20:00, Sun 11:00–17:00, Stall Street).

East of Pulteney Bridge

No. 5 Restaurant serves classic French and Mediterranean cuisine in a stylish setting (£16 main courses with vegetables, daily 12:00–14:30 & 18:30–22:00, later on Fri–Sat, Mon–Tue are "bring your own bottle of wine" nights—no corkage fee, reservations smart on weekends, smoke-free, just over Pulteney Bridge at 5 Argyle Street, tel. 01225/444-499).

Rajpoot Tandoori, next door to No. 5, serves—by all assessments—the best Indian food in Bath. You'll hike down deep into a cellar where the plush Indian atmosphere and award-winning cooking makes paying the extra pounds palatable. The seating is tight and the ceilings low, but it's smoke-free and air-conditioned (£8 three-course lunch special, £10 plates, £20 dinners, daily 12:00–14:30 & 18:00–23:00, 4 Argyle Street, tel. 01225/466-833).

Yak Yeti Yak Restaurant, a fun Nepali place way down in the basement, is run by a cheerful, hardworking Nepali family that cooks up great traditional food at prices a Sherpa could handle (daily 12:00–14:00 & 18:00–22:00, plenty of vegetarian plates, 12A Argyle Street, tel. 01225/442-299).

The Boater offers a £5 lunch in its huge, pleasant beer garden overlooking the river. It's popular with rowdy twentysomethings for its good ales and riverside perch (lunch only 12:00–15:00, otherwise drinks only, Mon–Sat 11:00–23:00, Sun 12:00–20:30, 9 Argyle Street, tel. 01225/464-211).

Pastiche Bistro is feisty, warm, and minimalist, offering inexpensive English food in two rooms overlooking the river (£6 two-course lunch, £11 two-course dinner, just east of Pulteney Bridge at 16 Argyle Street, tel. 01225/442-323).

Between the Circus and Royal Crescent

Circus Restaurant, a good value, gives modern English cuisine a Mediterranean twist. You'll get meat, fish, or veggies with an intimate, candlelit, Mozartean ambience. The three-course dinner special for £20 includes tasty vegetables and a selection of fine desserts (Tue–Sun dinner only 18:30–22:00, closed Mon, reservations smart, 34 Brock Street, tel. 01225/318-918, Natasha serves while Adrian cooks).

Bistro Papillon is small, fun, and unpretentious, dishing up "modern-rustic cuisine from the south of France." It has cozy indoor and outdoor seating on a fine pedestrian lane (£8.50 two-course lunch specials, £15–20 two-course dinner specials, Tue–Sat 12:00–14:30 & 18:30–22:00, closed Sun–Mon, reservations smart, 2 Margaret's Buildings, tel. 01225/310-064).

TRANSPORTATION CONNECTIONS

Bath's train station is called Bath Spa (train info: tel. 08457-484-950). The National Express bus office (Mon–Sat 8:00–17:30, closed Sun, bus info: tel. 08705-808-080) is one block in front of the train station.

From London to Bath: To get from London to Bath and see Stonehenge to boot, consider an all-day organized **bus tour** from London (and skip out of the return trip; see page 577 in the London chapter).

From Bath to London: You can catch a **train** to London's Paddington Station (2/hr, 90 min, £44 one-way after 9:30, www.firstgreatwestern.co.uk), or save money—but not time—by taking the National Express **bus** to Victoria Station (nearly hourly, a little over 3 hours, one-way-£17.50, round trip-£23.50, www.nationalexpress.com).

From Bath to London's Airports: You can reach **Heathrow** directly and easily by National Express bus (hourly, 2.5 hrs, £33.50 one-way, tel. 08705-757-747) or by a train-and-bus combination (take hourly train to Reading, catch twice-hourly airport shuttle bus from there, allow 2.5 hours total, £43, cheaper for BritRail passholders). You can get to **Gatwick** by bus (hourly, 4.5 hrs, £26 one-way) or by train (hourly, 3 hrs, £30 one-way, transfer in Reading or Clapham Junction).

From Bath by Train to: Salisbury (2/hr, 1 hr), **Portsmouth** (hourly, 2–2.25 hrs), **Exeter** (2/hr, 2–3 hrs, 1–2 transfers), **Penzance** (1–3/hr, 4.5–5 hrs, 1–3 transfers), **Moreton-in-Marsh** (hourly, 2–3 hrs, 1–3 transfers), **York** (hourly, 4.5–5 hrs, 1–2 transfers), **Oxford** (hourly, 1.5 hrs, transfer in Didcot).

ITALY

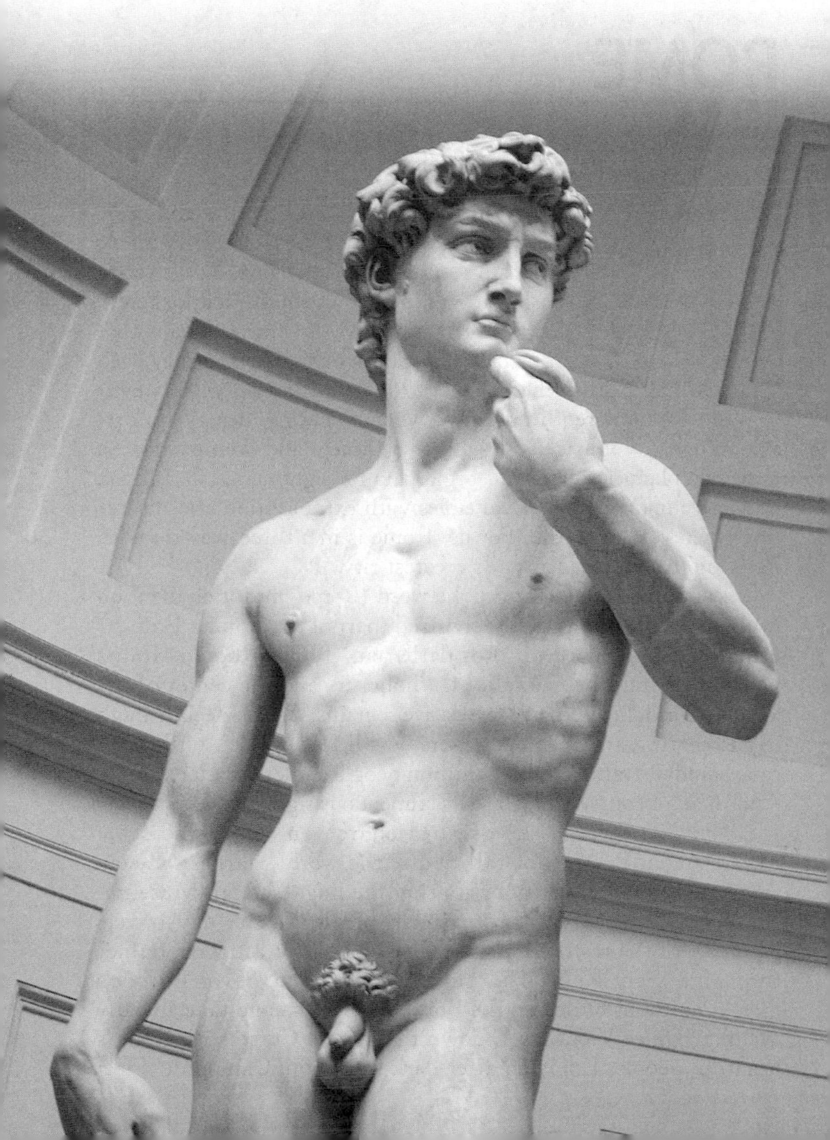

ROME

(Roma)

Rome is magnificent and brutal at the same time. It's a showcase of Western civilization, with astonishingly ancient sights. But if you're careless, you'll be run down or pickpocketed. You'll be frustrated by the kind of chaos that only an Italian can understand. You may even come to believe Mussolini was a necessary evil.

But Rome is required, and if your hotel provides a comfortable refuge; if you pace yourself; if you accept and even partake in the siesta plan; if you're well-organized for sightseeing; and if you protect yourself and your valuables with extra caution and discretion, then you'll do fine. For us, Rome is in a three-way tie with Paris and London as Europe's greatest city.

Two thousand years ago, the word "Rome" meant civilization itself. Everything was either civilized (part of the Roman Empire, Latin- or Greek-speaking) or barbarian. Today, Rome is Italy's political capital, the capital of Catholicism, and the center of the ancient world, littered with evocative remains. As you peel through its fascinating and jumbled layers, you'll find Rome's buildings, cats, laundry, traffic, and 2.6 million people endlessly entertaining. And then, of course, there are its stupendous sights.

Tour St. Peter's, the greatest church on earth, and scale Michelangelo's 328-foot-tall dome, the world's largest. Learn something about eternity by touring the huge Vatican Museum. You'll find the story of creation—bright as the day it was painted—in the restored Sistine Chapel. Do the "Caesar Shuffle" through ancient Rome's Forum and Colosseum. Savor Europe's most sumptuous building, the Borghese Gallery, and take an early evening "Dolce Vita Stroll" down the Via del Corso with Rome's beautiful people. Enjoy an after-dark walk from Campo de' Fiori to the Spanish Steps, lacing together Rome's Baroque and bubbly nightspots.

Planning Your Time

For most travelers, Rome is best done quickly. It's great, but huge (pop. 2.6 million) and exhausting. Time is normally short, and Italy is more charming elsewhere. To "do" Rome in a day, consider it as a side-trip from Orvieto or Florence, and maybe before the night train to Venice. Crazy as that sounds, if all you have is a day, it's one of the most exciting days Europe has to offer.

Rome in a Day: Start with the Vatican City (2 hours in the Vatican Museum and Sistine Chapel, 1 hour in St. Peter's), taxi over the river to the Pantheon (picnic on its steps), then hike over Capitol Hill, through the Forum, and to the Colosseum. Have dinner on Campo de' Fiori and dessert on Piazza Navona.

Rome in Two to Three Days: On the first day, do the "Caesar Shuffle" from the Colosseum to the Forum, then over Capitol Hill to the Pantheon. After a siesta, join the locals strolling from Piazza del Popolo to the Spanish Steps (see my recommended "Dolce Vita Stroll," page 695). On the second day, see Vatican City (St. Peter's, climb the dome, tour the Vatican Museum). Have dinner on the atmospheric Campo de' Fiori, then walk to the Trevi Fountain and Spanish Steps (see my recommended "Night Walk Across Rome," page 697). With a third day, add the Borghese Gallery (reservations required) and the National Museum of Rome.

ORIENTATION

Sprawling Rome actually feels manageable once you get to know it. The old core, with most of the tourist sights, sits in a diamond formed by the train station (in the east), the Vatican (west), Villa Borghese park (north), and the Colosseum (south). The Tiber River runs through the diamond from north to south. It takes about an hour to walk from the train station to the Vatican.

Consider Rome in these layers:

The ancient city had a million people. The best of the classical sights stand in a line from the Colosseum to the Pantheon. (See map on page 703.)

Medieval Rome was little more than a hobo camp of 50,000—thieves, mean dogs, and the pope, whose legitimacy required a Roman address. A colorful tangle of lanes, the medieval city lies between the Pantheon and the river.

Window-Shoppers' Rome twinkles with nightlife and ritzy shopping near Rome's main drag, Via del Corso—in the triangle formed by Piazza del Popolo, Piazza Venezia, and the Spanish Steps. (See "Dolce Vita Stroll" map, page 696.)

Rome

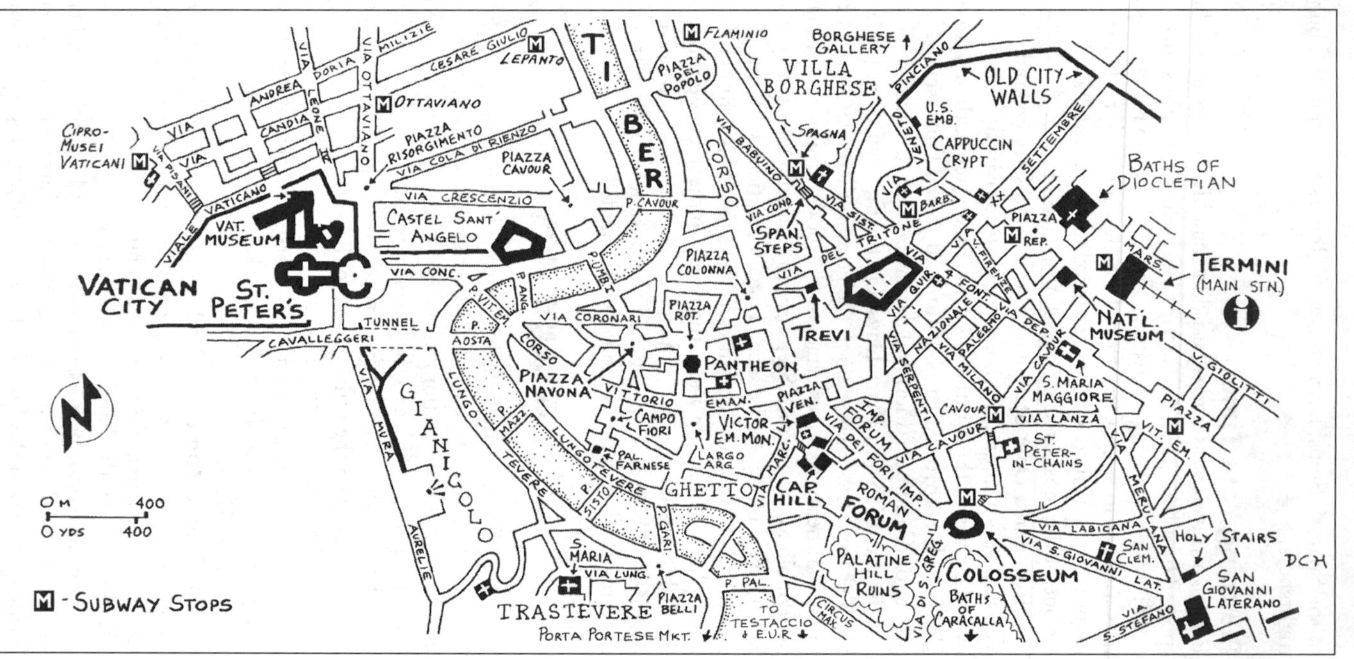

TERMINI (MAIN STN.)
BATHS OF DIOCLETIAN
NAT'L. MUSEUM
MARS.
PIAZZA REP.
OLD CITY WALLS
SETTEMBRE
CAPPUCCIN CRYPT
U.S. EMB.
PINCIANO
VIA VENETO
BARB.
BORGHESE GALLERY
VILLA BORGHESE
SPAGNA
SPAN. STEPS
VIA SIST.
TRITONE
VIA BABUINO
VIA COND.
FLAMINIO
PIAZZA DEL POPOLO
CORSO
PIAZZA COLONNA
TREVI
VIA QUIR.
4 FONT.
VIA V. FIRENZE
VIA DEP.
VIA NAZIONALE
PALERMO
VIA MILANO
VIA SERPENTI
VIA CAVOUR
CAVOUR
S. MARIA MAGGIORE
VIA LANZA
ST. PETER-IN-CHAINS
PIAZZA VIT. EM.
VIA MERULANA
V. GIOLITTI
HOLY STAIRS
SAN GIOVANNI LATERANO
SAN CLEM.
VIA LABICANA
VIA S. GIOVANNI LAT.
VIA S. STEFANO
DCH
COLOSSEUM
BATHS OF CARACALLA
VIA DI S. GREG.
IMP. FORUM
VIA DEI FORI IMP.
ROMAN FORUM
PALATINE HILL RUINS
CIRCUS MAX.
CAP. HILL
PIAZZA VEN.
VICTOR EM. MON.
PANTHEON
PIAZZA ROT.
LARGO ARG.
GHETTO
VIA MARC.
CAMPO FIORI
PAL. FARNESE
VITTORIO EMAN.
PIAZZA NAVONA
VIA CORONARI
CORSO
P. UMB. I
TIBER
P. CAVOUR
PIAZZA CAVOUR
LEPANTO
CESARE GIULIO
MILIZIE
OTTAVIANO
PIAZZA RISORGIMENTO
VIA COLA DI RIENZO
VIA CRESCENZIO
CASTEL SANT' ANGELO
P. ANG.
VIT. EM.
P.
AOSTA
VIA CONC.
TUNNEL
CAVALLEGGERI
LUNGO-TEVERE
LUNGOTEVERE
MAZZ.
SISTO
P. GARI.
P. PAL.
TO TESTACCIO & E.U.R.
PIAZZA BELLI
S. MARIA
VIA LUNG.
TRASTEVERE
PORTA PORTESE MKT.
GIANICOLO
VIA MURA AURELIE
VIA OTTAVIANO
VIA DORIA
VIA ANDREA
LEONE
CANDIA
VIA VATICANO
VAT. MUSEUM
ST. PETER'S
VATICAN CITY
VIALE
VIA PISANI
CIPRO-MUSEI VATICANI
0 M
400
0 YDS
400
M - SUBWAY STOPS

Vatican City, west of the Tiber, is a compact world of its own, with two great, huge sights: St. Peter's Basilica and the Vatican Museum. (See "Vatican City" map, page 725.)

Trastevere, the seedy, colorful, wrong-side-of-the-river neighborhood, is village Rome. This is the city at its crustiest—and perhaps most "Roman."

Baroque Rome is an overleaf that embellishes great squares throughout the town with fountains and church facades.

Since no one is allowed to build taller than St. Peter's dome, the city has no modern skyline. The Tiber River is basically ignored—after the last floods (1870), the banks were built up very high, and Rome turned its back on its naughty river.

Tourist Information

While Rome has several tourist information offices, the dozen or so TI kiosks scattered around the town at major tourist centers are handy and just as helpful. If all you need is a map, forget the TI and get one at your hotel or at a newsstand kiosk.

Rome has a helpful TI call center answered by English-speakers: 06-8205-9127 (daily 9:00–19:00, press 2 for English). Many travelers find this to be Rome's single best source of tourist information.

If you want to visit a TI in person, you'll find one in the airport at Terminal C (daily 8:00–19:00) and two at the Termini train station (daily 8:00–21:00, near a travel agency by track 24; another branch is outside the station, in a big glass building near the bus parking lot).

Smaller TIs (daily 9:00–18:00) include kiosks near the Forum (on Piazza del Tempio della Pace), at Via del Corso (on Largo Goldoni), in Trastevere (on Piazza Sonnino), on Via Nazionale (at Palazzo delle Esposizioni), at Castel Sant'Angelo (at Piazza Pia), at Santa Maria Maggiore Church, at Piazza Navonna (at Piazza delle Cinque Lune), and near the Trevi fountain (at Via del Corso and Via Minghetti).

At any TI, ask for a city map, a listing of sights and hours (in the free *Museums of Rome* booklet), and *Passepartout*, the free seasonal entertainment guide for evening events and fun. Don't book rooms through a TI; you'll save money by booking direct.

Roma c'è is a cheap little weekly entertainment guide with a useful English section (in the back) on musical events (€1.20, new edition every Thu, sold at newsstands, www.romace.it).

Websites: www.whatsoninrome.com (events and news), www.romaturismo.com (music, exhibitions, and events), www.wantedinrome.com (job openings and real estate, but also festivals and exhibitions), and www.vatican.va (the pope's website).

Greater Rome

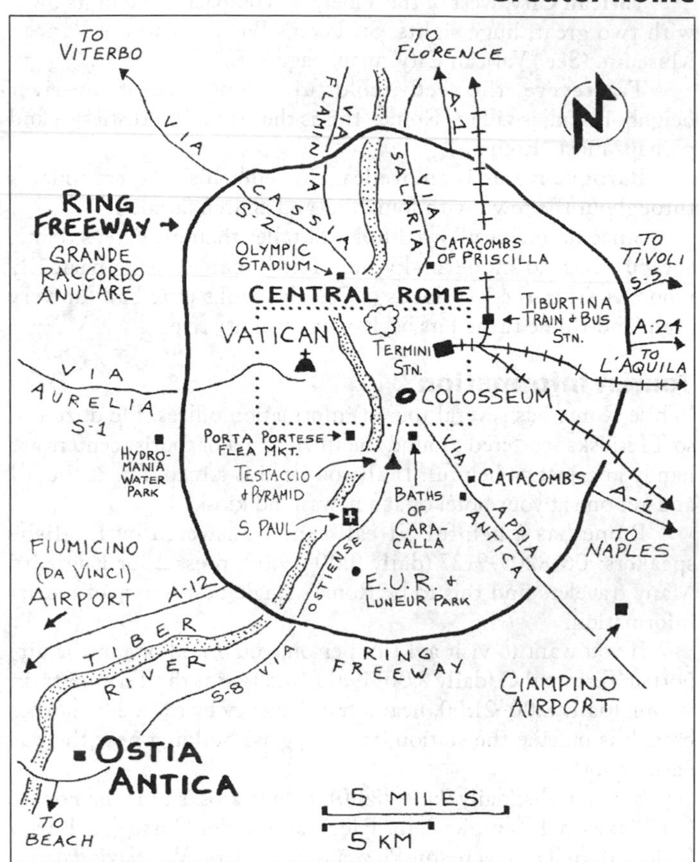

Rome Passes

The **Roma Pass** costs €18 and is valid for three days, covering public transportation and free or discounted entry to Roman sights. You get free admission to your first two sights, and then a discount on the rest within the three-day window. Sights covered (or discounted) by the pass include: Colosseum, Palatine Hill, Borghese Gallery, Capitol Hill Museum, all four branches of the National Museum of Rome, Museum of the Baths, Castel Sant'Angelo, Montemartini Museum, Altar of Peace, Museum of Roman Civilization, Etruscan Museum, Baths of Caracalla, Trajan's Market, and some of the Appian Way sights. If you'll be visiting any two of these sights in a three-day period, this money- and time-saver is a no-brainer (sold at participating sights and at the TIs at the airport and Termini station, www.romapass.it).

The **Archeologia Card,** which costs €22 and is valid for seven days, covers the Colosseum, Palatine Hill, Baths of Caracalla, Tomb of Cecilia Metella (on Appian Way), Villa of the Quintilli (barren Roman villa on the outskirts of Rome), and all four branches of the National Museum of Rome: Palazzo Massimo (the main branch), Museum of the Bath at the Baths of Diocletian (Roman inscriptions), Crypta Balbi (medieval art), and Palazzo Altemps (so-so sculpture collection). The combo-ticket saves you money if you plan to visit at least three of the major sights, such as the Colosseum, National Museum of Rome, and the Baths of Caracalla (sold at participating sights).

Arrival in Rome

By Train: Rome's main train station, **Termini,** is a minefield of tourist services: a TI (daily 8:00–21:00, near track 24), train info office (daily 7:00–21:00), ATMs, late-hours banks, 24-hour thievery, a café, and the handy, cheery Food Village Chef Express Self-Service (daily 11:00–22:30). Borri Books, near the front of the station, sells books in English, including popular fiction, Italian history and culture, and kids' books, plus maps upstairs (daily 7:00–23:00). In the modern mall downstairs (under the station), you'll find a grocery (oddly named Conad "Drug Store," daily 7:00–24:00) and a pharmacy (daily 7:30–22:00). Luggage deposit is along track 24 downstairs (€4 for up to 5 hours, €0.60/hr thereafter). The train to Leonardo da Vinci/Fiumicino Airport runs from tracks 28 and 29 (see "Rome's Airports," near the end of this chapter).

Termini is also a local transportation hub. The city's two Metro lines intersect at the Termini Metro station (downstairs). Buses (including the city orientation tours—see page 685) leave from the square directly in front of the main station hall. Taxis queue in front, along the right side of the square; avoid con men hawking "express taxi" services in unmarked cars (only use oncs marked with the word *taxi* and a phone number, also see page 684). To skip the long taxi line, simply hike out past the buses to the main street and hail one. The station has some sleazy sharks with official-looking business cards; avoid anybody selling anything at the station. From the train station, most of my accommodation listings are easily accessible by foot (for hotels near the Termini train station) or by Metro (for hotels in the Colosseum and Vatican neighborhoods).

By Bus: Long-distance buses (such as from Siena and Assisi) arrive at Rome's small **Tiburtina** station, which is on Metro line B, with easy connections to the Termini train station (a straight shot four stops away) and the entire Metro system.

By Plane: For information on Rome's airports and connections into the city, see "Rome's Airports" at the end of this chapter.

Dealing with (and Avoiding) Problems

Theft Alert: With sweet-talking con artists meeting you at the station, well-dressed pickpockets on buses, and thieving gangs of children at the ancient sites, Rome is a gauntlet of rip-offs. There's no great physical risk, but green or sloppy tourists will be scammed. Thieves strike when you're distracted. Don't trust kind strangers. Keep nothing important in your pockets. Be most on guard while boarding and leaving buses and subways. Thieves crowd the door, then stop and turn while others crowd and push from behind. The sneakiest thieves are well-dressed businessmen (generally with something in their hands); lately many are posing as tourists with fanny packs, cameras, and even Rick Steves' guidebooks. Scams abound: Don't give your wallet to self-proclaimed "police" who stop you on the street, warn you about counterfeit (or drug) money, and ask to see your cash. If a bank machine eats your ATM card, see if there's a thin plastic insert with a tongue hanging out that thieves use to extract it.

If you know what to look out for, the gangs of children picking the pockets and handbags of naive tourists are no threat, but an interesting, albeit sad, spectacle. Gangs of city-stained children (just 8–10 years old—too young to be prosecuted, but old enough to rip you off) troll through the tourist crowds around the Colosseum, Forum, Piazza Repubblica, and train and Metro stations. Watch them target tourists who are overloaded with bags or distracted with a video camera. The kids look like beggars and hold up newspapers or cardboard signs to confuse their victims. They scram like stray cats if you're onto them. A fast-fingered mother with a baby is often nearby. The terrace above the bus stop near the Colosseum Metro stop is a fine place to watch the action...and maybe even pick up a few moves of your own.

Reporting Losses: To report lost or stolen passports and documents or to make an insurance claim, you must file a police report (at Termini train station, with Polizia at track 1 or with Carabinieri at track 20; offices are also at Piazza Venezia). To replace a passport, file the police report, then go to your embassy (see below).

Embassies: The US Embassy is at Via Vittorio Veneto 119/A (Mon–Fri 8:30–12:30 & 14:00–17:30, closed Sat–Sun, 24-hour tel. 06-46741, www.usembassy.it), and the Canadian Embassy is at Via Zara 30 (tel. 06-445-981, www.canada.it).

Emergency Numbers: Police—tel. 113. Ambulance—tel. 118.

Hit and Run: Walk with extreme caution. Scooters don't need to stop at red lights, and even cars exercise what drivers call the "logical option" of not stopping if they see no oncoming traffic. As noisy gasoline-powered scooters are replaced by electric ones, they'll be quieter (hooray) but more dangerous for pedestrians. Follow locals like a shadow when you cross a street (or spend a good part of your visit stranded on curbs). When you do cross alone, don't be a deer in the headlights. Find a gap in the traffic and walk with confidence while making eye contact with the approaching driver—they won't hit you if they can tell where you intend to go.

Staying/Getting Healthy: The siesta is a key to survival in summertime Rome. Lie down and contemplate the extraordinary power of gravity in the Eternal City. I drink lots of cold, refreshing water from Rome's many drinking fountains (the Forum has three). There's a pharmacy (marked by a green cross) in every neighborhood, including a handy one in the Termini train station (daily 7:30–22:00, located downstairs at west end), and a 24-hour pharmacy on Piazza dei Cinquecento 51 (next to Termini train station on Via Cavour, tel. 06-488-0019). Embassies can recommend English-speaking doctors. Consider MEDline, a 24-hour home-medical service (tel. 06-808-0995, doctors speak English). Anyone is entitled to free emergency treatment at public hospitals. The hospital closest to the Termini train station is Policlinico Umberto 1 (entrance for emergency treatment on Via Lancisi, translators available, Metro: Policlinico). The American Hospital is a private hospital on the edge of town (Via Emilio Longoni 69, tel. 06-225-571).

Helpful Hints

Museums: Plan ahead. The marvelous Borghese Gallery requires reservations well in advance (see page 717). Reservations are also necessary for Nero's Golden House (see page 704). To avoid the long Vatican museum line, consider reserving a private tour (see page 729).

Churches: Churches generally open early (around 7:00–7:30), close for lunch (roughly 12:00–15:00), and close late (about 19:00). Kamikaze tourists maximize their sightseeing hours by visiting churches before 9:00 and seeing the major sights that stay open during the siesta (St. Peter's, Colosseum, Forum, Capitol Hill Museum, and National Museum of Rome), while Romans are taking it cool and easy.

Many churches have "modest dress" requirements, which means no bare shoulders, miniskirts, or shorts—for men, women, or children. This dress code is strictly enforced only at St. Peter's Basilica and St. Paul's Outside the Walls.

Internet Access: If your hotel doesn't offer free or cheap Internet access in their lobby, your hotelier can point you to the nearest

Internet café. The city's biggest is **easyInternetcafé,** centrally located on Piazza Barberini (cheap and open 24/7, 250 terminals, www.easyinternetcafe.com). A smaller branch is in Trastevere, on Piazza in Piscinula.

Bookstores: These stores (all open daily) sell travel guidebooks—**Borri Books** (at the Termini train station), **Feltrinelli International** (Via Vittorio Emanuele Orlando 84, Metro: Repubblica, tel. 06-482-7878), **Almost Corner Bookshop** in Trastevere (Via del Moro 45, tel. 06-583-6942), and the **Anglo American Bookshop** (Via della Vite 102, tel. 06-679-5222).

Laundry: Your hotelier can direct you to the nearest launderette. The **Bolle Blu** launderette chain comes with Internet access (usually open daily 8:00–22:00, about €7 to wash and dry a 15-pound load, near train station at Via Palestro 59 and at Via Principe Amedeo 116, tel. 06-446-5804).

Travel Agencies: You can get train tickets and railpass-related reservations and supplements at travel agencies, to avoid a trip to the train station. The cost is often the same, though sometimes there's a minimal charge. Your hotelier will know of a convenient agency nearby. The **American Express** office near the Spanish Steps sells train tickets (Mon–Fri 9:00–17:30, closed Sat–Sun, Piazza di Spagna 38, tel. 06-67641).

Getting Around Rome

Sightsee on foot, by city bus, by Metro, or by taxi. I've grouped your sightseeing into walkable neighborhoods. Make it a point to visit sights in a logical order. Needless backtracking wastes precious time.

Public transportation is efficient, cheap, and part of your Roman experience. (Note that public transportation is also covered—along with sightseeing deals—by the Roma Pass.) It starts running at about 5:30 and stops at about 23:30, sometimes as early as 21:00 for the Metro. After midnight, there are a few very crowded night buses, and taxis become more expensive and hard to get. Don't try to hail one—go to a taxi stand.

You can use the same ticket on the bus or the Metro (€1, good for 75 min, valid for one Metro ride—including transfers—and unlimited buses); you can also buy an all-day bus/Metro pass (€4, good until midnight) or a one-week transit pass (€16—about the cost of two taxi rides). You can buy tickets and passes at newsstands, tobacco shops (*tabacchi*, marked by a black-and-white *T* sign), and major Metro stations and bus stops, but not on board. Stamp your ticket before using it (machines are near subway turnstiles and on buses—watch others and imitate). If the validation machine won't work, you can write the date, time, and bus number on the ticket. For more information, visit www.atac.roma.it or call 800-431-784.

Rome's Metro

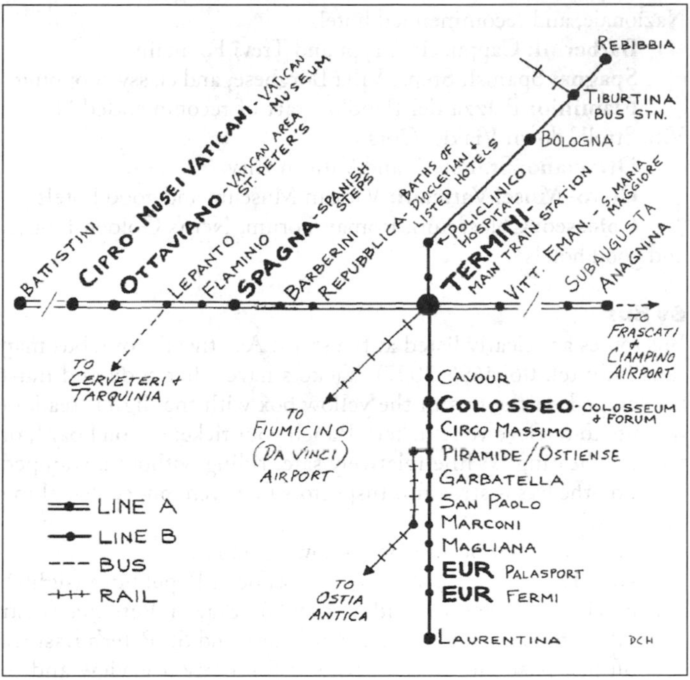

It's smart to buy an all-day pass or a Roma Pass, or to stock up on tickets early on. That way, you don't have to run around searching for an open *tabacchi* when you spot your bus approaching. Metro stations have no human ticket-sellers, and the machines are either broken or require exact change (it helps to put in smallest coin first).

Buses (especially the touristy #64) and the Metro are havens for thieves and pickpockets. Assume any commotion is a thief-created distraction. If one bus is packed, there's likely a second one on its tail with far fewer crowds and thieves. Once you know the bus system, it's easier than searching for a cab.

By Metro

The Roman subway system (Metropolitana, or "Metro") is simple, with two clean, cheap, fast lines that intersect at the Termini train station. Note that first and last compartments are generally the least crowded.

While much of Rome is not served by its skimpy subway, the following stops are helpful.

Termini: Train station, National Museum of Rome, and recommended hotels

Repubblica: Baths of Diocletian/Octagonal Hall, Via Nazionale, and recommended hotels

Barberini: Cappuccin Crypt and Trevi Fountain

Spagna: Spanish Steps, Villa Borghese, and classy shopping

Flaminio: Piazza del Popolo, start of recommended "Dolce Vita Stroll" down Via del Corso

Ottaviano: St. Peter's and Vatican City

Cipro–Musei Vaticani: Vatican Museum and good hotels

Colosseo: Colosseum, Roman Forum, Nero's Golden House, and good hotels

By Bus

Bus routes are clearly listed at the stops. Ask the TI for a bus map (bus info: tel. 06-4695-2027). Tickets have a bar code and must be stamped on the bus in the yellow box with the digital readout (be sure to retrieve your ticket). Punch your ticket as you board, or you are cheating. While relatively safe, riding without a stamped ticket on the bus is stressful. Inspectors fine even innocent-looking tourists €52.

Here are a few buses worth knowing about:

#64: Termini (train station), Piazza della Repubblica (sights), Via Nazionale (recommended hotels), Piazza Venezia (near Forum), Largo Argentina (near Pantheon), and St. Peter's Basilica (get off just past the tunnel). Ride it for a city overview and to watch pickpockets in action (can get horribly crowded, awkward for female travelers uncomfortably close to male strangers).

#40: This express bus following the #64 route is especially helpful—fewer stops, crowds, and pickpockets.

#8: This tram connects Largo Argentina with Trastevere (get off at Piazza Belli, just after crossing the Tiber River).

#62: Largo Argentina to St. Peter's Square.

#81: San Giovanni in Laterano, Colosseum, Largo Argentina, and Piazza Risorgimento (Vatican).

#H: Express connecting Termini train station and Trastevere, with a few stops on Via Nazionale (for Trastevere, get off at Piazza Belli, just after crossing the river).

#492: Stazione Tiburtina (bus station), Piazza Barberini, Piazza Venezia, Piazza Cavour (Castel Sant'Angelo), and Piazza Risorgimento (Vatican).

#271: Trastevere (from across Ponte Sisto bridge) to the Vatican (Piazza Risorgimento).

#571: Express from Via Cavalleggeri (near St. Peter's Square) to the Colosseum.

#714: Termini (train station), Santa Maria Maggiore, San Giovanni in Laterano, and Terme di Caracalla (Baths of Caracalla).

Rome's Public Transportation

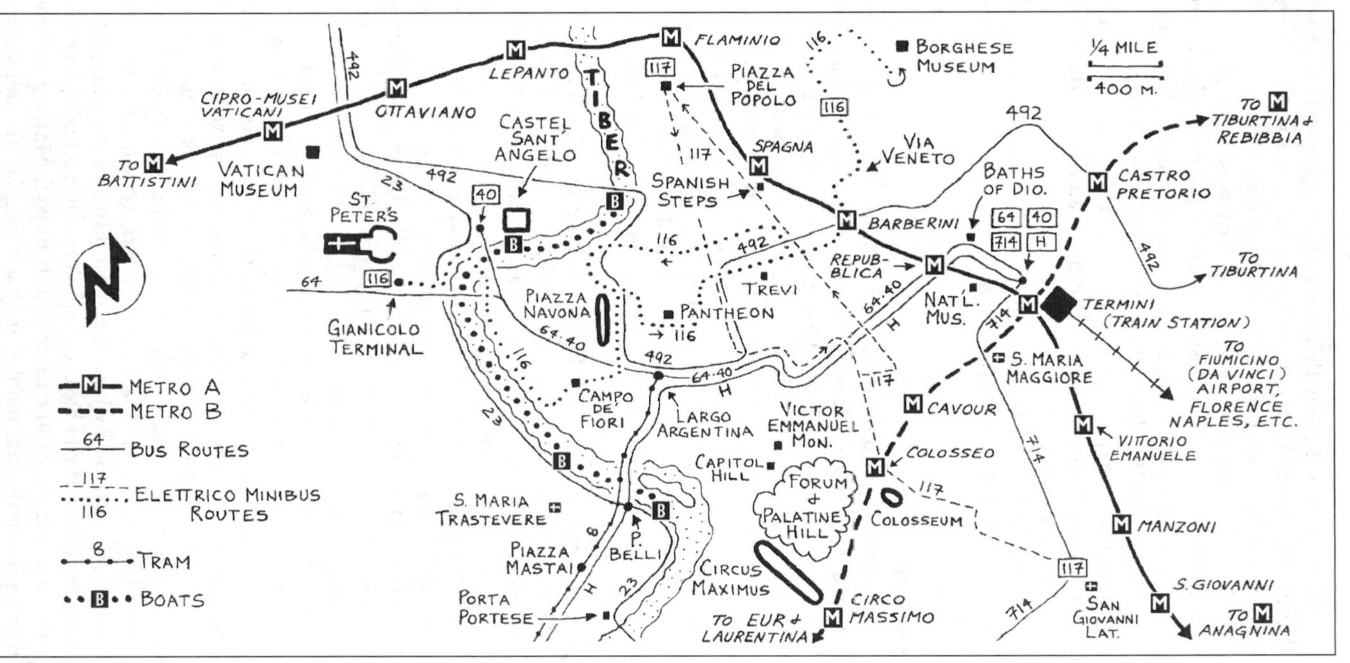

#23: Links Vatican with Trastevere, stopping at Porta Portese (Sunday flea market), Trastevere (Piazza Belli), Castel Sant'Angelo, and Vatican Museum (nearest stop is Via Leone IV).

Rome has cute *elettrico* minibuses that wind through the narrow streets of old and interesting neighborhoods (daily, fewer on Sun). These are handy for sightseeing and fun for simply joyriding:

***Elettrico* #116:** Through the medieval core of Rome: Ponte Vittorio Emanuele II (near Castel Sant'Angelo) to Campo de' Fiori, then to Piazza Barberini via the Pantheon, and finally through the scenic Villa Borghese park.

***Elettrico* #117:** San Giovanni in Laterano, Colosseo, Via dei Serpenti, Trevi Fountain, Piazza di Spagna, and Piazza del Popolo.

By Taxi

I use taxis in Rome more often than in other cities. They're reasonable and useful for efficient sightseeing in this big, hot metropolis. Taxis start at about €2.50, then charge about €1 per kilometer (surcharges: €1 on Sun, €2.75 for nighttime hours of 22:00–7:00, €1 for luggage, €7.25 extra for airport, tip by rounding up to the nearest euro). Sample fares: train station to Vatican-€9; train station to Colosseum-€6; Colosseum to Trastevere-€7. Three or four companions with more money than time should taxi almost everywhere. It's tough to wave down a taxi in Rome. Find the nearest taxi stand by asking a passerby or a clerk in a shop, "*Dov'è una fermata dei taxi?*" (doh-VEH OO-nah fehr-MAH-tah DEHee TAHK-see). Some taxi stands are listed on my maps. To save time and energy, have your hotel or restaurant call a taxi for you; the meter starts when the call is received (generally adding a euro or two to the bill). To call a cab on your own, dial 06-3570, 06-4994, or 06-88177. It's routine for Romans to ask the waiter in a restaurant to call a taxi when they ask for the bill. The waiter will tell you how many minutes you have to enjoy your coffee.

Beware of corrupt taxis. If hailing a cab on the street, be sure the meter is restarted when you get in (should be around €2.50; it may be higher if you called for the taxi). Many meters show both the fare and the time elapsed during the ride—and some tourists pay €8.30 for an eight-and-a-half-minute trip (more than the fair meter rate). When you arrive at the train station or airport, beware of hustlers conning naive visitors into unmarked rip-off "express taxis." Only use official taxis, with a *taxi* sign and phone number marked on the door. By law, they must display a multilingual official price chart. If you have any problems with a taxi, point to the chart and ask the cabbie to explain it to you. Making a show of writing down the taxi number (to file a complaint) can motivate a driver to quickly settle the matter. Tired travelers arriving at the airport will likely find it less stressful to take the airport shuttle to their hotel, or catch the train to the Termini train station and take the Metro or a cheaper taxi from there (see page 680 for details on the shuttle and train).

By Car with Driver

You can hire your own private car with driver through **Autoservizi Monti Concezio,** run by gentle, capable, and English-speaking Ezio (car-€35/hr, minibus-€40/hr, 3-hr minimum, mobile 335-636-5907 or 349-674-5643, www.montitours.com, concemon @tin.it).

By Boat

Tourist-laden boats slowly float their way down the Tiber—trying to re-energize the city's neglected river (single ride-€1, day pass-€2.30, tour-€12, boats depart hourly, daily 8:00–19:30, maybe until 24:00 in summer, tel. 06-678-9361, www.battellidiroma .it). The stops for the boats change regularly, but the route always runs between the Ponte Duca d'Aosta and Calata Anguillara (Isola Tiburtina) bridges—ask the TI or your hotel about current stops.

TOURS

Rome has many good, highly competitive tour companies. I've listed my favorites here, but without a lot of details on their offerings. Before your trip, spend some time on their websites to get to know your options, as each company has a particular teaching and guiding personality. Some are highbrow, and others are less scholarly. It's sometimes required, and always smart, to book a spot in advance (easy on the Web). While it may seem like a splurge to have a local or an American expat show you around, it's a treat that makes brutal Rome suddenly your friend.

Context Rome—Americans Paul Bennett and Lani Bevacqua offer walking tours for travelers with longer-than-average attention spans. Their orientation walks lace together lesser-known sights from antiquity to the present. Tours vary in length from two to four hours and range in price from €25 to €60. Try to book in advance, since their groups are limited to six and fill up fast (tel. 06-482-0911, US tel. 888-467-1986, www.contextrome.com). They also offer orientation chats in your hotel which can be well worth the price (€50/1 hr).

If you're interested in weeklong classes on Rome, look into the **American Institute for Roman Culture**—an innovative, educational organization run by Tom Rankin and his colleague, archaeologist Darius Arya (www.romanculture.org).

Enjoy Rome—This English-speaking information service offers a half-dozen walking tours (€24, 3 hours) and a bike tour (€25, 3.5 hours, includes bike). They provide a free, useful city guide and an informative website (Mon–Fri 8:30–19:00, Sat 8:30–14:00, closed Sun, three blocks north of Termini train station, Via Marghera 8a, tel. 06/445-1843, fax 06/445-0734, www.enjoyrome.com, info@enjoyrome.com).

Rome Walks—The licensed guides give tours in fluent English to small groups (generally 10 people). Sample tours: Colosseum/Forum/Palatine Walk (€52, includes admission to Colosseum, 3 hours), Scandal Tour (€60, 2 hours to dig up the dirt on Roman emperors, royalty, and popes), Vatican City Walk (€57, includes admission to Vatican Museum, 4 hours), a Twilight Rome Evening Walk (€25, all the famous squares with lively people scenes, 2 hours), and a Jewish Ghetto and Trastevere walk (€40, explore Rome's back streets, 3 hours). They also do pricier, private tours to far-flung places such as Orvieto (wine and olives), Ostia Antica, the Appian Way, and the Catacombs (mobile 347-795-5175, www.romewalks.com, info@romewalks.com, Annie Frances Gray).

Roman Odyssey—This expat-led tour company offers various two- to three-hour €25 walks led by native English speakers who are licensed guides (tel. 06-580-9902, mobile 328-912-3720, www.romanodyssey.com, Rahul).

Through Eternity—This company offers several walking tours, all led by native English speakers who strive to bring the history to life. The tours, which run nearly daily and are limited to groups of 20, do not include entry fees to museums or sights. Tours include St. Peter's and the Vatican Museum (€40, 5 hours); the Colosseum and Roman Forum (€25, 2.5 hours); and Rome at Twilight (€25, nightly). They also offer private tours of Rome, Tivoli, and Pompeii (tel. 06-700-9336, mobile 347-336-5298, 10 percent discount if booked online, www.througheternity.com, info@througheternity.com, Rob Allyn).

Private Guides—Consider a personal tour. Any of the tour companies I list can provide a guide (about €50/hr). I work with Francesca Caruso, a licensed Italian guide who speaks excellent English, loves to teach and share her appreciation of her city, and has contributed generously to this book. She has a broad range of expertise and can tailor a walk to your interests (€100 for 2 hours or more—she happily stretches the tour to half a day for eager students, individuals, and small groups, chris.fra@mclink.it).

Hop-on, Hop-off Tours—Several different agencies, including the ATAC public bus company, run hop-on, hop-off tours around Rome. You can hop off at a sight, do your sightseeing, then catch a later bus. These tours are constantly evolving and offer varying combinations of sights, so it's best to check their websites or call ahead for details. Here is a brief description of the tours available.

CitySightseeing Roma: These colorfully decorated buses run hourly and make six stops: at Piazza Santa Maria Maggiore, at Piazza Venezia, near Trastevere at Piazza di Monte Savello, near the Pantheon at Corso Vittorio Emanuele, near Vatican City at Via della Conciliazione, and at Piazza del Popolo (adults-€12, children-€6, purchase ticket from driver, valid for 24 hours, daily 9:30–17:30, recorded commentary, tel. 06-228-3957, www.roma.city-sightseeing.it).

Ciao Roma: This double-decker, hop-on hop-off bus tour loops through Rome for two hours, starting at the Termini train station. It has 13 stops, including the Colosseum, the Vatican sights, Piazza Navona, and Altar of Peace, among others (€19, buy tickets at Ciao Roma office in Termini station, runs hourly, daily 9:00–18:00, recorded narration, tel. 06-4878-6218, US tel. 800-621-2259).

Trambus Open 110: Operated by the ATAC city bus lines, the ATAC city bus #110 tour offers an orientation tour on big, red, double-decker buses with an open-air upper deck. In less than two hours, you'll have 80 sights pointed out to you (by a live guide in English and up to three other languages). While you can hop on and off, the service can be erratic (mobbed midday, not ideal in bad weather). It's best to think of this as a two-hour quickie orientation with scant information and lots of images. The 11 stops include Via Veneto, Via Tritone, Altar of Peace, Piazza Cavour, St. Peter's Square, Corso Vittorio Emanuele (for Piazza Navona), Piazza Venezia, Colosseum, and Via Nazionale. Bus #110 departs every 30 minutes—at the top and bottom of the hour—from in front of the Termini train station (runs daily 8:40–20:30, tel. 06-4695-2252, www.trambusopen.com). Buy the €13 ticket at platform D in front of the train station (red-topped kiosk in the middle of where the buses park).

Archeobus: This air-conditioned minibus runs hourly from the Termini train station out to the Appian Way. This is a handy way to see the sights down this ancient Roman road, but it can be frustrating for various reasons (sometimes crowded, service can be sporadic, not ideal for hopping on and off). The trip includes a basic, uninspired two-hour tour (longer if there's traffic) in Italian and English (€8, daily 9:30–16:50, hourly departures from station and Piazza Venezia, buy ticket at platform D in front of station, tel. 06-4695-4695).

Bus and Boat: This transportation combo makes nine stops on land and six stops on the Tiber. Bus stops include St. Peter's Basilica, Ponte Sant'Angelo, Piazza Barberini, the Colosseum, and Piazza Venezia (buses run hourly 9:00–19:00). The boat runs between Isola Tiberina and Ponte Duca d'Aosta, both of which are also bus stops (€13, buy ticket from driver, valid for 24 hours, recorded commentary, tel. 06-678-8454).

SELF-GUIDED WALKS

Here are three walks that give you a moving picture of Rome, an ancient yet modern city. You'll walk through history ("Roman Forum Walk"), take a refreshing early-evening stroll ("The Dolce Vita Stroll"), and enjoy the thriving night scene ("Night Walk Across Rome").

Roman Forum Walk

The Forum was the political, religious, and commercial center of the city. Rome's most important temples and halls of justice were here. This was the place for religious processions, political demonstrations, elections, important speeches, and parades by conquering generals. As Rome's empire expanded, these few acres of land became the center of the civilized world.

Cost, Hours, Location: Free, daily 8:30–19:00 (last entrance 18:15), Metro: Colosseo, tel. 06-3996-7700. A €4 unexciting yet informative audioguide helps decipher the rubble (rent at gift shop at entrance on Via dei Fori Imperiali). Guided tours in English are offered nearly hourly (€3.50); ask for information at the ticket booth at Palatine Hill (near Arch of Titus). Street vendors at several ancient sites sell small *Rome: Past and Present* books with plastic overlays that restore the ruins (marked €11, offer less).

• *Walk through the entrance nearest the Colosseum, hiking up the ramp marked* Via Sacra. *Stand next to the triumphal...*

❶ Arch of Titus (Arco di Tito): The arch commemorated the Roman victory over the province of Judaea (Israel) in A.D. 70. The Romans had a reputation as benevolent conquerors who tolerated the local customs and rulers. All they required was allegiance to the empire, shown by worshipping the emperor as a god. No problem for most conquered people, who already had half a dozen gods on their prayer lists anyway. But Israelites believed in only one god and it wasn't the emperor. Israel revolted. After a short but bitter war, the Romans defeated the rebels, took Jerusalem, sacked their temple, and brought home 50,000 Jewish slaves...who were forced to build this arch (and the Colosseum).

• *Start down the Via Sacra into the Forum. After about 20 yards, turn right and follow a path uphill to the three huge arches of the...*

❷ Basilica of Constantine (a.k.a. Basilica Maxentius): Yes, these are big arches. But they represent only one third of the original Basilica of Constantine, a mammoth hall of justice. The arches were matched by a similar set along the Via Sacra side (only a few squat brick piers remain). Between them ran the central hall, which

Roman Forum Walk

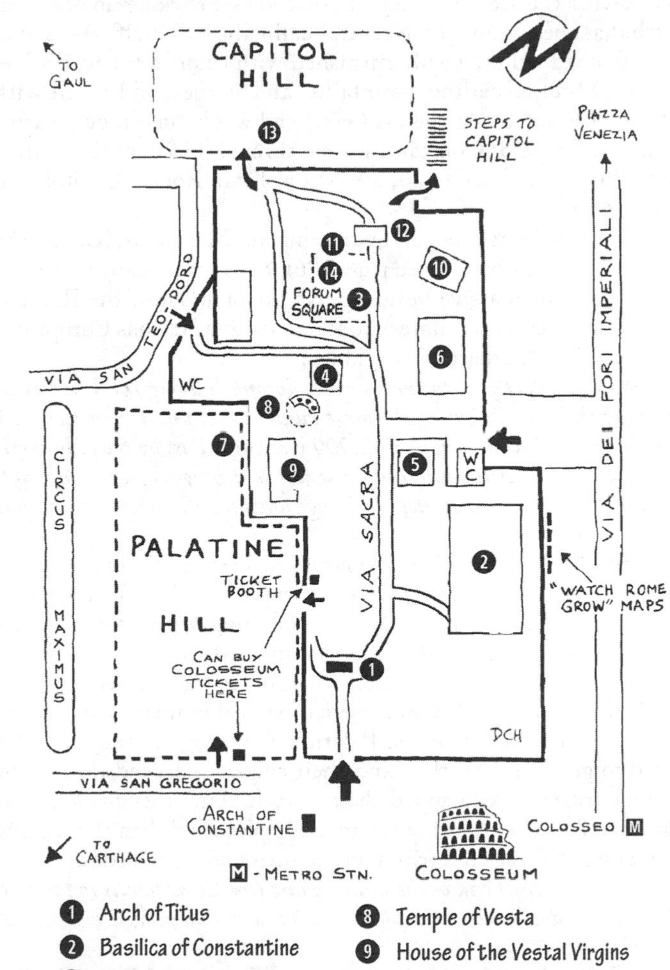

1. Arch of Titus
2. Basilica of Constantine
3. Forum's Main Square
4. Temple of Julius Caesar
5. Temple of Antoninus Pius & Faustina
6. Basilica Aemilia
7. Caligula's Palace
8. Temple of Vesta
9. House of the Vestal Virgins
10. Curia (Senate House)
11. Rostrum
12. Arch of Septimius Severus
13. Temple of Saturn
14. Column of Phocas

was spanned by a roof 130 feet high—about 55 feet higher than the side arches you see. (The stub of brick you see sticking up began an arch that once spanned the central hall.) The hall itself was as long as a football field, lavishly furnished with colorful inlaid marble, a gilded bronze ceiling, fountains, and statues, and filled with strolling Romans. At the far (west) end was an enormous marble statue of Emperor Constantine on a throne. (Pieces of this statue, including a man-size hand, are on display in Rome's Capitol Hill Museum.)

The basilica was begun by the emperor Maxentius, but after he was trounced in battle (see page 706), the victor—Constantine—completed the massive building. No doubt about it, the Romans built monuments on a more epic scale than any previous Europeans, wowing their "barbarian" neighbors.

• *Now stroll deeper into the Forum, downhill along the Via Sacra, through the trees. Many of the large basalt stones under your feet were walked on by Caesar Augustus 2,000 years ago. Pass by the only original bronze door still swinging on its ancient hinges (green, on right) and continue between ruined buildings until the Via Sacra opens up to a flat, grassy area.*

❸ **The Forum's Main Square:** The original Forum, or main square, was this flat patch about the size of a football field, stretching to the foot of Capitol Hill. Surrounding it were temples, law courts, government buildings, and triumphal arches.

Rome was born right here. According to legend, twin brothers Romulus (Rome) and Remus were orphaned in infancy and raised by a she-wolf on top of the Palatine. Growing up, they found it hard to get dates. So they and their cohorts attacked the nearby Sabine tribe and kidnapped their women. After they made peace, this marshy valley became the meeting place and then the trading center for the scattered tribes on the surrounding hillsides.

• *At the near (east) end of the main square (the Colosseum is to the east) are the foundations of a temple now capped with a peaked wood-and-metal roof...*

❹ **The Temple of Julius Caesar (Tempio del Divo Giulio, or "Ara di Cesare"):** Julius Caesar's body was burned on this spot (under the metal roof) after his assassination. Peek behind the wall into the small apse area where a mound of dirt usually has fresh flowers—given to remember the man who, more than any other, personified the greatness of Rome.

Caesar (100–44 B.C.) changed Rome—and the Forum—dramatically. He cleared out many of the wooden market stalls and began to ring the square with even grander buildings. Caesar's house was located behind the temple, near that clump of trees. He walked right by here on the day he was assassinated ("Beware the Ides of March!" warned a street-corner Etruscan preacher).

Rome—Republic and Empire (500 B.C.–A.D. 500)

Ancient Rome spanned about a thousand years, from 500 B.C. to A.D. 500. During that time, Rome expanded from a small tribe of barbarians to a vast empire, then dwindled slowly to city size again. For the first 500 years, when Rome's armies made her ruler of the Italian peninsula and beyond, Rome was a republic governed by elected senators. Over the next 500 years, a time of world conquest and eventual decline, Rome was an empire ruled by a military-backed dictator.

Julius Caesar bridged the gap between republic and empire. This ambitious general and politician, popular with the people because of his military victories and charisma, suspended the Roman constitution and assumed dictatorial powers in about 50 B.C., and in a few years was assassinated by a conspiracy of senators. His adopted son, Augustus, succeeded him, and soon "Caesar" was not just a name but a title.

Emperor Augustus ushered in the Pax Romana, or Roman peace (from A.D. 1–200), a time when Rome reached her peak and controlled an empire that stretched even beyond Eurail—from Scotland to Egypt, from Turkey to Morocco.

Though he was popular with the masses, not everyone liked Caesar's urban design or his politics. When he assumed dictatorial powers, he was ambushed and stabbed to death by a conspiracy of senators, including his adopted son, Brutus *("Et tu, Brute?")*.

The funeral was held here, facing the main square. The citizens gathered, and speeches were made. Mark Antony stood up to say (in Shakespeare's words), "Friends, Romans, countrymen, lend me your ears. I come to bury Caesar, not to praise him." When Caesar's body was burned, the citizens who still loved him threw anything at hand on the fire, requiring the fire department to come put it out. Later, Emperor Augustus dedicated this temple in his name, making Caesar the first Roman to become a god.

• *Behind and to the left of the Temple of Julius Caesar are the 10 tall columns of the...*

❺ **Temple of Antoninus Pius and Faustina:** The respected Emperor Antoninus Pius (A.D. 138–161) built this temple—originally called the Temple of Faustina—in honor of his late beloved wife. After the emperor's death, the temple became a monument to them both.

The 50-foot-tall Corinthian (leafy) columns must have been awe-inspiring to out-of-towners who grew up in thatched huts. Although the temple has been inhabited by a church, you can still see the basic layout—a staircase led to a shaded porch (the

Rome Falls

Remember that Rome lasted 1,000 years—500 years of growth, 200 years of peak power, and 300 years of gradual decay. The fall had many causes, among them the barbarians who pecked away at Rome's borders. Christians blamed the fall on moral decay. Pagans blamed it on Christians. Socialists blamed it on a shallow economy based on the spoils of war. (Republicans blamed it on Democrats.) Whatever the reasons, the far-flung empire could no longer keep its grip on conquered lands, and it pulled back. Barbarian tribes from Germany and Asia attacked the Italian peninsula and even looted Rome itself in A.D. 410, leveling many of the buildings in the Forum. In 476, when the last emperor checked out and switched off the lights, Europe plunged into centuries of ignorance, poverty, and weak government—the Dark Ages.

But Rome lived on in the Catholic Church. Christianity was the state religion of Rome's last generations. Emperors became popes (both called themselves "Pontifex Maximus"), senators became bishops, orators became priests, and basilicas became churches. The glory of Rome remains eternal.

columns), which admitted you to the main building (now a church) where the statue of the god sat. Originally, these columns supported a triangular pediment decorated with sculptures.

Picture these columns whitewashed, with gilded capitals, supporting brightly painted statues in the pediment, and the whole building capped with a gleaming bronze roof. The stately gray rubble of today's Forum is a faded black-and-white photograph of a 3-D Technicolor era. (Also picture the Forum covered with dirt as high as the green door—as it was until excavated in the 1800s.)

• *There's a ramp next to the Temple of A. and F. Walk halfway up it and look to the left to view the...*

❻ **Basilica Aemilia:** A basilica was a Roman hall of justice. In a society that was as legal-minded as America is today, you needed a lot of lawyers—and a big place to put them. Citizens came here to work out matters such as inheritances and building permits, or to sue somebody.

Notice the layout. It was a long, rectangular building. The stubby columns all in a row form one long, central hall flanked by two side aisles. Medieval Christians required a larger meeting hall for their worship services than Roman temples provided, so they used the spacious Roman basilica (hall of justice) as the model for their churches. Cathedrals from France to Spain to England, from Romanesque to Gothic to Renaissance, all have the same basic floor plan as a Roman basilica.

• *Return again to the Temple of Julius Caesar. To the right of the temple are the three tall Corinthian columns of the Temple of Castor and Pollux. Beyond that is Palatine Hill—the corner of which may have been...*

❼ **Caligula's Palace (a.k.a. the Palace of Tiberius):** Emperor Caligula (ruled A.D. 37–41) had a huge palace on Palatine Hill overlooking the Forum. It actually sprawled down the hill into the Forum (some supporting arches remain in the hillside), with an entrance from within the Temple of Castor and Pollux.

Caligula was not a nice person. He tortured enemies, stole senators' wives, and parked his chariot in handicap spaces. But he and Rome's other luxury-loving emperors also added to the glory of the Forum, each one trying to make his mark on history.

• *To the left of the Temple of Castor and Pollux, find the remains of a small, white circular temple...*

❽ **The Temple of Vesta:** This was Rome's most sacred spot. Rome considered itself one big family, and this temple represented a circular hut, like the kind that Rome's first families lived in. Inside, a fire burned, just as in a Roman home. And back in the days before lighters and butane, you never wanted your fire to go out. As long as the sacred flame burned, Rome would stand. The flame was tended by priestesses known as Vestal Virgins.

• *Around the back of the Temple of Vesta, you'll find two rectangular brick pools. These stood in the courtyard of...*

❾ **The House of the Vestal Virgins:** The Vestal Virgins lived in a two-story building surrounding a central courtyard with these two pools at one end. Rows of statues to the left and right marked the long sides of the building. This place was the model—both architecturally and sexually—for medieval convents and monasteries.

Chosen from noble families before they reached the age of 10, the six Vestal Virgins served a 30-year term. Honored and revered by the Romans, the Vestals even had their own box opposite the emperor in the Colosseum.

As the name implies, a Vestal took a vow of chastity. If she served her term faithfully—abstaining for 30 years—she was given a huge dowry, honored with a statue (like the ones at left), and allowed to marry (life begins at 40?). But if they found any Virgin who wasn't, she was strapped to a funeral car, paraded through the streets of the Forum, taken to a crypt, given a loaf of bread and a lamp...and buried alive. Many women suffered the latter fate.

• *Head to the Forum's west end (opposite the Colosseum). You'll pass by a space that was left open by design—kind of a proto-piazza. Consider how the piazza is still a standard part of any Italian town—reflecting and accommodating the gregarious and outgoing nature of the Italian people since Roman times. Stop at the big, well-preserved brick building (on right) with the triangular roof and look in.*

❿ **The Curia (Senate House):** The Curia was the most important political building in the Forum. While the present building dates from A.D. 283, this was the site of Rome's official center of government since the birth of the republic. Three hundred senators, elected by the citizens of Rome, met here to debate and create the laws of the land. Their wooden seats once circled the building in three tiers; the Senate president's podium sat at the far end. The marble floor is from ancient times. Listen to the echoes in this vast room—the acoustics are great.

Rome prided itself on being a republic. Early in the city's history, its people threw out the king and established rule by elected representatives. Each Roman citizen was free to speak his mind and have a say in public policy. Even when emperors became the supreme authority, the Senate was a power to be reckoned with. (Note: Although Julius Caesar was assassinated in "the Senate," it wasn't here—the Senate was temporarily meeting across town.) The Curia building (A.D. 280) is well-preserved, having been used as a church since early Christian times. In the 1930s, it was restored and opened to the public as an historic site.

A statue and two reliefs inside the Curia help build our mental image of the Forum. The statue, made of porphyry marble in about A.D. 100, with its head, arms, and feet missing, was a tribute to an emperor, probably Hadrian or Trajan. The two relief panels may have decorated the Rostrum. Those on the left show people (with big stone tablets) standing in line to burn their debt records following a government amnesty. The other shows the distribution of grain (Rome's welfare system), intact architecture, and the latest fashion in togas.

• *Go back down the Senate steps to the metal guardrail and find a 10-foot-high wall at the base of Capitol Hill marked...*

⓫ **Rostrum (Rostra):** Nowhere was Roman freedom more apparent than at this "Speaker's Corner." The Rostrum was a raised platform, 10 feet high and 80 feet long, decorated with statues, columns, and the prows of ships *(rostra)*.

On this stage, Rome's orators, great and small, tried to draw a crowd and sway public opinion. Mark Antony rose to offer Caesar the laurel-leaf crown of kingship, which Caesar publicly (and hypocritically) refused while privately becoming a dictator. Men such as Cicero railed against the corruption and decadence that came with the city's newfound wealth. In later years, daring citizens even spoke out against the emperors, reminding them that Rome was once free. Picture the backdrop these speakers would have had—a mountain of marble buildings piling up on Capitol Hill.

• *The big arch to the right of the Rostrum is the...*

⓬ **Arch of Septimius Severus:** In imperial times, the Rostrum's voices of democracy would have been dwarfed by images of empire such as the huge, six-story-high Arch of Septimius Severus (A.D. 203). The reliefs commemorate the African-born emperor's battles in Mesopotamia. Near ground level, see soldiers marching captured barbarians back to Rome for the victory parade. Despite Severus' efficient rule, Rome's empire was crumbling under the weight of its own corruption, disease, decaying infrastructure, and the constant attacks by foreign "barbarians."

• *Pass underneath the Arch of Septimius Severus and turn left. On the slope of Capitol Hill are the eight remaining columns of the...*

⓭ **Temple of Saturn:** These columns framed the entrance to the Forum's oldest temple (497 B.C.). Inside was a humble, very old wooden statue of the god Saturn. But the statue's pedestal held the gold bars, coins, and jewels of Rome's state treasury, the booty collected by conquering generals.

• *Standing here, at one of the Forum's first buildings, look east at the lone, tall...*

⓮ **Column of Phocas:** This is the Forum's last monument (A.D. 608), a gift from the powerful Byzantine Empire to a fallen empire—Rome. Given to commemorate the pagan Pantheon's becoming a Christian church, it's like a symbolic last nail in ancient Rome's coffin. After Rome's 1,000-year reign, the city was looted by Vandals, the population of a million-plus shrank to 10,000, and the once-grand city center—the Forum—was abandoned, slowly covered up by centuries of silt and dirt. In the 1700s, an English historian named Edward Gibbon overlooked this spot from Capitol Hill. Hearing Christian monks singing at these pagan ruins, he looked out at the few columns poking up from the ground, pondered the "Decline and Fall of the Roman Empire," and thought, "Hmm, that's a catchy title...."

The Dolce Vita Stroll

This is the city's chic stroll, from Piazza del Popolo (Metro: Flaminio) down a wonderfully traffic-free section of Via del Corso, and up Via Condotti to the Spanish Steps each evening around 18:00 (Sat and Sun are best). Shoppers, people-watchers, and flirts on the prowl fill this neighborhood of Rome's most fashionable stores (open after siesta 16:30–19:30). Throughout Italy, early evening is the time to stroll.

Start on **Piazza del Popolo.** The delightfully car-free square is marked by an obelisk that was brought to Rome by Augustus after he conquered Egypt. (It used to stand in the Circus Maximus.) In medieval times, this area was just inside Rome's main entry.

The Baroque church of **Santa Maria del Popolo,** on the square, contains Raphael's Chigi Chapel (KEE-gee, third chapel on left) and two paintings by Caravaggio (the side paintings in

The Dolce Vita Stroll

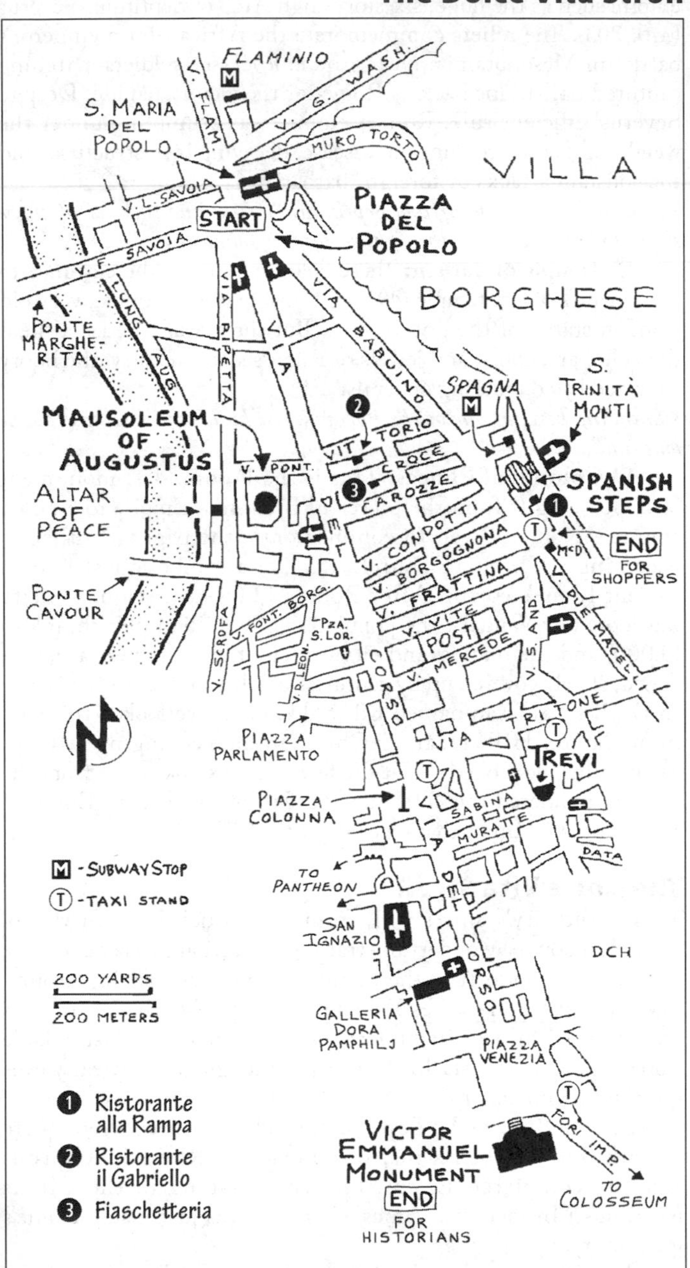

chapel left of altar). The church is open daily (Mon–Sat 7:00–12:00 & 16:00–19:00, Sun 8:00–13:30 & 16:30–19:30, next to gate in the old wall, on far side of Piazza del Popolo, to the right as you face gate).

From Piazza del Popolo, shop your way down **Via del Corso.** If you need a rest or a viewpoint, join the locals sitting on the steps of various churches along the street.

At Via Pontefici, historians turn right and walk a block to see the massive, rotting, round-brick **Mausoleum of Augustus,** topped with overgrown cypress trees. Beyond it, next to the river, is Augustus' Altar of Peace, or Ara Pacis, now located within a protective glass-walled museum.

From the mausoleum, return to Via del Corso and the 21st century, continuing straight until **Via Condotti.** Shoppers should take a left to join the parade to the **Spanish Steps.** The streets that parallel Via Condotti to the south (Borgognona and Frattini) are just as popular. You can catch a taxi home at the taxi stand a block south of the Spanish Steps (at Piazza Mignonelli, near American Express and McDonald's).

Historians: Ignore Via Condotti and forget the Spanish Steps. Stay on Via del Corso, which has been straight since Roman times, a half mile down to the Victor Emmanuel Monument. Climb Michelangelo's stairway to his glorious (especially when floodlit) square atop Capitol Hill. From the balconies at either side of the mayor's palace, catch the lovely views of the Forum as the horizon reddens and cats prowl the unclaimed rubble of ancient Rome.

Night Walk Across Rome: Campo de' Fiori to the Spanish Steps

Rome can be grueling. But a fine way to enjoy this historian's rite of passage is an evening walk that laces together Rome's floodlit night spots and fine urban spaces with real-life theater vignettes.

Sitting so close to a Bernini fountain that traffic noises evaporate; jostling with local teenagers to see all the gelato flavors; observing lovers straddling more than the bench; jaywalking past *polizia* in flak-proof vests; and marveling at the ramshackle elegance that softens this brutal city for those who were born here and can imagine living nowhere else—these are the flavors of Rome best tasted after dark.

Start this mile-long walk at the **Campo de' Fiori** (Field of Flowers), my favorite outdoor dining room after dark (see "Eating," page 755). The statue of Giordano Bruno, an intellectual heretic who was burned on this spot in 1600, marks the center of this great and colorful square. Bruno overlooks a busy produce market in the morning and strollers after sundown. This neighborhood is still known for its free spirit and occasional demonstrations. When the statue of Bruno was erected in 1889, local riots overcame Vatican protests against honoring a heretic. Bruno faces his nemesis, the Vatican Chancellory (the big white building in the corner a bit to his right), while his pedestal reads: "And the flames rose up." Check out the reliefs on the pedestal for scenes from Bruno's trial and execution.

At the east end of the square (behind Bruno), the ramshackle apartments are built right into the old outer wall of ancient Rome's mammoth Theater of Pompey. This entertainment complex covered several city blocks, stretching from here to Largo Argentina. Julius Caesar was assassinated in the Theater of Pompey, where the Senate was renting space.

The square is lined with and surrounded by fun eateries. Bruno faces **Ristorante la Carbonara,** the only real restaurant on the square. The **Forno,** next door to the left (7:30–20:00), is a popular place for hot and tasty take-out *pizza bianco* (pizza bread with cheese but no sauce). Step in to at least observe the frenzy as pizza is sold hot out of the oven. You can order an *etto* (100 grams) by pointing, then take your snack to the counter to pay. The **Taverna** and **Vineria** bars on the square are fine for drinks and people-watching.

If Bruno did a hop, step, and jump forward, then turned right on Via dei Baullari and marched 200 yards, he'd cross the busy Corso Vittorio Emanuele and find **Piazza Navona.** Rome's most interesting night scene features street music, artists, fire-eaters, local Casanovas, ice cream, fountains by Bernini, and outdoor cafés (worthy of a splurge if you've got time to sit and enjoy Italy's human river).

This oblong square retains the shape of the original racetrack that was built by the emperor Domitian. (To see the ruins of the original entrance, exit the square at the far—or north—end, then take an immediate left, and look down to the left 25 feet below the current street level.) Since ancient times, the square has been a center of Roman life. In the 1800s, the city would flood the square to cool off the neighborhood.

The **Four Rivers Fountain** in the center is the most famous fountain by the man who remade Rome in Baroque style, Gian Lorenzo Bernini. Four burly river gods (representing the four continents that were known in 1650) support an Egyptian obelisk that once stood on the ancient Appian Way. The water of the world gushes everywhere. The Nile has his head covered, since the headwaters were unknown then. The Ganges holds an oar. The Danube turns to admire the obelisk, which Bernini had moved here from a stadium on the Appian Way. And the Río de la Plata from Uruguay tumbles backward in shock, wondering how he ever made the top four. Bernini enlivens the fountain with horses plunging through

Night Walk Across Rome

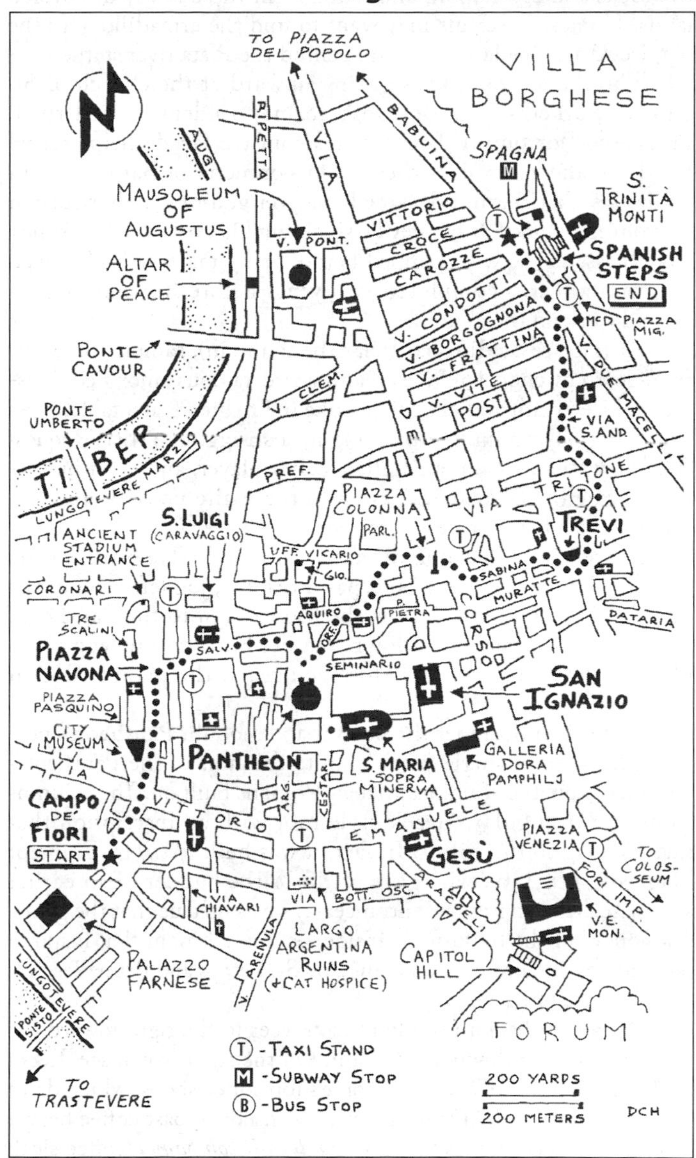

TO PIAZZA DEL POPOLO
VILLA BORGHESE
RIPETTA
VIA
BABUINA
SPAGNA
AUG.
MAUSOLEUM OF AUGUSTUS
S. TRINITÀ MONTI
V. PONT.
VITTORIO
CROCE
CAROZZE
SPANISH STEPS
END
ALTAR OF PEACE
V. CONDOTTI
V. BORGOGNONA
MCD
PIAZZA MIG.
V. FRATTINA
V. VITE
PONTE CAVOUR
V. CLEM.
POST
V. DUE MACELLI
VIA S. AND.
PONTE UMBERTO
TIBER
LUNGOTEVERE MARZIO
PREF.
DEM
TRITONE
PIAZZA COLONNA
VIA
S. LUIGI (CARAVAGGIO)
ANCIENT STADIUM ENTRANCE
PARL.
TREVI
UFF. VICARIO
GIO.
SABINA
MURATTE
CORONARI
AQUIRO
P. PIETRA
CORSO
DATARIA
TRE SCALINI
SALV.
ORF.
PIAZZA NAVONA
SEMINARIO
SAN IGNAZIO
PIAZZA PASQUINO
CITY MUSEUM
PANTHEON
S. MARIA SOPRA MINERVA
GALLERIA DORA PAMPHILJ
VIA
ARG.
CESTARI
CAMPO DE' FIORI
START
VITTORIO
EMANUELE
PIAZZA VENEZIA
GESÙ
TO COLOSSEUM
FORI IMP.
VIA CHIAVARI
VIA
BOTT. OSC.
ARACOELI
V.E. MON.
LARGO ARGENTINA RUINS (+CAT HOSPICE)
V. ARENULA
PALAZZO FARNESE
CAPITOL HILL
LUNGOTEVERE
PONTE SISTO
FORUM
T - TAXI STAND
M - SUBWAY STOP
B - BUS STOP
200 YARDS
200 METERS
DCH
TO TRASTEVERE

the rocks and exotic flora and fauna from these newly discovered lands. Homesick Texans may want to find the armadillo. (It's the big, weird armor-plated creature behind the Plata river statue.)

The Plata river god is gazing upward at the church of St. Agnes, worked on by Bernini's former student turned rival, Francesco Borromini. Borromini's concave facade helps reveal the dome and epitomizes the curved symmetry of Baroque. Tour guides say that Bernini designed his river god to look horrified at Borromini's work. Or he may be shielding his eyes from St. Agnes' nakedness, as she was stripped before being martyred. However, the fountain was completed two years before Borromini even started work on the church.

At the **Tre Scalini** bar (near the fountain), sample some *tartufo* "death by chocolate" ice cream, world-famous among connoisseurs of ice cream and chocolate alike (€4 to go, €8 at a table, open daily). Seriously admire a painting by a struggling artist. Request "Country Roads" from an Italian guitar player, and don't be surprised when he knows it. Listen to the white noise of gushing water and exuberant café-goers.

Leave Piazza Navona directly across from Tre Scalini café, go east past rose peddlers and palm readers, jog left around the guarded building, and follow the brown sign to the Pantheon. The Pantheon is straight down Via del Salvatore (cheap pizza place on left a few yards before you reach the piazza, WC at McDonald's).

Sit for a while under the floodlit and moonlit **Pantheon's** portico. The 40-foot single-piece granite columns of the Pantheon's entrance show the scale the ancient Romans built on. The columns support a triangular, Greek-style roof with an inscription that says "M. Agrippa" built it. In fact, it was built *(fecit)* by Emperor Hadrian (A.D. 120), who gave credit to the builder of an earlier structure. This impressive entranceway gives no clue that the greatest wonder of the building is inside—a domed room that inspired later domes, including Michelangelo's St. Peter's and Brunelleschi's Duomo (in Florence).

With your back to the Pantheon, veer to the right toward the Albergo Abruzzi down Via Orfani. On the right, you'll see **Tazza d'Oro Casa del Caffè,** one of Rome's top coffee shops, which dates back to the days when this area was licensed to roast coffee beans. Locals come here for its fine *granita di caffè con panna* (coffee slush with cream). Look back at the fine view of the Pantheon from here. Then take Via Orfani uphill to Piazza Capranica.

Piazza Capranica is home to the big, plain, Florentine Renaissance–style Palazzo Capranica (directly opposite as you enter the square). Big shots, like the Capranica family, built stubby towers on their palaces—not for any military use, but just to show off. Leave the piazza to the right of the palace, between the palace and the church. The street Via Aquiro leads to a sixth-century B.C. **Egyptian obelisk** (taken as a trophy by Augustus after his victory in Egypt over Mark Antony and Cleopatra). The obelisk was set up as a sundial. Walk the zodiac markings to the front door of the guarded parliament building. To your right is Piazza Colonna, where we're heading next—unless you like gelato...

A short detour to the left (past Albergo National) brings you to Rome's most famous *gelateria*. **Giolitti's** is cheap for take-out or elegant and splurge-worthy for a sit among classy locals (open daily until very late, Via Uffici del Vicario 40); get your gelato in a cone *(cono)* or cup *(coppetta)*.

Piazza Colonna features a huge second-century column honoring Marcus Aurelius. The big, important-looking palace houses the headquarters for the deputies (or cabinet) of the prime minister. The **Via del Corso** is named for the Berber horse races—without riders—that took place here during Carnevale until the 1800s when a horse trampled a man to death in front of a horrified queen. Historically the street was filled with meat shops. When it became Rome's first gaslit street in the 1800s, these butcher shops were banned and replaced by classier boutiques, jewelers, and antique dealers. Nowadays most of Via del Corso is closed to traffic every evening and becomes a wonderful parade of Romans out for a stroll (see "Dolce Vita Stroll," earlier).

Cross Via del Corso, Rome's noisy main drag. Continue through the Y-shaped Galleria del Sordi shopping gallery, forking to the right (but if you're out past 20:00, walk to the right past the gallery and take the first left), and head down Via dei Sabini to the roar of the water, light, and people of the Trevi Fountain.

The **Trevi Fountain** shows how Rome took full advantage of the abundance of water brought into the city by its great aqueducts. This watery Baroque avalanche was completed in 1762 by Nicola Salvi, hired by a pope who was celebrating the reopening of the ancient aqueduct that powers it. Salvi used the palace behind the fountain as a theatrical backdrop for the figure of "Ocean," who represents water in every form. The statue surfs through his wet kingdom—with water gushing from 24 spouts and tumbling over 30 different kinds of plants—while Triton blows his conch shell. (From here, the water goes underground, then bubbles up again at Bernini's Four Rivers Fountain in Piazza Navona.)

The magic of the square is enhanced by the fact that no streets directly approach it. You can hear the excitement as you approach, and then—bam—you're there. The scene is always lively, with lucky Romeos clutching dates while unlucky ones clutch beers. Romantics toss a coin over their shoulder, thinking it will give them a wish and assure their return to Rome. That may sound silly, but every year I go through this touristic ritual...and it actually seems to work.

Take some time to people-watch (whisper a few breathy *bellos* or *bellas*) before leaving. Face the fountain, then go past it on the right down Via delle Stamperia to Via del Triton. Cross the busy street and continue 100 yards. Veer right at Via S. Andrea, a street which changes its name to Via Propaganda before ending at the Spanish Steps.

The **Piazza di Spagna,** with the very popular Spanish Steps, is named for the Spanish Embassy to the Vatican, which has been here for 300 years. It's been the hangout of many Romantics over the years (Keats, Wagner, Openshaw, Goethe, and others). The British poet John Keats pondered his mortality, then died in the pink building on the right side of the steps. Fellow Romantic Lord Byron lived across the square at #66.

The Sinking Boat Fountain at the foot of the steps, built by Bernini or his father, Pietro, is powered by an aqueduct. All of Rome's fountains are aqueduct-powered; their spurts are determined by the water pressure provided by the various aqueducts. This one, for instance, is much weaker than Trevi's gush.

The piazza is a thriving night scene. Window-shop along Via Condotti, which stretches away from the steps. This is where Gucci and other big names cater to the trendsetting jet set.

Facing the Spanish Steps, you can walk right about a block to tour one of the world's biggest and most lavish McDonald's (salad bar, WC). There's a taxi stand in the courtyard outside McDonald's; or, if you'd prefer, the Spagna Metro stop (usually open until 23:30, but can close as early as 21:00) is just to the left of the Spanish Steps, ready to zip you home.

SIGHTS

From the Colosseum Area to Capitol Hill

The core of the ancient city, where the grandest monuments were built, is between the Colosseum and Capitol Hill. The following sights are listed in roughly geographical order from the Colosseum area to Capitol Hill. Except for the small St. Peter-in-Chains Church and the Time Elevator Roma, the sights date from ancient Rome.

▲St. Peter-in-Chains Church (San Pietro in Vincoli)—Built in the fifth century to house the chains that held St. Peter, this church is most famous for its Michelangelo statue. Check out the much-venerated chains under the high altar, then focus on mighty *Moses* (free, daily 7:00–12:30 & 15:00–19:00, until 18:00 in winter, modest dress required; the church is a 15-minute, uphill, zigzag walk from the Colosseum, or a shorter, simpler walk from the Cavour

Ancient Rome

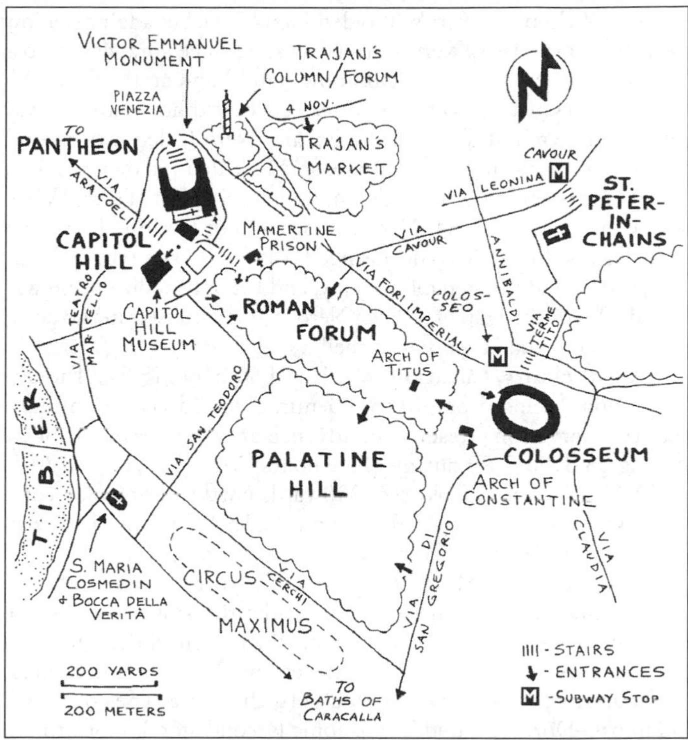

Metro stop—exiting the Metro stop, go up a steep flight of steps, take a right at the top, and walk a block to church). Note that this isn't the famous St. Peter's Basilica, which is in Vatican City.

Pope Julius II commissioned Michelangelo to build a massive tomb, with 48 huge statues, crowned by a grand statue of this egomaniacal pope. The pope had planned to have his tomb placed in the center of St. Peter's Basilica. When Julius died, the work had barely been started, and no one had the money or necessary commitment to Julius to finish the project. Michelangelo finished one statue—*Moses*—and left a few unfinished statues: Leah and Rachel flanking Moses in this church, the *Prisoners* (now in Florence's Accademia), and the *Slaves* (now in Paris' Louvre).

This powerful statue of Moses—mature Michelangelo—is worth studying. The artist worked on it in fits and starts for 30 years. Moses has received the Ten Commandments. As he holds the stone tablets, his eyes show a man determined to stop his tribe from worshipping the golden calf and idols...a man determined to win salvation for the people of Israel. Why the horns? Centuries ago, the Hebrew word for "rays" was mistranslated as "horns."

▲Nero's Golden House (Domus Aurea)—The underground remains of Emperor Nero's "Golden House" are but a faint shadow of ancient grandeur. Nero's massive estate once sprawled across the valley (where the Colosseum now stands) and up the hill, with the original entrance to the gold-leaf-encrusted house all the way over at the Arch of Titus in the Forum. Nero (ruled A.D. 54–68) was Rome's most notorious emperor. He killed his own mother, kicked his pregnant wife to death, and crucified St. Peter. When Rome burned in A.D. 64, Nero was accused of torching it to clear land for his domestic building needs. The Romans rebelled, the Senate declared him a public enemy, and his only noble option was suicide. With the help of a slave, Nero stabbed himself in the neck, crying, "What an artist dies in me!"

Cost, Hours, Location: €5 plus €1.50 booking fee, Tue–Fri 10:00–16:00, closed Sat–Mon, 50-min escorted visit with mandatory reservation. Reserve in advance at www.pierreci.it or by calling 06-3996-7700 during office hours (Mon–Sat 9:00–13:30 & 14:30–17:00), Metro: Colosseo, 200 yards northeast of Colosseum, through a park gate, up a hill, and on the left). Any unsold tickets are sold that day at the Colosseum ticket office.

▲▲▲Colosseum (Colosseo)—This 2,000-year-old building is *the* great example of Roman engineering. The Romans pioneered the use of concrete and the rounded arch, which enabled them to build on this tremendous scale. While the essential structure is Roman, the four-story facade is decorated with the three types of Greek columns—Doric (ground level), Ionic (second story), Corinthian, and, on the top, half-columns with a mix of all three. Built when the Roman Empire was at its peak in A.D. 80, the Colosseum represents Rome at its grandest. The Flavian Amphitheater (its real name) was an arena for gladiator contests and public spectacles. When killing became a spectator sport, the Romans wanted to share the fun with as many people as possible, so they stuck two theaters together to create a freestanding amphitheater. The outside (where slender cypress trees stand today) was decorated with a 100-foot-tall bronze statue of Nero that gleamed in the sunlight. The final structure was colossal—a "coloss-eum," the wonder of its age. It could accommodate 50,000 roaring fans (100,000 thumbs). The whole thing was topped with an enormous canvas awning that could be hoisted across by armies of sailors to provide shade for the spectators—the first domed stadium. This was where ancient Romans, whose taste for violence was the equal of modern America's, enjoyed their *Dirty Harry* and *Terminator.* Gladiators, criminals, and wild animals fought to the death in every conceivable scenario. The floor of the Colosseum is missing, exposing underground passages. Animals were kept in cages beneath the arena floor, then lifted up in elevators. Released at floor level, the animals would pop out from behind blinds into the arena—the gladiator didn't know where, when, or by what he'd be attacked.

Cost, Hours, Location: €11 ticket also includes Palatine Hill and special exhibits (ticket valid all day, or—if purchased after 13:30—for 24 hours). The Colosseum is also covered (or discounted) by the Roma Pass, and covered by the Archeologia Card. Audioguides are available at the ticket office (€4.50 for 2 hours of use). Guided one-hour tours in English depart several times per day between the hours of 9:45 and 17:15 (€3.50). Taking this tour allows you to skip the ticket line. The Colosseum is open daily 9:00–18:15, until 15:30 in winter (tel. 06-3996-7700). Metro: Colosseo.

Like at the Forum, vendors outside the entrance of the Colosseum sell handy little *Rome: Past and Present* books with plastic overlays to un-ruin the ruins (marked €11, price soft, offer less). A WC is behind the Colosseum (facing ticket entrance, go right; WC is under stairway). Caution: For a fee, the incredibly crude modern-day gladiators snuff out their cigarettes and pose for photos. They take easy-to-swindle tourists for too much money. Watch out if you tangle with these guys (they're armed...and accustomed to getting as much as €100 from naive tourists).

Avoid Long Lines: The lines in front of the Colosseum are for buying tickets, not for actually entering the sight. (Once you have your ticket, you can muscle through this ticket-buying crowd, head left up the passage for groups, and go directly to the turnstile, which never has a line.) Instead of waiting in the long Colosseum ticket line (sometimes as long as an hour), consider one of these alternatives:

1. Buy your ticket at either of the two rarely crowded Palatine Hill entrances near the Colosseum—there's one inside the Forum (near the Arch of Titus) and another on Via di San Gregorio (facing Forum entry, with Colosseum at your back, go left on street). The ticket includes entry to both the Colosseum and Palatine Hill.

2. Consider buying the Roma Pass or Archeologia Card at a less-crowded sight, and then use it to bypass the line at the Colosseum.

3. Book a tour with a guide. Tickets for official tours, offered by the Colosseum's guides, are purchased inside the Colosseum near the ticket counter. Tell the guard that you want to purchase a guided tour and he will usher you toward the ticket booth. Some walking-tour companies have guides that will approach you, offering tours that include the admission fee and allow you to skip the line. This will cost you a few extra euros (€15 for the tour, including the €11 Colosseum ticket), but can save time. Beware: It can be hard for you to instantly judge the length of the line, because it's

tucked into the Colosseum arcade. American students working for the guides might tell you that there's a long line, when sometimes there is none at all. Also note that you may buy a tour ticket, only to get stuck waiting for them to sell enough tickets to assemble a group.

▲Arch of Constantine—The arch, next to the Colosseum, marks one of the great turning points in history—the military coup that made Christianity mainstream. In A.D. 312, Emperor Constantine defeated his rival Maxentius in the crucial Battle of the Milvian Bridge. The night before, he had seen a vision of a cross in the sky. Constantine—whose mother and sister were Christians—became sole emperor and legalized Christianity. With this one battle, a once-obscure Jewish sect with a handful of followers was now the state religion of the entire Western world. In A.D. 300, you could be killed for being a Christian; later, you could be killed for not being one. Church enrollment boomed.

This newly restored arch is like an ancient museum. By decorating it with exquisite carvings of high Roman art—works that glorified previous emperors—Constantine put himself in their league. Fourth-century Rome may have been in decline, but Constantine clung to its glorious past.

▲▲▲Roman Forum (Foro Romano)—This is ancient Rome's birthplace and civic center, and the common ground between Rome's famous seven hills (free, daily 8:30–19:00, last entry at 18:15, Metro: Colosseo, tel. 06-3996-7700). A €4 audioguide helps decipher the rubble (rent at gift shop at entrance on Via dei Fori Imperiali). Guided tours in English are offered nearly hourly (€3.50); ask for information at the ticket booth at Palatine Hill (near Arch of Titus). See my self-guided walk on page 688.

▲▲▲Palatine Hill (Monte Palatino)—The hill above the Forum contains scant remains of the imperial palaces and the foundations of Rome, from Iron Age huts to the legendary house of Romulus (under corrugated tin roof in far corner). We get our word "palace" from this hill, where the emperors chose to live. The Palatine was once so filled with palaces that later emperors had to build out. (Looking up at it from the Forum, you see the substructure that supported these long-gone palaces.) The Palatine museum has sculptures and fresco fragments but is nothing special. From the pleasant garden, you'll get an overview of the Forum. On the far side, look down into an emperor's private stadium and then beyond at the dusty Circus Maximus, once a chariot course. Imagine the cheers, jeers, and furious betting.

While many tourists consider the Palatine Hill just extra credit after the Forum, it offers an insight into the greatness of Rome that's well worth the effort. (And, if you're visiting the Colosseum, you've got a ticket whether you like it or not.)

Cost, Hours, Location: €11 ticket also includes the Colosseum. If you purchase the ticket after 13:30, you may use it the next day to see the Colosseum (but not to return to the Palatine). Entry is also covered (or discounted) by the Roma Pass and covered by the Archeologia Card. It's open daily 9:00–19:00 (last entry at 18:15, museum closes at 18:30, Metro: Colosseo). The main entrance and ticket office—which also sells Colosseum tickets, enabling smart sightseers to avoid that long line—is near the Arch of Titus and Colosseum. Another Palatine entrance is on Via di San Gregorio.

Audioguides cost €4 (must leave ID). Guided tours in English are offered once daily (€3.50); ask for information at the ticket booth.

▲Mamertine Prison—This 2,500-year-old, cistern-like prison, which once held the bodies of Saints Peter and Paul, is worth a look (donation requested, daily 9:00–19:00, at the foot of Capitol Hill, near Forum's Arch of Septimius Severus). When you step into the room, ignore the modern floor and look up at the hole in the ceiling, from which prisoners were lowered. Then take the stairs down to the level of the actual prison floor. Downstairs, you'll see the column to which Peter was chained. It's said that a miraculous fountain sprang up in this room so that Peter could convert and baptize his jailers, who were also subsequently martyred. The upside-down cross commemorates Peter's upside-down crucifixion.

Imagine humans, amid fat rats and rotting corpses, awaiting slow deaths. On the walls near the entry are lists of notable prisoners (Christian and non-Christian) and the ways they were executed: *strangolati*, *decapitato*, *morto per fame* (died of hunger). The sign by the Christian names reads, "Here suffered, victorious for the triumph of Christ, these martyr saints."

▲Trajan's Column, Market, and Forum (Colonna, Foro, e Mercati de Traiano)—This offers the grandest column and best example of "continuous narration" from antiquity. Over 2,500 figures scroll around the 140-foot-high column, telling of Trajan's victorious Dacian campaign (circa A.D. 103, in present-day Romania), from the assembling of the army at the bottom to the victory sacrifice at the top. The ashes of Trajan and his wife were once held in the base while the sun once glinted off a polished bronze statue of Trajan at the top. (Today, St. Peter is on top.) Study the propaganda that winds up the column like a scroll, trumpeting Trajan's wonderful military exploits. You can see this close up for free (always open and viewable, just off Piazza Venezia, across the street from the Victor Emmanuel Monument). Viewing balconies once stood on either side, but it seems likely Trajan fans came away only with a feeling that the greatness of their emperor and empire was beyond comprehension. This column marked **Trajan's Forum,** which was built to handle the shopping needs of a wealthy city of over a million. Commercial, political, religious, and social activities all mixed in the forum.

For a fee, you can go inside **Trajan's Market** (boring) and part of Trajan's Forum. The market was once filled with shops selling goods from all over the Roman Empire (€6.20, covered or discounted by Roma Pass, Tue–Sun 9:00–14:00, ticket office closes 1 hour earlier, closed Mon, tel. 06-679-0048). Trajan's Column is just a few steps off Piazza Venezia, on Via dei Fori Imperiali, across the street from the Victor Emmanuel Monument. Trajan's Forum stretches southeast of the column toward the Colosseum. The entrance to Trajan's Market is uphill from the column on Via IV Novembre.

Time Elevator Roma—This cheesy and overpriced show is really just for kids (aged 5 and over). It starts with a stand-up Italian-only 15-minute intro, followed by a 30-minute, multi-screen show with seats jolting through the centuries. Equipped with headphones, you get nauseous in a comfortable, air-conditioned theater as the history of Rome unfolds before you—from the founding of the city, through its rise and fall, to its Renaissance rebound, and up to the present (€11, daily 11:00–19:30, shows every 30 min, no kids under 5, Via dei S.S. Apostoli 20, just off Via del Corso, 3-min walk from Piazza Venezia, tel. 06-9774-6243, www.time-elevator.it).

Capitol Hill Area

There are several ways to get to the top of Capitol Hill (also called Capitoline Hill and Campidoglio). If you're coming from the north (from Piazza Venezia), take Michelangelo's impressive stairway to the right of the big, white Victor Emmanuel Monument. Coming from the south (the Forum), take either the steep staircase or the winding road, which converge near the top of the hill at a great Forum overlook, she-wolf statue, and refreshing water fountain. Block the spout with your fingers, and water spurts up for drinking. Romans, who call this *il nasone* (the big nose), joke that a cheap Roman boy takes his date out for a drink at *il nasone.* Near the *nasone* is a back-door entrance to the Victor Emmanuel Monument (described later in this section).

▲▲Capitol Hill (Campidoglio) and Museum—This hill, once the religious and political center of ancient Rome, is still the home of the city's government. The mayoral palace and the twin buildings housing the Capitol Hill Museum (listed below) border Michelangelo's Renaissance square. The square's centerpiece is a copy of the famous equestrian statue of Marcus Aurelius (the original is in the Capitol Hill Museum).

Michelangelo intended that people approach the square from

Capitol Hill Area

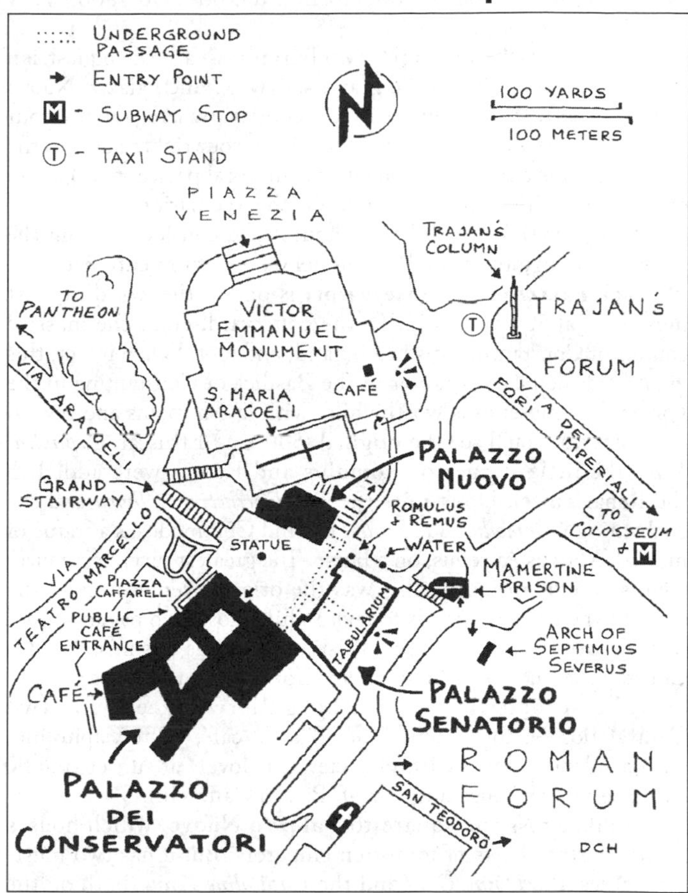

his grand stairway off Piazza Venezia. From the top of the stairway, you see the new Renaissance face of Rome, with its back to the Forum. Michelangelo gave the buildings the "giant order"—huge pilasters make the existing two-story buildings feel one-storied and more harmonious with the new square. Notice how the statues atop these buildings welcome you and then draw you in. The terraces just downhill (past either side of the mayor's palace) offer grand views of the Forum.

▲▲Capitol Hill Museum (Musei Capitolini)—This museum encompasses two buildings (Palazzo dei Conservatori and Palazzo Nuovo) and the underground vacant Tabularium, which has a panoramic overlook of the Forum (€8 ticket covers both buildings, €10 combo-ticket includes Montemartini Museum, covered or discounted by Roma Pass, Tue–Sun 9:00–20:00, closed

Mon, last entry 1 hour before closing, tel. 06-3996-7800, www.museicapitolini.org).

To identify the museum's two buildings, face the equestrian statue (with your back to the grand stairway). The Palazzo Nuovo is on your left, the Palazzo dei Conservatori (where you buy your ticket and start your self-guided tour) is on your right, closer to the river. Ahead is the Palazzo Senatorio (mayoral palace, not open to public); below it—and out of sight—is the Tabularium.

Buy your ticket (valid for 3 hours) and consider renting the good €4 audioguide at the Palazzo dei Conservatori entrance.

The **Palazzo dei Conservatori** is one of the world's oldest museums, at 500 years old. In the courtyard, enjoy the massive chunks of Constantine: his head, hand, and foot. When intact, this giant held the place of honor in the Basilica of Constantine in the Forum. The museum is worthwhile, with lavish rooms and several great statues. You'll see the original (500 B.C.) Etruscan *Capitoline Wolf* (the little statues of Romulus and Remus were added in the Renaissance). Don't miss the *Boy Extracting a Thorn* and the enchanting *Commodus as Hercules.* Behind Commodus is a statue of his dad, Marcus Aurelius, on a horse. The greatest surviving equestrian statue of antiquity, this was the original centerpiece of the square (where a copy stands today). While most such pagan statues were destroyed by Dark Age Christians, Marcus was mistaken for Constantine (the first Christian emperor) and therefore spared.

The second-floor painting gallery—except for two Caravaggios—is forgettable. The adjacent café, Caffè Capitolino, with a splendid patio with city views, is lovely at sunset (public entrance for non-museumgoers off Piazza Caffarelli).

Walk across the square to **Palazzo Nuovo,** which houses mostly portrait busts of forgotten emperors. But it has two must-see statues: the *Dying Gaul* and the *Capitoline Venus* (both on the first floor up).

Head downstairs to the **Tabularium.** Built in the first century B.C., this once held the archives of ancient Rome. The word *Tabularium* comes from "tablet," on which the Romans wrote their laws. You won't see any tablets, but you will see a superb head-on view of the Forum from the windows.

When you're ready to leave Capitol Hill, here are a couple of different options for reaching nearby sights:

Shortcut from Capitol Hill to Victor Emmanuel Monument: There's a clever little back-door access from the top of Capitol Hill directly to the top of the Victor Emmanuel Monument, saving you lots of uphill stair-climbing. Go up the wide steps in the left corner of the Capitol Hill Square (if facing the Forum, the back-door entry is near the drinking fountain and she-wolf statue—follow signs to *terrazze*), pass through the iron gate at the top of the steps, and enter the small unmarked door at #13 on the right. You'll find yourself at the top of the monument with vast views, a café, and the entrance to the Museum of the Risorgimento (see "Victor Emmanuel Monument" later in this section). If you don't take this shortcut, you might decide to...

Descend from Capitol Hill to Piazza Venezia: Leaving Capitol Hill, head down the stairs leading to Piazza Venezia. At the bottom of the stairs, look left several blocks down the street to see a condominium actually built upon the surviving ancient pillars and arches of Teatro Marcello.

Still at the bottom of the stairs, look up the long stairway to your right (which pilgrims climb on their knees) at the Santa Maria in Aracoeli church for a good example of the earliest style of Christian churches. While pilgrims find it worth the climb, sightseers can skip it. The contrast between this climb-on-your-knees ramp to God's house and Michelangelo's grand and elegant stairs leading to Capitol Hill (which you just came down) illustrates the changes Renaissance humanism brought civilization. As you walk toward Piazza Venezia, look down into the ditch on your right to see the ruins of an ancient apartment building from the first century A.D.; part of it was transformed into a tiny church (faded frescoes and bell tower). Rome was built in layers—almost everywhere you go, there's an earlier version beneath your feet.

Piazza Venezia—This vast square is the focal point of modern Rome. The Via del Corso, which starts here, is the city's axis, surrounded by Rome's classiest shopping district. In the 1930s, Benito Mussolini whipped up Italy's nationalistic fervor here from a balcony above the square (to your left with your back to Victor Emmanuel Monument). Fascist masses filled the square screaming, "Four more years!"—or something like that. Mussolini lied to his people, mixing fear and patriotism to push his country to the right and embroil the Italians in expensive and regrettable wars. In 1945, they shot and hung Mussolini from a meat hook in Milan.

Victor Emmanuel Monument—This oversized monument to Italy's first king, built to celebrate the 50th anniversary of the country's unification in 1870, was part of Italy's push to overcome the new country's strong regionalism and to create a national identity. Open to the public, it offers a grand view of the Eternal City (free, 242 punishing steps to the top—unless you take the shortcut from Capitol Hill described above).

Romans think of the 200-foot-high, 500-foot-wide monument not as an altar of the fatherland, but as "the wedding cake," "the typewriter," or "the dentures." It wouldn't be so bad if it weren't sitting on a priceless acre of ancient Rome and if they had chosen better marble (this is too in-your-face white and picks up the pollution horribly). Soldiers guard Italy's Tomb of the Unknown Soldier as the eternal flame flickers. At the tomb, stand with your back to the flame and see how Via del Corso bisects Rome.

The Victor Emmanuel Monument houses a little-visited **Museum of the Risorgimento** explaining the movement and war that led to the unification of Italy in 1870 (free, daily 9:00–19:00, café).

Pantheon Area

To get to the Pantheon, you can walk (15-min walk from the Forum), take a taxi, or catch a bus. Bus #64 carries tourists and pickpockets daily and frequently between the Termini train station and Vatican City, stopping at Largo Argentina, a few blocks south of the Pantheon. The *elettrico* minibus #116 runs between Campo de' Fiori and Piazza Barberini via the Pantheon (daily, fewer on Sun).

▲▲▲Pantheon—For the greatest look at the splendor of Rome, antiquity's best-preserved interior is a must (free, Mon–Sat 8:30–19:30, Sun 9:00–18:00, holidays 9:00–13:00, tel. 06-6830-0230). Because the Pantheon became a church dedicated to the martyrs just after the fall of Rome, the barbarians left it alone, and the locals didn't use it as a quarry. The portico is called "Rome's umbrella"—a fun local gathering in a rainstorm. Walk past its one-piece granite columns (biggest in Italy, shipped from Egypt) and through the original bronze doors. Sit inside under the glorious skylight and enjoy classical architecture at its best.

The dome, 142 feet high and wide, was Europe's biggest until the Renaissance. Michelangelo's dome at St. Peter's, while much higher, is about three feet narrower. The brilliance of this dome's construction astounded architects through the ages. During the Renaissance, Brunelleschi was given permission to cut into the dome (see the little square hole above and to the right of the entrance) to analyze the material. The concrete dome gets thinner and lighter with height—the highest part is volcanic pumice.

This wonderfully harmonious architecture greatly inspired Raphael and other artists of the Renaissance. Raphael, along with Italy's first two kings, chose to be buried here.

As you walk around the outside of the Pantheon, notice the "rise of Rome"—about 15 feet since it was built. The nearest WCs are at McDonald's and at bars on the square. You'll find perhaps Rome's most exuberant gelato at Gelateria della Palma, two blocks in front of the Pantheon (Via della Maddalena 20). For lunch or dinner ideas, see page 757.

▲▲Churches near the Pantheon—The **Church of San Luigi dei Francesi** has a magnificent chapel painted by Caravaggio (free, Fri–Wed 7:30–12:30 & 15:30–19:00, Thu 8:00–12:30, sightseers should avoid Mass at 7:30 and 19:00). The only Gothic church in Rome is

Pantheon Area

Santa Maria sopra Minerva, with a little-known Michelangelo statue, *Christ Bearing the Cross* (free, Mon–Sat 7:30–19:00, Sun 8:00–13:00 & 15:00–19:00, on a little square behind Pantheon, to the east). The **Church of St. Ignazio,** several blocks east of the Pantheon, is a riot of Baroque illusions with a false dome (free, daily 7:00–12:30 & 16:00–19:00). A few blocks away, across Corso Vittorio Emanuele, is the rich and Baroque **Gesù Church,** headquarters of the Jesuits in Rome (daily 7:00–12:30 & 16:00–19:15). Modest dress is recommended at all churches.

▲Galleria Doria Pamphilj—This gallery, filling a palace on Piazza del Collegio Romano, offers a rare chance to wander through a noble family's lavish rooms with the prince who calls this downtown mansion home. Well, almost. Through an audioguide, the prince lovingly narrates his family's story, including how the Doria Pamphilj (pahm-FEEL-yee) family's cozy relationship with the pope inspired the word "nepotism." Highlights include paintings by Caravaggio, Titian, and Raphael, and portraits of Pope Innocent X by Diego Velázquez (on canvas) and Gian Lorenzo Bernini (in marble). The fancy rooms of the palace are interesting, with a mini-Versailles–like hall of mirrors and paintings lining the walls to the ceiling in the style typical of 18th-century galleries (€8, includes worthwhile audioguide, Fri–Wed 10:00–17:00, closed Thu, from Piazza Venezia walk 2 blocks up Via del Corso and take a left, Piazza del Collegio Romano 2, tel. 06-679-7323, www.doriapamphilj.it).

Piazza di Pietra (Piazza of Stone)—This square was actually a quarry set up to chew away at the abandoned Roman building. You can still see the holes that hungry medieval scavengers chipped into the columns to steal the metal pins that held the slabs together (2 blocks toward Via del Corso from Pantheon).

▲Trevi Fountain—This bubbly Baroque fountain, worth ▲ by day and ▲▲ by night, is a minor sight to art scholars...but a major nighttime gathering spot for teens on the make and tourists tossing coins. (For more information, see page 701.)

East Rome, near the Train Station

These sights are within a 10-minute walk of the train station. By Metro, use the Termini stop for the National Museum and the Piazza Repubblica stop for the rest.

▲▲▲National Museum of Rome (Museo Nazionale Romano Palazzo Massimo alle Terme)—This museum houses the greatest collection of ancient Roman art anywhere. It's a historic yearbook of Roman marble statues with some rare Greek originals. On the ground floor alone, you can look eye-to-eye with Julius and Augustus Caesar, Alexander the Great, and Socrates.

On the second floor, along with statues and busts showing such emperors as Trajan and Hadrian, you'll see the best-preserved Roman copy of the *Greek Discus Thrower*. Statues of athletes like this commonly stood in the baths, where Romans cultivated healthy bodies, minds, and social skills. Other statues on this floor once stood in the pleasure gardens of the Roman rich—surrounded by greenery, with the splashing sound of fountains, the statues all painted in bright, lifelike colors. Though executed by Romans, the themes are mostly Greek, with godlike humans and human-looking gods.

The second floor features a collection of frescoes and mosaics that once decorated Roman villas. The frescoes—in black, red, yellow, and blue—show a few scenes of people and animals, but are mostly architectural designs, with fake columns and "windows" that "look out" on landscape scenes.

Finally, descend into the basement to see fine gold jewelry, dice, an abacus, and vault doors leading into the best coin collection in Europe, with fancy magnifying glasses maneuvering you

East Rome

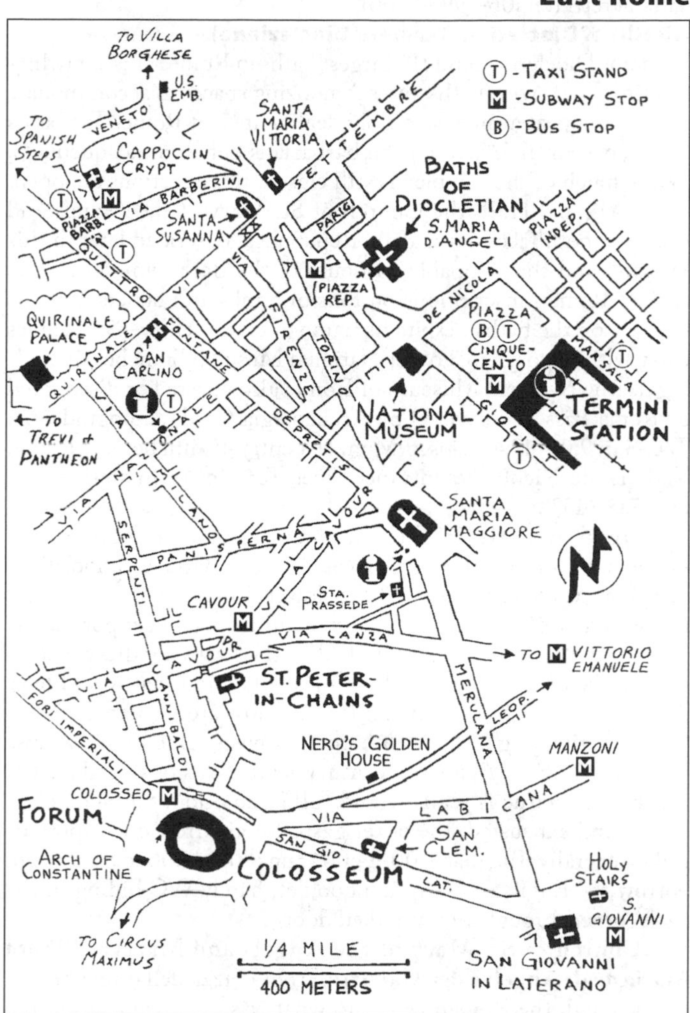

through cases of coins from ancient Rome to modern times.

Cost and Hours: €9 (includes entry to 3 other National Museum branches within 3 days: Museum of the Bath at the Baths of Diocletian, Palazzo Altemps, and Crypta Balbi), also covered (or discounted) by Roma Pass and covered by Archeologia Card. Open Tue–Sun 9:00–19:45, closed Mon, last entry 45 minutes before closing. An audioguide costs €4 (€2.50 with Archeologia Card, rent at ticket counter). The museum is about 100 yards from the Termini train station. As you leave the station, it's the sandstone-brick building on your left. Enter at the far end, at Largo di

Villa Peretti (tel. 06-3996-7700).

▲Baths of Diocletian (Terme di Diocleziano)—Around A.D. 300, Emperor Diocletian built the largest baths in Rome. This sprawling meeting place, with baths and schmoozing spaces to accommodate 3,000 bathers at a time, was a big deal in ancient Rome. The baths functioned until 537, when the barbarians cut Rome's aqueducts. While much of the complex is still closed, three sections are open: the Octagonal Hall, the Church of St. Mary of the Angels and Martyrs (both face Piazza della Repubblica, described later in this section), and the skippable Museum of the Bath, which displays ancient Roman inscriptions on tons of tombs and tablets, but has nothing on the baths despite its name (museum entry-€9, includes entry within 3 days to 3 other National Museum branches, including nearby National Museum of Rome; also covered or discounted by Roma Pass and covered by Archeologia Card, audioguide-€4, Tue–Sun 9:00–19:45, closed Mon, last entry 45 min before closing, Viale E. de Nicola 79, entrance faces Termini train station, tel. 06-4782-6152).

Octagonal Hall: The Aula Ottagona, or Rotunda of Diocletian, was a private gymnasium in the Baths of Diocletian. The floor would have been 23 feet lower (look down the window in the center of the room). The graceful iron grid supported the canopy of a 1928 planetarium. Today, the hall's a gallery, showing off fine bronze and marble statues—the kind that would have decorated the baths of imperial Rome. Most are Roman copies of Greek originals...gods, athletes, portrait busts. One merits a close look: the *Boxer at Rest* (first century B.C.). Textbook Hellenistic, this bronze statue is realistic and full of emotion. Slumped over, losing, and exhausted, the boxer gasps for air (free, open sporadically, generally Tue–Sat 9:00–14:00, Sun 9:00–13:00, closed Mon, borrow the English-description booklet, handy WC hiding in the back corner through an unmarked door).

Church of St. Mary of the Angels and Martyrs (Santa Maria degli Angeli e dei Martiri): From Piazza della Repubblica, step through the Roman wall into what was the great central hall of the baths and is now a church (since the 16th century) that was designed by Michelangelo. When the church entrance was moved to Piazza Repubblica, the church was reoriented 90 degrees, turning the nave into long transepts and the transepts into a short nave. The 12 red-granite columns still stand in their ancient positions. The classical floor was 15 feet lower. Project the walls down and imagine the soaring shape of the Roman vaults (free, Mon–Sat 7:00–18:30, Sun 7:00–19:30, closed to sightseers during Mass).

▲Santa Maria della Vittoria—This church houses Bernini's statue of a swooning *St. Teresa in Ecstasy* (free, Mon–Sat 7:00–12:00 & 15:30–19:00, closed Sun, about 5 blocks northwest of Termini train station on Largo Susanna, Metro: Repubblica).

Once inside the church, you'll find St. Teresa to the left of the altar. Teresa has just been stabbed with God's arrow of fire. Now, the angel pulls it out and watches her reaction. Teresa swoons, her eyes roll up, her hand goes limp, she parts her lips...and moans. The smiling, cherubic angel understands just how she feels. Teresa, a 16th-century Spanish nun, later talked of the "sweetness" of "this intense pain," describing her oneness with God in ecstatic, even erotic, terms.

Bernini, the master of multimedia, pulls out all the stops to make this mystical vision real. Actual sunlight pours through the alabaster windows; bronze sunbeams shine on a marble angel holding a golden arrow. Teresa leans back on a cloud and her robe ripples from within, charged with her spiritual arousal. Bernini has created a little stage-setting of heaven. And watching from the "theater boxes" on either side are members of the family that commissioned the work.

Santa Susanna Church—The home of the American Catholic Church in Rome, Santa Susanna holds Mass in English daily at 18:00 and on Sunday at 9:00 and 10:30. Their excellent website in English, www.santasusanna.org, contains tips for travelers and a long list of convents that rent out rooms. They arrange papal audiences (see page 724) and have an English library that includes my Venice, Florence, and Rome guidebooks (Mon–Fri 9:00–12:00 & 16:00–19:00, closed Sat–Sun, Via XX Settembre 15, near recommended Via Firenze hotels, Metro: Repubblica, tel. 06-4201-4554).

North Rome: Villa Borghese and Nearby Via Veneto

▲Villa Borghese—Rome's scruffy "Central Park" is great for people-watching (plenty of modern-day Romeos and Juliets). Take a rowboat out on the lake or visit the two museums listed below.

▲▲▲Borghese Gallery (Galleria Borghese)—This plush museum, filling a cardinal's mansion in the park, was recently restored and offers one of Europe's most sumptuous art experiences. You'll enjoy a collection of world-class Baroque sculpture, including Bernini's *David* and his excited statue of Apollo chasing Daphne, as well as paintings by Caravaggio, Raphael, Titian, and Rubens. The museum's slick mandatory reservation system keeps the crowds at a manageable size.

The essence of the collection is the connection of the Renaissance with the classical world. Notice the second-century Roman reliefs with Michelangelo-designed panels above either end of the portico as you enter. The villa was built in the early 17th century by the great art collector Cardinal Scipione Borghese, who wanted to prove that the glories of ancient Rome were matched by

North Rome

the Renaissance.

In the main entry hall, opposite the door, notice the thrilling relief of the horse falling (first century A.D., Greek). Pietro Bernini, father of the famous Gian Lorenzo Bernini, completed the scene by adding the Renaissance-era rider.

Each room seems to feature a Baroque masterpiece. The best of all is in Room III: Bernini's *Apollo and Daphne*. It's the perfect Baroque subject—capturing a thrilling, action-filled moment. In the mythological story, Apollo races after Daphne. Just as he's about to reach her, she turns into a tree. As her toes turn to roots and branches spring from her fingers, Apollo is in for one rude surprise. Walk slowly around. It's more air than stone.

Cost and Hours: €8.50, includes €2 reservation fee, covered or discounted by Roma Pass (except the reservation fee), Tue–Sun 9:00–19:00, closed Mon. No photos are allowed.

Reservations: Reservations are mandatory and easy to get in English online (www.ticketeria.it) or by phone: call 06-328-101 (if you get an Italian recording, press 2 for English; office hours Mon–Fri 9:00–18:00, Sat 9:00–13:00, office closed Sat in Aug and Sun year-round). Every two hours, 360 people are allowed to enter the museum. Entry times are 9:00, 11:00, 13:00, 15:00, and 17:00. Reserve a minimum of several days in advance for a weekday visit, at least a week ahead for weekends. Reservations are tightest at 11:00 and on weekends. When you reserve, request a day and time, and you'll get a claim number. While you'll be advised to come 30 minutes before your appointed time, I was told you can arrive 10 minutes beforehand. After that, you become a no-show, and your ticket is sold to stand-bys.

If you don't have a reservation, try calling to see if there are any openings, or just show up and hope for a cancellation. No-shows are released a few minutes after the top of the hour. Generally, out of 360 reservations, a few will fail to show (but more than a few may be waiting to grab them). You're most likely to land a stand-by ticket at 13:00. Visits are strictly limited to two hours. Concentrate on the ground floor, but leave yourself 30 minutes—any time during your visit—for the paintings of the Pinacoteca upstairs (highlights are marked by the audioguide icons). The fine bookshop and cafeteria are best visited outside your two-hour entry window.

Tours: Guided English tours are offered at 9:10 and 11:10 for €5; reserve with entry reservation (or consider the excellent audioguide tour for €5).

Getting There: The museum is in the Villa Borghese park. A taxi can get you within 100 yards of the museum (tell the cabbie your destination: gah-leh-REE-ah bor-GAY-zay). Getting to the museum by public transportation can be confusing, and requires a walk in the park. From the Spagna Metro stop, an escalator carries you up into the park, where you follow signs for 10 minutes. To avoid missing your appointment, allow yourself plenty of time to find the place.

Etruscan Museum (Villa Giulia Museo Nazionale Etrusco)—The Etruscan civilization thrived in this part of Italy around 600 B.C., when Rome was an Etruscan town. The Etruscan civilization is fascinating, but the Villa Giulia Museum is extremely low-tech and in a state of disarray. I don't like it, and fans of the Etruscans will prefer the Vatican Museum's section. Still, the Villa Giulia does have the famous "husband and wife sarcophagus" (a dead couple seeming to enjoy an everlasting banquet from atop their tomb—sixth century B.C. from Cerveteri); the *Apollo from Veii* statue (of textbook fame); and an impressive room filled with gold sheets of Etruscan printing and temple statuary from the Sanctuary of Pyrgi (€4, covered or discounted by Roma Pass, Tue–Sun 9:00–19:30, closed Mon, closes earlier off-season, Piazzale di Villa Giulia 9, tel. 06-322-6571).

▲Cappuccin Crypt—If you want to see artistically arranged bones, this is the place. The crypt is below the church of Santa Maria della Immacolata Concezione on Via Veneto, just up from Piazza Barberini. The bones of more than 4,000 monks who died between 1528 and 1870 are in the basement, all lined up for the delight—or disgust—of the always-wide-eyed visitor. The soil in the crypt was brought from Jerusalem 400 years ago, and the monastic message on the wall explains that this is more than just a macabre exercise: "We were what you are...you will become what we are now." *Buon giorno.* Pick up a few of Rome's most interesting postcards (donation requested, Fri–Wed 9:00–12:00 & 15:00–18:00, closed Thu, Metro: Barberini, tel. 06-487-1185). Just up the street, you'll find the American Embassy, Federal Express, Hard Rock Café, and fancy Via Veneto cafés filled with the poor and envious looking for the rich and famous.

Altar of Peace (Ara Pacis)—In 9 B.C., after victories in Gaul and Spain, Emperor Augustus celebrated the beginning of the Pax Romana (the Roman Empire at peace) by building this "altar of peace." Augustus himself walked up these stairs into the rectangular marble building, sacrificed an animal on the altar, and burned its body to thank the gods for his victory over political rivals and foreign lands. Other sacrifices were offered here—notice there's a hole in the roof to let out smoke, and there are drain holes for the blood at the base of the walls.

The sacrificial temple is decorated with excellent reliefs in the Greek Hellenistic style. At the main entrance, relief panels show the wolf's cave where Rome was born (left panel) and legendary Aeneas about to sacrifice a sow (right). The north and south walls show the dedication ceremonies, featuring a parade of senators, Vestal Virgins, and the imperial family.

In the south frieze, find Augustus himself, near the head of the parade, with his head covered by his robe in the style of a priest. (It's easy to spot Augustus—his body is sliced in half vertically by missing stone.) Augustus is followed by a half-dozen bigwigs and priests (with spiked hats). Next comes the man shouldering the sacrificial axe, followed by Augustus' son-in-law Agrippa, who's also hooded. A little boy tugs on Agrippa's toga while looking toward (most likely) Livia, Augustus' wife. Beside Livia is Tiberius, her son by a previous marriage, who became emperor when Agrippa died young.

On the monument's back side (east), a goddess suckles Romulus and Remus—an image which has become an unofficial symbol of Italy.

The Altar of Peace was originally located east of here, along today's Via del Corso. Over the centuries, various chunks were unearthed and scattered until Mussolini began the push to collect them and reconstruct them here. The project progressed in fits and starts until 2006, when the Altar of Peace was finally reopened to the public, housed in a modern (and therefore controversial) museum designed by a non-Italian (and therefore controversial) architect from America, Richard Meier. Today, it's a memorable combination of Roman grandeur and Greek elegance (€6.50, covered or discounted by Roma Pass, Tue–Sun 9:00–19:00, closed Mon, a long block west of Via del Corso on Via di Ara Pacis, on east bank of river near Ponte Cavour, nearest Metro: Spagna).

Catacombs of Priscilla (Catacombe di Priscilla)—For the most intimate catacombs experience, many prefer this smaller, more obscure option to the crowded catacombs on the Appian Way (San Callisto and San Sebastian). The Catacombs of Priscilla, which used to be situated under the house of a Roman noble family, were used for some of the most important burials during antiquity. Best of all, because they're on the opposite side of town from the most popular catacombs, you'll have them mostly to yourself. You'll actually be in the care of a nun with a flashlight as you walk through the evocative chambers claimed to show the first depiction of Mary with Jesus (€5, Tue–Sun 8:30–12:00 & 14:30–17:00, closed Mon, beyond Villa Borghese on Piazza Crati at Via Salaria 430, bus #63 from Largo Argentina or €10 taxi ride, tel. 06-862-06272, www.catacombedipriscilla.com). For more on catacombs, see "Catacombs," page 740.

West Rome: Vatican City Area

▲▲▲St. Peter's Basilica—There is no doubt: This is the richest and most impressive church on earth. To call it vast is like calling God smart. Marks on the floor show where the next-largest churches would fit if they were put inside. The ornamental cherubs would dwarf a large man. Birds roost inside, and thousands of people wander about, heads craned heavenward, hardly noticing each other. Don't miss Michelangelo's *Pietà* (behind bulletproof glass) to the right of the entrance. Bernini's altar work and seven-story-tall bronze canopy *(baldacchino)* are brilliant.

For a quick walk through the basilica, follow these points (see map on next page):

❶ The atrium is larger than most churches. Notice the historic doors (the Holy Door, on the right, won't be opened until the next Jubilee Year, in 2025).

St. Peter's Basilica

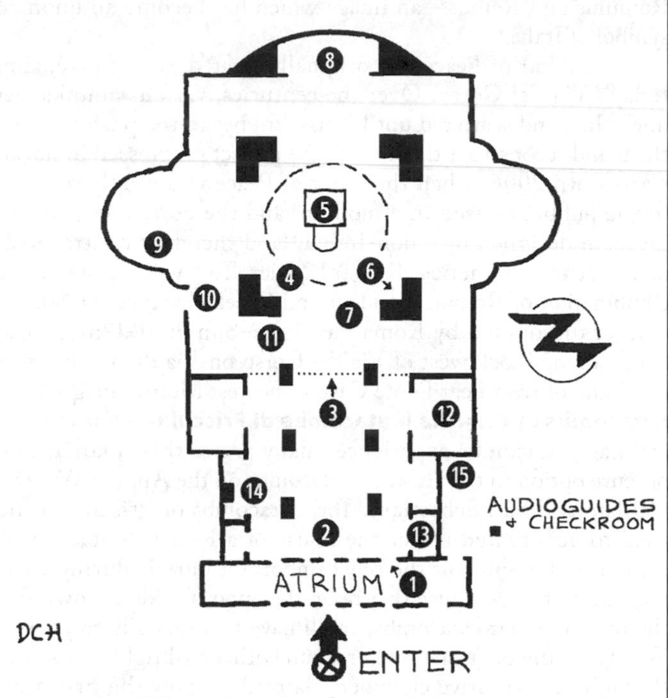

1. Holy Door
2. Charlemagne's Coronation Site, A.D. 800
3. Extent of original "Greek Cross" Church Plan
4. St. Andrew Statue & View of Dome
5. Main Altar (Directly over Peter's Tomb)
6. Stairs Down to Crypt (Entrance May Move)
7. St. Peter Statue (With Kissable Toe)
8. BERNINI—Dove Window & "Throne of Peter"
9. St. Peter's Crucifixion Site
10. Museum Entrance
11. RAPHAEL—Transfiguration (Mosaic Copy)
12. Blessed Sacrament Chapel
13. MICHELANGELO—Pietà
14. Elevator to Roof and Dome-Climb (Possible Indoor Location)
15. Elevator to Roof and Dome-Climb (Possible Outdoor Location)

❷ The purple, circular porphyry stone marks the site of Charlemagne's coronation in A.D. 800 (in the first St. Peter's church that stood on this site). From here, get a sense of the immensity of the church, which can accommodate 95,000 worshippers standing on its six acres.

❸ Michelangelo planned a Greek-cross floor plan rather than the Latin-cross standard in medieval churches. A Greek cross, symbolizing the perfection of God, and by association the goodness of man, was important to the humanist Michelangelo. But accommodating large crowds was important to the Church in the fancy Baroque age, which followed Michelangelo, so the original nave length was doubled. Stand halfway up the nave and imagine the stubbier design Michelangelo had in mind.

❹ View the magnificent dome from the statue of St. Andrew. See the vision of heaven above the windows: Jesus, Mary, a ring of saints, rings of angels, and, on the very top, God the Father.

❺ The main altar sits directly over St. Peter's tomb and under Bernini's 70-foot-tall bronze canopy.

❻ The stairs lead down to the crypt to the foundation, chapels, and tombs of popes (including the simple tomb of John Paul II).

❼ The statue of St. Peter, with an irresistibly kissable toe, is one of the few pieces of art that predate this church. It adorned the first St. Peter's church.

❽ St. Peter's throne and Bernini's starburst dove window is the site of a daily Mass (Mon–Sat at 17:00, Sun at 17:30).

❾ St. Peter was crucified here when this location was simply "the Vatican Hill." The obelisk now standing in the center of St. Peter's square marked the center of a Roman racecourse long before a church stood here.

❿ For most, the treasury (in the sacristy) is not worth the admission.

⓫ The church is filled with mosaics, not paintings. Notice the mosaic version of Raphael's Transfiguration.

⓬ Blessed Sacrament Chapel.

⓭ Michelangelo sculpted his Pietà when he was 24 years old. (A pietà is a work showing Mary with the dead body of Christ taken down from the cross.) Michelangelo's mastery of the body is obvious in this powerfully beautiful masterpiece. Jesus is believably dead, and Mary, the eternally youthful "handmaiden" of the Lord, still accepts God's will...even if it means giving up her son.

The Holy Door (to the right of the *Pietà*, covered in gray concrete with a gold cross) won't be opened again until Christmas Eve, 2024, the dawn of the next Jubilee Year. Every 25 years, the Church celebrates an especially festive year derived from the Old Testament idea of the Jubilee Year (originally every 50 years), which encourages new beginnings and the forgiveness of sins and debts.

Vatican City

This tiny independent country of little more than 100 acres, contained entirely within Rome, has its own postal system, armed guards, helipad, mini-train station, and radio station (KPOP). Politically powerful, the Vatican is the religious capital of 1.1 billion Roman Catholics. If you're not a Catholic, become one for your visit.

The pope is both the religious and secular leader of Vatican City. For centuries, locals referred to him as "King Pope." Italy and the Vatican didn't always have good relations. In fact, after unification (in 1870), when Rome's modern grid plan was built around the miniscule Vatican, it seemed as if the new buildings were designed to be just high enough so no one could see the dome of St. Peter's from street level. Modern Italy was created in 1870, but the Holy See didn't recognize it as a country until 1929, when the pope and Mussolini signed the Lateran Pact, giving sovereignty to the Vatican and a few nearby churches.

Like every European country, Vatican City has its own versions of the euro coin. You're unlikely to find one in your pocket, though, as they are snatched up by collectors before falling into actual circulation. After John Paul II's passing, the coins were redesigned to feature a portrait of the new pope, Benedict XVI.

Small as it is, Vatican City has two huge sights: St. Peter's Basilica (with Michelangelo's *Pietà*) and the Vatican Museum (with the Sistine Chapel). A helpful TI is just to the left of St. Peter's Basilica (Mon–Sat 8:30–19:00, closed Sun, tel. 06-6988-1662; Vatican switchboard tel. 06-6982, www.vatican.va). The thief-infested bus #64 and the safer #40 express bus both stop near the basilica. The closest Metro stops are a 10- to 15-minute walk away from either sight: For St. Peter's, it's Ottaviano; for the Vatican Museum, it's Cipro–Musei Vaticani.

The Vatican post office, with offices on St. Peter's Square (next to TI) and in the Vatican Museum, is more reliable than Italy's mail service (Mon–Sat 8:30–19:00). The stamps are a collectible bonus. Vatican stamps are good throughout Rome, but to use the Vatican's mail service, you need to mail your cards from the Vatican; write your postcards ahead of time. (Note that the Vatican won't mail cards with Italian stamps.)

Seeing the Pope: Your best chances for a sighting are on Sunday and Wednesday. The pope usually gives a blessing at noon on Sunday from his apartment on St. Peter's Square (except summer, when he speaks at his summer residence at Castel Gandolfo, 25 miles from Rome; train leaves Rome's Termini station). St. Peter's is easiest (just show up) and, for most, enough of a "visit." Those interested in a more formal appearance (but not more intimate) can get a ticket for the Wednesday general audience (at 10:30) when the pope, arriving in his bulletproof

Vatican City Overview

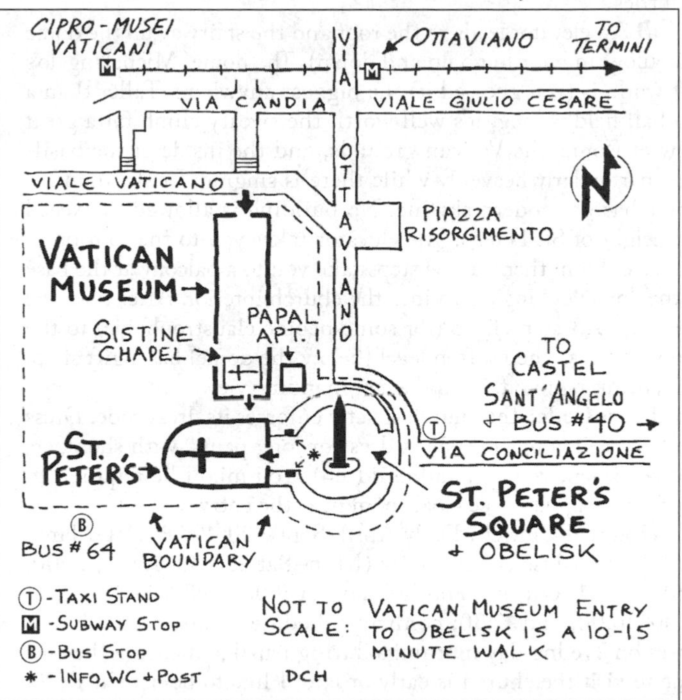

Popemobile, greets and blesses the crowds at St. Peter's from a balcony or canopied platform on the square (except in winter, when he speaks at 10:30 in the 7,000-seat Aula Paola VI Auditorium, next to St. Peter's Basilica). While anyone can observe from a distance, you need a ticket to actually get close to the papal action. Tickets are free and easy to get, but must be picked up the day before—on Tuesday for the Wednesday service. Your hotelier may be able to arrange a ticket for you; or you can contact Santa Susanna Church (they get the ticket and you pick it up on Tue at their church between 17:00 and 18:45, Via XX Settembre 15, near recommended Via Firenze hotels, Metro: Repubblica, tel. 06-4201-4554, www.santasusanna.org); or you can go to St. Peter's Basilica on Tuesday and wait in a long line for a ticket (Swiss Guards hand out tickets from their station at the Bronze Doors, just to the right of the basilica, after 12:00 on Tue). To find out the pope's schedule or to book a free spot for the Wednesday general audience (either for a seat on the square or in the auditorium), call 06-6988-4631. If you only want to see the Vatican—but not the pope—minimize crowd problems by avoiding these times.

In the Jubilee Year 2000, Pope John Paul II tirelessly—and with significant success—promoted debt relief for the world's poorest countries.

⓮ An elevator leads to the roof and the stairway up the dome (€6, allow an hour to go up and down). The dome, Michelangelo's last work, is (you guessed it) the biggest anywhere. Taller than a football field is long, it's well worth the sweaty climb for a great view of Rome, the Vatican grounds, and the inside of the basilica—particularly heavenly while there is singing. Look around—Rome has no modern skyline. No building is allowed to exceed the height of St. Peter's. The elevator takes you to the rooftop of the nave. From there, a few steps take you to a balcony at the base of the dome looking down into the church interior. After that, the one-way, 323-step climb (for some people claustrophobic) to the cupola begins. The rooftop level (below the dome) has a gift shop, WC, drinking fountain, and a commanding view.

Dress Code: The church strictly enforces its dress code: Dress modestly—in a not-too-short dress or long pants, with shoulders covered (men, women, and children). You might be required to check any bags at a free cloakroom near the entry.

Hours of Church: Daily April–Sept 7:00–19:00, Oct–March 7:00–18:00. Mass is held daily (Mon–Sat at 8:30, 10:00, 11:00, 12:00, and 17:00; Sun and holidays at 9:00, 10:30, 11:30, 12:10, 13:00, 16:00, and 17:30; confirm schedule locally). The church closes on Wednesday mornings during papal audiences. The best time to visit the church is early or late; I like to be here at 17:00, when the church is fairly empty, sunbeams can work their magic, and the late-afternoon Mass fills the place with spiritual music.

Tours: The Vatican TI conducts free 90-minute tours of St. Peter's (depart daily from TI at 14:15, many days also at 15:00, confirm schedule at TI, tel. 06-6988-1662). Audioguides can be rented near the checkroom (€5).

Tours are the only way to see the Vatican Gardens; book at least a day in advance by calling 06-6988-4676 (€12; Tue, Thu, and Sat at 10:00; tours start at Vatican Museum tour desk and finish on St. Peter's Square).

To tour the Necropolis of St. Peter's and the saint's tomb, call the Excavations Office at 06-6988-5318 a minimum of a week before your visit (€10, 2 hours, office open Mon–Sat 9:00–17:00). The Crypt is open for free to the public, but this tour gets you closer to St. Peter's tomb.

Cost and Hours of Dome: The view from the dome is worth the climb (€6 elevator plus 323-step climb, allow an hour to go up and down, daily April–Sept 8:00–17:45, Oct–March 8:00–16:45).

▲▲▲Vatican Museum (Musei Vaticani)—The four miles of displays in this immense museum—from ancient statues to Christian frescoes to modern paintings—are topped by the Raphael Rooms and Michelangelo's glorious Sistine Chapel. (If you have binoculars, bring them.)

Even without the Sistine, this is one of Europe's top three or four houses of art. It can be exhausting, so plan your visit carefully, focusing on a few themes. Allow two hours for a quick visit, three or four for time to enjoy it. The museum has a nearly impossible-not-to-follow one-way system. Tip: The Sistine Chapel has an exit (optional) that leads directly to St. Peter's Basilica, saving you the 10-minute walk back to the Vatican Museum exit; if you want to squirt out after seeing the Sistine, see the Pinacoteca painting gallery first (described below) and don't get an audioguide (which needs to be returned at the entry/exit).

Start, as civilization did, in **Egypt and Mesopotamia.** Next, the Pio Clementino collection features **Greek and Roman statues.** Decorating its courtyard are some of the best Greek and Roman statues in captivity, including the *Laocoön* group (first century B.C., Hellenistic) and the *Apollo Belvedere* (a second-century Roman copy of a Greek original). The centerpiece of the next hall is the *Belvedere Torso* (just a 2,000-year-old torso, but one that had a great impact on the art of Michelangelo). Finishing off the classical statuary are two fine fourth-century porphyry sarcophagi. These royal purple tombs were made (though not used) for the Roman emperor Constantine's mother and daughter. They were Christians—and therefore outlaws—until Constantine made Christianity legal (A.D. 312). The tombs, crafted in Egypt at a time when a declining Rome was unable to do such fine work, have details that are fun to study.

After long halls of tapestries, old maps, broken penises, and fig leaves, you'll come to what most people are looking for: The Raphael Rooms (or *stanza*) and Michelangelo's Sistine Chapel.

These outstanding works are frescoes. A fresco (meaning "fresh" in Italian) is technically not a painting. The color is mixed into wet plaster, and, when the plaster dries, the painting is actually part of the wall. This is a durable but difficult medium, requiring speed and accuracy, as the work is built one patch at a time.

After fancy rooms illustrating the "Immaculate Conception of Mary" (in the 19th century, the Vatican codified this hard-to-sell doctrine, making it a formal part of the Catholic faith) and the triumph of Constantine (with divine guidance, which led to his conversion to Christianity), you enter rooms frescoed by **Raphael** and his assistants. The highlight is the newly restored *School of Athens*. This is remarkable for its blatant pre-Christian classical orientation, especially since it originally wallpapered the apartments of Pope Julius II. Raphael honors the great pre-Christian thinkers—Aristotle, Plato, and company—who are portrayed as the leading artists of Raphael's day. The bearded figure of Plato is Leonardo da Vinci. Diogenes, history's first hippie, sprawls alone in bright blue on the stairs, while Michelangelo broods in the foreground—supposedly added later. Apparently, Raphael snuck a peek at the Sistine Chapel and decided that his arch-competitor was so good he had to put their personal differences aside and include him in this tribute to the artists of his generation. Today's St. Peter's was under construction as Raphael was working. In the *School of Athens*, he gives us a sneak preview of the unfinished church.

Next (unless you detour through the refreshingly modern Catholic art section) is the brilliantly restored **Sistine Chapel.** This is the pope's personal chapel and also the place where, upon the death of the ruling pope, a new pope is elected (as in April of 2005). The College of Cardinals meets here and votes four times a day until a two-thirds-plus-one majority is reached or a new pope is chosen.

The Sistine is famous for Michelangelo's pictorial culmination of the Renaissance, showing the story of creation, with a powerful God weaving in and out of each scene through that busy first week. This is an optimistic and positive expression of the High Renaissance and a stirring example of the artistic and theological maturity of the 33-year-old Michelangelo, who spent four years on this work.

Later, after the Reformation wars had begun and after the Catholic army of Spain had sacked the Vatican, the reeling Church began to fight back. As part of its Counter-Reformation, a much older Michelangelo was commissioned to paint the *Last Judgment* (behind the altar). Brilliantly restored, the message is as clear as the day Michelangelo finished it: Christ is returning, some will go to hell and some to heaven, and some will be saved by the power of the rosary.

In the recent and controversial restoration project, no paint was added. Centuries of dust, soot (from candles used for lighting and Mass), and glue (added to make the art shine) were removed, revealing the bright original colors of Michelangelo. Photos are allowed (without a flash) elsewhere in the museum, but as part of the deal with the company who did the restoration, no photos are allowed in the Sistine Chapel.

For a shortcut, a small door at the rear of the Sistine Chapel—likely labeled "Exit for private tour groups only"—allows groups and individuals (without an audioguide) to escape directly to St. Peter's Basilica. If you exit here, you're done with the museum. The Pinacoteca is the only important part left. Consider doing it at the start. Otherwise it's a 10-minute heel-to-toe slalom through tourists from the Sistine Chapel to the entry/exit.

After this long march, you'll find the **Pinacoteca** (the Vatican's small but fine collection of paintings, with Raphael's *Transfiguration,* Leonardo's unfinished *St. Jerome,* and Caravaggio's *Deposition*), a cafeteria (long lines, uninspired food), and the underrated early-Christian art section, before you exit via the souvenir shop.

Cost, Hours, Information: €13, March–Oct Mon–Fri 10:00–16:45, Sat 10:00–14:45; Nov–Feb Mon–Sat 10:00–13:45; closed Sun except last Sun of the month (when it's free, crowded, and open 9:00–13:45). Last entry is about 75 minutes before the closing time. The Sistine Chapel closes before the museum does.

The museum is closed on many holidays (mainly religious ones) including, for 2008: Jan 1 (New Year's), Jan 6 (Epiphany), Feb 11 (Vatican City established), March 19 (Saint Joseph), March 23–24 (Easter Sunday and Monday), May 1 (Labor Day and Ascension Thursday), June 15 (Corpus Christi Day), June 29 (Saints Peter and Paul), Aug 15 plus either Aug 14 or 16—it varies year to year (Assumption of the Virgin), Nov 1 (All Saints' Day), Dec 8 (Immaculate Conception), and Dec 25–26 (Christmas). Other holidays may pop up—search for "closed dates" at www.vatican.va.

The museum is generally hot and crowded. The most crowded days are Saturday, the last Sunday of the month, Monday, rainy days, and any day before or after a holiday closure. Afternoons or Wednesday mornings before 11:00 are best. On days the museum closes at 16:45, arriving by 13:00 works well. Most mornings, there's a line to get in that stretches around the block. (Stuck in the line? Figure about a 10-min wait for every 100 yards.) Modest dress (no short shorts or bare shoulders) is appropriate and often required. Museum tel. 06-6988-3860 or 06-6988-1662.

Tours: Both **private tour companies** and **private guides** offer guided tours of the museum, allowing you to skip the long ticket-buying line. For a listing of several companies, see page 685. These tours can be expensive—shop around for the best deal.

There are also English tours with a **Vatican guide,** but these are extremely difficult to join—they can book up as much as a year in advance (for details, see www.vatican.va). If you don't hear back, they're full.

If you rent a €6 audioguide (available at the top of the ramp/escalator), you lose the option of taking the shortcut from the Sistine Chapel to St. Peter's (audioguides must be returned at museum entrance).

▲Castel Sant'Angelo—Built as a tomb for the emperor; used through the Middle Ages as a castle, prison, and place of last refuge for popes under attack; and today, a museum, this giant pile of ancient bricks is packed with history (€5, covered or discounted by Roma Pass, Tue–Sun 9:00–18:00, closed Mon, audioguide-€4, near Vatican City, Metro: Lepanto or bus #64, tel. 06-3996-7600).

Ancient Rome allowed no tombs within its walls—not even the emperor's. So Emperor Hadrian grabbed the most commanding position just outside the walls and across the river and built a towering tomb (circa A.D. 139) well within view of the city. His mausoleum was a huge cylinder (210 by 70 feet) topped by a cypress grove and crowned by a huge statue of Hadrian himself riding a chariot. For nearly a hundred years, Roman emperors (from Hadrian to Caracalla, in A.D. 217) were buried here.

In the year 590, the Archangel Michael appeared above the mausoleum to Pope Gregory the Great. Sheathing his sword, the angel signaled the end of a plague. The fortress that was Hadrian's mausoleum eventually became a fortified palace, renamed for the "holy angel."

Castel Sant'Angelo spent centuries of the Dark Ages as a fortress and prison, but was eventually connected to the Vatican via an elevated corridor at the pope's request (1277). Since Rome was repeatedly plundered by invaders, Castel Sant'Angelo was a handy place of last refuge for threatened popes.

Touring the place is a stair-stepping workout. After you walk around the entire base of the castle, take the small staircase down to the original Roman floor (following the route of Hadrian's funeral procession). In the atrium, study the model of the mausoleum as it was in Roman times. From here, a ramp leads to the right, spiraling 400 feet. At the end of the ramp, a bridge crosses over the room where the ashes of the emperors were kept. From here, the stairs continue out of the ancient section and into the medieval structure (built atop the mausoleum) that housed the papal apartments. Don't miss the Sala del Tesoro (Treasury), where the wealth of the Vatican was locked up in a huge chest. (*Do* miss the 58 rooms of the military museum.) From the pope's piggy bank, a narrow flight of stairs leads to the rooftop and perhaps the finest Rome view anywhere—pick out landmarks as you stroll around.

Ponte Sant'Angelo—The bridge leading to Castel Sant'Angelo was built by Hadrian for quick and regal access from downtown to his tomb. The three middle arches are actually Roman originals, and a fine example of the empire's engineering expertise. The statues of angels (each bearing a symbol of the passion of Christ—nail, sponge, shroud, and so on) are Bernini-designed and textbook Baroque. In the Middle Ages, this was the only bridge in the area that connected St. Peter's and the Vatican with downtown Rome. Nearly all pilgrims passed this bridge to and from the church. Its shoulder-high banisters recall a tragedy: During a Jubilee Year festival in 1450, the crowd got so huge that the mob pushed out the original banisters, causing nearly 200 to fall to their deaths.

Southwest Rome: Trastevere

Trastevere is the colorful neighborhood across *(tras)* the Tiber *(Tevere)* River. Trastevere (trahs-TAY-veh-ray) offers the best look at medieval-village Rome. The action unwinds to the chime of the church bells. Go there and wander. Wonder. Be a poet. This is Rome's Left Bank.

This proud neighborhood was long a working-class area. Now that it's becoming trendy, high rents are driving out the source of so much color. Still, it's a great people scene, especially at night. Stroll the back streets (for restaurant recommendations, see page 754).

Getting There: Trastevere is on the west side of the Tiber River, south of Vatican City and across the river from the Forum and Capitol Hill area. To get there by foot from Capitol Hill, cross the Tiber on Ponte Cestio (over Isola Tiberina). You can also take tram #8 from Largo Argentina, or bus #H from Termini train station and Via Nazionale (get off at Piazza Belli). From the Vatican (Piazza Risorgimento), it's bus #23 or #271.

Linking Trastevere with the "Night Walk Across Rome": You can walk from Trastevere to Campo de' Fiori to link up with the beginning of my "Night Walk Across Rome" (page 697): From Trastevere's church square (Piazza di Santa Maria), take Via del Moro to the river and cross at Ponte Sisto, a pedestrian bridge that has a good view of St. Peter's dome. Continue straight ahead for one block. Take the first left, which leads down Via di Capo di Ferro through the scary and narrow darkness to Piazza Farnese, with the imposing Palazzo Farnese. Michelangelo contributed to the facade of this palace, now the French Embassy. The fountains on the square feature huge, one-piece granite hot tubs from the ancient Roman Baths of Caracalla. One block from there (opposite the palace) is the atmospheric square of Campo de' Fiori.

▲Santa Maria in Trastevere Church—One of Rome's oldest churches, this was made a basilica in the fourth century, when Christianity was legalized (free, daily 7:00–21:00). It was the first church dedicated to the Virgin Mary. The portico (covered area just outside the door) is decorated with fascinating ancient fragments filled with early Christian symbolism. Most of what you see today dates from around the 12th century, but the granite columns come from an ancient Roman temple, and the ancient basilica floor plan (and ambience) survive. The striking 12th-century mosaics behind the altar are notable for their portrayal of Mary—the first to show her at the throne with Jesus in Heaven. Look below the scenes from the life of Mary to see ahead-of-their-time mosaics (by Cavallini, from 1300), predating the Renaissance by 100 years.

The church is on Piazza di Santa Maria. While today's fountain is from the 17th century, there has been a fountain here since Roman times.

Trastevere

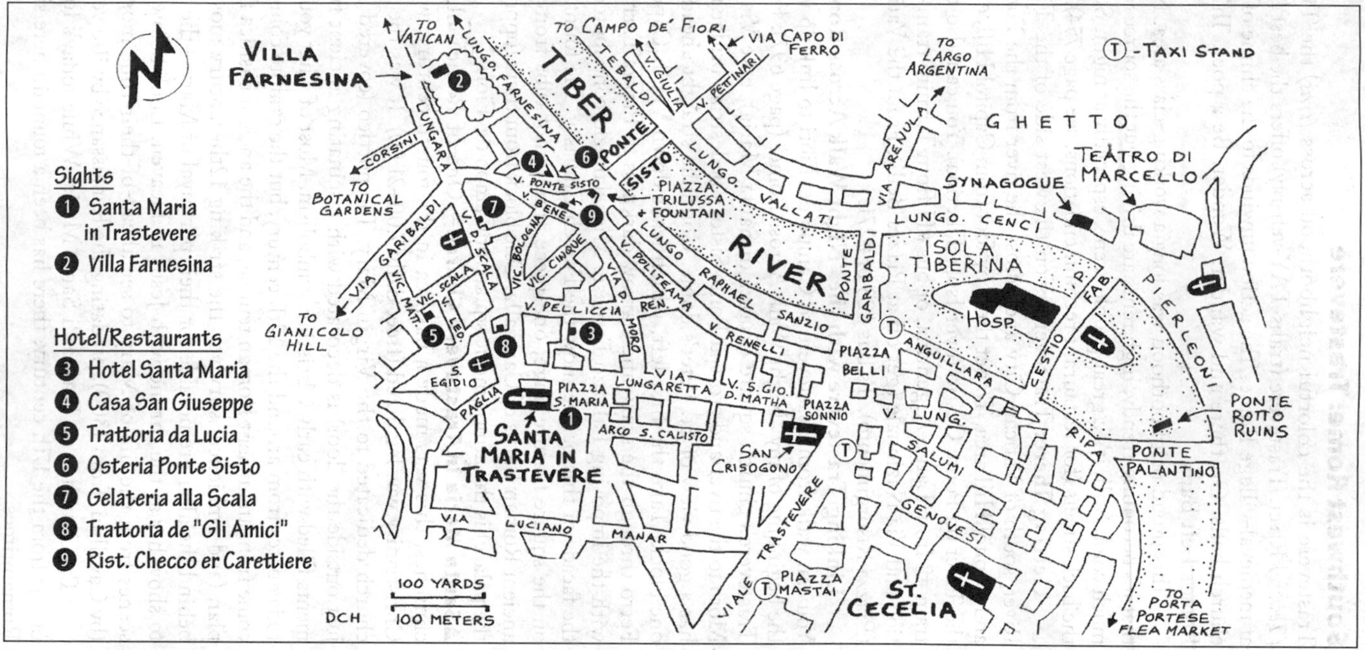
Sights
1 Santa Maria in Trastevere
2 Villa Farnesina
Hotel/Restaurants
3 Hotel Santa Maria
4 Casa San Giuseppe
5 Trattoria da Lucia
6 Osteria Ponte Sisto
7 Gelateria alla Scala
8 Trattoria de "Gli Amici"
9 Rist. Checco er Carettiere
T -Taxi Stand
Villa Farnesina
To Vatican
Lungo. Farnesina
Tiber
To Campo de' Fiori
Tebaldi
V. Giulia
V. Pettinari
Via Capo di Ferro
To Largo Argentina
Via Arenula
Ghetto
Synagogue
Teatro di Marcello
Lungara
Corsini
To Botanical Gardens
Ponte Sisto
V. Ponte Sisto
Piazza Trilussa + Fountain
Lungo. Vallati
Lungo. Cenci
V. Bene.
Via Garibaldi
V. D. Scala
Vic. Bologna
Vic. Cinque
Via D. Moro
V. Politeama
Lungo Raphael
River
Ponte Garibaldi
Isola Tiberina
Hosp.
P. Fab
Pierleoni
Cestio
Vic. Matt.
Vic. Scala
V. Leo.
To Gianicolo Hill
V. Pelliccia
Ren.
Sanzio
V. Renelli
Piazza Belli
Anguillara
S. Egidio
Paglia
Piazza S. Maria
Via Lungaretta
V. S. Gio. D. Matha
Piazza Sonnio
V. Lung.
Ponte Rotto Ruins
Santa Maria in Trastevere
Arco S. Calisto
San Crisogono
Salumi
Ripa
Ponte Palantino
Via Luciano
Manar
Viale Trastevere
Genovesi
Piazza Mastai
St. Cecelia
To Porta Portese Flea Market
100 Yards
100 Meters
DCH

▲Villa Farnesina—This sumptuous 16th-century Renaissance villa, built for a wealthy Sienese banker, is decorated with paintings by Baldassare Peruzzi and a lovesick Raphael (€5, Mon–Sat 9:00–13:00, closed Sun, Via della Lungara).

Porta Portese Flea Market (Mercato delle Pulci)—For antiques and fleas, this is the granddaddy of markets. This Sunday-morning market is long and spindly, running between the actual Porta Portese (a gate in the old town wall) and the Trastevere train station. Starting at Porta Portese, walk through the long, tacky parade of stalls selling cheap bras and shoes. Along the way, check out the con artists with the shell games. Each has shills in the crowd "winning big money" to get suckers involved. Hang on to your wallet—literally, in your front pocket. This is a den of thieves. The heart of the market for real flea-market junk (hiding a few little antique treasures) is the area from Piazza Ippolito Nievo to the Trastevere station (6:30–13:00 Sun only, on Via Portuense and Via Ippolito Nievo; to get to the market, catch bus #75 from Termini station or tram #3 from Largo Argentina; get off the bus or tram on Viale Trastevere and walk toward the river—and the noise).

Near Trastevere: Jewish Quarter

From the 16th through the 19th centuries, Rome's Jewish population was forced to live in a cramped ghetto at an often-flooded bend of the Tiber River. While the medieval Jewish ghetto is long gone, this area—just across the river and towards Capitol Hill from Trastevere—is still home to Rome's synagogue and fragments of its Jewish heritage.

Synagogue (Sinagoga) and Jewish Museum (Museo Ebraico)—Rome's modern synagogue stands proudly on the spot where the medieval Jewish community lived in squalor for over 300 years. The site of a historic visit by Pope John Paul II, this synagogue features a fine interior and a museum filled with artifacts of Rome's Jewish community (€7.50, includes synagogue and museum; May–Sept Sun–Thu 10:00–19:00, Fri 9:00–16:00, closed Sat; Oct–April Sun–Thu 10:00–17:00, Fri 9:00–14:00, closed Sat; on the riverbank road called Lungotevere dei Cenci near the bridge crossing Isola Tiberina, tel. 06-6840-0661).

South Rome

▲St. Paul's Outside the Walls (Basilica San Paolo Fuori le Mura)—This was the last major construction project of Imperial Rome (c. 380) and the largest church in Christendom until St. Peter's. After a tragic 19th-century fire, St. Paul's was rebuilt in the same general style and size as the original. Step inside and feel as close as you'll get in the 21st century to experiencing a monumental Roman basilica. Marvel at the ceiling, and imagine

South Rome

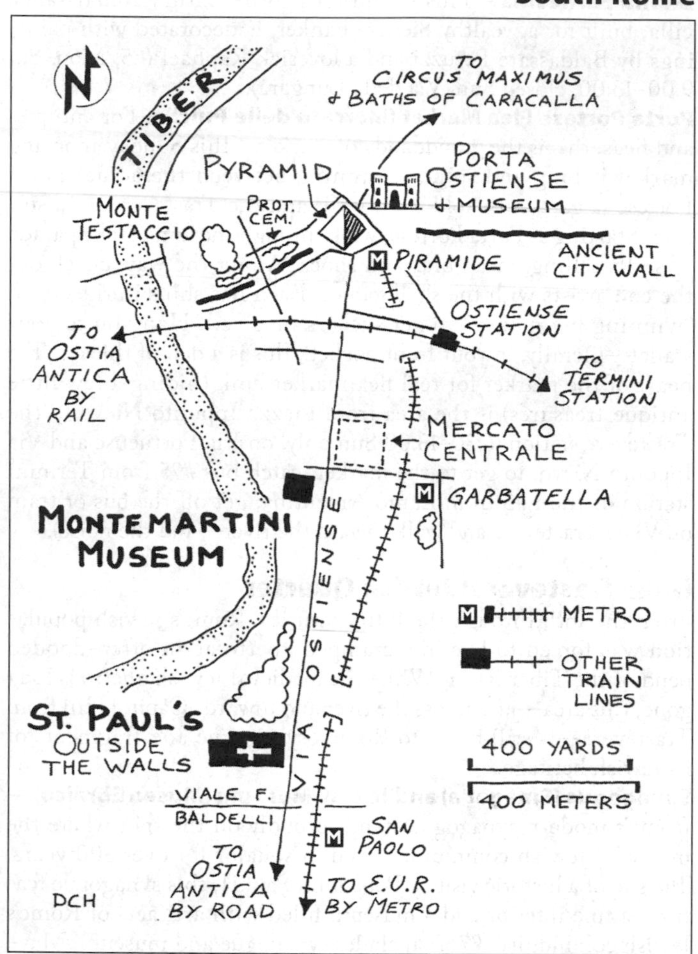

building it with those massive wood beams in A.D. 380.

It feels sterile, but in a good way—like you're already in heaven. Along with St. Peter's Basilica, San Giovanni in Laterano, and Santa Maria Maggiore, this church is part of the Vatican rather than Italy. The church is built upon the supposed grave of St. Paul, whose body is buried under the altar. (Paul was decapitated two miles from this spot, and his head is at San Giovanni in Laterano.)

Alabaster windows light the vast interior, and fifth-century mosaics decorate the triumphal arch leading to the altar. Mosaic portraits of 264 popes, from St. Peter to the present, ring the place—with blank spots ready to depict future popes. Pope #265—

Benedict XVI—should show up here any day now; find John Paul II (to right of the high altar: *Jo Paulus II*) and John Paul I (to his right, with a reign of 1 month and 3 days). Wander the ornate yet peaceful cloister—decorated with fragments from early Christian tombs and sarcophagi of people who wanted to be buried close to Paul (cloister closed 13:00–15:00).

The courtyard leading up to the church is typical of early Christian churches—even the first St. Peter's had this kind of welcoming zone (free, daily 7:00–18:00, modest dress code enforced, Via Ostiense 186, Metro: San Paolo).

▲Montemartini Museum (Musei Capitolini Centrale Montemartini)—This museum houses a dreamy collection of 400 ancient statues, set evocatively in a classic 1932 electric power plant, among generators and *Metropolis*-type cast-iron machinery. While the art is not as famous as the collections you'll see downtown, the effect is fun and memorable—and you'll encounter absolutely no tourists (€4.20, covered or discounted by Roma Pass, combo-ticket includes Capitol Hill Museum, Tue–Sun 9:00–20:00, closed Mon, last entry one hour before closing, Via Ostiense 106, a short walk from Metro: Garbatella, tel. 06-3996-7800, www.museicapitolini.org).

Baths of Caracalla (Terme di Caracalla)—Inaugurated by Emperor Caracalla in A.D. 216, this massive bath complex could accommodate 1,600 visitors at a time. Today it's just a shell—a huge shell—with all of its sculptures and most of its mosaics moved to museums. You'll see a two-story, roofless brick building surrounded by a garden, bordered by ruined walls. The two large rooms at either end of the building were used for exercise. In between the exercise rooms was a pool flanked by two small mosaic-floored dressing rooms. Niches in the walls once held statues.

In its day, this was a remarkable place to hang out. For ancient Romans, bathing was a social experience. The Baths of Caracalla functioned until Goths severed the aqueducts in the sixth century. In modern times, grand operas are performed here (€5, covered by Archeologia Card and discounted or covered by Roma Pass, Mon 9:00–14:00, Tue–Sun 9:00–19:30, last entry one hour before closing, audioguide-€4, good €8 guidebook can be read in shaded garden while sitting on a chunk of column, Metro: Circus Maximus, plus a 5-min walk south along Via delle Terme di Caracalla, tel. 06-3996-7700). The baths' statues are displayed elsewhere: several are in Rome's Octagonal Hall, and the immense *Toro Farnese* (a marble sculpture of a bull surrounded by people) snorts in Naples' Archaeological Museum.

Testaccio—In the gritty Testaccio neighborhood, four fascinating but lesser sights cluster at the Piramide Metro stop. Working-class since ancient times, the Testaccio neighborhood has recently gone

Testaccio

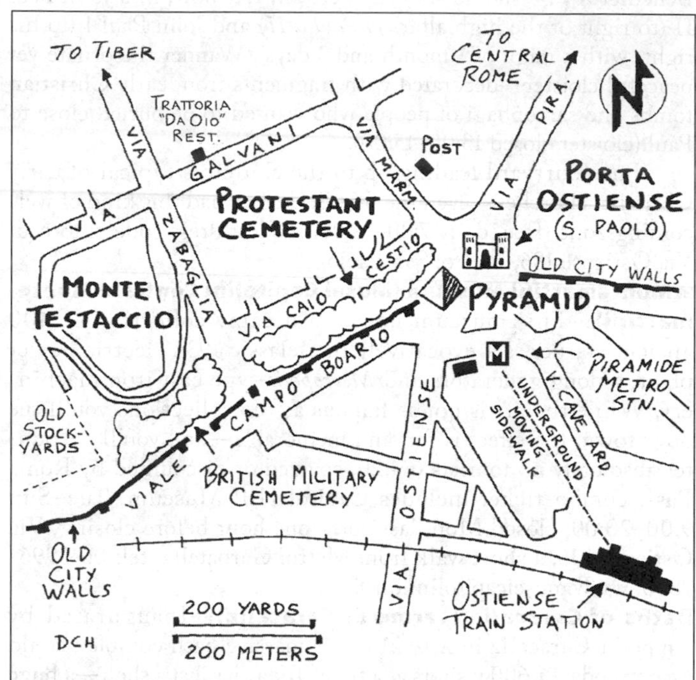

trendy-bohemian. Visitors wander through an awkward mix of yuppie and proletarian worlds, not noticing—but perhaps sensing—the "Keep Testaccio for the Testaccians" graffiti. This has long been the neighborhood of slaughterhouses, and its restaurants are renowned for their ability to cook up the least palatable part of the animals...the fifth quarter. For a meal you won't forget, try **Trattoria "Da Oio" A Casa Mia** (Mon–Sat 12:30–15:00 & 19:30–23:30, closed Sun, Via Galvani 43, tel. 06-578-2680).

High-end shoe and clothing boutiques are moving into the neighborhood, and this is now one of the best areas in Rome to have shoes custom-made. The Testaccio market (in the center) is hands-down the best, most authentic outdoor food market in Rome. This is where Romans shop while tourists flock to Campo de' Fiori.

Pyramid of Gaius Cestius: The Mark Antony/Cleopatra scandal (c. 30 B.C.) brought exotic Egyptian styles into vogue. A rich Roman magistrate, Gaius Cestius, had this pyramid built as his tomb. Made of brick covered in marble, it was completed in just 330 days (as stated in its Latin inscription) and fell far short of Egyptian pyramid standards. It was later incorporated into the Aurelian Wall, and it now stands as a marker to the entrance of

Testaccio (next to the Piramide Metro stop).

Porta Ostiense: This formidable gate (also next to Piramide Metro stop) is from the Aurelian Wall, begun in the third century under Emperor Aurelius. The wall, which encircled the city, was 12 miles long and 26 feet high, with 14 main gates and 380 72-foot-tall towers. Most of what you'll see today is circa A.D. 400, but the barbarians reconstructed the gate later, in the sixth century. If you climb up (enter nearest the pyramid), you can enjoy a free ramble along the ramparts and exhibits and models of Ostia Antica (Rome's ancient port) and the Ostian Way. (For more on the wall, visit the Museum of the Walls at Porta San Sebastian; see "Ancient Appian Way," later in this chapter.)

Protestant Cemetery: The Cemetery for the Burial of Non-Catholic Foreigners (Cimitero Acattolico per gli Stranieri al Testaccio) is a tomb-filled park, running along the wall just beyond the pyramid. The cemetery is also the only English-style landscape (rolling hills, calculated vistas) in Rome, and a favorite spot for quiet picnics and strolls. From the Piramide Metro stop, walk between the pyramid and the Roman gate on Via Persichetti, then go left on Caio Cestio to the gate of the cemetery. Ring the bell to get inside (donation box, Mon–Sat 9:00–16:40, until 15:40 in winter, closed Sun).

Originally, none of the Protestant epitaphs were allowed to make any mention of heaven. Signs direct visitors to the graves of notable non-Catholics who died in Rome since 1738. Many of the buried were diplomats. And many, such as the poets Shelley and Keats, were from the Romantic age. They came on the Grand Tour and—"captivated by the fatal charms of Rome," as Shelley wrote—never left. Head left toward the pyramid to find Keats' tomb, in the far corner. Keats died in his twenties, unrecognized. He wanted to be unnamed on a tomb that read, "Young English Poet, 1821. Here lies one whose name was writ in water." (To see Keats' tomb if the cemetery is closed, look through the tiny peephole on Via Caio Cestio, 10 yards off Via Marmarata.)

From inside the cemetery (nearest the pyramid), look down on Matilde Talli's cat hospice (flier at the gate). Volunteers use donations to care for these "Guardians of the Departed" who "provide loyal companionship to these dead."

Notice the beige travertine post office from 1932 (across the big street from cemetery). This is textbook Mussolini-era fascist architecture. The huge X design on the stairwells celebrates the 10th anniversary of the dictator's reign.

Monte Testaccio: Just behind the Protestant Cemetery (as you leave, turn left and continue 2 blocks down Caio Cestio) is a 115-foot-tall ancient trash mountain. It's made of broken *testae*—earthenware jars used to haul mostly oil 2,000 years ago, when this was a gritty port warehouse district. For 500 years, rancid oil vessels were discarded here. Slowly, Rome's lowly eighth hill was built. Because the caves dug into the hill stay cool, trendy bars, clubs, and restaurants compete with gritty car-repair places for a spot. The neighborhood was once known for a huge slaughterhouse and a Gypsy camp that squatted inside an old military base. Now it's home to the Testaccio Village, a site for concerts and techno-raves. The night scene at Monte Testaccio after 21:00 is youthful and lively with restaurants and clubs (Metro: Piramide).

Ancient Appian Way (Via Appia Antica)

Since the fourth century B.C., this has been Rome's gateway to the East. The wonder of its day, the Appian Way was the largest, widest, fastest road ever, called the "Queen of Roads." Eventually, this most important of Roman roads stretched 430 miles to the port of Brindisi—where boats sailed for Greece and Egypt. Twenty-nine such roads fanned out from Rome. Just as Hitler built the autobahn system in anticipation of empire maintenance, the emperors realized the military and political value of a good road system. A central strip accommodated animal-powered vehicles, and elevated sidewalks served pedestrians. The first section (near Rome) was perfectly straight, and lined with tombs and funerary monuments. Imagine a funeral procession passing under the pines and cypresses and past a long line of pyramids, private mini-temples, altars, and tombs.

Hollywood created the famous image of the Appian Way lined with the crucified bodies of Spartacus and his gang of slave rebels. This image is only partially accurate—Spartacus was killed in battle.

Today the road and the landscape around it are preserved as a cultural park, providing one of the best respites from the city for strolling or biking—especially on Sundays, when its active stretch closest to the city is closed to traffic and opened to people.

Tourist's Appian Way: The road starts less than two miles south of the Colosseum at the massive San Sebastian Gate. The **Museum of the Walls,** located at the gate, offers an interesting look at Roman defense and a chance to scramble along a stretch of the ramparts (€2.60, covered or discounted by Roma Pass, Tue–Sun 9:00–14:00, closed Mon, last entry 30 min before closing, tel. 06-7047-5284). A mile and a half down the road are the two most historic and popular catacombs, those of San Callisto and San Sebastian, described later in this section. (More intimate, less crowded, and at the other end of town—north of the Villa Borghese—are the Catacombs of Priscilla; see page 721.)

Besides the two main catacombs, the Appian Way offers additional catacombs, ruins, and tombs. As you head north on

Appian Way

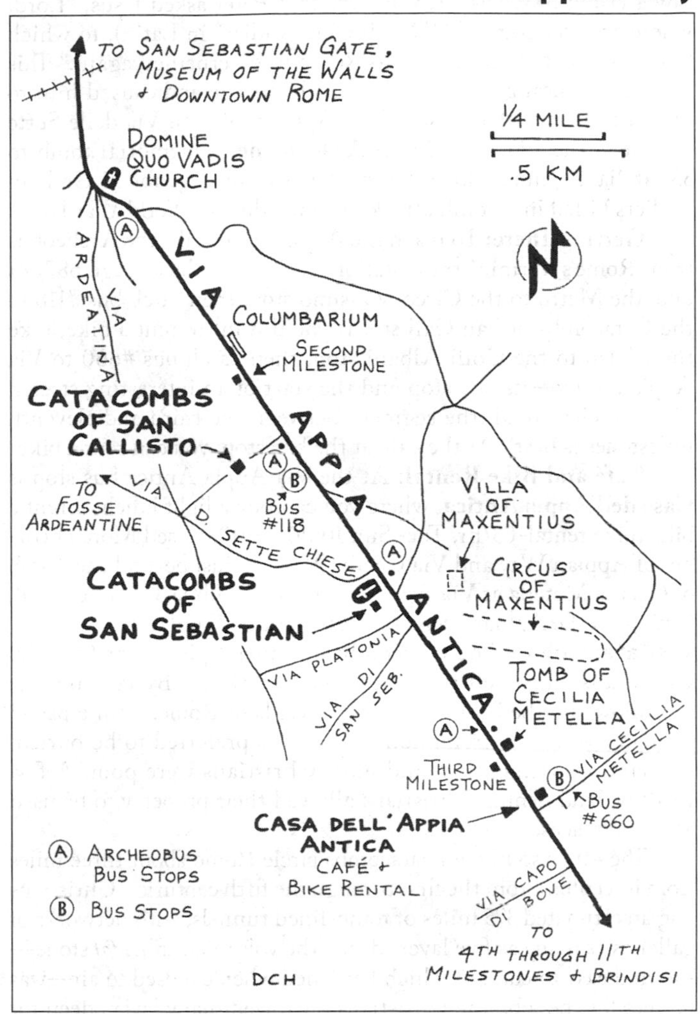

the Appian Way (from its intersection with Via Cecilia Metella) towards the Catacombs of San Sebastian, you can't miss on the right the massive cylindrical **Tomb of Cecilia Metella** (€2, covered by Archeologia Card), one of the best preserved of the many tombs of prominent Romans that line the road. Just past the tomb on the right are the ruins of the **Villa and Circus of Maxentius** (the emperor defeated by Constantine in A.D. 312). Farther along the Appian Way, past the Catacombs of San Sebastian and San Callisto, you'll see the **Church of Domine Quo Vadis,** built on the spot where Peter, while fleeing the city to escape Nero's persecution, saw a vision of Christ. It was here that Peter asked Jesus, "Lord, where are you going?" ("Domine quo vadis?" in Latin), to which Christ replied, "I am going to Rome to be crucified again." This miraculous sign gave Peter faith and courage and caused him to return to Rome. And just off the Appian Way on Via delle Sette Chiese is the evocative **Fosse Ardeantine,** a memorial tomb to 335 Italians gunned down by the Nazis as revenge for 32 German soldiers killed in a bomb attack in Rome during World War II.

Getting There: To reach the Appian Way, take the Archeobus from Rome's Termini train station (see "Archeobus," page 687) or take the Metro to the Circo Massimo stop, then catch bus #118 to the Catacombs of San Callisto. If you'll want to rent a bike, take the Metro to the Colli Albani stop, then catch bus #660 to Via Appia Antica—its last stop and the start of an interesting stretch of the ancient road (the segment between the third and eleventh milestones is best). At the café at the bus stop, you can rent a bike.

Café and Bike Rental: At the Via Appia Antica bus stop is **Casa dell'Appia Antica,** where you can buy a light lunch or rent a bike (bike rental-€3/hr, Tue–Sun 10:00–18:00, closed Mon, at corner of Appian Way and Via Cecilia Metella, just beyond the Tomb of Cecilia Metella at Via Appia Antica 175, mobile 338-3465-440). Biking on the Appian Way is a treat (best on Sundays).

▲▲Catacombs—The catacombs are burial places for (mostly) Christians who died in ancient Roman times. By law, no one was allowed to be buried within the walls of Rome. While pagan Romans were into cremation, Christians preferred to be buried. But land was expensive, and most Christians were poor. A few wealthy, landowning Christians allowed their property to be used as burial places.

The 40 or so known catacombs circle Rome about three miles from its center. From the first through the fifth centuries, Christians dug an estimated 375 miles of tomb-lined tunnels, with networks of galleries as many as five layers deep. The volcanic tuff *(tufo)* stone—soft and easy to cut, but which hardened when exposed to air—was perfect for the job. The Christians burrowed many layers deep for two reasons: to get more mileage out of the donated land, and to be near martyrs and saints already buried there. Bodies were wrapped in linen (like Christ's). Since they figured the Second Coming was imminent, there was no interest in embalming the body.

When Emperor Constantine legalized Christianity in A.D. 313, Christians had a new, interesting problem: There would be no more persecuted martyrs to bind them together and inspire them. Instead, the early martyrs and popes assumed more importance, and Christians began making pilgrimages to their burial places in the catacombs.

In the 800s, when barbarian invaders started ransacking the

tombs, Christians moved the relics of saints and martyrs to the safety of churches in the city center. For a thousand years, the catacombs were forgotten. Around 1850, they were excavated and became part of the Romantic Age's Grand Tour of Europe.

When abandoned plates and utensils from ritual meals were found, 18th- and 19th-century Romantics guessed that persecuted Christians hid out in these candlelit galleries. This legend grew—even though it was untrue. By the second century, more than a million people lived in Rome, and the 10,000 early Christians no longer had to camp out in the catacombs. They hid in plain view, melting into obscurity within the city itself.

The underground tunnels, while empty of bones, are rich in early Christian symbolism, which functioned as a secret language. The dove represented the soul. You'll see it quenching its thirst (worshipping), with an olive branch (at rest), or happily perched (in paradise). Peacocks, known for their "incorruptible flesh," embodied immortality. The shepherd with a lamb on his shoulders was the "good shepherd," the first portrayal of Christ as a kindly leader of his flock. The fish was used because the first letters of these words—"Jesus Christ, Son of God, Savior"—spelled "fish" in Greek. And the anchor is a cross in disguise. A second-century bishop had written on his tomb: "All who understand these things, pray for me." You'll see pictures of people praying with their hands raised up—the custom at the time.

Catacomb tours are essentially the same; which one you take is not important. The **Catacombs of San Callisto** (a.k.a. Callixtus), the official cemetery for the Christians of Rome and the burial place of third-century popes, is the most historic. Sixteen bishops (early popes) were buried here. Buy your €5 ticket and wait for your language to be called. They move lots of people quickly. If one group seems ridiculously large (more than 50 people), wait for the next tour in English (Thu–Tue 8:30–12:00 & 14:30–17:30, closed Wed and Feb, closes at 17:00 in winter, Via Appia Antica 110, tel. 06-5130-1580). Dig this: The catacombs have a website—www.catacombe.roma.it—that focuses mainly on San Callisto, featuring photos, site info, and history.

The **Catacombs of San Sebastian** (Sebastiano) are 300 yards farther south down the road (€5, Mon–Sat 8:30–12:00 & 14:30–17:30, closed Sun and Nov, closes at 17:00 in winter, Via Appia Antica 136, tel. 06-785-0350).

SLEEPING

The absolute cheapest beds in Rome are €20 in small, backpacker-filled hostels. A nicer hotel (around €130 with a bathroom and air-con) provides an oasis and refuge, making it easier to enjoy this

Sleep Code

(€1 = about $1.30, country code: 39)
S = Single, **D** = Double/Twin, **T** = Triple, **Q** = Quad, **b** = bathroom, **s** = shower only. Breakfast is included in all but the cheapest places. Unless I note otherwise, the staff speaks English. You can assume a hotel takes credit cards unless you see "cash only" in the listing.

To help you sort easily through these listings, I've divided the rooms into three categories based on the price for a standard double room with bath:

$$$ **Higher Priced**—Most rooms €180 or more.
$$ **Moderately Priced**—Most rooms between €120–180.
$ **Lower Priced**—Most rooms €120 or less.

intense and grinding city. If you're going door to door, prices are soft—so bargain. Built into a hotel's official price list is a kickback for a room-finding service or agency; if you're coming direct, they pay no kickback and may lower the price for you. Many hotels have high-season (mid-March–June, Sept–Oct) and low-season prices. If traveling outside of peak times, ask about a discount. Room rates are lowest in sweltering August. Easter, September, and Christmas are most crowded and expensive. On Easter (March 23 in 2008) and other major religious holidays, the entire city can get booked up.

Traffic in Rome roars. With the recent arrival of double-paned windows and air-conditioning, night noise is not the problem it once was. Even so, light sleepers who ask for a *tranquillo* room will likely get a room on the back...and sleep better.

As you look over the listings, you'll notice that many hotels promise special prices to my readers who book directly (without using a room-finding service, which takes a commission). To get these rates, mention this book when you reserve, then show the book upon arrival. During slow times, rooms might be offered for even less than listed. To get the best price, first ask the price, then request the discount with the book. Many places prefer hard cash. "Rack rates" (the highest rates a hotel charges) are much higher.

Most hotels are eager to connect you with a shuttle service to the airport. It's reasonable and easy for departure, but upon arrival, I just catch a cab or the train into the city.

Almost no hotels have parking, but nearly all have a line on spots in a nearby garage (about €24/day).

Bed-and-breakfasts are booming in Rome, offering comfy doubles in the old center for €75–110. The Beehive is a good contact for booking B&Bs in Rome (www.cross-pollinate.com, page 746).

Although I list only five, Rome has many convents that rent out rooms. See the Church of Santa Susanna's website for a long list (www.santasusanna.org, select "Coming to Rome," then "Convents"). At convents, the beds are twins and English is often in short supply, but the price is right.

Consider these nun-run places, all listed in greater detail below: the expensive but divine **Casa di Santa Brigida** (near Campo de' Fiori), the **Suore di Santa Elisabetta** and the **Istituto Il Rosario** (both near Basilica Santa Maria Maggiore), **Casa San Giuseppe** (secular but convent-owned, in Trastevere), and the most user-friendly of all, **Casa per Ferie Santa Maria alle Fornaci dei Padri Trinitari** (near the Vatican).

Via Firenze

I generally stay on Via Firenze because it's safe, handy, central, and relatively quiet. It's a 10-minute walk from the Termini train station and the airport shuttle, and two blocks beyond Piazza della Repubblica and the TI. The Defense Ministry is nearby, so you've got heavily armed guards watching over you all night.

The neighborhood is well-connected by public transportation (with the Repubblica Metro stop nearby). Virtually all the city buses that rumble down Via Nazionale (#64, #70, #115, #640, and the #40 express) take you to Piazza Venezia (Forum) and Largo Argentina (Pantheon). From Largo Argentina, electric trolley #8 goes to Trastevere (get off at first stop after crossing the river) and the #64 bus (jammed with people and thieves) and the #40 express bus both continue to St. Peter's.

A 24-hour **pharmacy** near the recommended hotels is Farmacia Piram (Via Nazionale 228, tel. 06-488-4437).

$$ Hotel Oceania is a peaceful slice of air-conditioned heaven. This 15-room, manor house–type hotel is spacious and quiet, with spotless, tastefully decorated rooms, run by a pleasant father-and-son team. While Armando (the dad) serves world-famous coffee, Stefano (the son) works to give their hotel all the extra touches, including a plasma TV in the lounge for guests to watch classic movies set in Rome...and Italy episodes from my TV series (Sb-€118, Db-€148, Tb-€178, Qb-€198, 25 percent less in Aug and winter, large roof terrace, family suite, Via Firenze 38, third floor, tel. 06-482-4696, fax 06-488-5586, www.hoteloceania.it, info@hoteloceania.it; Anna, Radu, and Enrico round out the staff).

$$ Hotel Aberdeen, which perfectly combines high quality and friendliness, is warmly run by Annamaria, with support from cousins Sabrina and Cinzia and sister Laura. The 37 comfy, modern, air-conditioned, and smoke-free rooms are a terrific value. Enjoy the frescoed breakfast room (Sb-€92, Db-€140, Tb-€155, Qb-€190, 30 percent less in Aug and winter, check website for

Hotels in East Rome

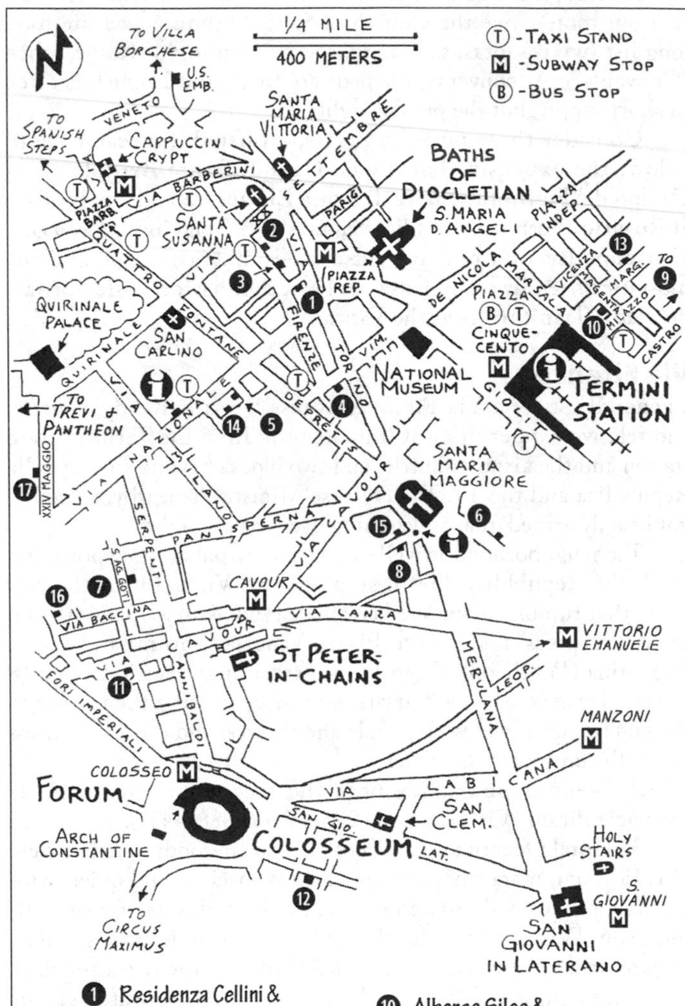

1. Residenza Cellini & Residence Adler
2. Hotels Oceania & Nardizzi
3. Hotel Aberdeen
4. Hotel Sonya
5. Hotel Pensione Italia
6. Hotel Montreal
7. Istituto Il Rosario
8. Suore di Santa Elisabetta
9. To Gulliver's Place B&B
10. Albergo Sileo & Fawlty Towers Hostel
11. Hotel Paba
12. Hotel Lancelot
13. The Beehive Hostel
14. Gulliver's House Hostel
15. Casa Olmata Hostel
16. Hotel Nerva
17. Hotel Giardino

deals, Via Firenze 48, tel. 06-482-3920, fax 06-482-1092, www.travel.it/roma/aberdeen, hotel.aberdeen@travel.it).

$$ Residenza Cellini is a gorgeous 11-room place that feels like the guest wing of a neoclassical palace. It offers "ortho/anti-allergy beds" and four-star comforts and service (Db-€170, larger Db-€190, Tb-€195–215, family apartment-€215, extra bed-€25, €35 less in Aug and mid-Nov–mid-March, air-con, terrace, elevator, Internet access, Via Modena 5, tel. 06-4782-5204, fax 06-4788-1806, www.residenzacellini.it, residenzacellini@tin.it, Barbara, Gaetano, and Donato).

$$ Residence Adler offers breakfast on a garden patio, wide halls, and eight quiet, simple, air-conditioned rooms in a good location. It's run the old-fashioned way by a charming family (Db-€125, Tb-€160, Qb-€190, Quint/b-€195, 5 percent off if you pay with cash, 15 percent less in Aug and winter, elevator, Via Modena 5, second floor, tel. 06-484-466, fax 06-488-0940, www.hoteladler-roma.com, info@hoteladler-roma.com, Alessandro).

$ Hotel Nardizzi Americana offers 33 pleasant, air-conditioned rooms—some with garden views—which are a fine value. This loosely run place also has a delightful rooftop terrace (Sb-€95, Db-€120, Tb-€145, Qb-€160, 15 percent discounts for off-season and long stays, additional 10 percent off with cash, elevator, Internet access, Via Firenze 38, fourth floor, tel. 06-488-0035, fax 06-488-0368, www.hotelnardizzi.it, info@hotelnardizzi.it).

Between Via Nazionale and Santa Maria Maggiore

$$ Hotel Sonya is small and family-run but impersonal, with 23 well-equipped rooms, a central location, and decent prices (Sb-€90, Db-€130, Tb-€145, Qb-€165, Quint/b-€185, 5 percent less if you pay cash, 30 percent less off-season, air-con, elevator, faces the opera at Via Viminale 58, Metro: Repubblica or Termini, tel. 06-481-9911, fax 06-488-5678, www.hotelsonya.it, info@hotelsonya.it, Francesca).

$ Hotel Pensione Italia, in a busy, interesting, and handy locale, is placed safely on a quiet street next to the Ministry of the Interior. Thoughtfully run by Andrea, Sabrina, Nadine, and Gabriel, it has 31 comfortable, clean, bright, non-smoking rooms (Sb-€80, Db-€120, Tb-€155, Qb-€180, all rooms 30 percent less mid-July–Aug and Nov–mid-March, air-con-€10 extra per day, elevator, Internet access, Via Venezia 18, just off Via Nazionale, Metro: Repubblica or Termini, tel. 06-482-8355, fax 06-474-5550, www.hotelitaliaroma.com, info@hotelitaliaroma.com). They also have eight decent annex rooms across the street.

$ Hotel Montreal, run with care, is a bright, solid, business-class place with 27 rooms on a big street a block southeast of Santa

Maria Maggiore (Sb-€95, Db-€120, Tb-€150; in July–Aug and Jan-Feb rates drop to Db-€95, Tb-€130; air-con, elevator, Internet access, good security, Via Carlo Alberto 4, 1 block from Metro: Vittorio Emanuele, 3 blocks west of Termini train station, tel. 06-445-7797, fax 06-446-5522, www.hotelmontrealroma.com, info@hotelmontrealroma.com).

$ Suore di Santa Elisabetta is a heavenly Polish-run convent with a peaceful garden and tidy rooms. Often booked long in advance, it's a super value (S-€38, Sb-€46, D-€61, Db-€79, Tb-€101, Qb-€122, Quint/b-€132, 23:00 curfew, elevator, fine view roof terrace, a block southwest of Santa Maria Maggiore at Via dell'Olmata 9, Metro: Termini or Vittorio Emanuele, tel. 06-488-8271, fax 06-488-4066, ist.it.s.elisabetta@libero.it).

$ Casa Olmata is a ramshackle, laid-back backpackers' place a block southwest of Santa Maria Maggiore, midway between the Termini train station and Colosseum (dorm beds-€20, S-€38, D-€57, family room-€61, laundry service, Internet access, video rentals, games, rooftop terrace with views and nearly free dinner parties, famous twice-weekly spaghetti parties, communal kitchen, Via dell'Olmata 36, third floor, Metro: Vittorio Emanuele, tel. 06-483-019, fax 06-486-819, www.casaolmata.com, info@casaolmata.com, Mirella and Marco).

$ Gulliver's House Rome, run by helpful Simon and Sara, is a fun little hostel in a safe and handy location. Its 24 beds in cramped quarters work fine for backpackers. They host English-language movie evenings nightly in their lounge—you can start off the evening with my TV shows on Rome (€22 per bunk in 8-bed dorm, €25 per bunk in 6-bed dorm, one D-€75, cash only, includes breakfast, closed 12:00–16:00, 1:00 curfew, small kitchen, Via Palermo 36, tel. 06-481-7680, www.gulliversh ouse.com, stay@gullivershouse.com).

$ Gulliver's Place B&B, run by Gulliver's House Rome, has five fun, nicely decorated rooms in a large, secure building next to a university (D-€80, Db-€90, Tb-€120, less off-season, air-con, elevator, east of Termini train station, Viale Castro Pretorio 25, Metro: Castro Pretorio, www.gulliversplace.com, stay@gulliversplace.com).

Sleeping Cheaply, Northeast of the Train Station

The cheapest beds in town are northeast of the Termini train station (Metro: Termini). Some travelers feel this area is weird and spooky after dark, but these hotels feel plenty safe. With your back to the train tracks, turn right and walk two blocks out of the station.

$ The Beehive gives vagabonds—old and young—a cheap, clean, and comfy home in Rome, thoughtfully and creatively run by a friendly young American couple, Steve and Linda. They offer six great-value, artsy-mod double rooms (D-€75) and an eight-bed dorm (€22 bunks, Internet, private garden terrace, cheery café, 2 blocks north of Termini train station at Via Marghera 8, tel. 06-4470-4553, www.the-beehive.com, info@the-beehive.com). Steve and Linda also run a B&B booking service (private rooms and apartments in the old center of Rome, Florence, and Venice; rates start at €30 per person, check out your options at www.cross-pollinate.com).

$ Albergo Sileo, with shiny chandeliers, has a contract to house train conductors who work the night shift—so its 10 simple, pleasant rooms are usually rentable from 19:00 to 9:00 only (though sometimes you can get one for the full day). If you can handle this, it's a wonderful value. During the day, they store your luggage, and though you won't have access to a room, you're welcome to shower or hang out in the lobby or bar (D-€55, Db-€65, Tb-€75, Db for 24 hours-€70 when available, elevator, Via Magenta 39, fourth floor, tel. & fax 06-445-0246, www.hotelsileo.com, info@hotelsileo.com, friendly Alessandro and Maria Savioli don't speak English, but their daughter Anna does).

$ Fawlty Towers Hostel is well-run and ideal for backpackers arriving by train. It offers 50 beds and lots of fun, games, and extras (4-bed coed dorms-€22 per person, S-€47, D-€65, Db-€80, Q-€90, includes sheets, from station walk a block down Via Marghera and turn right to Via Magenta 39, tel. & fax 06-4543-8781, www.fawltytowers.org, info@fawltytowers.org). Their nearby annex, Bubbles, offers similar beds and rates and shares the same reception desk.

Near the Colosseum

$$ Hotel Paba has seven rooms, chocolate-box-tidy and lovingly cared for by Alberta Castelli. Though it overlooks busy Via Cavour just two blocks from the Colosseum, it's quiet enough (Db-€135, extra bed-€40, 5 percent discount for cash, huge beds, breakfast served in room, air-con, elevator, Via Cavour 266, Metro: Cavour, tel. 06-4782-4902, fax 06-4788-1225, www.hotelpaba.com, info@hotelpaba.com).

$$ Hotel Lancelot is a homey refuge—a 60-room hotel with the ambience of a B&B. It's quiet and safe, with a shady courtyard, bar, communal sixth-floor terrace, and restaurant. Some rooms have private terraces big enough to host friends. Well-run by Faris and Lubna Khan, it's popular with returning guests (Sb-€115, Db-€175, Tb-€198, Qb-€235, €15 extra for first-floor terrace room, €20 extra for sixth floor, air-con, elevator, wheelchair access, parking-€15/day, behind Colosseum near San Clemente Church at Via Capo d'Africa 47, tel. 06-7045-0615, fax 06-7045-0640, www.lancelothotel.com, info@lancelothotel.com, Lubna speaks the Queen's English).

Near Campo de' Fiori

You'll pay a premium (and endure a little extra night noise) to stay in the old center. But each of these places is romantically set deep in the tangled back streets near the idyllic Campo de' Fiori and, for many, worth the extra money.

$$$ Casa di Santa Brigida overlooks the elegant Piazza Farnese. With soft-spoken sisters gliding down polished hallways, and pearly gates instead of doors, this lavish 23-room convent makes exhaust-stained Roman tourists feel like they've died and gone to heaven. If you don't need a double bed, this is worth the splurge (Sb-€110, twin Db-€190, 3 percent extra if you pay with credit card, air-con, tasty €20 dinners, roof garden, plush library, Monserrato 54, tel. 06-6889-2596, fax 06-6889-1573, hesselblad @tiscalinet.it, many of the sisters are from India and speak English). If you get no response to your fax or email within three days, consider that a "no."

$$ Hotel Smeraldo, with 50 rooms, is well-run, clean, and a great deal (Sb-€100, Db-€130, Tb-€150, 25 percent less off-season, buffet breakfast-€7, centrally controlled air-con, elevator, flowery roof terrace, Vicolo dei Chiodaroli 9, midway between Campo de' Fiori and Largo Argentina, tel. 06-687-5929, fax 06-6880-5495, www.smeraldoroma.com, albergosmeraldoroma@tin.it, Massimo).

$ Hotel in Parione, run by Hotel Smeraldo, crams 16 modern, high-ceilinged rooms into a tiny, adjacent building. It offers similar amenities and a fabulous location (Sb-€95, Db-€120, €25 less off-season, breakfast-€7 extra, air-con, elevator, roof terrace, Via dei Chiavari 32, tel. 06-6880-2560, fax 06-683-4094, www.inparione.com, info@inparione.com).

In the Jewish Quarter

$$ Hotel Arenula, with 50 decent rooms, is the only hotel in Rome's old Jewish ghetto. While it has the ambience of a gym and attracts lots of students, it's a fine value in the thick of old Rome (Sb-€95, Db-€128, Tb-€149, about 25 percent less off-season, extra bed-€21, air-con, just off Via Arenula at Via Santa Maria de' Calderari 47, tel. 06-687-9454, fax 06-689-6188, www.hotelarenula.com, hotel.arenula@flashnet.it, Rosanna).

Near the Pantheon

These places are buried in the pedestrian-friendly heart of ancient Rome, each within a four-minute walk of the Pantheon. You'll pay more here—but you'll save time and money by being exactly where you want to be for your early and late wandering.

$$$ Hotel Nazionale, a four-star landmark, is a 16th-century palace that shares a well-policed square with the Parliament building. Its 92 rooms are accentuated by lush public spaces, fancy bars, a uniformed staff, and a marble-floored restaurant. It's a big, stuffy hotel with a revolving front door, but it's a worthy splurge if you want security, comfort, and ancient Rome at your doorstep (Sb-€210, Db-€325, giant deluxe Db-€450, extra person-€65; less in Aug, winter, and when slow—check online for summer and weekend discounts; air-con, elevator, Piazza Montecitorio 131, tel. 06-695-001, fax 06-678-6677, www.nazionaleroma.it, hotel @nazionaleroma.it).

$$$ Albergo Santa Chiara is big, solid, and hotelesque, offering marbled elegance (but basic furniture) and all the hotel services in the old center. Its ample public lounges are dressy and professional, and its 100 rooms are quiet and spacious (Sb-€145, Db-€200, Tb-€250, book online to get these special Rick Steves rates, check website for other deals, elevator, behind Pantheon at Via di Santa Chiara 21, tel. 06-687-2979, fax 06-687-3144, www .albergosantachiara.com, info@albergosantachiara.com).

$$$ Hotel Due Torri, hiding out on a tiny, quiet street, is a little overpriced but beautifully located. It feels professional yet homey, with an accommodating staff, generous public spaces, and 26 comfortable rooms (Sb-€118, Db-€190, family apartment-€250 for 3 and €275 for 4, air-con, Vicolo del Leonetto 23, a block off Via della Scrofa, tel. 06-6880-6956, fax 06-686-5442, www .hotelduetorriroma.com, hotelduetorri@interfree.it).

Near Piazza Venezia

To locate these hotels, see the map on page 744.

$$ Hotel Giardino, thoughtfully run by Englishwoman Kate (and Sergio), offers 11 pleasant rooms in a central location three blocks northeast of Piazza Venezia. With no central lobby and a small breakfast room, it suits travelers who prize location over big-hotel amenities (March–mid-July and Sept–mid-Nov: Sb-€85, Db-€130; mid-July–Aug and mid-Nov–Feb: Sb-€60, Db-€90; check website for specials, air-con, double-paned windows, on a busy street off Piazza di Quirinale, Via XXIV Maggio 51, tel. 06-679-4584, fax 06-679-5155, www.hotel-giardino-roma.com, info @hotel-giardino-roma.com).

$ Istituto Il Rosario is a peaceful, well-run Dominican convent renting 40 rooms to both pilgrims and tourists in a good neighborhood (S-€39, Sb-€49, Db-€84, Tb-€115, Qb-€150, 23:00 curfew, roof terrace, midway between the Quirinale and Colosseum near bottom of Via Nazionale at Via Sant'Agata dei Goti 10, bus #40 or #64 from Termini, tel. 06-679-2346, fax 06-6994-1106, irodopre@tin.it).

Hotels in the Heart of Rome

Trastevere

Colorful and genuine in a gritty sort of way, Trastevere is a treat for travelers looking for a less touristy and more bohemian atmosphere. Choices are few here, but by trekking across the Tiber, you can have the experience of being comfortably immersed in old Rome. To locate the following two places, see the map on page 732.

$$$ Hotel Santa Maria sits like a lazy hacienda in the midst of Trastevere. Surrounded by a medieval skyline, you'll feel as if you're on some romantic stage set. Its 19 small but well-equipped, air-conditioned rooms—former cells in a cloister—are all on the ground floor, as are a few suites for up to six people. The rooms circle a gravelly courtyard of orange trees and stay-awhile patio furniture (Db-€180, Tb-€220, you must pay cash and stay at least three nights to get these 20–25 percent discounted rates; you'll pay more for shorter stays and credit-card payment, smaller discounts off-season, free loaner bikes and Internet access for guests, face church on Piazza Maria Trastevere and go right half a block to Vicolo del Piede 2, tel. 06-589-4626, fax 06-589-4815, www.htlsantamaria.com, hotelsantamaria@libero.it, Stefano).

$$ Casa San Giuseppe is down a characteristic, laundry-strewn lane with views of Aurelian walls. While convent-owned, it's a secular place renting 25 plain but peaceful, spacious, and spotless rooms (Sb-€110, Db-€150, Tb-€180, Qb-€210, street-facing rooms are noisy, air-con, elevator, parking-€10, just north of Piazza Trilussa, Vicolo Moroni 22, tel. 06-5833-3490, fax 06-5833-5754, casasangiuseppe@virgilio.it).

Near the Vatican Museum

Sleeping near the Vatican is expensive, but some enjoy calling this neighborhood home. Even though it's handy to the Vatican (when the rapture hits, you're right there), everything else is a long way away.

$$$ Hotel Sant'Anna is pricey, but located on a charming pedestrian street that fills up with restaurant tables at dinnertime. Its 20 comfy rooms, decorated with classical themes, are somewhere between tasteful and too much (Sb-€160, Db-€220; Db discounted to €150 in July–Aug, winter, and slow times; any time of year, ask for 10 percent Rick Steves discount; air-con, elevator, courtyard, Borgo Pio 133, near intersection with Mascherino, a couple blocks from entrance to St. Peter's, tel. 06-6880-1602, fax 06-6830-8717, www.hotelsantanna.com, santanna@travel.it, Viscardo).

$$$ Hotel Bramante sits like a grand medieval lodge in the shadow of the fortified escape wall that runs from the Vatican to Castel Sant'Angelo. The public spaces and 16 thoughtfully appointed rooms are generously sized, with rough wood beams and high ceilings (Sb-€160, Db-€220, Tb-€230, Qb-€240, air-con, no elevator, Vicolo delle Palline 24, tel. 06-6880-6426, fax 06-681-33339, www.hotelbramante.com, hotelbramante@libero.it, Maurizio and Loredana).

$$$ Hotel Alimandi Vaticano, facing the Vatican Museum, is beautifully designed. Run by the Alimandi family (see next listing), it features four stars, 24 spacious rooms, and all the modern comforts you can imagine (Sb-€160, standard Db-€190, big Db with 2 double beds-€220, Tb-€250, 5 percent discount with cash, air-con, elevator, Viale Vaticano 99, Metro: Cipro–Musei Vaticani, tel. 06-397-45562, fax 06-397-30132, www.alimandi.com, hotelali@hotelalimandie.191.it).

$$ Hotel Alimandi is a good value, run by the friendly and entrepreneurial Alimandi brothers—Paolo, Enrico, and Luigi—

Hotels and Restaurants in the Vatican Area

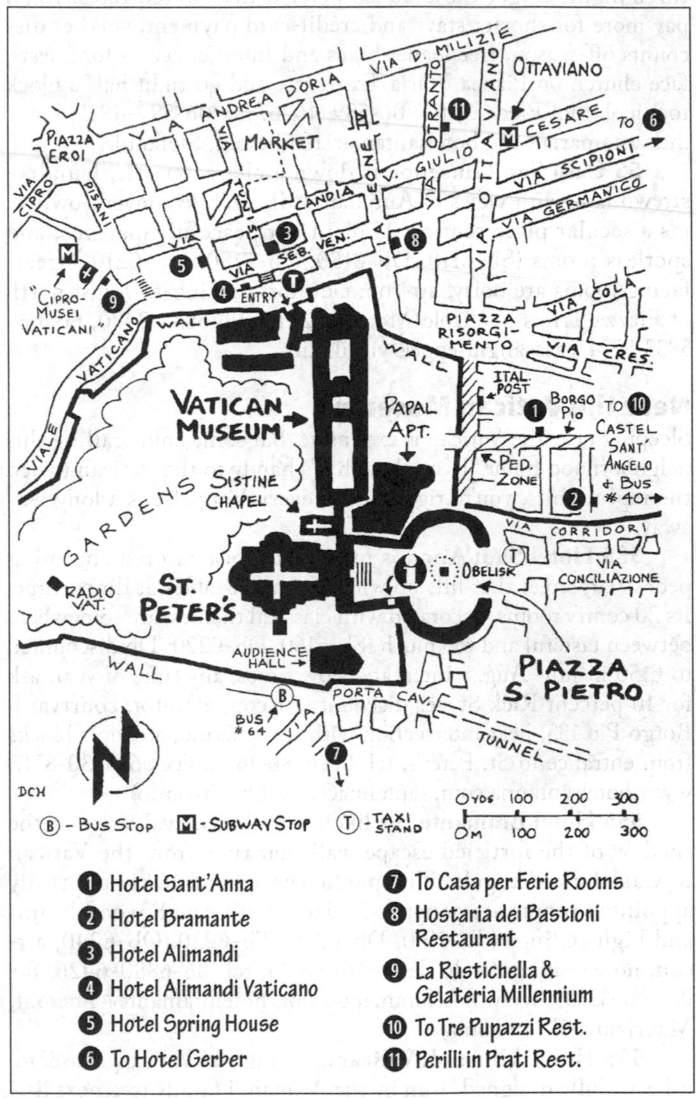

and the next generation, Marta, Irene, Barbara, and Germano. Their 35 rooms are air-conditioned, modern, and marbled in white (Sb-€90, Db-€160, Tb-€190, 5 percent discount for cash, closed Jan–mid-Feb, elevator, grand buffet breakfast served in great roof garden, small gym, pool table, piano lounge, down the stairs directly in front of Vatican Museum, Via Tunisi 8, Metro: Cipro–Musei Vaticani, reserve by phone, tel. 06-3972-6300, toll-free in Italy tel. 800-122-121, fax 06-3972-3943, www.alimandi.com, alimandi@tin.it). They offer free airport pick-up and drop-off for guests staying at either of their hotels, though you must reserve when you book your room and wait for a scheduled shuttle (every two hours, ask about schedule when you reserve).

$$ Hotel Spring House, part of the Best Western chain, has a hotelesque feel and 51 attractive rooms—some with terraces, some which connect to make a family room (standard Db-€165, superior Db-€195, Tb-€200, Qb-€215, discount July–Aug and Jan–Feb, air-con, elevator, Wi-Fi, free loaner bikes, Via Mocenigo 7, two blocks from Vatican Museum, Metro: Cipro–Musei Vaticani, tel. 06-3972-0948, fax 06-3972-1047, www.hotelspringhouse.com, info@hotelspringhouse.com, Stefania).

$$ Hotel Gerber, set in a quiet residential area, is modern and air-conditioned, with 27 well-polished, businesslike rooms (two S without air-con-€60, Sb-€105, Db-€140, Tb-€160, Qb-€180; 15 percent discount in low season; Via degli Scipioni 241, at intersection with Ezio, a block from Metro: Lepanto, tel. 06-321-6485, fax 06-321-7048, www.hotelgerber.it, info@hotelgerber.it, Peter, Simonetta, and friendly dog Kira).

$ Casa per Ferie Santa Maria alle Fornaci dei Padri Trinitari houses pilgrims and secular tourists with simple class just a short walk south of the Vatican in 54 stark, identical, utilitarian, mostly twin-bedded rooms. This is the most user-friendly convent-type place I found. Reserve as far in advance as possible—they're often booked up a year in advance (Sb-€60, Db-€90, Tb-€125, air-con, elevator; take bus #64 from Termini train station to San Pietro train station, then walk 100 yards north along Via della Stazione di San Pietro to Piazza Santa Maria alle Fornaci 27; tel. 06-393-67632, fax 06-393-66795, www.trinitaridematha.it, cffornaci@tin.it).

EATING

Romans spend their evenings eating rather than drinking, and the preferred activity is simply to enjoy a fine, slow meal, buried deep in the old city. Rome's a fun and cheap place to eat, with countless little eateries serving memorable €20 meals.

Although I've listed a number of restaurants, I recommend that you just head for a scenic area and explore. Piazza Navona, the Pantheon area, Campo de' Fiori, and Trastevere are neighborhoods packed with characteristic eateries. Sitting with tourists on a famous square, enjoying the scene, works fine. (As my Roman friend explained: "When you're in a bad restaurant, the best way to survive is bread, olive oil, and salt.") But for more of a local flavor, consider my recommendations. In general, I'm impressed by how small the price difference is from a mediocre restaurant to a fine one. You can pay about 20 percent more for double the quality.

Trastevere

Colorful Trastevere is now pretty touristy. Still, Romans join the tourists to eat on the rustic side of the Tiber River. Start at the central square (Piazza Santa Maria). Then choose: Eat with tourists enjoying the ambience of the famous square, or wander the back streets in search of a mom-and-pop place with barely a menu. My recommendations are within a few minutes' walk of each other (between Piazza Santa Maria Trastevere and Ponte Sisto; see map on page 732).

Trattoria de "Gli Amici" serves good food on a super square (reservations smart—popular with dressy locals) or fine interior for a fair price while employing locals with disabilities. At this "Inn of the Friends," waiters with disabilities do their work with a unique passion. Each is paired with a volunteer aide from the Community of Sant'Egidio. Pictures on the walls show what can be accomplished by mentally disabled people who are successfully integrated into the community like this (€7 pastas, €9 *secondi*, Mon–Sat from 19:30, closed Sun, 2 blocks off main square at Piazza Sant'Egidio 6, tel. 06-580-6033).

Trattoria da Lucia lets you enjoy simple, traditional food at a good price in a great scene. It offers the quintessential, rustic, 100 percent Roman Trastevere dining experience and has been family-run since World War II. You'll meet Renato, his uncle Ennio, and Ennio's mom—pictured on the menu in the 1950s (cheap, Tue–Sun 12:30–15:30 & 19:30–24:00, cash only, closed Mon, homey indoor or evocative outdoor seating, Vicolo del Mattonato 2, tel. 06-580-3601, some English spoken).

Osteria Ponte Sisto, small and Mediterranean, specializes in Neapolitan cuisine with a menu that changes often. Just outside the tourist zone, it caters mostly to Romans and offers beautiful desserts and a fine value, but be careful when ordering the unpriced fish dishes (daily 12:30–15:00 & 19:30–24:00, Via Ponte Sisto 80, tel. 06-588-3411). It's easy to find: Crossing Ponte Sisto (pedestrian bridge) toward Trastevere, continue across the little square (Piazza Trilussa) and you'll see it on the right.

Ristorante Checco er Carettiere is a big, classic, family-run place that's been a Trastevere fixture for three generations. While a bit pricey, you'll eat well among lots of fun commotion (€13 pastas, €16 *secondi*, daily 12:30–15:00 & 19:30–23:30, Via Benedetta 10/13, tel. 06-580-0985).

Gelateria alla Scala is a terrific little ice cream shop that dishes up delightful cinnamon *(cannella)* and oh-wow pistachio (daily 12:00–24:00, Piazza della Scala 51, across from the church on Piazza della Scala). Seek this place out.

On and near Campo de' Fiori

While it is touristy, Campo de' Fiori offers a sublimely romantic setting. And, since it's so close to the collective heart of Rome, it remains popular with locals. For greater atmosphere than food value, circle the square, considering your choices. Bars and pizzerias seem to overwhelm the square. The **Taverna** and **Vineria** (#16 and #15) offer good perches from which to people-watch and sip a glass of wine.

Ristorante la Carbonara has the ultimate Campo de' Fiori setting, with dressy waiters and superb on-the-square seating. While the service gets mixed reviews, the food and Italian ambience are wonderful (€10 pastas, €15 *secondi*, Wed–Mon 9:00–15:30 & 16:30–24:00, closed Tue, Campo de' Fiori 23, tel. 06-686-4783). Meals on small surrounding streets may be a better value, but they lack that Campo de' Fiori magic.

Ostaria da Giovanni ar Galletto is nearby, on the more elegant and peaceful Piazza Farnese. It has an upscale local crowd, pleasant outdoor seating, and reasonable prices. Say hi to Angelo, who's committed to serving fine food. Regrettably, service can be horrible and single diners aren't treated very well. Still, if you're in no hurry and ready to savor my favorite *al fresco* setting in Rome, this is a good bet (Mon–Sat 12:15–15:00 & 19:30–23:00, closed Sun, tucked in corner of Piazza Farnese at #102, tel. 06-686-1714).

Osteria Enoteca al Bric is a mod bistro-type place run by a man who loves to cook and serve good wine. Wine-case lids decorate the wall like happy memories. With candlelit grace and no tourists, it's perfect for the wine snob in the mood for pasta and fine cheese. Aficionados choose their bottle from the huge selection lining the walls near the entrance. Beginners order fine wine by the glass with help from the waiter when they order their meal (daily 12:30–15:00 & from 19:30 for dinner, closed Mon June–Sept, reserve after 20:30, 100 yards off Campo de' Fiori at Via del Pellegrino 51, tel. 06-687-9533). Al Bric offers my readers a special "Taste of Italy for Two" deal (fine plate of mixed cheese and meat with two glasses of full-bodied red wine and a pitcher of water) for €22 from 19:30, but you may need to finish by 20:30. This could be a light meal if you're kicking off an evening stroll, a substantial appetizer, or a way to check this place out for a serious meal later.

Filetti de Baccala, a tradition for many Romans, is basically a fish bar with paper tablecloths and cheap prices. Its grease-stained, hurried waiters serve old-time favorites—fried cod fillets, a strange bitter *puntarelle* salad, and their antipasto (delightful anchovies

Restaurants in the Heart of Rome

with butter)—to nostalgic locals (Mon–Sat 17:00–22:30, closed Sun, cash only, a block east of Campo de' Fiori tumbling onto long tables in a tiny and atmospheric square, Largo dei Librari 88, tel. 06-686-4018). Study what others are eating and order by pointing. Nothing is expensive (see the menu on wall). Urchins can get a cod stick to go and sit on the barnacle church doorsteps just outside. Say *ciao* to Marcello, who runs the place like a swim coach.

Trattoria der Pallaro, which has no menu, has a slogan: "Here, you'll eat what we want to feed you." Paola Fazi—with a towel wrapped around her head turban-style—and her family serve up a five-course meal of typically Roman food for €21, including wine, coffee, and a tasty mandarin juice. Make like Oliver Twist asking for more soup and get seconds on the juice (daily 12:00–15:00 & 19:00–24:00, indoor/outdoor seating on quiet square, a block south of Corso Vittorio Emanuele, down Largo del Chiavari to Largo del Pallaro 15, tel. 06-6880-1488).

Hostaria Costanza has crisp-vested waiters, a local following, and lots of energy. You'll eat traditional Roman cuisine on a ramshackle patio or inside under arches from the ancient Pompeo Theater (Mon–Sat 12:30–15:00 & 19:30–23:30, closed Sun, Piazza Paradiso 63, tel. 06-686-1717).

Piazza Pasquino

Between Campo de' Fiori and Piazza Navona, these three bustling places have low prices and a happy clientele. As they are neighbors and each is completely different, check out all three before choosing.

Cul de Sac is packed with enthusiastic locals cobbling together fun meals from an Italian dim sum–type menu of traditional dishes (daily 12:00–16:00 & 18:00–24:00, often crowded, a block southwest of Piazza Navona on Piazza Pasquino). **L'Insalata Ricca,** next door, is a popular chain that specializes in hearty and healthy €7 salads and much less healthy pizzas (daily 12:00–15:45 & 18:45–24:00, Piazza Pasquino 72, tel. 06-6830-7881). **Ristorante Terra di Siena** is more traditional, with a Tuscan passion for meat (Mon–Sat 12:00–15:00 & 19:00–23:30, closed Sun, Piazza Pasquino 77, tel. 06-6830-7704).

Dining near the Pantheon

Ristorante da Fortunato is an Italian classic, with fresh flowers on the tables, and white-coated, black-tie waiters politely serving good meat and fish to local politicians, foreign dignitaries, and tourists with good taste. Don't leave without perusing the photos of their famous visitors—everyone from former Iraqi Foreign Minister Tariq Aziz to Bill Clinton seems to have eaten here. The outdoor seating is fine for watching the river of Roman street life flow by. For a dressy night out, this is a reliable choice. When it comes to cuisine, Fortunato is a master of simple elegance (surprisingly reasonable, plan to spend €45, Mon–Sat 12:30–15:00 & 19:30–23:30, closed Sun, a block in front of the Pantheon at Via del Pantheon 55, tel. 06-679-2788).

Cheap and Colorful near the Pantheon

Eating on the square facing the Pantheon is a temptation (there's even a McDonald's that offers some of the best outdoor seating in town), and I'd consider it just to relax and enjoy the Roman scene.

Restaurants near the Pantheon

But if you walk a block or two away, you'll get less view and better food. Here are some suggestions:

Ristorante Enoteca Corsi is a wine shop that grew into a thriving lunch-only restaurant. The Paiella family serves straightforward, traditional cuisine at great prices to an appreciative crowd of office workers. Check the blackboard for daily specials (gnocchi on Thursday, fish on Friday, and so on). Friendly Ilaria and Manuela welcome diners to step into their wine shop and pick out a bottle. For the cheap take-away price, plus a euro or two, they'll uncork it at your table. With €5 pastas, €8.50 main dishes, and fine wine at a third the price you'd pay in normal restaurants, this is a superb value (Mon–Sat 12:00–15:00, closed Sun, a block toward the Pantheon from the Gesù church at Via del Gesù 87, tel. 06-679-0821).

Miscellanea is run by much-loved Mikki, who's on a mission to keep foreign students well-fed. You'll find cheap pasta, hearty and fresh €3 sandwiches, and a long list of €6 salads. Mikki often tosses in a fun little extra, including—if you have this book on the table—a free glass of Mikki's "sexy wine" (homemade from *fragolina*—strawberries). This place is popular with American students on foreign study programs (daily 11:00–24:00, indoor/outdoor seating, a block toward Via del Corso from the Pantheon at Via delle Paste 110).

Osteria da Mario, a homey little mom-and-pop joint with a no-stress menu, serves traditional favorites in a fun, homey little dining room or on tables spilling out onto a picturesque old Roman square (Mon–Sat 13:30–15:30 & 19:30–23:00, closed Sun, from the Pantheon walk 2 blocks up Via Pantheon, go left on Via delle Coppelle, take first right to Piazza delle Coppelle 51, tel. 06-6880-6349).

Restaurant Coco is a perfect place for a quick and atmospheric lunch with friendly service. They put out a wonderful €10 lunch buffet on weekdays. After grazing through the great selection of tempting dishes, you'll sit on the square among a produce market, watching local politicians stroll in and out of their dining hall across the way (classy indoor and rustic outdoor seating; €10–€12 Sun—gets you a big main plate, bread, dessert, water and coffee; daily 12:30–15:30, Piazza delle Coppelle 54, tel. 06-6813-6545).

Le Coppelle Taverna is good—especially for pizza—with a checkered-tablecloth ambience (daily 12:30–15:00 & 19:30–23:30, Via delle Coppelle 39, tel. 06-6880-6557).

Cafeteria Brek, on Largo Argentina just south of the Pantheon, is an appealing self-service restaurant with a modern, efficient atmosphere and cheap prices (daily 12:00–15:30 & 19:00–22:15, skip the sandwiches and pizza slices downstairs and go to the cafeteria upstairs, northwest corner of square, Largo Argentina 1, tel. 06-6821-0353).

Picnic on the Pantheon Porch: **Antica Salumeria** is an old-time *alimentari* (grocery store, daily 8:00–21:00) on the Pantheon square. Eduardo speaks English and will help you assemble your picnic: artichokes, mixed olives, bread, cheese, meat, and wine (with plastic glasses). While you can create your own (sold by the weight, more fun, and cheaper), they also sell quality ready-made sandwiches. Now take your peasant's feast over for a temple-porch picnic. Enjoy the shade at the base of a column and munch your meal. For dessert...

Gelato

Three fine gelaterias are within a two-minute walk of the Pantheon. Rome's most famous and venerable ice-cream joint is **Gelateria Caffè Pasticceria Giolitti** (with cheap take-away prices and elegant Old World seating, just off Piazza Colonna and Piazza Monte Citorio at Via Uffici del Vicario 40, tel. 06-699-1243). Another good option is **Gelateria della Palma** (daily 8:00–24:00, 2 blocks directly in front of the Pantheon at Via della Maddalena 20). Bright with neon and filled with every type of candy imaginable, kids of all ages will enjoy their huge selection of colorful, tasty gelati. However, taste purists look down on bright colors. For mellower hues and more traditional quality, try **Crèmeria Monteforte**, facing the right side of the Pantheon (Tue–Sun 11:00–24:00, closed Mon, Via della Rotonda 22).

Near the Spanish Steps

To locate these restaurants, see the "Dolce Vita Stroll" map on page 696.

Ristorante il Gabriello is inviting and small—modern under medieval arches—and offers a peaceful and local-feeling respite from all the top-end fashion shops in the area. Claudio serves with charisma, while his brother cooks creative Roman cuisine using fresh, organic products from his wife's farm. Simply close your eyes and point to anything on the menu (pastas-€9, *secondi*-€12; dinner only, Mon–Sat 19:00–23:30, closed Sun, air-con, dress respectfully—no shorts please, reservations smart, Via Vittoria 51, three blocks from Spanish Steps, tel. 06-6994-0810). Italians normally just trust the waiter and say "Bring it on." Tourists are understandably more cautious, but you can be trusting here. Invest €40 (not including wine) in "Claudio's Extravaganza," and he'll shower you with edible kindness.

Fiaschetteria, lively and simple, serves €8 plates of traditional Italian cuisine with good indoor and outdoor seating (closed Sun, Via della Croce 39).

Ristorante alla Rampa, just around the corner from the touristy crush of the Spanish Steps, offers Roman cooking, indoor/outdoor ambience at a moderate price, and impersonal service. They take no reservations, so arrive by 19:30, or be prepared to wait. For a simple meal, go with the €9 *piatto misto all'ortolana*—a self-service trip to their antipasto spread with meat, fish, and veggies. Even though you get just one trip to the buffet, this can be a meal in itself (Mon–Sat 12:00–15:00 & 18:00–23:00, closed Sun, 100 yards east of Spanish Steps at Piazza Mignanelli 18, tel. 06-678-2621).

Near the Trevi Fountain

To locate these restaurants, see map on page 756.

L'Antica Birreria Peroni is Rome's answer to a German beer-hall. Serving hearty mugs of the local Peroni beer and lots of just plain fun, beer-hall food, the place is a hit with locals for a cheap night out (Mon–Sat 12:00–24:00, closed Sun, midway between Trevi Fountain and Capitol Hill, a block off Via del Corso at Via di San Marcello 19, tel. 06-679-5310).

Ristorante Pizzeria Sacro e Profano fills an old church with spicy south Italian (Calabrian) cuisine and some pricey, exotic dishes. Run with enthusiasm and passion by Pasquale and friends, this is just far enough away from the Trevi mobs. Their hearty €13 antipasti plate offers a delightful montage of Calabrian taste treats—plenty of food for a light, memorable meal (Mon–Sat 12:00–15:00 & 18:00–24:00, closed Sun, a block off Via del Tritone at Via dei Maroniti 29, tel. 06-679-1836). For dessert...

Around the corner, **Gelateria San Crispino,** well-respected by locals, serves particularly tasty, gourmet gelato using creative ingredients such as balsamic vinegar, pear, and cinnamon (Wed–Mon 12:00–24:00, closed Tue, Via della Panetteria 42, tel. 06-679-3924).

Eating Cheaply Between the Colosseum and St. Peter-in-Chains Church

You'll find good views but poor value in the restaurants directly behind the Colosseum. To get your money's worth, eat at least a block away. Here are two handy eateries at the top of Terme di Tito (a block uphill from Colosseum, near St. Peter-in-Chains church—of Michelangelo's *Moses* fame; see page 762).

Caffè dello Studente is a lively spot popular with local engineering students attending the nearby U. of Rome. Pina, Mauro, and their perky daughter Simona (speaks English, but you can teach her some more) give my readers a royal welcome and serve typical *bar gastronomia* fare: toasted sandwiches and simple pastas and pizzas. You can get your food to go *(da portar via)*; stand up and eat at the crowded bar; sit at an outdoor table and wait for a menu; or—if it's not busy—show this book when you order at the bar and sit without paying extra at a table (Mon–Sat 7:30–21:00, Sun 9:00–18:00, tel. 06-488-3240).

Ostaria da Nerone, next door, is more of a restaurant: less friendly and more aggressive. Their €7.50 antipasti plate is the best value; add €2 and you get meat and shellfish (Mon–Sat 12:00–15:00 & 19:00–23:00, closed Sun, indoor/outdoor seating, Via delle Terme di Tito 96, tel. 06-481-7952, run by Teo).

Restaurants in East Rome

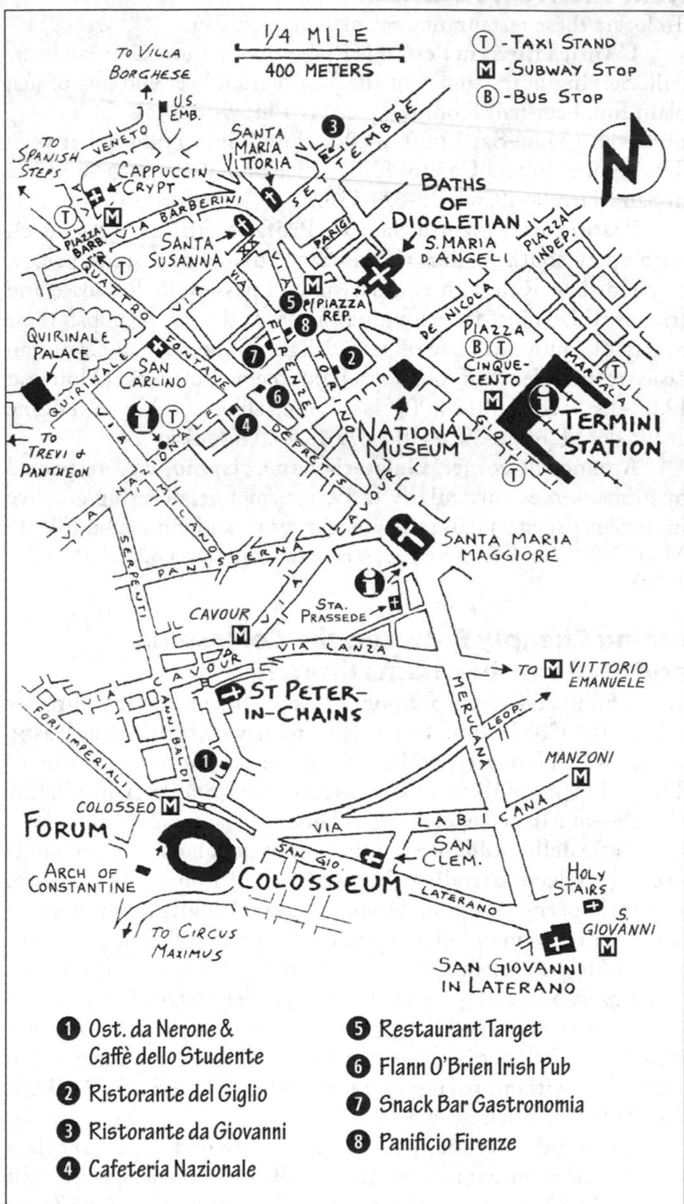

Munching near Via Firenze

You have plenty of eating options near my recommended hotels on Via Firenze.

Ristorante del Giglio is a circa-1900 place with a long family tradition of serving traditional Roman dishes (though the quality can be uneven). You'll eat in a big hall of about 20 tables with dressy locals and tourists following the recommendations of nearby hotels (€8 pastas, €15 *secondi*, Mon–Sat 12:00–15:00 & 19:00–23:00, closed Sun, Via Torino 137, tel. 06-488-1606).

Ristorante da Giovanni is a reasonable, budget option that has fed locals and hungry travelers now for 50 years (simple but filling €14 fixed-price meal, Mon–Sat 12:00–15:00 & 19:00–22:30, closed Sun and in Aug, just off Via XX Settembre at Via Antonio Salandra 1, tel. 06-485-950).

Cafeteria Nazionale, with woody elegance, offers light lunches—including salads—at fair prices. It's noisy with local office workers being served by frantic red-vested waitstaff (Mon–Sat 7:00–20:00, closed Sun, Via Nazionale 26–27, at intersection with Via Agostino de Pretis, tel. 06-4899-1716). Their lunch buffet is a delight but gets picked over early (small dish-€7.50, Mon–Sat 12:00–15:00).

Restaurant Target has decent pizza and pasta and slow service (Mon–Sat 12:00–15:30 & 19:00–24:00, Sun 19:00–24:00, indoor/outdoor seating, Via Torino 33, tel. 06-474-0066).

The **McDonald's** restaurants on Piazza della Repubblica (free piazza seating outside), Piazza Barberini, and Via Firenze offer air-conditioned interiors and salad bars.

Flann O'Brien Irish Pub is an entertaining place for a light meal (of pasta or something *other* than pasta, such as grilled beef, served early and late, when other places are closed), fine Irish beer, live sporting events on TV, and perhaps the most Italian crowd of all. Walk way back before choosing a table (daily 7:30–24:00, Via Nazionale 17, at intersection with Via Napoli, tel. 06-488-0418).

Snack Bar Gastronomia is a local joint with one table and a booming take-out business—especially popular for its Greek-style yogurt with fruit and honey (€3–5, confirm price before ordering as there are several versions; fresh meat or veggie sandwiches, salads, freshly squeezed juices, daily 7:00–24:00, Via Firenze 34).

Panificio Firenze offers take-out pizza, sandwiches, and an old-fashioned *alimentari* (grocery) with everything you'd need for a picnic. It's such a favorite with locals that it doesn't even need a sign (Mon–Fri 7:00–19:00, Sat until 14:00, closed Sun, across the street from Snack Bar Gastronomia at Via Firenze 51–52, tel. 06-488-5035).

Near the Vatican Museum and St. Peter's

Avoid the restaurant pushers handing out fliers near the Vatican: bad food and expensive menu tricks. Try any of these instead (see map on page 752).

Perilli in Prati is bright, modern, and just far enough away from the tourist hordes. While friendly Lucia and Massimo specialize in pizza and grilled meats, the highlight is their excellent €7.50 lunch buffet on weekdays (Mon–Fri 12:30–15:00 & 19:30–23:30, Sat 19:30–23:30, closed Sun, one block from Ottaviano Metro stop, Via Otranto 9, tel. 06-370-0156).

Hostaria dei Bastioni, run by Antonio and his family, has tasty food and friendly service. It's conveniently located midway on your hike from St. Peters' to the Vatican Museum, with noisy street-side seating and a quiet interior. The house fettuccine and the risotto with seafood are good (pastas-€6, *secondi*-€8–12, no cover charge, Mon–Sat 12:00–15:30 & 19:00–23:00, closed Sun, at corner of Vatican wall, Via Leone IV 29, tel. 06-3972-3034).

La Rustichella serves a sprawling *antipasti* buffet (€7 for a single meal-sized plate). Arrive when they open at 19:30 to avoid a line and have the pristine buffet to yourself (Tue–Sun 12:30–15:00 & 19:30–23:00, closed Mon, near Metro: Cipro–Musei Vaticani, opposite church at end of Via Candia, Via Angelo Emo 1, tel. 06-3972-0649). Consider the fun and fruity **Gelateria Millennium** next door.

Viale Giulio Cesare is lined with cheap **Pizza Rustica** shops, self-serve places, and inviting eateries. Restaurants such as **Tre Pupazzi** (Mon–Sat 12:00–15:00 & 19:00–23:00, closed Sun, tel. 06-686-8371), which line the pedestrian-only Borgo Pio—a block from Piazza San Pietro—are worth a look.

Turn your nose loose in the wonderful **Via Andrea Doria** open-air market, three blocks north of the Vatican Museum (Mon–Sat roughly 7:00–13:30, until 16:30 Tue and Fri except summer, corner of Via Tunisi and Via Andrea Doria). If the market is closed, try the nearby **IN's supermarket** (Mon–Sat 8:30–13:30 & 16:00–20:00, closed Thu eve and Sun, a half block straight out from Via Tunisi entrance of open-air market, Via Francesco Caracciolo 18).

Testaccio

For restaurant location, see the map on page 736.

Trattoria "Da Oio" A Casa Mia serves good-quality, inexpensive, traditional cuisine to a local crowd. It's an upbeat little eatery where you understand the Testaccio passion for the "fifth quarter." (Testaccio, dominated for centuries by its slaughterhouses, is noted for restaurants expert at preparing undesirable meat parts.) The menu is a minefield of soft meats (Mon–Sat 12:30–15:00 & 19:30–23:30, closed Sun, Via Galvani 43, tel. 06-578-2680).

TRANSPORTATION CONNECTIONS

Termini is the central station (see "Arrival in Rome" on page 677; Metro: Termini). Tiburtina is the bus station (on Metro line B, 4 Metro stops away from train station; Metro: Tiburtina).

From Rome by Train to: Venice (roughly hourly, 5–8 hrs, overnight possible), **Florence** (at least hourly, 2 hrs, many stop at Orvieto en route), **Assisi** (2/hr, 2–3 hrs), **Pisa** (at least hourly, 3–4 hrs), **La Spezia** (10/day, 4 hrs, overnight option), **Milan** (at least hourly, 4–7 hrs, overnight possible), **Naples** (at least hourly, 1.5–2 hrs), **Brindisi** (6/day, 6–9 hrs, overnight possible), **Amsterdam** (7/day, 20 hrs, overnight unavoidable), **Bern** (6/day, 9 hrs, plus several overnight options), **Frankfurt** (7/day, 14 hrs, plus several overnight options), **Munich** (4/day, 11 hrs, plus several overnight options), **Nice** (6/day, 10 hrs, overnight possible), **Paris** (3/day, 13–16 hrs, plus several overnight options, important to reserve ahead), **Vienna** (3/day, 13–15 hrs, plus several overnight options).

From Rome by Bus to: Assisi (2–4/day, 3 hrs), **Siena** (10/day, 3 hrs), **Sorrento** (1–2/day, 4 hrs; this is the quickest and easiest way to go straight to Sorrento).

Rome's Airports

Rome's two airports—Fiumicino (a.k.a. Leonardo da Vinci) and the small Ciampino—share the same website (www.adr.it).

Fiumicino Airport

Rome's major airport has a TI (daily 8:00–19:00, tel. 06-8205-9127, press 2 for English), ATMs, banks, luggage storage, shops, and bars.

A slick, direct **train** connects the airport and Rome's central Termini train station in 30 minutes. Trains run twice hourly in both directions from roughly 6:00 to 23:00 (double-check train times if you have a late-night or early-morning flight to catch). From the airport's arrival gate, follow signs to *Stazione/Railway Station*. Buy your ticket from a machine or the Biglietteria office (€9.50). Make sure the train you board is going to the central "Roma Termini" station, not "Roma Orte" or others. Once you arrive at Termini, the TI will be on your left along track 24.

Going from the Termini train station to the airport, trains depart at about :22 and :52 past the hour, usually from track 28 or 29; to reach these tracks, take a long 10-minute walk along track 24 to the end of the station (near the corner of Giovanni Giolitti and Via Lamarmora, moving walkways are inside the building to the right on the lower level). Check the departure boards for "Fiumicino Aeroporto"—the local name for the airport—and confirm with an official or a local on the platform that the train is indeed going to the airport (€9.50, buy ticket from computerized ticket machines, any *tabacchi* shop in station, or at the desk near entrance to track 26). Read your ticket: If it requires validation, stamp it in the yellow machine near the platform before boarding. Know whether your plane departs from terminal A, B, or C.

Shuttle van services run to and from the airport. Consider **Rome Airport Shuttle** (€30 for one or two people, extra people €6 each, 30 percent more late night or early morning, tel. 06-4201-4507 or 06-420-13469, www.airportshuttle.it).

Your hotel can arrange a **taxi** to the airport at any hour for about €40. To get from the airport into town cheaply by taxi, try teaming up with any tourist also just arriving (most are heading for hotels near yours in the center). Be sure to wait at the taxi stand. Avoid unmarked, unmetered taxis; these guys will try to tempt you away from the taxi stand line-up by offering an immediate (rip-off) ride.

For **airport information,** call 06-65951. To inquire about flights, call 06-6595-3640 (Alitalia: tel. 06-2222, British Airways: tel. 06-5249-2800, SAS: tel. 06-6501-0771, Continental: tel. 06-6605-3030, Delta: toll-free tel. 800-477-999, KLM/Northwest: tel. 199-414-199, Swiss International: tel. 848-868-120, United: tel. 848-800-692).

Ciampino Airport

Rome's smaller airport (tel. 06-794-941) handles budget airlines, such as easyJet or Ryanair, and charter flights. To get to downtown Rome from the airport, you can take the LILA/Cotral bus (2/hr, 40 min) to the Anagnina Metro stop, where you can connect by Metro to the stop nearest your hotel. Rome Airport Shuttle (listed above) also offers service to and from Ciampino. The Terravision Express Shuttle connects Ciampino and Termini, leaving every 20 minutes (€7 one-way, €11.50 round-trip, www.terravision.it).

Civitavecchia Cruise Ship Port

Twice-hourly trains connect the cruise-ship port of Civitavecchia, about 45 miles northwest of Rome, and Rome's Termini station in 75 minutes (€12). To reach the Civitavecchia train station from the port, take the free shuttle bus to the port entrance, and walk about 10–15 minutes along the seaside road. Some shuttle buses may take you all the way to the station—ask. To reach the port from the station, turn right after you exit. Local taxis also run between the port and the train station (tel. 0766-26121 or 0766-24251).

VENICE

(Venezia)

Soak all day in this puddle of elegant decay. Venice is Europe's best-preserved big city. This car-free urban wonderland of a hundred islands—laced together by 400 bridges and 2,000 alleys—survives on the artificial respirator of tourism.

Born in a lagoon 1,500 years ago as a refuge from barbarians, Venice is overloaded with tourists and is slowly sinking (unrelated facts). In the Middle Ages, the Venetians, becoming Europe's clever middlemen for East-West trade, created a great trading empire. By smuggling in the bones of St. Mark (San Marco) in A.D. 828, Venice gained religious importance as well. With the discovery of America and new trading routes to the Orient, Venetian power ebbed. But as Venice fell, her appetite for decadence grew. Through the 17th and 18th centuries, Venice partied on the wealth accumulated through earlier centuries as a trading power.

Today, Venice is home to about 65,000 people in its old city, down from a peak population of nearly 200,000. While there are about 500,000 in greater Venice (counting the mainland, not counting tourists), the old town has a small-town feel. Locals seem to know everyone. To see small-town Venice away from the touristic flak, escape the Rialto-San Marco tourist zone and savor the town early and late without the hordes of vacationers day-tripping in from cruise ships and nearby beach resorts. A 10-minute walk from the madness puts you in an idyllic Venice few tourists see.

Planning Your Time

Venice is worth at least a day on even the speediest tour. Hyper-efficient train travelers take the night train in and/or out.

Venice Overview

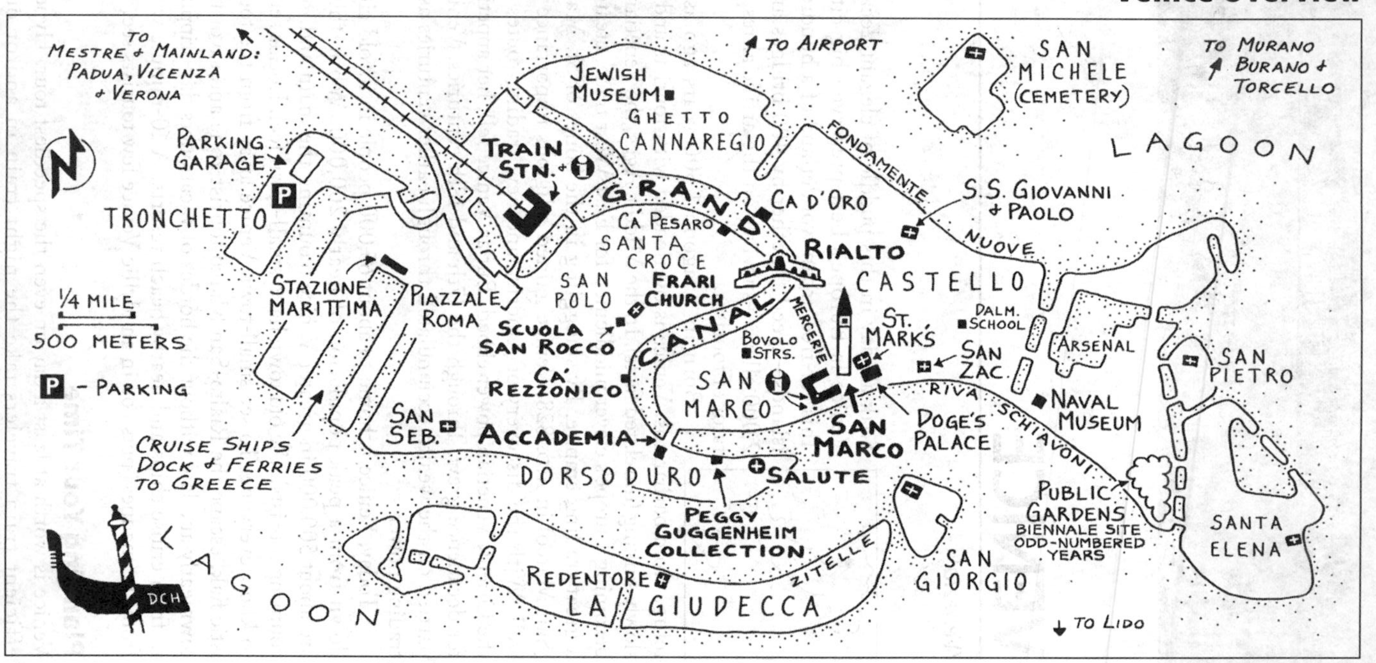

Sleep in the old center to experience Venice at its best: early and late. For a one-day visit, cruise the Grand Canal, do the major sights on St. Mark's Square (the square itself, Doge's Palace, and St. Mark's Basilica), see the Frari Church (Chiesa dei Frari) for art, and wander the backstreets on a pub crawl). Venice's greatest sight is the city itself. Make time to simply wander. While doable in a day, Venice is worth two. It's a medieval cookie jar, and nobody's looking.

ORIENTATION

The island city of Venice is shaped like a fish. Its major thoroughfares are canals. The Grand Canal winds through the middle of the fish, starting at the mouth where all the people and food enter, passing under the Rialto Bridge, and ending at St. Mark's Square (Piazza San Marco). Park your 21st-century perspective at the mouth and let Venice swallow you whole.

Venice is a car-less kaleidoscope of people, bridges, and odorless canals. The city has no major streets, and addresses are hopelessly confusing. There are six districts: San Marco (most touristy), Castello (behind San Marco), Cannaregio (from the train station to the Rialto), San Polo (other side of the Rialto), Santa Croce (the "eye" of the fish, east of the train station), and Dorsoduro (the belly of the fish and southernmost district of the city). Each district has about 6,000 address numbers.

To find your way, navigate by landmarks, not streets. Many street corners have a sign pointing you to *(per)* the nearest major landmark, such as San Marco, Accademia, Rialto, and Ferrovia (train station). Obedient visitors stick to the main thoroughfares as directed by these signs and miss the charm of back-street Venice.

Tourist Information

There are TIs at the **train station** (daily 8:00–18:30, crowded and surly); at **St. Mark's Square** (daily 9:00–15:30; with your back to St. Mark's Basilica, it's in far left corner of the square); and near the **St. Mark's Square vaporetto boat stop** on the lagoon (daily 10:00–18:00, sells vaporetto tickets). Smaller offices are at **Piazzale Roma** and the **airport** (daily 9:30–19:30). For a quick question, save time by phoning 041-529-8711. The TI's official website is www.turismovenezia.it.

At any TI, pick up the two free pamphlets that list museum hours, exhibitions, and musical events (in Italian and English). Confirm your sightseeing plans. Ask for the fine brochures outlining three offbeat Venice walks.

The free entertainment guide ***Un Ospite di Venezia*** (a listing of events, nightlife, museum hours, train and vaporetto schedules, emergency telephone numbers, and so on) is available at fancy hotel reception desks (www.aguestinvenice.com).

More Websites on Venice: www.veniceforvisitors.com, www.museiciviciveneziani.it (civic museums in Venice), www.venicexplorer.net (interactive maps), and www.meetingvenice.it.

Maps: Of all places, Venice requires a good map. Hotels give away lousy freebies. The TI sells a simple one that isn't much better. Bookshops, newsstands, and postcard stands sell a wider range of maps; the €3 maps are pretty bad, but if you spend €6, you'll get a map that shows you everything. Invest in a good map and use it—this can be the best €6 you'll spend in Venice.

Arrival in Venice

A two-mile-long causeway (with highway and train lines) connects Venice to the mainland. Mestre, the sprawling mainland industrial base, has fewer crowds, cheaper hotels, and plenty of cheap parking lots, but no charm. Don't stop in Mestre unless you're parking your car or transferring trains.

By Train: Trains to Venice stop at either Venezia Mestre (on the mainland) or at the Santa Lucia station on the island of Venice itself. If your train only stops at Mestre, worry not. Shuttle trains regularly connect Mestre's station with Venice's Santa Lucia station (6/hr, 10 min).

Venice's **Santa Lucia train station** plops you right into the old town on the Grand Canal, an easy vaporetto boat ride or fascinating 40-minute walk to St. Mark's Square. Upon arrival, skip the station's crowded TI, because the two TIs at St. Mark's Square are better, and it's not worth a long wait for a minimal map (buy a good one from a newsstand with no wait). Confirm your departure plan (stop by train info desk or just study the *partenze*—departure—posters on walls).

Consider storing unnecessary heavy bags, although lines for **baggage check** may be very long (platform #14, €3/12 hrs, €10/24 hrs, daily 6:00–24:00, no lockers).

Walk straight out of the station to the canal. On your left is the dock for ***vaporetti*** #82 (fast boat down Grand Canal) and #52 (goes clockwise around island of Venice). To your right is the dock for #1 (slow boat down Grand Canal) and #51 (goes counterclockwise around Venice). See the hotel listings in "Sleeping" (on page 799) to find out which boat to catch to get to your hotel. Buy a €5 ticket (or €12 24-hour pass) at the ticket window and hop on a boat. If you're taking #82 or #1, confirm that it's heading downtown (direction: Rialto or San Marco). Some boats only go as far as Rialto *(solo Rialto)*, so check with the conductor.

By Car: The freeway dead-ends at Venice, near several parking lots on the edge of the island. The most central lot, San Marco,

Arrival in Venice

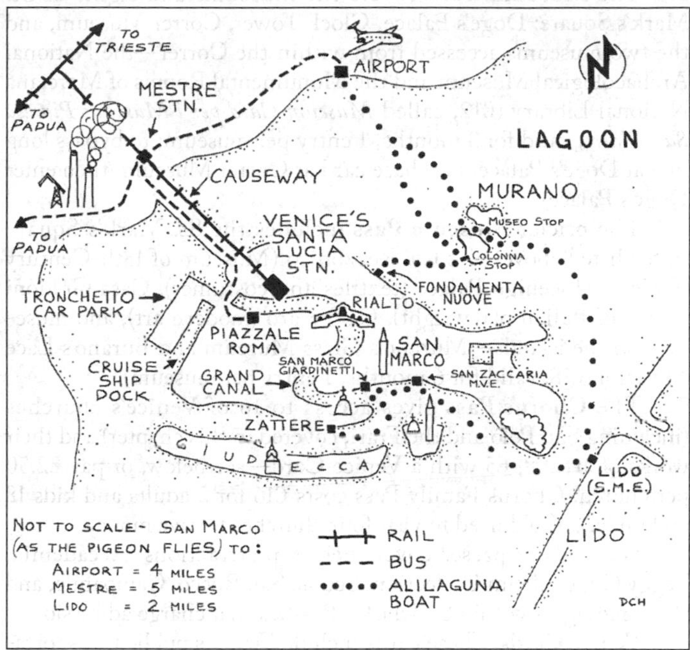

is very busy and too expensive. Follow the green lights directing you to an alternative parking lot with space, probably Tronchetto (across the causeway and on the right), which has a huge, multistoried garage (€20/day, tel. 041-520-7555). From there, avoid the travel agencies masquerading as TIs, and head directly for the vaporetto docks for the boat connection (#82) to the town center. Don't let taxi boatmen con you out of the relatively cheap €5 vaporetto ride.

Parking in Mestre is easy and cheap (open-air lots cost €5/day Mon–Fri, €10/day Sat–Sun, across from Mestre train station, easy shuttle-train connections to Venice's Santa Lucia Station—6/hr, 10 min). There are also huge and economical lots in Verona, Padua, and Vicenza.

By Plane: For information on Venice's airport and connections into the city, see page 824.

Passes for Venice

To help control (and confuse?) its flood of visitors, Venice offers cards and passes that cover some museums and/or transportation. For most visitors, the simple Museum Card (the Doge's Palace/Correr Museum combo-ticket) or Museum Pass will do. Passes are sold at participating sights.

The **Museum Card** covers the museums and sights of St. Mark's Square: Doge's Palace, Clock Tower, Correr Museum, and the two museums accessed from within the Correr—the National Archaeological Museum and the Monumental Rooms of Marciana National Library (€12, called *Museum Card per i Musei di Piazza San Marco,* valid for 3 months, 1 entry per museum; to bypass long line at Doge's Palace, purchase card at Correr Museum, then enter Doge's Palace).

The pricier **Museum Pass** includes the St. Mark's Square sights listed above, plus Ca' Rezzonico (Museum of 18th-Century Venice), Mocenigo Palace (textiles and costumes), Casa Goldoni (home of Italian playwright), Ca' Pesaro (modern art), and museums on the islands—Murano's Glass Museum and Burano's Lace Museum (€18, valid for 6 months, 1 entry per museum).

The **Chorus Pass** gives access to 16 of Venice's churches (including San Polo and the Frari, covered in this chapter) and their works of art (€8, €5 with a Venice Card—see below, or pay €2.50 per church; Chorus Family Pass costs €16 for 2 adults and kids 18 and under). You'd need to visit four churches to save money.

No cards or passes cover these top attractions: Accademia, Peggy Guggenheim Collection, Scuola San Rocco, Campanile, and the three sights within St. Mark's Basilica that charge admission.

Venice Cards: These cards include Venice's public transportation, public toilets, and, if you get the "orange" version, some sights. Personally, I don't think these are worth the bother, but here's the information: The **Blue Venice Card** covers all your vaporetto rides, plus entry to public toilets (€17/1 day, €34/3 days, €52/7 days, cheaper for "Juniors" under 30). The **Orange Venice Card** includes transportation and toilets, as well as the museums covered by the Museum Pass—so it's like getting a Blue Venice Card and a Museum Pass (€29/1 day, €54/3 days, €76/7 days, cheaper for "Juniors" under 30). To order either card, book online for a 5 percent discount at www.venicecard.it (tel. 041-2424 for information). Better yet, if all you want is a vaporetto pass, get a 24-hour pass for €12 at any vaporetto dock; described under "Getting Around Venice," later in this section.

"Rolling Venice" Youth Discount Pass: To those under age 30, this worthwhile pass (€4/1 day, €15/3 days) gives discounts on sights and transportation, plus information on cheap eating and sleeping. It is sold at kiosks at major vaporetto stops, including Ferrovia (train station), Rialto, Accademia, and San Marco–Vallaresso (St. Mark's Square).

Helpful Hints

Rip-offs, Theft, and Help: The dark, late-night streets of Venice are safe. Even so, pickpockets (often elegantly dressed) work the crowded main streets, docks, and *vaporetti* (wear your money belt and carry your daybag in front). Your biggest risk of pickpockets is actually inside St. Mark's Basilica. A service called Counter of Tourist Mediation handles complaints about local crooks, but does not give out information (tel. 041-529-8710, complaint.apt@turismovenezia.it).

Medical Help: Venice's hospital is a 10-minute walk from both the Rialto and San Marco neighborhoods, located on Fondamenta dei Mendicanti toward Fondamenta Nuove. Take vaporetto #41 from San Zaccaria–Jolanda to Ospedale stop (tel. 041-529-4111).

Crowd Control: Crowds can be a serious problem at the Accademia (to minimize crowds, go early or late, or call 041-520-0345 to reserve tickets in advance); St. Mark's Basilica (try going early or late, or you can skip the line if you have a bag to check—see "St. Mark's Basilica," page 787); Campanile (go early or late—it's open until 21:00 July–Aug); and the Doge's Palace. For the Doge's Palace, you have three options for avoiding the ticket-sales line: Buy your Museum Card or Museum Pass at the Correr Museum (then step right up to the Doge's Palace turnstile, thus skipping the long line); visit at 17:00 (if it's April–Oct), when lines disappear; or book a Secret Itineraries Tour (see page 791). All of the sights that have crowd problems (St. Mark's Basilica, Doge's Palace, and Accademia) get more crowded when it rains.

Get Lost: Accept the fact that Venice was a tourist town 400 years ago. It was, is, and always will be crowded. While 80 percent of Venice is, in fact, not touristy, 80 percent of the tourists never notice. Hit the back streets. Venice is the ideal town to explore on foot. Walk and walk to the far reaches of the town. Don't worry about getting lost. Get as lost as possible. Keep reminding yourself, "I'm on an island, and I can't get off." When it comes time to find your way, just follow the directional arrows on building corners or simply ask a local, *"Dov'è San Marco?"* ("Where is St. Mark's?"). People in the tourist business (that's most Venetians) speak some English. If they don't, listen politely, watch where their hands point, say, *"Grazie,"* and head off in that direction. If you're lost, pop into a hotel and ask for their business card—it comes with a map and a prominent "You are here."

Take Breaks: Venice's endless pavement, crowds, and tight spaces are hard on the tourist. Schedule breaks in your sightseeing. Grab a cool place to sit down, relax, and recoup—meditate on a pew in an uncrowded church, or buy a cappuccino and a fruit cup in a café.

Etiquette: Walk on the right and don't loiter on bridges. Picnicking is technically forbidden (keep a low profile). Dress modestly. Men should keep their shirts on. (Women, too.) When visiting St. Mark's Basilica or other major churches, men, women, and even children must cover their knees and shoulders (or risk being turned away). Remove hats when entering a church.

Be Prepared to Splurge: Venice is expensive for locals as well as tourists. The demand is huge, supply is limited, and running a business is costly. Things just cost more here; everything must be shipped in and hand-trucked to its destination. Perhaps the best way to enjoy Venice is just to succumb to its charms and blow a lot of money.

Public Toilets: There are handy public WCs near St. Mark's Square, the Rialto Bridge, and the Accademia Bridge. You'll find public pay toilets near most major landmarks. Use free toilets—in a museum you're visiting or a café you're eating in—when you can.

Pigeon Poop: If bombed by a pigeon, resist the initial response to wipe it off immediately—it'll just smear into your hair. Wait until it dries and flake it off cleanly.

Water: Venetians pride themselves on having pure, safe, and tasty tap water piped in from the foothills of the Alps. You can actually see the mountains from Venice's bell towers on crisp, clear winter days.

Lingo: *Campo* means square, *campiello* is a small square, *calle* is street, *fondamenta* is the road running along a canal, *rio* is a small canal, *rio terra* is a street that was once a canal and has been filled in, and *ponte* is a bridge.

Services

Money: The plentiful ATMs are the easiest way to go. If you must exchange currency, be aware that bank rates vary. The American Express change desk is just off St. Mark's Square (see "Travel Agencies," later in this section). Non-bank exchange bureaus, such as Exacto, will charge you $10 more than a bank for a $200 exchange.

Internet Access: You'll find handy little Internet places all over town. They're equally good.

Post Office: A large post office is just outside the far end of St. Mark's Square (the end farthest from the basilica; Mon–Fri 8:30–14:00, Sat 8:30–13:00, closed Sun, shorter hours off-season). The main P.O. is near the Rialto Bridge (on St. Mark's side, Mon–Sat 8:30–18:30, closed Sun). Use post offices only as a last resort, as simple transactions can take 45 minutes if you get in the wrong line. You can buy stamps from tobacco shops and mail postcards from any of the red postboxes around town.

Bookstores: Libreria Studium stocks all the English-language guidebooks (including mine) just a block behind St. Mark's Basilica (Mon–Sat 9:00–19:30, Sun 10:00–14:00, Calle de la Canonica, tel. 041-522-2382).

Laundry: I list several laundry options below, but your hotelier can direct you to one nearest your hotel. A modern **self-service *lavanderia*** is near St. Mark's Square on Ruga Giuffa at #4826 (daily 8:30–23:00, shorter hours Oct–May, next to recommended Hotel al Piave, tel. 347-870-6452, run by Massimo). **Lavanderia Gabriella** is also near St. Mark's Square (€14/load wash and dry, Mon–Fri 8:00–12:30, closed Sat–Sun; Rio Terra Colonne 985, with your back to the door of San Zulian Church go over Ponte dei Ferali, then take first right down Calle dei Armeni, then first left onto Rio Terra Colonne; tel. 041-522-1758). A **self-service launderette** near the train station is a few steps from the recommended hotel Albergo Marin—see page 811 for directions (daily 7:30–22:30, last wash at 21:30, Chiaverete di San Simon 665a/b, San Polo, tel. 348-301-7457).

Travel Agencies: If you need to get train tickets, make seat reservations, or arrange a *cucetta* (koo-CHET-tah—a berth on a night train), you can avoid a time-consuming trip to the crowded train station by using a downtown travel agency. All can give advice on cheap flights. Note that you'll get a far better price if you're able to book at least a week in advance. Consider booking flights for later in your trip while you're here (and the good news is that for flights within Europe, you don't have to buy a round-trip ticket to get the best price).

Kele & Teo Viaggi e Turismo is reliable and handy, selling train tickets with no fees (Mon–Fri 8:30–18:00, Sat 9:00–12:00, closed Sun, at Ponte dei Bareteri on the Mercerie midway between the Rialto Bridge and St. Mark's Square, tel. 041-520-8722, www.keleteo.com, incoming@keleteo.com).

American Express books flights, sells train tickets, and makes train reservations (Mon–Fri 9:00–17:30, closed Sat–Sun, about 2 blocks off St. Mark's Square en route to Accademia at Salizada San Moisè, 1471 San Marco, tel. 041-520-0844).

Oltrex, just one bridge past the Bridge of Sighs, sells train and plane tickets and happily books train reservations for a €2 fee (daily 9:00–19:00, Riva degli Schiavoni 4192, tel. 041-524-2828).

Church Services: The **San Zulian Church** (the only church in Venice that you can actually walk around) offers a Mass in English at 9:30 (daily May–Sept, Sun only Oct–April, 2 blocks toward Rialto off St. Mark's Square). Gregorians enjoy the sung Gregorian Mass on Sundays at 11:00 (plus Mon–Sat at 8:00) at the **Church of San Giorgio Maggiore** (on island of San Giorgio Maggiore, visible from Doge's Palace, see page 793). Call 041-522-7827 to confirm times.

Haircuts: I've been getting my hair cut at Coiffeur Benito for 16 years. Benito is an artist—actually a "hair sculptor"—and a cut here is a fun diversion from the tourist grind (€19.50 for women, €16.50 for men, Tue–Fri 8:30–13:00 & 15:30–19:30, Sat 8:30–13:00 only, closed Sun and Mon, behind San Zulian Church near St. Mark's Square, Calle S. Zulian Già del Strazzariol 592a, tel. 041-528-6221).

Getting Around Venice

By Vaporetto: The public transit system is a fleet of motorized bus-boats called *vaporetti*. They work like city buses except that they never get a flat, the stops are docks, and if you get off between stops, you might drown.

For most travelers, only two lines matter: #1 is the slow boat, which takes 45 minutes to make every stop along the entire length of the Grand Canal (leaves every 10 min); #82 is the fast boat that zips down the Grand Canal in 25 minutes (leaves every 20 min), stopping mainly at Tronchetto (parking lot), Piazzale Roma (bus station), Ferrovia (train station), Rialto Bridge, San Tomà (Frari Church), Accademia Bridge, San Marco (west end of St. Mark's Square), and San Zaccaria (east end of St. Mark's Square). Some #82 boats go only as far as Rialto *(solo Rialto)*—check with the conductor before boarding.

It's a simple system, but there are a few quirks. Some stops have just one dock for boats going in both directions, while others have docks across the canal from each other—one side of the canal if you're going upstream, the other side for downstream, or well-marked docks side by side: one serving upstream, one downstream. Electric reader boards on busy docks indicate which boats are coming next and when. Signs on board indicate upcoming stops.

Some lines don't run early or late. For example, the #82 fast vaporetto often doesn't leave the San Marco–Vallaresso stop (at St. Mark's Square) until 9:15; if you're trying to get from St. Mark's Square to the train station to catch an early train, you'd need to take slow #1 instead, which begins its runs from San Marco–Vallaresso at 4:25. If there's any doubt, ask a ticket-seller or conductor. If you plan to ride a lot of *vaporetti*, consider picking up the most current ACTV timetable (free at ticket booths, in English and Italian, www.actv.it).

Tickets are €5 each (though it's just €2 one-way to the island of San Giorgio). They're good for 60 minutes in one direction; you can hop on and off at stops during that time. Technically, you're not

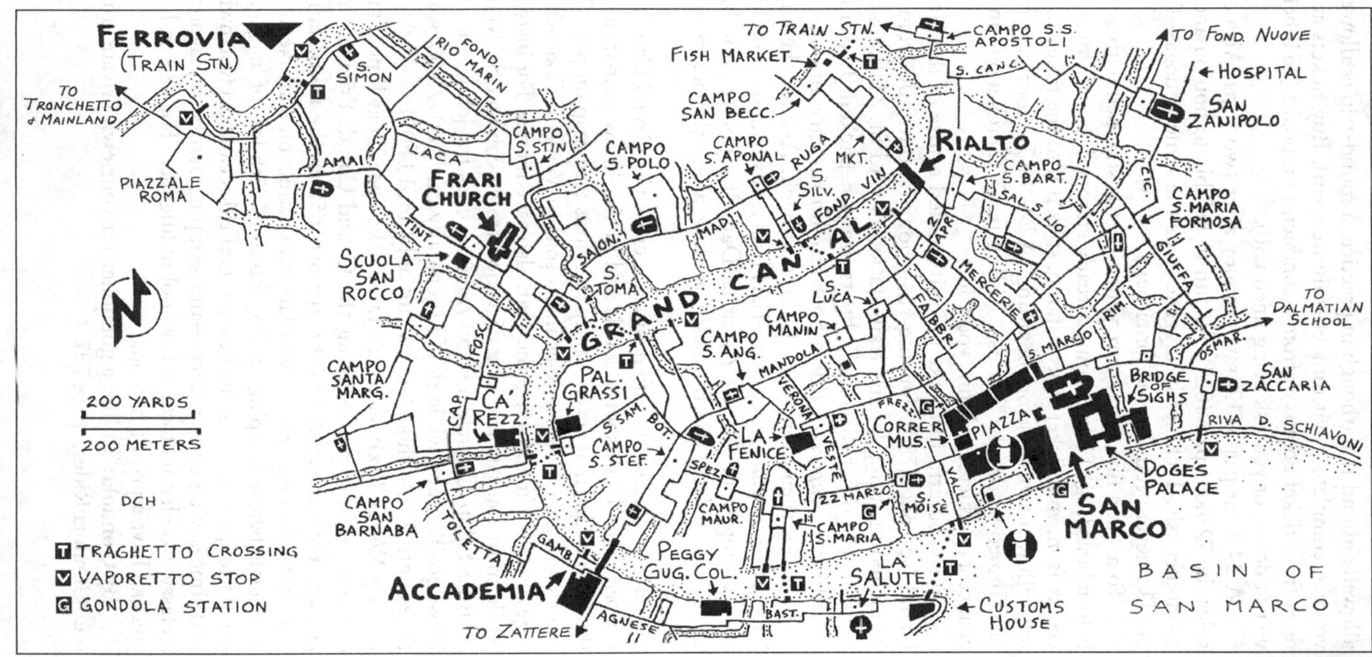
Venice
Ferrovia (Train Stn.)
To Tronchetto & Mainland
S. Simon
Rio Fond. Marin
Piazzale Roma
Amai
Laca
Campo S. Stin
Frari Church
Tint.
Scuola San Rocco
Campo S. Polo
Saon.
S. Toma
Mad.
Campo S. Aponal
Ruga
S. Silv.
Mkt.
Fond. Vin
Campo San Becc.
Fish Market
To Train Stn.
Campo S.S. Apostoli
S. Canc.
Rialto
Campo S. Bart.
Sal. S. Lio
2 Apr.
Mercerie
Fabbri
S. Luca
Grand Canal
Campo Manin
Campo S. Ang.
Mandola
Verona
Fosc.
Campo Santa Marg.
Cap.
Ca' Rezz.
Pal. Grassi
S. Sam. Bot.
Campo S. Stef.
La Fenice
Veste
Spez.
Campo Maur.
22 Marzo
Campo S. Maria
S. Moisè
Frezz.
Correr Mus.
Piazza
Vall.
Campo San Barnaba
Toletta
Gamb.
Accademia
To Zattere
Agnese
Peggy Gug. Col.
Bast.
La Salute
Customs House
San Marco
Doge's Palace
Bridge of Sighs
Riva D. Schiavoni
San Zaccaria
Osmar.
S. Marco
Rim.
Giuffa
C.C.
Campo S. Maria Formosa
To Dalmatian School
San Zanipolo
Hospital
To Fond. Nuove
Basin of San Marco
200 Yards
200 Meters
DCH
Traghetto Crossing
Vaporetto Stop
Gondola Station

allowed a round-trip (though in practice, a round-trip is allowed if you can complete it within a 60-minute span). Buy tickets at the dock from ticket booths or from a conductor on board (do it before you sit down, or you risk being fined €30).

A 24-hour pass (€12) saves money after two trips. Also consider the 72-hour pass (€25). It's fun to be able to hop on and off spontaneously. Technically, luggage costs the same as dogs—€5—but I've never been charged for either.

To avoid a fine, make sure your ticket is stamped with a time before boarding. Tickets come already stamped, but if, for whatever reason, your ticket lacks a stamp, stick it into the time-stamping yellow machine before boarding. A 24- or 72-hour pass must be stamped before the first use. Riding free? There's a one-in-ten chance a conductor will fine you €30.

For vaporetto fun, take my self-guided cruise of the Grand Canal (see page 780). During rush hour (about 9:00 from the Tronchetto parking lot and train station toward St. Mark's, about 17:00 in the other direction), boats are jam-packed. If you like joyriding on *vaporetti*, ride a boat around the city and out into the lagoon, then over to the Lido, and back. Ask for the circular route—*circulare* (cheer-koo-LAH-ray). It's usually the #51 or #52, leaving from the San Zaccaria–Danieli vaporetto stop (near the Doge's Palace) and from all the stops along the perimeter of Venice.

By *Traghetto*: Only four bridges cross the Grand Canal, but *traghetti* (gondolas) shuttle locals and in-the-know tourists across the Grand Canal at seven handy locations (see map on page 770; routes also marked on pricier maps sold in Venice). Take advantage of these time-savers—they can also save money. For instance, while most tourists take the €5 vaporetto to connect St. Mark's with La Salute Church, a €0.50 *traghetto* does the job just as well. Most people stand while riding (generally run 6:00–20:00, sometimes until 23:00, though a few run only until 14:00).

By Water Taxi: Venetian taxis, like speedboat limos, hang out at most busy points along the Grand Canal. Prices, which average €50 (about €90 to the airport, €50 to the train station, with extra fees for very early or late runs), are a bit soft. Negotiate and settle before stepping in. For travelers with lots of luggage or small groups who can split the cost, taxi rides can be a worthwhile and time-saving convenience—and skipping across the lagoon in a classic wooden motorboat is a cool indulgence. For €80 an hour, you can have a private taxi boat tour.

By Gondola: To hire a gondolier for your own private cruise, see "Gondola Rides," page 797.

TOURS

Avventure Bellissime Venice Tours—This company offers a selection of historic and entertaining walks, including the basic St. Mark's Square introduction called the Original Venice Walking Tour, offered daily at 11:00. Their other walks include Cannaregio and the Jewish Ghetto; San Polo and Dorsoduro (called Original Hidden Venice Walk); Doge's Palace (includes Secret Itineraries); Ghosts and Legends; Secret Doge's Palace; and Secret Gardens (€20–25 per person, cheaper for returnees and students, €5 discount for Rick Steves' readers who book online, group size 8–20, most tours last 2 hours and run rain or shine, English only—guides are native-speaking expats, tel. 041-520-8616, mobile 340-050-2444, see www.tours-italy.com for details, info@tours-italy.com, Monica or Jonathan). The company also runs day trips to the Dolomites, Veneto hill towns, and Palladian villa tours (€110–165, €10 discount for saying "Rick sent me," max 8 people).

Their 70-minute Grand Canal boat tour, offered daily at 16:30 (€40), is good. Tours are limited to about eight passengers (sitting awkwardly in a taxi not designed for sightseeing). You'll enjoy a fascinating, relaxing look at the wonders of the Grand Canal as well as the intimate back canals with a motor-mouthed (and interesting) guide. The departure is timed to give photographers the best possible light.

Classic Venice Bars Tour—Debonair local guide Alessandro Schezzini is a connoisseur of Venetian *bacari*—classic old bars serving traditional *cicchetti* (local munchies). He offers evening tours that involve sampling a snack and a glass of wine at three different *bacari*. The fee—€30 per person—includes wine, *cicchetti*, and a chat with Alessandro, who will answer all of your questions about Venice (April–Oct Wed and Sat at 18:00, other evenings and off-season by request and with demand, 6–8 per group, tours must have at least 6 people, meet at top of Rialto Bridge, call or email a day or two in advance to confirm, mobile 335-530-9024, venische@libero.it).

Venicescapes—Michael Broderick's private theme tours of Venice are intellectually demanding and beyond the attention span of most mortal tourists. Rather than a "sightseeing tour," consider your time with Michael a rolling, graduate-level lecture. Michael's challenge: To help visitors gain a more solid understanding of Venice. For a description of his various itineraries, see www.venicescapes.org (book well in advance, tours last 4–6 hours, €275 for 2, €50 per person after that, plus admissions and transportation, tel. 041-520-6361, info@venicescapes.org).

Local Guides—Licensed guides are carefully trained and love explaining Venice to visitors. The following companies and guides give excellent tours to individuals, families, and small groups. If you organize a small group from your hotel at breakfast to split the cost (€65/hr with 2-hour minimum), the fee becomes quite reasonable.

Elisabetta Morelli is reliable, personable, and informative, giving good insight into daily life in Venice (€60/hr, tours last 2–3 hours, tel. 041-526-7816, mobile 328-753-5220, bettamorelli@inwind.it).

Venice With a Guide is a co-op of 10 equally good guides (www.venicewithaguide.com).

Walks Inside Venice is a group of three women who are enthusiastic about their teaching (Cristina: tel. 335-229-714, Roberta: tel. 347-253-0560, Sara: tel. 348-341-5421, www.walksinsidevenice.com, info@walksinsidevenice.com).

Alessandro Schezzini isn't a licensed Italian guide (and is therefore unable to take you into actual sights), but he does a great job getting you beyond the clichés and into offbeat Venice (€90/2.5 hrs, listed earlier in "Classic Venice Bars Tour"). He also does Ghost Tours for spooky evening fun.

SELF-GUIDED CRUISE

Welcome to Venice Grand Canal Cruise

For a ▲▲▲ joyride, introduce yourself to Venice by boat. Cruise the Canal Grande from Tronchetto (parking lot) or Ferrovia (train station) all the way to St. Mark's Square.

You can ride boat #1 (slow and ideal, 45 min) or #82 (too fast to comfortably follow this tour, 25 min). When catching either boat, confirm that you're on a "San Marco via Rialto" boat (some boats finish at the Rialto Bridge, others take a non-scenic outside route). The conductor announces *"Solo Rialto!"* for boats going only as far as Rialto. You do not want boats heading for Piazzale Roma. Note that the San Marco vaporetto stop is actually called San Marco-Vallaresso.

The best seats are in the open air—if you can't snag a front seat, lurk nearby and take one when it becomes available or find an outside seat at the stern or along the railing. This ride has the best light and fewest crowds early or late. Twilight is magic. After dark, chandeliers light up the building interiors. While Venice is a barrage on the senses that hardly needs a narration, these notes give the cruise a little meaning and help orient you to this great city. Some city maps (on sale at postcard racks) have a handy Grand Canal map on the back.

Overview

The Grand Canal is Venice's "Main Street." At more than two

Venice's Grand Canal

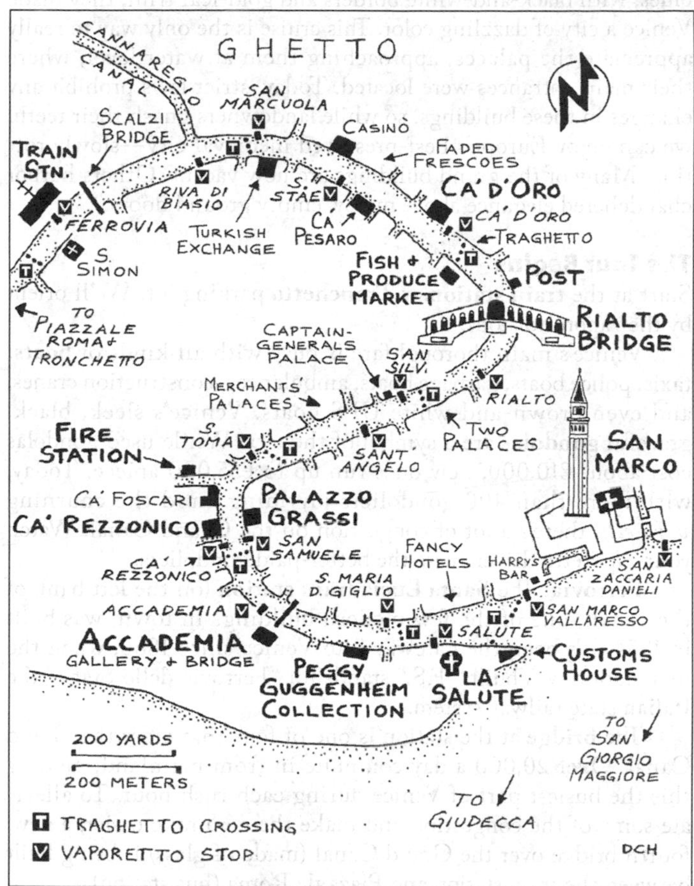

miles long, almost 150 feet wide, and nearly 15 feet deep, it's the biggest canal with the most impressive palaces. The canal is the remnant of a river that once spilled from the mainland into the Adriatic. The sediment it carried formed barrier islands that cut off the sea, forming a lagoon. Venice was built on the marshy islands of the former delta, sitting on more than a million trees piled together, reaching below the mud to the solid clay. Much of the surrounding countryside was deforested; trees were exported and consumed locally to fuel the furnaces of Venice's booming glass industry, to build Europe's biggest merchant marine, and to prop up this city in the mud.

Venice is a city of palaces, dating from the days when it was the world's richest city. The most lavish palaces formed a grand chorus line along the Grand Canal. Once frescoed in reds and blues, with black-and-white borders and gold-leaf trim, they made Venice a city of dazzling color. This cruise is the only way to really appreciate the palaces, approaching them at water level, where their main entrances were located. Today, strict laws prohibit any changes in these buildings, so while landowners gnash their teeth, we can enjoy Europe's best-preserved medieval city—slowly rotting. Many of the grand buildings are now vacant. Others harbor chandeliered elegance above mossy, empty ground floors.

The Tour Begins

Start at the **train station** or **Tronchetto** parking lot. We'll orient by the vaporetto stops.

Venice's main thoroughfare is busy with all kinds of **boats:** taxis, police boats, garbage boats, ambulances, construction cranes, and even brown-and-white UPS boats. Venice's sleek, black, graceful **gondolas** are a symbol of the city. While used gondolas cost about €10,000, new ones run up to €35,000 apiece. Today, with more than 400 gondoliers joyriding amid the churning *vaporetti*, there's a lot of congestion on the Grand Canal. Watch your vaporetto driver curse the better-paid gondoliers.

Ferrovia: The **Santa Lucia train station** (on the left bank of the canal), one of the few modern buildings in town, was built in 1954. It's been the gateway into Venice since 1860, when the first station was built. "F.S." stands for "Ferrovie dello Stato," the Italian state railway system.

The **bridge** at the station is one of four that cross the Grand Canal. Over 20,000 a day commute in from mainland, making this the busiest part of Venice during each rush hour. To alleviate some of the congestion and make the commute easier, a new, fourth bridge over the Grand Canal (made of glass) is being built between the train station and Piazzale Roma (bus station).

Opposite the train station, atop the green dome of **San Simeone Piccolo** church, Saint Simeon waves *ciao* to whoever enters or leaves the "old" city.

Riva di Biasio: Just past the Riva di Biasio stop, look left down the broad **Cannaregio Canal.** The twin, pale-pink, six-story "skyscrapers" are reminders of how densely populated the world's original **ghetto** was. Set aside as the local Jewish quarter in 1516, the area (located behind the San Marcuola stop) became extremely crowded. This urban island developed into one of the most closely knit business and cultural quarters of all the Jewish communities in Italy, and gave us our word ghetto (from *geto,* the copper foundry located here). For more information, visit the Jewish Museum in this neighborhood (see page 796).

San Marcuola: The gray **Turkish "Fondaco" Exchange** (right side, opposite San Marcuola vaporetto stop) is considered the oldest house in Venice. Its horseshoe arches and roofline of triangles-and-dingleballs are reminders of its Byzantine heritage. Turkish traders in turbans docked here, unloaded their goods into the warehouse on the bottom story, then went upstairs for a home-style meal and a place to sleep. Venice in the 1500s was very cosmopolitan, welcoming every religion and ethnicity...so long as they carried cash.

Venice's **Casinò** (left-hand side) is housed in the palace where German composer Richard *(The Ring)* Wagner died in 1883. See his distinct, strong-jawed profile in the white plaque on the brick wall. In the 1700s, Venice was Europe's Vegas, with casinos and prostitutes everywhere. Today, this elegant Casinò welcomes men in ties and ladies in dresses. *Casinòs* ("little houses") have long provided Italians with a handy escape from daily life.

San Stae: Opposite the San Stae stop, look for the **faded frescoes** (left bank, on lower story). Imagine the facades of the Grand Canal at their finest. As colorful as the city is today, it's still only a sepia-toned snapshot of a long-gone era of lavishly decorated and brilliantly colored palaces. This is the stop for the Ca' Pesaro International Gallery of Modern Art (see page 794).

Ca' d'Oro: The lacy **Ca' d'Oro,** or "House of Gold" (left bank, just before the vaporetto stop), is the best example of Venetian Gothic architecture on the canal. Its three stories offer different variations on balcony design, topped with a spiny white roofline. Venetian Gothic mixes traditional Gothic (pointed arches and round medallions stamped with a four-leaf clover) with Byzantine styles (tall, narrow arches atop thin columns), filled in with Islamic frills. Like all the palaces, this was originally painted and gilded to make it even more glorious than it is now. *Ca'* means "house." Because only the house of the doge (Venetian ruler) could be called a palace *(palazzo)*, all other palaces are technically *Ca'*. Today the Ca' d'Oro is a museum, but, other than temporary exhibits, there's little to see inside (see page 796).

Farther along, on the right, the outdoor arcade of the **fish and produce market** bustles with people in the morning but is quiet the rest of the day. This is a great scene to wander through—even though European hygiene standards recently required a less-colorful remodeling job. Find the ***traghetto*** gondola ferrying shoppers back and forth, standing like Washington crossing the Delaware.

The huge **post office** (left side, just before the Rialto Bridge), with *servizio postale* boats moored at its blue posts, was the German Exchange, the trading center for German metal merchants, in the early 1500s. The building's top story has a rare sight in frilly Venice—square windows. In the distance, rising above the post office, you can see the golden angel of the Campanile (bell tower) at St. Mark's Square, where this tour will end.

As the canal bends, we pass beneath the impressive Rialto Bridge. Singing gondoliers love the acoustics here: *"O sole mio..."*

Rialto: A major landmark of Venice, the **Rialto Bridge** is lined with shops and tourists. Constructed in 1588, it's the third bridge built on this spot. With a span of 160 feet and foundations stretching 650 feet on either side, the Rialto was an impressive engineering feat in its day. Earlier Rialto Bridges could open to let big ships in, but not this one. When this new bridge was completed, much of the Grand Canal was closed to shipping and became a canal of palaces.

Rialto, a separate town in the early days of Venice, has always been the commercial district, while San Marco was the religious and governmental center. Today, a winding street called the Mercerie connects the two, providing travelers with human traffic jams and a mesmerizing gauntlet of shopping temptations. The restaurants that line the canal feature great views, midrange prices, and low-quality food.

San Silvestro: On the left side, opposite the vaporetto stop, **two palaces stand side by side,** with stories the same height, creating the effect of one long balcony.

We now enter a long stretch of important **merchants' palaces,** each with proud and different facades. Since ships couldn't navigate beyond the Rialto Bridge to reach the section of the Grand Canal you just came from, the biggest palaces—with the major shipping needs—lie ahead.

Palaces like these were multifunctional: ground floor for the warehouse, offices and showrooms upstairs on the "noble floor" (with big windows designed to allow maximum light in), and living quarters on the top.

Sant'Angelo: Just past the Sant'Angelo stop (ahead on the right, with twin obelisks on the rooftop) stands the **palace of a 15th-century captain general** of the sea. These Venetian equivalents of five-star admirals were honored with twin obelisks decorating their palaces. This palace flies three flags: those of Italy (green-white-red), the European Union (blue with ring of stars), and Venice (the lion).

Notice how many buildings have a foundation of waterproof white stone *(pietra d'Istria)* upon which the bricks sit high and dry. Many canal-level floors are abandoned; the rising water level takes its toll. The **posts**—historically painted gaily with the equivalent of family coats of arms—don't rot under water. But the wood at the waterline does.

Take a deep whiff of Venice. What's all this nonsense about stinky canals? All I smell is my shirt. By the way, how's your captain? Smooth dockings? To get to know him, stand up in the bow and block his view.

San Tomà: After the San Tomà stop, look down the side canal (on the right, before the bridge) to see the traffic light, the **fire station,** and the fireboats ready to go.

We now prepare to round the corner and double back toward St. Mark's. The impressive **Ca' Foscari** (right side) dominates the bend in the canal. Its four stories get increasingly ornate as they rise from the water—from simple Gothic arches at water level, to Gothic with a point, to Venetian Gothic arches topped with four-leaf clovers, to still more medallions and laciness that look almost Moorish. Wow.

These days, when buildings are being renovated, huge murals with images of the building mask the ugly scaffolding. Corporations sponsor these multistory covers, hiding the scaffolding for the goodwill—and the publicity.

Ca' Rezzonico: The grand, heavy, white **Ca' Rezzonico,** directly at the stop of the same name, houses the Museum of 18th-Century Venice (see page 794). Across the canal is the cleaner and leaner **Palazzo Grassi,** the last major palace built on the canal, erected in the late 1700s. Today it showcases special exhibitions.

Accademia: The wooden **Accademia Bridge** crosses the Grand Canal and leads to the **Accademia** art museum (right side), filled with the best Venetian paintings (see page 793). The bridge was put up in 1932 as a temporary one. Locals liked it, so it stayed. Cruising under the bridge, you'll get a classic view of the domed La Salute Church ahead.

The low white building among greenery (on the right, between the bridge and the church) is the **Peggy Guggenheim Collection.** The American heiress "retired" here, sprucing up the palace that had been abandoned in mid-construction; the locals call it the *"palazzo non finito."* Peggy willed the city her fine collection of modern art (see page 793).

Salute: A crown-shaped dome supported by scrolls stands atop **La Salute Church** (see page 794). This Church of Saint Mary of Good Health was built to thank God for delivering Venetians from the devastating plague of 1630 (which had killed about a third of the city's population).

Across the canal (left side), several **fancy hotels** have painted facades that hint at the canal's former glory.

As the Grand Canal opens up into the lagoon, the last building on the right with the golden ball is the 16th-century **Customs House** (Dogana da Mar, not open to the public). Its two bronze Atlases hold a statue of Fortune riding the ball. Arriving ships stopped here to pay their tolls.

As you prepare to disembark at the San Marco–Vallaresso stop, look from left to right out over the lagoon. On the left, a wide harborfront walk leads past the town's most elegant hotels to the green area in the distance. This is the public garden, the largest of Venice's few parks, which hosts the Biennale art show every odd year (next one is in 2009). Farther in the distance is the **Lido,** the island with Venice's beach. It's tempting, with sand and casinos, but its car traffic breaks into the medieval charm of Venice.

The ghostly white church that seems to float is the architect Andrea Palladio's **San Giorgio Maggiore.** It's just a vaporetto ride away (#82 from the San Zaccaria–M.V.E. stop; see page 793). Across the lagoon (to your right) is a residential island called **Giudecca.**

San Marco–Vallaresso: Get off at the San Marco–Vallaresso stop. Directly ahead is **Harry's Bar.** Hemingway drank here when it was a characteristic no-name *osteria* and the gondoliers' hangout. Today, of course, it's the overpriced hangout of well-dressed Americans who don't mind paying triple for their Bellinis (peach juice with Prosecco—a sparkling white wine) to make the scene. While Harry's Bar is a non-sight, one of Europe's great experiences—St. Mark's Square—is just a long block up the waterfront.

SIGHTS

St. Mark's Square

For information on Venice's Museum Card and pricier Museum Pass, which cover most of the sights on the square, see page 771.

▲▲▲St. Mark's Square (Piazza San Marco)—This grand square is surrounded by splashy historic buildings and sights (each one described in more detail below): St. Mark's Basilica, the Doge's Palace, the Campanile (bell tower), and the Correr Museum. The square is filled with music, lovers, pigeons, and tourists by day, and is your private rendezvous with the Venetian past late at night, when Europe's most magnificent dance floor is *the* romantic place to be.

With your back to the church, survey one of Europe's great urban spaces, and the only square in Venice to merit the title "Piazza." Nearly two football fields long, it's surrounded by the offices of the republic. On the right are the "old offices" (16th-century Renaissance). At left are the "new offices" (17th-century Baroque). Napoleon, after enclosing the square with the more simple and austere Neoclassical wing across the far end, called this "the most beautiful drawing room in Europe."

For a slow and pricey evening thrill, invest about €15 (including the cover charge for the music) in a glass of wine or coffee at one of the elegant cafés with the dueling orchestras. For an unmatched experience that offers the best people-watching, it's worth the small splurge. But if all you have is €1, buy a bag of pigeon feed and become popular in a flurry. (To control the poopulation, the city adds bird birth control to the feed.) To get the flock airborne, toss your sweater in the air.

The **Clock Tower** (Torre dell'Orologio), built during the Renaissance in 1496, marks the entry to the main shopping drag, called the Mercerie, which connects St. Mark's Square with the Rialto. From the piazza, you can see the bronze men (Moors) swing their huge clappers at the top of each hour. In the 17th century, one of them knocked an unsuspecting worker off the top and to his death—probably the first-ever killing by a robot. Notice one of the world's first "digital" clocks on the tower facing the square (with dramatic flips every five min). The Clock Tower reopened in 2007 to visitors who have reserved ahead for the mandatory tour (€12; covered by Museum Card or Museum Pass, tours in English Mon–Wed at 9:00, 10:00, and 11:00; Thu–Sun 13:00, 14:00, and 15:00; reserve by phoning tel. 041-520-9070 or online at www.museicivicivenezianI.it).

Venice's best TI is in the far left corner of the square (daily 9:00–15:30), and a €1 WC is 30 yards beyond St. Mark's Square (see *Albergo Diorno* sign marked on pavement, WC open daily 9:00–17:30). Another TI is on the lagoon (daily 10:00–18:00, walk toward the water by the Doge's Palace and go right, €1 WCs nearby).

▲▲▲St. Mark's Basilica (Basilica di San Marco)—Built in the 11th century to replace an earlier church, this basilica's distinctly Eastern-style architecture underlines Venice's connection with the Byzantine Empire (which protected it from the ambition of Charlemagne and his Holy Roman Empire). It's decorated with booty from returning sea captains—a kind of architectural Venetian trophy chest. The interior glows mysteriously with gold mosaics and colored marble. Since about A.D. 830, the saint's bones have been housed on this site.

Cost and Hours: The basilica is free (except for the "Additional Sights" described below) and open Mon–Sat 9:45–17:00 (until 16:30 off-season), Sun 14:00–16:00 (tel. 041-522-5205). The line can be very long during peak season. No photos are allowed inside.

Bag Check: While small purses are allowed inside the church, larger bags and backpacks are not. Check them for free at the nearby Ateneo S. Basso, a former church (open roughly Mon–Sat 9:30–17:30, Sun 14:00–16:30; from Piazzetta dei Leoncini to the left of basilica, head down Calle S. Basso, second door on your right). Those with a bag to check actually get to skip the line. Here's how it works: Drop by Ateneo S. Basso. Leave your bag (for up to one hour) and pick up the tag. Two people per tag are allowed to go to the basilica's gatekeeper and scoot directly in (ahead of the line). After touring the church, come back and pick up your bag.

Dress Code: To enter the church, modest dress is required

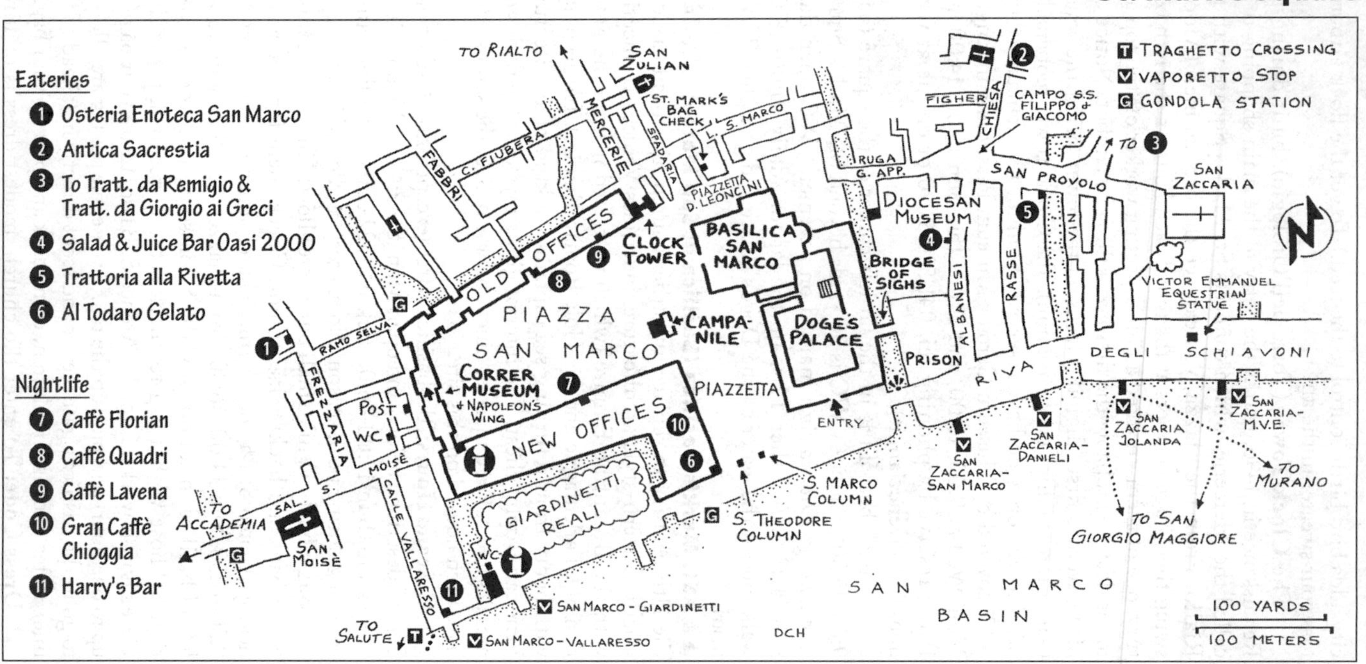
St. Mark's Square
Eateries
1 Osteria Enoteca San Marco
2 Antica Sacrestia
3 To Tratt. da Remigio & Tratt. da Giorgio ai Greci
4 Salad & Juice Bar Oasi 2000
5 Trattoria alla Rivetta
6 Al Todaro Gelato
Nightlife
7 Caffè Florian
8 Caffè Quadri
9 Caffè Lavena
10 Gran Caffè Chioggia
11 Harry's Bar
T Traghetto Crossing
V Vaporetto Stop
G Gondola Station
To Rialto
San Zulian
St. Mark's Bag Check
L. S. Marco
Mercerie
Spadaria
Fabbri
C. Fiubera
Piazzetta D. Leoncini
Ruga G. App.
Figher
Chiesa
Campo S.S. Filippo & Giacomo
To 3
San Provolo
San Zaccaria
Diocesan Museum
Vin
Rasse
Albanesi
Bridge of Sighs
Victor Emmanuel Equestrian Statue
Degli Schiavoni
Riva
Prison
Basilica San Marco
Clock Tower
Old Offices
Piazza San Marco
Campanile
Doge's Palace
Piazzetta
Entry
Correr Museum & Napoleon's Wing
New Offices
Ramo Selva
Post
WC
Frezzaria
Moisè
Sal. S. Moisè
San Moisè
To Accademia
Calle Vallaresso
Giardinetti Reali
S. Marco Column
S. Theodore Column
San Zaccaria-San Marco
San Zaccaria-Danieli
San Zaccaria Jolanda
San Zaccaria-M.V.E.
To Murano
To San Giorgio Maggiore
San Marco Basin
San Marco - Giardinetti
San Marco - Vallaresso
To Salute
DCH
100 Yards
100 Meters

even of kids (no shorts or bare shoulders). People who ignore the dress code hold up the line while they plead fruitlessly with the dress-code police.

Theft Alert: St. Mark's Basilica is the most dangerous place in Venice for pickpocketing—inside, it's always a crowded jostle.

Tours: In the atrium, see the schedule board that lists free English guided tours (schedules vary, but generally May–Oct Tue, Wed, and Thu at 11:00, 1 hour, meet guide just to the right of main doors).

Inside the Church: St. Mark's Basilica has 43,000 square feet of Byzantine mosaics, the best and oldest of which are in the atrium (turn right as you enter and stop under the last dome—this may be roped off, but dome is still visible). Facing the church, gape up (it's OK, no pigeons) and read the story of Adam and Eve that rings the bottom of the dome. Now, facing the piazza, look domeward for the story of Noah, the ark, and the flood (two by two, the wicked being drowned, Noah sending out the dove, a happy rainbow, and a sacrifice of thanks).

Step inside the church (the stairs on the right lead to the bronze horses in the San Marco Museum, described below—save these for later). Notice the marble floor richly decorated in mosaics. As in many Venetian buildings, because the best foundation pilings were made around the perimeter, the floor rolls. As you shuffle under the central dome, look up for the Ascension. As you follow the one-way tourist route, consider stopping off at the Treasury and the Golden Altarpiece, described below.

Additional Sights: Three separate exhibits inside each charge admission: the **San Marco Museum** (€3, Mon–Sat 9:45–16:30, Sun 9:45–16:00), the **Treasury** (€2, includes audioguide, same hours as church), and the **Golden Altarpiece** (€2, same hours as church).

In the **San Marco Museum** (Museo di San Marco) upstairs, you can see an up-close mosaic exhibition, a fine view of the church interior, a view of the square from the balcony with bronze horses, and (inside, in their own room) the original horses. These well-traveled horses, made during the days of Alexander the Great (fourth century B.C.), were taken to Rome by Nero, to Constantinople/Istanbul by Constantine, to Venice by crusaders, to Paris by Napoleon, back "home" to Venice when Napoleon fell, and finally indoors and out of the acidic air. The staircase up to the museum is in the atrium, near the basilica's entrance, marked by a sign that says *Loggia dei Cavalli, Museo.*

San Marco's **Treasury** (ask for the included and informative audioguide when you buy ticket) and **Golden Altarpiece** give you the best chance outside of Istanbul or Ravenna to see the glories of the Byzantine Empire. Venetian crusaders looted the Christian city of Constantinople and brought home piles of lavish loot (perhaps the lowest point in Christian history until the advent of TV evangelism). Much of this plunder is stored in the Treasury (Tesoro) of San Marco. As you view these treasures, remember that most were made around A.D. 500, while Western Europe was stuck in the Dark Ages. Beneath the high altar lies the body of St. Mark ("Marce") and the Golden Altarpiece (Pala d'Oro), made of 250 blue-backed enamels with religious scenes, all set in a gold frame and studded with 15 hefty rubies, 300 emeralds, 1,500 pearls, and assorted sapphires, amethysts, and topaz (c. 1100). Both of these sights are interesting and historic, but neither is as much fun as two bags of pigeon feed.

▲▲▲Doge's Palace (Palazzo Ducale)—The seat of the Venetian government and home of its ruling duke, or doge, this was the most powerful half-acre in Europe for 400 years.

The Doge's Palace was built to show off the power and wealth of the Republic and remind all visitors that Venice was number one. In typical Venetian Gothic style, the bottom has pointy arches and the top has an Eastern or Islamic flavor. Its columns sat on pedestals, but in the thousand years since they were erected, the palace has settled into the mud and the bases have vanished.

Enjoy the newly restored facades from the **courtyard.** Notice a grand staircase (with nearly naked Moses and Paul Newman at the top). Even the most powerful visitors climbed this to meet the doge. This was the beginning of an architectural power trip. The doge, the elected-for-life duke or leader of this "dictatorship of the aristocracy," lived with his family on the first floor near the halls of power. From his living quarters (once lavish, now sparsely furnished), you'll follow the one-way route through the public rooms of the top floor, finishing with the Bridge of Sighs and the prison. The place is wallpapered with masterpieces by Veronese and Tintoretto. Don't worry much about the great art. Enjoy the building.

In Room 12, the **Senate Room,** the 120 senators met, debated, and passed laws. From the center of the ceiling, Tintoretto's *Triumph of Venice* shows the city in all her glory. Lady Venice, in heaven with the Greek gods, stands high above the lesser nations, who swirl respectfully at her feet with gifts.

The **Armory**—a dazzling display originally assembled to intimidate potential adversaries—shows remnants of the military might that the empire employed to keep the East–West trade lines open (and the local economy booming). Squint out the window to see Palladio's San Giorgio Maggiore and, to the left in the distance, the tiny green dome at Venice's Lido (beach).

The giant **Hall of the Grand Council** (175 feet long, capacity 2,600) is where the entire nobility met to elect the senate and doge. Ringing the room are portraits of 76 doges (in chronological order). One, a doge who opposed the will of the Grand Council, is blacked out. Behind the doge's throne, you can't miss Tintoretto's monsterpiece, *Paradise,* the largest oil painting in the world. Christ and Mary are surrounded by a heavenly host of 500 saints. Its message to electors who met here: Make wise decisions and you'll ultimately join that holy crowd.

Cross the covered **Bridge of Sighs** over the canal to the **prisons** (at the fork in the route, descend the stairs rather than continuing right into a cell or you'll miss the basement altogether and end up at the bookshop at the end of the palace visit). In the privacy of his own home, a doge could sentence, torture, and jail his opponents secretly. Circle the cells. Notice the carvings made by prisoners—from olden days up until 1930—on some of the stone windowsills of the cells, especially in the far corner of the building.

Cross back over the Bridge of Sighs, pausing to look through the marble-trellised windows at all of the tourists.

Cost: €12 for Museum Card, includes admission to the Correr Museum (also covered by €18 Museum Pass). If the line is long at the Doge's Palace, buy your ticket at the Correr Museum across the square. With that, you can go directly through the Doge's turnstile without waiting in the long line.

Hours: Daily April–Oct 9:00–19:00, Nov–March 9:00–17:00, last entry one hour before closing.

Tours: Consider the €5 audioguide or the Secret Itineraries Tour, which takes you into palace rooms otherwise not open to the public (€16; in English at 9:55, 10:45, and 11:35; 75 min, call 041-291-5911 to reserve tour same day or a day in advance, or call 041-520-9070 if more than 2 days in advance). You must book in advance, and arrive 20 minutes early to check in—there's no need to wait in line, just *"scusi"* your way to the information desk in the room before the ticket counter. While the tour skips the main halls inside, it finishes inside the palace and you're welcome to visit the halls on your own.

▲▲Correr Museum (Museo Civico Correr)—This uncrowded museum gives you a good overview of Venetian history and art. In the Napoleon Wing, you'll see fine Neoclassical sculpture by Canova. Then peruse armor, banners, and paintings re-creating festive days of the Venetian republic. The upper floor lays out a good overview of Venetian art, including several paintings by the Bellini family. And just before the cafeteria is a room filled with traditional games. There are English descriptions and breathtaking views of St. Mark's Square throughout (€12 Museum Card also includes the Doge's Palace, also covered by €18 Museum Pass, daily April–Oct 9:00–19:00, Nov–March 9:00–17:00, last entry 1 hour before closing, enter at far end of square directly opposite basilica, tel. 041-240-5211).

▲**Campanile (Campanile di San Marco)**—This dramatic bell tower replaced a shorter lighthouse, once part of the original fortress/palace that guarded the entry of the Grand Canal. The lighthouse crumbled into a pile of bricks in 1902, a thousand years after it was built. Ride the elevator 300 feet to the top of the reconstructed bell tower for the best view in Venice. For an ear-shattering experience, be on top when the bells ring (€6, daily July–Aug 9:00–21:00, Sept–June 9:00–19:00). The golden angel at the top always faces into the wind. Lines are longest at midday; beat the crowds and enjoy crisp morning air at 9:00, or try in the early evening (around 18:00).

▲**La Fenice Opera House (Gran Teatro alla Fenice)**—During Venice's glorious decline in the 18th century, this was one of seven opera houses in the city. A 1996 arson fire completely gutted the theater, but La Fenice (the phoenix) has risen from the ashes, thanks to an eight-year effort to rebuild the historic landmark according to photographic archives of the interior. To see the results, you need to either attend an evening performance or take a guided tour. Tours last 45 minutes and run twice a day in English, but there's no set schedule and tour-group sizes are limited, so reserve ahead (€7, booking office open daily 9:30–18:30, tel. 041-2424, www.teatrolafenice.it).

Behind St. Mark's Basilica

Diocesan Museum (Museo Diocesano)—This little-known museum circles a peaceful Romanesque courtyard immediately behind the basilica (just before the Bridge of Sighs). It's filled with plunder from the Venetian Empire that never found a place in St. Mark's (free, but may charge admission for temporary exhibits, Mon–Sat 10:00–12:30—may be open longer if there's a special exhibition, closed Sun, tel. 041-522-9166).

▲**Bridge of Sighs**—Connecting two wings of the Doge's Palace high over a canal, this enclosed bridge was popularized by travelers in the Romantic 19th century. Supposedly, a condemned man would be led over this bridge on the way to the prison, take one last look at the glory of Venice, and sigh. While overhyped, the bridge is undeniably tingle-worthy—especially after dark, when the crowds have dispersed and it's just you and floodlit Venice. It's around the corner from the Doge's Palace: Walk toward the waterfront, turn left along the water, and look up the first canal on your left.

Church of San Zaccaria—This historic church is home to a sometimes-waterlogged crypt, a Bellini altarpiece, Tintoretto painting, and the final resting place of St. Zechariah, the father of John the Baptist (free, €1 to enter crypt, €0.50 coin to light up Bellini's altarpiece, Mon–Sat 10:00–12:00 & 16:00–18:00, Sun 16:00–18:00 only, 2 canals behind St. Mark's Basilica).

Across the Lagoon from St. Mark's Square

▲San Giorgio Maggiore—This is the dreamy island you can see from the waterfront by St. Mark's Square. The striking church, designed by Palladio, features art by Tintoretto and good views of Venice (free entry to church, daily May–Sept 9:30–12:15 & 14:30–18:00, Oct–April 9:30–12:35 & 14:30–16:30, closed Sun 11:00–12:00 to sightseers during Mass, Gregorian Mass sung Mon–Sat at 8:00, Sun at 11:00). The church's bell tower costs €3 and is accessible by elevator until 30 minutes before church's closing time. To reach the island from St. Mark's Square, take the five-minute vaporetto ride on #82 from the San Zaccaria–M.V.E. stop (the San Zaccaria dock farthest from the Bridge of Sighs, just beyond the big equestrian statue). But to get there for the 8:00 Gregorian Mass, take the vaporetto from the nearby San Zaccaria–Jolanda dock.

Dorsoduro District

▲▲Accademia (Galleria dell'Accademia)—Venice's top art museum, packed with highlights of the Venetian Renaissance, features paintings by the Bellini family, Titian, Tintoretto, Veronese, Tiepolo, Giorgione, Canaletto, and Testosterone. It's just over the wooden Accademia Bridge. Expect long lines in the late morning because they allow only 300 visitors in at a time; visit early or late to miss crowds, or call 041-520-0345 to book tickets at least a day in advance (€7.50, Mon 8:15–14:00, Tue–Sun 8:15–19:15, shorter hours off-season, last entry 45 min before closing, no photos allowed, tel. 041-522-2247). The dull audioguide costs €4 (€6 for double set or €6 for PalmPilot) and doesn't let you fast-forward to the works you want to hear about; you have to listen to the whole spiel for each room. One-hour guided tours in English are €5 (or €7 for two people, Sat–Sun at 11:00).

At the Accademia Bridge, there's a decent canalside pizzeria (Pizzeria Accademia Foscarini—see page 818) and a public WC at the base of the bridge.

▲▲Peggy Guggenheim Collection—The popular museum of far-out art, housed in the American heiress' former retirement palazzo, offers one of Europe's best reviews of the art of the first half of the 20th century. Stroll through styles represented by artists whom Peggy knew personally—Cubism (Picasso, Braque), Surrealism (Dalí, Ernst), Futurism (Boccioni), American Abstract Expressionism (Pollock), and a sprinkling of Klee, Calder, Duchamp, and Chagall (€10, Wed–Mon 10:00–18:00, closed Tue, last entry 15 min before closing, audioguide-€5, guidebook-€18, free and mandatory baggage check, pricey café, photos allowed only in garden and terrace—a fine and relaxing perch overlooking Grand Canal, near Accademia, Dorsoduro 704, tel. 041-240-5440, www.guggenheim-venice.it). The place is staffed by international interns working on art-related degrees.

▲La Salute Church (Santa Maria della Salute)—The impressive church with a crown-shaped dome was built and dedicated to the Virgin Mary by grateful survivors of the 1630 plague (free, daily 9:30–12:15 & 14:30–17:30, tel. 041-274-3928 to confirm). It's a 10-minute walk from Accademia Bridge, or a vaporetto ride (stop: Salute) from near St. Mark's Square—catch it at the San Marco–Valleresso dock near the TI and Harry's Bar.

▲Ca' Rezzonico (Museum of 18th-Century Venice)—This grand Grand Canal palazzo offers the best look in town at the life of Venice's rich and famous in the 1700s. Wander under ceilings by Tiepolo, among furnishings from that most decadent century, enjoying views of the canal and paintings by Guardi, Canaletto, and Longhi (€6.50, covered by €18 Museum Pass, April–Oct Wed–Mon 10:00–18:00, Nov–March Wed–Mon 10:00–17:00, closed Tue, last entry 1 hour before closing, audioguide-€4 for one person or €6 for two, free and mandatory baggage check, located at Ca' Rezzonico vaporetto stop, tel. 041-241-0100).

Santa Croce District

▲▲▲Rialto Bridge—One of the world's most famous bridges, this distinctive and dramatic stone structure crosses the Grand Canal with a single confident span. The arcades along the top of the bridge help reinforce the structure...and offer some enjoyable shopping diversions, as does the **market** surrounding the bridge (souvenir stalls open daily, produce market closed Sun, fish market closed Sun–Mon).

▲Ca' Pesaro International Gallery of Modern Art—This museum features 20th-century art in a 17th-century canalside palazzo. The collection is strongest on Italian (especially Venetian) artists, but also presents a broad array of other well-known artists. Highlights are Klimt's beautiful/creepy *Judith II*, Kandinsky's *White Zig Zags*, a colorful nude by Bonnard, and Chagall's portrait of his hometown rabbi, *The Rabbi of Vitebsk* (€5.50, covered by €18 Museum Pass, April–Oct Tue–Sun 10:00–18:00, Nov–March Tue–Sun 10:00–17:00, closed Mon, last entry 1 hour before closing, located at San Stae vaporetto stop, tel. 041-524-0695).

San Polo District

▲▲Frari Church (Chiesa dei Frari)—My favorite art experience in Venice is seeing art *in situ*—the setting for which it was designed—and my favorite example is the Chiesa dei Frari. The Franciscan "Church of the Brothers" and the art that decorates it is warmed by the spirit of St. Francis. It features the work of three great Renaissance masters: Donatello, Giovanni Bellini, and Titian—each showing worshippers the glory of God in human terms.

In **Donatello's wood carving of St. John the Baptist** (just to the right of the high altar), the prophet of the desert—dressed in animal skins and nearly starving from his diet of bugs 'n' honey—announces the coming of the Messiah. Donatello was a Florentine working at the dawn of the Renaissance.

Bellini's *Madonna and Child with Saints and Angels* painting (in the chapel farther to the right) came later, done by a Venetian in a more Venetian style—in soft focus, without Donatello's harsh realism. While Renaissance humanism demanded Madonnas and saints that were accessible and human, Bellini places them in a physical setting so beautiful it creates its own mood of serene holiness. The genius of Bellini, perhaps the greatest Venetian painter, is obvious in the pristine clarity, rich colors (notice Mary's clothing), believable depth, and reassuring calm of this three-paneled altarpiece. It's so good to see a painting in its natural setting.

Finally, glowing red and gold like a stained-glass window over the high altar, **Titian's *The Assumption of Mary*** sets the tone of exuberant beauty found in the otherwise sparse church. Titian the Venetian—a student of Bellini—painted steadily for 60 years... you'll see a lot of his art. As stunned apostles look up past the swirl of arms and legs, the complex composition of this painting draws you right to the radiant face of the once-dying, now-triumphant Mary as she joins God in heaven.

Be comfortable discreetly freeloading off passing tours. For many, these three pieces of art make a visit to the Accademia Gallery unnecessary (or they may whet your appetite for more). Before leaving, check out the Neoclassical, pyramid-shaped tomb of Canova and (opposite that) the grandiose tomb of Titian. Compare the carved marble Assumption behind Titian's tombstone portrait with the painted original above the high altar.

Cost, Hours, Information: €2.50, covered by €8 Chorus Pass, Mon–Sat 10:00–18:00, Sun 13:00–18:00 but closed Sun in Aug (last entry 15 min before closing, no visits during services, audioguides-€1.60/1 set, €2.60/2 sets). Modest dress is recommended. Church info: tel. 041-272-8618. The church often hosts evening **concerts** (€15, tickets sold at the church; for concert details, look for fliers, call 041-272-8611, or check www.basilicadeifrari.it).

▲▲Scuola San Rocco—Sometimes called "Tintoretto's Sistine Chapel," this lavish meeting hall, next to the Frari Church, has some 50 large, colorful Tintoretto paintings plastered to the walls and ceilings. The best paintings are upstairs, especially the *Crucifixion* in the smaller room. View the neck-breaking splendor with one of the mirrors *(specchio)* available at the entrance (€7, includes informative audioguide, daily April–Oct 9:00–17:30, Nov–March 10:00–16:00, last entry 30 min before closing, or see a concert here—tickets run €15–30—and enjoy the art as an evening bonus, tel. 041-523-4864, www.scuolagrandesanrocco.it).

Church of San Polo—This nearby church, which pales in comparison to the two sights listed above, is worth a visit for art-lovers. One of Venice's oldest churches (from the ninth century), San Polo features works by Tintoretto, Veronese, and Tiepolo and son (€2.50, covered by €8 Chorus Pass, Mon–Sat 10:00–17:00, closed Sun, last entry 15 min before closing).

Cannaregio District

Jewish Ghetto—The word "ghetto" comes from *geto*, which means "foundry" in the Venetian dialect. In 1516, Venice forced its Jews to live on an undesirable and easy-to-isolate island that was once home to the city's foundry. Restricted within their tiny neighborhood (the Ghetto Nuovo, or "New Ghetto"), they expanded upward, building six-story "skyscrapers" which stand today. The main square, Campo di Ghetto Nuovo, must have been quite a scene, with 70 shops ringing it and all of Venice's Jewish commerce compressed onto this one spot. The island's two bridges were locked up at night, when only Jewish doctors—coming to the aid of Venetians—were allowed to come and go. Eventually the ghetto community outgrew its original island, and the ghetto spread to adjacent blocks. As late as the 1930s, 12,000 Jews called Venice home, but today there are only 200—and only a handful live in the actual Ghetto. Of the original five synagogues, only two are still active. You can spot them (with their five windows) from the square, but to visit them you have to book a tour through the Jewish Museum.

This original ghetto becomes most interesting after touring the **Jewish Museum** (Museo Ebraico), with a humble two-room collection of silver and cloth worship aids and artifacts of the old community (€3, June–Sept Sun–Fri 10:00–17:00, Oct–May Sun–Fri 10:00–16:30, closed Sat and Jewish holidays, Campo di Ghetto Nuovo, tel. 041-715-359). Synagogue tours in English are offered hourly (€8.50, 30 min, June–Sept Sun–Fri 10:30–17:30, Oct–May until 16:30, contact museum for details).

Ca' d'Oro—This "House of Gold" palace, fronting the Grand Canal, is quintessential Venetian Gothic (Gothic seasoned with Byzantine and Islamic accents). Inside, there's little to see aside from special exhibitions (€5, Mon 8:15–14:00, Tue–Sun 8:15–19:15, free peek through hole in door of courtyard, Calle Ca' d'Oro 3932).

Castello District

Dalmatian School (Scuola Dalmata di San Giorgio)—This "school" (which means "meeting place") is a reminder that Venice was Europe's most cosmopolitan place in its heyday. It was here that the Dalmatians (from the present-day country of Croatia) worshipped in their own way, held neighborhood meetings, and worked to preserve their culture. The chapel on the ground floor happens to have the most exquisite Renaissance interior in Venice, with a cycle of paintings by Carpaccio ringing the room; be sure to pick up the English descriptions to the right of the entrance (€3, Tue–Sat 9:30–12:30 & 15:30–18:30, Sun 9:30–12:30, closed Mon, last entry 30 min before closing, between St. Mark's Square and Arsenale, on Calle dei Furlani, 3 blocks southeast of Campo San Lorenzo, tel. 041-522-8828).

Santa Elena—For a pleasant peek into a completely non-touristy, residential side of Venice, walk or catch vaporetto #1 from St. Mark's Square to the neighborhood of Santa Elena (at the fish's tail). This 100-year-old suburb lives as if there were no tourism. You'll find a kid-friendly park, a few lazy restaurants, and beautiful sunsets over San Marco.

EXPERIENCES

Gondola Rides

A rip-off for some, this is a traditional must for romantics. Gondoliers charge about €75–80 for a 40-minute ride during the day; from 19:30 on, figure on €95–105 (for *musica*—singer and accordionist—it's an additional €35). You can divide the cost—and the romance—among up to six people per boat, but you'll need to save two seats for the musicians if you choose to be serenaded. Note that only two seats (the ones in back) are next to each other. If you want to haggle, you'll find softer prices on back lanes where single gondoliers hang out, rather than at the bigger departure points. Establish the price and duration before boarding, enjoy your ride, and pay only when you're finished.

Gondolas cost lots more after 20:00 but are also more romantic and relaxing under the moon. Glide through nighttime Venice with your head on someone's shoulder. Follow the moon as it sails past otherwise unseen buildings. Silhouettes gaze down from bridges while window glitter spills onto the black water. You're anonymous in the city of masks, as the rhythmic thrust of your striped-shirted gondolier turns old crows into songbirds. This is extremely relaxing (and, I think, worth the extra cost to experience at night). Since you might get a narration plus conversation with your gondolier, talk with several and choose one you like who speaks English well. Women, beware...while gondoliers can be extremely charming, local women say that anyone who falls for one of these Romeos "has slices of ham over her eyes."

For cheap gondola thrills during the day, stick to the €0.50 one-minute ferry ride on a Grand Canal *traghetto.*

NIGHTLIFE

Venice is quiet at night, as tour groups stay in the cheaper hotels of Mestre on the mainland, and the masses of day-trippers return to their beach resorts. **Gondolas** cost more, but are worth the extra expense (see page 797). *Vaporetti* are uncrowded, and it's a great time to cruise the Grand Canal on the slow boat #1.

Venice has a busy schedule of events, festivals, and entertainment. Check at the TI for listings in publications such as the free *Un Ospite di Venezia* magazine (monthly, bilingual, available at top-end hotels, www.aguestinvenice.com).

Concerts—Take your pick of traditional Vivaldi concerts in churches throughout town. Homegrown Vivaldi is as trendy here as Strauss is in Vienna and Mozart is in Salzburg. In fact, you'll find frilly young Vivaldis all over town hawking concert tickets. The TI has a list of this week's Baroque concerts (tickets from €18, shows start at 21:00 and generally last 90 min). You'll find posters in hotels all over town. There's music most nights at Scuola San Teodoro (east side of Rialto Bridge) and San Vitale Church (north end of Accademia Bridge), among others. Consider the venue carefully. The general rule of thumb: Musicians in wigs and tights offer better spectacle, musicians in black-and-white suits are better performers. For the latest on church concerts, check at any TI or visit www.turismovenezia.it.

St. Mark's Square—For tourists, St. Mark's Square is the highlight, with lantern light and live music echoing from the cafés. Just being here after dark is a thrill, as **dueling café orchestras** entertain. Every night, enthusiastic musicians play the same songs, creating the same irresistible magic. Hang out for free behind the tables (which allows you to move easily on to the next orchestra when the musicians take a break), or spring for a seat and enjoy a fun and gorgeously set concert. If you sit a while, it can be €15 well spent (for a drink and the cover charge for music). Dancing on the square is free (and encouraged).

Streetlamp halos, live music, floodlit history, and a ceiling of stars make St. Mark's magic at midnight. You're not a tourist, you're a living part of a soft Venetian night...an alley cat with money. In the misty light, the moon has a golden hue. Shine with the old lanterns on the gondola piers, where the sloppy lagoon splashes at the Doge's Palace...reminiscing.

SLEEPING

Virtually all of my recommended hotels are central. See the maps (on pages 801, 804, and 807) for hotel locations. I've listed rooms in three neighborhoods: the Rialto action, St. Mark's bustle, and the quiet Dorsoduro area behind the Accademia art museum. Hotel websites are particularly valuable in Venice, because they often come with a map.

Reserve a room as soon as you know when you'll be in town. Hotels in Venice are usually booked up on Carnevale (Jan 29–Feb 5 in 2008), Easter and Easter Monday (March 23–24 in 2008), April 25 (St. Mark's Day), May 1 (Labor Day), November 1 (All Saints' Day)—and on Fridays and Saturdays year-round. If everything's full, don't despair. Call a day or two in advance and fill in a cancellation. If you arrive on an overnight train, your room may not be ready so early in the morning. Drop your bag at the hotel and dive right into Venice.

Venetian hoteliers are hard to pin down. They're experts at perfect price discrimination: They list a huge range of rates for the same room (e.g., €90–160) and refuse to give a firm price, enabling them to judge the demand and charge accordingly. Once they know what the market will bear, they max it out. Also, hotels are being squeezed by the very popular online-booking services (which take about a 20 percent commission). Between wanting to keep their gouging options open for high-season weekends and trying to recover these online commissions, hoteliers set their rack rates (the highest rates a hotel charges) sky-high.

My listings are more likely to give a straight price. I've assured hoteliers that my readers will book direct, so they'll get 100 percent

Sleep Code

(€1 = about $1.30, country code: 39)

S = Single, **D** = Double/Twin, **T** = Triple, **Q** = Quad, **b** = bathroom, **s** = shower only. Breakfast is included, credit cards are accepted, and English is spoken unless otherwise noted. Air-conditioning, when available, is usually only turned on in summer.

To help you easily sort through these listings, I've divided the rooms into three categories based on the price for a standard double room with bath:

$$$ Higher Priced—Most rooms €180 or more.
$$ Moderately Priced—Most rooms between €130–180.
$ Lower Priced—Most rooms €130 or less.

of what you pay; therefore, you'll get the fair net rate. I've listed only prices for peak season: April, May, June, September, and October. Prices will be higher during festivals, and virtually all places drop prices from November through March (except during Carnevale and Christmas) and in July and August.

Near St. Mark's Square

East of St. Mark's Square

Located near the Bridge of Sighs, just off the Riva degli Schiavoni waterfront promenade, these places rub drainpipes with Venice's most palatial five-star hotels. Ride the vaporetto to San Zaccaria (#51 from train station, #82 from Tronchetto parking lot).

$$$ Hotel Campiello, lacy and bright, was once part of a 19th-century convent. Ideally located 50 yards off the waterfront, its 16 rooms offer a tranquil, friendly refuge for travelers who appreciate comfort and professional service (Sb-€130, Db-€200, strict cancellation penalties enforced, air-con, elevator; from the waterfront street—Riva degli Schiavoni—take Calle del Vin, between pink Hotel Danieli and Hotel Savoia e Jolanda, to #4647, Castello; tel. 041-520-5764, fax 041-520-5798, www.hcampiello.it, campiello@hcampiello.it; family-run for four generations: sisters Monica and Nicoletta, and Thomas).

$$ Locanda al Leon has 14 posh, 18th-century Venice-style rooms just off Campo S.S. Filippo e Giacomo (Db-€140, bigger Db-€165, air-con, Campo S.S. Filippo e Giacomo 4270, Castello, tel. 041-277-0393, fax 041-521-0348, www.hotelalleon.com, leon @hotelalleon.com, Giuliano and Marcella). From the San Zaccaria vaporetto stop, take Calle dei Albanesi (two streets left of pink Hotel Danieli). The hotel is at the far end of the street on the left.

$$ Locanda Correr offers five elegant rooms with silk wallpaper and gilded furniture, decorated in classic 17th-century Venetian style with all the amenities on a quiet street a few blocks from St. Mark's Square and Campo S.S. Filippo e Giacomo (Db-€140, air-con, Calle Figher 4370, Castello, tel. 041-277-7847, fax 041-277-5939, www.locandacorrer.com, info@locandacorrer.com). From the San Zaccaria vaporetto stop, take the street to the right of the Bridge of Sighs to Campo S.S. Filippo e Giacomo, continue on Calle drio la Chiesa, then left down Calle Figher, past Hotel Castello.

$$ Hotel Fontana is a two-star, family-run place with 14 rooms and lots of stairs on a touristy square two bridges behind St. Mark's Square (Sb-€110, Db-€160, family rooms, air-con, 10 percent discount with cash, quieter rooms on garden side, 2 rooms have terraces for €10 extra, Campo San Provolo 4701, Castello; tel. 041-522-0579, fax 041-523-1040, www.hotelfontana.it,

Hotels near St. Mark's Square

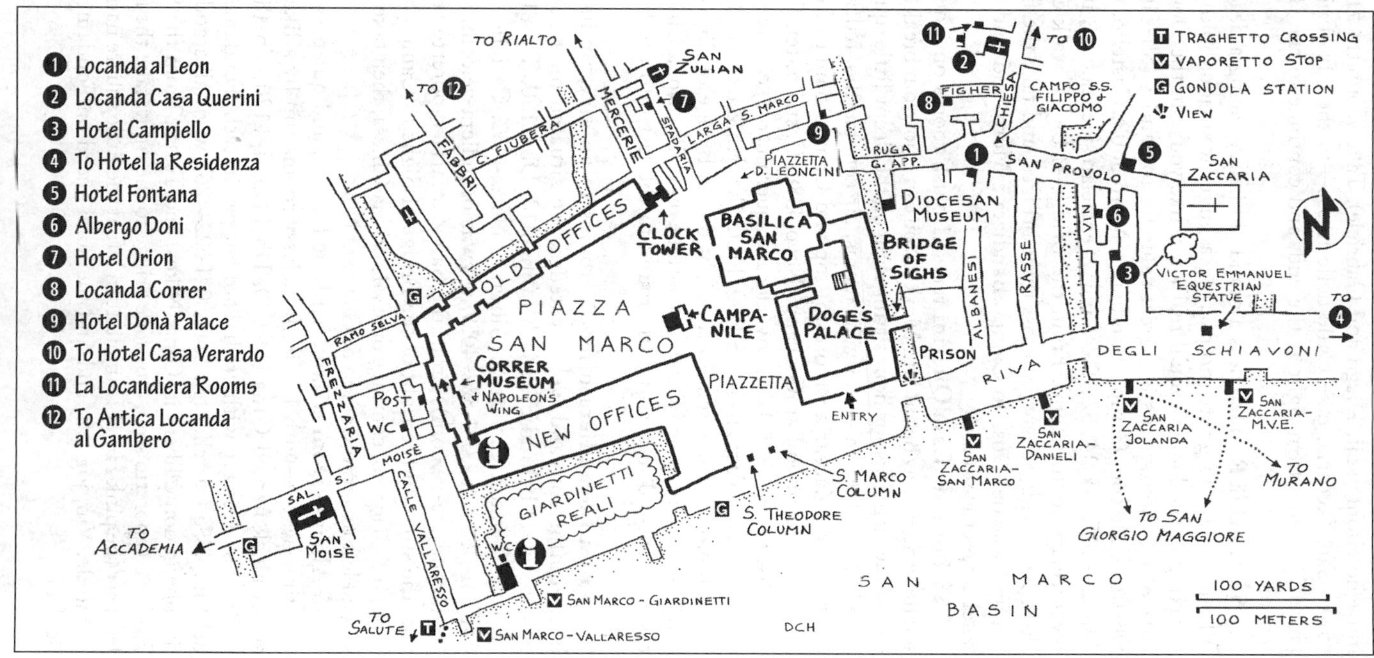

info@hotelfontana.it, Diego and Gabriele). Take vaporetto #1 or #51 to San Zaccaria, take Calle delle Rasse—to the left of pink Hotel Danieli—turn right at the end, and continue to the first square.

$$ Hotel la Residenza is a grand old palace facing a peaceful square. Its 15 great rooms ring a huge, luxurious lounge. Relaxing in the lounge, you'll really feel like you're in the Doge's Palace after hours. This is a great value for romantics (Sb-€100, Db-€160, air-con, Campo Bandiera e Moro 3608, Castello, tel. 041-528-5315, fax 041-523-8859, www.venicelaresidenza.com, info@venicelaresidenza.com). From the Bridge of Sighs, walk east along Riva degli Schiavoni, cross three bridges, and take the first left up Calle del Dose to Campo Bandiera e Moro, and find the hotel across the square.

$$ Locanda Casa Querini rents 11 plush rooms on a quiet square tucked away behind St. Mark's. You can enjoy your breakfast or a sunny picnic/happy hour sitting right on the sleepy little square (Db-€120–150, €5 more for view rooms, air-con, gazebo, halfway between San Zaccaria vaporetto stop and Campo Santa Maria Formosa at Campo San Giovanni Novo 4388, Castello, tel. 041-241-1294, fax 041-241-4231, www.locandaquerini.com, casaquerini@hotmail.com, Patrizia and Silvia). From the San Zaccaria vaporetto stop, take the street to the right of the Bridge of Sighs to Campo S.S. Filippo e Giacomo, continue on Calle drio la Chiesa, take the second left, and curl around to the left into the little square.

$$ La Locandiera offers 11 rooms in an airy, immaculate, comfortable and well-located haven situated on a quiet, bright square behind St. Mark's (Sb-€110, Db-€160, Tb-€190, air-con, elevator, Campo S. Giovanni Novo 4432, Castello, tel. 041-241-0664, fax 041-522-4059, www.lalocandiera-ve.com, info@lalocandiera-ve.com). From the San Zaccaria vaporetto stop, take the street to the right of the Bridge of Sighs to Campo S.S. Filippo e Giacomo, continue on Calle drio la Chiesa, then take the second left to get to Campo S. Giovanni Novo.

$ Albergo Doni is dark, hardwood, clean, and quiet—a bit of a time-warp—with 13 dim but classy rooms run by a likable smart aleck named Gina (D-€90, Db-€115, T-€120, Tb-€155, ceiling fans, reserve with credit card but pay in cash, Fondamenta del Vin, 4656 Castello, tel. & fax 041-522-4267, www.albergodoni.it, albergodoni@libero.it, Gina, Nikos, and Tessa). From the San Zaccaria vaporetto stop, cross one bridge to the right, take the first left past the pink Hotel Danieli, turn left at the little square named Ramo del Vin, jog left, and find the hotel ahead on Fondamenta del Vin.

North of St. Mark's Square

$$ Hotel Orion has 18 neat-as-a-pin, relaxing, and spacious rooms. Just off St. Mark's Square, it's a tranquil escape from the bustling streets (Db-€165, 5 percent discount with cash, air-con, Spadaria 700a, San Marco, tel. 041-522-3053, fax 041-523-8866, www.hotelorion.it, info@hotelorion.it, cheery Massimiliano and Stefano). From St. Mark's Square, walk to the left of the basilica's facade, then turn left on Spadaria; the hotel is just before the timbered overpass.

Near the Rialto Bridge

Vaporetto #82 quickly connects the Rialto with both the train station and the Tronchetto parking lot.

West of the Rialto Bridge

$$$ Locanda Sturion, with 11 rooms, air-conditioning, and all the modern comforts, is pricey because it overlooks the Grand Canal (Db-€250, canal-view rooms cost €60 extra, 10 percent discount with cash, family deals, piles of stairs, 100 yards from Rialto Bridge, opposite vaporetto dock, Calle del Sturion 679, San Polo, tel. 041-523-6243, fax 041-522-8378, www.locandasturion.com, info@locandasturion.com).

$ Albergo Guerrato, above a handy and colorful produce market two minutes from the Rialto action, is run by friendly, creative, and hardworking Roberto and Piero. Giorgio takes the night shift. Their 800-year-old building—with 24 spacious, air-conditioned, and charming rooms—is simple, airy, wonderfully characteristic (D-€90, Db-€120, top-floor "Guerratino" rooms go for Db-€135, Tb-€145, Qb-€170, 15 percent discount Nov–Feb and Aug, Calle drio la Scimia 240a, San Polo, tel. & fax 041-528-5927, www.pensioneguerrato.it, hguerrat@tin.it). Walk over the Rialto Bridge away from St. Mark's Square, go straight about three blocks, turn right on Calle drio la Scimia (not simply Scimia, the block before) and you'll see the hotel sign. My tour groups book this place for 50 nights each year. Sorry. The Guerrato also rents family apartments in the old center (great for groups of 4–8) for around €55 per person.

$$ Hotel al Ponte Mocenigo is off the beaten path—a 10-minute walk northwest of the Rialto Bridge—but it's a great value. This 16th-century Venetian palazzo has a garden terrace and 11 beautifully appointed, luxurious, and tranquil rooms (Sb-€70–100, Db-€90–150 depending on view and amenities, Santa Croce 2063, tel. 041-524-4797, fax 041-275-9420, www.alpontemocenigo.com, info@alpontemocenigo.com). Take vaporetto #1 to the San Stae stop, head inland on the right side of the church and take the first left down tiny Calle della Campanile; the hotel is on the right.

Hotels near the Rialto Bridge

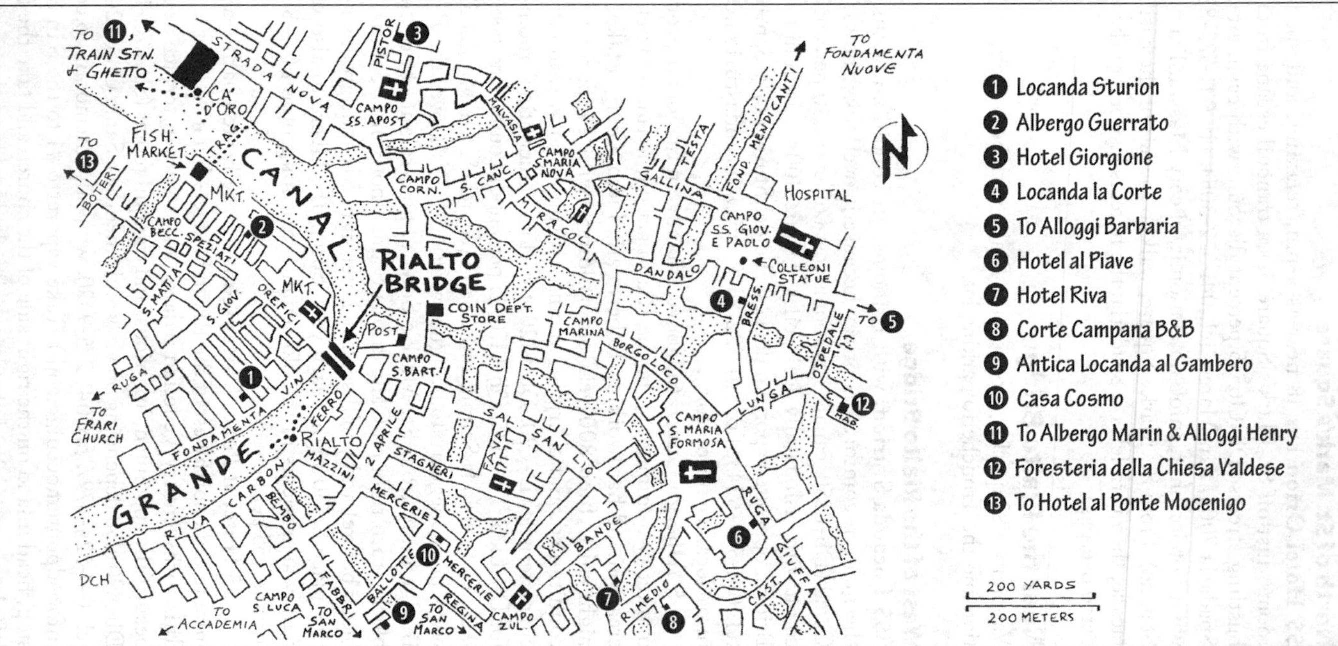

East of the Rialto Bridge

$$ Locanda la Corte, a three-star hotel, is perfumed with elegance. Its 16 attractive, high-ceilinged, wood-beamed rooms—done in pastels—circle a small, quiet courtyard (Sb-€120, standard Db-€150, superior Db-€170, 10 percent discount with cash, suites available, air-con, Castello 6317, tel. 041-241-1300, fax 041-241-5982, www.locandalacorte.it, info@locandalacorte.it, Marco and Raffaela). Take vaporetto #52 from the train station to Fondamenta Nuove, exit the boat to your left, follow the waterfront, and turn right after the second bridge to get to S.S. Giovanni e Paolo square. Facing the Rosa Salva bar, take the street to the left (Calle Bressana); the hotel is a short block away at #6317 before the bridge.

$ Alloggi Barbaria rents seven quiet, spacious, Ikea-style rooms with the basic comforts. Beyond Campo S.S. Giovanni e Paolo, it's a long walk from the action but a good value (Db-€110, extra bed-€30, family deals, air-con, tel. 041-522-2750, fax 041-277-5540, www.alloggibarbaria.it, info@alloggibarbaria.it, Giorgio and Fausto). Take vaporetto #52 to Ospedale stop, turn left as you get off the boat, then right down Calle de le Capucine to #6573 (Castello). Or, from the airport, take the Alilaguna speedboat to Fondamenta Nuove, turn left when you get off the boat, then right down Calle de le Capucine.

Southeast of the Rialto Bridge

$$$ Antica Locanda al Gambero, with 30 comfortable rooms, is extremely central but expensive, with impersonal service (Sb-€150, Db-€250, Tb-€290, air-con, Internet in lobby, Calle dei Fabbri 4687, San Marco, tel. 041-522-4384, fax 041-520-0431, www.locandaalgambero.com, hotelgambero@tin.it, Sandro). Take vaporetto #1 to Rialto stop and head inland (toward St. Mark's Square) down skinny Calle Bembo/Calle dei Fabbri. Or, from St. Mark's Square, go through Sotoportego dei Dai, then down Calle dei Fabbri. Gambero runs the pleasant, Art Deco–style La Bistrot on the corner, which serves old-time Venetian cuisine.

$$ Hotel al Piave, with 27 fine air-conditioned rooms above a bright and classy lobby, is fresh, modern, and comfortable. You'll enjoy the neighborhood and always get a cheery welcome (Db-€150, Tb-€200, family suites-€260 for 4 or €290 for 5, discount for cash; free Internet access off reception, Ruga Giuffa 4838/40, Castello, tel. 041-528-5174, fax 041-523-8512, www.hotelalpiave.com, info@hotelalpiave.com; Mirella, Paolo, and Ilaria speak English, faithful Molly doesn't). From the San Zaccaria vaporetto stop, take the street to the right of the Bridge of Sighs to Campo S.S. Filippo e Giacomo, and continue on Calle drio la Chiesa. Cross the bridge, continue forward, then turn left onto Ruga Giuffa until you find the Piave on your left at #4838/40.

$ Hotel Riva, with gleaming marble hallways and bright rooms, is romantically situated on a canal along the gondola serenade route. You could actually dunk your breakfast rolls in the canal (but don't). Sandro might hold a corner *(angolo)* room if you ask, and there are also a few rooms overlooking the canal. Ten of the 32 rooms come with air-conditioning for the same price—request one when you reserve (S-€70, Sb-€90, two D with adjacent showers-€100, Db-€120, Tb-€170, €10 extra for view, reserve with credit card but pay with cash only, Ponte dell'Angelo, tel. 041-522-7034, fax 041-528-5551, www.hotelriva.it, info@hotelriva.it). Facing St. Mark's Basilica, walk behind it on the left along Calle de la Canonica, take the first left (at blue *Pauly & C* mosaic in street), continue straight, go over the bridge, and angle right to the hotel at Ponte dell'Angelo.

$ Corte Campana B&B, run by enthusiastic and helpful Riccardo, rents three quiet rooms just behind St. Mark's Square, plus two apartments just around the corner (Db-€125, Tb or Tb apartment-€165, Qb or Qb apartment-€200, prices are soft, cash only, 2-night minimum stay, free Internet access at reception, Calle del Remedio 4410, Castello, tel. & fax 041-523-3603, mobile 389-272-6500, www.cortecampana.com, info@cortecampana.com). Facing St. Mark's Basilica, take Calle de la Canonica (left of church); turn left before the canal on Calle dell'Anzolo. Take the second right (onto Calle del Remedio), cross the bridge, and follow signs. Ring the bell at the black gate; the door is across the courtyard on the left wall, and the B&B is up three flights of stairs.

$ Casa Cosmo is a humble little five-room place run by Davide and his parents. While it comes with minimal services and no public spaces, it's air-conditioned, very central, inexpensive, and quiet, with a tiny terrace (Db-€110, no breakfast, Calle di Mezo 4976, San Marco, tel. & fax 041-296-0710, www.casacosmo.com, info@casacosmo.com). Take vaporetto #82 to Rialto; head inland on Larga Mazzini (which becomes Merceria after passing a square and a church), then turn right onto San Salvador, then immediately left onto tiny Calle di Mezo and find the hotel ahead on your right at #4976.

Near the Accademia Bridge

When you step over the Accademia Bridge, the commotion of touristy Venice is replaced by a sleepy village laced with canals. This quiet area, next to the best painting gallery in town, is a 15-minute walk from the Rialto or St. Mark's Square. For a shortcut between the Accademia neighborhood and St. Mark's Square, you can take a cheap €0.50 *traghetto* from Santa Maria del Giglio (daily 9:00–17:55). The fast vaporetto #82 connects the Accademia

Hotels near the Accademia Bridge

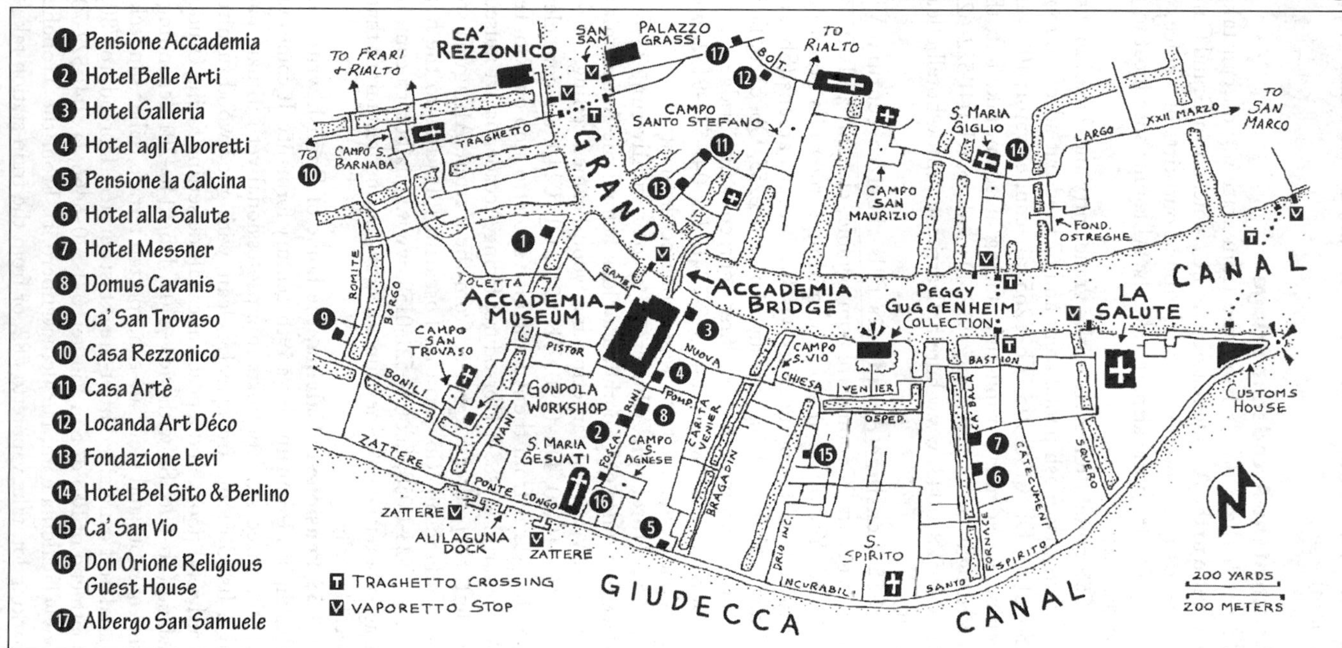

Bridge with both the train station (15 min) and St. Mark's Square (5 min).

South of the Accademia Bridge

To reach these hotels from the train station, you can take a vaporetto to the Accademia stop (more scenic, down Grand Canal) or the Zattere stop (less scenic, around outskirts of Venice, but faster). Or, from the airport, take the Alilaguna speedboat to the Zattere stop.

$$$ Hotel Belle Arti, with a grand entry and American hotel comforts, has plush public areas and 67 tired-but-adequate rooms (Sb-€120, Db-€180–215, Tb-€265, air-con, elevator; 100 yards behind Accademia art museum: facing museum, take left, then forced right, to Via Dorsoduro 912, Dorsoduro; tel. 041-522-6230, fax 041-528-0043, www.hotelbellearti.com, info@hotelbellearti .com).

$$$ Pensione Accademia fills the 17th-century Villa Maravege. Its 27 rooms are comfortable, elegant, and air-conditioned. You'll feel aristocratic gliding through its grand public spaces and lounging in its wistful, breezy gardens (Sb-€140, standard Db-€200, bigger "superior" Db-€255, Qb-€320, facing Accademia art museum, take first right, cross first bridge, go right to Dorsoduro 1058; tel. 041-523-7846, fax 041-523-9152, www .pensioneaccademia.it, info@pensioneaccademia.it).

$$$ Hotel agli Alboretti is a cozy, family-run, 23-room place in a quiet neighborhood a block behind the Accademia art museum. With red carpeting and wood-beamed ceilings, it feels classy (Sb-€110, Db-€190, Tb-€215, Qb-€240, air-con, elevator; 100 yards from the Accademia vaporetto stop on Rio Terra A. Foscarini at #884, Dorsoduro; facing Accademia art museum, go left, then forced right; or from the Zattere Alilaguna stop, head inland on Rio Terra A. Foscarini 100 yards to the hotel, tel. 041-523-0058, fax 041-521-0158, www.aglialboretti.com, info @aglialboretti.com). They run a nearby gourmet restaurant that's a local favorite.

$$ Pensione la Calcina, the home of English writer John Ruskin in 1876, maintains a 19th-century formality. It comes with all the three-star comforts in a professional yet intimate package. Its 33 rooms are squeaky clean, with good wood furniture, hardwood floors, and a peaceful canalside setting facing Giudecca Island (Sb-€96, Sb with view-€106, Db-€146–201 depending on size of room and view, air-con, rooftop terrace, killer sundeck on canal and canalside buffet-breakfast terrace, Dorsoduro 780, at south end of Rio di San Vio, tel. 041-520-6466, fax 041-522-7045, www.lacalcina.com, la.calcina@libero.it). From the Tronchetto parking lot, take vaporetto #82, or from the train station take #51 or #61, to Zattere (at vaporetto stop, exit right and walk along canal to hotel). Guests get a fine dinner at their La Piscina restaurant discounted to €22 (or to €32 for fresh fish menu). Guests are welcome to use the terrace outside of meal times without buying anything.

$$ Casa Rezzonico is a silent getaway far from the madding crowds. Its private garden terrace has perhaps the lushest grass in Italy, and its seven spacious rooms have views of this garden and of the adjacent canal (Sb-€120, Db-€150, Tb-€180, Qb-€220, some rooms with air-con, Fondamenta Gherardini 2813, Dorsoduro, tel. 041-277-0653, fax 041-277-5435, www.casarezzonico.it, info@casarezzonico.it). Take vaporetto #1 to the Ca' Rezzonico stop, head up Calle del Traghetto, cross Campo San Barnaba to the canal, and continue forward on Fondamenta Gherardini to #2813.

$$ Hotel alla Salute, a basic retreat buried deep in Dorsoduro with 50 rooms and indifferent owners, works for those wanting a quiet Venice residence (Db-€150, cheaper if you pay in cash, a few annex rooms have air-con, facing the Rio delle Fornace Canal near La Salute church, Salute 222, Dorsoduro, tel. 041-523-5404, fax 041-522-2271, www.hotelsalute.com, info@hotelsalute.com).

$$ Hotel Messner, a sprawling place popular with groups, rents 40 bright, newly refurbished rooms (half in main building, half in nearby, simpler annex), in a peaceful canalside neighborhood near La Salute Church. While remote, it has cheap and handy *traghetto* access to St. Mark's Square (Sb-€110, Db with air-con-€145, Db without air-con in annex-€115, Tb-€145, Qb-€160, peaceful garden, midway between lagoon and Grand Canal on Rio delle Fornace canal, Dorsoduro 216, tel. 041-522-7443, fax 041-522-7266, www.hotelmessner.it, messnerinfo@tin.it).

$ Hotel Galleria has nine tight, velvety rooms, most with views of the Grand Canal. Some rooms are quite narrow (S-€80, D-€110, Db-€120, big canal-view Db #8 and #10-€155, includes scant breakfast in room, fans, near Accademia art museum, and next to recommended Foscarini pizzeria, Dorsoduro 878a, tel. 041-523-2489, tel. & fax 041-520-4172, www.hotelgalleria.it, galleria@tin.it).

$ Ca' San Trovaso rents nine classy, spacious rooms split between the main hotel and a nearby annex. The location is peaceful, on a small canal (Sb-€90, Db-€115, bigger canal-view Db-€130, Tb-€145, breakfast in your room, fans, small roof terrace, Dorsoduro 1350/51, tel. 041-277-1146, fax 041-277-7190, www.casantrovaso.com, s.trovaso@tin.it, Mark and his son Alessandro). Take vaporetto #82 from the Tronchetto parking lot (or #51 from Piazzale Roma or the train station), get off at Zattere, exit left, and cross a bridge. Turn right at tiny Calle Trevisan (just past the white building with all the flags), cross another bridge, cross the adjacent bridge, take an immediate right, and then the first left.

$ Ca' San Vio is a tiny place run by the Ca' San Trovaso folks on a quiet canal with five fine air-conditioned rooms (small French bed Db-€100, bigger Db-€125, Tb-€140, breakfast in room, no public spaces, Calle delle Mende 531, Dorsoduro, tel. 041-241-3513, fax 041-241-3953, www.casanvio.com, info@casanvio.com, Roberto and Marco).

$ Don Orione Religious Guest House is a big cultural center dedicated to the work of a local man who became a saint in modern times. Filling an old monastery, it feels like a modern retreat center—clean, peaceful, and strictly run, with 50 rooms. It's beautifully located, comfortable, and a fine value (Sb-€70, Db-€116, Tb-€150, air-con, profits go to their mission work in the developing world, groups welcome, on the Giudecca Canal directly across from the Accademia Bridge facing Campo Sant'Agnese, Zattere 909a, Dorsoduro, tel. 041-522-4077, fax 041-528-6214, www.donorione-venezia.it, info@donorione-venezia.it).

$ Domus Cavanis, across the street from—and run by—Hotel Belle Arti (on page 808), is a big, dim, stark place renting 30 basic, dingy rooms (Sb-€66, Db-€110, Tb-€150, family rooms, includes breakfast at Hotel Belle Arti, air-con, elevator, Dorsoduro 895, tel. 041-528-7374, fax 041-528-0043, info@hotelbellearti.com).

North of the Accademia Bridge

$$ Hotel Bel Sito & Berlino, friendly for a three-star hotel, offers pleasing yet well-worn Old World character, 38 rooms, a peaceful courtyard, and a picturesque location—facing a church on a small square between St. Mark's Square and the Accademia (Sb-€100, Db-€164, air-con, elevator, some rooms with canal or church views; catch vaporetto #1 to Santa Maria del Giglio stop, take street inland to square, hotel is at far end to your right; Santa Maria del Giglio 2517, San Marco, tel. 041-522-3365, fax 041-520-4083, www.hotelbelsito.info, info@hotelbelsito.info).

$$ Locanda Art Déco is a charming little place. While the Art Deco theme is scant, a wrought-iron staircase leads from the inviting lobby to seven thoughtfully decorated rooms (Db-€165, 3-night minimum on weekends, 5 percent discount with cash, 2 family rooms, air-con, just north of the Accademia Bridge off Campo Santo Stefano at Calle delle Botteghe 2966, San Marco, tel. 041-277-0558, fax 041-270-2891, www.locandaartdeco.com, info@locandaartdeco.com, Judith).

$ Casa Artè has eight homey rooms with high ceilings, old-style Venetian furnishings, air-conditioning, and thoughtful touches in a red-velvet ambience. An annex contains eight peaceful, simpler rooms (Sb-€95, Db-€135, 10 percent discount with cash, family room sleeps up to 6, just north of Accademia Bridge, 100 yards west of Campo Santo Stefano on Calle de Frutariol 2900/01, San Marco, tel. 041-520-0882, fax 041-277-8395, www.casaarte .info, info@casaarte.info, Giancarlo).

$ Fondazione Levi, run by a foundation that promotes research on Venetian music, offers 18 quiet, institutional, yet comfortable and spacious rooms (Sb-€65, Db-€105, Tb-€124, Qb-€145, twin beds only, elevator, San Vidal 2893, San Marco, tel. 041-786-711, fax 041-786-766, foresterialevi@libero.it). It's 80 yards from the base of the Accademia Bridge on the St. Mark's side. From the Accademia vaporetto stop, cross the Accademia Bridge, take an immediate left, crossing the bridge Ponte Giustinian and going down Calle Giustinian directly to the Fondazione. Buzz the *Foresteria* door to the right.

$ Albergo San Samuele's 12 budget, basic, and spotless rooms are located in a crumbling historic palazzo just a few blocks from Campo Santo Stefano (S-€60, D-€90, Db-€125, cash only, Salizzada San Samuele 3358, San Marco, tel. 041-522-8045, fax 041-520-5165, www.albergosansamuele.it, info@albergosansamuele.it).

Near the Train Station

I don't recommend the train station area. It's crawling with noisy, disoriented tourists with too much baggage and people whose life's calling is to scam visitors out of their money. It's so easy just to hop a vaporetto upon arrival and get into the Venice of your dreams. Still, some like to park their bags near the station, and these two places work well.

$ Albergo Marin and its friendly, helpful staff offer 17 good-value, quiet, and immaculate rooms handy to the train station (Sb-€80, Db-€100, 5 percent discount with cash, fans on request, Ramo delle Chioverete #670B, Santa Croce, tel. 041-718-022, fax 041-721-485, www.albergomarin.it, info@albergomarin.it). From the station, cross the Grand Canal and turn immediately right. Take the first left, then the first right, then right again to Ramo delle Chioverete.

$ Alloggi Henry, a homey little family-owned hotel, has eight ramshackle rooms in a quiet neighborhood a five-minute walk from the train station (D-€80, Db-€90–100, no breakfast, Calle Ormesini 1506e, Cannaregio, tel. 041-523-6675, fax 041-715-680, www.alloggihenry.com, info@alloggihenry.com). From the station, follow Lista di Spagna, Rio Terra San Leonardo, and Rio Terra Farsetti, then take the second left on Calle Ormesini; the hotel's at #1506.

Big, Fancy Hotels

Here are three big, plush, four-star places with greedy, sky-high rack rates (around Db-€300) that often have great discounts (as low as Db-€160) for drop-ins, off-season travelers, or online booking through their website. If you want a sliding-glass-door, uniformed-receptionist kind of comfort and formality in the old center, these are worth considering: **$$$ Hotel Giorgione** (big, garish, shiny, near Rialto Bridge, www.hotelgiorgione.com); **$$$ Hotel Casa Verardo** (elegant and quietly parked on a canal behind St. Mark's, more stately, www.casaverardo.it); and **$$$ Hotel Donà Palace** (sitting like Las Vegas in the touristy zone just northeast of St. Mark's, see map on page 801, www.donapalace.it).

Cheap Dormitory Accommodations

$ Foresteria della Chiesa Valdese, warmly run by the Methodist Church, offers 60 beds in doubles and 3- to 10-bed dorms, halfway between St. Mark's Square and the Rialto Bridge. This run-down but charming old place has elegant ceiling paintings (dorm bed-€23, D-€60, Db-€76, includes breakfast, sheets, and lockers; must check in and out when office is open—9:00–13:00 & 18:00–20:00, Fondamenta Cavagnis 5170, Castello, tel. 041-528-6797, fax 041-241-6238, foresteriavenezia@diaconiavaldese.org). From Campo Santa Maria Formosa, walk past Bar all'Orologio to the end of Calle Lunga and cross the bridge onto Fondamenta Cavagnis.

$ Venice's **youth hostel,** on Giudecca Island, is crowded and inexpensive (€21 beds with sheets and breakfast in 12- to 16-bed dorms, cheaper for hostel members, office open daily 7:00–9:30 & 13:30–24:30, catch vaporetto #82 from station to Zittele, tel. 041-523-8211, can reserve online at www.hostelbooking.com). The budget cafeteria welcomes non-hostelers (nightly 18:00–23:00).

EATING

While touristy restaurants are the scourge of Venice, and most restaurateurs believe you can't survive in Venice without catering to tourists, there are plenty of places that are still popular with locals and respect the tourists who happen in. First trick: Walk away from triple-language menus. Second trick: Order the daily special. Third trick: For freshness, eat fish. Most seafood dishes are the local catch-of-the-day. Remember that the price of seafood and steak may be listed on the menu as "100 g" or "*l'etto*" (meaning you'll pay that price per 100 grams—about a quarter pound), or similarly, as "s.q." (according to quantity, meaning the weight of the piece).

For romantic—and usually pricey—meals along the water, see "Romantic Canalside Settings," page 820. For dessert, it's gelato (see later in this chapter).

Near the Rialto Bridge

North of the Rialto Bridge

These restaurants are located between Campo S.S. Apostoli and Campo S.S. Giovanni e Paolo.

Trattoria da Bepi is bright, alpine-paneled, and locally run. Owner Loris scours the market for just the best ingredients and takes good care of the hungry clientele (€30 meals, Fri–Wed 12:00–14:30 & 19:00–22:00, closed Thu, near Rialto, half a block north of Campo Santi Apostoli on Salizada Pistor, tel. 041-528-5031).

Osteria da Alberto has excellent €20 seafood dinners and €8 pastas (Mon–Sat 12:00–15:00 & 19:00–23:00, closed Sun, midway between Campo S.S. Apostoli and Campo S.S. Giovanni e Paolo, next to Ponte de la Panada on Calle Larga Giacinto Gallina, tel. 041-523-8153, run by Graziano and Giovanni).

***Cicchetti*, plus Pasta: Osteria al Bomba** is a *cicchetti* bar with a female touch. It's unusual (clean, no toothpicks, no cursing) and quite good, with lots of veggies. You can stand and eat at the bar, or oversee the construction of the house "*antipasto misto di cicchetti*" plate (€15, enough for 2), and then grab a seat at the long table to complete your pub crawl with a plate of pasta (daily 18:00–23:00, near Campo S.S. Apostoli, a block off Strada Nuova on Calle dell'Oca, tel. 041-520-5175). You'll find more pubs nearby, in the side streets opposite Campo Santa Sofia, across Strada Nuova.

East of the Rialto Bridge, near Campo San Bartolomeo

Osteria di Santa Marina, on the wonderful Campo Marina, serves pricey, near-gourmet food that's made with only the best seasonal ingredients. The quality food and classy ambience make this a good splurge (fun menu with €14 pastas and €25 *secondi,* Sun–Mon 19:30–21:30, Tue–Sat 12:30–14:30 & 19:30–21:30, reservations smart for dinner, eat indoors or outdoors on pleasant little square, midway between Rialto Bridge and Campo Santa Maria Formosa on Campo Marina, tel. 041-528-5239).

Osteria il Milion, with bow-tied waiters and dressy, candlelit tables indoors and out, is quietly situated next to Marco Polo's home. It's touristy but tasty—traditional Italian meals are about €25 (Thu–Tue 12:00–15:00 & 18:30–23:00, closed Wed; near Rialto Bridge, head north from Campo San Bartolomeo, over one bridge, take first right off San Giovanni Grisostomo before the church, walk under the sign *Corte Prima del Milion o del forno*, it's at #5841; tel. 041-522-9302).

***Cicchetti:* Osteria "Alla Botte" Cicchetteria** is packed with a young, local, bohemian-jazz clientele. It's good for a *cicchetti* snack with wine at the bar or for a light meal in the small back room—find the posted menus (Mon–Wed and Fri–Sat 10:00–15:00 & 17:30–23:00, Sun 10:00-15:00, closed Thu, 2 short blocks off

Restaurants near the Rialto Bridge

1. Trattoria da Bepi
2. Osteria da Alberto
3. Al Marcà
4. Osteria al Bomba
5. Ost. di Santa Marina
6. Osteria il Milion
7. Devil's Forest Pub
8. Cantina do Mori & Ostaria ai Storti
9. Antica Ostaria Ruga Rialto
10. Bancogiro & Osteria Naranzaria
11. Inishark Pub
12. Osteria al Diavolo e l'Acquasanta
13. Bácaro Jazz Venezia Wine Bar
14. To Tratt./Pizzeria Nono Risorto
15. Osteria "Alla Botte"
16. Rosticceria San Bartolomeo
17. Pasticceria Ponte delle Paste
18. Osteria al Portego
19. Rist. al Giardinetto
20. Bar all'Orologio
21. Cip Ciap Pizza & Osteria alle Testiere
22. Trattoria agli Artisti
23. Osteria al Mascaron
24. To Pizzerias l'Angelo & Al Vaporetto
25. Pizzeria Spizzico
26. La Boutique del Gelato
27. Michielangelo Gelato
28. Zanzibar Gelato
29. Desert Planet Bar
30. To Antica Birraria la Corte & La Rivetta

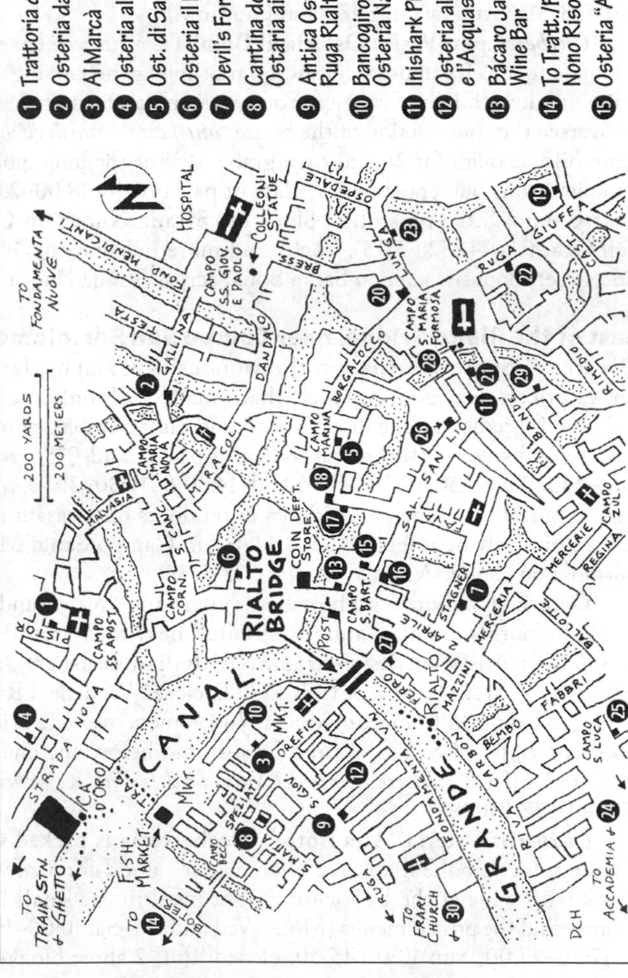

Campo San Bartolomeo in the corner behind the statue—down Calle de la Bissa, notice the "day after" photo showing a debris-covered Venice after the notorious 1989 Pink Floyd open-air concert, tel. 041-520-9775). Just around the corner from "Alla Botte" Cicchetteria is their wine shop *(enoteca)*, which sells quality bulk wine *(vino sfuso)* for about €2 per liter. Bring an empty water bottle or pick one up there, and select among several local wines such as pinot grigio, tocai, cabernet, or merlot to take on a picnic (Mon–Sat 10:00–13:00 & 16:00–20:00, closed Sun, Calle della Bissa 5529, San Marco, tel. 041-296-0596).

Rosticceria San Bartolomeo is a cheap—if confusing—self-service restaurant with a likeably surly staff. Take out, grab a table, or munch at the bar (good €6–7 pasta, great fried *mozzarella al prosciutto* for €1.30, delightful fruit salad, and €1 glasses of wine, prices listed on wall behind counter, no cover or service charge, daily 9:00–21:30, tel. 041-522-3569). To find this venerable budget eatery, imagine the statue on the Campo San Bartolomeo walking backwards 20 yards, turning left, and going under a passageway—now, follow him.

From Rosticceria San Bartolomeo, continue over a bridge to Campo San Lio. Here, turn left, passing Hotel Canada on your right and following Calle Carminati straight about 50 yards over another bridge. On the left is the pastry shop *(pasticceria)* Ponte delle Paste, and straight ahead is Osteria Al Portego (at #6015).

Pasticceria Ponte delle Paste is a feminine and pastel *salon de tè*, popular for its homemade pastries and pre-dinner drinks. Italians love taking 15-minute breaks to sip a *spritz* aperitif with friends before heading home after a long day's work. Ask sprightly Monica for a *spritz al bitter* (white wine, *amaro*, and soda water, €1.80; or choose from the menu on the wall) and munch some of the free goodies at the bar around 18:00 (daily 7:00–20:30, Ponte delle Paste).

Osteria al Portego is a friendly, local-style bar—one of the best in town—serving great *cicchetti* and good meals (Mon–Sat 10:30–15:00 & 18:00–22:00, closed Sun, Calle Malvasia 6015, Castello, tel. 041-522-9038). The *cicchetti* here can make a great meal, but you should also consider sitting down for an actual dinner. They have a fine menu.

Cicchetterie and Light Meals West of the Rialto Bridge

All of these places (except the last one—Nono Risorto) are within 200 yards of each other, in the neighborhood around the Rialto market. This area is very crowded by day but nearly empty after dark.

Cantina do Mori has been famous with locals (since 1462) and savvy travelers (since 1982) as a classy place for fine wine and *francobolli* (a spicy selection of 20 tiny, mayo-soaked sandwiches nicknamed "stamps"). Choose from the featured wines. Confirm the price, or they'll rip you off (Mon–Sat 12:00–20:30, closed Sun, stand-up only, arrive early before the *cicchetti* are gone, San Polo 429, tel. 041-522-5401). From Rialto Bridge, walk 200 yards down Ruga degli Orefici, away from St. Mark's Square—then left on Ruga Vecchia S. Giovanni, then right at Sotoportego do Mori.

Ostaria ai Storti offers lots of veggies, great prices, a homey feel, and a wonderful, fun place to congregate outdoors. Check out the photo of the market in 1909, below the bar (Mon–Sat 12:00–15:00 & 18:00–22:30, closed Sun, 20 yards from Cantina do Mori on Calle do Spade 819, tel. 041-214-2255).

Antica Ostaria Ruga Rialto, a.k.a. "the Ruga," is a local fixture where Marco serves great bar snacks and wine to his devoted clientele (daily 11:00–14:30 & 19:00–24:00, easy to find, just past the Chinese restaurant on Ruga Vecchia S. Giovanni 692, tel. 041-521-1243).

Osteria al Diavolo e l'Acquasanta, three blocks west of the Rialto Bridge, serves good—if pricey—pasta and makes a handy lunch stop for sightseers and gondola-riders. While they list *cicchetti* and wine by the glass on the wall, I'd come here for a light meal rather than for appetizers (Mon 12:00–14:30, Wed–Sun 12:00–14:30 & 19:00–21:30, closed Tue, hiding on a quiet street just off Ruga Vecchia S. Giovanni, on Calle della Madonna, tel. 041-277-0307).

Al Marcà, on Campo Cesare Battisti, is a literal hole-in-the-wall where young locals gather to grab drinks and little snacks. The father-and-son team clearly lists the prices for wine and sandwiches (Mon–Sat 9:00–15:00 & 18:00–21:00, closed Sun, located on empty part of square just below courthouse).

Bancogiro (Osteria da Andrea), a simple bar behind the Rialto market, has stark yet powerfully atmospheric outdoor seating overlooking the Grand Canal. Peruse their wine list and menu of creative pastas and entrées at the bar, or ask for a recommendation on a few strong local cheeses to go with your wine. Order and grab a table—worth the very reasonable cover charge (Tue–Sat 10:30–24:00, closed Mon, cash only, less than 200 yards from Rialto Bridge on Campo San Giacometto, San Polo 122, tel. 041-523-2061). Consider their €15 fish and vegetable plate.

Osteria Naranzaria, which shares a prime piece of Grand Canal real estate with Bancogiro a few doors towards the Rialto Bridge, is described later, under "Romantic Canalside Settings."

Trattoria Pizzeria Nono Risorto is unpretentious, inexpensive, youthful, and famous for some of the best pizza in town. You'll sit in a gravelly garden, under a leafy canopy, surrounded by a young, enthusiastic waitstaff and Italians enjoying huge salads, €9 pastas, and delicious €8 pizzas (€14 *secondi*, Thu 19:00–23:00, Fri–Tue 12:00–14:30 & 19:00–23:00, closed Wed; a 3-min walk from the Rialto fish market, find Campo San Cassiano and it's just over the bridge on Sotoportego de Siora Bettina; tel. 041-524-1169).

On or near Campo Santa Maria Formosa

These eateries can be found on the map on page 814.

Campo Santa Maria Formosa, a classic Venetian square, is a great place for a balmy outdoor meal of pizza and wine. **Bar all'Orologio** has a good setting and friendly service but mediocre freezer pizza (they're happy to let you split a pizza, Mon–Sat 6:00–23:00, closed Sun). To have a great pizza picnic on the square, cross the bridge behind the canalside *gelateria,* and grab a slice to go from **Cip Ciap Pizza** (Wed–Mon 9:00–21:00, closed Tue; facing *gelateria,* take bridge to the right; Calle del Mondo Novo). For a healthy snack, try the **fruit-and-vegetable stand** next to Campo Santa Maria Formosa's water fountain (Mon–Sat closes at about 19:30, closed Sun). Also on the square, the *gelateria* **Zanzibar** is perhaps too popular with tourists, but it's well-situated and the locals love it (daily 8:00–24:00, in winter 8:00–20:30).

Trattoria agli Artisti is efficient and friendly, with good food, especially the *frutti di mare*—spaghetti with seafood (Thu–Tue 12:00–15:00 & 18:00–22:30, closed Wed, half block off square down Ruga Giuffa at #4835, tel. 041-277-0029).

Ristorante al Giardinetto has white tablecloths, a formal-but-fun waitstaff, and a spacious, shady garden under a grapevine canopy. While it used to be set up for big tour groups—and still feels it—groups no longer come here, and the dining experience has improved (€9 pastas, €14 main courses, €2 *coperto*, closed Thu, at intersection of Ruga Giuffa and Calle Corona, tel. 041-528-5332).

Osteria alle Testiere is my most gourmet recommendation in Venice. Hugely respected, they are passionate about quality, serving up creative, artfully presented market-fresh seafood (there's no meat on the menu) and fine wine in what the chef calls a "Venetian Nouvel" style. Reservations are required for their three daily sittings: 12:30, 19:00, and 21:15. With only 22 seats, it's tight and homey yet elegant (€15 pastas, €24 *secondi*, plan on spending €50 for dinner, closed Sun–Mon, Calle del Mondo Novo 5801, tel. 041-522-7220).

Osteria al Mascaron is where I've come for 20 years to watch Gigi and his food-loving band of ruffians dish up rustic-yet-sumptuous pastas with steamy seafood (€13) to salivating local foodies. The €15 *antipasto misto* plate and two glasses of wine make a wonderful light meal (Mon–Sat 12:00–15:00 & 19:00–22:30, closed Sun, a block past Campo Santa Maria Formosa at Calle Longa Santa Maria Formosa 5225, tel. 041-522-5995).

In Dorsoduro

Near the Accademia Bridge

For locations, see the map on page 819.

Ristorante/Pizzeria Accademia Foscarini, next to the Accademia Bridge and Galleria, offers decent €7–8 pizzas in a great canalside setting. This place is both scenic and practical—I grab a quick lunch here on each visit to Venice (Wed–Mon 9:00–23:00 in summer, until 20:00 in winter, closed Tue, Dorsoduro 878C, tel. 041-522-7281).

Enoteca Cantine del Vino Già Schiavi is much loved for its €1 *cicchetti*. It's also a good place for a €2 glass of wine and appetizers (Mon–Sat 8:00–20:30, closed Sun, 100 yards from Accademia Gallery on San Trovaso canal; facing Accademia, take a right and then a forced left at the canal to the second bridge—S. Trovaso 992, tel. 041-523-0034). You're welcome to enjoy your wine and finger food while sitting on the bridge.

Ai Gondolieri is considered one of the best restaurants for meat—not fish—in Venice. Its sauces are heavy and prices are high, but gourmet carnivores love it (€17 pastas, €25 *secondi*, €5 cover, Wed–Mon 12:00–15:00 & 19:00–22:00, closed Tue, closed for lunch July–Aug, reservations smart, Dorsoduro 366 San Vio, behind Peggy Guggenheim Collection on east side of Rio delle Torreselle, tel. 041-528-6396).

Near Campo San Barnaba

A number of less-touristed restaurants cluster around this small square. From the Accademia, head northwest, following the curve of the Grand Canal. In five minutes, you'll spill out onto Campo San Barnaba (and the nearby Campo Santa Margherita). Follow the straight and narrow path (Calle Lunga San Barnaba) west of the square for more restaurants.

Casin dei Nobili (Pleasure Palace of Nobles) has a diverse, reasonably priced menu in a high-energy, informal, modern setting. The patio is filled with simple tables, happy tourists, and their inviting €10 daily specials (Tue–Sun 12:00–15:00 & 19:00–23:00, closed Mon, a half-block south of Campo San Barnaba, Calle delle Casin 2765, tel. 041-241-1841).

Ai Quattro Feri is a noisy, bustling, trattoria-style eatery, best for its catch-of-the-day seafood, especially the excellent grilled fish (€8 pastas, €12 *secondi*, Mon–Sat 12:30–15:00 & 19:30–23:00, closed Sun, just off the square on Calle Lunga San Barnaba 2757, tel. 041-520-6978).

Enoteca e Trattoria la Bitta, dark and woody, with a forgettable back patio, serves nicely presented traditional Venetian food with—proudly—no fish. Their small menu is clearly focused on quality cooking (€9 pastas, €14 *secondi*, dinner only, Mon–Sat

Restaurants near the Accademia Bridge

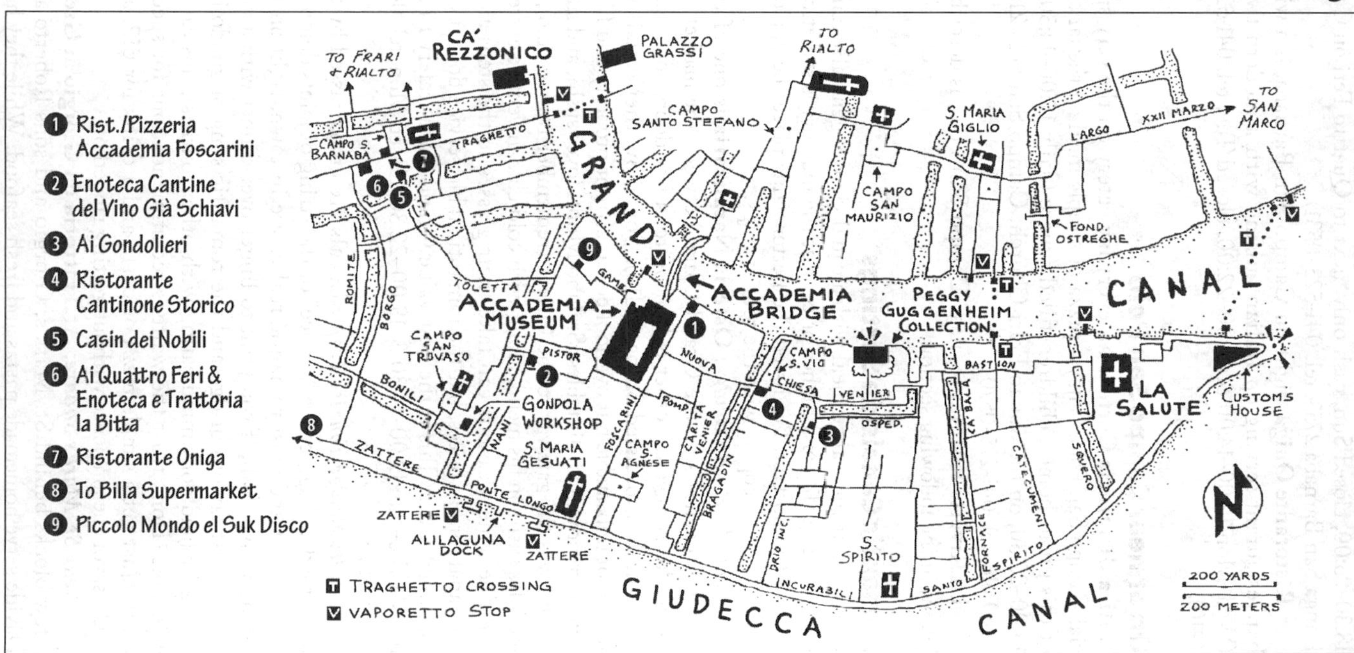

18:30–23:00, closed Sun, cash only, next to Quattro Feri on Calle Lunga San Barnaba 2753, tel. 041-523-0531).

Ristorante Oniga, right on Campo San Barnaba, is a wine bar/restaurant serving up Italian cuisine with a modern twist (Wed–Mon 12:00–14:00 & 19:00–22:00, closed Tue, tel. 041-522-4410).

On or near Campo San Polo

Antica Birraria la Corte is an everyday eatery on the very special Campo San Polo. Enjoy a pizza or simple meal on the far side of this great, homey, children-filled square (daily 12:00–14:30 & 19:00–22:30, on the way to Frari Church, Campo San Polo 2168, San Polo, tel. 041-275-0570).

La Rivetta Ristorante, near Campo San Polo, is described below, in the following section.

Romantic Canalside Settings

Of course, if you want a meal with a canal view, it generally comes with lower quality or a higher price. But the memory is sometimes the most important. I've listed the better-value places here, along with advice for coping with the tourist traps.

Near the Rialto Bridge: **Osteria Naranzaria** is one of two wonderful eateries on the Grand Canal between the market and the Rialto Bridge (the other is Bancogiro, a few doors down away from the Rialto, listed on page 814). Somehow they've taken a stretch of unbeatable but overlooked canalfront property and filled it with trendy candlelit tables. Stefano Monti loves sushi, and since Venice was the gateway to the Orient (remember Marco Polo), he includes sushi on his menu, along with cold cuts, inventive entrées, and fine wine. Peasants can take their glasses to the steps along the canal for bar prices, but the romantic table service doesn't cost that much extra. This is the best-value Grand Canal eatery I have found (Tue–Sun 12:00–14:30 & 19:00–22:30, closed Mon, tel. 041-724-1035).

Rialto Bridge Tourist Traps: Locals are embarrassed by the lousy food and aggressive "service" of the string of joints dominating the best and most romantic real estate in town, right on the Grand Canal. Still, if you want to linger over dinner with a view of the most famous bridge and the romantic song of gondoliers oaring by (and don't mind eating with other tourists), this can be enjoyable. Don't trust the waiter's recommendations for special meals. Just get a simple pizza or pasta and a drink for €12, and you'll savor the ambience without getting ripped off.

Near St. Mark's Square: At **Trattoria da Giorgio ai Greci,** a few blocks behind St. Mark's, Giorgio and sons Roberto and Davide serve homemade pastas and fresh seafood. While they have inside seating, you come here for the canalside dining—it's the best I've found anywhere in town. Call to reserve a canalside table (€17–21 tourist menus, daily 12:00–22:30, closed Mon in winter, 2 canals east of St. Mark's on Ponte dei Greci 4988, tel. 041-528-9780).

Near the Accademia Bridge: **Ristorante Cantinone Storico** sits on a peaceful canal in Dorsoduro between the Accademia Bridge and the Peggy Guggenheim Collection. It's dressy, specializes in fish and traditional Venetian dishes, has about a half-dozen tables on the canal, and is worth the splurge (€15 pastas, €20 *secondi*, €3 cover, Mon–Sat 12:30–14:30 & 19:30–21:30, later in summer, closed Sun, be wise and make reservations, on the canal Rio de S. Vio, tel. 041-523-9577).

Near Campo San Polo: **La Rivetta Ristorante** offers a canalside setting and well-priced Venetian cuisine. Consider *spaghetti al nero di seppie*—spaghetti in squid ink, or *fegato alla Veneziana*—calf liver and onions (daily 12:00–22:30, Calle di Mezo 1479, San Polo, tel. 041-523-1481).

Near St. Mark's Square

For the locations of these restaurants, see the "St. Mark's Square" map on page 788.

Osteria Enoteca San Marco offers beautifully presented "creative new Italian" cuisine with contemporary ambience in a classic medieval shell. They proudly offer fine wine by the glass. This place is pricey, but the food is always top quality (€40 meals, Mon–Sat 12:30–23:00, closed Sun, a long block west of St. Mark's Square at Frezzeria 1610, tel. 041-528-5242, Carlo and his white-aproned army speak English).

At **Salad and Juice Bar Oasi 2000,** hardworking, English-speaking Alessandro serves big salads, sandwiches, a few hot pasta dishes, and fresh-squeezed juice in a small student-cantina atmosphere just behind St. Mark's Basilica (Mon–Sat 8:00–20:00, closed Sun, off Calle San Provolo at Calle di Albanesi 4263, tel. 041-528-9937).

Trattoria alla Rivetta is a high-spirited hole-in-the-wall popular with gondoliers at lunch and mobbed with tourists at dinner. Even if they treat tourists as second-class eaters, pasta here for lunch is both a great meal and a great memory (daily 10:00–22:00, closed Mon–Tue in winter, just behind St. Mark's Basilica at the Ponte San Provolo bridge between Campo S.S. Filippo e Giacomo and Campo S. Provolo, tel. 041-528-7302). They also have bar munchies—see the *Prezzi al banco* price list on the wall by the bar.

Antica Sacrestia, a local institution, has à la carte choices and several different fixed-price meals: vegetarian, Venetian, tourist, seafood, fine pizza, and house specialties. I like the antipasto buffet, where you can help the waiter construct your €19 plate with all the local goodies, including great seafood, and call it a meal (Tue–Sun 12:00–15:00 & 18:30–22:30, closed Mon, on Calle della Sacrestia 4442, 2 blocks behind St. Mark's, tel. 041-523-0749, www.anticasacrestia.com).

Trattoria da Remigio is well-known for high-quality, serious Venetian cuisine. Its indoors-only setting is a bit dressy, with a mix of tourists and locals, and lots of commotion (Wed–Sun lunch from 12:30, dinner from 19:30, closed Mon–Tue, just past Rio dei Greci on a tiny square at the end of Calle Madonna, tel. 041-523-0089).

The **cafés on St. Mark's Square** offer music, inflated prices, and an unbeatable setting for a drink or light meal (for a description, see page 788).

Eating Elsewhere

Near the Train Station: For fast, cheap food near the station, consider **Brek,** a popular self-service cafeteria (after serving breakfast, it's open daily 11:30–22:00; with back to station, facing canal, go left on Rio Terra—it becomes Lista di Spagna in 2 short blocks. Lista di Spagna 124, tel. 041-244-0158).

Between the Station and North Venice: **Osteria al Bacco,** far beyond the crowds in a rustic Venetian setting, is worth the hike for its local cuisine (€35 for 3 courses and wine, Tue–Sun 19:00–22:00, Sun 12:00–14:00, closed Mon, reservations recommended, halfway between train station and the northernmost tip of Venice, Fondamenta Capuzine, Cannaregio 3054, tel. 041-717-493).

Midway Between the Station and Rialto: **Osteria la Zucca,** on the Rio del Megio canal, is hardworking, homey, and away from the crowds. You'll get good typical Venetian cuisine at a moderate price (€25 meals, Mon–Sat 12:30–14:30 for lunch, dinner guests usually have 2 seating choices—19:00 or 21:00, closed Sun, mostly indoors, reserve for canal windows, a few outdoor tables with one on the canal, midway between train station and Rialto Bridge at San Giacomo dell'Orio 1762, Calle Larga, Santa Croce, tel. 041-524-1570). A short block away is the square called San Giacomo dell'Orio—a breezy scene with trees, families at play, and a couple of simple trattorias offering basic food and classic, non-touristy, outdoor seating.

Cheap Meals

A key to cheap eating in Venice is **bar snacks**, especially stand-up mini-meals in out-of-the-way bars. Order by pointing. *Panini* (sandwiches) are sold fast and cheap at bars everywhere. Basic reliable ham-and-cheese sandwiches (white bread, crusts trimmed) come toasted—simply ask for "toast"; these make a great supplement to Venice's skimpy hotel breakfasts.

For budget eating, I like small ***cicchetti* bars** (see page 815). For speed, value, and ambience, you can get a filling plate of local appetizers at nearly any of the bars.

Pizzerias are cheap and easy—try for a sidewalk table at a scenic location.

Pizzeria l'Angelo serves up piping-hot pizza by the slice for under €2 or whole pizzas to go. Grab a beer or a soda and find a bench in nearby Campo Manin or Campo Sant'Angelo (Tue–Sun 11:30–22:00, closed Mon, Calle della Mandola 3711, tel. 041-277-1126). **Al Vaporetto Self-Service,** just across the street, is bright, efficient, and forgettable (€5 pastas, €6 *secondi*, Calle della Mandola). **Spizzico** is a cheap fast-food pizza shop on Campo San Luca. Here's a chance to compare American and Italian fast food—there's a Burger King nearby (between St. Mark's Square and the Rialto Bridge).

The **produce market** that sprawls for a few blocks just past the Rialto Bridge is a great place to assemble a picnic (best Mon–Sat 8:00–13:00, closed Sun). The adjacent fish market is wonderfully slimy. Side lanes in this area are speckled with fine little hole-in-the-wall munchie bars, bakeries, and cheese shops.

Gelato

For locations of first two places, see the "Restaurants near the Rialto Bridge" map on page 814. For the last place, see the "St. Mark's Square" map on page 788.

La Boutique del Gelato is considered the best *gelateria* in Venice (daily 10:00–20:00, closed Dec–Jan, 2 blocks off Campo Santa Maria Formosa on corner of Salizada San Lio and Calle Paradiso, next to Hotel Bruno, at #5727—just look for the crowd).

Late-Night Gelato: At the Rialto, try **Michielangelo,** just off Campo San Bartolomeo, on the St. Mark's side of the Rialto Bridge on Salizada Pio X (daily 10:00–23:00). At St. Mark's Square, the **Al Todaro** *gelateria* opposite the Doge's Palace is open late (daily 8:00–22:00, closes at 20:00 and on Mon in winter).

TRANSPORTATION CONNECTIONS

The train station can be crowded with long lines to buy train tickets and make fast-train and *cuccetta* reservations. Consider taking care of these tasks at downtown **travel agencies**—such as Kele & Teo Viaggi e Turismo (see page 775). The cost is the same or only slightly more (some agencies charge a small fee); it can be more convenient (if you find yourself near a travel agency while you're sightseeing); and the language barrier can be smaller than at the station's ticket windows. But many travelers find it's easiest to use the automatic ticket machines readily available at the station.

These gray-and-yellow touch-screen ***Biglietto Veloce*** (fast ticket) machines have an English option, issue train tickets, and allow payment in cash or by credit/debit card. You can also use the same machine to check train schedules.

From Venice by Train to: Padua (3–6/hr, 30 min), **Vicenza** (2/hr, 1 hr), **Verona** (2/hr, 90 min), **Ravenna** (about hourly, 3–4 hrs, transfer in Ferrara or Bologna and in Venice Mestre station), **Florence** (15/day, 3 hrs, may transfer in Bologna), **Dolomites** (12/day to Bolzano, 3–4 hrs, change in Verona, catch bus from Bolzano into mountains), **Milan** (about hourly, 3 hrs), **Monterosso/La Spezia/Cinque Terre** (8/day, 6–7 hrs, 1–3 changes), **Rome** (about hourly, 5–8 hrs, overnight possible), **Naples** (at least hourly, 7–8 hrs, 1–2 changes), **Brindisi** (6/day, 10–12 hrs, most change in Bologna), **Interlaken** (7/day, 7–10 hrs, 2–4 changes, overnight possible via Brig), **Munich** (5/day, 7 hrs, may change in Verona, overnight possible via Salzburg), **Paris** (1 direct night train/day, 12.5 hrs, important to reserve ahead; 3/day, 10–12 hrs with change in Milan), and **Vienna** (3/day, 1 direct day train 7 hrs, 10–12 hrs with 1–3 changes, overnight possible).

Marco Polo Airport

Venice's modern airport on the mainland, six miles north of the city, has a sleek wood-beam-and-glass terminal, with a TI (daily, 9:00–20:00), cash machines, car-rental agencies, and a few shops and eateries (airport info tel. 041-260-9250). Check with your hotel or in *Un Ospite di Venezia* (the free tourist information guide at fancy hotels) for phone numbers and websites for all airlines serving Marco Polo and nearby airports.

There are four ways for you to get between the airport and downtown Venice (described in detail below): the slow but reasonable Alilaguna boat, a faster and pricier Alilaguna boat (which goes nonstop to St. Mark's Square), the fastest and priciest water taxi, and the cheap shuttle bus to the edge of Venice (with easy connections to the Grand Canal *vaporetti*). Except for the fast boat and water taxi, expect a trip between the airport terminal and St. Mark's Square (San Marco) to take up to 90 minutes. When flying out of Venice, travelers are advised to get to the airport two or more hours before departure (even for flights within Europe), but I usually arrive about 90 minutes before takeoff and manage fine.

Alilaguna Water Bus: This is the simplest transportation to and from downtown Venice. A minor drawback is that you must walk (and carry your bags) eight minutes between the airport terminal and the boat dock (follow signs, level sidewalks are fine for wheeled bags).

The Alilaguna website (www.alilaguna.it) lists times and the various lines. These are the routes for the slow boats: The

Blue (BLU) Line stops at Fondamenta Nove and Ospedale (€6, on Venice's north shore), and San Zaccaria (€12, best for hotels east of St. Mark's Square); the Red Line stops at San Marco (St. Mark's Square) and then continues west to Zattere (€12, serving Dorsoduro hotels); and the Orange (ARANCIO) Line stops at Guglie near the train station (€12). From Venice to the airport, the first boat departs from San Marco-Giardinetti at 4:00 in the morning, with the last boat leaving at 22:25. Allow roughly 70–80 minutes for the trip, depending on your stop.

The fast Alilaguna Golden (ORO) Line zips nonstop to and from San Marco–Giardinetti in 35 minutes (€25, departs from San Marco–Giardinetti for the airport about hourly from 7:40–13:30).

Buy Alilaguna tickets and get more schedule information at the airport's Public Transport desk (to the left as you exit baggage claim), at the airport dock, or at any other vaporetto stop in Venice that has Alilaguna service. You can also purchase tickets on board (tel. 041-523-5775).

Water Taxi: Luxury taxi speedboats zip directly between the airport and your hotel in 30 minutes for €90 for up to four people. This can be a smart investment—especially for small groups and those with an early departure. Arrange at the airport's water-taxi desk when you arrive, or through your hotel the day before you leave. You'll have to schlep your bags for the eight-minute walk between the dock and the airport.

Buses: Blue ATVO shuttle buses connect the airport and the Piazzale Roma vaporetto stop at the head of the Grand Canal (€3, buy from driver, 2/hr, 20 min; buses leave airport 8:20–24:00 from platform 1 directly outside arrivals terminal, leave Piazzale Roma 5:00–20:40 from far side of the lot from Hotel S. Chiara, www.atvo.it). At the Piazzale Roma vaporetto stop, the slow vaporetto #1 or faster #82 (€6 for either) head to St. Mark's Square (see "Getting Around Venice," page 776).

FLORENCE

(Firenze)

Florence, the home of the Renaissance and birthplace of our modern world, is a "supermarket sweep," and the groceries are the best Renaissance art in Europe.

Get your bearings with a Renaissance walk. Florentine art goes beyond paintings and statues—there's food, fashion, and handicrafts. You can lick Italy's best gelato while enjoying some of Europe's best people-watching.

Planning Your Time

If you're in Italy for three weeks, Florence deserves at least a well-organized day. Make reservations at least a month in advance for the Uffizi Gallery (best Italian paintings anywhere) and a few days in advance for the Accademia (Michelangelo's *David*). You can have your hotelier make these reservations for you—request this service when booking your room (see page 850 for details).

For a day in Florence, see the Accademia, tour the Uffizi Gallery, visit the underrated Bargello (best statues), and do the Renaissance ramble (explained on page 835).

Art-lovers will want to chisel out another day of their itinerary for the many other Florentine cultural treasures. Shoppers and ice cream–lovers may need to do the same.

Plan your sightseeing carefully. The major sights—including the Uffizi and the Accademia—close on Monday. While many travelers spend several hours a day in lines, you can avoid this by making reservations or going late in the day. Places open at night are virtually empty.

Connoisseurs of smaller towns should consider taking the bus to Siena for a day or evening trip (75-min one-way, confirm when last bus returns). Siena is magic after dark.

ORIENTATION

The best of Florence lies mostly on the north bank of the Arno River. The main historical sights cluster around the red-brick dome of the cathedral (Duomo). Everything is within a 20-minute walk of the train station, cathedral, or Ponte Vecchio (Old Bridge). The less impressive but more characteristic Oltrarno area (south bank) is just over the bridge. Though small, Florence is intense. Prepare for scorching summer heat, kamikaze motor scooters, slick pickpockets, few WCs, steep prices, and long lines.

Tourist Information

There are three TIs in Florence: across from the train station, near Santa Croce Church, and on Via Cavour.

The TI across the square from the train station is most crowded—expect long lines (Mon–Sat 8:30–19:00, Sun 8:30–14:00; with your back to tracks, exit the station—it's across the square in wall near corner of church, Piazza Stazione 4, tel. 055-212-245). In the train station, avoid the Hotel Reservations "Tourist Information" window (marked *Informazioni Turistiche Alberghiere*) near the McDonald's; it's not a real TI, but a hotel-reservation business instead.

The TI near Santa Croce Church is pleasant, helpful, and uncrowded (Mon–Sat 9:00–19:00, Sun 9:00–14:00, shorter hours off-season, Borgo Santa Croce 29 red, tel. 055-234-0444).

Another winner is the TI three blocks north of the Duomo (Mon–Sat 8:30–18:30, Sun 8:30–13:30, closed Sun in winter, Via Cavour 1 red, tel. 055-290-832 or 055-23-320, international bookstore across street).

At any TI, pick up a free map (ask for the "APT" map and tear out the excellent center inset to keep handy in your pocket), a current museum-hours listing (extremely important, since no guidebook—including this one—has ever been able to accurately predict the hours of Florence's sights for the coming year), and any information on entertainment. The free, monthly *Florence Concierge Information* magazine lists museums, plus lots that I don't: concerts, markets, sporting events, church services, shopping ideas, bus and train connections, and an entire similar section on Siena. *The Florentine,* published every other Thursday, is a free newspaper for expats and tourists (in English; news, events, kids' activities, and cultural insights, download latest issue at www.theflorentine.net). Both of these English freebies are available at TIs and hotels all over town.

Greater Florence

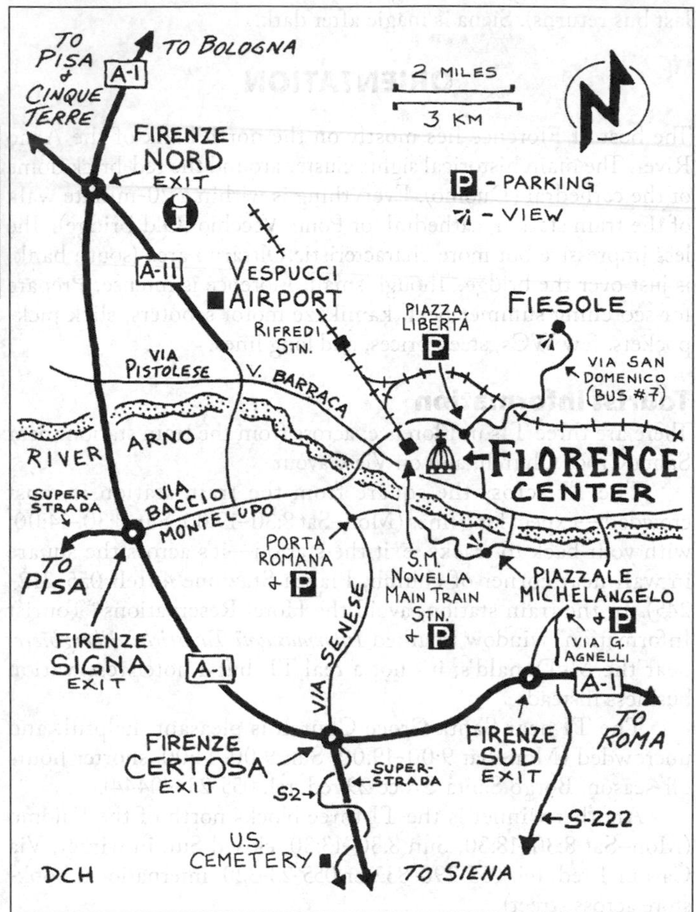

Arrival in Florence

By Train: Florence's Santa Maria Novella station soaks up time and generates dazed and sweaty crowds. If you arrive by train, there's no need to linger at the station. Extremely user-friendly, grayish-blue-and-yellow machines take euros and credit cards, and can display schedules, issue tickets, and even make reservations for railpass holders. You can also get tickets and train information for your next destination from travel agencies away from the congested station (such as American Express, see page 832). The fake "Tourist Information" office in the station (next to McDonald's) is actually a room-booking service funded by the hotels. The real TI is across the square from the station (see page 827).

With your back to the tracks, look left to see a 24-hour

Florence Overview

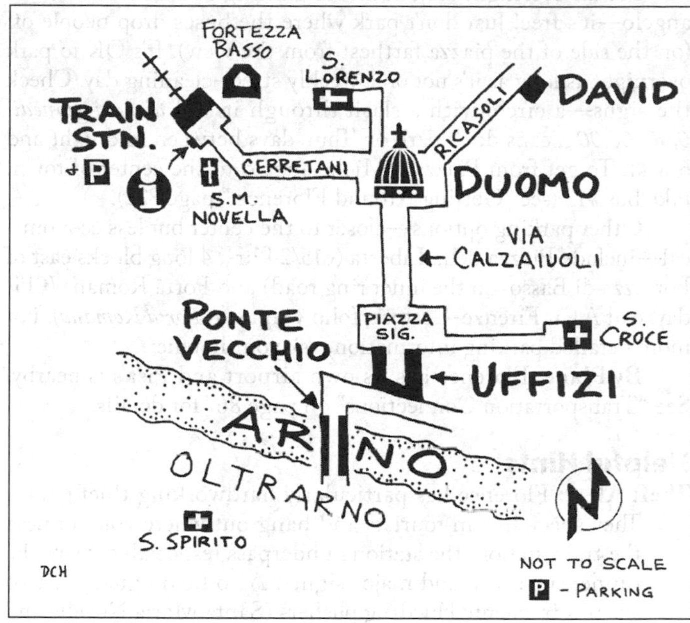

pharmacy (*Farmacia Comunale,* near McDonald's), city buses, and the entrance to the underground mall/passage that goes across the square to the Church of Santa Maria Novella. (Note: Pickpockets frequent this tunnel, especially the surface point near the church.) Baggage check is near track 16.

By Car: If you're taking the *autostrada* (north or south) to Florence, get off at the Certosa exit and follow signs to *Centro*; at Porta Romana, go to the left of the arch and down Via Francesco Petrarca. After driving around and trying to park in Florence, you'll understand why Leonardo never invented the car. Cars flatten the charm of the city.

Don't drive into the historic core of Florence. A system of cameras photographs every car entering the center. You must register your car with your hotel, whether you just drove in to drop off luggage or if you have parking reserved at your hotel. If you don't, a hefty fine will appear on your rental-car statement. If you go into the city beyond the ring road, even accidentally, you need to report your license-plate number to avoid the fine.

Non-residents are not allowed to park on the streets anywhere near or in the old center. Many hotels listed in this book have a few parking spots they can rent to guests in the center—most charge around €20 per day. In addition, the city has plenty of **parking lots.** For a short stay, park underground at the train station (€2–3/hr).

For an overnight stay, consider parking at Piazzale Michelangelo—it's free! Just don't park where the buses drop people off (on the side of the piazza farthest from the view). It's OK to park overnight as long as it's not on a weekly street-cleaning day. Check the signs—a circle with a slash through it and *dispari giovedi, 0,00-06,00* means don't park on Thursdays between midnight and 6 A.M. To get from Piazzale Michelangelo to the center of town, take bus #13 (see "Getting Around Florence," page 832).

Other parking options—closer to the center but less economical—include Piazza della Libertà (€15/24 hrs, 4 long blocks east of Fortezza di Basso, on the inner ring road) and Porta Romana (€15/day, exit A1 at Firenze-Certosa, follow signs to *Porta Romana*). For more detailed parking information, ask your hotelier.

By Plane: Florence has its own airport and Pisa's is nearby. See "Transportation Connections" on page 867 for details.

Helpful Hints

Theft Alert: Florence has particularly hardworking thief gangs. They specialize in tourists and hang out where you do: near the train station, the station's underpass (especially where the tunnel surfaces), and major sights. Also be on guard at two squares frequented by drug pushers (Santa Maria Novella and Santo Spirito). American tourists—especially older ones—are considered easy targets.

Medical Help: To reach a doctor who speaks English, call 055-475-411 (they answer 24/7, reasonable house calls to your hotel—arriving within an hour for €130, only €50 if you go to the clinic at Via L. Magnifico 59, near Piazza della Libertà when the doctor's in: Mon–Fri 11:00–12:00 & 17:00–18:00, Sat 11:00–12:00, house calls only on Sun, no appointment necessary). The TI has a list of English-speaking doctors. There are 24-hour pharmacies at the train station and near the Duomo on Borgo San Lorenzo.

Churches: Many churches now operate like museums, charging an admission fee to see their art treasures. Modest dress for men, women, and even children is required in some churches, and recommended for all of them—no bare shoulders, short shorts, or short skirts. Be respectful of worshippers and the art; don't use a flash. Churches usually close from 12:00 or 12:30 to 15:00 or 16:00.

Addresses: Street addresses list businesses in red and residences in black (color-coded on the actual street number and indicated by a letter following the number in printed addresses: r = red, no indication = black). *Pensioni* are usually black but can be either. The red and black numbers each appear in roughly consecutive order on streets but bear no apparent connection with each other. I'm lazy and don't concern myself with the distinction (if one number's wrong, I look for the other) and can easily find my way around.

Late-Hours Note: The Accademia, Uffizi, and Palatine Gallery/Royal Apartments in the Pitti Palace are open Tue–Sun until 18:50. Many other sights are open until 19:00: Museum of San Marco (Sat–Sun), Museum of Precious Stones (Thu), San Lorenzo Market (daily), Medici-Riccardi Palace (Thu–Tue), the Duomo's dome (Mon–Fri), Baptistery (Mon–Sat), Mercato Nuovo (daily), Palazzo Vecchio (Fri–Wed), and Leonardo Museum (daily). These sights are open until 19:30: Duomo Museum (Mon–Sat), Giotto's Tower (daily), the Boboli and Bardini Gardens in the Pitti Palace (daily, June–Aug only), and San Miniato Church (daily).

Internet Access: Internet Train is the dominant chain, with bright and cheery rooms, speedy computers, and long hours (daily 9:30–24:00, www.internettrain.it). Find branches at the train station (downstairs), Piazza della Repubblica (Via Porta Rossa 38 red), Piazza Santa Croce (Via de Benci 36 red), and Ponte Vecchio (Borgo San Jacopo 30 red). Two other Internet cafés are in the north of Florence, between the Duomo and the Accademia, near the Medici-Riccardi Palace: **Italian Point** (daily 9:00–20:00, Via Ricasoli 19 red) and **easyInternet** (daily 9:00–23:00, Via Ricasoli 23 red).

Bookstores: Local guidebooks (sold at kiosks) are cheap and give you a map and a decent commentary on the sights. For brand-name guidebooks in English, try **Feltrinelli International** (Mon–Sat 9:00–19:30, closed Sun, Via Cavour 20 red, a few blocks north of the Duomo and across the street from the TI and the Medici-Riccardi Palace on Via Cavour, tel. 055-219-524), **Edison Bookstore** (Mon–Sat 9:00–24:00, Sun 10:00–24:00, sells CDs and novels on Renaissance and a lot more on its four floors, facing Piazza della Repubblica, tel. 055-213-110), or **Paperback Exchange** (cheaper, all books in English, bring in your used book for a discount on a new one, Mon–Fri 9:00–19:30, Sat 10:00–19:30, closed Sun and Aug, just south of the Duomo on Via delle Oche 4 red, tel. 055-293-460).

Laundry: The **Wash & Dry Lavarapido** chain offers long hours and efficient, self-service launderettes at several locations (about €7 for wash and dry, daily 8:00–22:00, tel. 055-580-480). These are close to recommended hotels: Via dei Servi 105 (and a rival launderette at Via Guelfa 22 red, off Via Cavour; both near *David*); Via del Sole 29 red and Via della Scala 52 red (between train station and river); Via Ghibellina 143 red (Palazzo Vecchio); and Via dei Serragli 87 red (across the river in Oltrarno neighborhood).

Travel Agency: Get train tickets, reservations, and supplements at travel agencies rather than at the congested train station. The cost is often the same, though sometimes there's a minimal charge. Ask your hotel for the nearest travel agency, or try American Express.

American Express offers all the normal services, but is most helpful as an easy place to get your train tickets, reservations, supplements (all the same price as at the station), cell phone rental, or just information on trains (Mon–Fri 9:00–17:30, closed Sat–Sun, 3 short blocks north of Palazzo Vecchio on Via Dante Alighieri 22 red, tel. 055-50981).

Chill Out: Schedule several cool breaks into your sightseeing where you can sit, pause, and refresh yourself with a sandwich, gelato, or coffee.

Getting Around Florence

I organize my sightseeing geographically and do it all on foot.

If you take **buses,** a €1 ticket gets you one hour (€1.80/3 hrs, €4/24 hrs, buy in *tabacchi* shops or newsstands and validate on bus, or buy 1-hour tickets sold on bus for €1.50, route map available at TI, info tel. 800-424-500). Multiday passes are also available.

Florence requires a lot of walking. Its buses don't really cover the old center well. Fun little *elettrico* buses weave and circle around the old center from the station, and big buses rumble from the station and Piazza San Marco (near Museum of San Marco and many recommended hotels) to points beyond where most tourists go.

Of the many bus lines here are the only ones I found helpful: *elettrico* #D (from train station to Ponte Vecchio, joyriding through Oltrarno); *elettrico* #B (up and down the Arno River from Ognissanti to Santa Croce); lines #7, #31, and #32 (connecting the station, Duomo, and Piazza San Marco with #7 continuing on to Fiesole); and lines #12 and #13 (from station to Porta Romana, up to Piazzale Michelangelo, and on to Santa Croce).

Hop-on, hop-off bus tours stop at the major sights (see the next section, "Tours").

The minimum cost for a **taxi** ride is €4, or €6 after 22:00 and on Sundays (rides in the center of town should be charged as tariff #1). A taxi ride from the train station to Ponte Vecchio costs about €8.50. Taxi fares and supplements (e.g. €2 extra if you call a cab) are clearly explained on signs in each taxi.

TOURS

Note that big bus companies offer tours of Florence, but for most, the city is really best on foot. The outfits listed here are hardworking, creative, and offer a worthwhile array of organized sightseeing

Florence

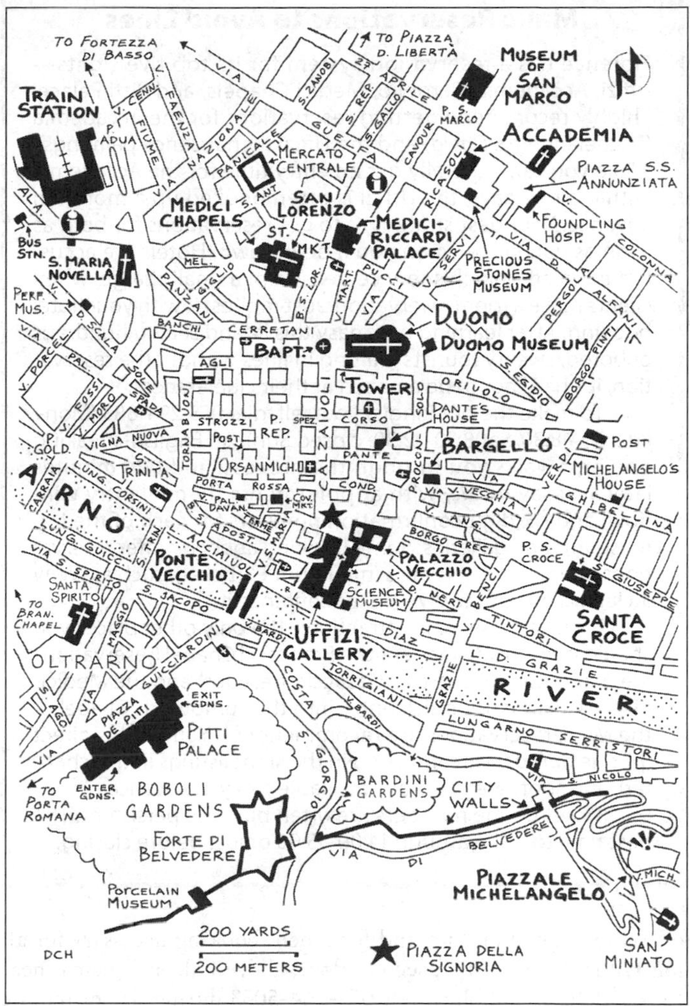

activities. Nearly all have guides available for private hire. Study their websites for details.

Walking Tours of Florence—This company offers a variety of tours (up to 12/day year-round) featuring downtown Florence, Uffizi highlights, and Tuscany day trips. Their guides are native English-speakers. The three-hour "Original Florence" walk hits the main sights but gets offbeat to weave a picture of Florentine life in medieval and Renaissance times. Tours go rain or shine with as few as two participants (€25 for 3-hour Original Florence walk daily at 9:15, office open Mon–Sat 8:00–18:00, Sun 8:30–13:30 but

Make Reservations to Avoid Lines

Florence has a reservation system for its top five sights—Uffizi, Accademia, Bargello, Medici Chapels, and Pitti Palace. I highly recommend getting reservations for the Accademia (Michelangelo's *David*) and the Uffizi (Renaissance paintings). While you can generally get an entry time for the Accademia within a few days, the Uffizi is often booked up a month in advance. Your best strategy is to get reservations for both as soon as you know when you'll be in town. Hotels are accustomed to offering this service free (or for a small charge) when clients make a room reservation. Just request it with your hotel booking. After learning how easy this is, and seeing hundreds of bored, sweaty tourists waiting in lines without the reservation, it's hard not to be amazed at their cluelessness.

To make the booking(s) yourself, dial 055-294-883 (Mon–Fri 8:30–18:30, Sat 8:30–12:30, closed Sun). An English-speaking operator walks you through the process, and two minutes later you say *grazie,* with appointments (15-min entry window) and six-digit confirmation numbers for each of the top museums and galleries. Some booking agencies offer reservations online for a hefty fee (minimum €5/ticket), such as www.tickitaly.com and www.weekendafirenze.it.

Besides these main attractions, the only other places you should book in advance are the Brancacci Chapel (reservations are mandatory to see the Masaccio frescoes) and the Medici-Riccardi Palace (for quick entry into the sumptuous Chapel of the Magi, reservations are recommended). You do this direct (phone numbers are included in the sight listings in this chapter), and spots are generally available a day in advance.

Ticket phone numbers are often busy; be persistent. The best time to call is around 14:00–15:00 or just before closing.

off-season closed on Sun and for lunch, booking necessary for all tours, Via dei Sassetti 1, second floor, above Odeon Cinema, near Piazza della Repubblica, tel. 055-264-5033 during day or mobile 329-613-2730 from 18:00–20:00, www.italy.artviva.com, staff@artviva.com). For schedule details, pick up their extensive brochure in your hotel lobby.

Florentia—Top-notch, private walking tours—geared for thoughtful, well-heeled travelers with longer than average attention spans—are led by local scholars. The tours range from introductory city walks and museum visits to in-depth thematic walks such as the Golden Age of Florence, the Medici Dynasty, and side-trips into Tuscany (tours start at €125 for 2 hours, reserve in advance, tel. 338-890-8625, US tel. 510-759-5059, www.florentia.org, info@florentia.org).

Context Florence—Started by the folks who run Context Rome, this group of graduate students and professors lead "walking seminars" as scholarly as Florentia's (above). Their tours include a three-hour Michelangelo seminar, an in-depth study of the artist's work and influence (€76/person) and a two-hour evening orientation stroll called the Florence Evening Transect (€35/person, tel. 06-482-0911, US tel. 888-467-1986, www.contextflorence.com, info@contextflorence.com, run by Lani Bevacqua and Paul Bennett).

Tuscany Tours—Run by Paola Migliorini and her partners, this group offers museum tours, city walking tours, and Tuscan excursions by van (you can tailor tours as you like). Go anywhere in the center of Florence by van and enjoy the city nearly sweat-free (€55/hr or €65/hr with 8-seat van, Via S. Gallo 120, tel. 055-472-448, mobile 347-657-2611, www.florencetour.com, info@florencetour.com).

Local Guides—Good guides include: Paola Barubiani and her partners at Walks Inside Florence (tel. 335-526-6496, www.walksinsideflorence.it, pbarub@tin.it) and Alessandra Marchetti (mobile 347-386-9839, aleoberm@tin.it).

Hop-on, Hop-off Bus Tours—Around town, you'll see big double-decker sightseeing buses double-parking at major sights. Tourists on the top deck can listen to brief recorded descriptions of the sights, snap photos, and enjoy an effortless drive-by look at the major landmarks. Tickets cost €20 (good for 24 hours, first bus at 9:30, last bus at 18:00, pay as you board). Tickets include two bus lines: Blue takes one hour with a trip up to Piazzale Michelangelo; Green takes two hours with a side-trip to Fiesole. As the name implies, you can hop off when you want and catch the next bus (every 30 min depending on the season). Hop-on stops include the train station, Duomo, and Pitti Palace (www.firenze.city-sightseeing.it).

Accidental Tourist—This tour company picks you up in a van for a day of cooking classes, hiking, biking, or wine-tasting, then drops you off back in Florence (prices vary, e.g. €85 for cooking class 9:30–17:00, book online in advance, allow 4 days for a reply to emails, US tel. 348-659-0040, www.accidentaltourist.com, info@accidentaltourist.com).

SELF-GUIDED WALK

A Renaissance Walk Through Florence

During the Dark Ages, it was especially obvious to the people of Italy—sitting on the rubble of Rome—that there had to be a brighter age before them. The long-awaited rebirth, or Renaissance, began in Florence for good reason. Wealthy because of its cloth

Renaissance Walk

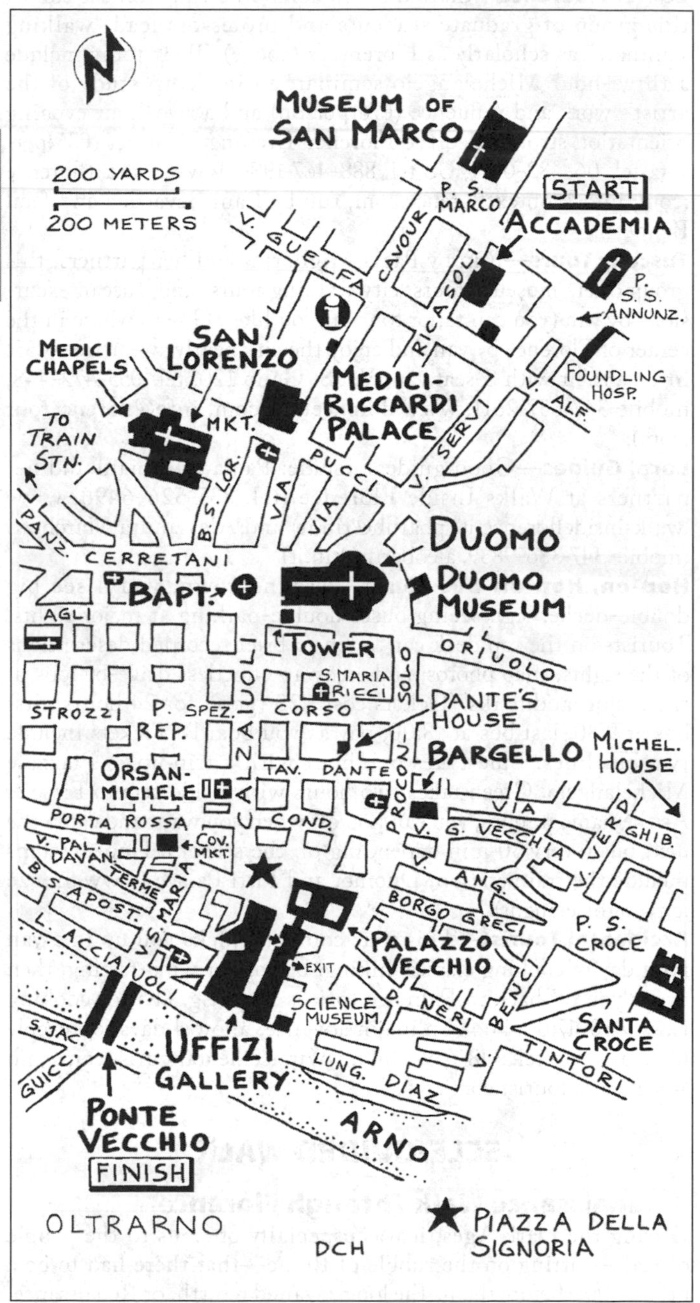
MUSEUM OF SAN MARCO
200 YARDS
200 METERS
START
ACCADEMIA
P. S. MARCO
P. S.S. ANNUNZ.
FOUNDLING HOSP.
MEDICI CHAPELS
SAN LORENZO
MEDICI-RICCARDI PALACE
TO TRAIN STN.
MKT.
DUOMO
DUOMO MUSEUM
CERRETANI
BAPT.
TOWER
S. MARIA RICCI
DANTE'S HOUSE
BARGELLO
MICHEL. HOUSE
STROZZI
P. REP.
ORSAN-MICHELE
PORTA ROSSA
COV. MKT.
PALAZZO VECCHIO
EXIT
SCIENCE MUSEUM
UFFIZI GALLERY
P. S. CROCE
SANTA CROCE
PONTE VECCHIO
FINISH
ARNO
OLTRARNO
DCH
PIAZZA DELLA SIGNORIA

industry, trade, and banking; powered by a fierce city-state pride (locals would pee into the Arno with gusto, knowing rival city-state Pisa was downstream); and fertile with more than its share of artistic genius (imagine guys like Michelangelo and Leonardo attending the same high school)—Florence was a natural home for this cultural explosion.

Take a walk through the core of Renaissance Florence by starting at the Accademia (home of Michelangelo's *David*) and cutting through the heart of the city to Ponte Vecchio on the Arno River.

At the Accademia, you'll look into the eyes of Renaissance man—humanism at its confident peak. Then walk to the cathedral (Duomo) to see the dome that kicked off the architectural Renaissance. Step inside the Baptistery to view a ceiling covered with preachy, flat, 2-D, medieval mosaic art. Then, to learn what happened when art met math, check out the realistic 3-D reliefs on the doors. The painter, Giotto, also designed the bell tower—an early example of a Renaissance genius excelling in many areas. Continue toward the river on Florence's great pedestrian mall, Via de' Calzaiuoli (or "Via Calz")—part of the original grid plan given to the city by the ancient Romans. Down a few blocks, compare medieval and Renaissance statues on the exterior of the Orsanmichele Church. Via Calz connects the cathedral with the central square (Piazza della Signoria), the city palace (Palazzo Vecchio), and the Uffizi Gallery, which contains the greatest collection of Italian Renaissance paintings in captivity. Finally, walk through the Uffizi courtyard—a statuary think tank of Renaissance greats—to the Arno River and Ponte Vecchio.

Sights on a Renaissance Walk Through Florence

▲▲▲Accademia (Galleria dell'Accademia)—This museum houses Michelangelo's *David* and powerful (unfinished) *Prisoners*. Eavesdrop as tour guides explain these masterpieces. More than with any other work of art, when you look into the eyes of *David*, you're looking into the eyes of Renaissance man. This was a radical break with the past. Man was now a confident individual, no longer a plaything of the supernatural. And life was now more than just a preparation for what happened after you died. Hello, humanism.

The Renaissance was the merging of art, science, and humanism. In a humanist vein, *David* is looking at the crude giant of medieval darkness and thinking, "I can take this guy." (David was an apt mascot for a town surrounded by big bully city-states.) Back on a religious track, notice *David*'s large and overdeveloped right hand. This is symbolic of the hand of God that powered David to slay the giant...and enabled Florence to rise above its crude neighboring city-states.

Beyond the magic marble are two floors of interesting pre-Renaissance and Renaissance paintings, including a couple of lighter-than-air Botticellis.

Cost, Hours, Location: €6.50, plus €3 fee for recommended reservation, Tue–Sun 8:15–18:50, closed Mon (last entry 45 min before closing, Via Ricasoli 60, tel. 055-238-8609). To avoid waiting in line, reserve ahead; see page 834 for details.

Nearby: Piazza S.S. Annunziata, behind the Accademia, displays lovely Renaissance harmony. Facing the square are two fine buildings: the 15th-century Santissima Annunziata church (worth a peek) and Brunelleschi's Hospital of the Innocents (Spedale degli Innocenti, not worth going inside), with terra-cotta medallions by Lucca della Robbia. Built in the 1420s, the hospital is considered the first Renaissance building.

▲▲Duomo (Santa Maria del Fiore)—Florence's Gothic cathedral (built 1300–1435) has the third-longest nave in Christendom. The noisy neo-Gothic facade (added later, from the 1870s) is covered with pink, green, and white Tuscan marble. Since nearly all of the cathedral's great art is stored in the nearby Duomo Museum, the best thing about the interior is the shade. The inside of the dome is decorated by one of the largest paintings of the Renaissance, a huge *Last Judgment* by Giorgio Vasari and Federico Zuccari.

Think of the confidence of the age: The Duomo was built with a hole awaiting a dome in its roof. This was before the technology to span it with a dome was available. No matter. They knew that someone soon could handle the challenge...and the local architect Brunelleschi did. The cathedral's claim to artistic fame is Brunelleschi's magnificent dome—the first Renaissance dome and the model for domes to follow.

Cost and Hours: Free entry to church (there's a cost to climb dome—see below), Mon–Wed and Fri–Sat 10:00–17:00 except first Sat of month 10:00–15:30, Thu 10:00–15:30, Sun 13:30–16:45, modest dress code enforced, tel. 055-230-2885. Note that the massive crowds that overwhelm the entrance in the morning usually clear out by afternoon.

▲Climbing the Duomo's Dome—For a grand view into the cathedral from the base of the dome, a peek at some of the tools used in the dome's construction, a chance to see Brunelleschi's "dome-within-a-dome" construction, a glorious Florence view from the top, and the equivalent of 463 plunges on a Stairmaster, climb the dome. When planning St. Peter's in Rome, Michelangelo rhymed (not in English), "I can build its sister—bigger, but not more beautiful" than the dome of Florence.

To avoid the *long*, dreadfully slow-moving line, arrive by 8:30 or drop by very late (€6, Mon–Fri 8:30–19:00, Sat 8:30–17:40 except first Sat of month 8:30–16:00, closed Sun, enter from outside church on north side, tel. 055-230-2885).

▲Giotto's Tower (Campanile)—The 270-foot bell tower has 50 fewer steps than the Duomo's dome, offers a faster, less crowded climb, and has a view of the Duomo to boot, but the cage-like top isn't great for photo ops (€6, daily 8:30–19:30, last entry 40 min before closing).

▲▲Duomo Museum (Museo dell'Opera del Duomo)—The underrated cathedral museum, behind the church (at Via del Proconsolo 9), is great if you like sculpture. It has masterpieces by Donatello (a gruesome wood carving of Mary Magdalene clothed in her matted hair, and the *cantoria,* a delightful choir loft bursting with happy children) and by Lucca della Robbia (another choir loft, lined with the dreamy faces of musicians praising the Lord). Look for a late Michelangelo *Pietà* (Nicodemus, on top, is a self-portrait), Brunelleschi's models for his dome, and the original restored panels of Ghiberti's doors to the Baptistery (€6, Mon–Sat 9:00–19:30, Sun 9:00–13:40, last entry 40 min before closing, one of the few museums in Florence open on Mon, tel. 055-230-2885).

If you find all this church art intriguing, look through the open doorway of the Duomo art studio, which has been making and restoring church art since the days of Brunelleschi (a block toward the river from the Duomo at Via dello Studio 23a).

▲Baptistery—Michelangelo said its bronze doors were fit to be the gates of paradise. Check out the gleaming copies of Lorenzo Ghiberti's bronze doors facing the Duomo. Making a breakthrough in perspective, Ghiberti used mathematical laws to create the illusion of receding distance on a basically flat surface.

The doors on the north side of the building were designed by Ghiberti when he was young; he'd won the honor and opportunity by beating Brunelleschi in a competition (the rivals' original entries are in the Duomo Museum).

Inside, sit and savor the medieval mosaic ceiling where it's always Judgment Day, and Jesus is giving the ultimate thumbs-up and thumbs-down (€3, interior open Mon–Sat 12:00–19:00, Sun 8:30–14:00; bronze doors are on the outside, so always "open"; original panels are in the Bargello Museum).

Orsanmichele Church—In the ninth century, this loggia (covered courtyard) was a market used for selling grain (stored upstairs). Later, it was closed in to make a church. Outside, check out the dynamic statue-filled niches, some with accompanying symbols from the guilds that sponsored the art. Donatello's *St. Mark* and *St. George* (on the northeast and northwest corners) step out boldly in the new Renaissance style. The interior has a glorious Gothic tabernacle (1359), housing the painted wooden panel depicting *Madonna delle Grazie* (1346). The iron bars spanning the vaults were the Italian Gothic answer to the French Gothic external buttresses (church is free, Tue–Sun 10:00–17:00, closed Mon, niche sculptures always viewable from the outside). The church sometimes hosts evening concerts (tickets sold on day of concert from door facing Via dei Calzaiuoli).

The museum upstairs, currently closed, holds many of the church's precious originals. Someday, tourists might be able to enjoy the fine statues by Ghiberti, Donatello, and company.

A block away, you'll find the...

▲Mercato Nuovo (a.k.a. the Straw Market)—This market loggia is how Orsanmichele looked before it became a church. Originally a silk and straw market, Mercato Nuovo still functions as a rustic yet touristy market today (at the intersection of Via Calimala and Via Porta Rossa). Prices are soft, but the San Lorenzo Market (see page 859) is much better for haggling. Notice the circled X in the center, marking the spot where people hit after being hoisted up to the top and dropped as punishment for bankruptcy. You'll also find *Porcellino* (a statue of a wild boar nicknamed "little pig"), which people rub and give coins to in order to ensure their return to Florence. This new copy, while only a few years old, already has a polished snout. Nearby, a wagon sells tripe (cow innards) sandwiches—a local favorite (daily 9:30–19:00).

▲Palazzo Vecchio—With its distinctive castle turret, this fortified palace, once the home of the Medici family, is a Florentine landmark. But if you're visiting only one palace interior in town, the Pitti Palace (see page 847) is better. The Palazzo Vecchio interior is worthwhile only if you're a real fan of Florentine history or of the artist Giorgio Vasari, who wallpapered the place with mediocre magnificence. The museum's most famous statues are Michelangelo's *Victory* and Donatello's bronze statue of *Judith and Holerfernes* (€6, €8 combo-ticket with Brancacci Chapel, Fri–Wed 9:00–19:00, Thu 9:00–14:00, ticket office closes one hour earlier, tel. 055-276-8224).

Even if you don't go to the museum, do step into the **free courtyard** behind the fake *David* just to feel the essence of the Medicis (you'll have to go through metal detectors but you don't have to pay). Until 1873, Michelangelo's *David* stood at the entrance, where the copy is today. While the huge statues in the square are important only as the whipping boys of art critics and as rest stops for pigeons, the nearby **Loggia dei Lanzi** has several important statues. Look for Cellini's bronze statue of Perseus holding the head of Medusa. The plaque on the pavement in front of the fountain marks the spot where the monk Savonarola was burned in MCDXCVIII, or 1498.

Children's Museum: The Museo dei Ragazzi in Palazzo Vecchio offers activities for children (ages 4 to teens) on a reservation-only basis. The kids can take a guided English tour with a historically costumed character, or make their own fresco on a souvenir tile (€6 plus €1–2/activity, family rates, no reservation fee, call center to reserve, daily 9:00–18:00, tel. 055-276-8224 or 055-276-8558).

Nearby: The square fronting the Palazzo Vecchio, Piazza della Signoria, is a tourist's world with pigeons, postcards, horse buggies, and tired hubbies. And, if it would make your tired hubby happy, the ritzy Café Rivoire—with the best view seats in town—is famous for its fancy desserts and hot chocolate (closed Sun).

▲▲▲Uffizi Gallery—This greatest collection of Italian paintings anywhere features works by Giotto, Leonardo, Raphael, Caravaggio, Rubens, Titian, and Michelangelo, and a roomful of Botticellis, including his *Birth of Venus.*

The museum is nowhere near as big as it is great. Few tourists spend more than two hours inside. The paintings are displayed on one comfortable U-shaped floor in chronological order, from the 13th through 17th centuries. The left wing—starring the Florentine Middle Ages to the Renaissance—is the best. The connecting corridor contains sculpture, and the right wing focuses on High Renaissance and Baroque.

Essential stops are (in this order): Gothic altarpieces (narrative, pre-Realism, no real concern for believable depth) including Giotto's altarpiece, which progressed beyond "totem-pole angels"; Uccello's *Battle of San Romano,* an early study in perspective (with a few obvious flubs); Fra Filippo Lippi's cuddly Madonnas; the Botticelli room, filled with masterpieces, including a pantheon of classical fleshiness and the small *La Calùnnia,* showing the glasnost of Renaissance free-thinking being clubbed back into the darker age of Savonarola; two minor works by Leonardo; the octagonal classical sculpture room with an early painting of Bob Hope and a copy of Praxiteles' *Venus de' Medici*—considered the epitome of beauty in Elizabethan Europe; a view of the Ponte Vecchio through the window—dreamy at sunset; Michelangelo's only surviving easel painting, the round *Holy Family;* Raphael's noble *Madonna of the Goldfinch;* Titian's voluptuous *Venus of Urbino;* and Duomo views from the café terrace (WC near café).

Cost, Hours, Reservations: €9.50, plus €3 for recommended reservation, Tue–Sun 8:15–18:50, last entry 45 minutes before closing, closed Mon (after entering the building, either take elevator or climb four long flights of stairs to reach the art).

As only 600 are allowed into the museum at a time, there are infamously long lines to get in. Avoid the two-hour peak-season wait by getting a reservation at least a month in advance (see page 834). Most hotels offer this service for free or for a €3–5 fee, if you request it when you book your room.

After you have your reservation (or voucher), go to the Uffizi 10 minutes before your appointed time. Walk briskly past the

200-yard-long ticket-buying line—pondering the IQ of this gang—to the reserve-ticket desk at door #3 (across the courtyard from the entry—see map) for those with reservations (labeled in English "Picking Up Service"), give your number (or voucher), pay (cash only), and scoot right in through door #1, close to the Palazzo Vecchio; one line for groups, one for individuals.

If you haven't called ahead, there are other ways to make an Uffizi reservation—sometimes for the same day, depending on availability: Try booking directly at the Uffizi (enter the left side of door #2, pay for ticket up front, same hours as museum); take a private tour of the museum with Walking Tours of Florence (booking required, see page 833); or for a hefty fee, you can reserve online through various agencies such as www.weekendafirenze.it or www.tickitaly.com. Sometimes, by the end of the day (an hour before closing), there are no lines and you can just walk right in.

In the Uffizi's Courtyard: Enjoy the courtyard (free), full of artists and souvenir stalls. The surrounding statues honor earth-shaking Florentines: artists (Michelangelo and Leonardo), philosophers (Machiavelli), scientists (Galileo), writers (Dante), and explorers (Amerigo Vespucci), and the great patron of so much Renaissance thinking, Lorenzo "the Magnificent" de' Medici.

▲Ponte Vecchio—Florence's most famous bridge is lined with shops that have traditionally sold gold and silver. A statue of Cellini, the master goldsmith of the Renaissance, stands in the center, ignored by the flood of tacky tourism. This is a romantic spot late at night. In fact, hanging over the edge of the bridge (on either side of the Cellini bust) are piles of padlocks. Guys demonstrate the enduring quality of their love by ceremonially taking their girls here, locking a lock, and throwing the key into the Arno. (But what's with the combination lock?)

Notice the "prince's passageway" above the bridge. In less secure times, the city leaders had a fortified passageway connecting the Vecchio Palace and Uffizi with the mighty Pitti Palace, to which they could flee in times of attack. This passageway, called the **Vasari Corridor,** is technically open to the public, but a visit is almost impossible to arrange, and if you do manage it, usually a disappointment (open "seasonally," try the museum reservation line, tel. 055-264-321).

SIGHTS

Near the Accademia

▲▲Museum of San Marco (Museo di San Marco)—One block north of the Accademia, this 15th-century monastery houses the greatest collection anywhere of frescoes and paintings by the early Renaissance master Fra Angelico. The ground floor features the monk's paintings, along with some works by Fra Bartolomeo. Upstairs are 43 cells decorated by Fra Angelico and his assistants. While the monk/painter was trained in the medieval religious style, he also learned and adopted Renaissance techniques and sensibilities, producing works that blended Christian symbols and Renaissance realism. Don't miss the cell of Savonarola, the charismatic monk who rode in from the Christian right, threw out the Medicis, turned Florence into a theocracy, sponsored "bonfires of the vanities" (burning books, paintings, and so on), and was finally burned himself when Florence decided to change channels (€4, Mon–Fri 8:15–13:50, Sat–Sun 8:15–19:00, but closed first, third, and fifth Sun and second and fourth Mon of each month, on Piazza San Marco, tel. 055-238-8608). While you can reserve an entrance time here, it's entirely unnecessary.

Museum of Precious Stones (Museo dell'Opificio delle Pietre Dure)—This unusual gem of a museum features mosaics of inlaid marble and stones. You'll see remnants of the Medici workshop from 1588, including 500 different precious stones, the tools used to cut and inlay them, and room after room of the sumptuous finished product. The helpful loaner booklet available next to the ticket window describes it all in English (€2, Mon–Wed and Fri–Sat 8:15–14:00, Thu 8:15–19:00, closed Sun, around corner from Accademia at Via degli Alfani 78, tel. 055-26511).

Heart of Florence

▲▲▲Bargello (Museo Nazionale)—This underappreciated sculpture museum is in a former police-station-turned-prison that looks like a mini-Palazzo Vecchio. It has Donatello's painfully beautiful *David* (the very influential first male nude to be sculpted in a thousand years), works by Michelangelo, and rooms of Medici treasures cruelly explained in Italian only (politely suggest to the staff that English descriptions would be wonderful). Moody Donatello, who embraced realism with his lifelike statues, set the personal and artistic style for many Renaissance artists to follow. The best works are in the ground-floor room at the foot of the outdoor staircase, and in the room directly above (€4, daily 8:15–13:50 but closed first, third, and fifth Sun and second and fourth Mon of each month, last entry 40 min before closing, Via del Proconsolo 4, tel. 055-238-8606).

▲▲Medici Chapels (Cappelle Medicee)—The chapel, containing Medici tombs, is drenched in lavish High Renaissance architecture and sculpture. The highlight is a chapel with interior decoration by Michelangelo, including the brooding *Night, Day, Dawn,* and *Dusk* statues (€6, daily 8:15–16:50 but closed the second and fourth Sun and the first, third, and fifth Mon of each month, tel. 055-238-8602).

Nearby: Behind the chapels on Piazza Madonna degli Aldobrandini is the lively **San Lorenzo Market,** with a scene that I find just as interesting. Take a stroll through the huge double-decker **Mercato Centrale** (central food market) one block north.

▲Medici-Riccardi Palace (Palazzo Medici-Riccardi)—Lorenzo the Magnificent's home is worth a look for its art. The tiny Chapel of the Magi contains colorful Renaissance gems like the *Procession of the Magi* frescoes by Benozzo Gozzoli. The Multimedia Room helps you navigate through details of Gozzoli's Magi frescoes, shown on a large video screen. The former library has a Baroque ceiling fresco by Luca Giordano, a prolific artist from Naples known as Fast Luke *(Luca fa presto)* for his ambidextrous painting abilities. While the Medicis originally occupied this 1444 house, in the 1700s it became home to the Riccardi family, who added the Baroque flourishes. As only eight people are allowed into the Chapel of the Magi every seven minutes, it's smart to call for a reservation if you want to avoid a wait (€5, Thu–Tue 9:00–19:00, closed Wed, Via Cavour 3, kitty-corner from Church of San Lorenzo, one long block north of Baptistery, tel. 055-276-0340).

▲Piazza della Repubblica and Nearby—This large square sits on the site of Florence's original Roman Forum. The lone column—nicknamed the belly button of Florence—once marked the intersection of the two main Roman roads. All that survives of Roman Florence is its grid street plan and this column. Look at the map (by the benches—where the old boys hang out to talk sports and politics) to see the ghost of Rome in its streets. Roman Florence was a garrison town—a rectangular fort with this square marking the intersection of the two main roads (Via Corso and Via Roma).

Today's piazza, framed by a triumphal arch, is a nationalistic statement celebrating the unification of Italy. Florence, the capital of the country (1865–1870) until Rome was liberated, lacked a square worthy of this grand new country. So the neighborhood here was razed to open up an imposing, modern forum surrounded by stately circa-1890 buildings.

The fancy La Rinascente department store, facing the Piazza della Repubblica, is one of the city's finest (WC on fourth floor, go up the stairs for the pricey café with an impressive view terrace).

▲▲Science Museum (Istituto e Museo di Storia della Scienza)—When we think of the Florentine Renaissance, we think of visual arts: painting, mosaics, architecture, and sculpture. But when the visual arts declined in the 1600s (abused and co-opted by political powers), music and science flourished in Florence. (The first opera was written here.) Florence hosted many breakthroughs in science, as you'll see in this fascinating collection of Renaissance and later clocks, telescopes, maps, and ingenious gadgets. Trace the technical innovations as modern science emerges from 1000 to 1900. One of the most talked-about bottles in Florence is the one here, which contains Galileo's finger. The first floor features various tools for gauging the world, from a compass and thermometer to Galileo's telescopes. The second floor delves into clocks, pumps, medicine, and chemistry. Loaner English guidebooklets are available. It's friendly, comfortably cool, never crowded, and just a block east of the Uffizi on the Arno River (€6.50, June–Sept Mon and Wed–Fri 9:30–17:00, Tue and Sat 9:30–13:00, closed Sun; Oct–May Mon and Wed–Sat 9:30–17:00, Tue 9:30–13:00, generally closed Sun but open second Sun of month 10:00–13:00; Piazza dei Giudici 1, tel. 055-265-311, www.imss.fi.it).

▲▲Church of Santa Maria Novella—The 13th-century Dominican church, just south of the train station, is rich in art. Along with crucifixes by Giotto and Brunelleschi, there's every textbook's example of the early Renaissance mastery of perspective: *The Holy Trinity* by Masaccio; it's opposite the side entrance. The exquisite chapels trace art in Florence from medieval times to early Baroque. The outside of the church features a dash of Romanesque (horizontal stripes), Gothic (pointed arches), Renaissance (geometric shapes), and Baroque (scrolls). Step in and look down the 330-foot nave for a 14th-century optical illusion (€2.50, Mon–Thu and Sat 9:30–17:00, Fri and Sun 13:00–17:00).

Nearby: Art lovers can seek out the adjacent **cloisters** (€2.70, includes meager church museum, entry to the left of the church's facade); the Chapel of the Spaniards is notable for Bonaiuto's fresco *Allegory of the Dominican Order*. A palatial **perfumery** (Farmacia de Santa Maria Novella) is around the corner 100 yards down Via della Scala at #16 (free but shopping encouraged, Mon–Sat 9:30–19:30, Sun 10:30–18:30, tel. 055-216-276). Thick with the lingering aroma of centuries of spritzes, it started as the herb garden of the Santa Maria Novella monks. Well-known even today for its top-quality products, it is extremely Florentine. Pick up the history sheet at the desk, and wander deep into the shop. From the back room, you can peek at one of Santa Maria Novella's cloisters with its dreamy frescoes and imagine a time before Vespas and tourists.

Dante's House (Casa di Dante)—Dante's house—actually a copy built near his house—reopened after a lengthy restoration, but is painfully lacking in artifacts, many of which were destroyed by a fire while in storage. The reopening releases Dante fans from the Purgatorio of waiting but falls short of Paradiso. The house's only valuable offering—not worth the entrance fee—is the exhibit of information panels that introduce visitors to the history of Florence within the context of Dante's life (€4, Tue–Sat 10:00–17:00, open sporadic hours on Sun, closed Mon, near the Bargello at Via S. Margherita 1, tel. 055-219-416).

Santa Croce and Nearby

▲▲Santa Croce Church—The 14th-century Franciscan church, decorated with centuries of precious art, holds the tombs of great Florentines (€5, Mon–Sat 9:30–17:30, Sun 13:00–17:30, slow-talking audioguide-€4, modest dress code enforced, tel. 055-246-6105).

The loud 19th-century Victorian Gothic facade faces a huge square ringed with tempting shops and littered with tired tourists. Escape into the church and admire its sheer height and spaciousness. Enter and head towards the front of the church. On your right is the **tomb of Galileo Galilei** (1564–1642). Having defied the Church by saying the earth revolved around the sun, his heretical remains were only allowed in the church long after his death. Directly opposite is the **tomb of Michelangelo Buonarroti** (1475–1564).

The first chapel to the right of the main altar features the famous fresco by Giotto of the *Death of Saint Francis.* With simple but eloquent gestures, Francis' brothers bid him a sad farewell, one of the first expressions of human emotion in modern painting.

At the end of the right transept, a door leads into the sacristy, where you'll find a rumpled bit of St. Francis' tunic *(Parte di Tunica)* and old sheets of music. In the bookshop, notice the photos of the devastating flood of 1966 high on the wall. Beyond that is the "leather school" that's really more of a touristy leather store. Exit between the Rossini and Machiavelli tombs into the cloisters. On the left, enter Brunelleschi's Pazzi Chapel, considered one of the finest pieces of Florentine Renaissance architecture.

▲Michelangelo's House (Casa Buonarroti)—Fans enjoy this house, which stands on property once owned by Michelangelo. It was built by the artist's grand-nephew, who turned it into a little museum honoring his famous relative. You'll see some of Michelangelo's early, less-than-monumental statues and a few sketches. Be warned: Michelangelo's descendants attributed everything they could to their famous relative, but very little here (beyond two marble relief panels and a couple of sketches) is actually by Michelangelo (€6.50, Wed–Mon 9:30–14:00, closed Tue, English descriptions, Via Ghibellina 70, tel. 055-241-752).

Leonardo Museum—This small, entrepreneurial venture is overpriced but fun for anyone who wants to actually crank the shaft and spin the ball bearings of Leonardo's genius inventions. While this exhibit has no actual historic artifacts, it shows about 30 of Leonardo's inventions made into models, each described in English. What makes this exhibit special is that you're encouraged to touch and play with the models—it's great for kids (€6, daily 10:00–19:00, Via dei Servi 66 red).

South of the Arno River

To locate these sights, see map on page 833.

▲▲Pitti Palace—The palace, several blocks southwest of the Ponte Vecchio, has three separate museums and two gardens. While reservations by phone are possible (tel. 055-294-883), they are not necessary. If there happens to be a long line at the palace, you can bypass it (and the line at the metal detector) for a fee: Head up to the front of the line to the quick reservations window (at the right-hand side of the facade), ask to enter immediately, and buy a ticket with the €3 reservation fee.

The **Palatine Gallery/Royal Apartments (Galleria Palatina)** is the biggie, featuring palatial room after chandeliered room, its walls sagging with masterpieces by 16th- and 17th-century masters including Rubens, Titian, and Rembrandt. Its Raphael collection is the second-biggest anywhere—the Vatican beats them by one. Included in the ticket is the **Modern Art Gallery,** which features Romantic, Neoclassical, and Impressionist works by 19th- and 20th-century Tuscan painters (€8.50, Tue–Sun 8:15–18:50, closed Mon, tel. 055-238-8614).

The **Grand Ducal Treasures (Museo degli Argenti)** is the Medici treasure chest, with jeweled crucifixes, exotic porcelain, gilded ostrich eggs, and so on, made to entertain fans of applied arts (€8; includes the mildly interesting Costume Museum, Porcelain Museum, Boboli Gardens, and Bardini Gardens; daily June–Aug 8:15–19:30, Sept–May 8:15–18:30, closed first and last Mon of month).

Behind the palace, the huge, landscaped **Boboli Gardens** and **Bardini Gardens** offer a shady refuge from the city heat (both gardens covered by Grand Ducal Treasures ticket). The recently reopened Bardini Gardens offer a belvedere with lovely panoramic city views. You can enter the Bardini Gardens at two different places:

1. When you exit the Boboli Gardens, head uphill, going around Forte di Belvedere, and then left down Costa di San Giorgio to the Bardini entrance on your right at #4 (it's a 10–15 min walk from the Pitti Palace). After visiting the garden, you can walk downhill and exit at what also serves as the lower entrance.

2. You can enter—or exit—the Bardini Gardens at Via de' Bardi 1 red, near Piazza de' Mozzi and the bridge called Ponte alle Grazie.

▲▲Brancacci Chapel—For the best look at Masaccio's works (he's the early Renaissance master who reinvented perspective), see his restored frescoes here. Instead of medieval religious symbols, Masaccio's paintings feature simple, strong human figures with facial expressions that reflect their emotions. The accompanying works of Masolino and Filippino Lippi provide illuminating contrasts.

Get reservations in advance (see below). Visits on the top of each hour include a free 40-minute English video on the history of the frescoes and the Biblical stories they represent. The doors close promptly when the video starts (first door on left past the ticket office/chapel entrance).

Cost, Reservations, Hours, Location: €4. Reservations—free and mandatory—are often available for the same day (dial 055-276-8224; it's frequently busy, but keep trying—the best time to call is around 14:00–15:00). Reservation times begin every 15 minutes, with a maximum of 30 visitors per time slot. You have 15 minutes in the actual chapel. The cost is €8 (includes Palazzo Vecchio, Mon and Wed–Sat 10:00–17:00, Sun 13:00–17:00, closed Tue, ticket office closes at 16:30). The chapel is in the Church of Santa Maria del Carmine, on Piazza del Carmine, in the Oltrarno neighborhood south of the Arno River. It's about a 15-minute walk or short taxi ride (about €8.50) from downtown Florence (e.g. Palazzo Vecchio).

The neighborhoods around the church are considered the last surviving bits of old Florence.

Santo Spirito Church—This church has a classic Brunelleschi interior and a painted, carved wooden crucifix attributed to Michelangelo. The sculptor donated this early work to the monastery in appreciation for allowing him to dissect and learn about bodies. Pop in for a delightful Renaissance space and a chance to marvel at a Michelangelo all alone (free, Thu–Sat and Mon–Tue 10:00–12:00 & 16:00–17:30, Wed 10:00–12:00, closed Sun to sightseers, Piazza Santo Spirito, tel. 055-210-030).

▲Piazzale Michelangelo—Overlooking the city from across the river (look for the huge statue of David), this square is worth the 30-minute hike, drive (free parking), or bus ride (either #12 or #13 from the train station) for the view of Florence and the stunning dome of the Duomo. Off the west side of the piazza is a somewhat hidden terrace, an excellent place to retreat from the mobs. After dark, the square is packed with local school kids licking ice cream and each other. About 200 yards beyond all the tour groups and teenagers is the stark, beautiful, crowd-free, Romanesque San Miniato Church.

▲San Miniato Church—This church was dedicated to a martyred saint who died on this hill. Its green-and-white marble facade is classic Florentine Romanesque. The church has wonderfully 3-D paintings, a plush ceiling of glazed terra-cotta panels by della Robbia, and a sumptuous Renaissance chapel (located front and center). For me, though, the highlight is the brilliantly preserved art in the sacristy (behind altar on right) showing the scenes from the life of St. Benedict (c. 1350) by a follower of Giotto. Drop a euro into the box to light the room (free, daily 8:00–19:30, 200 yards above Piazzale Michelangelo, bus #12 or #13 from train station, tel. 055-266-181).

EXPERIENCES

Gelato

Gelato is an edible art form. Italy's best ice cream is in Florence—one souvenir that can't break and won't clutter your luggage. But beware of scams at touristy joints on busy streets that turn a simple request for a cone into a €10 "tourist special" rip-off. A key to gelato appreciation is sampling liberally and choosing flavors that go well together. Ask, as the locals do, for *"Un assaggio, per favore?"* (A taste, please?; oon ah-SAH-joh pehr fah-VOH-ray) and *"Che si sposano bene?"* (What marries well?; kay see spoh-ZAH-noh BEN-ay).

Gelateria Carrozze is very good (daily 11:00–24:30, closes at 20:00 in winter; on riverfront 30 yards from Ponte Vecchio toward the Uffizi, Via del Pesce 3).

Gelateria dei Neri is a favorite worth tracking down (daily 11:00–24:00, try the *crostata*—a strawberry pie flavor, 2 blocks east of Palazzo Vecchio at Via dei Neri 20/22 red).

Gelateria Carabè, a stellar choice on a tourist thoroughfare, also serves up several flavors of luscious *granita*, Italian ices made with fresh fruit (daily 9:00–2:00 in the morning, between the Duomo and Accademia, Via Ricasoli 60 red). **Grom,** another *gelateria,* uses organic ingredients and only seasonal fresh fruit (daily 11:00–23:00, Via delle Oche 24a).

Vivoli's, which serves "only today's production," is the most famous (Tue–Sun 8:00–1:00 in the morning; closed Mon, closed Aug and Jan; opposite the Church of Santa Croce, go down Via Torta a block, turn right on Via Stinche). Before ordering, try a free sample of their rice flavor—*riso.*

If you want an excuse to check out the little village-like neighborhood across the river from Santa Croce, enjoy a gelato at the tiny no-name *gelateria* at Via San Miniato 5 red (just before Porta San Miniato).

SLEEPING

For hassle-free efficiency, I favor hotels and restaurants that are handy to your sightseeing activities. Nearly all of my recommended accommodations are located in Florence's downtown core.

The accommodations scene varies wildly with the season. Spring and fall are very tight and expensive, while mid-July through August is wide open and discounted. November through February is also generally empty. I've listed prices for peak season: April, May, June, September, and October.

Sleep Code

(€1 = about $1.30, country code: 39)
S = Single, **D** = Double/Twin, **T** = Triple, **Q** = Quad, **b** = bathroom, **s** = shower only. Breakfast is included, credit cards are accepted, and English is spoken unless otherwise noted. Air-conditioning, when available, is usually only turned on in summer.

To help you sort easily through these listings, I've divided the rooms into three categories based on the price for a standard double room with bath:

$$$ Higher Priced—Most rooms €165 or more.
$$ Moderately Priced—Most rooms between €110–165.
$ Lower Priced—Most rooms €110 or less.

With good information and an email or phone call beforehand, you can find a stark, clean, and comfortable double with breakfast and a private bath for around €100 (less at the smaller places, such as the *soggiorni*). You get elegance in peak season for €160. Some places listed are old and rickety, and I've described them as such.

Book ahead, especially for weekends and holidays. Hotels often fill up in advance on Easter (March 23 in 2008), April 25, May 1, June 24 (Florence's patron saint day), November 1, and on Fridays and Saturdays all year. Places will hold a room until early afternoon. If they say they're full, mention that you're using this book.

Museum-goers take note: When you book your room, you can usually ask your hotelier to book entry times for you to visit the popular Uffizi Gallery and the Accademia (Michelangelo's *David*). This service is fast, easy, and offered free (or at a small charge) by your hotel—the only requirement is advance notice. Ask them to make appointments for you any time the day after your arrival for the Uffizi and the Accademia. For details, see page 834.

Between the Station and Duomo

$$ Hotel Accademia is an elegant place with marble stairs, parquet floors, attractive public areas, 21 pleasant but pricey rooms, and a floor plan that defies logic (Db-€145, Tb-€175, 5 percent discount with cash, air-con, tiny courtyard, Via Faenza 7, tel. 055-293-451, fax 055-219-771, www.hotelaccademiafirenze.com, info@hotelaccademiafirenze.com).

$$ Residenza dei Pucci, a block north of the Duomo, has 12 tastefully decorated rooms—in soothing earth tones—with aristocratic furniture and tweed carpeting. It's fresh and bright

Florence Hotels

1. Hotel Aldobrandini
2. Hotel Accademia
3. Florence Dream Domus B&B
4. Residenza dei Pucci
5. Hotel Basilea
6. Casa Rabatti
7. Affitacamere Lucia Freda
8. Soggiorno Magliani
9. Hotel Loggiato dei Serviti
10. Hotel Morandi alla Crocetta
11. Hotel Enza & Locanda Pitti
12. Oblate Sisters of the Assumption
13. Hotel Pendini
14. Palazzo Niccolini al Duomo
15. Pensione Maxim
16. Soggiorno Battistero
17. Albergo Firenze
18. Hotel Torre Guelfa & Hotel Pensione Alessandra
19. In Piazza della Signoria B&B
20. Hotel Davanzati
21. Hotel Pensione Elite
22. Bellevue House
23. Hotel Sole
24. Hotel il Bargellino
25. Residenza il Villino
26. Hotel Dalí
27. Hotel Centrale

(Sb-€130, Db-€145, Tb-€165, Db suite with grand Duomo view-€207, €233 for four, Via dei Pucci 9, tel. 055-281-886, fax 055-264-314, www.residenzadeipucci.com, residenzadeipucci@residenzadeipucci.com).

$$ Hotel Centrale, with 20 spacious and recently renovated rooms, is indeed central (Db-€140, Tb-€172, air-con, elevator, Via dei Conti 3, tel. 055-215-761, fax 055-215-216, www.hotelcentralefirenze.it, info@hotelcentralefirenze.it).

$ Hotel Aldobrandini, a budget choice in a cheaply remodeled old palazzo, has 15 basic, clean rooms, with the San Lorenzo Market at its doorstep and the entrance to the Medici Chapels a few steps away (Ss-€40, Sb-€50, D-€65, Db-€80, €75 with cash, lots of night noise but has double-paned windows, fans, behind market stalls at Piazza Madonna degli Aldobrandini 8, tel. 055-211-866, fax 055-267-6281, www.hotelaldobrandini.it, info@hotelaldobrandini.it, Ignazio).

Near the Central Market

$$ Hotel Basilea has predictable three-star, air-conditioned comfort in its 38 modern rooms (Sb-€84, Db-€114, Tb-€160, elevator, terrace, Via Guelfa 41, near intersection with Via Nazionale—a busy street, ask for a room in the back, tel. 055-214-587, fax 055-268-350, www.hotelbasilea.net, basilea@dada.it).

$$ Florence Dream Domus B&B, with six precious little rooms, is well-run and appropriately named—you'll feel like a Medici princess settling into its doily world of aristocratic pastels (Db-€140, Tb-175, pricier bigger rooms, 2-night minimum, air-con, Via de Ginori 26, tel. 055-295-346, fax 055-267-5643, www.florencedream.it, info@florencedream.it).

$ Hotel Enza, which is basic, quirky, and hard-working, rents 19 decent rooms for a great value (S-€40, Sb-€50, D-€60, Db-€80, breakfast-€5, air-con except in doubles without bath, Via San Zanobi 45, tel. 055-490-990, fax 055-473-672, www.hotelenza.it, info@hotelenza.it).

$ Casa Rabatti is the ultimate if you always wanted to be a part of a Florentine family. Its four simple, clean rooms are run with motherly warmth by Marcella, who speaks minimal English. Seeing 10 years of my family Christmas cards on their walls, I'm reminded how long she has been keeping budget travelers happy (D-€50, Db-€60, €25 per bed in shared quad or quint, cash only, no breakfast, has fans, 5 blocks from station, Via San Zanobi 48 black, tel. 055-212-393, casarabatti@inwind.it).

If booked up, Marcella will put you up in her daughter's place nearby at Via Nazionale 20 (five big, airy rooms with fans, no breakfast, closer to the station). While daughter Patricia works, her mom runs the B&Bs. Getting bumped to Patricia's gives you slightly more comfort and slightly less personality...certainly not a net negative.

$ Affitacamere Lucia Freda is basic, clean, and cheap. Its four ground-floor-yet-quiet rooms share two bathrooms, a kitchenette, and a leafy garden terrace (S-€45, D-€50, T-€70, cash only, no breakfast, Via San Zanobi 76, but ring at #31, tel. 055-487-533, mobile 380-546-2386, luciafreda@libero.it, run by kind Lucia and son Claudio).

$ Locanda Pitti, tiny and funky with simple rooms, is run by a young couple (Db-€60, Tb-€90, air-con-€5, no breakfast, next to Hotel Enza at Via San Zanobi 43, tel. 055-462-7327, mobile 348-597-2670, www.roomsinflorence.it, info@roomsinflorence.it, Isabella and Marco).

$ Hotel Soggiorno Magliani is central and humble, with seven rooms that feel and smell like a great-grandmother's home (S-€39, D-€49, T-€65, cash only but secure reservation with credit card, no breakfast, a little traffic noise but has double-paned windows, near Via Guelfa at Via Santa Reparata 1, tel. 055-287-378, hotel-magliani@libero.it, run by the friendly duo Vincenza and her English-speaking daughter, Cristina).

East of the Duomo

$$$ Hotel Loggiato dei Serviti, at the most prestigious address in Florence on the most Renaissance square in town, gives you Old World romance with hairdryers. Stone stairways lead you under open-beam ceilings through this 16th-century monastery's classy public rooms. The 33 cells—with air-conditioning, TVs, mini-bars, and telephones—wouldn't be recognized by their original inhabitants. The hotel staff is both professional and warm (Sb-€120, Db-€180, family suites from €263, elevator, Piazza S.S. Annunziata 3, tel. 055-289-592, fax 055-289-595, www.loggiatodeiservitihotel.it, info@loggiatodeiservitihotel.it, Chiara and Simonetta). Ask for a room in the back to avoid piazza noise at night. When full, they rent five spacious and elegant rooms in a 17th-century annex a block away. While it lacks the monastic mystique, the rooms are bigger and gorgeous.

$$$ Hotel Morandi alla Crocetta, another former convent, envelops you in a 16th-century cocoon. Located on a quiet street, with 10 rooms, period furnishings, parquet floors, and wood-beamed ceilings, it takes you back a few centuries (Sb-€100, Db-€177, breakfast not worth €11, a block off Piazza S.S. Annunziata at Via Laura 50, tel. 055-234-4747, fax 055-248-0954, www.hotelmorandi.it, welcome@hotelmorandi.it). The hotel is well run by a terrific team: Claudio, Maurizio, Rolando, Paolo and Frank.

$$$ Palazzo Niccolini al Duomo is one of five elite Historic Residence Hotels in Florence. The lady of the house, Ginevra

Niccolini di Camugliano, actually greets the guests. The lounge is palatial and the 10 rooms are big and splendid, with original 16th-century frescos. If you have the money and want a Florentine palace to call home, this is a very good bet. Opened in 2003, it's a block from the Duomo (Db-€300, prices vary with the luxuriousness of the room, check online for last-minute deals, Via dei Servi 2, tel. 055-282-412, fax 055-290-979, www.niccolinidomepalace.com, info@niccolinidomepalace.com).

$$ Residenza il Villino is popular and friendly, with 10 rooms and a pleasant, peaceful little courtyard (Db-€130, Qb apartment-€150, 5 percent discount with cash, air-con, just north of Via degli Alfani at Via della Pergola 53, tel. 055-200-1116, fax 055-200-1101, www.ilvillino.it, info@ilvillino.it, Sergio, Elisabetta, and son Lorenzo).

$ Hotel Dalí (in all the guidebooks) has 10 decent, basic rooms in a nice location for a great price. Rare in this area and price range, the hotel has plenty of free parking (S-€40, D-€65, Db-€80, extra bed-€20, no breakfast, has fans, great for singles, 2 blocks behind the Duomo at Via dell'Oriuolo 17, tel. & fax 055-234-0706, hoteldali@tin.it, Marco).

$ Oblate Sisters of the Assumption run an institutional 20-room hotel in a Renaissance building with a dreamy garden, fine (if simple) rooms, and a quiet, prayerful ambience. The staff doesn't speak English; it's best to reserve by fax, using simple English that God only knows how they translate (S-€40, D-€76, T-€114, Q-€152, cash only, single beds only, elevator, Borgo Pinti 15, tel. 055-248-0582, fax 055-234-6291).

Near Piazza della Repubblica

These are the most central of my accommodations recommendations (and therefore a little overpriced). While worth the extra cost for many, given Florence's walkable core, nearly every hotel can be considered central.

$$ Hotel Pendini, a three-star hotel overlooking Piazza della Repubblica, has Old World tiles, chandeliers, 42 rooms, and high prices (Sb-€110, Db-€150, air-con, elevator, fine lounge and breakfast room, Via Strozzi 2, tel. 055-211-170, fax 055-281-807, www.hotelpendini.net, pendini@florenceitaly.net, Barbara).

$ Pensione Maxim, right on Via dei Calzaiuoli, is a big, institutional-feeling place as close to the sights as possible. Its halls are narrow, but the 26 basic rooms are comfortable and well-maintained. Their newer and even more sterile hotel is downstairs (Sb-€80, Db-€108, Tb-€138, Qb-€155, air-con, elevator, Via dei Calzaiuoli 11, tel. 055-217-474, fax 055-283-729, www.hotelmaximfirenze.it, hotmaxim@tin.it, father Paolo and daughters Nicola and Chiara).

$ Soggiorno Battistero, literally next door to the Baptistery, has seven simple, airy rooms, most with great views, overlooking the Baptistery and square (Sb-€75, Db-€98, Tb-€135, Qb-€145, 5 percent cash discount, breakfast served in room, air-con, double-paned windows, Wi-Fi, third floor, no elevator, Piazza San Giovanni 1, tel. 055-295-143, fax 055-268-189, www.soggiornobattistero.it, battistero@dada.it, lovingly run by Italian Luca and his American wife Kelly).

$ Albergo Firenze, a big, efficient place, offers 58 modern, basic rooms in a central locale two blocks behind the Duomo (Sb-€78, Db-€98, Tb-€132, Qb-€162, air-con, elevator, noisy, at Piazza Donati 4 across from Via del Corso 8, tel. 055-214-203, fax 055-212-370, www.hotelfirenze-fi.it, firenze.albergo@tiscali.it).

Near Piazza della Signoria and Ponte Vecchio

$$$ Hotel Torre Guelfa is topped by a fun medieval tower with a panoramic rooftop terrace and a huge living room. Its 29 pricey rooms vary wildly in size. Room #15, with a private terrace (€240), is worth reserving several months in advance (Sb-€120, standard Db-€185, Db junior suite-€230, family deals, air-con, elevator, a couple blocks northwest of Ponte Vecchio, at Borgo S.S. Apostoli 8, tel. 055-239-6338, fax 055-239-8577, www.hoteltorreguelfa.com, info@hoteltorreguelfa.com, Sabina, Giancarlo, Carlo, and Sandro).

$$$ In Piazza della Signoria B&B, overlooking Piazza della Signoria, is peaceful, classy, and homey at the same time. It comes with all the special touches and little extras you'd expect in a top-end American B&B (viewless Db-€200, view Db-€260, Tb-€280, family apartments, lavish bathrooms, tiny elevator, air-con, Via dei Magazzini 2, tel. 055-239-9546, mobile 348-321-0565, fax 055-267-6616, www.inpiazzadellasignoria.com, info@inpiazzadellasignoria.com, Sonia and Alessandro).

$$ Hotel Pensione Alessandra is 16th-century, tranquil, and sprawling, with 27 big, modern rooms (S-€67, Sb-€113, D-€113, Db-€150, T-€150, Tb-€196, Q-€165, Qb-€217, 5 percent discount with cash, air-con, Borgo S.S. Apostoli 17, tel. 055-283-438, fax 055-210-619, www.hotelalessandra.com, info@hotelalessandra.com, Andrea).

$$ Hotel Davanzati, bright and shiny with artistic touches, has 21 cheery rooms with all the comforts. It's a family affair, where friendly Tomasso and father Fabrizio also book dinners, museums, and excursions (Sb-€100, Db-€160, Tb-€215, 5 percent discount for payment in cash, PlayStation 2 and DVD player in every room, air-con, elevator, Via Porta Rossa 5, tel. 055-286-666, fax 055-265-8252, www.hoteldavanzati.it, info@hoteldavanzati.it).

Near the Train Station

Note: As with any big Italian city, the area around the train station is a magnet for hardworking pickpockets on alert for lost, vulnerable tourists with bulging moneybelts hanging out of their khakis.

$ Hotel Pensione Elite is run with warmth by sunny Nadia. It has 10 comfortable if plainly furnished rooms that can be slightly smoky (Ss-€70, Sb-€80, Ds-€75, Db-€90, Tb-€110, Qb-€130, breakfast-€6, air-con, fans, Via della Scala 12, second floor, tel. & fax 055-215-395, hotelelitefi@libero.it).

$ Bellevue House is a fourth-floor oasis (no elevator) with six spacious rooms flanking a long, mellow yellow lobby. It's a peaceful time-warp thoughtfully run by Rosanna and Antonio di Grazia (Db-€95 in April–June, Sept, and Oct; Db-€75 in off-season, 5 percent cash discount, includes breakfast in a street-level bar, Via della Scala 21, tel. 055-260-8932, mobile 333-612-5973, fax 055-265-5315, www.bellevuehouse.it, info@bellevuehouse.it).

$ Hotel Sole, a clean, cozy, non-English-speaking family-run place with eight bright, modern rooms, feels like a mini-hotel (Sb-€50, Db-€80, Tb-€110, 5 percent cash discount, no breakfast, air-con, elevator, 1:00 curfew, a block toward river from Piazza Santa Maria Novella at Via del Sole 8, tel. & fax 055-239-6094, htlsole@tiscali.it).

$ Hotel il Bargellino, run by Bostonian Carmel and her Italian husband Pino, has 10 summery rooms decorated with funky antique furniture and Pino's modern paintings, just a few blocks north of the train station. Guests are welcome to relax with Carmel on her big, breezy terrace (S-€45, D-€75, Db-€85, extra bed-€25, no breakfast, Via Guelfa 87, tel. 055-238-2658, www.ilbargellino.com, carmel@ilbargellino.com).

Oltrarno, South of the River

Across the river in the Oltrarno area, between the Pitti Palace and Ponte Vecchio, you'll still find small traditional crafts shops, neighborly piazzas, and family eateries. The following places are an easy walk from the Ponte Vecchio.

$$$ Hotel Silla, a classic three-star hotel with 35 cheery, spacious, pastel, and modern rooms, is a good value. It faces the river and overlooks a park opposite the Santa Croce Church (Db-€170, Tb-€210, air-con, Via dei Renai 5, tel. 055-234-2888, fax 055-234-1437, www.hotelsilla.it, hotelsilla@hotelsilla.it, Laura, Chiara and Stefano).

$$ Hotel la Scaletta, ramshackle and brimming in character, is a dark, cool place with 14 rooms, a narrow labyrinthine floor plan, senseless stairs, lots of Old World lounges, and a romantic, panoramic roof terrace (Sb-€100, Db-€140, Tb-€160, air-con, Via Guicciardini 13 black, 150 yards south of Ponte Vecchio, tel. 055-283-028,

Oltrarno Hotels

fax 055-283-013, www.hotellascaletta.it, info@hotellascaletta.it, Giovanna, Paolo, Andrea, and Fabrizio). To fully enjoy their wonderful roof terrace, consider their light "Taste of Tuscany" meal—fine cold cuts, bread, and wine—for €10 per person.

$$ Pensione Sorelle Bandini, a rickety 500-year-old palace on a perfectly Florentine square, has 12 cavernous rooms, museum-warehouse interiors, a musty youthfulness, a Renaissance balcony lounge-loggia with a view, and an ambience that—for romantic bohemians—can be a highlight of Florence (D-€115, Db-€139, T-€158, Tb-€190, cash only, elevator, Piazza Santo Spirito 9, tel. 055-215-308, fax 055-282-761, pensionebandini@tiscali.it).

$ Istituto Gould is a Protestant Church–run place with 41 clean and spartan rooms with twin beds and modern facilities (S-€36, Sb-€41, D-€50, Db-€58, Tb-€72, Qb-€84, no breakfast, quieter rooms in back, Via dei Serragli 49, tel. 055-212-576, fax 055-280-274, www.istitutogould.it, gould.reception@dada.it). You must arrive when the office is open (Mon–Fri 8:45–13:00 & 15:00–19:30, Sat 9:00–13:00 & 14:30–18:00, no check-in Sun or holidays).

$ Soggiorno Alessandra has five bright, comfy, and smallish rooms. With double-paned windows, you'll hardly notice the traffic noise (D-€70, Db-€75, Tb-€95, Qb-€125, air-con-€8 extra, just past the Carraia Bridge at Via Borgo San Frediano 6, tel. 055-290-424, fax 055-218-464, www.soggiornoalessandra.it, info@soggiornoalessandra.it, Alessandra).

$ Casa Santo Nome di Gesu is a grand 29-room convent whose sisters—Franciscan Missionaries of Mary—are thankful to rent rooms to tourists. Staying in this 15th-century palace, you'll be immersed in the tranquil atmosphere created by a huge peaceful garden, generous prayerful public spaces, and smiling nuns (D-€70, Db-€85, twin beds only, authentic breakfast room, cheap dinners, Piazza del Carmine 21, tel. 055-213-856, fax 055-281-835, www.fmmfirenze.it, info@fmmfirenze.it).

$ Ostello Santa Monaca, a cheap, well-run hostel, is a long block south of the Brancacci Chapel and attracts a young backpacking crowd (€17 beds with sheets, 4- to 20-bed rooms, 2:00 curfew, Via Santa Monaca 6, tel. 055-268-338, fax 055-280-185, www.ostello.it, info@ostello.it).

Away from the Center

$ Hotel Ungherese is good for drivers. It's northeast of the city center (near *stadio,* en route to Fiesole), with a nice backyard garden, easy street parking (€8/day), and quick bus access (#11 and #17) into central Florence (Sb-€55, Db-€100, extra bed-€20, air-con, Via G. B. Amici 8, tel. & fax 055-573-474, www.hotelungherese.it, info@hotelungherese.it). Ask for a room on the garden. They can recommend good eateries nearby.

$ Villa Camerata, classy for an IYHF hostel, is in a pretty villa on the outskirts of Florence (€17.50 per bed with breakfast, 4- to 12-bed rooms, must have hostel membership card, ride bus #17 to Salviatino stop, Via Righi 2, tel. 055-601-451, fax 055-610-300, firenze-hostelinfo.org).

EATING

To save money and time for sights, you can keep lunches fast and simple, eating in one of countless self-service places and pizzerias or just picnicking (try juice, yogurt, cheese, and a roll for €5). For good sit-down meals, consider the following. Remember, restaurants like to serve what's fresh. If you're into flavor, go for the seasonal best bets—featured in the *Piatti del Giorno* ("special of the day") sections of the menus.

North of the River

Near Santa Maria Novella and the Train Station

Trattoria al Trebbio serves traditional food with simple Florentine elegance at excellent prices in its candle-lit interior. Tables spill out onto a romantic little square—an oasis of Roman Trastevere-like charm (Wed–Mon 12:00–15:00 & 19:00–23:00, Tue 12:00–15:00 only, reserve for outdoor seating, half a block off of Piazza Santa Maria Novella at Via delle Belle Donne 47, tel. 055-287-089).

At **Osteria Belledonne,** you'll feel like you're eating dinner in a crowded terrarium piled high with decorative knickknacks. Old-fashioned Tuscan food is served on tight tables—a few tables hunker on the street. They take few reservations; arrive early or wait (daily 12:00–15:00 & 19:00–23:00, Via delle Belle Donne 16 red, tel. 055-238-2609, run by sprightly Giacinto).

Trattoria Marione serves sincerely home-cooked-style meals to a mixed crowd of tourists and locals in a happy, food-loving, and steamy ambience. Dinners run about €15 plus wine (daily 10:00–15:00 & 19:00–22:30, Via della Spada 27 red, tel. 055-214-756).

Trattoria Sostanza-Troia, characteristic and well-established, is famous for its beef. Hearty steaks and pastas are splittable. Whirling ceiling fans and walls strewn with old photos evoke earlier times, while the artichoke pies remind locals of grandma's cooking. Crowded, shared tables with paper tablecloths lend a bistro feel. They offer two dinner seatings, requiring reservations: one at 19:30 and one at 21:00 (dinners for about €30 plus wine, lunch Mon–Sat 12:30–14:00, closed Sun, closed Sat in off-season, Via del Porcellana 25 red, tel. 055-212-691).

Trattoria 13 Gobbi (13 Hunchbacks) is a trendy favorite, glowing with candles around a tiny garden. It serves beautifully presented, surprisingly reasonable Tuscan food on big, fancy plates to a dressy local crowd (daily 12:15–15:00 & 19:30–23:00, Via del Porcellana 9 red, tel. 055-284-015).

Near the Central and San Lorenzo Markets

For piles of picnic produce, people-watching, or just a rustic sandwich, try the huge **Central Market** (Mercato Centrale, Mon–Sat 7:00–14:00, closed Sun, a block north of San Lorenzo Market). The cheap eateries within the market can be more colorful than sanitary. Buy a picnic of fresh mozzarella cheese, olives, fruit, and crunchy bread to munch on the steps of the nearby Church of San Lorenzo, overlooking the bustling street market.

Each of the following market neighborhood eateries is distinct and within a hundred yards of each other. Scout about and choose your favorite.

At **Casa del Vino,** Florence's oldest operating wine shop, you can order a glass of wine from among 25 open bottles, and

Florence Restaurants

TO FORTEZZA DI BASSO
TO PIAZZA D. LIBERTÀ
TRAIN STATION
MUSEUM OF SAN MARCO
P. S. MARCO
ACCADEMIA
P. S.S. ANNUNZ.
P. ADUA
MERCATO CENTRALE
MEDICI CHAPELS
SAN LORENZO ST. MKT.
MEDICI-RICCARDI PALACE
FOUNDLING HOSP.
BUS STN.
S. MARIA NOVELLA
DUOMO
DUOMO MUSEUM
BAPT.
TOWER
CERRETANI
STROZZI
P. REP.
POST
CORSO
DANTE'S HOUSE
BARGELLO
ORSANMICH.
MICH. HOUSE
P. GOLD.
S. TRINITÀ
ARNO R.
COV MKT.
PALAZZO VECCHIO
PONTE VECCHIO
P. S. CROCE
SCIENCE MUSEUM
UFFIZI GALLERY
SANTA CROCE
OLTRARNO
200 YARDS
200 METERS
PIAZZA DELLA SIGNORIA
DCH
1 Osteria Belledonne
2 Trattoria al Trebbio
3 Trattoria Marione
4 Trattoria Sostanza-Troia
5 Trattoria 13 Gobbi
6 Trattoria Zà-Zà & Trattoria Mario's
7 Central Market & Trattoria la Burrasca
8 Osteria la Congrega
9 Gran Caffè San Marco
10 Self-Service Rist. Leonardo
11 Antico Ristorante il Sasso di Dante
12 Casa del Vino
13 Osteria Vini e Vecchi Sapori
14 Cantinetta dei Verrazzano & Ristorante Paoli
15 I Fratellini Wine & Sandwiches
16 Trattoria Icche C'è C'è
17 Osteria del Porcellino
18 Trattoria Nella
19 Café Rivoire
20 Osteria Vineria i'Brincello
21 Trattoria Nerone Pizzeria
22 Pasticceria Robiglio
23 Gelateria Carrozze
24 Gelateria dei Neri
25 Gelateria Carabè
26 Gelateria Grom
27 Vivoli's Gelateria
28 Il Centro Supermarcati

sip it alongside local workers on break. Owner Gianni (pronounced "Johnny"), whose family has owned the Casa for 70 years, also serves interesting *panini* (Mon–Fri 9:30–19:00, closed Sat–Sun, hidden behind stalls of the San Lorenzo Market on Via dell'Ariento 16 red).

Trattoria Zà-Zà is a fun, old, characteristic high-energy place facing the Central Market. Locals lament the invasion of tourists, but everyone's happy, and the food is still great. *Ribollita,* a Tuscan soup, is their specialty. Arrive early or make a reservation, especially for the wonderful outdoor piazza seating. Consider cobbling together a meal of different *antipasti* plates (daily 11:30–23:00, Piazza del Mercato Centrale 26 red, tel. 055-215-411).

Trattoria Mario's, next to Zà-Zà, has been serving marketgoers hearty lunches since 1953. Their simple formula: bustling service, old-fashioned good value, a lunch-only menu, and shared tables. It's *cucina casalinga*—home cooking. Mario's is extremely popular, so go early. If there's a line, put your name on the list (€4 pastas, €7 *secondi*, Mon–Sat 12:00–15:30, closed Sun, cash only, no reservations, Via Rosina 2, tel. 055-218-550).

Trattoria la Burrasca is Flintstone-chic, family-run, and ideal for Tuscan home cooking. It's small—10 tables—and often filled with our readers. Anna and Antonio Genzano have cooked and served here with passion since 1982. If Andy Capp were Italian, he'd eat here for special nights out. Everything is homemade except the desserts. And if you want good wine cheap, this is the place (Fri–Wed 12:00–15:00 & 19:00–22:30, closed Thu, Via Panicale 6 black, at north corner of Central Market, tel. 055-215-827, very little English spoken).

Osteria la Congrega brags it's "a Tuscan wine bar designed to help you lose track of time." In a fresh, romantic two-level setting, chef/owner Mahyar takes pride in his fun, easy menu featuring modern Tuscan cuisine, with top-notch meat and seasonal produce. He offers quality vegetarian dishes, creative salads, and an inexpensive but excellent house wine. With just 10 uncramped tables, reservations are required for dinner (€6 pastas, €12 nightly specials, daily 12:00–15:00 & 19:00–23:00, Via Panicale 43 red, tel. 055-264-5027). Mahyar offers fine wines by the glass (see list on blackboard).

Osteria Vineria i'Brincello is a bright, happy, no-frills diner with lots of spirit, friendly service, and few tourists during lunchtime. Notice the Tuscan daily specials on the blackboard hanging from the ceiling (daily 12:00–15:00 & 18:30–22:30, corner of Via Nazionale and Via Chaira at Via Nazionale 110 red, tel. 055-282-645).

Trattoria Nerone Pizzeria serves up cheap, hearty Tuscan dishes and just-okay pizzas. The lively, flamboyantly outfitted space was once the garden courtyard of a convent (€5 pastas, €10 *secondi*, daily 11:30–23:00, just north of Via Nazionale at Via Faenza 95-97 red, tel. 055-291-217).

Near the Accademia and Museum of San Marco

Pasticceria Robiglio, a classy little café, opens up its stately dining area for lunch on workdays. They have a small menu of daily pasta and *secondi* specials and seem determined to do things like they did in the elegant pre-tourism days (generous €8 plates, pretty pastries, good wines by the glass, smiling service, Mon–Fri 12:00–15:00, longer hours as a café, open Sat but no meals, closed Sun, a block towards the Duomo off Piazza S.S. Annunziata at Via dei Servi 112 red, tel. 055-212-784).

Gran Caffè San Marco, located on Piazza San Marco across from the entrance of the Museum of San Marco, might tempt you with its convenience and outdoor seating, but it churns out horrible cafeteria fare to cheap but tired tourists. Your best bet is to grab a *panino*—of which there are several vegetarian options—from their bar on the corner (no cover charge, self-service bar and restaurant, Piazza San Marco 11, entrance around the corner on Via Cavour near #50, tel. 055-215-833).

Picnic on the Ultimate Renaissance Square: There's a handy supermarket across from the Accademia *(David)* which happily makes sandwiches to your specs (Il Centro Supermarcati, Mon–Sat 8:00–20:00, Sun 9:00–19:00, Via Ricasoli 109). Choose your fresh bread and tasty meat and cheese (assembled and sold by the weight); embellish with some veggies, milk, yogurt, or juice; and hike around the block to Piazza S.S. Annunziata, the first Renaissance square in Florence. There's a fountain for washing fruit on the square. Grab a stony seat anywhere you like and savor one of my favorite cheap Florence eating experiences. (Or, drop by Pasticceria Robiglio, half a block from the square—see above—for a sandwich and juice to go.)

Near the Duomo

Self-Service Ristorante Leonardo is fast, cheap, air-conditioned, and handy, just a block from the Duomo, southwest of the Baptistery (€3.50 pastas, €5 main courses, Sun–Fri 11:45–14:45 & 18:45–21:45, closed Sat, upstairs at Via Pecori 5, tel. 055-284-446). Luciano (like Pavarotti) runs the place with enthusiasm.

Antico Ristorante il Sasso di Dante serves standard Tuscan fare in a surprisingly pleasant indoor/outdoor setting in the shadow of the Duomo (€18 two-course meals, always good vegetarian dishes and special menu of the day, daily 12:00–14:30 & 19:00–22:30, come early to snare front-row seats, Piazza delle Pallottole 6, tel. 055-282-113).

Near Palazzo Vecchio

Piazza della Signoria, the square facing Palazzo Vecchio, is ringed by beautifully situated yet touristy eateries. Don't waste a meal on probably microwaved food. The square's saving grace is dessert at the famous **Café Rivoire,** with its fancy desserts and thick hot chocolate. It has the top seating, service, and edibles on the square (Mon–Sat 7:40–24:00, closed Sun).

Osteria Vini e Vecchi Sapori, half a block north of Palazzo Vecchio, is a colorful hole-in-the-wall serving traditional food, including plates of mixed crostini (less than €1 each—step right up and choose at the bar) and €10 daily specials (Tue–Sat 12:30–3:00 & 19:30–22:00, Sun 12:30–3:00, closed Mon, Via dei Magazzini 3 red, facing the bronze equestrian statue in Piazza della Signoria, go behind its tail into the corner and to your left, run by Mario and Thomas).

Cantinetta dei Verrazzano is a long-established bakery/café/wine bar serving delightful sandwich plates in an elegant old-time setting, and hot focaccia sandwiches to go. Their *Specialità Verrazzano* is a fine plate of four little crostini (like mini bruschetta) featuring different local breads, cheeses, and meats (€7.50). The *Tagliere di Focacce* (confirm the €6 per person price), a sampler plate of mini-focaccia sandwiches, is also fun. Either of these dishes with a glass of Chianti makes a fine light meal. As office workers pop in for a quick bite, it's traditional to share tables at lunchtime (Mon–Sat 8:00–21:00, closed Sun, just off Via Calzaiuoli on a side street across from Orsanmichele Church at Via dei Tavolini 18, tel. 055-268-590).

I Fratellini is a rustic little eatery where the "little brothers" have served peasants 27 different kinds of sandwiches and cheap glasses of Chianti wine (see list on wall) since 1875. Join the local crowd, then sit on a nearby curb or windowsill to munch, placing your glass on the wall rack before you leave (€4 for sandwich and wine, Mon–Sat 8:00–20:00, closed Sun, 20 yards in front of Orsanmichele Church on Via dei Cimatori). Be adventurous with the menu (easy-order by number). Consider *Finocchiona* (the special local salami), *Lardo di Colonnata* (lard aged in Carrara marble), and *Cinghiale Piccante* (spicy wild boar) sandwiches. Order the most expensive wine they've corked (Brunello for €4). Bottles are labeled.

Ristorante Paoli serves wonderful local cuisine to loads of cheerful eaters under a richly frescoed Gothic vault. Because of its fame and central location, it's filled mostly with tourists, but for a classy, traditional splurge meal, this is my choice (Wed–Mon 12:00–14:30 & 19:00–22:30, closed Tue, reserve for dinner, €21 tourist menu, à la carte is pricier, midway between Piazza della Signoria and the Duomo at Via dei Tavolini 12 red, tel. 055-216-215). Salads are flamboyantly cut and mixed from a trolley right at your table. The walls are sweaty with memories that go back to 1824, and the service is flamboyant and fun-loving—but don't get taken. Confirm prices. Woodrow Wilson slurped spaghetti here (his bust looks down on you as you eat).

Trattoria Icche C'è C'è (ee-kay chay chay; dialect for "whatever is, is") is a small, family-style eatery where fun-loving Gino serves quality traditional meals (three-course €11 meals, not too touristy, Tue–Sun 12:30–14:30 & 19:00–24:00, closed Mon, midway between Bargello and river at Via Magalotti 11 red, tel. 055-216-589).

Osteria del Porcellino offers a romantic setting and a seasonal menu of Tuscan classics with a creative flair. This dark, dense, candlelit place is packed with a mix of locals and tourists and run with style and enthusiasm by friendly chef Enzo. In summer, they also have inviting outdoor seating in a secretive setting out back (€8 pastas, €18 *secondi*, daily 12:00–14:30 & 19:00–24:00, reserve for dinner, Via Val di Lamona 7 red, half a block behind Mercato Nuovo, tel. 055-264-148).

Trattoria Nella serves good, typical Tuscan cuisine at affordable prices. Arrive early or be disappointed—it's understandably popular. Save room for the *panna cotta* cooked cream dessert (€22 meals, Mon–Sat 12:00–15:00 & 19:00–22:00, Sun 19:00–22:00, 3 blocks northwest of Ponte Vecchio, Via delle Terme 19 red, tel. 055-218-925). Twin brothers Federico and Lorenzo carry on their dad's tradition of keeping their clientele well fed and happy.

Oltrarno, South of the River

Near Ponte Vecchio

Ristorante Bibo serves *"cucina tipica Fiorentina"* with a pink-tablecloth-and-black-bowtie dressiness, and leafy, candlelit outdoor seating. It's quiet and romantic, though the food can be bland (€15 three-course meal, leave this book face up on the edge of the table for a 15 percent discount, daily 12:00–14:30 & 19:00–22:30, Piazza Santa Felicita 6 red, tel. 055-239-8554, enthusiastic Tonino).

Golden View Open Bar is a lively, trendy place, good for a salad, pizza, or pasta with fine wine and a fine view of Ponte Vecchio and the Arno River. Reservations for window tables are recommended (reasonable prices, €10 pizzas and huge salads, daily 11:30–24:00, pizza and wine served even later, impressive wine bar, 50 yards upstream from Ponte Vecchio at Via dei Bardi 58, tel. 055-214-502, run by Francesco, Marco, and Tomaso). They have three zones: a river-side pizza place, a classier restaurant, and a jazzy lounge plus a wine bar. The live jazz (Sun, Mon, and Wed at 21:00) makes for a wonderful evening.

Oltrarno Restaurants

Via di Santo Spirito and Borgo San Jacopo

Several good and colorful restaurants line this multi-named street a block off the river in Oltrarno. I'd survey the scene before making a choice.

Trattoria Cammillo was formerly run by Cammillo, who is now slurping spaghetti in heaven. His granddaughter Chiara carries on the legacy, mixing traditional Tuscan and creative, modern cuisine. With a charcoal grill and a team of white-aproned waiters cranking out terrific food in a fun, noisy, dressy-but-down-to-earth ambience, this place is a hit (full dinners about €36 plus wine, Thu–Mon 12:00–14:30 & 19:30–22:30, closed Tue–Wed, reservations smart, Borgo San Jacopo 57 red, tel. 055-212-427).

Trattoria Angiolino serves good, old-fashioned local cuisine. Sit in the main hall rather than the stuffy side rooms (€20 for dinner plus wine, Tue–Sun 12:00–14:30 & 19:30–22:30, closed Mon, Via di Santo Spirito 36 red, tel. 055-239-8976).

Olio & Convivium Gastronomia Restaurant started as an elegant deli whose refined oil-tasting room has morphed into a romantic, aristocratic restaurant. Their three intimate rooms are surrounded by fine *prosciutti*, cheeses, and wine shelves. It's a gentle, friendly place with a quiet atmosphere and fine wines by the glass—a foodie's delight (€10 pastas, €15 *secondi*, Mon 10:00–15:00, Tue–Sat 10:00–15:00 & 17:30–22:30, Via di Santo Spirito 4, tel. 055-265-8198).

Trattoria Sabatino, farthest away and least touristy, is spacious and disturbingly cheap, with family character, red-checkered tablecloths, and a simple menu. A super place to watch locals munch, it's just outside the Porta San Frediano (medieval gate), a 15-minute walk from Ponte Vecchio (Mon–Fri 12:00–14:30 & 19:20–22:00, closed Sat–Sun, Via Pisana 2 red, tel. 055-225-955, little English spoken). If you eat here, let it be your reward after following my self-guided walk (on page 835).

Trattoria da Sergio, a tiny eatery about a block before Porta San Frediano, has homey charm and a strong local following. The food is on the gourmet side of home-cooking and therefore a bit more expensive but worth the little splurge (€9 pastas, €14 *secondi*, Tue–Sun 12:00–14:30 & 19:30–22:30, closed Mon, reservations smart for dinner, Borgo San Frediano 145 red, tel. 055-223-449).

Piazza Santo Spirito

This classic Florentine square (a bit seedy-feeling but favored by locals) has several popular little restaurants and bars that are open nightly. They offer good local cuisine, moderate prices, and impersonal service, with a choice of indoor or romantic on-the-square seating (reservations smart).

Lively **Borgo Antico** is the hit of the square, with enticing pizzas, big deluxe plates of pasta, a delightful setting, and a trendy and boisterous young local crowd (daily 12:00–24:00, best to reserve for a seat on the square, Piazza Santo Spirito 6 red, tel. 055-210-437). The quieter **Osteria Santo Spirito** has good seating on the square, a hip, eclectic interior, and cheap grub (Piazza Santo Spirito 16 red, tel. 055-238-2383).

Ricchi Caffè, next to Borgo Antico, has fine gelato, homemade desserts, shaded outdoor tables, and best of all, €3.50 pasta dishes at lunchtime (Mon–Sat 7:00–24:00, closed Sun, tel. 055-215-864). After noting the plain facade of the Brunelleschi church facing the square, step inside the café and pick your favorite picture of the many ways it might be finished.

Café Cabiria, on the other side of Borgo Antico, is a trendy local hangout with good, light meals, noisy 21st-century music, and a cozy Florentine-funky room in back (Wed–Mon 10:30–1:30, closed Tue, tel. 055-215-732).

Trattoria Casalinga, an inexpensive standby, comes with aproned women bustling around the kitchen. It's probably been too popular for too long, as the service has gotten a bit surly and it feels like every student group, backpacker, and Florentine artisan ends up here. But people seem to leave full and happy, with euros to spare for gelato (Mon–Sat 12:00–14:30 & 19:00–21:45, after 20:00 reserve or wait, closed Sun and all of Aug, just off Piazza Santo Spirito, near the church at Via dei Michelozzi 9 red, tel. 055-218-624).

TRANSPORTATION CONNECTIONS

From Florence by Train to: Pisa (2/hr, 1 hr), **Lucca** (9/day, 1.5 hrs), **Siena** (12/day, 1.75 hrs, more with transfer in Empoli; bus is better), **La Spezia** (for the Cinque Terre, 3/day direct, otherwise nearly hourly, 2.5 hrs or change in Pisa), **Milan** (12/day, 3 hrs), **Bolzano** (10/day, 4–6 hrs, change in Verona, some via Bologna as well), **Venice** (15/day, 3 hrs, may transfer in Bologna), **Assisi** (5/day, 2–2.5 hrs, more frequent with transfers, direction: Foligno), **Orvieto** (8/day, 2 hrs), **Rome** (2/hr, 2 hrs), **Naples** (7/day, 4 hrs), **Brindisi** (3/day, 11 hrs with change in Bologna), **Frankfurt** (3/day, 12 hrs), **Paris** (1/day, 12 hrs overnight, important to reserve ahead), **Vienna** (4/day, 9–10 hrs).

Buses: The SITA bus station, a block west of the Florence train station, is traveler-friendly. Schedules for regional trips are posted everywhere, and TV monitors show imminent departures. Bus service drops dramatically on Sunday. You'll find buses to: **San Gimignano** (€6, hourly, 1.25–2 hrs, change in Poggibonsi), **Siena** (€6.50, hourly, 75-min *corse rapide* buses are faster than the train, avoid the 2-hr *diretta* scenic but slow buses), and the **airport** (€4, buy ticket on bus, 2/hr, 20 min). Bus info: tel. 800-373-760 (Mon–Fri 8:30–18:30, Sat–Sun 8:30–12:30); some schedules are in the *Florence Concierge Information* magazine. Several buses cover San Gimignano and Siena in one big day-trip.

Taxi to Siena: If you don't want to mess with buses or trains, consider hiring a taxi to take you to nearby towns. For around €120, you can arrange a ride directly from your Florence hotel to your Siena hotel. For a small group or for people with more money than time, this can be a good value.

Airports

The **Amerigo Vespucci Airport,** several miles northwest of Florence, has a TI, cash machines, and car-rental agencies (airport info tel. 055-306-1300, flight info tel. 055-306-1700—domestic only, www.aeroporto.firenze.it). Frequent shuttle buses connect the airport with Florence's SITA bus station, a block west of the train station (€4, 2/hr, 30 min, from Florence runs 5:30–23:00, from airport 6:00–23:30). Allow about €20 for a taxi.

International flights often land at Pisa's **Galileo Galilei Airport** (also has TI and car-rental agencies, www.pisa-airport.com), a little over an hour from Florence by train (2/hr, 90 min). Flight info: 050-849-300.

Livorno Cruise Ship Port

If you're coming to Florence by cruise ship, you'll be getting off the boat in the coastal town of Livorno, Florence's official port and cruise ship dock, located about 60 miles west of the city.

A branch TI is open at the port in summer (tel. 0586-895-320). The main TI is located in the town center on Piazza Municipio (tel. 0586-204-611, www.costadeglietruschi.it). Livorno and Florence are most easily connected by train (15/day, 1.5 hrs, stops in Pisa, Lucca connection possible). Most cruise ships offer a shuttle to the train station; you can also take a taxi between the port and station for about €10.

THE CINQUE TERRE

The Cinque Terre (CHINK-weh TAY-reh), a remote chunk of the Italian Riviera, is the traffic-free, lowbrow, underappreciated alternative to the French Riviera. There's not a museum in sight. Just sun, sea, sand (pebbles), wine, and pure, unadulterated Italy. Enjoy the villages, swimming, hiking, and evening romance of one of God's great gifts to tourism. For a home base, choose among five *(cinque)* villages, each of which fills a ravine with a lazy hive of human activity—callused locals, sunburned travelers, and no Vespas. While the Cinque Terre is now discovered, I've never seen happier, more relaxed tourists.

The chunk of coast was first described in medieval times as "the five lands." In the feudal era, this land was watched over by castles. Tiny communities grew up in their protective shadows, ready to run inside at the first hint of a Turkish Saracen pirate raid. Marauding pirates from North Africa were a persistent problem until about 1400. Many locals were kidnapped and ransomed or sold into slavery, and those that remained built fires on flat-roofed watchtowers to relay warnings—alerting the entire coast to imminent attacks. The last major raid was in 1545.

As the threat of pirates faded, the villages prospered, catching fish and growing grapes. Churches were enlarged with a growing population. But until the advent of tourism in this generation, the towns remained isolated. Even today, traditions survive, and each of the five villages comes with a distinct dialect and its own proud heritage.

Sadly, a few ugly, noisy Americans are giving tourism a bad name here. Even hip, young locals are put off by loud, drunken tourists. They say, and I agree, that the Cinque Terre is an exceptional place. It deserves a special dignity. Party in Viareggio or Portofino, but be mellow in the Cinque Terre. Talk softly. Help keep it clean. In spite of the tourist crowds, it's still a real community, and we are guests. For ways to participate in preserving the area while experiencing it, see the Protect the Cinque Terre program under "Tours."

In this chapter, I cover the five towns in order from east to west, from Riomaggiore to Monterosso. Since I still get the names of the towns mixed up, I think of them by number: #1 Riomaggiore (a workaday town), #2 Manarola (picturesque), #3 Corniglia (on a hilltop), #4 Vernazza (the region's cover girl, the most touristy and dramatic), and #5 Monterosso (the closest thing to a beach resort of the five towns).

Planning Your Time

The ideal minimum stay is two nights and a completely uninterrupted day. The Cinque Terre is served by the local train from Genoa and La Spezia. Speed demons arrive in the morning, check their bags in La Spezia, take the five-hour hike through all five towns, laze away the afternoon on the beach or rock of their choice, and zoom away on the overnight train to somewhere back in the real world. But be warned: The Cinque Terre has a strange way of messing up your momentum. Frankly, staying anything less than two nights is a mistake that you'll likely regret.

The towns are just a few minutes apart by hourly train or boat. There's no checklist of sights or experiences—just a hike, the towns themselves, and your fondest vacation desires. Study this chapter in advance and piece together your best day, mixing hiking, swimming, trains, and a boat ride. For the best light and coolest temperatures, start your hike early.

Market days perk up the towns from 8:00 to 13:00 on Tuesday in Vernazza, Wednesday in Levanto, Thursday in Monterosso, and Friday in La Spezia.

The winter is really dead—most hotels close in December and January. Easter (March 23 in 2008) and July through August are peak of peak, the toughest time to find rooms. In spring, the towns can feel inundated with Italian school groups day-tripping on multi-day spring excursions (they can't afford to sleep in this expensive region). For more information on the region, see www.cinqueterre.it.

The Cinque Terre National Park

The creation of the Cinque Terre National Marine Park in 1999 has brought lots of money (all visitors pay a fee to hike the trails), new restrictions on land and sea to protect wildlife, and lots of concrete bolstering walkways, trails, beaches, breakwaters, and

The Cinque Terre

docks. Each village has a park-sponsored information center and two towns have tiny folk museums. The park is run by a powerful man—nicknamed "The Pharaoh" for his grandiose visions—who seems to double as Riomaggiore's mayor. (Powerful as he is, he can't seem to find a way for visitors between hotels to deposit their bags anywhere.) For the latest, see www.parconazionale5terre.it.

Cinque Terre Cards and Passes

Visitors hiking between the towns need to pay a **park entrance fee.** This fee keeps the trails safe and open, and pays for viewpoints, picnic spots, WCs, and more. The popular coastal trail generates enough revenue to subsidize the development of trails and outdoor activities higher in the hills.

You have two options (both valid until midnight on the expiration date):

The **Hiking Pass** costs €3 (includes map, kids under 4 free). It's valid for one day and covers all trails (but no buses or trains). Buy it at trailheads, at national park offices, and at most train stations (no validation required).

The **Cinque Terre Card** combines hiking privileges with free transportation. It covers the park entrance fee and shuttle buses, but no longer covers local trains. For more information, see www.parconazionale5terre.it.

It's sold at TIs inside train stations, but not at trailheads (€5/1 day, €8/2 days, €10/3 days, €20/7 days, kids 4–12 half-price, family cards available). The card comes with a map, information brochure, and train schedule. Validate your Cinque Terre Card at a train station by punching it in the yellow machine. The pass pays for itself if you hike, ride a train, and use a shuttle bus in a single day.

Getting Around the Cinque Terre

Within the Cinque Terre, you'll get around the villages more cheaply by train, but more scenically by boat.

By Train

Big, fast trains from elsewhere in Italy stop only at La Spezia and Monterosso, where you'll transfer to the milk-run Cinque Terre train. Don't bother with the TI in La Spezia.

Along the coast here, trains go in only two directions: "per (to) Genova" (the Italian spelling of Genoa) or "per La Spezia." Assuming you're on vacation, accept the unpredictability of Cinque Terre trains (they're often late, unless you are, too...in which case they're on time). Relax while you wait—buy a cup of coffee at a station bar. When the train comes (know which direction to look for: La Spezia or Genova), casually walk over and hop on. This is especially easy in Monterosso, with its fine café-with-a-view on track #1 (direction Milano/Genova).

By train, the five towns are just a few minutes apart. Know your stop. After the train leaves the town before your destination, go to the door and get ready to slip out before the mob packs in. Words to the wise for novice tourists, who often miss their stop: The stations are small and the trains are long, so you might have to get off deep in a tunnel. Also, the doors don't open automatically—you may have to flip open the handle of the door yourself. If a door isn't working, go quickly to the next car to leave. (When leaving a town by train, if you find the platform jammed with people, walk down the platform into the tunnel where things quiet down.)

It's cheap to buy individual train tickets to travel between the towns. Since a one-town hop costs the same as a five-town hop (around €1) and every ticket is good for six hours with stopovers, save money and explore the region in one direction on one ticket. Or buy a round-trip ticket from one end to the other of the region (e.g., round-trip from Monterosso to Riomaggiore and back)—it functions as a six-hour pass. Stamp the ticket at the station machine before you board. Riding without a validated ticket is very expensive if you meet a conductor. If you have a Eurailpass, don't spend one of your valuable flexi-days on the cheap Cinque Terre.

In general, I'd skip the train from Riomaggiore to Manarola (the trains are unreliable, and the 15-min Via dell'Amore stroll is a delight—see page 875 for more on this path).

Cinque Terre Train Schedule: Since the train is the Cinque Terre's lifeline, many shops and restaurants post the current schedule. Carry a copy of it—it'll come in handy. Note that fast trains leaving La Spezia zip right through the Cinque Terre, and stop only in Monterosso. But the trains on the following schedule (be sure to check for current times) will stop at all five Cinque Terre towns. Most trains run daily; a few trains run daily except Sunday, while others (not listed here) operate only on Sundays.

Trains generally leave La Spezia for the Cinque Terre villages at 7:12, 8:00, 10:00, 11:10, 12:10, 13:17, 14:10, 15:10, 16:10, 17:10, 18:10, 19:05, 20:18, 21:13, 23:10, and 00:20.

Going back to La Spezia, trains generally leave Monterosso at 6:33, 7:12, 8:24, 9:24, 10:24, 11:00, 12:04, 12:24, 13:25, 14:24, 15:24, 16:24, 17:24, 18:24, 19:24, 20:31, 22:30, 23:20, and 23:58 (same trains depart Vernazza about four minutes later).

Convenient TV monitors posted at several places in each station clearly show exactly what times the next trains are leaving in each direction (and if they're late, how late they are expected to be). I trust these monitors much more than my ability to read any printed schedule.

By Boat

From Easter through October, a daily boat service connects Monterosso, Vernazza, Manarola, Riomaggiore, and Portovenere. Boats provide a scenic way to get from town to town and survey what you just hiked. And boats offer the only efficient way to visit the nearby resort of Portovenere; the alternative is a tedious train/bus connection via La Spezia. In peaceful weather, the boats can be more reliable than the trains, but if seas are rough, they don't run at all. Because the boats nose in and tourists have to gingerly disembark onto little more than a plank, even a small chop can cancel some or all of the stops.

I see the tour boats as a syringe, injecting each town with a boost of euros. The towns are addicted, and they shoot up hourly through the summer. (Between 10:00 and 15:00—especially on weekends—masses of gawkers unload from boats, tour buses, and cruise ships, inundating the villages and changing the tenor of the region.)

Boats depart Monterosso about hourly (10:30–18:00), stopping at the Cinque Terre towns (except at Corniglia) and ending up an hour later in Portovenere. (The Portovenere–Monterosso boats run 9:00–17:00.) Single hops cost about €3 per town. Some towns are also connected by smaller boats and may honor the same tickets—ask. You can buy tickets at little stands at each town's harbor (tel. 0187-732-987 and 0187-818-440). An all-day boat pass, covering the Cinque Terre towns, is around €12. Boat schedules are posted at docks, harbor bars, Cinque Terre park offices, and hotels.

By Shuttle Bus

Shuttle buses connect each Cinque Terre town with distant parking lots and various points in the hills (for example, from Corniglia's beach and train station to its hilltop town center). Most rides cost €1.50—pick up schedules from a Cinque Terre park office or note the times posted on bus doors and at bus stops.

Hiking the Cinque Terre

All five towns are connected by good trails, although note that some portions are more strenuous. You'll experience the area's best by hiking all the way from one end to the other. While you can detour to dramatic hilltop sanctuaries, I'd keep it simple by following the easy red-and-white-marked low trail between the villages. The entire seven-mile hike can be done in about four hours, but allow five for dawdling. Germans (with their task-oriented *Alpenstock* walking sticks) are notorious for marching too fast through the region. (The non-German record for the entire five-town hike is by one of my tour guides: one hour, 52 minutes.) Take it slow...smell the cactus flowers and herbs, notice the lizards, listen to birds singing in the olive groves, and enjoy vistas on all sides.

Trails can be closed in bad weather or because of landslides. Remember that hikers need to pay a fee to enter the trails (see "Cinque Terre Cards and Passes," page 871). If hiking the entire five-town route, consider that the trails between Riomaggiore (#1), Manarola (#2), and Corniglia (#3) are easiest. The trail from Vernazza (#4) to Monterosso (#5) is the most challenging. For that hike, you might want to start in Monterosso in order to tackle the toughest section while you're fresh and to enjoy the region's most dramatic scenery as you approach Vernazza.

Maps aren't necessary for the basic coastal hikes described here. But for the expanded version of this hike (12 hours, from Portovenere to Levanto) and more serious hikes in the high country, pick up a good hiking map (about €5, sold everywhere), or see www.parconazionale5terre.it. To leave the park cleaner than when you found it, request a plastic bag *(sacchetto di plastica)* at any park information booth and pick up a little trail trash along the way. It would be great if American visitors—who get so much joy out of this region—were known for this good deed.

Riomaggiore-Manarola (20 min): Facing the front of the train station in Riomaggiore (#1), go up the stairs to the right, following signs for the Via dell'Amore. The film-gobbling promenade—wide enough for baby strollers—winds along the coast to Manarola (#2). While there's no beach here, stairs lead down to sunbathing rocks. A long tunnel and mega-nets protect hikers from mean-spirited rocks. The classy, park-run Bar & Vini A Pie de Ma wine bar—located at the Riomaggiore trailhead—offers light meals, awesome town views, and clever boat storage under the train tracks (for more info, see "Eating," page 883). There's also a scenic, peaceful cliffside bar on the Manarola end of the trail (daily in summer 9:00–24:00, until 20:00 off-season, light meals, drinks, picnic tables).

Manarola-Corniglia (45 min): The walk from Manarola (#2) to Corniglia (#3) is a little longer, more rugged, and less romantic than that from #1 to #2. To avoid the last stretch (switchback stairs leading up to the hill-capping town of Corniglia), catch the shuttle bus from Corniglia's train station (€1.50, free with Cinque Terre Card, 2/hr, usually timed to meet the trains).

Corniglia-Vernazza (90 min): The hike from Corniglia (#3) to Vernazza (#4)—the wildest and greenest of the coast—is very rewarding. From the Corniglia station and beach, zigzag up to the town (via the steep stairs, the longer road, or the shuttle bus). Ten minutes past Corniglia, toward Vernazza, you'll see Guvano beach far beneath you (the region's nude beach, see page 891). The scenic trail leads past a bar and picnic tables, through lots of fragrant and flowery vegetation, into Vernazza. If you need a break before reaching Vernazza, Franco's Ristorante La Torre has a small menu but big views (between meal times only drinks are served; see listing under "Eating," page 907).

Vernazza-Monterosso (90 min): The trail from Vernazza (#4) to Monterosso (#5) is a scenic, up-and-down-a-lot trek. Trails are rough (some readers report "very dangerous") and narrow, but easy to follow. Locals frown on camping at the picnic tables located midway. The views just out of Vernazza are spectacular.

Longer Hikes: Above the trails that run between the towns, higher-elevation hikes crisscross the region. Shuttle buses make the going easier, connecting villages and trailheads in the hills. Ask locally about the more difficult six-mile inland hike to Volastra. This tiny village, perched between Manarola and Corniglia, hosts the 5-Terre wine co-op. The Cantina Sociale is a third of a mile away from Volastra, in the hamlet of Groppo. If you take this high road between Manarola and Corniglia, allow two hours one-way.

In return, you'll get sweeping views and a closer look at the vineyards. Shuttle buses run about hourly to Volastra from Manarola and Corniglia (€2.50 or free with Cinque Terre Card, pick up schedule from park office); consider taking the bus up and hiking down.

Swimming and Kayaking

Every town has a beach or rocky place to swim. Monterosso has the biggest and sandiest, with paddleboats, beach umbrellas, and beach-use fees (but it's free where there are no umbrellas). Vernazza's is tiny—better for sunning than swimming. Manarola and Riomaggiore have the worst beaches (no sand), but Manarola offers the best deep-water swimming.

Wear your walking shoes and pack your swim gear. Several of the beaches have showers (no shampoo, please). Underwater sightseeing is full of fish—goggles are sold in local shops. Sea urchins can be a problem if you walk on the rocks. If you have swim shoes, this is the place to wear them.

You can rent kayaks in Riomaggiore, Vernazza, and Monterosso. (For details, see individual town listings in this chapter.) Some readers say kayaking can be dangerous—the kayaks tip easily, training is not provided, and lifejackets are not required. Mountain biking and horseback riding are possible (park info booths in each town have details on rentals and maps of trails high above the coast).

Tours

Local Guides—Paola Tommarchi leads hiking, wine-tasting, and town tours throughout the Cinque Terre for individuals or groups (€100/half-day tour, €165/day, mobile 333-798-7728, paolatomma1966@libero.it). Her friend, **Andrea Bordigoni,** is also good (mobile 347-972-3317, bordigo@inwind.it).

Ecotourism Program—The Protect the Cinque Terre program in Vernazza offers one- to three-day sessions that involve visitors in preserving the region for future generations. By working with local citizens, participants can help rebuild stone walls that support terraced fields, and clean up trails used by thousands of tourists. Group leaders share info on the local landscape, its inhabitants, and its cuisine (€390-890/couple, www.protectcinqueterre.com, alessandro@protectcinqueterre.com).

Sleeping in the Cinque Terre

If you think too many people have my book, avoid Vernazza. Monterosso is a good choice for the younger crowd (more nightlife) and rich, sun-worshipping softies (who prefer the comfort and ease of a real hotel). Hermits, anarchists, wine-lovers, and mountain goats like Corniglia. Sophisticated Italians and Germans choose Manarola. Riomaggiore is bigger than Vernazza and less resorty than Monterosso.

While the Cinque Terre is too rugged for the mobs that ravage the Spanish and French coasts, it's popular with Italians, Germans, and in-the-know Americans. Hotels charge more and are packed on holidays, in July and August, and on Fridays and Saturdays all summer. August weekends are worst. But €65 doubles abound throughout the year. For a terrace or view, you might pay an extra €20 or more.

Book ahead if you'll be visiting in July, August, on a weekend, or around a holiday. At other times, you can land a double room on any day by just arriving in town (ideally by noon) and asking around at bars and restaurants, or simply by approaching locals on the street. Many travelers enjoy the opportunity to shop around a bit and get the best price by bargaining. Private rooms—called *affitta camere*—are no longer an intimate stay with a family. They are generally comfortable apartments (often with small kitchens) where you get the key and come and go as you like, rarely seeing your landlord. Often landowners rent the buildings by the year to local managers, who then attempt to make a profit by filling them night after night with tourists.

For the best value, visit three private rooms and snare the best. Going direct cuts out a middleman and softens prices. Staying more than one night gives you bargaining leverage. Plan on paying cash. Private rooms are generally bigger and more comfortable than those offered by the pensions and offer the same privacy as a hotel room.

If you want the security of a reservation, make it at a hotel long in advance (smaller places generally don't take reservations that far ahead). Query by email, not fax. If you do reserve, honor your reservation (or, if you must cancel, do it as early as possible). Since people renting rooms usually don't take deposits, they lose money if you don't show up. Cutthroat room hawkers at the train stations might try to lure you away from a room that you've already reserved with offers of cheaper rates. Don't do it. You owe it to your hosts to stick with your original reservation.

Riomaggiore (Town #1)

The most substantial non-resort town of the group, Riomaggiore is a disappointment from the train station. But walk through the tunnel next to the train tracks (or ride the elevator through the hillside to the top of town), and you land in a fascinating tangle of pastel homes leaning on each other like drunken sailors.

ORIENTATION

Tourist Information

The TI and park information office are inside the train station (daily 6:30–22:00 in summer, until 20:00 in winter, tel. 0187-920-633). If the TI in the station is crowded, buy your hiking pass at the Cinque Terre park shop next door, or at the kiosk next to the stairs leading to the Via dell'Amore trail. The park shop provides eight computers with Internet access upstairs (daily 8:00–23:00 in summer, until 20:00 in winter). A less-formal information source is friendly and helpful Ivo, who runs the Bar Centrale (see "Eating," page 884).

Arrival in Riomaggiore

The bus shuttles locals and tourists up and down Riomaggiore's steep main street and continues to the parking lot outside of town (€1.50 one-way, €2.50 round-trip, free with Cinque Terre Card, 2/hr, just flag it down as it passes). The bus heads into the hills, where you'll find the region's top high-country activities (for details, see "Hikes," page 880).

Helpful Hints

Baggage Storage: You may be able to check your bags at the park information office (if not, complain, and see if you can store bags with Ivo at Bar Centrale, listed under "Eating," page 884).

Laundry: A self-service launderette is on the main street (daily 8:00–22:00, €3.50 wash, €3.50 dry, run by Edi's Rooms next door, Via Colombo 111).

SELF-GUIDED WALK

Welcome to Riomaggiore

Here's an easy loop trip that maximizes views and minimizes uphill walking.

• *Start at the train station (if you arrive by boat, cross beneath the tracks and take a left, then hike through the tunnel along the tracks to reach the station). You'll come to some...*

Colorful Murals: These murals, with subjects modeled after real-life Riomaggiorians, glorify the nameless workers who constructed the nearly 300 million cubic feet of dry stone walls (without cement). These walls run throughout the Cinque Terre, giving the region its characteristic *muri a secco* terracing for vineyards and olive groves. The murals, done by Argentinean artist Silvio Benedetto, are well-explained in English.

• *Head to the railway tunnel entrance, and ride the elevator to the top of*

Riomaggiore

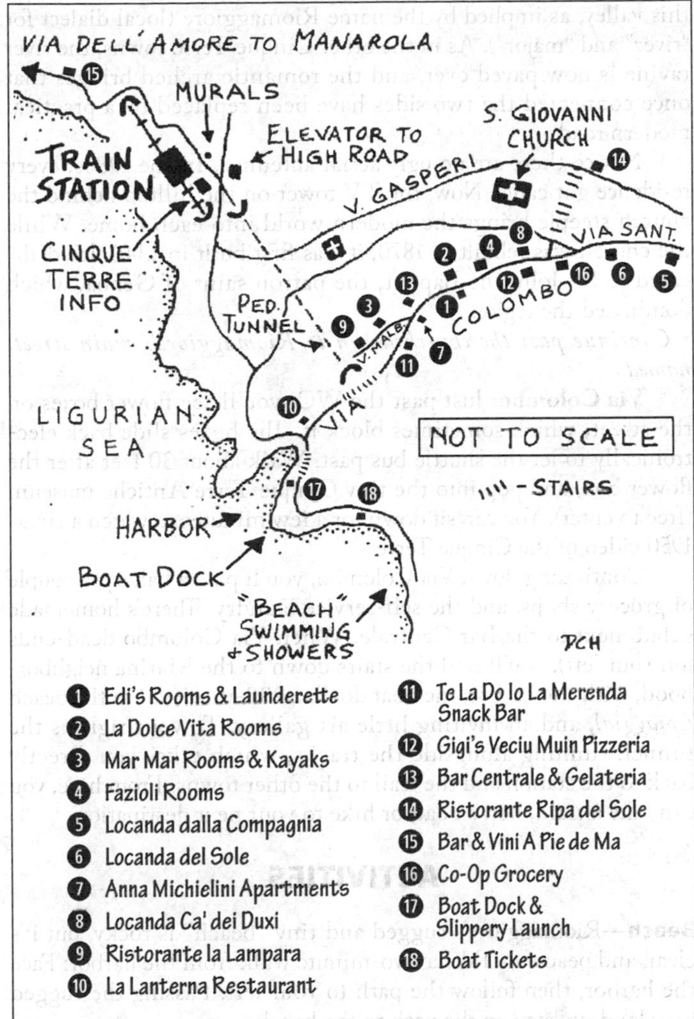

town (€0.50 or €1 family ticket, daily 8:00–19:45). You're at the...

Hilltop: Here at the top of town, you're treated to spectacular sea views. To continue the view-fest, go right, following the walkway (ignore the steps marked *Marina Seacoast* that lead to the harbor). It's a five-minute level stroll to the church. You'll pass under the city hall (flying two flags) with murals celebrating the heroic grape pickers and fishermen of the region (also by Silvio Benedetto).

• *Before reaching the church, pause to enjoy the...*

Town View: The major river of this region once ran through this valley, as implied by the name Riomaggiore (local dialect for "river" and "major"). As in the other Cinque Terre towns, the river ravine is now paved over, and the romantic arched bridges that once connected the two sides have been replaced by a practical modern road.

Notice there are no ugly aerial antennae. In the 1980s, every residence got cable. Now, the TV tower on the hilltop behind the church steeple brings the modern world into each home. While the church was rebuilt in 1870, it was first built in 1340. It's dedicated to St. John the Baptist, the patron saint of Genoa, which dominated the region.

• *Continue past the church down to Riomaggiore's main street, named...*

Via Colombo: Just past the WC, you'll see flower boxes on the street, which sometimes block it. The boxes slide back electronically to let the shuttle bus past. Walk about 30 feet after the flower box, and pop into the tiny Cinque Terre Antiche museum (free to enter). You can sit down for a few minutes to watch a circa-1950 video of the Cinque Terre.

Continuing down Via Colombo, you'll pass a bakery, a couple of grocery shops, and the self-service laundry. There's homemade gelato next to the Bar Centrale. When Via Colombo dead-ends (on your left), you'll find the stairs down to the Marina neighborhood, with the harbor, the boat dock, a 200-yard trail to the beach *(spiaggia)*, and an inviting little art gallery. To your right is the tunnel, running alongside the tracks, which takes you directly back to the station and the trail to the other towns. From here, you can take a train, hop a boat, or hike to your next destination.

ACTIVITIES

Beach—Riomaggiore's rugged and tiny "beach" is rocky, but it's clean and peaceful. Take a two-minute walk from the harbor: Face the harbor, then follow the path to your left. Passing the rugged boat landing, stay on the path to the beach.

Kayaks and Water Sports—Mar Mar rents kayaks (€5/hr for 1-person kayak, €10/hr for 2-person kayak) and offers boat excursions (cruising, €30/day per person for up to eight people, see their listing under "Sleeping," page 882). The town also has a diving center (scuba, snorkeling, boats, and kayaks; office under the tracks on Via San Giacomo, tel. 0187-920-011).

Hikes—Consider the cliff-hanging trail that leads from the beach to old WWII bunkers and a hilltop botanical garden (free entry with Cinque Terre Card). Another trail climbs scenically to the Madonna di Montenero sanctuary, high above the town. If you don't feel like hiking, ride the green shuttle bus from the town center to the sanctuary (12-min trip, details at park office). The park center and bar up top also offer horse rides and bike rentals.

NIGHTLIFE

With Ivo as master of ceremonies, **Bar Centrale** dominates the late-night scene in Riomaggiore. In the summer, **Bar & Vini A Pie de Ma,** at the beginning of the Via dell'Amore, has piles of charm and stays open until midnight. (See page 883 for details on these two bars.) And the marvelous **Via dell'Amore** trail welcomes romantics after dark. The trail is free after 19:30 and is lit only with subtle ground lighting so you can see the stars.

SLEEPING

Riomaggiore has arranged its private-room rental system better than its neighbors. But with organization (and middlemen) come higher prices. Several agencies—with regular office hours, English-speaking staff, and email addresses—line up within a few yards of each other on the main drag. Each manages a corral of local rooms for rent. These offices can close unexpectedly, so it's smart to settle up the day before you leave in case they're closed when you need to depart. Expect lots of stairs. Private parking will run you an extra €10–20. If you don't mind the hike, the street above town has safe, free overnight parking.

Room-Finding Services

$$$ Locanda del Sole has six basic and overpriced but sparkling-clean rooms with a shared and peaceful terrace. Located at the

Sleep Code

(€1 = about $1.30, country code: 39)
S = Single, **D** = Double/Twin, **T** = Triple, **Q** = Quad, **b** = bathroom, **s** = shower only. Unless otherwise noted, credit cards are accepted, English is spoken, and breakfast is included (except in Vernazza).

To help you sort easily through these listings, I've divided the rooms into three categories based on the price for a standard double room with bath:

$$$ Higher Priced—Most rooms €100 or more.
$$ Moderately Priced—Most rooms between €50–100.
$ Lower Priced—Most rooms €50 or less.

utilitarian edge of town, it's a five-minute walk to the center. The easy parking (€10/day in high season but often free) makes it especially appealing to drivers (Db-€90, €120 July–Aug, Via Santuario 114, tel. & fax 0187-920-773, mobile 340-983-0090, www.locandadelsole.net, info@locandadelsole.net, Enrico).

$$ Edi's Rooms rents 20 fine rooms and apartments, most with views. Edi and her partner Luana get my best business practices award for this town (Db-€55, apartment Db-€70–80, apartment Qb-€120–140, office open daily 9:00–20:00 in summer, winter 9:00–13:00 & 14:00–19:00, Via Colombo 111, tel. 0187-760-842, tel. & fax 0187-920-325, edi-vesigna@iol.it).

$$ Mar Mar Rooms offers 12 rooms, 10 apartments, and a mini-hostel, with American expat Amy smoothing communications (dorm bed-€20 per person in 4- or 8-bed room, Db-€60–90 depending on view, reception open 9:00–19:00 in season, 30 yards above train tracks on main drag next to Ristorante la Lampara at Via Malborghetto 4, tel. & fax 0187-920-932, www.5terre-marmar.com, marmar@5terre.com). Mar Mar also rents kayaks.

$$ La Dolce Vita, across from Edi's, offers five rooms and eight apartments (Sb-€20–30, Db-€40–60, cash only; open daily 9:30–19:30—if they're closed, they're full; Via Colombo 120, tel. & fax 0187-760-044, mobile 349-326-6803, www.dolcevita5terre.com, agonatal@interfree.it, Giacomo and Simone).

$$ Luciano and Roberto Fazioli rent nine rooms of variable quality while also running a basic, seven-bed mini-hostel (dorm bed-€20, €25 Fri–Sat or for 1-night stays, D and Db-€50–80 depending on season and view, cash only, office open daily 9:00–20:00, Via Colombo 94, tel. 0187-920-904, robertofazioli@libero.it).

$$ Locanda Ca' dei Duxi rents 10 good rooms—eight have air-conditioning—from an efficient little office on the main drag (Db-€70–100 depending on view and air-con, extra person-€20, open all year, Via Colombo 36, tel. & fax 0187-920-036, mobile 329-825-7836, www.duxi.it, info@duxi.it, Samuele).

Private Rooms and Hotels on Riomaggiore's Main Drag

$$ Locanda dalla Compagnia rents five modern rooms at the top of town, just 300 yards below the parking lot and the little church. All rooms—among the nicest in town—are on the same airy ground floor, sharing an inviting lounge. Franca runs it with Monica's help (Db-€80, winter Db-€50, air-con, mini-fridge, no view, Via del Santuario 232, tel. 0187-760-050, fax 0187-920-586, lacomp@libero.it).

$$ Anna Michielini rents five attractive no-sea-view apartments in the center. Two apartments have kitchens and can connect to sleep up to six (Db-€56–66, Tb-€99, Qb-€110, cheaper

Oct–mid-April and for longer stays, 2 nights preferred June–Sept, reserve with credit card but pay cash, across from Bar Centrale at Via Colombo 143—ring bell to open door, tel. & fax 0187-920-411, mobile 328-131-1032, michielinis@yahoo.it, friendly Daniela speaks good English but her mother speaks *solo Italiano*).

Cheap Beds in Riomaggiore

To sleep cheap, head to Riomaggiore, which has better options than the other four towns. **Mar Mar Rooms** and the **Faziolis** offer dorm beds for €20 in mini-dorms (see above for both). With a little luck, you and your partner could find yourselves all alone in an eight-bed room.

Ostello Mamma Rosa is your rock-bottom option (€15 per bed, she doesn't takes reservations but can always find you a room, no services, 30 yards in front of train station). Rosa and her husband greet arriving trains; don't let Rosa pirate you away if you already have reservations at another place.

EATING

Ristorante la Lampara, decorated like a ship, serves a *frutti di mare* pizza, *trenette al pesto,* and the aromatic *spaghetti al cartoccio*—€10 spaghetti with mixed seafood cooked in foil (daily 12:00–15:00 & 18:30–22:30, closed Tue in winter, just above tracks off Via Colombo at Via Malborghetto 10, tel. 0187-920 120).

La Lanterna is dressier and more expensive than Lampara. It's wedged into a niche in the Marina, overlooking the harbor under the tracks (daily 12:00–22:00, Via San Giacomo 10, tel. 0187-920-589).

Ristorante Ripa del Sole is the local pick for a nice night out, with the same prices and quality as the Lampara and Lanterna, but with a bit more elegance (Tue–Sun 12:00–14:00 & 19:00–21:30, closed Mon, 10-min hike above town, Via de Gasperi 282, tel. 0187-920-143).

Try **Te La Do Io La Merenda** ("I'll Give You a Snack") for a snack, pizza, or good takeout. Their counter is piled with an assortment of munchies, and they have pastas, roasted chicken, and focaccia sandwiches to go (daily 8:30–21:30, Via Colombo 171, tel. 0187-920-148). For cheap sit-down pizza, try **Gigi's Veciu Muin** (daily 12:00–14:30 & 18:30–23:00, closed Mon off-season, at Via Colombo 83, tel. 0187-920-487).

Bar & Vini A Pie de Ma, at the trailhead on the Manarola end of town, is great for a scenic light bite or quiet drink at night. Enjoying a meal at a table on its dramatically situated terrace provides an indelible Cinque Terre memory (daily 10:00–20:00 or later).

Groceries and delis on Via Colombo sell food to go, including pizza slices, for a picnic at the harbor or beach. The **Co-Op Grocery** is least expensive and will make sandwiches to go (Via Colombo 55).

Bar Centrale, run by sociable Ivo and his gang, is a good stop for breakfast and music. Ivo lived in San Francisco and speaks good English. He fills his bar with only the best San Franciscan rock and hosts a big party on the Fourth of July. During the day, Bar Centrale is a shaded place to relax with other travelers. At night, it offers the younger set the liveliest action in town. Ivo makes "better mojitos than you can get in Cuba," plucking fresh mint leaves for your drink from a plant growing on the counter (daily 7:30–24:00, closed Mon in winter, Via Colombo 144, tel. 0187-920-208). In a jam, Ivo may store your bag for the day. For the best gelato in town, go next door.

Manarola (Town #2)

Like Riomaggiore, Manarola is attached to its station by a 200-yard-long tunnel. During WWII air raids, these tunnels provided refuge and a safe place for rattled villagers to sleep. The town itself fills a ravine, bookended by its wild little harbor to the west and a diminutive church square to the east. A delightful and gentle stroll, from the church down to the harborside park, provides the region's easiest little vineyard walk.

ORIENTATION

Arrival in Manarola

A shuttle bus runs between the low end of Manarola's main street (at the *tabacchi* shop and newsstand) and the parking lot (€1.50 one-way, €2.50 round-trip, free with Cinque Terre Card, 2/hr, just flag it down).

To get to the dock and the boats that connect Manarola with the other Cinque Terre towns, find the steps to the left of the harbor view—they lead down to the ticket kiosk. Continue around the left side of the cliff (as you're facing the water) to catch the boats.

Helpful Hints

Baggage Storage: The Cinque Terre park office is in the train station, and may have bag storage—ask (daily 7:00–20:00, €0.50/hr, tel. 0187-760-511).

Public WC: They're on the opposite side of the building from the park office entrance.

SELF-GUIDED WALK

Welcome to Manarola

From the harbor, this 30-minute circular walk shows you the town and surrounding vineyards, and ends at a fantastic viewpoint.

• *Start down at the waterfront.*

The Harbor: Manarola is tiny and picturesque, a tumble of buildings bunny-hopping down its ravine to the fun-loving waterfront. Notice how the I-beam crane launches the boats. Facing the harbor, look to the right, at the hillside Punta Bonfiglio cemetery and park, with a bar in the middle. (Punta Bonfiglio is where this walk ends.)

The town's swimming hole is just below. Manarola has no sand, but offers the best deep-water swimming in the area. The first "beach" has a shower, ladder, and wonderful rocks. The second has tougher access and no shower, but feels more remote and pristine (follow the paved path toward Corniglia, just around the point). For many, the tricky access makes this beach dangerous.

• *Hiking inland up the town's main drag, you'll come to the train tracks covered by Manarola's new square, called...*

Piazza Capellini: Built in 2004, this square is an all-around great idea, giving the town a safe, fun zone for kids. Locals living too near the tracks also enjoy a little less noise. Check out the mosaic that displays the varieties of local fish in colorful enamel.

• *A few steps uphill, you'll find the...*

Sciacchetrà Museum: Run by the national park, it's hardly a museum. But pop in to its inviting room to see a tiny exhibit on the local wine industry (free, daily 10:30–17:30, 15-min video, English by request, 100 yards uphill from train tracks, across from the post office).

• *Hiking further uphill you can still hear...*

Manarola's Stream: As in Riomaggiore and Vernazza, Manarola's stream was covered over by a modern sewage system after World War II. Before that time, romantic bridges arched over its ravine. A modern waterwheel recalls the origin of the town's name—local dialect for "big wheel" (one of many possible derivations). Mills like this once powered the local olive oil industry.

• *Keep climbing until you come to the square at the...*

Top of Manarola: The square is faced by a church, an oratory—now a religious and community meeting place—and a bell tower, which served as a watch tower when pirates raided the town (the cupola was built once the attacks ceased). Behind the church is Manarola's well-run youth hostel—the only one in the Cinque Terre. To the right of the oratory, a lane leads to Manarola's sizable tourist-free zone.

Manarola

While you're here, check out the church. According to the white marble plague in its facade, the Parish Church of St. Lawrence dates from "MCCCXXXVIII" (1338). Step inside to see two paintings from the unnamed "Master of the Cinque Terre," the only painter of any note from the region. While the style is Gothic, the work dates from the late 15th century, long after Florence had entered the Renaissance.

• *Walk 20 yards below the church and find a wooden railing. It marks the start of a delightful stroll around the high side of town, and back to the seafront. This is the beginning of the...*

Manarola Vineyard Walk: Don't miss this experience. Simply follow the wooden railing, enjoying lemon groves and wild red valerian (a cousin to the herb used for valium). Along the way, you'll get a close-up look at the region's famous dry-stone walls and finely crafted vineyards (with dried-heather thatches to protect from the southwest winds). Smell the rosemary. Study the structure of the town, and pick out the scant remains of an old fort. Notice the S-shape of the main road—once a river bed—flowing through town. Take a look at the town's roofs; they're typically made of locally quarried slate, rather than tile.

The simple, wooden religious scenes that you'll likely see above on the hillside are the work of local resident Mario Andreoli. Before his father died, Mario promised him he'd replace the old cross on the family's vineyard. Mario's been adding figures ever since. After recovering from a rare illness, he redoubled his efforts. On religious holidays, everything's lit up: the Nativity, the Last Supper, the Crucifixion, the Resurrection, and more. Some of the scenes are left up year-round.

• *The trail ends at a T-intersection. Turn left. (A right takes you to the Corniglia trail.) Before descending back into town, take a right, detouring into...*

The Cemetery: Ever since Napoleon—who was king of Italy in the early 1800s—decreed that cemeteries were health risks, Cinque Terre's burial spots have been located outside of town. The result? The dearly departed generally get first-class sea views. Each cemetery—with its evocative yellowed photos and finely carved Carrara marble memorial reliefs—is worth a visit. (The basic structure for all of them is the same, but Manarola's is most easily accessible.)

In cemeteries like these, there's a hierarchy of four places to park your mortal remains: a graveyard, a condo *(loculo)*, a mini bone-niche *(ossario)*, or communal ossuary. Because of the tight space (except for the big communal ossuary), there's a time limit assigned to each. Unclaimed—and therefore unfunded—bones go into the ossuary in the middle of the chapel floor after about a generation. Traditionally, locals make weekly visits to loved ones here, often bringing flowers. The rolling stepladder makes access to top-floor *loculi* easy.

• *The Manarola cemetery is on Punta Bonfiglio. Walk just below it, to further out on the point, where you'll find an entertaining park/game area/bar with the...*

Best View on the Coast: At this spot, you can enjoy poster-perfect views of Manarola while you sip a coffee or munch a light lunch or picnic. The bench at the tip of the point offers perhaps the most commanding view of the entire region.

SLEEPING

(€1 = about $1.30, country code: 39)

Manarola has plenty of private rooms. Ask in bars and restaurants. There's a modern, three-star place halfway up the main drag, a pricey hotel on the harbor, and a cluster of options around the church at the peaceful top of the town (a 5-min hike from the train tracks). Manarola's handy shuttle-bus service makes it easy to get to and from your car (see "Arrival in Manarola," earlier in this chapter).

$$$ La Torretta is a trendy, upscale, 13-room place catering to a demanding clientele. It's a peaceful refuge with all the comforts for those happy to pay (Db-€100–150, on Piazza della Chiesa at Vico Volto 20, tel. & fax 0187-920-327, www.torrettas.com, torretta@cdh.it).

$$ Albergo ca' d'Andrean, run by Simone, is quiet, comfortable, and modern. While the welcome is formal at best, it has 10 big, sunny, air-conditioned rooms and a cool garden oasis complete with lemon trees (Sb-€67, Db-€90, breakfast-€6, cash only, send personal or traveler's check to reserve or call if you're already traveling, closed Nov–Christmas, up the hill at Via A. Discovolo 101, tel. 0187-920-040, fax 0187-920-452, www.cadandrean.it, cadandrean@libero.it).

$$ Marina Piccola offers 13 bright, slick rooms on the water—so they figure a warm welcome is unnecessary (Db-€90, no breakfast, air-con, Via Birolli 120, tel. 0187-920-103, fax 0187-920-966, www.hotelmarinapiccola.com, info@hotelmarinapiccola.com).

$ Casa Capellini rents three rooms: one has a view balcony, another a 360-degree terrace (Db-€50; €70 for the alta camera on the top, with a kitchen, private terrace, and knockout view; two doors down the hill from the church—with your back to the church, it's at 2 o'clock; Via Ettore Cozzani 12, tel. 0187-920-823 or 0187-736-765, www.casacapellini-5terre.it, casa.capellini@tin.it, Gianni and Franca don't speak English). Book long in advance.

$ Ostello 5-Terre, Manarola's modern and well-run hostel, stands like a Monopoly hotel above the church square and offers 48 beds in four- to six-bed rooms. It's smart to reserve at least a week in advance in high season. You book with your credit-card number; if you cancel with less than three days' notice, you'll be charged for one night. This is not a party hostel—quiet is greatly appreciated (May–Sept dorm beds-€23, Qb-€90; off-season dorm beds-€18, Qb-€72; closed Dec–mid-Feb, not co-ed except for couples and families, optional €3.50 breakfast and €6 dinner; in summer, office closed 13:00–17:00, rooms closed 10:00–17:00, 1:00 curfew; during off-season, office and rooms closed until 16:00, curfew at 24:00; open to all ages, laundry, safes, phone cards, Internet access, book exchange, elevator, great roof terrace and sunset views, Via B. Riccobaldi 21, tel. 0187-920-215, fax 0187-920-218, www.hostel5terre.com, ostello@cdh.it, well-managed by Nicola). They rent dorm rooms as doubles for €60 in low season.

EATING

Many hardworking places line the main drag. I like the Botto family's friendly **Trattoria Il Porticciolo** (€6 pastas, Thu–Tue 12:00–15:00 & 18:00–22:30, closed Wed, just below the train tracks at Via R. Birolli 92, tel. 0187-920-083). For harborside dining, **Marina Piccola** is the winner. While less friendly and a little more expensive, the setting is memorable (Wed–Mon 12:30–15:30 & 18:30–22:00, closed Tue, tel. 0187-920-923). The bar in the Punta Bonfiglio park offers light meals and the best views of Manarola.

Corniglia (Town #3)

This is the quiet town—the only one of the five not on the water—with a mellow main square. From the station, a footpath zigzags up nearly 400 stairs to the town. Or take the shuttle bus, generally timed to meet arriving trains (€1.50, free with Cinque Terre Card, 2/hr). Before leaving the bus, confirm departure times on the schedule posted on its door.

According to the (likely fanciful) local legend, the town was originally settled by a Roman farmer who named it for his mother, Cornelia (how Corniglia is pronounced). The town and its ancient residents produced a wine so famous that—some say—vases found at Pompeii touted its virtues. Regardless of the veracity of the legends, today wine remains Corniglia's lifeblood. Follow the pungent smell of ripe grapes into an alley cellar and get a local to let you dip a straw into a keg. Remote and less visited than the other Cinque Terre towns, Corniglia has fewer tourists, cooler temperatures, a few restaurants, a windy overlook on its promontory, and plenty of private rooms for rent (ask at any bar or shop, no cheaper than other towns).

SELF-GUIDED WALK

Welcome to Corniglia

We'll explore this tiny town—population 240—and end at a scenic viewpoint.

• *Begin near the bus stop, located in a...*

Town Square: The gateway to this community is "Ciappa" square, with an ATM, phone booth, and bus stop. Now that the Cinque Terre has been designated as a national park, the change has sparked a revitalization of the town. Corniglia's young generation might now stay put, rather than migrate into big cities the way locals did in the past.

• *Stroll the spine of Corniglia, Via Fieschi. In the fall, the smell of grapes*

Corniglia

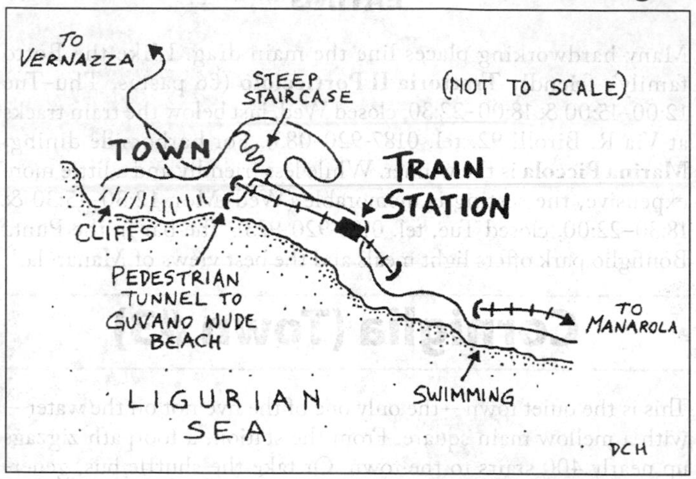

(on their way to becoming wine) wafts from busy cellars. Along the way on this main street, you'll see...

Corniglia's Enticing Shops: The enjoyable wine bar, **Enoteca Il Pirun**—named for the odd, old-fashioned pitcher used to pour (and drink) wine—is located in a cool cantina at Via Fieschi 115 (daily, tel. 0187-812-315). Sample any of the 30 local or national wines that friendly Mario offers by the glass (generally free), and have a light appetizer or salad. Mario doesn't speak English, but he tries.

Across from Enoteca Il Pirun, Alberto and Cristina's ***gelateria*** is the only—and therefore best—in town. Before ordering, get a free taste of Alberto's *miele di Corniglia* (made from local honey).

In the **Butiega shop** at Via Fieschi 142, Vincenzo and Lorenzo sell organic local specialties (daily 8:00–20:00). For picnickers, they offer €2.50 made-to-order sandwiches and a fun €3.50 *antipasto misto* to go. (There are good places to picnic farther along on this walk.)

• *Following Via Fieschi, you'll end up at the...*

Main Square: On Largo Taragio, tables from two bars and a trattoria spill around a WWI memorial and the town's old well. It once piped in natural spring water from the hillside to locals living without plumbing. What looks like a church is the Oratory of Santa Caterina. (An oratory is a kind of a spiritual clubhouse for a service group doing social work in the name of the Catholic Church. For more information see "Oratory of the Dead" on page 911.) Behind the oratory is a soccer field with benches and a viewpoint, a peaceful place for a picnic (less crowded than the end-of-town viewpoint, below).

• *Opposite the oratory, notice how steps lead steeply down on Via alla Marina to Corniglia's non-beach. It's a five-minute paved climb to sunning rocks, a shower, and a small deck (with a treacherous entry into the water). From the square, continue down Via Fieschi to the...*

End-of-Town Viewpoint: The Santa Maria Belvedere, named for a church that once stood here, marks the scenic end of Corniglia. This is a super picnic spot. From here, look high to the west, where the village of San Bernardino straddles a ridge (a good starting point for a hike; accessible by shuttle bus or long uphill hike from Vernazza). Below is the tortuous harbor, where locals ...ist their boats onto the cruel rocks.

ACTIVITIES

...own has rocky sea access below its train ...e a beach, it's all been washed away

... beach is in the opposite ... created by an 1893 ... The big news ... Italy in ...nd

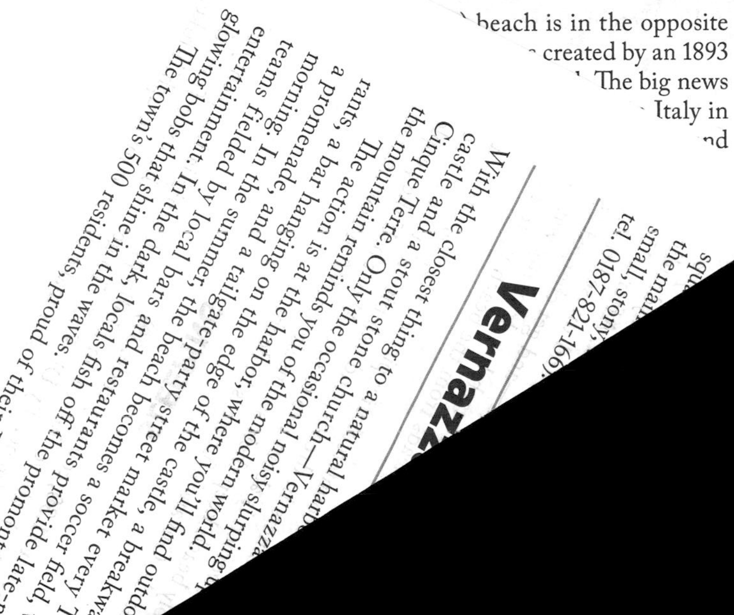

The town is riddled with meager places charging too much for their rooms, so it's almost never full.

$$ Cristiana Ricci (not the movie star) rents four small, clean, and peaceful rooms—two with kitchens and one with a terrace and sweeping view—just inland from the bus stop (Db-€60, Qb-€90, Via Fieschi 157, on main square, tel. 0187-812-541, mobile 338-937-6547, fax 0187-812-345, cri_affittacamere@virgilio.it). She also runs Bar Matteo, on the main square, and can meet you there. Her mom rents a few places in town for the same price.

$$ Villa Cecio feels like an abandoned hotel and rents eight well-worn rooms on the outskirts of town, all with no character or warmth (Db-€60, cash preferred, views, on main road 200 yards toward Vernazza, tel. 0187-812-043, fax 0187-812-138, www.cecio5terre.com, info@cecio5terre.com).

$$ Il Girasole, run by Stefano, rents three extremely humble rooms (overpriced at D-€45, Db-€55, Via Fieschi 93, tel. 0187-812-551, mobile 338-209-3565, www.corniglia.com). Stefano's pizzeria at Via Fieschi 109 serves as reception.

EATING

Corniglia has three decent restaurants. **Cecio,** above the town, has terrace seating with a view of the sea (closed Wed). The trattoria **La Lantera,** on the main square, is most atmospheric. Neither comes with particularly charming service. At **Bar Matteo,** Cristiana and Stefano offer light meals and Internet access (also on the main ...are). Restaurant **Osteria Mananan**—between the bus stop and ... square on Via Fieschi—serves the best food in town in its ... and elegant interior (closed Tue, no outdoor seating, ...

...za (Town #4)

...or—overseen by a ruined ... is the jewel of the ...p of the train by ... restau- ... ith brag, "Vernazza is locally owned. Portofino has sold out." Fearing the change it would bring, keep-Vernazza-small proponents stopped the construction of a major road into the town and region. Families are tight and go back centuries; several generations stay together. In the winter, the population shrinks, as many people return to more comfortable big-city apartments.

Leisure time is devoted to the *passeggiata*—strolling lazily together up and down the main street. Sit on a bench and study the passersby doing their *vasca* (laps). Explore the characteristic alleys, called *carugi*. Learn—and live—the phrase *"vita pigra di Vernazza"* (the lazy life of Vernazza).

ORIENTATION

Tourist Information

The TI/park information booth is in the train station (daily 6:30–22:00 in summer, until 19:30 in winter, tel. 0187-812-533). Public WCs are nearby in the station.

Arrival in Vernazza

A shuttle bus, generally with friendly English-speaking Beppe or Simone behind the wheel, runs from the top of the main street to the non-resident parking lot about 500 yards above Vernazza (€1.50, free with Cinque Terre Card, runs 8:30–19:30, 4/hr).

For a cheap and scenic round-trip joyride, with a chance to chat about the region with Beppe or Simone, stay on for the entire route for the cost of a normal ticket. You can also catch the bus to the two sanctuaries in the hills above town (€2.50 each way, free with Cinque Terre Card, 5/day, find schedule at park office and posted in train station). This high-country 40-minute loop gives you lots of scenery without having to hike.

Helpful Hints

Money: The town has two banks and two ATMs (in center and top of town).

Internet Access: The slick **Internet Point,** run by Alberto and Isabella, is in the village center (daily 9:30–23:00 in summer, until 20:00 in winter, high-speed line, Wi-Fi, will burn CDs to back up your digital photos for €8, sells international phone cards, tel. 0187-812-949). The **Blue Marlin Bar,** run by Massimo and Carmen, offers Internet access as well with longer hours (Fri–Wed 7:00–24:00, closed Thu, see "Eating," page 904).

Laundry: The nearest laundromats are in Monterosso and Riomaggiore.

Parking: Driving to Vernazza is a reasonable option because of the parking lot (€1.50/hr, €12/24 hrs, about 500 yards above town) and the hardworking shuttle service (connects the lot to the top of town every 15 min, see "Arrival in Vernazza," above).

Best Views: A steep five-minute hike in either direction from Vernazza gives you a classic village photo op (for the best light, head toward Corniglia in the morning, toward Monterosso in the evening). Franco's Ristorante La Torre, with a panoramic terrace, is at the tower on the trail toward Corniglia (listed under "Eating," page 907).

SELF-GUIDED WALKS

Welcome to Vernazza

This tour includes Vernazza's characteristic town squares, and ends on its scenic breakwater.

• *Walk uphill until you hit the parking lot, with a bank, a post office, and a barrier that keeps out all but service vehicles. Vernazza's shuttle buses run from here to the parking lot and into the hills. Walk to the tidy, modern square called...*

Fontana Vecchia: Named after a long-gone fountain, this is where older locals remember the river filled with townswomen doing their washing. Now they enjoy checking on the baby ducks. The trail leads up to the cemetery. Imagine the entire village trudging sadly up here during funerals.

• *Glad to be here in happier times, begin your saunter downhill to the harbor. Just before the* Pensione Sorriso *sign, on your right (big brown wood doors), you'll see the...*

Ambulance Barn: A group of volunteers is always on call for a dash to the hospital, 40 minutes away in La Spezia. Opposite from the barn is a big, empty lot. Like many landowners, the owner of Pension Sorriso had plans to expand, but since the 1980s, the government said no. While some landowners are frustrated, the old character of these towns survives.

• *A few steps farther along (past the town clinic and library), you'll see a...*

World Wars Monument: Look for a marble plaque in the wall to your left, dedicated to those killed in the World Wars. Not a family in Vernazza was spared. Listed on the left are soldiers *morti in combattimento,* who died in World War I; on the right is the World War II section. Some were deported to *Germania*; others—labeled *Part* (stands for *partigiani*, or partisans)—were killed while fighting against Mussolini. Cynics considered partisans less than heroes. After 1943, Hitler called up Italian boys over 15. Rather than die on the front for Hitler, they escaped to the hills. They become "resistance fighters" in order to remain free.

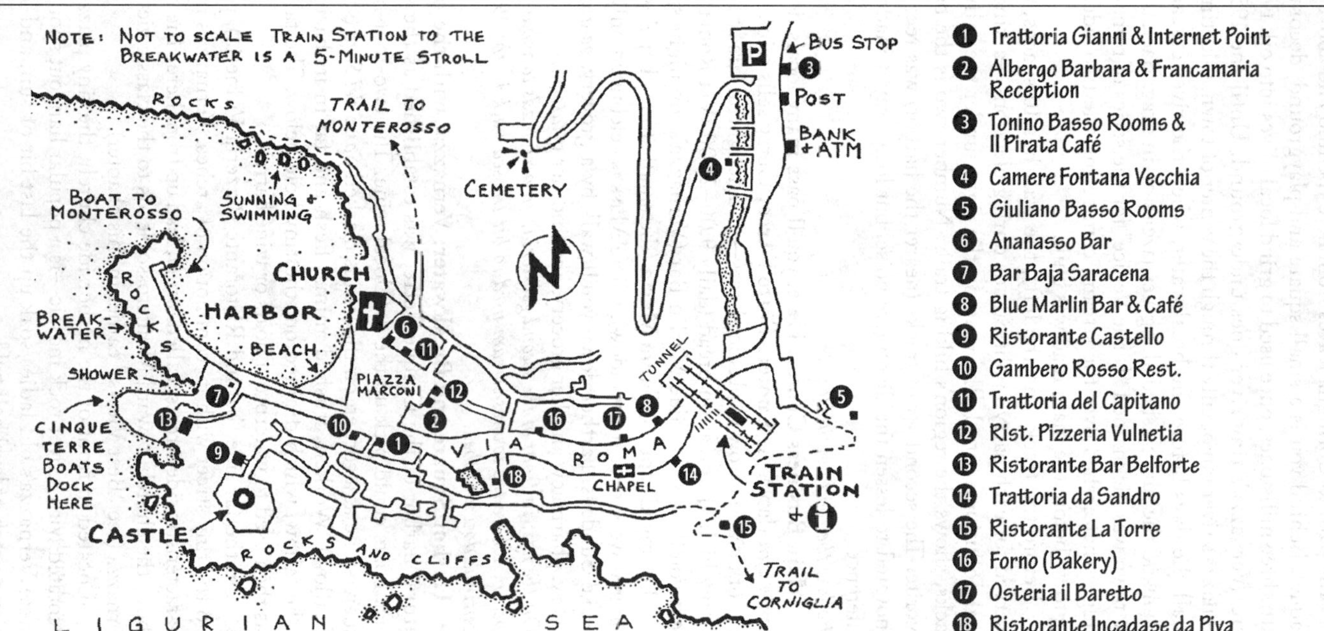
Vernazza
1 Trattoria Gianni & Internet Point
2 Albergo Barbara & Francamaria Reception
3 Tonino Basso Rooms & Il Pirata Café
4 Camere Fontana Vecchia
5 Giuliano Basso Rooms
6 Ananasso Bar
7 Bar Baja Saracena
8 Blue Marlin Bar & Café
9 Ristorante Castello
10 Gambero Rosso Rest.
11 Trattoria del Capitano
12 Rist. Pizzeria Vulnetia
13 Ristorante Bar Belforte
14 Trattoria da Sandro
15 Ristorante La Torre
16 Forno (Bakery)
17 Osteria il Baretto
18 Ristorante Incadase da Piva
Note: Not to scale Train Station to the Breakwater is a 5-Minute Stroll
Rocks
Trail to Monterosso
Cemetery
P
Bus Stop
Post
Bank + ATM
Boat to Monterosso
Sunning + Swimming
Church
Harbor
Beach
Piazza Marconi
Tunnel
Rocks
Break-water
Shower
Via Roma
Chapel
Train Station
Cinque Terre Boats Dock Here
Castle
Rocks and Cliffs
Trail to Corniglia
Ligurian Sea

The path to Corniglia leaves from here (behind and above the plaque). Behind you is a small square and playground, decorated with three millstones, once used to grind local olives into oil. From here, Vernazza's tiny river goes underground. Until the 1950s, Vernazza's river ran openly through the center of town. Old-timers recall the days before the breakwater, when the river cascaded down and the surf crashed along Vernazza's main drag. Back then, the town was nicknamed "Little Venice" for the series of romantic bridges that arched over the stream, connecting the two sides of the town before the main road was built.

Before the tracks (on the left), the wall has 10 spaces, one reserved for each party's political ads during elections—a kind of local pollution control. The **map** on the right, under the railway tracks, shows the region's hiking trails. Number two is the basic favorite. The second set of tracks (nearer the harbor) was recently renovated to lessen the disruptive noise, but locals say it made no difference.

• *Follow the road downhill to the...*

Main Business Center: Here, you'll pass many locals doing their *vasca* (laps). At **Enoteca Sotto l'Arco,** Gerry sells wine—he can cork it and throw in plastic glasses—and delightful jars of local pesto which are great on bread (daily 9:00–21:00, Via Roma 70). Next you'll pass the Blue Marlin Bar (Vernazza's top night spot) and the tiny **Chapel of Santa Marta** (the small stone chapel with iron grillwork over the window), where Mass is celebrated only on special Sundays. Farther down you'll walk by a grocery, *gelateria*, bakery, pharmacy, another grocery, and another *gelateria.*

• *On the left, in front of the second gelateria, an arch leads to what was a beach, where the town's stream used to hit the sea back in the 1970s. Continue down to the...*

Harbor Square and Breakwater: Vernazza, with the only natural harbor of the Cinque Terre, was established as the sole place boats could pick up the fine local wine. The two-foot-high square stone at a corner, on the left, is marked *Sasso del Sego* (stone of tallow). Workers crushed animal flesh and fat in its basin to make tallow, which drained out the tiny hole below. The tallow was then used to waterproof boats or wine barrels.

On the far side (behind Ristorante Pizzeria Vulnetia), peek into the tiny street with its commotion of arches. Vernazza's most characteristic side streets, called *carugi*, lead up from here. The trail (above the church, toward Monterosso) leads to the classic view of Vernazza (see "Best Views," earlier in this chapter).

Located in front of the harborside church, the tiny piazza—decorated with a river rock mosaic—is a popular hangout spot. It's where Vernazza's old ladies soak up the last bit of sun, and kids enjoy a patch of level ball field.

Vernazza's harborfront church is unusual for its strange entryway, which faces east (altar side). With relative peace and prosperity in the 16th century, the townspeople doubled the church in size, causing it to overtake a little piazza that once faced the west facade. From the square, use the "new" entry and climb the steps, keeping an eye out for the level necessary to keep the church high and dry. Inside, the lighter pillars in the back mark the 16th-century extension. Three historic portable crosses hanging on the walls are carried through town during Easter processions. They are replicas of crosses Vernazza ships once carried on crusades to the Holy Land.

• *Finish your town tour seated out on the breakwater (and consider starting the tour directly below).*

The Burned-Out Sightseer's Visual Tour of Vernazza

• *Sit at the end of the harbor breakwater (perhaps with a glass of local white wine or something more interesting from a nearby bar—borrow the glass, they don't mind), face the town, and see...*

The Harbor: In a moderate storm, you'd be soaked, as waves routinely crash over the *molo* (breakwater, built in 1972). Waves can even wash away tourists squinting excitedly into their cameras. (I've seen it happen.) Enjoy the new waterfront piazza—carefully. The red flag proudly flying above the breakwater signifies that Vernazza is one of Italy's 130 most beautiful towns.

The train line (to your left) was constructed in 1874 to tie together a newly united Italy, and linked Turin and Genoa with Rome. A second line (hidden in a tunnel at this point) was built in the 1920s. The yellow building alongside the tracks was Vernazza's first train station. You can see the four bricked-up alcoves where people once waited for trains.

Vernazza's fishing fleet is down to just a couple of fishing boats (with the net spools). Vernazzans are still more likely to own a boat than a car. Boats are on buoys, except in winter or when the red storm flag indicates bad seas (in which case they're allowed to be pulled up onto the square—which is usually reserved for restaurant tables). In the 1970s, tiny Vernazza had one of Italy's top water polo teams, and the harbor was their "pool." Later, when the league required a real pool, Vernazza dropped out.

The Castle: On the far right, the castle, which is now a grassy park with great views (and nothing but stones), still guards the town (€1 donation supports the local Red Cross, daily 10:30–19:30; from harbor, take stairs by Trattoria Gianni and follow signs to Ristorante Castello, tower is a few steps beyond). It was the town's lookout back in pirate days. The highest umbrellas mark the recommended Ristorante Castello (see page 905). The squat tower on the water is great for a glass of wine or a meal. From the breakwater, follow the rope to the Ristorante Belforte (see page 905), and pop inside, past the submarine-strength door. A photo of a major storm showing the entire tower under a wave (not uncommon in the winter) hangs near the bar.

The Town: Vernazza has two halves. *Sciuiu* (Vernazzan dialect for flowery) is the sunny side on the left, and *luvegu* (dank) is the shady side on the right. Houses below the castle were connected by an interior arcade—ideal for fleeing attacks. The "Ligurian pastel" colors are regulated by a commissioner of good taste in the regional government. The square before you is locally famous for some of the area's finest restaurants. The big red central house—on the site where Genoan warships were built in the 12th century—used to be a guardhouse.

Vernazza has the only natural harbor in the Cinque Terre. In the Middle Ages there was no beach or square. The water went right up to the buildings where boats would tie up, Venetian-style. Imagine what Vernazza looked like in those days, when it was the biggest and richest of the Cinque Terre towns. There was no pastel plaster, just fine stonework (traces of which survive above the Trattoria del Capitano). Apart from the added plaster, the general shape and size of the town has changed little in five centuries. Survey the windows and notice inhabitants quietly gazing back.

Above the Town: The small, round tower above the guardhouse—another part of the city fortifications—reminds us of Vernazza's importance in the Middle Ages, when it was a key ally of Genoa (whose archenemies were the other maritime republics, especially Pisa). Franco's Ristorante La Torre, just behind the tower, welcomes hikers finishing, starting, or simply contemplating the Corniglia–Vernazza hike, with great town views (between meal times, only drinks are served). Vineyards fill the mountainside beyond the town. Notice the many terraces. Someone—probably after too much of that local wine—calculated that the roughly 3,000 miles of dry stone walls built to terrace the region's vineyards have the same amount of stonework as the Great Wall of China.

Wine production is down nowadays, as the younger residents choose less physical work. But locals still maintain their tiny plots and proudly serve their family wines. The patchwork of local vineyards is atomized and complex because of inheritance traditions. Historically, families divided their land between their children. Parents wanted each child to get some good land. Because some lots were "kissed by the sun" while others were shady, the lots were split into increasingly tiny and eventually unviable pieces.

A single steel train line winds up the gully behind the tower. It is for the vintner's *trenino*, the tiny service train. Play "Where's *trenino?*" and see if you can find two trains. The vineyards once stretched as high as you can see, but since fewer people sweat in the fields these days, the most distant terraces have gone wild again.

The Church, School, and City Hall: Vernazza's Ligurian Gothic church, built with black stones quarried from Punta Mesco (the distant point behind you), dates from 1318. Note the gray stone marking the church's 16th-century expansion. The gray-and-red house above the spire is the local elementary school (about 25 children attend). High-schoolers go to the "big city": La Spezia. The red building to the right of the schoolhouse, a former monastery, is the City Hall. Vernazza and Corniglia function as one community. Through most of the 1990s, the local government was communist. In 1999, they elected a coalition of many parties working to rise above ideologies and simply make Vernazza a better place. Finally, on the top of the hill, with the best view of all, is the town cemetery.

ACTIVITIES

Tuesday Morning Market—Vernazza's meager business community is augmented Tuesday mornings (8:00–13:00) when a gang of cars and trucks pull into town for a tailgate market.

Beach—The harbor's sandy cove has sunning rocks and showers by the breakwater. There's also a ladder on the breakwater for deep-water access. A tiny *acqua pendente* (waterfall) cove, between Vernazza and Monterosso, is accessible by boat—when the service is available (ask at TI). Locals call it their *laguna blu*.

Kayaks—At the harbor, kayaks are rentable by the hour (June–Sept only, €4/hr for 1-person kayak, €8/hr for 2-person kayak).

Massage—In 2000, Kate Allen moved her massage table from London to the Cinque Terre. She provides a good therapeutic rubdown for €50 an hour in the clinic across from Pensione Sorriso (call for an appointment, cash only, 100 yards above Vernazza's train tracks, tel. 0187-812-537, katarinaallen@hotmail.com).

NIGHTLIFE

Vernazza's younger generation of restaurant workers lets loose after hours. They work hard through the tourist season, travel in the winter, speak English, and enjoy connecting with international visitors.

There are just a couple of places where you're likely to find action after Vernazza's restaurants close down. (See "Eating," page 904, for details on these restaurants and bars.) The local scene starts at the **Blue Marlin Bar.** Then, everyone migrates to **Ristorante Belforte,** which turns the old castle into a bar late in the evening (Thu–Sat only, closed in winter), with loud music and ample opportunity to dance with the locals. Then, the "after-after-hours" party moves down to the harbor.

For early-evening happy-hour fun, consider the **Ananasso Bar,** where every night, English-speaking Manuela serves munchies with cocktails for *aperitivi* (the pre-dinner happy hour that both locals and visitors enjoy). Its harborfront tables get the last sunshine of the day. At the top of the town, the Canoli brothers entertain their gang (of mostly tourists) at **Il Pirata delle Cinque Terre.**

For local music, hang out at **Ristorante Incadase da Piva** (tucked up the lane behind the pharmacy). When the cooking's done, Vernazza's troubadour, Piva, often gets out his guitar and sings traditional local songs as well as his own compositions.

SLEEPING

(€1 = about $1.30, country code: 39)

Vernazza, the essence of the Cinque Terre, is my top choice for a home base. There are two recommended pensions and piles of private rooms for rent.

These days, with so many rooms available, you can generally arrive without a reservation and find a place (except holidays such as Easter, weekends, and July–Aug). In fact, you can save money this way—or gain the chance to shop around and land a place with a terrace and a view for less. Drop by any shop or bar and ask; most locals know someone who rents rooms.

Even today, pirates lurk on the Cinque Terre. People recommended here are listed for their communication skills (they speak English, have email, are reliable with bookings) and because they rent several rooms. Consequently, my recommendations charge more than comparable rooms you'll find if you just arrive and shop around. Bold travelers who drop in without a reservation and shop around will likely save €10–20 per double per night—and often get a better place and view to boot. The real Vernazza gems are stray single rooms with no interest in booking in advance or messing with email.

Anywhere you stay here requires some climbing. Night noise can be a problem if you're near the station. Rooms on the harbor come with church bells (but only from 7:00–22:00). Unlike in other villages, prices do not include breakfast unless otherwise noted. For details see "Sleeping in the Cinque Terre," page 876.

Pensions

These pensions are listed on the map on page 895.

$$ Trattoria Gianni rents 23 small rooms just under the castle. The rooms are in two buildings—one funky, one modern—

up a hundred tight, winding spiral stairs. The funky ones, which may or may not have private baths, are artfully decorated à la shipwreck, with tiny balconies and grand sea views *(con vista sul mare)*. The new *(nuovo)*, comfy rooms lack views, but have modern bathrooms and a super-scenic, cliff-hanging guests' garden. Steely Marisa requires check-in before 16:00 or a phone call to explain when you're coming. Manuele (Gianni's son, who now runs the restaurant), Simona, and the staff speak a little English (S-€43, D-€61, D with small balcony-€65, Db-€78, Tb-€101, cancellations required 48 hours in advance or you'll be charged one night's deposit, closed Jan–Feb, Piazza Marconi 5, tel. & fax 0187-812-228, tel. 0187-821-003, www.giannifranzi.it, info@giannifranzi.it). Pick up your keys at Trattoria Gianni's restaurant/reception on the harbor square, and hike up scores of steps to funky old #41 or new and modern #47 at the top. If you arrive on Wednesday, when the restaurant is closed, pick up your keys at the *gelateria* by the grotto.

Cinque Terre

$$ Albergo Barbara, on the harbor square with nine simple but clean and modern rooms, is run by kindly, English-speaking Giuseppe and his Swiss wife, Patricia (D-€48, Db-€55–60, big Db with view-€80, fax or email credit card information to hold room but pay cash, 2-night stay preferred, fans, closed Dec–Feb, Piazza Marconi 30, tel. & fax 0187-812-398, mobile 338-793-3261, www.albergobarbara.it, albergobarbara@libero.it). The two big doubles on the main floor come with grand harbor views (top-floor doubles have small windows and small views). The office is on the top floor of the big, red, vacant-looking building facing the harbor.

Private Rooms *(Affitta Camere)*

Vernazza is honeycombed year-round with private rooms, offering the best values in town. Owners may be reluctant to reserve rooms far in advance. It's easiest to call a day or two ahead or simply show up in the morning and look around. Doubles cost €45–70, depending on the view, season, and plumbing. Most places accept only cash. Some have killer views, come with lots of stairs, and cost the same as a small dark place on a back lane over the train tracks. Little English is spoken at many of these places. If you call to let them know your arrival time (or call when you arrive, using the pay phone just below the station), they'll meet you at the train station.

Especially Well-Managed and Well-Appointed Rooms at the Top of Town

These accommodations are listed on the map on page 895.

$$$ Tonino Basso rents four super, clean, modern rooms—at a steep price. Each room has its own computer for free Internet access. He's located near the post office, in the only building in

Vernazza with an elevator. You get tranquility and air-conditioning, but no views. This is the only *affita camere* that takes credit cards (Sb-€60, Db-€100, Tb-€120, Qb-€150, call Tonino's mobile number upon arrival and he'll meet you, tel. 0187-821-264, mobile 335-269-436, fax 0187-812-807, toninobasso@libero.it). If you can't locate Tonino, his wife, Tania, works at the harborside Gambero Rosso restaurant.

$$ Camere Fontana Vecchia is a delightful place, with four bright, spacious, quiet rooms near the post office (no view). The only place in Vernazza with almost no stairs to climb and the sound of a babbling brook outside your window, it's a great value (D-€60, Db-€70, T-€90, Tb-€110, €5 less off-season, fans and heat, open all year, Via Gavino 15, tel. & fax 0187-821-130, mobile 333-454-9371, m.annamaria@libero.it, youthful and efficient Anna speaks English).

$$ Giuliano Basso rents four pleasant rooms just above town in the terraced wilds (sea views from terraces). Straddling a ravine among orange trees, it's an artfully decorated, Robinson Crusoe–chic wonderland, proudly built out of stone by Giuliano himself (Db-€70, larger Db and Db with air-con-€80, family room sleeps four-€130), fridge access, above train station—so with more train noise than others, mobile 333-341-4792, or have the Blue Marlin bar—see "Eating," page 904—contact him or his American partner Michele, www.cdh.it/giuliano, giuliano@cdh.it). Call to be met at the station. From Pensione Sorriso, hike up the Corniglia trail; 100 yards later, at the second Corniglia sign, follow the lane left.

Other Reliable Places Scattered Through Town and the Harborside

$$ Antonio and Ingrid Fenelli Camere rent three very central, comfy, and fairly priced rooms. Friendly Antonio—a hulking man in a huge white T-shirt and bathing suit—is a fixture on the village streets (small Db-€55, Db-€60, Tb-€80, apartment with terrace-€75, air-con, 10 steps above pharmacy at Via Carattino 2, tel. 0187-812-183).

$$ Memo Rooms offers three newly renovated, immaculate rooms overlooking the main street, in what feels like a miniature hotel. Enrica will meet you if you call upon arrival (Db-€65, Via Roma 15, tel. 0187-812-360, mobile 338-285-2385).

$$ Martina Callo rents four rooms overlooking the square, up plenty of steps near the silent-at-night church tower (room #1: Tb-€95 or Qb-€110 with harbor view; room #2: huge Qb family room with no view-€110; room #3: Db with grand view terrace-€75; room #4: roomy Db with no view-€55; ring bell at Piazza Marconi 26, tel. & fax 0187-812-365, mobile 329-435-5344, www.roomartina.com, roomartina@supereva.it).

$$ Elisabetta's Villino Azzurro has three ramshackle rooms with views. The lower room has a small window with a sea view; the two rooms upstairs come with view terraces; and the uppermost terrace has 360-degree views of town, the castello, the terraced hills, and the sea (Db-€50–62, Via Carattino 62, mobile 347-451-1834, www.elisabettacarro.it, carroelisabetta@hotmail.com).

$$ Nicolina rents four funky, lived-in rooms. The largest has a view; two others overlook Vernazza's main drag. Inquire at Pizzeria Vulnetia on the harbor square (viewless Db-€65, view Db-€70, Tb-€90, Qb with terrace and view-€130, Piazza Marconi 29, tel. & fax 0187-821-193, www.camerenicolina.it, camerenicolina.info@cdh.it).

$$ Rosa Vitali rents two apartments across from the pharmacy overlooking the main street. One, for up to three people, has a terrace and fridge (top floor); the other, for four, has windows and a full kitchen (Db-€75, Tb-€100, Qb-€120, €5 extra for 1-night stays, reception at Via Visconti 10 next to *gelateria* near the grotto, tel. 0187-821-181, mobile 340-267-5009, rosa.vitali@libero.it).

Other Private Rooms in Vernazza

I consider many of these places overpriced but reliable. Consider these options only if the places above are booked up:

$$$ Egi Rooms, run by English-speaking Egi Verduschi (pronounced "edgy"), offers three good, pricey rooms right in the center on the main drag (S-€70, D-€90, plush and designer Db-€120, Tb-€160, Qb-€180, across the street from *gelateria* just before harbor square on main drag at Via Visconti 9, tel. 0187-703-905, mobile 338-822-3202, egidioverduschi@libero.it).

$$ Francamaria rents four sharp, comfortable but expensive rooms. The two rooms above Trattoria Gianni's bar can be noisy in the evenings until 23:30 (Db-€75–95, Qb-€125–145, prices depend on view and season, Piazza Marconi 30, tel. 0187-812-002, mobile 328-711-9728, fax 0187-812-956, www.francamaria.com, francamaria@francamaria.com). Son Giovanni has three rooms of his own to rent (same prices but no views). Their reception is on the ground floor of the Albergo Barbara building.

$$ Affitta Camere Alberto Basso rents two rooms at a high price (Db-€75, run from Internet Point by Isabel, albertobasso@hotmail.com).

$$ Tilde's cheery and clean little room has a sea view (Db-€70, up Via Mazzini 9, mobile 339-298-9323, rasocri74@alice.it).

$$ Daria Bianchi offers three clean, spacious, and comfortable rooms near the station. Each has bright colors, worn carpeting, and either overlooks the main street or the inland hills (Db-€65, Qb-€100, tel. 0187-812-151, mobile 338-581-4688, www.vernazzarooms.com).

$$ Affitta Camere da Annamaria offers six basic rooms (avoid the two without views) with barnacled ambience up a series of comically tight spiral staircases (Db-€75 with town views and terrace, Db-€85 for top room with sea-view terrace; at pharmacy, climb up Via Carattino to #64; tel. 0187-821-082, mobile 349-887-8150).

More Options: **Filippo Rooms** (Db-€65, lots of rooms, tel. 0187-812-244), **Eva's Rooms** (Db-€50–70, air-con, tel. 0187-821-134, www.evasrooms.it, massimoeva@libero.it), **Sergio Callo Rooms** (Db-€75, Tb-€90, apartment sleeps up to three, tel. 0187-812-284, gemmina@5terre.com), **Armanda** (€70, no view, near castle, Piazza Marconi 15, tel. 0187-812-218, mobile 347-306-4760, www.armanda.it, info@armanda.it), **Manuela Moggia** (Db-€70, Qb-€110, top of town at Via Gavino 22, tel. 0187-812-397, mobile 333-413-6374), **Patrizia** (Db-€70, Qb-€100, four rooms, all with kitchens, on main street, tel. 0187-821-231, mobile 335-653-1563, fax 0187-812-907, bemili@libero.it), and **Villa Antonia** (Db-€70, 2 rooms on main drag, tel. 0187-821-143, mobile 333-971-5602).

EATING

Breakfast

Locals take breakfast about as seriously as flossing. A cappuccino and a pastry or a piece of focaccia does it. No accommodations come with breakfast. Instead, you have several fun options.

The two harborfront bars offer the most ambience. **Ananasso Bar** feels Old World, with low energy but a great location (toasted panini, pastries). Eat a bit cheaper at the bar (you're welcome to picnic on a bench or rock) or enjoy the best-situated tables in town (Fri–Wed 8:00 to late, closed Thu). **Bar Baja Saracena** has a chalkboard explaining their various set-price tourist *menùs* (€5–7 for breakfast, opens 7:30 Sat–Thu, closed Fri, located out on the breakwater, tel. 0187-812-113).

The **Blue Marlin Bar** (mid-town) serves a good array of clearly priced à la carte items and the only American-style eggs in town. It's run by Massimo with able help from his younger cousin, Stefano (Fri–Wed 7:00–24:00, closed Thu, open daily in Aug, just below station, tel. 0187-821-149). If awaiting a train, the Blue Marlin's outdoor seats beat the platform. The nearby bakery opens early, offering freshly made focaccia.

At **Il Pirata delle Cinque Terre,** dynamic Sicilian duo Gianluca and Massimo (twins, a.k.a. the Canoli Brothers) enthusiastically offer a great assortment of handcrafted, authentic Sicilian pastries. Their fun and playful service makes up for the lack of a view. Gianluca is a pastry artist, hand-painting fanciful sculptured marzipan. Their sweet pastry breakfasts are a hit, with a stunning array of hot-out-of-the-oven treats like *panzerotto* (made of ricotta, cinnamon, and vanilla, €1.50) and hot meat-and-cheese pies (€2.50). Other favorites include their *granitas*—slushees made from fresh fruit (daily 6:30–24:00, simple lunches and tasty dinners, by post office at top of town, Via Gavino 36, tel. 0187-812-047). While the atmosphere of the place seems like suburban Milano, it has a curious charisma among its customers—bringing Vernazza a welcome bit of Sicily.

Lunch and Dinner

If you enjoy Italian cuisine and seafood, Vernazza's restaurants are worth the splurge. All take pride in their cooking and have similar prices. Wander around at about 20:00 and compare the ambience, but don't wait too late to eat—many kitchens close at 22:00 since some of the workers have to catch the last train back home to La Spezia at 22:30. To get an outdoor table on summer weekends, reserve ahead. Expect to spend €10 for pastas, €12 for *secondi*, and €2 for a cover charge. Harbor-side restaurants and bars are easygoing. You're welcome to grab a cup of coffee or glass of wine and disappear somewhere on the breakwater, returning your glass when you're done.

Harborfront Options

Ristorante Castello is run by gracious and English-speaking Monica, her husband Massimo, kind Mario, and the rest of her family (you won't see mamma—she's busy personally cooking each *secondo*). Hike high above town to just below the castle for great seafood and regional specialties with commanding views (Thu–Tue 12:00–15:00 for lunch, 15:00–19:00 for drinks and snacks on cliff-hugging terrace, 19:00–22:00 for dinner, closed Wed and Nov–April, tel. 0187-812-296). Their *lasagna al pesto* and *ravioli di pesce* are time-honored family specialties and their *antipasto misto mare* is a sharable €15 treat for starters. Drop into Monica's new wine cantina and select the bottle of your choice.

Ristorante Belforte's chef Claudio—who previously cooked for a fancy resort-town restaurant—is the most experimental and creative cook in town. I enjoyed Claudio's *antipasto del nostro chef* (€28 for six plates—plenty for two people) and his *risotto del pirata* (and I generally don't like risotto). From the breakwater, follow a rope that leads up and around to the restaurant. You'll find a tangle of tables embedded in three levels of the lower part of the old castle. For the ultimate seaside perch, call and reserve one of four tables on the *fuori* (front terrace). But skip this place if the weather's bad, since most of Belforte's seating is outdoors. Explore the delightfully translated menu. The Belforte is also a good spot, even outside of mealtimes, for a romantic drink (Wed–Mon

12:00–22:00, closed Tue and Nov–March, tel. 0187-812-222). For info on late-night Belforte action, see "Nightlife," page 899.

Four Harborside Winners: These places—each with fine indoor and outdoor seating—fill the harborfront with happy eaters: **Gambero Rosso**, considered Vernazza's best restaurant, feels classy and costs only a few euros more than the others (Tue–Sun 12:00–15:00 & 19:00–22:00, closed Mon and Dec–Feb, Piazza Marconi 7, tel. 0187-812-265). **Trattoria del Capitano** might serve the best food for the money, including *tagliolini sul pesce*—white fish and delicate pasta—and their *zuppa provenzale*, a hearty Ligurian bouillabaisse (Wed–Mon 12:00–15:00 & 19:00–22:00, closed Tue except in Aug, closed Dec–Jan, tel. 0187-812-201, while Paolo speaks English, grandpa Giacomo doesn't need to). **Trattoria Gianni** is an old standby for locals and tourists alike, especially for well-prepared seafood and Tonino's steady, reliable, and friendly service (Thu–Tue 12:00–15:00 & 19:30–22:00, closed Wed except July–Aug, tel. 0187-812-228). The simpler **Ristorante Pizzeria Vulnetia** serves regional specialties and €8 pizzas (Tue–Sun 12:00–15:00 & 18:30–22:00, closed Mon, Piazza Marconi 29, tel. 0187-821-193).

Inland Restaurants

Several inland places manage to compete without the harbor ambience:

Trattoria da Sandro, on the main drag, mixes Genovese and Ligurian cuisine with friendly service. It can be a peaceful alternative to the harborside scene. Mario serves with panache while Alessandro cooks (Wed–Mon 12:00–15:00 & 19:00–22:00, closed Tue, just below train station, Via Roma 62, tel. 0187-812-223, Gabriella).

Antica Osteria Il Baretto is another solid bet for traditional cuisine, run by Simone, Zia, and family (closed Mon, indoor and outdoor seating, Via Roma 31).

Ristorante Incadase da Piva is a rare bit of old Vernazza. Charismatic Piva is known for his fine *tegame alla Vernazza* (typical Vernazzan dish with anchovies, tomatoes, and potatoes baked in the oven), *risotto con frutti di mare* (seafood risotto), and love of music. The town troubadour, he often serenades his guests when the cooking's done (tucked away 20 yards off the main drag, up a lane behind the pharmacy).

Other Eating Options

Il Pirata delle Cinque Terre is popular for breakfast, lunch (only sandwiches and light fare), dinner (pastas, salads, Sicilian specialities), and its homemade desserts and drinks (at the top of town; see "Breakfast," page 904, for complete description).

Franco's Ristorante La Torre, sitting humbly above Vernazza on the trail to Corniglia, offers a grand view, perfect peace, and especially romantic dinners at sunset. Hours can be sporadic so confirm he's open before hiking up (Wed–Mon 12:00–21:30, sometimes also open Tue, kitchen closes from 15:00–19:30 but drinks are served, tel. 0187-821-082, mobile 338-404-1181).

Pizzeria Baja Saracena (Saracen Bay) is where waiters take the pirate theme to heart, swinging in with earrings that blow in the wind. The bar has a dozen plastic tables on the breakwater and serves light meals throughout the day (€5–7 salads, €8 pizza, €4 glasses of *sciacchetrà*—sweet dessert wine, closed Fri, also see listing under "Breakfast," page 904).

Pizzerias, Sandwiches, Groceries, Gelato: The main street creatively fills tourists' needs. Two pizzerias stay busy, and while they mostly do take-out, each will let you sit and eat for the same cheap price. One has tables on the street, and the other (**Ercole**) hides a tiny terrace and a few tables out back. The **Blue Marlin Bar** offers a good selection of bruschetta, salad, pizza, and sandwiches (see listing under "Breakfast," page 904).

The **Forno** bakery has good focaccia and veggie tarts, and several bars sell sandwiches and pizza by the slice. Grocery stores also make inexpensive sandwiches to order (Mon–Sat 8:00–13:00 & 17:30–20:00, Sun 8:00–13:00). Tiny jars of pesto spread give elegance to picnics. The town's three *gelaterias* are good. What looks like Gelateria Amore Mio (near the grotto, mid-town), is actually **Gelateria Stalin**—founded in 1968 by a pastry chef with that unfortunate name. His niece Sonia and nephew Francesco now run it, and are generous with the *assaggiare* (free tastes, 24 flavors, sit there or take it to go).

Monterosso al Mare (Town #5)

This is a resort with cars, hotels, rentable beach umbrellas, crowds, and a thriving late-night scene. Monterosso—the only Cinque Terre town built on flat land—has two parts: A new town (called Fegina) with a parking lot, train station, and a TI, and an old town *(centro storico)*, which cradles Old World charm in its small, crooked lanes. In the old town, you'll find hole-in-the-wall shops, pastel townscapes, and a new generation of creative small businesspeople eager to keep their visitors happy.

A pedestrian tunnel connects the old with the new. But take a small detour around the point for a nicer walk. It offers a close-up view of two sights: a 16th-century lookout tower, built after the last serious pirate raid in 1545, and a Nazi "pillbox," a small, low, concrete bunker where gunners hid. (During World War II, nearby La Spezia was an important Axis naval base, and Monterosso was bombed while the Germans were here.)

Strolling the waterfront promenade, you can pick out each of the Cinque Terre towns decorating the coast. After dark they sparkle. Monterosso is the most enjoyable of the five for young travelers wanting to connect with other young travelers and looking for a little evening action. Even so, Monterosso is not a full-blown Portofino-style resort—and locals appreciate quiet, sensitive guests.

ORIENTATION

Tourist Information

The TI Proloco is next to the train station (Easter–Oct daily 9:30–18:30, closed Nov–Easter, exit station and go left a few doors, tel. 0187-817-506, Cristiana). The Cinque Terre has park offices on Piazza Garibaldi in the old town and in the train station in the new town (daily 8:00–22:00, until 20:00 in winter, tel. 0187-817-059, www.parconazionale5terre.it, parconazionale5terre@libero.it).

Arrival in Monterosso

Monterosso is 30 minutes off the freeway (exit: Carrodano). Parking is easy (except July, Aug, and summer weekends) in the huge beachfront guarded lot (€12/day). If that's full, there's a free lot about three miles up the hill, with an hourly shuttle-bus service. As you approach, save six miles of needless driving by deciding ahead of time whether to head into the old or new town. Pay attention to the fork that pops up three miles above town, directing cars to *Centro Storico* (old center, no parking available except for Villa Steno guests) or *Fegina* (the new town and parking, most likely where you want to go). Train travelers arrive in the new town, where it's a scenic 10-minute stroll to all the old-town action (leave station to the left, but for hotels in the new town, turn right out of station).

Shuttle buses run along the waterfront between the old town (Piazza Garibaldi, just beyond the tunnel), the train station, and the parking lot at the end of Via Fegina (*Campo Sportivo* stop). While the buses can be convenient, saving you a 10-minute schlepp with your bags, they only go once an hour, and are likely not worth the trouble (€1.50, free with Cinque Terre Card).

Helpful Hints

Medical Help: The town's bike-riding, leather-bag-toting doctor is Dr. Vitone (mobile 338-853-0949).

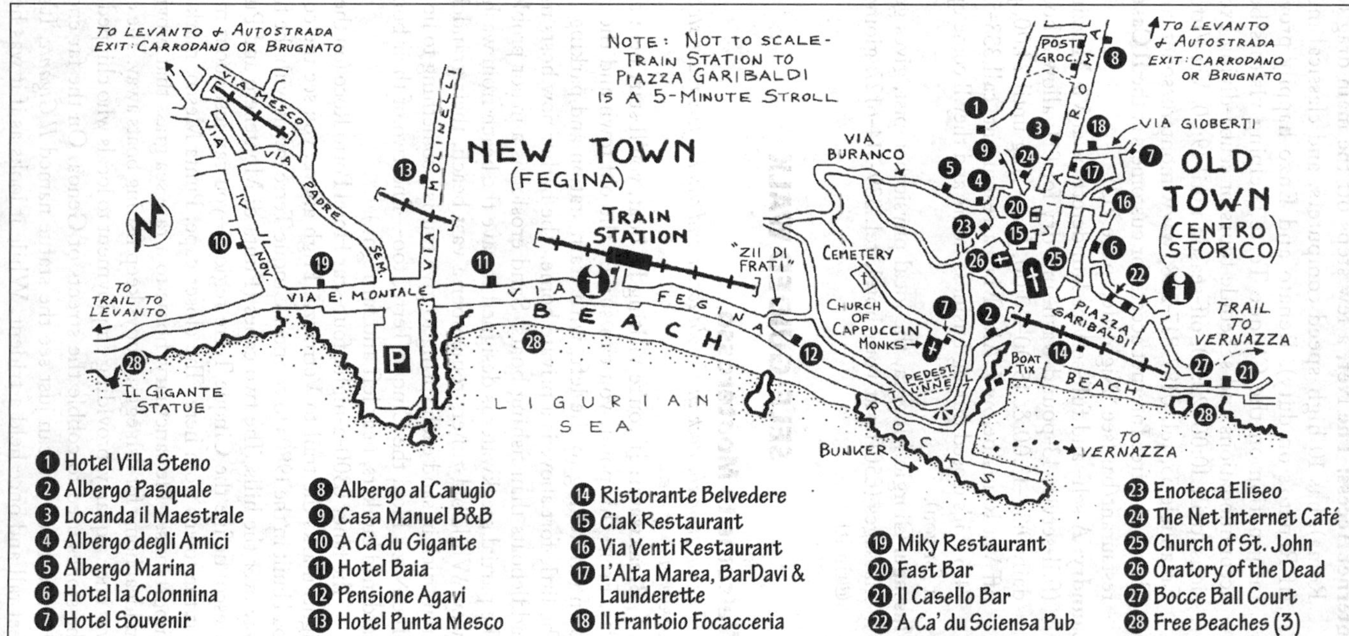
Monterosso al Mare
To Levanto & Autostrada Exit: Carrodano or Brugnato
Note: Not to scale - Train Station to Piazza Garibaldi is a 5-minute stroll
To Levanto & Autostrada Exit: Carrodano or Brugnato
Via Mesco
Via Padre
Via IV Nov.
Sem.
Via Molinelli
New Town (Fegina)
Train Station
"Zii di Frati"
Via E. Montale
Via Fegina
Beach
To Trail to Levanto
Il Gigante Statue
Ligurian Sea
Via Buranco
Cemetery
Church of Cappuccin Monks
Pedest. Tunnel
Bunker
Rocks
Boat Tix
Piazza Garibaldi
Beach
To Vernazza
Post
Groc.
Via Roma
Via Gioberti
Old Town (Centro Storico)
Trail to Vernazza
1 Hotel Villa Steno
2 Albergo Pasquale
3 Locanda il Maestrale
4 Albergo degli Amici
5 Albergo Marina
6 Hotel la Colonnina
7 Hotel Souvenir
8 Albergo al Carugio
9 Casa Manuel B&B
10 A Cà du Gigante
11 Hotel Baia
12 Pensione Agavi
13 Hotel Punta Mesco
14 Ristorante Belvedere
15 Ciak Restaurant
16 Via Venti Restaurant
17 L'Alta Marea, BarDavi & Launderette
18 Il Frantoio Focacceria
19 Miky Restaurant
20 Fast Bar
21 Il Casello Bar
22 A Ca' du Sciensa Pub
23 Enoteca Eliseo
24 The Net Internet Café
25 Church of St. John
26 Oratory of the Dead
27 Bocce Ball Court
28 Free Beaches (3)

Internet Access: The Net, a few steps off the main drag (Via Roma), has 10 high-speed computers, and classical music (if Renato's on duty). Renato and Enzo happily provide information on the Cinque Terre, helping visitors book accommodations and schedule tours or scuba-diving excursions (daily 10:00–22:00, off-season until 19:00, Via Vittorio Emanuele 55, tel. 0187-817-288, www.monterossonet.com). There's also free Internet access for customers at the **Il Casello** restaurant/bar (see "Nightlife," page 913).

Laundry: A self- and full-service launderette is at Via Mazzini 4 (full-service 13-pound wash-and-dry for €11, allow 2 hours, daily 9:30–13:00 & 15:00–20:00, June–Aug until 24:00, just off Via Roma below L'Alta Marea restaurant, call 333-525-7416 if it's closed during business hours and they'll come open it for you).

Massage: Giorgio Moggia, the local physiotherapist, gives good massages (€50/hr at your hotel, tel. 339-314-6127, giomogg@tin.it).

SELF-GUIDED WALK

Welcome to Monterosso

• *Hike out from the dock in the old town and climb a few rough steps to the very top of the...*

Breakwater: If you're visiting by boat, you'll start here anyway. From this point, you can survey the old town and the new town (stretching to the left, with train station and parking lot). The little fort above is a private home. The harbor now hosts more paddleboats than fishing boats. Sand erosion is a major problem. The partial breakwater is designed to save the beach from washing away. While old-timers remember a vast beach, their grandchildren truck in sand each spring to give tourists something to lie on. (The Nazis liked the Cinque Terre, too—find two of their bomb-hardened bunkers, near left and far right.)

The fancy €300-a-night, four-star Hotel Porto Roco (on the far right) marks the trail to Vernazza. High above, you see the costly road built in the 1980s to connect Cinque Terre towns with the freeway over the hills. The two capes (Punta di Montenero and Punta Mesco) define the Cinque Terre region—you can just about make out the towns from here. The closer cape, Punta Mesco, marks an important sea-life sanctuary, home to a rare sea grass that provides an ideal home for fish eggs. Buoys keep fishing boats away. The cape was once a quarry, providing employment to locals who chipped out the stones used to cobble the streets of Genoa. On the far end of the new town you can just see the statue named *Il Gigante.* It's 45 feet tall and once held a trident. While it looks as if it was hewn from the rocky cliff, it's actually made of reinforced concrete and dates from the beginning of the 20th century when it supported a dancing terrace for a *fin de siècle* villa. WWII bombs left the giant holding nothing but memories of Monterosso's glamorous age.

• *From the breakwater, walk to the old-town square (just past the train tracks and beyond the beach). Find the statue of a dandy holding what looks like a box cutter in...*

Piazza Garibaldi: The statue honors Giuseppe Garibaldi, the dashing firebrand revolutionary who, in 1870, helped unite the people of Italy into a modern nation. Facing Garibaldi, with your back to the sea, you'll see (from right to left) the City Hall (with the now-required European Union flag aside the Italian one), a big home and recreation center for poor and homeless elderly, and a park information center (in a building bombed in 1945 by the Allies, who were attempting to take out the train line). You'll also see the A Ca' du Sciensa pub (with historic town photos inside and upstairs, you're welcome to pop in for a look—see "Nightlife," page 913).

Just under the bell tower (with back to the sea, it's on your left) a set of covered arcades facing the sea is where the old-timers hang out (they see all and know all). The crenellated bell tower marks the church.

• *Go to church.*

Church of St. John the Baptist: This black-and-white church, with marble from Carrara, is typical of this region's Romanesque style. Note the lacy stone rose window above the entrance. The church dates from 1307—the proud inscription on the middle column inside reads "MilleCCCVII." Inside the church, on the left, find the high-water mark from a 1966 flood (the same month as the flood that devastated Florence).

• *Leaving the church, turn left immediately and go to church again.*

Oratory of the Dead: During the Counter-Reformation, the Catholic Church offset the rising influence of the Lutherans by creating brotherhoods of good works. These religious Rotary clubs were called "confraternities." Monterosso had two, nicknamed White and Black. This building is the oratory of the Black group, whose mission—as the macabre decor indicates—was to arrange for funerals and take care of widows, orphans, the shipwrecked, and the souls of those who ignore the request for a €1 donation. It dates from the 16th century, and membership has passed from father to son for generations. Notice the fine 17th-century carved choir stalls just inside the door. Look up on the ceiling to find the symbol of the confraternity: a skull, cross bones, and hourglass... death awaits us all.

• *Return to the beach and find the brick steps leading up to the hill-capping convent (starting between the train tracks and the pedestrian tunnel).*

The Switchbacks of the Monks: Follow the yellow brick road (OK, it's orange...but I couldn't help singing as I skipped skyward). Go constantly uphill until you reach a convent church, then a cemetery, in a ruined castle at the summit. The lane *(Salita dei Cappuccini)* is nicknamed *Zii di Frati* (switchbacks of the monks). Midway up the switchbacks, you'll see a statue of St. Francis and a wolf enjoying a grand view.

• *From here, backtrack 20 yards and continue uphill. When you reach a gate marked Convento e Chiesa Cappuccini, you have arrived. Go to church.*

Church of the Cappuccin Monks: The former convent (until recently a hotel) is now accommodating monks. Before stepping inside, notice the church's striped Romanesque facade. It's all fake. Tap it—no marble, just cheap 18th-century stucco. Sit in the rear pew. The high altarpiece painting of St. Francis can be rolled up on special days to reveal a statue of Mary, which stands behind it. Look at the statue of St. Anthony to the right and smile (you're on convent camera). Wave at the security camera—they're nervous about the precious painting to your left.

This fine painting of the Crucifixion is attributed to Antony Van Dyck, the Flemish master who lived and worked for years in nearby Genoa (though art historians suspect that, at best, it was painted by someone in the artist's workshop). When Jesus died, the earth went dark. Notice the eclipsed sun in the painting, just to the right of the cross. Do the electric candles work? Pick one up, pray for peace, and plug it in. (Leave €0.50, or unplug it and put it back.)

• *From the church, hike uphill to the cemetery that fills the remains of the castle, capping the hill. Look out from the gate and enjoy the view.*

Cemetery and Ruined Castle: In the Dark Ages, the village huddled within this castle. Slowly it expanded. Notice the town view from here—no sea. You're looking at the oldest part of Monterosso, huddled behind the hill, out of view of 13th-century pirates. Explore the cemetery, but remember that cemeteries are sacred and treasured places (as is clear by the abundance of fresh flowers). Ponder the black-and-white photos of grandparents past. Q.R.P. is *Qui Riposa in Pace* (a.k.a. R.I.P.). Rich families had their own little tomb buildings. Climb to the very summit—the castle's keep, or place of last refuge. Priests are buried in a line of graves closest to the sea, but facing inland—the town's holy sanctuary high on the hillside (above the road, hiding behind trees). Each Cinque Terre town has a lofty sanctuary, dedicated to Mary and dear to the village hearts.

• *From here, your tour's over—any trail leads you back into town.*

ACTIVITIES

Beaches—Monterosso's beaches, immediately in front of the train station, are easily the Cinque Terre's best and most crowded. This town is a sandy resort with everything rentable: lounge chairs, umbrellas, and paddleboats. Figure €15 to rent two chairs and an umbrella for the day. Light lunches are served by beach cafés to sunbathers at their lounge chairs. It's often worth the euros to enjoy a private beach. Beaches are free (and marked on the map on page 909) only where you see no umbrellas. The local hidden beach, which is free and generally less crowded, is tucked away under Il Casello restaurant at the east end of town, near the trailhead to Vernazza. The bocce ball court (next to Il Casello) is busy with the old boys enjoying their favorite pastime.

Kayaks—Bagni Stella Marina, next to the parking lot in the new town (train station side), rents kayaks (€8/hr for 1-person kayak, €12/hr for 2-person kayak, tel. 0187-817-209). The paddle to Vernazza is a favorite.

Shuttle Buses for High-Country Hikes—Monterosso's bus service (described in "Arrival in Monterosso," page 908) continues beyond the town limits. They do the heavy lifting, taking hikers to interesting trailheads in the nearby hills. They also go to Colle di Gritta, where you can hike back down to Monterosso via the Sanctuary of Soviore (1 hour, easy) or to Levanto via Punta Mesco (2.5 hours, strenuous). Rides cost €1.50 (free with Cinque Terre Card, pick up schedule from park office). For hiking details, ask at either park info booth (at the train station or Piazza Garibaldi).

Boat Rides—From the old-town harbor, boats run nearly hourly (10:30–17:00) to Vernazza, Manarola, Riomaggiore, and Portovenere. Schedules are posted in Cinque Terre park offices (for details, see page 873). A smaller boat connects Vernazza and Monterosso more frequently (2/hr).

NIGHTLIFE

Wander over to **Il Casello** for nightlife with a sea view. Enthusiastically run by Bacco, it's the best on-the-beach drinking spot—inexpensive and hip—with a creative and fun drink list. Built in about 1870 as the town's first train station, Il Casello overlooks the beach on the road toward Vernazza, with outdoor tables on a rocky outcrop sandwiched between old-town beaches. It's also a great place for a salad or sandwich during the day (daily 10:30–24:00, closed Oct–March, shorter hours outside June–Aug, tel. 0187-818-330).

A Ca' du Sciensa (The House of Sciensa) fills an old mansion with an antique dumbwaiter—a remnant from the days when servants toiled downstairs while the big shots wined and dined up top. This classy-yet-laid-back pub offers breezy square seating, bar action on the ground level, an intimate lounge upstairs, and discreet balconies overlooking the square to share with your best travel buddy. It's a good place for light meals (until 23:00) and plenty of drinks. Luca and Leo encourage you to wander around the place and enjoy the old Cinque Terre photo collection (daily 8:30–24:00, closed Wed off-season, Piazza Garibaldi 17, tel. 0187-818-233).

Enoteca Eliseo, the first wine bar in town, comes with operatic ambience. Eliseo and his wife, Mary, love music and wine. You can select a fine bottle from their shop shelf, and for €6 extra, enjoy it and the village action from their cozy tables. They serve munchies and light snacks. Wines sold by the glass *(bicchiere)* are posted (daily, closed Tue in winter, Piazza Matteotti 3, a few blocks inland behind church, tel. 0187-817-308).

BarDavi showcases owners Daniele's and Valeria's stylish knack for delicious entertainment. Each day after 17:00, they offer a "cocktails *con tapas*" deal: Buy a €6 drink or glass of wine and get a light meal's worth of good, local appetizers for free (daily 7:30–22:00, closed Tue Sept–June, under the arch on main drag, Via Roma 34, tel. 0187-817-019).

Fast Bar, where young travelers and night owls gather, is located on Via Roma in the old town. Customers mix travel tales with big, cold beers, and the crowd gets noisier as the night rolls on (sandwiches and snacks served until midnight, open nightly until 2:00).

SLEEPING

(€1 = about $1.30, country code: 39)
Monterosso, the most beach-resorty of the five Cinque Terre towns, offers maximum comfort and ease. The TI Proloco just outside the train station can give you a list of €30–35 per-person double rooms. To locate the hotels, see the map on page 909.

In the Old Town

$$$ Hotel Villa Steno is lovingly managed and features great view balconies, private gardens off some rooms, air-conditioning, and the friendly help of English-speaking Matteo and his wife, Carla. Of their 16 rooms, 12 have view balconies (Sb-€90, Db-€145, Tb-€170, Qb-€190, includes hearty buffet breakfast, Internet access, self-service laundry for guests, Via Roma 109, tel. 0187-817-028 or 0187-818-336, fax 0187-817-354, www.pasini.com, steno@pasini.com). It's a 10-minute hike (or €7 taxi ride) from the train station to the top of the old town. Readers get a free Cinque Terre info packet and a glass of the local sweet wine, *sciacchetrà,* when they check in—ask for it. The Steno has a tiny parking lot (free, but call to reserve a spot).

$$$ Albergo Pasquale is a modern, comfortable place, run by the same family as the Hotel Villa Steno (previous listing). It's just a few steps from the beach, boat dock, tunnel entrance to the new town, and train tracks. Noise is not a problem (same prices and welcome drink as Villa Steno; air-con, all rooms with sea view, Via Fegina 8, tel. 0187-817-550 or 0187-817-477, fax 0187-817-056, www.pasini.com, pasquale@pasini.com, Felicita and Marco).

$$$ Locanda il Maestrale rents six small, stylish rooms in a sophisticated and peaceful little inn. While renovated with all the modern comforts, it retains centuries-old character under frescoed ceilings. Its peaceful sun terrace overlooks the old town and Via Roma action (small Db-€100, Db-€130, suite-€170, less off-season, Via Roma 37, tel. 0187-817-013, mobile 338-4530-531, fax 0187-817-084, www.monterossonet.com, maestrale@monterossonet.com).

Two places, next door to each other on a quiet street, both push half-pension by bloating their B&B prices and offering dinner for just a few euros more. **$$$ Albergo Marina** has 25 decent rooms and a garden with lemon trees (Db-€100–130, €145 with optional dinner April–Oct, 5 percent discount with cash, elevator, air-con, free kayak and snorkel equipment, next door to Via Buranco 40, tel. & fax 0187-817-242 or 0187-817-613, www.hotelmarinacinqueterre.it, marina@cinqueterre.it). The not-as-nice **$$$ Albergo degli Amici** has 43 basic rooms (Db-€93–128, Db with optional half-pension-€185–213, no views from rooms, peaceful above-it-all view garden with lawn chairs, next door to Albergo Marina at Via Buranco 36, tel. 0187-817-544, fax 0187-817-424, www.hotelamici.it, amici@cinqueterre.it).

$$$ Hotel la Colonnina, a comfy, modern place with big rooms, is buried in the town's fragrant and sleepy back streets (Db-€115–125, cash only, air-con, elevator, great rooftop terrace, garden, Via Zuecca 6, tel. 0187-817-439, fax 0187-817-788, www.lacolonninacinqueterre.it, info@lacolonninacinqueterre.it, Paola). The hotel is in the old town by the train tracks, directly behind the statue of Garibaldi (take street to left of A Ca' du Sciensa one block up, hotel is to the right).

$$ Hotel Souvenir is Monterosso's cash-only backpacker's hotel. It has two buildings, each utilitarian but comfortable (one more stark than the other). The first is for students (S-€25, Sb-€30, D-€50, Db-€60, T-€75, no breakfast); the other is nicer and pricier, with a lounge and pleasant, leafy courtyard (Sb-€40, Db-€80, Tb-€120). Walk three blocks inland from the main old-town square to Via Gioberti 24 (tel. 0187-817-822, tel. & fax 0187-817-595, www.monterossonet.com, hotel_souvenir@yahoo.com).

$$ Albergo al Carugio is a simple, practical 10-room place in a big apartment-style building at the top of the old town. It's quiet, comfy-yet-forgettable, and run in an old-fashioned way (Db-€80 July–Aug, Db-€70 otherwise, Via Roma 100, tel. 0187-817-453).

$ Manuel's Guesthouse is a ramshackle place run by a ramshackle artist with five big, basic rooms and a grand view (Db-€50, less off-season, these discounted prices for Rick Steves' readers, cash only, honor-system beer and wine bar, €5/liter; in old town, up stepped lane, behind church at top of town, Via San Martino 39; tel. 328-842-6885 or 333-439-0809, www.manuelsguesthouse.com, send email to info@manuelsguesthouse.com).

In the New Town

Of these four, the first and last offer by far the best value for what you get—but they don't have a view. The middle two are tired, impersonal, and overpriced, cashing in on their seaside location, with varying levels of comfort.

$$$ A Cà du Gigante, despite its name, is a tiny yet classy refuge. About 100 yards from the beach (and surrounded by blocky apartments on a modern street), the interior is done with taste and modern comfort in mind (Db-€150, Db-suite €165, includes parking, air-con, Via IV Novembre 11, tel. 0187-817-401, fax 0187-817-375, www.ilgigantecinqueterre.it, gigante@ilgigantecinqueterre.it).

$$$ Hotel Baia (by-yah), overlooking the beach near the station, has high-ceilinged, dimly lit rooms, dark hallways, and impersonal staff. Of the hotel's 28 rooms, half have views. The best little two-chair view balconies are on top floors. Request a view room, since it's the same price (Db-€150, slow elevator, Via Fegina 88, tel. 0187-817-512, fax 0187-818-322, www.baiahotel.it, info@baiahotel.it).

$$$ Hotel Punta Mesco has 17 quiet, modern rooms without views, but 10 have little terraces (Db-€121, 5 percent discount with cash, air-con, free bike loan, free parking, exit right from station and take first right to Via Molinelli 35, tel. & fax 0187-817-495, www.hotelpuntamesco.it, info@hotelpuntamesco.it). For the price, it's the best comfort in town.

$$ Pensione Agavi has 10 bright, airy, tranquil, and quiet rooms, about half overlooking the beach near the big rock. This is not a place to party—it feels like an old hospital with narrow hallways (S-€40, Sb-€60, D-€80, Db-€100, no breakfast, cash only, refrigerators, turn left out of station to Fegina 30, tel. 0187-817-171, mobile 333-697-4071, fax 0187-818-264, www.paginegialle.it/hotelagavi, agavi@libero.it, spunky Hillary).

EATING

Ristorante Belvedere is *the* place for a good-value meal indoors or outdoors on the harborfront. Their *amfora bel vedere*—mixed seafood stew—is huge, and can easily be shared by up to four (€43). Share with your group and add pasta for a fine meal. It's energetically run by Fredrico and Roberto (daily 12:00–14:30 & 19:00–22:00, closed Tue off-season, on the harbor in the old town, tel. 0187-817-033).

L'Alta Marea offers special fish ravioli, the catch of the day, and huge crocks of fresh, steamed mussels. Young chef Marco cooks with charisma, while his wife, Anna, takes good care of the guests (Thu–Tue 12:00–15:00 & 18:30–22:00, open later in summer, closed Wed, Via Roma 54, tel. 0187-817-170). This place is quieter, buried in old town two blocks off the beach, and has covered tables out front for people-watching.

Ciak, a cut above its neighbors in elegance, is known for their three huge terra-cotta crocks for two, crammed with the day's catch and either accompanied by risotto or spaghetti, or swimming in a soup *(zuppa)*. Another popular choice is the seafood *antipasto* Lampara. Stroll a couple of paces past the outdoor tables up Via Roma to see what Ciak's got on the stove (Thu–Tue 12:00–14:00 & 19:00–21:30, closed Wed, tel. 0187-817-014).

Via Venti is a fun little trattoria, buried in an alley deep in the heart of the old town, where Papa Ettore creates imaginative seafood dishes using the day's catch and freshly-made pasta. Son Michele and Ilaria serve up delicate and savory gnocchi (tiny potato dumplings) with crab sauce, tender ravioli stuffed with fresh fish in a swordfish sauce, and unusual vegetarian items such as *risotto alle fragole* (strawberry risotto). There's nothing pretentious here...just good cooking, service, and price. From Piazza C. Colombo at the bottom of Via Roma, head down Via XX Settembre and follow it to the end to #32 (Fri–Wed 12:00–14:30 & 18:30–22:00, closed Thu, tel. 0187-818-347).

Miky is packed with locals who know their seafood and want to eat in a classy environment, but don't want to spend a fortune. For great food, this could be the best value in the entire Cinque Terre. It's clearly a family operation: Miky (dad), Simonetta (mom), and charming Sara (daughter) all work hard. All their pasta is "pizza pasta"—cooked normally but finished in a bowl that's encased in a thin pizza crust. They cook the concoction in a wood-fire oven to keep in the aroma. Miky's has the best wine list in the area, with most available by the glass if you ask (pastas-€10, *secondi*-€18, sweets-€5, Wed–Mon 12:00–15:00 & 19:00–23:00, closed Tue, reservations wise in summer, in the new town, 100 yards north of train station at Via Fegina 104, tel. 0187-817-608).

Light Meals, Take-Out Food, and Breakfast

Lots of shops and bakeries sell pizza and focaccia for an easy picnic at the beach or on the trail. At **Il Frantoio,** Simone makes tasty pizza to go or to munch perched on a stool (daily 9:00–14:00 & 16:00–19:30, just off Via Roma at Via Gioberti 1, tel. 0187-818-333).

Il Casello is the only place for a fun, light meal on a terrace overlooking the old town beach. With outdoor tables on a rocky outcrop—located between the old-town beaches—it's a good bet for a salad or sandwich (April–Sept daily 10:30–24:00, shorter hours outside June–Aug, closed Oct–March, tel. 0187-818-330).

BarDavi serves the best breakfast in town. They also make a €5 picnic box to go—ideal for the beach or for a hike. For a light lunch or dinner, try their €10 "international" buffet, or dine à la carte (see page 914).

TRANSPORTATION CONNECTIONS

Trains

The five towns of the Cinque Terre are on a pokey, milk-run train line (described in "Getting Around the Cinque Terre," page 872). Hourly trains connect each town with the others, La Spezia, and Genoa. While a few of these local trains go to more distant points (Milan or Pisa), it's much faster to change in La Spezia or Monterosso to a bigger train (local train info tel. 0187-817-458).

From La Spezia by Train to: Rome (10/day, 4 hrs), **Pisa** (hourly, 1 hr, direction: Livorno, Rome, Salerno, Naples, etc.), **Viareggio** (3–4/hr, 30–60 min), **Florence** (3/day direct, otherwise nearly hourly, 2.5 hrs or change in Pisa), **Milan** (hourly, 3 hrs direct or 4 hrs with change in Genoa), **Venice** (20/day, 5–7 hrs, 1–3 changes).

From Monterosso by Train to: Venice (8/day, 6–7 hrs, 1–3 changes), **Milan** (11/day, 3 hrs, change in Genoa), **Genoa** (hourly, 1.25 hrs), **Turin** (7/day, 3 hrs), **Pisa** (8/day, 1.5 hrs), **Sestri Levante** (hourly, 20–30 min, most trains to Genoa stop here), **La Spezia** (nearly hourly, 20 min), **Levanto** (nearly hourly, 6 min), **Santa Margherita Ligure** (hourly, 1 hr). For destinations in **France,** change trains in Genoa.

THE NETHERLANDS

AMSTERDAM

Amsterdam is a progressive way of life housed in Europe's most 17th-century city. Physically, it's built upon millions of pilings. But more than that, it's built on good living, cozy cafés, great art, street-corner jazz, stately history, and a spirit of live-and-let-live. It has 739,000 people and almost as many bikes. It also has more canals than Venice...and about as many tourists.

During its Golden Age in the 1600s, Amsterdam was the world's richest city, an international sea-trading port, and the cradle of capitalism. Wealthy, democratic burghers built a planned city of canals lined with trees and townhouses topped with fancy gables. Immigrants, Jews, outcasts, and political rebels were drawn here by its tolerant atmosphere, while painters such as young Rembrandt captured that atmosphere on canvas.

The Dutch are unique. They may be the world's most handsome people—tall, healthy, and with good posture—and the most open, honest, and refreshingly blunt. They like to laugh. As connoisseurs of world culture, they appreciate Rembrandt paintings, Indonesian food, and the latest French film—but with an unsnooty, blue-jeans attitude.

Approach Amsterdam as an ethnologist observing a strange culture. Stroll through any neighborhood and see things that are commonplace here but rarely found elsewhere. Carillons chime quaintly in neighborhoods selling sex, as young professionals smoke pot with impunity next to old ladies in bonnets selling flowers. Observe the neighborhood's "social control," where an elderly man feels safe in his home knowing he's being watched by the prostitutes next door.

Be warned: Amsterdam, a bold experiment in freedom, may

box your Puritan ears. Take in all of it, then pause to watch the sunset—at 10:00 p.m. during summer—and see the Golden Age reflected in a quiet canal.

Planning Your Time

Amsterdam is worth a full day of sightseeing on even the busiest itinerary. While the city has a couple of must-see museums, its best attraction is its own carefree ambience. The city's a joy on foot—and a breezier and faster delight by bike.

Amsterdam Overview

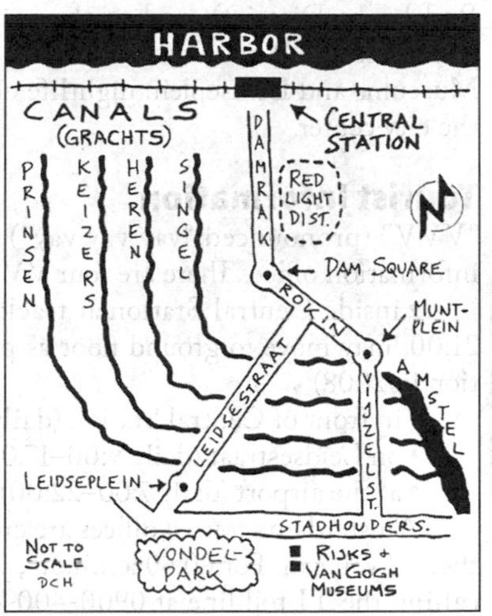

In the morning, see the city's two great art museums: the Van Gogh and the Rijksmuseum (cafeteria lunch). Walk from the museums to the Singel canal flower market, then take a relaxing hour-long, round-trip canal cruise from the dock at Spui (see "Tours," below). After the cruise, stroll through the peaceful Begijnhof courtyard and tour the nearby Amsterdam History Museum. Visiting the Anne Frank House after 18:00 will save you an hour in line (last entry is 20:30, or 18:30 Sept–March). Have a memorable dinner: try Dutch pancakes or a *rijsttafel*—an Indonesian smorgasbord.

On a balmy evening, Amsterdam has a Greek-island ambience. Stroll through the Jordaan neighborhood for the idyllic side of town and wander down Leidsestraat to Leidseplein for the roaring café and people scene. Tour the Red Light District while you're at it.

With extra time: With two days in Holland, I'd side-trip by bike, bus, or train to an open-air folk museum and visit Edam or Haarlem. With a third day, I'd do the other great Amsterdam museums.

ORIENTATION

(area code: 020)

Amsterdam's Central Train Station, on the north edge of the city, is your starting point, with the TI, bike rental, and trams branching out to all points. Damrak is the main north–south axis, connecting

Central Station with Dam Square (people-watching and hangout center) and its Royal Palace. From this main street, the city spreads out like a fan, with 90 islands, hundreds of bridges, and a series of concentric canals—named Herengracht (Gentleman's Canal), Keizersgracht (Emperor's Canal), and Prinsengracht (Prince's Canal)—that were laid out in the 17th century, Holland's Golden Age. Amsterdam's major sights are within walking distance of Dam Square.

To the east of Damrak is the oldest part of the city (today's Red Light District), and to the west is the newer part, where you'll find the Anne Frank House and the Jordaan neighborhood. Museums and Leidseplein nightlife cluster at the southern edge of the city center.

Tourist Information

"VVV" (pronounced "vay vay vay") is Dutch for "TI," a tourist information office. There are four VVV offices in Amsterdam:

• inside Central Station at track 2b (daily 8:00–20:00, until 21:00, may move to ground floor as part of train station construction in 2008)

• in front of Central Station (daily 9:00–17:00, most crowded)

• on Leidsestraat (daily 9:00–17:00, less crowded)

• at the airport (daily 7:00–22:00).

Amsterdam's tourist offices are crowded and inefficient—avoid them if you can. For €0.60 a minute, you can save yourself a trip by calling the TI toll line at 0900-400-4040 (Mon–Fri 9:00–17:00). Or, if you're staying in nearby Haarlem, ask the helpful, friendly, and rarely crowded Haarlem TI your Amsterdam questions, and pick up brochures there (see page 969).

At Amsterdam's TIs, consider buying a city map (€2) and any of the walking-tour brochures (€1.50 each, including *Discovery Tour Through the Center*, *The Former Jewish Quarter*, and *Walks Through Jordaan*). For entertainment, pick up the €2 *Day by Day* calendar; for additional entertainment ideas, see the free papers listed later in this chapter (under "Helpful Hints") and the Nightlife section (see page 946).

At Amsterdam's Central Station, GWK Change has hotel reservation windows whose clerks sell local and international phone cards and city maps (€2) and can answer basic tourist questions, with shorter lines (in west tunnel, at right end of station as you leave platform, tel. 020/627-2731).

Don't use the TI or GWK to book a room; you'll pay €5 per person and your host loses 13 percent—meaning you'll likely be charged a higher rate. The phone system is easy, everyone speaks English, and the listings in this book are a better value than the potluck booking you'd get from the TI.

***I amsterdam* Card:** This pricey card includes free entry to most city sights, discounts on other sights and attractions, two free canal boat tours, and unlimited use of the trams, buses, and metro (€33/24 hrs, €43/48 hrs, €53/72 hrs, sold at any TI, www.iamsterdamcard.com). While the pass covers most major Amsterdam museums—including the Van Gogh and the Rijksmuseum (but not the Anne Frank House)—it won't allow you to skip the lines at these popular sights. All but the most die-hard sightseers will get a better deal by buying individual or combo-tickets to various sights plus a transportation pass (see page 926). While these cards are sold at the TI, you can avoid the line by buying them at the GVB transit office across from Central Station.

Tourist Information Online: Visit www.visitamsterdam.nl (Amsterdam Tourism Board), www.amsterdam.nl (City of Amsterdam), and www.holland.com (Netherlands Board of Tourism).

Arrival in Amsterdam

By Train: Amsterdam swings, and the hinge that connects it to the world is its aptly named Central (Centraal) Station. Through 2010, expect a chaotic construction zone due to the station being renovated. The international ticket office should be at track 2, and luggage lockers are at the far east end of the building (from €5.70/24 hrs, daily 7:00–23:00, ID required).

Walk out the door of the station, and you're in the heart of the city. You'll nearly trip over trams ready to take you anywhere your feet won't. Straight ahead is Damrak street, leading to Dam Square. With your back to the entrance of the station, the TI and GVB public-transit offices are just ahead to your left. On your right is a vast, multistory bike garage, and bike rentals are to the far left as you exit.

By Plane: For details on getting from Schiphol Airport into downtown Amsterdam, see page 967.

Helpful Hints

Theft Alert: Tourists are considered green and rich, and the city has more than its share of hungry thieves—especially on trams and at the many hostels. Wear your money belt.

Emergency Telephone Number: Throughout the Netherlands, dial 112.

Street Smarts: Most canals are lined by streets with the same name. When walking around town, beware of the silent transportation—trams and bicycles. (Don't walk on tram tracks or pink/maroon bicycle paths.)

Sightseeing Strategies: To beat the lines at Amsterdam's most popular sights, plan ahead. You can bypass the main ticket-buyers' line at the Van Gogh Museum by buying an online ticket before you go (see page 932 for details). Friday night is a great time to visit the Van Gogh and the Rijks, which are both open until 22:00 to far smaller crowds. The Anne Frank House is open late every day—go in the early evening to escape the tourist crush (closes earlier in winter, see page 935 for details).

Many of Amsterdam's sights are currently undergoing renovations. Even if a sight is listed as reopening some time in 2008, always call to confirm.

Cash Only: Thrifty Dutch merchants hate paying fees to the credit-card companies; expect to pay cash in unexpected places, including post offices, grocery stores, train station windows, and some museums.

Shop Hours: Most shops are open Tuesday through Saturday from 10:00 to 18:00, and Sunday and Monday from 12:00 to 18:00. Some shops stay open later (21:00) on Thursdays. Supermarkets are generally open Monday through Saturday from 8:00 to 20:00, and are closed on Sundays.

Internet Access: It's easy at cafés all over town. The huge, impersonal **easyInternetcafé** near the Central Station offers hundreds of terminals with fast, cheap access (€2/hr, one block in front of the train station at Damrak 33, daily 10:00–20:00). The city's public library, **Openbare Bibliotheek Amsterdam,** has a central branch with free Internet access (18 terminals), cheap eats (€1.50 sandwiches and juice), and international newspapers (Mon 13:00–21:00, Tue–Thu 10:00–21:00, Fri 10:00–19:00, Sat 10:00–17:00, closed Sun, Prinsengracht 587, www.oba.nl). "Coffeeshops," which sell marijuana, usually also offer Internet access—letting you surf the Net with a special bravado.

English Bookstores: For fiction and guidebooks—including mine—try the **American Book Center** at Kalverstraat 125 (Mon–Sat 10:00–20:00, Sun 11:00–18:30, tel. 020/625-5537). Nearby, at Kalverstraat 185, **Waterstone's Booksellers** also sells British newspapers (Mon–Sat 10:00–20:00, Thu until 21:00, Sun 11:00–18:00, tel. 020/638-3821). Or try the huge and helpful **Scheltema,** near the Leidsestraat at Koningsplein 20 (Mon–Sat 10:00–18:00, Thu until 21:00, Sun 12:00–18:00; lots of English novels, guidebooks, and maps).

Free Papers: If you're interested in cutting-edge art, movies, and concerts (hip-hop, jazz, classical), pick up the *Amsterdam Weekly,* a free local English-language paper that's published every Wednesday. It's available at the bookstores listed above.

Entertainment: Pick up the *Day by Day* calendar at any TI (€2), call the Last Minute Ticket Shop (tickets for theater, classical music, and major rock shows, tel. 0900-0191, costs €0.40/min, www.lastminuteticketshop.nl), and check out the "Nightlife" section of this chapter (page 946).

Maps: The free and cheap tourist maps can be confusing, except for *Amsterdam Museums: Guide to 37 Museums* (includes tram info and stops, ask for it at the info desk at the big museums, such as the Van Gogh). If you want to buy a fancier map, consider paying a bit more (about €2) for a top-notch map. I like the *Carto Studio Centrumkaart Amsterdam* or, better yet, *Amsterdam: Go Where the Locals Go* by Amsterdam Anything.

Pharmacy: The shop named **DA** (Dienstdoende Apotheek) has all the basics—shampoo and toothpaste—as well as a pharmacy counter hidden in the back (Mon–Sat 9:00–22:00, Sun 11:00–22:00, Leidsestraat 74–76 near where it meets Keizersgracht, tel. 020/627-5351).

Laundry: Try **Clean Brothers Wasserij** in the Jordaan (daily 8:00–20:00 for €6 self-service, €8 drop-off—ready in an hour—Mon–Fri 9:00–17:00, Sat 9:00–12:00, no drop-off Sun, Westerstraat 26, one block from Prinsengracht, tel. 020/627-9888) or **Powders** near Leidseplein (daily 8:00–22:00, €6.50 self-service, €8.50 drop-off, Kerkstraat 56, one block south of Leidsestraat).

Holidays: Every year, **Queen's Day** (*Koninginnedag*, April 30) and **Gay Pride** (generally in June and August) bring crowds, fuller hotels, and higher room prices.

Amsterdam

Getting Around Amsterdam

The helpful GVB public-transit information office is in front of the Central Train Station (next to TI, daily 8:00–21:00, good detailed info on www.gvb.nl). Its free, multilingual *Public Transport Amsterdam Tourist Guide* includes a transit map and explains ticket options and tram connections to all the sights. In keeping with the Dutch mission to automate life, they'll tack on a €0.50 penalty if you buy your transit tickets from a human ticket seller, rather than from a machine. If you're stressed, jetlagged, or otherwise cranky, it's worth the fee for the personal assistance; ask which platform your train leaves from while you're at the ticket window.

By Bus, Tram, and Metro: Trams #2 *(Nieuw Sloten)* and #5 *(A'veen Binnenhof)* travel the north–south axis from Central Station to Dam Square to Leidseplein to Museumplein. Tram #1 (marked *Osdorp*) also runs to Leidseplein. At Central Station, these three trams depart from the west side of the Stationsplein (with the station behind you, the shelters for these lines are in front of a row of shops). Tram #14—which doesn't connect to Central Station—goes east–west (Westerkerk–Dam Square–Muntplein–Waterlooplein–Plantage). If you get lost in Amsterdam, 10 of the city's 17 trams take you back to Central Station.

The metro (underground train) is used mostly for commuting to the suburbs, but it does connect Central Station with some sights east of Damrak (Nieuwmarkt–Waterlooplein–Weesperplein).

You have various ticket options:

- **Individual tickets** cost €1.60 and give you an hour on the buses, trams, and metro system (on trams and buses, pay as you board; for the metro, buy tickets from machines).
- The **24-hour** (€6.30), **48-hour** (€10), or **72-hour** (€13) **tickets** give you unlimited transportation on Amsterdam's (and the Netherlands') public-transit network. Buy them at the GVB public-transit office (all versions available), at any TI, or as you board (24-hour version only costs €0.50 extra).
- **Strip tickets** *(strippenkaart)*, cheaper than individual tickets, are good on buses, trams, and the metro in Amsterdam and anywhere in the Netherlands. The further you go, the more strips you'll use: Any downtown ride in Amsterdam costs two strips (good for one hour of transfers). A card with 15 strips costs €6.70 (you can share them with your partner). Shorter strip tickets (2, 3, and 8) are sold on some buses and trams, but the per-strip cost is about double. It's cheapest to buy the 15-strip tickets at the GVB public-transit office, machines at the train station, bookstores, post offices, and airport, or at tobacco shops throughout the country. You can also buy them (for a little more) directly from the driver.

  Armed with your *strippenkaart*, board the tram (you may have to press a button to open the doors) and have your strip ticket stamped by a conductor/driver or a machine. For the machine, fold over the number of strips you need (2 for rides in central Amsterdam), stick that end in the slot, and it will stamp the time. To transfer (good for one hour), just show the conductor/driver your stamped *strippenkaart*.
- Along with its sightseeing perks, the ***I amsterdam* Card** offers unlimited use of the tram, bus, and metro for its duration (24, 48, or 72 hours—see above).

By Foot: The longest walk a tourist would take is an hour from Central Station to the Rijksmuseum. Watch out for silent but potentially painful bikes, trams, and crotch-high curb posts.

By Bike: Everyone—bank managers, students, pizza delivery boys, and police—uses this mode of transport. It's *the* smart way to travel in a city where 40 percent of all traffic rolls on two wheels. You'll get around town by bike faster than you can by taxi. On my last visit, I rented a bike for five days, chained it up outside my hotel, and enjoyed wonderful mobility. I highly encourage this for anyone who wants to get maximum fun per hour in Amsterdam. One-speed bikes, with "*brrringing*" bells, rent for about €8–10 per day (cheaper for longer periods) at any number of places—hotels can send you to the nearest spot.

MacBike, with 900 bikes and expanding, is the bike-rental powerhouse. It has a huge and efficient outlet at Central Station (€6/3 hrs, €8.50/24 hrs, more for three gears, no helmets, €50 deposit plus passport or credit-card imprint, daily 9:00–17:45, at east end of station—on the left as you're leaving, by the buses, tel. 020/624-8391, can reserve online, www.macbike.nl). They have two smaller, satellite stations at Leidseplein (Weteringschans 2, in Max Euweplein, tel. 020/528-7688) and Waterlooplein (Mr. Visserplein 2, tel. 020/620-0985). Return your bike to the station where you rented it. MacBike sells several pamphlets outlining bike tours in and around Amsterdam for €1.

Frederic Rent-a-Bike, near the Anne Frank House, has quality bikes and a helpful staff (€10/24 hrs, daily 9:00–18:00, Brouwersgracht 78, tel. 020/624-5509, www.frederic.nl).

No one wears helmets. For safety: Use arm signals, follow the bike-only traffic signals, stay in the obvious and omnipresent bike lanes, yield to traffic on the right, and fear oncoming trams and tram tracks. Carefully cross tram tracks at a perpendicular angle to avoid catching your tire in the rut. Warning: Police ticket bikers as drivers. Obey all traffic signals, and walk your bike through pedestrian zones. Fines for biking through pedestrian zones are reportedly €300.

By Boat: While the city is great on foot or bike, another option is the **Museum Boat,** which shuttles tourists from sight to sight on an all-day ticket. Tickets cost €15 (includes museum discounts). Sales booths in front of Central Station (and the boats) offer handy, free brochures with museum times and admission prices. The narrated boat ride takes two hours if you don't get off (about hourly, 12 stops, recorded narration, departures daily 10:00–17:00, discounted after 13:00 to €12.50, tel. 020/530-1090).

The nearby and similar **Canal Bus** offers 14 stops on three different boat routes (€17, ticket is valid until 12:00 the following day, departures daily 10:00–18:00, until 22:00 in summer, tel. 020/623-9886, www.canal.nl).

If you're looking for a floating nonstop tour, the regular canal tour boats (without the stops) give more information, cover more ground, and cost less (see "Tours," below). For do-it-yourself canal tours and lots of exercise, Canal Bus also rents "canal bikes" (a.k.a. paddleboats) near the Anne Frank House and Rijksmuseum (€8/hr per person, daily July–Aug 10:00–21:30, Sept–June 10:00–18:00).

By Taxi: Amsterdam's taxis are expensive (€3.50 drop, €2 per kilometer). You can wave them down, find a rare taxi stand, or call one (tel. 020/677-7777). Given the fine tram system, taxis are rarely a good value. You'll also see **bike taxis,** particularly near Dam Square and Leidseplein. Negotiate a rate for the trip before you board (no meter) and they'll wheel you wherever you want to go (€10/30 min, no surcharge for baggage or extra weight, sample fare from Leidseplein to Anne Frank House: about €6).

By Car: Forget it—all you'll find are frustrating one-way streets, terrible parking, and meter maids with a passion for booting cars wrongly parked.

TOURS

▲▲Canal Boat Tours—These long, low, tourist-laden boats leave continually from several docks around the town for a relaxing, if uninspiring, one-hour introduction to the city (with recorded headphone commentary). Select a boat tour for convenience based on the starting point, or if a particular tour is free and included with your *I amsterdam* Card (it covers Rederij Noord-Zuid and Holland International boats). Choose from one of these three companies:

Rondvaart Kooij is cheapest, and has the boats I prefer—all the seats face forward (€7, 4/hr in summer 10:00–22:00, 2/hr in winter 10:00–17:00, at corner of Spui and Rokin streets, about 10 min from Dam Square, tel. 020/623-3810, www.rederijkooij.nl).

Rederij Noord-Zuid departs from near Leidseplein (€10, 2/hr April–Oct 10:00–18:00, hourly Nov–March 10:00–17:00, tel. 020/679-1370, www.canal-cruises.nl).

Holland International offers a standard one-hour trip and a variety of longer tours (€10 60-min tour with recorded commentary, €15 90-min tour with live guide, 3/hr mid-March–Oct 9:00–22:00, 2/hr Nov–mid-March 10:00–18:00, blue boats depart from in front of Central Station, tel. 020/625-3035).

No fishing allowed—but bring your camera. Some prefer to cruise at night, when the bridges are illuminated.

Red Light District Tours—You have two walking-tour options for seeing Amsterdam's most infamous neighborhood with a guide.

Randy Roy's Red Light Tours consists of one expat American woman, Kimberley. She lived in the Red Light District for years, and she gives fun, casual, yet informative 90-minute walks through this fascinating and eye-popping neighborhood. While the actual information is light, you'll walk through various porn and drug shops and have an expert to answer your questions (€12.50 includes a drink in a colorful bar at the end, nightly at 20:00, Fri and Sat 22:00 tours meet in front of Victoria Hotel—in front of Central Station, mobile 06-4185-3288—call to reserve, www.randyroysredlighttours.com, kimberley@randyroysredlighttours.com).

Zoom Amsterdam Citywalk starts at a café in the Tower of Tears (located across from Central Station, to the southwest), where you listen to an initial 30-minute spiel about the history of the city. Then you'll hit the streets for another two hours to find out the complicated story behind the Red Light District, including some fascinating, locals-only info (such as the scams that unscrupulous bar owners use on the many young, male Brits who flock here). If you're curious about the area but would rather explore with a group, Zoom Amsterdam is a good way to go (€15, daily April–Oct at 17:00; book ahead at VVV, through hotel, or by calling 020/623-6302; www.zoomamsterdam.com, info@zoomamsterdam.com).

Bike Tours—The **Yellow Bike Guided Tours** company offers a three-hour city tour (€19, April–Oct Sun–Fri at 9:30 and 13:00, Sat at 9:30 and 14:00) and a six-hour, 22-mile tour of the countryside (€25, April–Oct daily at 11:00, both tours leave from Nieuwezijds Kolk 29, three blocks from Central Station, tel. 020/620-6940, www.yellowbike.nl). If you take their tour, you can rent the bike for the rest of the day at a discount (€50 deposit and passport required). **MacBike** also runs city bike tours (€12.50, Thu–Sun at 14:00, listed above).

Wetlands Safari, Nature Canoe Tours near Amsterdam—If you'd like to get some exercise and a dose of the *polder* country and village life, consider this five-hour tour. Majel Tromp, a friendly villager who speaks great English, takes groups limited to 15 people. The program: Meet at the VVV tourist information office outside Central Station at 9:30, catch a public bus, stop for coffee, take a 3.5-hour canoe trip (2–3 people per canoe) with several stops, tour a village by canoe, munch a rural canalside picnic lunch (included), then canoe and bus back into the big city by 14:30 (€33, May–mid-Sept Mon–Fri, reservations required, tel. 020/686-3445, mobile 06-5355-2669, www.wetlandssafari.nl, info@wetlandssafari.nl).

Adam's Apple Tours—This walking tour offers a two-hour, English-only look at the historic roots of Amsterdam. You'll have a small group and a caring guide, starting off at Central Station and ending up at Dam Square (€22.50; May–Sept Fri–Sun at 10:00, 12:30, and 15:00; call 020/616-7867 to confirm times and book, www.adamsapple.nl, Frank).

Private Guide—**Ab Walet** is a likeable, hardworking, and knowledgeable local guide who enjoys personalizing tours for Americans interested in knowing his city. He specializes in history and architecture, and exudes a passion for Amsterdam (€40/2 hrs, €80/4 hrs, for small groups of up to four people, on foot or by bike, tel. 020/671-2588, mobile 06-2069-7882, abwalet@yahoo.com). Ab also can take travelers to nearby towns.

Do-It-Yourself Bike Tour of Amsterdam—A day enjoying the bridges, bike lanes, and sleepy, off-the-beaten-path canals on your own one-speed is an essential Amsterdam experience. The real joys of Europe's best-preserved 17th-century city are the countless intimate glimpses it offers: the laid-back locals sunning on their porches under elegant gables, rusted bikes that look as if they've been lashed to the same lamppost since the 1960s, wasted hedonists planted on canalside benches, and happy sailors permanently moored, but still manning the deck.

For a good day trip, rent a bike at Central Station (see "By Bike" on page 926). Head west down Haarlemmerstraat, working your wide-eyed way down the Prinsengracht (drop into Café 't Papeneiland at Prinsengracht 2) and detouring through the small, gentrified streets of the Jordaan neighborhood before popping out at Westerkerk under the tallest spire in the city.

Pedal south to the lush and peaceful Vondelpark, then cut back through the center of town (Leidseplein to the Mint Tower, along Rokin street to Dam Square). From there, cruise the Red Light District, following Oudezijds Voorburgwal past the Old Church (Oude Kerk) to Zeedijk street, and return to the train station.

Then, you can escape into the countryside by hopping on the free ferry behind Central Station. In five minutes, Amsterdam will be gone, and you'll be rolling through your very own Dutch painting (get the €1 *Great Waterland Bicycle Tour* brochure from MacBike rental shop, described on page 927).

Prinsengracht via de Opstapper—For a quick, do-it-yourself public-bus tour along scenic Prince's Canal (Prinsengracht), catch Amsterdam's cute little Opstapper minibus. It arcs along the city's longest canal, offering clever budget travelers a very cheap and fun 20-minute experience that's faster than a touristy canal tour. The scenic bus ride goes where normal big buses can't fit (along the bumpy and cobbled canalside lanes), giving you a delightful look at the workaday city—without a tourist in sight. The high ride, comfortable seats, and big windows show you Amsterdam well. Grab a seat in the back for the best view.

From the train station, the minibus passes characteristic cafés in the Jordaan district, countless houseboats, and the whole gamut of gables (under a parade of leaning, Golden Age buildings complete with all the hooks and pulleys). Rolling along the Prinsengracht, you'll see the long line at the Anne Frank House just before the towering Westerkerk. You pass within a block of the thriving Leidseplein and Rijksmuseum before crossing the Amstel River to finish at the Waterlooplein flea market (near Rembrandt's House, Gassan Diamonds, and the metro station).

There are no stops—people just wave the bus down. The route follows the outside of the canal counterclockwise and returns clockwise along the inside. Any individual ticket is good for an hour. If you see something fun, just jump out—there's another bus in 10 minutes (€1.60 or 2 strips, 6/hr, 9 seats, Mon–Sat 7:30–18:30,

Amsterdam

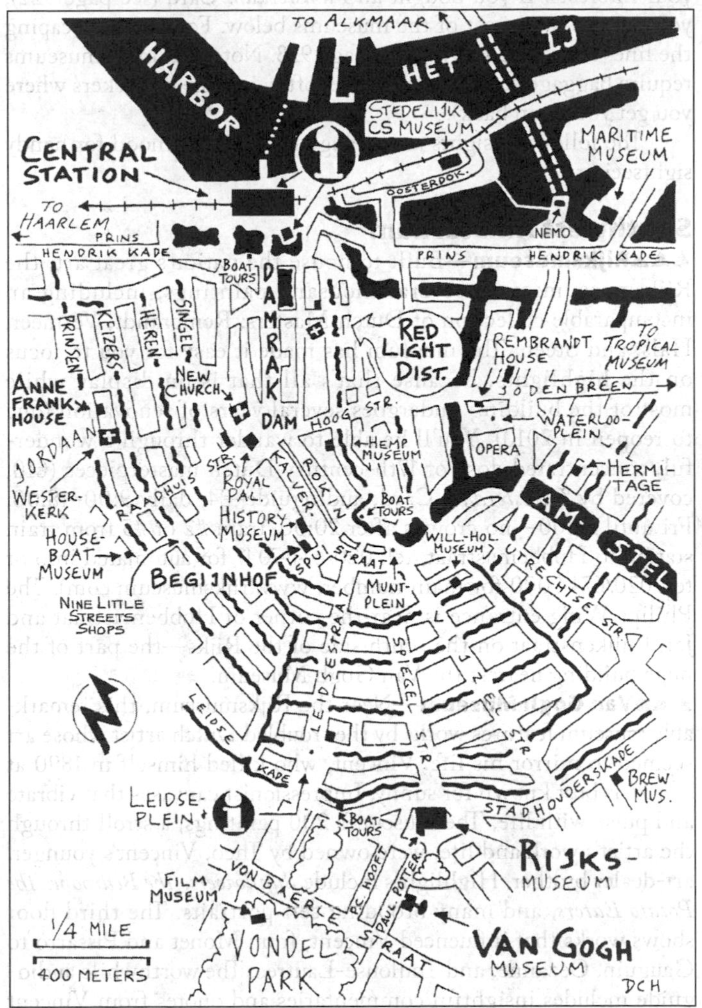

not Sun, can be muggy on hot days). Buses depart from a tiny lot in front of Victoria Hotel, across from Central Station, and finish at the Waterlooplein metro station (with subway trains coming every 2 min, returning you to Central Station in 3 min).

SIGHTS

One of Amsterdam's delights is that it has perhaps more small specialty museums than any other city its size. From houseboats to sex, from marijuana to Old Masters, you can find a museum to suit your interests. If you bought an *I amsterdam* Card (see page 922), you can use it at most of the museums below. For tips on escaping the lines at crowded sights, see page 923. Note that most museums require baggage check (usually free, often in coin-op lockers where you get your coin back).

The following sights are arranged by neighborhood for handy sightseeing.

Southwest Amsterdam

▲▲▲Rijksmuseum—Built to house the nation's great art, the Rijksmuseum owns several thousand paintings, including an incomparable collection of Dutch Masters: Rembrandt, Vermeer, Hals, and Steen. The museum has made it easy for you to focus on the highlights, because that's all that is on display while most of the building undergoes several years of renovation (due to reopen in 2010). You'll be able to wander through a wonderful, concentrated dose of 17th-century Dutch masterpieces (€10, covered by *I amsterdam* Card, audioguide-€4, daily 9:00–18:00, Fri until 22:00—no crowds after 20:00, tram #2 or #5 from train station to Hobbemastraat, tel. 020/674-7047 for automated info or tel. 020/674-7000 for main number, www.rijksmuseum.com). The Philips Wing entrance is near the corner of Hobbemastraat and Jan Luijkenstraat on the south side of the Rijks—the part of the huge building nearest the Van Gogh Museum.

▲▲▲Van Gogh Museum—Near the Rijksmuseum, this remarkable museum features works by the troubled Dutch artist whose art seemed to mirror his life. Vincent, who killed himself in 1890 at age 37, is best known for sunny, Impressionist canvases that vibrate and pulse with life. The museum's 200 paintings, a stroll through the artist's work and life, were owned by Theo, Vincent's younger, art-dealer brother. Highlights include *Sunflowers, The Bedroom, The Potato Eaters,* and many brooding self-portraits. The third floor shows works that influenced Vincent, from Monet and Pissarro to Gauguin, Cézanne, and Toulouse-Lautrec. The worthwhile audioguide includes insightful commentaries and quotes from Vincent himself. Temporary exhibitions fill the new wing, down the escalator from the ground floor lobby (€10, covered by *I amsterdam* Card, audioguide-€5, daily 10:00–18:00, Fri until 22:00—with no crowds in evening, Paulus Potterstraat 7, tel. 020/570-5200, www.vangoghmuseum.nl).

▲Museumplein—Bordered by the Rijks and Van Gogh museums and the Concertgebouw (classical music hall), this park-like square is interesting even to art-haters. Amsterdam's best acoustics are found underneath the Rijksmuseum, where street musicians perform everything from chamber music to Mongolian throat singing. Mimes, human statues, and crafts booths dot the square.

Southwest Amsterdam

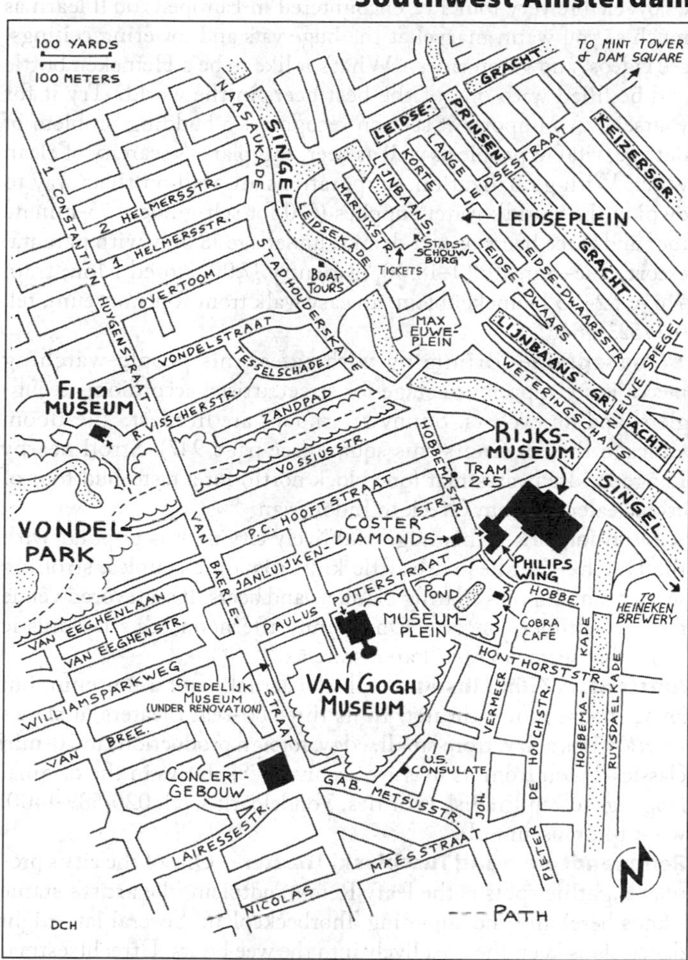

Skateboarders careen across a concrete tube, while locals enjoy a park bench or a coffee at the Cobra Café.

Nearby is **Coster Diamonds,** a handy place to see a diamond-cutting and polishing demo (free and interesting 30-min tours on request followed by sales pitch, popular for decades with tour groups, prices marked up to include tour guide kickbacks, daily 9:00–17:00, 2 Paulus Potterstraat, www.costerdiamonds.com). The tour at Gassan Diamonds is better (see "Southeast Amsterdam," later in this chapter), but Coster is convenient to the Museumplein scene.

▲Heineken Brewery—The leading Dutch beer is no longer brewed here, but this old brewery now welcomes visitors to a slick and entertaining beer-appreciation experience. It's the most enjoyable brewery tour I've encountered in Europe. You'll learn as much as you want, marvel at the huge vats and towering ceilings, see videos, and go on rides. "What's it like to be a Heineken bottle and be filled with one of the best beers in the world? Try it for yourself." An important section recognizes a budding problem of our age, vital to people as well as beer: this planet's scarcity of clean water. With globalization, corporations are well on their way to owning the world's water supplies (€10 for self-guided, 75-minute tour and three beers or soft drinks; under age 18 only with parental escort, Tue–Sun 10:00–18:00, last entry 17:00, closed Mon, tram #16 or #24 to Heinekenplein, an easy walk from Rijksmuseum, tel. 020/523-9666).

▲Leidseplein—Brimming with cafés, this people-watching mecca is an impromptu stage for street artists, accordionists, jugglers, and unicyclists. Sunny afternoons are liveliest. The Boom Chicago theater fronts this square (see page 947). Stroll nearby Lange Leidsedwarsstraat (one block north) for a taste-bud tour of ethnic eateries, from Greek to Indonesian.

▲▲Vondelpark—This huge and lively city park is popular with the Dutch—families with little kids, romantic couples, strolling seniors, and hippies sharing blankets and beers. It's a favored venue for free summer concerts. On a sunny afternoon, it's a hedonistic scene that seems to say, "Parents...relax."

Amsterdam Film Museum—This is actually not a museum, but an art-house movie theater. In its three 80-seat theaters, it shows several films a day, from small, edgy, foreign productions to 70-mm classics drawn from its massive archives (€8, always in the original language, often English subtitles, Vondelpark 3, tel. 020/589-1400, www.filmmuseum.nl).

Rembrandtplein and Tuschinski Theater—One of the city's premier nightlife spots is the leafy Rembrandtplein (the artist's statue stands here) and the adjoining Thorbeckeplein. Several late-night dance clubs keep the area lively into the wee hours. Utrechtsestraat is lined with upscale shops and restaurants.

The **Tuschinski Theater,** a movie palace from the 1920s (a half-block from Rembrandtplein down Reguliersbreestraat), glitters inside and out. Still a working theater, it's a delightful old place to see first-run movies. The exterior is an interesting hybrid of styles, forcing the round peg of Art Nouveau into the square hole of Art Deco. The stone-and-tile facade features stripped-down, functional Art Deco squares and rectangles, but is ornamented with Art Nouveau elements—Tiffany-style windows, garlands, curvy iron lamps, Egyptian pharaohs, and exotic gold lettering over the door. Inside (lobby is free), the sumptuous decor features red carpets, nymphs on the walls, and semi-abstract designs. Grab a seat in the lobby and watch the ceiling morph (Reguliersbreestraat 26–28).

Houseboat Museum (Woonbootmuseum)—In the 1930s, modern cargo ships came into widespread use—making small, sail-powered cargo boats obsolete. In danger of extinction, these little vessels found new life as houseboats lining the canals of Amsterdam. Today, 2,500 such boats—their cargo holds turned into classy, comfortable living rooms—are called home by locals. For a peek into this *gezellig* (cozy) world, visit this tiny museum. Captain Vincent enjoys showing visitors around the houseboat, which feels lived-in because, until 1997, it was (€3, covered by *I amsterdam* Card, March–Oct Tue–Sun 11:00–17:00, closed Mon; Nov–Feb Fri–Sun 11:00–17:00, closed Mon–Thu and most of Jan in 2008; on Prinsengracht, opposite #296 facing Elandsgracht, tel. 020/427-0750, www.houseboatmuseum.nl).

Central Amsterdam, near Dam Square

▲▲▲Anne Frank House—A pilgrimage for many, this house offers a fascinating look at the hideaway of young Anne during the Nazi occupation of the Netherlands. Anne, her parents, an older sister, and four others spent a little more than two years in a "Secret Annex" behind her father's business. While in hiding, 13-year-old Anne kept a diary chronicling her extraordinary experience. Acting on a tip, the Nazis arrested them in August 1944 and sent the group to concentration camps in Poland and Germany. Anne and her sister died of typhus in March 1945, only weeks before their camp was liberated. Of the eight inhabitants of the Secret Annex, only Anne's father, Otto Frank, survived. He returned to Amsterdam and arranged for his daughter's diary to be published in 1947. It was followed by many translations, a play, and a movie.

Pick up the English pamphlet at the door. The exhibit offers thorough coverage of the Frank family, the diary, the stories of others who hid, and the Holocaust. In summer, skip the hour-long daytime lines by arriving after 18:00 (last entry is 20:30) and visit after dinner (€7.50, not covered by *I amsterdam* Card, daily March 15–Sept 14 9:00–21:00, Sept 15–March 14 9:00–19:00, closed for Yom Kippur—October 9 in 2008, last entry 30 min before closing, strict, and baggage check required for large bags, Prinsengracht 267, near Westerkerk, tel. 020/556-7100, www.annefrank.org).

For an interesting glimpse of Holland under the Nazis, rent the powerful movie *Soldier of Orange* before you leave home.

Westerkerk—Near the Anne Frank House, this landmark church (free, generally open April–Sept Mon–Sat 10:00–15:00, closed Sun) has a barren interior, Rembrandt's body buried somewhere under the pews, and Amsterdam's tallest steeple.

The tower—which closed unexpectedly for renovation in 2006, but should be open by the time you read this book—can be seen by tour only and offers a grand city view. The tour guide,

Central Amsterdam

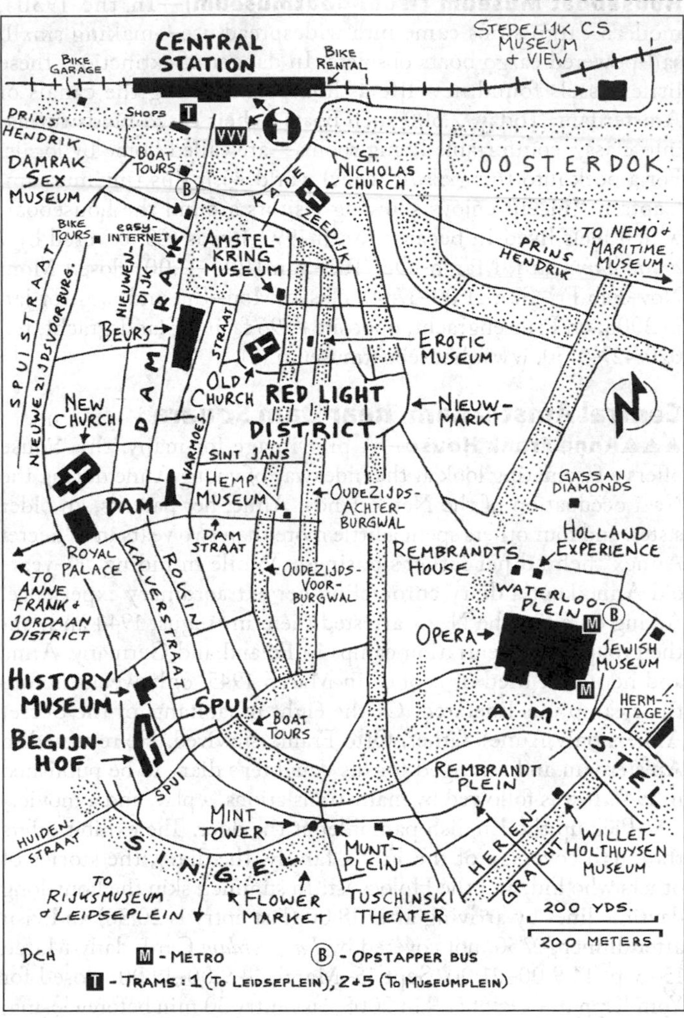

who speaks in English and Dutch, tells of the church and its carillon. Only five people are allowed at a time, so lines can be long (€5, 30 min, departures on the half hour, April–Sept Mon–Sat 10:00–17:30, last tour leaves at 17:30, closed Sun and Oct–March, call 020/624-7766 to confirm that it's open).

Royal Palace (Koninklijk Huis)—The palace, which should reopen in early 2008, is right on Dam Square. It was built as a lavish City Hall for Amsterdam, when the country was a proud new republic and Amsterdam was the richest city on the planet—awash in profit from trade. When constructed in 1648, this building was one of

Europe's finest, with a sumptuous interior. Today, it's the official (but not actual) residence of the queen (tel. 020/620-4060, www.koninklijkhuis.nl).

New Church (Nieuwe Kerk)—Barely newer than the "Old" Church (located in the Red Light District), this 15th-century sanctuary has an intentionally dull interior, after the decoration was removed by 16th-century iconoclastic Protestants seeking to unclutter their communion with God. This is where many Dutch royal weddings and all coronations take place, and it hosts temporary exhibits. While there's a steep €6–10 entrance fee to see the rotating exhibitions, you can still pop in to look at the vast interior between exhibits (€3, covered by *I amsterdam* Card, daily May–July 10:00–17:00, Aug–April 10:00–18:00, on Dam Square, tel. 020/638-6909, www.nieuwekerk.nl).

▲Begijnhof—Stepping into this tiny, idyllic courtyard in the city center, you escape into the charm of old Amsterdam. Notice house #34, a 500-year-old wooden structure (rare, since repeated fires taught city fathers a trick called brick). Peek into the hidden Catholic church, dating from the time when post-Reformation Dutch Catholics couldn't worship in public. It's opposite the English Reformed church, where the Pilgrims worshipped while waiting for their voyage to the New World (marked by a plaque near the door). Be considerate of the people who live around the courtyard (free, daily 8:00–17:00, on Begijnensteeg lane, just off Kalverstraat between #130 and #132, pick up flier at office near entrance,).

▲Amsterdam History Museum (Amsterdams Historisch Museum)—Follow the city's growth from fishing village to world trade center to hippie haven. Housed in a 500-year-old former orphanage, this creative and hardworking museum features Rembrandt's paintings, fine English descriptions, and a carillon loft. The loft comes with push-button recordings of the town bell tower's greatest hits, and a self-serve carillon "keyboard" that lets you ring a few bells yourself (€6, covered by *I amsterdam* Card, Mon–Fri 10:00–17:00, Sat–Sun 11:00–17:00, pleasant restaurant, next to Begijnhof, Kalverstraat 92, tel. 020/523-1822, www.ahm.nl). The museum's free pedestrian corridor—lined with old-time group portraits—is a powerful teaser.

Southeast Amsterdam

To reach the following sights from the train station, take tram #9 or #14. All of these sights (except the Tropical Museum) are close to each other and can easily be connected into an interesting walk, or better yet, a bike ride. Several of the sights in southeast Amsterdam cluster near the large square, Waterlooplein, dominated by the modern opera house. Most sights are covered by the *I amsterdam* Card.

Southeast Amsterdam

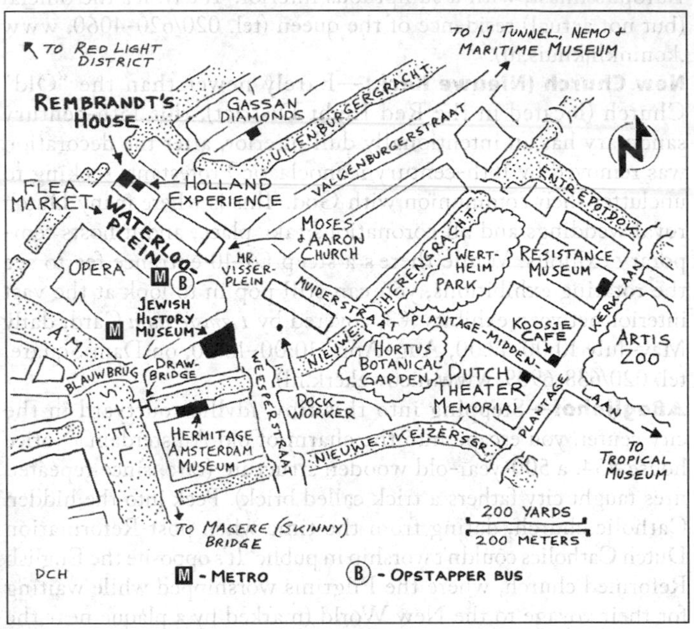

Waterlooplein Flea Market—For more than a hundred years, the Jewish Quarter flea market has raged daily except Sunday (at the Waterlooplein metro station, behind Rembrandt's House). The long, narrow park is filled with stalls selling cheap clothes, hippie stuff, old records, tourist knickknacks, and garage-sale junk.

▲Rembrandt's House (Rembrandthuis Museum)—A middle-aged Rembrandt lived here after his wife's death, as his popularity and wealth dwindled down to obscurity and bankruptcy (1639–1658). Tour the place this way: See the 10-minute introductory video (Dutch and English showings alternate); explore Rembrandt's reconstructed house (filled with exactly what his bankruptcy inventory of 1656 said he owned); imagine him at work in his reconstructed studio; marvel at his personal collection of exotic objects, many of which he included in paintings; ask the printer to explain the etching process (drawing in soft wax on a metal plate that's then dipped in acid, inked up, and printed); and then, for the finale, enjoy several rooms of original Rembrandt etchings. You're not likely to see a single painting, but the master's etchings are marvelous and well-described. I came away wanting to know more about the man and his art (€7.50, covered by *I amsterdam* Card, €13.50 combo-ticket includes *Holland Experience*—see below, daily 10:00–17:00, Fri until 21:00, Jodenbreestraat 4, tel. 020/520-0400, www.rembrandthuis.nl).

Holland Experience—Bragging "Experience Holland in 30 minutes," this 3-D movie takes you traveling through an idealized montage of Dutch clichés. There are no words, but lots of images (€8.50, €13.50 combo-ticket includes Rembrandt's House, daily 10:00–18:00, several shows a day alternating with a children's video, adjacent to Rembrandt's House at Jodenbreestraat 8, tel. 020/422-2233, www.holland-experience.nl). While it's a cheesy presentation (and the schedule, with showings only every couple of hours, can be frustrating), the *Experience* is relaxing and puts you in a Dutch frame of mind. The men's urinal is a trip to the beach. Plan for it. There's also a goofy chance to pose in a fake Red Light District window.

▲Diamonds—Many shops in this "city of diamonds" offer tours. These tours come with two parts: a chance to see experts behind magnifying glasses polishing the facets of precious diamonds, followed by a visit to an intimate sales room to see (and perhaps buy) a mighty shiny yet very tiny souvenir.

The handy and professional **Gassan Diamonds** facility fills a huge warehouse a block from Rembrandt's House. A visit here plops you in the big-tour-group fray (notice how each tour group has a color-coded sticker so they know which guide gets the commission on what they buy). You'll get a sticker, join a free 15-minute tour to see a polisher at work, and hear a general explanation of the process. Then you'll have an opportunity to sit down and have color and clarity described and illustrated with diamonds ranging in value from $100–30,000. Before or after, you can have a free cup of coffee in the waiting room across the parking lot (daily 9:00–17:00, Nieuwe Uilenburgerstraat 173, tel. 020/622-5333, www.gassandiamonds.com). Another company, Coster, also offers diamond demos, not as good as Gassan's, but handy if you're near the Rijksmuseum (see page 932).

▲Willet-Holthuysen Museum (a.k.a. Herengracht Canal Mansion)—This 1687 townhouse is a must for devotees of Hummel-topped sugar bowls and Louis XVI–style wainscoting. For others, it's a pleasant look inside a typical (rich) home with much of the original furniture and decor. Forget the history and just browse through a dozen rooms of beautiful and saccharine objects from the 19th century.

Upon entering, see photos of the owners during the house's heyday in the 1860s. The 15-minute video explains how the wealthy heiress Louise Holthuysen and the art-collecting bon vivant, Abraham Willet, got married and became joined at the hyphen, then set out to make their home the social hub of Amsterdam.

Picture the couple's servants in the kitchen—before electricity and running water—turning meat on the spit at the fireplace or filtering rainwater. Upstairs, where the Willet-Holthuysens entertained, wall paintings introduce you to Abraham's artistic tastes, showing scenes of happy French peasants and nobles frolicking in the countryside. Several rooms are done in the Louis XVI style, featuring chairs with straight, tapering legs (not the heavy, curving, animal-claw feet of earlier styles); blue, yellow, and purple-themed rooms; wainscoting ("wallpaper" covering only the lower part of walls); and mythological paintings on the ceiling.

The impressive ballroom contains a painting showing the room in its prime—and how little it's changed. Imagine Abraham, Louise, and 22 guests retiring to the Dining Room, dining off the 275-piece Meissen porcelain set; or chatting with friends in the Blue Room by the canal; or sipping tea in the Garden Room, gazing out at symmetrically curved hedges and classical statues. Up another flight is the bedroom, with a canopy bed and matching oak washstand and makeup table (and a chamber pot tucked under the bed).

When the widow Louise died in 1895, she bequeathed the house to the city, along with its collection of candelabras, snuff boxes, and puppy paintings (€4, covered by *I amsterdam* Card, Mon–Fri 10:00–17:00, Sat–Sun 11:00–17:00, take tram #4 or #9 to Rembrandtplein—it's a 2-min walk southeast to Herengracht 605, tel. 020/523-1870, www.willetholthuysen.nl). The museum lacks audioguides, but you can request a free blue notebook to learn more about the house's history.

▲Hermitage Amsterdam Museum—The famous Hermitage Museum in St. Petersburg, Russia, loans art to Amsterdam for display in the Amstelhof. Located on the Amstel River, this 17th-century former nursing home takes up a whole city block. The exhibit changes twice a year, and the museum closes for about a month in between shows—see website below for specifics (€7, covered by *I amsterdam* Card, daily 10:00–17:00, Nieuwe Herengracht 14, tram #4 to Rembrandtplein or #9 to Waterlooplein, tel. 020/531-8751, www.hermitage.nl).

Why is there Russian-owned art in Amsterdam? The Hermitage collection in St. Petersburg is so vast that they can only show about five percent of it at any one time. Therefore, the Hermitage is establishing satellite collections around the world. The one here in Amsterdam is the biggest, and will grow considerably as the museum takes over more of the Amstelhof. By law, the great Russian collection can only be out of the country for six months at a time, so the collection will always be rotating. Curators in Amsterdam make a point to display art that complements—rather than just repeats—what the city's other museums show so well.

De Hortus Botanical Garden—This is a unique oasis of tranquility within the city (no mobile phones are allowed, because "our collection of plants is a precious community—treat it with respect"). One of the oldest botanical gardens in the world, it dates from 1638, when medicinal herbs were grown here. Today, among its 6,000 different kinds of plants—most of which were collected by the Dutch East India Company in the 17th and 18th centuries—you'll find medicinal herbs, cacti, several greenhouses (one with a fluttery butterfly house—a hit with kids), and a tropical palm house. Much of it is described in English: "A Dutch merchant snuck a coffee plant out of Ethiopia, which ended up in this garden in 1706. This first coffee plant in Europe was the literal granddaddy of the coffee cultures of Brazil—long the world's biggest coffee producer" (€6, covered by *I amsterdam* Card; July–Aug Mon–Fri 9:00–21:00, Sat–Sun 10:00–21:00; Feb–June and Sept–Nov Mon–Fri 9:00–17:00, Sat–Sun 10:00–17:00; Dec–Jan Mon–Fri 9:00–16:00, Sat–Sun 10:00–16:00; Plantage Middenlaan 2A, tel. 020/625-9021, www.dehortus.nl).

▲Jewish Historical Museum (Joods Historisch Museum)—Four historic buildings have been joined by steel and glass to make one modern complex that tells the story of Amsterdam's Jews through the centuries, while serving as a good introduction to Judaism in general. There are several sections ("Jews in Amsterdam," children's museum, and temporary exhibits), but the highlight is the Great Synagogue. In 2006, the museum went through major renovations that included the restoration of the Great Synagogue and the addition of a new kosher café.

Enter the Great Synagogue, have a seat in the high-ceilinged synagogue, surrounded by religious objects, and picture it during its prime (1671–1943). The hall would be full for a service—men downstairs, women above in the gallery. On the east wall (the symbolic direction of Jerusalem) is the Ark, where they keep the scrolls of the Torah (the Jewish scriptures, including the first five books of the Christian Bible). The rabbi and other men, wearing thigh-length prayer shawls, would approach the Ark and carry the Torah to the raised platform in the center of the room. After unwrapping it from its drapery and silver cap, a man would use a *yad* (ceremonial pointer) to follow along while singing the text aloud.

Video displays around the room explain Jewish customs, from birth (circumcision) to puberty (the bar/bat mitzvah, celebrating the entry into adulthood) to marriage—culminating in the groom stomping on a glass while everyone shouts "Mazel tov!"(€7.50, covered by *I amsterdam* Card, daily 11:00–17:00, free audioguide but displays all have English explanations, Jonas Daniel Meijerplein 2, tel. 020/626-9945, www.jhm.nl.)

▲Dutch Theater (Hollandsche Schouwburg)—Once a lively theater in the Jewish neighborhood, and today a moving memorial, this building was used as an assembly hall for local Jews destined for Nazi concentration camps. On the wall, 6,700 family names pay tribute to the 104,000 Jews deported and killed by the Nazis. Some 70,000 victims spent time here, awaiting transfer to concentration camps. Upstairs is a small history exhibit with photos and memorabilia of some victims, putting a human face on the staggering numbers. Press the buttons on a model of the neighborhood to see round-up spots from the Nazi occupation. The ruined theater actually offers little to see but plenty to think about. Back on the ground floor, notice the hopeful messages that visiting school groups attach to the wooden tulips (free, daily 11:00–16:00, Plantage Middenlaan 24, tel. 020/531-0340, www.hollandscheschouwburg.nl).

▲▲Dutch Resistance Museum (Verzetsmuseum)—This is an impressive look at how the Dutch resisted their Nazi occupiers from 1940 to 1945. You'll see propaganda movie clips, study forged ID cards under a magnifying glass, and read about ingenious and courageous efforts—big and small—to hide local Jews from the Germans and undermine the Nazi regime.

The first dozen displays set the stage, showing peaceful, upright Dutch people of the 1930s living oblivious to the rise of fascism. Then—bam—it's May 1940 and the Germans invade the Netherlands, pummel Rotterdam, send Queen Wilhelmina into exile, and—in four short days of fighting—hammer home the message that resistance is futile. The Germans install local Dutch Nazis in power (the "NSB"), led by Anton Mussert.

Next, in the corner of the exhibition area, push a button to see photos of the event that first mobilized organized resistance. In February 1941, Nazis start rounding up Jews from the neighborhood, killing nine protesters. Amsterdammers respond by shutting down the trams, schools, and businesses in a massive two-day strike. (This heroic gesture is honored today with a statue of a striking dockworker on the square called Jonas Daniel Meyerplein, where Jews were rounded up). The next display makes it clear that this brave strike did little to save 100,000 Jews from extermination.

Turning the corner into the main room, you'll see numerous exhibits on Nazi rule and the many ways the Dutch resisted it: vandals turning Nazi V-for-Victory posters into W-for-Wilhelmina, preachers giving pointed sermons, schoolkids telling "Kraut jokes," printers distributing underground newspapers (such as *Het Parool*, which became a major daily paper), counterfeiters forging documents, and ordinary people hiding radios under floorboards and Jews inside closets. As the war progressed, the armed Dutch Resistance became bolder and more violent, killing German occupiers and Dutch collaborators. In September 1944, the Allies liberate Antwerp, and the Netherlands starts celebrating...too soon.

The Nazis dig in and punish the country by cutting off rations, plunging West Holland into the "Hunger Winter" of 1944–1945 in which 20,000 die. Finally, it's springtime. The Allies liberate the country, and at war's end, Nazi helmets are turned into Dutch bedpans.

Besides the history lesson, this thought-provoking exhibit examines the moral dilemmas of life under oppressive rule: Is it right to give money to poor people if the charity is run by Nazis? Should I quit my government job when the Nazis take control, or stay on to do what good I can? If I disagree with my government, is it okay to lie? To vandalize? To kill? (€5.50, covered by *I amsterdam* Card, Tue–Fri 10:00–17:00, Sat–Mon 12:00–17:00, well-described in English, no flash photos, tram #9 from station, Plantage Kerklaan 61, tel. 020/620-2535, www.verzetsmuseum.org.)

Two recommended restaurants (Plancius and Café Koosje) are adjacent to the museum (see page 962) and Amsterdam's famous zoo is just across the street.

▲Tropical Museum (Tropenmuseum)—As close to the Third World as you'll get without lots of vaccinations, this imaginative museum offers wonderful re-creations of tropical-life scenes and explanations of Third World problems (largely created by Dutch colonialism and the slave trade). Ride the elevator to the top floor, and circle your way down through this immense collection, opened in 1926 to give the Dutch a peek at their vast colonial holdings. Don't miss the display case where you can see and hear the world's most exotic musical instruments. The Ekeko cafeteria serves tropical food (€7.50, covered by *I amsterdam* Card, daily 10:00–17:00, tram #9 to Linnaeusstraat 2, tel. 020/568-8215, www.tropenmuseum.nl).

Northeast Amsterdam

Stedelijk Museum CS—This modern-art museum, temporarily located on the second and third floors of the towering post office building, features art that would normally be displayed in the actual Stedelijk Museum building (near the Rijksmuseum), which is under renovation until fall 2008. The fun, far-out, refreshing collection consists of post-1945 experimental and conceptual art. The famous masterpieces in its permanent collection—works by Picasso, Chagall, Cézanne, Kandinsky, and Mondrian—will not be on display until the museum moves back into its regular home, so expect funky temporary exhibits instead (€9, covered by *I amsterdam* Card, daily 10:00–18:00, just east of Central Station—to the left as you exit—look for the *Post CS* building in a sea of construction at Oosterdokskade 5, on second floor, tel. 020/573-2911, www.stedelijk.nl).

Best Amsterdam Viewpoint: In the post office, where the temporary galleries of the Stedelijk Museum are currently located, you can take the elevator to the 11th floor to see the best view of the city for free. (The Westerkerk's tower, near the Anne Frank House, offers a similarly good view, but costs €5 and may be closed for renovation.) Café 11 is a trendy nightspot that doubles as an eatery during the day.

Connecting Stedelijk CS to NEMO (described below): A convenient metal pedestrian bridge links these two museums—look for it to the east of Stedelijk CS or to the west of NEMO.

NEMO (National Center for Science and Technology)—This kid-friendly science museum is a city landmark. Its distinctive copper-green building, jutting up from the water like a sinking ship, has prompted critics to nickname it the *Titanic*. Designed by Italian architect Renzo Piano (known for Paris' Pompidou Center and Berlin's Potsdamer Platz complex), the building's shape reflects its nautical surroundings as well as the curve of the underwater tunnel it straddles.

Several floors feature permanent and rotating exhibits that allow kids (and adults) to explore topics such as light, sound, and gravity, and play with bubbles, topple giant dominoes, and draw with lasers. Whirring, room-sized pinball machines reputedly teach kids about physics. English explanations are available. Up top is a restaurant with a great city view, as well as a sloping terrace that becomes a "beach" in summer, complete with lounge chairs, sandbox, and lively bar. On the bottom floor is an inexpensive cafeteria offering €3 sandwiches (€11.50, not covered by *I amsterdam* Card, includes rooftop beach in July–Aug, €2.50—beach only July–Aug; Tue–Sun 10:00–17:00, generally closed Mon but open daily July–Aug; Oosterdok 2, above entrance to IJ tunnel, tel. 0900-919-1100—€0.35/min, www.e-nemo.nl). It's a 15-minute walk from Central Station or bus #22 to Kadijksplein stop. The roof terrace—which is open later than the museum in the summer—is generally free and open to the public off-season (Sept–June).

Netherlands Maritime Museum (Nederlands Scheepvaart-museum)—This huge collection of model ships, maps, and sea-battle paintings—which will be closed from through 2009 for major renovations—fills the 300-year-old Dutch Navy Arsenal. Given the Dutch seafaring heritage, I expected a more interesting museum; let's hope the renovations perk up the place (€9, covered by *I amsterdam* Card; mid-June–mid-Sept daily 10:00–17:00; mid-Sept–mid-June Tue–Sun 10:00–17:00, closed Mon; English explanations, don't waste your time with 30-min movie, bus #22 or #42 to Kattenburgerplein 1, tel. 020/523-2222, www.scheepvaartmuseum.nl).

Red Light District

▲▲Amstelkring Museum (Our Lord in the Attic)—While Amsterdam has long been known for its tolerant attitudes, 16th-century politics forced Dutch Catholics to worship discreetly. Near the train station in the Red Light District, you'll find a fascinating hidden Catholic church filling the attic of three 17th-century merchants' houses. Don't miss the silver collection and other exhibits of daily life from 300 years ago (€7, covered by *I amsterdam* Card, Mon–Sat 10:00–17:00, Sun and holidays 13:00–17:00, closed Jan 1 and April 30, Oudezijds Voorburgwal 40, tel. 020/624-6604, www.museumamstelkring.nl).

▲▲Red Light District—Europe's most touristed ladies of the night tease and tempt, as they have for centuries here, in 450 display-case windows around Oudezijds Achterburgwal and Oudezijds Voorburgwal, surrounding the Old Church (Oude Kerk, see below). Drunks and druggies make the streets uncomfortable late at night after the gawking tour groups leave (about 22:30), but it's a fascinating walk between noon and nightfall.

The neighborhood, one of Amsterdam's oldest, has hosted prostitutes since 1200. Prostitution is entirely legal here, and the prostitutes are generally entrepreneurs, renting space and running their own businesses. Popular prostitutes net about €500 a day (for what's called S&F in its abbreviated, printable form, costing €25–50 per customer), fill out tax returns, and even pay union dues.

The **Prostitution Information Center,** open to the public, offers a small €1.50 booklet that answers most of the questions tourists have about the Red Light District (free, Tue–Sat 12:00–17:00, closed Sun–Mon, facing Old Church at Enge Kerksteeg 3, www.pic-amsterdam.com).

Sex Museums—Amsterdam has two sex museums: one in the Red Light District, and another a block in front of Central Station on Damrak street. While visiting one can be called sightseeing, visiting both is hard to explain. Here's a comparison:

The **Erotic Museum** in the Red Light District is less offensive. Its five floors rely heavily on badly dressed dummies of prostitutes in various acts. It also has a lot of uninspired paintings, videos, phone sex, old photos, and sculpture (€5, daily 11:00–24:00, Fri–Sat until 2:00 in the morning, along the canal at Oudezijds Achterburgwal 54, tel. 020/627-8954).

The **Damrak Sex Museum** goes farther, telling the story of pornography from Roman times through 1960. Every sexual deviation is revealed in various displays, and the nude and pornographic art is a cut above that of the other sex museum. Also interesting are the early French pornographic photos and memorabilia from Europe, India, and Asia. You'll find a Marilyn Monroe tribute and some S&M displays, too (€3, daily 9:30–23:00, Damrak 18, a block in front of Central Station, tel. 020/622-8376).

Old Church (Oude Kerk)—This 14th-century landmark—the needle around which the Red Light District spins—has served as a reassuring welcome-home symbol to sailors, a refuge to the downtrodden, an ideological battlefield of the Counter-Reformation, and today, a tourist sight with a dull interior (€5, covered by *I amsterdam* Card, Mon–Sat 11:00–17:00, Sun 13:00–17:00, www.oudekerk.nl).

▲**Hash, Marijuana, and Hemp Museum**—This is a collection of dope facts, history, science, and memorabilia (€5.70, daily 11:00–22:00, Oudezijds Achterburgwal 148, tel. 020/623-5961, www.hashmuseum.com). While small, it has a shocking finale: the high-tech grow room, in which dozens of varieties of marijuana are cultivated in optimal hydroponic (among other) environments. Some plants stand five feet tall and shine under the intense grow lamps. The view is actually through glass walls into the neighboring Sensi Seed Bank Grow Shop, which sells carefully cultivated seeds and all the gear needed to grow them. (Both the museum and the Seed Bank may move 50 yards north in 2008, if the city grants them permits.)

The **Cannabis College**, "dedicated to ending the global war against the cannabis plant through public education," is a half block away (free, daily 11:00–19:00, Oudezijds Achterburgwal 124, tel. 020/423-4420, www.cannabiscollege.com).

NIGHTLIFE

Amsterdam hotels serve breakfast until 11:00 because so many people—visitors and locals—live for nighttime in Amsterdam.

On summer evenings, people flock to the main squares for drinks at outdoor tables. Leidseplein is the glitziest, surrounded by theaters, restaurants, and nightclubs. The slightly quieter Rembrandtplein (with adjoining Thorbeckeplein) is the center of gay discos. Spui features a full city block of bars. And Nieuwmarkt, on the east edge of the Red Light District, is a bit rough, but is probably the most local.

The Red Light District (particularly Oudezijds Achterburgwal) is less sleazy in the early evening, almost carnival-like, as the neon comes on and the streets fill with Japanese tour groups. But it starts to feel scuzzy after about 22:30.

Information: Pick up one of these free papers for listings of festivals and performances of theater, film, dance, cabaret, and live rock, pop, jazz, and classical music. ***Amsterdam Weekly*** is a free, local English-language paper that lists cutting-edge art, movies, and concerts (available in bookstores every Wed, see list on page 924). The irreverent ***Boom!*** has the lowdown on the youth and nightlife scene, and is packed with practical tips and countercultural insights (includes €3 discount on the Boom Chicago R-rated comedy theater act described below, available at TIs and many bars). ***Uitkrant*** is in Dutch, but it's just a calendar of events, and anyone can figure out the name of the event and its date, time, and location (available at TIs and many bars).

There's also *What's On in Amsterdam, Time Out Amsterdam,* the Thursday edition of many Dutch papers, and the *International Herald Tribune*'s special Netherlands inserts (all sold at newsstands).

The Last Minute Ticket Shop at Stadsschouwburg Theater (daily 12:00–19:30, Leidseplein 26, tel. 0900-0191—€0.40/min, www.lastminuteticketshop.nl) is the best one-stop-shopping box office for theater, classical music, and major rock shows. They also sell half-price, same-day (after 12:00) tickets to certain shows.

Music—You'll find classical music at the Concertgebouw (free 12:30 lunch concerts on Wed Sept–mid-June, no concerts mid-June–Aug; arrive at 12:00 for best first-come, first-serve seating; at far south end of Museumplein, tel. 020/671-8345, www.concertgebouw.nl) and at the former Beurs (on Damrak). For opera and dance, try the opera house on Waterlooplein (tel. 020/551-8100). In the summer, Vondelpark hosts open-air concerts.

Two rock music (and hip-hop) clubs near Leidseplein are Melkweg (Lijnbaansgracht 234a, tel. 020/531-8181, www.melkweg.nl) and Paradiso (Weteringschans 6, tel. 020/626-4521, www.paradiso.nl). They present big-name acts that you might recognize if you're younger than I am.

Jazz has a long tradition at the Bimhuis nightclub, east of the Red Light District (concerts Thu–Sat, Oude Schans 73–77, tel. 020/788-2150, www.bimhuis.nl).

The nearby town of Haarlem offers free pipe organ concerts on Tuesdays in summer at its 15th-century church, the Grote Kerk (at 20:15 mid-May–mid-Oct, see page 971).

Comedy—An R-rated comedy improv act, **Boom Chicago** was started 13 years ago by a group of Americans on a graduation tour. They have been entertaining tourists and locals alike ever since. The show is a series of rude, clever, and high-powered improvisational skits offering a raucous look at Dutch culture and local tourism (€19.50–22, 25 percent discount with *I amsterdam* Card, Sun–Fri at 20:15, Fri also at 23:30, Sat at 19:30 and 22:45; ticket office open Mon–Thu 11:00–20:30, Fri–Sat 11:00–23:30, closed Sun; fewer shows Jan–March, in 300-seat Leidseplein Theater, optional meal and drink service, enter through the skinny Boom Bar, Leidseplein 12, tel. 020/423-0101, www.boomchicago.nl). They do *Best of Boom* (a collection of their greatest hits over the years) as well as new shows for locals and return customers.

Theater—Amsterdam is one of the world centers for experimental live theater (much of it in English). Many theaters cluster around the street called the Nes, which stretches south from Dam Square.

Movies—It's not unusual for movies at many cinemas to be sold out—consider buying tickets during the day. Catch modern movies in the 1920s setting of the classic Tuschinski Theater (between Muntplein and Rembrandtplein, described on page 934). The Amsterdam Film Museum, which has some evening showings, shows artsy cult films from Europe's cinematic cutting edge (Vondelpark 3, tel. 020/589-1400, www.filmmuseum.nl, see page 934).

Museums—Several of Amsterdam's museums stay open late. The Anne Frank House is open daily until 21:00 in summer (April–Aug) and until 19:00 the rest of the year. The Rijksmuseum and Van Gogh Museum are open on Fridays until 22:00—sometimes with music—with wine and beer for sale. The Hash, Marijuana, and Hemp Museum is open daily until 22:00. And there are the sex museums (Erotic Museum daily until 24:00, Damrak Sex Museum daily until 23:00).

Skating After Dark—While there hasn't been a good canal freeze since 1996, Amsterdammers still get their skating fix on wheels every Friday night in summer. Huge groups don inline skates and meet at the Film Museum in Vondelpark (at 20:00 or 20:30). Tourists can roll along; there's a skate-rental shop at the far end of the park (Vondel Tuin Rental, daily 11:00–24:00, €5/hr; price includes helmet, wrist guards, and knee guards; at southeastern edge of park, tel. 020/664-5091, www.vondeltuin.nl).

SLEEPING

Greeting a new day by descending steep stairs and stepping into a leafy canalside scene—graceful bridges, historic gables, and bikes clattering on cobbles—is a fun part of experiencing Amsterdam. But Amsterdam is a tough city for budget accommodations, and any room under €140 will have rough edges. Still, you can sleep well and safely in a great location for €100 per double.

Amsterdam is jammed during tulip season (late March–mid-May), convention periods, Queen's Day (April 30), Gay Pride (generally in June and August), and on summer weekends. Some hotels will not take weekend bookings for people staying fewer than two or three nights.

Around just about every corner in downtown Amsterdam, you'll see construction: cranes for big transportation projects and small crews of bricklayers repairing the wobbly, cobbled streets that line the canals. Canalside rooms can come with great views—and early-morning construction-crew noise. If you're a light sleeper, ask the hotelier for a quiet room in the back.

Parking in Amsterdam is even worse than driving. You'll pay €32 a day to park safely in a garage—and then hike to your hotel.

Sleep Code

(€1 = about $1.30, country code: 31, area code: 020)
S = Single, **D** = Double/Twin, **T** = Triple, **Q** = Quad, **b** = bathroom, **s** = shower only. Nearly everyone speaks English in the Netherlands. Credit cards are accepted, and prices include breakfast and tax unless otherwise noted.

To help you easily sort through these listings, I've divided the rooms into three categories, based on the price for a standard double room with bath:

$$$ Higher Priced—Most rooms €140 or more.
$$ Moderately Priced—Most rooms between €80–140.
$ Lower Priced—Most rooms €80 or less.

If you'd rather trade big-city action for small-town coziness, consider sleeping in Haarlem, 15 minutes away by train (see page 969).

Near the Train Station

$$$ Ibis Amsterdam Hotel is a modern, efficient, 187-room place towering over Central Station and a multistory bicycle garage. It offers a central location, comfort, and good value, without a hint of charm (Db-€135–145, Db-€163–173, includes breakfast, check Website for deals, book long in advance, air-con, non-smoking rooms available, Stationsplein 49, tel. 020/638-9999, fax 020/620-0156, www.ibishotel.com, h1556@accor-hotels.com). When business is slow, they often rent rooms to same-day drop-ins for €115.

$$ Amstel Botel, the city's only remaining "boat hotel," is a shipshape floating hotel with 175 rooms (Sb/Db-€89, Tb-€119, worth the extra €5 per room for canal view, breakfast-€10, elevator, 400 yards from Central Station, on your left as you leave station, you'll see the sign and the big white boat at Oosterdokskade 2–4, tel. 020/626-4247, fax 020/639-1952, www.amstelbotel.nl, info@amsterdambotel.nl). The boat may chug to a new location in 2008 to steer clear of the major construction project around the station.

Between Dam Square and the Anne Frank House

$$$ Hotel Toren is a chandeliered, historic mansion in a pleasant, quiet, canalside setting in downtown Amsterdam. This splurge, run by Eric and Petra Toren, is classy yet friendly, and two blocks northeast of the Anne Frank House. It's the least expensive four-star in town and a great value (Sb-€135, Ds-€150, Db-€195, deluxe Db-€240, Tb-€225, prices decrease in winter, go direct for these prices, 5 percent tax, breakfast buffet-€12, air-con, Keizersgracht

Amsterdam Hotels

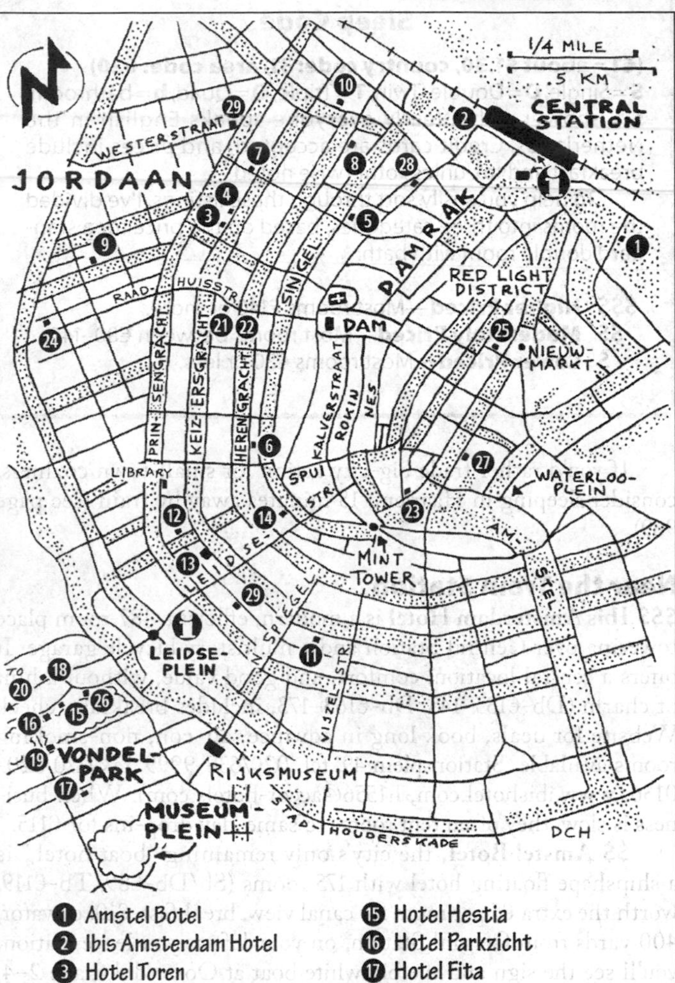

1. Amstel Botel
2. Ibis Amsterdam Hotel
3. Hotel Toren
4. Canal House Hotel
5. Hotel Brouwer
6. Hotel Ambassade
7. Truelove Antiek & Guesthouse
8. Chic and Basic Amsterdam
9. Hotel van Onna
10. Frederic Rent-a-Bike Guestrooms
11. Hotel Keizershof
12. Hotel de Leydsche Hof
13. Wildervanck B&B
14. The Waterfront Hotel
15. Hotel Hestia
16. Hotel Parkzicht
17. Hotel Fita
18. Hotel Alexander
19. Hotel Piet Hein
20. To Hotel Filosoof & Tulips B&B
21. Hotel Aspen
22. Hotel Pax
23. Hotel Résidence Le Coin
24. The Shelter Jordan
25. The Shelter City
26. Stayokay Vondelpark Hostel
27. Stayokay Stadsdoelen Hostel
28. Aivengo Youth Hostel
29. Launderettes (2)

164, tel. 020/622-6352, fax 020/626-9705, www.hoteltoren.nl, info@hoteltoren.nl). The capable and friendly staff is a great source of local advice.

$$$ Canal House Hotel, a few doors down, offers a plush 17th-century atmosphere rich with history. Above generous and elegant public spaces, tangled, antique-filled halls lead to 26 tastefully appointed rooms. Evenings come with candlelight and soft music (Db-€150–190, prices depend on room size, elevator, Keizersgracht 148, tel. 020/622-5182, fax 020/624-1317, www.canalhouse.nl, info@canalhouse.nl).

$$$ Hotel Ambassade, lacing together 60 rooms in 10 houses, is amazingly elegant and fresh, sitting aristocratically on the Herengracht. Its public rooms are palatial, with a library, antique furnishings, and modern art (Sb-€185, Db-€195–225, Db suite-€295–350, Tb-€255, extra bed-€30, 5 percent tax, breakfast-€16—and actually worth it, elevator, free Internet access in lobby, Herengracht 341, tel. 020/555-0222, www.ambassade-hotel.nl, info@ambassade-hotel.nl).

$$ Hotel Brouwer, a woody and homey old-time place situated tranquilly but centrally on the Singel canal, rents eight rooms up lots of very steep stairs (Sb-€55, Db-€90, Tb-€110, cash only, non-smoking rooms, small elevator, located between Central Station and Dam Square, near Lijnbaanssteeg at Singel 83, tel. 020/624-6358, fax 020/520-6264, www.hotelbrouwer.nl, akita@hotelbrouwer.nl).

$$ Chic and Basic Amsterdam, part of a trendy hotel chain, is a fine mix of comfort, value, and a great location near Central Station. View rooms are pricier and breezier. Cheaper, windowless rooms in the center of the hotel can get stuffy in summer (Db-€110–145, attic sofa-bed suite sleeps four-€145–180, prices go through the roof for Queen's Day and Gay Pride, always free coffee, fans on request, tangled floor plan connecting three canalside buildings, garage parking-€25, Herengracht 13, tel. 020/522-2345, fax 020/522-2389, www.chicandbasic.com).

In and near the Jordaan

$$ At **Truelove Antiek & Guesthouse,** a room-rental service, you'll feel like you're staying at your Dutch friends' house while they're out of town. Sean and Paul—who run a tiny antique store on Prinsenstraat—have 16 rooms and apartments in houses sprinkled throughout the northern end of the Jordaan neighborhood. The apartments are stylish and come with kitchens and pull-out beds (Sb-€110, Db-€130, Qb apartments-€150, prices soft in winter and midweek, non-smoking, two-night minimum on weekends, pick up keys in store at Prinsenstraat 4 or—if arriving after 17:00—call ahead and Sean can meet you at Central Station with keys and a map, store tel. 020/320-2500, mobile 062-480-5672, fax 084-711-4950, www.truelove.be, trueloveantiek@zonnnet.nl).

$$ Hotel van Onna, smoke-free and professional-feeling, has 41 simple, industrial-strength rooms. While the beds can feel like springy cots and the lights are dim, the price is right, and the leafy location makes you want to crack out your easel. Loek van Onna, who has slept in the building—probably on a cot—all his life, runs the hotel (Sb-€45, Db-€90, Tb-€135, cash only, reserve only by phone, in the Jordaan at Bloemgracht 104, tel. 020/626-5801, www.hotelvanonna.com).

$ Frederic Rent-a-Bike Guestrooms, with a bike-rental shop as the reception, is a collection of private rooms on a gorgeous canal just outside the Jordaan, a five-minute walk from Central Station. Frederic has amassed about 100 beds, ranging from dumpy €70 doubles to spacious and elegant apartments (from €46 per person). Some places are ideal for families and groups of up to six. He also rents houseboat apartments. All are displayed on his website (book with credit card but pay with cash, two-night minimum, no breakfast, Brouwersgracht 78, tel. 020/624-5509, www.frederic.nl). His excellent bike shop is open daily 9:00–17:30 (€10/24 hrs).

B&Bs near the Leidseplein

The area around Amsterdam's rip-roaring nightlife center (Leidseplein) is colorful, comfortable, and convenient. These canalside mom-and-pop places are within a five-minute walk of rowdy Leidseplein, but are in generally quiet and typically Dutch settings.

$$ Hotel de Leydsche Hof is a hidden gem located on a canal. Its two large, well-designed rooms are a symphony in white, overlooking a tree-filled backyard. Gentlemanly Frits and elegant Loes (you'll see photos from her modeling days throughout the house) give their home a royally stylish air. Understandably popular, this place books up far in advance, but you might get lucky if your timing's right (Db-€95, 2–3-night stays preferred, includes breakfast, cash only, Leidsegracht 14—don't confuse it with noisy shopping street Leidsestraat a block south, tel. 020/638-2327, mobile 065-125-8588, www.freewebs.com/leydschehof, loespiller@planet.nl).

$$ Wildervanck B&B, run by Helene and Sjoerd Wildervanck, offers two rooms in an elegant, 17th-century canal house (big Db on first floor-€125, Db with twin beds on ground floor-€105, extra bed-€25, family deals, breakfast in their pleasant dining room, family has three little girls, Keizersgracht 498, on Keizersgracht canal just west of Leidsestraat, tel. 020/623-3846, fax 020/421-6575, www.wildervanck.com, info@wildervanck.com). As it's in a busy area, you may get some bar noise at night.

$$ Hotel Keizershof is wonderfully Dutch, with six bright, airy rooms in a 17th-century canal house. A very steep spiral staircase leads to rooms named after old-time Hollywood stars. The enthusiastic hospitality of Mrs. de Vries and her daughter, Hanneke, give this place a friendly, almost small-town charm (S-€55, D-€75–80, Ds-€90, Db-€110, 2-night minimum stay, strictly non-smoking; tram #16, #24, or #25 from Central Station; Keizersgracht 618, where Keizers canal crosses Nieuwe Spiegelstraat, tel. 020/622-2855, fax 020/624-8412, www.hotelkeizershof.nl).

Near the Mint Tower, in the City Center

These two hotels are on either side of the Mint Tower; both are a two-minute walk to the Flower Market and a five-minute walk to the Rembrandtsplein. They are approximately halfway between Dam Square and the big museums (Rijks and Van Gogh).

$$$ Hotel Résidence Le Coin offers no-nonsense but larger-than-average rooms complete with small kitchenettes. You won't get canal views here—just a good, solid, sleepable room in an all-business hotel (Sb-€110, Db-€130-145, Qb-€218, extra bed-€35, breakfast-€10, by the University at Nieuwe Doelenstraat 5, tel. 020/524-6800, fax 020/524-6801, www.lecoin.nl, lecoin@holding.uva.nl).

$$$ The Waterfront Hotel, a block up busy Leidsestraat and just west of Koningsplein, has 10 tight rooms (the canalside ones are slightly roomier), indifferent management, lots of steep stairs, and a good location by the Singel canal (Sb-€110, Db-€125–135, view Db-€155, Tb-€185, Singel 458, tel. & fax 020/421-6621, www.waterfront.demon.nl, info@hotelwaterfront.nl).

Near Vondelpark and Museumplein

These options cluster around Vondelpark in a safe neighborhood. Though they don't have a hint of Old Dutch or romantic canalside flavor, they're reasonable values and only a short walk from the action. Many are in a pleasant nook between rollicking Leidseplein and the park, and most are a 5- to 15-minute walk to the Rijks and Van Gogh museums. They are easily connected with Central Station by trams #1, #2, and #5.

$$$ Hotel Fita has 16 bright, fresh rooms located 100 yards from the Van Gogh Museum (Sb-€90, two small basement Db-€125, Db-€135–150, Tb-€190, discounts for multiple nights—ask when you book, free laundry service, free Wi-Fi, elevator, seriously non-smoking, Jan Luijkenstraat 37, tel. 020/679-0976, fax 020/664-3969, www.fita.nl, info@fita.nl, joking and affable owner Hans).

$$$ Hotel Piet Hein offers comfortable renovated rooms with a swanky nautical atmosphere (Sb-€95–105, Db-€145–165, extra bed-€30, expensive Wi-Fi available—€12.50/24-hour pass,

Hotels and Restaurants near Museumplein

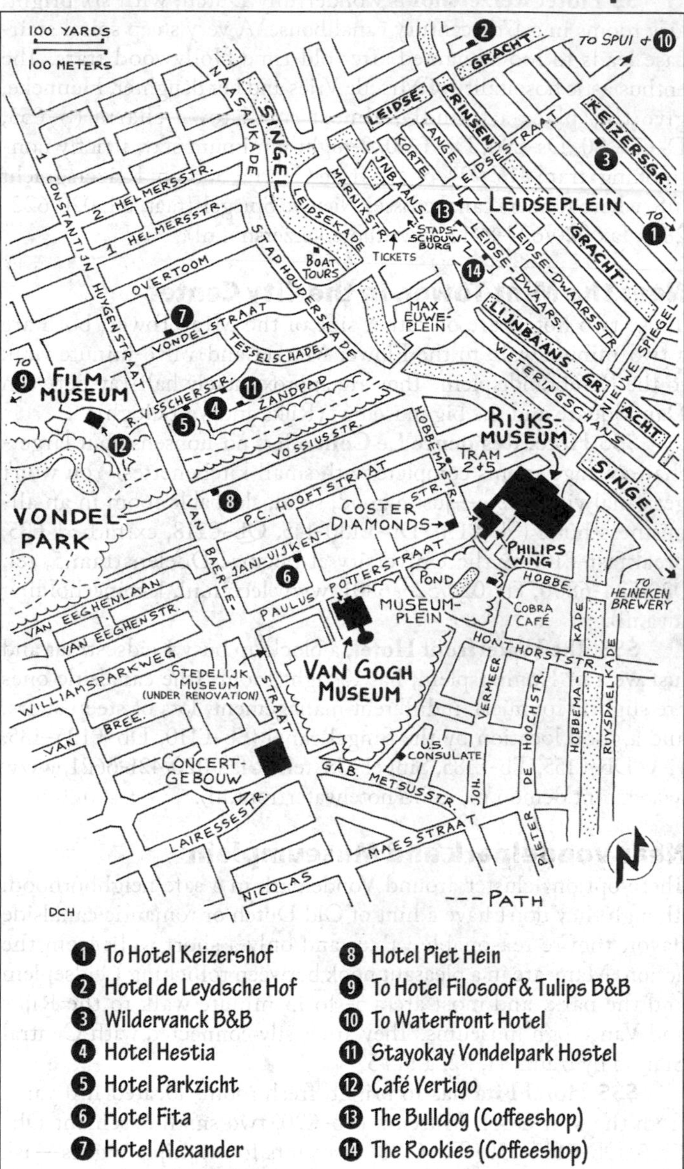

Amsterdam

Vossiusstraat 52–53, tel. 020/662-7205, www.hotelpiethein.nl, info@hotelpiethein.nl).

$$$ Hotel Filosoof greets you with Aristotle and Plato in the foyer and classical music in its generous lobby. Its 38 rooms are decorated with themes; the Egyptian room has a frieze of hieroglyphics. Philosophers' sayings hang on the walls, and thoughtful travelers wander down the halls or sit in the garden, rooted in deep discussion. The rooms are small, but the hotel is endearing (Db-€130–155, Tb-€183, elevator, three-minute walk from tram line #1, get off at Jan Pieter Heijestraat, Anna Vondelstraat 6, tel. 020/683-3013, fax 020/685-3750, www.hotelfilosoof.nl, reservations@hotelfilosoof.nl).

$$ Hotel Alexander is a modern, newly renovated, 32-room hotel on a quiet street. Some of the rooms overlook the garden patio out back (Sb-€80–95, Db-€120–135, includes breakfast, prices soft in winter, free Internet in lobby and Wi-Fi throughout the hotel, elevator, tel. 020/589-4020, fax 020/589-4025, www.hotelalexander.nl, info@hotelalexander.nl).

$$ Hotel Hestia, on a safe and sane street, is efficient and family-run, with 18 clean, airy, and generally spacious rooms (Sb-€82, very small Db-€98, standard Db-€117–135, Tb-€160, Qb-€188, elevator, Roemer Visscherstraat 7, tel. 020/618-0801, fax 020/685-1382, www.hotel-hestia.nl, info@hotel-hestia.nl).

$$ Hotel Parkzicht, an old-fashioned place with extremely steep stairs, rents 13 big, plain rooms on a street bordering Vondelpark (S-€39, Sb-€49, Db-€78–90, Tb-€110–120, Qb-€120–130, closed Nov–March, some noise from neighboring youth hostel, Roemer Visscherstraat 33, tel. 020/618-1954, fax 020/618-0897, www.parkzicht.nl, hotel@parkzicht.nl).

$$ Tulips B&B, with a bunch of cozy rooms—some on a canal—is run by a friendly Englishwoman, Karen, and her Dutch husband, Paul. Rooms are clean, white, and bright, with red carpeting, plants, and flowers (D-€55–75, Db-€100, suite-€130, family deals, includes milk-and-cereal breakfast, cash only, prefer three nights for weekends, non-smoking and no shoes, south end of Vondelpark at Sloterkade 65, directions sent when you book, tel. 020/679-2753, fax 020/408-3028, www.bedandbreakfastamsterdam.net).

Cheap Hotels in the Center

Inexpensive, well-worn hotels line the convenient but noisy main drag between City Hall and the Anne Frank House. Expect a long, steep, and depressing stairway, with noisy rooms in the front and quieter rooms in the back.

$ Hotel Pax has 11 large, plain, but airy rooms with Ikea furniture—a lot like a Euro dorm room (S-€35–40, D-€65, Db-€80,

T-€80, Tb-€95, Q-€100, no breakfast, prices drop dramatically in winter, six rooms share two showers and two toilets, Raadhuisstraat 37, tel. 020/624-9735, run by go-getters Philip and Pieter).

$ Hotel Aspen, a few doors away and a good value for a budget hotel, has eight tidy, stark, and well-maintained rooms (S-€40, tiny D-€50–55, Db-€70–75, Tb-€95, Qb-€110, no breakfast, Raadhuisstraat 31, tel. 020/626-6714, fax 020/620-0866, www.hotelaspen.nl, info@hotelaspen.nl, run by Esam and his family).

Hostels in the Center

Amsterdam has a world of good, cheap hostels. Most are designed for the party crowd, but here are a few quieter options.

In the Jordaan: **The Shelter Jordan** is a scruffy, friendly, Christian-run, 100-bed place in a great neighborhood. While most of Amsterdam's hostels are pretty wild, this place is drug-free and alcohol-free, with boys on one floor and girls on another. These are Amsterdam's best budget beds, in 14- to 20-bed dorms (€19.50 per bed, €16 off-season, sheets-€2, €5 key deposit that's returned when you check out, includes hot breakfast, Internet access in lobby, non-smoking, near Anne Frank House, Bloemstraat 179, tel. 020/624-4717, www.shelter.nl, jordan@shelter.nl). The Shelter serves hot meals, runs a snack bar in its big, relaxing lounge, offers lockers, and leads nightly Bible studies.

In the Red Light District: **The Shelter City** is Shelter Jordan's sister—similar, but definitely not preaching to the choir (€19.50 per bed, includes sheets, all ages welcome, curfew, Barndesteeg 21, tel. 020/625-3230, fax 020/623-2282, www.shelter.nl, city@shelter.nl).

In Vondelpark: **Stayokay Vondelpark (IYHF)** is one of Amsterdam's top hostels (€19.50–30 per bed, D-€73.50–80, higher prices are for March–Oct, members save €2.50, family rooms, lots of school groups, 4–20 beds per room, €2 lockers, right on Vondelpark at Zandpad 5, tel. 020/589-8996, fax 020/589-8955, www.stayokay.com). Though Stayokay Vondelpark and Stayokay Stadsdoelen (listed below) are generally booked long in advance, occasionally a few beds open up each day at 11:00.

Near Waterlooplein: **Stayokay Stadsdoelen (IYHF),** smaller and simpler than its Vondelpark sister (listed above), has only large dorms and no private bathrooms, but is free of large school groups (€23.75–24.75 per bed, members save €2.50, Kloveniersburgwal 97, tel. 020/624-6832, fax 020/639-1035, www.stayokay.com).

Near Central Station: **Aivengo Youth Hostel** has 32 beds in two Moroccan-themed dorms (one for men, one for women). It's clean, new-feeling, and bare-bones, with no common room or lunch counter—but it's well-located, just a five-minute walk from Central Station (€20–22 per bed, includes sheets, maximum age

35, free Internet at its one terminal, Spuistraat 6 at Kattegat, tel. 020/421-3670).

EATING

Traditional Dutch food is basic and hearty, with lots of bread, cheese, soup, and fish. Lunch and dinner are served at American times (roughly 12:00–14:00 and 18:00–21:00).

Dutch treats include cheese, pancakes *(pannenkoeken)*, gin *(jenever)*, light, pilsner-type beer, and "syrup waffles" *(stroopwafels)*.

Experiences you owe your tongue in Holland: trying a raw herring at an outdoor herring stand, lingering over coffee in a "brown café," sipping an old *jenever* with a new friend, and consuming an Indonesian feast—a *rijsttafel*.

Budget Tips: Get a sandwich to go, and grab a park bench on a canal. Sandwiches *(broodjes)* of delicious cheese on fresh bread are cheap at snack bars, delis, and *broodjes* restaurants. Ethnic fast-food stands abound, offering a variety of meats wrapped in pita bread. Easy to buy at grocery stores, yogurt in the Netherlands (and throughout northern Europe) is delicious and often drinkable right out of its plastic container. Keep in mind that tipping is not necessary in restaurants (15 percent service is usually already included in the menu price), but a tip of about 5–10 percent is a nice reward for good service. In bars, rounding up to the next euro ("keep the change") is appropriate if you get table service, rather than order at the bar.

Restaurants: Of Amsterdam's thousand-plus restaurants, no one knows which are best. I'd pick an area and wander. The rowdy food ghetto thrives around Leidseplein; wander along Leidsedwarsstraat, Restaurant Row. The area around Spui canal and that end of Spuistraat is also trendy and not as noisy. For fewer crowds and more charm, find something in the Jordaan district. Most hoteliers keep a reliable eating list for their neighborhood and know which places keep their travelers happy.

Here are some handy places to consider.

On and near Spui, in the Center

Restaurant Kantjil en de Tijger is a thriving place, full of happy eaters who know a good value. The food is purely Indonesian; the waiters are happy to explain your many enticing options. Their three *rijsttafels* (traditional "rice tables" with 11–13 small courses) range from €20–30 per person (ask for a description of each). While they are designed for two people, there's plenty of food for more; three people can make a meal by getting a *rijsttafel* for two, and for good form, ordering a bowl of soup or light dish for the third person. They offer a multi-course €8 lunch special on the weekends, as well as an early-bird €9 dinner daily from 16:30–18:30 (dinner only Mon–Fri 16:30–23:00, lunch and dinner Sat–Sun 12:00–23:00, reserve ahead for dinner—this place is popular, mostly indoor with a little outdoor seating, non-smoking section, Spuistraat 291, tel. 020/620-0994).

Kantjil To Go, run by Restaurant Kantjil (listed above), is a tiny take-out bar serving up inexpensive but delicious Indonesian fare (€4–6 meals, vegetarian specials, daily 12:00–21:00, storefront at Nieuwezijds Voorburgwal 342, around the corner from the sit-down restaurant listed above, tel. 020/620-3074).

Restaurant Haesje Claes, popular with tour groups, offers traditional Dutch cooking in the center. It's the Dutch equivalent of T.G.I. Friday's: big, with fast service, edible food, and reasonable prices (€25 fixed-price meal, daily 12:00–22:00, Spuistraat 275, tel. 020/624-9998). The area around it is a huge and festive bar scene.

Near the Mint Tower

Café 't Gasthuys, one of Amsterdam's many brown cafés (so called for their smoke-stained walls), has a busy dumbwaiter cranking out light lunches, good sandwiches, and reasonably priced dinners. It offers a long bar, a fine secluded back room, peaceful canalside seating, and sometimes slow service (€9 lunch special, €11 dinner specials, daily 12:00–16:30 & 17:30–22:00; Grimburgwal 7—from the Rondvaart Kooij boat dock, head down Langebrugsteeg and it's one block down on the left; tel. 020/624-8230).

Restaurant Kapitein Zeppos, named for an old-time Belgian TV star, serves French-Dutch food amid dressy yet unpretentious 1940s ambience. With a recent expansion, they offer both a restaurant (upstairs, with waiters in nice suits) and a pub (downstairs, good Belgian beers on tap at the big wooden bar, occasional live music). The light lunch specials—soups and sandwiches—cost €5–10. Dinners go for about €17 in the pub, and for €25–30 in the classy restaurant (food served daily 11:00–15:30 & 17:30–23:00, pub stays open later for drinks, just off Grimburgwal at Gebed Zonder End 5—a small pedestrian alleyway, tel. 020/624-2057).

De Jaren Café ("The Years Café") is a chic yet inviting place—clearly a favorite with locals. Upstairs is the minimalist restaurant with a top-notch salad bar and a canal-view deck (serving €12–15 dinners after 17:30, including fish, meat, and veggie dishes, and salad bar). Downstairs is a modern Amsterdam café, great for light lunches (soups, salads, and sandwiches served all day and evening), or just coffee over a newspaper. On a sunny day, the café's canal-side patio is a fine spot to nurse a drink; this is also a nice place to go just for a drink in the evening (Sun–Thu 10:00–1:00 in the morning, Fri–Sat until 2:00, Nieuwe Doelenstraat 20–22, a long

Restaurants and Coffeeshops

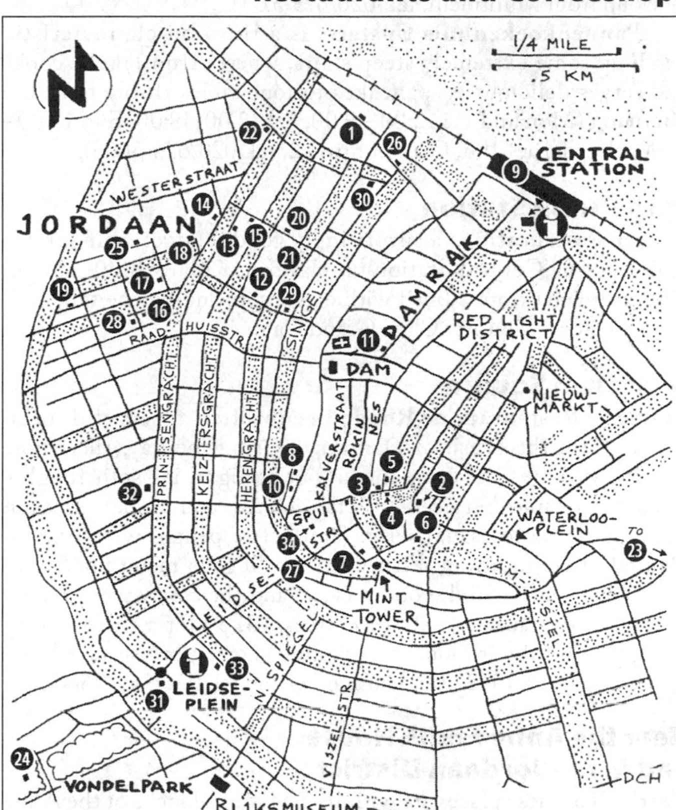

1 Toscana Italian Restaurant
2 Atrium University Cafeteria
3 Café 't Gasthuys
4 Pannenkoekenhuis Upstairs
5 Restaurant Kapitein Zeppos
6 De Jaren Café
7 La Place Cafeteria
8 Restaurant Haesje Claes
9 Stationsrestauratie
10 Rest. Kantjil en de Tijger
11 Brasserie Rest. de Roode Leeuw
12 Restaurant de Luwte
13 The Pancake Bakery
14 De Bolhoed
15 Ruhe Delicatessen
16 De Groene Lantaarn
17 Café Restaurant de Reiger
18 Café 't Smalle
19 Rest. Vliegende Schotel
20 Top Thai
21 Espresso Corner Bâton Brasserie
22 Café 't Papeneiland
23 To Rest. Plancius, Café Koosje & Taman Sari Restaurant
24 Café Vertigo
25 De Vrije Vork
26 Stubbe's Haring
27 Leidsestraat Eateries

Coffeeshops

28 Paradox
29 The Grey Area
30 Siberië Coffeeshop
31 The Bulldog
32 La Tertulia
33 The Rookies
34 The Dampkring

block up from Muntplein, tel. 020/625-5771).

Pannenkoekenhuis Upstairs is a tiny and characteristic perch up some extremely steep stairs, where Arno Jakobs cooks and serves delicious €7 pancakes to four tables throughout the afternoon (Mon and Fri 12:00–19:00, Sat 12:00–18:00, Sun 12:00–17:00, closed Tue–Thu, Grimburgwal 2, tel. 020/626-5603).

In the Train Station

Stationsrestauratie is a surprisingly good, budget, self-service option inside Central Station on platform 2 (daily 8:00–20:00). This entire platform is lined with eateries, including the tall, venerable, 1920s-style First Class Grand Café.

Near Dam Square

Brasserie Restaurant de Roode Leeuw offers a peaceful, calm respite from the crush of Damrak. During the day, the whole restaurant shares the same menu, but at night, it's split roughly in half, with finer service, cloth tablecloths, and higher prices in back, and a more casual setup (and better people-watching on Damrak street) up front. Either way, you'll get a menu filled with traditional Dutch food, good service, and the company of plenty of tourists (restaurant: €20–23 entrées, €31.50 for a three-course fixed-price meal with lots of intriguing choices; brasserie: €10–13 entrées; daily 12:00–22:00, Damrak 93–94, tel. 020/555-0666).

Near the Anne Frank House and in the Jordaan District

Nearly all of these places are within a few scenic blocks of the Anne Frank House, providing handy lunches and atmospheric dinners in Amsterdam's most characteristic neighborhood.

Restaurant de Luwte is romantic, located on a picturesque street overlooking a canal. It has lots of candles, a muted but fresh modern interior, a few cool outdoor canalside tables, and French Mediterranean cuisine (€20 entrées, €30 for a three-course fixed-price meal, big dinner salads for €16, daily 18:00–22:00, non-smoking section, Leliegracht 26–28, tel. 020/625-8548, Marko).

The Pancake Bakery serves good pancakes to tourists in a nothing-special, family atmosphere. The menu features a fun selection of ethnic-themed pancakes—including Indonesian, for those who want two experiences in one (€8–12 pancakes, splitting is OK, 25 percent discount with *I amsterdam* Card, daily 12:00–21:30, Prinsengracht 191, tel. 020/625-1333).

De Bolhoed has serious vegetarian and vegan food in a colorful setting that Buddha would dig (€5 lunches, €15 dinners, light lunches, daily 12:00–22:00, dinner starts at 17:00, Prinsengracht 60, tel. 020/626-1803).

De Groene Lantaarn ("The Green Lantern") is fun for fondue. The menu offers fish, meat, and cheese (Dutch and Swiss) with salad and fruit for €17–25 (Thu–Sun from 18:00, kitchen closes at 20:30, closed Mon–Wed, a few blocks into the Jordaan at Bloemgracht 47, tel. 020/620-2088).

Café Restaurant de Reiger must offer the best cooking of any *eetcafé* in the Jordaan. It's famous for its fresh ingredients and delightful bistro ambience. In addition to an English menu, ask for a translation of the €16–19 daily specials on the chalkboard. They're proud of their fresh fish. The café, which is crowded late and on weekends, takes no reservations, but you're welcome to have a drink at the bar while you wait (glass of house wine-€2.50). While there's a non-smoking section in front, the energy is with the smokers in the back room (Sat–Sun 11:00–15:30 & 18:00–22:30, Mon–Fri dinner only, veggie options, Nieuwe Leliestraat 34, tel. 020/624-7426, manager Edwin).

Café 't Smalle is extremely charming, with three zones where you can enjoy a light lunch or a drink: canalside, inside around the bar, and up some steep stairs in a quaint little loft. While the café is open daily until midnight, simple meals (salads, soup, and fresh sandwiches) are served only 12:00–17:00 (plenty of fine €2–3 Belgian beers on tap and interesting wines by the glass posted, at Egelantiersgracht 12 where it hits Prinsengracht, tel. 020/623-9617).

Restaurant Vliegende Schotel is a folksy, unvarnished little Jordaan eatery decorated with children's crayon art. Its cheap and fun menu features fish and vegetarian fare. Choose a table (I'd avoid the empty non-smoking section and eat with the regulars), and then order at the counter. Nothing trendy about this place—just locals who like healthful food and don't want to cook. The €8 *Vliegende Schotel* salad is a vegetarian extravaganza (€8–11 entrées, wine by the glass, daily 17:00–22:45, Nieuwe Leliestraat 162, tel. 020/625-2041).

De Vrije Vork, a neighborhood joint where hungry eaters share long wooden tables, serves breakfast, lunch, and buffet-style dinner. The mixed-salad plate is a bit of everything—from fresh mozzarella to red-beet coleslaw. You can stop in for just a *kopje koffee* or a €4 glass of wine (breakfast-€2 croissant with jam, €6 omelets, €8 lunchtime salads, €10 mix-and-match dinner buffet starts at 17:30, daily 10:00–23:00, cash only, Egelantiersstraat 122–124, tel. 020/320-4316).

Espresso Corner Bâton Brasserie, on the Herengracht canal, is a pleasant lunch spot for "de Croque Monsieur" (that's ham and cheese to you and me). Its three floors are cantilevered over each other in a pleasant, open-house design, but a few tables on the top floor have the best view of the canalside action outside (€6 sandwiches, Mon–Fri 8:00–18:00, Sat–Sun 9:00–18:00, Herengracht

82, tel. 020/624-8195).

Ruhe Delicatessen, run for decades by Mr. Ruhe, is the perfect late-night deli for a quick, cheap picnic dinner (daily 12:00–22:00, deli closes last three weeks in Aug for Mr. Ruhe's vacation, a block from recommended Hotel Toren at Prinsenstraat 13, tel. 020/626-7438).

Top Thai, a block from Hotel Toren, offers top-quality meals for under €20 (even cheaper for take-out), either to enjoy at their cozy, 10-table restaurant or carry out for a picnic (daily 16:30–22:30, good veggie options, Herenstraat 22, tel. 020/623-4633).

Toscana Italian Restaurant is the Jordaan's favorite place for good, inexpensive Italian cuisine, including pizza, in a woody Dutch-beer-hall setting (€4–8 pizza, €7 pastas, daily 16:30–24:00, Haarlemmerstraat 130, tel. 020/622-0353).

Drinks Only: A classic brown café with Delft tiles, **Café 't Papeneiland** has an evocative old stove, and a stay-awhile perch overlooking a canal with welcoming benches. It has been the neighborhood hangout since the 17th century (drinks but no food, overlooking northwest end of Prinsengracht at #2, tel. 020/624-1989). It feels a little exclusive; patrons who come here to drink and chat aren't eager to see it overrun by tourists. The café's name means "Papists' Island," since this was once a refuge for Catholics; there used to be an escape tunnel here for priests on the run.

Near the Dutch Resistance Museum

Restaurant Plancius, adjacent to the Dutch Resistance Museum, is a mod, handy spot for lunch, but service can be slow. Its good indoor and outdoor seating make it popular with the broadcasters from the nearby local TV studios (creative breakfasts, light €4–8 lunches and €15–18 dinners, daily 10:00–22:00, Plantage Kerklaan 61a, tel. 020/330-9469).

Café Koosje, located halfway between the Dutch Resistance Museum and the Dutch Theater, is a corner lunchtime pub ringed with outdoor seating. Inside, casual wooden tables and benches huddle under chandeliers, and the hip, young waitstaff serves beer and salads (big enough for two). It's a smoky, Dutch version of *Cheers* (€4 sandwiches, any sandwich can be turned into a huge and splittable €9.50 salad, Plantage Middenlaan 37, on the corner of Plantage Kerklaan, tel. 020/320-0817).

Taman Sari Restaurant is the local choice for Indonesian, serving hearty, quality €9.50 dinners and *rijsttafel* dinners for €16–22.50 (daily 17:00–23:00, Plantage Kerklaan 32, tel. 020/623-7130).

In Vondelpark

Café Vertigo—a surprisingly large complex of outdoor tables, an indoor pub, and an elegant, candlelit, back-room restaurant—offers a fun selection of excellent soups and sandwiches. The service can be slow, but if you grab an outdoor table, you can watch the world spin by (April–Sept daily 10:00–24:00; Oct–March Mon–Fri 11:00–24:00, Sat–Sun 10:00–24:00; beneath Film Museum, Vondelpark 3, call for dinner reservations in the indoor restaurant on weekends, tel. 020/612-3021).

Munching Cheap

Traditional fish stands sell €3 herring sandwiches and other salty treats, usually from easy-to-understand photo menus. **Stubbe's Haring,** where the Stubbe family has been selling herring for 100 years, is handy and well-established (Tue–Fri 10:00–18:00, Sat 10:00–17:00, closed Sun–Mon, at the locks where Singel canal boat arrives at the train station). Grab a sandwich and have a picnic canalside.

La Place, on the ground floor of the V&D department store, has an abundant, colorful array of fresh, appealing food served cafeteria-style. A multi-story eatery that seats 300, it has a nonsmoking section and a small outdoor terrace upstairs. Explore before you make your choice. This bustling spot has a lively market feel, with everything from made-on-the-spot beef stir-fry to fresh juice to veggie soups (€3 pizza and €4 sandwiches, Mon–Sat 10:00–20:00, Thu until 21:00, Sun 12:00–20:00, at the end of Kalverstraat near Mint Tower, tel. 020/622-0171). For fast and healthy take-out food (sandwiches, yogurt, fruit cups, and more), try the bakery on the department store's ground floor.

Atrium University Cafeteria, a three-minute walk from Mint Tower, feeds travelers and students from Amsterdam University for great prices, but only on weekdays (€6 meals, Mon–Fri 11:00–15:00 & 17:00–19:30, closed Sat–Sun; from Spui, walk west down Landebrug Steeg past canalside Café 't Gasthuys three blocks to Oudezijds Achterburgwal 237, go through arched doorway on the right; tel. 020/525-3999).

On Leidsestraat: This busy street offers plenty of starving-student options between the Prinsengracht and the Herengracht. You can window-shop these casual eateries, most of which offer better-than-average fast food for less than €5 a meal. You'll find NY Pizza (Leidsestraat 23, another location is at Spui 2, just across from the end of the Rokin Canal), Hot & Cold (#30, healthy sandwiches), Sanday's Sandwiches (#37), Bertolli Lucca Pasta (#54), and the Coffee Company (#80, drinks and snacks).

Supermarkets: You'll see **Albert Heijn** grocery stores all over town. Two helpful, central locations are right behind Dam Square at Nieuwezijds Voorburgwal 226 (daily 8:00–22:00, cash only, tel. 020/421-8344) and near the Flower Market and Mint Tower, at Koningsplein 4 (same hours, cash only, tel. 020/624-5721).

SMOKING

A third of Dutch people smoke tobacco. You don't have to like it, but expect it—in restaurants, bars, bus stops, almost everywhere. Holland has a long tradition as a smoking culture, being among the first to import the tobacco plant from the New World. Tobacco shops glorify the habit, yet the Dutch people are among the healthiest in the world. Tanned, trim, firm, 60-something Dutch people sip their beer, take a drag, and ask me why Americans murder themselves with Big Macs.

Still, their version of the Surgeon General is finally waking up to the drug's many potential health problems. Since 2002, warning stickers bigger than America's are required on cigarette packs, and some of them are almost comically blunt, such as: Smoking will make you impotent...and then you die. (The warnings prompted gag stickers like, "If you can read this, you're healthy enough," and "Life can kill you.")

Smoking was recently prohibited on trains. It's unclear how much this will be obeyed or enforced.

Throughout the Netherlands, you'll see "coffeeshops"—pubs selling marijuana. The minimum age for purchase is 18. Coffeeshops can sell up to five grams of marijuana per person per day. Locals buy marijuana by asking, "Can I see the cannabis menu?" The menu looks like the inventory of a drug bust. Display cases show various joints or baggies for sale. The Dutch usually include a little tobacco in their prerolled joints (though a few coffeeshops sell joints of pure marijuana). To avoid the tobacco, smokers roll their own (cigarette papers are free with the purchase, dispensed like toothpicks) or borrow a pipe or bong. Baggies of marijuana usually cost €10–15, and a smaller amount means better quality.

Most of downtown Amsterdam's coffeeshops feel grungy and foreboding to anyone over 30. Pot should never be bought on the street in Amsterdam, and don't smoke marijuana openly while walking down the street. Well-established coffeeshops are considered much safer, and coffeeshop owners have an interest in keeping their trade safe and healthy. They warn Americans—unused to the strength of the local stuff—to try a lighter leaf. In fact, they are generally very patient in explaining the varieties available. The neighborhood places (and those in small towns around the countryside) are much more inviting to people without piercings, tattoos, and favorite techno artists. I've listed a few places with a more pub-like ambience for Americans wanting to go local, but within reason. For locations, see the map on page 959.

Paradox is the most *gezellig* (cozy) coffeeshop I found—a mellow, graceful place. The managers, Ludo and Jan, and their staff are patient with descriptions, and happy to walk you through all your options. This is a rare coffeeshop that serves light meals. The juice is fresh, the music is easy, and the neighborhood is charming. Colorful murals with bright blue skies are all over the walls, creating a fresh and open feeling (loaner bongs, games, daily 10:00–20:00, two blocks from Anne Frank House at Eerste Bloemdwarsstraat 2, tel. 020/623-5639, www.paradoxamsterdam.demon.nl).

The Grey Area coffeeshop—a hole-in-the-wall spot with three tiny tables—is a cool, welcoming, and smoky place appreciated among local aficionados as winner of Amsterdam's Cannabis Cup awards. Judging by the autographed photos on the wall, many famous Americans have dropped in (say hi to Willie Nelson). You're welcome to just nurse a bottomless cup of coffee (Tue–Sun 12:00–20:00, closed Mon, they close relatively early out of consideration for their neighbors, between Dam Square and Anne Frank House at Oude Leliestraat 2, tel. 020/420-4301, www.greyarea.nl, run by two friendly Americans, Steven and Jon, who know the value of a bottomless cup of coffee).

Siberië Coffeeshop is a short walk from Central Station, but feels cozy, with a friendly canalside ambience. Clean, big, and bright, this place has the vibe of a not-too-far-out Starbucks (daily 11:00–23:00, free Internet access, helpful staff, English menu, Brouwersgracht 11, tel. 020/623-5909, www.siberie.nl).

La Tertulia is a sweet little mother-and-daughter-run place with pastel decor and a cheery terrarium ambience (Tue–Sat 11:00–19:00, closed Sun–Mon, sandwiches, brownies, games, Prinsengracht 312, www.coffeeshopamsterdam.com).

The Bulldog is the high-profile, leading touristy chain of coffeeshops. These establishments are young but welcoming, with reliable selections. They're pretty comfortable for green tourists wanting to just hang out for a while. The flagship branch, in a former police station right on Leidseplein, is very handy, offering fun outdoor seating where you can watch the world skateboard by (daily 10:00–1:00 in the morning, later on Fri–Sat, Leidseplein 17, tel. 020/625-6278, www.bulldog.nl). They opened up their first café (on the canal near the Old Church in the Red Light District) in 1975.

The Rookies, a block east of Leidseplein along "Restaurant Row," is one of the rare coffeeshops that sells individual, prerolled, decent-quality joints of pure marijuana—with no tobacco (€5.50, daily 10:00–1:00 in the morning, Fri–Sat until 3:00 in the morning, Korte Leidsedwarsstraat 14, www.rookies.nl).

The Dampkring, a rough-and-ready constant party, is one of very few coffeeshops that also serve alcohol. It's a high profile and busy place, filled with a young clientele, but the owners still take the time to explain what they offer. Scenes from the movie *Ocean's*

Twelve were filmed here (daily 11:00–22:00, later on Fri–Sat, close to Spui at Handboogstraat 29, tel. 020/638-0705).

TRANSPORTATION CONNECTIONS

Amsterdam's train-information center can require a long wait. Save lots of time by getting train tickets and information in a small-town station (such as Haarlem), at the airport upon arrival, or from a travel agency.

You have two options for buying train tickets in the Netherlands: at a ticket window (costs €0.50 extra), or at an automated machine (no extra charge). Some machines have instructions only in Dutch, and you can pay in euros (no credit cards). Frustratingly, the newer machines—which have instructions in English—accept only Dutch debit cards (no cash, Visa, or MasterCard). If you're having trouble, visit the yellow information booth, or enlist the help of any official-looking employee (most wear portable computers with timetables) to help you with train departure times, or to navigate your way through the older, Dutch-only machine menus. If ticket lines are short and your frustration level high, pay the extra €0.50 to buy your ticket at the window.

Remember, you can use *strippenkaart* on any train that travels within the Netherlands. If you have a Eurail pass and Amsterdam is your first stop, get it validated at the international train office at platform #2 (take a number and expect a wait).

By Train to: Schiphol Airport (6/hr, 20 min, €3.60, have coins handy to buy from a machine to avoid lines), **Haarlem** (6/hr, 15 min, €3.60 one-way, €6.20 same-day round-trip), **The Hague/Den Haag** (6/hr, 50 min, may require switch in Leiden to get to main station), **Delft** (6/hr, 50–60 min), **Arnhem** (2/hr, 75 min, transfer likely), **Rotterdam** (4/hr, 1 hr), **Bruges** (hourly, 3.5 hrs, transfer in Brussels or Antwerp's central station; transfer can be timed closely—be alert and check with conductor), **Brussels** (hourly, 3 hrs, €30–42.50), **Ostende** (hourly, 4 hrs, change in Antwerp), **London** (hourly, 6 hrs, with transfer to Eurostar Chunnel train in Brussels, Eurostar discounted with railpass, www.eurostar.com), **Copenhagen** (hourly, 15 hrs, requires multiple transfers), **Frankfurt** (hourly, 4–5.5 hrs, some are direct, others involve transfer in Köln or Duisburg), **Munich** (7/day, 7–8 hrs, transfer in Frankfurt or Düsseldorf), **Bonn** (10/day, 3 hrs, some direct but most transfer in Köln), **Bern** (5/day, 9 hrs, 1 direct but most transfer in Mannheim), **Paris** (5/day, 5 hrs, requires fast Thalys train from Brussels with €14.50 supplement, www.thalys.com).

By Bus: If you don't have a railpass, the cheapest way to get to Paris is by bus (Eurolines buses make the 8-hour trip every 2 hours, about €50–65 round-trip, compared to €100 second-class by train; check online for deals, bus station in Amsterdam at Julianaplein 5, Amstel Station, 5 stops by metro from Central Station, tel. 020/560-8788, www.eurolines.com).

Amsterdam's Schiphol Airport

Schiphol (SKIP-pol) Airport, like most of Holland, is English-speaking, user-friendly, and below sea level.

Information: Schiphol flight information (tel. 0900-7244-7465) can give you flight times and your airline's Amsterdam phone number for reconfirmation before going home (€0.45/min to climb through its phone tree—or visit www.schiphol.nl). To reach the airlines directly, call: KLM and Northwest, tel. 020/649-9123 or 020/474-7747; Martinair, tel. 020/601-1222; SAS, tel. 0900-746-63727; American Airlines, tel. 06/022-7844; British Airways, tel. 023/554-7555; and easyJet, tel. 023/568-4880.

Services: The ABN/AMRO **banks** offer fair exchange rates (in arrivals and lounge area). The GWK **public-transit office** is located in Schiphol Plaza. Surf the **Internet** and make phone calls at the Communication Centre on the top level of lounge 2 (daily 6:00–20:00, behind customs—not available once you've left the security checkpoint). Convenient luggage **lockers** are at various points around the terminal—and a big bank of them is on the bottom floor—allowing you to leave your bag at the airport on a lengthy layover (both short-term and long-term lockers).

If you have extra time to kill at Schiphol, check out some **fine art,** actual Dutch Masters by Rembrandt, Vermeer, and others. The Rijksmuseum loans a dozen or so of its minor masterpieces from the Golden Age to the unique airport museum "Rijksmuseum Amsterdam Schiphol," a little art gallery behind the passport check at Holland Boulevard between piers E and F. Yes, this is really true (free, daily 7:00–20:00). To escape the crowds in the airport, follow signs for the *Panorama Terrace* to the third floor, where you'll find a quieter, full-of-locals cafeteria, a kids' play area, and a view terrace where you can watch planes come and go while you nurse a coffee.

Transportation Connections: The airport has a train station of its own. You can validate your Eurailpass and hit the rails immediately, or, to stretch your railpass, buy an inexpensive ticket into Amsterdam today and start the pass later.

From Schiphol Airport to Amsterdam: There's a direct **train** to Amsterdam's Central Station (every 10 min, 20 min, €3.60). The Connexxion **shuttle bus** takes you to your hotel neighborhood; since there are various routes, ask the attendant which works best for your hotel (2/hr, 20 min, €12 one-way, €19 round-trip, one route stops at Westerkerk near Anne Frank House and many recommended hotels, bus to other hotels may cost a couple euros more, departs from lane A7 in front of airport, tel. 020/653-4975, www.airporthotelshuttle.nl). Allow about €45 for a **taxi** to downtown Amsterdam.

From Schiphol Airport to Haarlem: The big red #300 **bus** is direct, stopping at Haarlem's train station and near the Market Square (4/hr, 40 min, €5.80—buy ticket from driver, or use 7 strips of a *strippenkaart*, departs from lane B2 in front of airport). The **train** is slightly cheaper and just as quick, but you'll have to transfer at the Amsterdam-Sloterdijk station (4/hr, 40 min, €5.10). Figure about €45 to Haarlem by taxi.

From Schiphol Airport by Train to: The Hague/Den Haag (2/hr, 30 min), **Delft** (4/hr, 45 min, transfer in The Hague or Leiden), **Rotterdam** (3/hr, 45 min). International trains to Belgium run every hour: **Brussels** (2.5 hrs), **Bruges** (3.5 hrs, change in Antwerp or Brussels).

HAARLEM

Cute and cozy, yet authentic and handy to the airport, Haarlem is a fine home base, giving you small-town warmth overnight, with easy access (15 min by train) to wild and crazy Amsterdam during the day.

Bustling Haarlem gave America's Harlem its name back when New York was New Amsterdam, a Dutch colony. For centuries, Haarlem has been a market town, buzzing with shoppers heading home with fresh bouquets, nowadays by bike.

Enjoy the market on Monday (clothing) or Saturday (general), when the square bustles like a Brueghel painting, with cheese, fish, flowers, and families. Make yourself at home; buy some flowers to brighten your hotel room.

ORIENTATION

(area code: 023)

Tourist Information

Haarlem's TI (VVV), at the train station, is friendlier, more helpful, and less crowded than Amsterdam's, so ask your Amsterdam questions here. They also offer train-travel advice and sell tickets for destinations in the Netherlands, Belgium, and Germany (April–Sept Mon–Fri 9:00–17:30, Sat 10:00–16:00, closed Sun; Oct–March Mon–Fri 9:30–17:00, Sat 10:00–14:00, closed Sun; tel. 0900-616-1600—€0.50/min, helpful parking brochure). The €1 *Holiday Magazine* is not necessary, but it's free if you buy the fine €2 town map. The TI also sells a €2 self-guided walking-tour map for overachievers. The little yellow computer terminal on the curb outside the TI prints out free maps anytime. (It's fun...just dial the street and hit "print." Drivers will also find these terminals stationed at roads coming into town.)

Arrival in Haarlem

By Train: As you walk out of Haarlem's train station (lockers available), the TI is on your right and the bus station is across the street. Two parallel streets flank the train station (Kruisweg and Jansweg). Head up either street, and you'll reach the town square and church within 10 minutes. If you need help, ask a local person to point you toward the Grote Markt (Market Square).

By Car: Parking is expensive on the streets (€2.50/hr) and cheaper in several central garages (€1.50/hr). Three main garages let you park overnight for €2 (at the train station, near the Teylers Museum—follow signs to the museum, and near the Frans Hals Museum—again, follow signs).

By Plane: For details on getting from Schiphol Airport into Haarlem, see page 980.

Helpful Hints

Blue Monday: Most sights are closed on Monday, except the church.

Money: The handy GWK currency exchange office at the train station offers fair rates (Mon–Fri 8:00–20:00, Sat 9:00–17:00, Sun 10:00–17:00).

Internet Access: Try **Hotel Amadeus** (overlooking Market Square, €1.20/15 min) or nearly any **coffeeshop** (if you don't mind marijuana smoke). Perhaps the cheapest place in town is **Suny Teletechniques** (€2/hr, daily 10:00–24:00, near train station at Lange Herenstraat 4, tel. 023/551-0037).

Post Office: It's at Gedempte Oude Gracht 2 (Mon–Fri 9:00–18:00, Sat 10:00–13:30, closed Sun, has ATM).

Laundry: My Beautiful Launderette is handy and cheap (€6 self-service wash and dry, daily 8:30–20:30, €9 full service available Mon–Fri 9:00–17:00, near V&D department store at Boter Markt 20).

Bike Rental: You can rent bikes at the train station (€7.50/day, €50 deposit and passport number, Mon–Sat 6:00–24:00, Sun 7:30–24:00).

Local Guide: For a historical look at Haarlem, consider hiring Walter Schelfhout (€75/2-hr walk, tel. 023/535-5715, schelfhout@dutch.nl).

Best View: In the top-floor restaurant of the V&D department store (La Place—see page 980), you get wraparound views of the city as you sip your €2 self-serve tea.

Bulb Flower Parade: On Saturday, April 26, 2008, an all-day Bulb Flower Parade of floats, decorated with real blossoms, wafts through eight towns, including Haarlem. The floats are parked in Haarlem at Gedempte Oude Gracht overnight, when they're illuminated, and through the next day (for more details, see www.bloemencorso.info).

SIGHTS AND EXPERIENCES

▲▲Market Square (Grote Markt)—Haarlem's Market Square, where 10 streets converge, is the town's delightful centerpiece...as it has been for 700 years. To enjoy a coffee or beer here, simmering in Dutch good living, is a quintessential European experience. In a recent study, the Dutch were found to be the most content people in Europe. In another study, the people of Haarlem were found to be the most content in the Netherlands. Observe. Sit and gaze at the church, appreciating the same scene Dutch artists captured in oil paintings that now hang in museums.

Just a few years ago, trolleys ran through the square, and cars were parked everywhere. But today, it's a people zone, with market stalls filling the square on Mondays and Saturdays, and café tables dominating on other days.

This is a great place to build a picnic with Haarlem finger foods—raw herring, local cheese (Gouda and Edam), a *frikandel* (little corn-dog sausage), french fries with mayonnaise, *stroopwafels* (waffles with built-in syrup), *poffertjes* (little sugar doughnuts), or one of many different ethnic foods (falafel, *shoarma,* Indonesian dishes).

▲Church (Grote Kerk)—This 15th-century Gothic church (now Protestant) is worth a look, if only to see Holland's greatest pipe organ (from 1738, 100 feet high). Its 5,000 pipes impressed both Handel and Mozart. Note how the organ, which fills the west end, seems to steal the show from the altar. Quirky highlights of the church include a replica of Foucault's pendulum, the "Dog-Whipper's Chapel," and a 400-year-old cannonball.

To enter, find the small *Entrée* sign behind the church at Oude Groenmarkt 23 (€2, Mon–Sat 10:00–16:00, closed Sun to tourists, tel. 023/553-2040).

Consider attending (even part of) a **concert** to hear the Oz-like pipe organ (regular free concerts Tue at 20:15 mid-May–mid-Oct, additional concerts Thu at 15:00 late June–Aug, concerts nearly nightly at 20:15 during the organ competition in July, confirm schedule at TI or at www.bavo.nl; bring a sweater—the church isn't heated).

▲▲Frans Hals Museum—Haarlem is the hometown of Frans Hals, the foremost Dutch portrait painter of the 17th-century Golden Age. This refreshing museum—an almshouse for old men back in 1610—displays many of his greatest paintings, done in his

Haarlem

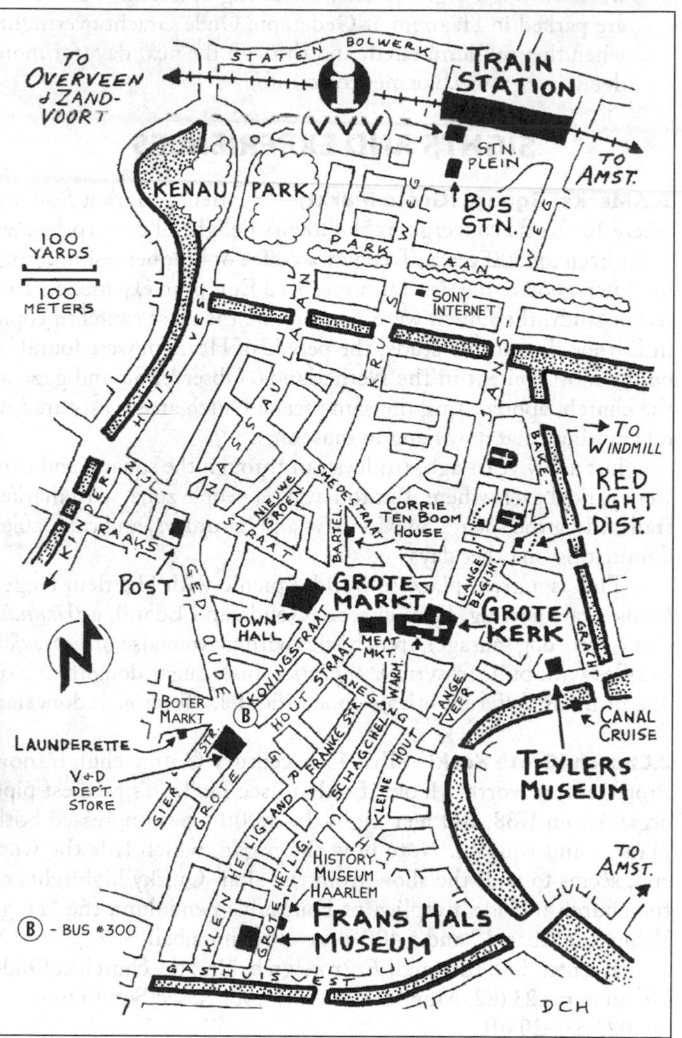

nearly Impressionistic style. Stand eye-to-eye with life-size, life-like portraits of Haarlem's citizens—brewers, preachers, workers, bureaucrats, and housewives—and see the people who built the Golden Age, then watched it start to fade.

Along with Frans Hals' work, the museum features Pieter Brueghel's painting *Dutch Proverbs,* illustrating 72 Dutch proverbs. To peek into old Dutch ways, identify some with the help of the English-language key. Also look for the 250-year-old dollhouse on display in a former chapel (€7, Tue–Sat 11:00–17:00, Sun

12:00–17:00, closed Mon, Groot Heiligland 62, tel. 023/511-5775, www.franshalsmuseum.nl).

History Museum Haarlem—This small museum, across the street from the Frans Hals Museum, offers a glimpse of old Haarlem. Request the English version of the 10-minute video, low-key Haarlem's version of a sound-and-light show. Study the large-scale model of Haarlem in 1822 (when its fortifications were still intact), and enjoy the "time machine" computer and video display that show you various aspects of life in Haarlem at different points in history (€2, Tue–Sat 12:00–17:00, Sun 13:00–17:00, closed Mon, Groot Heiligland 47, tel. 023/542-2427). The adjacent architecture center (free) may be of interest to architects.

Corrie ten Boom House—Haarlem is home to Corrie ten Boom, popularized by *The Hiding Place*, her inspirational book and the movie that followed, about the ten Boom family's experience protecting Jews from the Nazis. Corrie ten Boom gives the other half of the Anne Frank story—the point of view of those who risked their lives to hide Dutch Jews during the Nazi occupation (1940–1945).

The clock shop was the ten Boom family business. The elderly father and his two daughters—Corrie and Betsy, both in their 50s—lived above the store and in the brick building attached in back (along Schoutensteeg alley). Corrie's bedroom was on the top floor at the back. This room was tiny to start with, but then the family built a second, secret room (only about a foot deep) at the very back—"the hiding place," where they could hide six or seven Jews at a time.

Devoutly religious, the family had a long tradition of tolerance, having for generations hosted prayer meetings here in their home for both Jews and Christians.

The Gestapo, tipped off that the family was harboring Jews, burst into the ten Boom house. Finding a suspicious number of ration coupons, the Nazis arrested the family, but failed to find the six Jews in the hiding place (who later escaped). Corrie's father and sister died while in prison, but Corrie survived the Ravensbruck concentration camp to tell her story in her memoir.

The ten Boom House is open only for 60-minute English tours—check the sign on the door for the next start time; the tours are mixed with preaching (donation accepted, April–Oct Tue–Sat tours begin at 10:00 and the last tour is at 15:30, Nov–March Tue–Sat first tour at 11:00 and last at 14:30, closed Sun–Mon, 50 yards north of Market Square at Barteljorisstraat 19; the clock-shop people get all wound up if you go inside—wait in the little side street at the door, where hourly tour times are posted; tel. 023/531-0823, www.corrietenboom.com).

▲Teylers Museum—Famous as the oldest museum in Holland, Teylers is a time-warp experience, filled with all sorts of fun curios for science buffs: fossils, minerals, primitive electronic gadgetry, and examples of 18th- and 19th-century technology. This place feels like a museum of a museum. They're serious about authenticity here: The presentation is perfectly preserved, right down to the original labels. Since there was no electricity in the olden days, you'll find no electric lighting...if it's dark outside, it's dark inside. The museum's benefactor, Pieter Teyler van der Hulst, was a very wealthy merchant who willed his estate, worth the equivalent of €80 million today, to a foundation whose mission was to "create and maintain a museum to stimulate art and science." The museum opened in 1784, six years after Teyler's death (his last euro was spent in 1983—now it's a national museum.). Add your name to the guest book that goes back literally to before Napoleon's visit here. The oval room—a temple of science and learning—is the core of the museum; the art gallery hangs paintings in the old style. While there are no English descriptions, there is an excellent audioguide (€5.50, Tue–Sat 10:00–17:00, Sun 12:00–17:00, closed Mon, Spaarne 16, tel. 023/531-9010, www.teylersmuseum.nl).

De Adriaan Windmill—Haarlem's old-time windmill, located just a 10-minute walk from the station and Teylers Museum, welcomes visitors with a short video, little museum, and fine town views (€2, Wed–Fri 13:00–16:00, Sat–Sun 10:00–16:00, closed Mon–Tue, Papentorenvest 1, tel. 023/545-0259, www.molenadriaan.nl).

Canal Cruise—Making a scenic 50-minute loop through and around Haarlem with a live guide who speaks up to four languages, these little trips by Woltheus Cruises are more relaxing than informative (€7, May–Sept daily departures at the top of each hour from 12:00–17:00, closed Mon in April and Oct, no tours Nov–March, across canal from Teylers Museum at Spaarne 11a, tel. 023/535-7723, www.woltheuscruises.nl).

Red Light District—Wander through a little Red Light District as precious as a Barbie doll—and legal since the 1980s (2 blocks northeast of Market Square, off Lange Begijnestraat, no senior or student discounts). Don't miss the mall marked by the red neon sign reading *'t Steegje* (free, on Begijnesteeg). The nearby *'t Poortje* (office park) costs €6.

NIGHTLIFE

Haarlem's evening scene is great. The bars around the Grote Kerk and Lange Veerstraat are colorful and lively, and you'll find plenty of music. The best show in town: the café scene on Market Square. In good weather, café tables tumble happily out of the bars.

For trendy local crowds, sip a drink at **Café Studio** on Market

Square (daily 12:00–2:00 in the morning, next to Hotel Carillon, tel. 023/531-0033). **Grand Café XO** is another hip nightspot on the square (daily 10:00–24:00, Grote Markt 8, tel. 023/551-1350). Tourists gawk at the old-fashioned, belt-driven ceiling fans in **Café 1900** near the Corrie ten Boom House (daily 9:00–00:30, live music Sun night except in July, Barteljorisstraat 10, tel. 023/531-8283).

SLEEPING

The helpful Haarlem TI, just outside the train station, can nearly always find you a €25 bed in a private home (for a €6-per-person fee, plus a cut of your host's money, two-night minimum). Avoid this if you can; it's cheaper to reserve by calling direct. Nearly every Dutch person you'll encounter speaks English.

Haarlem is most crowded in April (in 2008, particularly Easter weekend—March 22–23, for the flower parade on April 26, and on Queen's Day on April 30), May, July, and August.

The listed prices include breakfast (unless otherwise noted) and usually include the €2-per-person-per-day tourist tax. To avoid this town's louder-than-normal street noises, forgo views for a room in the back. Hotels and the TI have a useful parking brochure.

In the Center

Hotels and B&Bs

$$$ Hotel Lion D'Or is a classy, 34-room business hotel with all the professional comforts and a handy location. Expect a proficient welcome (Db-€155, Fri–Sat Db-€110, extra bed-€20, soft prices in off-season, air-con, Internet access for a fee, some non-smoking rooms, elevator, across the street from train station at Kruisweg 34, tel. 023/532-1750, fax 023/532-9543, www.goldentulip.com, reservations@hotelliondor.nl).

Haarlem

Sleep Code

(€1 = about $1.30, country code: 31, area code: 023)
S = Single, **D** = Double/Twin, **T** = Triple, **Q** = Quad, **b** = bathroom, **s** = shower only. Credit cards are accepted unless otherwise noted.

To help you easily sort through these listings, I've divided the rooms into three categories, based on the price for a standard double room with bath:

$$$ Higher Priced—Most rooms €100 or more.
$$ Moderately Priced—Most rooms between €65–100.
$ Lower Priced—Most rooms €65 or less.

Haarlem Hotels and Restaurants

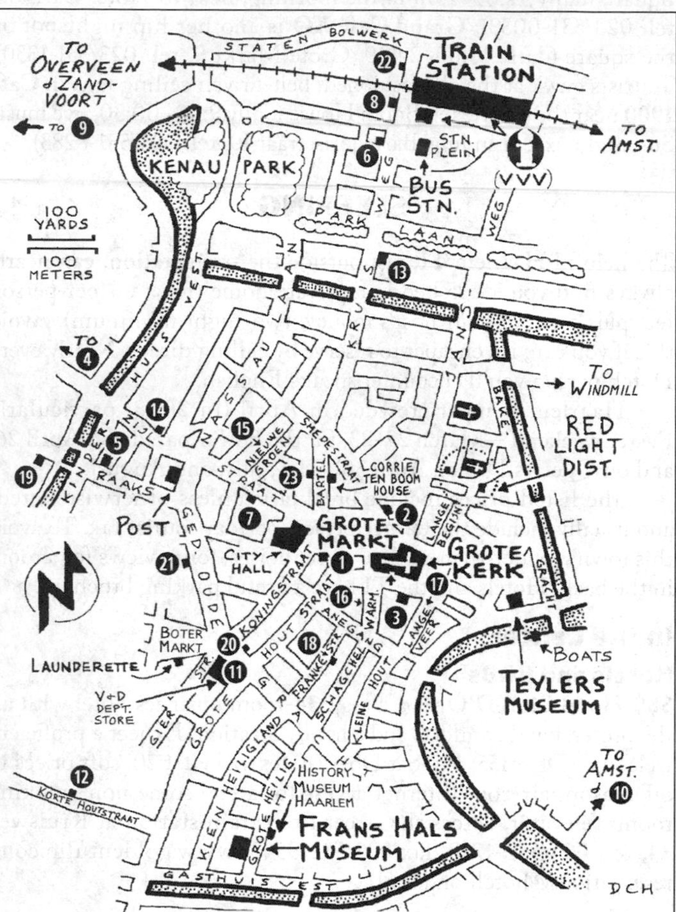

1. Hotel Amadeus & Grand Café XO
2. Hotel Carillon & Café Studio
3. Joops Hotel
4. To B & B House de Kiefte
5. Die Raeckse Hotel
6. Hotel Lion D'Or
7. Hotel Caruso
8. Indrapoera Hotel
9. To Stayokay Haarlem Hostel
10. To Hotel Haarlem Zuid
11. La Place Cafeteria
12. Fondue Rest. "in 't Goede Uur"
13. Pannenkoekhuis de Smikkel
14. Eko Eet Café
15. Vincent's Eethuis
16. Jacobus Pieck Eetlokaal & Friethuis de Vlaminck
17. La Plume & BastiJan Rest.
18. De Lachende Javaan Rest.
19. De Buren Eetlokaal
20. Pizzeria-Rist. Venezia
21. DekaMarkt Supermarket
22. Albert Heijn Supermarket
23. Café 1900

$$ Hotel Amadeus, on Market Square, has 15 small, bright, and basic rooms, some with views of the square. This characteristic hotel, ideally located above an early 20th-century dinner café, is relatively quiet, especially if you take a room in the back. Its lush old lounge/breakfast room on the second floor overlooks the square, and Mike and Inez take good care of their guests (Sb-€60, Db-€85, Tb-€110, includes tax, two-night stay and cash get you a 5 percent discount, 10-min walk from train station, steep climb to lounge and then an elevator, Grote Markt 10, tel. 023/532-4530, fax 023/532-2328, www.amadeus-hotel.com, info@amadeus-hotel.com). The hotel also has Internet access for a fee (€1.20/15 min, 25 percent discount with this book).

$$ Joops Hotel, with 29 comfortable rooms in an American-style hotel and 34 rooms in apartment buildings nearby, is located just behind the Grote Kerk (Db-€85, Fri–Sat Db-€95, breakfast buffet-€9.50, Internet access for a fee, Oude Groenmarkt 20, tel. 023/532-2008, fax 023/532-9549, www.joopshotel.com, info@joopshotel.com). Joops also rents studios with kitchenettes for 2–4 people (€105–150 depending on season and number of people).

$ Bed-and-Breakfast House de Kiefte is your get-into-a-local-home budget option. Marjet (mar-yet) and Hans, a frank, interesting Dutch couple who speak English well, rent four bright, cheery, non-smoking rooms (rates include breakfast and travel advice) in their quiet 1892 home (Ds-€55, T-€76, Qs-€98, Quint/b-€115, cash only, two-night minimum, very steep stairs, family loft sleeps up to five, kids older than 4 welcome, Coornhertstraat 3, tel. 023/532-2980, mobile 06-5474-5272, housedekiefte@gmx.net). It's a 15-minute walk or €7 taxi ride from the train station and a five-minute walk from the center. From Market Square, walk to the right of the town hall, go straight out Zijlstraat over the bridge, and take a left on the fourth street.

Rooms in Restaurants

These places are all run as sidelines by restaurants, and you'll know it by the style of service and rooms. Lobbies are in the restaurant and there are no public spaces. Still, they are handy and—for Haarlem—inexpensive.

$$ Hotel Carillon overlooks the town square and comes with a little traffic and bell-tower chimes. Many of the 20 rooms—all of which were renovated in 2006—are small, and the stairs are st-e-e-e-p. The front rooms come with more street noise and great town-square views (tiny loft S-€38–40, Db-€78–80, Tb-€99, Qb-€108, 5 percent discount for readers if claimed when booking, no elevator, 10-min walk from train station, Grote Markt 27, tel. 023/531-0591, fax 023/531-4909, www.hotelcarillon.com, info@hotelcarillon.com).

$$ Hotel Caruso rents 15 huge, plain, bright, mod rooms—which may suffer from a little commotion from revelers below—above its Italian restaurant (Db-€95, Tb-€110, Qb-€120, Zijlstraat 56, tel. 023/542-1420, www.hotelrestaurantcaruso.nl).

$$ Indrapoera Hotel, a humid little place with too much carpeting, has eight cheap, handy rooms across the street from the train station (Db-€75, trains stop by midnight, Kruisweg 18, tel. 023/532-0393, yeh@yeh.speedxs.nl, Yeh family).

$$ Die Raeckse Hotel, family-run and friendly, is not as central as the others and has less character and more traffic noise—but its 21 rooms are decent and comfortable. Ask for a quiet room (Sb-€55, Db-€65–85 depending on size, Tb-€85–105, Qb-€100–125, 10 percent discount for 2-night stay except in Aug, includes breakfast, Raaks Straat 1, tel. 023/532-6629, fax 023/531-7937, www.die-raeckse.nl, dieraeckse@zonnet.nl). A big, cheap parking garage is across the street.

Near Haarlem

$$ Hotel Haarlem Zuid, with 300 very American rooms, is sterile but a good value for drivers. It sits in an industrial zone a 20-minute walk from the center, on the road to the airport (Db-€82, breakfast-€12, elevator, free parking, laundry service, fitness center-€5, inexpensive hotel restaurant, Toekanweg 2, tel. 023/536-7500, fax 023/536-7980, www.hotelhaarlemzuid.nl, info@hotelhaarlemzuid.valk.nl). Bus #300 (runs every 10 min) conveniently connects the hotel with the train station, Market Square, and the airport.

$ Stayokay Haarlem, completely renovated and with all the youth-hostel comforts, charges €22–27 for beds in four-, six-, and eight-bed dorms. They also rent simple €60 doubles (€2.50 less for members, includes sheets and breakfast, daily 7:30–24:00, Jan Gijzenpad 3, two miles from Haarlem station—take bus #2 from station, or a 10-min walk from Santpoort Zuid train station, tel. 023/537-3793, fax 023/537-1176, www.stayokay.com/haarlem, haarlem@stayokay.com).

EATING

In or near the Train Station

Pancakes for lunch or dinner? **Pannenkoekhuis de Smikkel** serves a selection of more than 50 pancakes for a meal (meat, cheese, etc.) and dessert. The €8 pancakes can fill two (daily 12:00–21:00, Sun from 16:00, 2 blocks in front of station, Kruisweg 57, tel. 023/532-0631).

Enjoy a sandwich or coffee surrounded by trains and 1908 architecture in the **Stations Café** (daily 6:30–20:30, between tracks #3 and #6 at the station).

On or near Zijlstraat

Eko Eet Café is great for fish dishes or a cheery, tasty vegetarian meal (€12–18 plates, daily 11:30–21:30, Zijlstraat 39, tel. 023/532-6568).

Vincent's Eethuis, the cheapest restaurant in town, offers basic Dutch food—and occasional special dishes from Indonesia and elsewhere—and a friendly staff. This former St. Vincent's soup kitchen now feeds more gainfully employed locals than the poor (two €5.75 daily plates to choose from, Mon–Fri 16:30–19:30, closed Sat–Sun, Nieuwe Groenmarkt 22).

Between Market Square and Frans Hals Museum

Jacobus Pieck Eetlokaal is popular with locals for its fine-value "global cuisine," good salads, and peaceful garden courtyard (€9.50 plate of the day, great €6 sandwiches at lunch, Mon 10:00–17:00, Tue–Sat 10:00–22:00, closed Sun, cash only, Warmoesstraat 18, behind church, tel. 023/532-6144).

Friethuis de Vlaminck is your best bet for a cone of old-fashioned fresh "Flemish fries" (€2, daily until 18:00, Warmoesstraat 3, behind church, tel. 023/532-1084). Be creative with their dazzling array of sauces.

Pizzeria-Ristorante Venezia, run for 10 years by the same Italian family from Bari, is the place to go for pizza or pasta (€8–17 meals, pizza from €7.50, daily 13:00–23:00, facing V&D department store at Verwulft 7, tel. 023/531-7753).

La Plume Restaurant steakhouse is noisy, with a happy, local, and carnivorous crowd (€12–18 meals, daily from 17:30, Lange Veerstraat 1, tel. 023/531-3202). The relaxing outdoor seating faces the church and a lively pedestrian mall.

BastiJan serves good Mediterranean cuisine in an atmosphere of youthful elegance (€20 meals, 4-course dinner for €25, Tue–Sun from 18:00, closed Mon, Lange Veerstraat 8, tel. 023/532-6006).

De Lachende Javaan ("The Laughing Javanese") serves the best Indonesian food in town, in a spacious, classy, and woody dining area (I'd avoid their upstairs seating). Their €18–22 *rijsttafels* are excellent (Tue–Sun 17:00–22:00, closed Mon, Frankestraat 27, tel. 023/532-8792).

De Buren Eetlokaal, fun and traditional, offers an old-time ambience and good Franco-Dutch food to an enthusiastic local crowd. It's just outside the center near several recommended accommodations (€10–14 meals, Thu–Mon 16:00–22:00, closed Tue–Wed, Brouwersvaart 146, tel. 023/532-7078).

Fondue Restaurant "in 't Goede Uur" ("in the Good Hour") is a romantic, 12-table place with classical music on the most charming street in Haarlem. Reservations are required (€17 cheese fondue, Tue–Sun 17:00–24:00, closed Mon, cash only, Korte Houtstraat 1, tel. 023/531-1174).

La Place dishes up fresh, healthy, budget food with Haarlem's best view. Sit on the top floor or roof garden of the V&D department store (Mon 11:00–18:00, Tue–Sat 9:30–18:00, Thu until 21:00, closed Sun except for first Sun of month 12:00–17:00, large non-smoking section, Grote Houtstraat 70, on corner of Gedempte Oude Gracht, tel. 023/515-8700).

Picnics: Shoppers have two good choices—the **DekaMarkt supermarket** near Market Square (Mon 10:00–20:00, Tue–Wed 8:30–20:00, Thu–Fri 8:30–21:00, Sat 8:30–20:00, closed Sun, Gedempte Oude Gracht 54, between V&D department store and post office) or the **Albert Heijn supermarket** near the train station (Mon–Sat 8:00–20:00, closed Sun, cash only, Kruisweg 10).

TRANSPORTATION CONNECTIONS

From Haarlem by Train to: Amsterdam (6/hr, 15 min, €3.60 one-way, €6.20 same-day round-trip), **The Hague** (4/hr, 35 min), **Delft** (2/hr, 40 min), **Rotterdam** (2/hr, 50 min, may require change in Leiden), **Hoorn** (2/hr, 1 hr), **Alkmaar** (2/hr, 45 min), **Brussels** (hourly, 2.75 hrs, transfer in Rotterdam), **Bruges** (1–2/hr, 3.5 hrs, requires transfer).

To Schiphol Airport: Your options are the **bus** (4/hr, 40 min, €5.80 or 7 *strippenkaart* strips, bus #300, departs from Haarlem's train station in "Zuidtangent" lane), **train** (4/hr, 40 min, transfer at Amsterdam-Sloterdijk station, €5.10), or **taxi** (about €45).

SPAIN

BARCELONA

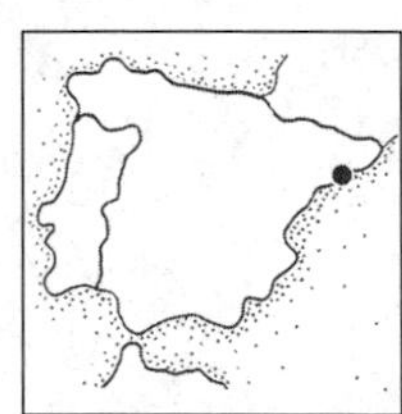

Barcelona is Spain's second city, and the capital of the proud and distinct region of Catalunya. With Franco's fascism now ancient history, Catalan flags wave once again. And the local language and culture are on a roll in Spain's most cosmopolitan and European corner.

Barcelona bubbles with life in its narrow Barri Gòtic alleys, along the grand boulevards, and throughout the chic, grid-planned, new part of town, called Eixample. While Barcelona had an illustrious past as a Roman colony, Visigothic capital, 14th-century maritime power, and—in more modern times—a top Mediterranean trading and manufacturing center, it's most enjoyable to throw out the history books and just drift through the city. If you're in the mood to surrender to a city's charms, let it be in Barcelona.

Planning Your Time

Located in the far northeast corner of Spain, Barcelona makes a good first or last stop for your trip. Now with the AVE train, Barcelona is only 4.5 hours away from Madrid.

You could sandwich Barcelona between flights. From the US, it's as easy to fly into Barcelona as it is to land in Madrid, Lisbon, or Paris. Those renting a car can cleverly start here, fly (or train) to Madrid, and see Madrid and Toledo, all before picking up their car—saving on several days' worth of rental fees.

On the shortest visit, Barcelona is worth one night, one day, and an overnight train ride or evening flight out. The Ramblas is two different streets by day and by night. Stroll it from top to bottom in the evening and again the next morning, grabbing breakfast on a stool in a market café. Wander the Barri Gòtic (BAH-ree

Barcelona Overview

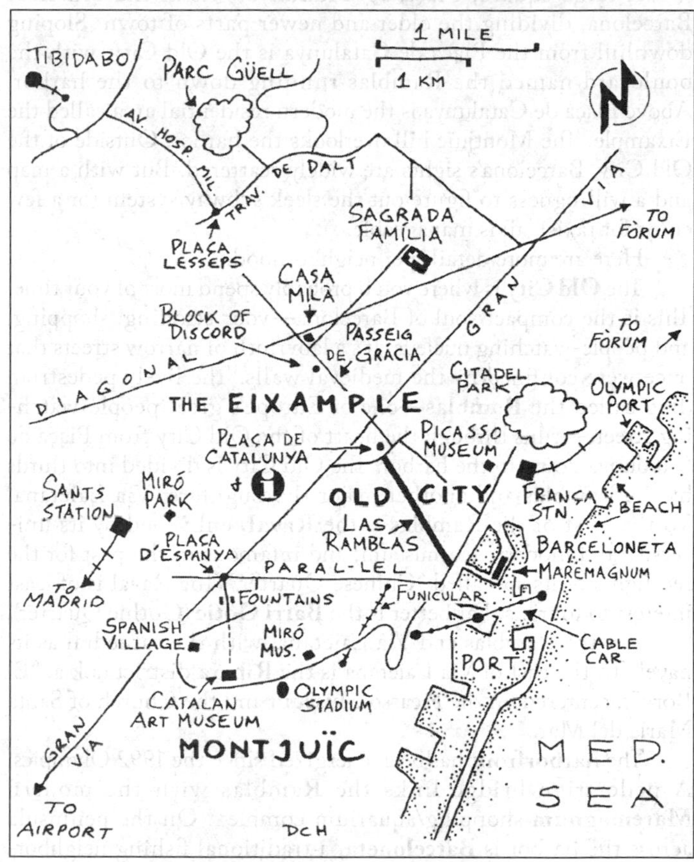

GOH-teek), see the cathedral, and have lunch in the Eixample (eye-SHAM-plah). The top two sights in town, Antoni Gaudí's Sagrada Família church and the Picasso Museum, are usually open until 20:00 during the summer (Picasso closed Mon). The illuminated Magic Fountains on Montjuïc make a good finale for your day (Thu–Sun until 23:00 in summer).

Of course, Barcelona in a day is insane. To better sample the city's ample charm, spread your visit over two or three days.

ORIENTATION

Like Los Angeles, Barcelona is a basically flat city that sprawls out under the sun between the sea and the mountains. It's huge (1.5 million people), but travelers need only focus on four areas: the Old City, the harbor/Barceloneta, the Eixample, and Montjuïc.

A large square, Plaça de Catalunya, sits at the center of Barcelona, dividing the older and newer parts of town. Sloping downhill from the Plaça de Catalunya is the Old City, with the boulevard named the Ramblas running down to the harbor. Above Plaça de Catalunya is the modern residential area called the Eixample. The Montjuïc hill overlooks the harbor. Outside of the Old City, Barcelona's sights are widely scattered. But with a map and a willingness to figure out the sleek subway system (or a few euros for taxis), all is manageable.

Here are more details per neighborhood:

The **Old City** is where you'll probably spend most of your time. This is the compact soul of Barcelona—your strolling, shopping, and people-watching nucleus. It's a labyrinth of narrow streets that once were confined by the medieval walls. The lively pedestrian drag called the **Ramblas**—one of Europe's great people-watching streets—runs through the heart of the Old City from Plaça de Catalunya down to the harbor. The Old City is divided into thirds by the Ramblas and another major thoroughfare, Via Laietana. To the west of the Ramblas is the **Raval,** enlivened by its university and modern art museum, and infamous in the past for the red lights of its so-called "Chinese Quarter." The Raval is of least interest to tourists. Far better is the **Barri Gòtic** (Gothic Quarter), between the Ramblas and Via Laietana, with the cathedral as its navel. To the east of Via Laietana is the **Ribera** district (a.k.a. "El Born"), centered on the Picasso Museum and the Church of Santa Maria del Mar.

The **harborfront** has been energized since the 1992 Olympics. A pedestrian bridge links the Ramblas with the modern **Maremagnum** shopping/aquarium complex. On the peninsula across the harbor is **Barceloneta,** a traditional fishing neighborhood that's home to some good seafood restaurants and a string of sandy beaches. Beyond Barceloneta, a man-made beach, several miles long, leads east to a new commercial and convention district called the **Fòrum.**

North of the Old City, beyond the bustling hub of Plaça de Catalunya, is the elegant **Eixample** district—its grid plan softened by cut-off corners. Much of Barcelona's Modernista architecture is found here. To the north is the **Gràcia** district, and beyond that, Antoni Gaudí's **Parc Güell.**

The large hill overlooking the city to the west is **Montjuïc,** home to a variety of attractions including several excellent museums (Catalan Art, Joan Miró) and the Olympic Stadium.

Apart from your geographical orientation, you'll need to orient yourself linguistically to a language distinct from Spanish. While Spanish ("Castilian") is widely spoken, the native tongue in this region is Catalan—as different from Spanish as Italian.

Tourist Information

There are several useful **city TIs** in Barcelona: at the **airport** (daily 9:00–21:00, offices in both terminal A and terminal B, tel. 934-784-704); at **Sants Train Station** (Mon–Fri 8:00–20:00, Sat–Sun 8:00–14:00, near track 6); and at **Plaça de Catalunya** (daily 9:00–21:00, on main square near recommended hotels—look for red sign, tel. 932-853-832). Most of these TIs have a room-finding service and sell phone cards and tickets for the Tourist Bus (described in "Getting Around Barcelona," page 987). The TI on Plaça de Catalunya also offers some guided walks (see "Tours," page 988). Throughout the summer, young, red-jacketed tourist-info helpers appear in the most touristy parts of town.

The two **all-Catalunya TIs** work fine for the entire region and even Madrid. You'll find them at **Passeig de Gràcia** (Mon–Sat 10:00–19:00, Sun 10:00–14:00, on Plaça de Joan Carlos I, at the intersection of Diagonal and Passeig de Gràcia, Passeig de Gràcia 107, tel. 932-384-000) and on **Plaça de Sant Jaume** (Mon–Fri 9:00–20:00, Sat 10:00–20:00, Sun 10:00–14:00, in the City Hall/Ajuntament building).

At any TI, pick up the free, small city map (the large €1.20 map is unnecessary), the brochure on public transport, and the free quarterly *See Barcelona* guide (practical information on museum hours, restaurants, transportation, history, festivals, and so on).

Articket Card: You can get into seven art museums and their temporary exhibits with this ticket, including the recommended Picasso Museum, Casa Milà, Catalan Art Museum, and Fundació Joan Miró (€20, valid for six months, sold at TIs and participating museums, www.articketbcn.org). If you're planning to go to three or more of the museums, this time-saver pays for itself. To skip the line, show your Articket Card to someone at the info desk or to the ticket taker, and they'll help you get your entrance ticket pronto.

Barcelona Card: This card covers public transportation (buses, Metro, Montjuïc funicular, and *golondrina* harbor tour) and includes free admission to minor sights and discounts on major sights (€23/2 days, €28/3 days, €31/4 days, €34/5 days, sold at TIs and El Corte Inglés department store).

Arrival in Barcelona

By Train: Although many international trains use the França Station, all domestic (and some international) trains use Sants Station. Both França and Sants have baggage lockers and subway stations: França's subway is Barceloneta (2 blocks away), and Sants' is Sants Estació (under the station). Sants Station has a good TI, a world of handy shops and eateries, automated train-ticket vending machines, and a classy, quiet Sala Euromed lounge for travelers with first-class reservations (TV, free drinks, study tables, and coffee bar). Take the Metro or a taxi to your hotel. Most trains traveling to or from France stop at the subway station Passeig de Gràcia, just a short walk from the center (Plaça de Catalunya, TI, hotels); you can get off there.

By Plane: Barcelona's **El Prat de Llobregat Airport,** eight miles southwest of town, has a post office, pharmacy, left-luggage office, plenty of good cafeterias in the gate areas, and ATMs (avoid the gimmicky machines before the baggage carousels; instead, use the bank-affiliated ATMs at the far-left end of the arrivals hall as you face the street).

The airport is connected cheaply and quickly to downtown by **Aerobus** (immediately in front of arrivals lobby, 3/hr until 24:00, 30 min to Plaça de Catalunya, buy €3.75 ticket from driver) or by the RENFE **train** (line 10; at the airport, walk through overpass to train station; 2/hr at about :00 and :30 after the hour, 20 min to Sants Station, 25 min to Passeig de Gràcia, and 30 min to Estació de França, €2.40 or buy a T10 Card at the airport and use it for this trip—see "Getting Around Barcelona," page 987). A **taxi** between the airport and downtown costs about €20. Airport info: tel. 932-983-838.

By Car: Barcelona's parking fees are outrageously expensive (the one behind Boquería market charges €23/day). You won't need a car in Barcelona because the public transportation is so good.

Helpful Hints

Theft Alert: You're more likely to be pickpocketed here—especially on the Ramblas—than about anywhere else in Europe. Most of the crime is nonviolent, but muggings do occur. Be on guard. Leave valuables in your hotel and wear a money belt.

Street scams are easy to avoid if you recognize them. Most common is the too-friendly local who tries to engage you in conversation by asking for the time, talking sports, asking whether you speak English, and so on. If you suspect the person is more interested in your money than your time, ignore him and move on. Beware of thieves posing as lost tourists who ask for your help. A typical street gambling scam is the pea-and-carrot game, a variation on the shell game. The people winning are all ringers, and you can be sure that you'll lose if you play. Also beware of groups of women aggressively selling carnations, people offering to clean off a stain from your shirt, and people picking things up in front of you on escalators. If you stop for any commotion or show on the Ramblas, put your hands in your pockets before someone else does. Assume any scuffle is simply a distraction by a team of thieves.

US Consulate: It's at Passeig Reina Elisenda 23 (for passport services: Mon–Fri 9:00–13:00, closed Sat–Sun, tel. 932-802-227, emergency after-hours tel. 915-872-200).

Emergency Phone Numbers: Police—092, Emergency—061, directory assistance—010.

Pharmacy: A 24-hour pharmacy is near La Boquería market at #98 on the Ramblas.

American Express: The AmEx office is at Las Ramblas 74 (daily 9:00–24:00, banking services only, opposite Liceu Metro station, tel. 900-994-426; for credit-card concerns, call 900-941-413).

Internet Access: EasyInternetcafé—with piles of computers, zippy access (€1.50/hr), drinks, and munchies—has two central locations: One is a half block west of Plaça de Catalunya on Ronda Universitat, and the other is near the seedy bottom of the Ramblas at #31 (both open daily 8:00–24:00).

Getting Around Barcelona

By Public Transit: Barcelona's Metro, among Europe's best, connects just about every place you'll visit. It has five color-coded lines. Rides cost €1.20. Given the excellent Metro service, it's unlikely you'll take a local bus (also €1.20). The T10 Card for €6.65 gives you 10 tickets (sharable, good for all Metro and local bus lines as well as the separate FGC line and RENFE train lines, including thc airport). Full- and multi-day passes are also available (€5/1 day, €9.20/2 days, €13.20/3 days). Pick up the TI's guide to public transport.

By Tourist Bus: The handy Tourist Bus (Bus Turistic) offers two multi-stop circuits in colorful double-decker buses (red route covers north Barcelona—most Gaudí sights; blue route covers south—Barri Gòtic, Montjuïc) with live multilingual guides (44 stops, 2 hours per route, daily 9:00–22:00 in summer, 9:00–21:00 in winter, buses run every 6–30 min, most frequent in summer). Ask for a brochure (which has a good city map) at the TI or at a pick-up point (buy tickets on bus or at TI). One-day (€18) and two-day (€22) tickets include 10–20 percent discounts on the city's major sights and walking tours, which will likely save you half the cost of the Tourist Bus.

By Taxi: Barcelona is one of Europe's best taxi towns. Taxis are plentiful (there are more than 10,000) and honest (whether they like it or not—the light on top shows which tariff they're charging). They're also reasonable (€1.45 drop charge, €1 per kilometer, these "*Tarif* 2" rates are in effect 6:00–22:00, pay higher "*Tarif* 1" rates off-hours, luggage-€1/piece, other fees posted in window). Save time by hopping a cab (figure €4 from Ramblas to Sants Station).

TOURS

Walking Tours—The TI at Plaça de Catalunya offers great guided walks through the Barri Gòtic in English only (€9, daily at 10:00, 2 hours, groups limited to 35, departs from the TI, buy your ticket 15 minutes early at the TI desk—not from the guide). A local guide will explain the medieval story of the city as you walk from Plaça de Catalunya through the cathedral neighborhood, finishing at the City Hall on Plaça de Sant Jaume. The TI also offers a 90-minute Picasso walk, taking you through the streets of his youth and early career and finishing in the museum (€11, includes museum admission, Tue–Sun at 10:30, departs from Plaça de Catalunya). There are also gourmet walks (Fri and Sat at 11:00) and Modernisme walks (Fri and Sat at 16:00).

Local Guides—The Barcelona Guide Bureau is a co-op with about 20 local guides who give personalized four-hour tours starting at €225 (per person price drops as group gets bigger); Joana Wilhelm and Carles Picazo are excellent (Via Laietana 54, tel. 932-682-422 or 933-107-778, www.bgb.es).

SELF-GUIDED WALKS

Most visitors to Barcelona spend much of their time in the twisty, atmospheric Old City. These two walks will give meaning to your wandering. The first begins at Barcelona's main square, and leads you down the city's main drag, and one of Europe's best public spaces: the Ramblas. The second walk starts at the same square, but guides you into the heart of the Barri Gòtic, to the neighborhood around Barcelona's impressive cathedral.

The Ramblas Ramble: From Plaça de Catalunya down the Ramblas

A ▲▲▲ sight, Barcelona's central square and main boulevard exert a powerful pull. Many visitors spend the majority of their time doing laps on the Ramblas. While the allure of the Ramblas is fading (as tacky tourist shops and fast-food joints replace its former elegance), this is still a fun people zone that offers a good introduction to the city. See it, but be sure to venture further afield. Here's a top-to-bottom orientation walk.

Plaça de Catalunya: This vast central square divides old and new Barcelona. It's also the hub for the Metro, bus, airport shuttle, and both Tourist Bus routes (red northern route leaves from El Corte Inglés—described below, blue southern route from the west side of the square). The grass around its fountain is the best public place in town for serious necking. Overlooking the square, the huge **El Corte Inglés** department store offers everything from

From Plaça de Catalunya down the Ramblas

NOT TO SCALE-
PLAÇA DE CATALUNYA TO COLUMBUS MONUMENT IS A 30 MIN. WALK
TO "BLOCK OF DISCORD"
RAMBLA DE CATALUNYA
PASSEIG DE GRÀCIA
BLUE TOURIST BUS
PLAÇA DE CATALUNYA
EL CORTE INGLÉS
CAFÉ ZÜRICH
Catalunya
CANALETES FOUNTAIN
AEROBUS, RED TOURIST BUS + TAXIS
AV. PORTAL DE L'ANGEL
SANTA ANNA
ACADEMY OF SCIENCE
CANUDA
BIRDS
ROMAN ACROPOLIS
CAFÉ GRANJA VIADER
BAROQUE CHURCH
BAGUES JEWELRY SHOP
CARME
Liceu
PORTAFERRISSA
CULTURAL INFO PALAU VIRREINA
LA BOQUERÍA MARKET
FLOWERS
CIGAR SHOP + EROTIC MUSEUM
CARDENAL
HOSP.
"UMBRELLA" BLDG.
ESCRIBA CAFÉ
FERRAN
TO PLAÇA DE S. JAUME
S. PAU
BARRIO XINES
MIRÓ MOSAIC
LICEU OPERA HOUSE
Liceu
PLAÇA REIAL
NOU RAMBLA
Drassanes
PALAU GÜELL
ESCUDELLERS
MARITIME MUSEUM
COLUMBUS MONUMENT
PASSEIG COLÓM
DCH
GOLONDRINAS BOATS
HARBOR
RAMBLA DE MAR
- METRO STATIONS
TO MAREMAGNUM
1
2
3
4
5
6

bonsai trees to a travel agency, plus one-hour photo developing, haircuts, and cheap souvenirs (Mon–Sat 10:00–22:00, closed Sun, pick up English directory flier, supermarket in basement, ninth-floor terrace cafeteria/restaurant has great city view—take elevator from entrance nearest the TI, tel. 933-063-800).

Four great boulevards radiate from Plaça de Catalunya: the Ramblas, the fashionable Passeig de Gràcia (top shops, noisy with traffic), the cozier, but still fashionable, Rambla de Catalunya (most pedestrian-friendly), and the stubby, shop-filled, and delightful traffic-free Avinguda Portal de l'Angel. Homesick Americans can even find a Hard Rock Cafe. Locals traditionally start or end a downtown rendezvous at the venerable Café Zürich.

• *Cross the street from the café to...*

❶ **The Top of the Ramblas:** Begin your ramble 20 yards down at the ornate fountain (near #129).

More than a Champs-Elysées, this grand boulevard takes you from rich (at the top) to rough (at the port) in a one-mile, 30-minute stroll. You'll raft the river of Barcelonan life past a grand opera house, elegant cafés, retread prostitutes, brazen pickpockets, power-dressing con men, artists, street mimes, an outdoor bird market, great shopping, and people looking to charge more for a shoeshine than what you paid for the shoes.

Grab a bench and watch the scene. Open up your map and read some history into it: You're about to walk right across medieval Barcelona, from Plaça de Catalunya to the harbor. Notice how the higgledy-piggledy street plan of the medieval town was contained within the old town walls—now gone, but traced by a series of roads named Ronda (meaning "to go around"). Find the Roman town, occupying about 10 percent of what became the medieval town—with tighter roads yet around the cathedral. The sprawling, modern grid plan beyond the Ronda roads is from the 19th century. Breaks in this urban waffle show where a little town was consumed by the growing city. The popular Passeig de Gràcia was literally the road to Gràcia (once a separate town, now a characteristic Barcelona neighborhood).

Rambla means "stream" in Arabic. The Ramblas used to be a drainage ditch along the medieval wall that once defined what's now called the Barri Gòtic (Gothic Quarter). "Las Ramblas" is plural, a succession of five separately named segments, but address numbers treat it as a single long street.

You're at Rambla Canaletes, named for the fountain. The black-and-gold **Fountain of Canaletes** is the starting point for celebrations and demonstrations. Legend says that a drink from the fountain ensures that you'll return to Barcelona one day. All along the Ramblas, you'll see newspaper stands (open 24 hours, selling phone cards) and ONCE booths (selling lottery tickets that support Spain's organization of the blind, a powerful advocate for the needs of people with disabilities).

Got some change? As you wander downhill, drop coins into the cans of the human statues (the money often kicks them into entertaining gear). Warning: Wherever people stop to gawk, pickpockets are at work.

• *Walk 100 yards downhill to #115 and the...*

❷ **Rambla of the Little Birds:** Traditionally, kids bring their parents here to buy pets, especially on Sundays. Apartment-dwellers find birds, turtles, and fish easier to handle than dogs and cats. If you're walking by at night, you'll hear the sad sounds of little tweety birds locked up in their collapsed kiosks.

Along the Ramblas, buildings with balconies that have flowers are generally living spaces; balconies with air-conditioners generally indicate offices. The Academy of Science's clock (at #115) marks official Barcelona time—synchronize. The Champion supermarket (at #113) has cheap groceries and a handy deli with cooked food to go.

A recently discovered **Roman necropolis** is in a park across the street from the bird market, 50 yards behind the big, modern Citadines Hotel (go through the passageway at #122). Local apartment-dwellers blew the whistle on contractors, who hoped they could finish their building before anyone noticed the antiquities they had unearthed. Imagine the tomb-lined road leading into the Roman city of Barcino 2,000 years ago.

• *Another 100 yards takes you to Carrer del Carme (at #2), and a...*

❸ **Baroque Church:** The big Betlem church fronting the boulevard is Baroque, unusual in Barcelona. Note the Baroque-style sloping roofline, ball-topped pinnacles, and the scrolls above the entrance. While Barcelona's Gothic age was rich (with buildings to prove it), the Baroque age hardly left a mark. (The city's importance dropped when New World discoveries shifted lucrative trade to ports on the Atlantic.)

The **Bagues** jewelry shop, across Carrer del Carme from the church, is known for its Art Nouveau jewelry (exactingly duplicated from the c. 1898 molds of Masriera displayed in the window; buzz to get inside). At the shop's side entrance, step on the old-fashioned scales (free, in kilos) and head down the narrow lane opposite (behind the church, 30 yards) to a place expert in making you heavier. **Café Granja Viader** (see page 1023) has specialized in baked and dairy delights since 1870. (For more sweets, follow "A Short, Sweet Walk"—on page 1030—which begins at the intersection in front of the church.)

• *Stroll through the Ramblas of Flowers to the subway stop marked by the red* M *(near #100), and...*

❹ **La Boquería:** This lively produce market at #91 is an explosion of chicken legs, bags of live snails, stiff fish, delicious oranges, and sleeping dogs (Mon–Sat 8:00–20:00, best mornings after 9:00, closed Sun). Wander through—as local architect Antoni Gaudí used to—and gain inspiration. The Conserves shop sells 25 kinds of olives (straight in, near back on right, 100-gram minimum, €0.20–0.40). Full legs of ham *(jamón serrano)* abound; *Paleta Ibérica de Bellota* are the best, and cost about €120 each. Beware: *Huevos del toro* are bull testicles—surprisingly inexpensive...and oh so good. Drop by a café for an *espresso con leche* or breakfast (*tortilla española*—potato omelet).

For a quick bite, visit the **Pinotxo Bar** (just to the right as you enter the market), where flamboyant Juan and his family are busy feeding shoppers. (Getting Juan to crack a huge smile and a thumbs-up for your camera makes a great shot...and he loves it.) The stools nearby are a great perch for enjoying both your coffee and the people-watching. The market and lanes nearby are busy with great little eateries (see page 1027).

The **Museum of Erotica** is your standard European sex museum—neat if you like nudes and a chance to hear phone sex in four languages (€7.50, daily June–Sept 10:00–22:00, shorter hours Oct–May, across from market at #96).

At #100, **Gimeno** sells cigars (appreciate the dying art of cigar boxes). Go ahead, do something forbidden in America but perfectly legal here...buy a Cuban (singles from €1). Tobacco shops sell stamps and phone cards—and plenty of bongs and marijuana gear (the Spanish approach to pot is very casual).

Farther down the Ramblas at #83, the **Art Nouveau Escriba Café** is an ornate world of pastries, little sandwiches, locally popular chocolates, and fine coffee. Opened in 1820 (as shown on the facade), it was remodeled in the Modernista style (daily 8:30–21:00, indoor/outdoor seating, tel. 933-016-027).

Fifty yards farther, find the much-trod-upon anchor mosaic, a reminder of the city's attachment to the sea. Created by noted abstract artist Joan Miró, it marks the midpoint of the Ramblas. (The towering Columbus Monument in the distance—hidden by trees—is at the end of this hike.) From here, walk down to the **Liceu Opera House** (tickets on sale Mon–Fri 14:00–20:30, tel. 902-533-353; 45-minute €6 tour in English daily at 10:00; 20-min €4 version from upper balcony—escorted but not guided, sometimes with no light—daily at 11:30, 12:00, and 13:00; tel. 934-859-914, www.liceubarcelona.com). From the Opera House, cross the Ramblas to Café de l'Opera for a beverage (#74). This bustling café, with Modernista (that is, old-timey) decor and a historic atmosphere, boasts that it's been open since 1929, even during the Spanish Civil War.

• *Continue to #46; turn left down an arcaded lane to a square filled with palm trees...*

❺ **Plaça Reial:** This elegant, Neoclassical square has a colonial (or maybe post-colonial) ambience. It comes complete with old-fashioned taverns, modern bars with patio seating, a Sunday coin and stamp market (10:00–14:00), Gaudí's first public works (the two colorful helmeted lampposts), and characters who don't need the palm trees to be shady. **Herbolari Ferran** is a fine and aromatic shop of herbs, with fun souvenirs such as top-quality saffron, or *safra* (Mon–Sat 9:30–14:00 & 16:30–20:00, closed Sun, downstairs at Plaça Reial 18). The small streets stretching toward the water from the square are intriguing, but less safe.

Back across the Ramblas, **Palau Güell**, which was closed through 2007, offers an enjoyable look at a Gaudí interior (Carrer Nou de la Rambla 3–5, tel. 933-173-974). This apartment was the first (1886) of Gaudí's innovative buildings, with a parabolic front doorway that signaled his emerging, non-rectangular style. Skip the climb to this less-interesting rooftop if you plan to see Casa Milà.

• *Farther downhill, on the right-hand side, is the...*

❻ **Bottom of the Ramblas:** The neighborhood to your right, Barri Xines, is the world's only Chinatown with nothing even remotely Chinese in or near it. Named for the prejudiced notion that Chinese immigrants go hand-in-hand with poverty, prostitution, and drug dealing, the neighborhood's actual inhabitants are poor Spanish, Arab, and Roma (Gypsy) people. At night, the Barri Xines is frequented by prostitutes, many of them transvestites, who cater to sailors wandering up from the port. A nighttime visit gets you a street-corner massage—look out. Better yet—stay out.

The bottom of the Ramblas is marked by the city's giant medieval shipyards (now the impressive Maritime Museum) and the Columbus Monument (both are described under "On the Harborfront, at the Bottom of the Ramblas," page 997). And just beyond the Columbus Monument, **La Rambla del Mar** ("Rambla of the Sea") is a modern extension of the boulevard into the harbor. A popular wooden pedestrian bridge—with waves like the sea—leads to Maremagnum, a soulless Spanish mall with a cinema, huge aquarium, restaurants (including the recommended Tapasbar Maremagnum; see page 1027), and piles of people. Late at night, it's a rollicking youth hangout. It's a worthwhile stroll.

The Barri Gòtic: From Plaça de Catalunya to the Cathedral

Barcelona's Barri Gòtic, or Gothic Quarter, is a bustling world of shops, bars, and nightlife packed between hard-to-be-thrilled-about 14th- and 15th-century buildings. The section near the port

Barcelona's Old City

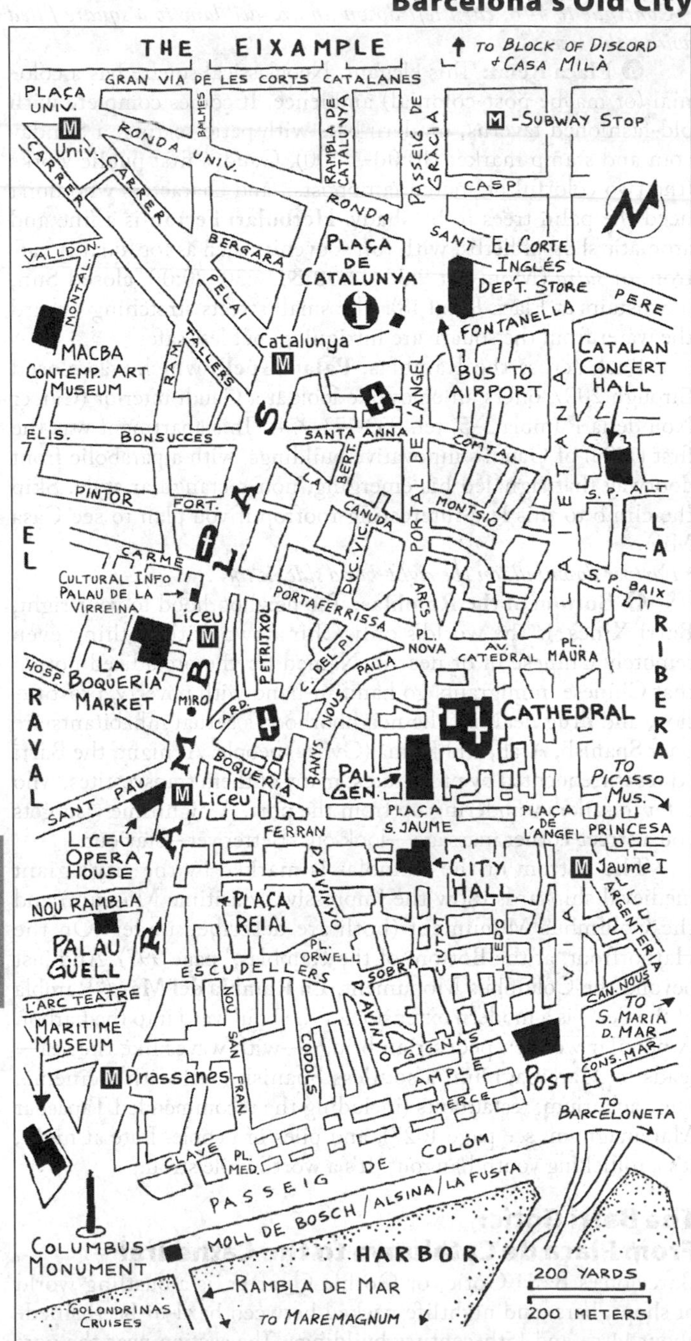
THE EIXAMPLE
TO BLOCK OF DISCORD & CASA MILÀ
GRAN VIA DE LES CORTS CATALANES
PLAÇA UNIV.
Univ.
M -SUBWAY STOP
RONDA UNIV.
BALMES
RAMBLA DE CATALUNYA
PASSEIG DE GRÀCIA
CARRER
CASP
RONDA
SANT
VALLDON.
BERGARA
PLAÇA DE CATALUNYA
EL CORTE INGLÉS DEP'T. STORE
MONTAL.
PELAI
PERE
FONTANELLA
TALLERS
RAM.
MACBA CONTEMP. ART MUSEUM
Catalunya
BUS TO AIRPORT
CATALAN CONCERT HALL
ELIS.
BONSUCCES
SANTA ANNA
COMTAL
PINTOR
FORT.
LA
BERT.
CANUDA
MONTSIO
PORTAL DE L'ANGEL
S.P. ALT
EL
LA
CARME
CULTURAL INFO PALAU DE LA VIRREINA
DUC. VIC.
ARCS
S.P. BAIX
PORTAFERRISSA
Liceu
PETRITXOL
PL. NOVA
AV. CATEDRAL
PL. MAURA
RIBERA
HOSP.
LA BOQUERÍA MARKET
C. DEL PI
PALLA
MIRO
CARD.
NOUS
CATHEDRAL
RAVAL
BOQUERIA
BANYS
PAL. GEN.
TO PICASSO MUS.
SANT PAU
Liceu
PLAÇA S. JAUME
PLAÇA DE L'ANGEL
PRINCESA
LICEU OPERA HOUSE
FERRAN
AVINYO
CITY HALL
Jaume I
ARGENTERIA
NOU RAMBLA
PLAÇA REIAL
VIA LAIETANA
RAMBLAS
PALAU GÜELL
PL. ORWELL
CIUTAT
LLEDO
ESCUDELLERS
SOBRA
CAN. NOUS
L'ARC TEATRE
TO S. MARIA D. MAR
MARITIME MUSEUM
NOU SAN FRAN.
CODOLS
GIGNAS
CONS. MAR
Drassanes
AMPLE
POST
MERCE
TO BARCELONETA
CLAVE
PL. MED.
PASSEIG DE COLÓM
PASSEIG ALSINA/LA FUSTA
MOLL DE BOSCH/ALSINA/LA FUSTA
COLUMBUS MONUMENT
HARBOR
200 YARDS
200 METERS
RAMBLA DE MAR
GOLONDRINAS CRUISES
TO MAREMAGNUM

is generally dull and seedy. But the area around the cathedral is a tangled-yet-inviting grab-bag of undiscovered courtyards, grand squares, schoolyards, Art Nouveau storefronts, baby flea markets on Thursdays, musty junk shops, classy antique shops (on Carrer de la Palla), street musicians strumming Catalan folk songs, and balconies with domestic jungles behind wrought-iron bars. Go on a cultural scavenger hunt. Write a poem. This self-guided walk gives you a structure, covering the main sights and offering a historical overview before you get lost.

• *Start on Barcelona's bustling main square...*

Plaça de Catalunya: This square is the center of the world for seven million Catalan people. The square (described at the start of my Ramblas self-guided walk, above) is decorated with the likenesses of important Catalans. From this square, walls that contained the city until the 19th century arc around in each direction to the sea. Looking at your map of Barcelona, you'll see a regimented waffle design—except for the higgledy-piggledy old town corralled by these walls.

The city grew with its history. Originally a Roman town, Barcelona was ruled by the Visigoths from the fall of Rome until 714, when the Moors arrived (they were, in turn, sent packing by the French in 801). Finally, in the 10th century, the Count of Barcelona unified the region, and the idea of Catalunya came to be. The area between Plaça de Catalunya and the old Roman walls (circling the smaller ancient town, down by the cathedral) was settled by churches, each a magnet gathering a small community outside the walls (or "extra muro"). Around 1250, when these "extra muro" communities became numerous and strong enough, the king agreed to invest in a larger wall, and Barcelona expanded. This outer wall was torn down in 1859 and replaced by a series of circular boulevards (named Rondas).

• *From Plaça de Catalunya's TI, head downhill, crossing the busy street into a broad pedestrian boulevard called...*

Avinguda Portal de l'Angel: This boulevard is named for the big gate in the medieval wall that once stood here, called the "Gate of the Angel." The gate was crowned by an angel who kept the city safe from plagues and who bid voyagers safe journey as they left the security of the city. Imagine the fascinating scene here at the Gate of the Angel, where Barcelona stopped and the wilds began.

Walking down the Avinguda Portal de l'Angel, you may detour a half block left on **Carrer de Santa Anna,** where a lane on the right leads into a courtyard facing one of those "extra muro" churches, with a fine cloister and simple, typically Romanesque facade.

Continuing down the main boulevard, you reach a fork in the road with a blue-tiled **fountain.** This was once a freestanding well—in the 17th century, it was the last watering stop for horses before leaving town. Take the left fork to the cathedral, past the Architects' House with its Picasso-inspired frieze. Enter the square, where you'll stand before two bold towers—the remains of the old Roman wall that protected a smaller Barcino, as the city was called in ancient times. The big stones at the base of the towers are actually Roman. The wall stretches left of the towers, incorporated into the Bishop's Palace (which you'll enter from the other side later).

• *The sights from here on are located on the map on page 999. Walk around—past the modern bronze letters* BARCINO *and the mighty facade of the cathedral (which we'll enter momentarily)—and go inside the...*

Bishop's Palace (Palau Episcopal): Visitors are welcome inside this palace, which today functions as the city archives (its front door faces the wall of the church). It's a good example of a Renaissance nobleman's palace. Notice how the century-old palm tree seems to be held captive by urban man. Inside you can see the Roman stones up close. Upstairs affords a good view of the cathedral's exterior—textbook Catalan Gothic (plain and practical, like this merchant community) next to textbook Romanesque (the smaller, more humble church adjacent on the right—which you'll visit entering from the church's cloister later).

• *Now enter the...*

Cathedral of Barcelona (Catedral de Barcelona): This huge house of worship is worth a look. Its vast size, peaceful cloister, and many ornate chapels—each one sponsored by a local guild—are impressive. For a self-guided tour, see "Cathedral of Barcelona" listing on page 998.

• *After visiting the cathedral's cloister, exit and walk to the tiny lane ahead on the right (Carrer de Montjuïc de Bisbe). This leads to the cute...*

Plaça Sant Felip Neri: This square serves as the playground of an elementary school bursting with youthful energy. The Church of Sant Felip Neri, which Gaudí attended, is still pocked with bomb damage from the Civil War. As a stronghold of democratic, anti-Franco forces, Barcelona saw a lot of fighting. The shrapnel that damaged this church was meant for the nearby Catalan government building (Palau de la Generalitat, described below).

Study the medallions on the wall. Guilds powered the local economy, and the carved reliefs here show that this building must have housed the shoemakers. In fact, on this square you'll find a fun little Shoe Museum (see page 1001).

• *Circle the block back to the cathedral's cloister and take a right, walking along Carrer del Bisbe to the huge...*

Palau de la Generalitat: For nearly 600 years, this spot has been the home of the Catalan government. Through good times and bad, the Catalan spirit has survived, and this building has housed its capital.

• *Continue along Carrer del Bisbe to...*

Plaça de Sant Jaume (jow-mah): On this stately central square of the Barri Gòtic, once the Roman forum, has been the seat of city government for 2,000 years. Today the two top governmental buildings in Catalunya face each other: the Barcelona City Hall (Ajuntament; free, Sun 10:00–13:30), and the seat of the autonomous government of Catalunya (Palau de la Generalitat, described above). From these balconies, the nation's leaders (and soccer heroes) greet the people on momentous days.

• *Take two quick left turns from the corner of Carrer Bisbe, and climb Carrer del Paridís about 100 yards to the summit of...*

"Mont" Taber: A millstone in the corner marks ancient Barcino's highest elevation, a high spot in the road called Mount Taber. A plaque on the wall says it all: "Mont Taber, 16.9 meters." Step into the courtyard for a peek at a surviving corner of the imposing **Roman temple** (Temple Roma d'August) which once stood here on Mont Taber, keeping a protective watch over Barcino (free, daily 10:00–14:00 & 16:00–20:00).

• *Continue down Carrer del Paridís back to the cathedral, take a right, and go downhill about 100 yards to...*

Plaça del Rei: The Royal Palace sat on this "King's Square" (a block from the cathedral) until Catalunya became part of Spain in the 15th century. Then it was the headquarters of the local Inquisition. In 1493, a triumphant Christopher Columbus, accompanied by six New World natives (whom he called "Indians") and several pure-gold statues, entered the Royal Palace. King Ferdinand and Queen Isabel rose to welcome him home, and honored him with the title "Admiral of the Oceans."

• *Your tour is over. Nearby, just off Plaça del Rei, is another sight—the City History Museum (described on page 1001). Or simply wander and enjoy Barcelona at its Gothic best.*

SIGHTS

Barcelona's Old City

I've divided Barcelona's Old City sights into three neighborhoods: near the harbor, at the bottom of the Ramblas; the Cathedral and nearby (Barri Gòtic); and the Picasso Museum and nearby (La Ribera).

On the Harborfront, at the Bottom of the Ramblas

Two great waterfront picnic spots are on the harbor steps or aboard one of the *golondrinas* cruises (described on the next page).

▲Maritime Museum (Museu Marítim)—Barcelona's medieval shipyard, the best-preserved in the entire Mediterranean, is an impressive museum covering the salty history of ships and navigation from the 13th to the 20th centuries. Its huge halls evoke the 14th-century days when Catalunya was a naval and shipbuilding power, cranking out 30 huge galleys a winter. As in the US today, military and commercial ventures mixed and mingled as Catalunya built its trading empire. The excellent included audioguide tells the story (€6, €6.70 combo-ticket includes Columbus Monument, daily 10:00–20:00, last entry at 19:00, tel. 933-429-920). Your ticket also gets you into the old-fashioned sailing ship *Santa Eulàlia*, docked in the harbor across the street.

Columbus Monument (Monument a Colóm)—Marking the point where the Ramblas hits the harbor, this 200-foot-tall monument built for an 1888 exposition offers an elevator-assisted view from its top (€2.30, daily June–Sept 9:00–20:30, May and Oct 9:00–20:00, Nov–April 10:00–18:30). It was here in Barcelona that Ferdinand and Isabel welcomed Columbus home after his first trip to America. It's ironic that Barcelona would so honor the man whose discoveries ultimately led to its downfall as a great trading power.

***Golondrinas* Cruises**—At the foot of the Columbus Monument, tourist boats called *golondrinas* offer 30-minute unguided harbor tours (€4, daily 12:00–19:00, tel. 934-423-106, www.lasgolondrinas.com) and longer, 90-minute tours up the coast to the new Fòrum complex and back (€9.70, also unguided, no stops, 6/day, daily 11:30–17:30).

Cathedral of Barcelona

Barcelona's cathedral (Catedral de Barcelona) is worth ▲. Most of the construction on this vast church took place in the 14th century, during the glory days of the Catalan nation. The facade was humble, so in the 19th century, the proud local bourgeoisie redid it in a more ornate neo-Gothic style.

Cost, Hours, Location: Strangely, even though the cathedral is free to enter daily 8:00–13:30 and 17:15–19:30, you have to pay €4 to enter between 13:30–17:15 (cloisters open daily 9:00–13:00 & 17:15–19:00; tel. 933-151-554). The dress code is sometimes strictly enforced; don't wear tank tops, short shorts, or short skirts just in case.

Getting There: The huge, can't-miss-it cathedral is in the center of the Barri Gòtic, on Plaça de la Seu. For an interesting way to reach the cathedral from Plaça de Catalunya, and some commentary on the surrounding neighborhood, see my self-guided walk of the Barri Gòtic on page 993.

➲ **Self-Guided Tour:** The cathedral's spacious interior—characteristic of Catalan Gothic buildings—is supported by

Barcelona's Cathedral Neighborhood

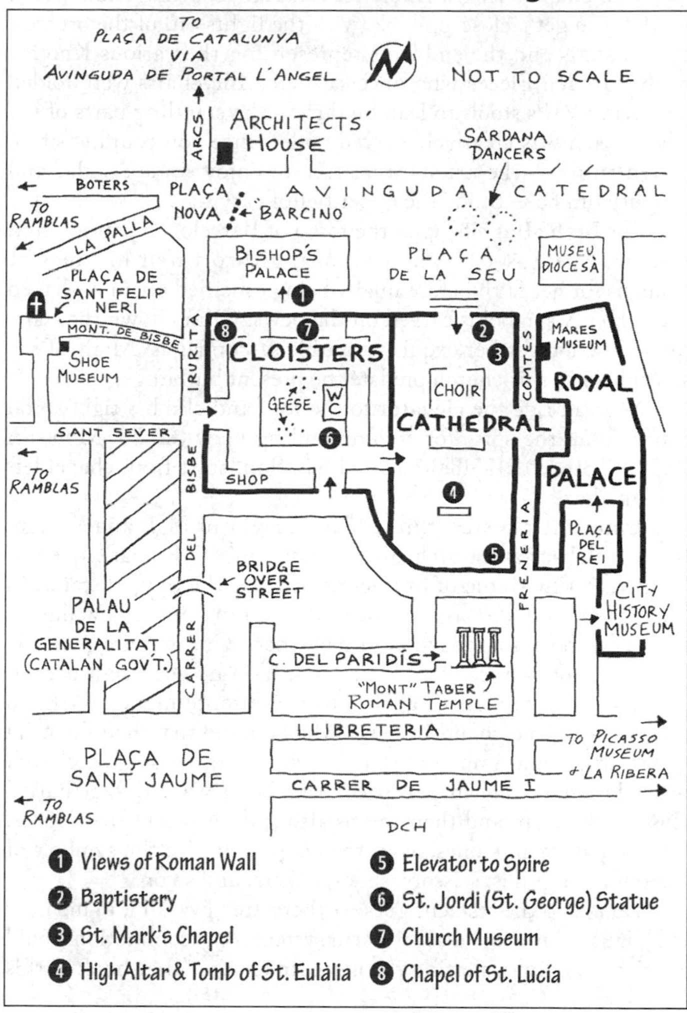

buttresses. These provide walls for 28 richly ornamented **chapels.** Typical of medieval churches, the cathedral has an "ambulatory" plan—allowing worshippers to amble around to the chapel of their choice. While the main part of the church is fairly plain, the chapels, sponsored by local guilds, show great wealth. Located in the community's most high-profile space, they provided a kind of advertising to illiterate worshippers. Find the logos and symbols of the various trades represented. The Native Americans that Columbus brought to town were supposedly baptized in the first chapel on the left.

The chapels ring a finely carved 15th-century **choir** *(coro)*. For €2, you get a close-up look (with the lights on) of the ornately carved stalls and the emblems representing the various Knights of the Golden Fleece who once sat here. The chairs were folded up, giving VIPs stools to lean on during the standing parts of the Mass. Each was creatively carved and—since you couldn't sit on sacred things—the artists were free to enjoy some secular and naughty fun here. Study the upper tier of carvings.

The **high altar** sits upon the tomb of Barcelona's patron saint, Eulàlia. She was a 13-year-old local girl tortured 13 times by Romans for her faith before finally being crucified on an X-shaped cross. Her X symbol is carved on the pews. Climb down the stairs for a close look at her exquisite marble sarcophagus. Many of the sarcophagi in this church predate the present building.

You can ride the **elevator** to the roof and climb a tight spiral staircase up the spire for a commanding view (€2.20, Mon–Fri 10:30–12:30 & 17:15–18:00, closed Sat–Sun, start from chapel left of high altar).

Enter the **cloister** (through arch, right of high altar). From there, look back at the arch, an impressive mix of Romanesque and Gothic. A tiny statue of St. George slaying the dragon stands in the garden. Jordi (George) is one of the patron saints of Catalunya, and by far the most popular boy's name here. Cloisters are generally found in monasteries. But this church has one because it needed to accommodate more chapels—to make more money. With so many wealthy merchants in town (who believed that their financial generosity would impress God and win them favor), the church needed more private chapel space. Merchants wanted to be buried close to the altar, and their tombs also spill over into the cloister. On the pavement stones, as in the chapels, notice the symbols of the trades or guilds: scissors, shoes, bakers, and so on.

Long ago the resident **geese**—there are always 13, in memory of Eulàlia—functioned as an alarm system. Any commotion would get them honking, alerting the monk in charge. They honk to this very day.

From the statue of St. Jordi, circle to the right (past a WC hidden on the left). The skippable little €1 **museum** (far corner) is one plush room with a dozen old religious paintings. In the corner, built into the cloister, is the dark, barrel-vaulted, Romanesque Chapel of Santa Lucía, a small church that predates the cathedral. People hoping for good eyesight (Santa Lucía's specialty) leave candles outside. Farther along, the Chapel of Santa Rita (her forte: impossible causes) usually has the most candles.

In the Barri Gòtic, near the Cathedral

For an interesting route from Plaça de Catalunya to the Cathedral neighborhood, see my self-guided walk of the Barri Gòtic on page 993. And if you're in town on a weekend, don't miss the *sardana* dances.

Shoe Museum (Museu del Calçat)—Shoe-lovers enjoy this two-room shoe museum, watched over by a we-try-harder attendant. The huge shoe at the entry is designed to fit the foot of the Columbus Monument at the bottom of the Ramblas (€2.50, Tue–Sun 11:00–14:00, closed Mon, 1 block beyond outside door of cathedral cloister, behind Plaça de G. Bachs on Plaça Sant Felip Neri, tel. 933-014-533).

City History Museum (Museu d'Història de la Ciutat)—For a walk through the history of the city, take an elevator down 65 feet (and 2,000 years) to stroll the streets of Roman Barcelona. You'll see sewers, models of domestic life, and bits of an early Christian church. Then, an exhibit in the 11th-century count's palace shows you Barcelona through the Middle Ages (€4; June–Sept Tue–Sat 10:00–20:00, Sun 10:00–15:00, closed Mon; Oct–May same hours but closed for lunch 14:00–16:00; Plaça del Rei, tel. 933-151-111).

▲▲Catalan Concert Hall (Palau de la Música Catalana)—This concert hall, finished in 1908, features the best Modernista interior in town (by Lluís Domènech i Muntaner). Inviting arches lead you into the 2,000-seat hall. A kaleidoscopic skylight features a choir singing around the sun, while playful carvings and mosaics celebrate music and Catalan culture. Admission is by tour only and starts with a relaxing 20-minute video (€8, 50-min tours in English, daily every hour 10:00–15:30, maybe later, about 6 blocks northeast of cathedral, tel. 932-957-200). To get a spot on an English guided tour, you must reserve in advance: you can drop by earlier in the day or up to a week in advance (ticket office open 9:30–15:30). Ask about concerts (300 per year, inexpensive tickets available, www.palaumusica.org).

Picasso Museum (Museu Picasso)

This is the best collection in the country of the work of Spaniard Pablo Picasso (1881–1973), and—since he spent his formative years (age 14–21) in Barcelona—it's the best collection of his early works anywhere. The museum is easily worth ▲▲▲. By seeing his youthful, realistic art, you can more fully appreciate the artist's genius and better understand his later, more challenging art. The collection is scattered through several connected Gothic palaces, six blocks from the cathedral in the Ribera district (for more on this area, see "In La Ribera, near the Picasso Museum," below).

Cost, Hours, Location: €6, free on first Sun of month, covered by Articket Card, Tue–Sun 10:00–20:00, closed Mon, Montcada 15, ticket office at #21, Metro: Jaume I, tel. 932-563-000, www.museupicasso.bcn.es. The ground floor has a required bag check, as well as a handy array of other services (bookshop, WC, and cafeteria). This generally crowded museum is quieter at about 14:00 and 18:00.

Hungry? The museum itself has a good café. The café at the Museum of Textiles across the street is good for a light meal in its inviting courtyard. And just down the street is a neighborhood favorite for tapas, El Xampanyet (see page 1028).

Background: Picasso's personal secretary amassed a huge collection of his work and bequeathed it to the city. Picasso, happy to have a fine museum showing off his work in the city of his youth, added to the collection throughout his life. (Sadly, since Picasso vowed never to set foot in a fascist, Franco-ruled Spain, and died two years before Franco, the artist never saw the museum.)

In La Ribera, near the Picasso Museum

There's more to the Ribera neighborhood than just the Picasso Museum. While the nearby, waterfront Barceloneta district was for the working-class sailors, La Ribera housed the wealthier shippers and merchants. Its streets are lined with their fine mansions—which, like the much-appreciated Church of Santa Maria del Mar, were built with shipping wealth.

La Ribera (also known as "El Born") is separated from the Barri Gòtic by Via Laietana, a street built through the Old City in the early 1900s to alleviate growing traffic problems. From the Plaça Jaume I (where the nearest Metro stop is), cross this busy street to enter an up-and-coming zone of lively and creative restaurants and nightlife. The Carrer de l'Argenteria (literally, "Goldsmiths Street"—streets in La Ribera are named after the workshops that used to occupy them) runs diagonally from the Plaça Jaume I straight down to the Church of Santa Maria del Mar.

Just beyond the church is a long square, the Passeig del Born (formerly a jousting square, as its shape indicates). This is the neighborhood center and a popular springboard for exploring tapas bars, fun restaurants, and nightspots in the narrow streets all around. Wandering around here at night, you'll find piles of inviting and intriguing little restaurants (I've listed my favorites in "Eating," page 1028). Enjoy a glass of wine on the square facing the church, or consider renting a bike here for a pedal down the beach promenade to the Fòrum. From behind the church, the Carrer de Montcada leads two blocks to the Picasso Museum (described above). The street's mansions—built by rich shippers centuries ago—now house galleries, shops, and even museums. In fact, the Picasso Museum itself consists of five such mansions laced together.

▲Church of Santa Maria del Mar—This church is the proud centerpiece of La Ribera. "Del Mar" means "of the sea"... and

Barcelona's La Ribera

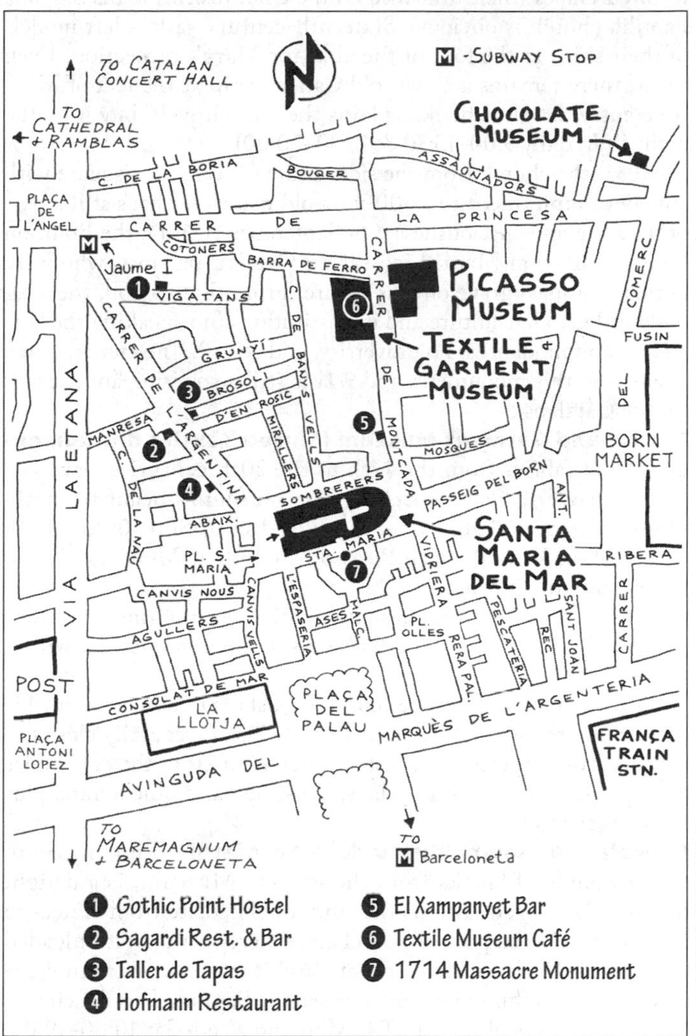

that's where the money came from. The proud shippers built this church in only 55 years, so it has a harmonious style considered pure Catalan Gothic. As you step in, notice the figures of workers carved into the big front doors. During the Spanish Civil War (1936–1939), the Church sided with the conservative forces of Franco against the people. In retaliation, the working class took their anger out on this church, burning all of its wood furnishings and decor (carbon still blackens the ceiling). Today it's stripped down—naked in all its Gothic glory. The tree-like columns inspired Gaudí (their influence on the columns inside his Sagrada Família church is obvious). Sixteenth-century sailors left models of their ships at the foot of the altar for Mary's protection. Even today, there remains a classic old Catalan ship at the feet of Mary (free entry, €3 guidebook explains the church well, buy it by the main altar, daily 9:00–13:30 & 16:30–20:00).

Exit the church from the side, and you arrive at a square with a modern **monument** to a 300-year-old massacre that's still a part of the Catalan consciousness. On September 11, 1714, the Bourbon king ruling from Madrid massacred Catalan patriots, who were buried in a mass grave on this square. From that day on, the king outlawed Catalan culture and its institutions (no speaking the language, no folk dances, no university, and so on). The eternal flame burns atop this monument, and 9/11 is still a sobering anniversary for the Catalans.

Textile and Garment Museum (Museu Tèxtil i d'Indumentària)—If fabrics from the 12th to the 20th centuries leave you cold, consider a *café con leche* on the museum's beautiful patio (museum entry €3.50, Tue–Sat 10:00–18:00, Sun 10:00–15:00, closed Mon, 30 yards from Picasso Museum at Montcada 12–14, www.museutextil.bcn.es).

It's free to enter the museum's patio—an inviting courtyard with a WC and coffee shop that's outside the museum but within the walls.

On Sunday nights, the museum hosts **jazz concerts** on this patio when the weather permits (21:00–23:00, generally closed in winter). You can stand and listen for free, or sit at the café tables for a pleasant meal (€5–10 salads, couscous, and quiche fare, plus €5 cover charge).

Chocolate Museum (Museu de la Xocolata)—This museum, only a couple of blocks from the Picasso Museum, is a delight for chocolate-lovers. It tells the story of chocolate from Aztecs to Europeans via the port of Barcelona, where it was first unloaded and processed. Even if you're into architecture more than calories, don't miss this opportunity to see the Sagrada Família church finished—and ready to eat (€4, Mon and Wed–Sat 10:00–19:00, Sun 10:00–15:00, closed Tue, Carrer Comerç 36, tel. 932-687-878, www.museuxocolata.com).

The Eixample

Wide sidewalks, hardy shade trees, chic shops, and plenty of Art Nouveau fun make the Eixample a refreshing break from the Old City. Uptown Barcelona is a unique variation on the common grid-plan city. Barcelona snipped off the building corners to create light and spacious eight-sided squares at every intersection. For the best Eixample example, ramble Rambla de Catalunya (unrelated to the more famous Ramblas) and pass through Passeig de Gràcia (described below, Metro for Block of Discord: Passeig de Gràcia, or Metro for Casa Milà: Diagonal).

The 19th century was a boom time for Barcelona. By 1850, the city was busting out of its medieval walls. A new town was planned to follow a grid-like layout. The intersection of three major thoroughfares—Gran Via, Diagonal, and Meridiana—would shift the city's focus uptown.

The Eixample, or "Expansion," was a progressive plan in which everything was made accessible to everyone. Each 20-block-square district would have its own hospital and large park, each 10-block-square area would have its own market and general services, and each five-block-square grid would house its own schools and day-care centers. The hollow space found inside each "block" of apartments would form a neighborhood park.

While much of that vision never quite panned out, the Eixample was an urban success. Rich and artsy big shots bought plots along the grid. The richest landowners built as close to the center as possible. For this reason, the best buildings are near the Passeig de Gràcia. While adhering to the height, width, and depth limitations, they built as they pleased—often in the trendy new Modernista style.

Gaudí's Art and Architecture

Barcelona is an architectural scrapbook of the galloping gables and organic curves of hometown boy Antoni Gaudí (1852–1926). A devoted Catalan and Catholic, he immersed himself in each project, often living on-site. At various times, he called Parc Güell, Casa Milà, and the Sagrada Família home.

▲▲▲Sagrada Família (Holy Family)—Gaudí's most famous and persistent work is this unfinished landmark church. He worked on it from 1883 to 1926. Since then, construction has moved forward in fits and starts. (But over 30 years of visits, I've seen considerable progress.) Even today, the half-finished church is not expected to be completed for another 50 years. One reason it's taking so long is that the temple is funded exclusively by private donations and entry fees. Your admission helps pay for the ongoing construction.

Cost, Hours, Location: €8, €7 with Tourist Bus ticket, €9 combo-ticket includes Gaudí Museum in Parc Güell, daily April–Sept 9:00–20:00, Oct–March 9:00–18:00, Metro: Sagrada Família puts you right on the doorstep, tel. 932-073-031, www.sagradafamilia.org.

Tours: The 50-minute English tours cost €3.50 (6/day April–Oct, Nov–March usually Fri–Mon only). Or rent the good, 70-minute audioguide (also €3.50).

The Construction Project: There's something powerful about

Modernista Sights

an opportunity to feel a community of committed people with a vision working on a church that will not be finished in their lifetime (as was standard in the Gothic age). Local craftsmen often cap off their careers by spending a couple of years on this exciting construction site. The church will trumpet its completion with 18 spires: A dozen "smaller" 330-foot spires (representing the apostles) will stand in groups of four and mark the three entry facades of the building. Four taller towers (dedicated to the four Evangelists) will surround the two tallest, central towers: a 400-foot-tall tower of Mary and the grand 550-foot Jesus tower, which will shine like a spiritual lighthouse—visible even from out at sea. A unique exterior ambulatory will circle the building, like a cloister turned inside out. If there's any building on earth I'd like to see, it's the Sagrada Família...finished.

➲ **Self-Guided Tour:** To get the whole story, follow this commentary.

• *Begin facing the western side of the church (where you'll enter).*

Passion Facade: This facade is full of symbolism from the Bible. The story of Christ's Passion unfolds in the shape of a Z, from bottom to top. Find the stylized Alpha and Omega over the door; Jesus—hanging on the cross—with an open book (the word of God) for hair; and the grid of numbers adding up to 33 (Jesus' age at the time of his death). The distinct face of the man below and just left of Christ is a memorial to Gaudí.

When Gaudí died in 1926, only the stubs of four spires stood above the building site. The rest of the church has been inspired by Gaudí's vision but designed and executed by others. Gaudí knew he wouldn't live to complete the church and recognized that later architects and artists would rely on their own muses for inspiration. This artistic freedom was amplified in 1936, when Civil War shelling burned many of Gaudí's blueprints. Judge for yourself how the recently completed and controversial Passion facade by Josep María Subirachs (b. 1927) fits with Gaudí's original formulation (which you'll see downstairs in the museum).

Now look high above: The colorful ceramic caps of the columns symbolize the mitres (formal hats) of bishops. This is only a side entrance. The nine-story apartment flat to the right will be torn down to accommodate the grand front entry of this church. The three facades—Passion, Nativity, and Glory—will chronicle Christ's life from birth to death to resurrection.

• *Go inside the church, entering the...*

Construction Zone (the Nave): The cranking cranes, rusty forests of rebar, and scaffolding require a powerful faith, but the Sagrada Família offers a fun look at a living, growing, bigger-than-life building. Part of Gaudí's religious vision was a love for nature. He said, "Nothing is invented; it's written in nature." His columns blossom with life, and little windows let light filter in like the canopy of a rain forest, giving both privacy and an intimate connection with God. The U-shaped choir hovers above the nave, tethered halfway up the columns. It's estimated that the proposed central tower (550 feet tall) will require four underground support pylons, each consisting of 8,000 tons of cement. Take the elevator on the Passion side (€2) or the stairs on the Nativity side (free, often miserably congested, most likely closed in hot weather) up to the dizzy lookout that bridges two spires. You'll get a great view of the city and a gargoyle's-eye perspective of the loopy church.

• *Outside, just after exiting the building, you'll encounter the...*

Nativity Facade (east side): This, the only part of the church essentially finished in his lifetime, shows Gaudí's original vision. Mixing Gothic-style symbolism, images from nature, and Modernista asymmetry, it is the best example of Gaudí's unmistakable cake-in-the-rain style. The sculpture shows scenes from the birth and childhood of Jesus, along with angels playing musical instruments. You can love it, hate it, or adopt a love/hate attitude to it, but you can't deny that it is unique.

• *Before leaving, head downstairs (into the church basement, or crypt) to the...*

Museum: The museum displays physical models used for the church's construction. As you wander, you'll notice that they don't always match the finished product—these are ideas, not blueprints set in stone. Original architectural sketches are in a dimly lit room. Photos show the construction work as it was when Gaudí died in 1926, and how it's progressed over the years. See how the church's design is a fusion of nature, architecture, and religion. The columns seem light, with branches springing forth and capitals that look like palm trees. An exhibition compares nature, waves, shells, mushrooms, and so on to Gaudí's work. Find the hanging model showing how Gaudí used gravity to calculate the perfect parabolas incorporated into the church design (the mirror above this model shows how the right-side-up church is derived from this). You'll also peek into a busy workshop where the slow-and-steady building pace is maintained.

Gaudí lived on the site for more than a decade and is buried in the crypt. A window allows you to look down into the neo-Gothic 19th-century crypt (which is how the church began) to see Gaudí's tomb. There's a move afoot to make Gaudí a saint. Perhaps someday, this tomb will be a place of pilgrimage. Gaudí—a faithful Catholic whose medieval-style mysticism belied his Modernista architecture career—was certainly driven to greatness by his passion for God. When undertaking a lengthy project, he said, "My client"—meaning God—"is not in a hurry."

▲▲Casa Milà (La Pedrera)—This Gaudí exterior laughs down on the crowds filling Passeig de Gràcia. Casa Milà, also called La Pedrera (The Quarry), has a much-photographed roller coaster of melting-ice-cream eaves. This is Barcelona's quintessential Modernista building and Gaudí's last major work (1906–1910) before dedicating his final years to the Sagrada Família.

You can visit three sections of Casa Milà: the apartment, attic, and rooftop. Buy the €8 ticket to see all three (all covered by Articket Card). Two elevators take you up to either the apartment or the attic and rooftop. Normally you're directed to the apartment, but if you arrive late in the day, go to the attic/rooftop elevator first, to make sure you have enough time to enjoy Gaudí's works and the views.

The apartment elevator whisks you to the *Life in Barcelona 1905–1929* exhibit (good English descriptions). Then, walk through the sumptuously furnished Art Nouveau apartment. Upstairs in the attic, wander under parabola-shaped brick arches and enjoy a multimedia exhibit of models, photos, and videos of Gaudí's works. A stairway leads to the fanciful rooftop, where chimneys play volleyball with the clouds. From here, you can see Gaudí's other principal works: the Sagrada Família to the west, Casa Batllò to the south, and Parc Güell to the north (daily 10:00–20:00, free 60-minute audioguide, Passeig de Gràcia 92, Metro: Diagonal, tel. 934-845-530).

At the ground level of Casa Milà, poke into the dreamily painted original entrance courtyard. The first floor hosts free art exhibits. During the summer, a concert series called "Pedrera by Night" features live music—jazz, flamenco, tango—a glass of champagne, and the chance to see the rooftop illuminated (€10, July–Sept Fri–Sat at 22:00, tel. 934-845-900).

If you're hungry, stop by the recommended La Bodegueta, a long block away (daily lunch special, see "Eating," below).

▲Block of Discord—Four blocks from Casa Milà, you can survey a noisy block of competing late-19th-century facades. Several of Barcelona's top Modernista mansions line Passeig de Gràcia (Metro: Passeig de Gràcia). Because the structures look as though they are trying to outdo each other in creative twists, locals nicknamed the block between Consell de Cent and Arago the "Block of Discord." First (at #43) and most famous is Gaudí's **Casa Batllò,** with skull-like balconies and a tile roof that suggests a cresting dragon's back; Gaudí based the work on the popular St. Jordi (George) legend, in which he slays the dragon (daily 9:00–20:00; €16 includes main floor, roof, and decent audioguide—but entering Casa Milà is much cheaper and better). By the way, if you're tempted to snap your photos from the middle of the street, be careful—Gaudí died under a streetcar.

Next door, at **Casa Amatller** (#41), check out architect Josep Puig i Cadafalch's creative mix of Moorish- and Gothic-inspired architecture and iron grillwork, which decorates a step-gable like those in the Netherlands.

On the corner (at #35), **Casa Lleó Morera** has a wonderful interior highlighted by the dining room's fabulous stained glass. The architect, Lluís Domènech i Muntaner, also did the Catalan Concert Hall (you'll notice similarities).

The perfume shop halfway down the street has a free and interesting little perfume museum in the back. La Rita restaurant, just around the corner on Carrer Arago, serves a fine three-course lunch for a great price at 13:00 (see "Eating," below).

▲Parc Güell—Gaudí fans enjoy the artist's magic in this colorful park. Gaudí intended this 30-acre garden to be a 60-residence housing project—a kind of gated community. As a high-income housing development, it flopped. But as a park, it's a delight, offering another peek into the eccentric genius of Gaudí. Notice the mosaic medallions that say "park" in English, reminding folks that this is modeled on an English garden.

Cost, Hours, Location: Free, daily 10:00–20:00, tel. 932-130-488. The red Tourist Bus or bus #24 from Plaça de Catalunya leaves you a few blocks away, or a €6 taxi drops you right at the gate.

If you're taking the Metro (which is likely if you're coming from Sagrada Família), get off at the Lesseps stop; to avoid the 20-minute tiring, uphill walk to the park, don't follow the *Parc Güell 1300 metros* sign; instead, exit left out of the Metro station, cross the streets Princep d'Astúries and Gran de Grácia, and catch bus #24 (on Gran de Grácia), which takes you to the park's side entrance in five to 10 minutes.

➲ **Self-Guided Tour:** As you wander the park, imagine living here a century ago—if this gated community succeeded and was filled with Barcelona's wealthy. Stepping past fancy gate houses (which now hold a good bookshop), you walk by Gaudí's wrought-iron gas lamps (1900–1914)—his dad was a blacksmith, and he always enjoyed this medium.

Climb the grand stairway past the ceramic dragon fountain. At the top, drop by the "Hall of 100 Columns," housing a produce market for the neighborhood's 60 mansions. The fun columns—each different, made from concrete and rebar, topped with colorful ceramic, and studded with broken bottles and bric-a-brac—add to the market's vitality.

After shopping, continue up. Look left, down the playful "pathway of columns" that support a long arcade. Gaudí drew his inspiration from nature, and this arcade is like a surfer's perfect tube. From here, continue up to the terrace. Sit on a colorful bench—designed to fit your body ergonomically—and enjoy one of Barcelona's best views. Look for the Sagrada Família church in the distance. Gaudí was an engineer as well. He designed a water-catchment system by which rain hitting this plaza would flow into and through the columns from the market below and power the park's fountains.

When considering the failure of Parc Güell as a community development, also consider that it was an idea a hundred years ahead of its time. Back then, high-society ladies didn't want to live so far from the cultural action. Today, the surrounding neighborhoods are some of the wealthiest in town, and a gated community here would be a big hit.

The skippable **Center for Interpretation of Parc Güell** (Centre d'Interpretació), at the park's main entrance, shows Gaudí's building methods plus maps, photos, and models of the park (€2, daily 11:00–15:00, tel. 933-190-222).

The small **Gaudí Museum** in the middle of the park is more worthwhile than the Center. While sparse, it comes with some interesting Gaudí furniture and a chance to wander through a model home used to sell the others. Gaudí lived here for 20 years, until his father died. His humble artifacts are mostly gone (€4, €9 combo-ticket includes Sagrada Família, daily April–Sept 10:00–20:00, Oct–March 10:00–18:00).

▲Palau Güell—This building, which was closed in 2007 and may reopen in 2008, offers a good chance to see a Gaudí interior. Curvy.

Montjuïc

Montjuïc ("Mount of the Jews"), overlooking Barcelona's hazy port, has always been a show-off. Ages ago it had an impressive fortress. In 1929, it hosted an international fair, from which most of today's sights originated. And in 1992, the Summer Olympics directed the world's attention to this pincushion of attractions once again.

Getting to Montjuïc: You have several options. The simplest is to take a **taxi** directly to your destination (about €7).

Here are more ways to reach Montjuïc, all of which drop you off at the base of a funicular below the Castle of Montjuïc: by the **blue Tourist Bus** route (see "Getting Around Barcelona," page 987); by **public bus** (take #50 from the corner of Gran Via and Passeig de Gràcia, or #55 from Plaça de Catalunya, next to Caja de Madrid building); or by **Metro** (to the Paral-lel stop, exit direction Non de la Rambla for the funicular).

By bus or Metro, you'll arrive at the base of **funicular**—take it up to Montjuïc (covered by a Metro ticket, every 10 min, 9:00–22:00, the number of minutes until next departure posted at start of entry tunnel). From the top of the funicular, it's a two-minute walk to the Joan Miró museum and a 10-minute stroll to the Catalan Art Museum.

The **bus** marked *Parc Montjuïc* also loops around the sights, starting at Plaça d'Espanya, and going to the Catalan Art Museum, the Joan Miró museum, the funicular, and the Castle of Montjuïc.

From the port, the most scenic way to Montjuïc is via the **cable car,** called the 1929 Transbordador Aereo (tel. 934-430-859).

I've listed the two museums in a logical sightseeing order—from higher up (Fundació Joan Miró, reach by funicular) to lower down (Catalan Art Museum)—but note that if you want to visit only the Catalan Art Museum, you can skip the funicular and instead take the Metro to Plaça d'Espanya and ride the escalators up to the museum.

▲Fundació Joan Miró—Showcasing the talents of yet another Catalan artist, this museum has the best collection of Joan Miró art anywhere. You'll also see works by other Modern artists (such as *Mercury Fountain* by the American sculptor Alexander Calder). If you don't like abstract art, you'll leave here scratching your head, but those who love this place are not faking it...they understand

Montjuïc

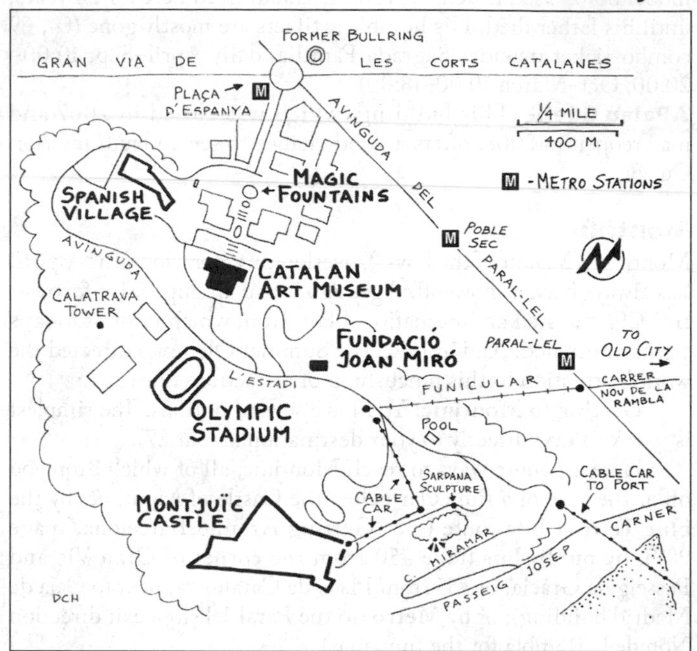

the genius of Miró and the fun of abstract art.

As you wander, consider this: Miró believed that everything in the cosmos is linked—colors, sky, stars, love, time, music, dogs, men, women, dirt, and the void. He mixed childlike symbols of these things creatively, as a poet uses words. It's as liberating for the visual artist to be abstract as it is for the poet: Both can use metaphors rather than being confined to concrete explanations. Miró would listen to music and paint. It's interactive, free interpretation. He said, "For me, simplicity is freedom."

Here are some tips to help you enjoy and appreciate Miró's art: 1) meditate on it; 2) read the title (for example, *The Smile of a Tear*); 3) meditate on it again. Repeat the process until you have an epiphany. There's no correct answer—it's pure poetry. Devotees of Miró say they fly with him and don't even need drugs. You're definitely much less likely to need drugs if you take advantage of the wonderful audioguide, included with admission (€7.50, covered by Articket Card, May–Sept Tue–Sat 10:00–20:00—but closes at 19:00 Oct–June, Thu until 21:30, Sun 10:00–14:30, closed Mon, 200 yards from top of funicular, Parc de Montjuïc, tel. 934-439-470, www.bcn.fjmiro.es).

Olympic Stadium (Estadi Olímpic)—For two weeks in the summer of 1992, the world turned its attention to this stadium (between the Catalan Art Museum and the Fundació Joan Miró at Passeig Olímpic 17). Redesigned from an earlier 1929 version, the stadium was updated, expanded, and officially named for Catalan patriot Lluís Companys i Jover. The XXV Olympiad kicked off here on July 25, when an archer dramatically lit the Olympic torch—which still stands high at the end of the stadium overlooking the city skyline—with a flaming arrow. Over the next two weeks, Barcelona played host to the thrill of victory (mostly at the hands of Magic Johnson, Michael Jordan, Larry Bird, and the rest of the US basketball "Dream Team") and the agony of defeat (i.e., the nightmares of the Dream Team's opponents). Hovering over the stadium is the memorable, futuristic Calatrava Communications Tower, used to transmit Olympic highlights and lowlights around the world. Aside from the memories of the medals, today's Olympic Stadium offers little to see today...except when it's hosting a match for Barcelona's other soccer team, RCD Espanyol, or a game of the NFL Europe's Barcelona Dragons.

▲▲Catalan Art Museum (Museu Nacional d'Art de Catalunya)—The big vision for this wonderful museum is to showcase Catalan art from the 10th century through about 1930. Often called "the Prado of Romanesque art" (and "MNAC" for short), its highlight is Europe's best collection of Romanesque frescos (€8.50, includes audioguide, covered by Articket Card, free first Sun of month, open Tue–Sat 10:00–19:00, Sun 10:00–14:30, closed Mon; in massive National Palace building above Magic Fountains, near Plaça d'Espanya—take escalators up; tel. 936-220-376, www.mnac.es).

As you enter, pick up a map (helpful for such a big and confusing building). The left wing is Romanesque, and the right wing is Gothic, exquisite Renaissance, and Baroque. Upstairs is more Baroque, plus modern art, photography, and more.

The MNAC's rare, world-class collection of **Romanesque** art came mostly from remote Catalan village churches in the Pyrenees (saved from unscrupulous art dealers—including many Americans). The Romanesque wing features frescoes, painted wooden altar fronts, and ornate statuary. This classic Romanesque art—with flat 2-D scenes, each saint holding his symbol, and Jesus (easy to identify by the cross in his halo)—is impressively displayed on replicas of the original church ceilings.

In the **Gothic** wing, fresco murals give way to vivid 14th-century wood-panel paintings of Bible stories. A roomful of paintings by the Catalan master Jaume Huguet (1412–1492) deserves a look, particularly his altarpiece of Barcelona's patron saint, George.

For a break, glide under the huge dome (which once housed an ice-skating rink) over to the air-conditioned cafeteria. This was the prime ceremony room and dance hall for the 1929 International Exposition. Then, from the big ballroom, ride the glass elevator upstairs, where the **Modern** section takes you on a delightful walk from the late 1800s to about 1930—kind of a Catalan Musée d'Orsay, showing off the best of local art during this exciting period. You start with Modernisme (furniture complements the empty spaces you likely saw in Gaudí's buildings), then Impressionists, *fin de siècle* fun, and Art Deco. It's refreshing to be introduced to Catalan artists.

Upstairs you'll also find photography (with a bit on how photojournalism came of age covering the Spanish Civil War), seductive sofas, and the chic Oleum restaurant, with vast city views.

▲Magic Fountains (Font Màgica)—Music, colored lights, and huge amounts of water make an artistic and coordinated splash on summer nights at Plaça d'Espanya (20-min shows start on the half-hour Fri–Sat 19:00–21:00, Thu–Sun in summer until 23:00; from the Espanya Metro station, walk toward the towering National Palace).

Spanish Village (Poble Espanyol)—This tacky five-acre model village uses fake traditional architecture from all over Spain as a shell to contain gift shops. Craftspeople do their clichéd thing only in the morning (not worth your time or €7.50, www.poble-espanyol.com). After hours, it's a popular local nightspot.

Castle of Montjuïc—The castle offers great city views from its fortress (€1, April–June daily 10:00–14:00, July–Sept daily 10:00–20:00, Oct–March Sat–Sun only 10:00–14:00) and a military museum (€2.50, Tue–Sun 10:00–20:00, closed Mon). The seemingly endless museum houses a dull collection of guns, swords, and toy soldiers. An interesting section on the Spanish-American War of 1898 covers Spain's valiant fight against American aggression (from its perspective). Unfortunately, there are no English descriptions. Those interested in Jewish history will find a fascinating collection of ninth-century Jewish tombstones.

The castle itself has a fascist past rife with repression. It was built in the 18th century by the central Spanish government to keep an eye on Barcelona and stifle citizen revolt. When Franco was in power, the castle was the site of hundreds of political executions.

NIGHTLIFE

Refer to the *See Barcelona* guide (free from TI) and ask about the latest at a TI. Major sights open until 20:00 include the Picasso Museum (closed Mon), Gaudí's Sagrada Família (open daily, until 18:00 Nov–March), Casa Milà (daily), and Parc Güell (daily). On Thursday, Montjuïc's Joan Miró museum stays open until 21:30 (otherwise open May–Sept Tue–Sat until 20:00).

Many lesser sights also stay open until 20:00, such as La Boquería market (Mon–Sat), the Maritime Museum (daily), Columbus Monument (daily May–Oct), City History Museum (Tue–Sat), Church of Santa Maria del Mar (daily), Casa Batllò (daily), Gaudí Museum (daily April–Sept), the Castle of Montjuïc (daily July–Sept), and Citadel Park (daily). The Magic Fountains on Plaça d'Espanya make a splash on weekend evenings (Fri–Sat, plus Thu in summer). The Tourist Bus (Bus Turistic) runs until 22:00 every day in summer.

For music, consider a performance at Casa Milà ("Pedrera by Night" summer concert series, see page 1008), the Liceu Opera House (page 992), or the Catalan Concert Hall (page 1001). There are many nightspots around Plaça Reial (such as the popular Jamboree).

Palau de la Virreina, an arts-and-culture TI, offers information on Barcelona cultural events—music, opera, and theater (Mon–Sat 10:00–20:00, Sun 10:00–15:00, Ramblas 99, see map on page 989).

SLEEPING

Book ahead. Barcelona is Spain's most expensive city. Still, it has reasonable rooms. Cheap places are more crowded in summer; fancier business-class hotels fill up in winter and offer discounts on weekends and in summer. When considering relative hotel values,

Sleep Code

(€1 = about $1.30, country code: 34)
S = Single, **D** = Double/Twin, **T** = Triple, **Q** = Quad, **b** = bathroom, **s** = shower only. Unless otherwise noted, credit cards are accepted, English is spoken, and prices listed do not include the 7 percent tax or breakfast (ranging from simple €3 spreads to €18 buffets).

To help you easily sort through these listings, I've divided the rooms into three categories, based on the price for a standard double room with bath (during high season):

$$$ **Higher Priced**—Most rooms €150 or more.
$$ **Moderately Priced**—Most rooms between €100–150.
$ **Lower Priced**—Most rooms €100 or less.

While many of my recommendations are on pedestrian streets, night noise can be a problem (especially in cheap places, which have single-pane windows). For a quiet night, ask for *"tranquilo"* rather than *"con vista."*

you can often get modern comfort for about the same price (€100) as you'll pay for ramshackle charm (and only a few minutes' walk from the Old City action). The TI at Plaça de Catalunya has a room-finding service, though it's cheaper to go direct.

Business-Class Comfort near Plaça de Catalunya

These hotels have sliding glass doors leading to plush reception areas, air-conditioning, and perfectly sterile modern bedrooms. Most are on big streets within two blocks of Barcelona's exuberant central square. As business-class hotels, they have hard-to-pin-down prices that fluctuate wildly. I've listed the average rate you'll pay. But in summer and on weekends, it seems the supply often far exceeds the demand, and many of these places lower prices to around €100—always ask for a deal.

$$$ Hotel Catalonia Albinoni, the best located of all, elegantly fills a renovated old palace with wide halls, hardwood floors, and 74 rooms. It overlooks a thriving pedestrian boulevard. Front rooms have views; balcony rooms on the back are quiet and come with sun terraces (Db-€170, extra bed-€35, family rooms, air-con, elevator, a block down from Plaça de Catalunya at Avinguda Portal de l'Angel 17, tel. 933-184-141, fax 933-012-631, www.hoteles-catalonia.com, albinoni.reservas@hoteles-catalonia.es).

$$$ Hotel Duques de Bergara boasts four stars. It has splashy public spaces, slick marble and hardwood floors, 150 comfortable rooms, and a garden courtyard with a pool a world away from the big-city noise (Sb-€155, Db-€192, Tb-€227, air-con, elevator, a half block off Plaça de Catalunya at Carrer de Bergara 11, tel. 933-015-151, fax 933-173-442, www.hoteles-catalonia.es, duques@hoteles-catalonia.es).

$$$ Nouvel Hotel, in an elegant, Victorian-style building on a handy pedestrian street, is less business-oriented and offers more character than the others listed here. It boasts royal lounges and 78 comfy rooms (Sb-€97, Db-€160, includes breakfast, air-con, Carrer de Santa Ana 18, tel. 933-018-274, fax 933-018-370, www.hotelnouvel.com, info@hotelnouvel.com).

$$ Hotel Occidental Reding, on a quiet street a five-minute walk west of the Ramblas and Plaça de Catalunya action, is a slick place renting 44 rooms at a very good price (Db-€120, extra bed-€59, air-con, elevator, near Metro: Universitat, Gravina 5–7, tel. 934-121-097, fax 932-683-482, www.occidental-hoteles.com, reding@occidental-hoteles.com).

$$ Hotel Duc de la Victoria, with 156 rooms, is professional yet friendly, buried in the Barri Gòtic just three blocks off the Ramblas (Db-€100–150 depending on occupancy, superior rooms—bigger and on a corner with windows on 2 sides—are worth €15 extra, air-con, elevator, Duc de la Victoria 15, tel. 932-703-410, fax 934-127-747, www.nh-hotels.com, nhducdelavictoria@nh-hotels.com).

$$ Hotel Lleó is well-run, with 90 big, bright, and comfortable rooms and a great lounge (Db-€120 but flexes way up with demand, summer Db special-€100, extra bed-about €25, air-con, elevator, Wi-Fi and Internet in lounge, 2 blocks west of Plaça de Catalunya at Carrer de Pelai 22, tel. 933-181-312, fax 934-122-657, www.hotel-lleo.com, reservas@hotel-lleo.es).

$$ Hotel Atlantis is solid, with 50 rooms and great prices for the location (Sb-€90, Db-€107, Tb-€125, breakfast-€8, air-con, elevator, Wi-Fi and Internet in lobby, Carrer de Pelai 20, tel. 933-189-012, fax 934-120-914, www.hotelatlantis-bcn.com, info@hotelatlantis.com).

Hotels with "Personality" on or near the Ramblas

The first three hotels—Hotel Continental Barcelona, Hotel Toledano, and Hostal Residencia Capitol—overlook the Ramblas and are in the same building at the top of the Ramblas, very near Plaça de Catalunya. They offer classic, tiny-view balcony opportunities if you don't mind the noise.

My last three listings—España, Peninsular, and Opera—are a few blocks away, on a seedy but safe street about halfway down the Ramblas. These places are generally family-run, with ad-lib furnishings, more character, and much lower prices. Only the Jardí offers a quaint square buried in the Barri Gòtic ambience—and you'll pay for it.

$ Hotel Continental Barcelona has an inviting lounge with a great Ramblas-view balcony. Its comfortable rooms come with double-thick mattresses, wildly clashing carpets and wallpaper, and perhaps one too many clever ideas (they're laden with microwaves, fridges, and strange Tupperware drawers). Choose between your own little Ramblas-view balcony or a quieter back room (S-€75, Db-€85, twin Db-€95, Db with balcony-€105, extra bed-€20, includes tax, air-con, elevator, Internet in lobby, Ramblas 138, tel. 933-012-570, fax 933-027-360, www.hotelcontinental.com, barcelona@hotelcontinental.com). José's free breakfast and all-day snack-and-drink bar makes this a better deal than the price suggests.

$ Hotel Toledano, overlooking the Ramblas, is stark and basic, popular with backpackers and dust-bunnies. Small, folksy, but with unpredictable plumbing, it's warmly run by Albert Sanz, his father Juan, Dani, and trusty Daniel on the night shift (Sb-€39, Db-€64, Tb-€81, Qb-€90; front rooms have petite Ramblas-view balconies, back rooms have no noise—request your choice when you call; some rooms have air-con, free Internet in lobby, Rambla de Canaletas 138, tel. 933-010-872, fax 934-123-142, www.hoteltoledano.com,

Hotels near the Ramblas

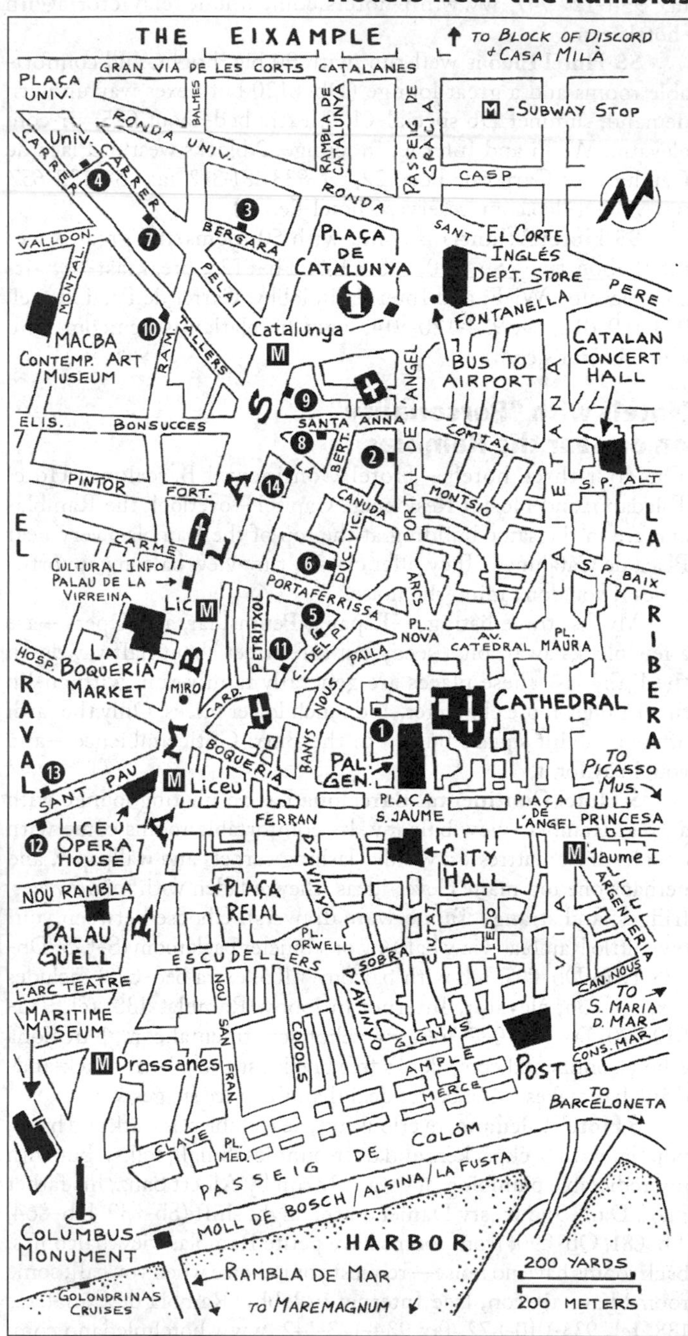

Hotel Key

1 Hotel Neri	9 Hotel Continental Barcelona, Hotel Toledano & Hostal Residencia Capitol
2 Hotel Catalonia Albinoni	10 Hostería Grau
3 Hotel Duques de Bergara	11 Hotel Jardí
4 Hotel Occidental Reding	12 Hotel España
5 Hostal Malda	13 Hotel Peninsular & Hostal Opera
6 Hotel Duc de la Victoria	14 Hostal Campi
7 Hotels Lleó & Atlantis	
8 Nouvel Hotel	

reservas@hoteltoledano.com). The Sanz family also runs **Hostal Residencia Capitol** one floor above—quiet, plain, no air-conditioning, cheaper, and also appropriate for backpackers (S-€28, D-€41, Ds-€47, Q-€61, 5-bed room-€69).

$ Hostería Grau is homey, family-run, and almost alpine. Its 25 clean and woody rooms are a few blocks off the Ramblas in the colorful university district (S-€33, D-€57, Db-€80, 2-bedroom family suites-€120, fans, air-con planned, Internet in lobby, 200 yards up Carrer dels Tallers from the Ramblas at Ramelleres 27, tel. 933-018-135, fax 933-176-825, www.hostalgrau.com, reservas @hostalgrau.com, Monica). The first two floors have ceilings a claustrophobic seven feet high, then things get tall again.

$ Hotel Jardí offers 40 clean, remodeled rooms on a breezy square in the Barri Gòtic. Many of the tight, plain, comfy rooms come with petite balconies (€15 extra) and enjoy an almost Parisian ambience. It's a good deal only if you value the cute square location. Book well in advance, as this family-run place has an avid following (Sb-€70, small interior Db-€80, Db-€86, Db with square-view terrace-€96, extra bed €12, breakfast-€6, air-con, elevator, halfway between Ramblas and cathedral at Plaça Sant Josep Oriol 1, tel. 933-015-900, fax 933-425-733, www.hoteljardi-barcelona.com, reservations@hoteljardi-barcelona.com).

$ Hotel España is in a big, creaky, circa-1900 building with 84 rooms and lavish public spaces still sweet with Art Nouveau decor by locally popular Modernista architect Domènech i Muntaner. While it's 50 yards off the Ramblas on a borderline-seedy street, it feels safe (Sb-€55–65, Db-€90–105, Tb-€105–135, includes tax and breakfast, air-con, elevator, near Metro: Liceu at Carrer Sant Pau 9, tel. 933-181-758, fax 933-171-134, www.hotelespanya.com, hotelespanya@hotelespanya.com).

$ Hotel Peninsular, farther down the same creepy-at-night street, is a unique and thoughtfully run value in the old center. A former convent, the 80 still-basic and thinly furnished rooms—

once nuns' cells—gather prayerfully around a bright, peaceful courtyard (Sb-€54, Db-€75, Tb-€90, prices include tax and breakfast and are the same year-round, air-con, elevator, Carrer Sant Pau 34, tel. 933-023-138, fax 934-123-699, www.hpeninsular.com, reservas@hpeninsular.com, Alex and Augustin).

$ Hostal Opera, with 70 stark rooms 20 yards off the Ramblas, is clean, simple, and modern (Sb-€43, Db-€63, no breakfast, air-con only in summer, elevator, Internet in lobby, Carrer Sant Pau 20, tel. 933-188-201, www.hostalopera.com, info@hostalopera.com). The street can feel seedy at night, but it's safe, and the hotel is very secure.

Chic and Posh, Deep in the Barri Gòtic

$$$ Hotel Neri is sophisticated, with 22 rooms spliced into the ancient stones of the Barri Gòtic overlooking an overlooked square a block from the cathedral. Opened in 2003, it has big plasma-screen TVs, pricey modern art on the bedroom walls, and dressed-up people in its gourmet restaurant (Db-€250, suites-€360, breakfast-€22, air-con, elevator, rooftop tanning deck, St. Sever 5, tel. 933-040-655, fax 933-040-337, www.hotelneri.com, info@hotelneri.com).

Humble, Cheaper Places Buried in the Old City

$ Hostal Campi is big, quiet, and ramshackle. This easygoing, old-school spot rents 24 rooms a few doors off the top of the Ramblas. The streets can be noisy, so request a quiet room in the back (D-€48, Db-€56, T-€65, Tb-€76, no breakfast but you're welcome to picnic in their fine salon, Canuda 4, tel. & fax 933-013-545, hcampi@terra.es, friendly Sonia, Margarita, and Nando).

$ Hostal Malda rents the best cheap beds I found in the old center. With 25 rooms above a small shopping mall near the cathedral, it's a time-warp—quiet and actually charming. Good-natured Aurora speaks no English and takes no reservations...good luck (S-€15, D-€30, T-€45, 100 yards up Carrer del Pi from delightful Plaça Sant Josep Oriol, Carrer del Pi 5, tel. 933-173-002).

$ Gothic Point Hostel is youthful, fun, and super-efficient, with 150 beds in the trendy Ribera district a block from the Picasso Museum. Rooms are coed, with eight to 12 beds. Each bunk bed has a little curtained area for privacy with a locker (€20 per bed, sheets-€2, includes breakfast, free Internet in lobby, open 24 hours but quiet after 23:00, roof terrace, Carrer Vigatans 5, tel. 932-687-808, www.gothicpoint.com). **Sea Point Hostel** is their sister hostel, on the beach nearby (Plaça del Mar 4, tel. 932-247-075, www.seapointhostel.com).

Hotels in Barcelona's Eixample

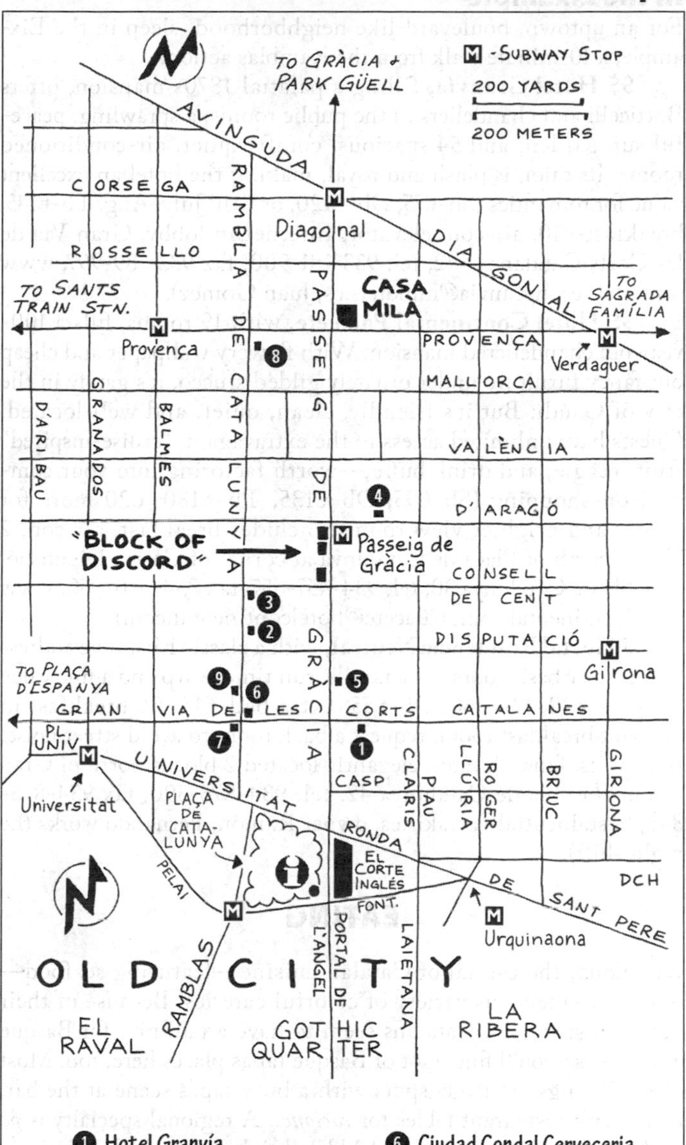

1. Hotel Granvía
2. Hotel Continental Palacete
3. Hostal Residencia Neutral
4. La Rita Restaurant
5. "QU QU" Quasi Queviures
6. Ciudad Condal Cerveceria
7. La Tramoia Braseria
8. La Bodegueta
9. El Raco

In the Eixample

For an uptown, boulevard-like neighborhood, sleep in the Eixample, a 10-minute walk from the Ramblas action.

$$ Hotel Granvía, filling a palatial 1870s mansion, offers Botticelli and chandeliers in the public rooms; a sprawling, peaceful sun garden; and 54 spacious, comfy, quiet, air-conditioned rooms. Its salon is plush and royal, making the hotel an excellent value for romantics (Sb-€75, Db-€120, or €110 July–Aug, Tb-€145, breakfast-€10, air-con, elevator, Internet in lobby, Gran Via de les Corts Catalanes 642, tel. 933-181-900, fax 933-189-997, www.nnhotels.es, hgranvia@nnhotels.es, Juan Gomez).

$$ Hotel Continental Palacete, with 19 rooms, fills a 100-year-old chandeliered mansion. With flowery wallpaper and cheap but fancy furniture under ornately gilded stucco, it's gaudy in the city of Gaudí. But it's friendly, clean, quiet, and well-located. Guests have unlimited access to the extravagant, "cruise-inspired" fruit, veggie, and drink buffet—worth factoring into your comparison-shopping (Sb-€95, Db-€135, Tb-€180, €20 more for bigger and brighter view rooms, includes breakfast, air-con, 2 blocks north of Plaça de Catalunya at corner of Carrer Diputació, Rambla de Catalunya 30, tel. 934-457-657, fax 934-450-050, www.hotelcontinental.com, palacete@hotelcontinental.com).

$ Hostal Residencia Neutral, with a classic Eixample address and 28 very basic rooms, is a family-run time-warp and a fine value (tiny Ss-€30, Ds-€48, Db-€55, extra bed-€15, €6 breakfast in pleasant breakfast room, request a back room to avoid street noise, thin walls, fans, elevator, elegantly located 2 blocks north of Gran Via at Rambla de Catalunya 42, tel. 934-876-390, fax 934-876-848, hostalneutral@arrakis.es, owner Ramón, Fernando works the night shift).

EATING

Barcelona, the capital of Catalan cuisine—featuring seafood—offers a tremendous variety of colorful eateries. Because of their common struggles, Catalans seem to have an affinity for Basque culture—so you'll find a lot of Basque tapas places here, too. Most of my listings are lively spots with a busy tapas scene at the bar, along with restaurant tables for *raciones*. A regional specialty is *pa amb tomaquet* (pah ahm too-MAH-kaht), bread topped with a mix of crushed tomato and olive oil.

I've listed mostly practical, characteristic, colorful, and affordable restaurants. The city is thriving with trendy and chic new eateries, and foodies will do well to get local advice or explore the Ribera area for a fine dinner. Many restaurants close in August (or July), when the owners take a vacation.

Eating Simply yet Memorably near the Ramblas

Taverna Basca Irati serves 40 kinds of hot and cold Basque *pintxos* for €1.60 each. These are open-faced sandwiches—like sushi on bread. Muscle in through the hungry local crowd. Get an empty plate from the waiter, and then help yourself. Every few minutes, a waiter prances proudly by with a platter of new, still-warm munchies. Grab one as they pass by...it's addictive. You pay on the honor system: you're charged by the number of toothpicks left on your plate when you're done. Wash it down with a €2 glass of Rioja (full-bodied red wine), €2.40 Txakolí (sprightly Basque white wine), or €1.60 *sidra* (apple wine) poured from on high to add oxygen and bring out the flavor (daily 11:00–24:00, a block off the Ramblas, behind arcade at Carrer Cardenal Casanyes 15, Metro: Liceu, tel. 933-023-084).

Restaurant Elisabets is a happy little neighborhood eatery packed with antique radios and popular with locals for its "home-cooked," three-course €8 lunch special. Stop by for lunch, survey what those around you are enjoying, and order what looks best (Mon–Sat 13:00–16:00, closed Sun, 2 blocks west of Ramblas on far corner of Plaça Bonsucces at Carrer Elisabets 2, tel. 933-175-826, run by Pilar).

Café Granja Viader is a quaint time-capsule place, family-run since 1870. They boast to be the first dairy business to bottle and distribute milk in Spain. This feminine place—specializing in baked and dairy delights, toasted sandwiches, and light meals—is ideal for a traditional breakfast (note the "Esmorzars" specials posted). Try a glass of *orxata* (or *horchata*—*chufa* nut milk, summer only), *llet mallorquina* (Majorca-style milk with cinnamon, lemon, and sugar), *crema catalana* (crème brûlée, their specialty), or *suis* ("Switzerland"—hot chocolate with a snowcap of whipped cream). It's a block off the Ramblas behind El Carme church (and an easy stop along my Ramblas walk, page 988; Sun–Mon 17:00–20:45, Tue–Sat 9:00–13:45 & 17:00–20:45, Xucla 4, tel. 933-183-486).

La Poma is popular with tired tourists for its good pizza, pasta, and salads in a bright, modern setting at the top of the Ramblas. Enjoy the comfortable views of all the Ramblas action, from street level or upstairs (daily 9:00–24:00, Ramblas 117, tel. 933-019-400).

Veggie Options: See "Vegetarian Eateries near Plaça de Catalunya and the Ramblas," below.

Picnics: Shoestring tourists buy groceries at **El Corte Inglés** (Mon–Sat 10:00–22:00, closed Sun, supermarket in basement, Plaça de Catalunya) and **Champion Supermarket** (Mon–Sat 10:00–22:00, closed Sun, Ramblas 113).

Barcelona's Barri Gòtic Restaurants

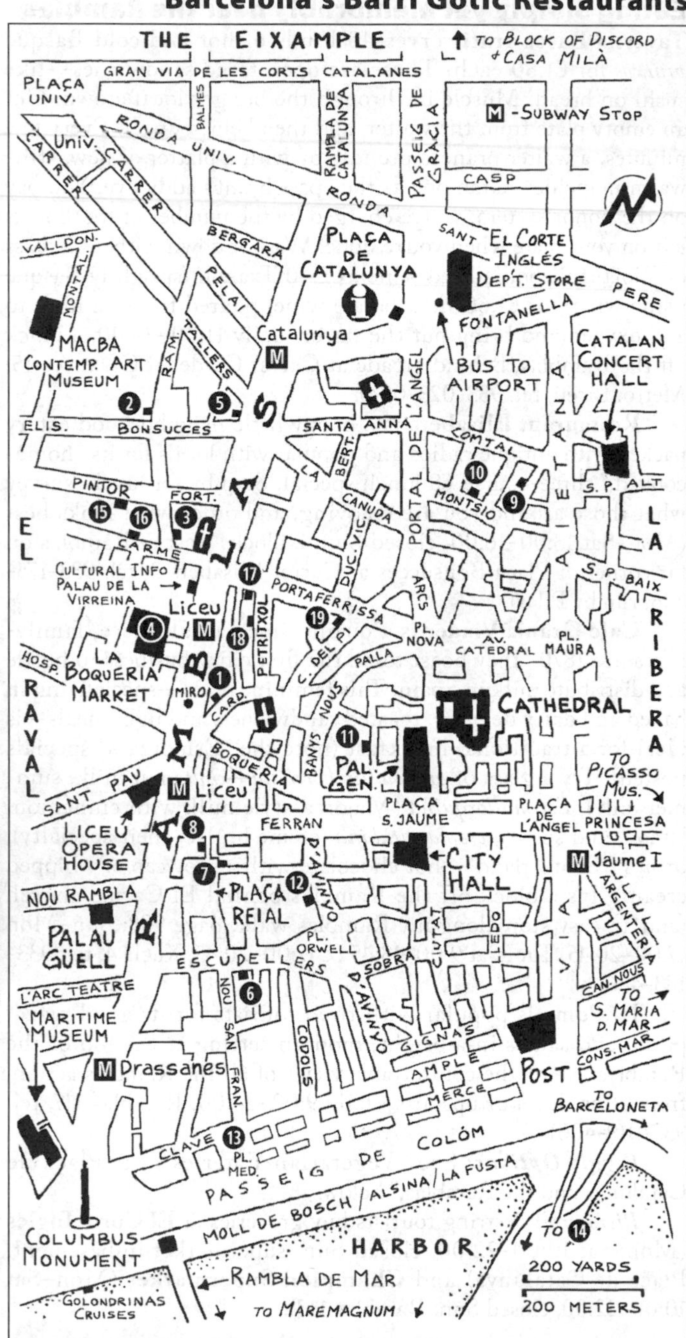

Restaurant Key

1. Taverna Basca Irati & Juicy Jones
2. Restaurant Elisabets
3. Café Granja Viader
4. La Boquería Market Eateries
5. La Poma & Champion Supermarket
6. La Fonda
7. Les Quinze Nits
8. La Crema Canela
9. La Dolça Herminia
10. Els Quatre Gats
11. El Pintor Restaurante
12. Agut d'Avignon Restaurante
13. Carrer Mercè Tapas Bars
14. To Tapasbar Maremagnum
15. Biocenter Veggie Rest.
16. Fresc Co Veggie Cafeteria
17. Casa Colomina Sweet Shop
18. La Pallaresa Granja-Xocolateria
19. Fargas Chocolate Shop

Dining (Real Restaurants) in the Barri Gòtic

Popular Chain Restaurants: Barcelona is enjoying a chain of five bright, modern restaurants (all with different names). These are a hit for their modern, artfully presented Spanish and Mediterranean cuisine, crisp ambience, and unbeatable prices. Because of their three-course €8 lunches and €15–20 dinners (both with wine), all are crowded with locals and in-the-know tourists. My favorite of the bunch is **La Crema Canela,** which feels cozier than the others and is the only one that takes reservations (daily 13:30–15:45 & 20:00–23:30, Passatge de Madoz 6, 30 yards north of Plaça Reial, tel. 933-182-744). The rest don't take reservations and are notorious for long lines at the door—arrive 30 minutes before opening, or be prepared to wait. The first two (along with La Crema Canela) are within a block of the Plaça Reial; the third is near the Catalan Concert Hall: **La Fonda** (daily 13:00–15:30 & 20:30–23:30, Carrer dels Escudellers 10, tel. 933-017-515); **Les Quinze Nits** (daily 13:00–15:45 & 20:30–23:30, on Plaça Reial at #6—you'll see the line, tel. 933-173-075); and **La Dolça Herminia** (2 blocks toward Ramblas from Catalan Concert Hall at Carrer de les Magdalenes 27, tel. 933-170-676). The fifth restaurant in the chain, **La Rita,** is described under "In the Eixample," below.

Els Quatre Gats, Picasso's hangout (and where he first showed off his paintings), retains its bohemian feel and serves quality, good-value meals in spite of its tourist crowds. Before Els Quatre Gats was founded in 1897, the idea of a café for artists was mocked as a place where only *quatre gats*—"four cats," meaning "crazies"—would go. Today diners enjoy a vaguely Parisian ambience with a rollicking crowd (of mostly tourists) surrounded by mementos from the Art Nouveau era (€10 three-course lunch, €10 salads, €15 plates, daily 8:30–24:00, live piano from 21:00, Carrer de Montsió 3, tel. 933-024-140).

El Pintor Restaurante serves one of the best €30 dinners in town. Dining here, you'll enjoy Catalan cuisine under medieval arches and rough brick, with candles and friendly service (daily 13:30–16:30 & 20:00–24:00, reserve ahead for evening, from Plaça de Sant Jaume walk north on Carrer Sant Honorat to #7, tel. 933-014-065).

Agut d'Avignon Restaurante has a country elegance and serves traditional Catalan and North Spanish cuisine to a dressy local clientele that knows good food (€11.50 fixed-price lunch offered Mon–Fri, €10–20 plates, daily 13:00–15:30 & 21:00–23:30, reservations smart, a block from Plaça de Sant Jaume in a dead-end alley off Carrer d'Avinyó 8 at Calle de la Trinidad 3, tel. 933-026-034).

Tapas on Carrer Mercè in the Barri Gòtic

Barcelona boasts great *tascas*—colorful local tapas bars. Get small plates (for maximum sampling) by asking for "tapas," not the bigger "*raciones.*" Glasses of *vino tinto* go for about €0.50. While trendy uptown restaurants are safer, better-lit, and come with English menus and less grease, these places will stain your journal. The neighborhood's dark, the regulars are rough-edged, and you'll get a glimpse of a crusty Barcelona from before the affluence hit.

From the bottom of the Ramblas (near the Columbus Monument), hike east along Carrer Clave. Then follow the small street that runs along the right side of the church (Carrer Mercè), stopping at the *tascas* that look fun. For a montage of edible memories, wander Carrer Mercè west to east and consider these spots, stopping wherever looks most inviting:

La Pulpería serves up fried fish, octopus, and *patatas bravas,* all with Galician Ribeiro wine. Tapas at the tables in back cost €1 extra. A few steps down the street, at **Casa del Molinero,** you can sauté your chorizo *al diablo* ("devil sausage"). It's great with *pa amb tomaquet* (tomato bread). Across the street, **La Plata** keeps things wonderfully simple, serving extremely cheap plates of sardines (€1.25), little salads (€1.10), and small glasses of keg wine (€0.50). **Tasca el Corral** serves mountain favorites from northern Spain, such as *queso de cabrales* (very moldy cheese) and chorizo (spicy sausage) with *sidra* (apple wine sold by the €4 bottle). **Sidrería Tasca La Socarrena** (at #21) is the only place that serves hard cider by the glass. At the end of Carrer Mercè, **Cerveceria Vendimia** serves up tasty clams and mussels (hearty *raciones* for €3 a plate—they don't do smaller portions, so order sparingly). Their *pulpo* (octopus) is more expensive and is the house specialty. Carrer Ample and Carrer Gignas, the streets parallel to Carrer Mercè inland, have more refined bar-hopping possibilities.

In and near La Boquería Market

Try eating at La Boquería market at least once (#91 on the Ramblas). Like all farmers' markets in Europe, this place is ringed by colorful, good-value eateries. Lots of stalls sell fun take-away food—especially fruit salads and fresh-squeezed fruit juices. There are several good bars around the market busy with shoppers munching at the counter (breakfast, tapas all day, coffee). The market, and most of the eateries listed here (unless noted), are open Monday through Saturday from 8:00 until 20:00 and closed on Sunday.

Pinotxo Bar is just to the right as you enter the market. It's a great spot for coffee, breakfast (spinach tortillas, or whatever's cooking with toast), or tapas. Fun-loving Juan and his family are La Boquería fixtures. Grab a stool across the way to sip your drink with people-watching views.

Kiosko Universal Bar is popular for its great prices on wonderful fish dishes (€10 fixed-price meals with different fresh-fish options, better before 12:30 but always packed, tel. 933-178-286). As you enter the market from the Ramblas, it's all the way to the left on the first alley. If you see people waiting, ask who's last in line *("¿El último?")*.

Restaurant la Gardunya, at the back of the market, offers tasty meat and seafood meals made with fresh ingredients bought directly from the market (€12.50 fixed-price lunch includes wine and bread, €15.50 dinner specials don't include wine, Mon–Sat 13:00–16:00 & 20:00–24:00, closed Sun, mod seating indoors or outside watching the market action, Carrer Jerusalem 18, tel. 933-024-323).

Casa Guinart is an "I love food and wine" kind of place serving fine light meals and great wine by the glass since 1899. The menu lists *flautas* (flute-sized sandwiches) and *xapatas* (bigger sandwiches). Check for the day's posting of wines. Some of the tables come with fine Ramblas views (Mon–Sat 9:00–21:00, closed Sun, on uphill corner of the market facing the Ramblas at Ramblas 95, tel. 933-178-887).

Bar Terrace Restaurant Ra is a lively terrace immediately behind the market with outdoor tables offering a view of the parking lot and happy eaters. At lunch they serve one great salad/pasta/wine meal for €11. If you feel like eating a big salad under an umbrella...this is it (daily 10:00–12:30 & 13:30–16:00 & 21:00–24:00, fancier menu at night, tel. 615-959-872).

Out at Sea—Maremagnum

Tapasbar Maremagnum is a big, rollicking, sports-bar kind of tapas restaurant, great for large groups. It's a fun way to end your Ramblas walk, featuring breezy harbor views and good local food with an emphasis on the sea (daily 11:00–24:00, a 10-minute stroll past the Columbus Monument straight out the dock on Moll d'Espanya, tel. 932-258-180).

In the Ribera District, near the Picasso Museum

La Ribera, the hottest neighborhood in town, sparkles with eclectic and trendy as well as subdued and classy little restaurants hidden in the small lanes surrounding the Church of Santa Maria del Mar. While I've listed a few well-established tapas bars that are great for light meals, to really dine, simply wander around for 15 minutes and pick the place that tickles your gastronomic fancy. I think anyone saying they know what's best in this area is kidding themselves—it's changing too fast and the choices are too personal. One thing's for sure: There are a lot of talented and hardworking restaurateurs with plenty to offer. Consider starting your evening off with a glass of fine wine at one of the *enotecas* on the square facing the Church of Santa Maria del Mar. Sit back and admire the pure Catalan Gothic architecture. My first three listings are all on the main drag, Carrer de l'Argenteria.

Sagardi offers a wonderful array of Basque goodies—tempting *pinchos* and *montaditos* at €1.30 each—along its huge bar. Ask for a plate and graze. You can sit on the square with your plunder for a few cents extra. Wash it down with Txakolí, a Basque white wine poured from the spout of a huge wooden barrel into a glass as you watch. Sagardi's back restaurant features excellent grilled meats and is a worthwhile splurge (bar open daily 12:00–24:00, restaurant open daily 12:00–16:00 & 19:30–24:00, Carrer de l'Argenteria 62–4, tel. 933-199-993).

Taller de Tapas ("Tapas Workshop") is an upscale, trendy tapas bar and restaurant that dishes up sophisticated morsels and light meals in a medieval-stone yet mod setting or on the square. This is favored by local office workers who aren't into the Old World Gothic stuff (little sandwiches until 12:30, then tapas, Mon–Sat 8:30–24:00, Sun 12:00–24:00, Carrer de l'Argenteria 51, tel. 932-688-559).

Hofmann is a renowned cooking school with an excellent if pricey restaurant. The four-course, €32 lunches are made up of just what the students are working on that day—so there's no choice. Dinners can easily cost twice as much. Save room (and euros) for the incredible desserts. Reservations are recommended, because locals love this place (Mon–Fri 13:30–15:15 & 21:00–23:15, closed Sat–Sun and Aug, Carrer de l'Argenteria 74–78, tel. 933-195-889, www.hofmann-bcn.com). When your meal's done, ask for a tour of the impressive kitchen.

El Xampanyet, a characteristic and often congested family-run bar with a fun-loving staff, specializes in tapas and anchovies. A *sortido* (assorted plate) of *carne* (meat) or *pescado* (fish) costs about

€6 with *pa amb tomaquet* (bread topped with tomato). While it's filled with tourists during the sightseeing day, it's a local favorite after dark (Tue–Sat 12:00–16:00 & 19:00–23:30, Sun 12:00–16:00, closed Mon, a half block beyond the Picasso Museum at Montcada 22, tel. 933-197-003). Don't be put off by the seafood from a tin... Catalans like it this way.

Vegetarian Eateries near Plaça de Catalunya and the Ramblas

Biocenter, a Catalan soup-and-salad restaurant popular with local vegetarians, takes its cooking very seriously and feels a bit more like a real restaurant than most (€8 lunches, Mon–Sat 13:00–17:00, Thu–Sat also 20:00–23:00, closed Sun, 2 blocks off the Ramblas at Pintor Fortuny 25, Metro: Catalunya, tel. 933-014-583).

Fresc Co, bright and cheery, offers a healthy buffet in a sleek and efficient cafeteria. For one cheap price (€8 until 18:00, then €10), you get a drink (one alcoholic or unlimited soft drinks) and all the salad (some with chicken or turkey), pasta, soup, pizza, and dessert you want. The hearty buffet is more appetizing than most. Choose between two locations (both open daily 12:30–24:00, tel. 933-016-837): west of Plaça de Catalunya at Ronda Universitat 29, or a block off the Ramblas (near La Boquería market) at Carme 16.

Juicy Jones is a tutti-frutti vegan/vegetarian eatery with garish colors, a hip veggie menu (served downstairs), and a stunning array of fresh-squeezed juices served at the bar (lunch and dinner fixed price meal-€8, daily 13:00–24:00, Carrer Cardenal Casanyes 7). Pop in for a quick €3 "juice of the day."

In the Eixample

The people-packed boulevards of the Eixample (Passeig de Gràcia and Rambla de Catalunya) are lined with appetizing eateries featuring breezy outdoor seating. Many trendy and touristic tapas bars offer a cheery welcome and slam out the appetizers. The first listing is a normal restaurant. The next three are upscale tapas bars, most with plenty of seating and a restaurant feel.

La Rita is a fresh and dressy little restaurant serving Catalan cuisine near the Block of Discord. Their lunches—three courses with wine for €8 (served Mon–Fri from 13:00)—and dinners (€15, à la carte, daily from 20:30) are a great value (a block from Metro: Passeig de Gràcia, near corner of Carrer de Pau Claris and Carrer Arago at Arago 279, tel. 934-872-376). Like its four sister restaurants—described under "Dining (Real Restaurants) in the Barri Gòtic," above—it takes no reservations and its prices attract long lines, so arrive just before the doors open...or wait.

"QU QU" Quasi Queviures serves upscale tapas, sandwiches, or the whole nine yards—classic food served fast from a fun menu with modern decor and a high-energy sports-bar ambience. Walk through their enticing kitchen to get to the tables in back (daily 7:00–24:00, between Gran Via and Via Diputació at Passeig de Gràcia 24, tel. 933-174-512).

Ciudad Condal Cerveceria brags it serves the best *montaditos* (sandwiches) and beers in Barcelona. It's an Eixample favorite, with an elegant bar and tables plus good seating out on the Rambla de Catalunya for all that people-watching action. While it has no restaurant-type menu, the list of tapas and *montaditos* is easy, fun, and comes with a great variety (including daily specials). This place is a cut above your normal tapas bar, but with reasonable prices (daily until 24:00, facing the intersection of Gran Via and Rambla de Catalunya at Rambla de Catalunya 18, tel. 933-181-997).

La Tramoia is a *braseria* (lots of grilled specialties) with piles of cheap *montaditos* and tapas at the downstairs bar. The brasserie-style restaurant upstairs bustles with happy local eaters enjoying great food and Gran Via views (€8–12 plates, open daily, also facing the intersection of Gran Via and Rambla de Catalunya at Rambla de Catalunya 15, tel. 934-123-634).

La Bodegueta is an unbelievably atmospheric below-street-level bodega serving hearty wines, homemade vermouth, *anchoas* (anchovies), tapas, and *flautas*—sandwiches made with flute-thin baguettes. Its daily €8.50 lunch special of three courses with wine is served 13:00–16:00 (Mon–Sat 8:00–24:00, Sun 19:00–24:00, at intersection with Provenza, Rambla de Catalunya 100, Metro: Diagonal, tel. 932-154-894). A long block from Gaudí's Casa Milà, this makes a fine sightseeing break.

El Raco is a local favorite for pasta, pizza, crêpes, and salads (about €6 each) in a modern, air-conditioned, lively setting (daily 13:00–24:00, Rambla de Catalunya 25, tel. 933-175-688).

Sandwich Shops

Bright, clean, and inexpensive sandwich shops are proudly holding the cultural line against the fast-food invasion hamburgerizing the rest of Europe. You'll find great sandwiches at **Pans & Company** and **Bocatta,** two chains with outlets all over town. Catalan sandwiches are made to order with crunchy French bread. Rather than butter, locals prefer *pa amb tomaquet* (tomato bread). Study the instructive multilingual menu fliers to understand your options.

A Short, Sweet Walk

Let me propose this three-stop dessert. You'll try a refreshing glass of *orxata*, munch some *churros con chocolate*, and visit a fine *xocolateria,* all within a three-minute walk of each other in the Barri Gòtic just off the Ramblas. Start at the corner of Carrer Portaferrissa midway down the Ramblas. For the best atmosphere, begin your walk at about 18:00.

***Orxata* at Casa Colomina:** Walk down Carrer Portaferrissa to #8. Casa Colomina, founded in 1908, sells ice cream and the refreshing *orxata* (or *horchata*—a drink made from the *chufa* nut). Order a glass (€1.15) and ask to see and eat a *chufa* nut (a.k.a. earth almond or tiger nut). In winter, they sell homemade *turrón*—a variation of nougat made with almond, honey, and sugar, brought to Spain by the Moors 1,200 years ago. They sell it in big €6 slabs, but if you ask nicely, they might give you a sample *(muestra)* of *blando, duro,* and *yema*—soft, hard, and yolk (Mon–Sat 10:00–20:30, Sun 12:30–20:30, tel. 933-122-511).

***Churros con Chocolate* at La Pallaresa Granja-Xocolateria:** Continue down Carrer Portaferrissa, taking a right at Carrer Petrixol to this fun-loving *xocolateria*. Older, elegant ladies gather here for the Spanish equivalent of tea time—dipping their greasy *churros* into pudding-thick cups of hot chocolate (€4 for 5 *churros con chocolate*, daily 9:00–13:00 & 16:00–21:00, Carrer Petritxol 11, tel. 933-022-036).

Homemade Chocolate at Fargas: For your last stop, head for the ornate Fargas chocolate shop (Mon–Sat 9:30–13:30 & 16:00–20:00, closed Sun, continue down Carrer Petritxol to the square, hook left and up Carrer del Pi; it's on the corner of Portaferrissa and Carrer del Pi, tel. 933-020-342). Since the 19th century, gentlemen with walking canes have dropped by here for their chocolate fix. Founded in 1827, this is one of the oldest and most traditional chocolate places in Barcelona. Ask to see the old chocolate mill *("¿Puedo ver el molino?")*. They sell even tiny quantities (one little morsel) by the weight—don't be shy. A delicious chunk of the house specialty costs €0.40 (tray by the mill).

TRANSPORTATION CONNECTIONS

From Barcelona by Train to: Madrid (6/day, 4.5–6.5 hrs, about €60, plus 2 night trains, 9 hrs, about €35–45 plus berth cost; the high-speed AVE train reduces time but increases cost, reservation required), **Paris** (1/day, 12 hrs, about €130, night train, reservation mandatory), **Sevilla** (3/day, 8.5–11 hrs, about €50), **Granada** (2/day, 12 hrs, about €50), **Málaga** (2/day, 14 hrs, about €55), **Lisbon** (no direct trains, head to Madrid and then catch night train to Lisbon, 17 hrs, about €130), **Nice** (1/day, 12 hrs, about €65, change in Cerbère, or about €95 for change in Montpellier), **Avignon** (5/day, 6–9 hrs, about €40, or about €65 for change in Montpellier). Train info: tel. 902-240-202, www.renfe.es.

By Bus to: Madrid (18/day, 8 hrs, half the price of a train ticket, departs from station Barcelona Nord at Metro: Marina, tel.

902-260-606). Sarfa buses serve all the coastal resorts (tel. 902-302-025).

By Plane: Check the reasonable flights from Barcelona to Sevilla or Madrid. Vueling is Iberia's most popular discount airline (e.g., Barcelona–Madrid flights as low as €30 if booked in advance, tel. 902-333-933, www.vueling.com). Iberia (tel. 902-400-500, www.iberia.com) and Air Europa (tel. 902-401-501 or 932-983-907, www.aireuropa.com) offer €80 flights to Madrid. Also, for flights to other parts of Europe, consider British Airways (tel. 902-111-333, www.britishairways.com) and easyJet (tel. 902-299-992, www.easyjet.com). Airport info: tel. 932-983-838. For details on getting between downtown Barcelona and the airport, see "Arrival in Barcelona—By Plane," page 986.

MADRID

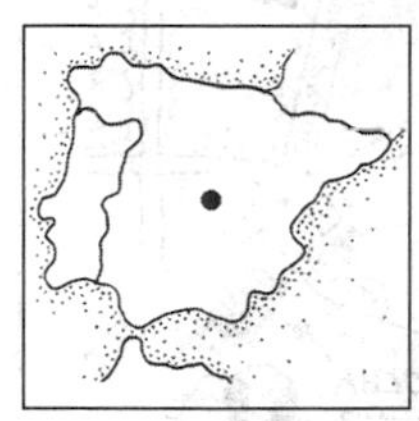

Today's Madrid is upbeat and vibrant, still enjoying a post-Franco renaissance. You'll feel it. Even the living-statue street performers have a twinkle in their eyes.

Madrid is the hub of Spain. This modern capital—Europe's highest, at more than 2,000 feet—has a population of 2.8 million. Like its people, the city is relatively young. In 1561, King Philip II decided to move the capital of his empire from Toledo to Madrid. One hundred years ago, Madrid had only 400,000 people—so the majority of today's Madrid is modern sprawl surrounding an intact, easy-to-navigate historic core.

The city's ambitious plans include the creation of a pedestrian street crossing the city from the Prado to the Royal Palace (the section from the Prado to Plaza Ángel has been completed) and a new macro-train station near Puerta del Sol (which will keep that subway station under construction until 2008). By installing posts to keep cars off sidewalks, making the streets safer after dark, and restoring old buildings, Madrid is working hard to make the city more livable...and fun to visit. In an effort to win the 2012 Olympics, Madrid began some massive city improvement building projects. Even though they lost out, the construction—which many locals believe is profitable for corrupt city officials who are getting kickbacks—continues as if they won.

Tourists are the real winners. Dive headlong into the grandeur and intimate charm of Madrid. The lavish Royal Palace, with its gilded rooms and frescoed ceilings, rivals Versailles. The Prado has Europe's top collection of paintings. The city's huge Retiro Park invites you for a shady siesta and a hopscotch through a mosaic of lovers, families, skateboarders, pets walking their masters, and

Madrid

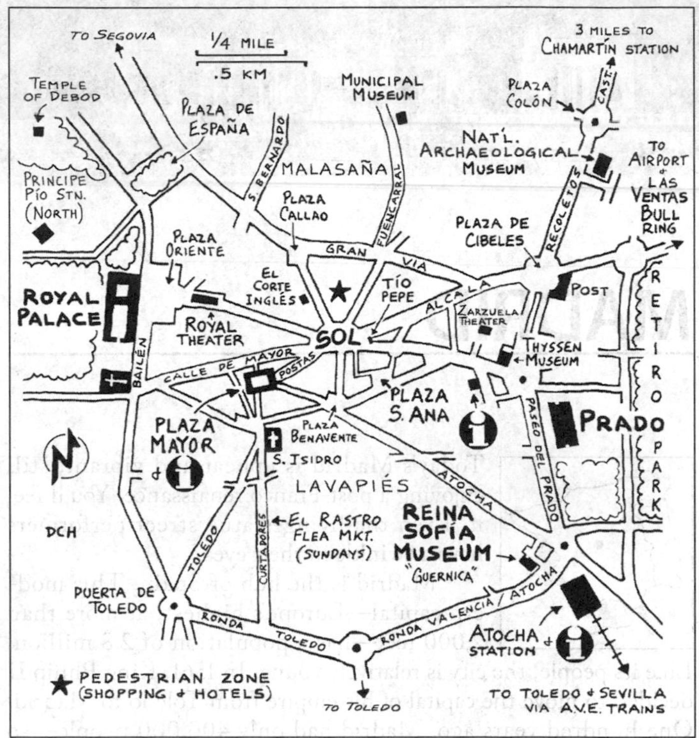

expert bench-sitters. Save time for Madrid's elegant shops and people-friendly pedestrian zones. On Sundays, cheer for the bull at a bullfight or bargain like mad at a mega-size flea market. Lively Madrid has enough street-singing, bar-hopping, and people-watching vitality to give any visitor a boost of youth.

Planning Your Time

Divide your time between Madrid's top three attractions: the Royal Palace (worth a half day), the Prado museum (also worth a half day), and its bar-hopping contemporary scene. On a Sunday (Easter–Oct), consider allotting extra time for the flea market and/or a bullfight.

Madrid is worth two days on even the fastest trip. I'd spend them this way:

Day 1: Take a brisk, 20-minute good-morning-Madrid walk from Puerta del Sol to the Prado (from Puerta del Sol, walk three blocks south to Plaza del Ángel, then take the pedestrian walkway to the Prado along Huertas street). Spend the rest of the morning at the Prado, then take an afternoon siesta in Retiro Park, or tackle modern art at the Centro de Arte Reina Sofía (Picasso's *Guernica*) and/or the Thyssen-Bornemisza Museum. Have dinner at 20:00, with tapas around Plaza Santa Ana.

Day 2: Follow my "Welcome to Madrid" self-guided walk (see page 1042), tour the Royal Palace, and have lunch near Plaza Mayor. Your afternoon is free for other sights or shopping. Be out at the magic hour—before sunset—when beautifully lit people fill Madrid.

Note that many top sights are closed on Monday, including the Prado and Thyssen-Bornemisza Museum; sights remaining open on Monday include the Royal Palace (open daily) and Centro de Arte Reina Sofía (closed Tue).

ORIENTATION

Puerta del Sol marks the center of Madrid. No major sight is more than a 20-minute walk or a €4 taxi ride from this central square. The Royal Palace (to the west) and the Prado Museum and Retiro Park (to the east) frame Madrid's historic center. This zone can be covered on foot. Southwest of Puerta del Sol is a 17th-century district with the slow-down-and-smell-the-cobbles Plaza Mayor and memories of pre-industrial Spain. North of Puerta del Sol runs Calle de Gran Vía, and between the two are lively pedestrian shopping streets. Gran Vía, bubbling with expensive shops and cinemas, leads to the modern Plaza de España. Between Puerta del Sol and the Atocha Train Station stretches the colorful, up-and-coming multiethnic Lavapiés district (see the "The Lavapiés District Tapas Crawl," page 1074).

Tourist Information

Madrid has five TIs: on **Plaza Mayor** (daily 9:00–20:30, air-con, four Internet terminals, tel. 915-881-636); near the **Prado Museum** (Mon–Sat 9:00–20:00, Sun 9:00–14:00, Duque de Medinaceli 2, behind Palace Hotel, tel. 914-294-951); at **Chamartín Train Station** (Mon–Sat 8:00–20:00, Sun 8:00–15:00, tel. 913-159-976); at the **Atocha Train Station** (daily 9:00–21:00); and at the **airport** (daily 8:00–20:00, at Terminal 1 in arrival hall and Terminal 2 in baggage area before you go through customs, tel. 913-058-656). During the summer, small temporary stands pop up at touristed places such as Puerta del Sol and Plaza de España.

The general tourist information number is 915-881-636 (or pricier toll call: tel. 902-100-007; www.munimadrid.es).

At any TI, pick up a map and confirm your sightseeing plans. The TI's free *Public Transport* map is very well-designed for travelers' needs, and has the most detailed map of the center. Get this and use it. TIs have the latest on bullfights and zarzuela (light

Spanish opera). Only the most hyperactive travelers could save money buying the **Madrid Card,** which covers 40 museums and the Madrid Vision bus tour mentioned in "Tours," below (€38/24 hrs, €48/48 hrs, €58/72 hrs).

For entertainment listings, the TI's printed material is not very good. Pick up the Spanish-language weekly entertainment guide ***Guía del Ocio*** (€1, sold at newsstands). It lists daily live music ("Conciertos"), museums ("Museos"—with the latest times and special exhibits), restaurants (an exhaustive listing), kids' activities ("Los Ninos"), TV schedules, and movies (*"V.O."* means original version, *"V.O. en ingles sub"* means a movie is played in English with Spanish subtitles rather than dubbed).

If you're heading to **other destinations in Spain,** ask any Madrid TI for free maps and brochures (ideally in English). Since many small-town TIs keep erratic hours and run out of these pamphlets, get what you can in Madrid. You can get schedules for buses and some trains, and thus avoid unnecessary trips to the various stations. The TI's free and amazingly informative *Mapa de Comunicaciones España* is a road map of Spain that lists all the tourist offices and highway SOS numbers. (If they're out, ask for the route map sponsored by the Paradores hotel chain, the camping map, or the golf map.)

For tips on sightseeing, hotels, and more, visit www.madridman.com, run with passion by American Scott Martin.

Arrival in Madrid

By Train: Madrid's two train stations, Chamartín and Atocha, are both on subway lines with easy access to downtown Madrid. Each station has all the services. Chamartín handles most international trains. Atocha generally covers southern Spain, including the AVE trains to Sevilla and Toledo. Both stations offer long-distance trains *(largo recorrido)* as well as smaller, local trains (*regionales* and *cercanías*) to nearby destinations. To travel between Chamartín and Atocha, skip the subway (which involves a transfer); the *cercanías* trains are faster (6/hr, 12 min, €1.20, free with railpass or any train ticket to Madrid—show it at ticket window in the middle of the turnstiles, departs from Atocha's track 2 and generally Chamartín's track 2 or 3—but check the *Salidas Inmediatas* board to be sure).

Chamartín Station: The **TI** is opposite track 19. The impressively large Centro de Viajes/Travel Center customer-service office is in the middle of the building. You can relax in the Sala VIP Club if you have a first-class railpass and first-class seat or sleeper reservations (near track 12, next to Centro de Viajes). The station's Metro stop is Chamartín. (If you arrive by Metro at Chamartín, signs to *Información* lead to the lobby. Signs to *Vías* send you directly to the platforms.)

Greater Madrid

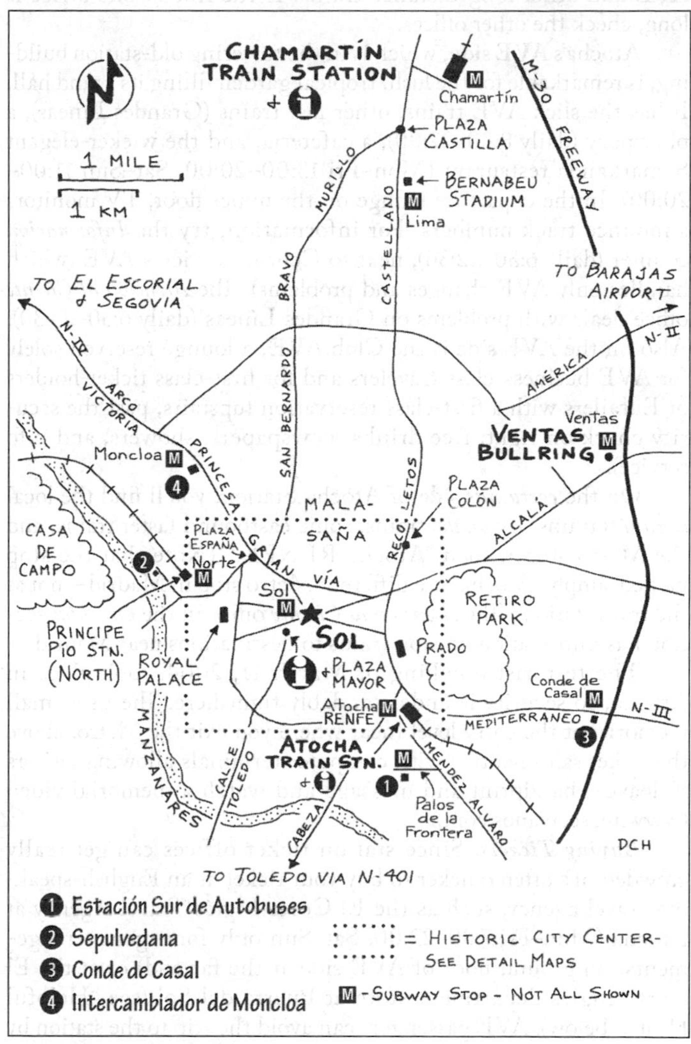

Atocha Station: The station is split into two halves: an AVE side (mostly long-distance trains) and a *cercanías* side (mostly local trains, nearest the Metro). These two parts are connected by a corridor of shops. Each side of the station has separate schedules and customer-service offices. The **TI,** which is in the AVE side, offers tourist info, but no train info (daily 9:00–21:00). There are three ticket offices at Atocha: The *cercanías* side has a small office for local trains and a big one for major trains (such as AVE). The AVE side has a pleasant, airy *Taquillas* office which also sells tickets for

AVE and other long-distance trains. If the line at one office is long, check the other offices.

Atocha's **AVE side**, which is in the towering old-station building, is remarkable for the lush, tropical garden filling its grand hall. It has the slick AVE trains, other fast trains (Grandes Líneas), a pharmacy (daily 8:00–22:00), a cafeteria, and the wicker-elegant Samarkanda restaurant (Mon–Fri 13:00–20:00, Sat–Sun 11:00–20:00). In the departure lounge on the upper floor, TV monitors announce track numbers. For information, try the *Información* counter (daily 6:30–22:30), next to Centro Servicios AVE (which handles only AVE changes and problems). The *Atención al Cliente* office deals with problems on Grandes Líneas (daily 6:30–23:30). Also on the AVE side is the Club AVE, a lounge reserved solely for AVE business-class travelers and for first-class ticket-holders or Eurailers with a first-class reservation (upstairs, past the security check on right; free drinks, newspapers, showers, and info service).

On the ***cercanías*** **side** of Atocha Station, you'll find the local *cercanías* trains, *regionales* trains, some eastbound faster trains, and the Metro stop named "Atocha RENFE." (Note that the stop named simply "Atocha" is a different Metro stop in Madrid—not at the train station.) The *Atención al Cliente* office in the *cercanías* section has information only on trains to destinations near Madrid.

The terrorist bombing of March 11, 2004, took place in Atocha, so security is understandably tight here. There's a small memorial at the entry level (near where you exit the Metro, above the ticket sales booths) with computer terminals allowing visitors to leave a handprint and message and watch a memorial video (www.mascercanos.com).

Buying Tickets: Since station ticket offices can get really crowded, it's often quicker to buy your ticket at an English-speaking travel agency, such as the El Corte Inglés Travel Agency at Atocha (Mon–Fri 7:00–22:00, Sat–Sun only for urgent arrangements, on ground floor of AVE side at the far end) or at the El Corte Inglés department store at Puerta del Sol (see "Helpful Hints," below). AVE passengers can avoid the trip to the station by reserving ahead by phone: Call 902-240-202 three days in advance, make a reservation, and pick up your ticket just before departure.

By Plane: For information on Madrid's Barajas Airport, see the end of this chapter.

Helpful Hints

Theft Alert: Be wary of pickpockets, anywhere, anytime. Areas of particular risk are Puerta del Sol (the central square), El Rastro (the flea market), Gran Vía (the paseo zone: Plaza del Callao to Plaza de España), the Ópera Metro station (or anywhere on the Metro), the airport, and any crowded streets. Assume a fight or any commotion is a scam to distract people about to become victims of a pickpocket. Wear your money belt. The small streets north of Gran Vía are particularly dangerous, even before nightfall. Muggings occur, but are rare. Victims of theft can call 902-102-112 for help (English spoken, once you get connected to a person).

Prostitution: Diverse by European standards, Madrid is spilling over with immigrants from South America, North Africa, and Eastern Europe. Many young women come here, fall on hard times, and end up on the streets. While it's illegal to make money from someone else selling sex (i.e., pimping), prostitutes get away with selling it directly on the street (€27, FYI). Calle de la Montera (leading from Puerta del Sol to Plaza Red de San Luís) is lined with what looks like a bunch of high-school girls skipping out of school for a cigarette break. Again, don't stray north of Gran Vía—while the streets may look inviting...this area is a meat-eating flower.

Embassies: The US Embassy is at Serrano 75 (tel. 915-872-200); the Canadian Embassy is at Nuñez de Balboa 35 (tel. 914-233-250).

One-Stop Shopping: The dominant local department store is **El Corte Inglés,** which takes up several huge buildings in the commercial pedestrian zone just off Puerta del Sol (Mon–Sat 10:00–22:00, closed Sun, navigate with the help of the info desk near the door of the main building—the tallest building with the biggest sign). They give out fine, free Madrid maps. In the main building, you'll find two handy travel agencies (see listing below), a post office, and a supermarket with a fancy "Club del Gourmet" section in the basement. Across the street is its Librería branch—a huge bookstore and six floors of music and home electronics, with a box office for tickets to whatever's on in town. Locals figure you'll find anything you need at El Corte Inglés.

Internet Access: There are plenty of centrally located places to check your email. Consider **NavegaWeb** (daily 9:00–24:00, Gran Vía 30) and the noisy, coin-operated **Zahara** (Mon–Fri 9:00–24:00, Sat–Sun 9:00–24:00, corner of Gran Vía and Mesoneros). Near Plaza Santa Ana (and great if you're waiting for the tapas crawl action to heat up), **Cyber Total** has plenty of fast terminals (€2/hr), disk-burning services, and helpful staff (daily 10:00–22:00, Calle Espoz y Mina 17, tel. 915-322-622). If you'd like to simultaneously wash clothes and surf, see "Laundry," below.

Bookstores: For books in English, try **NFAC Callao** (Calle Preciados 8, tel. 915-956-100), **Casa del Libro** (English on ground floor in back, Gran Vía 29, tel. 915-212-219), and **El Corte Inglés** (guidebooks and some fiction, in its Librería branch kitty-corner from main store, fronting Puerta del Sol—see listing above).

Laundry: Onda Blu will wash, dry, and fold your laundry for €5, including soap (Mon–Fri 9:30–22:00, Sat–Sun 10:30–19:00, self-service available, change machine, four Internet terminals, León 3, east of Plaza Santa Ana, tel. 913-695-071, Ana).

Travel Agencies: The grand department store, El Corte Inglés, has two travel agencies (air and rail tickets, but not reservations for railpass-holders, €2 fee, on first and seventh floors, Mon–Sat 10:00–22:00, closed Sun, just off Puerta del Sol, tel. 915-213-858).

Getting Around Madrid

If you want to use Madrid's excellent public transit, my two best tips are: Pick up and study the fine *Public Transit* map/flier (available at TIs), and take full advantage of the cheap 10-ride Metrobus ticket deal (see below).

By Metro: The city's broad streets can be hot and exhausting. A subway trip of even a stop or two saves time and energy. Madrid's Metro is simple, speedy, and cheap (€1.50/ride, runs 6:00–1:30 in the morning, www.metromadrid.es or www.ctm-madrid.es). The 10-ride Metrobus ticket can be shared by several travelers and works on both the Metro and buses (€6.15, sold at kiosks, tobacco shops, and in Metro). Insert your ticket in the turnstile (it usually shows how many rides remain on it), then retrieve it as you pass through. Stations offer free maps *(Madrid by Underground).* Navigate by subway stops (shown on city maps). To transfer, follow signs to the next subway line (numbered and color-coded). The names of the end stops are used to indicate directions. Green *Salida* signs point to the exit. Using neighborhood maps and street signs to exit smartly can save lots of walking. And watch out for thieves.

By Bus: City buses, while not as easy as the Metro, can be useful (€1 tickets sold on bus, or €6.15 for a 10-ride Metrobus ticket—see above; bus maps at TI or info booth on Puerta del Sol, buses run 6:00–24:00).

By Taxi: Madrid's 15,000 taxis are reasonably priced and easy to hail. Threesomes travel as cheaply by taxi as by Metro. After the €1.75 drop charge, the per-kilometer rate depends on the time: *Tarifa 1* (€0.75/kilometer) should be charged Mon–Sat 6:00–22:00; *Tarifa 2* (€0.90/kilometer) is valid after 22:00 and on Sundays. If your cabbie uses anything rather than *Tarifa 1* on weekdays (shown as an isolated "1" on the meter), you're being cheated. Rates can be higher if you go outside of Madrid. Other legitimate charges include the €4.50 supplement for the airport, the €2.40 supplement for train or bus stations, and €13.50 per hour for waiting. A ride from the Royal Palace to the Prado costs about €4.

TOURS

Madrid Vision Hop-On, Hop-Off Bus Tours—Madrid Vision offers three different hop-on, hop-off circuits of the city: historic, modern, and monuments. Buy a ticket from the driver (€14.50/1 day, €19/2 days) and you can hop from sight to sight and route to route as you like, listening to a recorded English commentary along the way. Each route has about 15 stops and takes about 90 minutes, with buses departing every 10 or 20 minutes. The three routes intersect at the south side of Puerta del Sol and in front of Starbucks across from the Prado (daily 10:00–21:00, longer in summer, shorter in winter, tel. 917-791-888).

Walking Tours—British expatriate Stephen Drake-Jones gives entertaining, informative walks of historic old Madrid almost nightly. A historian with a passion for the memory of the Duke of Wellington (the man who stopped Napoleon), Stephen is the founder and chairman of the Wellington Society. For €30, you become a member of the society for one year and get a free two-hour tour that includes stops at two bars for local drinks and tapas (morning and evening departures). Chairman Stephen takes you back in time to sort out Madrid's Hapsburg and Bourbon history. Eccentric Stephen likes his wine—if that's a problem, skip the tour. Tours start at the statue of García Lorca at the lower end of Plaza Santa Ana (maximum 10 people, call 609-143-203 to confirm tour and reserve a spot, chairman@wellsoc.org). Members of the Wellington Society can also take advantage of Stephen's helpline (if you're in a Spanish jam, call him to translate and intervene) and assistance by email (for questions on Spain, your itinerary, and so on). Stephen also does specialized walks, private tours, play-by-play bullfight visits, and day trips to great spots in the countryside for small groups (about €275 per couple, €350 per small group, see www.wellsoc.org for details).

LeTango Tourist Services—Carlos Galvin, a Spaniard who speaks flawless English (and has led tours for my groups since 1998) and his American wife, Jennifer, offer private tours in Madrid and other parts of Spain. Carlos mixes a market walk in the historic center with a culinary-and-tapas crawl to get close to the Madrileños, their culture, and their food. His walk gives a fine 2.5-hour orientation and introduction to the fascinating and tasty culture of Madrid (€75 per person including tapas and drinks, minimum 2 people, alcohol-free version, family-friendly). Carlos also offers an array of comprehensive travel services that include organizing itineraries and booking hotels, bullfights, admissions, and tours anywhere in Spain (tel. 915-223-928, mobile 661-752-458, www.letango.com, info@letango.com).

Private Guides—Inés Muniz Martin is a good local guide (€130 for up to 3.5 hours, or €165 on weekends and holidays, tel. 912-366-471, www.immguidedtours.com, info@immguidedtours.com). Hernan Amaya Satt directs a group of guides who take individuals on Madrid walks (€140/5 hrs for up to 8 people, mobile 680-450-231, www.madridmuseumtours.com, info@easygoing.org).

Big-Bus City Sightseeing Tours—Julia Travel offers standard guided bus tours departing from Gran Vía 68 (near Plaza de España, no reservations required—just show up 15 min before departure, tel. 915-599-605, www.juliatravel.com). Their city tours include a three-hour Madrid tour with a live guide in two or three languages (€17, one shopping stop, no museum visits, daily at 9:15 and 15:00) and "Madrid by Night" (€12.50, 2-hour floodlit overview, Mon–Sat at 20:30, none Sun).

Julia Travel also runs multiple day-trip tours to destinations near Madrid. The Valley of the Fallen and El Escorial tour is particularly efficient, given the lousy bus connections for this route (€43, 4.5 hours, makes the day trip easy—blitzing both sights with a commentary en route and no time-stealing shopping stops, Tue–Sun at 9:00 and most days at 15:00, none Mon). Three trips include Toledo: one of the city itself (€55, full day, daily departure at 9:15, return by 17:30), one of Madrid and Toledo together (€45, half-day in Toledo plus panoramic 3-hour Madrid tour, daily at 9:00), and a marathon tour of El Escorial, Valley of the Fallen, and Toledo (€87, full day, Tue–Sun at 9:00, none Mon). Note that the rushed Toledo tours skip the town's one must-see sight, the cathedral... but not the long shopping stops, because the shops give kickbacks to the guides. And even though the buses are air-conditioned, the all-day Toledo trip is just too hot to enjoy in summer (June–Sept).

SELF-GUIDED WALK

Welcome to Madrid: From the Puerta del Sol to the Royal Palace

Connect the sights with the following commentary. Allow an hour for this half-mile walk. Begin at Madrid's central square, Puerta del Sol (Metro: Sol).

Puerta del Sol: Named for a long-gone medieval gate with the sun carved onto it, bustling Puerta del Sol is worth ▲▲. It's a hub for the Metro, buses, political demonstrations, and pickpockets.

• *Stand by the statue of King Charles III and survey the square.*

Because of his enlightened urban policies, Charles III (who ruled until 1788) is affectionately called "the best mayor of

From Puerta del Sol to the Royal Palace

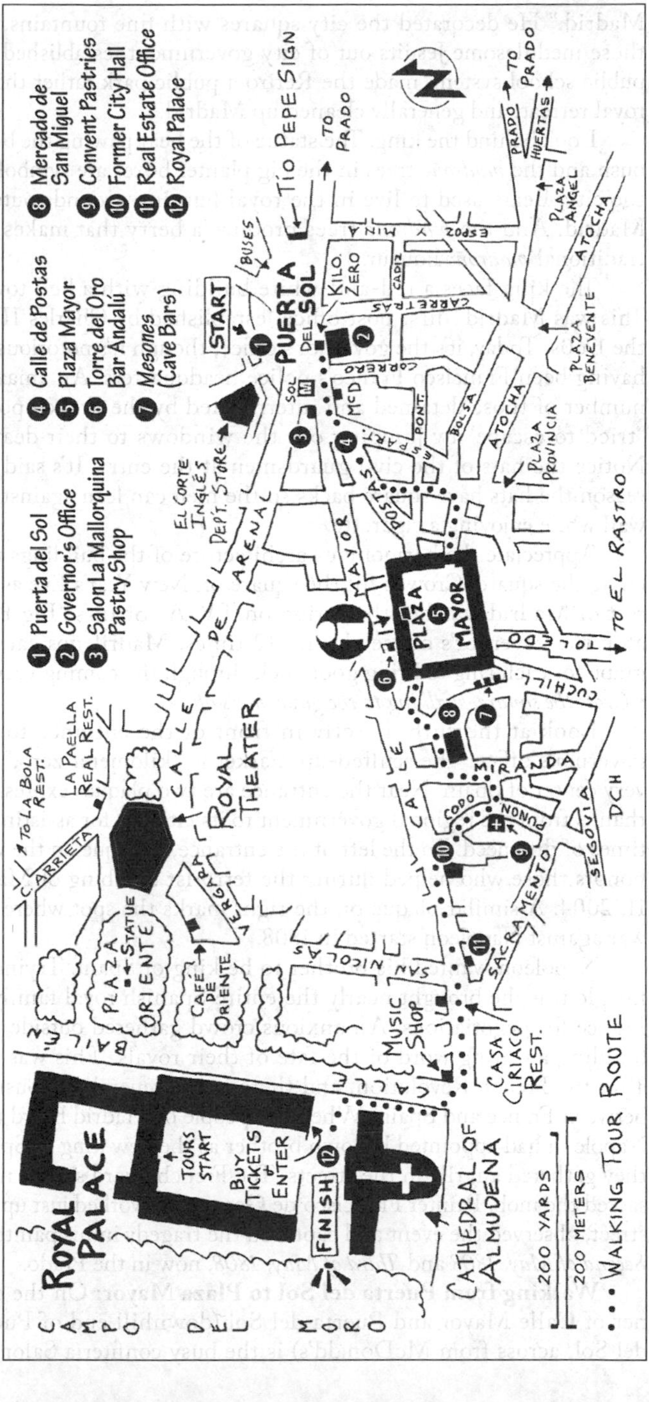

1. Puerta del Sol
2. Governor's Office
3. Salon La Mallorquina Pastry Shop
4. Calle de Postas
5. Plaza Mayor
6. Torre del Oro Bar Andalú
7. *Mesones* (Cave Bars)
8. Mercado de San Miguel
9. Convent Pastries
10. Former City Hall
11. Real Estate Office
12. Royal Palace

200 YARDS

200 METERS

• • • WALKING TOUR ROUTE

Madrid." He decorated the city squares with fine fountains, got those meddlesome Jesuits out of city government, established the public school system, made the Retiro a public park rather than a royal retreat, and generally cleaned up Madrid.

Look behind the king. The statue of the bear pawing the berry bush and the *madroño* trees in the big planter boxes are symbols of the city. Bears used to live in the royal hunting grounds outside Madrid. And the *madroño* trees produce a berry that makes the traditional *madroño* liqueur.

The king faces a red-and-white building with a bell tower. This was Madrid's first post office, established by Charles III in the 1760s. Today, it's the governor's office, though it's notorious for having been Francisco Franco's police headquarters. An amazing number of those detained and interrogated by the Franco police "tried to escape" by jumping out the windows to their deaths. Notice the hats of the civil guardsmen at the entry. It's said the reason the hats have square backs so the men can lean against the wall while enjoying a cigarette.

Appreciate the harmonious architecture of the buildings that circle the square. Crowds fill the square on New Year's Eve as the rest of Madrid watches the action on TV. As Spain's "Big Ben" atop the governor's office chimes 12 times, Madrileños eat one grape for each ring to bring good luck through the coming year.

• *Cross the square, walking to the governor's office.*

Look at the curb directly in front of the entrance to the governor's office. The scuffed-up marker is "kilometer zero," the very center of Spain. Near the entrance are two plaques expressing thanks from the regional government to its citizens for assisting in times of dire need. To the left of the entrance, a plaque on the wall honors those who helped during the terrorist bombing of March 11, 2004. A similar plaque on the right marks the spot where the war against Napoleon started in 1808.

Napoleon wanted his brother to be king of Spain. Trying to finagle this, he brought nearly the entire Spanish royal family to France for negotiations. An anxious crowd gathered outside this building awaiting word of the fate of their royals. This was just after the French Revolution, and there was a general nervousness between France and Spain. When the people of Madrid heard that Napoleon had appointed his own brother as the new king of Spain, they gathered angrily in the streets. The French guard simply massacred the mob. Painter Francisco de Goya, who worked just up the street, observed the event and captured the tragedy in his paintings *Second of May, 1808* and *Third of May, 1808,* now in the Prado.

Walking from Puerta del Sol to Plaza Mayor: On the corner of Calle Mayor and Puerta del Sol (downhill end of Puerta del Sol, across from McDonald's) is the busy confitería Salon La

Mallorquina (daily 9:00–21:15). Go inside for a tempting peek at racks with goodies hot out of the oven. The shop is famous for its sweet, cream-filled Napolitana pastry (€1). Or sample the Madrid specialty, *rosquillas* (*tontas* means "silly"—plain, and *listas* means "all dressed up"—with icing, €0.50 each).

From inside the shop, look back toward the entrance and notice the tile above the door with the 18th-century view of Puerta del Sol. Compare this with today's view out the door. This was before the square was widened, when a church stood where the *Tío Pepe* sign stands today. The French used this church to detain local patriots awaiting execution. (The venerable *Tío Pepe* sign, advertising a famous sherry for more than 100 years, was Madrid's first billboard.)

• *Cross busy Calle Mayor, round McDonald's, and veer up the pedestrian alley called Calle de Postas.*

The street sign shows the post coach heading for that famous first post office. Medieval street signs included pictures so the illiterate could "read" them. Fifty yards up the street, at Calle San Cristóbal, is Pans & Company, a popular sandwich chain. While Spaniards consider American fast food unhealthy—both culturally and physically—the local fast-food chains seem to be more politically and nutritionally correct.

• *From here, hike up Calle San Cristóbal.*

Within two blocks, you'll pass the local feminist bookshop (Librería Mujeres) and reach a small square. At the square, notice the big, brick 17th-century Ministry of Foreign Affairs building (with the pointed spire)—originally a jail for rich prisoners who could afford the cushy cells.

• *Turn right, and walk down Calle de Zaragoza under the arcade into the...*

Plaza Mayor: This square, rated ▲, was built in 1619. It's a vast, cobbled, traffic-free chunk of 17th-century Spain. Each side of the square is uniform, as if a grand palace were turned inside out. The statue is of Philip III, who ordered the square's construction. Upon this stage, much Spanish history has been played out: bullfights, fires, royal pageantry, and events of the gruesome Inquisition. Reliefs serving as seatbacks under the lampposts tell the story. During the Inquisition, many were tried here—suspected heretics, Protestants, Jews, and Muslims whose "conversion" to Christianity was dubious. The guilty were paraded around the square before their execution, wearing billboards listing their many sins (bleachers were built for bigger audiences, while the wealthy rented balconies). Some were slowly strangled as they held a crucifix, hearing the reassuring words of a priest as this life was squeezed out of them. Others were burned.

The square is painted a democratic shade of burgundy—the

result of a citywide vote. Since Franco's death in 1975, there's been a passion for voting here. Three different colors were painted as samples on the walls of this square, and the city voted for its favorite.

A stamp-and-coin market bustles here on Sundays from 10:00 to 14:00; on any day, it's a colorful and affordable place to enjoy a cup of coffee. Throughout Spain, lesser *plazas mayores* provide peaceful pools in the river of Spanish life. The TI (daily 9:00–20:30, wonderfully air-conditioned with free Internet access) is under the building on the north side of the square, the Casa de la Panadería, decorated with painted figures (it once housed the Bakers' Guild).

• *For some interesting, if gruesome, bullfighting lore, drop by the...*

Torre del Oro Bar Andalú: This bar is a good spot for a drink to finish off your Plaza Mayor visit (northwest corner of square, to the left of the Bakers' Guild). The bar has *Andalú* (Andalusian) ambience and an entertaining staff. Warning: They push expensive tapas on tourists. But buying a beer is safe and painless—just order a *caña* (small beer, shouldn't cost more than €2.30). The price list posted outside the door makes your costs perfectly clear. Consider taking a break at one of their sidewalk tables (or at any café/bar terrace facing Madrid's finest square). The scene is well worth the extra euro you'll pay for the drink.

The interior of the Torre del Oro bar is a temple to bullfighting, festooned with gory decor. Notice the breathtaking action captured in the many photographs. Look under the stuffed head of Barbero the bull. At eye level, you'll see a *puntilla,* the knife used to put a bull out of his misery at the arena. This was the knife used to kill Barbero. The plaque explains: weight, birthdate, owner, date of death, which matador killed him, and the location. Just to the left of Barbero, there's a photo of Franco with a very famous bullfighter. This is Manuel Benítez Pérez—better known as El Cordobés, the Elvis of bullfighters and a working-class hero. At the top of the stairs to the WC, find the photo of El Cordobés and Robert Kennedy—looking like brothers. At the end of the bar in a glass case is the "suit of lights" the great El Cordobés wore in his ill-fated 1967 fight. With Franco in attendance, El Cordobés went on and on, long after he could have ended the fight, until finally the bull gored him. El Cordobés survived; the bull didn't. Find another photo of Franco with El Cordobés at the far end, to the left of Segador the bull. Under the bull is a photo of El Cordobés' illegitimate son kissing a bull. Disowned by El Cordobés senior, yet still using his dad's famous name after a court battle, the new El Cordobés is one of this generation's top fighters.

Strolling from Plaza Mayor to the Royal Palace: Leave Plaza Mayor on Calle Ciudad Rodrigo (to your right as you exit the bull bar). You'll pass a series of fine turn-of-the-20th-century storefronts and sandwich joints, such as Casa Rúa, famous for their

Heart of Madrid

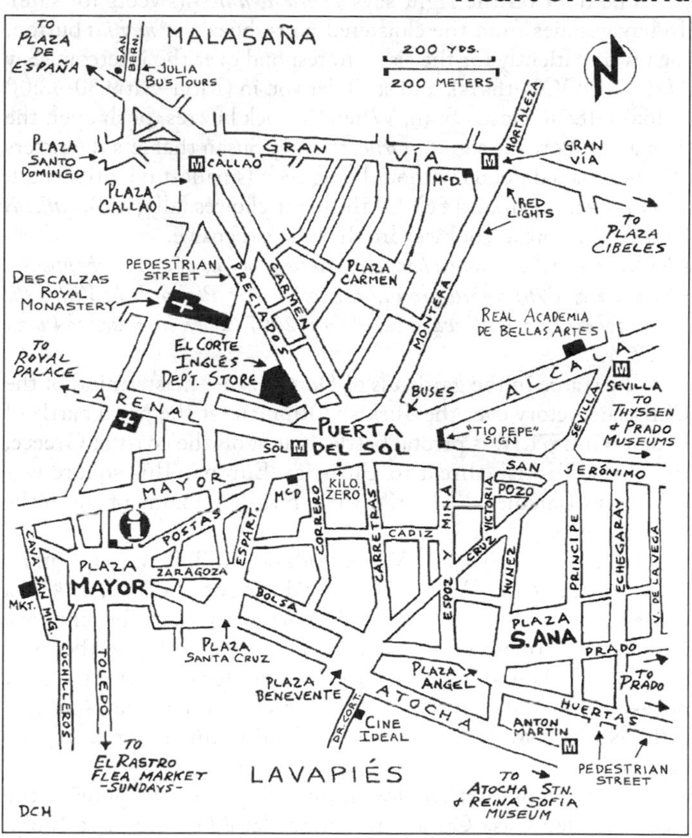

cheap *bocadillos de calamares*—fried squid-rings on a roll.

From the archway, you'll see the covered Mercado de San Miguel (green iron posts, on left). Before you enter the market, look left down the street called Cava de San Miguel. If you like sangria and singing, come back at about 22:00 and visit one of the *mesones* that line the street. These cave-like bars stretch way back and get packed with locals out on cheap dates who—emboldened by sangria, the setting, and Spain—might suddenly just start singing. It's a lowbrow, electric-keyboard, karaoke-type ambience, best on Friday and Saturday nights.

Wander through the produce market and consider buying some fruit (Mon–Fri 9:00–14:30 & 17:15–20:15, Sat 9:00–14:30, closed Sun).

• *Leave the market on the opposite (downhill) side and follow the pedestrian lane left. At the first corner, turn right and cross the small plaza to the modern brick convent.*

The door on the right says *venta de dulces* (sweets for sale). To buy goodies from the cloistered nuns, buzz the *monjas* button, then wait patiently for the sister to respond over the intercom. Say "*dulces*" (DOOL-thays), and she'll let you in (Mon–Sat 9:30–13:00 & 16:00–18:30, closed Sun). When the lock buzzes, push open the door and follow the sign to *torno,* the lazy Susan that lets the sisters sell their baked goods without being seen (smallest quantity: half, or *medio,* kilo—around €6). Of the many choices (all good), *galletas* (orange shortbread cookies) are the least expensive.

• *Follow Calle del Codo (where those in need of bits of armor shopped—see the street sign) uphill around the convent to Plaza de la Villa, the square where City Hall was located until 2007 (when it moved to Plaza de Cibeles).*

The statue in the garden is of Don Bazán—mastermind of the Christian victory over the Turkish Ottomans at the naval battle of Lepanto in 1571. This pivotal battle, fought off the coast of Greece, ended the Turkish threat to Christian Europe. This square was the heart of medieval Madrid, though little remains of the 14th-century town.

From here, busy Calle Mayor leads downhill for a couple more blocks to the Royal Palace. Halfway down (on the left), at #75, a real-estate office *(inmobiliaria)* advertises apartments for rent (*piso* is a large apartment or condo, priced by the month—in the hundreds or low thousands of euros) and condos for sale (with six-digit prices). To roughly convert square meters to square feet, multiply by 10. Notice how for large items, locals still think in terms of *pesetas* ("pts").

A few steps further down, on a tiny square opposite the recommended Casa Ciriaco restaurant (at #84—see page 1068), a statue memorializes the 1906 anarchist bombing that killed 23 people as the royal couple paraded by on their wedding day. While the crowd was throwing flowers, an anarchist (what terrorists used to be called) threw a bouquet lashed to a bomb from a balcony of #84 (the building was a hotel at the time). Gory photos of the event hang inside the restaurant (to the right of the entrance).

• *Continue down Calle Mayor. Within a couple of blocks, you'll come to a busy street, Calle de Bailen.*

The Garrido-Bailen music store is *the* place to stock up on castanets, unusual flutes, and Galician bagpipes. Across the busy street is Madrid's Cathedral of Almudena, built between 1883 and 1993. Its exterior is a contemporary mix, and its interior is neo-Gothic, with a refreshingly modern and colorful ceiling, glittering 5,000-pipe organ, and the 12th-century coffin (empty, painted leather on wood, in a chapel behind the altar) of Madrid's patron saint, Isidro. Isidro, a humble peasant, loved the handicapped and performed miracles. Forty years after he died, this coffin was opened and his body was found miraculously preserved, which convinced the pope to canonize him as the patron saint of Madrid and of farmers, with May 15 as his feast day.

Next to the cathedral is the **Royal Palace.**

• *When you're finished, you may want to...*

Return to Puerta del Sol: With your back to the palace, face the equestrian statue of Philip IV and (beyond the statue) the Neoclassical **Royal Theater** (Teatro Real, rebuilt in 1997). On your left, the **Madrid Tower** skyscraper marks the Plaza de España. Walk behind the Royal Theater (on the right, passing Café de Oriente—a favorite with theatergoers) to another square, where you'll find the Ópera Metro stop and Calle de Arenal, which leads back to Puerta del Sol.

SIGHTS

Royal Palace (Palacio Real)

Europe's third-greatest palace (after Versailles and Vienna's Schönbrunn), with arguably the most sumptuous original interior, is packed with tourists and royal antiques. It's worth ▲▲.

After a fortress burned down on this site in the 18th century, King Philip V commissioned this huge palace as a replacement. Though he ruled Spain for 40 years, Philip V was very French. (The grandson of Louis XIV, he was born in Versailles, and preferred speaking French.) He ordered this palace to be built as his own Versailles (although his wife's Italian origin had a tremendous impact in the style). It's big—more than 2,000 rooms, with tons of luxurious tapestries, a king's ransom of chandeliers, priceless porcelain, and bronze decor covered in gold leaf. While these days the royal family lives in a mansion a few miles away, this place still functions as a royal palace, and is used for formal state receptions, royal weddings, and tourists' daydreams.

The lions you'll see throughout were symbols of power. The Bourbon kings considered previous royalty not up to European par, and this palace—along with their establishment of a Spanish porcelain works and tapestry works—was their effort to raise the bar.

Cost, Hours, Location: €8 without a tour, €9 with a 60-minute tour; April–Sept Mon–Sat 9:00–19:00, Sun 9:00–16:00; Oct–March Mon–Sat 9:30–18:00, Sun 9:00–15:00; last tickets sold one hour before closing. The palace can close without warning if needed for a royal function; call a day ahead to check: tel. 914-548-800. The palace is most crowded on Wednesdays, when it's free for locals. Arrive early to minimize lines. To get to the palace, take bus #3 from Puerta del Sol, or if arriving by Metro, get off the Ópera stop. At the palace, there's a WC just past the ticket booth (men will enjoy the beer-stein urinals—all the rage in Madrid).

Touring the Palace: A simple one-floor, 24-room, one-way circuit is open to the public. You can wander on your own or join an English-language tour (check time of next tour and decide as you buy your ticket; the English-language tours depart about every 20 min, not worth a long wait). The tour guides, like the museum guidebook, show a passion for meaningless data. The €2.30 audioguides are much more interesting; if you enjoy sightseeing cheek-to-check, crank up the volume and share the audioguide with your companion. The armory (€3.40, described below) and the pharmacy (included in your ticket) are in the courtyard.

Madrid's Museum Neighborhood

Three great museums, all within a 10-minute walk of each other, cluster in east Madrid: El Prado (Europe's top collection of paintings), the Thyssen-Bornemisza Museum (a baron's collection of European art, from the old masters to the moderns), and the Centro de Arte Reina Sofía (modern art, including Picasso's famous *Guernica*). Note that the Prado and Reina Sofía are free on Sunday (and anytime for those under 18); the Prado and Thyssen-Bornemisza are closed Monday; and the Reina Sofía is closed Tuesday.

Prado Museum

With more than 3,000 canvases, including entire rooms of masterpieces by superstar painters, the Prado (PRAH-doh) is overwhelming. But pick up the free English floor plan as you enter, which will help. Rated ▲▲▲, the Prado is *the* place to enjoy the great Spanish painter, Francisco de Goya, and it's also the home of Diego Velázquez's *Las Meninas,* considered by many to be the world's finest painting, period. In addition to Spanish works, you'll find paintings by Italian and Flemish masters, including Hieronymus Bosch's delightful *Garden of Delights* altarpiece.

Cost and Hours: €6, free all day Sun, and free anytime to anyone under 18 and non-Americans over 65 (because the US doesn't offer Spanish seniors any discounts, Yankee seniors don't get discounts here). Open Tue–Sun 9:00–20:00, closed Mon, last entry 30 min before closing.

Location: It's at the Paseo del Prado. The Banco de España and Atocha Metro stops are each a five-minute walk from the museum. Cabs picking you up at the Prado are likely to overcharge—insist on the meter.

Special Exhibits and the Prado Expansion: The Prado prides itself on its grand special exhibits. While special exhibit admission is generally included in the museum price (and free on Sun, when the Prado is free), you must endure the longer lines by entering from the top floor of the Goya (north) entrance. Special

Madrid's Museum Neighborhood

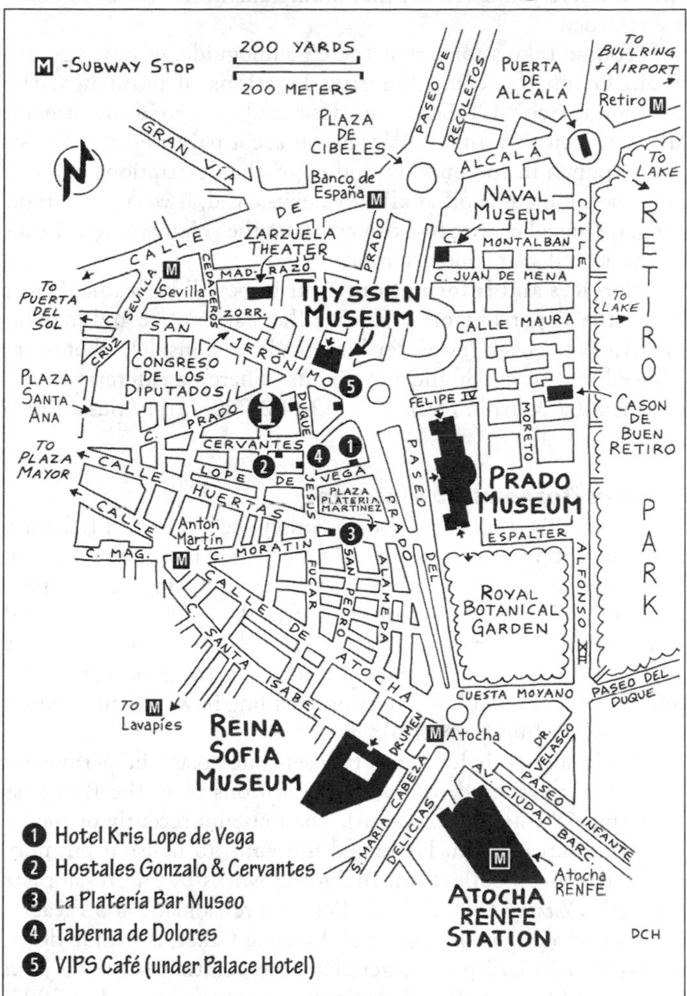

exhibits cause curators to jumble the museum's layout. The expansion project in the works now will give special exhibits their own wing, finally bringing stability to the museum's permanent collection. In the meantime, pick up a detailed map when you enter the museum, consider renting the audioguide recommended below, and enlist the help of a guard if you're unable to find a particular work of art.

Crowd-Beating Tips: The Murillo (south) entrance—at the end closest to the Atocha Train Station—often has shorter lines. Note that special exhibits (see above) can make it tricky for you to choose where you enter the museum. Lunchtime (14:00–16:00) is less crowded.

Tours: Take a tour, rent the €3 audioguide, or buy a guidebook. Given the ever-changing locations of paintings, the audioguide (with 120 paintings described) is a good investment, allowing you to wander. When you see a painting of interest, simply punch in the number and enjoy the description. You can drop the audioguide off at all three exits. And, if you're on a tight budget, remember that two can crank up the volume, listen cheek-to-cheek, and share one machine.

Services and Information: Your bags will be scanned (just like at the airport) before you leave them at the free and mandatory baggage check (no water bottles allowed inside). Photos are allowed, but no flash and no tripods. There's a cafeteria in the basement (at Murillo end). Tel. 913-302-800, http://museoprado.mcu.es.

Thyssen-Bornemisza Museum

Locals call this stunning museum simply the Thyssen (TEE-sun). Rated ▲▲, it displays the impressive collection that Baron Thyssen (a wealthy German married to a former Miss Spain) sold to Spain for $350 million. It's basically minor works by major artists and major works by minor artists (major works by major artists are in the Prado). But art-lovers appreciate how the good baron's art complements the Prado's collection by filling in where the Prado is weak (such as Impressionism).

Each floor is divided into two separate areas: the permanent collection (numbered rooms) and additions from the Baroness since the 1980s (lettered rooms). The museum recently opened a new wing (creating an L-shaped museum) to house even more of the Baroness' collection, including works by Impressionists (Monet's *Charing Cross Bridge*), Post-Impressionists, and Picasso. After purchasing your high-tech barcode ticket, continue down the wide main hall past larger-than-life paintings of King Juan Carlos and Queen Sofía, alongside the Baron (who died in 2002) and his art-collecting Baroness, Carmen. Pick up two museum maps (one for numbered rooms, another for lettered rooms) at the info desk. Ascend to the top floor and work your way down, taking a delightful walk through art history. Visit the rooms on each floor in numerical and alphabetical order, from Primitive Italian (Room 1) to Surrealism and Pop Art (Room 48). Afterwards, if you're heading to Centro de Arte Reina Sofía and you're tired, hail a cab at the gate to zip straight there.

Cost and Hours: €6 (€9 if there's a special exhibition); children under 12 free, Tue–Sun 10:00–19:00, closed Mon, last entry 30 min before closing.

Location: The museum is kitty-corner from the Prado at Paseo del Prado 8 in Palacio de Villahermosa (Metro: Banco de España).

Services and Information: Free baggage check, €4 audioguide, café, shop, no photos, tel. 914-203-944, www.museothyssen.org.

Centro de Arte Reina Sofía

This former public hospital (Madrid's first) shows off an exceptional collection of modern art, rated ▲▲. The permanent collection of modern art is on the second and fourth floors; the rotating exhibits are on the first and third floors. Ride the fancy glass elevator to the second floor and follow the room numbers for art chronologically displayed from 1900 to 1940. The fourth floor continues the collection, from 1940 to 1980.

The museum is most famous for Pablo Picasso's *Guernica* (second floor, Room 6), an epic painting showing the horror of modern war. Notice the two rooms of studies Picasso did for *Guernica*, filled with iron-nail tears and screaming mouths. *Guernica* was displayed in New York City until Franco's death, and now it reigns as Spain's national piece of art. After pondering the destruction of war, visit the room furthest back from the painting (confusingly, also numbered 6) to see photos of Picasso creating this masterpiece.

The museum also houses an easy-to-enjoy collection by other modern artists, including more of Picasso and a mind-bending room of works by Salvador Dalí (Room 10). Room 12 is a treat for movie buffs: Two films by Surrealist director Luis Buñuel (who had help from friends Dalí and the poet Federico García Lorca) play continuously. Enjoy a break in the shady courtyard before leaving.

Cost and Hours: €6, free Sat afternoon after 14:30 and all day Sun, always free to those under 18 and over 65. Even if admission is free when you visit, grab a ticket anyway—guards at the elevator check for them. The museum is open Mon and Wed–Sat 10:00–21:00, Sun 10:00–14:30, closed Tue.

Location: It's across from the Atocha Train Station at Santa Isabel 52; look for the exterior glass elevators (Metro: Atocha).

Services and Information: Good brochure, no tours in English, hardworking audioguide-€4, no photos, free baggage check. The *librería* on the first floor has a larger selection of Picasso and Surrealist reproductions than the main gift shop at the entrance. Tel. 914-675-062, www.museoreinasofia.es.

Near the Prado

▲Retiro Park (Parque del Buen Retiro)—Once the private domain of royalty, this majestic park has been a favorite of Madrid's commoners since Charles III decided to share it with his subjects in the late 18th century. Siesta in this 300-acre, green-and-breezy escape from the city. At midday on Saturday and Sunday, the area around the lake becomes a street carnival, with jugglers, puppeteers, and lots of local color. These peaceful gardens offer great picnicking and people-watching. From the Retiro Metro stop, walk to the big lake (El Estanque), where you can cheaply rent a rowboat. Past the lake, a grand boulevard of statues leads to the Prado.

Royal Botanical Garden (Real Jardín Botánico)—After your Prado visit, you can take a lush and fragrant break in this sculpted park. Wander among trees from around the world. The flier in English explains that this is actually more than a park—it's a museum of plants (€2, daily 10:00–21:00, until 18:00 in winter, entry opposite Prado's Murillo/south entry, Plaza de Murillo 2).

Naval Museum (Museo Naval)—This museum tells the story of Spain's navy, from the Armada to today, in a plush and fascinating-to-boat-lovers exhibit (free, no English anywhere, Tue–Sun 10:00–14:00, closed Mon, a block north of the Prado across boulevard from Thyssen-Bornemisza Museum, Paseo del Prado 5, tel. 915-239-884, www.museonavalmadrid.com). Because this is a military facility, you'll need to show identification (your passport) to get in.

Elsewhere in Madrid

Descalzas Royal Monastery (Monasterio de las Descalzas Reales)—Madrid's most visit-worthy monastery was founded in the 16th century by Philip II's sister, Joan of Hapsburg (also known as Joanna and Juana). She's buried here. The monastery's chapels are decorated with fine art, Rubens-designed tapestries, and the heirlooms of the wealthy women who joined the order (the nuns were required to give a dowry). Because this is still a working Franciscan monastery, tourists can visit only when the nuns vacate the cloister (€8, Tue–Thu 10:30–12:45 & 16:00–17:45, Sat 10:30–12:45, closed Sun–Mon & Fri, Plaza de las Descalzas Reales 3, near the Ópera Metro stop and just a short walk from Puerta del Sol, Metro: Ópera, tel. 914-548-700).

▲National Archaeological Museum (Museo Arqueológico Nacional)—This fine museum gives you a chronological walk on one convenient floor through the story of Iberia. With a rich collection of artifacts (but a maddening refusal to describe anything in English), it shows off the wonders of each age: Celtic pre-Roman, Roman, a fine and rare Visigothic section, Moorish, Romanesque, and beyond (€3, free Sat afternoon and Sun; open Tue–Sat 9:30–20:30, Sun 9:30–15:00, closed Mon; Calle Serrano 13, Metro: Serrano or Colón, tel. 915-777-912). Outside, underground in the museum's garden, is an underwhelming replica of northern Spain's Altamira Caves (big on bison), giving you a faded peek at the skill of the cave artists who created the originals 14,000 years ago.

Municipal Museum (Museo Municipal)—Follow the history of Madrid in old paintings and models (but no English). As you enter, notice Pedro de Ribera's fine Baroque door featuring St. James the Moor Slayer. The 10-minute video (continually playing, no words) gives a relaxing and vivid visual trip through the city's story (free, Tue–Fri 9:30–20:00, Sat–Sun 10:00–14:00, closed Mon, Calle Fuencarral 78, Metro: Tribunal or Bilbao, tel. 915-888-672).

▲Clothing Museum (Museo del Traje)—This museum shows the history of clothing from the 18th century until today. In a cool and air-conditioned chronological sweep, the museum's one floor of exhibits includes regional ethnic costumes, a look at how bullfighting and the French influenced styles, accessories through the ages, and Spanish flappers. The only downside of this marvelous modern museum is that it's a long way from anything else of interest (€3, Tue–Sat 9:30–19:00, Sun 10:00–15:00, closed Mon, Avenida Juan Herrera 2; Metro: Moncloa and a longish walk, bus #46, or taxi; tel. 915-497-150).

▲Chapel of San Antonio de la Florida—In this simple little Neoclassical chapel from the 1790s, Francisco de Goya's tomb stares up at a splendid cupola filled with his own proto-Impressionist frescoes. He frescoed this using the same unique technique that he used for his "dark paintings." Use the mirrors to enjoy the drama and energy he infused into this marvelously restored masterpiece (free, Tue–Fri 10:00–14:00 & 16:00–20:00, Sat–Sun 10:00–14:00, closed Mon, Glorieta de San Antonio de la Florida, tel. 915-420-722). This chapel is a five-minute walk down Paseo de San Antonio de la Florida from Metro Príncipe Pío and the Sepulvedana bus station (which serves Segovia). If you're day-tripping to Segovia from Madrid, it's easy to stop by before or after your trip.

Royal Tapestry Factory (Real Fábrica de Tapices)—Have a look at traditional tapestry-making (€3, Mon–Fri 10:00–14:00, closed Sat–Sun and Aug, some English tours, Calle Fuenterrabia 2, Metro: Menendez Pelayo, take Gutenberg exit, tel. 914-340-550). You can actually order a tailor-made tapestry (starting at $10,000).

Temple de Debod—In 1968, Egypt gave Spain its own ancient temple. It was a gift of the Egyptian government, which was grateful for Franco's help in rescuing monuments that had been threatened by the rising Nile waters above the Aswan Dam. Consequently, Madrid is the only place I can think of in Europe where you can actually wander through an intact original Egyptian temple—complete with fine carved reliefs from 200 B.C. (free; April–Sept Tue–Fri 10:00–14:00 & 18:00–20:00, Sat–Sun 10:00–14:00, closed Mon; Oct–March Tue–Fri 9:45–13:45 & 16:15–18:15, Sat–Sun 10:00–14:00, closed Mon). Set in a romantic park that locals love for its great city views (especially at sunset), the temple—as well as its art—is well-described. Popular as the view may be, the uninspiring "grand Madrid view" only causes me to wonder why anyone would build a city here.

Cable Car (Teleférico)—For city views, ride this cable car from downtown over Madrid's sprawling city park to Casa de Campo (€3.25 one-way, €4.65 round-trip, April–Aug daily from noon, Sept–March Sat–Sun only, departs from Paseo del Pintor Rosales, a short walk from Metro: Plaza de España, tel. 915-417-450, www.teleferico.com). Do an immediate round-trip to skip Casa de Campo's strange mix of rental rowboats, prostitutes, addicts, a zoo, and an amusement park. The family-friendly bits of the park are far from the cable-car terminus.

EXPERIENCES

▲▲Bullfight—Madrid's Plaza de Toros hosts Spain's top bullfights on Sundays and holidays from March through mid-October, and nearly every day during the San Isidro festival (May through early June—often sold out long in advance). Fights start between 17:00 and 21:00 (early in spring and fall, late in summer). The bullring is at the Ventas Metro stop (a direct 10-min Metro ride to the end of the line from Puerta del Sol, tel. 913-562-200, www.las-ventas.com).

Bullfight tickets range from €3.50 to €100. There are no bad seats at the Plaza de Toros; paying more gets you in the shade and/or closer to the gore. (The action often intentionally occurs in the shade to reward the expensive-ticket holders.) To be close to the bullring, choose areas 8, 9, or 10; for shade: 1, 2, 9, or 10; for shade/sun: 3 or 8; for the sun and cheapest seats: 4, 5, 6, or 7. Note these key words: *corrida*—a real fight with professionals; *novillada*—rookie matadors and younger bulls. Getting tickets through your hotel or a booking office is convenient, but they add 20 percent or more and don't sell the cheap seats. There are two booking offices; call both before you buy: at Plaza del Carmen 1 (daily 9:30–13:00 & 16:30–19:00, tel. 915-312-732, run by English-speaking José, who also sells soccer tickets) and at Calle Victoria 3 (daily 10:00–14:00 & 17:00–19:00, tel. 915-211-213). To save money (20 percent), you can stand in the ticket line at the bullring. Except for important bullfights—or during the San Isidro festival—there are generally plenty of seats available. About a thousand tickets are held back to be sold in the five days leading up to a fight, including the day of the fight. Scalpers hang out before the popular fights at the Calle Victoria booking office. Beware: Those buying scalped tickets are breaking the law, and can lose the ticket with no recourse.

For a dose of the experience, you can buy a cheap ticket and just stay to see a couple of bullfights. Each fight takes about 20 minutes, and the event consists of six bulls over two hours.

Madrid's **Bullfighting Museum** (Museo Taurino) is not as good as Sevilla's or Ronda's (free, Tue–Fri and Sun 9:30–14:30, closed Sat and Mon and early on fight days, at the back of bullring, tel. 917-251-857).

Football—Madrid, like most of Europe, is enthusiastic about soccer (which they call football). The legendary Real Madrid team plays to a spirited local crowd Saturdays and Sundays from September through May (tickets from €30—sold at bullfight box offices listed above, stadium at Metro: Bernabeu).

NIGHTLIFE

Disco dancers may have to wait until after midnight for the most popular clubs to even open, much less start hopping. Spain has a reputation for partying very late, not ending until offices open in the morning. If you're people-watching early in the morning, it's actually hard to know who is finishing their day and who's just starting it. Even if you're not a party animal after midnight, make a point to be out with the happy masses, luxuriating in the cool evening air between 22:00 and midnight. The scene is absolutely unforgettable.

▲▲▲Paseo—Just walking the streets of Madrid seems to be the way the Madrileños spend their evenings. Even past midnight on a hot summer night, whole families with little kids are strolling, enjoying tiny beers and tapas in a series of bars, licking ice cream, and greeting their neighbors. A good area to wander is along Gran Vía (from about Metro: Callao to Plaza de España). Or start at Puerta del Sol, and explore in the direction of Plaza Santa Ana. See "The Madrid Pub-Crawl Dinner (for Beginners)" on page 1071.

▲▲Zarzuela—For a delightful look at Spanish light opera that even English-speakers can enjoy, try zarzuela. Guitar-strumming Napoleons in red capes; buxom women with masks, fans, and castanets; Spanish-speaking pharaohs; melodramatic spotlights; and aficionados clapping and singing along from the cheap seats, where the acoustics are best—this is zarzuela...the people's opera. Originating in Madrid, zarzuela is known for its satiric humor and surprisingly good music. You can buy tickets at Theater Zarzuela, which alternates between zarzuela, ballet, and opera throughout the year (€10–30, box office open 12:00–18:00 for advance tickets or until showtime for that day, Jovellanos 4, near the Prado, Metro: Banco de España, tel. 915-245-400, http://teatrodelazarzuela.mcu.es). Madrid puts on live zarzuela events in the Royal Palace gardens summer evenings (ask the TI for details). The TI's monthly guide has a special zarzuela listing.

▲Flamenco—While Sevilla is the capital of flamenco, Madrid has two easy and affordable options.

Taberna Casa Patas attracts big-name flamenco artists. You'll quickly understand why this intimate (30-table) and smoky venue is named "House of Feet." Since this is for locals as well as tour groups, the flamenco is contemporary and may be jazzier than your notion—it depends on who's performing (€26 for Mon–Thu at 22:30, €31 for Fri–Sat at 21:00 and 24:00, closed Sun, 75–90 min, price includes cover and first drink, reservations smart, no flash cameras, Cañizares 10, tel. 913-690-496, www.casapatas.com). Its restaurant is a logical spot for dinner before the show (€30 dinners, Mon–Sat from 20:00). Or, since it's three blocks south of the recommended Plaza Santa Ana tapas bars, this could be your post-tapas-crawl entertainment.

Las Carboneras, more downscale, is an easygoing, folksy little place a few steps from Plaza Mayor with a nightly hour-long flamenco show (€29 includes an entry and a drink, €52 gets you a table up front with dinner and unlimited cheap drinks if you reserve ahead, Mon–Thu at 22:30 and often at 21:00, Fri–Sat at 21:00 and 23:00, closed Sun, earlier shows possible if a group books, reservations recommended, Plaza del Conde de Miranda 1, tel. 915-428-677).

Regardless of what your hotel receptionist may want to sell you, other flamenco places—such as Arco de Cuchilleros (Calle de los Cuchilleros 7), Café de Chinitas (Calle Torija 7, just off Plaza Mayor), Corral de la Morería (Calle de Morería 17) and Torres Bermejas (off Gran Vía)—are filled with tourists and pushy waiters.

Mesones—Just west of Plaza Mayor, the lane called Cava de San Miguel is lined with *mesones:* long, skinny, cave-like bars famous for drinking and singing late into the night. If you were to toss lowbrow locals, Spanish karaoke, electric keyboards, crass tourists, cheap sangria, and greasy calamari into a late-night blender and turn it on, this is what you'd get. It's generally lively only on Friday and Saturday, but you're welcome to pop in to several bars (such as Guitarra, Tortilla, or Boquerón) and see what you can find.

Late-Night Bars—If you're just picking up speed at midnight, and looking for a place filled with old tiles and a Gen-X crowd, power into **Bar Viva Madrid** (daily 13:00–3:00 in the morning, downhill from Plaza Santa Ana on Calle Manuel Fernández y González, tel. 914-293-640). The same street has other late-night bars filled with music. Or hike on over to **Chocolatería San Ginés** (described below) for a dessert of *churros con chocolate.*

Movies—During Franco's days, movies were always dubbed into Spanish. Movies in Spain remain about the most often dubbed in Europe. To see a movie with its original soundtrack, look for *V.O.* (meaning "original version"). **Cine Ideal,** with nine screens, is a good place for the latest films in V.O. (€7, 5-min walk south of Puerta del Sol at Calle del Dr. Cortezo 6, tel. 913-692-518 for info). For extensive listings, see the *Guía del Ocio* entertainment guide (€1 at newsstands) or a local newspaper.

SLEEPING

Madrid has plenty of centrally located budget hotels and *pensiones.* You'll have no trouble finding a sleepable double for €35, a good double for €70, and a modern, air-conditioned double with all the comforts for €100. Prices are the same throughout the year, and it's almost always easy to find a place. Anticipate full hotels only during May (the San Isidro festival, celebrating Madrid's patron saint with bullfights and zarzuelas—especially around his feast day on May 15) and the last week in September (conventions). In July and August, prices can be softer—ask about promotional deals. All of the accommodations I've listed are within a few minutes' walk of Puerta del Sol.

With all of Madrid's street noise, I'd request the highest floor possible. Also, twin-bedded rooms are generally a bit larger than double-bedded rooms for the same price. Madrid hoteliers rarely offer a cash discount. During slow times, drop-ins can often score a room in business-class hotels for just a few euros more than the budget hotels (which don't have prices that fluctuate as wildly with demand).

Sleep Code

(€1 = about $1.30, country code: 34)

S = Single, **D** = Double/Twin, **T** = Triple, **Q** = Quad, **b** = bathroom, **s** = shower only. Unless otherwise noted, credit cards are accepted, English is spoken, and breakfast is *not* included. In Madrid, the 7 percent IVA tax is sometimes included in the price.

To help you easily sort through these listings, I've divided the rooms into three categories, based on the price for a standard double room with bath during high season:

$$$ **Higher Priced**—Most rooms €100 or more.
$$ **Moderately Priced**—Most rooms between €70–100.
$ **Lower Priced**—Most rooms €70 or less.

Fancier Places in the Pedestrian Zone Between Puerta del Sol and Gran Vía

Reliable and away from the seediness, these hotels are good values for those wanting to spend a little more. Their formal prices may be inflated, but some offer weekend and summer discounts when it's slow. Drivers will pay about €24 a day in garages. Use Metro: Sol for all but Hotel Opera (Metro: Ópera). For locations, see the map on page 1061.

$$$ Hotel Regente is big and traditional, with 154 tastefully decorated and comfortable air-conditioned rooms, generous public spaces, a great location, and a good value (Sb-€63, Db-€105, Tb-€128, 20 percent cheaper Fri–Sun, tax not included, breakfast-€8, midway between Puerta del Sol and Plaza del Callao at Mesonero Romanos 9, tel. 915-212-941, fax 915-323-014, www.hotelregente.com, info@hotelregente.com).

$$$ Hotel Liabeny rents 220 plush, spacious, business-class rooms offering all the comforts (Sb-€100, Db-€130, Tb-€155, 10 percent cheaper mid-July–Aug and Fri–Sat, tax not included, breakfast-€13, air-con, sauna, gym, off Plaza del Carmen at Salud 3, tel. 915-319-000, fax 915-327-421, www.liabeny.es, reservas@hotelliabeny.es).

$$$ Hotel Preciados, a four-star business hotel, has 73 fine, sleek, and modern rooms, as well as a breakfast room and elegant lounges. It's well-located and reasonably priced for the luxury it provides (Db-€130, prices are often soft, checking Web specials or dropping in will likely snag a room for around €100, just off Plaza de Santo Domingo at Calle Preciados 37, tel. 914-544-400, fax 914-544-401, www.preciadoshotel.com, preciadoshotel@preciadoshotel.com).

$$$ Hotel Opera, a serious and modern hotel with 79 classy rooms, is located just off Plaza Isabel II, a four-block walk from Puerta del Sol toward the Royal Palace (Sb-€100, Db-€134, Db with big view terrace-€147, Tb-€175, tax not included, buffet breakfast-€10, air-con, elevator, free Internet in lobby, ask for a higher floor—there are eight—to avoid street noise, Cuesta de Santo Domingo 2, Metro: Ópera, tel. 915-412-800, fax 915-416-923, www.hotelopera.com, reservas@hotelopera.com). Hotel Opera's cafeteria is understandably popular. Also consider their "singing dinners"—great operetta music with a delightful dinner—offered nightly at 22:00 (average price-€60, reservations wise, call 915-426-382).

$$ Hotel Carlos V, a Best Western with 67 classy, high-ceiling rooms and an elegant breakfast and lounge, is a fair value. Its central location off Preciados pedestrian street makes it convenient—but ask for an inside room to avoid street noise (Sb-€80–90, standard Db-€90, larger "superior" view Db–€112, Tb-€130, air-con,

Madrid's Center—Hotels and Restaurants

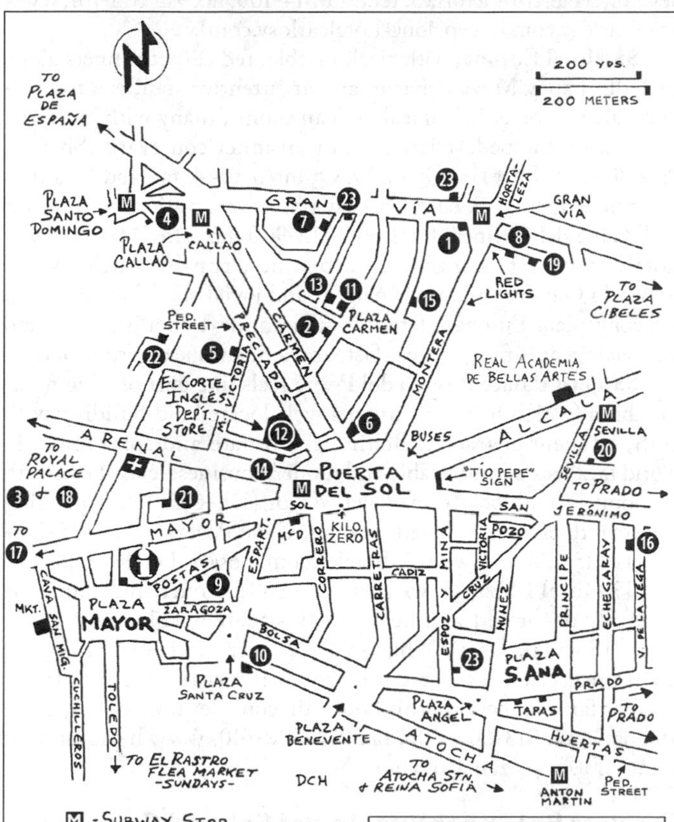

For eateries near Plaza Mayor and Plaza Santa Ana, please see those maps.

1. Hostal Res. Louis XV & Hostal Metropol
2. Hotel Liabeny
3. To Hotel Opera
4. Hotel Preciados
5. Hotel Carlos V
6. Hotel Europa & Cafeteria
7. Hotel Regente
8. Hostal Aliste & Pension Marina Santa
9. Petit Palace Posada del Peine
10. Hotel Plaza Mayor
11. Hostales at Calle de la Salud 13
12. El Corte Inglés Cafeteria
13. Restaurante Puerto Rico
14. Casa Labra Taberna Restaurante
15. Artemisia II Veggie Rest.
16. Artemisia I Veggie Rest.
17. To Casa Ciriaco & La Paella Real Rest.
18. To La Bola Taberna
19. La Gloria de Montera Rest. & Fresc Co Buffet
20. La Finca de Susana
21. Chocolatería San Ginés
22. Chocolatería Valor
23. Internet Cafés (3)

elevator, Maestro Victoria 5, tel. 915-314-100, fax 915-313-761, www.hotelcarlosv.com, recepcion@hotelcarlosv.com).

$$ Hotel Europa, with sleek marble, red carpet runners along the halls, happy Muzak charm, and an attentive staff, is a tremendous value. It rents 103 squeaky-clean rooms, many with balconies overlooking the pedestrian zone or an inner courtyard (Sb-€64, Db-€80–100, Tb-€113, Qb-€129, Quint/b-€144, tax and breakfast not included, air-con, elevator, easy phone reservations with credit card, Calle del Carmen 4, tel. 915-212-900, fax 915-214-696, www.hoteleuropa.net, info@hoteleuropa.net, run by Antonio and Fernando Garaban and their helpful and jovial staff, Javi and Jim). The convenient Europa cafeteria/restaurant next door is a lively and convivial scene—fun for breakfast, and a fine value any time of day.

$$ Petit Palace Posada del Peine feels like part of a big modern chain (which it is), but fills its well-located old building with fresh, efficient character. Behind the ornate and sparkling Old World facade is a comfortable and modern business-class hotel with 69 rooms just a block from Plaza Mayor (Db-€85–130 depending on demand, tax not included, air-con, Calle Postas 17, tel. 915-238-151, fax 915-232-993, www.hthoteles.com, pos@hthoteles.com).

$$ Hotel Plaza Mayor, with 34 solidly outfitted rooms, is tastefully decorated and beautifully situated a block off Plaza Mayor (Sb-€60, Db-€80, bigger Db corner room-€90, Tb-€110, buffet breakfast-€8, 5 percent discount if you reserve directly by email or fax and mention this book, air-con, elevator, Wi-Fi, Calle Atocha 2, tel. 913-600-606, fax 913-600-610, www.h-plazamayor.com, info@h-plazamayor.com).

Cheaper Bets near Puerta del Sol and Gran Vía

These accommodations are also in or near the handy pedestrian zone between Puerta del Sol and Gran Vía. The first two (Acapulco and Triana) are by far the best (and priciest). The Isabel, Arcos, Aliste, and Marina Santa are your best cheap-bed options (with youth-hostel prices, yet hotel privacy).

At Calle de la Salud 13

These are all in the same building at Calle de la Salud 13, overlooking Plaza del Carmen—a little square with a sleepy, almost Parisian ambience.

$ Hostal Acapulco rents 16 bright rooms with air-conditioning and all the big hotel gear. The neighborhood is quiet enough that it's smart to request a room with a balcony (Sb-€45, Db-€55, Tb-€73, elevator, free Internet access in lobby, fourth floor, tel. 915-311-945, fax 915-322-329, www.hostalacapulco.com, hostal_acapulco@yahoo.es, Ana and Marco).

$ Hostal Triana, also a fine deal, is bigger—with 40 rooms—and offers a little less charm for a little less money (Sb-€37, Db-€50, Tb-€65, includes taxes, rooms facing the square have air-con and cost €3 extra, other rooms have fans, elevator, free Wi-Fi, first floor, tel. 915-326-812, fax 915-229-729, www.hostaltriana.com, triana@hostaltriana.com, Victor González).

Old-Fashioned, Granny-Run Places: These two tiny, five-room *pensiones*—both run by non-English-speaking little old ladies—reek of the 1950s (their business cards have the new phone codes penned in, and there's no hint of email or even fax). You can reserve by phone only a day in advance, and you must pay in cash. They're clean, quiet, reasonably friendly, and air-conditioned. Both are located on the third floor, which is served by an elevator, and you step right out onto a great square. If you're looking for cheap beds in a great locale, assuming you can communicate enough to reserve a room, these places are unbeatable: **$ Hostal Isabel** (Sb-€35, Db-€43, Tb-€45, tel. 915-217-326, Beatrice) and **$ Pension Arcos,** which has a tiny roof terrace, a nice little lounge, and has been in the Hernández family since 1936 (Db-€36, tel. 915-324-994, Anuncia and Sabino).

More Cheap Sleeps

At Caballero de Gracia 6: These two *hostales* (which share the same building near Gran Vía Metro) are quiet, plain, and dreary, yet safe, on a quiet street a block past thc unthreatening prostitutes of Calle de la Montera: **$ Hostal Aliste** (11 rooms on third floor, Sb-€30, D-€30–33, Db-€40–43, extra bed-€10, air-con €5 extra, elevator, tel. 915-215-979, h.aliste@teleline.es, Manuela's son Edward speaks English) and the humble **$ Pension Marina Santa** (nine rooms on second floor, D-€30, Db-€40, elevator, tel. 915-327-074, Lydia).

$ Hostal Residencia Louis XV is a big, plain, well-run, and clean place offering a good value. It's on a quiet eighth floor (there's an elevator). You'll find it where prostitute-lined Calle de la Montera hits noisy Gran Vía. It can be smoky, so if that's an issue, request a non-smoking room. They also run the 36-room Hostal Jerez—similar in every way except the name—located on the floor below (Sb-€42, Db-€55, Tb-€70, includes tax, air-con, elevator, Calle Montera 47, seventh floor, tel. 915-221-350, fax 915-221-021, www.hrluisxv.net, reservas@hrluisxv.net).

$ Hostal Metropol is a big, colorful, and very youthful youth hostel with 130 beds beautifully located at the noisy corner of Calle de la Montera and Gran Vía a few minutes' walk from Puerta del Sol (bed-€18, 3–5 beds per room, includes sheets and breakfast, free Internet access, Calle de la Montera 47, first floor, tel. 915-212-935, fax 915-212-934, www.metropolhostel.com, info@metropolhostel.com).

Near the Prado

To locate the following three places, please see "Madrid's Museum Neighborhood" map on page 1051.

$$$ Hotel Kris Lope de Vega is your best business-class hotel value near the Prado. A four-star place that opened in 2000, it's a "cultural-themed" hotel inspired by the 17th-century writer Lope de Vega. With 60 rooms, it feels cozy and friendly for a formal business-class hotel (Sb-€108, Db-€140, Tb-€182, one child sleeps free, prices about 20 percent lower Fri–Sun and during most of the summer, air-con, elevator, Internet access in lobby, parking-€18/day, Calle Lope de Vega 49, tel. 913-600-011, fax 914-292-391, www.krishoteles.com, krislopedevega@krishoteles.com).

At Cervantes 34: Two fine budget *hostales* are at Cervantes 34 (Metro: Anton Martín—but not handy to Metro). Both are homey, with inviting lounge areas; neither serve breakfast. **$ Hostal Gonzalo**—with 15 spotless, comfortable rooms, well-run by friendly and helpful Javier—is deservedly in all the guidebooks. Reserve in advance (Sb-€45, Db-€52, Tb-€63, elevator, third floor, tel. 914-292-714, fax 914-202-007, www.hostalgonzalo.com, hostal@hostalgonzalo.com). Downstairs, the nearly as polished **$ Hostal Cervantes,** also with 15 fine rooms, is likewise good (Sb-€45, Db-€55, Tb-€70, includes tax, cheaper when slow and for longer stays, Wi-Fi and Internet access, second floor, tel. 914-298-365, fax 914-292-745, www.hostal-cervantes.com, correo@hostal-cervantes.com, Fabio and Christian).

EATING

In Spain, only Barcelona rivals Madrid for tastebud thrills. You have three dining choices: an atmospheric sit-down meal in a well-chosen restaurant; an unmemorable, basic sit-down meal; or a stand-up meal of tapas in a bar or four. Many restaurants are closed in August (especially through the last half). Madrid has famously good tap water, and waiters willingly serve it free—just ask for *agua del grifo.*

Eating Cheaply North of Puerta del Sol

See the map on page 1061 for locations.

Restaurante Puerto Rico fills a long, congested hall by serving good meals for great prices to smart locals (€8.50 three-course fixed-price meal, Mon–Sat 13:00–16:30 & 20:30–24:00, closed Sun, Chinchilla 2, between Puerta del Sol and Gran Vía, tel. 915-219-834).

Hotel Europa Cafetería is a fun, high-energy scene with a mile-long bar, traditionally clad waiters, great people-watching, local cuisine, and a fine €10 fixed-price lunch (daily 7:30–24:00, next to Hotel Europa—listed on page 1062, 50 yards off Puerta del Sol at Calle del Carmen 4, tel. 915-212-900). The menu lists three price levels: bar, table, or outside, on the terrace. While you pay a premium for the outdoor seating, it's a big hit with people-watchers.

El Corte Inglés' seventh-floor cafeteria is fresh, modern, and understated. While not particularly cheap, it's popular with locals (Mon–Sat 10:00–22:00, closed Sun, non-smoking section, just off Puerta del Sol at intersection of Preciados and Tetuán.

Casa Labra Taberna Restaurante is famous as the birthplace of the Spanish Socialist Party in 1879...and as a spot for great cod. Packed with Madrileños, it's a wonderful scene with three distinct sections: the stand-up bar (cheapest, with two lines: one for munchies, the other for drinks), a peaceful little sit-down area in back (a little more expensive but still cheap; good €6 salads), and a fancy restaurant (€20 lunches). Their tasty little €1 *Tajada de Bacalao* (cod) dishes put it on the map. The waiters are fun to joke around with (Mon–Sat 11:00–15:30 & 18:00–23:00, closed Sun, a block off Puerta del Sol at Calle Tetuán 12, tel. 915-310-081).

La Gloria de Montera Restaurante, a mod Spanish bistro with white tablecloths and a minimalist-library ambience, serves good food to locals (€7 fish and meat plates, daily 13:15–16:00 & 20:30–23:45, no reservations—arrive early or put your name on the list, a block from Gran Vía and Metro: Red de San Luis at Caballero de Gracia 10, tel. 915-234-407). Their sister restaurant, **La Finca de Susana,** is also extremely popular for the same reasons (daily 13:00–15:45 & 20:30–23:45, go early—line starts forming at about 20:00, just east of Puerta del Sol at Calle Arlabán 4, tel. 913-693-557).

Fresc Co is the place for a cheap, modern, fast, and buffet-style meal. It's a chain with a winning plan: a long, appealing salad and buffet bar with one cheap price for all-you-can-eat, including dessert and a drink (€8 lunch, €10 dinner, daily 12:30–24:00, air-con, Caballero de Gracià 8, tel. 915-216-052).

Vegetarian: **Artemisia II** is a hit with vegetarians who like good, healthy food in a smoke-free room without the typical hippie-ambience that comes with most veggie places (great €10.50 three-course fixed-price lunch Mon–Fri only, open daily 13:30–16:00 & 21:00–24:00, 2 blocks north of Puerta del Sol at Tres Cruces 4, a few steps off Plaza del Carmen, tel. 915-218-721). **Artemisia I,** II's older sister, is located two blocks east of Plaza Santa Ana at Ventura de la Vega 4, off San Jerónimo (same hours, tel. 914-295-092).

On or near Plaza Mayor

Madrileños enjoy Plaza Mayor (without its high costs) by grabbing a bite to go from a nearby bar and just planting themselves somewhere on the square to eat (squid sandwiches are popular—

Eating near Plaza Mayor

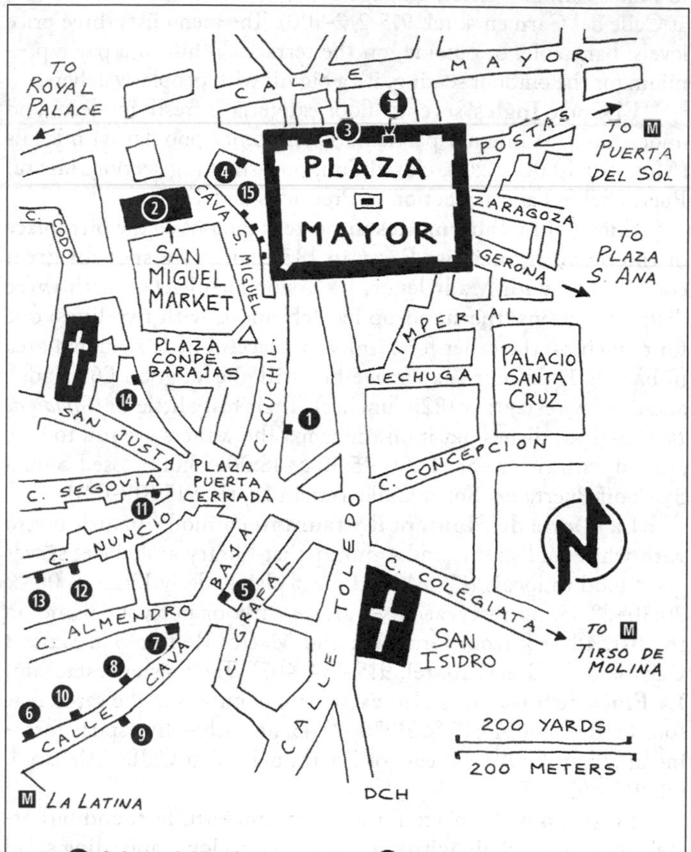

1. Sobrino del Botín
2. Mercado de San Miguel
3. Torre del Oro Bar Andalú
4. Casa Rúa
5. Posada de la Villa
6. Giangrossi Helado Artesanal Ice Cream
7. Julian de Tolosa
8. Taberna Los Lucio
9. Casa Lucio
10. Taberna Tempranillo
11. El Madroño
12. Taberna Los Austrias
13. Taberna de los 100 Vinos
14. Las Carboneras (Flamenco)
15. *Mesones* (Cave Bars)

described below). But for many tourists, dinner at a sidewalk café right on the Plaza Mayor is worth paying a premium for (consider Cervecería Pulpito, southwest corner of the square at #10).

Squid Sandwich: Plaza Mayor is famous for its *bocadillos de calamares*. For a tasty €2 squid-ring sandwich, line up at **Casa Rúa** at Plaza Mayor's northwest corner, a few steps up Calle Ciudad Rodrigo (daily 9:00–23:00). Hanging up behind the bar is a photo-advertisement of Plaza Mayor from the 1950s, when the square contained a park.

Bullfighting Bar: The **Torre del Oro Bar Andalú** on Plaza Mayor has walls lined with grisly bullfight photos). While this place is good for drinks, you pay a premium for the tapas and food... the cost of munching amidst all that bullephenalia while enjoying their excellent Plaza Major outdoor seating (daily 8:00–15:00 & 18:00–24:00).

Hemingway Haunt: **Sobrino del Botín** is a hit with many Americans because "Hemingway ate here" (daily 13:00–16:00 & 20:00–24:00, Cuchilleros 17, a block downhill from Plaza Mayor, tel. 913-664-217). It's touristy, pricey (€30 average meals), and the last place Papa would go now...but still, people love it, and the food is excellent (roast suckling pig is the specialty). If phoning to make a reservation, choose between the downstairs (for dark, medieval-cellar ambience) or upstairs (for a still-traditional, but airier and lighter elegance). While this restaurant boasts that it's the oldest in the world (dating from 1725), a nearby restaurant teases, "Hemingway never ate here."

On Calle Cava Baja, South of Plaza Mayor

Few tourists frequent this traditional neighborhood—Barrio de los Austrias, named for the Hapsburgs. It's three minutes south of Plaza Mayor, or a 10-minute walk from Puerta del Sol. Lined with a diverse array of restaurants and tapas bars, the street called Cava Baja is clogged with Madrileños out in search of a special meal. I've listed a few standards, but there are always excellent new eateries opening up. For a good, authentic Madrid dinner experience, take time to survey the many options along this street—between the first and last listings described below—and choose your favorite. A key wine-drinking phrase: *mucho cuerpo* (full-bodied).

Posada de la Villa serves Castilian cuisine in a 17th-century posada. This sprawling, multi-floor restaurant has dressy tables under open beams, which give it a rustic elegance. Peek into the big oven to see the baby pigs about to make some diner happy (roast suckling pig and lamb are the house specialties; €30 meals, Mon–Sat 13:00–16:00 & 20:00–24:00, closed Sun and Aug, Calle Cava Baja 9, tel. 913-661-860). If you're not going to Toledo or Sevilla, this is the place to try roast suckling pig or lamb.

Julian de Tolosa is classy, pricey, elegantly simple, and popular with natives who know good food. They offer a small, quality menu of Navarra's regional cuisine, from T-bone steak *(chuletón)* to red *tolosa* beans in a spacious, dressy, and sane setting (€40 meals, Mon–Sat 13:30–16:00 & 21:00–24:00, Sun 13:30–16:00, Calle Cava Baja 18, tel. 913-658-210).

Taberna Los Lucio is a jam-packed bar serving good tapas, salads, *huevos estrellados* (scrambled eggs with fried potatoes), and wine (Wed–Mon 13:00–16:00 & 20:30–24:00, closed Tue, Calle Cava Baja 30, tel. 913-662-984). Their basement is much less atmospheric.

Casa Lucio is a favorite splurge among power-dressing Madrileños. While the king and queen of Spain eat in this elegant place, it's accessible to commoners. This could be the best place in town for a special night out and a full-blown meal (€40 for dinner, daily 13:00–16:00 & 21:00–24:00, Calle Cava Baja 35; unless you're the king or queen, reserve several days in advance—and don't even bother on weekends; tel. 913-653-252).

Taberna Tempranillo, ideal for hungry wine-lovers, offers tapas and 250 kinds of wine. Wines available by the glass are listed on the board. With a phrasebook in hand or a spirit of adventure, use their fascinating menu to assemble your dream meal. It's packed and full of commotion—the crowds can be overwhelming. Arrive by 20:00 or plan to wait (daily 13:00–15:30 & 20:00–24:00, closed Aug, Cava Baja 38, tel. 913-641-532).

Ice Cream Finale: **Giangrossi Helado Artesanal** is a popular chain considered to serve some of Madrid's best ice cream. This Giangrossi—which has a plush white leather lounge and lots of great flavors—is a fun way to finish your dining experience in this area. It's just 50 yards from the La Latina Metro stop (Cava Baja 40, tel. 902-444-130).

Near the Royal Palace

Casa Ciriaco is popular with Madrileños who appreciate good traditional cooking (€30 meals, Thu–Tue 13:30–16:00 & 20:30–24:00, closed Wed and Aug, air-con, halfway between Puerta del Sol and the Royal Palace at Calle Mayor 84, tel. 915-480-620). It was from this building in 1906 that an anarchist bombed the royal couple on their wedding day (for details, see page 1048; for location, see map on page 1043). A photo of the carnage is inside the front door.

La Bola Taberna, touristy but friendly and tastefully elegant, specializes in *cocido Madrileño*—Madrid stew. The €18 stew consists of various meats, carrots, and garbanzo beans in earthen jugs. It's big enough to split—which they'll let you do, as long as the second person orders something small, like a salad. The stew is served as two courses: First you enjoy the broth as a soup, then you dig into the meat and veggies (Mon–Fri lunch seatings 13:30–15:30, evenings 20:30–23:00, closed Sat–Sun, cash only, midway between the Royal Palace and Gran Vía at Calle Bola 5, tel. 915-476-930).

La Paella Real Restaurante ("Royal Paella Restaurant") is considered a top spot for "a proper paella." While you'll see this saffron-rice specialty from Valencia served all over town, paella requires a special oven and big pan in order to cook it correctly. For your paella experience, enjoy this venerable and dressy spot (€14 per person for hearty portions—minimum of two, Tue–Sun 13:00–16:00 & 19:30–22:30, closed Mon, allow a good 30 min for your meal to arrive, between Puerta del Sol and the palace at Plaza de la Ópera, Arrieta 2, see map on page 1043 for location, tel. 915-420-942).

Near the Prado

Each of the three big art museums has a decent cafeteria. Or choose from these restaurants, all within a block of the Prado. To locate the following three places, please see "Madrid's Museum Neighborhood" map on page 1051.

La Platería Bar Museo is a hardworking little café/wine bar with a good menu for tapas, light meals, and hearty salads (listed as *raciones* and *1/2 raciones* on the chalkboard). Its tables spill onto the leafy little Plaza de Platerías de Martínez (daily 8:00–24:00, air-con, directly across busy boulevard Paseo del Prado from Atocha end of Prado, tel. 914-291-722).

Taberna de Dolores, a winning formula since 1908, is a commotion of locals enjoying €2.50 *canapés* (open-face sandwiches), tasty *raciones* of seafood, and *cañas* (small beers) at the bar or at a few tables in the back (daily 11:00–24:00, Plaza de Jesús 4, tel. 914-292-243).

VIPS is a bright, popular chain restaurant, handy for a cheap and filling salad. Engulfed in a big bookstore, this is a high-energy, no-charm eatery (daily 9:00–24:00 in the morning, across the boulevard from northern end of Prado, under Palace Hotel). In 2001, Spain's first Starbucks opened next door.

Fast Food and Picnics

Fast Food: For an easy, light, cheap meal, try **Rodilla**—a popular sandwich and salad chain with a shop on the northeast corner of Puerta del Sol at #13 (Mon–Fri 9:30–23:00, Sat 10:00–23:00, Sun 11:00–23:00). **Pans & Company,** with shops throughout Madrid and Spain, offers healthy, tasty sandwiches and pre-packaged salads (daily 9:00–24:00, locations at Puerta del Sol, on Plaza Callao, at Gran Vía 30, and many more).

Breakfast in Madrid

As most hotels don't include breakfast (and many don't even serve it), you may be out on the streets first thing looking for a place. Non-touristy places only offer a hot drink and a pastry, with perhaps a potato omelet and sandwiches (toasted cheese, ham, or both). Touristy places will have a *desayuno* menu with various ham and eggs deals. Try *churros* once (see below). Starbucks, a temptation to many for its familiarity, is always nearby. Get advice from your hotel staff for their favorite breakfast place.

Picnics: The department store **El Corte Inglés** has well-stocked meat and cheese counters downstairs (Mon–Sat 10:00–22:00, closed Sun). Downtown Madrid's neighborhood market, **Mercado de San Miguel,** is a perfect place to assemble a cheap picnic. How about breakfast surrounded by early-morning shoppers in the market's café? (Mon–Fri 9:00–14:30 & 17:15–20:15, Sat 9:00–14:30, closed Sun; to reach the market from Plaza Mayor, face the colorfully painted building and exit from the upper left-hand corner.)

Churros con Chocolate

Those not watching their cholesterol will want to try the deep-fried doughy treats called *churros* (or the thicker *porras*), best enjoyed by dipping them in pudding-like hot chocolate. While many *chocolaterías* offer the dunkable fritters, *churros* are most delicious when consumed fresh out of the greasy cauldron.

Chocolaterías Valor is a modern chain that does *churros* with pride and gusto. A few minutes' walk from nearly all my hotel recommendations, it's a fine place for breakfast (€3.50 *churros con chocolate*, Mon–Fri 8:00–24:00, Sat–Sun 9:00–24:00, a half-block below Plaza Callao and Gran Vía at Postigo de San Martín 7, tel. 915-229-288). With a Web address like www.amigosdelchocolate.com, you know where their heart is.

Chocolatería San Ginés is a classy institution, much loved by Madrileños for its *churros con chocolate* (€3). Dunk your *churros* into the chocolate pudding, as locals have done here for more than 100 years. While quiet before midnight, it's packed with the disco crowd in the wee hours; the popular dance club Joy Eslava is next door (Mon–Tue 18:00–7:00 in the morning, Wed–Sun 9:30–7:00 in the morning; from Puerta del Sol, take Calle de Arenal 2 blocks west, turn left on book-lined Pasadizo de San Ginés, and you'll see the café—it's at #5; tel. 913-656-546).

Tapas

Tapa-Hopping on Calle del Nuncio (near Calle Cava Baja)

El Madroño ("The Berry Tree," a symbol of Madrid) is a fun tapas bar that preserves a bit of old Madrid. A tile copy of Velázquez's famous *Drinkers* grins from its facade. Inside, look above the stairs for photos of 1902 Madrid. Study the coats of arms of Madrid through the centuries as you try a *vermut* on tap and a €2 sandwich. Or ask to try the *licor de madroño;* a small glass *(chupito)* costs €1.20 (€8.20 fixed-price lunch, quieter tables in the back, Tue–Sun 9:00–17:00 & 20:00–24:00, closed Mon, Plaza Puerta Cerrada 7, tel. 913-645-629). While indoor seating is bright and colorful, the sidewalk tables come with great people-watching.

Taberna Los Austrias, two blocks away, serves tapas, salads, and light meals on wood-barrel tables (daily 12:00–16:00 & 20:00–24:00, more formal seating in back, Calle Nuncio 17).

Taberna de los 100 Vinos, the "Tavern of 100 Wines," is extremely hip and popular. This classy wine bar serves top-end tapas and fine wine by the glass—see the chalkboard. Eat creative, non-traditional delicious €3.75 *pinchos* standing up, or sit down for excellent €15 *raciones.* For those in search of some fine local wine, this is the place (Tue–Sat 13:00–16:00 & 20:00–24:00, closed Sun–Mon, Calle Nuncio 17).

The Madrid Pub-Crawl Dinner (for Beginners)

For maximum fun, people, and atmosphere, go mobile for dinner: Do the "tapas tango," a local tradition of going from one bar to the next, munching, drinking, and socializing. Tapas are the toothpick appetizers, salads, and deep-fried foods served in most bars. Madrid is Spain's tapas capital—tapas just don't get any better. Grab a toothpick and stab something strange—but establish the prices first, especially if you're on a tight budget or at a possible tourist trap. Some items are very pricey, and most bars push larger *raciones,* rather than smaller tapas. The real action begins late (around 20:00). But for beginners, an earlier start, with less commotion, can be easier. In good old-fashioned bars, a drink comes with a free tapa. The litter on the floor is normal; that's where people traditionally toss their trash and shells. Don't worry about paying until you're ready to go. Then ask for *la cuenta* (the bill).

If done properly, a pub crawl can be a highlight of your trip. Before embarking upon this culinary adventure, learn a little about tapas, the tasty treats you'll encounter. Your ability to speak a little Spanish will get you a much better (and less expensive) experience.

Prowl the area between Puerta del Sol and Plaza Santa Ana. There's no ideal route, but the little streets (in this book's map)

Plaza Santa Ana Pub Crawl

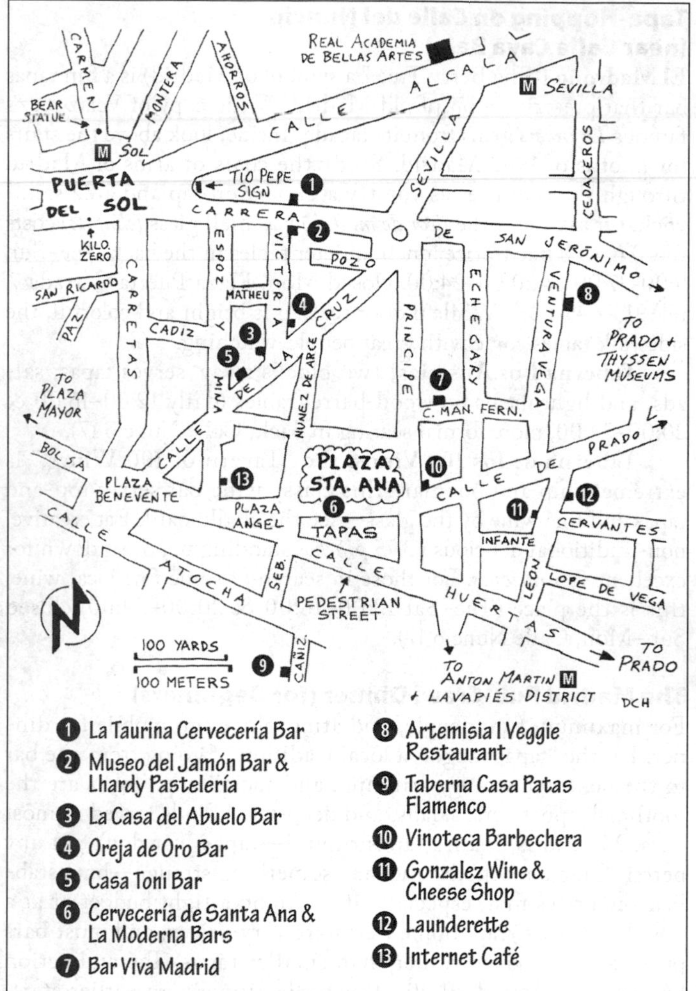

between Puerta del Sol, San Jerónimo, and Plaza Santa Ana hold tasty surprises. Nearby, the street Jesús de Medinaceli is also lined with popular tapas bars. Below is a six-stop tapa crawl. These places are good, but don't be afraid to make some discoveries of your own. The more adventurous should read this crawl for ideas, and skip directly to the advanced zone (Lavapiés), described below.

• *From Puerta del Sol, walk east a block down Carrera de San Jerónimo to the corner of Calle Victoria. Across from the Museo del Jamón (Museum of Ham), you'll find...*

1. La Taurina Cervecería: This is a bullfighters' Planet Hollywood (daily 8:00–24:00, air-con). Wander among trophies and historic photographs. Each stuffed bull's head is named, along with his farm, awards, and who killed him. Among the many gory photos, study the first post: It's Che Guevara, Orson Welles, and Salvador Dalí, all enjoying a good fight. Around the corner, the Babe Ruth of bullfighters, El Cordobés, lies wounded in bed. The photo above and below shows him in action. I enjoyed the art. Then, inspired, I went for the *rabo de toro* (bull-tail stew, €12.50)—and regretted it. A good, basic dish here is *chorizos a la sidra* (spicy sausage in cider, €7) with a beer. If a fight's on, it'll be packed with aficionados gathered around the TV.

• *Across the street, just left of the Museo del Jamón, is the...*

2. Lhardy Pastelería: Offering a taste of Old World charm in this district of rowdy pubs, this place has been a fixture since 1839 for Madrileños wanting to duck in for a cup of soup or a light snack with a fortified wine. Step right in, and pretend you're an aristocrat back between the wars. Serve yourself. You'll pay as you leave (on the honor system). Help yourself to the silver water dispenser (free), a line of elegant bottles (each a different Iberian fortified wine: sherry, port, and so on, €1.80 per glass), a revolving case of meaty little pastries (€0.80 each), and a fancy soup dispenser (chicken broth consommé-€1.80, or €2.30 with a splash of sherry... local style—bottles in the corner, help yourself; daily 9:30–15:00 & 17:00–21:30, Carrera de San Jerónimo 8).

• *Now duck into the...*

3. Museo del Jamón (Museum of Ham): This frenetic, cheap, stand-up bar (with famously rude service) is an assembly line of fast and simple *bocadillos* and *raciones*. It's tastefully decorated—unless you're a pig (or a vegetarian). Take advantage of the easy photo-illustrated menus that show various dishes and their prices. The best ham is the pricey *jamón ibérico*—from pigs who led stress-free lives in acorn-strewn valleys. Just point and eat, but be specific: A plate of low-end *jamón blanco* portion costs only €2, while *jamón ibérico* costs €12. For a small sandwich, ask for a *chiquito* (€0.70, or €3.10 for *ibérico*). If on a budget, don't let them sell you the *ibérico* (daily 9:00–24:00, sit-down restaurant upstairs, air-con).

• *Next, forage halfway up Calle Victoria to the tiny...*

4. La Casa del Abuelo: This is where seafood-lovers savor sizzling plates of tasty little *gambas* (shrimp) and *langostinos* (prawns). Try *gambas a la plancha* (grilled shrimp, €6.50) or *gambas al ajillo* (ahh-HHEEE-yoh, shrimp version of escargot, cooked in oil and garlic and ideal for bread dipping, €7) and a €1.80 glass of sweet red house wine (daily 11:30–15:30 & 18:30–23:30, Calle Victoria 12).

• *Across the street is...*

5. Oreja de Oro: The "Golden Ear" is named for what it sells—sautéed pigs' ears (*oreja,* €3). While oinker ears are a Madrid specialty, this place is Galician, so people also come here for *pulpo* (octopus, €12), *pimientos de Padrón* (sautéed miniature green peppers—my favorite plate of the entire crawl, €3.50), and the distinctive *ribeiro* (ree-BAY-roh) wine, served Galician-style, in characteristic little ceramic bowls (to disguise its lack of clarity). Jaime is a frantic one-man show who somehow gets everything just right. Have fun here.

• *For a finale, continue uphill and around the corner to...*

6. Casa Toni: This is the spot for refreshing bowls of gazpacho—the cold tomato-and-garlic soup (€1.80, available all year but only popular when temperatures soar). Their specialties are *berenjena* (deep-fried slices of eggplant, €4) and *champiñones* (sautéed mushrooms, €4.50; open daily 11:30–16:00 & 18:00–23:30, closed July, Calle Cruz 14).

More Options: If you're hungry for more, and want a trendy, up-to-date, pricier tapas scene, head for Plaza Santa Ana, with lively bars spilling out onto the square. Survey the entire scene. Consider **Cervecería de Santa Ana** (tasty tapas with two zones: rowdy, circa-1900 beer-hall and classier sit-down) and **La Moderna** (wine, good tapas, pâté, and cheese plates—all with quality ingredients). **Naturbier** is a local microbrewery. **Vinoteca Barbechera,** at the downhill end of the square, has an inviting menu of tapas and fine wines by the glass (indoor and outdoor seating).

Gonzalez, a venerable gourmet cheese and wine shop with a circa 1930s interior, offers a genteel opportunity to enjoy a plate of first-class cheese or meat and a fine glass of wine with friendly service and a fun setting. Their assortment of five Spanish cheeses—more than enough for two—is a cheese lover's treat (Tue–Sat 9:00–24:00, closed Sun–Mon, three blocks past Plaza Santa Ana at Calle Leon 12, tel. 914-295-618).

The Lavapiés District Tapas Crawl (for the Adventurous)

A neighborhood called Lavapiés is emerging as a colorful magnet for people-watching. This is where the multiethnic tapestry of Madrid society enjoys pithy, cheap, seedy-yet-fun-loving life on the streets. Neighborhoods like this typically experience an evolution: initially they're so cheap that only the immigrants, downtrodden, counter-culture types live there. The diversity and color they bring attracts those with more money. Businesses erupt to cater to those bohemian/trendy tastes. Rents go up. Those who gave the area the colorful liveliness in the first place can no longer afford to live there. They move out and here comes Starbucks. For now, Lavapiés is edgy yet comfortable enough for most.

This district has almost no tourists. Old ladies with their tired bodies and busy fans hang out on their tiny balconies as they have for 40 years watching the scene. Shady types lurk on side streets (don't venture off the main drag, don't show your wallet or money, and don't linger on Plaza Lavapiés).

For food, you'll find all the various kinds of tapas bars described earlier in "The Madrid Pub-Crawl Dinner (for Beginners)," plus great Indian and Moroccan eateries. I've listed a couple of places that appealed to me...but explore your options. I'd recommend taking the entire walk once, then backtracking and eating at the place or places that appeal to you.

From the Anton Martin Metro stop (or Plaza Santa Ana), walk down Calle Ave Maria (on its way to becoming Calle Ave Allah) to Plaza Lavapiés (where old ladies hang out with the swarthy drunks and a mosaic of cultures treat this square as a communal living room; Metro station here), and then up Calle de Lavapiés to the newly remodeled square, Plaza Tirso de Molina (Metro stop). This square was once plagued by drug addicts. Now with flower kiosks and a playground, it's homey and inviting. This is a fine example of the vision for Madrid's public spaces.

On Calle Ave Maria: **Bar Melos** is a thriving dive jammed with a hungry and nubile local crowd. It's famous for its giant patty melts called *Zapatillas de Lacon y Queso* (because they're the size and shape of a *zapatilla* or slipper, €7 feeds at least two, Ave Maria 44, smoky tables in back). **Nuevo Café Barbieri,** one of a dying breed of smoky mirrored cafés with a circa-1940 ambience, offers classical music in the afternoon and jazz in the evening. Coffee sippers enjoy a menu of loaner books (Ave Maria 45).

On Calle de Lavapiés: At Calle de Lavapiés 44, consider a fun cluster of three places: **Indian Restaurant Shapla** (good €8 fixed-price meal), **Tetería Lakutubia** (atmospheric tea house), and **Montes Wine Bar** (countless wines open and served by the glass, good tapas, crawl under the bar to get to the WC).

TRANSPORTATION CONNECTIONS

By Train

Remember that Madrid has two main train stations: Chamartín and Atocha. At the Atocha Station, AVE and other long-distance trains depart from a different area than local *cercanías* trains (see "Arrival in Madrid," page 1036).

AVE Trains: Spain's AVE (AH-vay) bullet train opens up some good itinerary options. Currently the AVE is handiest for visiting **Sevilla** (and, on the way, **Córdoba**). The basic Madrid–Sevilla second-class AVE fare is €47 to €71, depending upon departure time (the almost-as-fast TALGO is €12 less; first-class

AVE costs €101 and comes with a meal). Consider this exciting day trip to Sevilla from Madrid: 7:00-depart Madrid, 8:45–12:40-in Córdoba, 13:30–21:00-in Sevilla, 23:30-back in Madrid. AVE also runs most of the route between Madrid and **Barcelona;** as tracks are completed, minutes are shaved off that journey (and euros are added to the price). You can now zip to Toledo in 30 minutes by AVE (€8). For the latest, pick up the AVE brochure at the station, or check out www.renfe.es/ave. Prices vary with times and class, and Eurailpass-holders get a big discount (e.g., Madrid to Sevilla is only €9 second-class, only at RENFE ticket windows). Reserve each AVE segment ahead (tel. 902-240-202 for Atocha AVE info).

From Madrid by Train to: Toledo (nearly hourly, 30-min AVE from Atocha), **Segovia** (9/day, 2 hrs, both Chamartín and Atocha stations), **Ávila** (hourly, 1.5–2 hrs, from Chamartín and Atocha), **Salamanca** (6/day, 2.5 hrs, from Chamartín), **Santiago** (3/day, 8.5–13 hrs, includes night train, from Atocha), **Barcelona** (6/day, 4.5–6.5 hrs, mostly from Atocha, plus 2 night trains, 9 hrs; the high-speed AVE connection reduces time but increases cost), **Granada** (2/day, 6 hrs), **Sevilla** (hourly, 2.5 hrs by AVE; 2 slower TALGO trains/day, 3.5 hrs; both from Atocha), **Córdoba** (18 AVE trains/day, 2 hrs, from Atocha, 12 TALGO trains/day, 2 hrs), **Málaga** (7/day, 4 hrs, from Atocha), **Lisbon** (1/day departing at 22:45, 10 hrs, pricey overnight Hotel Train from Chamartín), **Paris** (1/day, 13.5 hrs, 1 direct overnight—a €130 Hotel Train, €119 in winter, from Chamartín). General train info: tel. 902-240-202.

Madrid's Barajas Airport

Ten miles east of downtown, Madrid's modern Barajas airport has four terminals (#1, 2, and 3 are connected by long indoor walkways, and are an 8-minute walk apart). The Metro is in Terminal 2. Newer Terminal 4 consists of two sections—the main T-4 and its separate satellite T-4S. To get to Terminal 4, you need to take a 10-minute shuttle-bus trip (see below) from the other three terminals, and the bus and subway stops. For more information about navigating this massive airport, go to www.aena.es.

Make sure you get the right terminal: International flights use T-1 or T-4. T-1 is served by British Midland, Continental, Delta, easyJet, KLM, Lufthansa, SAS, US Airways, and others. T-4 serves American, British Air, Iberia, Virgin Express, Vueling, and more.

At Terminal 1, you'll find a helpful English-speaking **TI** (marked *Oficina de Información Turística,* Mon–Sat 8:00–20:00, Sun 9:00–14:00, tel. 913-058-656); **ATMs;** a **flight info office** (marked simply *Information* in airport lobby, open 24 hours daily, tel. 902-353-570); a **post-office** window; a **pharmacy;** lots of **phones** (buy a phone card from the nearby machine); a few scattered **Internet** terminals (small fee); **eateries;** a **RENFE office** (where you can get train info and buy long-distance train tickets, daily 8:00–21:00, tel. 902-240-202); and on-the-spot **car-rental agencies** (see above). Super-modern Terminal 4 offers essentially the same services (www.aena.es).

A **green shuttle bus** connects terminals 1, 2, and 3 with Terminal 4 (free, leaves from departure level, 6/hr, 10 min). A new Metro station is in the works to T-4 (may be completed in 2007).

Iberia, Spanair, and Air Europa are Spain's airlines, connecting a reasonable number of cities in Spain, as well as international destinations (ask for best rates at travel agencies). Vueling is the most popular discount airline in Iberia (e.g., Madrid–Barcelona flight as cheap as €30 if booked in advance, tel. 902-333-933, www.vueling.com).

Getting Between the Airport and Downtown

By Public Bus: Bus line #200 shuttles travelers between airport terminals 1, 2, and 3 (departing from arrival level every 10 minutes, runs 6:00–24:00) and the Metro stop Avenida de América (northeast of historical center) in about 20 minutes. From the Metro stop, you can connect to your hotel by taking the Metro or hopping a taxi. Bus #204 serves Terminal 4 the same way. The trip costs only €1 (buy ticket from driver; or get a shareable 10-ride Metrobus ticket for €6.15 at a tobacco shop—for more info, see "Getting Around Madrid," pagc 1040).

By Minibus Shuttle: The AeroCity shuttle bus provides door-to-door transport in a seven-seat minibus with up to three hotel stops en route. The €19 fee covers up to three people per trip, and is a good value for two or three people with luggage that they don't want to haul on public transportation. Extra passengers pay more (runs 24 hours, price includes 1 piece of luggage and 1 carry-on per person, payment in cash, tel. 917-477-570, www.aerocity.com). They also offer a €36 private shuttle service for up to three people (your hotel can book it for you).

By Metro: The subway costs the same as the public bus, but involves two transfers (€1; or use a ticket from the 10-ride, €6.15 Metrobus ticket). The airport's futuristic Aeropuerto Metro stop (notice the cash machines, subway info booth, and huge lighted map of Madrid) is in Terminal 2. Access the Metro at the check-in level; to reach the Metro from Terminal 1's arrivals level, stand with your back to the baggage claim, then go to your far right, up the stairs, and follow red-and-blue Metro diamond signs to the station (8-min walk). To get to Puerta del Sol, take line #8 for 12 minutes to Nuevos Ministerios, then continue on line #10 to Tribunal, then line #1 to Puerta del Sol (30 min more total); or exit at Nuevos Ministerios and take a €5 taxi or bus #150 straight to Puerta del Sol.

By Taxi: For a taxi between the airport and downtown, allow €25 during the day *(Tarifa 1)* or €35 at night and on Sundays *(Tarifa 2)*. Insist on the meter. The €4.50 airport supplement is legal. Plan on getting stalled in traffic. For more on taxis—and corrupt cabbies—see "Getting Around Madrid," page 1040.

SWITZERLAND

GIMMELWALD

and the BERNER OBERLAND

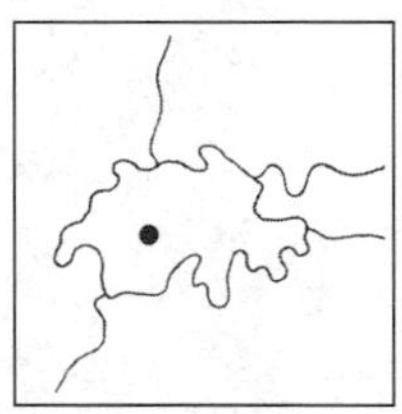

Frolic and hike high above the stress and clouds of the real world. Take a vacation from your busy vacation. Recharge your touristic batteries high in the Alps, where distant avalanches, cowbells, the fluff of a down comforter, the whistle of marmots, and the crunchy footsteps of happy hikers are the dominant sounds. If the weather's good (and your budget's healthy), ride a gondola from the traffic-free village of Gimmelwald to a hearty breakfast at Schilthorn's 10,000-foot-elevation, revolving Piz Gloria restaurant. Linger among alpine whitecaps before riding, hiking, or parasailing down 5,000 feet to Mürren and home to Gimmelwald.

Your gateway to the rugged Berner Oberland is the grand old resort town of Interlaken. Near Interlaken is Switzerland's open-air folk museum, Ballenberg, where you can climb through traditional houses from every corner of this diverse country.

Ah, but the weather's fine and the Alps beckon. Head deep into the heart of the Alps, and ride the cable car to the stop just this side of heaven—Gimmelwald.

Planning Your Time

Rather than tackle a checklist of famous Swiss mountains and resorts, choose one region to savor: the Berner Oberland.

Interlaken is the administrative headquarters and a fine transportation hub. Use it for business—banking, post office, laundry, shopping—and as a springboard for alpine thrills. (Note that at higher altitudes, many hotels, restaurants, and shops are closed between Easter and late May.) At your hotel, pick up a free guest card for small discounts on some museums and sights (such as the Swiss Open-Air Folk Museum at Ballenberg).

With decent weather, explore the two areas that tower above either side of the Lauterbrunnen Valley, south of Interlaken: Kleine Scheidegg/Jungfrau and Mürren/Schilthorn. To check the weather, call the Interlaken TI (tel. 033-826-5300), ask a local, or visit www.swisspanorama.com (entire area), www.jungfraubahn.ch (for icy Jungfraujoch, accessed by train), or www.schilthorn.ch (for Schilthorn peak, accessed by lift).

The best overnight options are the rustic hamlet of Gimmelwald, the resort town of Mürren, or (for accommodations without the expense and headache of mountain lifts) the village of Lauterbrunnen, on the valley floor. Ideally, spend three nights, with a day exploring each side of the valley.

For the fastest look, consider a night in Gimmelwald, breakfast at the Schilthorn, an afternoon doing the Männlichen–Wengen hike, and an evening or night train out. What? A nature-lover not spending the night high in the Alps? Alpus interruptus.

Getting Around the Berner Oberland

For more than 100 years, this region has been the target of nature-worshipping pilgrims. And Swiss engineers and visionaries have made the most exciting alpine perches accessible...

By Lifts and Trains: Part of the fun—and most of the expense—here is riding the many lifts (gondolas and cable cars). Generally lifts are not covered by train passes, but a Swiss railpass gives you a 50 percent discount on even the highest lifts (without the loss of a flexi-day of your pass); 25 percent discount with Eurail and other passes. Ask about discounts for early-morning and late-afternoon trips, youths, seniors, families, groups, and those staying a while. The Junior Card for families pays for itself in the first hour of trains and lifts: Children under 16 travel free with parents (20 SF/one child, 40 SF/two or more children; available at Swiss train stations). Get a list of discounts and the free fare and time schedule at any Swiss train station. If you're staying a week, you can save money with the **Berner Oberland Pass** (220 SF, includes 3 days of unlimited travel and 4 days of half-price fares on all trains, buses, and lifts) or the **Jungfraubahnen Pass** (190 SF, or 140 SF with Swiss Pass, covers 6 days of unlimited transportation in Jungfrau region except pricey Jungfraujoch train, tel. 033-828-7233).

Study the "Alpine Lifts in the Berner Oberland" chart on page 1083. Lifts generally go at least twice hourly, from about 7:00 until about 20:00 (sneak preview: www.jungfraubahn.ch). For a complete schedule of all trains, lifts, buses, and boats, pick up the regional timetable (2 SF at any station).

By Car: Lauterbrunnen, Stechelberg, Isenfluh, and Interlaken are all accessible by car. You can't drive to Gimmelwald, Mürren,

Berner Oberland

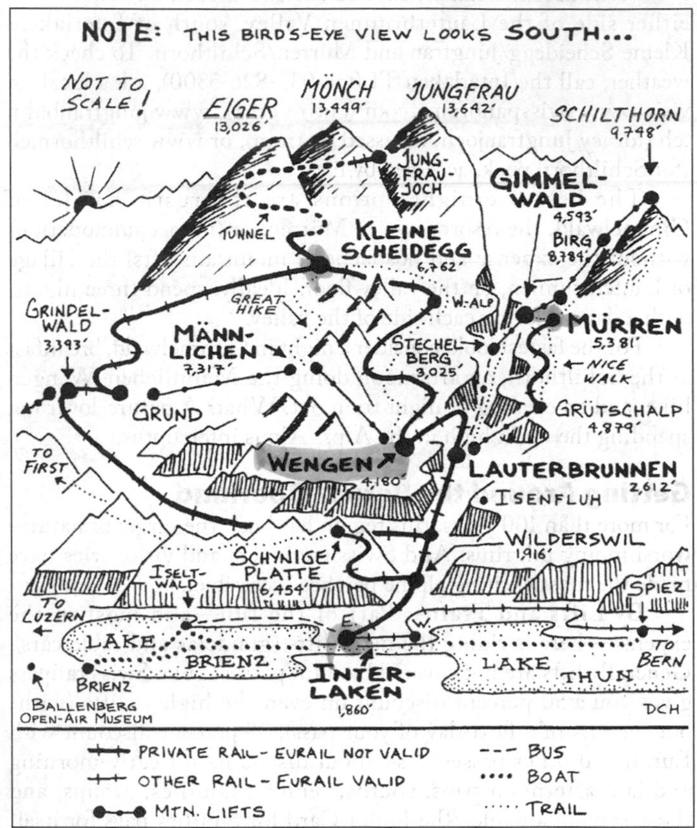

Wengen, or Kleine Scheidegg—but don't let that stop you from staying up in the mountains; park the car and zip up on a lift. To catch the lift to Gimmelwald, Mürren, and the Schilthorn, park at the cable-car station in Stechelberg (parking: 2 SF/2 hrs, 6 SF/day, see page 1110 for more information). To catch the train to Wengen or Kleine Scheidegg, park at the train station in Lauterbrunnen (parking: 2 SF/2 hrs, 9 SF/day).

Interlaken

When the 19th-century Romantics redefined mountains as something more than cold and troublesome obstacles, Interlaken became the original alpine resort. Ever since, tourists have flocked to the Alps "because they're there." Interlaken's glory days are long gone, its elegant old hotels eclipsed by the new, more jet-setty

Alpine Lifts in the Berner Oberland

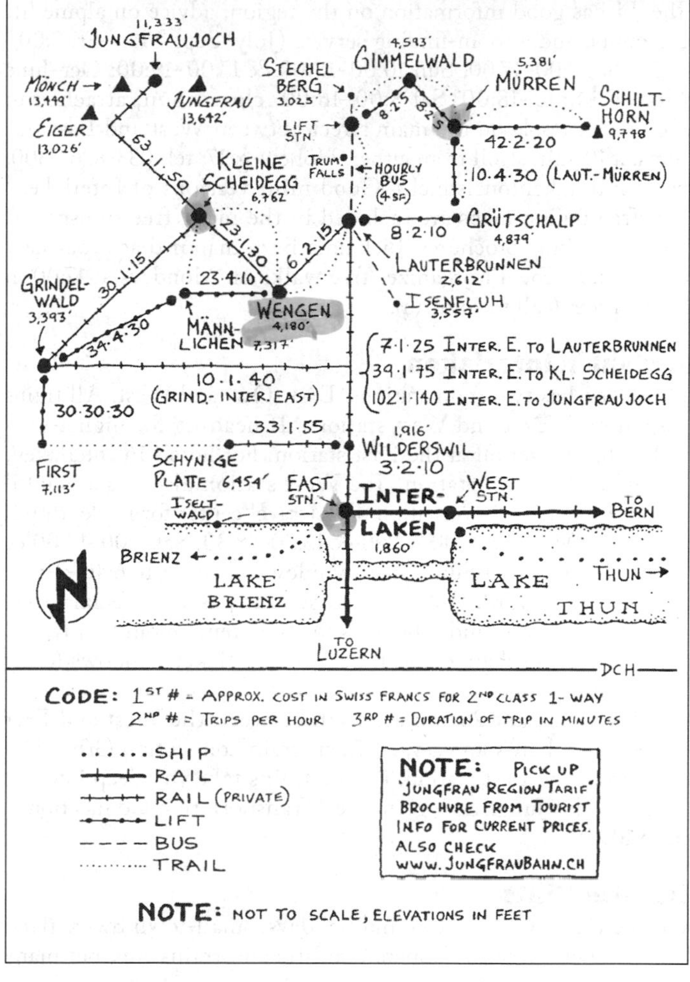

alpine resorts. Today, its shops are filled with chocolate bars, Swiss Army knives, and sunburned backpackers.

ORIENTATION

Efficient Interlaken (pop. 5,500) is a good administrative and shopping center. Take care of business, give the town a quick look, and view the live TV coverage of the Jungfrau and Schilthorn weather in the window of the Schilthornbahn office on the main street (at Höheweg 2). Then head for the hills. Stay in Interlaken only if you suffer from Alptitude sickness.

Tourist Information

The TI has good information on the region, advice on alpine lift discounts, and a room-finding service (July–Sept Mon–Fri 8:00–18:30, Sat 8:00–17:00, Sun 10:00–12:00 & 17:00–19:00; Oct–June Mon–Fri 8:00–18:00, Sat 8:00–16:00, closed Sun; attached to Hotel Metropole on the main street between West and East stations, a 10-min stroll from either, Höheweg 37; tel. 033-826-5300, www.interlakentourism.ch). Good mini-versions of Interlaken/Jungfrau region maps are included in the many free transportation and hiking brochures. Pick up a Bern map if that's your next destination. The TI organizes free walks on Mondays at 17:00 in the summer (call to confirm).

Arrival in Interlaken

Interlaken has two train stations: East (Ost) and West. All trains stop at both East and West stations. If heading for higher-altitude villages, get off at the East station. For hotels in Interlaken, get off at the West station. The West station also has a helpful and friendly train information desk (travel center for in-depth rail questions: Mon–Fri 9:00–12:00 & 13:30–18:30, Sat 9:00–12:00 & 13:30–17:00, closed Sun; ticket windows open daily 6:40–21:00; tel. 033-826-4750). Ask about discount passes, special fares, railpass discounts, and schedules for the scenic mountain trains. There's a fair exchange booth next to the ticket windows (daily 6:40–20:00).

It's a pleasant 20-minute walk between the West and East stations, or there's an easy, frequent train connection (3/hr, 2.80 SF). From the East station, private trains take you deep into the mountainous Jungfrau region (see "Transportation Connections," page 1094).

Helpful Hints

Closed Days: On Sundays and holidays, small-town Switzerland is quiet. Hotels are open, and lifts and trains run, but many stores are closed.

Telephones: Phone booths cluster outside the post office near the West station. For efficiency, buy a phone card from a newsstand or train station ticket window. (If you'll be staying in Gimmelwald, note that its sole public phone—at the gondola station—takes only cards, not coins.)

Laundry: Friendly Helen Schmocker's **Wäscherei** has a change machine, soap, English instructions, and a riverside location (open daily 7:00–22:00 for self-service: load-6 SF; open for full service Mon–Fri 8:00–12:00 & 13:30–18:00, Sat until 16:00, closed Sun, drop off in the morning and pick up that afternoon: load-12 SF; from the main street take Marktgasse over two bridges to Beatenbergstrasse 5, tel. 033-822-1566).

Local Guidebook: Don Chmura's Lauterbrunnen guidebook gives history, folk life, flora, fauna, and hiking information (sold throughout the Lauterbrunnen Valley, 8 SF).

Bike Rental: You can rent bikes at either train station (23 SF/half day, 31 SF/day, 5 SF less with Eurailpass or Swiss Pass, daily 8:30–12:00 & 13:00–18:30).

SELF-GUIDED WALK

Welcome to Interlaken

Most visitors use Interlaken as a springboard for high-altitude thrills (and rightly so). But the town itself has history and scenic charm, and is worth a short walk. This 45-minute stroll circles from the West train station down the main drag to the big meadow, past the casino, along the river to the oldest part of town (historically a neighboring town called Unterseen), and back to the station.

• *From the West train station, walk along...*

Bahnhofstrasse: This main drag, which turns into Höheweg as it continues east, cuts straight through the town center from the West train station to the East station. The best Swiss souvenir shopping is along this Bahnhofstrasse stretch (things get more expensive on the Höheweg stretch, near the fancy hotels). Tchibo makes the best take-out coffee in town (Starbucks-style). At the roundabout is the handy post office (with free public WCs) and Loeb, Interlaken's only department store. Just behind the post office on Marktgasse, the hardware store stocks real cowbells (both ornate and plain). At Höheweg 2, the TV in the window of the Schilthornbahn office shows the weather up top.

• *On your right is...*

Höhematte Park: This "high meadow," or Höhematte (but generally referred to simply as "the park"), marks the beginning of Interlaken's fancy hotel row. Hotels like the Victoria-Jungfrau hearken back to the days when Interlaken was *the* original alpine resort. The first grand hotels were built here to enjoy the views of the Jungfrau in the distance. (Today, the Jungfraus getting the most attention are next door, at Hooters.)

The park originated as farmland of the monastery that predated the town (marked today by the steeples of both the Catholic and Protestant churches—neither of any sightseeing interest). The actual **monastery site** is now home to the City Hall, courthouse, and city administration building. With the Reformation in 1528, the monastery was shut down, and its land was taken by the state. Later, when the land was being eyed by developers, the town's leading hotels and business families bought it and established that it would never be used for commercial buildings (a very early example of smart town planning). There was talk of building a parking lot under it, but the water table here, between the two lakes, is too high. Today, this is a fine place to stroll, hang out on the park benches or at Restaurant Schuh, and watch the parasailors gracefully land.

From the park, turn left into the grounds of **Casino Kursaal,** where, at the top of each hour, dwarfs ring the toadstools on the flower clock. The Kursaal, originally a kind of 19th-century fat farm, is now both a casino (passport but no tie required) and a convention center that hosts musical events and nightly folklore shows through the summer (fun yodeling with lots of audience participation, details at the TI).

• *Follow the path left of the Kursaal to the river (huge public swimming pool just over the river). Walk downstream under the train track and cross the pedestrian bridge, stopping in the middle to enjoy the view.*

Aare River: The Aare River is Switzerland's longest. It connects Lake Brienz and Lake Thun (with an 18-foot altitude difference—this short stretch has quite a flow). Then it tumbles out of Lake Thun, heading for Bern and ultimately into the Rhine. Its level is controlled by several sluices. In the distance, a church bell tower marks a different parish and the neighborhood of Unterseen, which shares the town's name, but in German: *Unterseen* means "lower lakes." Behind the spire is the pointy summit of the Niesen (like so many Swiss peaks, capped with a restaurant and accessible by a lift). Stroll downstream along the far side of the river to the church spire. The delightful riverside walk is lined by fine residences. Notice that your Jungfrau view now includes the Jungfraujoch observation deck (the little brown bump in the ridge just left of the peak).

• *At the next bridge, turn right to the town square lined with 17th-century houses on one side and a modern strip on the other.*

Unterseen: This was a town when Interlaken was only a monastery. The church is not worth touring. A block away, the (generally empty) **Town History Museum/Museum of Tourism** shows off classic posters, fascinating photos of the construction of the Jungfraujoch, and exhibits on folk life, crafts, and winter sports—all well-described in English (5 SF, May–mid-Oct Tue–Sun 14:00–17:00, closed Mon and mid-Oct–April, Obergasse 26).

Return to Station: From Unterseen, cross the river on Spielmatte, and you're a few minutes' walk from your starting point. On the second bridge, notice the border between the two towns, or parishes, marked by their respective heraldic emblems (each with an ibex, or wild mountain goat). A block or so later, on the left, is the Marktplatz. The river originally ran through this square. The town used to be called "Aaremühle" ("Aare mill") for the mill that was here. But in the 19th century, town fathers made a key marketing decision: Since "Aaremühle" was too difficult for English tourists to pronounce, they changed the name to "Interlaken."

SIGHTS AND ACTIVITIES

Near Interlaken

Boat Trips—"Interlaken" is literally "between the lakes" of Thun and Brienz. You can explore these lakes on a lazy boat trip (8/day mid-June–mid-Sept, fewer off-season, free with Eurailpass or Eurail Selectpass but uses a flexi-day, schedules at TI or at BLS Travel Center in West station, tel. 033-826-4760 or 033-334-5211). The boats on **Lake Thun** (10/day, 2 hours to Thun, 4 hours return, 51 SF round-trip) stop at the St. Beatus Höhlen caves (30 min away, see below) and two visit-worthy towns: Spiez (1 hour) and Thun (1.75 hours). The boats on **Lake Brienz** (3 hours, 36 SF round-trip) stop at the super-cute village of Iseltwald (45 min away) and at Brienz (1.25 hours away, near Ballenberg Open-Air Folk Museum—described below).

St. Beatus Höhlen caves on Lake Thun can be visited with a guided tour (17 SF, 60 min, 2/hr, April–mid-Oct daily 10:30–17:00, closed mid-Oct–March, tel. 033-841-1643, www.beatushoehlen.ch). The best excursion plan: Ride the bus from Interlaken (20-min ride, line #21, depart West station at :19 past the hour); tour the caves; take the short, steep hike down to lake; and return by boat (8.40 SF one-way, 30 min to Interlaken, see above).

Adventure Trips—For the adventurer with money and little concern for personal safety, several companies offer high-adrenaline trips such as rafting, canyoning (rappelling down watery gorges), bungee jumping, and paragliding. Costs range from 160 SF to 205 SF (river rafting plus bungee jump-205 SF, paragliding-160 SF, tandem hang gliding-180 SF). Interlaken companies include Alpin Raft (tel. 033-823-4100, www.alpinraft.com) and Outdoor Interlaken (tel. 033-826-7719, www.outdoor-interlaken.ch). For an overview of your options, visit www.interlakenadventure.com or study the racks of brochures at most TIs and hotels (everyone's getting a cut of this lucrative industry).

Recent fatal accidents jolted the adventure-sport business in the Berner Oberland, leading to a more professional respect for the risks involved. In May 2000, an American died bungee jumping from the Stechelberg–Mürren cable car (the operator used a 180-meter rope for a 100-meter jump). In July 1999, 21 tourists died canyoning on the Saxetenbach River, 10 miles from Interlaken; they were battered and drowned by a flash flood filled with debris. (The monument just outside Wilderswil on the Saxeten Road is stirring.) Enjoying nature up close comes with risks. Adventure

Interlaken

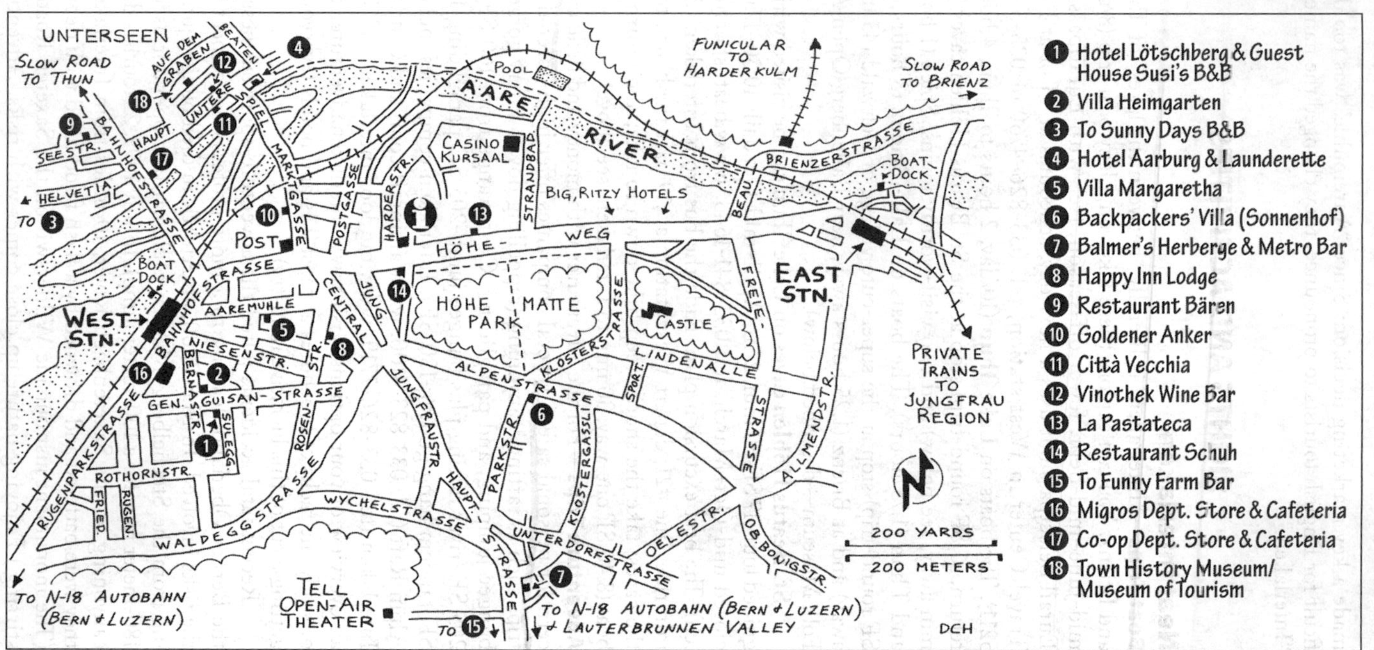
Interlaken
1 Hotel Lötschberg & Guest House Susi's B&B
2 Villa Heimgarten
3 To Sunny Days B&B
4 Hotel Aarburg & Launderette
5 Villa Margaretha
6 Backpackers' Villa (Sonnenhof)
7 Balmer's Herberge & Metro Bar
8 Happy Inn Lodge
9 Restaurant Bären
10 Goldener Anker
11 Città Vecchia
12 Vinothek Wine Bar
13 La Pastateca
14 Restaurant Schuh
15 To Funny Farm Bar
16 Migros Dept. Store & Cafeteria
17 Co-op Dept. Store & Cafeteria
18 Town History Museum/ Museum of Tourism
Unterseen
Slow road to Thun
Funicular to Harder Kulm
Slow road to Brienz
Private trains to Jungfrau Region
200 yards
200 meters
DCH
Aare River
Pool
Casino Kursaal
Big, Ritzy Hotels
East Stn.
Castle
Höhe Matte
Höhe Park
West Stn.
Post
Boat Dock
To N-18 Autobahn (Bern + Luzern)
To N-18 Autobahn (Bern + Luzern) + Lauterbrunnen Valley
Tell Open-Air Theater
Bahnhofstrasse
Brienzerstrasse
Marktgasse
Postgasse
Harderstr.
Strandbad
Höheweg
Jungfraustr.
Alpenstrasse
Klosterstrasse
Klostergassli
Lindenalle
Freiestrasse
Allmendstr.
Ob. Bönigstr.
Oelestr.
Unterdorfstrasse
Parkstr.
Hauptstrasse
Wychelstrasse
Waldeggstrasse
Rosenstrasse
Centralstr.
Niesenstr.
Bernastr.
Gen. Guisan-Strasse
Sulegg.
Rothornstr.
Rugen.
Fried.
Rugenparkstrasse
Aaremuhle
Seestr.
Helvetia
Spiel.
Untere
Beaten.
Auf dem Graben

sports increase those risks dramatically. Use good judgment.

▲▲Swiss Open-Air Folk Museum at Ballenberg—Across Lake Brienz from Interlaken, the Swiss Open-Air Museum of Vernacular Architecture, Country Life, and Crafts in the Berner Oberland is a rich collection of traditional and historic farmhouses from every region of the country. Each house is carefully furnished, and many feature traditional craftspeople at work. The sprawling 50-acre park, laid out roughly as a huge Swiss map (Italian Swiss in the south, Appenzell in the east, and so on), is a natural preserve providing a wonderful setting for this culture-on-a-lazy-Susan look at Switzerland.

The Thurgau house (#621) has an interesting wattle-and-daub (half-timbered construction) display, and house #331 has a fun bread museum and farmers' shop. There's cheesemaking (near the east entry), traditional farm animals (like very furry-legged roosters, near the merry-go-round in the center), and a chocolate shop (under the restaurant on the east side).

An outdoor cafeteria with reasonable prices is inside the west entrance, and fresh bread, sausage, mountain cheese, and other goodies are on sale in several houses. Picnic tables and grills with free firewood are scattered throughout the park.

The little wooden village of Brienzwiler (near the east entrance) is a museum in itself, with a lovely pint-size church.

Cost, Hours, Information: 18 SF, half-price after 16:00, 16 SF with guest card, covered by Swiss Pass. A RailAway combo-ticket, available at either Interlaken station, includes transportation to and from Ballenberg and your admission (38 SF from West station, 35.20 SF from East, add 12.60 SF to return by boat instead). The houses are open daily May–Oct 10:00–17:00, but the park stays open later. Craft demonstration schedules are listed just inside entry. Use the 2-SF map/guide. The more expensive picture book is a better souvenir than guide. Tel. 033-952-1030, www.ballenberg.ch.

Getting There from Interlaken: Take the train from either of Interlaken's train stations to Brienz (hourly, 30 min, 8.60 SF one-way from West station). From Brienz, catch a bus to Ballenberg (10 min, 3.20 SF one-way) or hike (45 min, slightly uphill). Consider returning by boat (Brienz boat dock next to train station, one-way to Interlaken-21 SF). Trains also run occasionally from Interlaken to Brienzwiler, a 20-min uphill walk to the museum (every 2 hours, 30 min, 9.80 SF one-way from West station).

Castles and Forts—A few impressively well-kept and welcoming old castles in the Interlaken area are worth considering for day trips by boat, bus, or car.

Thun Castle (Schloss Thun), built between 1180 and 1190 by the Dukes of Zähringer, has a five-floor historical museum offering insights into the cultural development of the region over a period of some 4,000 years. From the corner turrets of the castle, you are rewarded with a spectacular view of the city of Thun, the lake, and the Alps (7 SF, 5 SF with guest card, April–Oct daily 10:00–17:00, Feb–March daily 13:00–16:00, Nov–Jan Sun only 13:00–16:00, www.schlossthun.ch).

Hünegg Castle (Schloss Hünegg) in Hilterfingen (farther along Lake Thun, towards Interlaken) contains a museum exhibiting furnished rooms from the second half of the 19th century. The castle is situated in a beautiful wooded park (8 SF, 7 SF with guest card, mid-May–mid-Oct Mon–Sat 14:00–17:00, Sun 10:00–12:00 & 14:00–17:00, closed off-season, www.schlosshuenegg.ch).

Oberhofen Castle (Schloss Oberhofen) is for those interested in gardens. Its beautifully landscaped park with exotic trees is a delight (free, mid-March–mid-Nov daily from 9:00 until dusk, closed in winter). The museum in the castle depicts domestic life in the 16th through 19th centuries, including a Turkish smoking room and a medieval chapel (7 SF, 5 SF with guest card, mid-May–mid-Oct Mon 14:00–17:00, Tue–Sun 11:00–17:00, closed off-season, tel. 033-243-1235).

For a more modern fort, consider visiting the **WWII Swiss Infantry Bunker** in Beatenbucht. From the cable car station there, walk uphill for five minutes to the first bend, keep straight for 10 yards, and walk behind the camouflage at the first right turn.

NIGHTLIFE

For counterculture with a reggae beat, check out **Funny Farm** (past Balmer's Herberge hostel, in Matten). The young frat-party dance scene rages at the **Metro Bar** at Balmer's (bomb-shelter disco bar, with cheap drinks and a friendly if loud atmosphere). For a stylish wine bar with local yuppies, check in at the **Vinothek,** across from Città Vecchia in Unterseen (see "Eating," below). If you can't sleep and are waiting for your prunes, try **Restaurant Schuh** on the park.

SLEEPING

I'd head for Gimmelwald, or at least Lauterbrunnen (20 min by train or car). Interlaken is not the Alps. But if you must stay...

$$$ Hotel Lötschberg, with a sun terrace and 21 wonderful rooms, marked its 100th anniversary in 2006. It's run by English-speaking Susi and Fritz and is the best real hotel value in town. Happy to dispense information, these gregarious folks pride themselves on a personal touch that sets them apart from other hotels (Sb-120 SF, Db-165 SF, big Db-185 SF, extra bed-30 SF,

Sleep Code

(1.25 SF = about $1, country code: 41)
S = Single, **D** = Double/Twin, **T** = Triple, **Q** = Quad, **b** = bathroom, **s** = shower only. Unless otherwise noted, credit cards are accepted, English is spoken, and breakfast is included.

To help you sort easily through these listings, I've divided the rooms into three categories, based on the price for a standard double room with bath:

$$$ Higher Priced—Most rooms 150 SF or more.
$$ Moderately Priced—Most rooms between 90–150 SF.
$ Lower Priced—Most rooms 90 SF or less.

family deals, rates about 15 percent cheaper mid-Oct–April, closed Nov–March, non-smoking, elevator, Internet access, kitchen open to guests, laundry service, bike rental; 5-min walk from West station: leaving station, turn right, after Migros at the circle go left to General-Guisanstrasse 31; tel. 033-822-2545, fax 033-822-2579, www.lotschberg.ch, hotel@lotschberg.ch). Effervescent Fritz offers cooking classes and organizes guided adventures. He does tandem hang gliding almost every day with one of his guests (guests fly with Fritz at a discount, about 20 SF cheaper than any other deal in town).

$$ Guest House Susi's B&B is Hotel Lötschberg's no-frills, cash-only annex, run by Fritz and Susi, offering nicely furnished, cozy rooms (Sb-105 SF, Db-135 SF; apartment with kitchenette 105 SF/2 people, 185 SF/4–5 people—minimum 3-night stay; prices about 20 percent cheaper mid-Oct–April, closed Nov–March, same contact info as Hotel Lötschberg, above).

$$ Sunny Days B&B, a homey, nine-room place in a residential neighborhood, is run by Dave from Britain (Sb-98–110 SF, Db-110–148 SF, prices vary with season and view, extra bed about 40 SF, Nov–late-April all rooms 100–120 SF, Internet access; exit left out of West station and take first bridge to your left, after crossing the bridges turn left on Helvetiastrasse and go 3 blocks to #29; tel. 033-822-8343, www.sunnydays.ch, mail@sunnydays.ch).

$$ Hotel Aarburg offers 13 plain, peaceful rooms in a beautifully located but run-down old building a 10-minute walk from the West station (Sb-70 SF, Db-120 SF, 10 SF more in July–Aug, next to launderette at Beatenbergstrasse 1, tel. 033-822-2615, fax 033-822-6397, hotel-aarburg@quicknet.ch).

$$ Villa Heimgarten is a fine 1902 house in a quiet, handy location. While not particularly cozy, it rents seven basic rooms at a good price (Sb-50 SF, Db-90 SF, T-110 SF, Q-140 SF, 6-bed room-195 SF, the whole house can be rented for bigger groups, cash strongly preferred, garden, playground, 5-min walk from West station, across from Hotel Lötschberg at Bernastrasse 7, tel. 033-821-0963, fax 033-822-7479, www.villaheimgarten.ch, villaheimgarten@bluewin.ch).

$ Villa Margaretha, run by English-speaking Frau Kunz Joerin, offers the best cheap beds in town. It's like grandma's big Victorian house on a residential street. Keep your room tidy, and you'll have a friend for life (D-86 SF, T-129 SF, Q-172 SF, the 3 rooms share a big bathroom, 2-night minimum, closed Oct–April, cash only, no breakfast served but dishes and kitchenette available, lots of rules to abide by, go up small street directly in front of West station to Aarmühlestrasse 13, tel. 033-822-1813).

$ Backpackers' Villa (Sonnenhof) Interlaken is a creative guest house run by a Methodist church group. It's fun, youthful, and great for families, without the frat-party scene of Balmer's Herberge (listed below). Travelers of any age feel comfortable here (D-98 SF, T-135 SF, Q-156 SF, dorm beds in 5- to 7-bed rooms with lockers and sheets-35 SF per person, 5 SF more per person for rooms with toilets and Jungfrau-view balconies, includes breakfast, kitchen, garden, movies, small game room, Internet access, laundry, bike rental, free admission to public swimming pool/spa, no curfew, open all day but reception open only 7:00–11:00 & 16:00–22:00, 10-min walk from either station, across the park from TI, Alpenstrasse 16, tel. 033-826-7171, fax 033-826-7172, www.villa.ch, mail@villa.ch).

$ Balmer's Herberge is many people's idea of backpacker heaven. This Interlaken institution comes with movies, table tennis, a cheap launderette (4 SF/load), bar, restaurant, swapping library, Internet access, tiny grocery, bike rental, excursions, a shuttle-bus service (which meets important arriving trains), and a friendly, hardworking staff. This little Nebraska is home for those who miss their fraternity. It can be a mob scene, especially on summer weekends (dorm bed-25–29 SF, S-43 SF, D-66 SF, T-99 SF, Q-132 SF, includes sheets and breakfast, non-smoking rooms, open year-round, emailed reservations recommended 5 days in advance except for dorm beds, Hauptstrasse 23, in Matten, 15-min walk from either train station, tel. 033-822-1961, fax 033-823-3261, www.balmers.com, mail@balmers.ch).

$ Happy Inn Lodge has 15 cheap backpacker rooms above a lively, noisy restaurant a five-minute walk from the West station (dorm bed-22 SF, S-40 SF, D-80 SF, T-90–105 SF, Q-120–140 SF, breakfast-8 SF, Rosenstrasse 17, tel. 033-822-3225, fax 033-822-3268, www.happyinn.com, info@happyinn.com).

EATING

Interlaken's two big department stores each feature reasonable self-service restaurants. **Migros** is across the street from West station (Mon–Thu 8:00–18:30, Fri 8:00–21:00, Sat 7:30–17:00, closed Sun); while the **Co-op** is across the river from the West station, on your right (Mon–Thu 8:00–18:30, Fri 8:00–21:00, Sat 7:30–17:00, closed Sun).

In Unterseen, the Old Town Across the River

Restaurant Bären, in a classic low-ceilinged building with cozy indoor and fine outdoor seating, is a great value for *Rösti,* fondue, raclette, fish, traditional sausage, and salads (20-SF plates, open daily, closed Mon off-season, from West station turn left on Bahnhofstrasse and go over the river a block to Seestrasse 2, tel. 033-822-7526).

Goldener Anker is the local hangout—smoky, with a pool table and a few unsavory types. If you thought Interlaken was sterile, you haven't been here. Jeannette serves and René cooks, just as they have for 25 years (hearty 20-SF salads, fresh vegetables, 3 courses for 17 SF, daily from 16:00, Marktgasse 57, tel. 033-822-1672). This place sometimes hosts small concerts, and has launched some of Switzerland's top bands.

Città Vecchia serves the best Italian food and Italian wine in town, with seating indoors or out, on a leafy square (pizza-15 SF, pasta-20 SF, plates-30 SF, Mon and Wed–Sat 10:00–14:00 & 17:30–23:30, Sun 10:00–23:30, closed Tue, on main square in Unterseen at Untere Gasse 5, tel. 033-822-1754, Rinaldo).

On or near the Main Drag

La Pastateca, at the top hotel in town (Victoria-Jungfrau), is very elegant. To sit on its terrace and watch the Jungfrau is one of the great Interlaken treats. To do it affordably, go with the super antipasto buffet (all you like from a huge spread of Italian-style treats, including lots of meat and seafood, 25 SF), or come for the "business lunch" (the buffet, plus a pasta of your choice, great bread and olive oil, bottled water, and coffee for 27 SF, available Mon–Fri 11:30–14:00). The service is formal and can be slow (daily 11:30–23:00, a block past TI, facing the park, tel. 033-828-2680).

Restaurant Schuh, formerly the Grand Café Schuh, retains its grand-café ambience on the best real estate in town (at the corner of the park, across from Hotel Metropole and TI). Meals are disappointing, but desserts are wonderful, and there's no better place to nurse a drink or coffee and watch the parasailors glide into the park (live schmaltzy music, newspapers, classy indoor and outdoor seating, Höheweg 56, tel. 033-822-9441).

TRANSPORTATION CONNECTIONS

Note that Interlaken is connected to Luzern and Montreux (on Lake Geneva) via the Golden Pass scenic rail route. Train info: toll tel. 0900-300-3004 (www.rail.ch).

From Interlaken East (Ost) by Train to: Lauterbrunnen (hourly, 20 min, 9.40 SF each way), **Spiez** (2/hr, 20 min), **Brienz** (1–2/hr, 30–40 min), **Bern** (2/hr, 50 min), **Zürich** and **Zürich Airport** (hourly, 2–2.25 hrs, most direct but some with transfer in Bern and/or Spiez), **Luzern** (hourly, 2 hrs), **Lugano** (hourly, 5 hrs, transfer in Luzern, Zürich, or Olten), **Zermatt** (hourly, 3.5 hrs, transfer in Spiez and Brig). While there are a few long trains from Interlaken, you'll generally connect from Bern.

From Bern by Train to: Lausanne (2/hr, 1.25 hrs), **Murten** (hourly, 40 min, some transfer in Kerzers), **Zürich** (2/hr, 1–1.25 hrs), **Zermatt** (hourly, 3.25 hrs, transfer in Brig), **Appenzell** (hourly, 3.25 hrs, transfer in Gossau), **Munich** (hourly, 6 hrs), **Frankfurt** (hourly, 4.5 hrs), **Salzburg** (4/day, 7.25 hrs, transfer in Zürich), **Paris** (6/day, 6 hrs).

From Interlaken to the Lauterbrunnen Valley

By Public Transportation to Gimmelwald: Take the train from the Interlaken East station to Lauterbrunnen (hourly, 20 min). From Lauterbrunnen, you have two options:

1. The faster, easier way—best in bad weather or at the end of a long day with lots of luggage—is to ride the postal bus from Lauterbrunnen station (3.80 SF, hourly bus departure coordinated with arrival of train, get off at Schilthornbahn stop) to Stechelberg and the base of the Schilthornbahn gondola station, where the gondola will whisk you in five thrilling minutes up to Gimmelwald (7.80 SF, departing at :10 and :40).

2. The more scenic route is to catch the cable car from Lauterbrunnen to Grütschalp, where a special scenic train *(Panorama Fahrt)* will roll you along the cliff to Mürren (total trip from Lauterbrunnen to Mürren: 30 min, 9.80 SF). From there, either walk a paved 30 minutes downhill to Gimmelwald, or walk 10 minutes across Mürren to catch the gondola down to Gimmelwald (7.80 SF).

By Car: You can drive to Lauterbrunnen and to Stechelberg; but you can't drive to Gimmelwald (park in Stechelberg and take the cable car) or to Mürren, Wengen, or Kleine Scheidegg (park in Lauterbrunnen and take the cable car to Mürren or the train to Wengen/Kleine Scheidegg). For drivers, the most direct route to Gimmelwald is via the cable car at Stechelberg. It's a 30-minute drive from Interlaken to the Stechelberg cable-car station (parking lot:

2 SF/2 hrs, 6 SF/day). Gimmelwald is the first stop above Stechelberg on the Schilthorn cable car (7.80 SF, 2/hr at :10 and :40). Note that the Schilthornbahn is closed for servicing for a week in early May and also from mid-November through early December. During this time, you'll ride the cargo cable car directly from Stechelberg to Mürren, where a small bus shuttles you down to Gimmelwald.

Gimmelwald

Saved from developers by its "avalanche zone" classification, Gimmelwald was (before tourism) one of the poorest places in Switzerland. Its traditional economy was stuck in the hay, and its farmers—unable to make it in their disadvantaged trade—survived only by Swiss government subsidies (and working the ski lifts in the winter). For some travelers, there's little to see in the village. Others (like me) enjoy a fascinating day sitting on a bench and learning why they say, "If heaven isn't what it's cracked up to be, send me back to Gimmelwald."

Take a walk through the town. The huge, sheer cliff face that dominates your mountain views is the Schwarzmönch ("Black Monk"). The three peaks above (or behind) it are, left to right, the Eiger, Mönch, and Jungfrau. While Gimmelwald's population has dropped in the last century from 200 to about 100 residents, traditions survive. Most Gimmelwalders have one of two last names: von Allmen or Feutz. They are tough and proud. Raising hay in this rugged terrain is labor-intensive. One family harvests enough to feed only about 15 cows. But they'd have it no other way, and, unlike the absentee-landlord town of Mürren, Gimmelwald is locally owned. (When word got out that urban planners wished to develop Gimmelwald into a town of 1,000, locals pulled some strings to secure the town's bogus avalanche-zone building code.) Those same folks are happy the masses go to touristy and commercialized Grindelwald, just over the Kleine Scheidegg ridge. Don't confuse Gimmelwald and Grindelwald—they couldn't be more different.

SELF-GUIDED WALK

Welcome to Gimmelwald

Gimmelwald, though tiny, with one zigzag street, gives a fine look at a traditional Swiss mountain community.

• *Start this quick walking tour at the...*

Cable-Car Station: When the lift came in the 1960s, the village's back end became its front door. Gimmelwald was, and still is, a farm village. Stepping off the cable car, you see a sweet

Gimmelwald

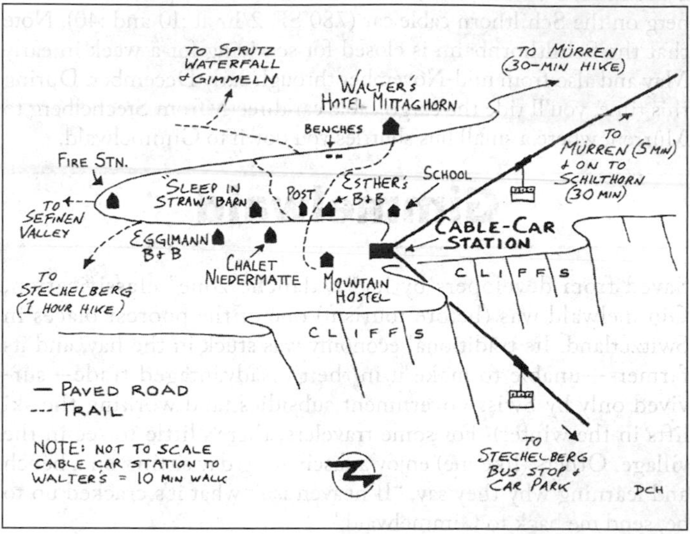

little hut. Set on stilts to keep out mice, the hut was used for storing cheese (the rocks on the rooftop keep the shingles on through wild winter winds). Behind the cheese hut stands the village schoolhouse. In Catholic Swiss towns, the biggest building is the church. In Protestant towns, it's the school. Gimmelwald's biggest building is the school (two teachers share one teaching position, 17 students, and a room that doubles as a chapel when the Protestant pastor makes his monthly visit). Don't let Gimmelwald's low-tech look fool you: In this school, each kid has his or her own website. In the opposite direction, just beyond the little playground, is Gimmelwald's Mountain Hostel (listed on page 1100).

• *Walk up the lane 50 yards, past the shower in the phone booth, to Gimmelwald's...*

"Times Square": The yellow alpine "street sign" shows where you are, the altitude (4,470 feet), and how many hours *(Std.)* and minutes it takes to walk to nearby points. Most of the buildings once housed two families and are divided vertically right down the middle. The writing on the post office building is a folksy blessing: "Summer brings green, winter brings snow. The sun greets the day, the stars greet the night. This house will keep you warm. May God give us his blessings." The date indicates when it was built or rebuilt (1911). Gimmelwald has a strict building code. For instance, shutters can only be natural, green, or white. Esther's farmer shop (10 yards uphill, always open, buy things on the honor system) is worth a look.

• *From this tiny intersection, we'll follow the town's main street (away from gondola station).*

Main Street: Walk up the road. Notice the announcement board: one side for tourist news, the other for local news. Cross the street and peek into the big new barn, dated 1995. This is part of the Sleep in Straw association, which rents out barn spots to travelers when the cows are in the high country. To the left of the door is a cow-scratcher. Swiss cows have legal rights (for example, in the winter, they must be taken out for exercise at least three times a week). This big barn is built in a modern style. Traditionally, barns were small (like those on the hillside high above) and closer to the hay. But with trucks and paved roads, hay can be moved more easily, and farm businesses need more cows to be viable. Still, even a well-run big farm hopes just to break even. The industry survives only with government subsidies.

• *Go just beyond the next barn. On your right is the...*

Water Fountain/Trough: This is the site of the town's historic water supply. Local kids love to bathe and wage water wars here when the cows aren't drinking from it. Now detour left down a lane about 50 yards (along a wooden fence and then past pea-patch gardens) to the next trough and the oldest building in town, Husmättli, from 1658. (The town's 17th-century buildings are mostly on the road zigzagging below town.) Study the log-cabin construction. Many are built without nails. The wood was logged up the valley and cut on the water-powered village mill (also below town). Gimmelwald heats with wood and, since the wood needs to age a couple of years to burn well, it's stacked everywhere.

• *Back on the paved road, continue uphill.*

Notice the cute cheese hut on the right (with alpine cheese for sale). It's full of strong cheese—up to three years old. On the left (at the B&B sign) is the home of Olle and Maria, the village schoolteachers. Maria runs the Lilliput shop (the "smallest shop with the greatest gifts"—handmade delights from the town and region, just ring the bell and meet Maria). Her son does a booming trade in sugar-coated almonds; her daughter competes with cookies.

• *Fifty yards farther along is the...*

Alpenrose: At the old schoolhouse, notice the big ceremonial cowbells hanging under the uphill eave. These swing from the necks of cows during the procession from the town to the high Alps (mid-June) and back down (about Sept 20). If the cows are gone, so are the bells—hanging from similar posts under the eaves of mountain huts in the high meadows.

• *At the end of town, notice the dramatic...*

Sefinen Valley: All the old homes in town are made from local wood cut from the left-hand side of this valley (shady side, slow-growing, better timber).

• *The road switches back at the...*

Gimmelwald Fire Station: The *Föhnwacht Reglement* sheet, posted on the fire station building, explains rules to keep the village from burning down during the fierce dry wind of the Föhn season. During this time, there's a 24-hour fire watch, and even smoking cigarettes outdoors is forbidden. Mürren was devastated by a Föhn-caused fire in the 1920s. Because villagers in Gimmelwald—mindful of the quality of their volunteer fire department—are particularly careful with fire, this is a rare village to not have had a terrible fire in its history.

Check out the other posted notices. This year's Swiss Army calendar tells reservists when and where to go. Every Swiss male does a 17-week stint in the military, then a few days a year in the reserves until about age 40. The *Schiessübungen* poster details the shooting exercises required this year. In keeping with the William Tell heritage, each Swiss man does shooting practice annually for the military (or spends three days in jail).

• *Take the...*

High Road to Hotel Mittaghorn: The resort town of Mürren hovers in the distance. And high on the left, notice the hay field with terraces. These are from WWII days, when Switzerland, wanting self-sufficiency, required all farmers to grow potatoes. Today, this is a festival of alpine flowers in season (best at this altitude in May and June).

• *Our walk is over. From Hotel Mittaghorn, you can return to Gimmelwald's "Times Square" via the stepped path.*

NIGHTLIFE

Evening fun in Gimmelwald is found at the **Mountain Hostel** (offering a pool table, Internet access, lots of young Alp-aholics, and a good chance to share information on the surrounding mountains). **Walter's bar** (in Hotel Mittaghorn) is a local farmers' hangout. When they've made their hay, they come here to play. Although they look like what some people would call hicks, they speak some English and can be fun to get to know. Sit outside (benches just below the rails, 100 yards down the lane from Walter's) and watch the sun tuck the mountaintops into bed as the moon rises over the Jungfrau. If this isn't your idea of nightlife, stay in Interlaken.

SLEEPING

(4,593 feet, 1.25 SF = about $1, country code: 41)
Gimmelwald is my home base in the Berner Oberland. To inhale the Alps and really hold them in, you'll sleep high in Gimmelwald,

too. Poor but pleasantly stuck in the past, the village has a creaky hotel, happy hostel, a couple of B&Bs, and even a website (www.gimmelwald.ch). The only bad news is that the lift costs 7.80 SF each way to get here.

$$ Maria and Olle Eggimann rent two rooms—Gimmelwald's most comfortable—in their quirky but alpine-sleek chalet. Maria and Olle, who job-share the village's only teaching position and raise three kids of their own, offer visitors a rare and intimate peek at this community (D-120 SF, Db with kitchenette-180 SF for 2 or 3 people, optional breakfast-20 SF, cash only, guarantee your reservation in advance with a check or wire transfer equal to half the cost of your stay, last check-in 19:30, 3-night minimum; from gondola continue straight for 200 yards along the town's only road, B&B on left; tel. 033-855-3575, oeggimann@bluewin.ch).

$$ Esther's B&B, overlooking the main intersection of the village, is like an upscale mini-hostel, with five clean, basic, and comfortable rooms sharing two bathrooms and a great kitchen (S-45–60 SF, big D-95–105 SF, Db-90–100 SF, big T-130–180 SF, Q-170–200 SF, family room for up to 5, cash only, 2-night stays preferred, breakfast with homemade bread-15 SF, non-smoking, tel. 033-855-5488, fax 033-855-5492, www.esthersguesthouse.ch, info@esthersguesthouse.ch, some English spoken). Esther also rents two four-person **apartments** with kitchenettes in the house next door (140 SF/2 people, 190 SF/4 people; balcony suite-150 SF/2 people, 200 SF/4 peoplc; extra bed-20 SF, check website for details).

$ Hotel Mittaghorn, the treasure of Gimmelwald, is run by Walter Mittler, a perfect Swiss gentleman. Walter's hotel is a classic, creaky, alpine-style place with memorable beds (if the bed's too lumpy or short, consider putting the mattress on the floor, or wear socks and drape the blanket over your feet), and a million-dollar view of the Jungfrau Alps. The hotel has three rooms with private showers and four rooms that share a shower (1 SF/5 min). Walter is careful not to let his place get too hectic or big, and he enjoys sensitive Back Door travelers. He runs the hotel with a little help from Rosemarie, from the village. To some, Hotel Mittaghorn is a fire waiting to happen, with a kitchen that would never pass code, bumpy beds, teeny towels, and minimal plumbing, run by an eccentric old grouch. These people enjoy Mürren, Interlaken, or Wengen, and that's where they should sleep. Be warned, you'll see more of my readers than locals here, but it's a fun crowd—an extended family (Db-80 SF, 6-SF surcharge per person for 1-night stays, cash only, open April–Oct). Reserve by telephone only, then reconfirm by phone the day before your arrival (tel. 033-855-1658, www.ricksteves.com/mittaghorn). Walter usually offers his guests a hearty 15-SF dinner at 19:30 (soup, main course, and dessert, by reservation only). Hotel Mittaghorn is at the top of Gimmelwald, a five-minute climb up the steps from the village intersection.

$ Chalet Niedermatte rents an apartment just 50 yards from the cable-car station (summer: Db-75 SF, Tb-100 SF, Qb-130 SF; winter: Db-130 SF, Tb-145 SF, Qb-160 SF; kitchen, laundry, reserve by email and then reconfirm by email 2–3 days before arrival, tel. 033-855-1662, rossbollen@hotmail.com, Liesi and Mani).

$ Mountain Hostel is a beehive of activity, as clean as its guests, cheap, and friendly. Phone ahead, or, to secure one of its 50 dorm beds the same day, call after 9:30 and leave your name. The hostel has low ceilings, a self-service kitchen, a mini-grocery, a free pool table, and healthy plumbing. It's mostly a college-age crowd; families and older travelers will probably feel more comfortable elsewhere. Petra Brunner has lined the porch with flowers. This relaxed hostel survives with the help of its guests. Read the signs *(Please Clean the Kitchen),* respect Petra's rules, and leave it tidier than you found it. The place is one of those rare spots where a congenial atmosphere spontaneously combusts, and spaghetti becomes communal as it cooks (23 SF per bed in 6- to 15-bed rooms, includes sheets, showers-1 SF, no breakfast, hostel membership not required, cash only, free Internet access, laundry, 20 yards from lift station, tel. & fax 033-855-1704, www.mountainhostel.com, reserve by email at mountainhostel@tcnet.ch).

$ Schlaf im Stroh ("Sleep in Straw") offers exactly that, in an actual barn. After the cows head for higher ground in the summer, the friendly von Allmen family hoses out their barn and fills it with straw and budget travelers. Blankets are free, but bring your own sheet, sleep sack, or sleeping bag. No beds, no bunks, no mattresses, no kidding. Esther fluffs up your hay each night (24 SF, 18 SF for kids ages 11–15, 10 SF for kids up to age 10, cash only, includes breakfast "barn service" and a single modern bathroom and showers, open late June–mid-Oct depending on grass and snow levels, almost never full, possible manure pile outside barn door; from lift, continue straight through intersection to big modern barn marked 1995 on the right; same contact info as Esther's B&B, above).

EATING

There are no restaurants in town, but you have a few options. The Mountain Hostel has a decent members' kitchen and makes great pizzas in the evenings (non-guests welcome). Hotel Mittaghorn serves dinner only to its guests (15 SF). Consider packing in a picnic meal from the larger towns. Mürren, a 30-minute hike away, has good restaurants and a grocery. If you need a few groceries and want to skip the hike to Mürren, you can buy the essentials—

noodles, spaghetti sauce, and candy bars—at the Mountain Hostel's reception desk. Local farmers sell their produce. Esther (at the main intersection of the village) sells cheese, sausage, bread, and Gimmelwald's best yogurt—but only until the cows go up in June.

Mürren

Mürren—pleasant as an alpine resort can be—is traffic-free and filled with bakeries, cafés, souvenirs, old-timers with walking sticks, GE employees enjoying incentive trips, and Japanese tourists making movies of each other. Its chalets are prefab-rustic. With help from a panorama, train, funicular, and cable car, hiking options are endless from Mürren. Sitting on a ledge 2,000 feet above the Lauterbrunnen Valley, surrounded by a fortissimo chorus of mountains, the town has all the comforts of home (for a price) without the pretentiousness of more famous resorts.

Historic Mürren, which dates from 1384, has been overwhelmed by development. Still, it's a peaceful town. There's no full-time doctor, no police officer (they call Lauterbrunnen if there's a problem), and no resident priest or pastor. (The Protestant church—up by the TI—posts a sign showing where the region's roving pastor preaches each Sunday.) There's not even enough business to keep a bakery open full-time (Mürren's bakery is open mid-June–Sept and Dec–April)—a clear indication that this town is either lively or completely dead, depending on the season. Keep an eye open for the "Milch Express," a tiny cart that delivers fresh milk and eggs to hotels and homes throughout town.

ORIENTATION

Mürren sits high on a ledge, overlooking the Lauterbrunnen Valley. You can walk from one end of town to the other in about 10 minutes.

There are two basic ways to get to Mürren: on the panoramic train from Grütschalp (connects via cable car to Lauterbrunnen); or on the cable car from Stechelberg (in the valley), which stops at Gimmelwald, Mürren, and continues up to the Schilthorn. The train and cable-car stations (which both have lockers) are at opposite ends of town.

Tourist Information: Mürren's TI can help you find a room and give hiking advice (July–Sept daily 8:30–19:00, Thu until 20:45, less off-season, above the village, follow signs to Sportzentrum, tel. 033-856-8686, www.wengen-muerren.ch). You can change money at the TI, or even better, use the ATM by the Co-op grocery.

Mürren

1. Anfi Palace Hotel
2. Hotel Alpina & Edelweiss Cafeteria
3. Hotel/Rest. Bellevue & Launderette
4. Hotel/Rest. Jungfrau
5. Hotel/Rest. Blumental
6. Eiger Guesthouse
7. Chalet Fontana
8. Chalet Helvetia
9. Chalet Böbs
10. Stägerstübli Restaurant
11. Restaurant Hotel Eiger
12. Top Apartments (Laundry)
13. Co-op Grocery
14. Päsci's Snack Bar Bistro

— Paved Road
--- Trail
Not to scale -
Cable-Car Stn.
to Train Stn. is
about 10 min. walk

Helpful Hints

R & R: The slick **Sportzentrum** (sports center) that houses the TI offers a world of indoor activities (13 SF to use pool and whirlpool; 8 SF for Gimmelwald, Lauterbrunnen, and Interlaken hotel guests; free for guests at Mürren hotels—ask your hotelier for a voucher; pool open Mon–Sat 13:00–18:45, Thu until 20:45, Sun 13:00–17:45, closed May and Nov–mid-Dec). In season, they offer squash, mini-golf, table tennis, and a fitness room.

Internet Access: Connect at the **TI** (see above) or **Eiger Guesthouse** (see "Sleeping," below, daily 8:00–23:00, across from train station, tel. 033-856-5460).

Bike Rental: You can rent mountain bikes at **Stäger Sport** (bikes with helmets-25 SF/half-day, 35 SF/day, daily 9:00–17:00, closed late Oct–mid-May, in TI/Sportzentrum, tel. 033-855-2355, www.staegersport.ch). Use caution on rough stretches.

Laundry: Hotel Bellevue has a self-service launderette in its basement (5 SF/wash, 5 SF/dry, daily 7:00–22:00). **Top Apartments** will do your laundry by request (25 SF/load, unreliable hours: Mon–Sat 9:00–11:00 & 15:00–17:00, closed Sun, behind and across from Hotel Bellevue, look for blue triangle, call first to drop off in morning, tel. 033-855-3706).

SELF-GUIDED WALK

Welcome to Mürren

Mürren has long been a top ski resort, but a walk across town offers a glimpse into its past. This stroll takes you through town on the main drag, from the train station (where you'll arrive if coming from Lauterbrunnen) to the cable-car station, then back up to the Allmendhubel funicular station.

• *Start at the...*

Train Station: The first trains pulled into Mürren in 1891. (A circa-1911 car is permanently parked at the Grütschalp station.) A display case inside the station shows an original car from the narrow-gauge, horse-powered line that rolled fancy visitors from here into town. The current station, built in 1964, comes with impressive engineering for heavy cargo. Look out back, where a small truck can be loaded up and driven away.

• *Wander into town along the main road.*

Stroll Under the Anfi Palace Hotel: The towering Anfi Palace Hotel was the "Grand Palace Hotel" until it burned in 1928. Its Jugendstil Hall is the finest room in Mürren. The small wooden platform on the left—looking like a suicide springboard—is the place where snow-removal trucks dump their loads over the cliff in the winter. Look back at the meadow below the station: This is a favorite grazing spot for chamois (the animals, not the rags for washing cars). Ahead, at Edelweiss Hotel, step to the far corner of the restaurant terrace for a breathtaking view stretching from the big three (Eiger, Mönch, and Jungfrau) to the lonely cattle farm in the high alp on the right. Then look down.

Next, the Haus Montana was where Kandahar ski boots were first made in 1933 (to give the necessary support to daredevils racing from the Schilthorn to the valley floor in Mürren's infamous Inferno race). Today, the still-respected Kandahar boots are made in nearby Thun.

• *Continue toward...*

Downtown Mürren: You'll pass the main intersection (where the small service road leads down to Gimmelwald) and the only grocery store in town (Co-op). The tiny fire barn (Feuerwehr) has a list showing the leaders of the volunteer force and their responsibilities. The old barn behind it on the right evokes the day, not so long ago, when the town's barns housed cows. Imagine Mürren with more cows than people.

• *Reaching the far end of Mürren, you come to the...*

Cable-Car Station: The first cable car (goes directly to Stechelberg) is for cargo, garbage, and the (reputedly) longest bungee jumping in the world. The other takes hikers and skiers up to the Schilthorn and down to Stechelberg via Gimmelwald.

• *Hiking back along the high road, you'll enter...*

Upper Mürren: You'll pass Mürren's two churches, the Allmendhubel funicular station, and the Sportzentrum (with swimming pool and TI).

• *Consider riding the...*

Mürren's Allmendhubel Funicular: A quaint-looking but surprisingly rewarding funicular (1912, renovated in 1999) carries nature-lovers from Mürren to a perch offering a Jungfrau view that (while much lower) rivals the Schilthorn. At the station, notice the 1920s bobsled. The restaurants here (full- and self-service) have awesome views.

Allmendhubel is particularly good for families: It's cheaper than the Schilthorn. The restaurant overlooks a great playground. And the entertaining children's hike—with rough and thrilling, kid-friendly alpine rides along the way—departs from here. This is also the departure point for the North Face hike and walks to Grütschalp (see "Hikes," page 1112).

SLEEPING

(5,381 feet, 1.25 SF = about $1, country code: 41)
Prices for accommodations are often higher during the ski season. Many hotels and restaurants close in spring, roughly from

Easter to early June, and any time between late September and mid-December.

$$$ Hotel Alpina is a simple, modern place with 24 comfortable rooms and a concrete feeling—a good thing, given its cliff-edge position (Sb-85 SF, Db-160 SF, Tb-200 SF, Qb-220 SF with awesome Jungfrau views and balconies, prices less off-season and without a view, family rooms, homey lounge, avoid their restaurant; exit left from train station, walk 2 min downhill; tel. 033-855-1361, fax 033-855-1049, www.muerren.ch/alpina, alpina @muerren.ch, Cecilia and her son Roger).

$$$ Hotel Bellevue has a homey lounge, solid woodsy furniture, a great view terrace, the hunter-themed Jägerstübli restaurant, and 17 great rooms at fair rates, all with balconies and views (Sb-110 SF, Db-190 SF, Internet access, tel. 033-855-1401, fax 033-855-1490, www.muerren.ch/bellevue, bellevue-crystal@bluewin .ch, Ruth and Othmar Suter).

$$$ Hotel Jungfrau offers 29 modern and comfortable rooms (with view: Sb-100–110 SF, Db-190–220 SF; no view: Sb-95–100 SF, Db-180–200 SF; elevator, near TI/Sportzentrum, tel. 033-856-6464, fax 033-856-6465, www.hoteljungfrau.ch, mail @hoteljungfrau.ch, Anne-Marie and Andres).

$$$ Hotel Blumental has 16 older but nicely furnished rooms and a fun, woodsy game/TV lounge (Sb-75–80 SF, Db-150–170 SF, 10 percent cheaper in Sept–Oct, higher prices are for July–Aug, all non-smoking rooms, attached restaurant—see listing below, tel. 033-855-1826, fax 033-855-3686, www.muerren.ch/blumental, blumental@muerren.ch, Ralph and Heidi, fourth generation in the von Allmen family).

$$ Eiger Guesthouse offers 14 good budget rooms. This is a friendly, creaky, easygoing home-away-from-home (S-60–65 SF, Sb-80–85 SF, D-100–110 SF, Db-130–140 SF, beds in 2- and 4-bunk rooms 40–45 SF, includes sheets and breakfast; closed Nov and for one month after Easter, across from train station, tel. 033-856-5460, fax 033-856-5461, www.eigerguesthouse.com, info@eigerguesthouse.com, well-run by Scotsman Alan and Swiss Véronique). The restaurant serves good, reasonably priced dinners (25 SF). Its poolroom—with public Internet access—is a popular local hangout. My Switzerland Alps TV show on DVD is available in the lobby.

$ Chalet Fontana, run by charming Englishwoman Denise Fussell, is a rare budget option in Mürren, with simple, crispy-clean, and comfortable rooms (35–45 SF per person in small doubles or triples with breakfast and shared bathrooms, price varies with size of room, 5 SF cheaper without breakfast; one apartment with kitchen and bathroom-120 SF/2 people, 150 SF/3 people; cash only, closed Nov–April, across street from Stägerstübli restaurant in town center, tel. 033-855-4385, mobile 078-642-3485, chaletfontana @muerren.ch). If no one's home, check at the Ed Abegglen shop next door (tel. 033-855-1245, off-season only).

$ Chalet Helvetia, run by Frau Hunziker, offers a homey, clean, two-bedroom apartment with bathroom, kitchen, separate entrance, and balcony from 40 SF per person (up to 4 people, no breakfast, 2-night minimum preferred, more expensive for 1-night stays, laundry service-10 SF/load; 200 yards below cable-car station on path to Gimmelwald, look for red *Zimmer* sign on right; tel. 033-855-4169, mobile 079-234-7867, chalet.helvetia@quicknet.ch).

$ Chalet Böbs, with terrific views, is the last house in Mürren on the road to Gimmelwald. Kitty and Albert, an alphorn player, rent three apartments: two that sleep four to five people (each with double bed, bunk bed, and twin bed) and one that sleeps two people (40 SF/person, 2-night minimum stay, kitchens, tel. 033-855-1463, mobile 078-633-6091, fax 033-855-4282, boebs@quicknet.ch).

EATING

Many of these restaurants are in or near my recommended hotels. Outside of summer and ski season, it can be hard to find any place that's open (ask around).

Stägerstübli is, hands down, *the* place to eat in town. It's the only real restaurant not associated with a hotel. Located in the town center, this 1902 building was once a tearoom for rich tourists, while locals were limited to the room in the back—the nicest dining area today (15–30 SF lunches and dinners, daily 11:30–22:00, Lydia). Sitting on its terrace, you know just who's out and about in town.

Päsci's Snack Bar Bistro has fun, creative, and inexpensive light meals; a good selection of salads, vegetarian dishes, coffees, teas, and pastries; and impressive views (take-out available, run by a serious chef—Päsci—and Fränzi, daily 9:00–18:00, at the Sportzentrum, overlooking the ice rink).

Hotel Blumental specializes in typical Swiss cuisine, but also has fish, international, and vegetarian dishes. Everything is homemade and fresh (daily specials 15–24 SF, fondue-19 SF, raclette-14.50 SF, pasta-15 SF, non-smoking section, tel. 033-855-1826, see "Sleeping," above).

Restaurant Hotel Jungfrau is a dressy ski lodge with a modern octagonal dining room and a fine view terrace (always a 10.50-SF salad bar, 50-SF four-course meal, 23-SF cheese fondue, veggie options, nightly from 18:30, near TI/Sportzentrum, tel. 033-856-6464, see "Sleeping," above).

The **Edelweiss self-serve cafeteria** offers lunch with the most cliff-hanging dining in town—incredible views (18.50-SF hearty salads, daily 10:30–20:30, more variety—including fondue—after 18:00, next to Hotel Alpina, see "Sleeping," above).

Restaurant Hotel Eiger is considered one of the better places in town, with a good chef, classy indoor seating, and a terrace with a view obstructed by the station (open daily, 20-SF plates, 29-SF fixed-price meal, enticing variety of 45-SF meat fondue dinners, tel. 033-856-5454). Note that this is not the same as **Eiger Guesthouse**—which also serves good, but simpler, food (see "Sleeping," above).

Hotel Bellevue is atmospheric, with three dining zones: view terrace, elegant indoor, and the Jägerstübli—a cozy, well-antlered hunters' room guaranteed to disgust vegetarians. This is your best bet for game, as they buy chamois and deer direct from local hunters (lamb or game-35 SF, cheaper options as low as 13 SF, mid-June–Oct daily 11:30–14:00 & 18:00–21:00, closed off-season, tel. 033-855-1401, see "Sleeping," above).

The **Co-op** is the only grocery store in town, with good picnic fixings and sandwiches (Mon–Fri 8:00–12:00 & 13:45–18:30, Sat until 17:00, closed Sun). Given restaurant prices, this place is a godsend for those on a tight budget.

Lauterbrunnen

Lauterbrunnen is the valley's commercial center and transportation hub. It boasts a train station (with lockers), cable car, bank, shops, and lots of hotels, and is the jumping-off point for Jungfrau and Schilthorn adventures. It's idyllic, in spite of the busy road and big buildings.

In 2006, the 114-year-old funicular between Lauterbrunnen and Grütschalp (which has a panorama train to Mürren) was closed due to shifting soil. A replacement cable car opened in January 2007.

ORIENTATION

Tourist Information: Stop by the friendly TI to check the weather forecast, use the Internet, or buy any regional train or lift tickets you need (July–Aug daily 9:00–18:00; Sept–June Mon–Fri 9:00–18:00, closed Sat–Sun; 1 block up from station, tel. 033-856-8568, www.wengen-muerren.ch).

Helpful Hints

Medical Help: Dr. Bruno Durrer is good and speaks English (tel. 033-856-2626).

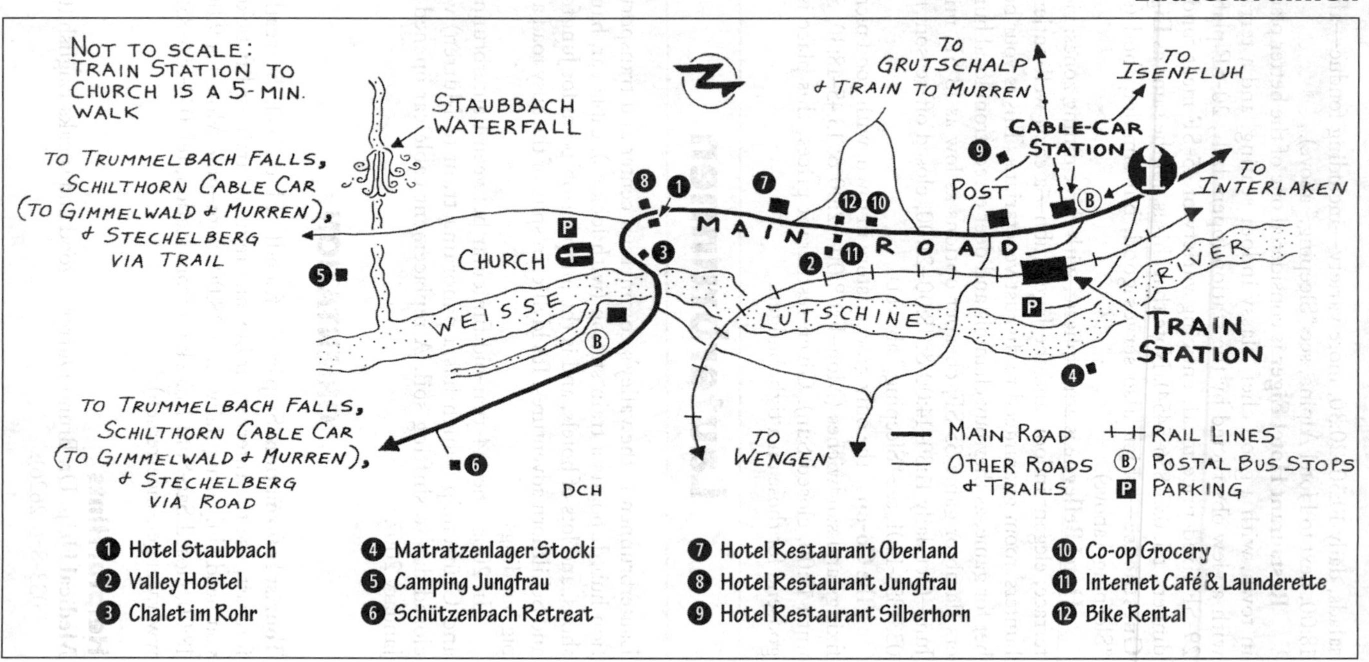
Lauterbrunnen
NOT TO SCALE: TRAIN STATION TO CHURCH IS A 5-MIN. WALK
STAUBBACH WATERFALL
TO TRUMMELBACH FALLS, SCHILTHORN CABLE CAR (TO GIMMELWALD & MURREN), & STECHELBERG VIA TRAIL
CHURCH
WEISSE
LUTSCHINE
MAIN ROAD
TO GRUTSCHALP & TRAIN TO MURREN
TO ISENFLUH
CABLE-CAR STATION
POST
TO INTERLAKEN
RIVER
TRAIN STATION
TO TRUMMELBACH FALLS, SCHILTHORN CABLE CAR (TO GIMMELWALD & MURREN), & STECHELBERG VIA ROAD
TO WENGEN
DCH
MAIN ROAD
OTHER ROADS & TRAILS
RAIL LINES
POSTAL BUS STOPS
PARKING
1 Hotel Staubbach
2 Valley Hostel
3 Chalet im Rohr
4 Matratzenlager Stocki
5 Camping Jungfrau
6 Schützenbach Retreat
7 Hotel Restaurant Oberland
8 Hotel Restaurant Jungfrau
9 Hotel Restaurant Silberhorn
10 Co-op Grocery
11 Internet Café & Launderette
12 Bike Rental

Internet and Laundry: Valley Hostel on the main street runs an Internet café and a small launderette (both daily 9:00–22:00, shorter hours Nov–April; 10 SF/load includes soap, don't open dryer door until machine is finished or you'll have to pay another 5 SF to start it again; tel. 033-855-2008).

Bike Rental: You can rent mountain bikes at **Imboden Bike** on the main street (25-SF/4 hrs, 35-SF/day; full-suspension—reserve ahead—45-SF/half-day, 65-SF/day; daily July–Aug 9:00–18:30, Sept–June 8:30–21:00, tel. 033-855-2114).

Grocery Store: The **Co-op** is on the main street (Mon–Fri 8:00–12:00 & 14:00–18:30, Sat 8:00–12:00 & 13:30–17:00, closed Sun).

SLEEPING

(2,612 feet, 1.25 SF = about $1, country code: 41)

$$ Hotel Staubbach, a big, Old World place—one of the first hotels in the valley (1890)—is being lovingly restored by hard-working American Craig and his Swiss wife, Corinne. Its 30 plain, comfortable rooms are family-friendly, there's a kids' play area, and the parking is free. Many rooms have great views (S-70 SF, Ss-80 SF, Sb-100 SF, D-90 SF, Db-120 SF, figure 50 SF/person in family rooms sleeping up to 6; 10 SF extra per room for 1-night stays, 10 SF extra for balcony rooms with valley view; elevator, 4 blocks up from station on the left, tel. 033-855-5454, fax 033-855-5484, www.staubbach.com, hotel@staubbach.com). Guests can watch a DVD of my TV show on the region in the lounge.

$ Valley Hostel is practical and comfortable, offering 70 inexpensive beds for quieter travelers of all ages, with a pleasant garden and the welcoming Abegglen family: Martha, Alfred, Stefan, and Fränzi (D with bunk beds-56 SF, twin D-64 SF, beds in larger family-friendly rooms-25 SF per person, breakfast-5 SF, most rooms have no sinks, non-smoking, kitchen available, cash only, 16-SF cheese fondue on request for guests 18:00–20:00, Wi-Fi, laundry, 2 blocks up from train station, tel. & fax 033-855-2008, www.valleyhostel.ch, info@valleyhostel.ch).

$ Chalet im Rohr—a creaky, old, woody firetrap of a place—has oodles of character (spiced with lots of Asian groups) and 50 beds in big one- to four-bed rooms that share six showers (27 SF per person, no breakfast, common kitchen, cash only, closed for 3 weeks after Easter, below church on main drag, tel. & fax 033-855-2182).

$ Matratzenlager Stocki is rustic and humble, with the cheapest beds in town (14 SF with sheets in easygoing little 30-bed co-ed dorm with kitchen, closed Nov–Dec, across river from station, tel. 033-855-1754, Frau Graf).

$ *Camping:* Two campgrounds just south of town provide 15–35-SF beds (in dorms and 2-, 4-, and 6-bed bungalows, no sheets, kitchen facilities, cash only, big English-speaking tour groups). **Mountain Holiday Park-Camping Jungfrau,** romantically situated beyond Staubbach Falls, is huge, well-organized by Hans, and also has fancy cabins (26 SF per person, tel. 033-856-2010, fax 033-856-2020, www.camping-jungfrau.ch). The park's shop, open to the public, has longer opening hours than other grocery stores in town (daily 7:30–12:00 & 16:00–20:00). **Schützenbach Retreat,** on the left just past Lauterbrunnen toward Stechelberg, is a simpler campground (tel. 033-855-1268, www.schutzenbach-retreat.ch).

EATING

At **Hotel Restaurant Oberland,** the Nolan family takes pride in serving tasty meals from a fun menu (daily 11:30–16:00 & 17:30–21:00, tel. 033-855-1241).

Hotel Restaurant Jungfrau, along the main street on the right-hand side, offers a wide range of specialties served by a friendly staff (daily 12:00–14:00 & 18:00–21:00, tel. 033-855-3434, run by Brigitte Melliger).

Hotel Restaurant Silberhorn is the local choice for a fancy meal out (fine indoor and outdoor seating, above the cable-car station, tel. 033-856-2210).

More in the Berner Oberland

SIGHTS AND ACTIVITIES

Lifts and Trains

The following lifts are both rated ▲▲▲. Doing at least one of them is an essential Berner Oberland experience.

The Schilthorn and a 10,000-Foot Breakfast

The Schilthornbahn carries skiers, hikers, and sightseers effortlessly to the 10,000-foot summit of the Schilthorn, where the Piz Gloria station awaits, with a solar-powered revolving restaurant, shop, and panorama terrace. Linger on top. Piz Gloria has a free "touristorama" film room with a multi-screen slide show and explosive highlights from the James Bond thriller that featured the Schilthorn (*On Her Majesty's Secret Service;* if it's not running, press the 007 button on the column in the middle of the room).

Watch paragliders set up, psych up, and take off, flying 45 minutes with the birds to distant Interlaken. (This is a tough launch point, but generally safe in the morning and late in the summer.) Walk along the ridge out back. This is a great place for a photo of you, the mountain climber.

When you ascend in the cable car, take a look at the altitude meter. (The Gimmelwald–Schilthorn hike is free, if you don't mind a 5,000-foot altitude gain.) Ask at the Schilthorn station for a cable-car souvenir decal (Schilthornbahn station in Stechelberg, tel. 033-856-2141). For another cheap thrill, ask the cable-car attendant to crank down the window (easiest on the Mürren–Birg section). Then stick your head out the window...and you're hang gliding.

You can ride up to the Schilthorn and hike down, but it's tough. For information on **hikes** from lift stations along the Schilthorn cable-car line, see "Hikes," page 1112. My favorite "hike" from the Schilthorn is simply along the ridge out back, to get away from the station and be all alone on top of an Alp.

Youth hostelers—not realizing that rocks may hide just under the snow—scream down the ice fields on plastic-bag sleds from the Schilthorn mountaintop. (There's an English-speaking doctor in Lauterbrunnen.)

Cost, Hours, Information: The early-bird and afternoon-special cable-car tickets (61 SF round-trip before 9:00 or after 15:30) take you from Gimmelwald to the Schilthorn and back at a discount (normal rate: 81 SF, or 96 SF from the Stechelberg car park; parking-2 SF/2 hrs, 6 SF/day). These same discounted fares are available all day long in the shoulder season (roughly May and Oct). Eurailpass and Swiss railpass holders—who get a 50 percent discount (a better deal than the early/late specials)—might as well go whenever they like, because there's no double discount. Lifts go twice hourly, and the ride (including two transfers) to the Schilthorn takes 30 minutes. For more information, including current weather conditions, see www.schilthorn.ch or call 033-826-0007.

Breakfast at 10,000 Feet: There's no à la carte—only a small breakfast for 15 SF (rolls and hot chocolate or coffee) or the James Bond breakfast for 22.50 SF (add egg, ham, and champagne; breakfast served 8:00–11:00). If you're going for breakfast before 9:00, consider an early-bird-plus-breakfast combo-ticket to save a few francs (round-trip from Gimmelwald: 74 SF with small breakfast/81 SF for James Bond breakfast; from Stechelberg: 85/92 SF). Ask for more hot drinks if necessary. If you're not revolving, ask them to turn on the mechanism.

Jungfraujoch

The literal high point of any trip to the Swiss Alps is a train ride through the Eiger to the Jungfraujoch. At 11,300 feet, it's Europe's highest train station. The ride from Kleine Scheidegg takes about an hour (sit on right side for better views), including two five-minute stops at stations actually halfway up the notorious North Face of the Eiger. You have time to look out windows and marvel at how people could climb the Eiger—and how the Swiss built this train more than a hundred years ago. The second half of the ride takes you through a tunnel inside the Eiger (some newer train cars run multilingual videos about the history of the train line).

Once you reach the top, study the Jungfraujoch chart to see your options (many of them are weather-dependent). There's a restaurant, history exhibit, ice palace (a cavern with a gallery of ice statues), and a 20-minute video that plays continuously. A tunnel leads outside, where you can ski (33 SF for gear and lift ticket), sled (free loaner discs with a 5 SF deposit), ride in a dog sled (8 SF, mornings only), or hike 45 minutes across the ice to Mönchsjochhütte (a mountain hut with a small restaurant). An elevator leads to the Sphinx observatory for the highest viewing point, from which you can see Aletsch Glacier—Europe's longest, at nearly 11 miles—stretch to the south. Remember that your body isn't used to such high altitudes. Signs posted at the top remind you to take it easy.

One of the best hikes in the region—from Männlichen to Kleine Scheidegg—could be combined with your trip up to the Jungfraujoch (see page 1117).

Cost, Hours, Information: The first trip of the day to Jungfraujoch is discounted; ask for a Good Morning Ticket, and return from the top by noon (Nov–April you can get Good Morning rates for the first or second train and stay after noon; train runs all year; round-trip fares to Jungfraujoch: from Kleine Scheidegg-104 SF, 80 SF for first trip of day—about 8:02; from Lauterbrunnen-154 SF, 130 SF for first trip—about 7:08; confirm times and prices, 50 percent discount for Eurailpass and Swiss railpass–holders). Pick up a leaflet on the lifts at a local TI, or call 033-828-7233 (www.jungfraubahn.ch). If it's cloudy, skip the trip; for a trilingual weather forecast from the Jungfraujoch, call 033-828-7931.

HIKES

There are days of possible hikes from Gimmelwald and Mürren. Many are a fun combination of trails, mountain trains, and cable-car rides. I've listed them based on which side of the Lauterbrunnen Valley they're on: west (the Gimmelwald/Mürren/Schilthorn side) or east (the Jungfrau side).

On the Gimmelwald (West) Side of the Lauterbrunnen Valley

Hikes from the Schilthorn

While several tough trails lead down from the Schilthorn, most visitors take the cable car round-trip simply for the views (see "Lifts and Trains," above). But if you're a serious hiker, consider walking all the way down (first hike) or part of the way down (second hike) back into Gimmelwald. Don't attempt to hike down from the Schilthorn unless the trail is clear of snow. Adequate shoes and clothing (weather can change quickly) and good knees are required. You can also visit the Sprutz Waterfall on your way to Gimmelwald.

From the Top of the Schilthorn—To hike downhill from the Piz Gloria revolving restaurant at the peak, start at the steps to the right of the cable, which lead along a ridge between a cliff and the bowl. As you pass huge rocks and shale fields, keep an eye out for the painted rocks that mark the scant trail. Eventually, you'll hit the service road (a ski run in the winter), which is steep and not very pleasant. Passing a memorial to a woman killed by lightning in 1865, you come to the small lake called Grauseeli. Leave the gravel road and hike along the lake. From there, follow the trail (with the help of cables when necessary) to scamper along the shale in the direction of Rotstockhütte (to Gimmelwald, see next hike) or Schilttal (the valley leading directly to Mürren; follow *Mürren/Rotstockhütte* sign painted on the rock at the junction).

▲▲Birg to Gimmelwald via Brünli—Rather than the very long hike all the way back down into Gimmelwald, I prefer the easier (but still strenuous) hike from the intermediate cable-car station at Birg. This is efficiently combined with a visit to the Schilthorn (from Schilthorn summit, ride cable car halfway down, get off at Birg, and hike down from there; buy the round-trip excursion early-bird fare—which is cheaper than the Gimmelwald–Schilthorn–Birg ticket—and decide at Birg if you want to hike or ride down).

The most interesting trail from Birg to Gimmelwald is the high one via Grauseeli Lake and Wasenegg Ridge to Brünli, then down to Spielbodenalp and the Sprutz waterfall. Warning: This trail is quite steep and slippery in places, and can take four hours. Locals take their kindergartners on this hike, but it can seem dangerous to Americans unused to alpine hikes. Do not attempt this hike in snow—which you might find at this altitude, even in the peak of summer. (Get local advice.)

From the Birg lift, hike toward the Schilthorn, taking your first left down and passing along the left side of the little Grauseeli lake. From the lake, a gravelly trail leads down rough switchbacks (including a stretch where the path narrows and you can hang onto a guide cable against the cliff face) until it levels out. When you see

Gimmelwald Area Hikes

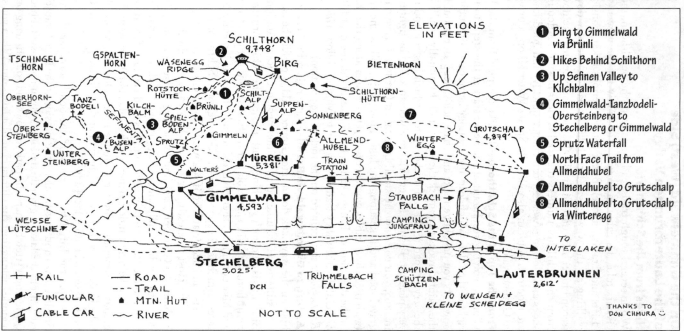

1. Birg to Gimmelwald via Brünli
2. Hikes Behind Schilthorn
3. Up Sefinen Valley to Kilchbalm
4. Gimmelwald-Tanzbodeli-Obersteinberg to Stechelberg or Gimmelwald
5. Sprutz Waterfall
6. North Face Trail from Allmendhubel
7. Allmendhubel to Grutschalp
8. Allmendhubel to Grutschalp via Winteregg

a rock painted with arrows pointing to Mürren and Rotstockhütte, follow the path to Rotstockhütte (traditional old farm with light meals and drinks, mattress loft with cheap beds), traversing the cow-grazed mountainside.

For a thrill, follow Wasenegg Ridge. It's more scary than dangerous if you're sure-footed and can handle the 50-foot-long "tightrope" section along an extremely narrow ledge with a thousand-foot drop. This trail gets you to Brünli with the least altitude drop. (The safer, well-signposted approach to Brünli is to drop down to Rotstockhütte, then climb back up to Brünli.) The barbed-wire fence leads to the knobby little summit, where you'll enjoy an incredible 360-degree view and a chance to sign your name on the register stored in the little wooden box.

A steep trail winds directly down from Brünli toward Gimmelwald and soon hits a bigger, easy trail. The trail bends right (just before the farm/restaurant at Spielbodenalp), leading to Sprutz. Walk under the Sprutz waterfall, then follow a steep, wooded trail that deposits you in a meadow of flowers at the top side of Gimmelwald.

Hikes from Gimmelwald

▲Up Sefinen Valley to Kilchbalm—An easy trail from Gimmelwald is up the Sefinen Valley (Sefinental). This is a good rainy-weather hike, as you can go as far as you like. After two hours and a gain of only 800 feet, you hit the end of the trail and Kilchbalm, a dramatic bowl of glacier fields. Note that snow can make this trail unsafe, even into the summer (ask locally for information), and there's no food or drink along the way.

From the Gimmelwald fire station, walk about 100 yards down the paved Stechelberg road. Leave it on the dirt Sefinental road, which becomes a lane, then a trail. You'll cross a raging river and pass a firing range where locals practice their marksmanship (Fri and Sat evenings; the *danger of fire* sign refers to live bullets). Follow signs to Kilchbalm into a forest, along a river, and finally to the glacier fields.

▲Gimmelwald–Tanzbodeli–Obersteinberg–Stechelberg/Gimmelwald—This eight-hour, 11-mile hike is extremely rewarding, offering perfect peace, very few people, traditional alpine culture, and spectacular views. (There's no food or drink for five hours, so pack accordingly.) As the trail can be a bit confusing, this is best done with a good map (buy locally).

About 100 yards below the Gimmelwald firehouse, take the Sefinental dirt road (described above). As the dirt road switches back after about 30 minutes, take the right turn across the river and start your ascent, following signs to Obersteinberg. After 90 minutes of hard climbing, you have the option of a side-trip to

Busenalp. This is fun if the goat and cow herder is there, as you can watch the traditional cheesemaking in action. (He appreciates a bottle of wine from hikers.) Trail markers are painted onto rocks—watch carefully. After visiting Busenalp, return to the main path.

At the *Obersteinberg 50 min/Tanzbodeli 20 min* signpost, head for Tanzbodeli ("Dancing Floor"). This is everyone's favorite alpine perch—great for a little romance, or a picnic with breathtaking views of the Obersteinberg valley. From here, you enter a natural reserve, so you're likely to see chamois and other alpine critters. From Tanzbodeli, you return to the main trail (there's no other way out) and continue to Obersteinberg. You'll eventually hit the Mountain Hotel Obersteinberg (see "Sleeping," page 1122; American expat Vickie will serve you a meal or drink).

From there, the trail leads to Hotel Tschingelhorn and back to Gimmelwald (2 hours total) or Stechelberg (bottom of Schilthorn cable car, 90 min total). About an hour later, you hit a fork in the trail and choose where you'd like your hike to end.

▲Sprutz Waterfall—The forest above Gimmelwald hides a powerful waterfall with a trail snaking behind it, offering a fun gorge experience. While the waterfall itself is not well-signed, it's on the Gimmelwald–Spielbodenalp trail. It's steep, through a forest, and can be very slippery when wet, but the actual crossing under the waterfall is just misty.

The hike up to Sprutz from Gimmelwald isn't worth the trip in itself, but it's handy when combined with the hike down from Birg and Brünli (see above) or the North Face Trail (see below). As you descend on either of these two hikes, the trail down to Gimmelwald splits at Spielbodenalp—to the right for the forest and the waterfall; to the left for more meadows, the hamlet of Gimmeln, and more gracefully back into Gimmelwald.

Hikes from Mürren/Allmendhubel

▲▲North Face Trail from Allmendhubel—For a pleasant, mainly downhill, two-hour hike (4 miles, from 6,385 feet to 5,375 feet), ride the Allmendhubel funicular up from Mürren (7.40 SF, much cheaper than Schilthorn, good restaurant at top). From there, follow the well-signed route circling around to Mürren (or cut off at Spielbodenalp, near the end, and descend into Gimmelwald via the Sprutz Waterfall). Just follow the blue signs. You'll enjoy great views, flowery meadows, mountain huts, and a dozen information boards along the way, describing the fascinating climbing history of the great peaks around you.

Along the trail, you'll pass four farms (technically "alps," as they are only open in the summer) that serve meals and drinks. Sonnenberg was allowed to break the all-wood code with concrete for protection against avalanches. Suppenalp is quainter. Lean against the house with a salad, soup, or sandwich and enjoy the view.

Notice how older huts are built into the protected side of rocks and outcroppings, in anticipation of avalanches. Above Suppenalp, Blumental ("Flower Valley") is hopping with marmots. Because hunters are not allowed near lifts, animals have learned that these are safe places to hang out—giving tourists a better chance of spotting them.

The trail leads up and over to a group of huts called Schiltalp. If the poles under the eve have bells, the cows are up. If not, the cows are still at the lower farm. Half the cows in Gimmelwald (about 100) spend their summers here. In July, August, and September, you can watch cheese being made and have a snack or drink. Thirty years ago, each family had its own hut. Labor was cheap and available. Today, it's a communal thing, with several families sharing the expense of a single cow herder. Cow herders are master cheesemakers, and have veterinary skills, too.

From Schiltalp, the trail winds gracefully down to Spielbodenalp—a farm with lots going on (open May–mid-Oct Fri–Wed, closed Thu, good menu, 31-SF dorm beds with breakfast). From there, you can finish the North Face trail (continuing down and left through meadows and the hamlet of Gimmeln, then back to Mürren, with more historic signposts); or cut off right (descending steeply through a thick forest and under the dramatic Sprutz Waterfall into Gimmelwald).

▲Allmendhubel/Mürren to Grütschalp—For a not-too-tough, two-hour walk with great Jungfrau views, ride the funicular from Mürren to Allmendhubel (6,344 feet) and walk to Grütschalp (a drop of about 1,500 feet), where you can catch the panorama train back to Mürren. An easier version is the lower Bergweg from Allmendhubel to Grütschalp via Winteregg and its cheese farm. For a super-easy family stroll with grand views, walk from Mürren just above the train tracks to either Winteregg (40 min, restaurant, playground, train station) or Grütschalp (60 min, train station), then catch the panorama train back to Mürren.

Hikes on the Jungfrau (East) Side of the Lauterbrunnen Valley

▲▲▲The Männlichen–Kleine Scheidegg Hike—This is my favorite easy alpine hike (2.5 miles, 1.5 hours, 900-foot altitude drop to Kleine Scheidegg). It's entertaining all the way, with glorious Jungfrau, Eiger, and Mönch views. That's the Young Maiden being protected from the Ogre by the Monk. (These days, that could be problematic.) Trails may be snowbound into June; ask about conditions at the lift stations or local TIs. If the Männlichen lift is closed, you can take the train straight from Lauterbrunnen to Kleine Scheidegg (see Jungfraujoch under "Lifts and Trains," page 1110).

If the weather's good, descend from Gimmelwald bright and early to Stechelberg. From here, get to the Lauterbrunnen train station by postal bus (3.80 SF, covered by Swiss Pass, bus is synchronized to depart with the arrival of each lift) or by car (parking at the large, multistory pay lot behind the Lauterbrunnen station-2 SF/2 hrs, 9 SF/day). At Lauterbrunnen, buy a train ticket to Männlichen (29 SF one-way). If hiking down from Männlichen to Wengen via Kleine Scheidegg (the complete hike described in this listing), you'll buy a ticket from Lauterbrunnen to Männlichen, then from Wengen back to Lauterbrunnen, for 32 SF. Sit on the right side of the train for great waterfall views on your way up to Wengen. In Wengen, walk across town (buy a picnic, but don't waste time here if it's sunny—you can linger after your hike) and catch the Männlichen lift to the top of the ridge high above you (lift departs every 15 min, beginning the first week of June). Note that the lift can be open even if the trail is closed; confirm that the trail is open before ascending.

From the top of Wengen–Männlichen lift station, turn left and hike uphill 20 minutes to the little peak (Männlichen Gipfel, 7,500 feet) for that king- or queen-of-the-mountain feeling. Then take an easy hour's walk—facing spectacular alpine panorama views—to Kleine Scheidegg for a picnic or restaurant lunch. To start the hike, leave the Wengen–Männlichen lift station to the right. Walk past the second Männlichen lift station (this one leads to Grindelwald, the touristy town in the valley to your left). Ahead of you in the distance, left to right, are the north faces of the Eiger, Mönch, and Jungfrau; in the foreground is the Tschuggen peak, and just behind it, the Lauberhorn. This hike takes you around the left (east) side of this ridge. Simply follow the signs for Kleine Scheidegg, and you'll be there in about an hour—a little more for gawkers, picnickers, and photographers. You might have to tiptoe through streams of melted snow—or some small snow banks, even well into the summer—but the path is well-marked, well-maintained, and mostly level all the way to Kleine Scheidegg.

About 35 minutes into the hike, you'll reach a bunch of benches and a shelter with incredible unobstructed views of all three peaks—the perfect picnic spot. Fifteen minutes later on the left, you'll see the first sign of civilization: Restaurant Grindelwaldblick, offering a handy terrace lunch stop with tasty, hearty, and reasonable food (open daily, closed Dec and May). After 10 more minutes, you'll be at the Kleine Scheidegg train station, with plenty of other lunch options (including Bahnhof Buffet).

From Kleine Scheidegg, you can catch the train to "the top of Europe" (see Jungfraujoch information, page 1111). Or head downhill, riding the train or hiking (30 gorgeous min to Wengernalp station, a little farther to the Allmend stop; 60 more steep min from there into the town of Wengen). The alpine views might be accompanied by the valley-filling mellow sound of alphorns and distant avalanches.

If the weather turns bad or you run out of steam, catch the train at any of the stations along the way. After Wengernalp, the trail to Wengen is steep and, though not dangerous, requires a good set of knees. Wengen is a good shopping town. (For accommodations, see "Sleeping in Wengen," page 1120.) The boring final descent from Wengen to Lauterbrunnen is knee-killer steep—catch the train.

▲▲Schynige Platte to First—The best day I've had hiking in the Berner Oberland was when I made this demanding six-hour ridge walk, with Lake Brienz on one side and all that Jungfrau beauty on the other. Start at Wilderswil train station (just above Interlaken) and catch the little train up to Schynige Platte (6,560 feet). The high point is Faulhorn (8,790 feet, with its famous mountaintop hotel). Hike to a small mini-gondola called "First" (7,110 feet), then ride down to Grindelwald and catch a train back to your starting point, Wilderswil. Or, if you have a regional train pass (or no car but endless money), take the long, scenic return trip to Gimmelwald: From Grindelwald, take the lift up to Männlichen, do the hike to Kleine Scheidegg and Wengen (see above), then head down into Lauterbrunnen and on to Gimmelwald.

For a shorter (3-hour) ridge walk, consider the well-signposted Panoramaweg, a loop from Schynige Platte to Daub Peak.

The alpine flower park (4 SF, 3 SF with guest card, at the Schynige Platte station) offers a delightful stroll through several hundred alpine flowers (best in summer) including a chance to see edelweiss growing in the wild.

Lowa, a leading local manufacturer of top-end hiking boots, has a promotional booth at the Schynige Platte station providing free loaner boots to hikers who'd like to give their boots a try. They are already broken in, but bring thick socks (or buy them there).

If hiking here, be mindful of the last lifts (which can be as early as 16:30). Climbing from First (7,113 feet) to Schynige Platte (6,454 feet) gives you a later departure down and less climbing.

Mountain Biking

Mountain biking is popular and accepted, as long as you stay on the clearly marked mountain-bike paths.

A good but challenging ride is the round-trip Mürren Loop that runs from Mürren to Gimmelwald, down the Sefinen Valley to Stechelberg, along the dreamy bike path left of the river to Lauterbrunnen, up by cable car to Grütschalp (bike costs same as person-7.80 SF), and back through a working cheese farm to Mürren.

You can rent bikes in Mürren (Stäger Sport, 35 SF/day includes helmet, daily 9:00–17:00, closed late Oct–mid-May, in TI/Sportzentrum, tel. 033-855-2355, www.staegersport.ch) or in Lauterbrunnen (Imboden Bike, 25 SF/4 hrs, 35 SF/day; call ahead to reserve a full-suspension bike: 45 SF/half-day, 65 SF/day; daily July–Aug 8:30–21:00, Sept–June 9:00–18:30, tel. 033-855-2114). The Lauterbrunnen shop is often open when the Mürren one isn't. It costs 2.50 SF per segment to take a bike onto the gondola.

You can also bike the Lauterbrunnen Valley from Lauterbrunnen to Interlaken. It's a gentle downhill ride via a peaceful bike path across the river from the road (don't bike on the road). Rent a bike at Lauterbrunnen (see above), bike to Interlaken, and return to Lauterbrunnen by train (to take bike on train, pay about 4 SF extra). Or rent a bike at either Interlaken station, take the train to Lauterbrunnen, and ride back.

SLEEPING AND EATING

In addition to my listings in Interlaken, Gimmelwald, Mürren, and Lauterbrunnen, consider these nearby places.

Sleeping in Wengen

(4,180 feet, 1.25 SF = about $1, country code: 41)

Wengen—a bigger, fancier Mürren on the other side of the valley—has plenty of grand hotels, many shops, tennis courts, minigolf, and terrific views. This traffic-free resort is an easy train ride above Lauterbrunnen and halfway up to Kleine Scheidegg and Männlichen, and offers more activities for those needing distraction from the scenery. Hiking is better from Mürren and Gimmelwald. The **TI** is one block from the station; go up to the main drag, turn left, and look ahead on the left (June–Sept and Dec–mid-April daily 9:00–18:00; mid-April–May and Oct–Nov Mon–Fri 9:00–18:00, closed Sat–Sun; Internet access in lobby; tel. 033-855-1414, www.wengen-muerren.ch).

Sleeping Above the Train Station

$$$ Hotel Berghaus, in a quiet area a five-minute walk from the main street, offers 19 rooms above a fine restaurant specializing in fish (Sb-86–117 SF, Db-172–234 SF, elevator, Internet access; call on phone at station hotel board for free pickup, or walk up street across from Bernerhof Hotel, bear right and then left at fork, 200 yards more past church on the left; tel. 033-855-2151, fax 033-855-3820, www.wengen.com/hotel/berghaus, berghaus@wengen.com, Fontana family).

$$$ Hotel Schönegg, on Wengen's main drag, is a centrally located splurge, decorated with antiques and old wood (Sb-100–110 SF, Db-200–220 SF; higher July–Aug: Sb-115–125 SF, Db-230–250 SF; non-smoking rooms, all rooms have balconies and great views, cozy family room with fireplace, Internet access in lobby, good restaurant with big terrace, look for big yellow hotel on main drag near TI, tel. 033-855-3422, fax 033-855-4233, www.hotel-schoenegg.ch, mail@hotel-schoenegg.ch, Herr und Frau Berthod).

Sleeping Below the Train Station

The first two listings are bright, cheery, family-friendly, and five minutes below the station: Leave the station toward the Co-op store, turn right and go under the rail bridge, bear right (paved path) at the fork, and follow the road down and around.

$$$ Bären Hotel, run by friendly Therese and Willy Brunner, offers 14 tidy rooms with perky, bright-orange bathrooms. Their newly renovated restaurant is bright and inviting, offering garden-fresh Swiss cuisine (daily specials for 15.50 SF; Sb-80 SF, Db-150 SF, Tb-210 SF, dinner-20 SF more, family rooms, Internet access, tel. 033-855-1419, fax 033-855-1525, www.baeren-wengen.ch, info@baeren-wengen.ch).

$$ Familienhotel Edelweiss has 25 bright rooms, lots of fun public spaces, a Christian emphasis, and a jittery Chihuahua named Speedy (Sb-70–75 SF, Db-140–150 SF, non-smoking, elevator, great family rooms, TV lounge, game room, meeting room, kids' playroom, tel. 033-855-2388, fax 033-855-4288, www.edelweisswengen.ch, edelweiss@vch.ch, Bärtschi family).

$$ Clare and Andy's Chalet (Trogihalten) offers three rustic, low-ceilinged rooms (1-room studio: Sb-56 SF, Db-90 SF; 2-room suite: Sb/Db-106 SF, Tb-145 SF, Qb-188 SF; 4-room flat: Tb-159 SF, Qb-192 SF, 6-bed apartment-294 SF; breakfast-15 SF, dinner by request-35 SF, 4-night minimum preferred, prices higher for shorter stays, cash only, all rooms with balconies; leave station to the left and follow paved path next to Bernerhof Hotel downhill, steep 5-min hike; tel. & fax 033-855-1712, mobile 079-423-7813, www.chaletwengen.ch, info@chaletwengen.ch, Clare is English, Andy is Swiss).

$ Backpackers' Old Lodge is centrally located and offers cheap beds (25 SF per bed with sheets in a 6-bed dorm; S-45 SF, D-90 SF, T-105 SF, Q-140, optional breakfast-7 SF, kitchens available; walk from station toward the Co-op store, before rail bridge turn left; tel. 033-855-1573, mobile 078-745-5850, www.oldlodge.ch, info@oldlodge.ch, Angela).

Sleeping and Eating at Kleine Scheidegg

(6,762 feet, 1.25 SF = about $1, country code: 41)

Confirm price and availability before ascending. Both places serve meals.

$$ Restaurant Bahnhof invites you to sleep face-to-face with the Eiger (dorm bed-51 SF with breakfast, 69 SF includes dinner as well, D-167 SF with breakfast and dinner; in the train station building, tel. 033-828-7828, fax 033-828-7830, www.roestizza.ch, info@bahnhof-scheidegg.ch).

$ Restaurant Grindelwaldblick, a 10-minute hike from the train station, really gets you up into the mountains (38 SF per bed in 12-bed room, includes sheets, closed Nov and May, tel. 033-855-1374, fax 033-855-4205, www.grindelwaldblick.ch).

Sleeping in Stechelberg

(3,025 feet, 1.25 SF = about $1, country code: 41)

Stechelberg is the hamlet at the end of Lauterbrunnen Valley, at the base of the lift to Gimmelwald, Mürren, and the Schilthorn.

$$ Hotel Stechelberg, at road's end, is surrounded by waterfalls and vertical rock, with a garden terrace and 20 quiet rooms—half in a creaky old building, half in a concrete, no-character newer building (D-86–104 SF, Db-130, Db with balcony-158 SF, T-147 SF, Tb-186 SF, Q-176 SF, Qb-234 SF, postal bus stops here, tel. 033-855-2921, fax 033-855-4438, www.hotel-stechelberg.ch, hotel@stechelberg.ch).

Sleeping in Obersteinberg

(5,900 feet, 1.25 SF = about $1, country code: 41)

$$ Here's a wild idea: **Mountain Hotel Obersteinberg** is a working alpine farm with cheese, cows, a mule shuttling up food once a day, and an American (Vickie) who fell in love with a mountain man. It's a 2.5-hour hike from either Stechelberg or Gimmelwald. They rent 12 primitive rooms and a bunch of loft beds. There's no shower, no hot water, and only meager solar-panel electricity. Candles light up the night, and you can take a hot-water bottle to bed if necessary (S-83 SF, D-166 SF, includes linen, sheetless dorm beds-66 SF, these prices include breakfast and dinner, without meals S-37 SF, D-74 SF, dorm beds-20 SF, closed Oct–May, tel. 033-855-2033). The place is filled with locals and Germans on weekends, but it's all yours on weekdays. Why not hike there from Gimmelwald and leave the Alps a day later?

Sleeping in Isenfluh

(3,560 feet, 1.25 SF = about $1, country code: 41)

The yellow postal bus takes you up on a spectacular road, through a long and narrow tunnel to the tiny hamlet of Isenfluh, which is even smaller than Gimmelwald and offers better views (3.80 SF one-way; from Lauterbrunnen train station: almost hourly at :50, from Interlaken: 4 buses/day; some buses require reservations—especially the first or last ride of the day, tel. 079-788-5120).

$$ Hotel Restaurant Waldrand has a decent restaurant (including great fresh salads) and four reasonable rooms (Db-140–160 SF, Tb-190 SF, cash only, includes breakfast, tel. 033-855-1227, fax 033-855-1392, www.hotel-waldrand.ch, info@hotel-waldrand.ch, Vreni and Urs Werthmüller).

APPENDIX

US Embassies and Consulates

Austria: US Embassy, Boltzmanngasse 16, Vienna, tel. 01/313-390; consular services at Parkring 12, tel. 01/313-397-535, www.usembassy.at

Belgium: US Embassy, Regentlaan 27 Boulevard du Régent, Brussels, tel. 02/508-2111, www.usembassy.be

Czech Republic: US Embassy, Tržiště 15, in the Little Quarter below the castle, Prague, tel. 257-022-000, www.usembassy.cz

France: US Embassy, 2 avenue Gabriel, to the left as you face Hôtel Crillon, Paris, Mo: Concorde, tel. 01 43 12 22 22; US Consulate, 2 rue St. Florentin, Paris, Mo: Concorde, tel. 01 43 12 22 22, www.amb-usa.fr

Germany: US Embassy, Neustädtische Kirchstrasse 4–5, Berlin, tel. 030/83050; consular services at Clayallee 170, tel. 030/832-9233, www.usembassy.de, consberlin@state.gov

Great Britain: US Embassy, 24 Grosvenor Square, Tube: Bond Street, London, tel. 020/7499-9000, www.usembassy.org.uk (also see Scotland, below)

Italy: US Embassy at Via Vittorio Veneto 119/A, Rome, tel. 06-46741, www.usembassy.it; US Consulate, Lungarno Vespucci 38, Florence, tel. 055-266-951, http://florence.usconsulate.gov/english

The Netherlands: US Embassy, Lange Voorhout 102, The Hague, tel. 070/310-2209, http://netherlands.usembassy.gov; US Consulate, Museumplein 19, Amsterdam, tel. 020/575-5309

Scotland: US Consulate, 3 Regent Terrace, Edinburgh, tel. 0131/556-8315, emergency tel. 0122/485-7097, www.usembassy.org.uk/scotland

Spain: US Embassy, Calle Serrano 75, Madrid, tel. 915-872-240, emergency tel. 915-872-200, www.embusa.es/cons/services.html

European Calling Chart

Just smile and dial, using this key:
AC = Area Code, LN = Local Number.

European Country	Calling long distance within...	Calling from the US or Canada to...	Calling from a European country to...
Austria	AC + LN	011 + 43 + AC (without the initial zero) + LN	00 + 43 + AC (without the initial zero) + LN
Belgium	LN	011 + 32 + LN (without initial zero)	00 + 32 + LN (without initial zero)
Bosnia-Herzegovina	AC + LN	011 + 387 + AC (without initial zero) + LN	00 + 387 + AC (without initial zero) + LN
Britain	AC + LN	011 + 44 + AC (without initial zero) + LN	00 + 44 + AC (without initial zero) + LN
Croatia	AC + LN	011 + 385 + AC (without initial zero) + LN	00 + 385 + AC (without initial zero) + LN
Czech Republic	LN	011 + 420 + LN	00 + 420 + LN
Denmark	LN	011 + 45 + LN	00 + 45 + LN
Estonia	LN	011 + 372 + LN	00 + 372 + LN
Finland	AC + LN	011 + 358 + AC (without initial zero) + LN	999 + 358 + AC (without initial zero) + LN
France	LN	011 + 33 + LN (without initial zero)	00 + 33 + LN (without initial zero)
Germany	AC + LN	011 + 49 + AC (without initial zero) + LN	00 + 49 + AC (without initial zero) + LN
Greece	LN	011 + 30 + LN	00 + 30 + LN
Hungary	06 + AC + LN	011 + 36 + AC + LN	00 + 36 + AC + LN
Ireland	AC + LN	011 + 353 + AC (without initial zero) + LN	00 + 353 + AC (without initial zero) + LN

European Country	Calling long distance within...	Calling from the US or Canada to...	Calling from a European country to...
Italy	LN	011 + 39 + LN	00 + 39 + LN
Montenegro	AC + LN	011 + 382 + AC (without initial zero) + LN	00 + 382 + AC (without initial zero) + LN
Netherlands	AC + LN	011 + 31 + AC (without initial zero) + LN	00 + 31 + AC (without initial zero) + LN
Norway	LN	011 + 47 + LN	00 + 47 + LN
Poland	LN	011 + 48 + LN (without initial zero)	00 + 48 + LN (without initial zero)
Portugal	LN	011 + 351 + LN	00 + 351 + LN
Slovakia	AC + LN	011 + 421 + AC (without initial zero) + LN	00 + 421 + AC (without initial zero) + LN
Slovenia	AC + LN	011 + 386 + AC (without initial zero) + LN	00 + 386 + AC (without initial zero) + LN
Spain	LN	011 + 34 + LN	00 + 34 + LN
Sweden	AC + LN	011 + 46 + AC (without initial zero) + LN	00 + 46 + AC (without initial zero) + LN
Switzerland	LN	011 + 41 + LN (without initial zero)	00 + 41 + LN (without initial zero)
Turkey	AC (if no initial zero is included, add one) + LN	011 + 90 + AC (without initial zero) + LN	00 + 90 + AC (without initial zero) + LN

- The instructions above apply whether you're calling a land line or mobile phone.
- The international access codes (the first numbers you dial when making an international call) are 011 if you're calling from the US or Canada, or 00 if you're calling from virtually anywhere in Europe (except Finland, where it's 999).
- To call the US or Canada from Europe, dial 00, then 1 (the country code for the US and Canada), then the area code and number. In short, 00 + 1 + AC + LN = Hi, Mom!

Switzerland: US Embassy, Jubilaeumsstrasse 93, Bern, tel. 031-357-7234, http://bern.usembassy.gov

Let's Talk Telephones

To make international calls, you need to break the codes: the international access codes and country codes (see below). For information on making local, long-distance, and international calls, see "Telephones" in this book's Introduction.

Country Codes

After you've dialed the international access code (011 if you're calling from the US or Canada; 00 if you're calling from Europe), dial the code of the country you're calling.

Austria—43
Belgium—32
Britain—44
Canada—1
Croatia—385
Czech Rep.—420
Denmark—45
Estonia—372
Finland—358
France—33
Germany—49
Gibraltar—350
Greece—30
Hungary—36
Ireland—353
Italy—39
Morocco—212
Netherlands—31
Norway—47
Poland—48
Portugal—351
Slovakia—421
Slovenia—386
Spain—34
Sweden—46
Switzerland—41
Turkey—90
US—1

Numbers and Stumblers

- Europeans write a few of their numbers differently than we do: 1 = 1, 4 = 4, 7 = 7. Learn the difference or miss your train.
- Europeans write dates as day/month/year (Christmas is 25/12/08).
- Except in Great Britain, commas are decimal points, and decimals are commas. A dollar and a half is 1,50. There are 5.280 feet in a mile.
- When counting with fingers, start with your thumb. If you hold up your first finger to request one item, you'll probably get two.
- What we Americans call the second floor of a building is the first floor in Europe.
- Europeans keep the left "lane" open for passing on escalators and moving sidewalks. Keep to the right.

Metric Conversion (approximate)

1 inch = 25 millimeters
1 foot = 0.3 meter
1 yard = 0.9 meter
1 mile = 1.6 kilometers
1 centimeter = 0.4 inch
1 meter = 39.4 inches
1 kilometer = 0.62 mile
32 degrees F = 0 degrees C
82 degrees F = about 28 degrees C
1 ounce = 28 grams
1 kilogram = 2.2 pounds
1 quart = 0.95 liter
1 square yard = 0.8 square meter
1 acre = 0.4 hectare

Temperature Conversion: Fahrenheit and Celsius

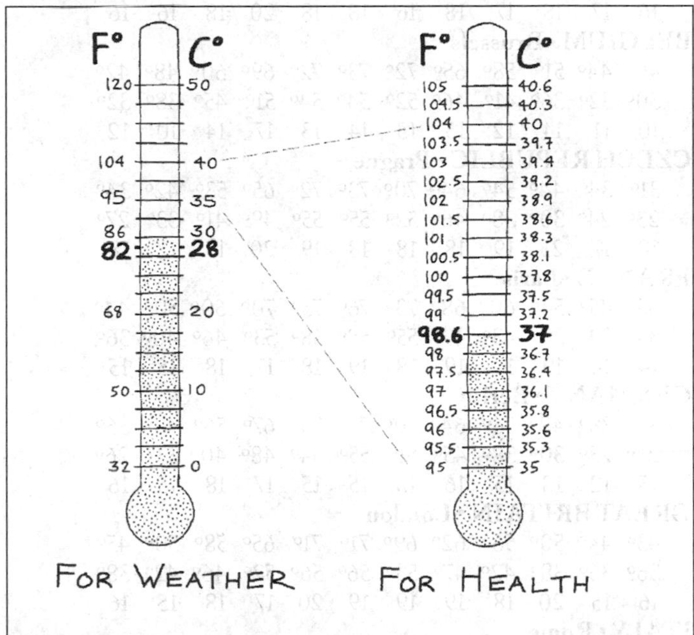

Europe takes its temperature using the Celsius scale, while we opt for Fahrenheit. For weather, remember that 28°C is 82°F—perfect. For health, 37°C is just right.

Climate

Here is a list of average temperatures (first line—average daily high; second line—average daily low; third line—days of no rain). This can be helpful in planning your itinerary, but I have never found European weather to be particularly predictable, and these charts ignore humidity.

	J	F	M	A	M	J	J	A	S	O	N	D
AUSTRIA • Vienna												
	34°	38°	47°	58°	67°	73°	76°	75°	68°	56°	45°	37°
	25°	28°	30°	42°	50°	56°	60°	59°	53°	44°	37°	30°
	16	17	18	17	18	16	18	18	20	18	16	16
BELGIUM • Brussels												
	40°	44°	51°	58°	65°	72°	73°	72°	69°	60°	48°	42°
	30°	32°	36°	41°	46°	52°	54°	54°	51°	45°	38°	32°
	10	11	14	12	15	15	14	13	17	14	10	12
CZECH REPUBLIC • Prague												
	31°	34°	44°	54°	64°	70°	73°	72°	65°	53°	42°	34°
	23°	24°	30°	38°	46°	52°	55°	55°	49°	41°	33°	27°
	18	17	21	19	18	18	18	19	20	18	18	18
FRANCE • Paris												
	43°	45°	54°	60°	68°	73°	76°	75°	70°	60°	50°	44°
	34°	34°	39°	43°	49°	55°	58°	58°	53°	46°	40°	36°
	14	14	19	17	19	18	19	18	17	18	15	15
GERMANY • Berlin												
	35°	38°	48°	56°	64°	70°	74°	73°	67°	56°	44°	36°
	23°	23°	30°	38°	45°	51°	55°	54°	48°	40°	33°	26°
	15	12	18	15	16	13	15	15	17	18	15	16
GREAT BRITAIN • London												
	43°	44°	50°	56°	62°	69°	71°	71°	65°	58°	50°	45°
	36°	36°	38°	42°	47°	53°	56°	56°	52°	46°	42°	38°
	16	15	20	18	19	19	19	20	17	18	15	16
ITALY • Rome												
	52°	55°	59°	66°	74°	82°	87°	86°	79°	71°	61°	55°
	40°	42°	45°	50°	56°	63°	67°	67°	62°	55°	49°	44°
	13	19	23	24	26	26	30	29	25	23	19	21
NETHERLANDS • Amsterdam												
	40°	42°	49°	56°	64°	70°	72°	71°	67°	57°	48°	42°
	31°	31°	34°	40°	46°	51°	55°	55°	50°	44°	38°	33°
	9	9	15	14	17	16	14	13	11	11	9	10
SPAIN • Madrid												
	47°	52°	59°	65°	70°	80°	87°	85°	77°	65°	55°	48°
	35°	36°	41°	45°	50°	58°	63°	63°	57°	49°	42°	36°
	23	21	21	21	21	25	29	28	24	23	21	21
SWITZERLAND • Bern												
	38°	42°	51°	59°	66°	73°	77°	76°	69°	58°	47°	40°
	29°	30°	36°	42°	49°	55°	58°	58°	53°	44°	37°	31°
	20	19	22	21	20	19	22	20	20	21	19	21

Hotel Reservation

To: ______________________ ______________________
hotel *email or fax*

From: ______________________ ______________________
name *email or fax*

Today's date: ____ / ____ / ____
day *month* *year*

Dear Hotel ______________________,
Please make this reservation for me:

Name: ______________________

Total # of people: ____ # of rooms: ____ # of nights: ____

Arriving: ____ / ____ / ____ My time of arrival (24-hr clock): ____
day *month* *year* (I will telephone if I will be late)

Departing: ____ / ____ / ____
day *month* *year*

Room(s): Single ___ Double ___ Twin ___ Triple ___ Quad ___

With: Toilet ___ Shower ___ Bath ___ Sink only ___

Special needs: View ___ Quiet ___ Cheapest ___ Ground Floor ___

Please email or fax confirmation of my reservation, along with the type of room reserved and the price. Please also inform me of your cancellation policy. After I hear from you, I will quickly send my credit-card information as a deposit to hold the room. Thank you.

____
Name

____
Address

____
City **State** **Zip Code** **Country**

Before hoteliers can make your reservation, they want to know the information listed above. You can use this form as the basis for your email, or you can photocopy this page, fill in the information, and send it as a fax (also available online at www.ricksteves.com/reservation).

INDEX

Travel smart...carry on!

The latest generation of Rick Steves' carry-on travel bags is easily the best—benefiting from two decades of on-the-road attention to what really matters: maximum quality and strength; practical, flexible features; and no unnecessary frills. You won't find a better value anywhere!

Rick Steves' Convertible Carry-On $99.95

Our roomy, versatile 9" x 21" x 14" carry-on has a large 2600 cubic-inch main compartment, plus four outside pockets (small, medium and huge) that are perfect for often-used items. Wish you had even more room to bring home souvenirs? Pull open the full-perimeter expando-zipper and its capacity jumps from 2600 to 3000 cubic inches. When you want to use it as a suitcase or check it as luggage (required when "expanded"), the straps and belt hide away in a zippered compartment in the back. It weighs just 3 lbs.

Rick Steves' Classic Back Door Bag $79.95

This ultra-light (1½ lbs.) version of our Convertible Carry-On features the same 9" x 21" x 14" dimensions and hideaway straps, but does not include a waistbelt or expandability. This is the bag that Rick lives out of for three months a year!

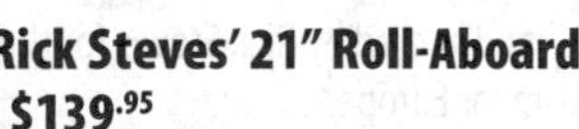

Rick Steves' 21" Roll-Aboard $139.95

Our sturdy 21" Roll-Aboard is rucksack-soft in front, but the rest is lined with a hard ABS-lexan shell to give maximum protection to your belongings. We've spared no expense on moving parts, splurging on an extra-long button-release handle and big, tough inline skate wheels for easy rolling on rough surfaces. It features the same 9" x 21" x 14" carry-on dimensions, pocket configuration and expandability as our Convertible Carry-On—and at 7 lbs. it's the lightest roll-aboard in its class.

Prices and features are subject to change.

For great deals on a wide selection of travel goodies, begin your next trip at the Rick Steves Travel Store!

Visit the Rick Steves Travel Store at
www.ricksteves.com

As the #1 authority on European travel, Rick gives you inside information on what to visit, where to stay, and how to get there—economically and hassle-free.

www.ricksteves.com

PHRASE BOOKS & DICTIONARIES

French
French, Italian & German
German
Italian
Portuguese
Spanish

MORE EUROPE FROM RICK STEVES

Europe 101
Europe Through the Back Door
Postcards from Europe

RICK STEVES' EUROPE DVDs

All 70 Shows 2000–2007
Britain
Eastern Europe
France & Benelux
Germany, The Swiss Alps & Travel Skills
Ireland
Italy
Spain & Portugal

PLANNING MAPS

Britain & Ireland
Europe
France
Germany, Austria & Switzerland
Italy
Spain & Portugal

CREDITS

Contributors

Steve Smith
Steve manages tour logistics for Rick Steves' Europe Through the Back Door and has co-authored France guidebooks with Rick for almost two decades. Fluent in French, he's lived in France on several occasions starting when he was seven, and has traveled there annually for the last 23 years.

Gene Openshaw
Gene is a writer, composer, and lecturer on art and history. Specializing in writing walking tours of Europe's cultural sights, Gene has co-authored eight of Rick's books. Gene lives near Seattle with his wife and daughter, and roots for the Mariners in good times and bad.

Honza Vihan
Honza, co-author of Rick's book on Prague, grew up roaming the Czech countryside in search of the Wild West. Once the borders opened, he set off for South Dakota. His journey took him to China, Honduras, India, and Iran. Honza lives in Prague with his wife and grandmother, is studying for a PhD in Chinese, and leads Rick Steves' tours through Eastern Europe.

Researchers

Amanda Buttinger
Amanda moved to Madrid in 1998 thinking she'd be there a year. Her first reason to stay was to learn more Spanish. Then she discovered the perfect *café con leche*, travel writing, sunny city walks, massage, and professional wine tasting.

Jennifer Hauseman
Jennifer Hauseman, an editor and researcher for Rick Steves, originally hails from the East Coast, but has since become an honorary Seattleite. While in the Low Countries, Jen enjoyed researching by bike with Rick, sampling vending-machine *stroopwafels*, and being mistaken for a Nederlandse in and around Amsterdam.

Trina Kudlacek
Trina was a university lecturer, but left it behind for what she calls a career in higher education: researching books and guiding tours for Rick Steves. A native of Kansas, she splits her time between Hawai'i and Italy (where she's even spent a summer renting kayaks in Vernazza).

Kristen Kusnic
Kristen Kusnic, lover of all things French, leads tours and researches guidebooks for Rick Steves. She lived for a year each in the south of France and Berlin, becoming fluent in French, German, and red wine. When she's not in Europe, Kristen calls Seattle home.

Susana Minich
Susana Minich was born in Czechoslovakia, grew up in Switzerland, and now divides her time between Spain and Seattle. She has been guiding tours for Rick Steves since 1999. She's multilingual and has a degree in Art History with two minors: Architecture and Chocolate.

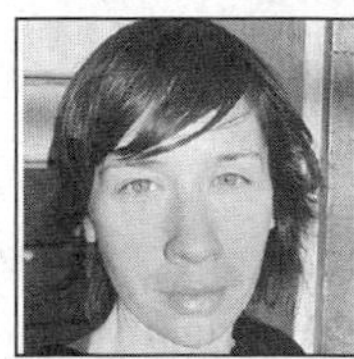

Amanda Scotese
Amanda Scotese freelances as a journalist and editor in San Francisco. Her travels in Italy include a stint selling leather jackets in Florence's San Lorenzo Market, basking in the Sicilian sun, and of course, helping out with Rick Steves' guidebooks and tours.

Heidi Sewell
Heidi Sewell lived in Italy for two years, learning to speak Italian and roll her own pasta. When she's not leading tours and scouring the Italian Peninsula for Back Doors worthy of Rick Steves' guidebooks, she resides in Seattle with her husband Ragen.

Karoline Vass
Karoline Vass was born and raised in Munich, Germany. Passionate about anything alpine, she made her way to Seattle via the Swiss Alps and the Rocky Mountains. When not researching guidebooks and leading tours, she makes her living as a freelance violist.

IMAGES

Location	Photographer
Austria	
Full-page image: Vienna—St. Peter's Church	Cameron Hewitt
Vienna—Schönbrunn Palace	Cameron Hewitt
Salzburg	Rick Steves
Hallstatt	David C. Hoerlein
Belgium	
Full-page image: Bruges Canal	Rick Steves
Bruges	David C. Hoerlein
Czech Republic	
Full-page image: Prague—Charles Bridge	Cameron Hewitt
Prague—View of Prague Castle	Cameron Hewitt
France	
Full-page image: Paris—*Venus de Milo*, Louvre Museum	Rob Unck
Paris—Louvre Museum	Rick Steves
Provence—Pont du Gard	Rick Steves
The French Riviera—Nice	David C. Hoerlein
Germany	
Full-page image: Munich—Marienplatz	Dominic Bonuccelli
Bavaria—Neuschwanstein Castle	Dominic Bonuccelli
Rothenburg	David C. Hoerlein
Rhine River	Dominic Bonuccelli
Berlin—Gendarmenmarkt	Cameron Hewitt
Great Britain	
Full-page image: London's British Museum	Rick Steves
London—Houses of Parliament	Rick Steves
Bath—Pulteney Bridge	Lauren Mills

Italy

Full-page image: Florence—Michelangelo's *David*	Rick Steves
Rome—Piazza Navona	Rick Steves
Venice—Church of San Giorgio Maggiore	David C. Hoerlein
Florence—Piazzale Michelangelo	Rick Steves
The Cinque Terre—Corniglia	Rick Steves

Netherlands

Full-page image: Amsterdam	Rick Steves
Amsterdam	Rick Steves
Haarlem—Market Square	Rick Steves

Spain

Full-page image: Moorish Arches	David C. Hoerlein
Barcelona—Montjuïc	David C. Hoerlein
Madrid—Retiro Park	David C. Hoerlein

Switzerland

Full-page image: Gimmelwald	Dominic Bonuccelli
Gimmelwald	Cameron Hewitt

Rick Steves' Guidebook Series

Country Guides

Rick Steves' Best of Europe
Rick Steves' Best of Eastern Europe
Rick Steves' Croatia & Slovenia
Rick Steves' England
Rick Steves' France
Rick Steves' Germany & Austria
Rick Steves' Great Britain
Rick Steves' Ireland
Rick Steves' Italy
Rick Steves' Portugal
Rick Steves' Scandinavia
Rick Steves' Spain
Rick Steves' Switzerland

City and Regional Guides

Rick Steves' Amsterdam, Bruges & Brussels
Rick Steves' Florence & Tuscany
Rick Steves' Istanbul
Rick Steves' London
Rick Steves' Paris
Rick Steves' Prague & the Czech Republic
Rick Steves' Provence & the French Riviera
Rick Steves' Rome
Rick Steves' Venice

Rick Steves' Phrase Books

French
German
Italian
Spanish
Portuguese
French/Italian/German

Other Books

Rick Steves' Europe Through the Back Door
Rick Steves' Europe 101: History and Art for the Traveler
Rick Steves' Postcards from Europe
Rick Steves' European Christmas

(Avalon Travel Publishing)

Avalon Travel Publishing
a member of the Perseus Books Group
1400 65th Street, Suite 250
Emeryville, CA 94608

Printed in the US by Worzalla
First printing August 2007

For the latest on Rick Steves' lectures, guidebooks, tours, public television series, and public radio show, contact Europe Through the Back Door, Box 2009, Edmonds, WA 98020, 425/771-8303, fax 425/771-0833, www.ricksteves.com, rick@ricksteves.com.

ISBN-10: 1-56691-852-9
ISBN-13: 978-1-56691-852-7
ISSN: 1096-7702

Europe Through the Back Door Managing Editor: Risa Laib
ETBD Editors: Cathy McDonald, Jennifer Madison Davis, Jennifer Hauseman
Avalon Travel Publishing Senior Editor and Series Manager: Madhu Prasher
Avalon Travel Publishing Project Editor: Kelly Lydick
Editorial: Patrick Collins
Indexer: Stephen Callahan
Production & Typesetting: McGuire Barber Design
Interior Design: Laura Mazer, Jane Musser, Amber Pirker
Cover Design: Kari Gim, Laura Mazer
Cover Art Manager: Laura VanDeventer
Maps and Graphics: David C. Hoerlein, Laura VanDeventer, Lauren Mills, Barb Geisler, Mike Morgenfeld
Front Matter Color Photos: Page i: Venice, Italy © Rick Steves; Page xiv: Arnhem Open-Air Museum in the Netherlands © Dominic Bonuccelli, page xvi: Salzburg Cathedral, Germany © Dominic Bonuccelli
Cover Photos: Front image: Parisian Café, Paris, France © Carol Ries; back image: Gimmelwald Goat, Switzerland © Dominic Bonuccelli